BOOKS BY DIONE LUCAS

THE CORDON BLEU COOK BOOK

THE DIONE LUCAS MEAT AND POULTRY COOKBOOK
Dione Lucas and Ann Roe Robbins

THE GOURMET COOKING SCHOOL COOKBOOK
Dione Lucas with Darlene Geis

THE DIONE LUCAS BOOK OF FRENCH COOKING
Dione Lucas and Marion Gorman

THE DIONE LUCAS
BOOK OF FRENCH COOKING

THE DIONE LUCAS
BOOK OF FRENCH COOKING

by Dione Lucas and Marion Gorman

Illustrated by Joseph S. Patti

LITTLE, BROWN AND COMPANY — BOSTON — TORONTO

FIRST EDITION

T 11/73

Library of Congress Cataloging in Publication Data

Lucas, Dione, 1909-1971.
    The Dione Lucas book of French cooking.

    1. Cookery, French. I. Gorman, Marion, joint
author. II. Title.
[TX719.L783 1973]   641.5'944   73-13750
ISBN 0-316-53517-6

Published simultaneously in Canada by Little, Brown & Company (Canada) Limited

PRINTED IN THE UNITED STATES OF AMERICA

T HIS BOOK is a collection of most of the classic French and international recipes which have been interpreted for the home in my classes over the last thirty years.

This compendium, therefore, is dedicated to all of my students.

I would also like to honor the memory of my teacher, M. Henri Pellaprat, for over fifty years head of the famous Cordon Bleu school in Paris. He bridged the life line of culinary art from La Belle Époque to mid-twentieth century and from the professional kitchen to the home.

DIONE LUCAS
Diplomate de Cordon Bleu

Cookery is one of the humanities whose entire philosophy is in step with the progress of civilization throughout the centuries, reflecting the development of man as surely through a recipe as through the Capitularies of Charlemagne or the Code Napoleon.

RAYMOND OLIVER
Gastronomy of France

B EFORE YOU BEGIN TO COOK any of these recipes, please observe these bon mots.

(1) ORIENTATION. Please read the recipe through from beginning to end before planning to prepare it.

(2) HAVE THE INGREDIENTS READY. The procedure assumes that all items listed as ingredients have been prepared and measured as directed, and are at hand before taking the first step of the procedure.

(3) SUBSTITUTE INGREDIENTS. It is better not to prepare a dish than to substitute an ingredient. Unless stated, no substitutes are advisable.

(4) MEASUREMENTS. All spoon and cup measurements are level, except when stated otherwise.

(5) COOKING TIMES. All time periods are estimates. If you are preparing a recipe for the first time, regardless of your experience or expertise, by all means please allow plenty of time for preparation, and keep a close watch to avoid overcooking.

(6) STOCK BASES. Many sauce, soup, fish, poultry, and meat recipes call for the use of chicken or fish stock. It is assumed that connoisseurs of cooking in the French manner have supplies of fresh or frozen stock on hand. See Chicken Stock (page 35) and Fish Stock (page 36).

INTRODUCTION

A PHILOSOPHY OF COOKING

Preparation of a meal requires skill and patience, and the results mean the difference between eating to exist, and the satisfaction that comes from one of the major pleasures of life.

Cooking is an art, and the kitchen cannot be regarded as a scientific laboratory. "Tender loving care" should be on the bottom of every recipe, a part of every ingredient in it. This is artistic involvement. A cook is working with life materials and must develop a feeling for what each ingredient will do in a recipe.

This sensitivity and reverence toward food reflects the French culinary environment in which evolved the style of cooking known as classic French cooking. Its essence is the use of high quality raw materials, cooked simply but perfectly to enhance their natural flavor. Its basis is a set of principles and practices that have been refined and refined, and have withstood the tests of time and experience. To translate these classic principles of French cuisine into successful, workable methods for the American home kitchen has been the purpose of my endeavor.

Uniquely, French home cooking, from the provinces, begat the eventual culinary classics of this civilization because the dishes were a natural, honest derivation of their particular locale and environment — root elements that have satisfied the human attitude as well as the appetite.

In 1942 I arrived in America filled with love of the art of classic cookery, and respect for it too, for classic cookery offers intellectual appreciation of food. I soon felt I had discovered America in another way, a way that I believed offered great opportunity and satisfaction. I was bursting with inspiration when, even in wartime, I saw an abundance of beautiful natural resources so sadly misunderstood.

Nowhere was there a pattern or mode of cuisine in any significant respect. With my education at L'École du Cordon Bleu, a full chef's apprenticeship at the Drouant Restaurant in Paris, and a partnership experience in operating Le Petit Cordon Bleu school and restaurant in London, I would try to interpret the classic dishes of French cuisine for America — with American materials, in very dissimilar American home kitchens, with an entirely different set of tools and equipment.

The most successful way to reproduce the great French classical dishes in American kitchens could not be the same as one would follow in professional restaurant cookery, nor, for that matter, in the home kitchens in France. This process of interpretation and refinement of great dishes like Quenelles de Brochet Nantua, or the simple omelet, has been my preoccupation in this wonderful land of America all these years. The reward has been to see the growth of an absolute force in American cuisine. If there is any formal cuisine in America, it comes from the gradual adaptation of the French classics to the resources of this country. Through these years the number of cooking schools has increased greatly, and bookstores are bulging with cookbooks.

This is just fine. It demonstrates acute awareness and interest, from which will grow more interest in ever finer cooking — and eating.

The Human Element

I like this story about the human element in cooking, told me by my good friend Henry Sell, editor-at-large for *Town & Country Magazine* and ambassador of good will for one of my most favorite cities, Venice. With Janet Leckie, Henry created the best tinned pâté short of Strasbourg foie gras — their widely distributed Sell's Liver Pâté, originally created to make profitable use of surplus pork livers and other inexpensive and highly nutritious products, then adjusted for taste in the kitchens of the Waldorf Astoria Hotel. By the time they sold the formula and business to a major canner, production was in millions of tins each month, and Janet was always on the working floor directing the flow with her know-how. But the new owners could not seem to get the smooth kitchen-quality emulsion that had made the pâté famous, and Janet searched desperately for the difference. She remembered only one thing: in the old days, at a rest point in the cooking, she had walked to the window, looked out, and come back. Her "walk to the window" was rechecked — seventy slow steps to the window, look out, and take seventy slow steps back — and behold, the pâté was correct! That human element, her intuitive timing, converted into the mathematics of food engineering, made all the difference.

YOUR COMPENDIUM AND HOW IT WORKS

Among my most precious possessions are two yellowed French school composition books. They contain the recipes of classic French cuisine as I learned them at L'École du Cordon Bleu and during my apprenticeship at the Drouant Restaurant in Paris. My former students may remember these school composition books as the authority consulted when an infrequent dish was requested in a class lesson, perhaps some special provincial dish that interested a student because he'd visited the region of origin in France (I remember one such was the Clafouti). A glimpse of the original method would set the memory wheels turning, and we would interpret the dish in our cooking class.

This compendium is intended to serve others in the same way my yellow composition books served me — to provide a collection of class recipes for the many people who learned to cook in my school, and to make these time-tested (thirty years) recipes available to new people who are interested in fine cooking.

The organization of this book and the recipe presentation reflect my teaching method — along with the list of ingredients and the procedure for each recipe, I tried to inculcate the idea of the dish, the nature of the food, and the necessary measure of human involvement — tender loving care.

Teaching was my original purpose in the cooking field, and I have loved it the most of all my cooking activities. I have always given individual lessons, each student choosing his dish and preparing it. With no more than six students in a class at any one time, I can stand next to each one and show each hand-to-hand how to prepare a dish — how to stir, how to roll out pastry and line a flan ring, how to "serve up" the dish, to garnish it, to make it beautiful to the beholder.

This book is not an attempt to teach basic cooking procedures or methods via "correspondence course." Frankly, there is no substitute for actual cooking lessons, if only to learn one's way through basic techniques of handling food. Today there are many excellent cooking classes in the United States, and I urge anyone who has not done so to attend a few classes; it will be reassuring to see the correct way to use a whisk, how to beat egg whites and heavy cream, how to brown meat correctly, how to make basic classic sauce preparations (is there anyone who still does not make mayonnaise at home?). Knowing the basics will instantly cast off petty frustration and make whatever degree of cooking involvement you choose a pleasurable activity.

Each recipe is intended to be a built-in cooking lesson, within the scope described above. Mainly what is meant by "built-in" is freedom from a multitude of referrals to basic procedures or preparations elsewhere in the book. I have always felt that a major put-off of some cookbooks is to describe the preparation of a complex dish by referrals to other parts of the book for the proper sauce, etc. Obviously, some referrals are necessary — the step-by-step methods for tying, boning, and carving poultry, the basic omelet preparation (which would otherwise be repeated in every savory omelet recipe), the basic pastry shell preparation, and others. But there are as few as possible, and most of the recipes in this book are self-contained.

In the seemingly identical preparations given in detail from recipe to recipe, however, there is often some little difference. However tiny, it may be just the touch that adapts a basic sauce or flan shell, for example, to the needs of a particular dish. In cooking these dishes year after year in my school and restaurant operations, I often discovered a way to change the balance of ingredients just a little, or revise a technique, that would be the miracle we were looking for.

The independence of each recipe is also designed for those people who, God bless them, just want to open a cookbook and cook. Cooking may not be their thing; but if they are going to the trouble, they want the result to be successful. Many people attended a few of my classes for just this reason.

The Recipe Format

(1) THE NAME. If the dish is French or has found its way into the French chef's repertoire, the name is given in French; if of another nationality, the original name is used. English translations (when appropriate) appear below the title.

A brief description of the dish, if it is not already implied in the name, is given, where it may be helpful to the reader. These descriptions and any urgent information about the recipe (such as an extra long preparation time) appear in the text before the list of ingredients.

(2) HAVE THE INGREDIENTS READY. Anyone who ever attended a Dione Lucas cooking lesson knows this is step number one. Do not start to cook anything until you have assembled all the ingredients in readiness to "go onstage" — the onions chopped, the bouquet garni assembled, the flour measured, or the butter at the proper temperature.

Every class of mine began with the students seated around a table where they would write the recipes as I dictated them. Side queries were answered while the students wrote, and throughout the whole lecture period, as I spoke, my hands were assembling the preparation trays for the dishes to be made in that session.

Each preparation tray was actually a jelly roll pan on which all the ingredients for a particular dish were assembled. On the tray for a Poulet Marengo, for example, would be the chicken, tomatoes prepared as directed, measured chicken stock, sliced mushrooms, boiled lobster, prepared croûtons, eggs, and chopped chives. Handy in the work area would be the staple ingredients — butter, brandy, chopped garlic, salt, white pepper in a mill, meat glaze, tomato paste, potato flour, dry sherry, cayenne pepper, and vegetable oil.

The trays were prepared in the interest of time and efficiency, but they also demonstrated to students the speed and smoothness with which the most complicated dish could be prepared — with joy, without frustration — when the ingredients were ready. Not to acquire the preparation tray habit invites disaster — a finished omelet in the pan and no garnishes ready, or a striped bass poached to perfection and no eggs for the Sauce Mousseline to accompany this kingly dish!

In a word, cooking can be fun if the whole symphony of ingredients is at your fingertips ready for you to lift the baton.

(3) PROCEDURE. Here are incorporated many of the little attentions that make a fine dish great without becoming tedious — the little nuances as well as the general method. Former students will remember how we would identify the kind and size of each pan needed (a small tin-lined copper pan, or a large heavy pot) or the size of whisk, the degree of vitality with which something should be stirred, and even the type of serving dish (I adore shiny copper casseroles). This was all an extension of my own training in the classic methods and traditions, and as far as is feasible the recipes in this book include these instructions.

Directions in the recipe are arranged in order of performance, including when to turn on the oven. Allowing time for the oven to heat to the proper temperature before putting in the masterpiece should ward off more cooking disappointments than you can imagine.

In most recipes, the procedure section includes advice on how to present the finished product for serving — the kind of dish, the garnishes, the sauce. Here again your own artistry can gleam. No chef with heart arranges a dish precisely the same way every time, and from season to season, place to place, ingredients have different qualities. The point of classic cookery is to emphasize the natural beauty and quality of food.

(4) NET. The cook needs some idea of the quantity a given recipe will produce, which in most of these recipes is given in terms of "servings." The number of servings may vary from the stated amount depending upon their size, the scope of the rest of the menu, the appetites of the diners, and the tendency of the family to raid the refrigerator or pantry when some delicious homemade dish is resting there.

MENU COMPOSITION
To keep you healthy, wealthy, and wise

"Appetite really is synonymous with eye. We have a buffet display each day, but I don't let people order a lot of food. The days of big dinners are gone. A piece of melon or madrilène, roast duckling, cheese and fruit are enough."

This is the advice of Le Pavillon Restaurant (Stuart Levin), one of the finest temples of French cuisine in the United States. It expresses perfectly the contemporary attitude about menu composition, whether we are selecting a meal at a restaurant or composing a meal at home.

In this framework it is important — and pleasurable — to take the extra bit of time to prepare a beautiful dish well, and further enhance your effort by surrounding it with very simple courses. If you serve a rich lobster bisque, accompany it with a simple entrée and dessert. If you are in the mood to dazzle with a gloriously rich dessert (and doesn't everyone need this frivolity once in a while?), have a simple first course and entrée. Or balance a lusty Boeuf Bourguignonne with a light first course and, to finish the meal, cheese and perhaps a cold ripe syrupy pear.

Informed menu planning is the first step in good eating. The primary ingredient in this operation is you — your knowledge, taste, and judgment. Here are a few basic pointers for planning the main meal of the day, whether it is lunch or dinner.

(1) A family meal — even a meal with guests — requires only two, three or four courses.

(2) Balance is the key to good menu planning. There should be a balance of complex and simple foods — only one rich or substantial course, with a balancing light, refreshing, natural quality in the others.

(3) The menu should reflect a contrast in textures — chewy, crunchy, purée, or fibrous.

(4) The menu should also reflect a contrast in flavor and color — a light sauce and a dark sauce; never two lights or two darks in succession. Color should vary from course to course.

(5) It is best to serve the salad as a separate course, either as an hors d'oeuvre or after the entrée. The vinegar in the dressing will not mix favorably with your sauce or wine.

(6) In French cuisine, vegetables are either a garnish with the main fish, meat, or poultry course, in which case they are small accompaniments, or are a separate course so that their special composition may be properly enjoyed — Petits Pois à la Française, for example, which is too substantial to serve with a filling meat or poultry dish, or Eggplant Provençale or asparagus.

(7) A cheese tray following the main course or salad course is de rigueur with Europeans and is being served more and more in America. (Various cheese trays are described in the cheese chapter.) Cheese draws the palate to contentment following the filling parts of the meal, after which a touch of dessert (if you wish) and coffee offer a final happy frill.

(8) Know the best natural foods of the season in your own locality, and plan menus around them. Avoid using packaged frozen or long-distance imported items if you are blessed with local produce.

During the spring, summer and fall most localities in the United States can offer local produce. Ask and search for the skinny little carrots just pulled from the ground in the first yield in the spring, the slightly underdeveloped green peas sweet with flavor, the perky scallions and spring lettuces. Every day throughout these seasons whole menus should be planned to take advantage of the lovely fresh garden vegetables and fruit, whether from your own garden or the local truck farm or greengrocer. It's a challenge to fit all the fruit — strawberries, raspberries, cantaloupes, watermelons, blueberries, blackberries, peaches, nectarines, cherries, plums — into the program; not to mention the fresh herbs — dill, Italian parsley, basil, tarragon — and the variety of garden lettuces, home-grown tomatoes — big beefsteaks, Italian plum, and cherry size — baby beets, green beans that really snap, skinny firm cucumbers, smooth juicy green and red peppers, corn on the cob, zucchini and summer squash, marble-size potatoes . . . glory! glory! glory!

In the late fall and winter there is ample time to savor a whole different grouping — the apples, eggplant, cauliflower, potatoes, pears, chestnuts, all the right produce to go with the feast of the hunt or the stick-to-the-ribs ragoût.

Keep seasonality in mind, too, with fish, seafood, and meats. Ask your fish market about when to expect seasonal specialties — delicate little bay scallops, smelts, soft-shell crabs, all the delicacies of the sea which have limited periods of availability.

As to meats, more and more Americans are discovering the gastronomical pre-eminence of young lamb and veal, of which the French and Italians have long been large consumers and connoisseurs. Most baby lambs are slaughtered in March for the Easter season. This is the time to enjoy this exquisite food — save your beef bird menus for January.

(9) For a meal with guests, never serve a dish which you have not prepared successfully at least once before. The vagaries of culinary elements are many and unexpected, and even the great chefs who produce the extraordinary feasts of the high gourmet societies, such as the Chevaliers du Tastevin and the Commanderie de Bordeaux, test their grande cuisine dinners at least twice, using the same staff who will be preparing the final dinner.

(10) In the section on Marketing there is a suggested weekly menu planning form which has been used successfully in setting up a week's program of meals. In planning menus for a week, remember that there are many good dishes for which the ingredients can be purchased and either partially or fully cooked several days in advance. The opportunity to precook and freeze is an important modern contribution to the art of French cooking (other important contributions are plastic wrap and the electric blender). Be sure to check the section on Freezing before freezing any dish for the first time.

Menu Worksheets

Here is a suggested worksheet which may help in planning menus within the framework of the above ground rules. The purpose of these categorical groupings is to demonstrate that every main meal need not have an hors d'oeuvre or a salad or a vegetable. We have filled in one as an example. You might try the others — just to demonstrate the method.

Basic Main Meal Menu Patterns

	COURSE	DISH
(A)	1. Soup	Pot-au-Feu — broth
	2. Poultry	Pot-au-Feu — chicken/beef/vegetables
	3. Salad	Tossed greens/simple vinaigrette
	4. Dessert	Clafouti (with cherries or plums)
(B)	1. Soup	
	2. Meat	
	3. Dessert	
(C)	1. Hors d'oeuvres	
	2. Meat	
	3. Salad	
	4. Pastry	
(D)	1. Meat	
	2. Salad	
	3. Cheese	
	4. Fruit	
(E)	1. Salad	
	2. Meat	
	3. Cheese	
	4. Fruit	
(F)	1. Separate vegetable	
	2. Meat	
	3. Salad	
	4. Dessert	
(G)	1. Fish	
	2. Salad	
	3. Cheese	
	4. Dessert	
(H)	1. Soup	
	2. Poultry	
	3. Separate vegetable	
	4. Dessert	
(I)	1. Meat	
	2. Cheese	
	3. Fruit	

If you have the "staff" and prefer more elaborate meals, perhaps to show off some of your wine collection to guests, here are a few patterns which I believe are as far as the home dinner party should venture.

More Elaborate Home Menu Patterns

COURSE	DISH

(A) 1. Hors d'oeuvres
    2. Seafood
    3. Poultry or game
    4. Salad
    5. Cheese
    6. Dessert

(B) 1. Hors d'oeuvres
    2. Meat
    3. Salad
    4. Cheese
    5. Pastry

(C) 1. Hors d'oeuvres
    2. Fish
    3. Meat
    4. Cheese
    5. Dessert

(D) 1. Soup
    2. Fish or shellfish
    3. Meat
    4. Salad
    5. Cheese
    6. Dessert

As you can see, the above patterns offer all kinds of planning flexibility. The main principle is balance — in flavors, textures, and color. Servings should be modest so as not to embarrass the timid nibblers who do not eat lustily. You will have the charm to make it easy for the happy eater to accept second helpings.

ONE FAMILY — ONE MENU. There should never be two menus in a family, one for the adults and a bland, very bland one for the children. I agree with the French way with children at the table. There's nothing wrong with giving children properly prepared food right from the very beginning, exactly what the parents eat.

Don't explain, "You may not like this, darling." Just serve the child as you do everyone else at the table; treat him as an equal. If you continue, soon he will be enjoying your menu and educating his palate rather than desensitizing it.

Cooking in the classic manner improves your chances of converting your child to an adult menu. Children especially love pure fresh food; and pure fresh food, whether served raw or cooked in a way that maintains its fresh quality, is a primary requisite of classic cookery.

FREEZING RAW AND COOKED FOODS
Advance planning potential

The freezer helps you make good eating possible every day of the week and at the same time confine your marketing to a once-a-week basis. With a general awareness of which fresh foods and cooked dishes will or will not freeze successfully, you can intelligently plan certain more elaborate dishes for the latter part of your weekly menu. These can be cooked or partially prepared several days in advance, and stored in the freezer. You may also prepare basic ingredients such as stocks, butters, doughs, or even crêpes to have on hand.

Please do not misunderstand, however. My classes have heard me repeat ad infinitum that the very best is always the very fresh, and I maintain this position. Basically, nothing (except food to be served frozen, of course) is improved by freezing.

Here are a few basic principles on freezing foods, followed by notes about the freezing potential for each food category you will be considering in your menu planning.

(1) Since nothing is improved by freezing, do not make large quantities of food for freezing except when it fits into a plan for use.

(2) Slightly overseason food to be frozen.

(3) Do not freeze any preparation that contains gelatine or aspic. Aspic clouds when frozen.

(4) Do not freeze any preparation that contains eggs, neither sauces bound with egg nor custard types (except ice cream).

(5) Anything bound with butter freezes well — basic butters, compound butters, and butter creams.

(6) Doughs and many baked pastries freeze nobly (see also under Pastries, below).

Stocks, Sauces, and Basic Cooking Agents

Stocks freeze very well and may be kept in a frozen state for at least three months. If you make a large quantity of basic stock, and strain and store it in the freezer in small covered plastic containers, you can always achieve instant "miracle" cooking. (You'll feel just a little smug being able to make a quick rice pilaff cooked in homemade chicken stock!) These handy little containers of homemade stock with frozen-in flavor are the modern substitute for that basic element in original French cuisine, the simmering stockpot on the back of the stove from which marvelous sauces were born.

Many sauces can be prepared ahead of time and frozen successfully, and leftover sauces (Demi-Glace, Bordelaise) can be saved for use on an omelet or to sauce a chop. (1) Brown, white, fish, and vegetable sauces will freeze well provided they do not contain gelatine or egg. Many white sauces, the velouté type, are bound with egg yolk, so be careful. (2) No egg-base sauces such as mayonnaise will freeze successfully. (3) No need to freeze sauces of the vinaigrette type; they will last a long time in the refrigerator, preserved by their oil content. (Also store pure olive oil, which is very delicate and sensitive, in the refrigerator so that it does not become rancid. It will cloud, but that does not harm it.) (4) Dessert sauces that contain egg or juicy fruit should not be frozen. Dessert glazes, usually made with preserves, store well in the refrigerator. Fruit syrup made with citrus rind (page 68) will keep superbly in the refrigerator for many months.

All whipped butters freeze successfully. Sweet butter should always be stored in the freezer because it is most susceptible to other flavors and odors. "Fancy" butters stored in the freezer can make you a wonder chef; for example, a quick broiled steak garnished with an herby Bercy butter (which is simply rolled up in foil and frozen; whenever you want to use it just slice off a half-dollar shape and lay it, frozen, on the hot cooked steak or chop). Garlic butter may be frozen and used at will, with half a loaf or a whole one. Pan butters like Beurre Noir and Beurre à la Meunière would usually not be available for freezing except as part of a leftover.

Certain fresh herbs may be stored in the freezer for a few weeks. The sometimes hard-to-find fresh tarragon freezes satisfactorily. To prepare it, wrap two or three sprigs in a little piece of foil, like a packet. Make up as many of these packets as you want to freeze. Chives freeze well for a few weeks also. Parsley seems to be available fresh everywhere. Dill does not freeze very well; if you have some extra fresh sprigs it would be better to dry them.

Hors d'Oeuvres

Many hors d'oeuvres can be prepared ahead of time, partially or fully, and frozen. To determine whether a recipe might freeze well, please check under the food category the hors d'oeuvre is made of.

Egg dishes, for example, generally do not freeze successfully, but Quiche Lorraine, after it has been baked, freezes just fine! (I often froze it for my restaurant operations.) Bake it just a little underdone and cool, then freeze it. Thaw it by warming it in a moderate oven (350°) and let it brown a little.

Certain prepared meats, like pâtés and the various stuffed salami cornucopias, freeze excellently.

Plain crêpes and unfilled cream puffs (to be filled before serving) and prepared puff paste hors d'oeuvres, like Palmiers de Fromage, also hold their identity in the freezer.

History does not record the successful freezing of a baked soufflé.

Soups

Many soups maintain their flavor and consistency when frozen, and thus, for the joy of more homemade soups, I encourage advance preparation and freezing of these soups. Any cream soup or potage type (of the hot or iced category) can be frozen, but be sure not to add any cream and final egg or egg yolk liaison until the soup is thawed, reheated, and ready to serve. Then stir the soup into the egg liaison.

Plain consommé, ungarnished and without aspic, may be frozen. Add the garnish when ready to serve.

Cooked Egg Dishes

Not freezable!

Fish and Shellfish

Fresh-caught fish may be frozen, although I can't imagine why anyone would want to. Better to eat such a treasure right away, and give some to friends to share. If you do freeze fresh fish, first scale and gut it, wash it in cool water, and rub it with lemon juice and salt. Seal in a strong plastic bag and freeze quickly.

Raw shrimp may be frozen, sealed in covered plastic containers, but home freezing of other seafood is not recommended.

Lobster and crab may be plain-cooked in court-bouillon, the flesh removed from the shell, dried on a towel, and frozen dry in plastic containers.

Quenelles for Quenelles de Brochet freeze beautifully. Prepare them up to the point when they would be poached, and instead of poaching wrap each cork-shaped quenelle in plastic wrap and freeze. When you are ready to make this classic dish, thaw the quenelles at room temperature and poach them according to the recipe.

Poultry

All fresh dressed poultry (also game birds), whole or in sections, including the suprêmes (breasts), may be frozen for the sake of expediency. I have in mind my basic point that nothing is improved by freezing — particularly poultry, whose total sum of flavor when it is fresh is often not enough.

When freezing a whole dressed chicken or other poultry, remove the paper package of neck, liver, and gizzard that is usually in the cavity; then dry and tie the chicken according to the standard procedure (page 342) to keep it compact when frozen. Seal it in a plastic bag. Later, if you plan to poach the chicken as is, just remove it from the bag and put it into the stockpot in its frozen state. If you plan to roast or sauté it, thaw it completely, dry it thoroughly, and prepare it according to the recipe.

To freeze fresh poultry pieces, wrap each one snugly in plastic wrap. If possible, avoid freezing chicken breasts — used in so many delicious combinations in French cuisine — because their flavor is so delicate. Chicken livers may be put in a covered plastic container and frozen.

The following types of poultry dishes may be partially cooked, cooled, and then frozen in the tightly covered plastic containers:

Plain roast unstuffed poultry or leftover cooked poultry. (Freeze dry.)

Many sauté and casserole dishes, which have a stock-base sauce. Partially cook these up to the point of (but excluding) the garnish. Vegetables, mushrooms, or whatever garnish is part of the dish should be prepared and incorporated in the dish just prior to serving. Again, do not freeze dishes which have gelatine, aspic, or egg in the preparation.

Most suprême (breast) dishes freeze well, again providing the sauce does not contain gelatine, aspic, or egg. Chicken Kiev freezes excellently. (Imagine dashing home late and being able to lay out an elegant little dinner of golden brown deep-fried Poulet à la Kiev, garnished with ten-minute Parisienne potatoes, a salad, some cheese and fruit!) To freeze Chicken Kiev, prepare through the step of encasing the sticks of butter and herbs in the rolled breast meat. Seal the ends of the rolled chicken breasts by tucking them in and pressing them. Do not coat, but wrap each piece in plastic wrap and carefully lay on a small flat tray or cardboard. Wrap the whole trayful in a plastic bag and freeze. When you wish to serve your Kiev's, thaw them a little, then proceed as in the recipe with coating and deep-frying.

Meat (Beef, Veal, Lamb, Pork and Ham, and Furred Game)

Except for ground meat, which does not freeze successfully, raw beef, lamb, pork, venison, and tongue may be frozen. Rub the meat with a little salt, or oil, then wrap in freezer paper, seal in a plastic bag, and freeze.

Raw veal should not be frozen. It is very delicate, and the flavor will be lost.

Marrowbones, veal knuckles, and calves' feet, for stocks and sauces, can be kept in the freezer indefinitely.

Cooked meat dishes have about the same freezing potential as poultry dishes. The ragoûts, daubes, all casserole types, freeze quite well, again except for those which contain gelatine, aspic, or egg. Cook the dish to be frozen up to the point of adding the garnish. Cool, and store in tightly covered plastic containers in the freezer. Prepare and add the garnish after the dish has been gently reheated for serving.

Boeuf Bourguignonne freezes famously well. This can be one of your end-of-the-week instant surprise dishes.

Vegetables and Fruits

The goodness of dishes prepared in the French manner is due largely to the principle of using fresh raw ingredients. In all my experience there has everywhere been enough fresh produce available to avoid the need for frozen vegetables and fruits.

If you have an overly abundant garden and want the gratification of serving up your own garden peas when the ground is covered with snow, these may indeed be frozen. A few vegetables that may be frozen raw reasonably well are green beans (topped and tailed), garden peas (shelled), brussels sprouts (trimmed), okra, and lima beans (shelled). To freeze these vegetables, wash them thoroughly and blanch them.

To blanch vegetables for freezing, put them in a pan, cover them with cold water, bring the water to a boil, and drain immediately. Cool the vegetables, then put in tightly covered plastic containers or sealed plastic bags, and freeze.

Do not try home-freezing fresh spinach; it needs commercial fast-freeze methods.

The freezing of fresh fruit is not recommended.

Breads, Pastry, Cakes, and Other Doughs

The following doughs can be frozen: bread dough, brioche dough; Pâté Feuilletée (puff paste), after the fourth turn; Pâté à Foncer (basic short pastry). To bake, thaw these doughs just enough so you can roll them out and/or shape them. It is best to keep them as cold as possible.

Fresh-baked breads, both yeast and non-yeast types, freeze well. Cool the bread and wrap it in foil, then seal in a plastic bag and freeze. To prepare it for use, preheat the oven to 400°, remove the bread from the plastic bag and put it in the oven still securely wrapped in foil. In a few minutes all the lovely aroma of fresh bread baking will return; you were able to catch that wonderful perfume and lock it in a safe! Frozen baked bread may be thawed at room temperature, also.

Tarts and pies freeze well unless they contain juicy fruit (either in the filling, like apple pie, or as the top decoration, like Tarte aux Fraises). Puff pastries, like Pithiviers, and unfilled cream puffs will freeze.

Plain cakes, genoese and sponge, undecorated, freeze very well. Seal them in plastic bags and store in the freezer until you are ready to assemble and/or decorate the finished dessert.

Butter cream and cakes sandwiched and frosted with butter cream and/or chocolate decorations (rounds, shavings, cornucopias) freeze excellently. Actually, it is recommended to store the finished dessert in the deep freezer until a few minutes before it is to be served.

Plain crêpes freeze well. If you are making crêpes for dessert, make some extra for a savory a few days hence, such as Crêpes Niçoise.

All petits fours, including Petits Fours Secs, à la Crème, and Fruits Déguisées, can be successfully frozen. Store them carefully in a plastic container so they will not be marred or broken.

Desserts

Let's check off the types:

Custard: No.

Bavarian cream: No. (The freezer is used to quick-set these preparations; then they are stored in the refrigerator.)

Mousses: Yes. The Normandy Chocolate Mousse keeps its visual and flavorful beauty in the freezer very well.

Sabayons: No.

Cold soufflés: No.

Other Foods

Salads hold beautifully in refrigeration — not a freezer — for a few hours to a day. That's all.

Some pastas freeze very well, such as a prepared lasagna dish with sauce, filled ravioli, and filled canelloni.

Cheese — refrigerate, yes; freeze, generally no, unless your supplier advises you about a specific type.

MARKETING
Selection and storage

Here is a simple procedure through which your marketing can contribute to the economy and efficiency of your kitchen and help you reach the ultimate in good eating. Whether you are the chef de cuisine in your house or an infrequent specialist, self-disciplining yourself into a routine similar to the following one will help.

(1) PREPARE A "NOTE-PAD MENU." If you cook every day, prepare a menu (listing all the dishes) for each meal you expect to cook during the week. Review the Freezing section and include dishes that may be cooked partially or completely and frozen. These can be programmed for the latter part of the week and prepared at your convenience. If you are cooking one meal, jot down the dishes to be served for that menu.

(2) PREPARE A MARKETING LIST. Divide this list into columns or sections based on where you market; for example: butcher (meats), fish market (fish and seafood), greengrocer (fresh vegetables and fruit), supermarket or general grocer (staples), specialty shops as required (bread, cheese, wine, a gourmet specialty shop for truffles, etc.).

(3) TRANSLATE THE MENU INGREDIENTS INTO THE MARKETING LIST. The way to do this is to check the recipe for each dish on each day's menu, and itemize the ingredients under the proper resource (store). Of course exclude staples you have on hand, but be sure to check them all. Result: A compact, organized marketing list (whether you visit the stores or telephone), assuring you that precisely what you need will be on hand with a minimum expenditure of time and effort.

In addition to the benefits of time and assurance, there is definite economy in this method of marketing. You need purchase no more of a perishable item than you need (4 ounces of firm white mushrooms, or 2 medium-size ripe tomatoes), and you have set the stage for the preparation of a great meal with more ease and facility than those ordinary ones that are made with "the back of the hand."

Try to confine your marketing to once, or at most twice, a week. When the supplies have been purchased, store the dry goods. Next remove the paper wraps from the meat, put it in freezer wrap, and store it in the refrigerator if it is to be used in the next day or two, or freezer if planned for later in the week. (Naturally, the meats to be frozen are those that freeze successfully; see the Freezing section.)

Clean and prepare all the greens and vegetables immediately to be ready for instant use; that is, clean and dry well all the leafy greens, including parsley, and put them in plastic bags ready for the salad bowl. Remove all other vegetables from paper bags, clean them if necessary, and put them in the vegetable tray.

There are busy families, including working couples, of my acquaintance who follow this weekly marketing procedure, and after the supplies are stored and ready, post the week's menus in the kitchen for all to see, including the resident sommelier. This helps in producing a lovely relaxed meal, with proper selection of wine, and adequate time allowed for the wine and you to breathe. The final ingredient of the art of good eating is conversation, and you are in a frame of mind to make it as pleasant and stimulating as your well-prepared meal.

Here are a few suggestions about the selection of foods on your marketing list.

(1) Long before ecology became a cause, many will recall, I was urging people to seek out and buy only pure, fresh foods. Sometimes this is not easy, but one should not plan to serve fresh peas or corn in January. There are always beautiful vegetables in season, and in winter good produce from Florida, Mexico, or California is shipped to all parts of the country. Be principled in demanding quality and freshness. It is your right and your duty.

(2) Itemize the ingredients on your marketing list in the same words used in the recipe — "firm white mushrooms" or "crisp fresh watercress" or "whole dressed chicken" — surprising that a butcher would send a cut-up chicken, but they do. These notes help even if you are the shopper yourself.

(3) Don't hesitate to pick over or dig underneath the dried, bruised greens, fruits or vegetables to be selective, even if the store objects; what is involved is your body and your money.

MENU PLAN

Week of:

DAY	MEAL	MENU	WINE

MARKETING LIST

Week of:

MEAT	GENERAL GROCER OR SUPERMARKET
FISH	
GREENGROCER	
	SPECIALTIES

(4) Cheeses are an important food that store well in the refrigerator and can be purchased to cover a period of several weeks. Enjoy the fun of visiting a good cheese shop and exploring different kinds of cheeses in addition to your standard favorites. The same with wine — many of you know the added measure of good living when the family lives a wine life with little wines as well as big wines (see the Wine section for suggestions on maintaining a modest supply of wine for family use).

(5) After the shopping is completed, staple the cash register tapes or bills to it for a record to help you maintain your food expenditures on a businesslike basis. If you do any business entertaining at home, this record with your weekly menu plan sheet are helpful with the tax department to support your home entertainment expense.

(6) If you are exploring the world of wines, the file of your past menus showing what wines were consumed when is an interesting record that helps to educate one's "wine memory."

(7) A weekly menu form and marketing list which an associate and I once designed (see pages 19 and 20) have been in regular use by practicing home cooks ever since and function well.

YOUR KITCHEN IS YOUR STUDIO
Arranging and equipping your kitchen

All the recipes in this book can be — and have been — produced in modest apartment kitchens. Therefore, the subject of equipping and arranging your kitchen, which is the studio for your cooking art and should be thought of as such, is a matter of degree but not of substitution. One may not be able to accommodate or afford the whole battery of copper saucepans; but I expect any interested home chef will insist on one good-quality average-size tin-lined copper saucepan rather than those "sets of pans" that seem to find a market in bridal showers and Christmas "solutions."

Here are my suggestions for Utopia. Start building slowly. Insist on what you want, and little by little you will have a kitchen that will work for you. If indeed you would explore a fairly wide repertoire of classic dishes, the inventory of equipment provided in this chapter will put you in a "ready" situation for all encounters. On the other hand, those with more modest objectives are advised to select their favorite dishes, gradually acquire the appropriate equipment to prepare those dishes, and build their batterie de cuisine as they build their expertise.

Kitchen Garb

An artist's smock is absolutely the best kitchen fashion for the home chef, male or female. It is better than an apron — your clothes are completely protected and you can cook whenever you want to without worrying about changing clothes. Wear comfortable shoes (or scuffs that may be left in the kitchen) to complete the ensemble.

Stove

Choose a stove with four burners, a large oven, and a separate rotisserie and broiler. Gas or electric, as you prefer.

Refrigerator

Either gas or electric, but you will be glad to have the maximum size your kitchen will accommodate — there never seems to be enough refrigerated storage space or freezing space, and ice plays a large part in cooking. The freezing compartment should be big enough (particularly if you do not have a separate freezer) to accommodate a large tray or mold when you are working with cold-set dishes and puff pastry.

Freezer

A separate freezer unit, with shelves, is ideal in a kitchen. You can store so many basic materials (and reduce your marketing time to once a week or less), so many prepared materials (starting with your basic white stock and fish stock), and so many delicious dishes prepared partially or wholly in advance and frozen. Throughout this book you will find freezing used frequently in the preparation procedures. The freezing compartment of the refrigerator will do, but a separate freezer is a joy.

Work Surface and Other Fittings

Your work surface, whether a table or counter top, is your "drawing board" or your "desk." Properly equipped, it is an extension of you. It should be large, with shelves and a drawer within reach. Part of the surface should be made of hardwood, so that it can be used as a chopping block, and part of marble, which is the best surface for preparing pastry doughs. A magnetic bar for knives can be attached to the side, and a few hooks for hanging whisks, rotary beater, cleavers, etc. If possible, have the work surface the proper height for the person most frequently using it.

The electric mixer and scales can be on the work surface if it is large enough and strongly supported.

I always recommend having one wall of the kitchen covered with pegboard for hanging saucepans, molds, wire baskets, or any other kitchen utensils — proper kitchen equipment and utensils are a joy to look at.

Open shelves for storage are best for keeping track of what staples are on hand.

You'll want an electric mixer with two bowls, a rotary whisk that skims the sides and bottom of the bowl when it beats (some beaters reach only the middle of the mixture, and a pastry arm, meat chopper, and juicer attachments. You'll also want an electric blender, a set of scales with dram weights and one with ounce and pound weights, and a pasta machine.

Wooden Equipment

1 thick large chopping board
1 thinner chopping board, exclusively for fish
1 meat and poultry carving board
1 large salad bowl (or glass or porcelain)
1 small chopping bowl and mincer knife
2 small, 2 medium, and 2 large wooden spoons (boxwood or beech-wood)
2 medium-size flat wooden spatulas (boxwood or beechwood)
1 large wooden mallet
1 pair wooden salad spoons

Knives and Spatulas

All knives should be steel, not stainless steel.
2 small paring knives
1 medium-size and 1 large chopping knife
1 small saw knife (serrated edge), for tomatoes
1 medium-size thin-bladed knife, for filleting fish and kitchen carving
1 carborundum rod (for sharpening knives)
1 fish slice
1 large spatula
1 wide medium-size spatula
1 very small spatula
6 rubber scrapers

Small Equipment

1 ice pick
2 large metal kitchen serving spoons
1 large slotted kitchen spoon
1 carving fork
1 steel fork
1 large and 2 small larding needles
2 sets measuring spoons
6 tablespoons
6 teaspoons
2 regular-size forks
3 wire mesh strainers — large, medium, small

1 medium-size conical strainer (passoire chinois)
1 food mill (moulin à légumes) with coarse, medium, and fine sieves
1 mandoline (for thin-slicing)
1 flour sifter
1 sugar sifter
2 sifter cups
1 baster
1 rotary whisk
1 small and 1 medium-size wire whisk
1 large piano-wire whisk
1 pair kitchen shears
1 pair medium-size scissors
1 large pair meat tongs
3 metal bowls — large, medium, small
1 large and 1 medium melon baller
1 potato parer
1 corkscrew
1 bottle opener
4 metal skewers
1 china pestle and mortar, medium size
1 meat cleaver
1 colander
1 cheese grater
1 nutmeg grater
1 can opener
1 candy thermometer
1 deep-fat frying thermometer
2 pepper mills (one for white peppercorns and one for black)
1 soup ladle
1 skimmer
1 timer

Pots and Pans

2 small tin-lined copper pans (4 ounces and 8 ounces), for heating brandy or wine
1 copper (or heavy enamel) butter pan (1-cup size)
4 tin-lined copper saucepans (1 quart, 2 quarts, 2½ quarts, 3½ quarts) with covers
1 whistling teakettle
1 unlined copper pan, for sugar syrup and caramel
2 copper sauté pans (medium-size and large) with covers
1 copper mixing bowl, 12-inch diameter
1 omelet pan*
3 heavy aluminum frying pans (7½, 10½, 12½ inches across the top)

*My preferred omelet pan is 7 inches across the bottom, 10½ inches across the top, and is made of heavy (¼ inch) aluminum, with a 9-inch heat-resistant handle. May I suggest that your omelet pan be kept in the most unlikely spot in the kitchen, with a clear label saying: To be used only for omelets or pancakes ON PAIN OF THE GALLOWS.

4 French or Belgian heavy enamel-coated dutch ovens (2 quarts and
  4 quarts, round; 4 quarts and 6 quarts, oval)
1 aluminum vegetable steamer
1 fish kettle, at least 24 inches long
2 roasting pans (medium and large) with racks
1 large stockpot (marmite) with cover (12 quarts)
4 heavy aluminum saucepans (4½ quarts, 2¾ quarts, and two 1½
  quarts) with covers
1 deep fryer with basket

Molds and Baking Pans

2 jelly roll pans, 11 by 17 inches
2 large baking sheets
4 loaf pans (two 10-inch, two 6-inch)
2 springform pans (9-inch and 10-inch) 3 inches high
2 layer cake pans (8-inch diameter)
1 kugelhopf mold
12 madeleine molds
3 flan rings (8, 9, and 10 inches in diameter)
1 charlotte mold
2 pie tins (8 and 10 inches)
1 set of tiny cutters (for garnishes)
2 sets cookie cutters (one set round, one fluted)
12 3-inch tartlet tins
36 1-inch tartlet tins
1 fish mold
1 oblong pâté form (12 inches long)
2 ring molds (8-inch and 9½-inch diameter)

China, Earthenware, and Glass

1 series of earthenware mixing bowls
2 series of measuring cups (quart, pint, cup)
2 oval heatproof glass or earthenware baking dishes (one small and
  one large)
3 earthenware casseroles (large, medium, small)
2 screw-top glass jars (quart and pint)
1 double boiler (heat resistant glass preferred, especially for poaching
  eggs); for a bain-marie (water bath), see page 000.
6 onion soup pots
4 soufflé dishes (3 cups, #5; 1 quart, #6; 1½ quarts, #7; 2 quarts,
  #8)
6 3¼-inch ramekins
8 white or brown china custard cups (for pots de crème or chocolate
  mousse)
1 cone-type drip coffee-maker and filter papers
1 series heavy glass mixing bowls
12 ovenproof glass custard cups (6 small, 6 medium)
6 large ovenproof glass custard dishes

1 large glass or porcelain salad bowl

Pastry Equipment

3 plastic-lined canvas pastry bags (16-inch)
Assortment of plain round pastry tubes
Assortment of star pastry tubes
Baba and dariole molds, cream horns, large and small brioche molds
1 French rolling pin
3 wire cake racks (1 large, 2 small)
1 long chocolate roll board
2 1-inch and 2 2-inch pastry brushes (I prefer good-quality paint-brushes with natural bristles

Serving Platters

2 flat earthenware platters (10-inch and 12-inch)
2 earthenware or copper casseroles (2 quarts and 4 quarts) with covers
1 14-inch oval copper au gratin or heatproof glass platter
1 10-inch oval flat copper au gratin
2 round copper au gratins or earthenware serving dishes (8-inch and 10½-inch)
2 12-inch flat platters, for cakes, tarts, or molded desserts

Miscellaneous Equipment

2 balls of string (cotton string and butcher's cord)
12 thick dishcloths
24 good-quality drying cloths
Large packet of cheesecloth
Wax paper, aluminum foil, plastic wrap, paper towels
Steel wool
Steel wool soap pads
1 wire salad basket or a salad dryer
2 sizes of plastic storage bags
1 foot-opening garbage receptacle with supply of plastic garbage bags
I bucket
Mild liquid soap
Strong liquid cleaner
Liquid bleach
Various sizes of storage containers for the refrigerator and freezer
2 stiff-bristle brushes (for scrubbing mussels, etc.)

Dry Foods Storage Cabinet

5 pounds all-purpose flour
5 pounds granulated sugar (keep both flour and sugar in large labeled canisters)

1 pint jar potato flour
1 quart jar superfine sugar
1 quart jar confectioners sugar
1 quart jar salt (Kosher salt is preferred)
1 pint jar light brown sugar
1 pint jar dark brown sugar
1 quart jar long-grain converted rice
1 quart jar Carolina rice
1 pound jar blanched whole almonds
1 pint jar shelled walnuts
1 pint jar dry breadcrumbs (page 69)
1 pint jar dry white breadcrumbs (page 69)
2 cans Italian tomato paste
4 2-ounce jars beef extract (meat glaze)
1 package cake flour (without baking powder)
1 small can baking powder
1 small package baking soda
1 package cream of farina
1 can dry mustard
1 small packet rock salt
1 jar black peppercorns
1 jar white peppercorns
1 small jar cayenne pepper
1 jar ground cardamom seed
1 jar ground cinnamon
1 jar cinnamon sticks
1 jar whole allspice
1 jar whole cloves
1 jar whole nutmeg
1 jar bay leaves
1 jar paprika
1 jar dried thyme
1 jar rosemary leaves
1 jar leaf saffron
2 vanilla beans
1 package dried mushrooms
1 pint jar seeded black raisins
1 pint jar dried currants
1 pint jar seedless white raisins
1 small jar instant coffee
1 box of envelopes of unflavored gelatine
1 jar (1 or 2 quarts) good vegetable oil
1 bottle vanilla extract
1 quart jar tarragon vinegar (preferably homemade, page 74)
1 quart jar good red wine vinegar (preferably homemade, page 74)
1 12-ounce jar red currant jelly
1 12-ounce jar apricot jam
1 12-ounce jar grape jelly
1 12-ounce jar seedless black raspberry jam

At all times one should find in the refrigerator:

1 dozen large fresh eggs
1 pound sweet butter (in freezer compartment)
1 pound salt butter
1 pint sealed container of clarified butter
1 quart milk
1 pint light cream
½ pint heavy cream
1 pint jar mayonnaise (homemade, pages 52-53)
1 pint jar vinaigrette dressing (pages 62-63)
6 hard-boiled eggs
1 pound sliced bacon (in freezer compartment)
1 large screw-top bottle of water for drinking
1 quart bottle pure olive oil
1 pound regular-grind coffee
Vegetables, properly cleaned and wrapped
Fruit, properly cleaned and wrapped
Ample supply of ice cubes
Cheeses
Dijon mustard
1 pint jar freshly grated Parmesan cheese

Bain-marie (Water Bath)

In professional parlance, a water bath is called bain-marie. It is a container half filled with hot water into which another container with food is set for the purpose of controlled gentle heat. One use of a water bath is to keep foods hot without further cooking. The container of food is placed in the water bath, which is kept hot over very low heat or a pilot light. A water bath is also used to cook certain delicate dishes which would disintegrate, dry out, or separate if cooked over direct heat. One example is an egg-base sauce such as Hollandaise, Béarnaise, or Sabayon. Use a shallow frypan or sauté pan; half fill it with hot water; set it over low heat, and stand the bowl in which the sauce is to be made in the water bath. (A double boiler could also be used for this purpose.)

Similarly, soufflés, pâtés, mousses, and custards are cooked in a water bath in the oven. Use a roasting pan, half fill it with hot water, set the food dish (or dishes) in the bath, and put the whole assembly in the oven.

WEIGHTS AND MEASURES CONVERSION TABLE

INGREDIENT	WEIGHT		MEASURE*	
	Ounces	Pounds	Tablespoons	Cups
Butter	1		2	
Sugar	1		1	
Flour	1		2	
Flour	1		2	
Gelatine	¼		1 envelope†	
Dried yeast	¼		1 envelope	
Jam or jelly	1		1	
Fresh breadcrumbs	2			1
Parmesan cheese, grated	4			1
Mixed nuts, chopped	5			1
Candied peel	5			1
Seedless raisins	5¾			1
Currants	5			1
Chocolate pieces	6			1
Candied fruit	7			1
Soft brown sugar	7			1 (packed)
Butter	8			1
Lard	8			1
Dry breadcrumbs		1		4
Coffee (unground)		1		2½
Lentils, split peas, dried beans		1		2
Rice		1		2¼ to 2½
Brown (moist) sugar		1		2¼ (packed)
Confectioners sugar, sifted		1		3½
Granulated sugar		1		2¼
Flour (sifted)		1		4
Butter or other fat		1		2

*3 teaspoons = 1 tablespoon   2 pints = 1 quart
 4 tablespoons = ¼ cup   †1 envelope = ¾ tablespoon
 2 cups = 1 pint

OVEN TEMPERATURE
(Fahrenheit)

Very slow or very cool or warm	200°-250°
Slow or cool	250°-300°
Very moderate	300°-350°
Moderate	350°-375°
Moderately hot to hot	375°-400°
Hot to very hot	425°-450°
Very hot	450°-500°

STOCK, SAUCES, AND
BASIC COOKING AGENTS

A NYONE WHO IS GOING TO DO any real cooking must make a batch of chicken stock and a batch of fish stock, and freeze it, and have it on hand to use" (Dione Lucas, ad infinitum).

For the home kitchen, I believe, far too much emphasis is placed on specific definitions of the various types and permutations of sauces. Rather than such memorizing, let us learn the basic principles of French cuisine to guide our understanding and appreciation so that its contributions can be applied (but not necessarily copied) to serve our needs, with our resources.

Stocks unquestionably are the foundation (the French "fond") of provincial and haute cuisines in French gastronomic culture, but one cannot expect any home to keep on hand the variety of chicken, veal, beef, game and fish stocks used in professional kitchens. My philosophy is to adapt the goodness of French cuisine to the home kitchen. I have formulated a "universal" chicken stock (page 35), really a chicken-veal stock, for use whenever any poultry or meat stock is required. This has always been my method in teaching as well as in my restaurant operations, and presumably the results have been acceptable. I have never used a commercial stock base or consommé, nor is it condoned. In this day and age we are looking for ways to save time and yet enjoy natural living; the fundamental chicken-veal stock is one good solution.

For the American home, like the French home, the dish that produces the best-flavored stock is Pot-au-Feu (pot on the fire) — chicken, beef, and vegetables slowly cooked in lots of water with a bouquet garni. There is more than enough stock for the Pot-au-Feu meal, and the excess may be frozen and used for sauces and other soups. Or a simple stockpot (page 35) is no trouble while you attend to other matters, even go to a movie, as it gently smiles over very low heat and its aroma fills the house with the meaning of home. When the infusion of the ingredients into the water is complete, quickly strain the stock, cool, and pour it into plastic containers. Freeze and use it as needed. The bonus is a cup of hot broth to sip when you feel like it.

With frozen chicken stock or fish stock on hand, the whole spectrum of sauces is easy. In my classes the basic brown sauce, Bordelaise sauce, chicken and fish velouté sauces were emphasized. From these many, many specialty sauces develop. The recipes in this book demonstrate how a simple good sauce may vary from dish to dish, picking up the character of each one. This is why, in this book, most recipes using sauces described in the Sauces chapter have their own versions of the sauces rather than cross-references. You can experience this creativity by knowing the basic sauce form and adapting it to the personality of the dish you are preparing.

No cuisine has glorified fish and shellfish more than the French, and half the glory must go to the fish sauces these people have developed from fish stock. Fish markets will actually give you fish heads and bones, which make the best fish stock (page 36). Dry white wine is the chief liquid of fish stock (or a good share of it). The marriage is amazing. Freeze fish stock, too, and in minutes you can have an exquisite white wine sauce for the first delicate bay scallops of the season.

The French culinary repertoire also gives us the fabulous family of egg-base sauces — Sauce Hollandaise, Mousseline, Béarnaise, the mayonnaises, Rémoulade, and the dessert Sabayon — and all those in between. If you follow carefully the recipes for these gentle, delicate sauces, they will not curdle. They must be prepared quickly — you can make an elegant sauce for steak, such as Sauce Béarnaise, in less time and with less expense than if you use the canned variety.

Mayonnaise is the great commercial hi-jink on the American public — a sauce so easily, quickly, and economically prepared at home, and with much more quality. Please, I urge everyone who has never tried my recipe, prepare Mayonnaise I or II just once! If you have a large enough vessel, in five minutes you can make enough mayonnaise to last you all summer. Keep it in the refrigerator. When you wish to use it, thin it with cream or milk. (Never add cream or milk when it is just made except to thin it for immediate use.)

The divine butters are classed as sauces. I hope you will read my notes on salt and sweet butter (page 56); they are so important in cooking. Then on to the compound butters — exquisite White Butter Sauce, classic Beurre à la Meunière for fresh fish, perky Bercy Butter, which can be frozen and is another instant elegant touch to your steaks.

The classic vinaigrettes are in this chapter, and the piquant Sauce Mignonnette for oysters and clams. In oyster country along the west coast of France oysters are usually served with Sauce Mignonnette, a couple of broiled baby sausages on the side, and thin slices of dark bread spread with sweet butter. If you are in Brittany, you will enjoy with them a well-chilled glass of Muscadet; if you are farther down the coast around Bordeaux, a fine bottle of chilled Graves.

Dessert sauces are dangerous; they are so good that left in the refrigerator, they risk being sampled out of business before the meal is presented. Besides the classic egg and fruit sauces, my Sour Cream Sauce (Sauce Smitane) and Fruit Syrup Sauce seemed to be permanent hits with my classes and restaurant patrons.

Other basic cooking agents in French culinary practice appear in this chapter. (English terms for them are used unless the French has been adopted into English, like "au gratin" or "panade.") It is important to know any recipe author's attitude about the most basic ingredients, like salt and pepper, even scalded milk.

Here are a few important notes about sauces:

(1) Never drown an individual serving in sauce. What is wanted is a subtle emphasis to enhance the main ingredient of the dish. Better to spoon a little sauce on the side of a serving of fish, meat, or poultry, or just a "ribbon" across the top.

(2) Most sauces with a brown stock base will keep for weeks in the refrigerator in a tightly covered container. Once you've made a batch, save the rest, and use a spoonful with an omelet, or escalopes de veau, etc.

(3) Mayonnaises, vinaigrettes, and fruit sauces will also keep for weeks. (You can build an inventory of leftover sauces in the refrigerator, and your family will be convinced you are Merlin the magician when you whip out the homemade mayonnaise, or spoon luscious fruit syrup over grapefruit and orange sections.)

BASIC STOCKS AND SEASONING AGENTS

BOUQUET GARNI

Bouquet of Herbs

As a general rule, a bouquet garni is made with one or two aromatic herbs and two basic herbs like parsley or bay leaf. An all-purpose bouquet could be made of a bay leaf, 2 pieces celery leaf, 2 sprigs parsley, and 1 sprig thyme (or tarragon or dill, according to the purpose of the herbs). Tie them all together with a long string so they can be quickly and easily removed before the dish has finished cooking. In a stockpot they are usually tied in a piece of cheesecloth.

Certain aromatic herbs relate best to specific foods: thyme for meats, tarragon for chicken and poultry, dill for fish, basil for tomatoes and fish, oregano with all the hot spicy sausages. There are obviously other combinations and uses, but these are the basic ones.

Try to use fresh herbs rather than dried, and if you are using dried cut down a little on the quantity. Dried herbs should be wrapped up in a little muslin bag.

FONDS BLANC DE VOLAILLE

White Chicken Stock

This is the basic chicken stock called for in the recipes in this book. With the veal knuckle, it is a good all-purpose stock. It is the stock base for all brown sauce and white sauce recipes that require stock. This stock can be made periodically, put in plastic containers, and frozen until needed.

2 pounds chicken wings, backs, and/or raw chicken bones

1 knuckle of veal, cracked
4 quarts cold water

2 small carrots, sliced
2 yellow onions, sliced
2 leeks, sliced
1 stalk celery, cut in 2-inch pieces
1 whole clove stuck into 1 small
    white onion
Bouquet garni (1 large bay

leaf, 2 sprigs parsley, 3 pieces
celery leaf, 2 sprigs fresh
tarragon or thyme, if
available)
1 tablespoon salt
12 white peppercorns

Put the chicken pieces and/or bones into a large stockpot (7 to 8 quart size) with the veal knuckle. Cover with the water and bring slowly to a boil. Reduce to a simmer and carefully remove all the scum. Add the carrots, onions, leeks, celery, clove-and-onion, bouquet garni (tied in cheesecloth), salt and peppercorns. Simmer very gently 2½ hours (not a bubbling boil; the surface should just "smile"). Strain the stock through a strainer or a colander which has been lined with a wet kitchen towel, pour into containers, cool, and put in the freezer. When it is thoroughly chilled, remove any fat solidified on the top. This delicious stock is ready for use or may be stored in the freezer. NET: 3 to 4 quarts.

COURT BOUILLON

Poaching Liquid for Fish and Shellfish

1 carrot, thinly sliced
2 yellow onions, thinly sliced
2 tablespoons salt butter
½ cup dry sherry
4 cups water
1 cup dry white wine

1 teaspoon salt
6 white peppercorns
Bouquet garni (bay leaf, 2 or 3
    sprigs parsley, celery leaf, dill
    or tarragon if you like)

Cook the carrots and onions in the butter without browning. Add the other ingredients and bring to a boil. Cool the court bouillon a bit before poaching fish in it (see Fish chapter). NET: 1 quart.

FUMET DE POISSON

Fish Stock

This recipe makes a lovely concentrated stock to use as the base for fish and seafood sauces. It may be stored and frozen in covered plastic containers.

2 pounds fish bones (sole, bass
    or scrod; never use salmon
    or red fish)
2 tablespoons salt butter
Approximately ½ pound
    mushroom peelings and stems,
    coarsely chopped
2 teaspoons salt
A little freshly grated nutmeg
2 teaspoons lemon juice
1 small white onion, chopped

2 stalks celery, sliced
1 small carrot, sliced
1½ cups dry white wine
4 cups water
Bouquet garni (bay leaf,
    2 celery leaves, 2 sprigs
    parsley and, if you like, 2
    sprigs fresh dill)
6 white peppercorns, freshly
    cracked

Melt the butter in a heavy sauté pan. Add the mushroom peelings and stalks. Sprinkle with a little of the salt and the nutmeg and lemon juice. Sauté briskly 2 to 3 minutes, then stir in the onion, carrot, celery, wine, and water. Add the fish bones and bring slowly to a boil. Add the bouquet garni, the rest of the salt, and the cracked peppercorns. Simmer 30 to 45 minutes. Pour the stock through a fine strainer and cool it. NET: 1 quart.

This is the basic aspic. For a lighter aspic, use a lighter chicken stock (made without a veal knuckle). For a fish aspic, use fish stock.

2 tablespoons unflavored
  gelatine
4 cups chicken stock
1 tablespoon tomato paste

¼ cup dry white wine
3 egg whites, beaten to
  soft peaks

Combine all the ingredients in a 3 to 4 quart tin-lined copper or heavy enamel pan. Beat with a whisk over slow heat until the mixture comes to a rolling boil. Remove from the heat and let it stand absolutely still for 15 minutes. Slowly pour through a strainer that has been lined with a wet kitchen towel. Store in the refrigerator. Aspic must not be frozen (it will cloud).

For a firmer aspic, increase the gelatine. The amount depends on how much the stock has jellied while chilling and before being clarified for aspic. NET: 2¾ cups.

CHOPPED ASPIC. Pour the aspic into a layer cake pan and let it set. Turn it out of the pan onto wax paper and chop it into fine dice.

Meat glaze is made from boiled-down pan juices from a roast (chicken, veal, beef, etc.). There are very good commercial meat glazes (sometimes marketed as beef extract).

SAUCES

When you want to serve a fine roast of beef, chicken, veal, etc., with its pan juices, begin by putting the basic basting liquids, such as wine, stock, or water, in the roasting pan and baste with the frequency directed in the recipe. Before each basting add a small quantity of the same liquid, swirl it in the pan to lift the glaze, and then baste. When your roast is done, you will have a beautiful gravy.

Strain the gravy through a fine strainer, put it into another pan, and beat vigorously with a little wire whisk to incorporate any fat there may be. This fat then functions as the thickener in the gravy. If there is too much fat, either skim it off with a spoon or throw in a lump of ice.

SAUCE BRUNE OR SAUCE ESPAGNOLE

With the addition of 1 cup whipped cream, stirred in spoonful by spoonful, this sauce can be used in a famous pheasant dish (Faisan Vallée d'Auge). It can also be used with 1 cup sour cream for Filet de Boeuf Orloff.

Basic Brown Sauce

2 tablespoons pure olive oil
4 tablespoons salt butter
1 onion, sliced
2 stalks celery, sliced
1 carrot, sliced
Handful of mushroom
    trimmings and stems
3 tablespoons all-purpose flour
1 tomato with skin on, sliced

2 teaspoons tomato paste
1 teaspoon meat glaze
1½ cups chicken stock
    (page 35)
¼ cup dry sherry
1 teaspoon red currant jelly
Salt (if needed)
Freshly cracked white pepper
1 small bay leaf

Melt the oil and butter in a pan. Add the onion, carrot, and celery. Brown slowly. Add the mushroom stems and trimmings. Cook a little longer. Add the flour and brown very slowly, stirring occasionally. Stir in the tomato, tomato paste, meat glaze, stock, dry sherry, and currant jelly. Season with salt and pepper and bring to a boil. Add the bay leaf and simmer very gently 45 minutes. Put through the blender or a very fine strainer. NET: 1½ cups.

DEMI-GLACE

Rich Brown Sauce

4 chicken livers
2 tablespoons salt butter
1 teaspoon finely chopped garlic
3 tablespoons Cognac or
    good brandy
1 teaspoon tomato paste
1 teaspoon meat glaze
3 teaspoons potato flour
1⅓ cups chicken stock
    (page 35)

¼ cup Marsala wine
1 teaspoon guava or red currant
    jelly
A little white pepper, freshly
    cracked
2 marrowbones
1 cup dry white wine
1 bay leaf
1 small piece of celery with leaf
A few peppercorns

Brown the chicken livers in 1 tablespoon very hot butter. Add the garlic. Heat the brandy in a small copper pan. Flame, and carefully pour it over the chicken livers. Remove the livers, and add 1 tablespoon butter to the pan. Stir in, off the heat, the tomato paste, meat glaze, and potato flour. When smooth, mix in the chicken stock, Marsala, jelly, and white pepper (no salt). Stir over the fire until it comes to a boil. Put back the whole chicken livers. Heat another pan, dry. Brown the marrowbones in it quickly on each end. Add the white wine, bay leaf, celery leaf, and peppercorns. Bring to a boil. Add all this mixture to the first sauce. Boil down to a nice, fairly thick sauce. Strain. Remove the marrow from the bones, crush, and add to the sauce. Slice and add the chicken livers. NET: 2 cups.

This rich brown sauce is made with marrow and red wine.

2 chicken livers
1 teaspoon and 1 tablespoon
   salt butter
2 tablespoons Cognac or good
   brandy
1 teaspoon tomato paste
1 teaspoon meat glaze
2 teaspoons potato flour
¼ cup dry sherry
1¼ cups chicken stock

    (page 35)
1 teaspoon red currant jelly
Freshly cracked white pepper
2 marrowbones
1 cup dry red wine
1 bay leaf
1 small piece celery
1 bruised clove garlic
1 or 2 black peppercorns

Brown the chicken livers in 1 teaspoon hot butter. In a separate little pan, heat the brandy, ignite and pour it over the livers. Remove them and add 1 tablespoon butter to the pan. Stir in, off the heat, the tomato paste, meat glaze, potato flour, sherry, chicken stock, jelly, and a little white pepper. Stir over the heat until it comes to a boil, and put back the chicken livers. Heat another pan, dry. Quickly brown the marrowbones, then add the red wine, bay leaf, celery, garlic, and peppercorns. Bring to a boil, stir into the first pan, and boil the combined mixture down to a creamy consistency. Strain. Chop the livers and add to the sauce. Remove the marrow from the bones, crush, and stir into the sauce. NET: 2 cups.

A piquant sauce to be served with game. If you happen to have a game bird carcass, like pheasant or grouse, put that in also, and cook it in the sauce.

Pepper Sauce

8 tablespoons salt butter
2 chicken livers
⅓ cup Madeira
1 teaspoon meat glaze
1 teaspoon tomato paste
3 teaspoons potato flour
2 cups chicken stock
   (page 35)
¼ cup finely chopped celery
¼ teaspoon finely chopped
   garlic

¼ cup tarragon vinegar
¼ cup dry red wine
Bouquet garni (bay leaf and
   1 sprig each of thyme and
   parsley)
1 carrot, sliced
1 onion, sliced
¼ cup Cognac or good brandy
10 mixed black and white
   peppercorns
1 teaspoon red currant jelly

Heat a small heavy pan dry, then add 1 teaspoon butter. Place the chicken livers in the pan without touching each other and brown quickly on each side. In a separate little pan heat the Madeira, light it and pour it flaming over the chicken livers. Remove the livers and add 1 tablespoon butter to the pan. Stir in, off the heat, the meat glaze, tomato paste, and potato flour. Stir in the chicken stock, celery, and garlic. Stir gently over low heat until it comes to a boil. Return the chicken livers to the sauce and add the tarragon vinegar, red wine, bouquet of herbs, carrot and onion, brandy, black and white peppercorns, and the game bird carcass, if you have one. Simmer all together gently 45 minutes. Strain through a fine strainer. Return the strained sauce to the pan and stir in, bit by bit, the rest of the butter and the red currant jelly. NET: 2½ cups.

SAUCE AU MADÈRE

Madeira Sauce

This marvelously rich brown sauce may be used with steaks, roasts, and leftover meats of any kind.

8 tablespoons salt butter
2 chicken livers
⅓ cup Madeira
1 teaspoon meat glaze
1 teaspoon tomato paste
3 teaspoons potato flour

2 cups chicken stock
   (page 35)
¼ cup finely chopped celery
¼ teaspoon finely chopped
   garlic
1 teaspoon red currant jelly

Heat a small heavy pan dry, then add 1 teaspoon butter. Place the chicken livers in the pan without touching each other and brown quickly on each side. In a separate little pan, heat the Madeira, ignite, and pour it flaming over the chicken livers. Remove the livers and add 1 tablespoon butter to the pan. Stir in, off the heat, the meat glaze, tomato paste, and potato flour. Stir in the chicken stock, celery, and garlic. Return the pan to low heat and stir gently until it comes to a boil. Return the chicken livers to the sauce. Simmer gently 45 minutes. Strain through a fine strainer. Return the sauce to the pan and stir in, bit by bit, the rest of the butter and the red currant jelly. NET: 2 cups.

SAUCE PÉRIGUEUX

Madeira Sauce with Chopped Truffle

2 teaspoons salt butter
4 chicken livers
1 cup Madeira
2 tablespoons tomato paste
1 teaspoon meat glaze
4 teaspoons potato flour
4 cups chicken stock
   (page 35)

1 bay leaf
2 sprigs celery leaf
6 peppercorns
1 teaspoon salt
1 teaspoon red currant jelly
1 calf's foot
1 finely chopped black truffle

Heat the butter in a small heavy pan. Quickly brown the chicken livers on each side and remove from the pan. Add 2 tablespoons Madeira to the pan and stir in, off the heat, the tomato paste, meat glaze, and potato flour. Mix in the stock and stir the sauce over low heat until it comes to a boil, then add the rest of the Madeira, and the bay leaf, celery, peppercorns, salt, currant jelly, and calf's foot. Return the chicken livers to the sauce. Simmer very gently 1½ hours. Strain through a fine strainer. Add the chopped truffle to the strained sauce. The chicken livers also may be chopped and added to the sauce; otherwise they can be used for an omelet filling. NET: 1 quart.

There are a variety of piquant sauces. You can add capers, or chopped black olives, or finely diced fresh pineapple.

2 cups thin Bordelaise Sauce
   (made with half the normal
   quantity of potato flour,
   page 39)
½ cup tarragon vinegar

1 tablespoon sugar
1 tablespoon honey
1 teaspoon red currant jelly
¼ cup Madeira

Prepare the thin Bordelaise sauce. In a separate pan, boil down the vinegar, sugar, and honey to one-half. Add this mixture to the Bordelaise sauce with the currant jelly and Madeira. NET: 1½ cups.

A jellied brown sauce for coating cold dishes.

4 tablespoons vegetable oil
1 cup combined sliced onion,
   carrot, and celery
4 tablespoons all-purpose flour
1 tomato, sliced
A few mushroom stems or caps
2 teaspoons meat glaze
1 tablespoon red currant jelly

2 teaspoons tomato paste
2 cups chicken stock
   (page 35)
½ cup dry sherry
2 tablespoons Cognac or good
   brandy
1 tablespoon unflavored gelatine

Heat the vegetable oil in a small deep pan. Add the sliced onion, carrot, and celery, and cook very slowly until they are soft but not brown. Add the flour and continue to cook slowly until the flour is dark brown. Remove the pan from the heat and stir in the sliced tomato, mushroom stems or caps, meat glaze, jelly, and tomato paste. Pour on the chicken stock, dry sherry, and brandy. Return the pan to low heat and stir until it comes to a boil. Simmer the sauce very gently about 10 to 12 minutes. Rub it through a strainer. Dissolve the gelatine in about 2 tablespoons of the sauce, then mix it back into the rest of the sauce. The sauce is now ready for coating. Coat immediately. If the mixture sets in the pan, reheat, and proceed to coat again. NET: 2½ cups.

MUSTARD CREAM SAUCE

This sauce is a simple pan glaze to which heavy cream, shallots, and mustard are added to give it a unique character. It adds a piquancy to calf's liver or kidneys, chicken livers, or lamb kidneys. (See the recipe for Foie de Veau à la Moutarde, page 509.)

2 tablespoons salt butter
1 teaspoon tomato paste
1 teaspoon meat glaze
2½ cups heavy cream
2 teaspoons finely chopped shallots
1 teaspoon finely chopped garlic

1 egg yolk
½ teaspoon potato flour
1 teaspoon dry mustard
2 teaspoons Dijon mustard
2 tablespoons light cream
1 tablespoon chopped fresh tarragon (optional)

Melt the butter in a sauté pan. Add the tomato paste and meat glaze, and mix well. Very slowly, over low heat, stir in the heavy cream. When it all has been blended, add the chopped shallots and garlic. In a small bowl, mix the egg yolk with the potato flour, dry mustard, Dijon mustard, and light cream. Remove the sauce from the heat and stir this mixture into it. Add the chopped tarragon. Gently reheat the sauce, but do not allow it to boil. NET: 2½ cups.

SAUCE BÉCHAMEL

Cream Sauce

This basic sauce should not be made too far ahead of the time you plan to use it.

4 tablespoons salt butter
4 tablespoons all-purpose flour
1 teaspoon salt

A few grains cayenne pepper
1 cup milk
3 tablespoons heavy cream

Melt the butter in a small heavy pan. Add the flour (off the heat). Stir over very low heat and cook a little, without covering the pan and taking great care not to brown the flour. Remove from the heat again and stir in the milk, salt, and pepper. Over low heat, stir the sauce until it comes to a boil and simmer gently 2 to 3 minutes. Mix in the heavy cream. Strain the sauce through a fine strainer. Cover tightly with a piece of plastic wrap until ready to use. NET: 1½ cups.

SAUCE MORNAY

Cheese Sauce

This is a basic cream sauce (Béchamel) with cheese added.

6 tablespoons salt butter
6 tablespoons all-purpose flour
2 teaspoons Dijon mustard
1 teaspoon dry mustard
½ teaspoon salt
A few grains cayenne pepper
2 cups milk
1 small sprig celery leaf

1 bay leaf
⅓ cup freshly grated Parmesan cheese
⅓ cup freshly grated imported Swiss cheese
⅓ cup light cream
2 tablespoons sweet butter

Melt the salt butter in a small heavy pan. Off the heat, stir in the flour. Mix in the Dijon mustard, dry mustard, salt, and cayenne pepper. Stir in the milk, and add the celery leaf and bay leaf. Return the pan to low heat and bring the mixture to a boil. Instantly remove the bay leaf and celery leaf. Stir in the cheeses and light cream, and simmer 5 minutes. Add the sweet butter bit by bit, stirring constantly. NET: 1½ cups.

This is a basic cream sauce (Béchamel) with onion purée added. For a richer sauce, stir in, bit by bit, 2 teaspoons sweet butter.

SAUCE SOUBISE

Onion Sauce

4 large Bermuda onions
1½ cups milk
4 tablespoons salt butter
4 tablespoons all-purpose flour
1 teaspoon salt

⅛ teaspoon cayenne pepper
3 tablespoons heavy cream
⅛ teaspoon freshly grated
   nutmeg

Peel the onions, cut into slices, and simmer them gently in the milk until soft. Then purée the mixture in a blender. Melt the butter in a small heavy pan. Off the heat, stir in the flour. Return the pan to low heat and cook the mixture gently 2 to 3 minutes without browning the flour. Add (off the heat) the salt and pepper, then the onion purée. Bring to a boil and simmer 2 to 3 minutes. Strain the sauce and stir in the heavy cream and nutmeg. NET: 2 cups.

This is the basic Chicken Velouté Sauce used in many poultry and meat dishes in French cuisine. In most of my recipes for dishes traditionally accompanied by a velouté, the sauce is further enriched with cream, butter, and/or egg yolk (usually the full sauce recipe is given with the recipe for the dish). In classic cookery definitions, a velouté with heavy cream and sweet butter added is called a Sauce Suprême; a velouté with egg yolk added is a Sauce Allemande. In the general term, they are both veloutés; this basic velouté is the "mother sauce." If it is made ahead of time, cover the pan with plastic wrap and stir the sauce from time to time with a small wire whisk to avoid a skin forming on top.

*VELOUTÉ
DE VOLAILLE*

Chicken Velouté

6 tablespoons sweet butter
6 tablespoons all-purpose flour
Salt

A few grains cayenne pepper
2 cups chicken stock
   (page 35)

Melt the butter in a small tin-lined copper pan, but do not allow it to brown. Off the heat, stir in the flour. Add a very little salt and cayenne pepper. Stir the mixture over low heat until it becomes frothy without browning (about 2 minutes). Remove the pan from the heat and stir in the chicken stock. Return the pan to moderate heat, bring the sauce to a boil, and allow it to simmer very slowly 10 minutes. It will be thick enough to coat. NET: 1½ cups.

SAUCE CHAUD-FROID BLONDE

White Chaud-Froid Sauce

A jellied white sauce for coating cold dishes — chicken, fish, or eggs.

2 tablespoons vegetable oil
6 tablespoons water
3 tablespoons all-purpose flour
1 tablespoon unflavored gelatine

⅛ teaspoon cayenne pepper
1 teaspoon salt
1¼ cups milk
2 tablespoons light cream

In a heavy pan, gently warm the oil and water together. In a separate bowl mix the flour, gelatine, salt, and cayenne pepper until completely blended, then stir the mixture into the warm oil and water. Carefully mix in the milk. Stir over low heat, bring to a boil, then remove the mixture from the heat. Put the pan over a bowl of ice and stir until it is at the point of setting. Mix in the light cream. The chaud-froid is now ready to use for coating. Use it immediately. If the mixture sets in the pan, reheat and proceed again as above. NET: 1½ cups.

VELOUTÉ SAUCE GRAND VÉFOUR

A very delicate, enriched velouté sauce, to use over chicken ballotine or mousse preparations.

8 tablespoons sweet butter
½ teaspoon very finely chopped garlic
2 finely chopped baby white onions
3 tablespoons all-purpose flour
2 tablespoons dry white wine
1 tablespoon dry sherry

1 cup chicken stock (page 35)
¼ cup light cream
2 egg yolks
1 tablespoon Cognac or good brandy
2 tablespoons heavy cream
4 tablespoons heavy cream, whipped

VELOUTÉ DE POISSON OR SAUCE VIN BLANC

In a mixer, cream the sweet butter until it is very light and fluffy. Add the garlic and onions. Beat well. Put the mixture into a heavy or tin-lined copper pan over moderate heat. Stir with a wooden spoon until the onion is a little soft but still a little crisp. Stir in, off the heat, the flour, white wine, sherry, and chicken stock. Stir over low heat until it thickens a little. Add the light cream, bring to a boil, and simmer 5 minutes. In a separate bowl, mix the egg yolks with the brandy and 2 tablespoons heavy cream. Pour the sauce onto the egg yolk mixture, beating all the time. Return the sauce to the pan and reheat it without boiling. Fold in the whipped cream. NET: 1½ cups.

Fish Velouté Sauce or White Wine Sauce

I have rarely prepared a fish stock without white wine. Therefore, in my recipes the terms Fish Velouté Sauce and White Wine Sauce are used interchangeably. They are both the same basic formula of fish stock made with white wine in the stock.

3 tablespoons salt butter	1¼ cups fish stock (page 36)
3 tablespoons all-purpose flour	⅓ cup light cream
Salt to taste	1 tablespoon sweet butter
A few grains cayenne pepper	

Melt the salt butter in a tin-lined copper pan. Stir in (off the heat) the flour. Season with salt and cayenne pepper, and stir in the strained fish stock. Stir over the fire until it thickens. Add the light cream, bring to a boil, and add the sweet butter bit by bit. Simmer gently about 5 minutes. NET: 1½ cups.

Shrimp butter (pulverized shrimps and/or shells and butter) can also be stirred into a Béchamel sauce for another variation. "Nantua" means with shrimp (or crayfish) purée.

1 pound fish bones, head, and skin	Salt
½ cup dry white wine	6 whole peppercorns, black and white
2 cups water	6 ounces raw shrimp
1 small onion, sliced	8 tablespoons sweet butter
2 stalks celery, sliced	3 tablespoons all-purpose flour
1 small carrot, sliced	A few grains cayenne pepper
Bouquet garni (2 sprigs parsley, 1 bay leaf, 1 sprig fresh dill if available)	¼ cup heavy cream
	½ teaspoon tomato paste

Put the fish skin, bones, head into a pan with the wine and the water, and bring very slowly to a boil. Skim off the scum. Add the sliced onion, carrot, and celery, the bouquet garni, ½ teaspoon salt, and peppercorns. Simmer very gently 45 minutes. Strain. Add the raw shrimps (with the shells on) and simmer gently until they blush. Strain, and set the shrimps aside. Melt 2 tablespoons butter in a tin-lined copper pan. Stir in (off the heat) the flour. Season with a little salt and cayenne pepper. Mix in about 1¼ cups of the strained fish stock. Stir over moderate heat until it comes to a boil. Reserve 4 whole shrimps. Slice the rest with their shells and put them in a blender. Add the tomato paste, the rest of the butter, and half the velouté sauce you have just made. Blend until absolutely smooth and rub through a fine strainer. Return the sauce with the shrimp to the rest of the sauce in the pan and stir over low heat till it comes to a boil. Add the heavy cream. Shell and devein the 4 whole shrimps, cut them into thin slices, and add to the sauce. NET: 1½ cups.

SAUCE NANTUA

Shrimp Sauce
(Velouté Base)

SAUCE CARDINAL

Sauce Cardinal, a pink lobster sauce with a velouté base, is made exactly the same way as Sauce Nantua, except that you use the shell and meat of a small cooked lobster in place of the shrimp shells and meat. Reserve about a third of the lobster meat for slicing into the finished sauce. Cut the lobster shell in small pieces with kitchen shears before putting it in the blender. (Specifically, you may follow the recipe for Lobster Butter, page 59.)

SAUCE NORMANDE

Normandy Sauce (with oyster juice)

This sauce accompanies the classic Sole Normande.

8 tablespoons salt butter
6 tablespoons all-purpose flour
Salt
A few grains cayenne pepper
2 cups fish stock (page 36)
½ cup oyster juice (drained from the oysters used in Sole Normande)
3 tablespoons mushroom juice
(cook stems and trimmings with a little water, lemon juice, and salt; strain before using)
2 egg yolks
2 tablespoons dry sherry
6 tablespoons heavy cream
2 teaspoons sweet butter

Melt the salt butter in a tin-lined copper pan. Off the heat, stir in the flour. Season with salt and cayenne pepper. Mix in the fish stock, oyster juice, and mushroom juice. Stir over low heat until the mixture comes to a boil. In a separate bowl, mix the egg yolks with the dry sherry. Add the heavy cream. Stir a little of the warm sauce into the egg yolk mixture; then stir it all into the rest of the sauce. Simmer gently 5 to 10 minutes. (Do not allow the sauce to boil or it will separate.) Bit by bit, add the sweet butter (to make the sauce shiny). NET: 2 cups.

SAUCE BERCY

Bercy Sauce

Made with wine and herbs, this is nice with eggs, fish, meats.

1 cup dry white wine
¼ cup dry sherry
⅓ cup fish stock (page 36) (if you have none, water or even chicken stock will do)
2 tablespoons salt butter
2 tablespoons finely chopped fresh shallots
2 tablespoons finely chopped fresh chives
2 teaspoons chopped fresh
tarragon
½ teaspoon finely chopped fresh garlic
Salt
Freshly cracked white pepper
3 egg yolks
1 teaspoon potato flour
2 tablespoons Cognac or good brandy
⅓ cup heavy cream

Put the white wine, sherry, and fish stock into a saucepan. Bring to a boil. In another saucepan, melt the butter and add the shallots, chives, tarragon, and garlic. Season with a little salt and pepper. Cook gently 1 to 2 minutes. Stir into the wine mixture and bring to a boil. In a small bowl mix the egg yolks with the potato flour, beat well, and add the brandy and heavy cream. Beat the wine and herb liquid into the egg yolk mixture and return the sauce to the pan, beating all the time. Gently reheat, but do not allow to boil or it will separate. NET: 1 cup.

SAUCE ARMORICAINE

This sauce is an extention of a mirepoix mixture (page 72), with ingredients added. It is used primarily with Lobster à l'Armoricaine.

2 tablespoons salt butter
1 cup each of finely diced
   mushrooms, carrots, turnips,
   and green beans
Salt
Freshly cracked white pepper
1 cup diced skinned tomato
1 teaspoon finely chopped garlic
Pan juices from 1 sautéed lobster

Preheat the oven to 350°. Melt the butter in a heavy pan. Add the mushrooms and stir until they are coated with butter. Put the carrots in a layer on top of the mushrooms, then a layer of turnips and a layer of green beans. Sprinkle with salt and pepper. Add the diced tomato, garlic, and lobster pan juices. Cover the vegetables with a piece of buttered wax paper. Cover the pan and bake 25 to 30 minutes. NET: 2 cups.

SAUCE BOLOGNESE

Italian Fresh Tomato and Meat Sauce

8 tablespoons salt butter
2 cups finely chopped yellow
   onion
1 teaspoon finely chopped garlic
1 pound ripe tomatoes, skinned
   and cut into eighths
1½ pounds ground lean beef
2 tablespoons tomato paste
1 tablespoon chopped fresh
   parsley
1 tablespoon chopped fresh
   oregano or 1 teaspoon dried
Salt
Freshly cracked black pepper
¼ cup good Chianti wine

Heat the butter in a heavy sauté pan. When it is foaming, stir in the chopped onion and garlic, and cook over low heat until the onion is lightly brown. Add the tomatoes and simmer gently until they are slightly mushy. Crumble the ground raw beef over the top of the tomato mixture and stir it into the sauce until well-blended. Mix in the tomato paste, parsley, and oregano. Season with salt and freshly cracked black pepper, then stir in the Chianti. Simmer the sauce over low heat, very gently, 45 minutes. NET: 2 to 3 cups thick sauce.

SAUCE BOUCHÈRE

The "bouchère" is the butcher's wife. This is a delicious meat sauce with tomato, onion, and celery. It may be used with fresh noodles or any pasta.

2 tablespoons pure olive oil
4 tablespoons salt butter
1 cup finely chopped onion
½ cup finely chopped celery
2 teaspoons finely chopped
  garlic
2 tablespoons tomato paste
2 large ripe tomatoes, skinned
  and chopped
1 pound ground beef
1 teaspoon meat glaze
1 tablespoon chopped fresh
  parsley
Salt to taste
Freshly cracked white pepper

Melt the olive oil and butter in a heavy sauté pan. Add the chopped onion, celery, and garlic. Stir briskly until they begin to brown. Add the tomato paste, chopped tomatoes, and ground beef. When the mixture is well blended, add the meat glaze, parsley, salt, and pepper. Simmer all together gently 30 to 45 minutes. NET: 2 cups.

SAUCE TOMATE I

*Tomato Sauce I
(with fresh tomatoes)*

4 tablespoons salt butter
1 teaspoon finely chopped garlic
4 large firm ripe tomatoes
2 tablespoons tomato paste
Salt
Freshly cracked black pepper
2 tablespoons all-purpose flour
3 cups water or chicken stock
  (page 35)

Slice 3 tomatoes with the skins on and set aside. Skin the fourth tomato, cut it into quarters, and remove the seeds. Rub the pith (seed parts) through a strainer and reserve the juice. Cut the pulp sections into fine shreds. Melt 3 tablespoons salt butter in a saucepan. Add the chopped garlic and cook over low heat 2 minutes. Add the sliced tomatoes and tomato paste, season with salt and pepper, and cook briskly over medium heat 2 minutes with the pan covered. Off the heat, stir in the flour. Add the water or chicken stock, return the pan to low heat, and stir the sauce until it comes to a boil. Strain it through a fine strainer, return it to the saucepan, and let it simmer gently 5 minutes. Stir in 1 tablespoon salt butter bit by bit, then the strained fresh tomato juice and the tomato cut into fine shreds. NET: About 4 cups.

SAUCE TOMATE II

*Tomato Sauce II
(with tomato paste)*

4 tablespoons salt butter
1 tablespoon all-purpose flour
Salt
Freshly cracked white pepper
3 tablespoons tomato paste
½ teaspoon finely chopped
  garlic
1½ cups chicken stock
  (page 35)

Melt 2 tablespoons salt butter in a saucepan. Off the heat, stir in the flour, and season with salt and pepper. Mix in the tomato paste, chopped garlic, and chicken stock. Stir the sauce over low heat until it comes to a boil. Add the rest of the butter bit by bit, and gently simmer the sauce 5 minutes. NET: About 1 cup.

SAUCE HOLLANDAISE I

Classic Method

2 egg yolks
¼ teaspoon salt
A few grains cayenne pepper
2 tablespoons tarragon vinegar

2 tablespoons heavy cream
6 tablespoons frozen sweet
  butter, cut in pieces
2 or 3 drops fresh lemon juice

Put the egg yolks into a small bowl — earthen or heatproof glass; never use metal or plastic. Add the salt, cayenne pepper, and tarragon vinegar. Mix well with a little whisk and add the cream. Set the bowl in a shallow pan of hot water over low heat. Beat the mixture with the whisk until it is as thick as you want it. (You have to get it to the desired thickness before adding butter.) Add the frozen sweet butter bit by bit, stirring all the time. Stir in the lemon juice drop by drop (too much will spoil the sauce). When the sauce is done, cover it with plastic wrap, and it can stand all day in a pan of lukewarm water. (Hollandaise curdles only if it cools and sets. It is important to keep the water warm. A pilot light is about the right heat.) NET: 1 cup.

SAUCE HOLLANDAISE II

"Assured" Method

"Assured" Hollandaise differs from classic Hollandaise in quality because you put a little arrowroot in to help thicken the sauce. This Hollandaise will not separate.

3 egg yolks
1 tablespoon tarragon vinegar
A few grains cayenne pepper

½ teaspoon salt
12 tablespoons sweet butter
½ teaspoon arrowroot

Put the egg yolks in a mixer and beat until they are very light and fluffy. Add the vinegar and cayenne pepper and continue beating. Add the salt and beat some more. Melt the butter in a pan — get it quite hot, but not brown. When the egg yolks are really thick, take the bowl away from the mixer and pour the melted butter in slowly, stirring constantly with a wire whisk. Add the arrowroot last, little by little. NET: 1 cup.

SAUCE MOUSSELINE I

Classic Method

Hollandaise with reduced fish stock, lightened with whipped cream.

1 cup fish stock (page 36)

1 whole egg

2 egg yolks

6 tablespoons sweet butter

1 tablespoon dry sherry

½ cup heavy cream, whipped

Reduce the fish stock to one-third its original quantity. Cool a little and put it in a medium-size bowl with the whole egg, egg yolks, and dry sherry. Set the bowl in a shallow pan of hot water over low heat. Beat with a rotary egg beater until the sauce thickens, then add the butter bit by bit. Remove from the heat and gently fold in the whipped cream. NET: 1 cup.

SAUCE MOUSSELINE II

1 cup fish stock (page 36)

12 tablespoons sweet butter

5 egg yolks

¾ cup heavy cream, whipped

Salt, if needed

Quick Method

Boil the fish stock down to 4 tablespoons. Beat the egg yolks in a mixer until they are light and fluffy. Slowly add the reduced fish stock. Add salt, if needed, and beat until the yolks are very thick. Heat the butter and bring it just to a boil. Remove the egg yolk mixture from the mixer and pour the melted butter slowly into it, stirring constantly with a whisk. Have the cream whipped to a very thick consistency and carefully fold it into the sauce. NET: 1 cup.

SAUCE BÉARNAISE

A Hollandaise type of sauce with vinegar and herbs, for meat or fish. Serve it separately with steak or whatever you wish. It can be made ahead of time and kept in a pan of warm water, covered with a piece of plastic wrap.

2 egg yolks

2 teaspoons finely chopped fresh tarragon

2 tablespoons tarragon vinegar

A good dash of cayenne pepper

2 teaspoons finely chopped shallot

3 tablespoons heavy cream

8 tablespoons frozen sweet butter, cut into small pieces

A tiny bit of garlic, finely chopped

2 or 3 drops fresh lemon juice

A tiny speck of meat glaze

1 tablespoon finely chopped fresh parsley

A tinier bit of tomato paste

Put the egg yolks in a medium-size bowl. Mix in the tarragon vinegar, cayenne pepper, and 2 tablespoons heavy cream. Stand the bowl in a pan of hot water over low heat. Stir with a little whisk until it is as thick as you want it. Add the frozen sweet butter bit by bit, stirring all the time with the small whisk (don't beat). Add 1 tablespoon heavy cream and the lemon juice, parsley, tarragon, shallot, garlic, meat glaze, and tomato paste. NET: 1 cup.

A spicy version of caper sauce, good with lamb or mutton.

1 tablespoon pure olive oil
2 tablespoons plus 2 teaspoons
   sweet butter
½ teaspoon meat glaze
½ teaspoon tomato paste
1 teaspoon tarragon vinegar
3 tablespoons all-purpose flour
1 teaspoon dry mustard
½ teaspoon ground cardamom

seed
1¼ cups light cream
2 tablespoons whipped cream
2 tablespoons capers
1 egg yolk mixed with 1 tablespoon dry sherry
1 tablespoon light cream or
   milk

Melt the olive oil and 2 tablespoons sweet butter in a saucepan. Add, off the heat, the meat glaze, tomato paste, vinegar, flour, dry mustard, and cardamom seed. Mix to a smooth paste. Still off the heat, add the light cream. Stir the sauce over low heat until it comes to a boil. Stir in the 2 teaspoons of sweet butter bit by bit, then the whipped cream, capers, mixed egg yolk and dry sherry, and the finishing tablespoon of light cream or milk. Gently reheat the sauce but do not boil it. NET: 1¾ cups.

A Hollandaise type of sauce, with mushrooms and white truffle, this is for ham only.

3 tablespoons salt butter
4 firm white mushrooms, thinly
   sliced
3 shallots, finely chopped
1 teaspoon chopped garlic
Salt
Freshly cracked white pepper
1 teaspoon lemon juice plus 1
   or 2 drops
1 white truffle, sliced

1 teaspoon chopped tarragon
   leaves
1 tablespoon Cognac or good
   brandy
3 egg yolks
2 tablespoons heavy cream
A few grains cayenne pepper
8 tablespoons frozen sweet
   butter, cut into small pieces

Melt the salt butter in a sauté pan. Add the mushrooms, shallots, and garlic. Season with salt and pepper and add 1 teaspoon lemon juice. Cook briskly 2 to 3 minutes. Add the sliced truffle and chopped tarragon. Flame with the brandy and cook another minute or two. Pour the juice from the pan (about 3 tablespoons) through a strainer into a bowl (set the mushroom mixture aside). Add the egg yolks to the bowl, beat together with the juice, and add the heavy cream. Season with salt and a little cayenne pepper. Set the bowl in a shallow pan of hot water over low heat. Beat with a whisk until the mixture is thick. Add the frozen sweet butter bit by bit, and the drops of lemon juice. Mix the mushroom mixture into the sauce. If you have made the sauce ahead of time, cover the bowl with plastic wrap and keep it in a pan of warm water. NET: 1 cup.

SAUCE FOYOT

A Hollandaise type of sauce with meat glaze, vinegar, and herbs, that is excellent served over poached eggs or sautéed sweetbreads.

3 egg yolks
2 tablespoons tarragon vinegar
3 tablespoons heavy cream
12 tablespoons frozen sweet
   butter
2 teaspoons meat glaze
1 tablespoon chopped fresh

   tarragon
1 tablespoon chopped fresh
   parsley
2 teaspoons chopped shallots
1 teaspoon finely chopped garlic
Few grains cayenne pepper

Put the egg yolks into a small bowl. Stir in the vinegar, then the cream. Stand the bowl in a pan of hot water over low heat. Beat the mixture quickly until it begins to thicken; then add the butter bit by bit. Heat the meat glaze a little and mix it into the sauce. Lastly, add the tarragon, parsley, shallots, garlic, and cayenne pepper. NET: 1 cup.

SAUCE MOUTARDE

Mustard Sauce

An egg-base sauce highly seasoned with mustard and excellent with broiled or sautéed fish, beef, ham, kidneys, or whatever you like.

4 tablespoons salt butter, melted
3 tablespoons all-purpose flour
2 egg yolks
1 teaspoon salt
⅛ teaspoon cayenne pepper
2 teaspoons lemon juice
2 egg whites, beaten to soft

   peaks
8 tablespoons frozen sweet
   butter, cut into small pieces
2 teaspoons Dijon mustard
1 teaspoon dry mustard
1 tablespoon dry sherry

In a medium-size bowl mix the melted salt butter, flour, egg yolks, salt, cayenne pepper, lemon juice, and beaten egg whites. Stand the bowl in a shallow pan of hot water over low heat. Beat with a whisk until thick. Add the sweet butter bit by bit. Mix in the two mustards and dry sherry. Mix until smooth. If the sauce is too thick, dilute it with a little cream. Serve warm. NET: 1 cup.

SAUCE MAYONNAISE I

Basic Mayonnaise Sauce

2 egg yolks
1 teaspoon salt
A few grains cayenne pepper
½ teaspoon dry mustard

1 teaspoon Dijon mustard
2 teaspoons lemon juice
1 tablespoon tarragon vinegar
1½ cups vegetable oil

Put the egg yolks in an electric mixer bowl and beat well. Add the salt, cayenne pepper, and mustards, and mix well. Beat in the lemon juice and tarragon vinegar. Slowly beat in the vegetable oil (at the start, literally drop by drop until the sauce begins to thicken). If the mayonnaise sauce becomes too thick, it can be thinned with a little light cream. NET: 1¾ cups.

TO RECONSTITUTE MAYONNAISE. If mayonnaise should curdle, add 2 to 3 tablespoons boiling water. In another bowl, stir together 1 whole egg, a little salt, a bit of Dijon mustard, and beat until creamy. Then add the curdled mayonnaise to this mixture drop by drop while you continue beating. (It will do no good to merely add more egg yolks.)

TO USE MAYONNAISE FOR COATING. If you are using any of the mayonnaise sauces to coat fish, add unflavored gelatine in the following manner. Dissolve 1 teaspoon unflavored gelatine in 2 tablespoons boiling water. Cool to room temperature. Mix thoroughly into 1 cup mayonnaise.

SAUCE MAYONNAISE II

Rich Mayonnaise Sauce

2 egg yolks
1 teaspoon salt
A few grains cayenne pepper
1/2 teaspoon dry mustard
1 teaspoon Dijon mustard

1 tablespoon tarragon vinegar
1 1/2 cups vegetable oil
1 hard-boiled egg yolk,
    rubbed through a fine strainer
2 to 3 tablespoons heavy cream

Put the raw egg yolks in an electric mixer bowl and beat well. Add the salt, cayenne pepper, mustards, and mix well. Add the tarragon vinegar and mix well. Slowly beat in the vegetable oil (literally drop by drop until it begins to thicken). Mix the strained hard-boiled egg yolk and heavy cream into the finished, thickened sauce. NET: 1 3/4 cups.

MAYONNAISE À L'AIL

Garlic Mayonnaise

1 cup basic mayonnaise
1 teaspoon finely chopped garlic
1 teaspoon Worcestershire sauce

1/2 teaspoon curry powder
1 or 2 drops lemon juice

Mix all the ingredients together well. NET: 1 cup.

MAYONNAISE À LA MOUTARDE

Mustard Mayonnaise

2 egg yolks
Pinch of sugar
1 teaspoon salt (scant)
1/8 teaspoon cayenne pepper
1 teaspoon dry mustard

1 teaspoon Dijon mustard
1 tablespoon tarragon vinegar
1 cup vegetable oil
1 to 2 tablespoons light cream

Put the egg yolks into an electric mixer bowl and beat well. Add the sugar, salt, cayenne pepper, mustards, and mix well. Add the tarragon vinegar and mix well. Slowly beat in the vegetable oil (literally drop by drop until it begins to thicken). Add the cream according to how you wish to use this sauce, thick or thin. NET: 1 cup.

SAUCE VERTE

Green Sauce (Mayonnaise)

This sauce can be used for coating fish (see below) and also served separately with salmon, bass, scrod, and other seafood.

1 pound fresh spinach
2 egg yolks
1 teaspoon salt
1/8 teaspoon cayenne pepper

1 tablespoon tarragon vinegar
1 cup vegetable oil
2 tablespoons heavy cream

Wash the spinach very well and put it in a heavy pan. Wilt it quickly over a high flame (do not add water), then drain well and purée it in an electric blender. Chill. Put the egg yolks in an electric mixer bowl and beat well. Add the salt, cayenne pepper, vinegar, and mix well. Slowly beat in the vegetable oil (literally drop by drop until it begins to thicken). Mix in spinach purée to attain the desired shade of green, then mix in the cream. NET: 1 1/3 cups.

TO USE FOR COATING. This sauce can be set with a little unflavored gelatine to use for coating fish. To 1 cup Sauce Verte, add 2 teaspoons unflavored gelatine dissolved in 2 tablespoons boiling water and cooled.

SAUCE RÉMOULADE

Rémoulade Sauce

2 egg yolks
1 teaspoon salt
1/8 teaspoon cayenne pepper
1 teaspoon dry mustard
2 teaspoons Dijon mustard
1 tablespoon tarragon vinegar
1 cup vegetable oil
2 tablespoons chopped capers

1 tablespoon chopped sour gherkins
1 tablespoon finely chopped parsley
2 teaspoons finely chopped fresh tarragon
2 or 3 drops lemon juice
2 tablespoons heavy cream

Put the egg yolks in an electric mixer bowl and beat well. Add the salt, cayenne pepper, mustards, and mix well. Slowly beat in the vinegar, then the vegetable oil (literally drop by drop until the sauce begins to thicken). Stir in the chopped capers, sour gherkins, parsley, tarragon, lemon juice, and heavy cream, and mix well. NET: 1 cup.

SAUCE GRIBICHE

Another great sauce for cold fish and seafood.

4 hard-boiled egg yolks, rubbed through a fine strainer
1/2 teaspoon salt
1/8 teaspoon cayenne pepper
2 teaspoons Dijon mustard
1/2 teaspoon dry mustard
2 tablespoons tarragon vinegar
1/2 cup pure olive oil

1 tablespoon chopped parsley
1 tablespoon chopped fresh thyme
1 tablespoon chopped sour gherkins
2 hard-boiled egg whites, cut into fine dice

Put the hard-boiled egg yolks, salt, cayenne pepper, and mustards in an electric mixer bowl and mix well with a wooden spoon. With the electric beater, slowly mix in the vinegar, then the olive oil, drop by drop. Mix in the herbs and sour gherkins. Stir in the finely diced hard-boiled egg whites. NET: ¾ cup.

SAUCE TARTARE

Tartar Sauce

2 raw egg yolks
1 teaspoon salt
2 hard-boiled egg yolks,
 rubbed through a fine strainer
⅛ teaspoon cayenne pepper
1 teaspoon dry mustard
1 teaspoon Dijon mustard
1 tablespoon tarragon vinegar

1 cup vegetable oil
1 tablespoon chopped capers
1 tablespoon chopped sour
 gherkins
1 tablespoon chopped parsley
1 tablespoon chopped green
 celery leaves
2 tablespoons heavy cream

Put the raw egg yolks and salt in an electric mixer bowl and beat well. Add the strained hard-boiled egg yolks, cayenne pepper, and mustards, and mix well. Slowly beat in the vinegar, then the vegetable oil very slowly, drop by drop until the sauce is really thick. Add the rest of the ingredients and mix well. NET: About 1½ cups.

SAUCE MALTAISE

An egg-base sauce flavored with fresh orange juice and rind, excellent with asparagus or artichokes.

3 egg yolks
5 tablespoons cold fresh orange
 juice
2 teaspoons lemon juice
Finely grated rind of 1 orange
1 teaspoon tarragon vinegar

1 teaspoon sugar
Pinch of salt
12 tablespoons frozen sweet
 butter, cut into small pieces
2 tablespoons Curaçao liqueur

Put the egg yolks, orange juice, lemon juice, grated orange rind, vinegar, sugar, and salt in the top of a double boiler. Beat with an egg beater over hot water to a creamy consistency. Bit by bit add the sweet butter, then the liqueur. Keep the sauce warm over warm water (not hot) until you are ready to serve it. NET: ¾ cup.

COLD SAUCE

Here is a heavenly variation of mayonnaise to serve with cold salmon, trout, turbot, and other fish.

1 cup basic mayonnaise
3 egg whites, stiffly beaten

1 cup sour cream
Grated rind of 1 lemon

Fold the beaten egg whites into the sour cream, then mix into the basic mayonnaise. Add the grated lemon rind. Serve very cold. NET: 2 cups.

BUTTERS

Salt butter is used for browning meat, poultry, game, and fish. It is also used to sauté vegetables and, in a few cases, fruit. Also use salt butter in beurre manié, the butter and flour base for thickening sauces.

Sweet (unsalted) butter is much richer and more delicate than salt butter and should be used in enriching cream and velouté sauces, soups, Hollandaise and Béarnaise sauces, all flavored butters, and is strongly recommended for cakes and pastry. *Frozen sweet butter* is recommended for sauces of the Hollandaise type because the frozen bits slow down the rate at which the butter is blended in, making the sauce lighter and fluffier.

Sweet butter is not used for browning purposes because it burns quickly.

Sweet butter should be stored in the freezer because it can become rancid quickly. It is a very perishable food and will take on the flavor of any food with which it comes into contact. Therefore, when it is stored, it should be well wrapped in wax paper or any other suitable wrapping, and it is advisable to keep it in a tightly sealed jar.

When serving butter with bread, only sweet butter should be used, I believe.

HOMEMADE BUTTER

With an electric mixer, homemade butter is so simple it just isn't funny. One is apt to forget about the cream being beaten (churned). One day I was beating cream by hand, over ice, and somebody came to ask me something. Absorbed in the conversation, I went on beating the cream. Suddenly it felt very queer; I looked down, and I had butter! You can make butter without even knowing you are making it.

To make butter, mix 2 to 3 cups heavy cream (at room temperature) with 1 teaspoon lemon juice and ½ teaspoon salt. Beat in the mixer until they transform into butter. Remove the solid of butter and wash it in ice water. Knead it really well in the water. Then, if you've got butter pats, pat the butter into a shape, or make balls or sticks or whatever you like. Or put into molds if you have them. NET: ¼ to ½ pound.

BEURRE CLARIFIÉ

Clarified Butter

This butter is used for frying. To make it, melt 8 tablespoons salt or sweet butter slowly over a low flame and add a few drops of lemon juice. Pour the mixture into a small cup and put it in the refrigerator. When it is set, use the solid yellow top. Discard the milky whey. NET: 3 ounces (6 tablespoons).

Use beurre manié for thickening sauces, gravies, etc. To make it, mix 4 tablespoons salt butter and 4 tablespoons all-purpose flour together into a smooth paste.

BEURRE MANIÉ

Kneaded Butter

Serve with sole, mackerel, salmon, and other fish.

BEURRE À LA MAÎTRE D'HÔTEL

Maître d'Hôtel Butter

8 tablespoons sweet butter
1 teaspoon chopped parsley
1 teaspoon lemon juice

Salt to taste
Freshly cracked white pepper

Beat the butter to a cream with a wooden spatula, and work in the parsley and lemon juice by degrees. Season with salt and pepper. Shape into a roll about the diameter of a half dollar, wrap in plastic wrap, and store in the freezer. To serve, lay thin slices of the butter on the hot fish. NET: 4 ounces (8 tablespoons).

A very delicate sauce. Serve with poached turbot, sole, salmon, and other fish and shellfish.

SAUCE AU BEURRE BLANC

White Butter Sauce

2 tablespoons finely chopped
*   shallots*
4 tablespoons white wine
*   vinegar*
¼ teaspoon salt

1 tablespoon freshly cracked
*   white pepper*
32 tablespoons (1 pound) frozen
*   sweet butter, cut into small*
*   pieces (about ½ inch square)*

Put the shallots, wine vinegar, salt, and pepper in a small pan. Bring to a boil and reduce the liquid quickly until it measures 2 tablespoons. Strain into the top of a double boiler over hot water. Add the butter piece by piece, beating constantly with a little wire whisk. (The sauce will soon begin to thicken. Do not add more butter until the previous chunk has dissolved.) Continue beating until all the butter has been added and the sauce has the same consistency as Hollandaise. Serve at once. NET: 1½ cups.

A simple white butter sauce, to serve with poached turbot or other fine fish.

BEURRE BLANC

White Butter

8 tablespoons sweet butter (at
*   room temperature)*
½ teaspoon very finely chopped

garlic
2 finely chopped baby white
*   onions*

Beat the butter in a mixer until it is creamy, actually very light and fluffy. Add the garlic and onions. Beat the mixture well, put it in a tin-lined copper or heavy pan over moderate heat, and stir with a wooden spoon until the onion is a little soft but still a little crisp. The warm butter should be frothy and white. Serve at once. NET: ½ cup.

BEURRE NOIR

Brown Butter

This is generally served with capers to accompany poached fish, eggs, brains, roes.

8 tablespoons salt butter
Juice of half a lemon
½ teaspoon salt

¼ teaspoon freshly cracked
    white pepper

Put the butter in a small pan and stir over very low heat until it becomes very dark (but not burned). Add the lemon juice, salt, and pepper, and stir well. NET: ½ cup.

BEURRE À LA MEUNIÈRE

Meunière Butter

This sauce is made in the same pan in which the fish has been sautéed.

4 tablespoons dry white wine
1 tablespoon finely chopped
    shallots
¼ teaspoon finely chopped
    garlic

Salt
Freshly cracked white pepper
6 tablespoons salt butter
Juice of half a lemon

When the fish is removed from the pan, add the dry white wine, then the shallots, garlic, salt and pepper. Cook for a minute or two, stirring constantly with a whisk. Continue stirring and add the butter bit by bit. Last, add the lemon juice and stir well. To serve, spoon a little of the butter over or on the side of the fish. (Sometimes it is nice to add a teaspoon of chopped fresh parsley or other herbs before serving, depending on what the sauce is for.) NET: ½ cup.

BEURRE AUX FINES HERBES

Herb Butter

4 sprigs fresh tarragon
6 sprigs parsley
2 sprigs celery leaf

8 tablespoons sweet butter
1 teaspoon salt
A few grains cayenne pepper

Plunge all the herbs into boiling water for a minute or two. Drain well and remove the leaves from the stalks. Pound the leaves with a pestle and mortar. Put them in a small cloth and squeeze out all of the moisture. If necessary, chop them a little finer on a board. Beat the butter in an electric mixer until it is creamy. Add the herbs, salt, and cayenne pepper. Wrap the butter in wax paper or plastic wrap in a long sausage shape. Freeze. Use as a spread on canapés or lay a thin slice over broiled chops or fish. NET: 4 ounces (8 tablespoons).

A superb herbed butter to serve with grilled steak or entrecôte.

4 tablespoons beef marrow
½ cup white wine vinegar
2 tablespoons chopped shallots
8 tablespoons salt butter

Salt to taste
Freshly cracked white pepper
A few drops lemon juice

Lightly poach the beef marrow in plain boiling salt water until it is just cooked. Drain, chill, cut it into small dice, and set aside. Put the vinegar and shallots in a small pan and cook until the shallots are just soft. In an electric mixer, beat the butter until it is light and creamy; add the salt, pepper, and lemon juice. Carefully combine the shallot mixture and creamed butter. Add the diced beef marrow. Serve a dollop of this butter on top of each steak. This butter may also be wrapped in plastic wrap or foil in a long sausage shape, and frozen. To serve, lay thin slices over individual servings of the meat or fish. NET: ½ cup.

This is a versatile butter, used to fill snails for Escargots à la Bourguignonne as well as for garlic bread. It is excellent served with broiled cod or mackerel.

8 tablespoons salt butter
1 teaspoon finely chopped garlic
1 teaspoon chopped fresh basil
    or parsley

1 teaspoon Worcestershire sauce
Salt
Freshly cracked white pepper

Beat the butter in an electric mixer until it is creamy. Add the chopped garlic and beat well. Add the Worcestershire sauce, basil or parsley, salt and pepper to taste. NET: 4 ounces (8 tablespoons).

8 tablespoons sweet butter
6 anchovy fillets
½ teaspoon lime juice

½ teaspoon freshly cracked
    white pepper

Beat the butter in an electric mixer until it is creamy. Mix in the anchovies, lime juice, and pepper. Roll up in wax paper and foil, freeze, and use when needed. NET: 4 ounces (8 tablespoons).

This butter is for making a hot lobster sauce, as for Sauce Cardinal or Bisque d'Homard. Added to 1½ to 2 cups of fish velouté sauce, it will produce a Sauce Cardinal. Use only the soft shells such as the head, body, and little claws; do not use the large claws.

8 tablespoons sweet butter
1 small lobster (1 pound),
   cooked (meat, coral, and soft
   shells)
½ teaspoon salt

A few grains cayenne pepper
A little of the fish velouté sauce
   to be combined with the
   lobster butter

Beat the butter in a mixer until it is creamy. Coarsely chop the lobster meat, coral, and soft shells. Put them and the creamed butter in the blender with the salt and pepper and a little of the prepared velouté sauce. Pulverize the mixture to a smooth cream, then rub it through a fine vegetable strainer. To complete the sauce (as for Sauce Cardinal or Bisque d'Homard), stir this butter bit by bit into the liquid. NET: Approximately 1 cup.

BEURRE DE HOMARD (À FROID)

Lobster Butter (cold)

This butter can be used as a canapé spread or with hot broiled fish.

8 tablespoons sweet butter
Meat from the large claws of a
   cooked lobster, finely
   chopped, and a little of the

soft shell
¼ cup heavy cream
Salt to taste
A few grains cayenne pepper

Beat the butter in an electric mixer until it is creamy. Add the finely chopped lobster. Crush the lobster shell in a blender and add to the butter mixture. Add the cream and blend until quite smooth. Season with salt and the cayenne pepper. Rub through a fine strainer. NET: ¾ cup.

ANCHOVY AND TOMATO BUTTER

For cod, haddock, salmon.

8 tablespoons sweet butter
1 teaspoon tomato paste
½ teaspoon finely chopped
   garlic
4 anchovy fillets, chopped

½ teaspoon chopped mixed
   herbs
Paprika
Salt to taste
Freshly cracked white pepper

Beat the butter in an electric mixer until it is creamy, and add in the other ingredients (the paprika is for color). Mix well. Chill. NET: 4 ounces (8 tablespoons).

ORANGE BUTTER

Serve on broiled fish or poultry.

1 garlic clove, bruised
8 tablespoons salt butter

Grated rind of 1 orange
1 tablespoon fresh orange juice

½ teaspoon paprika
1 tablespoon shredded orange
 rind (which has been

blanched in boiling water)
Salt to taste
Freshly cracked white pepper

Rub the mixer bowl with the bruised clove of garlic. Beat the butter in this bowl until it is light and creamy. Add the other ingredients (the paprika adds color), mix well, and chill. NET: 4 ounces (8 tablespoons).

1 pound fresh spinach
½ pound sorrel (or another
 ½ pound spinach and 1
 teaspoon lemon juice)

8 tablespoons salt butter
1 tablespoon chopped fresh dill
Salt to taste
Freshly cracked white pepper

BEURRE VERT

Green Butter

Blanch the spinach and sorrel in boiling water. Drain well and rub through a fine strainer or purée in an electric blender. Beat the butter in an electric mixer until it is light and creamy. Mix the purée and dill into the butter. Season with salt and pepper. Chill. NET: 8 ounces (about 1 cup).

For herring or mackerel.

1 garlic clove, bruised
8 tablespoons salt butter
1 teaspoon Dijon mustard
½ teaspoon dry mustard
A few drops each of dry white

wine, tarragon vinegar,
 tomato catsup
Salt to taste
Freshly cracked white pepper

BEURRE DE MOUTARDE

Mustard Butter

Rub the mixer bowl with the bruised garlic clove. Beat the butter in this bowl until it is creamy. Add the mustards, wine, vinegar, and catsup. Mix well. Season with salt and pepper. Chill. NET: 4 to 5 ounces (8 to 10 tablespoons).

MARINADES AND SALAD DRESSINGS

For salad dressings, see also the mayonnaises in the Sauces section, starting on page 52.

To season and tenderize meat and game.

Salt

Freshly cracked white pepper

MARINADE CRUE

Uncooked Marinade

3 yellow onions, thinly sliced
1 carrot, thinly sliced
2 whole cloves
1 bay leaf
1 garlic clove, bruised
4 sprigs parsley

10 peppercorns, black and white
   mixed
2 cups dry white or red wine
¼ cup tarragon vinegar
½ cup pure olive oil

Rub the meat to be marinated all over with salt and freshly cracked white pepper. Lay it in an earthenware dish and cover with the onions, carrot, cloves, bay leaf, garlic, parsley, and peppercorns. Mix the wine, vinegar, and olive oil together in a pan, warm it a little, and pour over the meat. Allow the meat to marinate 2 to 3 days in the refrigerator; baste and turn it frequently. NET: 1 quart.

MARINADE CUITE

Cooked Marinade

For meat and game.

2 tablespoons salt butter
1 carrot, sliced
2 yellow onions, sliced
1 garlic clove, bruised
Bouquet garni (1 bay leaf, 4
   sprigs parsley)

1 cup water
2 tablespoons pure olive oil
½ cup dry white or red wine
4 tablespoons tarragon vinegar
4 white peppercorns
Salt to taste

Melt the butter in a heavy pan. Add the carrot, onions, garlic, and bouquet garni. Cook a few minutes. Add the other ingredients and simmer until the liquid is reduced to about one-third. Allow the mixture to cool before pouring it over the meat or game, which should stand in it 24 hours. NET: 3 to 4 cups.

SAUCE VINAIGRETTE I

Simple Vinaigrette Sauce

This is the basic French salad dressing.

1 clove garlic, bruised
1 teaspoon kosher salt
   or ½ teaspoon regular
   granulated salt
½ teaspoon freshly cracked
   white pepper
½ teaspoon dry mustard

1 teaspoon Dijon mustard
2 tablespoons pure olive oil
1 teaspoon fresh lemon juice
2 tablespoons tarragon or wine
   vinegar
4 tablespoons vegetable oil

Rub the inside of the salad bowl with the bruised garlic clove. Put in the salt, pepper, mustards, and olive oil. Stir vigorously with a wooden spoon. Slowly add the vinegar and lemon juice. Last, add the vegetable oil, drop by drop, stirring constantly. Place cleaned and well-dried salad greens on top of the dressing. (Your salad may sit in the refrigerator several hours this way.) When ready to eat, toss and serve. NET: ½ cup.

This dressing may be kept in a tightly closed screw-top jar in the refrigerator up to about two months.

1 teaspoon kosher salt or ½ teaspoon regular granulated salt	1 teaspoon Dijon mustard
½ teaspoon freshly cracked black peppercorns	½ teaspoon fresh lemon juice
½ teaspoon freshly cracked white peppercorns	2 tablespoons tarragon vinegar
½ teaspoon granulated sugar	2 tablespoons pure olive oil
½ teaspoon dry mustard	8 tablespoons vegetable oil
	1 raw egg
	½ teaspoon finely chopped garlic

Put all the ingredients into a 1-pint screw-top jar. Close tightly. Shake very well. Store the jar in the refrigerator. NET: About 1 cup.

SAUCE VINAIGRETTE II

Compound Vinaigrette Sauce

This dressing keeps well in the refrigerator.

1 teaspoon kosher salt or ½ teaspoon regular granulated salt	2 tablespoons tarragon vinegar
1 teaspoon mixed black and white peppercorns, coarsely cracked	7 tablespoons vegetable oil
½ teaspoon superfine sugar	3 tablespoons pure olive oil
½ teaspoon dry mustard	1 raw egg
1 teaspoon Dijon mustard	1 hard-boiled egg, finely diced
1 teaspoon fresh lemon juice	2 ounces imported Roquefort cheese, finely diced
	½ teaspoon finely chopped garlic or 1 teaspoon finely chopped shallots

Put the ingredients into a 1-pint screw-top jar. Shake very well. Serve over tossed greens. NET: ¾ cup.

SAUCE ROQUEFORT

Roquefort Cheese Dressing

This dressing keeps a long time in the refrigerator.

¼ cup pure olive oil	shallots
½ cup vegetable oil	1 teaspoon finely chopped white onion
2 tablespoons tarragon vinegar	A few capers
1 tablespoon Dijon mustard	1 teaspoon kosher salt or ½ teaspoon regular granulated salt
1 tablespoon finely chopped parsley	½ teaspoon freshly cracked black pepper
1 teaspoon finely chopped fresh thyme	
1 teaspoon finely chopped	

Put all the ingredients in a 1-pint screw-top jar. Shake well. NET: ¾ cup.

SAUCE RAVIGOTE

SAUCE MIGNONNETTE

Coarse-ground pepper in lemon and lime juice, for raw oysters or clams.

2 teaspoons white peppercorns   *Juice of 2 limes*
1 teaspoon black peppercorns   *Juice of 2 lemons*

Coarsely crack the peppercorns with a pestle and mortar. Mix with the lime and lemon juice. Serve this in a little bowl surrounded by fresh oysters or clams on the half shell. NET: 4 to 5 tablespoons.

DESSERT SAUCES

CRÈME À L'ANGLAISE OR SAUCE VANILLE

Vanilla Custard Sauce

This sauce may be served either hot or cold.

4 egg yolks   *Half a vanilla bean, split and*
½ cup superfine sugar   *scraped inside*
1½ cups light cream   *Optional: 1 cup whipped cream*

Put the egg yolks, sugar, and the scraping of the vanilla bean in a mixer bowl. Beat until light and fluffy. Put the cream with the vanilla pod into a tin-lined copper pan and bring to a boil. Remove from the heat and pour very slowly into the egg yolk mixture, beating constantly with a whisk. Return the mixture to the pan. Stir over very low heat until the custard coats the back of a silver spoon. Pour it into a sauce bowl at once. If desired, 1 cup of plain whipped cream may be folded into the sauce. NET: 1⅓ cups.

CRÈME CHANTILLY

Whipped Cream with Vanilla and Confectioners Sugar

Heavy cream should always be whipped over ice to ensure that it will not sour in the process. Generally speaking, heavy cream doubles in bulk when it is whipped.

2 cups heavy cream   *Scraping from 2 inches vanilla*
4 tablespoons confectioners   *bean (or 2 teaspoons vanilla*
* sugar*   *essence)*

Pour the heavy cream into a large round-bottom metal bowl and set it over another bowl or pan filled with crushed ice, or ice cubes. Beat the cream with a large piano wire whisk until it begins to thicken. Then add the sugar and the vanilla bean scraping or vanilla essence. Continue beating until the cream holds its shape. Be careful not to beat it too long, or it will separate. Store the whipped cream, covered with plastic wrap, in the refrigerator until ready for use, but no longer than 2 to 3 hours. NET: 4 cups whipped cream.

1 cup granulated sugar

¼ teaspoon cream of tartar

⅓ cup plus 1 tablespoon water

Combine the sugar, ⅓ cup water, and cream of tartar in an unlined copper pan. Stir over low heat until the sugar is dissolved. Increase the heat and allow the mixture to cook to a medium caramel color, without stirring. Then instantly remove the pan from the heat and set it in a bowl of cold water to stop further cooking. Stir in 1 tablespoon cold water. Cool the sauce before using it, and add more water if it is too thick. NET: About ¾ cup.

Caramel Sauce

This is a rich chocolate sauce. For an even richer one add the whipped cream.

12 ounces dark sweet chocolate

1 ounce bitter chocolate

1 cup light cream

6 tablespoons frozen sweet

butter

1 teaspoon vanilla extract or

1 tablespoon light rum

Optional: ¾ cup whipped cream

Chocolate Sauce

Cut the sweet and bitter chocolate into pieces and put them into a small heavy pan. Add the light cream and stir over very low heat until the chocolate is melted and smooth. Then add the sweet butter bit by bit. Flavor with vanilla or rum. Serve hot or cold. NET: 1½ cups.

For use with beignets soufflés, puddings, and other desserts.

1½ 12-ounce jars apricot jam
   (superior quality)

Juice of 1 lemon

Grated rind of 1 lemon

½ cup superfine sugar

⅓ cup Sauternes (sweet white
   wine)

Apricot Sauce

Combine the ingredients in a saucepan and stir over low heat until the mixture is dissolved. Let it simmer very gently 15 minutes and stir it occasionally. Put the finished sauce through a fine wire strainer. Serve either warm or cold. NET: About 2 cups.

For use with beignets soufflés, puddings, and other desserts.

1 jar (12 ounces) seedless black
   raspberry jam (superior quality)

5 tablespoons Framboise
   (raspberry brandy)

3 teaspoons lemon juice

Black Raspberry Sauce

Combine the jam, 4 tablespoons Framboise, and lemon juice in a saucepan. Stir the mixture over very low heat until it dissolves. Just before serving, flame the sauce with another tablespoon of Framboise, warmed. Serve warm or cold. NET: About 1½ cups.

SAUCE AUX FRUITS FRAIS: FRAISES, FRAMBOISES, PÊCHES

Fresh Fruit Sauce: Strawberry, Raspberry, Peach

Fragrant fruit sauces with whole chunks of fresh fruit, to use with Coeur à la Crème, puddings, ice creams, crêpes, and other basic desserts.

STRAWBERRY
2 cups fresh hulled strawberries
¼ cup Framboise (raspberry brandy)
1 cup seedless black raspberry jam (superior quality)

RASPBERRY
2 cups fresh raspberries
1 cup red currant jelly

¼ cup light rum

PEACH
3 cups thinly sliced fresh peaches
1 cup apricot jam (superior quality)
¼ cup Drambuie (Scottish liqueur)

STRAWBERRY. If the strawberries are large, cut them into halves or quarters. Put them in a bowl and sprinkle with the Framboise. Dissolve the jam over low heat and strain it over the strawberries. Mix the berries with the jam and chill at least 1 hour before serving. NET: 3 cups.

RASPBERRY. Clean the raspberries and put them in the refrigerator to chill well. Put the jelly in a saucepan and dissolve it over low heat. Mix in the rum, strain, and set the liquid in the refrigerator to chill thoroughly. In order to keep the fresh raspberries as whole as possible in the sauce, mix them with the currant jelly mixture just before serving (not before). Both ingredients should be well chilled. NET: 2½ cups.

PEACH. Put the thinly sliced fresh peaches in a bowl and sprinkle the Drambuie over them. Dissolve the jam over low heat in a small saucepan and rub it through a fine wire strainer. (If the apricot purée is too thick, add a little boiling water.) Mix the apricot sauce with the sliced peaches and chill the combined mixture at least 1 hour. NET: 3 cups.

FRUIT GLAZES: APRICOT AND CURRANT

Fruit glazes are used to finish off fruit tarts and occasionally cakes, as well as to fill layered cakes. Apricot and currant are the most useful.

APRICOT GLAZE
¾ cup apricot jam (superior quality)
1 tablespoon Cognac, good brandy, Kirsch, dry sherry, or other suitable liqueur

RED CURRANT JELLY GLAZE
½ cup red currant jelly (superior quality)
1 tablespoon Framboise (raspberry brandy)

APRICOT GLAZE. Combine the jam and the brandy, sherry, or liqueur in a little pan and dissolve the jam over low heat. Stir so that it does not burn. When the jam is dissolved, put it through a fine wire strainer. Cool the glaze a little and use as instructed for the particular dish. NET: About ½ cup.

RED CURRANT JELLY GLAZE. Heat the jelly in a little pan over low heat until it dissolves. Mix in the Framboise. Put the mixture through a fine wire strainer. Cool it a little and use as instructed for the particular dish. NET: ½ cup.

SAUCE SMITANE

Sour Cream Sauce

This is a delicious zesty garnish with fruit-filled pastries, or with plain poached apples or pears. Serve it icy cold with hot or cold desserts.

1 cup sour cream
⅓ cup superfine sugar
Grated rind of 1 lemon
¼ teaspoon freshly grated

nutmeg
¼ teaspoon ground cinnamon
¾ cup heavy cream, whipped

Put the sour cream in a bowl with the sugar, lemon rind, nutmeg, and cinnamon. Fold these ingredients through the cream well, using a rubber scraper. Then fold in the whipped cream. Chill thoroughly. NET: 2 cups.

SAUCE SABAYON I

Sabayon Sauce I (with brandy or liqueur)

For use with soufflés, crêpes, and some puddings. It should be prepared just before serving to present it at its frothiest, even though we do include a little arrowroot, the most delicate of all starch thickening agents, to help it hold up a little longer.

1 egg
2 egg yolks
4 tablespoons superfine sugar
½ teaspoon arrowroot
2 tablespoons any good brandy

or liqueur (such as Grand Marnier, Cognac, Kirsch, Framboise, dry sherry, rum, Madeira, and of course the traditional Marsala)

Combine all the ingredients in a medium-size bowl and mix with a wire whisk. Set the bowl in a shallow pan half filled with hot water over low heat. Beat the mixture with a rotary beater until it becomes very frothy and holds its shape. Use as directed by the recipe for the dish this sauce is to accompany. NET: About ¾ cup.

SAUCE SABAYON II

Sabayon Sauce II (with lemon or orange zest)

For use with companionable soufflés, crêpes, and certain puddings — see the preceding recipe. The rind, or exterior peel, of citrus fruits (lemons, oranges, limes) contains the oil or essence of the fruit. Therefore in French culinary parlance it is often called "zeste" which is a lovely word for describing the vitality the citrus rind gives to food (as it also does to perfume).

2 eggs
4 egg yolks
9 tablespoons superfine sugar
½ teaspoon arrowroot

2 tablespoons fresh lemon juice
    (or orange juice)
4 teaspoons grated lemon rind
    (or orange rind)

The procedure is just the same as for Sauce Sabayon I, above. NET: About 1 cup.

SAUCE MOUSSELINE

Mousseline Sauce (for desserts)

A sabayon sauce with whipped cream. It may be served warm or chilled.

1 egg
2 egg yolks
4 tablespoons superfine sugar
Tiny pinch of salt

½ cup heavy cream, whipped
2 tablespoons Grand Marnier
    (or any choice of liqueur or
    rum)

Combine the egg and egg yolks in a small bowl with the sugar and salt. Blend together with a small wire whisk. Set the bowl in a shallow pan half filled with hot water over low heat. Beat the mixture with a rotary beater until it holds its shape. Add the Grand Marnier and beat some more. Remove the bowl from the hot water and carefully fold in the whipped cream. NET: About 1½ cups.

SIROP DES FRUITS

Fruit Syrup

A very successful tart sugar syrup for a fresh fruit bowl.

2 oranges
2 lemons
2 limes

2 cups sugar
½ teaspoon cream of tartar
3 cups water

Remove the rind from the fruit with a potato peeler. Cut it into very fine shreds crosswise and put it into a heavy pan with the sugar, water, and cream of tartar. Stir over low heat until the sugar dissolves. Simmer slowly until it reaches a light syrupy consistency. Put the syrup in a covered container and store in the refrigerator. Spoon over a fresh fruit bowl just before serving. NET: 1½ cups.

OTHER BASIC AGENTS AND PREPARATIONS

DRY BREADCRUMBS FOR SPRINKLING OVER AU GRATIN DISHES. Leftover pieces of French bread can be saved and left to dry out. Or they can be dried in a slow oven. Coarsely cut the pieces of dry bread and put them in an electric blender. Blend until they are fine as you want them. Store the breadcrumbs in an airtight jar and use as needed.

WHITE BREADCRUMBS FOR DEEP-FRYING. For coating foods to be fried in deep fat, white breadcrumbs will give you much better results than others. Take a large loaf of sturdy white bread and trim off the crusts. (Let the crusts dry out to make brown crumbs for au gratin, etc.) Cut the loaf into thin slices and spread them on baking sheets. Put them to dry overnight in a cool oven. (With a gas oven, the pilot flame or "keep warm" indicator is enough.) Be sure that the bread slices are completely dried. Put them through a coarse meat chopper and store in an airtight jar.

FRIED BREADCRUMBS. For ½ cup fried breadcrumbs, melt 2 tablespoons salt butter or 2 tablespoons bacon fat in a frypan. Add ½ cup dry breadcrumbs and stir and fry until the butter or fat is absorbed and the breadcrumbs are a golden brown. Take care not to let them scorch.

The primary ingredient for all forms of croûtons is good sturdy white bread, either the sandwich loaf shape or the French baguette shape. Toasted croûtons may be prepared in advance and stored for considerable time in a sealed plastic bag or airtight jar.

The following are the basic types of croûtons called for in the recipes in this book:

LARGE CROUTONS. Cut the bread for large croûtons into whatever shapes you need: thick slices (French bread) for soups; squares to serve as a base for serving a tournedos; rectangles for lining in dishes like Pommes Charlotte; rounds for a base or garnish; triangles for a garnish, stuck around a casserole or platter.

For the thick slices of French bread, leave the crust on. For the other shapes, made with sandwich bread, trim off the crusts with a sharp straight-blade knife. Cut diagonally for triangles, in 2 or 3 oblong strips for rectangles, or with a large round cutter for rounds. To *toast*, arrange the pieces of bread on a baking sheet and toast on both sides in a moderate oven. To *fry*, cook the pieces of bread in foaming butter in a frypan on both sides, until they are golden brown. (Do not let the butter burn.) Drain on paper towels.

SMALL CROUTONS. These are cubes of bread about ⅜ or ¼ inch square, either toasted or fried. They are usually used to garnish soups or in Caesar salad.

Using a very sharp, large, straight-blade French knife, cut off all the crusts from slices of sandwich bread. Cut the bread into uniform cubes. To *toast*, scatter the cubes on a baking sheet and toast them in a moderate oven (350°–375°), turning them once or twice to brown them evenly. To *fry*, for 1 cup croûtons, heat 2 tablespoons salt butter or bacon fat in a frypan. When it is foaming, put in the croûtons. Fry them until they are golden brown all over, stirring constantly so that they brown evenly and don't burn. Drain on paper towels.

TINY CROUTONS. About ⅛ inch square, these cubes of bread are either toasted or fried. They are used to garnish soups, or in omelets or scrambled eggs.

Using a very sharp, large, straight-blade French knife, cut off all the crusts from slices of sandwich bread. Then slice each slice horizontally, to make 2 very thin slices of bread. (There is now very thinly sliced Melba toast bread which is thin enough to use). Carefully, with the sharp knife, cut the thin slices into tiny cubes. Toast or fry tiny croûtons the same way as small croûtons, above.

CROUSTADES

For a toasted bread shell in which food may be served (croustade), see Champignons en Croûte, page 603. For another type of croustade, the toasted bread platform on which game fowl are often served, see Faisan Rôti Classique, page 423.

PLAIN GRILLED OR MELBA TOAST

Cut a loaf of sturdy sandwich bread into very thin slices and trim off the crusts. (Or simply slice a skinny loaf of French bread, leaving on the crust; or use, if available, a special Melba toast loaf.) Lay the slices of bread on a baking sheet and bake slowly in a preheated 325° oven until they are a light golden color and crisp. This toast can be stored in an airtight tin.

FAIRY TOAST

Like Melba toast. Make 2 slices of sandwich bread (with crusts removed) from 1 slice, or use thin-slice Melba toast bread, and cut them into halves diagonally. Toast on a baking sheet in a preheated 325° oven until they are light golden in color. This toast is very delicate and must be handled carefully. It, too, can be stored in an airtight tin.

MORNAY TOAST

Cheese Toast

Cut a loaf of sturdy sandwich bread into wafer-thin slices and remove the crusts. (Or simply slice a skinny loaf of French bread, but do not remove the crust; or use a special Melba toast loaf.) Lay the slices on a baking sheet. Brush them with a little melted salt butter and sprinkle generously with freshly grated Parmesan cheese. Dust with paprika and 1 or 2 grains of cayenne pepper. Brown in preheated 325° oven. When done, these may be stored in an airtight tin.

AU GRATIN

"Au gratin" is the term applied to a savory dish which is covered with a sauce, sprinkled with breadcrumbs, freshly grated Parmesan cheese and melted butter, and put under a hot broiler to brown. This use of dry breadcrumbs and freshly grated Parmesan cheese appears in dish after dish in many categories of French cooking; for example, in many sautéed dishes. The "finish" should enhance the beautiful dish it presents. That is why we have always used and always specify "freshly grated Parmesan cheese" in every recipe.

Freshly grated Parmesan cheese is so easy to have on hand, and far more economical, fresher, more moist, and more fragrant than the already grated commercial packages. Just buy a chunk of good imported Parmesan cheese at the cheese shop or the Italian grocer's. Grate a supply on a hand grater or a Mouli grater and store it in an airtight jar in the refrigerator. It is ready for instant use.

Breadcrumbs, homemade, are the answer to leftover French bread, and again much fresher and better than the commercial packages. The method is described in the Breadcrumbs recipe above.

Melted butter, for a few drops on a gratin, or to brush over a steak or chop, or to brush out a baking dish, should be instantly available. I have always suggested that a little butter warmer be on hand, which makes it convenient to melt the tiniest bit of butter whenever you need it.

BEST DEEP-FRY FAT

Have ready 6 pounds beef suet (kidney fat) and 2 cups cold water. Preheat the oven to 250°. Chop the suet in large chunks and put them in a large pan. Cover with cold water. Cook the fat in the oven until it is rendered (melted). Strain carefully. Set aside to solidify. Lift the solidified fat off and store it in the refrigerator. To use, melt it in your fryer or sauté pan. NET: About 2 pounds.

TO CLEAN THE FAT FOR REUSE. If you wish to fry fish one day and pineapple the next, the fat must be cleaned before you reuse it. Put 2 to 3 cups of the used fat in a saucepan, add a peeled potato cut in thick slices and an unpeeled quartered apple, and boil gently 10 minutes. Strain through a fine conical strainer and chill. (The potato draws off the impurities, and the apple sweetens the fat.)

DUXELLES

An excellent chopped mushroom mixture used as stuffing for mushroom caps, artichokes, small joints of meat, etc. The ham in the recipe may be omitted.

2 cups finely chopped fresh   Optional: 2 ounces boiled ham,
   mushrooms   finely diced
2 tablespoons salt butter   1 tablespoon tomato paste
2 tablespoons chopped onion   Salt
1 teaspoon finely chopped   Freshly cracked white pepper
   shallot

Put the chopped mushrooms into a cloth and squeeze out all the liquid. In a small sauté pan, melt the butter. Add the mushrooms, onion, and shallot. Season with salt and pepper and sauté for a few minutes. When the mixture begins to brown a little, add the ham. Cook a little longer. Mix in the tomato paste. Cover the mixture with a piece of buttered wax paper and simmer for a few minutes. NET: 1½ cups.

MIREPOIX

This chopped vegetable mixture can be used as a stuffing for poached fish or sautéed veal scallops, as a garnish for broiled lamb chops, or as the base for Sauce Armoricaine.

2 tablespoons salt butter   green beans
1 cup each of finely diced mush-   Salt
   rooms, carrots, turnips, and   Freshly cracked white pepper

Preheat the oven to 350°. Melt the butter in a heavy pan. Add the mushrooms and stir until they are coated with butter. Put the carrots in a layer on top of the mushrooms, then add a layer of turnips and a layer of green beans. Sprinkle with salt and pepper. Cover the vegetables with a piece of buttered wax paper. Cover the pan and bake 25 to 30 minutes. NET: 1½ cups.

FARCES

Forcemeats or Stuffings

In its broadest sense, a forcemeat is any mixture used as a food stuffing — and when one surveys the use of stuffings in French cuisine, the category must be viewed broadly. However, the term is generally applied to savory dishes.

As with sauces, the permutations of the basic types of forcemeat are endless, with the forcemeat (like the sauce) adapted to the personality of a given dish. Therefore my recipes for forcemeat are given with the recipe for the entire dish.

The following paragraphs describe the basic types of forcemeat used in French cuisine and provide a recipe reference for each type. For example, if you wish a basic chopped or ground meat stuffing for a turkey, you could use the forcemeat recipe under Poulet Rôti Farci (increasing the quantity to fit the turkey, of course).

FORCEMEAT OF FINELY CHOPPED MEAT OR SEAFOOD, BOUND WITH WHOLE EGG. A primary forcemeat preparation is to combine finely chopped or ground meat, or seafood, with seasonings and bind the mixture with whole raw egg. Examples of this type of forcemeat are in recipes for Choux Farci and Poule Farcie au Pot (chopped or ground meat), Poulet Rôti Farci (pork sausage), and Filets de Soles Walewska (seafood).

MOUSSELINE (FINE) FORCEMEAT. A refined mixture is made by mixing finely ground meat, poultry, or fish with raw unbeaten egg white and rubbing it through a fine strainer. Then beat the mixture over ice with the slow addition of cream. A quicker method is to combine the ground meat and raw unbeaten egg whites in a mixer and beat well. Then, continuing to beat, slowly add the cream, literally drop by drop. The mixture may become quite thin and runny (which is less likely when it is beaten over ice), but can be restored to workable thickness with the addition of 1 to 2 teaspoons salt. (The advantage of this method is less time and effort; the result is not so delicate and fine as the whisking over ice method.) Examples of mousseline forcemeat are in recipes for Filets de Soles Joinville (salmon), Rôti de Veau Farci and the quenelles in Daube de Veau (veal), Galantine de Faisan à la Gelée (veal and pork), and Ballotine de Volaille à la Régence (poultry).

PANADE FORCEMEAT. Forcemeat bound with a paste mixture (see Panade, below) produces the smoothest of all forcemeats. In this procedure, a panade is prepared and chilled. The meat must be finely ground and beaten with raw egg white and then cream, after which it is combined with the panade. Finally, the whole mixture is rubbed through a fine strainer, to become the texture of thick purée. Examples of panade forcemeat are in recipes for Quenelles de Brochet (fish) and Cotelettes de Volaille Vicomtesse (poultry).

FORCEMEATS MADE WITH VEGETABLES, RICE, EGGS, ETC. The recipes in this book will disclose many stuffings with other primary ingredients, such as chopped mixed vegetables, hard-boiled eggs and herbs, rice, mushrooms, chestnuts, pâtés.

PANADE

A panade mixture is used to bind quenelles, forcemeats, or hot savory mousses of any kind.

6 tablespoons water
2 tablespoons vegetable oil
4 tablespoons all-purpose flour

1 tablespoon unflavored
   gelatine
1 cup milk

In a saucepan warm the water and vegetable oil. Mix the flour and gelatine together in a little bowl. Off the heat, add the flour and gelatine to the water and oil. Then add the milk. Stir over low heat until the mixture boils. Pour onto a plate and chill the panade before adding it to the preparation in which it is to be used.

ROUX

Flour and Butter Thickening Agent

The general procedure for preparing a roux is to first melt the butter in a pan, then add the flour and stir the mixture over heat until it is blended. Then the rest of the ingredients for a sauce or other preparation are added.

If the roux is to thicken a *white* sauce or soufflé mixture, for example, the butter and flour are blended over low heat and cooked a little, but they must not brown. If the roux is to thicken a *dark* sauce or other mixture, the flour and butter are blended over higher heat and permitted to brown and take on a browned (not burned) flavor.

HERB VINEGAR OR TARRAGON VINEGAR

Your own homemade herb vinegars will be better than commercial ones. The way to do it is as follows: Fill glass bottles or screw-top jars with fresh tarragon or any fresh herbs you wish to use. (Literally stuff the jars with herbs.) Fill the jar to the top with cider vinegar. Seal tightly and keep in a dark place at least a month before using. Each time a little is used, replace with more cider vinegar. By the time the bottle is a year old you will have the most wonderful vinegar.

WINE VINEGAR

Collect any "leftover" dry white wines and dry red wines in separate containers. Keep them in a warm room. When a thick film, called the mother, has formed, seal tightly in screw-top jars and put in a cool place for two months. Strain through a jelly bag and add an equal amount of good (unturned) red or white wine, whichever you are using.

HERBS AND SPICES OR AROMATICS

Perfumery should be classed as one of the great civilized arts and the French the masters of it. Development of the olfactory sense is elusive, indefinable, and mysterious. Secret perfume formulas of flowers, spices, plants and oils joined with the oil of the body communicate a personal impression that often defies words. In this very same way artistic and intelligent use of an herb or spice joined to food will lift up the soul of that particular dish. Also, of course, too heavy or misunderstood use of herbs can be as offensive as a person wearing too much of the wrong perfume. Overkill!

Herbs and spices function as the "top note" in French cookery, and the way in which one uses them is a strong reflection of taste and sensitivity. In order to use herbs and spices properly it is essential to understand them. There are excellent literary discussions about herbs. One reference I recommend highly is Craig Claiborne's *An Herb and Spice Cook Book*. The whole subject is too voluminous to expand upon here, but I will briefly express my position on the use of herbs and spices as practiced in these recipes.

Herbs (Leaf Type and Root Type)

(1) Wherever called for, herbs are important to the personality of the recipe. The bouquet garni is but one example of the pre-eminence of herbs in the foundation of classic cookery. Fresh herbs are always preferred.

(2) I assume that anyone who has an opportunity will grow fresh herbs in the garden, or backyard, or in a window box. And I think all serious connoisseurs should grow pots of herbs in the kitchen (in addition to the garden, if you have one). The wonderful aromatics from a few pots of fresh growing herbs in the kitchen will waft extra inspiration through your culinary temple the year around. It is not possible to describe the happy sense of one-upmanship you will feel as you trim a few tarragon leaves off the pot in the middle of winter, or pick off a few basil leaves to accent a fresh, sliced tomato.

If you have a garden, please try to plant some chervil. It is the most "beautiful" of all herbs, and fresh chervil is rarely found commercially in this country. It is the favorite in French herb selections. Chervil looks like delicate parsley leaf and is much more delicate in flavor.

(If you do successfully raise some chervil in your garden, prepare a green salad with lots of whole chervil leaves in it with Boston lettuce and a simple French vinaigrette dressing. You can't have a better salad! Romaine is too coarse with chervil; the lettuce must be either Bibb or Boston.)

(3) These are the herbs called for most frequently in my recipes:

LEAF TYPE	
Basil	Rosemary
Bay leaf	Sage
Celery leaf	Savory
Chervil	Tarragon
Chives	Thyme
Dill	Watercress
Fennel	
Marjoram	ROOT TYPE
Mint	Garlic
Oregano	Leeks
Parsley	Baby white onions
Hamburg parsley	Yellow onions
Italian parsley	Scallions
	Shallots

(4) Except for parsley, fresh herbs are still not so universally avail-

able as we might wish, but the situation is improving. There are more and more specialty food stores in the cities that sell little packets of fresh tarragon, dill, thyme, or chives the year round. Small ethnic groceries are often an excellent source, especially Italian shops.

If certain herbs must be used dried, the dried leaf is preferred to powdered or ground types. When dried leaf forms are used, use one-half the quantity of the fresh herb ingredient.

The only herbs I would ever consider using in dried form are bay leaf, marjoram, oregano, rosemary, sage, and thyme. All the others are usually available fresh year-round. If you cannot find them fresh, my advice is to substitute another fresh herb that you believe would be appropriate. (For Tarragon Chicken, Poulet à l'Estragon, if you can't obtain fresh tarragon leaves, the dish obviously cannot be prepared properly; the very essence of the dish is in the aromatic quality of the fresh tarragon herb.)

(5) *Fines herbes* is one of the classic garnishes. The traditional fines herbes includes parsley, chervil, tarragon, and chives. In my own adaptation, as in Omelette Fines Herbes, I like to use any two of the traditional leaf herbs plus two root herbs, preferably shallot and a touch of garlic. Chop them all together a little, and the bouquet is ambrosia! The fines herbes garnish must always be made with fresh herbs.

(6) GARLIC. Always use fresh garlic; never dried! To chop garlic, peel a few garlic cloves and chop them coarsely. Sprinkle the coarsely chopped garlic with about 1 teaspoon salt (to avoid sticking to the knife). Mix the garlic with the salt on the chopping board. Proceed to chop the garlic very fine. To crush it even finer, press it down with the tip of a knife.

Spices

(1) A knowledge of spices and their far-flung origins can add romance to your cooking activity and art to your dish. As with herbs, the way in which you use spices can be a real clue to your talent. Therefore it is a good idea (and fascinating reading) to learn something about spices and how they perform.

(2) The spices and other seasonings called for most frequently in this book are:

Allspice (whole)
Capers
Cardamom (preferably seeds, otherwise ground)
Cayenne pepper (ground)
Cinnamon (stick and ground)
Cloves (whole and ground)
Curry powder (a ground blend)
Ginger (candied, ground, and root)
Juniper berries (whole)

Mace (ground)
Mustard (hot dry and Dijon)
Nutmeg (always whole, to be grated as needed)
Paprika (ground)
Peppercorns, black and white (always whole, to be cracked as needed; see paragraph on Pepper below)
Saffron (always leaf form, to be crushed as needed)

Salt (see paragraph on Salt
  below)
Tabasco (liquid)

Turmeric (ground)
Vanilla (bean and extract)

(3) Purchase the smallest quantity of spice possible at any one time. Spices are used sparingly, and ideally they should not sit around for more than a year.

(4) PEPPER (POIVRE). Black peppercorns are the whole dried pepper berry. White peppercorns are the inner core, or seed, of the black peppercorn. Cayenne pepper is finely ground *hot* red pepper.

My recipes limit cayenne pepper to a few grains used when you want just a touch of bite but no specks of any kind showing, as in smooth white sauces. For most other purposes my preference is to use freshly cracked white pepper. It is a little more delicate than black pepper and less likely to show specks. When a definite pepper statement is desired, such as in certain salads, or in the stockpot or court bouillon, a few whole or cracked black peppercorns are used.

It is a good idea to have a black pepper mill and a white pepper mill on your work counter along with a little container of kosher or regular salt. Cayenne pepper can be kept in a jar on the spice shelf.

Never use preground pepper; the essence (flavor) of the pepper is gone. Pepper is like any other living food — just compare the bouquet (aroma) of freshly cracked pepper to preground.

(5) SALT (SEL). My preference is to use coarse kosher salt for all cooking uses. It tends to give a lighter, more delicate salt flavor; it seems to enhance the flavor of the food rather than "salt" the flavor of the food. However, in this book we bow to majority usage and give the salt ingredient in quantities for regular granulated salt. If you, too, are a kosher salt user, as most of my former students are, double the quantity given in the recipe. Incidentally, salt is never placed on a purist gourmet table. It should not be needed; the seasoning should be just right. A pepper mill is available, since pepper should be added to food just before eating.

VANILLA SUGAR

Granulated sugar flavored with vanilla is used when the merest suggestion of vanilla is desired, usually in a dessert. To prepare vanilla sugar, place about half a vanilla bean or the pod only in a cup of sugar. Allow the combination to stand at least 1 hour. A supply of vanilla sugar may be maintained in a jar in this manner for any length of time. Use the sugar as called for in the particular recipe.

PRALIN

Praline, Praline Powder

2 cups granulated sugar
½ teaspoon cream of tartar

1½ cups blanched almonds

Brush a jelly roll pan or baking sheet lightly with vegetable oil. Combine the ingredients in an unlined copper pan and put it over moderate heat. As the sugar begins to melt, turn the mixture with a metal spoon. When the whole mixture is caramelized to a rich medium caramel color, pour it onto the oiled jelly roll pan.

The praline will quickly set and become brittle. When it is cooled and hard, break it into chunks small enough to put into an electric blender. Pulverize the praline in the blender according to the texture desired: coarse and chunky (as for ice cream) or powdered (as for soufflés and sauces). Praline powder may be stored indefinitely in a screw-top jar in the refrigerator. NET: About 3 cups.

SCALDED MILK

Primarily in the preparation of custards, milk or cream must be "scalded" when it is added to the egg or egg yolk mixture. To scald, bring milk or cream slowly to a boil and remove it immediately from the heat. Do not boil milk unless a recipe specifically instructs the procedure.

SOUR MILK

There are three ways to "manufacture" sour milk. (1) Put lemon rind and a large slice of pumpernickel bread in warm milk for 1 hour; then strain. (2) Dilute sour cream with skim milk. (3) Add 2 teaspoons vinegar to 1 cup sweet milk and let it stand a few minutes at room temperature.

CARAMEL COLORING

This is used only to give any savory brown sauce a good appearance and does not alter the flavor. It is very handy to keep a small bottle of it in the refrigerator. To make it, put 2 cups granulated sugar, ½ teaspoon cream of tartar, and ¼ cup water in a small heavy pan, preferably an unlined copper pan. Stir over high heat until the sugar dissolves, then allow to boil until it becomes very dark caramel in color. Add ½ cup water to reduce it to a light syrupy consistency. If it becomes too thick when chilled, add a little more water.

BLANCHED VEGETABLES, FRUITS, ETC.

To "blanch" means to cover the raw food with cold water, bring it to a boil, and usually drain immediately. The French method is to blanch vegetables before cooking them according to the particular recipe (see page 569). The purpose of blanching a vegetable is generally to remove all trace of bitterness or to make vegetables such as lettuces and leeks more pliable (to facilitate cleaning and shaping them).

Certain offals are blanched, such as sweetbreads, to make it easier to remove the skin.

Tomatoes and peaches are quickly blanched (by pouring boiling water over them and counting to 10) to remove the skins.

Wine is the warm blood that courses through the veins of French cooking. It is the essence that expresses life and goodness in a dish of food. When wine is called for in this book, it is as necessary for that particular dish as are salt or eggs when they are listed; there is no substitute.

Today, when one can purchase a perfectly good bottle of American Burgundy or Chablis in any neighborhood, not even economy is an excuse for omitting the wine ingredient. Inexpensive dry red Burgundies and dry white Chablis, among the others listed below, are quite good for everyday cooking and drinking — better than the average Algerian wine that many contemporary French homes must accept as "vin ordinaire" (everyday wine).

The following paragraphs are on general techniques and procedures for cooking with wine and spirits.

(1) DRY AND SWEET WINES. Please use the kind of wine specified in the recipe; the flavor balance can be destroyed entirely if you do not. Substitution of a sweet white Sauternes for a dry white wine in a fish stock, for instance, would be disaster. Some general types:

Dry white wine: Chablis, Pinot Chardonnay, Muscadet, Pouilly-Fuissé, Swiss whites, Graves, Portuguese Dao white, Italian Soave.

Dry red wine: Burgundy, Pinot Noir, Beaujolais, Cabernet Sauvignon, Portuguese Dao red.

Sweet white wine: Sauternes.

"Sweet red wine." Although the term "sweet red wine" is rarely, if ever, used, it is employed here for comparison, to identify the sweet character of such wines as port, Marsala, and Madeira. These wines are frequently used in combination with dry wine in a sauce, and are used sparingly, a tablespoon or two, or ¼ cup. Please do not ever use port, Marsala, or Madeira as the ingredient when dry red wine is specified.

Rosé wine is rarely, if ever, used in cooking. Its character is too indefinite to provide the desired top note of a white or a red.

Sherry is a lovely enhancement in cooking and in many savory dishes in this book we include a dash of dry sherry. In a few dishes we want the character of cream sherry, and specify it.

(2) QUALITY OF COOKING WINE. Never use a wine in cooking that you wouldn't drink. A wine "just for cooking," and presumably not good for drinking, won't glorify your cooking at all.

(3) FLAVOR HARMONIZING WITH WINE. Most commonly, dry white wines are used in fish and chicken dishes, dry red wines in cooking red meats, dry sherry in soups and creamed dishes, sweet wines in fruit sauces and syrups. There are famous exceptions like Coq au Vin, however.

(4) METHOD OF COOKING WITH WINE. Wine in a cooked dish must be cooked with other ingredients so that it marries with the total composition. If the wine (or spirit) is to be added at the end of the preparation, it should be flamed (see paragraph below on flaming). Either cooking or flaming dissipates the alcohol so that you do not get a "raw" taste. You want the essence and refinement that is the contribution of wine in cooking. Never drown foods in wine; what is wanted is subtlety.

WINE: THE INGREDIENT

Also Spirits and Liqueurs

(5) SPIRITS AND LIQUEURS IN COOKING. Cognac or good brandy is the most frequently used spirit in cooking. In this book, when brandy appears as an ingredient, which is frequently, a good grape brandy is meant, and Cognac is preferred. All sorts of other spirits are used throughout this collection, in savory and in sweet dishes, in sauces, fillings, and pastry doughs, for the unique character that each contributes to the dish.

Usually a spirit is flamed when added to a preparation, which burns off all the alcohol and leaves the flavor concentrate (see flaming technique below). Because the real purpose in using a spirit is to obtain its flavor character or zest, and not to provide dramatic pyrotechnics, it is very important to use good spirits. Only a little is used in any recipe; therefore cooking with this somewhat expensive product is not extravagant.

Some of the wonderful spirits used in cooking are:

NAME	DISTILLED ESSENCE OF
Cognac, Armagnac, Marc	Grapes
Calvados	Apples
Framboise (eau de vie)	Raspberries
Kirsch	Cherries
Crème de Cassis	Black currants
Gin	Juniper berries
Rum	Molasses
Rye whiskey	Rye (which gives a distinct rye tang)
Scotch whiskey	Malted barley (which gives a smoky peat character)
Grand Marnier	A bouquet of Cognac and bitter orange spirits

(6) FLAMING WINE OR SPIRITS. The flaming of wine or spirits properly takes place in the kitchen and not at the table, because the spirit is usually added early in the preparation of a dish. The safest and surest way to flame a wine or spirit when adding it to a preparation is as follows.

Put the measured quantity of spirit in a separate little pan (for example, a 1-cup copper saucepan). When you are ready to add it to your dish, warm it in its separate pan and ignite it (if the surrounding gas flame hasn't already done that for you). Carefully pour the flaming spirit over the food it is to join. Let the flame burn out, then proceed with the preparation. (It is a good idea to keep a little copper saucepan near your stove just for this purpose.)

(7) THE KITCHEN WINE RACK. In addition to the family wine cellar, you will find it convenient to keep in a little rack in the kitchen a few wines that are basic in cooking. My suggested inventory is 1 bottle each of Cognac (or other good grape brandy), dry red wine (light Burgundy type), dry white wine (light Chablis or Loire type), dry sherry, Marsala, Madeira, Grand Marnier, rum, Framboise, Kirsch, and Calvados.

HORS D'OEUVRES

Hors d'oeuvres are mini-servings of food that tantalize the palate, taste good, and are presented with special attractiveness — a definition often reiterated in my cooking classes. A mystery in American cuisine is how the name for this category of French gastronomy ever became linked with the questionable institution of the cocktail party and its soggy strips of spongy white bread spread with unsavory dips, dry smoked salmon, straight-from-the-can anchovy paste, sticky canned caviar, and other spreads which defy identification. These creations, always called canapés, have no connection with a real French canapé, which is always toasted or fried, with a garnish that meets the above specifications.

This twentieth-century social rite of the cocktail party is an exercise in misery and endurance — crowded, smoke-filled rooms, standing up, moving about, balancing handbag, drink, cigarette, and tidbit while projecting animated conversation in shouting tones. Nowhere in literature on authentic French gastronomy does one find any reference to food of this kind for eating (one can't call it a meal, really). It is totally antagonistic towards the appreciation of culinary art.

Maybe this has all been part of an era that is on its way out, and we can now rediscover the real meaning of hors d'oeuvres as the French originated the category, and make it step one in our new quest for honest food. Add to the chichi canapé the "creative" dip, and let's discard both from our vocabulary and our cuisine. Then let us move to the fine art of serving and eating real raw vegetables beautifully served in cartwheel arrangements with homemade vinaigrette, raw scallops marinated in lemon-lime-orange juices, a lovely homemade spinach tart, simple cold homemade meat loaf (pâté maison) with sour gherkins, or perfect hard-boiled eggs coated with mustard mayonnaise. Actually, the Russians, in their zakuski, offer one of the best interpretations of the serving of hors d'oeuvres at a predinner social gathering. The zakuski is a buffet of appetizing savory dishes which can be nibbled in concert with conversation and drink, much like the Scandinavian smorgasbord.

Drawing upon the finest aspects of hors d'oeuvres in the style of French gastronomy, I believe that the contemporary position of hors d'oeuvres might best be regarded as follows.

(1) Hors d'oeuvres should stimulate the appetite. This means awaken the taste buds, stimulate the salivary glands, and excite the mind for the meal that is to come.

(2) In the French milieu, hors d'oeuvres usually precede the luncheon meal. In most contemporary U.S. life styles, the main meal and the only meal taken at home is dinner in the evening. Therefore, hors d'oeuvres should be construed nowadays as an option for a first course, other options being soup, a light fish, a seafood dish, salad, or vegetable, eaten either at or pre-table with an apéritif or wine.

(3) If one must sponsor a "cocktail gathering," it is most gracious to offer an attractive buffet of real food, with little plates, and arrange for groupings of chairs and little café tables, so that some guests may sit for a spell.

(4) Except for very grand formal occasions, hors d'oeuvres are not necessary preceding a dinner party. If one wishes to accompany a predinner aperitif with snack tidbits, they should be simple and limited, such as a few dishes of fresh nuts, or little cheese Palmiers. The exception is fresh black caviar, which should be served with plain toast and lemon.

(5) Hors d'oeuvres in the home can frequently be prepared with leftovers — a bit of lobster, a chunk of cold cucumber, a little Roquefort, a few slices of salami, partnered with a wedge or two of tomato, hard-boiled eggs, or minced and stuffed into mushroom caps or pastry scraps dusted with grated cheese.

(6) Hors d'oeuvres should be slightly more seasoned or piquant than most main dishes, and taken in small quantities.

(7) Keep hors d'oeuvres simple, to express their natural goodness. As the first course of a family meal, for instance, nothing beats a plate of asparagus in season with clarified butter, or cold mussels with homemade Rémoulade Sauce. Build to the more complicated flavors to come in the main course or in the dessert.

(8) Do not underrate the necessity of beauty and eye appeal in the presentation of hors d'oeuvres. Sight is important in gastronomy; it should invite all the other senses into great anticipation of the meal that will follow. Hors d'oeuvres should be attractively shaped and decorated, and served on an attractive serving dish or tray. But above all, the presentation should not be contrived or decorated with inedible or unrelated items.

OEUFS À LA PARISIENNE

Eggs Parisian Style (cold)

Hard-boiled eggs stuffed with chive butter and served on a tomato half, the whole coated with an anchovy mayonnaise.

6 hard-boiled eggs   _6 tablespoons sweet butter_

1 tablespoon chopped fresh
   chives
Salt
Few grains cayenne pepper
6 firm ripe tomatoes (skinned)
Freshly cracked white pepper
A little granulated sugar
½ teaspoon finely chopped
   garlic

ANCHOVY MAYONNAISE
1 egg
1 egg yolk
½ teaspoon salt
Few grains cayenne pepper

1 teaspoon Dijon mustard
3 tablespoons tarragon vinegar
1½ cups vegetable oil
4 tablespoons pure olive oil
6 anchovy fillets
1 tablespoon unflavored gelatine
3 tablespoons milk
1 teaspoon tomato paste
½ cup light cream

GARNISH
4 fresh red radishes
2 teaspoons chopped fresh
   parsley
2 lemons

Carefully shell the eggs. (If done ahead of time, store the shelled eggs in a strong solution of lemon juice and cold water.) Drain well. Cut them in half lengthwise and remove the yolks. Rub the yolks through a coarse strainer. Beat the butter in a mixer until it is light and creamy. Add the chopped chives and strained egg yolks, season with salt and cayenne pepper. Refill the egg white halves with this mixture. Cut the skinned tomatoes in half horizontally, and sprinkle the top of each half with a little salt, pepper, sugar, and garlic. Place a stuffed egg half (cut side down) on top of each tomato half. Place them on a cake rack on a jelly roll pan and carefully coat each one with the following anchovy mayonnaise.

ANCHOVY MAYONNAISE. Put the whole egg and egg yolk in a mixer and beat well. Add the salt, cayenne pepper, and mustard. Continue beating and slowly add the vinegar, vegetable oil, and olive oil (at the start, drop by drop; when it begins to thicken, the oils can be added a little faster). Pulverize the anchovy fillets with a pestle and mortar and add to the mayonnaise. Put the gelatine in a small pan with the milk. Soak the gelatine a few minutes to soften, and then stir it over low heat until it dissolves. Cool a little and slowly mix into the mayonnaise. Add the tomato paste and enough of the light cream to bring the mayonnaise to a coating consistency.

Carefully coat the eggs and tomatoes with the mayonnaise. Put them in the refrigerator to set. To serve, garnish each egg top with a thin slice of radish. Sprinkle the tops with a little chopped parsley. Arrange on a serving dish and surround with thin half-slices of lemon.

OEUFS AU FOIE GRAS

Eggs Stuffed
with Liver Pâté (cold)

6 eggs, hard-boiled
A little lemon juice and cold
   water
8 tablespoons sweet butter
2½ ounces fine liver pâté

Salt
Freshly cracked white pepper
2 tablespoons Cognac or good
   brandy
12 small rounds of buttered

pumpernickel bread　　　　　　　　*Sprigs of fresh watercress*
12 small rounds of black olive

Chill the hard-boiled eggs. Shell them and cut them carefully in half lengthwise. Remove the yolks, taking care not to break the whites. Place the whites in a bowl of cold water with a little lemon juice in it. Rub the yolks through a fine strainer. Cream the butter in an electric mixer. Add the pâté to the mixer and beat well. Season with salt and white pepper. Add the brandy and beat well. Mix in the strained egg yolks. Put this mixture into a pastry bag fitted with a large star tube. Drain the egg whites on paper towels. Anchor them cut side up on rounds of buttered pumpernickel bread and arrange them on a long, narrow oval platter. Carefully fill them with the pâté mixture. Decorate the tops with small rounds of black olive, and garnish the platter with sprigs of fresh crisp watercress. NET: 4 to 6 servings.

OEUFS POCHÉS À LA BOUR-GUIGNONNE

Eggs Poached in Red Burgundy (hot)

4 cups red Burgundy or other dry red wine
Salt
24 baby white onions, peeled and blanched
6 tablespoons salt butter
2 tablespoons chopped fresh parsley

Freshly cracked black pepper
24 baby white mushrooms
A little lemon juice
6 eggs
3 tablespoons all-purpose flour
6 large croûtons of bread, fried in pure olive oil until golden brown (page 69)

Heat the red wine with a little salt. Add the blanched baby white onions and simmer gently until just soft. Drain the onions, and toss them in a little melted butter and chopped parsley. Sauté the baby white mushrooms in a little butter, lemon juice, salt and pepper. Strain the wine and return it to the pan. Bring it to a simmer. Break one egg into a cup. Stir the wine until it makes a deep whirlpool, slide the egg into the bottom of the whirlpool, and let it cook 3½ minutes. Remove it from the wine with a slotted spoon and slide it into a bowl of warm water until ready to serve. Poach all the eggs in this manner.

When all the eggs are poached, strain the wine once more and boil it down to 1½ cups. Mix the flour with 3 tablespoons butter and add this roux, bit by bit, to the reduced wine. Simmer the sauce 10 minutes. Put the mushrooms and onions in a shallow copper casserole. Drain the eggs and place them carefully on top of the mushrooms and onions. Spoon the wine sauce over them. Sprinkle the top with a little chopped fresh parsley. Surround the casserole with the croûtons of fried bread. NET: 6 servings.

OEUFS À LA RUSSE

Jellied Poached Eggs on Russian Salad (cold)

For these poached eggs in aspic you will need 6 chilled dariole molds (small oval-shaped tins). If you like, serve the jellied eggs without the Russian salad.

6 eggs
½ cup tarragon vinegar
4 cups water
2 teaspoons salt
4 cups aspic (from chicken stock, recipe on page 37)
6 small thin slices of boiled ham, cut into diamond shapes
3 hard-boiled eggs

RUSSIAN SALAD
1½ cups each of finely chopped

carrots, green beans, and turnips
1½ cups each of green peas and baby lima beans
1 egg yolk
½ teaspoon dry mustard
1½ teaspoons salt
A few grains cayenne pepper
1 tablespoon tarragon vinegar
1 cup vegetable oil
1 tablespoon unflavored gelatine
4 tablespoons hot milk

To poach the eggs, put the vinegar, water, and salt in the top of a double boiler. Bring to a rolling boil, then reduce to a gentle simmer. Break an egg into a cup. Stir the simmering liquid with a slotted spoon to form a deep whirlpool, and carefully slide the egg into the center of the whirlpool. Let it poach 3½ minutes. Remove it with the slotted spoon and place it in a bowl of ice water. Cook all the eggs the same way. Have the chilled dariole molds ready. Dissolve the aspic in a pan over low heat, then stir it over a bowl of ice until it is at the point of setting. Pour about a third of it into the molds and put them in the refrigerator to set. Dip each diamond of ham into the aspic and set it in the middle of the mold. Place a poached egg in each mold, if necessary trimming the white with scissors to fit. Pour another third of the aspic into the molds and chill them. Pour the rest of the aspic into a shallow pan and chill it until firm.

RUSSIAN SALAD. Barely cook the chopped vegetables in plain salted water; they should be a little crisp. Drain them well, mix them together lightly in a bowl, and chill while you prepare a mayonnaise sauce as follows. In a mixer bowl, beat the egg yolk, mustard, salt, and cayenne pepper until thick. Slowly add the vinegar and vegetable oil, beating constantly. Dissolve the gelatine in the milk, let cool a little, and add to the mayonnaise sauce. Mix this sauce with the cooked vegetables. Pack them into a plain round mold, such as a springform cake pan, and put in the refrigerator to set.

To serve, unmold the vegetables on a round silver platter by wrapping the mold with a hot wet cloth. Remove the jellied poached eggs from the molds by sliding a small knife around the edge and giving the mold a light knock. Arrange the eggs around the edge of the platter. Chop the remaining aspic on a piece of wax paper and pipe or spoon it around the edge of the platter. Chill before serving. NET: 6 servings.

CAMEMBERT GLACÉ

8 ounces Camembert cheese
¼ cup dry white wine
¼ cup heavy cream

Salt
A few grains cayenne pepper
2 tablespoons dry white

Iced Camembert (cold)

breadcrumbs (page 69)
¾ cup freshly grated Parmesan
cheese

A little paprika
A few sprigs fresh crisp
watercress

Rub the cheese through a wire sieve or fine strainer, rind and all. In an electric mixer, beat the cheese until it is almost liquid with the wine, cream, salt, cayenne pepper, and breadcrumbs. Freeze. When it is solid, cut into bite-size pieces and roll them in the grated Parmesan cheese and paprika. Stick a toothpick into each piece. Serve on a small round platter garnished with the fresh watercress. NET: 12 to 16 pieces.

FONDUE DE FROMAGE

Cheese Fondue (hot)

This is the classic Swiss recipe. The fondue can also be made with Bock beer in season instead of dry white wine. But of course if you decide to use Bock beer, you should first test it for excellence in the traditional Swiss-German manner. Put on your lederhosen, then pour a small puddle of beer on a varnished wooden stool. Sit on the stool for about 30 minutes and then rise slowly. If the stool rises with you, the Bock beer is of excellent quality and should make a nice flavorful fondue.

4 cups imported Swiss Gruyère
cheese, cut into dice
1 large garlic clove
2 cups dry white wine
(preferably Neuchatel)
1 teaspoon salt
½ teaspoon freshly cracked

white pepper
½ teaspoon freshly grated
nutmeg
2 tablespoons all-purpose flour
¼ cup Kirsch
1 long loaf of French bread

Spread the diced Gruyère cheese on a large tray and allow to dry overnight, if possible. Heat a heavy pan. When the pan is hot, rub it out with the clove of garlic, then put into it the cheese, wine, salt, pepper, and nutmeg. Stir over low heat without stopping until the cheese has just melted. Mix the flour into the Kirsch and stir it into the cheese. If the melted cheese is too thick, add a little more white wine. Serve in a chafing dish. Cut the French bread into slices or large cubes, toast them on each side, and serve separately in a basket, with long fondue forks. NET: Serves 8 as a first course, 4 as a main course.

PETITES BOULES DE FROMAGE

*Little Mixed
Cheese Balls (cold)*

A way to serve cheese balls, when they are well chilled, is to put a cocktail stick into each ball and stick it into a beautiful head of red or green cabbage.

12 tablespoons salt butter
8 ounces cream cheese
1 teaspoon dry mustard
½ teaspoon curry powder

1 tablespoon Worcestershire
sauce
1 teaspoon Tabasco sauce
1 teaspoon soya sauce

Salt
A few grains cayenne pepper
4 ounces Roquefort cheese
1 cup walnut meats, finely

chopped
1 cup almonds, blanched,
browned, and ground

Cream the butter and divide it in half. Cream the cream cheese and add half the butter to it with the mustard, curry powder, Worcestershire, Tabasco, soya sauce, salt to taste, and cayenne pepper. Mix well and chill. Rub the Roquefort cheese through a strainer and mix it well with the other half of the butter and a little salt and cayenne pepper. Chill. When both cheese mixtures are chilled firm, form into balls about the size of a very small walnut. Roll the Roquefort cheese balls in the ground almonds and the cream cheese balls in the finely chopped walnut. Chill the balls thoroughly before serving. NET: 24 to 30 balls.

These finger-size cheese pastries may be made in advance and kept in an airtight tin to be handy for tidbits.

12 tablespoons salt butter
6 ounces all-purpose flour
3 ounces freshly grated
　Parmesan cheese
1 hard-boiled egg yolk, rubbed
　through a fine strainer

2 ounces ground almonds
½ teaspoon salt
A few grains cayenne pepper
1 raw egg yolk
1 tablespoon ice water

*PETITES
TARTINES
AU FROMAGE*

Austrian Cheese Cakes
(cold)

Preheat the oven to 350°. In a bowl, rub the butter into the flour with your fingertips until it resembles coarse cornmeal. (There is a greater proportion of butter to flour in this pastry than in regular short pastry; therefore one must work quickly to get it to a crumbly, not pasty, state.) Add to the pastry the grated cheese, strained hard-boiled egg yolk, ground almonds, salt, and cayenne pepper. Mix the raw egg yolk with the ice water. Add it to the other ingredients, and work up quickly to a firm dough. Roll out the dough ¼ inch thick on a lightly floured board. Using a 1-inch cookie cutter, cut all the dough into rounds. Place them on an ungreased baking sheet. Bake until they are a delicate golden brown, 20 to 30 minutes. Gently remove them from the pan, cool, and store in an airtight tin. NET: 18 to 24 small cakes.

This is the correct way to serve fine caviar. The best malossol beluga caviar is such a rare and wonderful food that it would be a crime to hide any of its superb natural flavor.

　At the Drouant Restaurant in Paris, where I apprenticed as a chef, fine caviar was served in two ways. The first, my favorite, is to put the fresh caviar in a small silver or crystal bowl and place the bowl in a larger one of crushed ice which is set on a flat platter. Serve it with lemons cut in half, thinly sliced trimmed plain toast, and a small

*CAVIARE
CLASSIQUE*

Classic Caviar (cold)

dish of excellent sweet butter. The other very acceptable alternative was to serve it with very thin slices of buttered rye or whole wheat bread, and garnishes of finely chopped white onion, finely chopped fresh parsley, strained hard-boiled egg yolk, and finely chopped hard-boiled egg white, all placed in small mounds around the bowl of caviar.

CLAMS AU NATUREL

Clams on the Half-Shell (cold)

48 littleneck clams or 24 cherrystone clams
½ cup cornmeal (for soaking)
Crushed ice (enough to cover
   4 serving plates)
Freshly cracked black and white

pepper
2 lemons, cut in half
Thin slices of whole wheat or
   pumpernickel bread spread
   with sweet butter

Wash the clams thoroughly in several waters, then cover them with clear water, sprinkle with the cornmeal, and leave them in this bath at least 3 hours, or preferably overnight. This procedure will whiten the clams and rid them of most of the sand as well as the black liquid in their stomachs. When ready to prepare, wash them in clear water again.

To open hard-shell clams, cover them with tepid water and let them stand 5 minutes. They will then open slightly. Carefully lift up a clam, quickly insert an oyster knife between the shells, and cut through the muscle holding the shells together. Try to save the clam juice as you open them because the juice contains much of the flavor.

Cover 4 plates with crushed ice. Arrange 6 clams on the bed of crushed ice on each plate. Serve with freshly cracked black and white pepper, half a lemon per serving, and a plate of thin slices of whole wheat or pumpernickel bread spread with excellent sweet butter. NET: 4 servings.

BROILED CLAMS ON THE HALF-SHELL, GARLIC BUTTER

Clams prepared in this manner are also very good sprinkled with finely shredded crisp cooked bacon. Large mussels can also be prepared in this manner.

48 littleneck clams or 24 cherrystone clams
½ cup cornmeal (for soaking)
Coarse rock salt
8 tablespoons sweet butter

1 teaspoon finely chopped garlic
1 tablespoon finely chopped
   fresh parsley
Salt
Freshly cracked white pepper

Wash, soak, and open the clams as in the preceding recipe. In an electric mixer bowl, beat the butter with the chopped garlic, parsley, and salt and pepper to taste. Roll this butter in wax paper and freeze it. Cover a large flat metal platter with coarse rock salt. Set the clams on the half-shell on this platter. When the butter is a solid roll, place a slice of the butter on each clam. Put the platter of clams under a hot broiler for 4 minutes. Remove, and serve piping hot. NET: 4 servings.

24 littleneck clams on the half-
   shell
1 teaspoon finely chopped garlic
6 tablespoons Herb Butter

(page 58)
4 large slices toast, cut in
   quarters

CLAMS AUX
FINES HERBES

*Clams on the Half-Shell
with Herb Butter (hot)*

Place the clams on a baking sheet. Put a speck of finely chopped garlic on top of each. Put a small portion of the herb butter on each clam. Place the clams under a hot broiler for 2 to 3 minutes. Arrange the clams on a hot platter and garnish around the edge with snippets of toast. (Snippets are pieces of toast cut in the shape of tiny isosceles triangles.) NET: 4 servings.

This recipe should be started 48 hours before serving.

12 salt herrings
1 quart milk
18 whole peppercorns, black and
   white mixed
3 bay leaves, crumbled
4 sprigs fresh thyme, chopped
6 baby white onions, chopped

1 lemon, thinly sliced
3/4 cup pure olive oil
1/2 cup tarragon vinegar
1 1/2 cups sour cream
Freshly cracked black pepper
1/2 teaspoon lemon juice
4 shallots, finely chopped

*FILETS DE
HARENGS SAURS
MARINÉS
À LA CRÈME*

*Salt Herring Fillets
in Sour Cream (cold)*

Wash the salt herrings in cold water. Carefully remove the skin, center bone, heads, and tails. Place the fillets in a shallow earthenware bowl and cover them with the milk. Cover the bowl with cheesecloth and let it stand 24 hours.

Drain the fillets from the milk. Have a deep oval dish ready. Put two fillets in the dish, scatter over them a few peppercorns, a little bay leaf, thyme, and onion, and two thin slices of lemon. Sprinkle well with olive oil and repeat this procedure until all the fillets have been used. Gently and thoroughly mix the vinegar and sour cream together with a rubber scraper. Add a little freshly cracked black pepper and the lemon juice. Completely cover the herring fillets with the sour cream mixture, cover the dish again with cheesecloth, and allow the herrings to marinate at least 24 hours. Serve very cold, with very finely chopped shallots on the top. NET: 12 servings.

These kippered herring pieces, rolled in bacon, are coated in a delicate warm sauce.

2 smoked kippered herrings

6 thin slices bacon

*CANAPÉS
NORDAISES*

A few slices white bread

SAUCE
3 egg yolks
2 tablespoons salt butter
1 cup light cream

3 tablespoons freshly grated
   Parmesan cheese
Salt to taste
A little freshly cracked white
   pepper

Preheat the oven to 350°. Skin and bone the kippers and cut in small finger-size pieces. Cut the bacon into enough pieces to wrap each piece of kipper in bacon. Place the wrapped kipper on a baking sheet and bake 10 minutes. While the kippers are in the oven, trim the bread and cut into pieces about the size of the kipper fillets. Toast the bread. Remove the kippers from the oven and arrange one on each piece of toast. Place them on a hot flat dish and keep them warm. Put the sauce ingredients in the top of a double boiler. Stir over low heat until the mixture thickens (do not allow it to get too hot or it will curdle). Add a little more cream if it does become too thick. Carefully spoon this sauce over each piece of kipper and brown quickly under the broiler just before serving. NET: About 24 individual servings.

MOULES FARCIES

Stuffed Mussels (hot)

These mussels are stuffed with a salpicon of shallots and red pepper, grilled under the broiler, and served on the half-shell.

24 large mussels
1 teaspoon dry mustard
1 slice bacon
6 shallots, finely chopped
1 red pepper, seeded and finely
   diced
½ cup fried breadcrumbs (page
   69)

Salt
Freshly cracked black pepper
1 tablespoon finely chopped
   parsley
½ cup freshly grated Parmesan
   cheese
6 tablespoons salt butter
Rock salt

Preheat the oven to 350°. Wash the mussels well in cold water with the dry mustard. Put them in a shallow baking dish and bake until the shells are well opened. Remove and cool a little. Discard the top shell of each mussel. Place the mussels (in the shell) on a bed of rock salt on an ovenproof serving platter, and set aside. Cut the bacon slice into very fine shreds, sauté until crisp, scoop out of the pan, and drain on a paper towel. Cook the shallots in the bacon fat until they begin to brown, then add the red pepper, bacon, 2 tablespoons fried bread-crumbs, the chopped parsley, and a little salt and pepper. Mix well. Put a teaspoon of this mixture in the bottom of each shell. Place the mussel on it and cover with more of the mixture. Sprinkle the mussels with the Parmesan cheese; melt the butter and pour a little on each. Brown the mussels under a hot broiler. The mussels may be left on the bed of rock salt for serving. NET: 4 servings.

This style of cooking mussels is a favorite one.

1 quart large mussels
1 teaspoon dry mustard
1 bay leaf
1 onion, sliced
1 carrot, sliced
1 stalk celery, sliced
Salt to taste
6 black peppercorns
½ cup dry white wine

RÉMOULADE SAUCE
2 egg yolks
1 teaspoon dry mustard

1 teaspoon Dijon mustard
½ teaspoon salt
A few grains cayenne pepper
1 tablespoon tarragon vinegar
¼ cup pure olive oil
¾ cup vegetable oil
1 tablespoon capers, chopped
1 tablespoon finely chopped
    sour gherkins
1 tablespoon finely chopped
    fresh herbs (parsley, thyme,
    tarragon)

*Mussels with
Rémoulade Sauce (cold)*

Scrub the mussels well in cold water with the mustard in it. Put them in a pan with the bay leaf, onion, carrot, celery, salt, peppercorns, and wine. Bring slowly to a boil, cover, and simmer 5 minutes. Remove the top shell from the mussels and arrange them on a platter. Strain the liquid, boil it down to 1 tablespoon in quantity, and set it aside.

RÉMOULADE SAUCE. Beat the yolks in the mixer. Add the salt, mustards, cayenne pepper, and the reserved liquid from the mussels. Beat well. When the mixture is thick, add the vinegar drop by drop. Then add the olive oil and the vegetable oil, at first drop by drop, until the sauce becomes thick. Keep beating it throughout. Add the capers, gherkins, and herbs. If the sauce is too thick, add a little light cream.

Coat the mussels with this sauce, and serve them very cold. NET: 4 servings.

16 oysters and 8 oyster half-
    shells
Juice of 1 lemon
Salt
Freshly cracked white pepper
2 tablespoons salt butter

2 tablespoons all-purpose flour
A few grains cayenne pepper
1¼ cups dry white wine
2 tablespoons heavy cream
2 tablespoons freshly grated
    Parmesan cheese

*Oysters Baked
in the Shell (hot)*

Place 2 oysters in each shell. Sprinkle them with lemon juice, salt, and pepper.

SAUCE. Melt the butter in a saucepan. Off the heat add the flour, cayenne pepper and salt to taste. In a separate little pan reduce the dry white wine to half quantity. Add it to the roux and stir until the sauce thickens. Add the heavy cream and the grated Parmesan cheese. Bring to a boil and simmer gently 3 to 4 minutes.

Spoon a little of the sauce over the oysters and put them under a hot broiler for about 4 to 5 minutes. If desired, pipe a crisscross of very cold shrimp butter (page 152) over each before serving. NET: 4 servings.

HUÎTRES CASINO

Oysters Casino (hot)

12 oysters on the half-shell
Lemon juice
Salt
A few grains cayenne pepper
8 slices bacon
½ cup freshly grated
   Parmesan cheese

2 tablespoons chopped fresh
   parsley
¾ cup dry breadcrumbs
   (page 69)
8 tablespoons salt butter
Rock salt

Loosen each oyster on its shell, sprinkle with a little lemon juice, and season with salt and cayenne pepper. Cut 6 slices bacon into fine shreds and fry until crisp. Drain and reserve the fat. Sprinkle the shredded bacon over the top of each oyster. Fry the breadcrumbs in the bacon fat. Mix them with cheese and parsley. Spoon some of the crumb mixture on each oyster. Cut the remaining slices of raw bacon into 4 pieces each. Place a small piece of bacon on each oyster. Put a little chunk of salt butter on the bacon. Cover an ovenproof serving platter with rock salt. Place the oysters in their shells on the salt. Brown under a hot broiler for 4 minutes and serve hot in the same dish. NET: 4 servings.

OYSTERS ROCKEFELLER

This famous dish consists of broiled oysters on the half-shell, covered with a spinach purée and laced with Pernod.

16 oysters on the half-shell
4 tablespoons Pernod (liqueur)
Salt
Freshly cracked white pepper
1 cup sour cream
1 teaspoon finely chopped garlic
¾ pound raw spinach

3 tablespoons breadcrumbs
5 tablespoons freshly grated
   Parmesan cheese
3 tablespoons melted salt butter
½ cup heavy cream, whipped
Rock salt

Remove the oysters from their shells. Put them in a bowl and sprinkle them with 1 tablespoon Pernod and a little salt and pepper. Mix half the sour cream with half the garlic and a little salt and pepper, and put some of this mixture into each oyster shell. Put the oysters back in their shells. Put the raw spinach through a fine meat chopper. Mix it with the remaining sour cream and garlic and salt and pepper. Spoon this mixture over the oysters. Sprinkle them with the breadcrumbs and grated cheese. Dot with the melted butter. Cover the bottom of an ovenproof serving platter with rock salt. Set the oysters on the salt. Brown them under a very hot broiler. Sprinkle them with the rest of the Pernod. Put 1 teaspoon plain whipped cream on the top of each and scorch the cream topping under a very hot broiler. NET: 4 servings.

I personally like the way smoked salmon is served in Scotland. The smoked salmon has very little saltiness and is very thinly sliced. Slices of smoked salmon are laid on a plate, not overlapping, with a few capers, half a fresh lemon, and wafer-thin slices of whole wheat bread spread with sweet butter.

Fine smoked sturgeon may be served in the same manner.

SAUMON FUMÉ

Smoked Salmon (cold)

This preparation should be started 24 hours in advance. It is served in small scallop shells.

1 pound sea or bay scallops
Juice of 2 limes
Juice of 1 orange
Grated rind of 1 lemon, 1 lime, and half an orange

Salt to taste
A little freshly cracked white pepper
2 tablespoons Curaçao (liqueur)
Lime slices

Slice the raw scallops thinly. Mix all the other ingredients together and add the sliced scallops. Allow them to marinate overnight in the refrigerator. To serve, arrange the sliced scallops on small scallop shells, and serve ice cold. Garnish with a thin slice of lime on each. NET: 4 to 6 servings.

COQUILLES SAINT-JACQUES EN SEVICHE

Scallops Marinated in Citrus Juices (cold)

This preparation should be started a day in advance. You'll need four snail platters and tongs.

24 snails (1 package)
24 snail shells
½ cup combined sliced onion, carrot, and celery
1 garlic clove, bruised
1 cup good red Burgundy wine
¼ cup pure olive oil
2 whole cloves
8 peppercorns, black and white mixed
1 bay leaf

HERB BUTTER
12 tablespoons sweet butter
1½ teaspoons finely chopped garlic
½ cup finely chopped shallots
2 tablespoons finely chopped fresh parsley
2 tablespoons finely chopped fresh chives
2 teaspoons finely chopped fresh thyme
1 teaspoon lemon juice
Salt to taste
Freshly cracked white pepper

ESCARGOTS À LA BOUR-GUIGNONNE

Snails with Garlic and Herb Butter (hot)

Open the can of snails and put the snails in a small earthenware dish or crock. Over the top scatter the sliced onion, carrot, and celery, and the bruised garlic clove. Pour over the Burgundy and the olive oil. Add the cloves, peppercorns, and the bay leaf, broken in half. Mix well, cover, and keep in the refrigerator overnight. Continue next day when you are almost ready to serve the snails.

HERB BUTTER. Cream the butter in a mixer until very light and fluffy. Mix in the chopped garlic, shallots, parsley, chives, and thyme. (If fresh thyme is not available, use ½ teaspoon dried thyme leaf soaked 10 minutes in 1 tablespoon water and drained before using.) Also add the lemon juice and season well with salt and pepper.

Preheat the oven to 350°. Put a teaspoon of the herb butter in the bottom of each snail shell, then insert one of the marinated snails and fill the opening with more of the butter. Arrange the stuffed shells on a proper snail platter and cook them 8 to 9 minutes in the oven. Serve them very hot with fresh French bread. NET: 4 servings.

PETITS FOURS EN HORS D'OEUVRES

Miniature Seafood Hors d'Oeuvres on Skewers (hot)

1 boiled lobster (about 1 pound)	12 shelled oysters
½ pound raw shrimps (shelled)	½ pound bacon, thinly sliced
¼ pound sea scallops	4 tablespoons salt butter
12 shelled clams	1 teaspoon finely chopped garlic

Remove the meat from the lobster and cut it into small bite-size pieces. Cut the shrimps in half. If the scallops are large, cut them in half. Wrap each piece of seafood, including the whole clams and oysters, in a small, thin piece of bacon. Thread this assortment of seafood onto small skewers and place them on a wire rack on a jelly roll pan. Melt the butter with the chopped garlic and brush the skewers with it. Broil each side 3 minutes under a hot broiler. NET: 4 to 6 servings.

SHRIMPS IN DILL

1 pound shelled boiled shrimps	1 tablespoon fresh lemon juice
2 tablespoons chopped fresh dill	Salt
1 tablespoon pure olive oil	A few grains cayenne pepper
3 tablespoons vegetable oil	A few crisp perfect lettuce leaves
1 tablespoon fresh lime juice	

Cut the shrimps into thin slices. Mix all the other ingredients together and add the sliced shrimps. Chill thoroughly. Serve on lettuce leaves. NET: 4 to 6 servings.

CRÊPES CANARI D'OR

Thin Pancakes Filled with Cherrystone Clams

These pancakes are a first course dish. Melted butter will make more delicate crêpes than vegetable oil, but they may stick in the pan, which is less likely with vegetable oil.

8 tablespoons all-purpose flour	About 1 cup milk
¼ teaspoon salt	2 tablespoons cool melted
1 egg	salt butter or vegetable oil
1 egg yolk	½ teaspoon dry mustard

FILLING

7 tablespoons salt butter
3 tablespoons dry white wine
Salt
A few grains cayenne pepper
1½ cups shelled cherrystone
    clams, cut into small dice
2 shallots, finely chopped
1 teaspoon finely chopped garlic
1 tablespoon chopped fresh
    chives
4 tablespoons sour cream

MUSTARD SAUCE

4 egg yolks
4 tablespoons sweet butter,
    cut into little pieces
2 tablespoons freshly grated
    Parmesan cheese
1 teaspoon dry mustard
2 tablespoons Cognac or
    good brandy
1 cup light cream
Salt to taste
A few grains cayenne pepper

In a small bowl combine the flour, salt, egg and egg yolk, and 4 table-spoons milk. With a little wire whisk, beat the mixture until it is smooth. Mix in the butter or vegetable oil and dry mustard, then add enough milk to make the batter the consistency of light cream. Cover the bowl with plastic wrap and leave it in the refrigerator at least 30 minutes. Heat an omelet pan very hot (a dot of butter dropped in it should sizzle and brown). Rub the inside with salt butter, using a wad of wax paper. Take up some batter in a ladle and cover the bottom of the pan with a 4 to 5 inch crêpe. Brown the crêpe on one side, turn it over with a spatula, and brown it on the other side. Pile one crêpe on top of the other as you make them. If the batter thickens, add more milk. It should just coat the back of a metal spoon.

FILLING. Melt 3 tablespoons salt butter in a sauté pan. Stir in the wine, salt, cayenne pepper, clams, chopped shallots, garlic, and chives. Cook slowly, over low heat, for 4 minutes. Add 4 tablespoons butter and the sour cream. Continue to cook gently over low heat until the additional butter is melted and the mixture is well blended.

MUSTARD SAUCE. Combine all the ingredients in the top of the double boiler. Set over simmering water over low heat and cook, stirring with a whisk or wooden spoon, until the mixture is thick.

Have ready a buttered au gratin dish. Spread a little filling on each crêpe, roll them up like little cigars, and arrange them in the au gratin dish. Spoon the sauce over them and brown quickly under a hot broiler. Serve immediately. NET: 4 to 6 servings.

---

3 large leeks
Salt
½ cup shelled cooked shrimps
2 hard-boiled egg yolks
Freshly cracked white pepper
1 tablespoon chopped fresh
    parsley

SAUCE VERTE

2 raw egg yolks
½ teaspoon Dijon mustard
½ teaspoon dry mustard
1 teaspoon salt
⅛ teaspoon cayenne pepper
Pinch of sugar
1 cup vegetable oil
1 tablespoon vinegar, lemon

POIREAUX AUX CREVETTES, SAUCE VERTE

Leeks Stuffed with
Shrimps, Green
Mayonnaise

juice, or dry white wine
½ cup spinach purée (cooked

spinach well drained and
puréed in the electric blender)

GREEN MAYONNAISE (SAUCE VERTE). Put the egg yolks in a mixer bowl. Beat well with the two mustards, salt, pepper, and sugar. Beating all the time, add the vegetable oil very slowly, drop by drop until it begins to thicken, then a little faster. Then beat in the vinegar, lemon juice or wine, and the spinach purée.

Remove the outside leaves of the leeks. Wash the leeks very well and cut the white parts into 2-inch pieces. Put into salted cold water, bring to a boil, and simmer 5 minutes. Drain and dry thoroughly. Chop the shrimps very fine. Pound or mince with the hard-boiled egg yolks and pepper. Bind the shrimp with a spoonful of green mayonnaise. Add the chopped parsley and salt if needed. When the leeks are cold, split them down the middle. Fill them with this stuffing. Arrange on a dish, cover with green mayonnaise, and serve very cold. NET: 4 servings.

DATTES AU LARD

Broiled Dates Stuffed with Almonds and Wrapped in Bacon (hot)

24 pitted dates
24 blanched almonds
½ teaspoon salt
1 teaspoon freshly cracked
  white pepper

½ teaspoon freshly grated
  nutmeg
1 teaspoon dry mustard
½ cup Cognac or good brandy
12 thin slices bacon

Stuff the almonds into the dates. Put them in a bowl with the salt, pepper, nutmeg, and mustard. Mix well. Add the brandy, mix again, and allow to marinate for 2 to 3 hours (or longer). Cut the bacon slices in half and roll each around a date. Place on the broiler rack and broil under a hot flame 8 to 10 minutes, turning once after 4 minutes. A nice way to serve the dates is to spear them with little cocktail sticks and stick them into a red or green cabbage. Serve piping hot. NET: 6 servings.

ANGELS ON HORSEBACK

Bacon-Wrapped Baked Prunes Stuffed with Chicken Livers (hot)

12 large pitted prunes
Salt
Freshly cracked black pepper
2 teaspoons Dijon mustard
6 chicken livers
2 tablespoons salt butter

12 blanched almonds
6 thin slices bacon
12 small 1½-inch rounds thinly
  sliced white bread, fried in
  butter
Fresh crisp watercress (garnish)

Preheat the oven to 375°. Season the insides of the prunes with salt, pepper, and mustard. Sauté the chicken livers in very hot butter. Brown them on all sides and cut in half. Put a chicken liver half and a blanched almond inside each prune. Season on the outside with a little salt and pepper and roll each in a half-slice of bacon. Place on a baking sheet on a rack and bake until the bacon is crisp. Drain, and place each prune on a round of fried bread. Arrange them on a hot flat platter and garnish with watercress. NET: 12 canapés.

The classic and best way to serve this perfect food is in a plain simple manner. Put a slice of pure foie gras in an individual ramekin. Decorate it with a little strained hard-boiled egg yolk and creamed butter piped through a cornucopia. Serve with fresh French bread.

This pâté may be made with pheasant, duck . . . or chicken. You'll need a 10 or 12 inch pâté form.

PASTRY
3 cups all-purpose flour, sifted
½ teaspoon salt
3 egg yolks
12 tablespoons salt butter at
    room temperature
1 tablespoon pure olive oil
¾ to 1 cup ice water

FILLING
8 ounces thinly sliced fatback
6 ounces lean veal, finely ground
2 raw egg whites
¾ cup light cream

1 teaspoon salt
Freshly cracked white pepper
1 whole duck, pheasant, or
    chicken (about 3 pounds),
    completely boned (page 344)
1 6-ounce slice of lean ham
2 black truffles, coarsely
    chopped
2 ounces shelled blanched
    pistachio nuts
½ cup chicken aspic (page 37)
1 egg yolk beaten with 1
    tablespoon of milk

Sift the flour and salt together into a bowl. Make a well in the center and in it put the egg yolks, butter, and olive oil. Blend this together lightly with the fingertips to a smooth paste. Combine it with ice water to make a firm dough. Form into a ball, cover with a cloth, and let it rest 1 hour. Roll out three-quarters of the dough into a round or oval (depending on the shape of your pâté mold) large enough to line the mold with a half-inch overhang. It should be about ⅛ inch thick. Butter a bottomless pâté mold and place it on a buttered baking sheet. Line the mold with the dough, pressing it firmly against the sides and bottom. Trim the edges evenly, leaving a half-inch overhang.

Preheat the oven to 350° and prepare the filling. Line the inside of the pastry with three-quarters of the fatback. Put the veal in a small metal bowl over a bowl of ice. With a wire whisk, beat in the egg whites. Slowly add the light cream, drop by drop. Season with the salt and pepper. Beat well. Spread half of this mixture on the fatback. Cut the meat of the boned fowl and the slice of ham into thin strips. Lay them in the mold in alternate layers, sprinkling each layer with the chopped truffles and pistachio nuts. Cover the top with the rest of the veal mixture and slices of fatback. Brush the dough on the edge of the mold with cold water.

Roll out the remaining dough and cover the top of the mold with it. Press the edges down on the half-inch border of the bottom pastry and pinch together. Roll out the pastry scraps and cut out decorations such as leaves or flowers. Brush the top of the pâté with the mixed egg yolk beaten with the milk. Stick the decorative pieces of pastry on the top and brush them with the mixture. Make a small hole in the center of the pastry top to let the steam out as the pâté bakes. Bake 1½ hours. If the pastry begins to brown too much, cover it with foil. Remove the pâté from the oven, cool, and chill it. Dissolve the aspic. With a little paper funnel, slowly pour the dissolved aspic through the hole in the pastry to fill up the spaces inside the pâté. Return to the refrigerator to set. NET: 8 servings.

CORNETS DE JAMBON

Ham Cornucopias (cold)

For this dish you will need 12 small cornucopia molds.

12 small thin slices lean boiled ham	nutmeg
1 6-ounce slice lean boiled ham	1 teaspoon salt
3 tablespoons Madeira	A few grains cayenne pepper
10 tablespoons sweet butter	12 thin slices pumpernickel bread, each about the size of your cornucopia mold
1 teaspoon Dijon mustard	
1 teaspoon dry mustard	
¼ teaspoon mace	Fresh crisp watercress (for garnish)
½ teaspoon freshly grated	

Line 12 cornucopia molds with the thin slices of boiled ham. Trim off any excess ham with scissors. Put the excess ham and the 6-ounce piece of ham through a very fine meat chopper. Mix in the Madeira. Cream 8 tablespoons butter in an electric mixer until it is light and fluffy. Slowly add the ground ham. Mix in the mustards, mace, nutmeg, salt, and cayenne pepper. Put the mixture in an electric blender and pulverize it to a paste. Put it in a pastry bag fitted with a large star tube. Fill the ham-lined cornucopia molds. Chill them in the refrigerator. Spread the slices of pumpernickel bread with the rest of the butter. Turn the cornucopias out of the molds and place them on the bread. Serve with a garnish of fresh crisp watercress. NET: 12 servings.

CROQUE-MONSIEUR

French Toast Ham and Mushroom Sandwich with Hollandaise (hot)

6 slices sturdy white bread	2 tablespoons salt butter
2 eggs	4 tablespoons vegetable oil
Salt	¼ pound firm white mushrooms, sliced
Freshly cracked white pepper	
1 cup milk	6 tablespoons shredded boiled

ham
6 tablespoons freshly grated
   Parmesan cheese

HOLLANDAISE SAUCE
2 tablespoons tarragon vinegar
1 bay leaf

1 slice onion
2 whole peppercorns
1/4 cup dry white wine reduced
   by boiling to 1 tablespoon
2 egg yolks
3 tablespoons light cream
8 tablespoons sweet butter

Trim the crusts from the bread. Beat the eggs in a bowl with salt and pepper, then stir in the milk. Soak the trimmed bread slices in the egg mixture. Heat the salt butter and vegetable oil in a sauté pan, and fry the slices of soaked bread on each side until golden brown. Remove, set aside, and keep warm. Sauté the mushrooms 4 to 5 minutes in the same pan. Season with salt and pepper. Add the shredded ham and warm a little. Sandwich this mixture between the slices of fried bread (French toast). Cut each sandwich in 4 triangles and arrange these little sandwiches overlapping down a hot oval serving dish.

HOLLANDAISE SAUCE. Boil the vinegar down to half quantity with the bay leaf, onion, and peppercorns. Strain and add to the reduced white wine. Put the egg yolks, vinegar-wine mixture, and cream in the top of a double boiler, stir together, and set over simmering water, beating constantly until the sauce thickens. Then add the sweet butter bit by bit, beating each bit in thoroughly.

To serve, spoon the sauce over the little sandwiches, sprinkle with the grated cheese, and brown quickly under a hot broiler. NET: 6 servings.

A smooth light liver pâté.

1 pound pork liver
1 pound fatback
20 anchovy fillets
4 eggs
2 cups light cream
1 teaspoon freshly grated

nutmeg
1/2 teaspoon ground mace
2 teaspoons salt
1 teaspoon freshly cracked white
   pepper
1 pound bacon, thinly sliced

PÂTÉ DANOIS

Danish Liver Pâté
(cold)

Preheat the oven to 325°. Cut the pork liver and fatback into small pieces, and put them twice through a fine meat chopper. Crush the anchovy fillets with a pestle and mortar until smooth. Put the ground liver in a bowl with the anchovy paste, the eggs, cream, nutmeg, mace, salt, and pepper. Mix well, then blend in an electric blender until very smooth. Line two 1-pound loaf pans with bacon, fill with the liver mixture, and cover with more bacon. Wrap each pan tightly in aluminum foil, like a package. Place the pans in the oven in a large shallow pan half filled with hot water. Bake 1½ hours. Remove the pâté from the oven, cool, chill thoroughly, turn out of the pans, and slice. NET: About 4 dozen small slices.

PÂTÉ DE FOIE GRAS EN BRIOCHE

Liver Pâté in Brioche
(cold)

This is a classic presentation — a large fluted brioche stuffed with foie gras. It can also be made into little brioches filled with pâté. For this, reduce the baking time.

1¼ cups soft salt butter
4 cups all-purpose flour
1 tablespoon sugar
2 teaspoons salt
7 eggs, beaten
2 packages yeast

½ cup lukewarm water
4 ounces fine liver pâté (or pure foie gras)
1 egg, beaten with 1 teaspoon milk

Cream the butter in a mixer until it is light and fluffy. Remove the butter from the mixer bowl. Put 3 cups flour in the mixer. Add the sugar, salt, and beaten eggs. Beat all together until the dough is shiny. Add the creamed butter and beat a little more. Dissolve the yeast in the lukewarm water. Add it to 1 cup flour in a small bowl. Stir until it forms a ball. Knead it on a lightly floured board, turn it over, cut a crisscross on the top, and drop this ball into a bowl of lukewarm water. In a few minutes it will rise to the top of the water. Take it out with your hand, put it into the mixer bowl with the dough, and beat well. Place the brioche dough in a lightly floured bowl. Cover the bowl with a cloth, set it in a warm place, and let the dough rise to double its bulk. Break the rise by stirring it with your finger just once. Put the dough in the freezer until it is workable — not hard, not flabby.

Butter a large fluted brioche mold. On a lightly floured surface, roll about two-thirds of the dough into an oblong shape, then fold over and shape like a bag. Line the brioche mold with this dough. Fill the center with the liver pâté. Brush the edge of the dough with a little of the beaten egg and milk. Set the oven at 400°. Roll out all the remaining dough except a little ball for the topknot of the brioche. Cover the brioche with this dough, then make a hole in the center and put in the ball of dough for the topknot. Place the filled brioche on a baking sheet and cover with a cloth canopy. (Be sure the cloth does not touch the dough.) Allow to rise about 20 minutes. Carefully brush all over the top with the beaten egg and milk. Bake about 30 minutes, until it is golden brown. Serve cooled, at room temperature. NET: 6 to 8 servings.

PÂTÉ DE PORC

Pork Liver Pâté (cold)

1½ pounds pork liver
½ pound fatback
¼ cup Cognac or good brandy
2 eggs
Salt
Freshly cracked black pepper
½ pound piece of lean pork

¼ cup finely chopped shallots
2 tablespoons chopped fresh parsley
¼ teaspoon thyme
⅜ pound bacon, thinly sliced
1 bay leaf

Preheat the oven to 350°. Put the pork liver and fatback through a fine meat chopper twice. Heat the brandy in a little pan, ignite, and stir into the mixture with a wooden spoon. Beat the eggs, mix them in, and season the mixture with salt and pepper. Cut the piece of pork into long, thin strips. Mix the chopped shallots, parsley, thyme, salt, and pepper together. Roll the lean pork strips in this mixture and set aside. Line a loaf pan with bacon slices. Put in half the liver mixture, then the strips of pork, then the rest of the liver mixture. Lay the bay leaf on top and cover the top with strips of bacon. Wrap the pan tightly with foil, place it in the oven in a shallow pan half filled with hot water, and bake 1½ hours. Remove, cool a little, put a weight (such as a brick wrapped in foil) on it and chill well in the refrigerator. Turn out of the pan and cut as many slices as needed. Serve with toasted slices of French bread. NET: 6 to 8 servings.

PÂTÉ MAISON

Meat and Liver Pâté

½ pound bacon, thinly sliced
6 tablespoons water
2 tablespoons vegetable oil
4 tablespoons all-purpose flour
1 tablespoon unflavored gelatine
1 cup milk
1 pound ground lean veal
½ pound ground lean beef
½ pound ground lean pork
½ pound ground calves' liver
3 eggs, beaten

¼ teaspoon mace
Salt
Freshly cracked white pepper
1 teaspoon finely chopped garlic
½ teaspoon freshly grated
    nutmeg
4 chicken livers
¼ cup Cognac or good brandy
1 slice boiled ham, ¼ inch thick,
    cut into finger-size strips

Preheat the oven to 325°. Line a loaf pan with the bacon, reserving a few strips. Prepare a thick panade: Warm the water and vegetable oil in a saucepan and add, off the heat, the flour and gelatine mixed together. Then add the milk. Stir over low heat until the mixture boils. Pour on a plate and chill.

Put the ground meats in a mixer bowl. Add the cold panade, beaten eggs, mace, 2 teaspoons salt, 1 teaspoon pepper, chopped garlic, and nutmeg. Mix well. In a separate little bowl marinate the chicken livers in the brandy and a little salt and pepper for a few minutes. Fill the lined mold halfway with the ground meat mixture. On it put the chicken livers in a row with a few fingers of boiled ham on each side. Cover with the rest of the ground meat mixture, and top with a few strips of bacon. Wrap the filled loaf pan tightly with buttered foil. Place in the oven in a shallow pan half filled with hot water and bake 1 hour and 45 minutes. Remove from the oven, cool a little at room temperature, put a weight (such as a brick wrapped in foil) on top, and chill well in the refrigerator. To serve, arrange thin slices on a plate with thick slices of French bread and (if desired) chopped aspic (page 37). NET: 24 slices.

TERRINE DE FAISAN

Terrine of Pheasant (cold)

This recipe may also be followed for terrines of rabbit (lapin), hare (lièvre), or duck (caneton). It is a fine game pâté with whole strips of game in the center. It is nice to put it in the traditional game terrine with the shape of the animal head on the cover.

1 pheasant, skinned and boned	1 raw egg yolk
½ cup Cognac or good brandy	2 teaspoons chopped fresh
Freshly cracked white pepper	tarragon
2 garlic cloves, bruised	1 teaspoon finely chopped garlic
½ pound fatback or bacon,	¼ teaspoon ground allspice
thinly sliced	¼ teaspoon freshly grated
½ pound finely ground lean	nutmeg
pork	½ teaspoon ground cardamom
½ pound finely ground fat pork	seed
½ pound finely ground lean veal	2 teaspoons salt
2 tablespoons chopped fresh	⅓ cup heavy cream
chives	Thick paste mixture of flour
2 raw egg whites	and water

Cut the pheasant meat into strips ½ inch thick. Put into a small bowl with the brandy, 1 teaspoon cracked white pepper, and the garlic cloves. Mix well and allow to marinate at room temperature at least 1 hour.

Preheat the oven to 350°. Line a terrine or loaf pan with the thin slices of fatback or bacon. Put the ground meats in a mixer bowl and mix well with the chives, egg whites, egg yolk, tarragon, garlic, allspice, nutmeg, cardamom seed, salt, and 1 teaspoon freshly cracked white pepper. Add the heavy cream and mix again. Fill the mold with alternate layers of the ground meat mixture and pheasant strips, starting and ending with a ground meat layer. Cover the top of the terrine with more slices of fatback or bacon. Secure the lid with a paste of flour and water. (If using a loaf pan, wrap it well in foil.) Put the terrine in the oven in a shallow pan half filled with hot water and bake 3 hours. Cool gradually at room temperature; then refrigerate. If in a loaf pan, refrigerate with a weight (such as a brick wrapped in foil) on top of the terrine. Serve in slices, with strips of plain toast. NET: 24 slices.

RILLETTES DE TOURS

Potted Minced Pork and Duck (cold)

Rillettes offer a delicious alternative to Pâté Maison. They will stay fresh for many weeks. You will need 12 small earthenware pots or a large crock.

2 pounds pork loin (with bone)	leaves, 1 clove)
1 duck, boned and skinned	Salt
Bouquet garni wrapped in	Freshly cracked white pepper
cheesecloth (thyme, parsley,	Water
a piece of celery leaf, 2 bay	

Remove the pork loin from the bone. Cut up both the pork and duck meat into large dice. Place the diced meat and pork bone in a heavy pan with the bouquet garni, salt, and pepper. Barely cover with water. Cook very slowly until practically no liquid is left.

Put the cooked meats in a shallow bowl or pan and cool a little. Remove the bone and bouquet garni. Break up the meats with a large fork and spread on a platter. Chill, then work the mixture smooth with a fork. Fill small earthenware pots with the meat mixture and store in the rerigerator. Serve in the small earthenware pots, or spoon from a large crock, with toasted French bread and sour gherkins, if desired. NET: 12 small pots.

These cornets, with their assorted fillings, may be prepared as much as a week in advance, and frozen. Put them in the freezer on a tray until set; then put them in a plastic bag and store in the freezer.

12 very thin slices Italian salami
  (2 to 3 inches in diameter),
  with skin removed
12 cut-out ovals of thinly sliced
  pumpernickel or rye bread

ROQUEFORT FILLING
6 tablespoons salt butter
3 ounces Roquefort cheese,
  rubbed through a fine strainer
2 teaspoons dry sherry
Freshly cracked white pepper
12 raisins

LIVER PÂTÉ FILLING
6 tablespoons sweet butter

3 ounces fine liver pâté
1 tablespoon Cognac or good
  brandy
Salt
Freshly cracked white pepper
1 black truffle, cut in 12 pieces

CREAM CHEESE FILLING
6 tablespoons salt butter
4 ounces (¼ pound) cream
  cheese
1 teaspoon finely chopped garlic
A few drops Tabasco sauce
A few drops Worcestershire
  sauce

Each of the fillings will fill 12 cornets. To make the cornets, make a cut from the middle to the edge of each salami slice. Press each slice into a cornucopia (cornet) shape with your fingers. Chill the cornets while you prepare the filling. When the filling is made, spread the bread ovals with a little of it. Pipe the rest into the cornets (see directions for each, below).

ROQUEFORT. Cream the butter in a mixer until it is very light and fluffy. Mix in the strained cheese, sherry, and a little pepper (but no salt). Put the mixture into a pastry bag with a small plain tube. Fill each cornet, and decorate the top with a raisin.

LIVER PÂTÉ. Cream the butter in a mixer and add the liver pâté. Chill. Mix in the brandy and a little salt and pepper. Put the filling in a pastry bag with a small star tube. Pipe it into the cornets, ending with a swirl on the top. Put a dot of truffle on the end of each.

CREAM CHEESE. Cream the butter in a mixer, add the cream cheese, and beat well. Season with the garlic, Tabasco, and Worcestershire. Put the filling in a pastry bag with a small star tube and pipe it into the cornets, ending with a swirl on the top.

Arrange the cornets on the bread ovals. Chill well. NET: 12 cornets.

CANAPÉS À LA RICHELIEU

Artichoke Bottoms Stuffed with Sweetbreads and Veal Kidney (hot)

1 large veal kidney with its fat
1 pair sweetbreads
A little all-purpose flour
5 tablespoons salt butter
Salt
Freshly cracked black pepper
4 firm white mushrooms, finely chopped
A little lemon juice
2 tablespoons chopped fresh parsley
Grated rind of 1 lime
½ teaspoon finely chopped garlic
2 raw egg yolks
2 tablespoons fried breadcrumbs (page 69)
About ½ teaspoon sugar
6 cooked artichoke bottoms (1 can, usually)
6 rounds (same size as artichoke bottoms) of fried bread (page 69)

Preheat the oven to 375°. Roast the veal kidney with its fat left on. Remove the fat. Chill the kidney. Put the sweetbreads in cold water, bring to a boil, then plunge them into ice water. Remove and chill. When they are cold, skin them and remove the membrane, dry thoroughly on paper towels, and dust with a little flour. Sauté the sweetbreads in 2 tablespoons butter. Brown them on each side, season with a little salt and pepper, then cover and allow to cook very gently 12 to 15 minutes, turning them over at the halfway point. Chill the cooked sweetbreads, then put them and the fat from the roasted kidney through a fine meat grinder. Cut the kidney into very fine dice and mix it with the sweetbread and fat.

Sauté the chopped mushrooms in 1 tablespoon hot butter with a little lemon juice, salt, and pepper. Add to the sweetbread mixture with the parsley, grated lime rind, garlic, egg yolks, and fried breadcrumbs. Correct the seasoning and add about ½ teaspoon of granulated sugar. Fill the artichoke bottoms with this mixture. Mound the tops with the back of a spoon. Spoon a few drops of melted butter over each and brown under a hot broiler. Place on the rounds of fried bread and arrange down a hot au gratin dish for serving. NET: 6 servings.

ASPERGES AU BEURRE FONDU

Asparagus with Melted Butter (hot)

Most fresh asparagus in the United States is green asparagus. It should be washed, the tough ends cut off, and sprinkled generously with salt. To cook in the classic style, the spears should be tied in a bunch and wrapped in a piece of cheesecloth. Because asparagus is so delicate and must be crunchy when cooked, it is safest to cook it in a steamer. Steam only 4 to 5 minutes and remove immediately. Drain carefully, remove the cheesecloth and string, and arrange on squares of plain toast. (Asparagus should always be served on toast, whose function is to absorb any liquid. The toast is not eaten.) The melted butter should be clarified butter (page 56). If you want a sauce instead of melted butter, one of the best to serve with asparagus is Hollandaise sauce.

As to the right way to eat asparagus spears, I like the French and English manner, which is to lift the spears up in your fingers and eat them. Serve little fingerbowls with lemon and water afterward. The other way to eat asparagus is to cut the spears with a knife and fork, which to me removes all the glamour and delight, and in Europe is considered very bad table manners. Unfortunately, to eat asparagus with your fingers is often considered bad manners in the United States. I was once asked to leave a restaurant for this very reason.

Broccoli and cauliflower can also be prepared à la Polonaise, which means with hard-boiled eggs and brown butter.

ASPERGES À LA POLONAISE

Asparagus with Hard-Boiled Eggs and Brown Butter (hot)

20 to 24 spears fresh asparagus	chopped
4 squares plain toast	1 tablespoon finely chopped
4 tablespoons sweet butter	fresh parsley
4 tablespoons dry breadcrumbs	Salt
(page 69)	Freshly cracked white pepper
2 hard-boiled eggs, finely	

Prepare, cook, and drain the asparagus as in the preceding recipe. (For this number of spears, make two bunches in the steamer.) Arrange on the toast. Melt the butter in a little pan. Add the breadcrumbs and brown a little. Add the chopped hard-boiled eggs, parsley, and pepper. Spoon the butter over the middle of the asparagus and serve. NET: 4 servings.

To prepare whole globe artichokes for cooking, trim the stalk level at the bottom. With scissors, trim off all the points on the leaves.

Globe artichokes are best cooked in a steamer, if possible. Cook 10 to 12 minutes with a little water. They can be cooked in plain boiling water with lemon juice, but will require about 30 to 45 minutes. Drain cooked artichokes immediately on paper towels.

A classic way to serve artichokes warm is to remove all the small leaves in the center and the choke (thistle). Fill the center cavity with either clarified butter, seasoned with salt and pepper, or Hollandaise sauce. To serve cold, fill the center with vinaigrette sauce.

ARTICHAUTS ENTIERS BOUILLIS

Whole Globe Artichokes (hot or cold)

CÉLERI FARCI

Stuffed Celery (cold)

Sliced circles of celery stuffed with Roquefort and cream cheese, served on rounds of rye bread.

2 large stalks celery	1 teaspoon tomato paste
6 tablespoons salt butter	6 tablespoons Roquefort cheese
2 ounces cream cheese	18 thin slices rye bread
Salt	1 pimento
Freshly cracked black pepper	

Wash and dry the celery stalks. Cream 3 tablespoons butter in a bowl, add the cream cheese with a little salt and pepper, and color with a little tomato paste. In another bowl cream the rest of the butter. Rub the Roquefort cheese through a strainer and mix it into the butter with a little pepper, but no salt. Stuff one large stalk with the cream cheese mixture and the other with the Roquefort cheese mixture. Stick them together, wrap in wax paper, and chill. When the stuffed celery is thoroughly chilled, cut it into thin slices and place each slice on a round of rye bread. Decorate the top of each with a dot of pimento. NET: 18 small slices.

CÉLERI AU ROQUEFORT

Fresh Celery Chunks Stuffed with Roquefort Cheese

2 bunches celery	Salt
4 tablespoons sweet butter	Freshly cracked black pepper
1/4 pound Roquefort cheese	A little paprika
1 tablespoon Cognac or good brandy	A few crisp sprigs fresh watercress

Remove the best stalks of celery, wash them well, and cut into 1½-inch lengths. Freshen them in iced salted water. Drain them and dry well on paper towels. Cream the butter in the mixer until it is light and fluffy. Rub the Roquefort cheese through a fine strainer and beat it into the butter. Season with brandy, salt, and pepper, and beat well. Put the cheese mixture in a pastry bag fitted with a medium-size star tube (about #4 or #5) and pipe the mixture into the hollows of the pieces of celery. Sprinkle the tops with a little paprika, and chill well. Arrange the stuffed celery on a flat serving dish, garnish with crisp sprigs of watercress, and serve very cold. NET: 6 to 8 servings.

CÉLERI-RAVE RAVIGOTE

Celery Root (Celeriac), Finely Shredded, with Ravigote Sauce (cold)

4 knobs celery root	1/2 teaspoon salt
1 lemon	1/4 teaspoon cayenne pepper
	1 tablespoon Dijon mustard
RAVIGOTE SAUCE	1/2 teaspoon curry powder
2 hard-boiled egg yolks	1/4 cup pure olive oil
3 raw egg yolks	1 1/2 cups vegetable oil
2 tablespoons tarragon vinegar	Few drops lemon juice
2 tablespoons light cream	1/4 cup heavy cream, whipped

Skin the celery root. Cut it into very thin slices, then into very fine shreds. Plunge them for 3 minutes into boiling water. Drain at once, plunge into ice water with the juice of 1 lemon, and chill.

RAVIGOTE SAUCE. Rub the hard-boiled egg yolks through a fine strainer. Put the raw yolks in a mixer bowl. Beat in the strained hard-boiled yolks, vinegar, light cream, salt, cayenne pepper, mustard, and curry powder. Drop by drop, add the olive oil, then the vegetable oil, beating all the time. (As soon as the mixture is really thick, you can add the oil faster.) Beat in a few drops of lemon juice and chill thoroughly. Fold in the whipped cream.

Drain the shredded celery root and dry well in a cloth. Mix with the ravigote sauce and serve very cold in a small hors d'oeuvres dish with rusks or toasted slices of French bread. NET: About 6 servings.

SLICED CUCUMBERS STUFFED WITH MUSHROOM

1 long thin cucumber
6 ounces firm white mushrooms, finely chopped
2 tablespoons salt butter
1 teaspoon lemon juice
Salt
Freshly cracked black pepper
1 tablespoon chopped fresh dill

Cut off the top and bottom of the cucumber, skin it, and cut it into rounds about 1 inch thick. With a potato scoop, remove some of the center seed section and reserve these half-spheres. Soak the half-spheres in a little water about 30 minutes. Drain and dry thoroughly on paper towels. Sauté the mushrooms in the butter with the lemon juice, salt, and pepper. Add the chopped dill and cook briskly 3 to 4 minutes, keeping mixture dry. Chill. Spoon the mushroom mixture into the cucumber rounds. Cover with the cap of the cucumber (the half-sphere that was scooped out). Arrange on a platter over crushed ice and serve very cold. NET: 6 to 8 servings.

EGGPLANT CAVIAR

1 large eggplant
2 yellow onions, finely chopped
2 teaspoons finely chopped garlic
4 tomatoes, skinned and chopped
¾ cup pure olive oil
Salt
Freshly cracked black pepper
8 to 12 fingers of toast brushed with melted butter

Preheat the oven to 350°. Wrap the eggplant in a double piece of wax paper or foil brushed well with olive oil, and bake until soft. When done, unwrap the eggplant and carefully remove the skin. In a wooden bowl, chop the eggplant very fine, then mix in the chopped onion, garlic, and tomatoes. Continue chopping as you slowly add the olive oil, salt, and pepper. When the mixture is very fine and well mixed, chill it thoroughly. Serve it in a bowl on a bed of crushed ice with fingers of hot buttered toast. NET: 4 to 6 servings.

FRESH MELON

One of the most delicious ways to serve cantaloupe, honeydew, or Persian melon is in well-chilled wedges with a sprinkling of granulated sugar mixed with ground ginger (1 part ginger to 4 parts sugar).

Another way is to cut the melon in half, scoop out all the seeds, and remove the flesh with a melon baller. Mix the melon balls with chunks of fresh pineapple, whole strawberries, seeded white grapes, and mix with a little Fruit Syrup (page 68). Fill the melon shells with the mixed fruit and serve well chilled, garnished with grape leaves. For another garnish, dip whole unhulled strawberries into egg white and roll in granulated sugar. Dry, and arrange them around the melon. Other fruit can be sugared in the same manner and served on candy dishes for a party.

CHAMPIGNONS AUX ÉPICES

Spiced Mushrooms (cold)

Mushrooms prepared in this manner and placed in a screw-top jar will keep up to about 2 months in the refrigerator, and the flavor seems to improve with time.

1 pound firm white baby mushrooms
2 teaspoons lemon juice
½ cup pure olive oil
1 teaspoon finely chopped garlic
6 cardamom seeds, crushed with a pestle and mortar
½ teaspoon dry mustard
Salt
Freshly cracked white pepper
2 small pieces gingerroot
2 tablespoons chopped fresh parsley

Wash the mushrooms in cold water and 1 teaspoon lemon juice. Trim off the stems. Heat 3 tablespoons olive oil in a sauté pan. Put in the mushrooms with the garlic, cardamom seeds, mustard, salt, pepper, and 1 teaspoon lemon juice. Shake over high heat 4 to 5 minutes. Remove from the heat and add the gingerroot and the rest of the olive oil. Chill well before serving. Sprinkle with chopped parsley. NET: 4 servings.

CHAMPIGNONS FARCIS

Stuffed Mushrooms with Fried Parsley (hot)

This is an excellent way to use leftover ham, chicken, or shrimp.

6 large firm white mushrooms
4 tablespoons salt butter
1 cup finely chopped onion
½ cup finely chopped celery
½ cup finely diced cooked ham, chicken, or shrimp
Salt
Freshly cracked white pepper
⅓ cup dry breadcrumbs (page 69)
¼ cup freshly grated Parmesan cheese

FRIED PARSLEY
1 bunch crisp fresh parsley
Vegetable oil for deep-fryer

Carefully remove the stems from the mushrooms. Place the mushroom caps top down in a sauté pan with 1 tablespoon hot butter. Put a dot of butter in the center of each mushroom. Season each with a little salt and pepper and cook slowly a minute or two. Arrange the mushrooms on an ovenproof serving dish, and chill a little. Melt 1 tablespoon butter in a pan. Add the chopped onion and celery and brown lightly, stirring occasionally. Season with salt and pepper. Chop the mushroom stems very fine and add to the mixture. Cook 2 minutes and add the ham, chicken, or shrimp. Correct the seasoning and add 2 tablespoons breadcrumbs. Spoon this mixture into the mushroom caps, forming into little mounds. Sprinkle the tops with grated Parmesan cheese and the rest of the breadcrumbs, dot with butter, and brown under the broiler. Serve garnished with the fried parsley. NET: 6 servings.

FRIED PARSLEY. Heat the vegetable oil in the deep-fryer to 350°. Wash and thoroughly dry the parsley. Cut off the stalks. Wrap the parsley in paper towels and dry again. Put it in a metal basket and plunge it into the hot oil. Fry until crisp but not black. Drain and dry on paper towels.

These little tomatoes are stuffed with a mixture of garden vegetables.

1 pound cherry tomatoes
½ cup thick homemade
  mayonnaise (page 52)
2 teaspoons unflavored
  gelatine
2 tablespoons warm milk
2 cups combined finely chopped

cooked green beans, carrots,
  and turnips
½ cup finely chopped
  cucumber
1 medium-size tomato, skinned,
  seeded, and finely chopped
Bunch of fresh crisp watercress

TOMATES FARCIES

Stuffed Cherry Tomatoes (cold)

Cut off the tops of the cherry tomatoes and spoon out the insides. Dissolve the gelatine in the warm milk and mix it quickly into the mayonnaise. Mix all the vegetables together with this mayonnaise, and fill the cherry tomatoes with the mixture. Arrange them on a platter and garnish with watercress. NET: 4 to 6 servings.

This makes a lovely summer salad or hors d'oeuvres course.

To prepare a vegetable vinaigrette, try to have a good assortment of fresh peas, diced string beans, shredded carrots, asparagus tips, tiny florets of cauliflower, diced baby turnips, diced small leeks, shredded beets, sliced mushrooms.

Each vegetable for a vinaigrette should be barely cooked in a little salted water, with a little lemon juice added to retain the color. Drain and chill each cooked vegetable as soon as it is done. If mushrooms are used, cook them with a little lemon juice in the water, but no salt. If beets are used, cook them in a pressure cooker or steamer, skin them and shred them.

Mix each cooked vegetable, well chilled, with a good vinaigrette

COOKED VEGETABLES VINAIGRETTE

dressing (page 62). Arrange the vegetables in individual mounds on a round flat serving dish, and garnish with a little fresh crisp watercress.

RAW VEGETABLES VINAIGRETTE

1 cup coarsely grated carrots
1 cup coarsely grated beets
1 cup shredded cucumber pulp
4 tomatoes, skinned, seeded, and shredded

1 cup baby peas (raw also)
1 cup shredded white celery
1 cup sliced endive
Vinaigrette dressing (page 62)

Mix each vegetable individually with vinaigrette dressing. Arrange them in separate mounds on a flat serving dish. Or you may mix all the vegetables together with the vinaigrette, which makes a very colorful mosaic. Serve very chilled.

CANAPÉS, PASTRIES, CRÊPES, SOUFFLÉS

BEIGNETS DE FROMAGE

Cheese Fritters (hot)

½ cup water
4 tablespoons salt butter
½ cup all-purpose flour
2 eggs
½ teaspoon dry mustard
½ teaspoon Dijon mustard

¼ teaspoon baking powder
1 egg white
⅓ cup freshly grated Parmesan cheese
Vegetable oil for deep-fryer

Put the water and butter in a saucepan and bring to a rolling boil. Throw in the flour. Stir over low heat about 2 to 3 minutes, until the mixture comes away from the sides of the pan. Put the dough in a mixer bowl and beat in the eggs one at a time. Beat until the dough is very shiny. Mix in the mustards and baking powder. Beat the egg white to soft peaks and fold it into the mixture with the grated Parmesan cheese, lightly but thoroughly. Heat the vegetable oil in the deep-fryer to 375°. Put small teaspoonfuls of the dough into the hot fat, and cook until they are golden brown all over. Remove with a slotted spoon. Serve immediately on a warm napkin on a platter. NET: 4 to 6 servings.

BLINIS AU CAVIARE

Russian Pancakes with Caviar (hot)

1½ cups buckwheat flour (or 1 cup buckwheat flour and ½ cup fine groats, pulverized)
1 teaspoon sugar
½ teaspoon salt
1 egg
1 egg yolk

2 tablespoons cool melted sweet butter
½ package yeast, dissolved in ¼ cup lukewarm water
4 tablespoons lukewarm milk, plus more if necessary
Red and/ or black caviar

1 cup sour cream	(page 56)
½ cup clarified sweet butter	Salt butter (for omelet pan)

Sift together the flour, sugar, and salt. Add the egg and egg yolk, melted sweet butter, yeast dissolved in water, and warm milk. Mix together with a wire whisk until quite smooth. Add enough more warm milk to bring the batter to the consistency of heavy cream. Cover with a cloth and allow to rise (get puffy) 30 minutes in a warm place.

Heat an omelet pan very hot (a speck of butter should instantly sizzle and brown). Wipe the pan with salt butter, using a wad of wax paper. Spoon a large tablespoon of the batter into the pan and spread it thin, to about 4 inches in diameter. Brown one side, then the other. Make all the blini this way. To serve, cover a silver platter with a warm napkin and put the blini on it. Accompany it with little bowls of red and/or black caviar and sour cream, and a tiny little copper pan of warm clarified sweet butter. NET: Serves 6.

CANAPÉ CRACKERS

Tiny Cheese Pastries for Assorted Fillings

Recipes for several good fillings (liver pâté, red caviar, black caviar, and smoked salmon) are in the next recipe. Or use whatever filling you like. To make these pastries you need about 24 1-inch tartlet and/or barquette molds.

1 cup all-purpose flour	1 tablespoon Dijon mustard
6 tablespoons soft salt butter	1 teaspoon paprika
1 egg	1 teaspoon salt
¼ cup ice water	¼ teaspoon cayenne pepper
½ cup freshly grated Parmesan cheese	A little cool melted salt butter
	Raw rice (to anchor pastry)

Put the flour on a pastry board or marble slab. Make a well in the center, put all the other ingredients (except melted butter and rice) in the well, work them to a smooth paste, then work in the flour with the heel of your hand. Roll out the pastry very thin on a lightly floured surface. Line tiny little tartlet and/or barquette molds with the pastry. Prick the bottom of each with a fork. Brush with a little melted butter. Line with pieces of wax paper and anchor with raw rice. Place the molds on a baking sheet and put them in the freezer to chill thoroughly. Preheat the oven to 350°. Bake the pastries 15 to 20 minutes, until they are a golden brown. Remove from the oven and chill. Fill as in the next recipe, or however you wish. NET: About 24 little pastry shells.

FILLINGS FOR CANAPÉ CRACKERS

Each recipe will fill 24 1-inch tartlets, as made in the recipe for canapé crackers above. Chill the filled pastries before serving.

LIVER PÂTÉ FILLING
3 ounces fine liver pâté
4 tablespoons salt butter
A few grains cayenne pepper
Salt
1 black truffle, sliced and cut
  in diamond shapes

RED CAVIAR FILLING
½ cup red caviar
2 tablespoons finely chopped
  fresh chives
Very thin strips of lemon peel

BLACK CAVIAR FILLING
¼ cup black caviar
1 hard-boiled egg yolk, rubbed
  through a strainer
1 hard-boiled egg white, very
  finely chopped
2 tablespoons finely chopped
  fresh parsley

SMOKED SALMON FILLING
2 ounces smoked salmon
A few sprigs fresh crisp
  watercress

LIVER PÂTÉ. Cream the butter and add the liver pâté. Season with salt and cayenne pepper. Fill the molds in a dome shape with a small spatula. Decorate with small diamonds of truffle. Chill.

RED CAVIAR. Fill the molds with red caviar. Decorate with the chopped chives and lemon peel strips. Chill.

BLACK CAVIAR. Fill the molds with black caviar. Decorate with the parsley and the egg yolk and white. Chill.

SMOKED SALMON. Flatten the smoked salmon between pieces of wax paper until it is very thin. Cut into small strips the same length as the pastries. Roll each strip into a thin roll, put it in the pastry shell, and stick a tiny sprig of watercress at each end. Chill.

CROISSANTS AU JAMBON

Puff Pastry Crescents Filled with Ham (hot)

6 ounces boiled ham
1 tablespoon salt butter
1 tablespoon finely chopped
  shallot
½ teaspoon finely chopped
  garlic
2 tablespoons Marsala wine
Salt
A few grains cayenne pepper

1 tablespoon all-purpose flour
½ teaspoon dry mustard
1 teaspoon Dijon mustard
¼ cup chicken stock (page 35)
1 tablespoon heavy cream
½ pound puff pastry (half
  quantity of recipe, page 723,
  or use commercial dough)
1 egg, beaten

Put the ham through a coarse meat grinder. Then sauté the ground ham in the butter with the chopped shallot, garlic, Marsala, a little salt, and cayenne pepper. Sprinkle with the flour and mix in the mustards and chicken stock. Stir over low heat until the mixture thickens. Add the heavy cream and chill.

Preheat the oven to 400°. Roll out the puff pastry ⅛ inch thick. Cut it into triangles 4 inches on each side. Brush the triangle tips with water. Put a generous teaspoonful of the ham mixture on the wide end of each triangle. Roll up the triangle around the ham, starting from the wide end. Put the croissants on a wet baking sheet and bend each into a crescent. Put in the freezer for at least 30 minutes. Brush with beaten egg. Bake about 30 minutes, until golden brown. Serve hot. NET: 6 servings (12 to 18 croissants).

PALMIERS DE FROMAGE

Puff Pastry Palm Leaves with Cheese (hot or cold)

1 12-inch square of rolled-out puff pastry ⅛ inch thick (page 723, or use commercial dough)
¾ cup freshly grated Parmesan cheese
½ cup freshly grated Gruyère cheese
A few grains cayenne pepper
1 egg, beaten

Preheat the oven to 400°. Brush the rolled-out puff pastry all over with water. Sprinkle it generously with the grated cheeses (reserve a little Parmesan) and cayenne pepper. Roll up one side like a carpet, and stop at the middle. Roll the other side so that it meets the other roll at the middle. Cut the rolled dough in ½-inch slices and put them on a wet baking sheet. Flatten them with your hand so that they look like a palm leaf. Chill 30 minutes in the freezer. Bake 15 minutes, then turn them over, brush with beaten egg, the reserved Parmesan cheese and a little cayenne pepper, and bake another 10 minutes. NET: 24 palmiers.

PETITES CRÊPES AUX CLAMS

Little Pancakes with Clams, Deep-Fried (hot)

Crêpes batter (page 781)
Vegetable oil for deep-fryer
3 tablespoons freshly grated Parmesan cheese
½ cup dry breadcrumbs (page 69)
Fresh crisp watercress (for garnish)

CLAM FILLING
½ cup chopped mushrooms
A little hot butter
1 cup finely chopped raw clams, drained
½ cup sour cream
2 tablespoons chopped fresh parsley
Salt to taste
Freshly cracked white pepper
½ teaspoon finely chopped garlic
1 tablespoon freshly grated Parmesan cheese

Cook the crêpes according to the instructions on page 781, making them very thin and little, no more than 4 inches in diameter. Pile them one on top of the other. (Reserve about two tablespoons of batter.) Set aside while you prepare the filling.

CLAM FILLING. Sauté the chopped mushrooms in the butter. Then add the clams, sour cream, parsley, salt and pepper, garlic, and cheese. Mix together well.

Put a little of the clam mixture on each crêpe and spread it with a small spatula to within a half-inch of the edge. Roll each crêpe up tightly, starting from the end nearest you, and folding the sides in about a half-inch as you go, so the ends of the roll will be tucked in. Brush the rolled crêpes with the remaining batter and roll each one in breadcrumbs. Deep-fry the prepared crêpes in hot oil at 350° until they are golden brown all over. Drain well on paper towels. Pile the fried stuffed crêpes like little logs on a warm napkin on a flat hot serving dish. Sprinkle them with the rest of the grated cheese and garnish with fresh crisp watercress. NET: 6 servings.

PROFITEROLES AUX CRUSTACÉS

Tiny Cream Puffs with Crab or Shrimp (cold)

½ cup water
4 tablespoons salt butter
½ cup all-purpose flour
2 large or 3 small eggs
About ½ cup blanched slivered almonds

FILLING
½ cup chopped lump crabmeat or chopped boiled shrimps

8 tablespoons butter, creamed in mixer until light and fluffy
1 tablespoon sour cream
A few drops Tabasco sauce
A few drops Worcestershire sauce
½ teaspoon finely chopped garlic
Salt
Freshly cracked white pepper

Preheat the oven to 375°. Put the water and the salt butter in a saucepan and bring slowly to a boil, taking care that the butter dissolves as the water comes to a boil. Throw in the flour. Stir over low heat until the mixture comes away from the sides of the pan. Put the dough in a mixer bowl and beat in the eggs one at a time. Beat until very shiny. Chill the dough 10 to 20 minutes, then put it into a pastry bag fitted with a plain round tube (about #6). Pipe little mounds on an unbuttered baking sheet. Stick one almond sliver on top of each mound. Bake 25 minutes. Reduce the oven heat to 350° and leave the cream puffs 5 minutes, or until they dry out. Cool.

FILLING. Cream the butter in a mixer bowl until fluffy and light. Mix in the chopped crabmeat or shrimp, sour cream, Tabasco, Worcestershire, and chopped garlic. Season with a little salt and pepper.

Cut each little cream puff in half horizontally and fill them, using a tiny spoon. Put the tops back on them. Put them in little paper candy cups to serve, if desired. NET: 24 to 36 profiteroles.

QUICHE LORRAINE

Custard Tart with Cheese and Bacon (hot or cold)

2 cups all-purpose flour
Salt
12 tablespoons (¾ cup) sweet butter (at room temperature)
⅓ cup ice water
A little cool melted butter
2 cups raw rice (to anchor the pastry)
1 tablespoon dry breadcrumbs (page 69)
2 tablespoons plus ⅓ cup

freshly grated Parmesan cheese
1 pound bacon, sliced
3 whole eggs
2 egg yolks
1 teaspoon Dijon mustard
½ teaspoon dry mustard
¼ teaspoon freshly grated nutmeg
A few grains cayenne pepper
1 cup light cream, scalded

Preheat the oven to 375°. Put the flour in a bowl with ½ teaspoon salt. Cut the butter into pieces and rub it into the flour with the fingertips until it resembles coarse cornmeal. Work the mixture to a firm dough quickly with ⅓ cup ice water. Place a 10-inch flan ring on a baking sheet. Roll out all of the pastry and line the flan ring. Trim the top edge neatly. Prick all over the bottom surface lightly but not all the way through. Brush the pastry with a little melted butter, line it with a piece of wax paper, and anchor the paper with raw rice. Bake 30 minutes, remove the rice and wax paper, and bake another 10 minutes to finish the bottom crust. Reduce the oven temperature to 325°.

Sprinkle the bottom of the tart shell with the breadcrumbs mixed with 2 tablespoons grated cheese. Cut the sliced bacon into ¼-inch wide shreds and cook until crisp in a heavy pan. Strain and reserve the fat. Drain the bacon on paper towels and scatter about half of it on the crumb mixture in the tart shell. Put the eggs and egg yolks in a bowl and mix well with a whisk (but do not beat). Mix in ½ teaspoon salt, the mustards, nutmeg, and cayenne pepper. Add ⅓ cup of the strained bacon fat, ⅓ cup freshly grated Parmesan cheese, and the scalded light cream. Mix well and spoon this custard mixture into the tart shell. Bake the quiche at 325° about 30 minutes, until it is set. Remove from the oven and sprinkle the top of the quiche with the rest of the cooked shredded bacon. NET: 4 to 6 servings (as first course).

This recipe may be followed to prepare a lobster tart. If lobster is used, reserve one or two pieces of claw meat to garnish the tart after it is baked.

TARTE AUX CREVETTES

Shrimp Tart (hot or cold)

3 whole eggs
2 egg yolks
1 teaspoon Dijon mustard
1 teaspoon dry mustard
1 teaspoon salt
⅛ teaspoon cayenne pepper
⅓ cup freshly grated imported
    Swiss cheese
3 tablespoons and ⅓ cup
    freshly grated Parmesan
    cheese
8 tablespoons cool melted sweet
    butter

2½ cups scalded milk or light
    cream
¼ teaspoon finely chopped
    garlic
1½ cups chopped boiled
    shrimps
2 tablespoons dry breadcrumbs
    (page 69)
1 10-inch baked tart shell
1 tablespoon chopped fresh
    parsley
A little paprika
6 whole shrimps (for garnish)

Preheat the oven to 350°. Put the whole eggs and the egg yolks in a mixing bowl. Add the mustards, salt, and cayenne pepper. Stir with a whisk until blended (but do not beat). Mix in the Swiss cheese, ⅓ cup grated Parmesan cheese, and the butter. Pour in the scalded milk or cream. Add the garlic and the chopped shrimps. In a separate little bowl mix the breadcrumbs and 2 tablespoons grated Parmesan cheese. Sprinkle this over the bottom of the baked tart shell. Spoon the shrimp mixture into the shell and bake 30 minutes. Let it cool a little, then sprinkle with 1 tablespoon grated Parmesan cheese and the parsley and paprika. Thinly slice the 6 whole boiled shrimps and decorate the top of the tart. NET: 6 servings.

TARTE AUX ÉPINARDS

Spinach Tart (hot)

TART SHELL
2 cups all-purpose flour
1 teaspoon salt
12 tablespoons salt butter (at room temperature)
⅓ cup ice water
2 tablespoons melted salt butter
2 cups raw rice (to anchor the pastry)
2 tablespoons dry breadcrumbs (page 69)
2 tablespoons freshly grated Parmesan cheese

SPINACH FILLING
1 pound fresh spinach or 1 package frozen spinach
2 tablespoons salt butter
1 cup finely chopped onion
½ cup finely chopped celery
½ teaspoon finely chopped
garlic
Salt
Freshly cracked white pepper
1 tablespoon juniper berries, finely crushed
3 whole eggs
2 egg yolks
A few grains cayenne pepper
1 teaspoon Dijon mustard
8 tablespoons cool melted sweet butter
2¼ cups milk, scalded
2 to 3 tablespoons freshly grated Parmesan cheese

ONION RINGS
24 ½-inch raw onion rings
A little flour, beaten egg, and dry breadcrumbs
Vegetable oil for deep-fryer

Preheat the oven to 350°. Put the flour in a bowl with the salt. Rub the butter into the flour with the fingertips until it resembles coarse cornmeal. Add the ice water and work up quickly to a firm dough. Roll out the dough and line a 10-inch flan ring or pie tin. Trim the top edge neatly. Prick all over the bottom with a fork, and brush it all over with the melted butter. Line with a piece of wax paper and put the raw rice on the paper to hold it down. Bake 30 minutes, remove the rice and paper, and return the tart shell to the oven for another 10 minutes. When done, remove from the oven, mix the breadcrumbs with the grated cheese, and sprinkle over the shell.

SPINACH FILLING. Wash the spinach very well and drain thoroughly. Put it in a large pan with 2 tablespoons water and wilt it quickly over high heat. Drain, and press out all liquid with a heavy weight. Chop it fine. Melt the salt butter in a heavy pan. Add the chopped onion, celery, and garlic. Sauté 3 to 4 minutes, then add the salt, pepper, crushed juniper berries, and chopped spinach. Mix the eggs and egg yolks in a bowl. Add salt, cayenne pepper, and the mustard. Stir with a whisk until blended, but do not beat. Mix in the sweet butter. Add the scalded milk, then the spinach mixture. Spoon this into the tart shell and sprinkle the top with a little grated Parmesan cheese. Bake 30 minutes, until the custard is set. Remove from the oven and allow to stand for a moment.

ONION RINGS. Dip the onion rings in the flour, brush with beaten egg, and cover with breadcrumbs. Fry in hot vegetable oil in a deep-fryer at 375° until golden brown. Drain on paper towels.

Arrange the onion rings overlapping around the top of the spinach tart. Sprinkle with a little more grated Parmesan cheese and serve hot. NET: 4 to 6 servings (as first course).

JALOUSIE DE HOMARD

Puff Pastry Tart with Lobster (hot)

Meat of a 1-pound boiled lobster
2 tablespoons salt butter
Salt
A few grains cayenne pepper
2 tablespoons Cognac or good brandy
1 tablespoon all-purpose flour
⅓ cup sour cream
2 teaspoons chopped fresh dill
½ pound puff pastry (half the recipe, page 723, or use commercial dough)
1 egg, beaten

Chop the lobster meat fine. Melt the butter in a small sauté pan. Add the lobster with a little salt and cayenne pepper. Shake over low heat 1 to 2 minutes. In a separate little pan heat the brandy, ignite, and pour over the lobster. Sprinkle the lobster with the flour and stir in the sour cream and dill. Spread the mixture on a plate and chill.

Roll out the puff pastry ⅛ inch thick and cut it into two rectangles the same size. Fold one in half lengthwise and cut it like a paper frill, slicing the folded edge crosswise into ½-inch strips but leaving the other side intact. Place the solid rectangle on a wet baking sheet, brush the edges with water, and put the lobster filling down the center of it. Unfold the "jalousie" rectangle and place it on top. Press the edges to secure the top to the bottom. Chill thoroughly in the freezer, at least 30 minutes. Preheat the oven to 400° while it is chilling. Brush the chilled pastry with beaten egg and bake about 30 minutes, until golden brown. Serve on a warm napkin on a platter. NET: 4 to 6 servings.

TARTE AUX MORILLES

Tart with Morels (Wood Mushrooms) (hot)

TART SHELL
1 teaspoon salt
2 cups all-purpose flour
12 tablespoons (¾ cup) sweet butter
½ cup cold sour cream
About 2 cups raw rice (to anchor pastry)

MOREL FILLING
¼ pound thinly sliced bacon
½ pound morels (in can)
2 tablespoons salt butter
A little lemon juice
Salt
Freshly cracked black pepper
6 ounces imported Swiss cheese, cut into small dice
¼ cup freshly grated Parmesan cheese
2 cups heavy cream
3 whole eggs

2 egg yolks
¼ teaspoon freshly grated
   nutmeg

2 tablespoons dry breadcrumbs
   (page 69)

Sift the salt and the flour together into a bowl. Cut 8 tablespoons (½ cup) of the sweet butter into small pieces and rub into the flour. Add enough sour cream to bind the mixture together. On a lightly floured surface, roll out the pastry into a long strip. Cut the remaining butter into small pieces and scatter them over the pastry. Fold the dough in three. Roll again into a long strip. Fold in three again. Wrap in wax paper and a cloth and chill in the refrigerator at least 2 hours.

Preheat the oven to 425°. Roll out the chilled pastry about ¼ inch thick. Line a 10-inch flan ring with it. Prick the bottom with a fork. Line the inside of the pastry shell with a piece of wax paper and anchor it down with raw rice. Bake 20 to 25 minutes. Remove from the oven and remove the rice and wax paper. Reduce the oven temperature to 300°.

MOREL FILLING. Cut the bacon into fine shreds and sauté until crisp. Drain and set aside. Drain the liquid from the morels, slice them, and sauté in the salt butter with a little lemon juice, salt, and pepper. Add the bacon and diced Swiss cheese to the sautéed mushrooms. Scald the heavy cream and cool it a little. Mix the eggs and egg yolks in a bowl and add the scalded cream. Season with salt, pepper, and the grated nutmeg. Sprinkle the breadcrumbs on the baked tart shell. Spread the mushroom mixture on top of them. Spoon in the egg and cream mixture.

Bake the filled tart until it is barely firm to the touch. Turn off the heat and leave the tart in the oven until quite well set. Remove from the oven, sprinkle with the grated Parmesan cheese, and serve hot.
NET: 6 servings (as first or main course).

TARTE AUX OIGNONS

Onion Tart (hot)

This tart can be made with leeks (Tarte aux Poireaux) instead of the Bermuda onions.

1 10-inch tart shell, baked (page
   726)
2 tablespoons dry breadcrumbs
   and 2 tablespoons grated
   Parmesan cheese, mixed
2 tablespoons salt butter
3 Bermuda onions, sliced ½ inch
   thick
3 whole eggs
2 egg yolks
1 teaspoon dry mustard
1 teaspoon Dijon mustard
1 teaspoon salt

¼ teaspoon cayenne pepper
½ teaspoon freshly grated
   nutmeg
⅓ cup cool melted salt butter
   or bacon fat
⅓ cup freshly grated imported
   Swiss cheese
¼ cup freshly grated Parmesan
   cheese
2½ cups milk, scalded
24 small onion rings (for
   garnish)
A little flour, beaten egg, and

dry breadcrumbs (for deep-fried onion rings)
Vegetable oil for deep-fryer

1 tablespoon chopped fresh parsley

Preheat the oven to 350°. Place the baked tart shell on a baking sheet. Sprinkle the bottom of the tart shell with the Parmesan cheese and breadcrumb mixture. Melt 2 tablespoons salt butter in a saucepan. Add the sliced Bermuda onions and cook until soft. In a separate bowl mix the eggs and egg yolks with a whisk. Stir in the mustards, salt, cayenne pepper, and nutmeg. Blend well but do not beat. Mix in the cool melted butter or bacon fat and the Swiss cheese, scalded milk, and cooked Bermuda onions. Spoon the mixture into the tart shell and bake 20 minutes.

ONION RINGS. Dust the 24 small onion rings with flour, dip them in beaten egg, and coat them in breadcrumbs. Heat some vegetable oil in a deep-fryer to 375°. Fry the onion rings until golden brown. Drain them on paper towels.

Arrange the onion rings overlapping on the baked onion tart. Sprinkle with the grated Parmesan cheese, and chopped fresh parsley. Serve warm. NET: 6 servings.

These little pastry shells can be baked in advance and kept in a tightly covered metal container for some time. The recipe for the fillings follows this one for the shells.

1 cup all-purpose flour
½ teaspoon salt
½ teaspoon finely grated lemon rind
6 tablespoons salt butter
3 tablespoons water (or dry

vermouth, or whiskey), well chilled
A little melted butter
A little raw rice (to anchor pastry)

TARTELETTES OU BARQUETTES GARNIES

Savory Garnished Tartlets or Barquettes (cold)

Preheat the oven to 350°. Have ready 2 to 3 dozen little tartlet and barquette molds. Sift the flour with the salt into a bowl. Add the lemon rind. Cut the butter in pieces and rub it into the flour with the fingertips until it resembles coarse cornmeal. Work the dough up to a firm paste with the very cold liquid. Roll the pastry out on a lightly floured surface until it is very thin. Line the little molds with the pastry and press it down firmly. Brush each mold with melted butter, line with a little piece of wax paper, and fill with raw rice. Place the molds on a baking sheet and bake 8 to 10 minutes, until golden brown. Remove the pastry shells from the molds. NET: 24 to 36 little pastry shells.

Each of the following fillings should fill all the little pastry shells in the preceding recipe.

LIVER PÂTÉ FILLING
4 tablespoons salt butter
2½ ounces fine liver pâté
1 teaspoon finely chopped
    shallot
1 tablespoon Cognac or good
    brandy
Salt
Freshly cracked white pepper
1 hard-boiled egg

ROQUEFORT CHEESE
4 tablespoons salt butter
¼ pound Roquefort cheese
2 tablespoons Cognac or good
    brandy, whiskey, or dry
    sherry
A few grains cayenne pepper
Thin slices of green stuffed

olive or black olive (for
garnish)

CHIPPED BEEF
¼ pound chipped beef
A few grains cayenne pepper
2 tablespoons whipped cream
Thin slices green stuffed olive
    or black olive (for garnish)

CREAM CHEESE AND ALMOND
4 tablespoons salt butter
¼ pound cream cheese
A few drops Tabasco sauce
A few drops Worcestershire
    sauce
2 teaspoons gin
¼ cup finely chopped blanched
    browned almonds

LIVER PÂTÉ (TARTELETTE DE PÂTÉ). Cream the butter in an electric mixer until it is light and fluffy. Set aside 1 tablespoon. To the rest, add the pâté, shallot, brandy, salt, and pepper. Mix well. Fill the little pastries, using a small spatula. Chill them well in the freezer. Rub the hard-boiled egg yolk through a strainer, mix it with the reserved tablespoon of creamed butter, and season with a little salt and pepper. Make a little wax paper cornucopia and put the yolk mixture in it. Cut a tiny hole in the point of the cornucopia and pipe through it a line of egg yolk mixture across the top of each little filled pastry. Chop the egg white very, very fine and decorate one side of each pastry with it.

ROQUEFORT CHEESE (TARTELETTE AU ROQUEFORT). Cream the butter in a mixer until it is very light and fluffy. Rub the cheese through a strainer and mix it with the creamed butter. Add the liquid and a little cayenne pepper, but no salt. Put the mixture in a pastry bag fitted with a plain #4 or #5 tube. Fill the little pastry shells, shaping the filling like little onion spires. Decorate each top with an olive slice.

CHIPPED BEEF (TARTELETTE AU BOEUF FUMÉ). Chop the chipped beef very, very fine. Season with cayenne pepper and mix in the whipped cream. With a small spatula, fill the pastries with this mixture and decorate the tops with olive slices.

CREAM CHEESE AND ALMOND (TARTELETTE À LA CRÈME). Cream the butter in a mixer until it is very light and fluffy. Add the cream cheese and beat well. Add the Tabasco, Worcestershire, and gin. With a small spatula fill the little pastries with this mixture. Cover the tops with the chopped almonds.

SOUFFLÉ
AU CAMEMBERT

A most interesting cheese soufflé with one of my favorite cheeses, Camembert.

Camembert Cheese
Soufflé (hot)

2 tablespoons salt butter
3 tablespoons all-purpose flour
Salt
A few grains cayenne pepper
¾ cup milk
2 ounces Camembert cheese

3 tablespoons freshly grated
    Parmesan cheese
1 teaspoon dry mustard
4 egg yolks
6 egg whites

Preheat the oven to 375°. Butter a 4-cup soufflé dish (#6) and tie a band of buttered wax paper around the outside. The wax paper collar should rise about 3 inches above the top of the dish. (Preparation of soufflé dish, page 787.) Melt the butter in a saucepan. Off the heat stir in the flour, salt, and cayenne pepper. Add the milk and stir over low heat until the mixture thickens; do not allow it to boil. Remove from the heat. Rub the Camembert cheese through a strainer and stir it into the flour mixture. One by one mix in the Parmesan cheese, mustard, and each egg yolk. Beat the egg whites to soft peaks and fold into the mixture. Spoon the mixture into the soufflé dish. Stand the filled dish in a roasting pan half filled with hot water. Set it in the oven and bake 1 hour. Remove from the oven and water bath, remove the paper collar, and serve at once. NET: 4 servings.

SOUFFLÉ
EN SURPRISE

Cheese Soufflé with
Poached Eggs (hot)

2 tablespoons dry breadcrumbs,
    fried in a little butter (page
    69)
5 tablespoons salt butter
3 tablespoons all-purpose flour
Salt
A few grains cayenne pepper
1 cup milk
¾ cup freshly grated Parmesan

    cheese
4 eggs, separated
6 eggs, not separated
½ cup finely chopped onion
1 teaspoon finely chopped garlic
3 ripe tomatoes, skinned and
    sliced
Freshly cracked white pepper

Preheat the oven to 375°. Butter a 6-cup oblong baking dish and dust it out with the fried breadcrumbs. Melt 3 tablespoons butter in a small saucepan. Off the heat stir in the flour, a little salt and cayenne pepper. Add the milk and stir over low heat until the sauce thickens. Then mix in ¼ cup grated Parmesan cheese and 4 egg yolks, one at a time. Beat the 4 egg whites to soft peaks and fold them into the yolk mixture. Put half this soufflé mixture in the baking dish and on it make an impression with the back of a wet tablespoon in six places, evenly spaced. Drop an egg in each.

Sauté the chopped onion and garlic 1 to 2 minutes in 2 tablespoons butter, then add the sliced tomatoes and season well with salt and freshly cracked white pepper. Shake over high heat 3 minutes. Put a tablespoon of the tomato mixture on top of each egg, and cover with the remaining half of the soufflé mixture. Sprinkle the top with ½ cup grated Parmesan cheese. Bake 15 minutes. Serve at once. NET: 6 servings.

SOUPS

A SPLENDID IDEA for a meal — a bowl of thick soup, hot French bread, runny Brie cheese, topped off with a wine-soaked peach. I predict that soup-making will be revived as an art in America by our young intellectuals, the prime movers in the groundswell to question, discover, and produce (if they must) honest, natural foods and cooking. No longer almost forgotten, except as lore, will be the humble beginnings of soup, the gurgling pot on the back of Grandma's stove whence came all the potages, soupes, and ragoûts, too, that featured the "whatever available" from the family potager (kitchen-garden). Most people today never had that kind of grandma.

Invariably in my classes the student who chose to make a soup was soon the center of attraction to the rest of the class. There is a special wholesomeness and quality of "good earth" in homemade soup, and people are discovering this in the new quest for the real and honest thing. Why else must the commercial canners try so hard to convince us of their "homemade" or "kitchen-made" quality?

Many people today have never known homemade soup. We have the "soup-can generation," but this is an educated, inquisitive generation who are now looking for an honest loaf of bread and a bowl of soup of recognizable flavor. Hence we can survey all the rules and myths about soup, take the best of the past, and start with new concepts, as we launch the great homemade soup revival.

Here's some background information to help us contemplate the primary soup lesson.

(1) There is a choice of types of soups. *Bouillon* is the basic stock or broth which has been strained but not clarified. *Consommé* is bouillon or strained stock which has been clarified with beaten egg white. *Jellied consommé* is, obviously, cold consommé, which should always be well chilled. *Potages* are puréed vegetable soups and strained cream soups. *Bisques* are strained shellfish soups in which the shells have been pulverized for maximum essential flavor. *Soupe* is usually a broth with vegetables and bits of meat or fish. The word is

often used generically in culinary references. *Chowders* are strictly American, and Americans can be proud of this contribution to the soup art. They are made with clams and clam broth, or fish and fish broth, and there's also corn "chowder." *Garbure* is a thick, lusty vegetable and meat soup indigenous to Béarn, a certain region of France. *Iced cream and vegetable soups* are potages which are thoroughly chilled. Usually, if they are to be served chilled, they are made with vegetable oil instead of butter.

(2) Any of these soups are quick and easy to prepare *if:* (a) You have your supply of homemade frozen stock on hand. When you observe this fundamental, you are ready to make *instant soup* with a stock base at any time. (b) You use your electric blender. This appliance is a boon to the preparation of delicious potages and bisques. No longer is it necessary to pound the lobster or shrimp shells with clenched fist and elbow grease. The electric blender pulverizes the shells or purées whole vegetables in minutes. In most cases the use of a strainer is also eliminated.

(3) Homemade soups (except consommés which contain a garnish or aspic) freeze successfully. Cook a batch of soup whenever you want to and freeze it. When you want to serve it, thaw and gently warm it, and it will be as fresh and fragrant as the day you made it. Soups can be kept a long time in the freezer.

(4) Soup is no longer a fixed course in the meal. If you want to serve it as an hors d'oeuvre, your ingenuity will be applauded. The great chef Albert Stockli, creator of the Four Seasons and Forum of the Twelve Caesars in New York, created an important luncheon menu with the traditional onion soup as a stand-up hors d'oeuvre — served as a "taste" rather than a full serving, in mini-onion soup pots. If you want a gutsy soup for the main course, followed by a salad, cheese, and fruit, you will be forever remembered as a warm, thoughtful human being. Don't be afraid to use soups whenever and however you wish.

(5) Though no beverage is necessary, there are appropriate wines to accompany soups of definite character. A few examples are Meursault or Puligny Montrachet with bisques, Meursault with onion soup, Gewurtztraminer with pea soup with ham, sherry in and with turtle soup or Potage Saint-Germain, and Beaujolais with pot-au-feu.

(6) In menu planning, keep color, texture, and taste in mind in choosing the soup; how does it complement the rest of the menu?

(7) Serving soup at the correct temperature is very important to the enjoyment of each type of soup. Serve *hot clear soups* boiling hot; serve *hot clear soups with garnishes* very hot but not boiling; serve *hot cream soups* moderately hot but never boiling; and serve *iced clear and iced cream soups* ice cold (ideally in a glass or metal bowl embedded in crushed ice).

(8) If you are serving soup at the start of a meal, either as an hors d'oeuvre or sit-down soup course before the entrée, the soup should introduce your fellow diners to what is coming. For example, a cream soup would precede roast chicken and chocolate mousse. A clear soup would be the best prelude to filets de soles with Hollandaise, or tour-

nedos, and a baked dessert or soufflé, Never serve a heavy soup before a delicate dish.

(9) In vegetable soups and purées, the art is to highlight the delicate flavor of the fresh vegetable. Therefore, never use strong meat or game stocks with vegetable soups; use only chicken stock or water, or for richness — cream.

(10) Herbs are rarely used in soups. They are too strong and pungent, and dull the taste buds. A green soup would be an exception. Garnishes of chopped herbs should be sparing.

(11) Sherry and Madeira are the wines most regularly used *in* soups; the purpose is to make the stock stronger and more flavorsome. There are others, as dry white wine in bisques and onion soup.

(12) Tiny croûtons, crisped in the oven or delicately fried in sweet butter, are a good textural contrast for soups. Also fairy toast, Mornay toast, miniature crisp cream puffs (the tiniest possible), and all the many different custard garnishes enhance soup.

(13) To operate your own soup kitchen you will need a large heavy metal or copper marmite for cooking stock slowly and gently, a heavy enamel-coated iron pan for cooking vegetable soups, a tin-lined copper pan for clarifying stocks, wooden spoons, large metal spoons for stirring clear stocks, whisks, a moulin à légumes, and an electric blender.

(14) To serve your soups you want a tureen. If you don't have one, please urge some friend or relative (or spouse) to give you a handsome one for a present, either earthenware or metal. My preferred dish for the individual serving has always been the wide soup plate rather than the bowl, particularly for very hot soups. For onion soup it is de rigueur to use small earthenware covered pots with little handles on them.

The first soup lesson is, in my philosophy, the classic Pot-au-Feu. Synonymous with hearth and home, the legendary grandmother's pot-on-the-fire, it literally gives forth one of the supreme meals, plus an extra supply of good all-purpose stock to produce more soups and sauces for all your cooking, and usually enough extra chicken meat for Crêpes Niçoise or chicken omelets.

The Pot-au-Feu is the easiest of all soups and meals to prepare, and during its long, slow simmer, the blended aromatics create an olfactory euphoria. Before too long they will join in a meal of warm fragrant broth with toasted French bread, and moist poached chicken and tender beef with a garniture of coarse salt, Dijon mustard, sour gherkins, and gently cooked fresh vegetables.

Every country has its traditional soups (the Russian bortsch, the Greek avgolemono, the Iranian yoghurt soup, our American clam chowder, Spain's gazpacho, Italy's minestrone). When you travel, your own philosophy of good taste will be enhanced if you taste them in their countries of origin. The Pot-au-Feu is the mother lode of classical French cooking, and its like is found among various peoples and locales. It has its variations in France, including the Poule-au-Pot which I offer in this book as a poultry dish (page 345); in Jewish cooking it is the much-loved chicken-in-the-pot; and it is not too distant from the New England boiled dinner. I would say it is the dish that offers the best guarantee to please the most people most of the time, which is quite an order (and an early political campaign theme of Henry IV in the sixteenth century).

CLEAR AND CREAM SOUPS

POT-AU-FEU

Broth with Chicken and Meat

This soup, garnished with little vegetables, gherkins, coarse salt, horseradish, and mustard, is a family meal. It also provides basic stock that can be frozen, and perhaps a supply of cooked chicken for other dishes. Pot-au-feu is made in a large (10 to 12 quarts) enamel stockpot. Put the stock that is not used in covered plastic containers and store in the freezer. Use it in any recipe calling for chicken or meat stock.

1 whole chicken, 2½ to 3 pounds
1½ pounds eye round of beef
3 or 4 marrowbones
1 calf's foot, split in half
1 knuckle of veal
1 small carrot, sliced
1 large yellow onion, cut in quarters
1 small white onion, stuck with 2 whole cloves
2 large stalks celery, cut in 1-inch pieces
1 garlic clove, bruised
2 leeks, cut in 3 pieces
Optional: 2 tomatoes, cut in quarters
Optional: A few mushroom trimmings and stems

1 slice lemon
Bouquet garni (2 sprigs parsley, 1 bay leaf, 1 sprig fresh tarragon, 1 sprig celery leaf)
12 black and white peppercorns, mixed
2 tablespoons salt
8 medium-size carrots and 8 medium-size turnips, cut into little olive shapes

FOR SERVING
A few sour gherkins
Coarse salt
Grated fresh horseradish
Dijon mustard
10 to 12 thin slices French bread, toasted

Tie the chicken with string (page 342). Fold a long strip of foil in half lengthwise, set the chicken on it lengthwise, and put this foil hammock into the stockpot, twisting each end of the foil up into a handle, so that later you can lift the chicken out easily. Tie the beef neatly with string and put it in the stockpot. Add the marrowbones, calf's foot, and knuckle of veal. Cover the contents of the pot with cold water and slowly bring it to a boil. Reduce the heat to a simmer, remove the scum, and add the sliced carrot, both onions, the celery, garlic clove, leeks (and tomatoes and mushrooms if desired), slice of lemon, peppercorns, and salt. Tie the bouquet garni in cheesecloth and fasten it to the handle of the pot. Let the pot simmer very gently 45 minutes. Remove the chicken, and continue simmering another 1¼ hours.

Then strain the stock through a colander lined with a damp cloth. Set aside the beef and marrowbones. Cook the little olive-shaped carrots and turnips (and any other vegetables you wish to serve with the pot-au-feu) in a little salted water until soft.

Serve the soup, garnished with marrow slices, separately, with the toasted French bread. Cut the chicken and beef into serving pieces and serve as the main course with the vegetables. This course is traditionally accompanied by sour gherkins, coarse salt, grated fresh horseradish, and Dijon mustard. NET: 8 servings.

For a Petite Marmite, which is served as a soup course only, the Pot-au-Feu stock is clarified to become consommé. It is served with bits of chicken, meat, and vegetables in it, instead of their being served separately as the main course, as for Pot-au-Feu. The Petite Marmite is accompanied by a bowl of freshly grated Parmesan cheese and toasted French bread.

5 cups stock from Pot-au-Feu
    recipe (page 130)
1 tablespoon tomato paste
⅓ cup dry white wine
¼ cup dry sherry
3 egg whites, beaten stiff
6 medium-size carrots, cut into
    little olive shapes
6 medium-size turnips, cut into
    little olive shapes
1 cup green beans, French-cut

¾ cup fresh baby peas
1 large stalk celery, cut in shreds
For each serving (also from the
    Pot-au-Feu recipe): 2 small
    squares each of white chicken
    meat, dark chicken meat, and
    beef, and 1 slice marrow
Bowl of freshly grated Parmesan
    cheese
Thin slices of French bread,
    toasted

Put the stock into a large tin-lined copper pan or an enamel pan with the tomato paste, white wine, sherry, and beaten egg whites. With a wire whisk, stir over low heat until the mixture comes to a rolling boil. Remove from the heat and let the pan stand 15 minutes without being moved. Line a colander with a cloth wrung out in cold water. Put the colander over a bowl. Slowly pour the stock through the cloth. This should give 4 cups clear consommé.

All the vegetables can be individually packaged in foil and plain-cooked in the same pot. Cover them with cold salted water, cook until just soft, and drain. Have ready warm individual earthenware marmite pots or soup bowls. Into each bowl put the pieces of chicken, beef, and marrow, and a few of each of the cooked vegetables. Ladle hot consommé over them. Serve with a bowl of freshly grated Parmesan cheese and thin slices of toasted French bread. NET: 6 servings.

CONSOMMÉ DE VOLAILLES

Chicken Consommé

This recipe is a simple way to clarify some of the chicken stock you have on hand, and makes a refined, nourishing, and delicious consommé to serve with one of the elegant garnitures in the following recipes.

5 cups chicken stock (page 35)
1 tablespoon tomato paste
1/3 cup dry white wine

1/4 cup dry sherry
3 egg whites, beaten stiff

Put the stock in a large tin-lined copper pan or enamel pan with the tomato paste, white wine, sherry, and stiffly beaten egg whites. With a wire whisk, stir over low heat until the mixture comes to a rolling boil. Remove from the heat and let the pan stand 15 minutes without being moved. Line a colander or strainer with a cloth wrung out in cold water. Put the colander over a bowl. Slowly pour the stock through the cloth. NET: 4 cups clear consommé.

CONSOMMÉ CÉLESTINE

Consommé with Shredded Pancakes (Crêpes)

Wrap extra crêpes in plastic and freeze for future use.

4 cups chicken consommé
   (above)

CRÊPES
8 tablespoons all-purpose flour
1 egg

1 egg yolk
2 tablespoons vegetable oil
1/2 teaspoon salt
1/2 teaspoon sugar
1 cup milk
1 tablespoon salt butter

CRÊPES. In a small bowl put the flour, egg and egg yolk, oil, salt, sugar, and 4 tablespoons of the milk. Beat with a little whisk until quite smooth. Then stir in the rest of the milk and set the batter in the refrigerator for a minimum of 30 minutes. Heat a small crêpe pan or omelet pan very hot. (A dot of butter dropped in it should sizzle and brown.) Rub the inside of the pan with the butter, using a thick wad of wax paper. Pour a thin coating of batter in the pan. Brown on one side, turn over, and brown on the other side. When all the pancakes have been made, cut enough of them into fine strips to garnish the consommé.

Reheat the consommé, add the shredded pancakes, and serve very hot. NET: 4 to 6 servings.

CONSOMMÉ JULIENNE

Consommé with Garnish of Mixed Vegetables (Cut into Matchsticks)

4 cups chicken consommé
   (above)
2 teaspoons chopped fresh
   parsley

JULIENNE
1 large carrot

1 medium-size white turnip
2 leeks
1 medium-size onion
12 green beans
1/2 head Boston lettuce
1 teaspoon sugar
1/2 teaspoon salt

Peel the carrot, turnip, leeks, and onion. Top and tail the green beans. Cut them all into very fine, even matchsticks. Cut the lettuce into very fine shreds. Bring a pan of salted water to a boil and plunge all these vegetables into boiling water for 5 minutes. Drain them, but not too well. Place them in a pan with the sugar and salt. Cover with a double piece of wax paper and the lid, and cook slowly 8 minutes. Add these vegetables to the consommé and reheat. Serve very hot. Sprinkle a little chopped parsley in each bowl. NET: 4 to 6 servings.

CONSOMMÉ MOSAIC

Consommé with Mosaic Garnish of Vegetables, Truffles, and Tongue

4 cups chicken consommé
   (page 132)
Fresh parsley

MOSAIC GARNISH
2 carrots

2 turnips
10 green beans
1 large truffle
2 ounces boiled tongue
2 hard-boiled egg whites

Peel the carrots and turnips, top and tail the green beans, and cut them all into very small dice. Wrap each vegetable separately in aluminum foil, and cook them together in the same pan of boiling salted water until they are just soft. Drain the vegetables and put them in the bottom of a warm soup tureen. Cut the tongue, truffle, and hard-boiled egg whites in the same very small dice and put them in the tureen. Reheat the consommé, pour it in the tureen, and serve very hot. Place a few leaves of parsley in each soup plate before serving the consommé. NET: 4 to 6 servings.

CONSOMMÉ AU PETITES PROFITEROLES

Consommé with Little Cream Puffs

How this is served: The consommé (which contains dry white wine and sherry) is served hot, in bowls. With it the guests are served a bottle of very good dry sherry and a bowl of hot baby profiteroles. The idea is for the guests to pour a little more sherry in their consommé and float a large tablespoonful of the hot profiteroles in it just before eating. It is a delightful "soup" course. The profiteroles may be made ahead of time and reheated in the oven.

4 cups chicken consommé
   (page 132)
1 bottle very good dry sherry

PROFITEROLES
¼ cup cold water

2 tablespoons salt butter
¼ teaspoon salt
A few grains cayenne pepper
¼ cup all-purpose flour
2 small eggs

PROFITEROLES. Preheat the oven to 375°. Put the cold water in a saucepan with the butter, salt, and cayenne pepper. Stir over low heat until it comes to a rolling boil. (The butter must melt at the same rate that the water comes to a boil.) Throw in the flour and stir until the mixture thickens and comes away from the sides of the pan. Put the dough in an electric mixer, add one egg, and beat well. Break the other egg in a small bowl and beat well but not until frothy. Reserve a quarter of the beaten egg and add the rest to the cream puff dough in the mixer. Beat until very shiny. Put it in a pastry bag fitted with a small round tube (#1). Pipe little dots of dough onto an unbuttered baking sheet. Brush the tops with the reserved beaten egg. Bake 20 to 25 minutes, until the cream puffs have risen and are a golden brown.

Remove the profiteroles from the oven and serve hot in a separate bowl, with the consommé. NET: 4 to 6 servings.

CONSOMMÉ AUX QUATRE FILETS

Consommé Garnished with Chicken, Tongue, Truffles, and Mushrooms

4 cups chicken consommé (page 132)

GARNISH
2 large firm white mushrooms, cut in thin slices
1 teaspoon lemon juice
Salt

A few grains cayenne pepper
½ cup cooked white chicken meat, cut in fine shreds
½ cup cooked tongue, cut in fine shreds
2 black truffles, cut in fine shreds

Cook the thinly sliced mushrooms in a little water with the lemon juice, salt, and cayenne pepper. Drain. Warm the consommé and add the mushrooms with the shredded chicken, tongue, and truffles. Reheat and serve very hot. NET: 4 to 6 servings.

CONSOMMÉ À LA ROYALE

Consommé with Garnish of Custard Cutouts

4 cups chicken consommé (page 132)

WHITE CUSTARD
3 egg whites, unbeaten

¼ teaspoon salt
A few grains cayenne pepper
¾ cup milk, scalded
1 teaspoon vegetable oil

WHITE CUSTARD. Preheat the oven to 300°. Stir (do not beat) the egg whites in a bowl over a bowl of crushed ice. Add the salt and cayenne pepper and continue stirring until the egg whites are smooth without being frothy. Stir the scalded milk quickly into the egg whites. Lightly oil a shallow pan or layer cake tin. Pour in the white custard mixture and place the tin in a roasting pan half filled with hot water. Cover the custard with a piece of lightly oiled wax paper. Bake until firm to the touch, approximately 45 minutes. Remove from the oven and chill. Unmold, and cut into small shapes with miniature cutters or cut into small squares with a sharp knife.

Reheat the consommé, add the custard cutouts, and serve very hot. NET: 4 to 6 servings.

5 cups chicken stock (page 35)
1 tablespoon tomato paste
1 sprig mint
¼ cup dry white wine
2 teaspoons lemon juice
3 raw egg whites
Salt
1 cup shredded raw spinach

1 cup shredded green lettuce
   (Boston or romaine)
1 tablespoon shredded cucumber
   rind
1 tablespoon fresh or frozen
   peas
¼ cup dry sherry

Put the chicken stock in a pan with the tomato paste, mint, wine and lemon juice. Beat the egg whites to soft peaks and add them to the pan. Stir the mixture with a whisk over low heat until it comes to a boil. Remove the pan from the heat and let it stand 15 minutes without being moved. Line a colander with a damp cloth and strain the mixture through it into a clean pan. Set aside this clarified stock (consommé). Blanch the shredded spinach, lettuce, and cucumber rind by plunging them in boiling salt water for 3 minutes. Drain and dry lightly in a cloth. Cook the peas in a little pan of boiling water until soft, and rub them through a small strainer. Add all these vegetables to the consommé. Stir in the dry sherry. Reheat and serve very hot. NET: 4 to 6 servings.

4 cups chicken consommé
   (page 132)

SPINACH CUSTARD
½ pound spinach leaves, with
   stalks removed

2 eggs
2 tablespoons vegetable oil
3 tablespoons all-purpose flour
Salt
A few grains cayenne pepper
½ cup milk

SPINACH CUSTARD. Wash the spinach leaves very, very well. Put them in a pan with salt and ¼ cup cold water. Cover and cook briskly 5 minutes. Drain and dry well. Rub the wilted spinach through a fine strainer, or put through a fine meat chopper. Set aside to cool. Beat the eggs lightly and add to the spinach purée. Preheat the oven to 300°. Heat the vegetable oil in a saucepan. Off the heat, add the flour, salt, and cayenne pepper. Pour in the milk and stir over low heat until it thickens. Mix in the strained spinach and egg mixture. Lightly oil a shallow layer cake tin and fill it with the spinach custard. Put this pan in a roasting pan half filled with hot water. Cover the custard with a piece of lightly oiled wax paper. Bake the custard in the water bath until it is firm to the touch, approximately 45 minutes. When the custard is cool, unmold it. Cut it into various shapes with miniature cutters or into small squares with a sharp knife.

Reheat the consommé, add the spinach custard cutouts, and serve very hot. NET: 4 to 6 servings.

APPLE AND CELERY SOUP

Apple and celery purée with chicken stock, garnished with a sautéed apple ring.

2 tablespoons salt butter
3 tablespoons vegetable oil
2 stalks celery, sliced
1 medium-size onion, sliced
1 carrot, sliced
6 medium-size apples

2 cups chicken stock (page 35)
1 teaspoon meat glaze
Salt
Fresh cracked white pepper
A little all-purpose flour

In a deep heavy pan, melt the butter with 1 tablespoon vegetable oil. Add the celery, onion, and carrot, and cook slowly for a few minutes. Slice 5 of the apples (do not peel or core them). Add them to the pan and cook fairly briskly until the apples are soft but not brown. Then mix in the chicken stock and meat glaze, season with salt and white pepper, and bring to a boil. Rub the soup through a fine strainer. Return the pureé to the pan, and reheat. Core and slice the remaining apple, but do not peel it. Dust the slices with a little flour and sauté in 2 tablespoons of hot oil until golden brown on both sides. Serve the soup garnished with a sautéed apple ring in each bowl. NET: 4 servings.

CRÈME DE CHAMPIGNONS

Cream of Mushroom Soup

14 tablespoons salt butter
1 tablespoon rice flour
3 cups chicken stock (page 35)
Salt
Freshly cracked white pepper
2 bay leaves

¾ pound firm white mushrooms
Juice of 1 lemon
2 egg yolks
¾ cup light cream
¼ cup heavy cream, whipped
1 cup fried croûtons (page 70)

Melt 6 tablespoons butter in a deep heavy pan over low heat. Off the heat, stir in the rice flour and mix in the chicken stock. Return to low heat and stir until the mixture comes to a boil. Season with salt and pepper and simmer 12 minutes. Add the bay leaves and set aside. Put the mushrooms through a fine meat chopper twice. In a saucepan, heat 8 tablespoons (¼ pound) butter until it begins to brown. Add the ground mushrooms, lemon juice, and salt and pepper. Cook very briskly 3 minutes. Stir the ground mushroom and butter mixture into the stock mixture and simmer gently 15 minutes. In a separate bowl mix the egg yolks with the light cream. Stir a little soup into the yolk mixture to temper it, then pour it all into the soup pot. Stir over very low heat 10 minutes without boiling. Remove the bay leaves. Serve the soup in individual bowls with 1 tablespoon of plain whipped cream on the top of each. Serve a separate bowl of fried croûtons. NET: 4 to 6 servings.

4 cups fresh shelled peas
1 cup chicken stock (page 35)
1½ cups milk, scalded
3 tablespoons rice flour or 1
    tablespoon all-purpose flour
6 tablespoons cold milk

1 teaspoon sugar
Salt
Freshly cracked white pepper
6 outside Boston lettuce leaves
2 egg yolks
4 tablespoons light cream

CRÈME CLAMART

Cream of Pea
and Lettuce Soup

Cook the peas in salted water until they are soft. Drain them well and rub through a fine strainer, or purée in an electric blender. Return the pea purée to the pan and stir in the chicken stock and the scalded milk. Bring the soup slowly to a boil. Mix the flour with the cold milk and stir this into the soup off the heat. Add the sugar, season with salt and pepper, and simmer gently 20 minutes. Cut the lettuce leaves into fine shreds, plunge into boiling water, drain and set aside. Put the egg yolks and light cream in the bottom of the soup tureen and mix well. Slowly pour in the soup, while you stir with a whisk. Add the shredded lettuce leaves and serve. NET: 4 to 6 servings.

The prevailing image of "cream of chicken soup" is an injustice to this rendition. Freshness and balance are the keys: stock, eggs, and cream. An equally exquisite and delicious alternative in hot weather is the cold version of Crème Cyrano (page 164).

CRÈME CYRANO

Cream of Chicken
Soup (hot)

6 tablespoons salt butter
1 tablespoon finely chopped
    white onion
1 tablespoon finely chopped
    celery heart
4 tablespoons all-purpose flour
4 cups chicken stock (page 35)
Salt
A few grains cayenne pepper

A little freshly grated nutmeg
4 teaspoons sweet butter
3 egg yolks
3 tablespoons dry sherry
½ cup light cream
¼ cup heavy cream, whipped
2 tablespoons chopped fresh
    chives

Melt the salt butter in a large heavy pan. Add the finely chopped onion and celery. Cook slowly until soft but not brown. Remove the pan from the heat and stir in the flour. Mix in the chicken stock. Season with salt, cayenne pepper, and a very few grains of freshly grated nutmeg. Stir over the heat until the soup comes to a boil. Then add, bit by bit, 4 teaspoons of sweet butter, stirring all the time, and simmer 10 minutes. Beat the egg yolks until they are light and lemony in color. Mix in the sherry and light cream. Put this mixture in the bottom of the soup tureen. Pour on the hot soup slowly, stirring all the time. Fold in the whipped cream and sprinkle the top with the chopped fresh chives. NET: 4 to 6 servings.

CRÈME OLGA

Cream of Raw Mushrooms and Scallions

Be very careful not to overcook this soup if it must be reheated. The essence is the freshness of the raw mushrooms and raw scallions infused in stock.

8 tablespoons salt butter
3 cups chopped scallions
Salt
Freshly cracked white pepper
½ cup all-purpose flour

3 cups chicken stock (page 35)
½ pound fresh mushrooms, sliced
1 cup light cream
¼ cup heavy cream, whipped

Melt 5 tablespoons butter in a heavy pan. Add the chopped scallions, season with salt and pepper, and cook very slowly until the scallions are soft. Off the heat, mix in the flour, then stir in the chicken stock. Stir over low heat until the soup comes to a boil. Add the sliced mushrooms (reserving about 8 very thin slices for garnish) and rub the mixture through a fine strainer or purée it in an electric blender. Return the purée to the pan and, over low heat, stir in the light cream. Correct the seasoning. Serve in individual bowls topped with a dollop of whipped cream carrying two thin slices of raw mushroom. NET: 4 servings.

L'OIGNON AU LAIT

Cream of Onion Soup

For the onion connoisseur, and who isn't? A purée of milky Bermuda onions textured with vermicelli, garnished with a ball of frozen sweet butter.

1½ pounds Bermuda onions, thinly sliced
2 leeks, washed and thinly sliced
½ teaspoon finely chopped garlic
1 teaspoon salt
8 tablespoons salt butter
Freshly cracked white pepper
3 tablespoons all-purpose flour
1 cup water
1 cup milk, scalded with 1 whole

nutmeg and 2 bay leaves
¼ cup vermicelli, boiled in plain water and drained
6 small balls frozen sweet butter (made with a small melon scoop)
1 teaspoon freshly grated nutmeg
½ skinny loaf French bread (for fairy toast, page 70)

Put the sliced onions on a platter and cover with the sliced leeks. Scatter the chopped garlic over them with the salt. Let stand 30 minutes.

Dissolve the salt butter in a heavy pan. Add the onion mixture and sprinkle well with freshly cracked white pepper. Cover the pan and cook very slowly until the onions are soft but not brown. Remove the pan from the heat and stir in the flour and water, then stir over low heat until the mixture comes to a boil. Scald the milk with the whole nutmeg and the bay leaves. Remove the nutmeg and bay leaves from the scalded milk and stir it into the soup. Rub the soup through a fine strainer or purée it in an electric blender. Return it to the pan and add the drained cooked vermicelli. Reheat slowly and carefully.

Serve in individual bowls. Float a ball of frozen sweet butter in each and sprinkle the top with freshly grated nutmeg. Serve with a separate tray of fairy toast. NET: 4 servings.

POTAGE
BONNE-FEMME

Leek and Potato Soup

The winter version of Vichyssoise, in a way; just as good and long a classic favorite.

4 tablespoons salt butter	Freshly cracked black pepper
4 Idaho-type potatoes, peeled and thinly sliced	1½ cups milk
	2 egg yolks
4 large leeks, washed and shredded	½ cup heavy cream
	2 tablespoons chopped fresh parsley
1½ cups water	
½ teaspoon Dijon mustard	½ cup fried croûtons (page 70)
Salt	

Melt the butter in a deep heavy pan. Add the sliced potatoes and three-quarters of the shredded leeks with ½ cup water, the mustard, and salt and pepper to season. Cover and cook over low heat until the vegetables are soft and mushy. Pour in the milk and 1 cup water and stir over low heat until the soup comes to a boil. Remove from the heat and let stand 15 minutes, then rub the mixture through a fine strainer or purée in an electric blender. Beat the egg yolks with the heavy cream in a separate little bowl. Stir the yolk mixture into the soup over low heat, but do not let the soup boil. Blanch the remaining shredded leeks in boiling water. Drain and dry on paper towels. Stir them into the soup. Sprinkle the soup with chopped parsley and serve with a separate bowl of fried croûtons. NET: 4 servings.

POTAGE CRÉCY

Purée of Carrot Soup

Carrots, onion, and potatoes provide excellent flavor balance in this classic.

4 large carrots	2 egg yolks
1 large yellow onion	1 cup light cream
4 Idaho-type potatoes	1 tablespoon chopped fresh chives
4 tablespoons salt butter	
1½ cups water	1 teaspoon chopped fresh parsley
Salt	
Freshly cracked white pepper	1½ cups fried croûtons (page 70)
1½ cups milk, scalded	

Peel the carrots, onion, and potatoes. Cut into thick slices and put in a heavy pan. Add the butter, water, and season with salt and pepper. Cover the pan and cook over moderate heat until all the vegetables are soft. Rub them through a very fine strainer or purée in an electric blender, and return them to the pan. Stir in the scalded milk. In a separate bowl mix the egg yolks with the cream and stir this into the soup. The soup may be reheated before serving, but it must not boil. To serve, ladle into bowls, sprinkle with the chives and parsley, and serve with a separate bowl of fried croûtons. NET: 4 servings.

POTAGE CRÈME D'ASPERGES

Cream of Fresh Asparagus Soup

Garnished with crisp delicate tips of asparagus.

3 tablespoons salt butter
24 spears fresh asparagus
1 cup chopped scallions
½ teaspoon finely chopped garlic
1 teaspoon lemon juice
Salt
Freshly cracked white pepper

4 tablespoons all-purpose flour
2 cups water
½ cup heavy cream
1 egg yolk mixed with 2 teaspoons heavy cream
2 tablespoons chopped fresh parsley

Slice the asparagus spears and set aside 18 nice tips. Melt the butter in a deep heavy pan. Add the sliced asparagus and the scallions, garlic, and lemon juice, and season with salt and pepper. Cover the pan and cook very slowly until mushy. Remove from the heat, stir in the flour and water, and stir over low heat until the soup comes to a boil. Simmer 10 minutes. Rub the soup through a fine strainer or purée it in an electric blender and return it to the pan. Cook the 18 asparagus tips in a little salted water until just soft but still crisp. Drain them and add to the soup. Mix in the heavy cream. Stir in the egg yolk mixed with heavy cream and the chopped parsley. Gently reheat but do not boil. NET: 4 servings.

POTAGE CRÈME DUBARRY

Cream of Cauliflower Soup

With a liaison of egg yolks, and textured with cauliflower florets, fresh chives, and fried croûtons.

1 large cauliflower
2 tablespoons lemon juice
6 tablespoons salt butter
4 tablespoons all-purpose flour
Salt
A few grains cayenne pepper
4 cups chicken stock (page 35)

½ cup milk, scalded
½ cup instant tapioca
2 egg yolks
½ cup heavy cream
1 tablespoon chopped fresh chives
1 cup fried croûtons (page 70)

Remove about ½ cup tiny florets from the cauliflower. Blanch them 4 to 5 minutes in boiling salted water with 2 teaspoons lemon juice. Drain and set aside. Slice the rest of the cauliflower and blanch 15 minutes with the rest of the lemon juice in boiling salted water. Drain. Dissolve the butter in a large heavy pan. Off the heat, stir in the flour and season with salt and cayenne pepper. Pour in the chicken stock and stir over low heat until the soup comes to a boil. Put the drained sliced cauliflower in this mixture. Continue cooking over low heat until the cauliflower is very soft. (Skim when necessary.) Rub the soup through a very fine strainer or purée it in an electric blender. Return it to the pan, add the scalded milk, and reheat. Add the tapioca and gently simmer until it is soft. In a warm tureen, mix the egg yolks with the heavy cream. Pour the hot soup slowly onto the yolk mixture, stirring all the time. Add the chopped fresh chives and cauliflower florets. Serve with a separate bowl of fried croûtons. NET: 4 servings.

POTAGE CRÈME D'ÉPINARDS

Cream of Fresh Spinach Soup

2 tablespoons salt butter
1 tablespoon finely chopped onion
½ pound well-cleaned raw spinach, finely chopped
2 tablespoons rice flour or 1 tablespoon all-purpose flour
Salt

Freshly cracked white pepper
1½ cups water
1 small bay leaf
Small lumps of salt butter
3 tablespoons heavy cream
About ½ cup tiny fried croûtons (page 70)

Melt 2 tablespoons salt butter in a large heavy pan. Add the chopped onion and cook 4 minutes. Stir in the chopped raw spinach, cover the pan, and cook slowly 7 to 8 minutes. Remove the pan from the heat and stir in the flour. Season with salt and pepper. Pour in the water and stir over low heat until the soup comes to a boil. Cover and simmer until the spinach is soft, then rub the mixture through a fine strainer or purée it in an electric blender. Return the soup to the pan with the bay leaf, lump of butter, and heavy cream. Adjust the seasoning. Reheat, but do not let the soup get too hot. Serve with tiny fried croûtons. NET: 4 servings.

POTAGE CRÈME DE LAITUES

Cream of Lettuce Soup

Finely shredded Boston lettuce in a rich, creamy suspension of sweet butter.

4 tablespoons salt butter
6 tablespoons rice flour
3 cups chicken stock (page 35)
4 small heads Boston lettuce
1 pinch baking soda
Salt

Freshly cracked white pepper
1 cup light cream
2 egg yolks
8 tablespoons sweet butter
1 teaspoon lemon juice
1 cup fried croûtons (page 70)

Melt the salt butter in a heavy pan. Off the heat stir in the rice flour. Return to the heat and cook slowly, without browning, for 2 minutes. Off the heat, stir in the chicken stock. Return to slow heat and bring to a boil. Cut 8 to 10 of the greenest leaves of the lettuce into very fine shreds. Plunge the shredded lettuce into boiling water with the baking soda, remove the pan from the heat, and let it stand 5 minutes. Drain the shredded lettuce, dry well in a cloth, and set aside. Cut the rest of the lettuce into fine shreds and add it to the soup with salt and pepper. Cook very slowly 1 hour. In a separate bowl, mix the egg yolks with the light cream. Remove the soup from the heat and stir in the yolk mixture. Cream the sweet butter with a little salt, pepper, and the lemon juice. Stir the butter into the soup bit by bit, and blend well. Add the blanched shredded lettuce leaves. Reheat very carefully, but do not boil. (This soup should be only a little more than warm; not hot.) Serve the soup in individual bowls, with a separate bowl of fried croûtons. NET: 4 servings.

POTAGE CRESSONIÈRE

Purée of Watercress Soup

The purée is mixed with a generous supply of whole fresh watercress leaves.

4 Idaho potatoes, peeled
1 large yellow onion, skinned
1 small heart of celery
4 tablespoons salt butter
2 cups water
3 teaspoons salt
1 teaspoon freshly cracked white pepper

12 tablespoons frozen sweet butter
1 bunch fresh watercress
¾ cup milk, scalded
3 egg yolks
3 tablespoons dry sherry
¾ cup light cream, scalded

Cut the potatoes, onion, and celery heart into ¼-inch slices. Heat the salt butter in a heavy pan. When it is foaming, put in the vegetables and shake them over high heat for 2 minutes. Add the water, salt, and pepper, and bring very slowly to a boil. Reduce the heat. Cut up the frozen sweet butter in 4 or 5 pieces and put them on top of the mixture. Put the lid on the pan and cook very slowly over low heat until the vegetables are soft. Remove the individual leaves from about half the bunch of watercress and set them aside. Off the fire, add the stalks and the rest of the watercress bunch to the potato mixture. Stir in the scalded milk. Rub the mixture through a fine strainer. Add the reserved whole leaves of the watercress to the purée. In a bowl, mix the egg yolks with the dry sherry and stir in the scalded cream. Stir a little of the soup into the egg yolk mixture to temper it, then pour it all slowly back into the soup pot, stirring all the time. Before serving, reheat but do not boil. NET: 4 to 6 servings.

POTAGE DURANT

Purée of Fresh Pea and Tapioca Soup with Finely Diced Carrots

4 cups fresh shelled peas
2 tablespoons salt butter
4 shallots, finely chopped
6 cups cold water
¼ cup instant tapioca

Salt
Freshly cracked white pepper
2 cups buttermilk
2 egg yolks
2 tablespoons cold milk

2 large carrots
4 tablespoons chopped fresh
  parsley

8 to 10 toasted thin slices of
  French bread

Cook the peas in an ample amount of salted water. When they are soft, drain and rub them through a fine strainer or purée them in an electric blender. Melt the butter in a heavy pan and cook the chopped shallots 2 minutes. Add the puréed peas and dilute with the cold water. Add the tapioca, salt, and white pepper. Stir over moderate heat until the mixture comes to a boil. Simmer gently until the tapioca is soft. In a bowl mix the egg yolks, buttermilk, and cold milk together. Slowly pour this into the soup, stirring constantly. Remove the soup from the heat. Cut the carrots in fine dice and cook until soft in boiling salted water. Add the carrots to the soup. Just before serving, sprinkle the bowls of soup with chopped parsley. Serve with a plate of thin slices of toasted French bread. NET: 6 to 8 servings.

12 tablespoons salt butter
2 medium-size yellow onions,
  finely chopped
½ teaspoon finely chopped
  garlic
1 teaspoon salt
Freshly cracked white pepper
½ teaspoon ground cardamom
  seed
2 packages frozen green peas
  or 5 cups fresh shelled peas

3¼ cups water
4 tablespoons all-purpose flour
¼ cup Cognac or good brandy
1 pound sorrel or spinach leaves,
  well washed (if spinach
  leaves, sprinkle with a little
  lemon juice)
1 cup milk, scalded
½ cup heavy cream, scalded
½ cup heavy cream, whipped

POTAGE FONTANGES

Purée of Pea and Sorrel Soup

Cream the butter in a mixer until it is light and fluffy. Add the chopped onion and garlic. Season with the salt, pepper, and cardamom seed. Mix well and put the mixture in a heavy pan. Cook slowly until the onions become soft without browning. Add the green peas and ¼ cup water. Cover the pan and cook until the peas are just soft, stirring occasionally. Remove from the heat and stir in the flour and 3 cups water. Stir over low heat until the soup comes to a boil. In a separate little pan, heat the brandy, ignite it, and pour it over the soup. Let the soup simmer gently for about 5 minutes. Remove the soup from the heat and add the sorrel or spinach leaves, stirring them in until they wilt. Rub the soup mixture through a fine strainer or purée it in an electric blender. Return it to the pan and stir in the scalded milk and heavy cream. Reheat. Serve in a warm tureen or individual bowls. With individual bowls, top each bowl of soup with a dollop of whipped cream and scorch under a hot broiler. NET: 6 servings.

POTAGE AUX GOURDES ET MARRONS

Purée of Squash and Chestnut Soup

This is a perfect winter soup, when acorn squash and chestnuts are plentiful.

3/4 pound raw chestnuts	Salt
2 or 3 acorn squashes	Freshly cracked white pepper
2 tablespoons vegetable oil	3 cups chicken stock
2 tablespoons salt butter	3 tablespoons heavy cream
1 small onion, sliced	2 tablespoons chopped fresh
1 carrot, sliced	parsley
1 stalk celery, sliced	Toasted slices of French bread

Cut the acorn squashes in quarters, remove the seeds, and cook them in boiling salted water until soft. Remove the skins and set the squash aside. Put the chestnuts in a pan, cover with cold water, bring to a boil, and boil 3 minutes. Remove from the heat and peel off both the outer and inner shells. Set the chestnuts aside.

Melt the oil and butter in a deep heavy pan. Add the sliced onion, carrot, and celery. Season with salt and pepper. Cook 3 minutes. Add the prepared chestnuts, cover with the chicken stock, and simmer gently until the vegetables and chestnuts are quite soft. If the stock reduces, add more stock. Rub the chestnut mixture with the boiled skinned acorn squash through a fine strainer or purée it in an electric blender. Return the purée to the pan. Gently reheat and stir in the heavy cream and parsley. Do not allow the soup to get too hot before serving. Serve with toasted slices of French bread. NET: 4 to 6 servings.

POTAGE GRAND DUC

Cauliflower and Onion Soup

Garnished with fresh chives and crisp fried croûtons.

2 small cauliflowers	Freshly cracked white pepper
1 tablespoon vegetable oil	3 tablespoons all-purpose flour
2 tablespoons salt butter	2 1/2 cups mixed milk and water
2 medium-size yellow onions, cut in eighths	1 bay leaf
1/4 teaspoon finely chopped garlic	1/2 cup heavy cream
3/4 cup water	2 teaspoons chopped fresh chives
Salt	A few fried croûtons (page 70)

Trim and core the cauliflowers and cut them into small pieces. Heat the oil and butter in a deep heavy pan. Add the cut-up cauliflower, onions, and garlic, and cook 2 to 3 minutes. Add 3/4 cup water, season with salt and pepper, cover, and cook over low heat until the cauliflower is mushy. Remove from the heat and stir in the flour and the mixed milk and water. Stir over low heat until the soup comes to a boil. Add the bay leaf and simmer 2 minutes. Rub the mixture through a fine strainer, or purée it in an electric blender, and return the purée to the pan. Stir in the heavy cream, correct the seasoning, and gently reheat. Garnish with the chopped chives and fried croûtons. NET: 4 servings.

This is an awfully good soup, one to build a meal around. Start the soup a day in advance.

1½ cups dry lentils
1 slice lemon
4 tablespoons salt butter
4 chicken livers
¼ pound bacon, sliced
1 medium-size yellow onion, finely chopped
1 teaspoon finely chopped garlic
3½ cups chicken stock (page 35)
¼ cup dry white wine
¼ cup Madeira wine
1 small bay leaf

1 small white onion stuck with 2 whole cloves
½ pound lean salt pork (in one piece)
½ cup light cream
¼ cup boiled ham or tongue, finely diced
2 egg yolks
2 tablespoons Cognac or good brandy
¼ cup heavy cream
1 cup fried croûtons (page 70)

Soak the lentils overnight in water with a slice of lemon in it. Change the water once or twice.

Heat the butter in a heavy pan and quickly brown the chicken livers on each side. Remove the livers from the pan. Cut the bacon into shreds, add it to the pan, and cook it briskly 1 to 2 minutes. Add the finely chopped onion and garlic and cook slowly 2 to 3 minutes without browning the onion too much. Drain the lentils and put them in the pan. Pour in the chicken stock, white wine, and Madeira and bring the soup to a boil. Add the bay leaf, the onion with cloves, and the piece of salt pork. Cover the soup and simmer it very gently until the lentils are soft. Remove the piece of salt pork and rub the soup through a fine strainer or purée it in an electric blender. Return the purée to the pan. Stir in the light cream and the ham or tongue. In the bottom of a warm tureen put the egg yolks, brandy, and heavy cream and mix them together. Pour the hot soup slowly onto the yolk mixture, stirring all the time. Serve from the tureen, with a separate bowl of hot fried croûtons. NET: 4 to 6 servings.

Favorite split pea soup slow-cooked with a ham bone, served with a few strands of vermicelli, whole fresh peas, and tiny fried croûtons. This soup should be started a day in advance.

1 pound dried split peas
6 cups water
4 ounces boiled ham, in large

dice
2 white onions, each stuck with 1 whole clove

1 ham bone
1 large carrot, sliced
8 tablespoons salt butter
2 whole leeks (including the
    greens), sliced
Salt
Freshly cracked white pepper
A little sugar
2 ounces vermicelli, broken a
    little, plain-boiled
½ cup finely shredded sorrel

(or substitute spinach with a
    little lemon juice)
½ cup milk, scalded
1 tablespoon finely chopped
    fresh parsley
½ cup fresh shelled peas (or
    frozen), barely cooked in a
    little salted water
1 cup tiny fried croûtons (page
    70)

Soak the split peas overnight in an ample amount of water. Drain and wash them thoroughly in several more waters. Put them in a heavy pan and pour over about 5 cups water. Add the boiled ham. Bring to a boil and remove any scum. Add the onions with cloves and the ham bone. Sauté the sliced carrot in 1 tablespoon butter and add it to the soup. Add the sliced leeks, salt, and pepper. Cover the pan and cook the soup 1½ hours over very low heat. Remove the ham bone. Rub the soup through a very fine strainer or purée it in an electric blender. Dilute the purée with about 1 cup boiling water (the consistency should be thick). Adjust the seasoning with salt, pepper, and a little sugar. Stir in 6 tablespoons butter, cut in pieces. Add the boiled vermicelli. Cook the sorrel (or spinach) in 1 tablespoon butter and add it to the soup. Stir in the scalded milk. Garnish the soup with the whole peas and chopped parsley. Serve with a bowl of tiny fried croûtons. NET: 6 servings.

POTAGE MARGUERITE

Red Kidney Bean Soup with Fresh Tomatoes

Soaked and softened kidney beans are cooked in stock or water with fresh tomatoes, and served with a separate bowl of freshly grated Parmesan cheese. This soup should be started a day in advance.

½ pound dry red kidney beans
4 tablespoons salt butter
1 carrot, sliced
1 onion, sliced
1 small turnip, sliced
4 tomatoes, peeled and cut in
    quarters
2 teaspoons tomato paste
Bouquet garni (1 bay leaf, 2

sprigs parsley, ½ teaspoon
    basil leaf, tied in cheesecloth)
Salt
Freshly cracked white pepper
6 cups chicken stock (page 35)
    or water
½ cup freshly grated Parmesan
    cheese

Soak the kidney beans at least 12 hours, then drain, rinse, and drain again. Melt the butter in a deep heavy casserole. Add the sliced carrot, onion, turnip, and the kidney beans. Shake the mixture over the heat for a few minutes. Add the tomatoes, tomato paste, bouquet garni, and season with salt and pepper. Pour in the stock or water. Simmer until the kidney beans are soft (approximately 2 hours). Remove the bouquet garni. Serve the soup with a separate bowl of freshly grated Parmesan cheese. NET: 6 servings.

In honor of General Antoine Parmentier, who must have been one of the best public relations experts in culinary history, to transform the rejected potato into a household word.

POTAGE PARMENTIER

Purée of Potato Soup

2 tablespoons salt butter
3 small leeks, cleaned well and
   cut in thin shreds
4 Idaho-type potatoes, peeled
   and cut in eighths
Salt
Freshly cracked white pepper

1½ cups water
¾ cup milk, scalded
2 egg yolks
½ cup light cream
8 tablespoons frozen sweet
   butter
1 cup fried croûtons (page 70)

Melt the salt butter in a heavy pan. Put the shredded leeks in the pan, cover, and cook very slowly, without browning, until they are nearly soft. Add the potatoes to the pan with the leeks and season with salt and pepper. Add the water and cook very slowly until the potatoes are quite soft. Rub the mixture through a fine strainer or purée it in an electric blender. Put the potatoe purée back in the pan and add the scalded milk. (If the soup is too thick, add a little boiling water.) Simmer 10 minutes. Remove any scum that might form on the top. In a warm soup tureen, mix the egg yolks and the light cream. Pour the soup slowly into the tureen, stirring all the time. Cut the sweet butter in little pieces, and stir them into the soup, bit by bit. Serve with the fried croûtons. NET: 4 servings.

A thick country soup of potatoes, onions, leeks, celery, and fresh spinach leaves.

POTAGE PROVENÇALE

4 large Idaho-type potatoes
2 large yellow onions
2 leeks
3 stalks celery
16 tablespoons frozen sweet
   butter
1 pound fresh spinach leaves,

   well washed
4 cups cold water
1 teaspoon salt
2 teaspoons freshly cracked
   white pepper
½ cup light cream, scalded

Skin and slice the potatoes and the onions. Wash and slice the celery and the leeks. Put these vegetables in a heavy pan with the water. Sprinkle with the salt and pepper. Put the frozen sweet butter on top, cover the pan, and cook slowly until the potatoes are mushy. Remove from the heat. Add the spinach leaves to the soup and stir with a wooden spoon until they are wilted. Then rub the mixture through a fine strainer or purée it in an electric blender. Return the purée to the pan and stir in the scalded light cream. Reheat, but do not boil. NET: 6 servings.

POTAGE SAINT-GERMAIN

Purée of Fresh Pea Soup

This is a great soup in the French repertoire.

2 cups shelled fresh peas
½ cup green part of leek, sliced
About 10 spinach leaves
About 10 lettuce leaves
2 or 3 sprigs fresh parsley
1 teaspoon sugar

5 tablespoons salt butter
Salt
Freshly cracked white pepper
2½ cups chicken stock (page 35) or water
¼ cup heavy cream

Put the peas and the sliced leek in a deep heavy casserole. Thoroughly wash and dry the spinach and lettuce leaves, cut them into shreds, and add to the casserole with the parsley, sugar, and 3 tablespoons butter. Season with salt and pepper. Pour in 1 cup stock or water. Bring to a boil quickly. Reduce the heat and cook very slowly. When the peas are soft, reserve 2 to 3 tablespoons whole peas (for garnish), and rub the rest of the mixture through a fine strainer or purée it in an electric blender. Return the purée to the casserole. Add the remaining 1½ cups stock or water. Stir until the soup comes to a boil. Then stir in, bit by bit, the heavy cream and 2 tablespoons butter. Add the reserved cooked whole peas and correct the seasoning. NET: 4 servings.

POTAGE SANTÉ

The classic potato and sorrel soup called "health soup."

2 tablespoons salt butter
4 or 5 Idaho-type potatoes, peeled and sliced
6 scallions, sliced
¾ cup water
Salt
Freshly cracked white pepper

½ pound sorrel, well washed and shredded (or substitute ½ pound spinach sprinkled with juice of 1 lemon)
2½ cups chicken stock (page 35)
1 cup light cream

Melt the butter in a large heavy pan. Add the sliced potatoes and scallions, water, and salt and pepper. Cover and cook slowly until the vegetables are mushy. Add the sorrel or spinach and cook 2 minutes; then add the stock and stir over low heat until the mixture comes to a boil. Rub the mixture through a strainer or purée it in an electric blender. Return the purée to the pan and stir in the light cream. Reheat and serve. NET: 4 servings.

This soup should be started a day in advance.

1 pound dry white beans or
    chick peas
A little lemon juice
1 onion, sliced
1 large carrot, sliced
1 stalk celery, sliced
Salt
Freshly cracked white pepper
Water

1 cup chicken stock (page 35)
4 tablespoons salt butter
2 cups milk
2 egg yolks
1 cup light cream
¼ cup fresh parsley or chervil
    leaves (whole)
1 cup fried croûtons (page 70)

*POTAGE
SOISSONNAISE*

---

*Purée of White Bean
or Chick Pea Soup*

Soak the beans overnight. Drain and wash well with a little lemon juice and clean water. Put the soaked beans in a heavy pan. Add the sliced onion, carrot, and celery. Season with salt and pepper. Cover with cold water to about an inch above the beans. Bring slowly to a boil and simmer gently until all the beans are soft. Rub the soup through a fine strainer or purée it in an electric blender, and return it to the pan. Add the chicken stock, milk, and a little extra salt and pepper. Bring slowly to a boil, stirring all the time. Stir in the butter, little by little. Put the egg yolks and light cream in the bottom of a warm tureen and mix them together. Slowly pour on the hot soup, stirring constantly. Float whole parsley leaves on the soup. Serve the fried croûtons separately. NET: 6 to 8 servings.

I don't know the origin of this soup, but it tastes very different from the usual conception of soup. It is very good!

4 large Idaho-type potatoes
2 cups water
Salt
Freshly cracked white pepper
½ pound salsify (oyster plant)
2 tablespoons tarragon vinegar

3 cups milk
1½ cups heavy cream
½ teaspoon freshly grated
    nutmeg
Crème Royale (white custard,
    page 134)

POTAGE SUZETTE

---

*Purée of Potato
and Salsify Soup*

First prepare the white custard (Crème Royale). While it is baking and cooling, get the soup ready. Peel the potatoes, cut them into eighths, and put them in a pan with 1 cup water. Add salt and pepper and cook slowly until the potatoes are mushy. Skin the salsify and cut into very thin slices. Cook it in 1 cup water with the vinegar until it is quite soft. Mix the cooked potatoes and salsify together and rub the mixture through a fine strainer or purée it in an electric blender. Put the purée in a heavy pan, adjust the seasoning with salt and pepper, and stir in the milk. Slowly bring the soup to a boil and remove from the heat.

When the custard is quite cold, stamp cutout rounds the size of a quarter with a small cookie cutter. Cut these in thin slices (for garnish). Put the heavy cream in a large bowl over a bowl of ice and beat until thick but not too stiff. Put the whipped cream in the bottom of a warm soup tureen. Slowly pour in the hot soup, stirring constantly with a wooden spoon. Sprinkle with the grated nutmeg and garnish with the white custard cutouts. NET: 4 to 6 servings.

POTAGE DE TOMATE ET CRABE

Fresh Tomato and Crabmeat Soup

Without the crab, this recipe is an excellent basic Cream of Tomato Soup.

2 tablespoons vegetable oil
1 tablespoon salt butter or
   bacon fat
1 baby white onion, thinly
   sliced
2 large ripe tomatoes, sliced,
   with skins left on
½ teaspoon finely chopped
   garlic
Salt
Freshly cracked white pepper
3 tablespoons all-purpose flour

2 tablespoons tomato paste
2½ cups fish stock (page 36)
   or chicken stock (page 35)
1 tablespoon chopped fresh dill
¾ cup light cream
2 medium-size ripe tomatoes,
   skinned, quartered, seeded,
   and cut into shreds
1 cup fresh flaked crabmeat
¼ teaspoon cayenne pepper
A little granulated sugar
Garlic bread (page 716)

Heat the vegetable oil and butter in a deep heavy pan. Add the sliced onion and cook 2 minutes over low heat. Add the sliced tomatoes, chopped garlic, salt and pepper. Stir well and cook 10 minutes over low heat. Remove the pan from the heat. Mix the flour with the tomato paste and stir it into the pan. Pour in the fish or chicken stock and stir over low heat until the mixture comes to a boil. Simmer 2 minutes. Pour the mixture in an electric blender and purée until it is absolutely smooth. Return the soup to the pan and stir in the chopped fresh dill, cream, tomato shreds, and crabmeat. Season with salt, cayenne pepper, and a few grains of sugar. Reheat the soup and serve it with hot garlic bread. NET: 4 servings.

POTAGE VÉRONIQUE

Purée of Green and Ripe Tomatoes, with Rice

1 pound ripe tomatoes
1 pound green tomatoes
4 tablespoons salt butter
2 small onions, finely chopped
1 tablespoon tomato paste
1 bay leaf
½ teaspoon finely chopped
   garlic
6 black peppercorns
Salt

Freshly cracked white pepper
3 cups chicken stock (page 35)
   or water
2 tablespoons plain-cooked rice
2 teaspoons chopped fresh
   parsley
2 teaspoons chopped fresh mint
1 teaspoon sugar
Garlic bread (page 716)

Slice all but one of the ripe tomatoes, leaving the skins on. Skin the remaining ripe tomato, cut it in quarters, and remove the seeds. Cut the pulp into fine shreds and set aside. Slice the green tomatoes, leaving the skins on. Melt the butter in a deep heavy pan, add the chopped onions, and cook 5 minutes. Add the sliced ripe and green tomatoes and cook briskly 3 to 4 minutes. Then add the tomato paste, bay leaf, chopped garlic, peppercorns, and a little salt. Cover and cook slowly 10 minutes, stirring occasionally. Rub the mixture through a fine strainer. Return the purée to the pan and add the chicken stock or water. Stir over moderate heat and bring to a boil. Add the cooked rice and simmer 15 minutes. Just before serving, mix in the shredded tomato, parsley, mint, and sugar. Serve with hot garlic bread. NET: 4 servings.

FISH AND SHELLFISH SOUPS

This rich and full-bodied soup should be the character, with the rest of the meal complementary.

BISQUE D'ECREVISSES OU BISQUE DE HOMARD

Shrimp or Lobster Bisque

1 pound raw shrimps (in shell)
14 tablespoons salt butter
2 shallots, finely chopped
½ teaspoon finely chopped garlic
1 carrot, finely sliced
½ cup finely diced green beans
Salt
Freshly cracked white pepper
1 tablespoon tomato paste
4 tablespoons all-purpose flour
½ cup light cream
¾ cup heavy cream
2 teaspoons chopped fresh parsley
2 egg yolks
3 tablespoons Cognac or good brandy

1 cup tiny fried croûtons (page 70)

COURT BOUILLON
3 or 4 fish carcasses (such as flounder or pike)
6 cups water
1½ cups dry white wine
½ cup dry sherry
1 large yellow onion, sliced
1 garlic clove, bruised
1 stalk celery, sliced
1 small carrot, sliced
1 bay leaf
1 or 2 sprigs fresh dill
1 sprig fresh parsley
6 black peppercorns
2 teaspoons salt

Make the court bouillon first. Put the fish carcasses in a pan with the water, dry wine, and sherry. Bring to a boil slowly. Reduce the heat to low and remove the scum. Add the onion, garlic, celery, carrot, bay leaf, dill, parsley, peppercorns, and salt. Simmer gently 1 hour over low heat. Strain the liquid and return it to the pan.

Put the raw shrimps into the court bouillon and cook briskly until they blush. Strain them out of the court bouillon and set both aside for a moment. Melt 6 tablespoons butter in a medium-size heavy pan. Add the chopped shallots, garlic, carrot, and green beans. Season with a little freshly cracked white pepper. Cover and cook 3 minutes over very low heat. Remove the pan from the heat and stir in the tomato paste, flour, and 6 cups of the boiled-down court bouillon. Bring slowly to a boil. Correct the seasoning and simmer very slowly 30 minutes. Stir in the light cream and ½ cup of the heavy cream.

SHRIMP BUTTER. Cream 8 tablespoons butter in a mixer bowl. Set aside a third of the cooked shrimps. Coarsely chop the remaining two-thirds of the shrimps, removing the feet and tails but keeping the shells on. Put the chopped shrimps and shells and the creamed butter in an electric blender with a little of the soup. Pulverize this to a smooth cream, then rub the mixture through a fine strainer.

Add this shrimp butter to the soup bit by bit, stirring all the time. Shell the remaining third of the shrimps and cut into thin slices cross-wise. Add the sliced shrimp to the soup with the chopped parsley. In a warm soup tureen, beat the egg yolks with the brandy and ¼ cup heavy cream. Pour the hot soup on to this egg mixture, stirring with the ladle all the time. (At this point do not reheat the soup to the boiling point.) Serve with a separate bowl of tiny fried croûtons. NET: 4 to 6 servings.

LOBSTER BISQUE (BISQUE DE HOMARD). Instead of 1 pound raw shrimps use a live lobster (about 1¾ pounds). Have the court bouillon bubbling when you put the lobster in. Substitute lobster meat and shell throughout, but use only the soft shell, such as the head and the little claws, cut up; not the large claws or the tail — it is extra hard.

CLAM AND OYSTER CHOWDER

Fresh clams, oysters, and cream — simple and good.

6 tablespoons salt butter	12 raw shelled clams
1 tablespoon vegetable oil	3 cups light cream
1 tablespoon chopped scallions	Salt
1 tablespoon chopped onion	A few grains cayenne pepper
¼ teaspoon finely chopped	2 tablespoons chopped fresh
garlic	parsley
12 raw shelled oysters	

Heat 2 tablespoons butter with the oil in a deep heavy pan until it is foaming. Add the scallions, onion, and garlic and cook 2 minutes. Cut the oysters and clams into pieces and put them in the pan, then pour on the cream and season with salt and cayenne pepper. Bring to a boil over low heat. Stir in 4 tablespoons butter bit by bit, so that it blends with the cream. Stir in the parsley, simmer a few minutes and serve. NET: 4 servings.

MANHATTAN CLAM CHOWDER WITH TOMATOES

A good honest soup that can be made in Kansas as well as New York.

3 ounces salt pork, cut into	1 large yellow onion, chopped
½-inch cubes	1 leek, washed and chopped

2 medium-size potatoes, peeled
   and cut into small cubes
4 large ripe tomatoes, skinned
   and coarsely chopped
1 stalk celery, chopped
1 green pepper, seeded and
   chopped
1 bay leaf

½ teaspoon thyme
5 cups water
12 large fresh clams, shelled,
   and the clam liquor
Salt
Freshly cracked white pepper
½ teaspoon caraway seeds
Water crackers or hot biscuits

Heat a large heavy pan, put in the cubed salt pork, and render a little of the fat. Put in the chopped onion and leek, and cook over moderate heat until they are lightly browned. Add the potatoes, tomatoes, celery, green pepper, bay leaf, thyme, water, and the liquor from the clams. Season with salt and pepper. Bring the mixture to a boil over moderate heat; reduce the heat and simmer gently 30 to 35 minutes, until the vegetables are tender. Cut the clams into small bits and add them to the soup. Add the caraway seeds and cook the soup 5 more minutes, over low heat. Serve with water crackers or hot biscuits. NET: 6 servings.

MY OYSTER STEW

The oysters are never cooked over heat — the most delicate way.

8 tablespoons salt butter
1 teaspoon finely chopped garlic
3 cups light cream (or whole
   milk)
Salt
Freshly cracked white pepper

24 large shelled oysters
1 cup heavy cream
Freshly cracked black pepper
Thin slices of French bread,
   toasted

Melt 1 tablespoon butter in a large heavy pan. Add the garlic and stir over low heat 3 to 4 minutes without browning it. Off the heat, stir in the light cream or milk. Season with salt and freshly cracked white pepper. Stir over low heat until it comes to a boil. Bit by bit, stir in 4 tablespoons butter, being careful that the butter completely blends with the cream with each addition. Take the pan off the heat, add the oysters, cover, and let stand 8 minutes off the heat. Divide the rest of the butter into 4 soup bowls. Whip the heavy cream over ice and divide it among the bowls. Slowly pour in the hot stew, distributing the oysters evenly. Sprinkle the tops with freshly cracked black pepper and serve immediately. Serve the toast separately. NET: 4 servings.

NEW ENGLAND CLAM CHOWDER

"Provincial American cooking" — a very good example.

2 tablespoons salt butter
1 Bermuda onion, finely chopped
1 teaspoon finely chopped

garlic
2 stalks celery, finely chopped
24 fresh shelled chowder clams

2 cups clam juice, fresh or
    canned
Salt
Freshly cracked black pepper
6 ounces salt pork, cut into
    small dice
2 Idaho-type potatoes, peeled
    and cut into small dice
2 cups light cream

4 tablespoons frozen sweet
    butter
1 tablespoon chopped fresh
    chives
1 tablespoon chopped fresh
    parsley
Freshly cracked white pepper
Coarse salt
3 small French rolls

Melt 1 tablespoon salt butter in a heavy pan. Add the chopped onion, garlic, and celery, and cook very slowly 4 minutes. Put the raw clams through a fine meat chopper. Add another tablespoon of salt butter to the pan, add the chopped clams, moisten with 4 tablespoons clam juice, and season with salt and black pepper. Cover and cook very slowly 10 to 15 minutes.

Blanch the salt pork in boiling water, strain, and sauté in a large heavy pan until nearly crisp. Plunge the diced potatoes into boiling water for 2 minutes. Drain, dry, and add to the salt pork. Pour in the rest of the clam juice, bring slowly to a boil, and simmer gently until the potatoes are soft. Remove the pan from the heat and mix in the chopped clams. Stir in the cream and continue stirring over the heat until the chowder comes to a boil. Cut the frozen sweet butter into 4 slices, ladle the soup into individual bowls, and float a slice of frozen butter on top of each. Sprinkle chopped chives and parsley, freshly cracked black and white pepper, and a very little coarse salt into each bowl. Cut the French rolls into very thin slices lengthwise, toast them quickly under a hot broiler, and serve on a napkin. NET: 4 servings.

POTAGE BILLI BI

*Cream of Mussel Soup
(hot or cold)*

A beautiful light soup hot or cold, invented at Maxim's in Paris.

1 quart mussels
1 teaspoon dry mustard
⅓ cup dry white wine
1 cup combined sliced onion,
    carrot, and celery
3 cups fish stock (page 36)
¼ cup all-purpose flour
8 tablespoons salt butter
Salt

Freshly cracked white pepper
2 egg yolks
⅓ cup dry sherry
1 cup light cream, scalded
1 tablespoon chopped fresh
    parsley
Thin slices of French bread,
    toasted

Thoroughly scrub the mussels in cold water with the mustard. Put them in a deep heavy pan with the dry white wine, sliced onion, carrot and celery, and fish stock. Bring slowly to a boil, cover, and simmer until the shells have opened (about 5 minutes). Discard any that don't open. Pour the contents of the pan through a fine strainer and reserve the liquid. Shell the mussels, remove the beards, and set them aside. Melt 6 tablespoons of salt butter in a clean pan. Off the heat, stir in the flour, then the strained stock. Return to low heat and stir until the soup comes to a boil. Correct the seasoning with salt and pepper. Put the egg yolks in a bowl and mix with the dry sherry. Stir in the scalded light cream. Pour some of the soup into the egg yolk mixture, stirring all the time, then pour it all back in the soup pot and mix well. Add the mussels and parsley. Serve hot or ice cold with toasted thin slices of French bread. NET: 4 servings.

POTAGE DIEPPOISE

Mussel and Shrimp Soup

"À la Dieppoise" means with mussels and shrimps.

1 quart large mussels
1 teaspoon dry mustard
3 cups fish stock (page 36)
   or good clam juice
2 tablespoons chopped fresh
   parsley
2 tablespoons Cognac or good
   brandy
6 tablespoons salt butter
5 tablespoons all-purpose flour

½ teaspoon finely chopped
   garlic
Salt
Freshly cracked black pepper
¾ cup light cream
½ cup shelled boiled shrimps
2 raw egg yolks
2 tablespoons water
1½ cups fried croûtons (page 70)

Scrub the mussels thoroughly in cold water with the mustard. Put them in a pan and pour in the fish stock. Bring slowly to a boil, cover, and simmer about 5 minutes (until the shells are open). Discard any unopened mussels. Drain, strain the stock, and set it aside. Shell the mussels and remove the beards. Mix the chopped parsley and brandy with the mussels and set them aside to keep warm. Melt the butter in a heavy pan. Stir in, off the heat, the flour and garlic. Season with salt and black pepper. Stir in the fish stock. Return the pan to the heat and stir until the mixture comes to a boil. Lower the heat and slowly stir in the cream. Cut the shrimps in thin slices and add them and the mussel mixture to the soup. Beat the egg yolks with the water. Remove the soup from the heat and slowly add the egg yolks, stirring all the time. Reheat but do not boil. Serve the fried croûtons separately. NET: 4 servings.

SPECIALTY SOUPS

BOULA BOULA

Very Rich Pea and Turtle Soup

An elegant character . . . for a special meal.

6 tablespoons salt butter
1 small onion, finely chopped
2 stalks celery, finely chopped

3 cups shelled green peas or 2
   packages frozen peas
Salt

Freshly cracked white pepper
¼ cup water
1 large can turtle soup, strained
(3 to 4 cups; reserve the

meat)
2 tablespoons all-purpose flour
1 cup heavy cream, whipped

Melt the butter in a large heavy pan. Add the chopped onion and celery. Stir and cook 2 minutes over low heat. Add the peas, a little salt and pepper, and the water. Stir and mix. Cover and cook over very low heat until the peas are soft. Remove the pan from the heat and stir in the flour and strained turtle stock. Stir over low heat until the mixture comes to a boil. Simmer gently 2 minutes. Purée the mixture in an electric blender. Return to the pan and, over very low heat, stir in the whipped cream, reserving 4 teaspoons of it for garnish. Cut the turtle meat into small dice and add to the soup. Top each bowl of soup with a teaspoon of whipped cream and serve. NET: 4 servings.

AVGOLEMONO SOUP

Greek Egg and Lemon Soup

The Greeks should be justly proud of this international favorite.

⅓ cup long-grain rice
6 cups chicken stock (page 35)
2 egg yolks

Juice of 1 large lemon
Salt
A few grains cayenne pepper

Wash the rice through several waters to remove all excess starch. Drain thoroughly. Put the chicken stock in a heavy pan and bring it to a boil. Add the rice, cover, and simmer very gently over low heat 30 minutes, or until the rice is very soft. In a separate bowl beat the egg yolks with the lemon juice until light and foamy. Slowly pour 1 cup of the hot chicken broth into the beaten egg yolks, stirring constantly. Remove the rest of the stock, still in the pan, from the heat, and when it stops boiling, stir the egg mixture into it. Correct the seasoning with salt and cayenne pepper. Serve the soup immediately, hot. NET: 4 to 6 servings.

POTAGE AUX POMMES

Apple Soup with Camembert Cheese Balls

4 tablespoons salt butter
½ teaspoon finely chopped garlic
1 teaspoon tomato paste
3 tablespoons all-purpose flour
4 cups chicken stock (page 35)
Salt
Freshly cracked white pepper

½ teaspoon chili pepper
¾ cup heavy cream
1 tablespoon chopped fresh chives
2 firm apples
Camembert cheese balls (Camembert Glacé, page 87)

Melt 2 tablespoons butter in a large heavy pan, add the chopped garlic, and cook 2 minutes. Off the heat, add the tomato paste and flour. Stir until smooth, then add the chicken stock. Return to low heat and stir until the mixture boils. Season with salt and pepper, add the chili pepper, cream and chives, mix well, and set aside. Skin, core, and cut the apples into bite-size pieces, and sauté in the rest of the butter until golden. Add them to the soup, reheat a little, and serve with a separate dish of frozen Camembert cheese balls. NET: 4 to 6 servings.

Green with ordinary fresh garden greens — spinach, sorrel, and kale or beet tops — and garnished with chopped hard-boiled egg.

5 cups chicken stock (page 35)
1 cup chopped raw spinach
1/2 cup chopped scallions
1/2 cup raw mixed greens (kale, sorrel, and/or beet tops)
Bouquet garni (parsley, Italian parsley, tarragon, chives, and
rosemary, tied in cheesecloth)
1 tablespoon all-purpose flour
5 tablespoons sour cream
Salt
Freshly cracked white pepper
4 hard-boiled eggs, finely chopped

Green Soup with Chopped Hard-Boiled Egg Garnish

Put the chicken stock in a large heavy pan and bring it to a boil. Add the spinach, scallions, mixed greens, and herbs, and simmer very slowly 1 hour. Remove from the heat and discard the herbs. Mix the flour and sour cream to a smooth paste and stir into the soup. Season with salt and pepper. Return to low heat and stir until the soup thickens and comes to a boil. Serve with a generous portion of chopped hard-boiled egg in each soup bowl. NET: 4 to 6 servings.

1 tablespoon salt butter
4 tablespoons vegetable oil
2 onions, finely sliced
2 turnips, shredded
2 carrots, shredded
1 stalk celery, finely sliced
2 parsnips, shredded
1 cup green beans, diced
4 cups chicken stock (page 35)
1/2 cup vermicelli, broken up
Salt
Freshly cracked white pepper
1 cup spinach leaves, coarsely chopped
1/2 cup frozen peas
3 tomatoes, skinned and sliced

Fresh Vegetable Soup

Melt the butter and oil in a deep heavy pan. Add the onions, turnips, carrots, celery, and parsnips. Stir and cook a few minutes, then add the green beans. Cook a few minutes longer, then add the chicken stock and vermicelli, and season with salt and white pepper. Cook until the vegetables are just tender. Add the spinach, peas, and tomatoes, continue cooking a little longer, correct the seasoning, and serve. NET: 4 to 6 servings.

WALNUT SOUP

Ground walnuts and sour cream are stirred into hot chicken soup which has been refined with egg yolks.

3 cups chicken stock (page 35)
1 tablespoon salt butter
2 tablespoons all-purpose flour
2 egg yolks, beaten
Salt

Freshly cracked white pepper
1 cup fresh shelled English
  walnuts
4 tablespoons sour cream

Put the stock in a heavy pan and bring it to a boil. Mix the butter and flour together. Off the heat, add the butter and flour paste to the stock bit by bit, stirring all the time. Still off the heat, stir in the egg yolks and season with salt and pepper. Crush the walnuts very fine in a wooden bowl (or in a blender) and mix the chopped nuts with the sour cream. Gently reheat the soup but do not boil. Remove from the heat and stir in the nut and sour cream mixture. Serve immediately. NET: 4 servings.

POTAGE BORTSCH À LA RUSSE

*Russian Bortsch
(hot or cold)*

Bortsch is the Russian equivalent of the French Petite Marmite. In every region of Russia there is a different kind of bortsch. This particular version comes from the southern part of Russia and was taught to me by a Russian lady. It may also be followed to make a meat bortsch by adding a piece of ham or corned beef. Serve hot or very cold.

½ cup thinly sliced onion
½ cup each of finely shredded
  carrot, parsnip, celery, and
  beet
6 cups chicken stock (page 35)
3 cups finely shredded green
  cabbage
2 teaspoons finely chopped
  garlic
Salt

Freshly cracked black pepper
1 large tomato, peeled, seeded,
  and shredded
2 tablespoons tomato paste
1 teaspoon sugar
1 large raw beet, coarsely
  chopped
2 tablespoons chopped fresh
  parsley
1 cup sour cream

Put the onion and shredded carrot, parsnip, celery, and beet in a large, deep heavy pot. Cover with the chicken stock. Add the garlic and season with salt and pepper. Simmer until the vegetables are about half cooked. Add the cabbage and cook a bit more. Add the tomato, tomato paste, sugar, and a little more salt and pepper. Simmer gently 45 minutes. Meanwhile, put the coarsely chopped beet in a small pan with cold water. Bring it to a boil and simmer a few minutes until the liquid is a good red. Strain and add the liquid to the bortsch for coloring. Serve the soup sprinkled with chopped fresh parsley and accompanied by a separate bowl of sour cream. NET: 4 to 6 servings.

Here is a "pot" of cabbage soup, slowly and evenly cooked in the oven with a soupçon of pork and green beans. Eat with a little freshly grated Parmesan.

SOUPE AU CHOU

Cabbage Soup

3 tablespoons salt butter
4 small onions, sliced
½ teaspoon finely chopped
    garlic
½ pound sliced bacon or salt
    pork, cut up coarsely
½ large green cabbage, chopped
5 cups chicken stock (page

35) or water
18 green beans, shredded
Salt
Freshly cracked white pepper
Toasted slices of French bread
½ cup freshly grated Parmesan
    cheese

Preheat the oven to 325°. Melt the butter in a deep heavy casserole. Add the onions, garlic, and bacon or salt pork. Sauté this mixture over low heat 5 minutes. Blanch the cabbage in boiling water (page 571), drain, and add it to the casserole. Pour in the stock or water and bring slowly to a boil. Season with salt and pepper. Cover and simmer 50 minutes in the oven, then add the green beans and continue cooking another 50 minutes. Remove from the oven and serve from the pot with the toasted bread slices floating on the top. Pass around a separate bowl of freshly grated cheese. NET: 4 to 6 servings.

This soup is from Iran, where yoghurt is called madzoon. The recipe was given me by an Iranian pupil. It should be started a day in advance.

MADZOON SOUP

Yoghurt Soup
(hot or cold)

1 cup pearl barley
6 cups chicken stock (page 35)
¼ cup chopped fresh parsley
4 cups madzoon (yoghurt)

1 tablespoon chopped mint
    (fresh if possible)
Salt
A few grains cayenne pepper

Soak the barley overnight in cold water. Drain and put it in a heavy pan. Pour in the chicken stock. Add the parsley and mint, and season with salt and cayenne pepper. Cover and cook over low heat about 1½ hours. When the barley is tender, slowly stir in the yoghurt and cook another 5 minutes. Serve hot, or chill in the refrigerator and serve very cold. NET: 6 to 8 servings.

I came across this interesting soup in a tiny café in Istanbul. A specialty of the house, it was brought to the table in a magnificent earthenware bowl from which we all ate with painted wooden ladles.

POTAGE AUX
AMANDES

Turkish Almond Soup

¾ cup blanched whole almonds,
    dried in a 350° oven but not
    browned

2½ cups chicken stock (page
    35)
2 small white onions, one of

them stuck with 2 whole
 cloves
1 small bay leaf
½ teaspoon ground coriander
 seed
1½ cups heavy cream
2 tablespoons salt butter
2 tablespoons all-purpose flour

1 tablespoon chopped fresh
 chives
4 shallots, finely chopped
2 egg yolks
Grated rind of 1 lemon
¼ teaspoon almond flavoring
¼ cup almond slivers, browned
 in the oven

Pulverize the whole almonds in an electric blender. Put them in a heavy pan and add the chicken stock, onions, and bay leaf. Simmer gently about 20 minutes. Remove both onions and the bay leaf. Add to the stock the coriander seed and 1 cup heavy cream. Cook 5 minutes and remove from the heat. Mix the butter and flour to a creamy paste and add the chopped chives and shallots. Stir this mixture into the soup bit by bit, and gently reheat. Put the egg yolks in a warm soup tureen with ½ cup heavy cream and the grated lemon rind and almond flavoring. Mix well and slowly pour the hot soup in, stirring constantly. Sprinkle the slivered almonds on the soup and serve. NET: 4 to 6 servings.

*SOUPE
À L'OIGNON,
GRATINÉE*

---

*Onion Soup with
Grated Cheese*

French onion soup was born of necessity, as most inspired ideas are. Riding back to Paris in the dead of night, and very hungry, Louis XIV and his party stopped at one of his many palaces for something to eat. They could find nothing except . . . onions, Champagne, and butter. Thus was born "onion soup" — a good way to use up your leftover Champagne.

This soup and the toast can be prepared a day or two ahead and warmed and assembled just before serving. It is nice to serve it in the traditional earthenware onion soup pots with little handles.

2 pounds yellow onions, skinned
8 tablespoons salt butter
1 teaspoon meat glaze
2 teaspoons potato flour
4 cups chicken stock (page 35)
¾ cup dry white wine or brut
 Champagne
Salt
Freshly cracked white pepper
2 tablespoons Cognac or good

brandy
1 teaspoon Dijon mustard
1 cup freshly grated Parmesan
 cheese
6 thick slices French bread (or
 1 per portion)
8 or 10 thin slices of French
 bread
Melted salt butter
A little cayenne pepper

Cut the onions in half and then in ½-inch slices. In a large heavy pan melt 4 tablespoons butter. Put in the sliced onions (no seasoning) and brown them slowly, stirring occasionally. (It is very important that the onions brown slowly.) When they are a rich golden brown, stir in, off the heat, the meat glaze, potato flour, chicken stock, and dry white wine. Season with salt and pepper. Return the mixture to low heat and bring it to a boil. In a mixer bowl cream 4 tablespoons butter. Mix in the brandy and mustard and stir into the soup bit by bit. Sprinkle a little grated Parmesan cheese over the top of the soup, put the lid on, and keep it warm (either in a warm oven or over a very low flame) until you are ready to serve it.

For the garnish, preheat the oven to 400°. Brush all the slices of French bread with a little melted butter and sprinkle with a little grated Parmesan cheese and 1 or 2 grains cayenne pepper per slice. Put the bread slices on a baking sheet and brown in the oven.

To serve, put a thick slice of French bread in the bottom of each individual soup bowl and spoon the onion soup over it. Sprinkle with more grated Parmesan cheese and a little melted butter. Brown under a hot broiler. Serve the thin pieces of toast separately with a bowl of grated Parmesan cheese. NET: 4 to 6 servings.

Parslied chicken soup with little chicken ravioli.

ZUPPA VERDE

Italian Green Soup

CHICKEN SOUP (STOCK)
6 chicken wings
1 pound chicken backs, wings, or other chicken bones for stock
About 3 quarts water
2 cups combined sliced onions, carrots, and celery
1 sprig fresh tarragon
1 small yellow onion stuck with 2 whole cloves
2 tomatoes, sliced
½ cup dry white wine
2 teaspoons salt
4 black peppercorns
½ cup combined finely chopped fresh parsley and chives

RAVIOLI
1 cup all-purpose flour
½ teaspoon salt
1 large (or 1½ small) egg
1 small egg, beaten

RAVIOLI FILLING
½ cup finely ground cooked chicken (from the stockpot)
1 tablespoon heavy cream
1 egg yolk
Salt
Freshly cracked white pepper

GARNISH
1 cup freshly grated Parmesan cheese

Put the chicken wings and bones in a deep heavy pan and cover them with the water. Bring to a boil and skim off any scum. Add the sliced onion, carrot, and celery, the onion with cloves, and the tomatoes, tarragon, wine, salt, and peppercorns. Simmer the stock very gently 1¼ hours. Remove the chicken meat from the wings and bones and strain the stock through a colander lined with a damp cloth. Return the strained stock to the pan and add the chopped parsley and chives.

CHICKEN RAVIOLI. Put the flour and salt in a bowl, make a well in the center, and break the egg in it. In a circular motion with the fingers of one hand, mix the egg gradually into the flour until it is a firm paste. Wrap the dough in a piece of plastic wrap and leave it in the refrigerator at least 30 minutes. Then roll it out to a very, very thin sheet. (You can use a pasta machine for this if you have one.) Divide the sheet of dough in half and mark (don't cut) one half into 2-inch squares. Brush the surface with a little beaten egg, and put a little marble-size ball of filling (below) in the center of each square. Cover with the reserved sheet of dough, and press it gently but firmly down around each filled area. Cut the dough into 2-inch filled squares. Firmly press the corners of each little ravioli.

FILLING. Put the chicken meat through a fine meat chopper. Mix it with the raw egg yolk and heavy cream. If the mixture is still too dry or stiff, moisten it with a very little bit of the chicken stock. Season well with salt and freshly cracked white pepper.

To finish, bring the soup to a boil and drop in the chicken ravioli. Simmer very gently 15 minutes, until the ravioli are cooked. Serve the soup with a large bowl of freshly grated Parmesan cheese. NET: 6 servings.

COLD SOUPS

BORTSCH GLACÉ

Iced Bortsch

4 cups chicken consommé (page 132)
2 cups grated raw beets
½ teaspoon finely chopped garlic

1 tablespoon chopped fresh dill
Salt
Freshly cracked white pepper
Small bowl of sour cream

Put the consommé in a pan. Add the grated beets. Bring to a boil, simmer 4 to 5 minutes, and strain. Chill thoroughly. Mix the chopped garlic, dill, salt, and pepper into the sour cream, and serve separately with the bortsch. NET: 4 servings.

CONSOMMÉ GLACÉ STROZZI

Cold Consommé with Tapioca

Superb and surprising — consommé whipped with tapioca to resemble whipped cream.

4 cups chicken consommé (page 132)
¾ cup instant tapioca

2 hard-boiled eggs, finely chopped
Crushed ice, for serving

Put the consommé and tapioca in a pan and bring slowly to a boil. Reduce to a simmer and cook about 20 minutes, until the tapioca is quite soft. Rub the mixture through a very fine strainer into a metal bowl over a bowl of crushed ice. Beat the consommé mixture with a wire whisk until it is quite cold and achieves a nice thick consistency. It should closely resemble whipped cream when it is finished. To serve, pile the whipped consommé into individual crystal soup bowls surrounded by crushed ice. Garnish the top of each with finely chopped hard-boiled egg. Serve very cold. NET: 4 servings.

CONSOMMÉ MADRILÈNE

Classic Iced Tomato Consommé

5 cups chicken stock (page 35)
4 tablespoons tomato paste
4 very ripe tomatoes (unpeeled), sliced
½ cup ground raw beef
¼ cup dry sherry
1 tablespoon sugar
3 egg whites, beaten stiff

1 tablespoon unflavored gelatine
¼ teaspoon paprika
⅛ teaspoon cayenne pepper
2 firm ripe tomatoes, skinned, seeded, and finely shredded or diced
1 tablespoon finely chopped tarragon and parsley (mixed)

Put the chicken stock into a large pan with the tomato paste, tomatoes, ground beef, sherry, sugar, stiffly beaten egg whites, and gelatine. Put the pan over low heat and beat with a wire whisk until the mixture comes to a rolling boil. Remove from the heat and let stand without moving it for 15 minutes. Line a colander with a damp cloth and strain the stock through it. Return the clarified stock (consommé) to the pan and add the paprika and cayenne pepper. Reheat for a moment. Remove from the heat, add the shredded or diced tomatoes, and chill thoroughly. When serving, sprinkle with fresh tarragon and parsley. NET: 4 servings.

CRÈME D'ASPERGES GLACÉ

Iced Cream of Asparagus Soup

24 spears fresh asparagus
⅓ cup vegetable oil
1 medium-size yellow onion, chopped
Salt
Freshly cracked white pepper
¼ cup all-purpose flour

2 cups chicken stock (page 35)
Optional: ¼ teaspoon ground cardamom
¾ cup light cream
¾ cup whipped cream (about ½ cup heavy cream)
Crushed ice, for serving

Cut off and discard the tough parts of the asparagus. Slice the tender parts of the asparagus, reserving about 12 nice tips. Heat the oil in a heavy pan, add the chopped onion, and cook 2 minutes. Add the sliced asparagus (but not the reserved tips). Season with salt and pepper, cover, and cook slowly until the asparagus is soft. Off the heat, stir in the flour, then mix in the chicken stock. Stir over the heat until the mixture comes to a boil. Correct the seasoning. (Sometimes it is nice to add ground cardamom seed at this point.) Simmer 15 minutes. Rub the mixture through a strainer or purée it in an electric blender. Chill thoroughly. Cook the reserved asparagus tips in a little water until just soft, and drain. Just before serving, mix the light cream and the asparagus tips in the soup. Serve very cold in chilled bowls, topped with a dollop of whipped cream and surrounded with crushed ice. NET: 4 servings.

CRÈME DE CONCOMBRES GLACÉ

Iced Cream of Cucumber Soup

4 long thin cucumbers
1 Bermuda onion, sliced
2 cups water
Salt
Freshly cracked white pepper

¼ cup rice flour or 2 tablespoons all-purpose flour
¾ cup heavy cream
1 tablespoon chopped fresh mint
Crushed ice, for serving

Cut off the tops and bottoms of the cucumbers and skin 2½ of them. Set the skinned half aside for garnish and slice all the rest. Put the sliced cucumbers in a pan with the sliced onion, add ½ cup water, season with a little salt and pepper, and simmer gently until the vegetables are soft. Off the heat, stir in the flour. Add 1½ cups water and bring the mixture to a boil over low heat. Purée the soup in an electric blender, correct the seasoning, and chill thoroughly. When ready to serve, stir in the heavy cream. Remove the seeds from the reserved cucumber and cut the pulp into shreds. Add the shredded cucumber and chopped fresh mint to the cold soup. Serve in chilled bowls, surrounded with crushed ice. NET: 4 servings.

CRÈME DE CHOU BROCOLI GLACÉ

Iced Cream of Broccoli Soup

Garnished with a dollop of whipped cream and fresh parsley.

⅓ cup vegetable oil
2 bunches broccoli, cleaned
 and sliced
1 Bermuda onion, sliced
2 stalks celery, sliced
Salt
Freshly cracked white pepper
About ½ cup water

2 tablespoons rice flour or 3
 tablespoons all-purpose flour
2 cups chicken stock (page 35)
1 cup light cream
½ cup heavy cream, whipped
1 tablespoon chopped fresh
 parsley
Crushed ice, for serving

Heat the oil in a heavy pan. Add the sliced broccoli, onion, and celery. Mix, season with salt and pepper, and sprinkle with a little water. Cover the pan and cook over low heat until the vegetables are mushy. Remove from the heat and stir in the flour and the chicken stock. Return to low heat and stir until the mixture comes to a boil. Purée the soup in an electric blender and return to the pan. Stir in the light cream. Reserve 4 teaspoons of the whipped cream for garnish and fold the rest of it into the soup. Chill the soup thoroughly. Serve it in bowls topped with a teaspoon of whipped cream and a sprinkling of chopped fresh parsley, and surrounded with crushed ice. NET: 4 servings.

CRÈME CYRANO FROID

Cold Chicken Custard Soup

This delicate soup mixture is as good hot as it is cold. For the hot version, use the recipe on page 137.

6 egg yolks
½ teaspoon salt

A few grains cayenne pepper
½ teaspoon dry mustard

1 teaspoon Dijon mustard
2 cups heavy cream
1 tablespoon potato flour
3 cups chicken stock (page 35)
2 teaspoons chopped fresh

tarragon
2 ounces very finely diced ham
   or chicken
Crushed ice, for serving

In a mixer bowl mix the egg yolks, salt, cayenne pepper, and mustards, and beat until the mixture is light and fluffy. Slowly mix in ½ cup heavy cream and the potato flour. Warm the chicken stock and add it, very slowly, to the egg yolk mixture, beating all the time. Transfer the custard soup mixture to a tin-lined copper pan. Stir it over low heat until it coats the back of a silver spoon, then put it in a bowl over ice and stir it until it chills. Lightly whip 1½ cups heavy cream and fold it into the chilled custard soup. Mix in the tarragon and diced ham or chicken. Serve in crystal bowls surrounded by crushed ice. NET: 4 to 6 servings.

Rhubarb, bananas, apple puréed with orange juice laced with rum.

6 stalks rhubarb, cut in pieces
⅓ cup superfine sugar
¼ cup water
1 teaspoon lemon juice
Juice of 1 lime
4 bananas, sliced
1½ cups fresh orange juice

Optional: ⅓ cup light rum
1 Golden Delicious apple,
   peeled, cored, and cut into
   small dice
2 thin slices lime, cut in half
Crushed ice, for serving

POTAGE DE FRUITS GLACÉ

Iced Fruit Soup

Preheat the oven to 325°. Put the rhubarb in a heavy pan. In a separate small pan, heat the sugar and water and stir until the sugar dissolves, then allow to cook to a light syrup without stirring. Pour this syrup over the rhubarb, add the lemon and lime juices, cover with a piece of wax paper, and bake 15 minutes. Remove from the oven and cool. Add the sliced bananas and purée the mixture in an electric blender until smooth. Mix in the orange juice and rum. Add the diced apple. Serve in chilled bowls surrounded with crushed ice. Float half of a very thin slice of lime on the top of each bowl. NET: 4 servings.

This is my salute to the wonderful pumpkin. If you happen to have a fresh pumpkin, you may purée it by cooking it and rubbing it through a fine strainer. Using the canned pumpkin saves time and, in this instance, is just as good.

⅓ cup vegetable oil
1 large yellow onion, finely
   chopped

4 tablespoons all-purpose flour
1 2-pound can pumpkin purée
2 teaspoons ground ginger

CRÈME DE POTIRON GLACÉE

Iced Cream of Pumpkin Soup

1 teaspoon salt
½ teaspoon freshly cracked
  white pepper
3 cups chicken stock (page 35)
1 cup light cream

½ cup heavy cream, whipped
½ teaspoon freshly grated
  nutmeg
Crushed ice, for serving

Heat the oil in a large heavy pan. Add the chopped onion and cook very slowly until the onion is soft without browning. Off the heat, stir in the flour, pumpkin purée, ginger, salt, pepper, and chicken stock. Stir the mixture over moderate heat until it comes to a boil. Stir in the light cream and simmer gently 10 minutes. Taste to correct seasoning. Chill thoroughly. Serve in bowls surrounded by crushed ice. Put a dollop of whipped cream on top of each serving of soup and sprinkle with freshly grated nutmeg. NET: 4 to 6 servings.

CRÈME DE TOMATES GLACÉE

Iced Tomato and Dill Soup

4 tablespoons vegetable oil
1 onion, finely chopped
1 teaspoon finely chopped garlic
1 small bunch fresh scallions,
  chopped, including the green
  tops
6 large ripe tomatoes (unpeeled),
  sliced
Salt
Freshly cracked black pepper

1 tablespoon tomato paste
4 tablespoons rice flour or 6
  tablespoons all-purpose flour
3 cups water
2 tablespoons chopped fresh dill
1 cup heavy cream
2 small tomatoes, skinned,
  seeded, and cut in fine shreds
Crushed ice, for serving

Heat the oil in a large heavy pan. Add the chopped onion and garlic, and cook a few minutes. Stir in the chopped scallions and unpeeled sliced tomatoes and season with salt and pepper. Cover the pan and cook over low heat 8 minutes. Remove from the heat and stir in the tomato paste and flour. Pour in the water, put the pan over moderate heat, and stir until the mixture comes to a boil. Simmer 10 minutes. Rub the mixture through a fine strainer, add the chopped dill, and chill the soup thoroughly. (This soup will keep very well for several days in the refrigerator, prepared up to this point.) Just before serving, stir in the heavy cream and shredded tomatoes. Serve in bowls surrounded by crushed ice. NET: 4 to 6 servings.

CRÈME DE TOPINAMBOURS GLACÉE

Iced Cream of Jerusalem Artichoke Soup, with Preserved Ginger

2 pounds Jerusalem artichokes
1 tablespoon tarragon vinegar
Salt
⅓ cup vegetable oil
1 Bermuda onion, sliced
2 stalks celery, sliced
2 leeks, sliced
Freshly cracked white pepper

¼ cup all-purpose flour
2½ cups chicken stock (page
  35)
1 teaspoon ground ginger
¾ cup heavy cream
2 tablespoons finely chopped
  preserved ginger
Crushed ice, for serving

Skin the artichokes, cut into thin slices, and put in a pan. Barely cover them with water, add the vinegar and 1 teaspoon salt. Bring quickly to a boil and drain. Heat the oil in a heavy pan. Add the sliced onion, celery, and leeks. Cook gently 10 minutes. Add the drained artichokes, salt, and pepper. Cook very gently until the vegetables are soft. Off the heat, stir in the flour, then the chicken stock. When smooth, stir over low heat until the mixture comes to a boil. Add the ground ginger and a little more salt and pepper. Simmer 10 to 15 minutes. Put the mixture through a fine strainer or purée it in an electric blender, then chill thoroughly. When it is chilled, mix in the heavy cream and preserved ginger. Serve in crystal bowls surrounded by crushed ice. NET: 4 servings.

GAZPACHO

Spanish Raw Vegetable Soup (cold)

All gazpacho recipes seem to vary, including mine. The following was the most successful in my class and restaurant use. No separate garnishes. The soup is *it*, and it will hold very well in the refrigerator for several hot summer days.

2 red peppers, seeded
3 green peppers, seeded
3 stalks celery
2 carrots
1 small white onion
1 red onion
3 cucumbers, peeled and seeded
3 large ripe tomatoes, skinned
   and seeded (strain the seeds
   and save the fresh juice)

1 teaspoon finely chopped garlic
7 cups good tomato juice
1/3 cup lemon juice
1/2 cup pure olive oil
2 teaspoons Tabasco
1 tablespoon sugar
1 teaspoon salt
2 teaspoons freshly cracked
   white pepper
Crushed ice, for serving

Chop (very fine) the red peppers, green peppers, celery, carrots, white onion, red onion, and cucumbers. Cut the tomatoes into fine shreds, then dice the shreds very fine. Put all the chopped vegetables and the chopped garlic in a large bowl. Pour in the tomato juice and the fresh tomato juice strained from the seeds. Add the lemon juice, olive oil, Tabasco, sugar, salt, and pepper. Thoroughly chill, for 24 hours if possible. Serve in bowls surrounded with crushed ice. NET: 8 to 10 servings.

POTAGE BATWINIA

Russian Iced Green Soup

1/4 cup vegetable oil
4 shallots, finely chopped
Salt
Freshly cracked black pepper
1 pound sorrel (or spinach
   sprinkled with the juice of
   a lemon)
2 pounds spinach

1 pound beet tops
1/2 cup dry white wine
2 cups water
2 teaspoons sugar
1 small dill pickle, cut into
   small dice
1 tablespoon chopped fresh
   tarragon

1 tablespoon chopped fresh dill
1 tablespoon chopped fresh
  parsley

2 hard-boiled egg yolks, rubbed
  through a fine strainer
Crushed ice, for serving

Heat the oil in a large heavy pan. Add the chopped shallots with a little salt and pepper. Cover and cook over low heat 3 minutes. Wash and drain the sorrel, spinach, and beet tops thoroughly. Cut them into fine shreds and add to the shallots in the pan. Cover and cook over low heat 3 minutes, or until the greens are just soft. Rub the mixture through a fine strainer or purée it in an electric blender. Add the wine, water, sugar, dill pickle, fresh herbs, and a little extra salt and pepper. Thoroughly chill the soup. Serve in bowls surrounded with crushed ice. Garnish the tops with a little strained hard-boiled egg yolk. NET: 4 servings.

ICED PEA AND CURRY SOUP

There's a cult of pea soup lovers. This is for them — in the summertime. It is garnished with diced chicken or turkey.

¼ cup plus 2 tablespoons
  vegetable oil
1 yellow onion, finely sliced
2 teaspoons curry powder
1 teaspoon salt
1½ teaspoons sugar
A few grains cayenne pepper
2 packages frozen green peas or
  4 cups fresh shelled peas
1¼ cups water
2 tablespoons rice flour or

1 tablespoon all-purpose flour
2 cups chicken stock (page 35)
⅛ teaspoon freshly grated
  nutmeg
⅛ teaspoon mace
½ cup light cream
½ cup heavy cream
1 tablespoon finely chopped
  fresh chives
3 ounces finely diced cooked
  turkey or chicken

Heat ¼ cup vegetable oil in a large heavy pan. Add the sliced onion and sauté until it is golden brown. Add the curry powder, salt, ½ teaspoon sugar, and cayenne pepper. Cook over very low heat 5 minutes. (Curry powder must always be cooked; it should never be served raw.) Add 2 tablespoons of vegetable oil to the pan. Add the peas and ¼ cup water. Cover and cook over very low heat until the peas are just soft. Remove from the heat and stir in the flour, chicken stock, and 1 cup water. Put the pan over moderate heat and stir until the mixture comes to a rolling boil. Add the nutmeg, mace, a little more cayenne, and 1 teaspoon sugar. Lower the heat and simmer 10 minutes. Rub the mixture through a fine strainer. Chill thoroughly. (The soup can be frozen at this point.) Immediately before serving, stir in the light and heavy cream. Serve in chilled crystal bowls, surrounded with crushed ice. Garnish with chopped fresh chives and diced turkey or chicken. NET: 4 servings.

Touched up with a little rum and frosted sprigs of fresh mint.

2 8-ounce cans freestone
   peaches or 2½ cups peeled
   and sliced fresh peaches
2 ripe fresh peaches, peeled
   and sliced
Juice and grated rind of 1 lemon
   and 1 lime

2 tablespoons light rum
Crushed ice, for serving

FROSTED FRESH MINT
A few sprigs fresh mint
A little raw egg white
2 tablespoons superfine sugar

Put the canned peaches (or 2½ cups fresh) in a blender with the juice and grated rind of the lemon and the lime. Blend until very smooth. Mix the 2 sliced ripe peaches into the puréed peaches. Chill thoroughly. Serve in cold crystal bowls surrounded with crushed ice. Sprinkle the top of the soup with light rum. For garnish, dip the fresh mint leaves in egg white, then in superfine sugar. Decorate each bowl with the mint leaves. NET: 4 servings.

This Vichyssoise can be made several days in advance of serving, as long as no cream is added. Add the cream immediately prior to serving. For an extra festive dish, an alternate garnish is finely shredded blanched carrot and black or red caviar.

4 large Idaho-type potatoes,
   peeled and sliced
4 large leeks, washed and sliced
2 stalks celery, sliced
1 Bermuda onion, sliced
1 cup water
Salt

Freshly cracked white pepper
4 cups chicken stock (page 35)
1½ cups light cream
¼ cup heavy cream
Small bowl of chopped fresh
   chives

Put the sliced vegetables in a heavy pan. Add the water, salt, and pepper. Bring the water to a boil, cover the pan, and cook very gently, stirring occasionally, until all the vegetables are soft. Stir in the chicken stock. Rub the mixture through a fine strainer or purée it in an electric blender. Correct the seasoning. Chill thoroughly. Stir in the light cream and the heavy cream. Serve very cold with a separate little bowl of chopped fresh chives. NET: 6 servings.

½ cup superfine sugar
1 tablespoon finely shredded
   orange rind
½ cup water
1 teaspoon potato flour
Juice of 2 lemons

Juice of 1 lime
2 cups fresh orange juice
2 cups weak China tea
Skinned sections of 1 large
   orange
Crushed ice, for serving cold

Combine the sugar, the shredded orange rind, and the water in a heavy pan. Stir the mixture over low heat until the sugar melts; then allow it to simmer until the orange rind is translucent. Mix the potato flour with the lemon and lime juice. Then stir it into the orange juice and the tea. Add the mixed juices to the sugar syrup in the pan and stir the combined mixture over low heat until it comes to a boil. Simmer it gently 5 to 6 minutes. Serve this soup hot with a few pieces of skinned orange sections in each bowl of soup. Or chill the soup thoroughly and serve it ice cold in small crystal bowls embedded in crushed ice. Garnish it with skinned orange sections. NET: 4 servings.

CRÈME DE CAROTTES GLACÉE

Iced Carrot Soup

A little glory for the carrot — onion, carrot, and rice puréed and enriched with egg yolk and cream.

1 tablespoon salt butter
1 Bermuda onion, sliced
6 carrots, thinly sliced
½ cup water
Salt
Freshly cracked white pepper
3 cups chicken stock (page 35)
2 tablespoons raw rice

¾ cup light cream
3 egg yolks
1 carrot, finely shredded and blanched (cover with cold water, bring to a boil, and drain)
½ cup heavy cream, whipped
A few grains cayenne pepper

Melt the butter in a pan and add the sliced onion, carrots, and water. Season with salt and pepper and cook slowly, over low heat, with the pan covered, until the vegetables are soft. Mix in the stock and bring it to a boil, then purée it in the electric blender until it is absolutely smooth. Return it to the pan, add the rice, cover the pan, and cook over low heat until the rice is very soft. Purée the mixture again in the blender and stir in the light cream. Beat the egg yolks in a mixer until they are light and lemony and thick. Pour the soup gradually into the yolks, beating all the time. Place the soup in the refrigerator and chill it thoroughly. When it is cold, fold in the blanched shredded carrot. When ready to serve, beat the heavy cream until it is stiff. Spoon the ice-cold soup into chilled individual bowls, embedded in ice. Float a dollop of whipped cream on top of each bowl. Sprinkle the whipped cream with a few grains of cayenne pepper. NET: 4 servings.

EGGS
AND THE OMELET

FOR A MOMENT, let us talk about the egg instead of the recipe. It's such a lovely thing to talk about. The egg is the mystique of life itself. "The oval body laid by the female of birds and other animal species, and containing the germ of a new individual, enclosed within a shell or strong membrane," says the Oxford English Dictionary.

Perhaps the egg is the soul of culinary art, if you project this idea into the thousands of ways eggs are used in cooking. There are in effect many, many ways of cooking with eggs. Limitless. Absolutely limitless.

"The ubiquitous egg . . . is a cook's best friend. There is the egg that binds; the egg that enriches; the egg that gives substance to a sauce; and the egg that gives a soufflé its splendor. Apart from the egg's protean ability to combine with other foods, it is — dressed in infinite variety — a meal in itself, as nutritious as a steak and at a fraction of the cost. For centuries immemorial, the creators of truly great dishes have devoted a large measure of their inventiveness and artistry to the ennoblement of the egg's unique flavor and consistency. But it takes an uncommon cook to do justice to the common egg. There are few abominations to equal an egg scrambled or fried to tough tastelessness. Chefs de cuisine of eminence have long considered the egg a worthy companion to the most sophisticated foods, fit to crown with Madeira sauce, to be poached in Burgundy, to rest on a purée of chestnuts, or to be covered with foie gras" (Dione Lucas in *House & Garden*, March 1956).

I think an egg is the universal food; but by itself it is cooked in so very few ways, which is sad. It is one of the most important elements in cooking. In this chapter I have tried to describe the ten basic ways of cooking an egg as differentiated in classic cookery. Each of these basic egg recipes, in itself, is a most superb dish.

Eggs are most frequently used here in America for breakfast, and they make the best luncheon dish. Could an "egg dish" ever be used in a dinner menu or a more formal meal? Yes, certainly, as a first course or instead of a fish course. For example, a favorite egg dish for a first course is a soufflé — cheese or vegetable types, or seafood. The difficulty, I guess, is that except for the hard-boiled egg, an egg must be cooked at the last minute and served quickly — the timing must be à point. So you must be sure of your guests — that you can immediately marshal them to the table when the egg dish is to be ready. But egg dishes are so awfully good, it is worth trying.

Egg Commentary

(1) I cannot emphasize too much the fact that *eggs ought to be cooked very, very quickly, or very, very gently,* but never for a long time, nor with very great heat. If there is great heat, the preparation has to be so quick that the heat doesn't have time to toughen and dry the egg.

(2) The *fresher* the egg is, the better. It is at its supreme best the minute it comes out of the hen. Someone once asked me if there is ever any time that a slightly aged egg is used? Never!

You can test the freshness of an egg by breaking it into a bowl. If the umbilical cord (the pale yellow cord) is broken, the egg is stale.

(3) The egg *absorbs flavor,* so must be protected from other flavors in the refrigerator. For instance, if you put an egg next to a melon, it would be almost impossible to eat.

(4) White versus brown eggs — I have no preference; both are exactly the same.

(5) TO SEPARATE EGGS. Tap the middle girth of the egg against a bowl or cup, to crack and notch it. Then, carefully, with the tips of the fingers, pull the eggshell into two halves. Gently but surely transfer the yolk from one half-shell to the other, back and forth, letting the white drop into the container. Take great care not to break the yolk.

(6) TO REMOVE DROPS OF EGG YOLK FROM SEPARATED EGG WHITE. If even a very little bit of yolk drops into the white, it must be removed or the white will not beat stiff. The yolk can be removed only by using one of the empty half-shells to scoop the bit of yolk out of the white. It is impossible to remove yolk from the white with anything but its own shell. A spoon is useless.

(7) TO MEASURE EGGS. Sometimes a recipe calls for 2 large or 3 small eggs, or half an egg. If it is necessary to use a fraction of an egg, the way to do it is to beat the egg a little and then measure the quantity needed. If "the weight of an egg" is called for, a scale must be used to establish the common measurement.

(8) LEFTOVER EGG YOLKS OR EGG WHITES. Either can be stored in a screw-top jar in the refrigerator. They will keep about a week. Try to keep the yolks whole. They can be used in a future sauce, or as a glaze to brush over pastry dough, or in some other dish. Put a little water over them so that the tops do not harden.

Egg whites may also be stored in a screw-top jar in the refrigerator. When you want to use them, measure out the individual whites by counting one "plop" as the total white of one egg.

(9) STIFFLY BEATEN EGG WHITES. The best way to beat egg whites is to put them into a large round-bottom metal bowl and beat them with a large piano wire whisk, beating just until you can turn the bowl upside down and they won't fall out.

Egg whites may be beaten in an electric mixer, but it is not possible to beat as much air into them as with a wire whisk. Beating maximum air into the whites is the principle of stiffly beaten egg whites.

Do not try to ensure their stiffness by beating them any longer than arriving at the point of stiffness. To do so will cause them to become dry and brittle, and it will be very difficult, if not impossible, to fold them smoothly into the preparation. That is why recipes frequently specify "soft peaks."

(10) EGG SIZE. All egg recipes are based on use of 2-ounce (large size) eggs. If you are using extra large or jumbo size eggs, extra cooking time should be allowed.

(11) TEMPERATURE. All recipes assume the eggs are refrigerator-cool.

BASIC EGG PREPARATIONS

Hard-boiled eggs, like cheese and wine, are a universal food that has nourished humanity throughout the centuries, on all manner of tables. Hard-boiled eggs are well established in grand cuisine, such as the "au simplicité" accompaniment for elegant caviar or a set piece like Oeufs Froids à l'Aurore. But the following touching tale best expresses the common language of the egg among all mankind.

A few years ago when my friend Lionel Braun spent a few days in a small village on the southern coast of Tunisia, he met an Arab camel boy, Bouden Abderrazak, from Kalaä Kebira. The boy, about twelve, was learning English in school, and Mr. Braun was expanding his French vernacular, and they exchanged lessons. When the time came for Mr. Braun to leave the village, his young friend Bouden, with camel in tow, came to bid him farewell and to offer him a gift "from the house of my father." It was a sack containing eight hard-boiled eggs and a bottle of olive oil made by Bouden's mother. This, he explained, was to sustain his friend on the long journey back to America.

Perhaps it's the mystique of the yolk that inspires all manner of cold and hot dishes with hard-boiled eggs. They are peeled and used whole, sliced, quartered, chopped, stuffed, and strained, and, of course, have their day in the sun on Easter Sunday.

The following recipe should give you perfect hard-boiled eggs — the whites delicate but set, the yolks also set and completely yellow, with no greenish tinge. Note that: (1) Salt in the cooking water helps keep the shells from cracking. (2) Eggs should never cook more than 10 minutes. When cooked longer, the yolks acquire a greenish or gray tinge on the outside and the whites take on an unpleasant odor. (3)

OEUFS DURS

Hard-Boiled Eggs

Plunging the hot eggs immediately into cold water slightly shrinks the egg away from the shell, which permits it to be peeled easily and smoothly.

Fresh eggs   Salt
Water   A little lemon juice (for storage)

Fill a deep pan with at least 2 to 3 inches of cold water, to cover the eggs. Add ½ teaspoon salt per egg to the water (to keep the shells from cracking). Bring the water to a boil and put the eggs into it. Reduce the heat so that the water is just simmering, and cook the eggs 10 minutes. Immediately remove them from the pan and plunge them into ice water.

If the eggs are to be used within a day or two, shell them and store them in the refrigerator in a bowl of water with a little lemon juice. If they are to be kept longer, store them in their shells in a bowl or jar of water in the refrigerator.

OEUFS MOLLETS

Soft-Boiled Eggs

Always use very fresh eggs for soft-boiled eggs. In a perfect soft-boiled egg, the white will be firm and not liquid; the yolk should be running. It differs from a coddled egg (see next recipe) in that the cooking method results in coddled eggs being a little more delicate and consistent than soft-boiled eggs.

Soft-boiled eggs are almost always served in their shell in an egg-cup. The diner eats the egg from the shell.

Very fresh eggs   Salt
Water

Fill a deep pan with at least 2 to 3 inches of water to cover the eggs. Add ½ teaspoon of salt per egg to the water to keep the shells from cracking. Bring the water to the boiling point. Reduce it to a simmer, carefully put the eggs in the water, and simmer them 3½ minutes. Remove the eggs from the water and give each one a little crack on the top to stop further cooking. Serve immediately in eggcups, with the larger end up.

OEUFS À LA COQUE

Coddled Eggs

Like the soft-boiled egg, a coddled egg is cooked in its shell in water, but the water is completely removed from the heat. A coddled egg must never boil or be over direct heat. It is cooked, or "coddled," by the gentle warmth of the water surrounding it, which results in a more delicately cooked egg than one which has been boiled. When a coddled egg has been properly cooked, the white has been just set through (it is not running), and the yolk is warm and liquid.

The coddled egg is always served with the shell removed (the shelling operation must be of the utmost gentleness). It can be served plain, or it can be served in the many ways in which the poached egg is served. In fact, most recipes for poached eggs and coddled eggs are interchangeable. Eggs cooked either way may be served on a purée of vegetables — such as chestnut, spinach, pea, carrot — with delectable sauces over them. Also, like poached eggs, they may be served cold, in little pastry cases, over a filling, on a macédoine or salad, or in aspics.

Very fresh eggs	*Salt*
Water	

Fill a deep heavy pan with 2 inches water or more, to cover the eggs. Add ½ teaspoon of salt per egg to the water to keep the shells from cracking. Bring the water to the boiling point. Lower the eggs into the boiling water, instantly removing the pan from the heat. Cover the pan and let it stand 9 minutes. Remove the eggs from the pan. Hold briefly under cold water and shell them carefully.

OEUFS POCHÉS

Poached Eggs

A poached egg differs from a coddled egg in that the poached egg is cooked out of its shell in vinegar and water. But the effect is the same; in both poached and coddled procedures, the yolk is not set and the white is just set through. Especially with poached eggs, it is important that the eggs be fresh.

The method for poaching given below is the most satisfactory one, but there are commercially produced special cookers (egg poachers) in which eggs are put in individual molds and simmered 3½ minutes. With this method one is less likely to have the yolk entirely surrounded by the white as in the first method, and the eggs are not so attractive and natural-looking.

As with coddled eggs, the uses for poached eggs are endless, as far as your imagination will carry you. To begin with, think of poached eggs, warm and plain, with a little butter, or in cold majesty, Oeufs en Gelée.

The best pan for poaching eggs is the top of a glass double boiler (it is just the right size and you can watch the progress of the egg). You will also need a slotted spoon, a custard cup, and a bowl of warm or ice water, depending on whether the eggs are to be used hot or cold.

Fresh eggs	*1 teaspoon salt*
2 tablespoons good tarragon	*Water*
vinegar	

Fill the top of a glass double boiler (or any other deep, narrow pan) three-quarters full with water. Add the vinegar and salt. Bring to a boil over high heat, then reduce the heat to a simmer.

Break 1 egg into a custard cup. (The yolk must stay whole. If it breaks, keep the egg for other uses and start again.) Hold the cup in one hand while you stir the simmering water with the slotted spoon with the other. As soon as you have a deep whirlpool, stop stirring and slide the egg from the custard cup into the center of the whirlpool. Leave it in the swirling, simmering water to poach 3½ minutes. (The white should neatly envelop the yolk. The yolk should not show.) Gently remove the egg with the slotted spoon and put it into the bowl of warm or cold water. If warm, the water should not be so hot as to continue cooking the egg. This water will also wash away the vinegar.

Poach all the eggs in this manner. They may be poached an hour or two ahead of time, as long as they are kept in water. When you are ready to use them, dry them on paper towels and carefully trim off any streamers with a pair of kitchen shears.

OEUFS FRITS

Fried Eggs

There are two distinct methods of frying eggs, one which may be termed the French way and the other the American or English way. The French cook includes under the heading of "frying" anything immersed and cooked in very hot fat (usually termed "deep fat"), which may be oil, lard, or butter. The American or English cook applies the term to anything that is cooked with the aid of oil, lard, or butter and generally at a much lower temperature.

From my point of view, the American or English way of frying an egg, with a small quantity of butter over moderate heat, keeps the lightness and the digestibility of the egg much better than the method at great heat. Generally speaking, 2 teaspoons butter per egg cooked in a correctly preheated pan over low heat for 3 minutes is sufficient for a perfect American-style fried egg. No seasoning should be added except at the table.

The French-style fried egg (see below) must be covered with white. The raw egg is usually dropped in a "puddle of hot fat" in the corner of a tilted sauté pan. For a true Poulet Marengo, French-style fried eggs are a must. Otherwise the two methods are interchangeable for most recipes calling for fried eggs. For those who like their eggs "sunny side up," the only way is the American way.

Fried Eggs American Style

Fresh eggs   *2 teaspoons salt butter per egg*

If you are frying more than 1 egg, have on hand plain round cookie cutters, about 2½ to 3 inches diameter. Heat a small heavy frypan until it is hot enough to make a speck of butter sizzle but not brown. Immediately put in the butter and let it dissolve. Maintain the heat so that the butter does not brown. If more than 1 egg is to be fried in the same pan, set the cookie cutters in the pan (1 for each egg). Break 1 egg into each cookie cutter frame. Fry the eggs gently until the whites have set, about 3 minutes. Remove the cookie cutters and then remove the eggs with a spatula. Serve immediately.

These are also called "turned eggs."

Fresh eggs   *About 2 tablespoons salt butter*

The eggs must be cooked one at a time. Heat a small heavy frypan or sauté pan until it is hot enough to make a speck of butter sizzle but not brown. Immediately put in the butter. Let the butter dissolve and become golden brown. Break 1 egg into a custard cup. With your left hand holding the handle of the pan, tilt the pan at an angle so that the butter is in a little puddle in the side. Slide the egg into the butter. When the white has set, carefully turn the egg over and cook the other side. Remove it from the fat with a slotted spoon or spatula. (If a particular recipe calls for the turned egg to be browned, do this very slowly, or the egg will become tough.) Continue to cook as many eggs as required in this manner. Set them on a warm plate until all of the eggs have been cooked.

OEUFS SUR LE PLAT AU FOUR (OEUFS MIROIR)

Baked or Shirred Eggs

Baked eggs are usually cooked and served in individual "sur le plat" dishes, the lovely French dishes with a handle on each side, or in individual-size gratins. They are also cooked in larger shallow baking dishes, when a larger quantity is prepared as a dish.

In English I prefer to call Oeufs sur le Plat by the term "baked eggs," which is the most precise description of the method by which they are cooked. (The Oxford English Dictionary defines "shirred eggs" as "poached in cream," which they characteristically are not, although cream or cream sauce may occasionally be used as a garnish.) Baked eggs are invariably served warm, or hot, and the list of sauces, garnishes, and other accompaniments with which they can be used is another volume. The seasoning, if no sauce accompanies them, should be left to the diner, as, naturally, salt and pepper would destroy the beauty of a perfect baked egg.

Fresh eggs   *1 teaspoon salt butter per egg*

Use individual or larger shallow baking dishes or gratins. Preheat the oven to 350°. Melt the butter for each egg in the dish. Break the eggs into the dish. Bake 4 to 5 minutes, until the whites are set — the yolks look as though they are covered with a veil. Remove the eggs from the oven and sprinkle the yolks with a little melted butter. They may be served as they are or garnished according to a particular recipe.

OEUFS BROUILLÉS

Scrambled Eggs

Of the many ways in which eggs can be prepared, there is none so liable to be unsatisfactory as scrambling. Correctly and at their most delicious, scrambled eggs (oeufs brouillés) should be creamy and moist; they should never have the slightest tinge of brown.

For the best plain scrambled eggs, I recommend using a double boiler rather than a sauté pan or frypan. However, both methods are given below. Either way, the technique is the same; and either way, the eggs should be served as soon as they reach a creamlike consistency and are just at the point of coagulation. At this point the scrambled eggs are at a delicate moment of perfection, and from then on they will begin to dry out, deteriorate, and, if left too long, become indigestible. If they cannot be served immediately, add a little heavy cream or sour cream just before removing them from the double boiler or pan (about 1 tablespoon of cream to every two eggs).

Scrambled eggs have great versatility because they produce so many interesting dishes when combined with almost all types of vegetables and a wide representation of fruits, meats, fish, and shellfish.

Fresh eggs
1 teaspoon salt butter per egg
Salt

Freshly cracked white pepper
Optional: A little heavy cream
or sour cream

As stated above, for the best plain scrambled eggs I recommend using a double boiler. Have the double boiler ready with simmering water in the bottom section. If you are using a sauté pan, make sure it is a heavy one. Put it over low heat.

Melt the butter in the top of the double boiler or in the heated sauté pan. Break the number of eggs to be scrambled into a small bowl. Give them just one or two quick stirs with a fork to break the yolks. Add them to the butter and season with a little salt and freshly cracked white pepper. Stir the eggs gently with a fork or wooden spoon until they coagulate; then immediately transfer them from the double boiler top or pan onto a serving dish. If desired, you may stir in a little heavy cream or sour cream just before removing them.

OEUFS EN COCOTTE

Baked Eggs in a Water Bath

Apart from the omelet, this is one of the most delicious ways of preparing eggs. The traditional cocotte is an individual-size porcelain or earthenware squatty-shape dish with a little handle. Equally traditional and perhaps a bit more classic is the ramekin, which looks like a miniature soufflé dish, about 3¼ inches in diameter. Oeufs en Cocotte are always cooked in individual-size containers, and they are always served in the container, never removed.

Recipes for Eggs en Cocotte usually combine a sauce or minced type of garnish with the egg. Some poached egg and scrambled egg recipes can also be served en cocotte. It is a very attractive way to serve egg dishes.

Fresh eggs
½ teaspoon melted salt butter
   per egg
Salt

Freshly cracked white pepper
2 tablespoons heavy cream per
   egg

Preheat the oven to 350°. Have ready a 3¼-inch ramekin or individual cocotte for each egg to be cooked. In a little pan, melt the butter and pour ½ teaspoon of it into each ramekin. Break 1 egg into each ramekin and season it with a little salt and freshly cracked white pepper. Put the cream in a small pan and bring it to a boil. Pour 2 tablespoons of it onto each egg.

Place the egg-filled ramekins in a shallow roasting pan. Pour about a ½-inch level of hot water into the pan, around the ramekins, and be sure no water gets into them. (This pan is now a bain marie or water bath.) Place it on the stove over very low heat and cook 3 minutes. Then lay a sheet of foil over the ramekins and place them with their water bath in the oven. Bake them 3 to 5 minutes, or until the whites are set. Remove them from the oven. The cooked egg en cocotte is served in its container on a folded napkin on a plate.

Eggs in timbales or molded eggs are baked in individual buttered dariole molds or baba molds. (Darioles are small oval-shaped metal molds and babas are small round metal molds.) They are cooked in exactly the same way as Oeufs en Cocotte — in a water bath in a moderate oven. The difference is in serving — eggs cooked in the metal molds are turned out of the molds on to the serving dish, and eggs en cocotte are served in the container in which they were cooked.

Molded eggs are necessarily combined with a filling; therefore, no recipe is given for a basic preparation of the egg only. This chapter does offer one of the classic Oeufs en Timbales dishes of French cuisine, with lobster meat and lobster coral (page 204).

OEUFS MOULÉS OU OEUFS EN TIMBALES

Molded Eggs or
Eggs in Timbales

The basic omelet is given extensive coverage in the separate section of this chapter devoted to the world of omelets, pages 205–229.

OMELETTES

Omelets

EGG DISHES

Boulangère means "baker's style." This dish is a sandwich fantasy — French dinner rolls stuffed with hard-boiled eggs, ham, and tongue (a hot dish).

OEUFS DURS BOULANGÈRE

---

6 small French dinner rolls

¾ cup clarified salt butter,

melted (page 56)
6 hard-boiled eggs
½ cup diced boiled ham
½ cup diced cooked tongue
1 teaspoon finely chopped garlic
2 tablespoons chopped fresh
   parsley

2 tablespoons chopped fresh
   chives
½ cup sour cream
1 tablespoon Dijon mustard
Salt
Freshly cracked black pepper
¼ cup pure olive oil

Cut a thin slice off the end of each roll. With a little knife or spoon remove all the white insides. Pour a little of the melted butter through each roll. Shell the hard-boiled eggs and chop them coarsely. Mix them with the diced ham and tongue. Put the rest of the butter in a little pan with the chopped garlic and warm them together 2 to 3 minutes. Put the chopped parsley and chives, sour cream, Dijon mustard, salt and pepper in a little bowl. Stir in the butter and garlic mixture and the chopped egg mixture, and mix well.

Preheat the oven to 350°. Stuff each hollowed-out dinner roll with the chopped egg filling. Heat the olive oil in a little pan and brush it all over the outside of the stuffed rolls. Wrap the rolls individually in aluminum foil and bake them 10 minutes. To serve, remove the foil and wrap each hot roll individually in a starched napkin. Serve piping hot. NET: 6 servings.

OEUFS DU CARÊME

Eggs Carême

A first course treat, served warm, these hard-boiled eggs with artichoke bottoms, pâté, and mushrooms are served with Bercy sauce.

6 hard-boiled eggs
6 cooked artichoke bottoms
   (canned)
½ cup pitted black olives
4 ounces fine liver pâté, well-
   chilled
¼ pound firm white mush-
   rooms, thickly sliced
3 tablespoons salt butter
1 teaspoon lemon juice
Salt
Freshly cracked black pepper

BERCY SAUCE
2 tablespoons salt butter
2 tablespoons finely chopped
   shallots
1 cup dry white wine
¾ cup chicken stock (page 35)
1 teaspoon chopped fresh
   tarragon
1 teaspoon finely chopped fresh
   parsley
Salt
Freshly cracked white pepper
1 tablespoon all-purpose flour
   mixed with 4 tablespoons
   sweet butter

Shell the hard-boiled eggs and cut each one lengthwise into 6 even wedges. Cut each artichoke bottom into 6 slices, and cut the olives in half. Cut the well-chilled liver pâté into thick dice. Sauté the sliced mushrooms briskly in the butter with the lemon juice, salt, and pepper. Mix the eggs, artichoke bottoms, olives, pâté, and mushrooms together in a bowl, then arrange them to cover the bottom of an au gratin dish. Set the dish aside.

BERCY SAUCE. Melt the butter in a saucepan. Add the shallots and cook them very slowly, over low heat, so they become soft but not brown. Add the wine, chicken stock, tarragon, and parsley. Season with salt and pepper and stir over low heat until the mixture comes to a boil. Off the heat, bit by bit, stir in the combined flour and sweet butter. Bring the sauce again to a boil and simmer over very low heat 10 minutes.

Spoon this sauce over the egg dish and serve at once. NET: 4 to 6 servings.

STUFFED EGGS
6 hard-boiled eggs
6 tablespoons sweet butter
2 teaspoons Dijon mustard
1 tablespoon sour cream
½ teaspoon salt
⅛ teaspoon cayenne pepper

WATERCRESS CREAM
3 bunches fresh watercress
1 cup sour cream
Salt
Freshly cracked white pepper
¼ teaspoon freshly grated
    nutmeg

MAYONNAISE SAUCE
1 whole egg
1 teaspoon salt
⅛ teaspoon cayenne pepper
½ teaspoon dry mustard
1 teaspoon Dijon mustard
1 teaspoon tomato paste
1½ tablespoons tarragon
    vinegar
¼ cup pure olive oil
1 cup vegetable oil
½ cup fresh tomato juice (made
    from 1 or 2 strained ripe
    tomatoes)
½ cup light cream
2 teaspoons unflavored gelatine
4 tablespoons boiling water

OEUFS FARCIS AU CRESSON

*Stuffed Eggs
on Watercress Cream
(cold)*

WATERCRESS CREAM. Reserve about 6 beautiful sprigs of crisp watercress for decoration. Remove all the hard stalks from the rest of the watercress, but leave the tender ones near the leaves. Plunge the watercress into a pan of boiling water, leave it there 2 minutes, then drain immediately in a colander. Press it down with a small plate to get it quite dry. Put it in a wooden chopping bowl and chop it fine. Transfer it to a mixing bowl and mix in the sour cream. Season with salt, pepper, and the nutmeg. Arrange the Watercress Cream in the form of a narrow bed down the center of a flat oval platter.

STUFFED EGGS. Shell the hard-boiled eggs and cut them in half lengthwise. Remove the yolks and rub them through a fine wire strainer. Cream the sweet butter in a mixer. Add the strained yolks and beat in Dijon mustard, sour cream, salt, and cayenne pepper. Fill the egg whites with the beaten yolk mixture and reshape them to resemble whole unstuffed eggs. Arrange the reassembled eggs on the bed of Watercress Cream.

MAYONNAISE SAUCE. Put into a mixer bowl the egg, salt, cayenne pepper, two mustards, and tomato paste. Beat well. Continue beating and, drop by drop, add the tarragon vinegar and olive oil. At this point the sauce should be very thick and the vegetable oil can be added a little faster (a slow stream). When all the oil has been added, mix in the fresh tomato juice and light cream. Dissolve the gelatine in the boiling water. Cool it a little, then mix it into the mayonnaise sauce.

To finish, coat each egg with the mayonnaise sauce, allowing the bed of watercress to show. (If there is any extra mayonnaise, it can be stored in the refrigerator for other uses.) Garnish the platter with the reserved sprigs of watercress. Chill thoroughly and serve. NET: 4 to 6 servings.

OEUFS FARCIS MAISON

Stuffed Eggs on Rice with Ham, Tongue, Green Beans (cold)

STUFFED EGGS
4 hard-boiled eggs
1 cup cooked green peas, rubbed through a strainer
12 tablespoons sweet butter, creamed until light and fluffy
2 tablespoons freshly grated Parmesan cheese
Salt
A few grains cayenne pepper

GARNISH
1 sour gherkin, sliced
1 pitted ripe olive, sliced
1 bunch crisp fresh watercress
4 small firm ripe tomatoes, skinned, cut in quarters, and seeded

RICE SALAD
2 cups plain cooked rice (page 675)
2 tablespoons shredded boiled ham
2 tablespoons shredded cooked tongue
½ cup sliced cooked green beans
Salt
Freshly cracked black pepper
1 teaspoon lemon juice
2 tablespoons vegetable oil
1 tablespoon tarragon vinegar

STUFFED EGGS. Shell the hard-boiled eggs and cut in half lengthwise. Remove the yolks. Put the whites aside in cold water. Rub the yolks through a fine wire strainer and put them in a mixer bowl with the peas, butter, and Parmesan cheese. Season with salt and cayenne pepper and beat well. Set this mixture aside.

RICE SALAD. Place the cooked rice in a bowl with the ham, tongue, and green beans. Season with salt and pepper, and add the lemon juice, oil, and tarragon vinegar. Mix the contents of the bowl with two forks.

Arrange the rice salad in a ring around the sides of a serving platter. Fill the center with the watercress. Drain the whites of the hard-boiled eggs on paper towels. Arrange them on the rice salad, spaced equally apart. Embed them a little in the rice. Put the yolk mixture into a pastry bag fitted with a #4 or #5 star tube. Pipe rosettes into the hollow of each egg white. Decorate each egg with a slice of gherkin or ripe olive. Surround the edge of the dish with the tomato sections. Chill the prepared platter thoroughly and serve. NET: 4 main course servings; 8 first course.

6 hard-boiled eggs
6 tablespoons sweet butter,
    creamed in a mixer until light
    and fluffy
½ cup heavy cream, whipped
1 tablespoon chopped fresh
    chives
1 tablespoon Dijon mustard
Salt
A few grains cayenne pepper
2 cups cooked white meat of
    chicken, cut into coarse
    shreds

1 small head Boston lettuce,
    washed and crisped

EGG SAUCE
2 raw egg yolks
Salt
A few grains cayenne pepper
4 hard-boiled egg yolks, rubbed
    through a fine strainer
4 tablespoons tarragon vinegar
2 cups vegetable oil
¾ cup light cream

OEUFS À LA REINE

Salad of Stuffed Eggs with Cold Chicken

STUFFED EGGS. Shell the hard-boiled eggs and cut them in half lengthwise or across. Remove the yolks and rub them through a coarse wire strainer. Add the strained yolks to the creamed butter with the whipped cream, chives, and Dijon mustard. Season with salt and cayenne pepper. Beat the mixture well. Fill the egg whites with the yolk mixture and reshape the whites to resemble unstuffed eggs. Chill them thoroughly in the refrigerator.

EGG SAUCE. Beat the raw egg yolks in a mixer bowl until they are light and fluffy. Season with salt and cayenne pepper. Add the 4 finely strained hard-boiled egg yolks and vinegar and beat well. Continue beating, and, drop by drop, add the vegetable oil. Then beat in the light cream.

Mix a little of the sauce into the shredded chicken, reserving a few selected shreds for garnish. Line a shallow glass salad bowl with crisp lettuce leaves. Arrange the shredded chicken over the lettuce. Arrange the stuffed eggs on the chicken. Coat the eggs with the sauce. Garnish the top of each egg with a criss-cross of shredded white meat of chicken. Chill thoroughly. NET: 6 servings.

6 ounces uncooked spaghetti
Salt
2 tablespoons vegetable oil
4 tablespoons salt butter
3 tablespoons all-purpose flour
Salt
A few grains cayenne pepper

1 cup milk plus 1 tablespoon
¼ cup heavy cream
2 raw egg yolks
6 hard-boiled eggs
¼ cup freshly grated Parmesan
    cheese
About 1 teaspoon paprika

OEUFS À LA TALLEYRAND

Hard-Boiled Eggs with Spaghetti and Cream Sauce (hot)

To cook the spaghetti, fill a large pan three-quarters full of water. Add 1 tablespoon salt and the vegetable oil, and bring the water to a rolling boil. Add the spaghetti and cook it 10 to 12 minutes, until it is al dente, just tender. Drain it thoroughly in a colander and transfer it to an au gratin dish. Mix in 1 tablespoon of butter and spread the spaghetti over the bottom of the dish.

Melt 2 tablespoons butter in a saucepan. Off the heat, stir in the flour and season with salt and cayenne pepper. Add 1 cup milk and stir over low heat until the sauce comes to a boil, then mix in the heavy cream. Bit by bit, stir in 1 tablespoon butter. Simmer the sauce very gently 5 minutes. Mix the raw egg yolks in a little bowl with 1 tablespoon of milk. Remove the sauce from the heat and carefully stir the yolk mixture into it. Slice the hard-boiled eggs and arrange the slices on the spaghetti in the au gratin dish. Cover the sliced eggs and spaghetti with the sauce. Sprinkle with the Parmesan cheese and paprika. Brown under a hot broiler and serve. NET: 4 servings.

OEUFS À LA TRIPE

Classic Hard-Boiled Eggs with Onions (hot)

7 tablespoons salt butter
6 large yellow onions, thinly sliced
6 hard-boiled eggs, shelled and thinly sliced
½ cup dry breadcrumbs (page 69)
3 tablespoons all-purpose flour
Salt

A few grains cayenne pepper
1 cup milk
2 tablespoons freshly grated Gruyère cheese
¼ cup freshly grated Parmesan cheese
½ teaspoon Dijon mustard
¼ cup heavy cream

Put 3 tablespoons of butter in a deep heavy pan. When the butter is foaming, add the sliced onions. Cook them until they are soft without browning. Have the hard-boiled eggs sliced and at hand. Butter a small, deep glass baking dish and dust it out with the breadcrumbs, reserving a little for the top. Fill the dish as follows: Put a layer of cooked onions in the bottom, then a layer of sliced hard-boiled eggs. Arrange alternate layers of onions and eggs until all the materials have been used.

Preheat the oven to 400°. Melt 2 tablespoons butter in a saucepan. Off the heat, stir in the flour and season with salt and cayenne pepper. Add the milk and stir the sauce over low heat until it comes to a boil. Mix in the Gruyère cheese, 1 tablespoon Parmesan, the Dijon mustard and heavy cream. Simmer gently 5 minutes.

Spoon the sauce over the eggs and onions in the dish. Sprinkle with the rest of the Parmesan and the reserved breadcrumbs, and dot with the remaining butter. Put the dish in the hot oven for a few minutes to warm and brown. Serve immediately. NET: 4 servings.

OEUFS MOLLET ARGENTEUIL

Soft-Boiled Eggs in Pastry Cases, with Fresh Asparagus Purée

TARTLET SHELLS
1½ cups all-purpose flour
2 hard-boiled egg yolks, rubbed through a fine wire strainer
½ cup freshly grated Parmesan cheese
2 teaspoons dry mustard

1 teaspoon salt
½ teaspoon paprika
8 tablespoons salt butter
1 egg, beaten
2 cups raw rice (to anchor pastry)

OEUFS MOLLET
*6 soft-boiled eggs, shelled (page
   176)*

ASPARAGUS PURÉE
*24 medium-size spears fresh
   asparagus*
Salt
6 tablespoons salt butter
4 tablespoons all-purpose flour
Salt

A few grains cayenne pepper
1 cup milk
½ cup heavy cream, whipped
*½ cup freshly grated Gruyère
   cheese*
*4 tablespoons freshly grated
   Parmesan cheese*
*2 tablespoons dry breadcrumbs
   (page 69)*
*2 tablespoons melted salt
   butter*

PASTRY. Preheat the oven to 375°. Put the flour, strained hard-boiled egg yolks, Parmesan cheese, mustard, salt, and paprika in a bowl. Cut the butter into pieces, add it to the dry ingredients in the bowl, and work it in with the tips of your fingers until the mixture resembles coarse cornmeal. Then add the beaten egg and, if necessary, a little ice water, and work the mixture up to a firm ball of dough. Chill the dough at least 30 minutes.

Have ready 6 tartlet tins. Roll the dough out fairly thin, cut it into large rounds with a fluted cutter (larger than the tins) and line the tartlet tins. Press a little piece of buttered wax paper into each lined tartlet tin. Fill it with raw rice or beans (to keep the shape of the shell while baking). Put the tins on a baking sheet and bake for 20 minutes. Remove the pastry from the oven, remove the paper and rice, and lift the pastry shells from the tins onto a wire rack to cool.

ASPARAGUS PURÉE. Cut the tips from the asparagus (about 1-inch lengths) and set aside for garnish. Cut the rest of the tender part of the asparagus spears into chunks and cook them in boiling salted water until they are very soft. Drain and rub them through a fine strainer, and set aside.

Put the asparagus tips in a small pan, cover them with water and a little salt. Bring the water to a boil, then drain the asparagus tips immediately. Brush them with a little melted butter and keep them warm for the garnish.

Melt 3 tablespoons butter in a saucepan. Off the heat, stir in the flour and season with salt and cayenne pepper. Add the milk and stir over low heat until the sauce comes to a boil. Let it simmer 3 minutes, then mix 2 to 3 spoonfuls into the asparagus purée.

Have the soft-boiled eggs prepared and shelled. Half fill the tartlet shells with asparagus purée, and place an egg on top of each prepared tartlet. Mix the rest of the asparagus purée into the remainder of the cream sauce with the Gruyère cheese. Fold in the whipped cream. Adjust the seasoning, if necessary. Coat each egg with the finished sauce. Decorate around the edge of the pastry shells with the reserved asparagus tips. Sprinkle the top with the Parmesan cheese and breadcrumbs. Dot with a little melted butter and brown under a hot broiler. Serve at once. NET: 6 servings.

OEUFS POCHÉS À L'ANDALOUSE

Green Peppers Stuffed with Poached Eggs and Rice (hot)

6 eggs
2 tablespoons tarragon vinegar
1 teaspoon salt
6 medium-size fresh sweet
  green peppers
4 tablespoons salt butter
6 chicken livers
½ cup pure olive oil
1 cup finely chopped onion
1 cup long-grain rice
2 cups chicken stock (page 35)
½ cup freshly grated Parmesan

cheese
A little melted butter

TOMATO SAUCE
4 tablespoons salt butter
1 teaspoon finely chopped garlic
4 firm ripe tomatoes
Salt
Freshly cracked black pepper
2 tablespoons all-purpose flour
3 cups water or chicken stock
2 tablespoons tomato paste

Poach the eggs as directed on page 177, using the vinegar and salt in the water, and as each egg is poached set it in a basin of warm water.

RICE. Preheat the oven to 350°. Heat 1 tablespoon butter in a deep heavy pan. Quickly brown the chicken livers in the pan. Remove them, then add the olive oil to the pan and heat it a little. Put in the chopped onion and cook it over low heat until translucent but not brown. Add the raw rice, mix it with the oil and onion, and cook another 2 minutes. Add the chicken stock and bring to a boil. Cover the pan firmly with the lid and bake 30 minutes. Remove it from the oven, slice the chicken livers, and stir them into the rice with 3 tablespoons butter and the grated cheese.

While the rice is cooking, prepare the peppers. Have ready a large pan of boiling water. Cut the tops off the peppers and plunge peppers and tops into the boiling water for 2 minutes, then drain. Remove the seeds without breaking the peppers. Dry the insides with a bit of cheesecloth, and put a few drops of melted butter in the bottom of each pepper.

TOMATO SAUCE. Slice three tomatoes with their skins on. Skin the fourth, quarter it and remove the seeds. Rub the seeds in a strainer and reserve the juice. Cut the pulp into fine shreds. Melt 3 tablespoons butter in a saucepan. Add the chopped garlic and cook over low heat 2 minutes. Add the 3 sliced tomatoes, season with salt and pepper, and cook briskly over medium heat 2 minutes with the lid on the pan. Remove the saucepan from the heat and stir in the flour. Add the water or chicken stock, return the pan to low heat, and stir until the sauce comes to a boil. Strain it through a fine strainer, return it to the saucepan, and let it simmer gently 5 minutes. Stir in another tablespoon of butter bit by bit. Stir in the strained fresh tomato juice and, last, add the tomato cut into fine shreds.

Have ready a heated oval au gratin dish. Drain the poached eggs on paper towels. Fill the peppers with a little of the rice mixture. Make a hole in the center of the rice filling and carefully insert a poached egg. Cover the egg with more rice, and cover the stuffed peppers with their caps. Arrange the stuffed peppers on the au gratin dish, pour the tomato sauce over them, and serve. NET: 6 servings.

Poached eggs on toasted English muffins and ham, with Hollandaise sauce.

6 eggs
2 tablespoons tarragon vinegar
Salt
3 English muffins
3 tablespoons melted salt butter
6 2-inch rounds of boiled ham
    ½ inch thick
1 tablespoon salt butter

HOLLANDAISE SAUCE
3 egg yolks

Salt
A few grains cayenne pepper
2 tablespoons tarragon vinegar
4 tablespoons light cream
12 tablespoons frozen sweet
    butter
4 drops lemon juice

GARNISH
6 thick slices black truffle

Poach the eggs as described on page 177, adding the vinegar and salt to the water. As each egg is poached, put it in a basin of warm water. Split the English muffins and spread each half with a little melted butter. Toast quickly under the broiler. Place a round of ham on each muffin half, with a tiny piece of butter on the ham. Return them to the broiler for another minute. Drain the poached eggs on paper towels. Trim off any streamers of egg white. Place a poached egg on top of each round of ham. Arrange the prepared muffins down the center of an oval au gratin dish, and keep it warm.

HOLLANDAISE SAUCE. Put the egg yolks in a small bowl with a little salt and cayenne pepper. Beat well with a small wire whisk. Mix in the vinegar and half the light cream. Stand the bowl in a shallow pan half filled with hot water over low heat. Continue beating with the whisk until the sauce thickens. Cut the frozen sweet butter into small pieces and beat it into the sauce bit by bit. Then add the lemon juice and the rest of the cream, and correct the seasoning.

Spoon the sauce over the eggs on the au gratin dish. Brown quickly under the broiler and place a slice of truffle on top of each serving. Serve at once. NET: 6 servings.

What French cuisine terms "black butter" is really dark brown. It must not be burned.

4 eggs
2 tablespoons tarragon vinegar
1 teaspoon salt

BEURRE NOIR
6 tablespoons salt butter

2 tablespoons capers
3 tablespoons dry white wine
Salt
Freshly cracked black pepper

Poach the eggs as described on page 177, using the vinegar and salt in the water. As each is poached, put it in a pan of warm water. When all the eggs are poached, drain them on paper towels. Trim off any streamers of egg white. Place the eggs on a hot flat serving dish and keep them warm.

BEURRE NOIR. Put the butter in a small sauté pan and cook it slowly until it is dark brown, stirring all the while with a small wire whisk. Continue stirring and add the capers, dry white wine, a little salt, and pepper.

Pour the sauce over the eggs and serve at once. NET: 4 servings.

OEUFS POCHÉS CLAMART

Poached Egg and Green Pea Tartlets, with Mayonnaise Sauce (cold)

CHEESE TARTLET SHELLS
1 cup all-purpose flour
5 tablespoons cool melted salt butter
3 raw egg yolks
2 tablespoons freshly grated Parmesan cheese
Salt
A few grains cayenne pepper
½ teaspoon paprika
2 tablespoons ice water
2 cups raw rice (to anchor pastry)

MAYONNAISE SAUCE
2 raw egg yolks
2 tablespoons tarragon vinegar
1 teaspoon Dijon mustard
½ teaspoon lemon juice
Scant ½ teaspoon salt
A few grains cayenne pepper
¾ cup vegetable oil

2 tablespoons heavy cream
2 tablespoons cooked peas from the filling preparation, rubbed through a fine wire strainer

POACHED EGGS
2 tablespoons tarragon vinegar
4 eggs
1 teaspoon salt

FILLING
2½ cups shelled green peas (fresh or frozen), plain-cooked and cooled
2 tablespoons heavy cream
1 to 2 tablespoons finely chopped fresh mint
Salt
Freshly cracked black pepper

GARNISH
1 bunch crisp fresh watercress

CHEESE TARTLET SHELLS. Preheat the oven to 375°. Have ready 4 individual-size tartlet tins. Put the flour in a bowl or on a marble slab. Make a well in the center. In the well put the butter, egg yolks, grated cheese, a little salt and the cayenne pepper, paprika, and ice water. Work them to a smooth paste, then work them into the flour. Roll the dough out fairly thin, cut it in large rounds with a fluted cutter (larger than the tins) and line the tins. Press a piece of buttered wax paper into each lined tin and fill it with raw rice to keep the shape of the shell while baking. Put the tins on a baking sheet and bake 20 minutes. Remove them from the oven, remove the paper and rice, lift the shells from the tins, and cool them on a wire rack.

MAYONNAISE SAUCE. Put the egg yolks in a mixer bowl, and beat until they are light and fluffy. Continue beating and add the vinegar, Dijon mustard, lemon juice, salt, and cayenne pepper. Slowly, drop by drop, beat in the vegetable oil. Last, beat in the heavy cream and strained peas. Chill the sauce in the refrigerator.

POACHED EGGS. Poach as described on page 177, using the vinegar and salt in the water. As each egg is poached, transfer it to a basin of cold water to chill.

FILLING. Mix the cooked peas with the other filling ingredients. Stir well together.

To assemble, place the baked tartlet shells on a flat serving platter. Fill each shell with the pea mixture. Lift the poached eggs from the cold water, drain, trim off any egg white streamers, and set the eggs on the peas. Spoon the mayonnaise sauce over them. Garnish each end of the serving platter with clusters of crisp fresh watercress. NET: 4 servings.

OEUFS POCHÉS FLORENTINE

Poached Eggs on Spinach with Mornay Sauce (hot)

3 pounds spinach
2 tablespoons salt butter
Salt
Freshly cracked black pepper
1 cup small croûtons (page 70)
6 eggs
2 tablespoons tarragon vinegar
⅓ cup freshly grated Parmesan
  cheese
2 tablespoons dry breadcrumbs
  (page 69)
1 tablespoon melted salt butter

MORNAY SAUCE
5 tablespoons salt butter
3 tablespoons all-purpose flour
1 cup milk
4 tablespoons spinach juice
  (from the cooked spinach)
1 teaspoon Dijon mustard
Salt
A few grains cayenne pepper
A few grains freshly grated
  nutmeg
⅓ cup light cream
⅓ cup freshly grated imported
  Swiss cheese

Wash the spinach thoroughly in several changes of water. Drain it, but not too well, and put it in a large pan with the butter and a little salt and pepper. Cook over high heat 2 to 3 minutes, until the spinach wilts. Stir and turn it, then drain it in a colander over a bowl. Reserve the juice. With a small plate, press out all the liquid and return the spinach to the pan to dry a little more. Chop it coarsely and mix in the croûtons. Arrange it on the bottom of an oval au gratin dish and keep it warm.

MORNAY SAUCE. Melt 3 tablespoons salt butter in a small heavy pan. Off the heat, stir in the flour. Cook over low heat 2 to 3 minutes. Remove the pan from the heat and mix in the milk and spinach juice. Add the Dijon mustard, salt, cayenne pepper, and nutmeg. Stir over low heat until the sauce comes to a boil. Add the light cream and Swiss cheese. Set the sauce aside and keep it warm.

Poach the eggs as described on page 177, using the vinegar and 1 teaspoon salt in the water. As each egg is poached, transfer it to a basin of warm water. When the eggs are done, drain them on paper towels. Trim off any egg white streamers. Arrange the eggs on the spinach in the au gratin dish. Spoon the sauce over the eggs and spinach. Sprinkle the top with the Parmesan cheese and breadcrumbs. Drizzle a little melted butter over the dish and brown under a hot broiler. NET: 6 servings.

OEUFS POCHÉS À LA FLORENTINE EN SAVARIN

Poached Eggs with Ring Mold Spinach Mousse, Bercy Sauce (hot)

1 cup Bercy Sauce (page 46)
6 eggs
2 tablespoons tarragon vinegar
1 teaspoon salt
6 (4-inch diameter) round fried croûtons (page 69)

SPINACH MOUSSE
2 pounds fresh spinach
Salt

3 tablespoons salt butter
5 tablespoons all-purpose flour
A few grains cayenne pepper
A little freshly grated nutmeg
1 cup milk
1 tablespoon sour cream
2 whole eggs
2 egg yolks
Butter for ring mold

Have the Bercy Sauce (page 46) ready and keep it warm.

SPINACH MOUSSE. Preheat the oven to 350°. Wash the spinach thoroughly in several waters. Drain it, but not too well, and put it in a large pan with 2 teaspoons salt and the nutmeg. Cook over high heat 2 to 3 minutes, until the spinach wilts. Stir and turn it, then drain it in a colander, using a small plate to press out all the liquid. Return the spinach to the pan to dry a little more, put it through a fine meat chopper, and set it aside. Melt the butter in a saucepan. Off the heat, stir in the flour and season with salt, cayenne pepper, and grated nutmeg. Mix in the milk. Stir over low heat until the sauce comes to a boil. Remove from the heat and mix in the sour cream, eggs, egg yolks, and ground spinach. Test the seasoning, and add more salt and pepper if necessary.

Generously butter a 4-cup ring mold. Fill it with the spinach mixture and cover with buttered wax paper. Stand the mold in a shallow roasting pan half-filled with hot water and put the pan in the oven. Bake about 1 hour, until the mousse is set. Remove the mold from the oven and let it stand at least 10 minutes before you turn it out.

POACHED EGGS. Poach as described on page 177, using the vinegar and salt in the water. As each egg is poached, transfer it to a basin of warm water to keep warm.

Have ready a hot flat serving dish. Slide the blade of a little knife around the edge of the spinach mold and turn it out onto the dish. Surround the ring with the croûtons. Drain the eggs and trim off any egg white streamers. Place an egg on each croûton. Pour a spoonful of Bercy Sauce over each egg. NET: 6 servings.

OEUFS POCHÉS EN GELÉE

Poached Eggs in Aspic (cold)

This is the classic poached eggs in aspic, with pâté de foie gras.

6 poached eggs
2 tablespoons tarragon vinegar
1 teaspoon salt
5 cups chicken aspic (page 37)
6 thin rounds of boiled ham, the size of a quarter

1 black truffle, sliced and cut into 6 rounds the size of a dime (chop the scraps)

PÂTÉ
6 tablespoons sweet butter
3 ounces bloc foie gras or fine

liver pâté	Salt
1 tablespoon Cognac	A few grains cayenne pepper

Chill 6 dariole molds (small oval metal molds).

PÂTÉ. Cream the butter in the electric mixer until it is light and fluffy. Add the foie gras or fine liver pâté and mix well. Continue beating and add the Cognac, a little salt, and the cayenne pepper. Put the mixture in a pastry bag fitted with a #3 or #4 star tube and set it in the refrigerator.

POACHED EGGS. Poach the eggs as described on page 177, using the vinegar and salt in the water. As each is poached, set it in a basin of ice water.

Put the aspic in a pan over a bowl of crushed ice. Stir until it is at the point of setting. Then put 1 tablespoon aspic in the bottom of each dariole mold. Put the molds on a tray and put them briefly in the refrigerator for the aspic to set. When it is set, decorate each mold as follows. Dip a round of truffle in aspic and place it in the center of the mold, then dip a round of ham in aspic and place it on the truffle. Return the molds to the refrigerator for a moment.

Drain the poached eggs and dry them well on paper towels. Trim off any egg white streamers. You want the eggs to look absolutely perfect. Carefully place an egg in each mold. On top of each egg, pipe a rosette of the prepared pâté. Return the molds to the refrigerator to chill well, then fill them to the top with more aspic that is on the point of setting, and return them to the refrigerator to become well set. (At the same time, chill a handsome silver platter for serving.) Put the remaining aspic in a layer cake tin and put it to set in the refrigerator. When it is firmly set, turn it out on a piece of wax paper on a cutting board, quickly chop it finely, and set it back in the refrigerator. Have ready the scraps of truffle which have been finely chopped. Slide a thin-bladed knife around the edge of each mold and then dip the molds for 1 minute in a little warm water. Turn the egg aspics out onto a piece of wax paper. Cover the bottom of the serving platter with the chopped aspic and sprinkle the finely chopped truffle all over it. Arrange the aspic molds on the chopped aspic. Refrigerate (but don't freeze) and serve when desired. NET: 6 servings.

*Ring Mold of Poached
Eggs in Aspic
with Tarragon (cold)*

6 eggs	A few grains cayenne pepper
2 tablespoons tarragon vinegar	1 tablespoon tomato paste
Salt	¼ cup dry sherry
3 egg whites	12 sprigs fresh tarragon
4 cups chicken stock (page 35)	6 thin rounds smoked tongue or
3 tablespoons unflavored	ham
gelatine	1 bunch crisp fresh watercress

Put a 4-cup ring mold in the refrigerator to chill. Poach the eggs as described on page 177, using the vinegar and 1 teaspoon of salt in the water. As each egg is poached, transfer it to a basin of cold water.

Beat the egg whites. Put the chicken stock in a tin-lined copper pan with the gelatine, a little salt and the cayenne pepper, tomato paste, sherry, and stiffly beaten egg whites. Put the pan over low heat and beat the mixture with a wire whisk until it comes to a rolling boil. Remove the pan from the heat and let it stand without moving it for 15 minutes. Pour the mixture into a bowl through a colander lined with a damp cloth. Set it over a bowl of ice and stir the aspic until it is on the point of setting. Fill the chilled ring mold half full of aspic and put it in the refrigerator to set.

Drain the poached eggs and dry them carefully on paper towels. Trim off any egg white streamers. Snip tarragon leaves for decoration from their stems, and place them in the shape of a sprig of tarragon in six places on the aspic in the ring mold. Place a poached egg on each tarragon decoration. Place the thin rounds of tongue or ham in the spaces between the eggs. Fill the mold with more aspic and put it in the refrigerator to set thoroughly. Put the remaining aspic in a small pan and let it set to be used for garnish.

Have ready a chilled flat serving dish. When ready to serve, dip the mold quickly in a bowl of warm water and turn it out onto the serving dish. Turn the remainder of the aspic out on a piece of wax paper on a cutting board. Chop it fine and garnish the dish with the chopped aspic, a few tarragon leaves, and clusters of crisp, fresh watercress. NET: 6 servings.

OEUFS POCHÉS GEORGETTE

*Poached Eggs
in Baked Potatoes
with Shrimp Sauce (hot)*

4 large Idaho-type potatoes
Salt
6 tablespoons salt butter
Freshly cracked white pepper
¾ cup milk
3 large ripe tomatoes, skinned
1 small white onion,
    finely sliced
½ pound shelled boiled
    shrimps, coarsely chopped

3 tablespoons all-purpose flour
1 teaspoon chopped fresh
    parsley or fresh chives or
    both
2 tablespoons heavy cream
4 eggs
2 tablespoons tarragon vinegar
2 tablespoons freshly grated
    Parmesan cheese
1 bunch crisp fresh watercress

Preheat the oven to 350°. Scrub the potatoes well, dry with paper towels, and rub them with a little salt. Bake 45 to 60 minutes, until soft. When they are baked, cut the tops off lengthwise. Scoop out most of the inside and rub it through a vegetable strainer. Put the strained potato in a mixer bowl and beat in 2 tablespoons butter, salt, pepper, and 2 tablespoons milk. Put the potato mixture in a pastry bag with a #3 or #4 star tube and keep it warm.

While the potatoes are baking, cut the tomatoes in quarters. Remove the seeds and rub them through a fine strainer, reserving the juice. Shred the tomato pulp. Melt 2 tablespoons butter in a sauté pan. Add the sliced onion and cook 4 minutes over low heat. Season with salt and pepper. Add the shrimps to the pan and sprinkle them with 1 tablespoon flour. Mix in the shredded tomato pulp and the strained juice. Add the chopped fresh parsley and/or chives. Bring the mixture to a boil over low heat, then remove from the heat and keep it warm.

Melt 1 tablespoon butter in a small saucepan. Off the heat stir in 2 tablespoons flour and add the rest of the milk. Stir the sauce over low heat until it comes to a boil. Bit by bit, stir in another tablespoon of butter, then stir in the heavy cream. Simmer the sauce 3 minutes, and keep it warm. Poach the eggs as described on page 177, using the vinegar and 1 teaspoon salt in the water. As each egg is poached, transfer it to a basin of warm water.

Have ready the scooped-out baked potatoes. Put 1 tablespoon of the shrimp mixture in the bottom of each potato shell. Drain the poached eggs on paper towels and fit an egg into each potato. Cover the egg with the sauce. Pipe a border of whipped potatoes around the top edge of each potato. Sprinkle the tops with freshly grated cheese and dot with a little butter. Brown the potatoes quickly under the broiler. Just before serving, garnish with the watercress. NET: 4 servings.

Vegetables for the macédoine: 1 cup each of baby lima beans, diced green beans, diced carrots, shelled green peas, diced turnips, diced cucumber pulp (no seeds), and diced tomato pulp (no seeds)
Salt
6 eggs
2 tablespoons tarragon vinegar
Freshly cracked white pepper

1 teaspoon lemon juice
6 sprigs crisp fresh watercress

MAYONNAISE SAUCE
3 egg yolks
½ teaspoon salt
A few grains cayenne pepper
1 teaspoon Dijon mustard
2 tablespoons tarragon vinegar
2 cups vegetable oil
½ cup light cream

OEUFS POCHÉS À LA MACÉDOINE

Poached Eggs on a Vegetable Macédoine, with Mayonnaise (cold)

Cook the vegetables (except cucumber and tomato) in a little boiling salted water until just tender and still crunchy. Drain. While they are cooling, poach the eggs as directed on page 177, using the vinegar and 1 teaspoon salt in the water. As each egg is poached, put it in a basin of ice water. Put all the vegetables in a large bowl and mix them together lightly with two forks. Season with salt, pepper, and lemon juice. Cover the bottom of a chilled au gratin dish with the vegetables. Drain the poached eggs on paper towels and trim off any egg white streamers. Arrange the eggs on the macédoine of vegetables, and chill the whole dish in the refrigerator.

MAYONNAISE SAUCE. Put the egg yolks in a mixer bowl with the salt, cayenne pepper, and Dijon mustard. Beat the mixture until it is light and fluffy. Continue beating and slowly add the vinegar, then the vegetable oil (drop by drop until it begins to thicken). Last, add the light cream to bring the sauce to a coating consistency. If necessary, add a little more cream.

Coat the poached eggs with the mayonnaise. Garnish the top of each egg with a sprig of fresh watercress. Chill thoroughly and serve. NET: 6 servings.

OEUFS POCHÉS SOUBISE

Poached Eggs
in Onion Purée (hot)

6 eggs
2 tablespoons tarragon vinegar
1 teaspoon salt
12 ¼-inch onion rings (re-
    served from the onions for
    the sauce)
A little flour, salt, and pepper
    for dusting
½ cup vegetable oil for frying

SOUBISE SAUCE
4 large Bermuda onions, finely

sliced except for 12 ¼-inch
    rings reserved for garnish
1 cup milk
1 garlic clove, crushed
4 peppercorns
1 bay leaf
Salt
3 tablespoons salt butter
2 tablespoons all-purpose flour
A few grains cayenne pepper
2 tablespoons heavy cream

SOUBISE SAUCE. Put the sliced onions (except the 12 reserved rings) in a pan with the milk, crushed garlic clove, peppercorns, bay leaf, and a little salt. Bring to a boil, reduce to very low heat, and simmer until the onions are soft. Remove the bay leaf and peppercorns and put the mixture through a fine strainer. In a separate saucepan melt 2 tablespoons butter. Off the heat, stir in the flour with a little salt and cayenne pepper. Add the strained onion mixture and stir over low heat until the sauce comes to a boil and thickens. Stir in 1 tablespoon butter, bit by bit, and the heavy cream. Simmer over very low heat 3 minutes. Keep the sauce warm.

Poach the eggs as described on page 177, using the vinegar and salt in the water. As each egg is poached, transfer it to a basin of warm water. Have ready a hot shallow serving dish. Drain the poached eggs on paper towels and trim off any egg white streamers. Arrange the eggs on the serving dish and spoon the soubise sauce over them.

GARNISH. Dust the reserved onion rings with a little flour, salt, and pepper. Heat the vegetable oil in a small pan. When it is very hot, fry the onion rings until they are golden brown. Drain them on paper towels.

Decorate the serving dish with fried onion rings. Serve at once. NET: 6 servings.

OEUFS FRITS AU BEURRE NOIR

Fried Eggs
with Brown Butter (hot)

6 eggs
Butter for frying
6 large croûtons of fried bread
    (page 69)

BROWN BUTTER
8 tablespoons salt butter

1 tablespoon finely chopped
    onion
Salt
Freshly cracked white pepper
½ cup capers
¼ cup tarragon vinegar

Fry the eggs American or French style, as described on pages 178-179. Arrange them on a hot shallow serving dish or au gratin dish. Have the croûtons ready. Beurre noir takes only a minute or two. To make it, heat the butter very slowly in a little sauté pan. Stir occasionally and let it turn dark brown, then add the other ingredients. Do not cook the sauce any longer. Pour it over the egg whites only, and garnish the dish with the fried croûtons. NET: 6 servings.

OEUFS FRITS
À L'ESPAGNOLE

Pure olive oil for frying
6 rounds ham or Canadian
 bacon (about 4-inch di-
 ameter)
6 eggs
Butter for frying

FRENCH TOAST
2 eggs
½ cup milk
Salt
A few grains cayenne pepper

6 large rounds white bread
 (about 4-inch diameter)

TOMATO SAUCE
4 tablespoons salt butter
1 tablespoon all-purpose flour
Salt
Freshly cracked white pepper
3 tablespoons tomato paste
½ teaspoon finely chopped
 garlic
1½ cups chicken stock (page 35)

Fried Eggs and Ham
on French Toast,
Tomato Sauce (hot)

FRENCH TOAST. With a wire whisk, mix the eggs and milk with a little salt and the cayenne pepper. When the mixture is well blended, dip the rounds of bread in it. Heat the olive oil in a sauté pan, and fry the egg-coated bread in it until golden brown on both sides. Arrange the toast on a hot flat serving dish and keep it warm.

TOMATO SAUCE. Melt 2 tablespoons butter in a saucepan. Off the heat, stir in the flour and season with salt and pepper. Mix in the tomato paste, garlic, and chicken stock. Stir over low heat until the sauce comes to a boil. Add the rest of the butter bit by bit, and gently simmer the sauce 5 minutes. Keep it warm.

Fry the rounds of ham or Canadian bacon in a little olive oil and place each on a round of French toast. Fry the 6 eggs in butter, American or French style (pages 178-179). Place a fried egg on each ham slice. Pour the tomato sauce over the eggs. Serve at once. NET: 6 servings.

OEUFS SUR LE
PLAT AUX
HARICOTS
DE LIMA

1½ pounds fresh young lima
 beans, shelled (about 1 cup),
 or use frozen lima beans
Salt
2 tablespoons salt butter
1 medium-size onion, sliced
1 teaspoon chopped fresh
 parsley

1 firm ripe tomato, skinned and
 cut into ½-inch slices
Freshly cracked white pepper
4 eggs
3 tablespoons heavy cream
2 tablespoons freshly grated
 Parmesan cheese

Baked Eggs
on Lima Beans
with Tomato (hot)

Preheat the oven to 350°. Put the lima beans in a pan with a little water and salt. Simmer until tender, and drain. Melt the butter in a sauté pan. Add the onion and cook over low heat until it is translucent. Add the lima beans, parsley, tomato, and salt and pepper. Shake over moderate heat for 2 minutes. Generously butter a small flat baking dish. Spread the lima bean mixture on it. Break each egg into a cup (to ensure unbroken yolks in the dish), then slide it onto the lima bean bed. Spoon the heavy cream over the yolks. Sprinkle with the grated cheese. Place the dish in the oven and bake 7 to 10 minutes, until the eggs are set. Serve immediately. NET: 4 servings.

OEUFS SUR LE PLAT FLAMENCO

Eggs Baked on a Bed of Tomatoes, Potatoes, and Sausage (hot)

2 Idaho-type potatoes, peeled and plain-cooked
4 tablespoons salt butter
3 frankfurters, skinned and cut into ¼-inch slices
2 tablespoons cooked shelled frozen or fresh green peas
2 whole canned pimentos, cut in large dice
Salt
Freshly cracked black pepper
2 firm ripe tomatoes, skinned and cut into ½-inch cubes
2 tablespoons chopped fresh parsley
4 eggs
2 tablespoons heavy cream
A few grains cayenne pepper

Preheat the oven to 350°. Cut the cooked potatoes into ½-inch cubes. Heat the butter in a sauté pan and add the potatoes and sliced frankfurters. Shake the pan over moderate heat until the potatoes begin to brown. Add the peas and pimentos to the pan with a little salt and pepper and cook 4 minutes. Add the cubed tomatoes and chopped parsley and mix all together. Spread the mixture on a flat earthenware baking dish. Break each egg into a cup (to ensure unbroken yolks in the dish) and gently slide it onto the vegetable and frankfurter mixture. Season with a little salt and pepper, place the dish in the oven, and bake until the eggs are set (7 to 10 minutes). Spoon the heavy cream over the top, sprinkle with a very little cayenne pepper, and serve at once. NET: 4 servings.

OEUFS SUR LE PLAT À LA GRECQUE

Eggs Baked on a Bed of Potato, Onion, Eggplant, Peppers, Tomatoes (hot)

4 firm white mushrooms, sliced
6 tablespoons salt butter
1 teaspoon lemon juice
1 Idaho-type potato
Salt
1 very small eggplant (about 4 ounces), cut in half, salted, and set aside 30 minutes)
2 tablespoons pure olive oil
Rind of 1 navel orange, cut into fine shreds
½ teaspoon finely chopped
garlic
2 medium-size yellow onions, cut into ½-inch dice
1 green and 1 red pepper, seeded and cut into ¼-inch dice
2 firm ripe large tomatoes, skinned and cut into ½-inch cubes
Freshly cracked white pepper
6 eggs

Preheat the oven to 350°. Quickly sauté the sliced mushrooms in 3 tablespoons butter and the lemon juice. Set them aside to keep warm. Peel the potato and cut it in quarters. Put it in a pan of cold salted water and slowly bring to a boil. Boil 3 minutes and drain. Cut the potato into ¼-inch dice. Rinse the eggplant, dry it on paper towels, and cut it into ½-inch dice. Heat the olive oil in a small sauté pan and quickly brown the eggplant. Melt 3 tablespoons butter in a large, heavy sauté pan. Add the orange rind and chopped garlic and cook over low heat 2 minutes. Add the potato and cook 3 minutes, then the onions and cook 2 minutes, then the green and red peppers and cook 2 minutes more. Mix in the sautéed eggplant and sautéed mushrooms and the cubed tomatoes. Season the mixture with salt and freshly cracked white pepper and arrange it on a large au gratin or baking dish. Make 6 indentations in the vegetable bed with the back of a large spoon. Taking care not to break the yolk, (break the egg into a cup first if you like), break an egg into each hollow. Place the dish in the oven and bake 7 to 10 minutes, or until the eggs are set. Serve at once. NET: 6 servings.

6 large firm white mushroom	CREAM PUFFS	
caps	½ cup water	
3 tablespoons salt butter	2 tablespoons salt butter	
1 teaspoon lemon juice	Pinch of salt	
6 slices bacon	½ cup all-purpose flour	
6 eggs	2 eggs	

OEUFS BROUILLÉS ALICE

Scrambled Eggs in Cream Puffs, with Mushrooms and Bacon (hot)

CREAM PUFFS. Put the water, butter, and salt in a little pan. Bring it slowly to a boil and throw in the flour. Remove from the heat and beat the paste until it is smooth and comes away from the sides of the pan. Then beat in the eggs one at a time (before adding the second egg, beat it a little and reserve a bit of it to brush the tops of the cream puffs). Beat the dough with a small wire whisk until it is smooth and shiny. Set it in the refrigerator to chill at least 30 minutes, and preheat the oven to 375°. Put the chilled cream puff dough into a pastry bag fitted with a #8 or #9 round tube. Pipe the dough onto a baking sheet in mounds for 6 large cream puffs (use all the dough). Brush the tops with the reserved egg. Bake the cream puffs 45 to 50 minutes, or until they are crisp and brown all over.

While the cream puffs are baking, sauté the mushroom caps quickly in the butter and lemon juice. Grill the bacon until it is crisp, and drain on paper towels. When the cream puffs are almost done, scramble the eggs in butter as directed on page 180. Cut the finished cream puffs in half horizontally, and fill them completely with the scrambled eggs. Reshape them, allowing a little of the scrambled egg filling to show. Arrange them on a hot flat serving dish. Garnish the dish with the mushroom caps and grilled slices of bacon. Serve immediately. NET: 6 servings.

OEUFS BROUILLÉS AUGUSTE

Scrambled Eggs with Peas, Mushrooms, and Swiss Smoked Beef (hot)

This dish is made with the delicious Bündnerfleisch, the Swiss specialty from the canton of the Grisons. Today it is available in most gourmet shops that deal in imported meats. It is unique in flavor and texture.

4 cups shelled green peas, fresh or frozen
Salt
2 cups thinly sliced firm white mushrooms
4 tablespoons salt butter
2 teaspoons lemon juice
1 hard-boiled egg yolk
1 cup finely shredded imported

Swiss dried smoked beef (Bündnerfleisch)
8 tablespoons melted salt butter
Freshly cracked black pepper
6 eggs
2 tablespoons chopped fresh parsley
6 large fried croûtons (page 69)

Cook the peas in salted water until tender. Drain and keep them warm. Sauté the mushrooms in the butter and lemon juice. Rub the egg yolk through a coarse strainer. Put the peas, mushrooms, smoked beef, and melted butter in a bowl, season with a little salt and pepper, and mix lightly together. Butter an oval au gratin dish. Put the pea mixture down one side of the dish and keep it warm. Scramble the eggs in butter (page 180) and fill the other side of the dish with them. Sprinkle them with the parsley and sprinkle the pea mixture with the egg yolk. Stick the fried croûtons around the sides of the dish and serve immediately. NET: 6 servings.

OEUFS BROUILLÉS CRESSFIELD

Scrambled Egg and Crab Meat Croûton Sandwich (hot)

½ cup heavy cream
4 tablespoons melted salt butter
1½ cups crab meat, flaked
Salt
A few grains cayenne pepper
6 eggs, scrambled (page 180)

12 large round croûtons of bread (4 to 5 inches diameter), fried in butter (page 69)
1 tablespoon chopped fresh chives

Put the heavy cream, melted butter, and crab meat into a sauté pan. Season with salt and cayenne pepper. Stir the mixture over very low heat until it is warmed. (Be very careful not to cook it too much, or the crab meat will become hard and tough.) Mix the crab meat mixture into the scrambled eggs. Arrange 6 of the fried croûtons on a hot flat serving dish. Cover each croûton with the egg and crab meat mixture. Top with another piece of fried bread, like a round sandwich. Sprinkle each serving with chopped fresh chives and serve at once, very hot. NET: 6 servings.

OEUFS BROUILLÉS AUX CREVETTES

Molded Scrambled Eggs with Shrimps, Tomato Sauce (hot)

6 eggs, scrambled (page 180)
2 raw eggs, beaten
1 cup shelled boiled shrimps,

finely sliced
4 tablespoons melted sweet butter

1 tablespoon chopped fresh
   chives

TOMATO SAUCE
4 tablespoons salt butter
2 tablespoons all-purpose flour
½ teaspoon finely chopped
   garlic

3 tablespoons tomato paste
Salt
Freshly cracked white pepper
1½ cups chicken stock
   (page 35)
1 large very ripe tomato,
   skinned, quartered, seeded,
   and shredded

Generously butter 8 dariole molds (small oval-shaped metal molds). Preheat the oven to 350°. Combine the scrambled eggs in a bowl with the shrimps and raw eggs. Mix together quite well. Put the melted sweet butter and chopped chives in a heavy sauté pan. Add the egg mixture and scramble very lightly. Fill the molds with the scrambled egg mixture. Set the filled molds in a shallow roasting pan and pour warm water around them about ½ inch deep. Cover them with a sheet of buttered wax paper. Put the pan in the oven, and bake the molds 15 minutes.

TOMATO SAUCE. Melt 2 tablespoons butter in a saucepan. Off the heat, stir in the flour, tomato paste, and chopped garlic. Season with salt and pepper and add the chicken stock. Stir the sauce over low heat until it comes to a boil. Bit by bit stir in the rest of the butter, and gently simmer the sauce 5 minutes. During the last minute of cooking, add the shredded tomato.

When the eggs are set, remove them from the oven. Slide a small sharp knife blade around the inside edge of each mold to loosen it. Turn the molds out onto a hot flat serving dish. Spoon the tomato sauce around the molds (not over them) on the bottom of the dish. Serve immediately. NET: 4 servings (2 molds per person).

6 large artichoke bottoms
   (canned)
½ cup chicken stock (page 35)
3 firm white mushrooms, thinly
   sliced and sautéed quickly in
   2 tablespoons butter and 1
   teaspoon lemon juice
½ cup freshly grated Gruyère
   cheese
4 tablespoons melted salt butter
6 eggs, scrambled (page 180)
¼ cup freshly grated Parmesan

cheese

BROWN SAUCE
2 tablespoons salt butter
2 teaspoons potato flour
2 teaspoons meat glaze
1 teaspoon tomato paste
½ cup dry red wine
½ cup Madeira wine
Freshly cracked white pepper
½ cup chicken stock (reserved)

Artichoke Bottoms
Filled with Scrambled
Eggs, Cheese,
Mushrooms (hot)

Put the artichoke bottoms in a small pan with the chicken stock and warm them a little over low heat. Drain them, reserving the chicken stock, and arrange them down a long flat serving dish. Have the scrambled eggs ready, and mix the mushrooms, Gruyère cheese, and 2 tablespoons melted butter into them. Pile the egg mixture into the artichoke bottoms, mounding the tops. Sprinkle with the Parmesan cheese. Sprinkle the rest of the melted butter over them.

BROWN SAUCE. Melt the butter in a saucepan. Off the heat, stir in the potato flour, meat glaze, and tomato paste. Add the dry red wine, Madeira, and the reserved chicken stock. Return the pan to low heat and stir until the sauce comes to a boil. Season with a little pepper and simmer 5 minutes.

Brown the filled artichoke bottoms quickly under the broiler. Pour the brown sauce around them. Serve at once. NET: 6 servings.

OEUFS BROUILLÉS MALTAISE

Orange Scrambled Eggs with Orange Sections and Orange Croûtons (hot)

2 navel oranges
4 eggs
2 tablespoons heavy cream
Salt
A few grains cayenne pepper

1 teaspoon tomato paste
2 tablespoons dry sherry
5 tablespoons salt butter
2 slices dry white bread
1 tablespoon fresh orange juice

Peel the rind from 1 orange with a potato parer and cut it into fine shreds. Put it in a little pan, cover with cold water, bring to a boil, and drain. Set the blanched rind aside. Cut both oranges into neat sections. Make sure that all membranes and white parts are removed. Put the eggs in a mixing bowl and beat them with a rotary beater. Add the heavy cream, season with salt and cayenne pepper, and beat again. With a wire whisk, mix in the tomato paste, sherry, and blanched shredded orange rind. Melt 3 tablespoons butter in a heavy sauté pan. Add the egg mixture and stir it slowly over low heat until it is thick and creamy (scrambled). Transfer it to a hot serving dish.

Trim the crusts from the bread. Cut the slices into 4 squares each (2 for each person). Melt 2 tablespoons butter in a little pan. Add the orange juice. Sauté the squares of bread briskly until they are brown and sticky on both sides. Arrange the sticky squares of orange croûtons at one end of the serving dish. Warm the orange sections in a little pan and place them on the other end of the dish. Serve at once. NET: 4 servings.

OEUFS BROUILLÉS MARIETTE

Eggs Scrambled with Fresh Tomatoes and Shrimps (hot)

4 eggs
Salt
Freshly cracked white pepper
2 tablespoons heavy cream
4 tablespoons salt butter
1 small white onion, chopped
1 firm white mushroom, sliced
½ cup shelled boiled shrimps,

sliced
2 firm ripe tomatoes, skinned and sliced
4 slices sturdy white bread (no crusts), toasted and brushed with melted butter
2 tablespoons freshly grated Parmesan cheese

Break the eggs into a bowl and mix them with a little salt and pepper and the heavy cream. Melt the butter in a heavy sauté pan. When it is foaming, add the onion and mushrooms. Cook 4 minutes over low heat. Add the shrimps and tomatoes and shake the pan over moderate heat 2 minutes. Then add the egg mixture, and stir it slowly over low heat with a metal or wooden spoon until it is thick and creamy. Arrange the buttered toast on a hot platter. Spoon the egg mixture on them and sprinkle with the grated cheese. Serve at once. NET: 4 servings.

OEUFS BROUILLÉS TURBIGO

Mushroom, Lamb Kidney, and Scrambled Eggs in Individual Brioches (hot)

6 small brioches, homemade
   (page 708) or commercial
2 tablespoons melted salt butter
6 lamb kidneys
2 tablespoons solid salt butter
½ teaspoon finely chopped
   garlic
¼ cup finely chopped shallots
Salt
Freshly cracked white pepper
6 firm white fresh mushroom
   caps
1 teaspoon tomato paste

1 teaspoon meat glaze
2 teaspoons potato flour
1 cup dry red wine (preferably
   Burgundy)
½ cup chicken stock (page 35)
6 eggs, scrambled (and covered
   to keep them moist)
   (page 180)
Salt
Freshly cracked white pepper
2 tablespoons chopped fresh
   parsley

Preheat the oven to 350°. Remove the caps from the brioches and scoop out all the soft insides (reserve the brioche tops). Pour 1 teaspoon of melted butter in the bottom of each brioche shell. Wrap each shell in aluminum foil and heat them in the oven 5 minutes.

Skin the lamb kidneys. Split them down the middle and remove the white cores. Heat 2 tablespoons butter in a sauté pan. When it is foaming, add the garlic and shallots. Brown the kidneys on both sides in the pan, then remove them, sprinkle with salt and pepper, and set aside. Brown the mushroom caps quickly in the same butter and set aside. Remove the pan from the heat and stir in the tomato paste, meat glaze, and potato flour. Add the red wine and chicken stock. Return the pan to low heat and stir until the sauce comes to a boil. Simmer 5 minutes.

Remove the brioches from the oven and take them out of the foil wraps. Place a mushroom cap in the bottom of each brioche, bottom side up, so that it will serve as a saucer. Place a lamb kidney in the hollow of each mushroom. Spoon the scrambled eggs on the kidneys, filling the brioches to the top. Put the brioche tops back on them. Arrange the filled brioches on a hot serving dish. Just before serving, spoon the sauce over them and sprinkle them with the parsley. NET: 6 servings.

OEUFS EN COCOTTE LORRAINE

Eggs with Bacon, Cheese, and Cream (hot)

3 slices raw bacon
3 thin 6-inch slices Gruyère
   cheese, cut in half
¾ cup heavy cream

6 eggs
Salt
Freshly cracked white pepper

Preheat the oven to 350°. Cut the bacon into very fine shreds crosswise and fry it until crisp. Drain and dry on a paper towel. Have ready 6 individual ramekins or cocottes and a large shallow pan of hot water about ½ inch deep. (See Oeufs en Cocotte, page 180.) Put a little of the bacon on the bottom of each ramekin (reserve about half the bacon). Then line each dish with a half-slice of Gruyère cheese, put 1 tablespoon heavy cream on the cheese, and break 1 egg on the heavy cream. Pour another tablespoon of heavy cream on the egg. Sprinkle with salt and a little freshly cracked pepper.

Set the ramekins in the pan of hot water. Place the pan in the oven and bake the eggs 6 minutes, or until they are just set. Remove the ramekins from the oven and sprinkle the tops with the rest of the crisp bacon. Place each ramekin on a folded napkin on a serving plate and serve at once. NET: 6 servings.

OEUFS EN COCOTTE SAGAN

Eggs with Calf's Brains (hot)

2 pairs calf's brains
A little lemon juice (½ lemon)
1 cup chicken stock (page 35)
½ cup heavy cream
4 tablespoons melted salt butter
Salt
Freshly cracked black pepper
6 eggs
¼ cup freshly grated Parmesan cheese

First prepare the calf's brains for cooking. Soak them in ice water and a little lemon juice about 30 minutes. Drain them and remove all the skin, using a small paring knife. Pat them dry with a paper towel.

Preheat the oven to 350°. Put the skinned calf's brains in a little pan and cover with the chicken stock. Simmer over low heat 10 minutes. Drain, and chill them a few minutes in the refrigerator. Cut them into ½-inch cubes, mix with ¼ cup heavy cream and 2 tablespoons melted butter, and season with salt and pepper. Have ready 6 ramekins or cocottes and a shallow pan of hot water about ½ inch deep. (See Oeufs en Cocotte, page 180.) Fill each ramekin halfway with the calf's brains and break 1 fresh egg on top. Sprinkle with a little salt and pepper. Spoon the remaining heavy cream over the egg and sprinkle with a little grated Parmesan cheese and melted butter. Set the ramekins in the water bath and bake 6 minutes. Remove from the oven. Place each hot ramekin on a folded napkin on a plate. Serve at once. NET: 6 servings.

OEUFS EN TIMBALE CARDINAL

Eggs in Timbales with Lobster Coral and Lobster Sauce (hot)

This dish is a classic in French cuisine. It offers one of the favorite delicacies, the coral of the lobster, in one of the most delicate methods of cooking, in a water bath in the oven. If you happen to have spent a dear sum for lobsters for another dish and another meal, this dish can be a dividend meal from the same lobster. Just save the coral and enough lobster meat for a half-cup chopped. The coral—the roe of the female lobster—turns bright red when cooked. Lobster liver, called tomalley, is also a delicacy and turns green when cooked. It is usually used to thicken a lobster sauce.

Butter for the molds
½ cup uncooked lobster coral
6 fresh eggs
Salt
A few grains cayenne pepper

LOBSTER SAUCE
4 tablespoons salt butter

2 tablespoons all-purpose flour
Salt
A few grains cayenne pepper
½ cup light cream
½ cup heavy cream
4 tablespoons Cognac or good
   brandy
½ cup chopped lobster meat

Preheat the oven to 350°. Generously butter 6 small timbale molds (darioles — oval metal molds). Chop the lobster coral very fine and use it to line the buttered molds. Break 1 egg into each coral-lined mold and sprinkle it with a little salt and cayenne pepper. Place the molds in a shallow roasting pan. Pour hot water about ¾ inch deep around the molds. Place the water bath with the molds in the oven and bake about 6 minutes (until the eggs are set).

LOBSTER SAUCE. Melt 2 tablespoons butter in a saucepan. Off the heat, stir in the flour and season with a little salt and cayenne pepper. Add the light cream and stir over low heat until the sauce comes to a boil. Then add the heavy cream, brandy, and chopped lobster meat. Stir in the remaining butter, bit by bit, and simmer the sauce very gently 2 to 3 minutes.

When the timbales are cooked, turn them out on a hot shallow serving dish. Pour the sauce around them (not over). Serve at once. NET: 6 servings.

THE OMELET
Savory and Dessert

A plain omelet is the most beautiful meal you can feed anybody. In less than ten minutes you can get a dinner together. Heat the pan, beat the eggs, and it shouldn't on the outside take you more than a minute and a half to cook and serve your omelet.

But to many, the omelet remains the enigma of the culinary art. Much has been written about *how* to make an omelet, but the question *"What* is an omelet?" seems to defy most food and cookbook scholars. My own brief definition is: An omelet should be layer upon layer of very light-textured cooked egg. The test of a good plain omelet is that it should seem to be melting in your mouth.

The omelet is a favorite subject for culinary rhetoric, advisements, and exhortations:

Escoffier: "There should be complete incorporation of the egg molecules . . . the whole mass should be smooth and soft . . . an omelet is really scrambled eggs enclosed in a coating of coagulated egg."

Larousse Gastronomique, where the omelet is not defined but is procedurally described from the ancient Roman "ova mellita," eggs beaten with honey according to Apicius in the third century *(De Re Coquinaria)*, to the basic plain omelet: "Beat 8 eggs in moderation. . . . Heat butter in a frying pan and add the eggs. Put on a high flame. Mix with a fork. Shake the eggs in the pan to ensure that the omelette is evenly cooked all over. Fold it over once and turn it upside down with one quick movement onto a warm dish."

Henri Pellaprat in *Modern French Culinary Art*, in an excellent synoptic description of how to make a basic omelet, defines the ultimate test: "The finished omelette must be soft and juicy inside."

André Simon and Robin Howe advise in *Dictionary of Gastronomy*: "For a good omelet, fresh eggs at room temperature are essential. Also important is a special heavy pan, reserved for the purpose, never washed but always rubbed with salt and oil after use." ("Room temperature" in England is much cooler than room temperature in America; hence our requirement that eggs be refrigerated in American recipes.)

Mrs. Beeton's *Book of Household Management* (1892) offers recipes for nine excellent omelets with the following instruction: "Stir the omelet with a spoon one way until the mixture thickens and becomes firm, and when the whole is set, fold the edges over, so that the omelet assumes an oval form; and when it is nicely brown on one side, and quite firm, it is done. To take off the rawness on the upper side, hold the pan before the fire for a minute or two and brown it with a salamander or hot shovel. Serve very expeditiously on a very hot dish, and never cook it until it is just wanted." (Mrs. Beeton's last sentence should precede every omelet recipe, even today.)

Brillat-Savarin in his classic *Physiology of Taste* reported on the curé's omelet for Madame Récamier: "Madame Récamier took care to praise its size, its roundness, and its form; from all these indications, it was unanimously concluded that it must have been excellent."

Brillat-Savarin remarked that for an omelet to be excellent it should never be made with less than twelve eggs. That was in the good old days when ranges were as large as houses and men had appetites to correspond — to say nothing of the fine biceps of the French chefs of those times. For this day and age I would say that not more than four eggs should be used; in other words, corresponding both to the size of the omelet pan and the range and the capacity of the person cooking it. It is always better to make individual omelets, as they are more certain to be perfect.

Hugo Ziemann and Mrs. F. L. Gillette expound omelets thoroughly in *The White House Cook Book* (1901). Hugo Ziemann was "then steward of the White House and his credits include being caterer for that Prince Napoleon who was killed while fighting the Zulus in Africa. He was afterward steward of the famous Hotel Splendide in

Paris. Later he conducted the celebrated Brunswick Café in New York, and still later he gave to the Hotel Richelieu, in Chicago, a cuisine which won the applause of even the gourmets of foreign lands. It was here that he laid the famous 'spread' to which the chiefs of the warring factions of the Republican Convention sat down in June 1888, and from which they arose with asperities softened, differences harmonized, and victory organized." (A replay of Talleyrand's ploy at the Congress of Vienna?)

On omelets in the White House, 1901: "Put a smooth, clean, iron frying pan on the fire to heat, meanwhile, beat four eggs very light, the whites to a stiff froth, and the yolks to a thick batter. Add to the yolks four tablespoonfuls of milk, pepper, and salt; and lastly, stir in the whites lightly. Put a piece of butter nearly half the size of an egg into the heated pan; turn it so that it will moisten the entire bottom, taking care that it does not scorch. Just as it begins to boil, pour in the eggs. Hold the frying pan handle in your left hand, and, as the eggs whiten, carefully, with a spoon, draw up lightly from the bottom, letting the raw part run out on the pan, till all be equally cooked; shake with your left hand, till the omelet be free from the pan, then turn with a spoon one half of the omelet over the other; let it remain a moment, but continue shaking, lest it adhere; toss to a warm platter held in the right hand, or lift with a flat, broad shovel; the omelet will be firm around the edge, but creamy and light inside."

For two hundred years writers and experts have beseeched cooks not to overcook omelets. Speaking for the modern school:

James Beard: "The French omelet should still be moist and soft on top when you roll it out of the pan. It will finish cooking with its own heat. A true French omelet is never flat or firm, but always soft."

Nicholas Roosevelt in *Creative Cooking:* "Omelet making will be easier if you have a clear idea of how a French omelet should look. The outside should be firm, but scarcely browned at all. The inside should be as soft as underdone scrambled eggs."

Mr. Roosevelt is one of the finest rhetoricians on food. I like "The best omelets are cooked in pans which are sacred to the omelet art." Indeed! Also, "After ten years' experience I still have trouble transferring an omelet from the pan to the serving dish without breaking it. But one should be comforted by the fact that it will taste just as good if it is not in its perfect and pristine shape. It goes without saying that omelets should be eaten immediately. Few egg dishes lose their charm more quickly when kept waiting."

Gerald Maurois in *Cooking with a French Touch* admonishes: "Never brown an omelet. It should, on the under side, be only faintly golden. Never overcook an omelet. And never cook it even one second in advance. Make your guests wait for the omelet."

Fernande Garvin in the little book *The Art of French Cooking* speaks of the real, authentic, classic omelet: "French omelets are famous for their smoothness and lightness. This is because the eggs are cooked very quickly and remain moist, as they should. Once the butter is hot, it takes not more than two minutes to make the omelet itself. . . .

There is in every French household an 'omelet skillet,' used only for that purpose."

My specialty is the omelet, which I make in a pan which has not been used for anything else in the forty years I have owned it. I have often been asked and interviewed about how this came to pass. My good friend Clementine Paddleford, one of the great food editors of this era, described the case rather well in the New York *Herald–Tribune* in 1961:

"Duck eggs, four dozen hand-blown duck eggs in a basket, hang by invisible wires in a sparkling plate glass window at 222 East 59th Street. In this busy block of little shops you might mistake the place for an egg and butter store. But look again. See that omelet bar? See the shop with copper cooking wares tucked into a corner? Beyond is a restaurant white and orange.

"Behind the omelet bar is Dione Lucas, who over the years has turned a parade of hundreds of thousands of eggs into omelets. There she is looking as trim and lovely as eighteen years ago when she opened her first Cordon Bleu Restaurant and cooking school on East 60th Street. . . . She is the gal who totes her omelet pan along in her suitcase wherever she goes.

"Dione and the egg have been friends for a quarter of a century. It was before the Second World War when Dione and Rosemary Hume had their first little restaurant in London featuring the omelet as the pièce de résistance, mainly because they had neither room nor equipment to prepare anything else. That was the real beginning. Omelets made the restaurant famous. There were omelets superb, served in many ways — plain, fines herbes, watercress with sour cream topping, onion, cheese, mushroom, ham, chicken liver, red caviar with sour cream — Dione serves the same omelets today."

When I first came to America from London during the Blitz with my two babies, I opened a small restaurant. Actually it was an omelet bar and cooking school. I chose this type of restaurant because it was very economical to open and to operate. We had only to break as many eggs as the customers ordered each day. And no one had ever had a restaurant here that specialized in omelets at that time. As in London, my first restaurant in America was called Au Petit Cordon Bleu. I also used to do omelet parties on order. An omelet bar would be set up and the guests would order the kind of omelet they wanted. The omelet was very well received, and thus it became my symbol.

Here is my basic omelet lesson as it has been taught to thousands of people who attended my classes, demonstrated on television and in group presentations around the world, and featured many times in magazines and newspapers. Before the actual recipe I always give a brief description of the basic requirements and procedures for making an omelet, so as not to confuse the nonprofessional chef with what may seem like more don't's than do's. The basic instructions serve as a check list of important factors, just in case there may be a problem after the first few trials.

The best way to learn to make an omelet is to make one — just dive in and do it. My teacher at l'Ecole du Cordon Bleu, M. Pellaprat, once told me, "After you make two thousand omelets, you might make a perfect one." This was his way of encouraging and inspiring his students, and I pass it on to you. Even with little mistakes, an omelet is a superb meal, and more so, if you made it!

Equipment

(1) THE OMELET PAN. You must have a pan you use only for omelets. It should be of very heavy cast aluminum or castiron. Never use a stainless steel, glass, or enameled pan, as the metal must be porous. The pan must have rounded sloping shoulders so that when you tilt it the egg mixture will slide easily from side to side when stirred. The best omelet pan on the market, which I recommend, measures 7 inches across the bottom, 10½ inches across the top, has a 9-inch heat-resistant handle, and is made of ¼-inch heavy aluminum. In this pan you can make a 1-, 2-, 3-, or 4-egg omelet very easily. Do not try to make a larger omelet in this pan; it would be too thick to cook through without toughening the bottom. If you want to make a larger omelet, for example up to 6 or 8 eggs, use a 12-inch pan; but do not try any omelet larger than this because you cannot make a really good omelet if it is too large.

Season a new omelet pan in the following manner: (a) Rub it thoroughly with steel wool. (b) Clean it well with vegetable oil. (c) Fill it to the top with vegetable oil, slowly heat the oil in the pan, and let it stand 48 hours at room temperature. (d) Pour off the oil (you can pour it back into the bottle) and rub the pan thoroughly with paper towels. (e) Put the pan over moderate heat and get it very hot for a few minutes. The omelet pan is now ready to cook omelets.

Care for the omelet pan properly, and it will improve with use and become the most precious piece of equipment in your kitchen. (a) Keep it extremely clean, but never wash it — water or any other liquid should never touch the omelet pan. Wipe it out after each use with vegetable oil. In the rare and unhappy event that an omelet sticks and the pan has to be cleaned, heat it gently first and then rub it out with plain fine steel wool. Use a clean cloth and vegetable oil to wipe off any steel wool that may be left there. (b) Never use the omelet pan for any other purpose except making of crêpes. When it is not being used for omelets or crêpes, it should always be left a little greasy with butter or wiped out with vegetable oil, wrapped in a plastic bag or in aluminum foil, and kept in a cool place. (c) The omelet pan must always be heated slowly, with nothing in it — heat it before the butter goes in.

(2) THE FORK. A four-tine dinner fork is the very best implement for making an omelet.

(3) OTHER EQUIPMENT. You need a bowl to beat the eggs in, a small

wire whisk for beating them (and, for sweet omelets a larger whisk, rotary beater or mixer), a small oval platter on which to turn out the omelet, either tin-lined copper or stainless steel, and plenty of paper towels by your side.

Ingredients

The eggs should be very fresh and refrigerated. (For an omelet you want a fresher egg than almost any other way of cooking — you can taste it more readily there. And not ever at room temperature, always refrigerated is the best rule — they are better for anything, cooking or eating. Eggs should be kept at a cool temperature as much as possible.)

The butter must be salt butter. The only other ingredients you need are a little cold water, salt, melted sweet butter (or for dessert omelets confectioners sugar), and freshly cracked pepper (or for dessert omelets superfine sugar).

Technique

Technique is outlined step by step in the two basic omelet recipes below (Basic Savory Omelet and Basic Dessert Omelet). Be sure to read the recipe through first, so that everything will be ready when you start.

OMELETTE NATURE

Basic Savory Omelet

The basic 3-egg savory omelet is for 1 serving.

BASIC SAVORY OMELET MIXTURE	ALSO
3 fresh eggs, refrigerator cool	*1 tablespoon salt butter*
1 teaspoon cold water	*A little melted sweet butter*
¼ teaspoon salt	*Freshly cracked white pepper*

(1) Heat the omelet pan. The pan should heat slowly over low to moderate heat. (You must not do this quickly; it would ruin the pan. This is important!) For savory omelets you want the pan hot enough so that a speck of butter dropped in the pan, as a test, will sizzle without browning. This is a key checkpoint.

(2) Break 3 eggs in a bowl. Add 1 teaspoon cold water and ¼ teaspoon salt. Beat the mixture with a wire whisk until very well mixed but not too frothy. The whites should be well blended with the yolks. (No pepper should be added until after the omelet is made.)

(3) Pour the egg mixture through a fine wire strainer into another bowl (to strain out the white cord). Wipe out the test butter with a dry paper towel. If the pan is at the correct temperature, proceed to make the omelet. If the pan is too hot, it must cool a bit and heat *slowly* again until it tests correctly.

(4) Proceed to make the omelet. Put 1 tablespoon salt butter in the

pan. Slide it around to coat the entire bottom. Add the strained egg mixture.

(5) Immediately begin to stir the egg mixture in circular motions with the flat of the fork in your right hand. At the same time, shake the pan briskly back and forth with your left hand. These two actions must be concurrent. (It's a good idea to practice this motion with your hands in the air in front of you, at waist level, moving your right hand in a circle at the same time you move your left hand straight back and forth. This may help to ingrain the coordination of "the omelet exercise."

(6) When you first put the egg mixture in the omelet pan, stir the eggs with the flat of the fork touching the bottom of the pan, moving the eggs all over the pan and away from the sides.

(7) When the eggs begin to set (like a custard firming), lift your fork and stir them only on the surface, always in circular motions. Spread out the mixture so that no holes are left on the bottom of the pan. (The result is not altogether unlike scrambled eggs, except that you are using mainly horizontal circular motions instead of turning motions. The aim is to achieve creamy layers of lightly set egg.)

(8) Let the omelet set for 1 second; then slide the tines of the fork all around the edge of the pan.

(9) Have a hot flat serving dish waiting at the side of the stove as you prepare to turn out the omelet. With your left hand, raise the handle of the omelet pan to tilt it. Give the pan a quick gentle knock on its side to loosen the omelet. Holding the tilted pan firmly, fold the omelet over on itself, with the side edge of the fork, tucking in the sides. Swiftly roll the folded omelet over and onto the serving dish. (The best way is to drop the fork, hold the dish (with a holder if it is very hot) near the lower edge of pan, and tip the two together.)

(10) Brush the omelet after it is on the serving dish with a little melted sweet butter and sprinkle it with a little freshly cracked pepper. (Never put pepper in the egg mixture; it discolors the eggs and does not give a good flavor. Pepper should always be freshly cracked, as close as possible to the moment of eating. Serve at once.

These ten steps comprise the whole basic procedure. The omelet should appear on the serving dish in the shape of a neat plump oval, with an even yellow surface. A perfect omelet should never have any brown marks on it. The whole cooking performance should take no more than 2 minutes; ideally it should be 1 to 1½ minutes, unless a filling is being added. (The world's record is 35 seconds.) Great care should be taken not to overcook the omelet. The correct serving dishes for savory omelets are small white porcelain oval baking dishes, or tin-lined copper or stainless steel. They can be thoroughly preheated in a warm oven to receive the omelet from the omelet pan. NET: 1 serving.

TO PREPARE TWO OR MORE OMELETS. Multiply the quantities in the Basic Savory Omelet Mixture by the number of omelets you wish to prepare. Prepare the whole amount of mixture at once and have it ready in a large bowl near the omelet pan. Use a ladle to put the proportionate amount of egg into the omelet pan, as you prepare the omelets one by one.

When preparing two or more omelets, it is impossible to keep them warm until all the omelets are prepared. They must be made and eaten as they are turned out of the pan.

FILLINGS AND GARNISHES. The list is endless and you will invent more. The instructions for adding fillings and garnishes to omelets are given with each specific omelet recipe because the method varies.

OMELETTE SOUFFLÉE

Basic Dessert Omelet (Soufflé Omelet)

The minimum basic dessert omelet recipe is for 2 servings. It is rather impossible and unlikely to prepare it for one.

BASIC DESSERT OMELET MIXTURE	ALSO
3 fresh eggs, refrigerator-cool and separated	1 tablespoon salt butter
	A little confectioners sugar
2 teaspoons superfine sugar	A metal skewer, heated red hot
1/8 teaspoon salt	

(1) Heat the omelet pan slowly over low to moderate heat, gradually raising the heat until a speck of butter dropped in the pan instantly turns brown (but not black). (The pan for a dessert omelet is hotter than for a savory omelet.) At the same time heat the broiler.

(2) Put the egg yolks, superfine sugar, and salt in a bowl and beat with a small wire whisk until the yolks are light and fluffy.

(3) Beat the egg whites to soft peaks, either in a copper beating bowl with a large wire whisk, in the electric mixer, or with a rotary beater.

(4) With a rubber scraper, carefully fold the beaten yolk mixture into the beaten whites.

(5) Wipe out the test butter with a dry paper towel. If the pan is at the correct temperature, proceed to make the omelet. If it is too hot (the butter turning black), the pan must cool a little and be retested.

(6) Proceed to make the omelet. Put the salt butter in the omelet pan. Spread it around the pan with a wad of paper towel. Immediately put the Basic Dessert Omelet Mixture in the pan and spread it with the fork to completely cover the pan.

(7) Stir only with the back of the fork and stir only the surface of the egg mixture. Do not let the fork touch the bottom of the pan, ever.

(8) Run the tines of the fork around the sides of the pan and when the bottom of the omelet appears golden brown and the top is the consistency of Sabayon Sauce, put the omelet under the broiler a minute or two to set the top.

(9) At this point you would add the filling, if one is to be included. The filling is put down the center of the omelet.

(10) Fold the omelet, using the fork. Slide it onto a hot flat metal serving platter.

(11) To serve the basic dessert omelet, dust the top heavily with confectioners sugar. Have ready a metal skewer heated red hot. Use it to make a large X on the sugar-sprinkled omelet. (When the dessert omelet is garnished or filled, the skewer singe is omitted.) To serve, use a large serving fork and spatula to divide into two servings. NET: 2 servings.

FILLINGS AND GARNISHES. Dessert omelets are usually filled or garnished with fruit. Frequently they are flamed with brandy, rum, or liqueurs.

OMELETTE À L'ARLÉSIENNE

Eggplant and Tomato Omelet

Basic Savory Omelet Mixture
  (for 1 omelet: 3 eggs, 1
  teaspoon cold water, ¼
  teaspoon salt)
1 tablespoon salt butter

FILLING FOR 4 OMELETS (the
  minimum quantity to cook
  properly)
1 very small eggplant

Salt
3 tablespoons vegetable oil
2 large ripe tomatoes, skinned
  and cut into ½-inch slices
1 tablespoon salt butter
½ teaspoon finely chopped
  garlic
Freshly cracked white pepper
1 teaspoon chopped fresh
  parsley

First prepare the filling. Slice the eggplant, leaving the skin on, and cut it into small dice. Spread it out on a platter, sprinkle generously with salt, and let it sit 30 minutes. Drain, rinse in cold clear water, and dry on paper towels.

Heat the vegetable oil in a sautè pan. Add the diced eggplant and cook briskly until it is golden brown. Remove the eggplant from the pan and put the butter into the pan. When it is foaming, add the tomatoes and garlic. Season with a little salt and pepper and cook briskly 2 minutes. Return the eggplant to the pan and mix with the tomatoes. Adjust the seasoning.

Prepare the Basic Savory Omelet Mixture according to the Basic Savory Omelet procedure (page 210). (Increase the quantities by the number of omelets you wish to serve). Have both the egg mixture and the eggplant mixture ready in separate bowls. Reserve about a fourth of the eggplant mixture in a separate bowl to use for garnish.

Make the omelet according to the Basic Savory Omelet procedure (page 210). When you are ready to fold the omelet over, put a fourth of the eggplant mixture in the center of the omelet. Fold the omelet over and slide it from the pan onto the serving plate. Cut a little slit on top of the omelet. Spoon in some of the reserved filling. Sprinkle the top with a little pepper and the parsley. Serve at once. NET: 1 serving, with filling for 3 others.

OMELETTE BENEDICTE

Omelet with Ham, Croûtons, and Hollandaise Sauce

In a press interview, when I was in charge of food at The Ginger Man Restaurant in Lincoln Center in New York, the subject was eggs and I was asked for my version of Eggs Benedict, one of the most popular luncheon dishes in New York. To quote:

"Do you know what I've done? I don't serve Eggs Benedict. We couldn't be bothered with it. But we specialize in omelets, and we make a Benedict omelet, which is absolutely delicious. We put into the omelet tiny diced cooked ham (having first soaked it in sherry) and little croûtons of bread; then the omelet is turned out, Hollandaise is poured over it, and it's browned under the broiler. It is very popular."

"I've never even heard of that before."

"I know, because I invented it. Everybody was asking for Eggs Benedict, and I just wasn't going to make it because you can get Eggs Benedict everywhere. But we have a new version, and it's been a resounding success."

"That's most unusual, Hollandaise *on* an omelet?"

"Not at all, because in France there are several omelets coated with Hollandaise, but I don't think that it has been done anywhere here, and it's really delicious!"

Basic Savory Omelet Mixture
  (for 1 omelet: 3 eggs, 1
  teaspoon cold water, ¼
  teaspoon salt)
1 tablespoon salt butter

FILLING FOR 1 OMELET
½ cup finely diced lean boiled
  ham
½ cup tiny fried croûtons (page
  70)

½ teaspoon salt butter

HOLLANDAISE SAUCE (*Generous
  for 1 omelet; ample for 2*)
2 egg yolks
¼ teaspoon salt
A few grains cayenne pepper
1 tablespoon tarragon vinegar
2 tablespoons heavy cream
8 tablespoons frozen sweet
  butter

First prepare the Hollandaise sauce. With a wire whisk, mix the egg yolks, salt, cayenne pepper, and tarragon vinegar in a small bowl until they are well blended. Mix in the heavy cream. Stand the bowl in a shallow pan of hot water over low heat. Beat the yolk mixture until it thickens. Cut the frozen sweet butter into little pieces, and add it, bit by bit, to the sauce, stirring all the while. Cover the sauce with a piece of plastic wrap and keep it warm.

Next, prepare the filling. Melt the butter in a small sauté pan, add the diced ham, and sauté briskly a few minutes. Add it to the croûtons and set the mixture aside.

Now prepare the Basic Savory Omelet Mixture according to the Basic Savory Omelet procedure (page 210). Preheat the broiler very hot. Heat the omelet pan. Just before you are ready to cook the omelet, mix the ham and croûtons into the egg mixture. Prepare the omelet according to the Basic Savory Omelet procedure and turn it out onto a hot serving dish. Spoon half the prepared Hollandaise sauce over the prepared omelet and quickly brown it under a hot broiler. Serve at once. NET: 1 serving, with sauce for another.

This filling has long been a favorite dish as a vegetable, served with a meat, or sausages. With the omelet, it is a sublime meal in itself, with all the warmth and goodness of a country kitchen.

OMELETTE BONNE FEMME

The Good Woman's Omelet, with Potato, Bacon, and Onion

Basic Savory Omelet Mixture (for 1 omelet: 3 eggs, 1 teaspoon cold water, ¼ teaspoon salt)
1 tablespoon salt butter
A little melted sweet butter

FILLING FOR 4 OMELETS (*the minimum quantity to cook properly*)
1 tablespoon salt butter
½ pound sliced bacon, cut crosswise into ½ inch shreds
2 medium-size yellow onions, sliced
2 small raw Idaho-type

potatoes, peeled, halved, and sliced ¼ inch thick
½ teaspoon salt
½ teaspoon freshly cracked white pepper
2 teaspoons chopped fresh parsley

GARNISH (OPTIONAL)
1 large yellow onion, cut in ½ inch slices
A little all-purpose flour (for dusting)
1 egg, beaten
¼ cup dry breadcrumbs
½ cup vegetable oil

First prepare the filling (if you do not need 4 omelets, the extra filling can be set aside for a lunch or snack). Have ready a deep heavy pan with a firm lid. Put the butter and shredded bacon in the pan. On the bacon put the onions, and on the onions the potatoes. Sprinkle the salt and pepper over the top. Cover the pan firmly with the lid. Cook over low heat 25 minutes; do not stir. When the filling is cooked, add the parsley, and mix it together with a wooden spoon.

Prepare the Basic Savory Omelet Mixture according to the Basic Savory Omelet procedure (page 210). (Increase the quantities by the number of omelets you plan to serve.) Then prepare the garnish. Separate the onion rings. Select 3 perfect ones for each omelet. Dust them lightly with flour, brush with beaten egg, and coat with dry breadcrumbs. Heat the vegetable oil very hot in a small pan. Put in 1 or 2 onion rings at a time and fry until they are golden brown, turning them over to cover both sides. Drain on paper towels and have them handy when you prepare the omelet.

Have both the egg mixture and the potato mixture ready in separate bowls. Prepare the omelet according to the Basic Savory Omelet procedure (page 210). When you are ready to fold the omelet over, put a fourth of the potato mixture in the center of the omelet. Fold the omelet over and slide it onto the hot serving plate. Brush the top with a little melted sweet butter and sprinkle with a little freshly cracked white pepper. Arrange 3 overlapping fried onion rings on the top of the omelet. Serve at once. NET: 1 serving, with filling for 3 others.

OMELETTE AU CAVIARE

Caviar Omelet

If you plan to serve caviar omelets as a first course, use only 2 eggs per person in the basic egg mixture.

Basic Savory Omelet Mixture
  (for 1 omelet: 3 eggs, 1
  teaspoon cold water, ¼
  teaspoon salt)
1 tablespoon salt butter
A little melted sweet butter

GARNISH
2 tablespoons black or red
  caviar

2 teaspoons finely chopped
  fresh parsley
2 teaspoons finely chopped
  white onion
2 tablespoons sour cream
2 teaspoons finely chopped
  hard-boiled egg white
2 teaspoons hard-boiled egg
  yolk, rubbed through a fine
  wire strainer

Prepare the Basic Savory Omelet Mixture according to the Basic Savory Omelet procedure (page 210). Cook the Basic Savory Omelet according to the same procedure and turn it out onto a hot serving dish. Brush the top of the omelet with melted sweet butter. Garnish as follows: At one side of the omelet put the caviar, between a little mound of chopped parsley and one of chopped white onion. At the other side of the omelet put the sour cream, between a little mound of chopped egg white and one of strained egg yolk. Serve at once. NET: 1 serving.

OMELETTE AUX CHAMPIGNONS

Mushroom Omelet

Basic Savory Omelet Mixture
  (for 1 omelet: 3 eggs, 1
  teaspoon cold water, ¼
  teaspoon salt)
1 tablespoon salt butter
A little melted sweet butter
Freshly cracked white pepper

FILLING
1 tablespoon salt butter
4 medium-size firm white
  mushrooms, thinly sliced
1 whole firm white mushroom
  cap, fluted if desired (for
  garnish)
1 teaspoon lemon juice
Salt
Freshly cracked white pepper

First prepare the mushroom filling. Heat the butter in a small sauté pan, add the whole cap and sliced mushrooms with the lemon juice, salt, and pepper, and cook briskly 3 minutes. Set the mushroom cap aside.

Prepare the Basic Savory Omelet Mixture according to the Basic Savory Omelet procedure (page 210). Just before you are ready to cook the omelet, mix the sautéed sliced mushrooms into the egg mixture. Cook the omelet according to the Basic Savory Omelet procedure and turn it out onto a hot serving dish. Brush the top with a little melted sweet butter, sprinkle with a little white pepper, and set the whole mushroom cap on the top. Serve at once. NET: 1 serving.

Basic Savory Omelet Mixture
    (for 1 omelet: 3 eggs, 1
    teaspoon cold water, ¼
    teaspoon salt)
1 tablespoon salt butter

FILLING
3 tablespoons salt butter
2 chicken livers
2 tablespoons Cognac or good
    brandy
2 firm white mushrooms, thinly

sliced.
½ teaspoon lemon juice
Salt
Freshly cracked white pepper
½ teaspoon tomato paste
½ teaspoon meat glaze
1 teaspoon potato flour
½ cup chicken stock (page 35)

GARNISH
2 teaspoons chopped fresh
    parsley, tarragon, or chives

OMELETTE CHASSEUR

Chicken Liver and Mushroom Omelet

First prepare the filling. Heat 1 tablespoon butter in a little pan and brown the chicken livers quickly. Heat the brandy in a separate little pan, ignite, and pour it over the livers. Remove the livers from the pan. Add 2 tablespoons butter to the pan in which they were browned. When it is foaming, add the mushrooms, lemon juice, salt, and pepper. Cook the mushrooms slowly 2 minutes. Remove the pan from the heat and stir in the tomato paste, meat glaze, and potato flour. Add the chicken stock and stir the mixture over low heat until it comes to a boil. Slice the chicken livers and put them in the pan with the mushrooms, with 1 teaspoon of the chopped fresh herbs.

Prepare the egg mixture according to the Basic Savory Omelet procedure (page 210). Have the egg mixture and chicken liver mixture ready in separate bowls. (Reserve about a fourth of the liver mixture in a separate little bowl for garnish.) Proceed to cook the omelet according to the Basic Savory Omelet procedure. Just before you are ready to fold it over, put the liver mixture in the center. Fold the omelet over and slide it onto the serving plate. Cut a little slit on top. Spoon in the reserved liver mixture and pour a little of the sauce around the omelet. Sprinkle over the top a little pepper and the rest of the chopped fresh herbs. Serve at once. NET: 1 serving.

Basic Savory Omelet Mixture
    (for 1 omelet: 3 eggs, 1
    teaspoon cold water, ¼
    teaspoon salt)
I tablespoon salt butter
A little melted sweet butter

1 sprig crisp fresh watercress
2 tablespoons sour cream

FILLING
½ cup fresh watercress leaves

OMELETTE AU CRESSON

Watercress Omelet

Prepare the Basic Savory Omelet Mixture according to the Basic Savory Omelet procedure (page 210). Just before you are ready to cook the omelet, stir the watercress leaves into the mixture. Cook the omelet according to the Basic Savory Omelet procedure and turn it out onto a hot serving dish. Brush the top with a little melted sweet butter and garnish with the sprig of watercress. Put the dollop of sour cream on the side of the omelet. Serve at once. NET: 1 serving.

OMELETTE AUX FINES HERBES

Omelet with Mixed Herbs

Basic Savory Omelet Mixture (for 1 omelet: 3 eggs, 1 teaspoon cold water, ¼ teaspoon salt
2 tablespoons salt butter
A little melted sweet butter
Freshly cracked white pepper

FILLING
1 teaspoon finely chopped shallot
⅛ teaspoon finely chopped garlic
2 tablespoons finely chopped parsley
2 teaspoons finely chopped fresh tarragon

For an Omelette aux Fines Herbes, always use a combination of two root herbs and two leaf herbs. Chop them fine, then chop them all together. The herbs listed are a sample — use green onions, chervil, chives, thyme, or whatever herbs you wish. When the chopped mixed herbs are ready, prepare the Basic Savory Omelet according to the procedure (page 210) up to the point of putting the butter in the pan. (For this omelet note that the butter is increased.) As soon as the butter is in the pan, immediately put in the chopped mixed herbs and instantly pour in the egg mixture. Stir the mixture with a fork and finish the omelet in the standard procedure. Brush the omelet with melted sweet butter, sprinkle with pepper, and serve at once. NET: 1 serving.

OMELETTE AU FOIE DE VOLAILLE

Chicken Liver Omelet

Basic Savory Omelet Mixture (for 1 omelet: 3 eggs, 1 teaspoon cold water, ¼ teaspoon salt)
1 tablespoon salt butter
Freshly cracked white pepper
1 teaspoon chopped fresh parsley

FILLING
3 chicken livers
1 teaspoon salt butter
2 tablespoons Cognac or good brandy
½ teaspoon tomato paste
½ teaspoon meat glaze
1 teaspoon potato flour
½ cup chicken stock (page 35)
2 tablespoons Madeira wine
¼ teaspoon red currant jelly

First prepare the filling. Heat the butter in a little pan and brown the chicken livers quickly. Heat 1 tablespoon brandy in a separate little pan, ignite, and pour it over the livers. Remove the livers from the pan. Add the other tablespoon of brandy to the pan. Off the heat, stir in the tomato paste, meat glaze, and potato flour. Mix in the chicken stock, Madeira, and currant jelly. Stir the sauce over low heat until it comes to a boil. Slice the chicken livers and put them back in the sauce. Simmer the sauce very gently 6 minutes.

Prepare the Basic Savory Omelet Mixture according to the Basic Savory Omelet procedure (page 210). Have both the egg mixture and liver mixture ready in separate bowls. Cook the Basic Savory Omelet according to the same procedure and turn it out onto the hot serving dish. Make an incision in the top and fill it with the chicken liver mixture. Spoon a little of the sauce around the omelet. Sprinkle the omelet with pepper and chopped parsley. Serve at once. NET: 1 serving.

Basic Savory Omelet Mixture
    (for 1 omelet: 3 eggs, 1
    teaspoon cold water, ¼
    teaspoon salt)
2 tablespoons salt butter
A little melted sweet butter
2 tablespoons sour cream

FILLING
¼ cup mixed finely chopped
    fresh parsley, tarragon,
    chives, a little shallot, and a
    speck of garlic
½ cup tiny croûtons fried in
    butter (page 70)

OMELETTE GRANDMÈRE

Omelet with Croûtons and Herbs

When you have assembled and chopped all of the herbs, mix them and chop them again, all together. Then mix them with the fried croûtons and have the mixture ready in a separate little bowl. Prepare the Basic Savory Omelet Mixture according to the Basic Savory Omelet procedure (page 210) and cook the omelet according to the same procedure up to the point of putting the butter in the omelet pan. (For this omelet note that the butter is increased.) As soon as the butter is in the pan, immediately put the mixed herbs and croûtons in the pan and instantly pour in the egg mixture. Stir the mixture with a fork and finish the omelet in the basic manner. Brush the top with the melted sweet butter and put a dollop of sour cream on the side. NET: 1 serving.

Basic Savory Omelet Mixture
    (for 1 omelet: 3 eggs, 1
    teaspoon cold water, ¼
    teaspoon salt)
1 tablespoon salt butter
A little melted sweet butter

Freshly cracked white pepper

FILLING
½ cup finely shredded sorrel
¼ cup heavy cream, whipped
A few grains cayenne pepper

OMELETTE À L'OSEILLE

Sorrel Omelet

Prepare the Basic Savory Omelet Mixture according to the Basic Savory Omelet procedure (page 210). Then mix the filling, and have it by your side in a little dish. Cook the omelet according to the Basic Savory Omelet procedure, but just before you are ready to fold it over, put the filling in the center, then fold the omelet over and slide it onto the serving plate. Brush the omelet with melted sweet butter, sprinkle with pepper, and serve at once. NET: 1 serving.

Basic Savory Omelet Mixture
    (for 1 omelet: 3 eggs, 1 tea-
    spoon cold water, ¼ teaspoon
    salt)

1 tablespoon salt butter
A little melted sweet butter
Freshly cracked white pepper

OMELETTE PARMENTIER

Potato Omelet

FILLING

1 small yellow onion, finely
  chopped

½ to ¾ cup thinly sliced cooked
  potatoes
1 tablespoon salt butter

Prepare the filling. Sauté the onion in the butter until it is light brown.
Add the potatoes and cook another 2 minutes. Prepare the Basic
Savory Omelet Mixture according to the Basic Savory Omelet procedure (page 210), and continue with that procedure, but as soon as
the butter is in the pan, immediately add the potato filling, then instantly pour in the egg mixture. Stir the potatoes and egg mixture
with a fork. Finish and serve the omelet in the basic manner. NET:
1 serving.

OMELETTE PRINCESSE

*Fresh Asparagus
Omelet*

Basic Savory Omelet Mixture
  (for 1 omelet: 3 eggs, 1 teaspoon cold water, ¼ teaspoon
  salt)
1 tablespoon salt butter

FILLING

1 cup cooked fresh asparagus
  tips
¼ cup cool melted clarified
  butter (page 56)
¼ cup freshly grated Parmesan
  cheese

Prepare the Basic Savory Omelet Mixture according to the Basic
Savory Omelet procedure (page 210). Just before you are ready to
cook the omelet, mix most of the asparagus tips into the egg mixture
(reserve a small group of perfect tips for garnish). Also add to the
egg mixture half the clarified butter and all the grated Parmesan
cheese. Cook the omelet according to the Basic Savory Omelet procedure and turn it out onto a hot serving dish. Decorate the top with
the reserved asparagus tips. Pour over the rest of the clarified butter.
Serve at once. NET: 1 serving.

OMELETTE AUX TRUFFES

Truffle Omelet

Basic Savory Omelet Mixture
  (for 1 omelet: 3 eggs, 1 teaspoon cold water, ¼ teaspoon
  salt)
1 tablespoon salt butter

FILLING

3 large truffles, black or white,
  thinly sliced
2 tablespoons Cognac
¼ cup cool melted clarified
  butter (page 56)

Slice the truffles very thin, sprinkle them with the Cognac and let
them marinate a little. Prepare the Basic Savory Omelet Mixture according to the Basic Savory Omelet procedure (page 210). Just before
you are ready to cook the omelet, mix the truffles with the Cognac
and half the clarified butter into the egg mixture. Cook the omelet
according to the Basic Savory Omelet procedure and turn it out onto
a hot serving dish. Pour the rest of the clarified butter over it. Serve
at once. NET: 1 serving.

Basic Savory Omelet Mixture
(for 1 omelet: 3 eggs, 1 teaspoon cold water, ¼ teaspoon
salt)
1 tablespoon salt butter
1 garlic clove, bruised
1 tablespoon chopped fresh
chives
2 teaspoons chopped fresh
tarragon

FILLING
3 firm white mushroom caps,
sliced
2 tablespoons salt butter
½ teaspoon lemon juice
3 artichoke bottoms, cut in thin
slices
Optional: 1 black truffle, sliced
Salt
Freshly cracked white pepper
¼ teaspoon meat glaze
4 tablespoons chicken stock
(page 35)

OMELETTE AUX ARTICHAUTS

Omelet with Artichoke Bottoms

First prepare the filling. Sauté the mushrooms in a little pan with 1 tablespoon butter and the lemon juice, salt, and pepper. Add to the pan the thinly sliced artichoke bottoms and the truffle (if you are using one). Season with salt and pepper. Mix the meat glaze with the chicken stock and add to the pan. Stir the mixture well over low heat, and allow it to simmer 3 to 4 minutes.

Rub the bowl in which you are going to beat the omelet eggs with the bruised clove of garlic. Prepare the Basic Savory Omelet Mixture according to the Basic Savory Omelet procedure (page 210), and proceed to cook the omelet according to the same procedure. When you are ready to fold it, spread the artichoke and mushroom mixture on top of the omelet in the pan, then fold and turn it out onto a hot serving dish. Sprinkle the chopped fresh chives and tarragon all over the top. Serve at once. NET: 1 serving.

Basic Savory Omelet Mixture
(for 1 omelet: 3 eggs, 1 teaspoon cold water, ¼ teaspoon
salt)
1 tablespoon salt butter

FILLING
¼ to ½ pound sliced raw bacon
(quantity depends on your
taste)

OMELETTE AU LARD

Bacon Omelet

Reserve 2 whole slices of bacon. Cut the rest into very thin shreds crosswise. Put them in a moderately hot sauté pan and cook slowly until very crisp, then strain and dry the crisp shreds on paper towels. Cook the reserved slices of bacon between two wire racks on a jelly roll pan in a hot oven until crisp. Remove and set aside on a paper towel.

Prepare the Basic Savory Omelet Mixture according to the Basic Savory Omelet procedure (page 210). Just before you are ready to cook the omelet, mix the shredded bacon into the egg mixture. Cook the omelet according to the Basic Savory Omelet procedure and turn it out onto a hot serving dish. Decorate the top with the bacon slices. Serve at once. NET: 1 serving.

PETITES OMELETTES AU CAVIARE

Six Little 1-Egg Caviar Omelets (an appetizer)

Basic Savory Omelet Mixture
(for 6 1-egg omelets: 6 eggs,
2 teaspoons cold water, ½ teaspoon salt)
2 tablespoons salt butter

GARNISH
⅓ cup black caviar, or ¾ cup
red caviar
A few drops lemon juice
1 cup thick sour cream
A few grains cayenne pepper

Preheat the oven to 225° (to use as a warming oven). Prepare the Basic Savory Omelet Mixture, using the quantities of ingredients as given above, according to the Basic Savory Omelet procedure (page 210). Then, following the Basic Savory Omelet procedure, make up 6 1-egg omelets without folding them over. Just cook them on each side quickly (like a fluffy fat pancake), without letting them brown. As you make them, place them on a wire rack on a jelly roll pan and set them in the oven, with the oven door open.

When all the little omelets have been made up, spread each one with a little caviar, sprinkle it with a little lemon juice, and fold it over. To serve, arrange the folded omelets down a hot serving dish. Put a dollop of sour cream on each omelet. Sprinkle a few grains of cayenne pepper on the cream. These little appetizer omelets should be served with well-chilled Vodka neat. NET: 6 1-egg omelets.

OMELETTE AU POULET

Chicken Omelet with Onion Cream Sauce

Basic Savory Omelet Mixture
(for 1 omelet: 3 eggs, 1 teaspoon cold water, ¼ teaspoon
salt)
1 tablespoon salt butter

FILLING
½ cup diced cooked white meat
of chicken
3 firm white mushroom caps,
sliced and sautéed in a little
butter
½ teaspoon potato flour
Salt
A few grains cayenne pepper
¼ cup chicken stock (page 35)
1 tablespoon heavy cream

1 tablespoon Cognac or good
brandy

SOUBISE SAUCE
2 tablespoons salt butter
½ tablespoon all-purpose flour
Salt
A few grains cayenne pepper
½ cup light cream
1 large yellow onion, thinly
sliced

GARNISH
2 tablespoons freshly grated
Parmesan cheese
¼ cup melted salt butter

First prepare the filling. In a small pan, combine the diced cooked chicken, sautéed mushrooms, salt, the cayenne pepper and potato flour, and blend well. Add the chicken stock and the heavy cream and simmer over low heat 1 to 2 minutes, then stir in the brandy. Set the mixture aside.

Next, prepare the Soubise sauce. In a little saucepan, melt 1 table-spoon butter. Off the heat, stir in the flour. Season with salt and cay-enne pepper and mix in the cream. Stir over low heat until the sauce comes to a boil. In a separate little pan, melt 1 tablespoon butter, add the onion, and cook it until it is mushy, but not brown. Purée the cooked onion and cream together in an electric blender.

Now prepare the Basic Savory Omelet Mixture according to the Basic Savory Omelet procedure (page 210). Preheat the broiler very hot. Cook the omelet according to the Basic Savory Omelet procedure, but just before you are ready to fold it, spread the diced chicken mixture on the omelet in the pan, then fold and turn it out onto a hot serving dish. Spoon the onion cream sauce over it. Sprinkle with the grated Parmesan cheese. Pour the melted butter over it and brown the omelet quickly under the hot broiler. Serve at once. NET: 1 serving.

This is a 4-egg omelet to serve 2 persons.

OMELETTE AUX ROGNONS D'AGNEAU

Omelet with Sautéed Lamb Kidneys and Sausages

4 eggs
1 teaspoon cold water
¼ teaspoon salt
1 tablespoon salt butter

GARNISH
3 lamb kidneys
2 tablespoons salt butter
4 firm white mushroom caps, sliced
2 drops lemon juice

Salt
Freshly cracked white pepper
½ teaspoon meat glaze
½ teaspoon tomato paste
1 teaspoon potato flour
½ cup chicken stock (page 35)
2 tablespoons dry sherry
4 cocktail sausages
1 teaspoon chopped fresh parsley

First prepare the garnish. Skin the lamb kidneys, cut them in half, and remove the core. Heat the butter in a small heavy sauté pan and put in the kidneys, cut side down. Brown them quickly on each side, remove, and set aside. Add the sliced mushrooms to the sauté pan with the lemon juice. Season with salt and pepper and sauté them briskly 2 to 3 minutes. Then stir in off the heat the meat glaze, tomato paste, and potato flour. When the paste is smooth, mix in the chicken stock and sherry. Stir over low heat until the mixture comes to a boil. Cut the kidneys and sausages into ½-inch slices and add them to the mushroom sauce in the pan. Simmer the whole mixture 1 to 2 minutes.

Mix and cook the omelet according to the Basic Savory Omelet procedure (page 210), but using 4 eggs. Turn it out onto a hot serving platter, cover it with the kidney mixture, and sprinkle the top with the chopped parsley. Serve at once. NET: 2 servings.

OMELETTE À L'OIGNON

Onion Omelet

Basic Savory Omelet Mixture (for 1 omelet: 3 eggs, 1 teaspoon cold water, ¼ teaspoon salt)
1 tablespoon salt butter

FILLING AND GARNISH
4 large yellow onions
2 tablespoons salt butter
Salt
Freshly cracked white pepper

A little all-purpose flour
1 egg, beaten
About ½ cup dry white bread-

crumbs (page 69)
Vegetable oil for deep-fryer

First prepare the onion filling and garnish. Cut the nicest onion into ¼-inch slices. Separate the slices and set aside 10 rings (of as even size as possible) for the garnish. Cut the rest of the onions into ½-inch slices. Heat the butter in a small sauté pan. Add all the onion to the pan except the 10 reserved rings. Season with salt and pepper, and sauté briskly until they are cooked and are a delicate golden brown. Set the pan aside. Dust the reserved onion rings all over in flour. Dip them in the beaten egg, then coat them in breadcrumbs. Heat the oil in the deep-fryer to 375° and fry the onion rings, one or two at a time. Remove them from the hot oil with a slotted spoon and drain them on paper towels.

Prepare and cook the omelet according to the Basic Savory Omelet procedure (page 210), but just before folding it, spread the sautéed onion mixture over the omelet in the pan. Fold the omelet over twice and turn it out onto a hot serving dish. Decorate the top with the deep-fried onion rings. NET: 1 serving.

PIPERADE

Basque Omelet
with Peppers, Onion,
Tomato

Basic Savory Omelet Mixture
  (for 2 omelets: 6 eggs, 2 teaspoons cold water, ½ teaspoon salt)
2 tablespoons salt butter

FILLING
3 small green peppers
2 sweet green (Italian) peppers
1 medium-size yellow onion,
  finely chopped
3 large tomatoes, skinned,

quartered, and seeded
½ teaspoon finely chopped
  garlic
Salt
Freshly cracked black pepper
3 tablespoons pure olive oil

GARNISH
2 snippets of toast per omelet
  (diagonal croûtons, page
  69)

First prepare the filling. Blanch all the peppers (put them in a pot, cover with cold water, bring slowly to a boil, drain, and plunge the peppers immediately into ice water). When they are chilled, cut them into quarters and remove the seeds; then cut them into very small shreds. Heat the olive oil in a sauté pan. Add the onion and shredded peppers. Cook over low heat until the onion begins to turn translucent, then add the seeded tomato sections and garlic. Season with salt and pepper and simmer briskly until the mixture is mushy. Have the snippets of toast prepared and ready.

Prepare and cook the omelets according to the Basic Savory Omelet procedure (page 210), mixing the quantity of ingredients given above but cooking the mixture one-half at a time. For each omelet, just before folding it, spread half the piperade mixture over the omelet in the pan, then fold the omelet over several times and turn it out onto a hot serving dish. Garnish on each side with a snippet of toast. Serve at once. NET: 2 servings.

Basic Savory Omelet Mixture
(for 2 omelets: 6 eggs, 2 teaspoons cold water, ½ tea-
spoon salt)
2 tablespoons salt butter

FILLING
6 ounces very thin slices
smoked salmon

BÉARNAISE SAUCE
2 egg yolks

1 tablespoon tarragon vinegar
Salt
A few grains cayenne pepper
2 tablespoons heavy cream
8 tablespoons frozen sweet
butter
1 tablespoon finely chopped
mixed herbs, including tarragon, parsley, thyme, and
shallots (if available)
2 drops lemon juice

OMELETTE AU SAUMON FUMÉ I

Smoked Salmon
Omelet I
(with Béarnaise Sauce)

First prepare the Béarnaise Sauce. Combine the egg yolks, vinegar, salt, and cayenne pepper in a small bowl and beat with a small whisk until well blended, then mix in the heavy cream. Stand the bowl in a shallow pan half full of hot water over low heat, and beat the yolk mixture until it thickens. Cut the frozen sweet butter into little pieces and add it, bit by bit, to the sauce, stirring all the while. Mix in the chopped herbs and lemon juice. Cover the sauce with a piece of plastic wrap and keep it warm.

Preheat the broiler very hot. Prepare and cook the omelets according to the Basic Savory Omelet procedure (page 210), mixing the quantity of ingredients above but cooking half at a time. Just before folding each omelet, spread half the smoked salmon on the omelet in the pan, then fold and turn the omelet out onto a hot serving dish. Spoon the Béarnaise Sauce over it and brown it quickly under the hot broiler. Serve at once. NET: 2 servings.

Basic Savory Omelet Mixture
(for 1 omelet: 3 eggs, 1
teaspoon cold water,
¼ teaspoon salt)
1 tablespoon salt butter

FILLING
3 thin slices smoked salmon

GARNISHES
1 tablespoon capers
2 tablespoons sour cream
A few grains cayenne pepper

ACCOMPANIMENT
Wafer-thin slices dark whole
wheat bread and sweet butter

OMELETTE AU SAUMON FUMÉ II

Smoked Salmon
Omelet II (with Sour
Cream and Capers)

Prepare and cook the omelet according to the Basic Savory Omelet procedure (page 210), but just before folding it, spread the smoked salmon on the omelet in the pan, then fold and turn the omelet out onto a hot serving dish. Sprinkle the top with the capers. On one side of the omelet put the sour cream and sprinkle it with the cayenne pepper. Serve immediately with a separate plate of the dark whole wheat bread and sweet butter. NET: 1 omelet.

OMELETTE D'ÉPINARDS

Spinach Omelet

Basic Savory Omelet Mixture (for 2 omelets: 6 eggs, 2 teaspoons cold water, ½ teaspoon salt)
2 tablespoons salt butter

FILLING
½ pound fresh spinach
1 cup heavy cream, whipped and seasoned with a little salt and cayenne pepper
Salt
A few grains cayenne pepper

First prepare the spinach. Wash the leaves in several changes of water and dry them thoroughly on paper towels. Cut them into very fine shreds, put the shreds in a bowl, and season them with salt and a little cayenne pepper.

Preheat the broiler very hot. Prepare and cook the omelets according to the Basic Savory Omelet procedure (page 210), adding the finely shredded raw spinach to the egg mixture, and cooking one-half the mixture at a time. As each omelet is cooked, turn it out onto a hot serving dish, cover it with half the seasoned whipped cream, brown it under a very hot broiler, and serve at once. NET: 2 servings.

OMELETTE AUX CREVETTES

Shrimp Omelet with Chopped Mixed Vegetables

This is a 4-egg omelet to serve 2 persons.

4 eggs
1 teaspoon cold water
¼ teaspoon salt
1 tablespoon salt butter

FILLING (MIREPOIX)
4 tablespoons salt butter
½ cup each of finely diced raw carrot, onion, celery, and

green beans
Salt
Freshly cracked white pepper
¼ teaspoon fresh thyme (less if using dry thyme)
2 tablespoons dry sherry
1 cup cooked shrimps, finely diced
¾ cup heavy cream, whipped

First prepare the mirepoix. Heat the butter in a small deep heavy pan with a tight lid. When it is just melted, add the finely diced raw vegetables. Season with salt, pepper, and the thyme. Pour in the dry sherry. Cover the mixture with buttered wax paper and the lid. Cook over low heat until the vegetables are just soft. Mix in the shrimps and set the filling aside.

Preheat the broiler very hot. Prepare and cook the omelet according to the Basic Savory Omelet procedure (page 210), but just before you are ready to fold it, cover it in the pan with the shrimp and vegetable mixture, then fold and turn the omelet out onto a hot serving platter. Cover the top of the omelet with the whipped cream, brown it quickly under the broiler, and serve at once. NET: 2 servings.

This filling may also be used with a Basic Savory Omelet Mixture.

Basic Dessert Omelet Mixture
    (for 1 omelet: 3 eggs sepa-
    rated, 2 teaspoons superfine
    sugar, ⅛ teaspoon salt)
1 tablespoon salt butter
A little confectioners sugar
Metal skewer, heated red-hot

Optional: ¼ cup light rum

FILLING
⅓ cup any good fruit preserves
    (jam or jelly)
Grated rind of 1 lemon

Jam or Jelly Soufflé
Omelet

For the filling, mix the preserves with the grated lemon rind. Prepare the Basic Dessert Omelet (page 212) through point #8 (the omelet has been under the broiler). Place the preserve mixture down the center of the omelet in the pan and finish as in the basic procedure, dusting the top with the confectioners sugar and crisscrossing with the red-hot skewer. If desired, heat the rum, pour it around the omelet, and ignite. NET: 2 servings.

Basic Dessert Omelet Mixture
    (for 1 omelet: 3 eggs sepa-
    rated, 2 teaspoons superfine
    sugar, ⅛ teaspoon salt)
1 tablespoon salt butter
A little confectioners sugar

FILLING
1 cup fresh hulled strawberries
¼ cup Framboise eau de vie
    (raspberry brandy)
2 tablespoons guava jelly or
    ½ cup heavy cream, whipped

Fresh Strawberry
Soufflé Omelet

FILLING. Steep the strawberries in the Framboise eau de vie at least 30 minutes. Drain, and reserve the drained Framboise. Mix the drained strawberries with the guava jelly or whipped cream.

Put the drained Framboise eau de vie in a little pan and have it at hand. Prepare the Basic Dessert Omelet (page 212) through point #8 (the omelet has been under the broiler). Put all the strawberry filling down the center of the omelet in the pan and finish the basic procedure, dusting the top liberally with confectioners sugar. Warm the drained Framboise, pour it around the omelet, and ignite. Serve at once. NET: 2 servings.

Basic Dessert Omelet Mixture
    (for 1 omelet: 3 eggs, sepa-
    rated, 2 teaspoons superfine
    sugar, ⅛ teaspoon salt)
1 tablespoon salt butter
A little confectioners sugar

FILLING
2 ounces dark sweet chocolate
⅓ cup light or dark rum
½ cup marron glacé bits

Soufflé Omelet
with Chestnuts and
Chocolate

Prepare the filling first. Cut the chocolate into pieces and put them in a pan with 2 tablespoons rum. Stir over very low heat until the chocolate dissolves. Add the marron glacé bits. Prepare the Basic

Dessert Omelet (page 212) through point #8 (the omelet has been under the broiler). Put all the filling down the center of the omelet in the pan and finish the basic procedure, dusting the top with the confectioners sugar. Warm the rest of the rum in a little pan, pour it around the omelet in the serving platter, and ignite. Serve at once. NET: 2 servings.

SOUFFLÉE OMELETTE AU RHUM

Rum Soufflé Omelet

Basic Dessert Omelet Mixture (for 1 omelet: 3 eggs, separated, 2 teaspoons superfine sugar, ⅛ teaspoon salt)
1 tablespoon salt butter
A little confectioners sugar

Large metal skewer, heated red hot

GARNISH
⅓ cup light rum

Prepare the Basic Dessert Omelet (page 212) through step #10 (it is on the hot platter). Warm the rum in a little pan. Pour it around the omelet and ignite it. Serve at once. NET: 2 servings.

DENTS DE LION

Lion's Teeth Omelet

Dramatic little soufflé omelets with big grins of strawberries and whipped cream (arranged to look like the teeth of a lion).

3 eggs
3 teaspoons superfine sugar
1 teaspoon arrowroot or corn-starch
⅛ teaspoon salt
1 tablespoon salt butter
1 cup heavy cream, whipped
2 tablespoons confectioners

sugar
1 teaspoon vanilla
20 whole hulled fresh firm red strawberries
½ cup red currant jelly, strained
Optional: ⅓ cup Framboise eau de vie (raspberry brandy)

Separate the eggs. Stir the superfine sugar and arrowroot or corn-starch into the yolks, and beat until very light and fluffy. Beat the egg whites to soft peaks and fold them into the yolk mixture. Set aside for a moment. Whip the heavy cream with the confectioners sugar and vanilla over a bowl of ice. Have the strawberries ready, cleaned and hulled, and the jelly strained. Heat the omelet pan according to the Basic Dessert Omelet procedure (page 212). When it is properly heated, rub it out with a little butter.

Put about 2 heaping tablespoons of the egg mixture on the omelet pan and make a round about 4 inches in diameter and ½ inch thick, like a pancake. Brown the omelet on one side. Turn it over and brown it on the other side. Remove it from the pan and put it on a wire cake rack. Prepare 4 little omelets in this manner. Have a long metal serving platter ready and assemble the dish as follows: Take an omelet in your hand and put 1 tablespoon whipped cream in the center. Fold the omelet over like a turnover, but don't press it down. Place the folded omelet on the serving platter. Around its open edge stand 5 whole strawberries which have been dipped in the strained currant jelly. Prepare all omelets in this fashion. When they are all on the serving platter, sprinkle them liberally with confectioners sugar. If desired, warm the Framboise eau de vie in a little pan. Pour it around the omelets and ignite. Serve at once. NET: 4 servings.

4 egg yolks	*4 egg whites*
Juice of 1 lemon	*½ cup confectioners sugar*
Grated rind of 2 lemons	*2 tablespoons salt butter*
3 teaspoons superfine sugar	*1 large metal skewer*

OMELETTE SOUFFLÉE AU CITRON

Lemon Soufflé Omelet

Preheat the broiler very hot. In a mixer bowl, combine the egg yolks, lemon juice, lemon rind, and superfine sugar, and beat the mixture at least 2 minutes, until it becomes light and fluffy. Beat the egg whites in a large metal bowl with a large wire whisk until they hold their shape. Fold the egg yolk mixture into the egg white mixture. Heat the omelet pan according to the Basic Dessert Omelet procedure (page 212), and follow that procedure (using 2 tablespoons salt butter in the pan) through to the end. NET: 2 servings.

FISH AND SHELLFISH

THE FRENCH PEOPLE gave the American people their symbol of *free* living in the Statue of Liberty that is the glory of New York harbor and of all America. The French also gave the Americans their symbol of *good* living in classic cookery, that art of glorifying the natural beauty and goodness of the provincial resources of one's own country — its lands, rivers, and coasts. Here, the French manner in how to prepare fish and shellfish reaches a classic purity.

The key to French perfection in fish cookery is lightness and restraint. Analyze any properly made fish or shellfish dish in French cuisine. The whole composition is designed to complement the delicate character of the food of the sea. The butters, the sauces, the garnishes should always be extra fresh and light so as to be sensitive to the essential flavor of the dish.

A moment of scholarly endeavor to understand and appreciate classic fish cookery can open up a whole new dimension of menu planning and dining especially suited to present life styles. Most fish dishes must be prepared within minutes. After a busy day one can purchase at the fish market a fresh trout or fillets of sole, some mussels or scallops, and prepare the most delicious meal in no more time than is required to broil a steak or chops, at less expense, and with more benefit to one's health and well-being.

Like the country of France, America is bounded by temperate and subtropical coasts and contains a great diversity of inland water bodies; in sum, both countries are blessed with a boundless variety of fish and crustaceans.

When I arrived in America, it was appalling to see how seldom seafood cookery was understood in American kitchens and restaurants. The natural result was that many Americans passionately disliked this food. It was always a special joy for me to see the wide-eyed wonderment of my students when a fish dish was prepared in class — the cooking processes and the sauces and garnishes absolutely a revelation to many of them. Students from Midwestern America especially, and the Great Lakes country in particular, where the most delicate fish used to abound until the tragedy of pollution, would describe to me the disastrous local "fish frys," where beautiful fresh-caught local fish were fried so thoroughly that you couldn't tell the fish either by taste or by appearance from the mélange of "French fried" potatoes! The other great American fish disaster would seem to be the weekly tuna fish casserole. Both have done great injustice to the American fish industry and the fish cuisine of a nation.

With air cargo, fresh fish and shellfish are available in all corners of the land. Americans interested in the French art of cooking fish are applying its fundamentals to their native product. The New England flounder substitutes superbly for the Dover sole; in fact, I recommend fresh flounder fillets rather than imported sole, which must be frozen. The brook trout of the Rocky Mountains are peerless, and the Gulf and West coasts are separate "paradisos" for fish and seafood cookery.

In planning the fish and seafood section of this book, the thought crossed my mind — if the Pot-au-Feu is the first cooking lesson for poultry, meat, sauce, and soup preparations, then the fish stew should be the first cooking lesson to get to know the fish and their friends. The most famous fish stew is, of course, La Bouillabaisse, credited to Marseilles. It is really a stew (or soup) of fish and shellfish available in the Marseilles region (but not necessarily, according to Raymond Oliver as he traces its development in his great essay on bouillabaisse in *French Gastronomy*. The bouillabaisse idea offers the pattern for a superb regional fish stew that can be made anywhere in America. Therefore, the very first recipe in this chapter is for bouillabaisse, and it is there for the purpose of getting to know fish.

If you are making bouillabaisse for the first time, plan to take a whole morning or afternoon to produce a great dish and, at the same time, really get to know and handle in your hands a whole whiting, bluefish, pike, a live lobster, raw shrimps, scallops, and mussels — whatever collection you are using. Your bouillabaisse will give you olfactory proof of how sublime a seafood stock can be, and it will demonstrate how little cooking time any of the foods of the sea actually require. "Fish and shellfish" is one of the most delicate types of food and its appreciation produces a higher acculturation of mind and taste buds. Preparing a bouillabaisse for the first time is a plunge, but it is a whole education in a great world of eating.

After that, fish will be a regular item on your weekly bill of fare. Indeed it does offer more variety than meats, in both species and culinary innovation. Next try one of the exquisite sole dishes — Filets de Soles Duglere, for instance. Before long, you will be a master of Quenelles de Brochet, one of the supreme tests of a good chef (an excellent quenelle should quiver like a custard on the serving plate). I love the story of a great American gentleman and international gourmet who took the eminent Louis Vaudable, owner of Maxim's Restaurant in Paris, to New York's Le Pavillon (under the regime of

Mr. Stuart Levin), unannounced, and ordered the Quenelles de Brochet Nantua as offered on the day's menu. The French gentleman pronounced them a worthy challenge to any in France! The supreme accolade . . . in America.

The very few classic principles in mastering le cuisine de poisson are:

(1) Buy the freshest fish and shellfish. Know your fishmonger. A fish market is a fascinating place, and the fishermen and their vendors are wonderful folk still dedicated to the human cause.

Classic cookery does not condone frozen fish and seafood.

(2) Cooking agents used with fish should be superfresh; the wines used in cooking should be light and dry. The slightest deviation in either category will be instantly discernible in the finished dish.

(3) Understand the fish and the recipe. In an age of intellect, it is also fascinating to acquire knowledge of the anatomy of a fish or crustacean, its habitat and life style (which contribute to flavor character and seasonality). Its relative elements are frequently reflected in the artistic idea of the recipe.

A fish velouté sauce served with sole is prepared with the liquid in which the fish was poached, thereby utilizing all the flavor of the fish. The sauce and the fish are married. If the fish is sautéed in butter or garnished with one of the classic butters, the butter absorbs its flavor almost as if by osmosis; it, too, restores all the fish flavor to the dish and enhances it. If the fish is deep-fried, it should be done so quickly that the hot fat merely seals the moisture and original flavor of the fish within its crisp egg and crumb coating.

(4) Never, never overcook fish and seafood. Do not be afraid to undercook fish. Remove it from the heat when it is still a little underdone. The heat of the dish and cooking mixture will continue the cooking, so that with this allowance, the fish should be just right when served.

In America, "bouillabaisse" translates into "superb regional fish stew." In it you should have both fat and lean fishes and a good representation of shellfish. This recipe is composed of examples of such types which are all usually available in most American cities. To be authentic and to produce the very best sauce, have the heads and tails left on the fish when you buy it. The fish should be only cleaned and gutted by the fish market.

BOUILLABAISSE I

MUSSELS
1½ dozen large mussels
1 teaspoon dry mustard
1 onion, sliced
1 piece celery, sliced
1 bay leaf
2 cups dry white wine

½ cup water
6 white peppercorns
2 teaspoons salt

LOBSTER
1 large live lobster (1½ to
    2 pounds) or 2 live lobsters,

¾ pound each
2 tablespoons vegetable oil
4 tablespoons salt butter
⅓ cup Cognac or good brandy

SAUCE
4 tablespoons salt butter
2 teaspoons finely chopped
    garlic
4 large ripe tomatoes, skinned
    and cut in cubes
Salt
Freshly cracked white pepper
1 tablespoon tomato paste
3 teaspoons potato flour
Strained stock in which the
    mussels were cooked

SHRIMPS
½ pound raw shrimps, shelled
    and deveined

FRESHWATER FISH
1 whole pike (1 to 2 pounds)
2 1-pound fillets of carp

OILY FISH
1 whole bluefish (1 to 2 pounds)
1 whole whiting (1½ pounds)

SCALLOPS
½ pound sea scallops

OTHER INGREDIENTS
½ cup Cognac or good brandy
1 skinny loaf French bread
1 tablespoon leaf saffron,
    pulverized with a pestle and
    mortar
Vegetable oil (to fry the bread
    slices)

MUSSELS. To clean the mussels, put them into a pan, cover with cold water, sprinkle over the dry mustard, and scrub them (see detailed instructions, page 320). Discard any opened mussels. Put the good mussels (closed ones) in a pan with the sliced onion, celery, bay leaf, white wine, water, peppercorns, and salt. Cover the pan and bring to a boil. Shake the pan a few minutes over brisk heat until the mussel shells open. Strain and reserve the mussel stock. Remove the top shell from each mussel. Set the mussels attached to their bottom shells aside.

LOBSTER. Split the head of the lobster at the cross in the shell, and cut all the way through the tail. Separate the head section from the tail. Remove the sac behind each eye. Cut off the claws, large and small. Cut the tail in 3 or 4 pieces, according to the size of the lobster. Heat the vegetable oil and butter in a large heavy pan. Add all the lobster pieces to the pan, including the head pieces. Cover the pan and cook the lobster 3 minutes. In a separate little pan heat the brandy, ignite, and pour it over the lobster. Cover the lobster again and cook over brisk heat until the shells are bright red. Remove the lobster pieces from the pan and set them aside.

SAUCE. Put the butter into the pan in which the lobster was cooked. When it is melted, add the chopped garlic and cubed tomatoes. Season with a little salt and freshly cracked white pepper. Cook over brisk heat until the tomato cubes begin to break down. Remove the pan from the heat. Mix the tomato paste with the potato flour and stir into the sauce in the pan. Then add all the strained stock in which the mussels were cooked. Return the pan to low heat and stir until the sauce comes to a rolling boil, then reduce to a simmer.

SHRIMPS. Leave the shrimps whole and add them to the sauce.

FISH. Wash the carp, bluefish, whiting, and pike in cold water and lemon juice and dry on paper towels. Cut the carp into 1½-inch slices, the pike into 2-inch pieces, and the bluefish into 2-inch pieces, and add them all to the sauce. (The whiting is more tender than the others and will disintegrate if it is cooked as long.)

SEA SCALLOPS. Add as is to the sauce.

Simmer the preparation in the pan 5 minutes at very, very low heat. Then cut the whiting into 1½-inch pieces and add to the sauce. Return the mussels and lobster pieces to the pan (first crack the large lobster claws). In a separate little pan heat ½ cup brandy, ignite, and pour it over the whole preparation. At this point do not cook the bouillabaisse any more until you are ready to serve it. Then warm it slowly and gently cook another 3 to 5 minutes if necessary.

CROÛTONS. Slice the loaf of French bread into 1-inch slices, on the bias. Sprinkle a few grains of the pulverized saffron on each slice. Heat some vegetable oil in a large frypan, and fry the slices of bread on the saffron side until they are golden brown. Sprinkle the tops of the slices with specks of saffron, turn them over, and fry the other sides until golden brown.

To serve the bouillabaisse, use large soup plates. Place 2 or 3 fried croûtons on the bottom of each plate and fill with pieces of fish, shellfish, and a little sauce. NET: 4 to 6 servings.

BOUILLABAISSE II

Another fish stew in the Marseillaise manner, using a different assembly of American fish than in the preceding recipe. Purist aficionados of La Bouillabaisse assert that the authentic dish is and must be indigenous to the coastal Mediterranean city of Marseilles because its character is produced by the concert of local fish and shellfish native to that coast and no other (the particular qualification is the craggy-looking fish called rascasse). Whatever may be the final judgment, the great debate on bouillabaisse has given the world an awareness of how good a simple fish pot can be wherever it is made. This one includes eel and mackerel (fat); sole, bass, and red snapper (lean); and, for shellfish, lobster, mussels, shrimps, and sea scallops.

FISH AND SHELLFISH
6 fillets of sole or flounder,
  rolled and tied
6 fillets of bass, rolled and tied
6 fillets of eel, cut into 2-inch
  pieces
2 medium-size red snappers,
  skinned, boned, and cut in
  quarters
2 mackerels, skinned and cut in
  quarters
1 pound sea scallops
1 pound raw shrimps, shelled

and deveined
2 small live lobsters (about
  ¾ pound each)
1 quart large mussels

OTHER INGREDIENTS
1 teaspoon dry mustard
1½ cups pure olive oil
1 large Bermuda onion, finely
  chopped
4 leeks (white parts), finely
  chopped
2 stalks celery, finely chopped

2 teaspoons finely chopped
  garlic
2 pounds ripe tomatoes, skinned
  and coarsely chopped
½ cup Cognac or good brandy
½ cup fresh parsley, coarsely
  chopped
1 teaspoon leaf saffron

3 cups boiling water
Salt
Freshly cracked white pepper
1 large bay leaf
3 large sprigs fresh dill or
  fennel
1 skinny loaf French bread

It is very important that all the ingredients be prepared and in readiness exactly as described above.

To clean the mussels, put them in a pan, cover with cold water, sprinkle the dry mustard over them and scrub them (see detailed instructions about mussels, page 320). Discard any opened mussels, and set the good (closed) mussels aside.

Split the lobsters in half, inserting a large chopping knife at the point of the cross in the shell of the head and cutting all the way through the head and the tail. Remove the sac behind each eye. Cut off the large and small claws, and crack the large claws. Cut the tail in 2 or 3 pieces.

Assemble the fish pot as follows: Heat ½ cup olive oil in a heavy pan large enough to contain all the fish and shellfish. Add the onion, leeks, and celery. Cover the pan and cook the vegetables 2 minutes over brisk heat. Add the garlic, tomatoes, and parsley. Cook another minute. Put all the fish and shellfish into the pan in the order given above: sole, bass, eel, red snapper, mackerel, sea scallops, shrimps, lobster pieces, and mussels. Cover the pan and cook 2 minutes over brisk heat. In a separate little pan warm the brandy, ignite, and pour it over the ingredients in the big pan. Then remove from the heat for a moment.

Crush the leaf saffron with a pestle and mortar and add it to the boiling water. Pour the saffron water into the pot, and season with salt and a little freshly cracked white pepper. Add the bay leaf and dill or fennel. Cover the pot and cook over low heat until the lobster shells are bright red. (This should require only a few minutes, no more than 7 to 8.) Take great care not to overcook the fish. Just before serving, pour in ¾ cup olive oil and warm the pot just a little.

Cut the French bread into 1½-inch slices, on the bias. Heat ¼ cup of olive oil in a frypan, and fry the slices on both sides until they are golden brown.

To serve the bouillabaisse in the provincial way, put one or two slices of the fried French bread on each of the soup plates and cover with juices from the fish pot. Arrange the pieces of fish and shellfish on a large hot platter, remembering to remove the string ties from the various fillets. (Or the fish and shellfish may be arranged on the soup plates.) NET: 8 to 10 servings.

In this dish, lobster, scallops, shrimps, and cod are served on skewers, with rice pilaff. You will need four skewers about 14 inches long.

1 boiled lobster, 1 to 1½
 pounds
1 pound bacon, thinly sliced
½ pound sea scallops
½ pound large boiled shrimps,
 shelled and deveined
½ pound fresh codfish
Salt
Freshly cracked white pepper

½ pound firm white
 mushrooms, medium size
A little lemon juice
A little vegetable oil
2 Bermuda onions
5 tablespoons salt butter
1 bunch crisp fresh watercress
Rice pilaff (page 675)

Remove the lobster meat from the shell. Cut each large claw in half, and the tail into four pieces. Wrap each piece of lobster in a half-slice of bacon and set aside. Wrap the raw sea scallops and boiled shrimps in half-slices of bacon the same way and set aside. Skin and bone the codfish, cut into 1½-inch squares, season with salt and pepper, and wrap them the same way. Cut the mushrooms in half, sprinkle with the lemon juice, and dip them in vegetable oil. Cut the Bermuda onions in quarters or eighths and separate the pieces. (When threading the skewers, use two pieces of onion together, dipped in vegetable oil.)

Have ready four long skewers. Thread all the seafood and vegetables onto the skewers, distributing them evenly and alternating flavors. Melt the butter slowly with the garlic in a little pan. Place the skewers on a broiler rack and brush them all over with the melted butter. Sprinkle with pepper. Broil under a hot flame 4 to 5 minutes on each side, then brush again with melted butter. Arrange them on a hot serving platter and garnish with watercress. Serve with a separate bowl of rice pilaff, or the skewers may be placed on a bed of rice pilaff. NET: 4 servings.

FISH

1 sea bass (about 2½ pounds)
2 large firm white mushrooms
½ pound fresh spinach
1 Bermuda onion, cut in eighths
½ pound raw fresh codfish (no
 skin or bones)
1 slice white bread (no crust)
1 teaspoon finely chopped
 garlic
¼ cup water
3 or 4 Bermuda onions, thinly
 sliced

½ cup vegetable oil
3 carrots, thinly sliced
¼ cup dry sherry
3 tablespoons salt butter
¼ cup dry red wine
Salt
Freshly cracked white pepper
4 hard-boiled eggs, finely
 chopped
2 tablespoons mixed finely
 chopped fresh herbs (tarragon, parsley, chives)

Preheat the oven to 375°. Bone the sea bass (see below) but leave the head on. Wash and dry thoroughly. Stuff it with the following mixture. Put the mushrooms, spinach, onion cut in eighths, and cod through a fine meat chopper. Put this mixture in a bowl with the slice of bread, which has been soaked in the ¼ cup water. Add the garlic, salt, and pepper. Fill the fish and sew it with fine thread.

Sauté the sliced onions in the vegetable oil. Spread them over the bottom of a baking dish. Put the stuffed sea bass on top of them. Blanch the sliced carrots in boiling water, drain, and return them to the pan with the sherry, 1 tablespoon salt butter, red wine, salt, and pepper. Cook 2 to 3 minutes, until the carrots are just soft. Spoon this over the fish and dot with butter. Cover the fish preparation with buttered wax paper and bake 30 minutes, removing the wax paper 10 minutes before finishing. Just before serving, sprinkle the fish generously with the chopped hard-boiled eggs and mixed herbs. NET: 4 to 6 servings.

TO BONE BASS. Remove the scales from the fish. (This may be done with a knife, but it is easier with a fish scaler.) Work from the tail toward the head, and don't forget to take off the fins. Cut the bass down the back. It may be a temptation to cut it down the belly, but only by splitting the back is it possible (1) to bone it, (2) to remove the inedible parts neatly, and (3) to stuff it. Proceed to remove the innards and bone the fish, but do not remove the skin.

BAR POCHÉ, SAUCE MOUSSELINE

Poached Bass with Mousseline Sauce

1 whole striped bass or
  whitefish
Lemon juice
Kosher salt
Butter
Sprigs of watercress
Paper-thin slices of lemon
Very finely chopped parsley
Paprika
Twists of lemon slices

COURT BOUILLON
A few mushroom stalks and
  peelings
2 tablespoons salt butter
2 shallots, finely chopped
2 garlic cloves, bruised
1 small piece celery, sliced
1 small yellow onion, sliced
½ teaspoon salt

2 cups dry white wine
¾ cup dry sherry
½ cup Cognac or good brandy
¼ cup water
8 black and white peppercorns,
  mixed
2 good-size sprigs of fresh dill
1 small bay leaf
1 piece celery leaf
1 sprig fresh parsley
2 slices lemon
1 whole clove

SAUCE MOUSSELINE
¼ cup of reduced fish stock
  (fumet, page 36)
1 whole egg
2 egg yolks
¼ cup heavy cream, whipped

Make the court bouillon first. Sauté the mushroom peelings and stalks in the butter with the shallots, garlic, celery, onion, and salt. Pour on the wine, sherry, brandy, and water. Add the peppercorns and the herbs, which have been tied together into a bouquet garni. Add the lemon and clove. Bring slowly to a boil and simmer 20 minutes.

Clean the fish carefully. Cut off all the fins. Slit the belly of the fish from tail to throat, and remove the innards and the skin around the air pocket. Wash the fish thoroughly in water and lemon juice, inside and out. Season the inside very well with kosher salt. Place the fish on a well-buttered rack in a fish kettle. Strain the hot rich court bouillon over it. Cover, and steam the fish slowly until the eye becomes clouded and opaque. Remove the fish on the rack. Strain the stock and put it in a small saucepan. Return the fish to the fish kettle to keep warm.

SAUCE MOUSSELINE. Boil the strained fish stock down to ¼ cup liquid (almost a glaze). Put the egg and egg yolks in a medium-size bowl and add the reduced stock. Put the bowl in a shallow pan of hot water over low heat. Beat the mixture with an egg beater until it is thick and light, then remove from the hot water and fold in the whipped cream.

Skin both sides of the fish carefully and cut off the fat. Place the fish, round side up, on a fish platter. Put a few fresh sprigs of watercress in the mouth, and a few clusters of watercress around the top of the platter and at the tail. Press half of each paper-thin slice of lemon in finely chopped parsley and the other half in paprika, and arrange them along the bottom of the platter. Down the body of the fish, put little twists of lemon. To serve, first cut servings from the top of the backbone, then lift and remove the backbone and serve the underside of the fish. Serve the sauce separately in a sauceboat. NET: 4 to 6 servings.

---

1 sea bass (1½ pounds)
A little lemon juice
½ cup dry white wine
Salt
Freshly cracked white pepper
8 tablespoons salt butter
3 tablespoons all-purpose flour
¾ cup milk
¼ cup heavy cream
1 tablespoon tomato paste
4 medium-size potatoes,

skinned and boiled
2 small eggs
3 tablespoons freshly grated
Parmesan cheese
2 tablespoons coarsely cut-up
boiled shrimps
A little flour
½ cup dry white breadcrumbs
Vegetable oil for deep-fryer
A few whole cloves

BAR THÉODORA

*Poached Sea Bass with
Shrimps and
Tomato Velouté Sauce*

Preheat the oven to 350°. Remove the dark skin from the sea bass. Leave the head and tail on. Wash in water with a little lemon juice and dry well. Place the fish on a well-buttered ovenproof dish and pour on the white wine. Season with a little salt and pepper. Cover with a piece of buttered wax paper and poach 20 to 25 minutes. Remove from the oven, place the fish on a serving dish; strain and reserve the liquid. Keep the fish warm.

SAUCE. Melt 3 tablespoons butter in a saucepan. Season with a little salt and pepper. Off the heat, stir in the flour. Pour in the strained liquid from the fish and stir over low heat until the sauce thickens. Pour in the milk and bring to a boil. Add the heavy cream. Bit by bit, add 2½ tablespoons butter, stirring constantly.

Reserve 2 tablespoons of this sauce. With the rest of it, coat the fish. In a small saucepan, put the 2 tablespoons sauce with the tomato paste and beat well. Bring to a boil. Make a little paper cornet, and fill it with this tomato paste mixture. Cut a very small piece off the bottom of the cornet and pipe red lines in large crisscrosses over the coated fish.

POTATOES. Beat the warm boiled potatoes in an electric mixer. Add 2½ tablespoons butter, 1 small egg, and the grated cheese and cut-up shrimps. Season with salt and a little pepper. Form the potato mixture into small pear shapes, using a spoon and your hand. Dust them lightly with flour. Beat the other small egg and brush the potato shapes with this egg, then roll them in the breadcrumbs. Fry them in deep fat at 375° until golden brown. Drain, and stick 1 whole clove on the top of each to form the pear stem.

Surround the fish with the potato garnish. NET: 4 servings.

BAR AU MOUSSE DE CREVETTES

Striped Bass Stuffed with Shrimp Mousse

1 striped bass (2½ to 3 pounds) boned by the fishmonger, or see page 240
2 tablespoons whiskey
Salt
A few grains cayenne pepper
1 tablespoon finely chopped shallots
1 tablespoon finely chopped celery
2 teaspoons finely chopped fresh dill
½ teaspoon finely chopped garlic
4 tablespoons melted salt butter
6 firm ripe tomatoes (small to medium-size), skinned and thinly sliced

SHRIMP MOUSSE
½ pound large raw shrimps
1 raw egg white
½ cup light cream
1 teaspoon salt
A few grains cayenne pepper

HOLLANDAISE SAUCE
3 egg yolks
1 tablespoon tarragon vinegar
2 tablespoons juice from the pan in which the fish was baked
1 tablespoon heavy cream
Salt
A few grains cayenne pepper
12 tablespoons frozen sweet butter
2 drops lemon juice

Wash the boned fish in cold water and dry it on paper towels. Spread it out on a board and brush it with whiskey. Preheat the oven to 350°.

SHRIMP MOUSSE. Shell the raw shrimps, devein them, and put the shrimp meat through a fine meat chopper. Put the finely ground shrimp in a mixer bowl, add the egg white, and beat well. Very slowly (drop by drop), add the light cream, beating constantly. Add the salt and cayenne pepper and beat until the mixture thickens. Mix into the mousse the finely chopped shallots, celery, dill, and garlic.

Spread the mousse on the bass. Fold over the flap and reshape the fish. Place it on a buttered baking dish, brush all over the top with most of the melted butter, and completely cover the fish with the thinly sliced tomatoes. Pour over the rest of the melted butter and sprinkle with a little salt and pepper. Cover the dish with a piece of wax paper and bake 25 to 30 minutes. When the fish is baked, remove it from the oven, remove the wax paper, and keep the fish warm while you make the sauce. Preheat the broiler.

HOLLANDAISE SAUCE. Combine the egg yolks, vinegar, and fish juices (from the baking dish) in a small bowl and mix with a small wire whisk. Beat in the heavy cream and season with salt and the cayenne pepper. Stand the bowl in a shallow pan half filled with hot water over low heat and beat until the mixture is thick. Cut the frozen sweet butter into small pieces and beat it into the sauce bit by bit. Last, add the lemon juice.

Spoon the Hollandaise over the fish, then brown the coated fish quickly under a hot broiler. Serve at once. NET: 4 servings.

---

4 Idaho-type potatoes	A few grains cayenne pepper	
2 pounds fresh cod	3 tablespoons grated imported	
1 cup fish stock (page 36)	Swiss cheese	
1 teaspoon finely chopped garlic	½ cup heavy cream	
½ cup chopped fresh parsley	8 tablespoons salt butter	
Salt	¼ cup dry breadcrumbs	

MERLUCHE MAISON

Baked Potato Shells Stuffed with Cod, Gratinée

Preheat the oven to 350°. Bake the potatoes until soft, about 1 hour. Remove, cool a little, and scoop out the insides. Reserve the potato shells. Mash the potato meal and set aside.

Poach the cod in the fish stock 20 minutes over medium heat. Remove from the pan, bone, and flake it. In an electric mixer, mix the flaked cod and mashed potatoes. Add the garlic, parsley, salt, and cayenne pepper. Then add half the Swiss cheese and all the heavy cream. Mix in half the butter and beat well.

Fill the potato shells with this mixture. Sprinkle the tops with the rest of the Swiss cheese and the breadcrumbs. Melt the rest of the butter and sprinkle it over the potatoes. Brown them under the broiler. NET: 4 servings.

---

2 pounds fresh cod, at least	1 teaspoon finely chopped garlic
1 inch thick	Salt
A little lemon juice	Freshly cracked pepper
¾ cup pure olive oil	2 tablespoons chopped fresh
A little all-purpose flour	parsley
3 pounds tomatoes	

CABILLAUD À LA BASQUE

Poached Fresh Cod with Tomatoes

Preheat the oven to 350°. Cut the cod into small steaks. Wash them in a little lemon juice and water and dry well on paper towels. In a sauté pan heat the olive oil until very hot. Dust the cod lightly with flour. Brown the cod steaks in the hot oil on each side. Arrange on a baking dish. Skin the tomatoes and cut them into eighths. Add them to the hot oil in the sauté pan with the garlic, salt, and pepper. Cook thoroughly until the tomatoes almost become a sauce, and spoon them over the cod. Bake the cod 15 minutes, sprinkle with the parsley, and serve. NET: 4 servings.

CABILLAUD MILANESE

Fresh Cod Steaks with Cheese on Tomato Coulis

4 small fresh cod steaks
A little all-purpose flour
Salt
Freshly cracked white pepper
1 egg, beaten
About ½ cup white bread-crumbs and grated Parmesan cheese, mixed
3 to 4 tablespoons vegetable oil or salt butter

1 lemon, sliced

TOMATO COULIS
4 large ripe tomatoes
Salt
Freshly cracked white pepper
1 tablespoon salt butter
1 teaspoon finely chopped garlic
1 small onion, chopped

TOMATO COULIS. Skin the tomatoes, cut into half-inch slices, and sprinkle with a little salt and pepper. Heat the butter in a pan. Add the chopped garlic and onion. Cook until just soft, then add the tomatoes and cook quickly 3 minutes.

Wash and dry the cod steaks. Dust them very lightly in flour, salt, and pepper. Brush with the beaten egg and roll in the mixed bread-crumbs and grated cheese. Cook in hot vegetable oil or salt butter until golden brown on each side. Serve on the tomato coulis with slices of lemon. NET: 4 servings.

CABILLAUD À L'AMÉRICAINE

Fresh Cod Sauté with Rice Pilaff

1 pound fresh cod
A little vegetable oil for frying
2 tablespoons salt butter
3 carrots, finely chopped
½ teaspoon finely chopped garlic
1 medium-size onion, finely chopped

½ cup dry white wine
½ cup Cognac or good brandy
1 teaspoon tomato paste
Pinch of paprika
½ cup water
Salt
Freshly cracked white pepper
Rice pilaff (page 675)

Skin and bone the cod and cut the fillets into 1½-inch pieces. Cover the bottom of a sauté pan with vegetable oil. Heat the oil very hot and boiling, and quickly fry the pieces of cod. Drain well on paper towels. In a separate sauté pan melt the butter, add the chopped carrots, garlic, and onion, and brown them. Add the wine, brandy, tomato paste, paprika, water, salt, and pepper. Simmer 20 minutes.

Add the fried fish and continue cooking 15 minutes. Serve with a rice pilaff. NET: 4 servings.

This dish, a charlotte mold of flaked cod, rice, red and green peppers and eggs, with cream sauce, should be started a day in advance.

2 pounds salt cod, soaked overnight in water
1 quart milk, warmed a little
½ cup pure olive oil
7 tablespoons salt butter
1 cup finely chopped onion
1½ cups long-grain rice
2 cups fish stock (page 36)

4 hard-boiled eggs, chopped
2 green peppers, finely chopped
2 red peppers, finely chopped
3 tablespoons all-purpose flour
Salt
A few grains cayenne pepper
2 tablespoons heavy cream

MORUE À L'ESPAGNOLE

Spanish Cod

Drain the cod and dry well. Pour the warm milk over it and let it soak another hour or two, then drain and flake it, reserving the milk.

Preheat the oven to 350°. Heat the olive oil in a pan with 1 table-spoon butter. (The pan should have a tight cover and be able to go in the oven.) Add the onion and cook 1 to 2 minutes. Add the rice and cover with the fish stock. Stir over moderate heat until it comes to a boil. Cover the pan tightly and cook 15 minutes in the oven. Generously butter a charlotte mold. Put in a layer of rice, then a layer of flaked cod, a layer of chopped hard-boiled egg, a layer of mixed chopped red and green peppers. Repeat the layers until the mold is filled, reserving about 2 tablespoons chopped red and green pepper for the sauce. Cover the mold with a piece of buttered wax paper, stand it in a shallow pan of hot water, and bake 20 minutes.

To make the sauce, reduce the milk the cod was soaked in to 1½ cups by boiling. In a small saucepan melt 6 tablespoons butter. Off the heat, stir in the flour and season with salt and a little cayenne pepper. Cook a minute or two without browning the flour. Stir in the reduced milk (off the heat). Return to low heat and stir until it comes to a boil. Stir in the heavy cream and the reserved chopped red and green pepper. When the mold is done, remove it from the oven and let it stand 5 minutes. Turn the mold out onto a hot flat serving dish and pour the sauce over it. NET: 4 to 6 servings.

This dish should be started a day in advance.

2 pounds salt cod
⅓ cup pure olive oil
3 yellow onions, finely sliced
2 leeks, finely sliced
3 garlic cloves, finely sliced
3 cups water

Salt
Freshly cracked white pepper
½ teaspoon leaf saffron
Bouquet garni (wrapped in
   cheesecloth), including
   thyme, parsley, 1 bay leaf

BOUILLABAISSE DE MORUE

Salt Cod Bouillabaisse

5 large potatoes
1 tablespoon chopped parsley
4 to 6 slices rye or pumpernickel bread which have been
rubbed with garlic and
toasted under the broiler

Soak the cod overnight in water or milk, changing the bath several times if very salty. Heat 3 tablespoons olive oil in a heavy pan. Add the onions, leeks, and garlic. Cook slowly 8 minutes without browning the vegetables. Add the water, salt, pepper, saffron, and bouquet garni. Bring to a boil and boil 5 minutes. Peel the potatoes, slice them in ½-inch rounds, and add to the pan. Skin the cod, cut it in 2-inch squares, and add to the pan. Add the rest of the olive oil and let the stew simmer 20 minutes. Remove the bouquet garni. Sprinkle the stew with the chopped parsley and arrange in a deep casserole. Serve in deep soup plates. Serve the rye toast separately. NET: 4 servings.

BRANDADE DE MORUE

Mousse of Salt Cod

This classic dish should be started a day in advance.

2 pounds salt cod
1 bay leaf
2 peppercorns
1 tablespoon lemon juice
8 tablespoons (4 ounces) salt
  butter
1 cup pure olive oil
2 cups potato purée (page 610)

3 tablespoons all-purpose flour
Salt
A few grains cayenne pepper
⅔ cup milk
2 tablespoons light cream
¾ cup heavy cream
6 large croûtons, fried in olive
  oil (page 69)

Soak the salt cod overnight in water or milk. If it is very salty, give it several baths. Be sure that all the salt has been soaked out of the fish before cooking it.

Preheat the oven to 350°. Put the fish in a baking dish and cover it with water. Add the bay leaf and peppercorns, cover with a piece of buttered wax paper, and cook 20 minutes. Drain the fish thoroughly and place it in a heavy sauté pan. Flake it as fine as possible with a wooden spoon. Add the lemon juice and the butter (except 2 tablespoons), cut in pieces. Heat the mixture gently, stirring all the time until the fish has absorbed all the butter. Then pound it thoroughly with a large pestle and mortar until the mixture is very smooth. Add the olive oil and potato purée alternately, bit by bit, mixing very well after each addition.

In a small saucepan melt 2 tablespoons butter. Stir in the flour, salt, and cayenne pepper. Cook a minute or two without browning. Off the heat, mix in the milk. Stir over low heat until it comes to a boil. Add the light cream. Beat this mixture slowly into the fish mixture with the pestle and mortar. Put the mixture in a sauté pan over very low heat and stir in the heavy cream, tablespoon by tablespoon. Pile in the form of a pyramid on a hot flat serving dish. Surround it with the large croûtons of bread fried in olive oil, and serve. NET: 4 to 6 servings.

6 small eels, skinned and filleted
  in 2-inch pieces
2 to 3 teaspoons lemon juice
6 tablespoons salt butter
1 yellow onion, finely chopped
2 shallots, finely chopped
1 garlic clove, bruised
Bouquet garni (fresh dill, 1 bay
  leaf, 3 sprigs parsley)
Salt
Freshly cracked black pepper

¾ cup Cognac or good brandy
1½ cups dry red wine
1 pound small fresh mushrooms
36 baby white onions
2 tablespoons all-purpose flour
A few grains cayenne pepper
Optional: A little caramel
  coloring (page 78)
1 tablespoon chopped parsley
4 to 6 large croûtons of fried
  bread (page 69)

*Eel Stewed in
Dark Brown Sauce*

Wash the eel fillets in a little lemon juice and water. Drain and dry well. In a heavy sauté pan put 1 tablespoon butter, the onion, shallots, garlic, bouquet garni, salt, and a little freshly cracked black pepper. Place the pieces of eel on top, heat just a little, and flame with the brandy. Pour the red wine in and cook over low heat 20 minutes. Place the eel in a casserole for serving, and reserve the liquid in the pan.

In a separate pan, sauté the small mushrooms in 1 tablespoon butter, 1 teaspoon lemon juice, and seasoning. Blanch the baby white onions in boiling water. Drain them and sauté until brown in 1 tablespoon butter. Scatter the mushrooms and the onions over the eel in the casserole. Mix the flour and 3 tablespoons butter, and add this bit by bit to the liquid the eel was cooked in. Season with salt and cayenne pepper, and bring the mixture to a boil over low heat. (A little caramel coloring may be added to the liquid to give it a deeper tone, but this is optional.) Pour the thickened liquid over the eel, sprinkle with chopped parsley, surround with the croûtons of fried bread, and serve. NET: 4 servings.

This dish of Scotch-style smoked haddock, made in a ring mold, should be started 6 hours or more in advance.

1 finnan haddie
5 tablespoons salt butter
4 tablespoons all-purpose flour
Salt
A few grains cayenne pepper
1 cup milk
3 eggs

1 egg white
2 fresh white mushrooms,
  finely chopped
1 cup fish fumet (page 36)
  or clam juice
¼ cup heavy cream
1 egg yolk

*MOLDED FINNAN
HADDIE WITH
MUSHROOM
SAUCE*

The finnan haddie should be big and fat. Soak it in cold water 5 hours at least, then simmer 12 minutes in fresh water. Skin, bone, and flake it with a fork. Make a cream sauce as follows. In a saucepan, melt 2 tablespoons butter. Off the heat, stir in 2 tablespoons flour, a little salt, and cayenne pepper. Pour in the milk and stir over low heat until the sauce comes to a boil. Let it cool a little.

Preheat the oven to 350°. Generously butter a ring mold. Beat the eggs and combine with the flaked fish, then beat the egg white and fold it into the mixture. Mix in the cream sauce and pour the mixture into the mold. Cover the mold with a piece of buttered wax paper, set it in a pan of hot water, and bake 40 minutes. Make the mushroom sauce in time to have it ready when the fish is cooked, as follows. Melt 1 tablespoon butter in a saucepan. Add the chopped mushrooms and cook briskly 3 minutes. Then add 2 tablespoons flour, a little salt, and cayenne pepper. Pour in the fish fumet and stir over low heat until the sauce comes to a boil. Add, bit by bit, 2 tablespoons butter. Simmer 10 minutes. In a little bowl mix the egg yolk with the heavy cream, and add to the sauce. Turn the mold out onto a serving dish, spoon the mushroom sauce over it, and serve. NET: 4 servings.

HARENGS CALAISIENNE

Herrings Stuffed with Hard-Boiled Eggs and Herbs, in Tomato Sauce

4 fresh herrings
2 hard-boiled eggs, finely chopped
1 teaspoon finely chopped garlic
Half a small white onion, finely chopped
1 tablespoon chopped fresh parsley
½ teaspoon oregano
Salt
Freshly cracked white pepper
1 slice white bread
½ cup fish fumet (page 36) or clam juice

1 tablespoon melted salt butter
1 lemon, cut in thin slices

FISH STOCK TOMATO SAUCE
4 tablespoons salt butter
Half a small white onion, sliced
1 bay leaf
6 whole peppercorns
2 tomatoes, with skins on, sliced
1 tablespoon tomato paste
1 tablespoon all-purpose flour
Salt
1 cup fish fumet (page 36) or clam juice

Preheat the oven to 350°. Remove the heads of the herrings. Split the herrings down the back with a sharp knife and carefully remove the bone. Remove the roe (if any) and reserve it. Wash and dry the herrings well. Put in a bowl the chopped hard-boiled eggs, chopped roe if any, garlic, onion, parsley, oregano, salt, and pepper. Soak the slice of bread in the fish fumet and add to the egg mixture. Fill the herrings with the mixture, place them on a buttered baking dish, and pour the melted butter over them. Cover with wax paper and bake 25 minutes. Remove, and keep them warm.

FISH STOCK TOMATO SAUCE. Melt 2 tablespoons butter in a pan. Add the sliced onion, bay leaf, peppercorns, tomatoes, and tomato paste. Cover the pan and cook slowly 10 minutes. Off the heat, stir in the flour. Add a little salt and the fish fumet. Stir over low heat until the sauce comes to a boil. Rub through a fine vegetable strainer and return to the pan. Stir in 2 tablespoons butter bit by bit.

To serve, pour the sauce on the bottom of the serving dish. Arrange the stuffed herrings on top. Garnish around the dish with thin slices of lemon. NET: 4 servings.

1 pair kippered herring (deli-
    cately salted and smoked)
2 tomatoes, skinned and sliced
¼ teaspoon freshly chopped
    garlic or 1 small white onion,
    chopped
2 tablespoons vegetable oil
2 tablespoons salt butter
3 tablespoons all-purpose flour

Salt
A few grains cayenne pepper
¾ cup milk
6 egg yolks
½ teaspoon dry mustard
1 tablespoon freshly grated
    Parmesan cheese
6 egg whites

SOUFFLÉ D'HARENG

Hot Kipper Soufflé

Preheat the oven to 350°. Simmer the kippered herring 5 minutes in water. Remove, bone, and flake with a fork. Cook the sliced tomatoes and onion or garlic in the vegetable oil. Mix the flaked kippered herring in the tomatoes, and set aside. Melt the butter in a saucepan. Off the heat, stir in the flour, salt, and cayenne pepper. Pour in the milk. Stir over low heat until the mixture thickens; do not boil. Remove from the heat and mix in the egg yolks, one by one, the mustard, and the grated cheese. Beat the egg whites to soft peaks. Fold into the egg yolk mixture, then fold in the kippered herring mixture. Generously butter a 6-cup soufflé dish. Tie a double band of buttered wax paper around the outside. (The wax paper should rise about 3 inches above the top of the soufflé dish; see page 787.) Pour the soufflé mixture into the dish, set it in a pan of hot water, and bake 30 to 40 minutes. Serve at once. NET: 4 to 6 servings.

8 mackerel fillets
1 teaspoon lemon juice
2 tablespoons salt butter,
    melted
Salt
A few grains cayenne pepper
2 tablespoons vegetable oil
½ teaspoon finely chopped
    garlic

6 large ripe tomatoes, skinned
    and cut in thick slices
3 egg yolks
3 teaspoons dry mustard
1 tablespoon tarragon vinegar
3 tablespoons heavy cream
6 tablespoons frozen sweet
    butter

MAQUEREAU À L'HOLLANDAISE MOUTARDÉE

Baked Mackerel with Mustard Hollandaise

Preheat the oven to 350°. Arrange the mackerel, with the skin left on, on a baking dish. Pour over it the lemon juice, melted salt butter, salt, and cayenne pepper. Cover with wax paper and bake 20 minutes. While the fish is cooking, heat the oil in a pan and add the garlic and tomato slices. Cook briskly 2 minutes. When the fish is cooked, arrange the tomatoes on a serving dish, put the mackerel fillets on top, and keep the dish warm.

MUSTARD HOLLANDAISE. Put the egg yolks in a bowl and mix well with the mustard, vinegar, a little salt and cayenne pepper, and 2 tablespoons heavy cream. Put the bowl in a shallow pan half filled with hot water over low heat. Beat until the sauce begins to thicken. Then add the frozen sweet butter bit by bit, beating continuously with a whisk. Last, add 1 additional tablespoon of heavy cream to bring the sauce to a pouring consistency.

Pour the sauce over the mackerel and brown under a hot broiler. NET: 4 servings.

PERCHE EN BIÈRE

Perch Braised in Beer and Honey Cake

4 small perch, cleaned and boned
12 tablespoons salt butter
3 Bermuda onions, finely chopped
1 stalk celery, finely chopped
Salt
Freshly cracked white pepper
1 piece (about 6 ounces) of honey or spice cake
2 12-ounce bottles beer
½ pound soft roe (cod or flounder)
A little all-purpose flour

Preheat the oven to 350°. In a heavy sauté pan heat 4 tablespoons butter. Add the Bermuda onions and celery. Season with salt and pepper, and cook slowly until nearly soft but not brown. Cut the honey cake into small cubes and add it to the pan. Arrange this mixture in the bottom of a covered baking dish. Place the cleaned and boned perch on the top. Pour the beer over them. Season with salt and pepper, cover the baking dish with the lid, and bake 20 minutes. Remove the fish from the oven and arrange them on a hot flat serving dish. Reduce (by boiling) the mixture in which the fish was cooked, until it is half quantity. Put it in a blender with the celery and onion, and blend until smooth. Return to a saucepan and, bit by bit, stir in 4 tablespoons butter. (This should make a nice coating sauce.) Spoon the sauce over the fish. Dry the roe on paper towels. Dip them in flour and sauté them in 4 tablespoons butter until golden brown. Arrange them on the coated perch, and serve. NET: 4 servings.

QUENELLES DE BROCHET, SAUCE VIN BLANC

Light Pike Dumplings in White Wine Sauce

The quenelles may also be coated with Sauce Nantua (see the next recipe).

¾ pound finely ground pike
Melted butter
Freshly grated Parmesan cheese

COURT BOUILLON
Head and bones of the pike
2 cups cold water
1 cup dry white wine
1 small piece celery, sliced
1 small onion, sliced
1 small bay leaf
6 white peppercorns

QUENELLES
1 cup water
12 tablespoons sweet butter
2½ teaspoons salt
1 cup all-purpose flour
2 large eggs
⅓ cup egg whites (unbeaten)
A few grains cayenne pepper
¼ teaspoon ground nutmeg
¼ cup heavy cream

SAUCE
5 tablespoons sweet butter
5 tablespoons all-purpose flour

Salt
A few grains cayenne pepper
1¼ cups strained court bouillon
   (above)
⅓ cup light cream
2 egg yolks

1 tablespoon dry sherry
2 tablespoons heavy cream
1 small black truffle, cut in
   shreds and marinated in
   1 tablespoon Cognac or good
   brandy

COURT BOUILLON. Put the head and bones of the pike in a pan with the cold water and white wine. Bring slowly to a boil. Reduce the heat to a simmer. Skim off all the scum. Add the celery, onion, bay leaf, and peppercorns. Simmer gently about 45 minutes. Strain through a cloth placed over a colander.

QUENELLES. Put the water in a small heavy pan with 4 tablespoons sweet butter and ½ teaspoon salt. (Cut the butter in pieces so that it melts as the water comes to a boil.) When the water is boiling, put in the flour, all at once. Stir over low heat until the mixture comes away from the sides of the pan. In a mixer beat 8 tablespoons sweet butter until light and creamy. Remove it from the mixer bowl (but don't wash the bowl). Put the cream puff dough in the mixer bowl. Beat in the eggs, one at a time, the unbeaten egg whites, the creamed butter, and the ground raw pike. Season with 2 teaspoons salt, the cayenne pepper, nutmeg, and heavy cream. Mix well. Put the mixture through the finest strainer of a vegetable mill. Chill it if you have time (it will be easier to form the quenelles), then form it into cork shapes, using a lightly floured board. Try not to get any wrinkles in the quenelles and don't coat them with too much flour.

Have ready a large pan of hot salted water (not boiling, just "smiling"). Drop the quenelles gently in the water. Cover the top of the water with a double thickness of paper towels to keep the quenelles moist. Poach gently until set. (In about 10 to 15 minutes the quenelles will rise to the top of the water. Do not at any time cover the pan except with the paper towels. The quenelles can be left in the hot, not boiling, water until you are ready to put them on a serving dish.)

SAUCE. In a saucepan melt 3 tablespoons of sweet butter. Off the heat, stir in the flour. Season with a little salt and cayenne pepper. Add the court bouillon and stir over low heat until the sauce thickens. Add the light cream. Bring to a boil, stirring constantly, and add the rest of the butter, bit by bit. Simmer about 5 minutes. In a medium-size bowl, beat the egg yolks and dry sherry. Stir in the heavy cream. Pour a little of the hot sauce into the egg yolk mixture, then return it all to the saucepan. Reheat, but do not boil. Stir in the shredded truffle.

Brush a hot serving platter with a little melted butter. Drain the quenelles and arrange them on the platter. Spoon the sauce carefully over the quenelles. Sprinkle the top with a little melted butter and freshly grated Parmesan cheese. Brown quickly under the broiler (not too long or the sauce will separate). NET: 4 to 6 servings.

QUENELLES DE BROCHET, SAUCE NANTUA

Light Pike Dumplings in Shrimp Sauce

The style of serving Quenelles de Brochet with Sauce Nantua has an established place among the great gourmet delights.

Prepare the quenelles exactly according to the preceding recipe for Quenelles de Brochet, Sauce Vin Blanc. Prepare the Nantua sauce according to the recipe on page 45.

To serve, brush a serving platter with a little melted butter. Drain the quenelles and arrange them on the platter. Spoon the Nantua sauce over the quenelles. Sprinkle with a little freshly grated Parmesan cheese and glaze briefly under a hot broiler.

SUPRÊMES DE BROCHET PARISIENNE

Larded Pike Fillets with Mushroom Garnish

The pike fillets are larded with fatback and truffle, and garnished with duxelles-stuffed mushroom caps. The dish should be started a day or two in advance of serving to allow the larded fillets to steep in the marinade. To make it, you will need one or two small larding needles.

4 large pike fillets (1 per
  serving)
1 lemon
2 ounces fatback or salt pork
1 large black truffle
⅓ cup Cognac or good brandy
1 cup dry white wine
⅓ cup Madeira wine
¼ cup finely chopped shallots
Bouquet garni (parsley, thyme,
  1 bay leaf)
Salt
Freshly cracked white pepper

MUSHROOM CAPS
2 tablespoons salt butter
8 firm white mushroom caps
1 teaspoon lemon juice
Salt

Freshly cracked white pepper
Freshly grated Parmesan cheese

DUXELLES
2 tablespoons salt butter
1 cup finely chopped fresh
  mushrooms
1 teaspoon lemon juice
Salt
Freshly cracked white pepper
A little all-purpose flour
4 tablespoons dry breadcrumbs
  (page 69)

SAUCE
2 egg yolks
½ cup heavy cream
Liquid in which the fish is
  cooked

Wash the pike fillets in lemon juice and water and dry them well on a cloth or paper towels. Cut the fatback or salt pork and the truffle into little strips the size of small thin matchsticks. Thread these strips into small larding needles and generously lard each fillet, using about the same quantity of fatback and truffle per fillet. Put several rows of strips through each. Arrange the larded fillets on a well-buttered baking dish. Pour over them the brandy, white wine, and Madeira, and sprinkle with the chopped shallots. Divide the bouquet garni, placing half the herbs at each end of the dish. Season with salt and a little pepper. Cover the dish with plastic wrap, set it in the refrigerator, and let the fillets steep in the marinade 1 or 2 days.

When you are ready to cook them, preheat the oven to 375°. Remove the plastic wrap, place the baking dish in the oven, and bake the fillets 25 to 30 minutes, basting them frequently with the liquid.

MUSHROOM CAPS. Heat the butter in a sauté pan and add the mushroom caps with the lemon juice, salt, and pepper. Sauté them briskly 2 minutes, remove from the pan, and set aside. Prepare the duxelles in the same pan. Add the butter to the pan, then the chopped mushrooms, and season with the lemon juice, salt, and pepper. Cook the mushrooms briskly 2 minutes, sprinkle well with flour, and add the breadcrumbs. Blend the mixture well, stirring it over low heat a minute or two.

Stuff the chopped mushroom mixture (duxelles) into the mushroom caps and dome the tops. Sprinkle generously with Parmesan cheese. When the fillets are out of the oven, arrange them on a heated serving platter or au gratin dish. Arrange the stuffed mushrooms along the sides of the dish. Strain the liquid in which the fillets were cooked and boil it down to half quantity. In a small saucepan, combine the egg yolks with the heavy cream and the reduced fish liquid. Stir the mixture over very low heat, without boiling, until it thickens. Spoon this sauce over the fillets and the stuffed mushrooms and brown quickly under a hot broiler. Serve immediately. NET: 4 servings.

BROCHET FARCI À LA TOUR D'ARGENT

Baked Whole Pike
Stuffed with
Salmon Mousse,
Hollandaise

1 whole pike (about 2½ pounds)
3 tablespoons Cognac or good
    brandy
4 tablespoons salt butter

SALMON MOUSSE STUFFING
1½ pounds salmon cut from
    tail or 1 pound center-cut
2 egg whites
1½ cups light cream
2 teaspoons salt
A few grains cayenne pepper

GARNISH
2 or 3 small ripe tomatoes, cored
    and cut in half

5 or 6 cooked shrimps
1 or 2 black truffles
5 or 6 firm white mushroom
    caps, fluted if desired
Butter
Lemon juice

HOLLANDAISE SAUCE
3 egg yolks
3 tablespoons tarragon vinegar
Salt
A few grains cayenne pepper
3 tablespoons light cream
8 tablespoons frozen sweet
    butter
2 drops lemon juice

Scale, clean, and bone the pike (see procedure for bass, page 240). Wash the fish in cold water and dry it on paper towels. Spread it out on a board and brush it with 1 tablespoon brandy.

SALMON MOUSSE. Skin and bone the salmon and put it through a fine meat chopper. Put the finely ground salmon in a mixer bowl, add the egg whites, and beat well. Continue beating and slowly, drop by drop, add the light cream, then the salt. Beat until the mixture is very thick, then season with a few grains of cayenne pepper.

Preheat the oven to 375°. Spread the salmon mousse on the pike, reserving a little for the garnish. Fold the flap over, reshape the pike, and transfer it to a buttered baking dish. Make 5 or 6 diagonal cuts across the skin on top. Melt the butter, add it to the rest of the brandy, and pour the mixture over the fish in the baking dish. Set the stuffed pike in the oven and bake 25 minutes. Pile up the reserved salmon mousse on top of the tomato halves for garnish. Place them on a small buttered baking dish, cover with a piece of buttered wax paper, and bake about 20 to 25 minutes with the fish.

Slice the truffles. Slit the shrimps lengthwise but not all the way through to the end. Insert a slice of truffle in each shrimp. Sauté the mushroom caps in a little butter and lemon juice.

HOLLANDAISE SAUCE. Mix the egg yolks and tarragon vinegar in a little bowl and season with salt and cayenne pepper. Add the light cream. Place the bowl in a shallow pan half filled with hot water over low heat. Continue stirring until the mixture becomes thick. Cut the sweet butter into little pieces and stir it into the sauce bit by bit. Last, add 2 drops lemon juice to the sauce. Cover the sauce with a piece of plastic wrap and keep it warm until ready for use.

To serve, arrange the baked fish on a warm heatproof serving platter, with the tomato halves and mushroom caps around it. Stick 1 shrimp with truffle slice in each of the diagonal cuts on the fish. Coat the fish with Hollandaise and brown it quickly (only a minute or two) under a hot broiler. Serve immediately. NET: 4 servings.

SAUMON À LA MATELOTE

Poached Salmon with Red Wine Sauce

1 pound salmon
Salt
Freshly cracked white pepper
4 tablespoons melted salt butter
1/4 cup dry red wine
1 cup water
1 onion, sliced
1 garlic clove, bruised
1 sprig fresh thyme
2 egg yolks
4 tablespoons frozen sweet
    butter

4 tablespoons heavy cream
Juice of half a lemon
3/4 cup baby white onions
    (cocktail size)
1/4 pound fresh button-size
    mushrooms
A little chopped fresh parsley

PUFF PASTRY CRESCENTS
1/2 cup scraps of puff paste
    (page 723)
1 egg, beaten

PUFF PASTRY CRESCENTS. Preheat the oven to 400°. Roll out the puff paste fairly thick and cut it in 2-inch crescent shapes with a fluted cutter. Place on a wet baking sheet, brush the tops with the beaten egg, chill, and bake 15 to 20 minutes. Remove from the oven and keep warm.

SALMON. Lower the oven heat to 350°. Skin, bone, and cut the salmon in pieces about 1½ inches square. Place them in an earthenware dish. Season with salt and pepper, pour the melted butter over them, and put them under the broiler for a few minutes. Pour in the wine and water and add the onion, garlic, and thyme. Cover with wax paper and poach in the oven 10 to 15 minutes. Remove, arrange the pieces of salmon in a heatproof serving dish, and strain and reserve the liquid.

sauce. Put the egg yolks in a medium-size bowl with ¼ cup of the reserved salmon liquid and the heavy cream. Put the bowl in a shallow pan half full of hot water and beat over low heat until it thickens. Add the frozen sweet butter bit by bit, and a drop or two of lemon juice. Cover with plastic wrap and keep warm.

mushrooms and onions. Skin and cook the baby onions in boiling salted water until barely soft. Drain. Wash the mushrooms, cut in quarters, and cook 4 minutes in a little butter, lemon juice, salt, and freshly cracked white pepper.

To serve, scatter the mushrooms and onions over the salmon. Pour over the sauce. Brown quickly under a broiler. Garnish with the puff pastry crescents and sprinkle the top with the parsley. net: 4 servings.

MOUSSE DE SAUMON NARONA

Fish Mold of Rich Salmon Mousse in Aspic with Mustard Sauce

2½ pounds salmon in one piece
¾ cup dry white wine
1½ cups water
1 bay leaf
6 peppercorns
2 teaspoons salt
8 tablespoons salt butter
¼ teaspoon crushed cardamom seed
Truffles or black olives, cut in half-slices
Pimento

PANADE
2 tablespoons vegetable oil
6 tablespoons warm water
4 tablespoons all-purpose flour
2 tablespoons unflavored gelatine
½ teaspoon salt
A few grains cayenne pepper
1½ cups milk
2 tablespoons heavy cream

ASPIC
3 egg whites

5 cups cold fish fumet (page 36) or chicken stock (page 35)
1 tablespoon tomato paste
⅓ cup dry sherry
3 tablespoons unflavored gelatine

MUSTARD SAUCE
2 egg yolks
½ teaspoon dry mustard
1 teaspoon Dijon mustard
A few grains cayenne pepper
⅛ teaspoon each of mace and nutmeg
¼ teaspoon very finely chopped garlic
1 tablespoon tarragon vinegar
½ teaspoon salt
2 teaspoons Cognac or good brandy
1 cup vegetable oil
3 tablespoons sour cream
¾ cup whipped cream (about ½ cup heavy cream)

First put the mold you plan to use in the freezer to get it very cold. (It is nice to use a fish-shaped mold.) Then put the salmon in a hammock of foil in a fish kettle, pour in the wine and water, and add the bay leaf, peppercorns, and salt. (The salmon must hang in the liquid to poach.) Bring very slowly to a boil, cover, and simmer very gently 45 minutes. When it is cool (cool it in the liquid if you have time), skin and bone it, put it through a fine meat chopper, and set it aside.

panade. Put the vegetable oil and water into a saucepan and bring to a boil. Mix the flour and gelatine together and stir into the water and oil. Add the salt and cayenne pepper. Off the heat, stir in the milk and cream. Stir over low heat until it comes to a rolling boil, then pour it onto a flat platter and chill.

SALMON MOUSSE. Beat the butter to a light cream in a mixer. Beat in the cooled panade little by little and beat well. Gradually beat in the ground salmon, add the cardamom seed, taste for seasoning, and set aside in the refrigerator.

ASPIC. Beat the egg whites to soft peaks. Put the stock into a pan with the other ingredients. (If the stock is not very gelatinous, use a little more gelatine.) Add the beaten egg whites, put the mixture over moderate heat, and beat it with a whisk until it comes to a rolling boil. Remove the pan from the heat and let it stand 15 minutes without moving it. Strain it through a damp cloth in a colander.

Pour some of the aspic into a layer cake pan and set it in the refrigerator to set, to be chopped for garnish. When you are ready to coat the mold, dissolve the rest of it (if it has jellied) in a tin-lined copper pan. Put the pan over a bowl of ice. Stir until it is on the point of setting, then pour some into the very cold mold and tip it around to cover the inside of the mold with a thin layer (¼ inch) of aspic. Outline each scale of the fish mold with a crescent of truffle or black olive. Cut a small round of truffle or olive for the eye, with a dot of pimento in the center. Line the mold again with a thin layer of aspic on the point of setting. Chill the mold a bit so that the aspic is firm. Spoon the salmon mousse into a large pastry bag fitted with a #9 star tube. Fill the mold with the salmon mousse, forcing it through the tube, moving from side to side in the mold, from head to tail, until the mold is filled. Put it in the freezer for a few minutes to set. Fill all the little spaces around the sides of the mousse and the mold with more aspic on the point of setting. Put it in the freezer just to set, then move it to the refrigerator. (Do not allow the aspic to freeze.) If any mousse is left over, it can be put into little baba molds to use as garnish. Put a slice of stuffed olive in the bottom of each mold, fill with mousse, and chill.

MUSTARD SAUCE. In a mixer bowl put the egg yolks, mustards, cayenne pepper, mace, nutmeg, garlic, vinegar, salt, and brandy. Beat thoroughly. Add the vegetable oil drop by drop, beating all the time. Remove from the mixer, fold in the sour cream and whipped cream, cover the bowl with plastic, and set it in the refrigerator to chill.

When you are ready to serve the mousse, slide a very small sharp knife around the edge of the mold. Turn the mold upside down on a cold serving platter, rub the top with a cloth wrung out in hot water, and gently lift it off the salmon. Surround it with chopped set aspic and, if you made them, the little mousse molds. Serve the mustard sauce icy cold in a separate bowl. NET: 4 to 6 servings.

COULIBIAC

Smoked Nova Scotia Salmon in Brioche

This is a delicious home-style version of the Russian coulibiac, of smoked salmon baked in brioche. (Purists will insist it be made with vesiga, which is the marrow from the backbone of the sturgeon, and not readily available.) Coulibiac is sometimes made with puff pastry, and the filling wrapped in crêpes before being enclosed in the pastry. Cooked fresh salmon may be used instead of smoked salmon. There is also a "Poor Man's Coulibiac" — homemade bread dough filled with meat loaf (page 488).

2 tablespoons dry breadcrumbs
   (page 69)
¼ cup cool melted salt butter
2 tablespoons chopped fresh dill
1 yellow onion, finely chopped
1 teaspoon finely chopped garlic
¾ cup sour cream
3 hard-boiled eggs, finely
   chopped
Freshly cracked white pepper
1 pound Nova Scotia smoked
   salmon, sliced

Lemon juice
1 egg, beaten

BRIOCHE DOUGH
1 package yeast
¼ cup lukewarm water
2 cups all-purpose flour
10 tablespoons salt butter
½ teaspoon salt
2 teaspoons sugar
3 large or 4 small eggs

BRIOCHE DOUGH. Dissolve the yeast in the water. Add it to ½ cup flour and stir with a rubber scraper to a firm ball. Turn out onto a lightly floured board and knead it until smooth. Cut a deep crisscross on the top and drop it into a small bowl of lukewarm water. Cream the butter in a mixer bowl. Remove the butter, and into the same bowl (no need to wash it) put 1½ cups flour, the salt, sugar, and eggs. Beat until well mixed. Add the creamed butter and mix well. Add the yeast, which will have risen to the top of the water. Mix all together thoroughly. Put the dough in a clean bowl that has been wiped out with a damp cloth and lightly floured. Cover with plastic wrap and cloth. Leave it to rise at room temperature until double in bulk. Break the rise by running your finger around the edge of the bowl. Put it in the freezer at least 2 hours, then turn it out onto a floured board. Roll out two-thirds of it and line a well-buttered loaf pan (reserve a third of the dough for the top).

FILLING. Preheat the oven to 375°. Mix the breadcrumbs with the melted butter. Add 1 tablespoon dill, the onion, and ½ teaspoon garlic. Sprinkle half this mixture over the bottom of the brioche in the pan. Put the sour cream, ½ teaspoon garlic, 1 tablespoon dill, the hard-boiled eggs, and a little pepper in a bowl, and mix well. Spread half the mixture in a layer over the crumb mixture. Sprinkle the slices of smoked salmon with a little lemon juice and pepper and roll up tightly. Arrange the rolls on the sour cream mixture, cover them with another layer of sour cream mixture, and finish with a layer of crumb mixture. At this point the pan should be almost full (if it isn't, you may put in another layer of sour cream).

Brush the edges of the brioche dough with beaten egg. Roll out the other piece of dough, cover the top of the pan with it, and tuck it in well. Cover the pan with a cloth canopy (the cloth should not touch the dough) and let it stand at room temperature 15 to 20 minutes. Brush the top with beaten egg. Bake 30 to 40 minutes, until it is well risen and a lovely brown on top. Remove, and let it stand about 5 minutes before sliding it out of the pan onto a hot white napkin on a hot platter. To serve, slice it. NET: 6 to 8 servings.

SAUMON, SAUCE VERTE

Cold Poached Salmon on Rice Salad, with Green Mayonnaise

2½ pounds salmon in one piece
Lemon juice
3 cups water
6 whole peppercorns
Plain-cooked rice (page 675)

½ cup French dressing
(vinaigrette, page 62)
Sauce Verte (page 54; make
1½ times the recipe)
1 cucumber, sliced

Preheat the oven to 350°. Skin and bone the salmon and put it in a baking dish. Sprinkle with a little lemon juice, salt, and the peppercorns, and pour in 3 cups water. Cover with buttered wax paper and bake 20 minutes. Drain and chill. Cut in 2-inch pieces and put in the refrigerator until needed.

RICE SALAD. Mix the cold cooked rice with the vinaigrette dressing.

Arrange the rice in a loaf shape on a chilled serving dish. Arrange the salmon pieces on it, and cover with the sauce. Garnish with crisp cucumber slices. NET: 4 servings.

MOUSSE DE SAUMON FROID

Cold Salmon Mousse

Pike or sole may be substituted for the salmon in this recipe. Or it may be made exactly the same way with ham, chicken, or veal, and coated with chicken or game aspic. The mousse is served in a soufflé dish and decorated with aspic and "tomato flowers."

¾ pound salmon
1 onion, sliced
1 carrot, sliced
1 bay leaf
½ cup dry white wine
1¾ cups water
15 tablespoons salt butter
3 tablespoons all-purpose flour
1 cup milk

Salt
A few grains cayenne pepper
2 tablespoons dry sherry
2 tablespoons heavy cream
1 cup fish aspic (page 37)
A few sprigs fresh parsley,
pressed flat
1 tomato

Place the salmon, onion, carrot, bay leaf, wine, and water in a pan. Bring slowly to a boil and simmer 15 to 20 minutes. Cool the fish in the liquid. While it is cooling, make the sauce.

BÉCHAMEL SAUCE. Melt 3 tablespoons butter in a pan. Off the heat, add the flour. Stir until smooth, and add the milk, salt, and cayenne pepper. Stir over low heat until it comes to a boil. Pour onto a plate to cool.

When the salmon is cool, skin and bone it and put it through a fine meat chopper. Cream 12 tablespoons butter in a mixer, and gradually beat in the ground salmon and 1½ cups of the cooled Béchamel sauce. Add the sherry, heavy cream, and a little extra salt and pepper. Mix well. Nearly fill a 1½-quart soufflé dish with the salmon mousse. Smooth over the top and chill.

Dissolve a little of the aspic in a pan, then put the pan over a bowl of ice and stir until the aspic is at the point of setting. Spoon a thin coating of aspic over the salmon mousse in the soufflé dish. Dip a few sprigs of pressed parsley into the aspic and arrange them around the top. Skin and seed the tomato, and cut the outer pulp into small flowerpot shapes. Dip these into the aspic and set them at the bottom of each sprig of parsley. Let the mousse set in a cool place, then fill up the rest of the dish with aspic. Let it set again, and serve (in the dish; it is not turned out). NET: 4 servings.

<hr>

Stuffed hard-boiled eggs are the garnish for this dish. Striped bass may be used instead of salmon trout.

TRUITE SAUMONÉE VOISIN

Cold Poached Salmon Trout Filled with Tartar Salmon Mousse

1 salmon trout (2½ to 3 pounds)
1½ cups dry white wine
2 cups water
Half a lime, sliced
1 stalk celery, sliced
1 small carrot, cut in half
1 small onion, cut in quarters
1 large sprig tarragon
7 peppercorns, black and white mixed
2 teaspoons salt

TARTAR SALMON MOUSSE
1 pound salmon (middle cut), cooked with the salmon trout
12 tablespoons sweet butter
6 ounces cream cheese
2 teaspoons finely chopped shallots
2 teaspoons very finely chopped fresh tarragon
½ teaspoon finely chopped garlic
2 teaspoons finely chopped green olive
2 teaspoons finely chopped fresh parsley
Salt

A few grains cayenne pepper
1 tablespoon Cognac or good brandy
½ cup plain whipped cream (¼ cup unwhipped)

GREEN MAYONNAISE
2 tablespoons parsley, coarsely chopped
2 tablespoons Cognac or good brandy
3 egg yolks
1 teaspoon dry mustard
½ teaspoon Dijon mustard
1 teaspoon salt
A few grains cayenne pepper
1 tablespoon tarragon vinegar
2 cups vegetable oil
⅔ cup pure olive oil
3 tablespoons heavy cream
1 tablespoon unflavored gelatine
4 tablespoons milk

GARNISH
4 hard-boiled eggs
2 tablespoons of the mousse mixture

Clean the salmon trout but leave the head and tail on. Put it in the fish kettle with the pound of salmon for the mousse. Pour in the wine and water, and add the lime, celery, carrot, onion, tarragon sprig, peppercorns, and salt. Cover the pan and bring very slowly to a boil.

Simmer gently 20 minutes (if you're using bass, 30 minutes). Allow the fish to cool in the liquid. Remove the salmon trout and very carefully skin and bone it, leaving the head and tail on. Set it aside and chill.

TARTAR SALMON MOUSSE. Skin and bone the cooled cooked piece of salmon. Put it through a fine meat chopper. In a mixer bowl, beat the butter until it is very light and creamy. Beat in the cream cheese and ground salmon, then add the shallots, chopped tarragon, garlic, green olive, and parsley. Season with salt and the cayenne pepper. Add the brandy and whipped cream and mix well.

Sandwich the salmon trout with the mousse, reserving a little of the mousse for the garnish. Reshape the fish and arrange on a serving dish. Chill.

GREEN MAYONNAISE. To make the green coloring, sprinkle the coarsely chopped parsley with the brandy. Put the parsley in the corner of a clean cloth and squeeze it out in a bowl to get the parsley essence. (Or purée it in a blender.) Set aside. Put the egg yolks in a mixer bowl and beat until light and fluffy. Add the mustards, salt, cayenne pepper, and vinegar. Beat in, very slowly, the vegetable oil and olive oil, drop by drop at the start. If the mayonnaise becomes too thick for coating, thin it with a little heavy cream. Add the green coloring. Put the gelatine in a small pan and add the milk. Stir over low heat until the gelatine is completely dissolved. Cool it a little, then slowly mix it into the mayonnaise. Coat the fish with this sauce.

GARNISH. Cut the eggs in half crosswise. (Slice a tip from the ends so the halves stand upright.) Rub the yolks through a strainer and mix into the mousse. Put the mixture into a pastry bag fitted with a star tube and fill the egg whites.

Surround the salmon trout with the stuffed eggs and chill thoroughly in the refrigerator. NET: 4 to 6 servings.

TRUITE SAUMONÉE REINE MARIE

Braised Salmon Trout with Eggplant and Mushrooms

2 pounds salmon trout in one
   piece or a whole trout
Salt
Freshly cracked white pepper
1 cup fish stock (page 36) or
   clam juice
2 cups dry red wine
Bouquet garni, including parsley
   and thyme
6 whole peppercorns
1 garlic clove, bruised
1 onion, sliced
1 small carrot, sliced
3 egg yolks

A few grains cayenne pepper
14 tablespoons salt butter
1 teaspoon tomato paste
½ cup heavy cream
1 eggplant, medium-size
5 or 6 firm ripe tomatoes,
   skinned, seeded, and cut
   into shreds
A little chopped mint, if
   available
5 or 6 firm white mushrooms,
   sliced
Juice of half a lemon

Preheat the oven to 350°. Wash and dry the salmon trout and place it on a buttered baking dish. Season with salt and pepper and add the fish stock, wine, bouquet garni, peppercorns, garlic, onion, and carrot. Cover with buttered wax paper and cook in the oven 45 minutes, basting occasionally. Remove from the oven and keep the salmon warm. Strain the liquid (stock) and boil down to ¼ cup.

SAUCE. Beat the egg yolks in a small bowl. Add the ¼ cup reduced stock. Season with a little salt and the cayenne pepper. Stand the bowl in a shallow pan of hot water over low heat, and beat until it thickens. Bit by bit, beat in 8 tablespoons butter, the tomato paste, and the cream. Cover with plastic wrap and keep warm.

GARNISH. Cut the eggplant in slanting slices about ½ inch thick. Put them in a bowl, salt them, and let stand 30 minutes. Drain and dry them, then sauté quickly in 2 tablespoons butter. Set aside and keep them warm. Sauté the tomatoes in another 2 tablespoons butter in the same pan. Add the mint and season with salt and pepper. In the same pan, add the mushrooms, a little lemon juice, and another 2 tablespoons butter. Sauté 5 to 6 minutes.

To serve, place the salmon trout on a serving dish. On each side arrange the eggplant slices, alternating with a tablespoon of sliced mushrooms and chopped tomatoes which have been mixed together. Spoon the sauce over the fish and glaze under the broiler. NET: 4 servings.

This is an interesting luncheon or supper dish, and good, too.

SARDINES
À LA BASQUE

Sardines with Peppers
and Vegetables
au Gratin

5 tablespoons salt butter
2 large carrots, finely chopped
1 pound baby white onions,
   sliced and separated in rings
¼ cup finely diced green beans
Salt
Freshly cracked white pepper
4 tomatoes, skinned, seeded,
  and diced
2 sweet red peppers, diced
  (canned are all right)
4 tins good quality sardines,
  skinless and boneless
1 tablespoon freshly grated
  Parmesan cheese

Melt 4 tablespoons salt butter in a pan. Add the carrots, onions, and green beans. Season with salt and pepper and stir well. Cover the pan with a piece of buttered wax paper and the lid, and cook slowly 5 to 6 minutes, stirring once or twice. Add the diced tomatoes and peppers. Place this mixture on the bottom of a serving dish. Arrange the sardines on it, slightly overlapping. Sprinkle with the grated cheese and 1 tablespoon melted butter. Brown under the broiler and serve. NET: 4 servings.

ALOSE ET
LAITANCE

Poached Shad with Roe
and Fresh Tomato
Sauce

1 shad, about 2½ pounds
Shad roe
½ cup dry white wine
½ cup water
Salt
6 whole peppercorns
4 tablespoons salt butter
4 tablespoons all-purpose flour

A few grains cayenne pepper
2 teaspoons chopped fresh basil
(1 teaspoon dried)
¼ cup fresh tomato pulp
(1 large tomato, skinned and

strained)
3 large ripe tomatoes, skinned
and chopped
4 large ripe tomatoes, skinned
and sliced ¼ inch thick

Preheat the oven to 350°. Scrape the scales of the shad if the fish market hasn't already done so, clean it inside and out, wash it quickly, and dry it with paper towels. Arrange it on a buttered baking dish and pour the wine and water over it. Sprinkle with salt and the peppercorns. Cover with buttered wax paper and cook 25 minutes in the oven. Remove, arrange on a serving dish, and keep it warm. Reserve the liquid. Melt 2 tablespoons butter in a saucepan. Off the heat, stir in the flour, a little salt, and the cayenne pepper. Strain the liquid in which the fish was cooked and add it to the pan with the basil and tomato pulp. Stir over low heat until the sauce comes to a boil. Add the chopped tomatoes and simmer 10 minutes. If the sauce is too thick, add a little water. Sauté the sliced tomatoes and the roe very quickly in 2 tablespoons butter. Pour the sauce over the fish, and garnish the dish with the roe and slices of sautéed tomato. NET: 4 servings.

RAIE AU BEURRE NOIR

Poached Skate with Brown Butter

2 pounds skate (or ray)
Juice of 1 lemon
1 cup water
Salt
Freshly cracked white pepper

4 tablespoons salt butter
2 tablespoons capers, chopped
1 pound baby potatoes, steamed
whole (page 612)

Preheat the oven to 350°. Cut the skate in thick strips and wash thoroughly in lemon juice and water. Arrange on a buttered baking dish and pour over it a little lemon juice, the water, salt, and pepper. Cover with wax paper and cook 20 to 25 minutes in the oven. Drain and arrange on a hot serving dish. Brown the butter very slowly in a pan. Add a squeeze of lemon juice, the capers, salt, and pepper. Spoon over the fish. Serve the skate with steamed baby potatoes. NET: 4 servings.

RAIE AU FROMAGE

Skate Poached in Milk with Cheese Sauce

2 pounds skate (or ray), cut into
pieces 1½ inch wide
A little lemon juice
2 cups milk
1 bay leaf
Salt
Freshly ground white pepper
2 cups baby white onions
8 tablespoons salt butter
4 tablespoons all-purpose flour

A few grains cayenne pepper
1 teaspoon Dijon mustard
½ teaspoon dry mustard
¾ cup freshly grated imported
Swiss cheese
½ cup freshly grated Parmesan
cheese
⅓ cup heavy cream
2 tablespoons dry breadcrumbs
(page 69)

Preheat the oven to 350°. Wash the pieces of skate in a little lemon juice and water. Dry them on paper towels and arrange on a lightly buttered baking dish. Scald the milk with the bay leaf and a little salt. Pour this over the skate and sprinkle with a little freshly ground white pepper. Cover with a piece of buttered wax paper and cook in the oven 25 minutes. Remove and arrange the skate on a buttered serving dish. Reserve the milk it was cooked in. Quickly blanch the onions in boiling water. Drain and sauté them in 2 tablespoons butter until golden. Scatter the onions over the skate.

SAUCE. In a small saucepan, melt 4 tablespoons butter. Off the heat, stir in the flour with a little salt and cayenne pepper. Cook over low heat a few minutes without browning. Again off the heat, add the two mustards and the reserved milk. Stir over low heat until it comes to a boil. Add the Swiss cheese and half the Parmesan. Mix well and simmer gently 2 to 3 minutes. Stir in the heavy cream.

Spoon the sauce over the fish, sprinkle the top with the breadcrumbs and the rest of the Parmesan cheese, and dot with 1 to 2 tablespoons butter. Brown under a hot broiler, and serve at once. NET: 4 servings.

---

2 pounds skate (or ray) steaks
A little lemon juice
1 cup fish stock (page 36) or
    clam juice
4 tablespoons salt butter
4 chicken livers
1/4 cup Cognac or good brandy
3 large navel oranges
1 teaspoon finely chopped garlic
1 teaspoon meat glaze
1 teaspoon tomato paste
2 teaspoons potato flour

2/3 cup orange juice
1/3 cup good orange marmalade
2 cups potato purée (page 610)
1 egg
2 tablespoons sweet butter
Salt
A few grains cayenne pepper
Flour, for coating
1 egg, beaten
Dry breadcrumbs, for coating
Vegetable oil for deep-fryer

RAIE À L'ORANGE

Poached Skate with
Orange Sauce and
Orange Potatoes

Preheat the oven to 325°. Wash the skate in lemon juice and water, dry on paper towels. Place the fish on a lightly buttered baking dish. Pour the fish stock over it and cover with buttered wax paper. Poach 25 minutes in the oven. Arrange the fish on a serving dish and reserve the liquid. Cut the rinds of two of the oranges into very fine shreds crosswise, and grate the rind of the third orange.

ORANGE SAUCE (this is a brown sauce, enriched by the pan glaze from the chicken livers). In a small heavy pan, heat 1 tablespoon salt butter. Quickly brown the chicken livers on each side, then remove and use them for something else. Add 2 more tablespoons salt butter to the pan. Off the heat, add the brandy, the shredded orange rind, and the garlic. Cook over low heat 3 to 4 minutes. Again off the heat, stir in the meat glaze, tomato paste, and potato flour, then the reserved stock from the fish, orange juice, and marmalade. Stir over low heat until the sauce comes to a boil. Simmer very gently for 30 minutes, then add the skinned sections of the three oranges.

ORANGE POTATOES. Put the warm mashed potatoes in a mixer bowl. Mix in the grated orange rind, the whole egg, sweet butter, a little salt, and the cayenne pepper. Spread the potato mixture on a plate and chill thoroughly. Form it into small cork shapes with a lightly floured hand, brush them with the beaten egg, roll in breadcrumbs, and fry in hot oil (375°) until they are a golden brown. Drain on paper towels.

Spoon the orange sauce over the fish and garnish with the potatoes. NET: 4 servings.

ÉPERLANS À LA BRETONNE

Smelts Baked in Vegetable Sauce

1 carrot
1 yellow onion
Salt
Freshly cracked white pepper
6 tablespoons salt butter
2 firm white mushrooms, sliced
1 stalk celery, finely chopped
2 teaspoons finely chopped garlic

¾ cup dry white wine
1 tablespoon chopped fresh parsley
Juice of a half-lemon
¼ cup water
8 to 10 smelts (gutted)
A few dry breadcrumbs (page 69)

Preheat the oven to 400°. Cut the carrot in small matchsticks and the onion in thin half-slices. Mix with a little salt and pepper and put into a pan with 2 tablespoons butter. Cover with wax paper and bake 7 to 8 minutes. Sauté the mushrooms and the chopped celery in 2 tablespoons butter. In a separate pan, cook the garlic with 1 tablespoon butter. Add the wine and allow to reduce to one-half in quantity. Add a little salt, pepper, the parsley, lemon juice, and water. Bring to a boil. Add the carrot and onion and the mushroom and celery mixtures to the liquid. Simmer 10 minutes. Put a little of this sauce in the bottom of a heatproof serving dish. Place the well-washed smelts on top. Sprinkle with a little salt and pour over the rest of the sauce. Sprinkle with breadcrumbs and dot with butter. Bake 15 minutes. NET: 4 servings.

ÉPERLANS FARCIS

Stuffed Smelts

I have always loved this touch of romantic rhetoric within the encyclopedic discipline of *Larousse Gastronomique*: "Freshly caught smelts have a fairly strong smell, similar to that of the violet. Some authorities, however, believe that smelts recall the scent of cucumbers rather than violets. One thing is certain, that this little fish is most delicate in flavor and that fried smelts are properly regarded as one of the finest of all fish dishes." This version is a sauté of boned smelts stuffed with chopped hard-boiled egg and onion, served on a bed of tomatoes, with Mustard Hollandaise. It is easy and fun to bone smelts. Try it!

8 medium-size whole smelts, not gutted, with heads and tails on
1 lemon
10 tablespoons salt butter
1 cup finely chopped yellow

onion
2 finely chopped hard-boiled eggs
2 tablespoons chopped fresh dill
Salt

Freshly cracked white pepper
A little all-purpose flour (for dusting)
1 egg, beaten
A few white dry breadcrumbs, for coating (page 69)
5 medium-size firm ripe tomatoes, skinned and sliced ½ inch thick
½ teaspoon finely chopped garlic

MUSTARD HOLLANDAISE SAUCE
2 egg yolks
A few grains cayenne pepper
1 teaspoon dry mustard
1 teaspoon Dijon mustard
2 teaspoons tarragon vinegar
2 tablespoons heavy cream
12 tablespoons frozen sweet butter cut into small pieces
2 drops lemon juice

Wash the smelts in lemon juice and water, and dry on paper towels. Then bone them as follows. Cut off the head and the tail, using a very sharp paring knife. Slide the tip of the knife just on top of the backbone on each side to loosen the flesh. Then, rolling the fish in your hands, work it free from the bone. Very carefully pull out the backbone, holding it firmly in the left hand. In no way should the smelt be slit (you want a "hollow" smelt). Bone all the smelts in this manner and set them aside.

STUFFING. Melt 1 tablespoon salt butter in a small sauté pan and add the onion. Cook the onion and let it brown a little, then add the chopped hard-boiled eggs, mix in the dill, and season with salt and a little pepper. Remove the pan from the heat and let the stuffing cool a little.

Put the stuffing into a pastry bag fitted with a small plain round tube (about #4 size). Fill the smelts (like hollow tubes) with this mixture, dividing it evenly. Reshape them and dust them all over lightly with flour, brush with the beaten egg, and roll in the breadcrumbs. Heat 7 tablespoons salt butter in a sauté pan until it is foaming and golden brown. Fry 1 or 2 smelts at a time until they are golden brown all over. Drain them on paper towels.

GARNISH. Heat 2 tablespoons salt butter in a shallow sauté pan. Put in the sliced tomatoes and finely chopped garlic and cook briskly over moderate heat 1 to 2 minutes, breaking up the tomatoes as little as possible.

MUSTARD HOLLANDAISE SAUCE. Combine the egg yolks in a small bowl with the cayenne pepper, and two mustards, and beat very well with a little wire whisk. Mix in the vinegar and cream. Stand the bowl in a shallow pan of hot water over moderate heat. Continue beating until the yolk mixture is thick. Beat the frozen sweet butter into the sauce bit by bit, then beat in the lemon juice.

Arrange the tomato garnish on the bottom of a heated oval baking dish. Place the fried stuffed smelts on tomatoes. Serve the Mustard Hollandaise sauce in a separate bowl. Serve immediately. NET: 4 servings of 2 smelts each.

FILETS DE SOLES ALPHONSE XIII

Sautéed Fillets of Sole with Eggplant and Green Peppers

2 small eggplants
Salt
6 fillets of sole or flounder
2 tablespoons all-purpose flour
Freshly cracked white pepper
8 tablespoons salt butter
4 tablespoons vegetable oil
1 pound ripe tomatoes, skinned,
    quartered, and seeded
1 small jar Italian sweet pep-
    pers, seeded and cut in shreds
1 teaspoon finely chopped
    mixed herbs (such as parsley,
    chives, tarragon)
1 tablespoon tomato paste
1 cup fish stock (page 36) or
    clam juice

Split the eggplants in half and cut into ½-inch slices. Make a few slits in the pulp with a sharp knife. Spread on a plate and sprinkle well with salt. Let steep 30 minutes.

Wash and dry the fillets of sole. Dust them lightly with 1 tablespoon flour seasoned with a little salt and pepper. Heat 4 tablespoons butter in a sauté pan and cook the fillets on each side until golden brown. Drain and keep them warm. Drain the eggplant and squeeze dry. In another sauté pan heat the vegetable oil. Fry the eggplant slices 4 minutes on each side. Drain and set aside. Heat 3 tablespoons butter in a pan and add the tomatoes, shredded sweet peppers, and chopped herbs. Season with salt and pepper and shake the pan over moderate heat 5 minutes.

For the sauce, melt 1 tablespoon salt butter in a saucepan and off the heat add 1 tablespoon flour. Season with a little salt and pepper. Add the tomato paste and stir until smooth. Add the fish stock and stir over low heat until it comes to a boil. To serve, arrange the eggplant slices on a serving dish. Spread the tomato mixture over the eggplant. Arrange the fillets of sole on the tomatoes. Serve the sauce separately. NET: 4 to 6 servings.

TO SKIN AND BONE A SOLE OR FLOUNDER. The fish should be gutted but with the head and tail left on.

(1) Remove the skin only from the side of the fish with the dark skin. Make a little slit near the tail. With the tip of the knife, loosen underneath the skin. Sprinkle the tail with a little salt. You can now slip your thumb under the skin and move it along to the end at the head. Then do the same on the other side of the backbone. Get a firm grip on the skin and pull it off, being very careful not to take the flesh with it. Cut the skin off at the head. Trim off the tail, leaving just a stub. Leave a little skin on the tip of the nose and the tail to show that it is a sole.

(2) Take a pair of scissors and trim off the outside fins on both sides. Leave the skin on the blind (white) side.

(3) On the side of the fish that has been skinned, with a very sharp little knife cut through the flesh down the center of the backbone. Cut the flesh away from the bone on both sides, leaving an attached ½-inch margin top and bottom of the body. Carefully remove the roe and use it in making fish stock. Slide the knife just under the bone at any point and loosen all the bones on each side. Cut out the bone with scissors. Be very careful when you actually loosen the center bone in order to lift the bone away from the body; there is very little

flesh on the back side. Cut the main bone through at the top and at the tail. (Wash the backbone and it may be used in making fish stock.) The fish is now boned and ready for stuffing.

8 small fillets of sole or flounder
and the bones of the fish
1 tablespoon lemon juice plus a
little extra for washing the
fish and cabbage
½ cup water
1 garlic clove, bruised
6 whole peppercorns
1 slice onion
1 small head green cabbage

8 tablespoons salt butter
Salt
Freshly cracked white pepper
2 tablespoons dry red wine
1 tablespoon all-purpose flour
1 cup milk
½ cup freshly grated Parmesan
cheese
2 tablespoons heavy cream

*Poached Fillets of Sole
with Cabbage and
Cheese Sauce*

Preheat the oven to 350°. Wash the sole in a little lemon juice and water. Dry well. Lay the fillets on a buttered baking dish. Add 1 table-spoon lemon juice, water, garlic, peppercorns, and onion slice. Cover with the bones and a piece of buttered wax paper. Poach 15 minutes in the oven. Strain the liquid and reduce it by boiling to 2 tablespoons in quantity.

CABBAGE. Cut the cabbage in quarters, remove the stalk, and shred the cabbage very fine. Soak it in lemon juice and water 30 minutes. Blanch by bringing to a boil from cold water, strain, and add 4 table-spoons of melted butter, salt, pepper, and the wine. Cover the pan with buttered wax paper and the lid. Simmer until the cabbage is tender without browning.

SAUCE. In a saucepan, melt 2 tablespoons butter. Off the heat, stir in the flour and season with salt and pepper. Pour in the milk and stir over low heat until it comes to a boil and thickens. Add 3 tablespoons of the grated cheese, the reduced liquid from the sole, and the heavy cream. Stir in, bit by bit, 2 teaspoons butter.

To serve, spread the cabbage on the bottom of a serving dish. Place the fillets of sole on the cabbage and spoon the sauce over them. Sprinkle with the remaining grated cheese, dot with a little butter, brown under a hot broiler, and serve immediately. NET: 4 servings.

8 fillets of sole or flounder
A little all-purpose flour (for
dusting)
Salt
Freshly cracked white pepper
6 tablespoons salt butter
5 tomatoes

2 teaspoons finely chopped
garlic
1 tablespoon vegetable oil
1 teaspoon chopped fresh
tarragon
¾ cup blanched, slivered
almonds

*Sautéed Fillets of Sole
with Almonds*

Wash and dry the fillets of sole. Dust them very lightly in flour seasoned with a little salt and pepper. Heat the butter in a sauté pan and brown the fillets very quickly on each side.

Preheat the oven to 400°. Skin the tomatoes and chop them coarsely. In another pan heat the vegetable oil and add the tomatoes and the garlic. Then add the tarragon, salt, and pepper. Arrange the tomatoes on a serving dish and place the sole on top. Brown the almonds in the oven. Put them in the pan the sole was cooked in. Sprinkle with salt, toss for 1 minute, then scatter them over the fish. NET: 4 to 6 servings.

FILETS DE SOLES ANDALOUSE

Poached Fillets of Sole with Anchovy and Tomatoes

2 large beefsteak tomatoes
4 tablespoons salt butter
Salt
Freshly cracked white pepper
½ teaspoon finely chopped garlic
4 fillets of sole or flounder

1½ cups fish stock (page 36) or clam juice
2 teaspoons tomato paste
2 teaspoons potato flour
8 anchovy fillets
1 tablespoon chopped fresh parsley

Preheat the oven to 350°. Place the tomatoes in a deep bowl, cover with boiling water, leave 10 seconds, drain, and cover with cold water. Remove the skins and cut the tomatoes in half horizontally. Heat 2 tablespoons butter in a sauté pan, cook the tomatoes a few minutes on each side, season with salt and pepper, and arrange them on an au gratin dish. Add the chopped garlic to the pan the tomatoes were cooked in. Cook 1 minute and spoon over each tomato half. Keep the tomatoes warm. Fold the fillets of sole in half and arrange them in a lightly buttered baking dish. Heat the fish stock and pour it over them. Cover with buttered wax paper and poach 10 minutes in the oven. Place a fillet of sole on each tomato half. Add 2 tablespoons butter to the pan the tomatoes were cooked in. Off the heat, stir in the tomato paste and potato flour. Strain the stock the fish was cooked in, add to the pan, and stir over low heat until the sauce comes to a boil. Simmer 10 minutes. Spoon the sauce over the fish and place 2 anchovy fillets crisscross over each fillet of sole. Sprinkle with the parsley, and serve. NET: 4 servings.

FILETS DE SOLES À L'ARMORICAINE

A Crown of Fillets of Sole with Lobster and Tomatoes

LOBSTER
2 small (1 pound) live lobsters
8 tablespoons salt butter
4 tablespoons Cognac or good brandy
6 ripe tomatoes, skinned and sliced
2 teaspoons finely chopped garlic

Salt
Freshly cracked white pepper
1 tablespoon tomato paste
¾ cup plain-cooked diced green beans
¾ cup plain-cooked diced carrots
¾ cup plain-cooked diced young turnips

SOLE

8 small fillets of sole (or
   flounder)
Juice of ½ lemon
Salt butter
Salt
A few grains cayenne pepper
1 cup dry white wine
¾ cup water
1 bay leaf
6 peppercorns
¼ cup combined sliced onion,
   carrot and celery

WHITE WINE SAUCE

6 tablespoons frozen sweet
   butter
Salt
A few grains cayenne pepper
6 tablespoons all-purpose flour
Fish stock reserved from the
   sole
½ cup light cream
2 egg yolks
2 tablespoons dry sherry
4 tablespoons heavy cream
A little freshly grated Parmesan
   cheese
A little melted salt butter

LOBSTER. Split the live lobsters in half, using a large French knife. Place the point of the knife at the little cross in the shell on the center of the head, and cut down through the lobster. Discard the small sacs behind the eyes. Remove the large vein in the tail. Cut off the large claws and cut a split up each side of the claw shell with kitchen scissors. Remove the small claws.

Heat 4 tablespoons butter in a deep heavy pan. Put in the 4 halves of lobster with the small and large claws on top. Cover the pan and cook over high heat 3 minutes. Remove the cover. Heat the brandy in a small pan, ignite, and pour it over the lobsters. Cover them again and cook over moderate heat 12 minutes, or until the shells are bright red. Remove the lobsters and keep them warm. Add 4 table-spoons butter to the juices in the lobster pan. Also add the tomatoes with the garlic, salt, and pepper, and cook the mixture briskly 5 minutes. Add the tomato paste and mix well. Then add the well-drained cooked beans, carrots, and turnips. Remove all the meat from the lobsters, cut it into chunks, and add it to this mixture. Cover the lobster and tomato mixture and keep it warm.

SOLE. Preheat the oven to 350°. Wash the fillets of sole in lemon juice and water and dry well on paper towels. Put a little nut of butter, salt, and a very few grains of cayenne pepper on each fillet and fold them over lengthwise with the skin side (white) out. Fold back the narrow end. Arrange the fillets in this fashion down a flat buttered baking dish. Pour over them the wine and water, and flavor with the bay leaf, peppercorns, and mixed onion, carrot, and celery. Cover the dish with buttered wax paper and poach in the oven 15 minutes. Remove them immediately (being careful not to overcook them) and arrange them in a crown on a round flat serving dish. Cover the dish with aluminum foil and keep the fish warm. Strain the liquid in which they were cooked and reserve it.

WHITE WINE SAUCE. Melt the sweet butter in a small tin-lined copper saucepan over low heat and season it with a little salt and the cayenne pepper. Off the heat, stir in the flour. Pour in the strained liquid from the sole, and stir the sauce over low heat until it comes to a boil. Add the light cream and simmer the sauce very gently 5 minutes. In a separate small bowl mix the egg yolks with the sherry. When the mixture is well blended, mix in the heavy cream. Pour a little of the hot sauce onto the egg yolk mixture, beating all the time, then mix it all back into the sauce. Mix well, and reheat the sauce, but do not allow it to boil.

Arrange the lobster and tomato mixture in the center of the crown of fillets of sole. Coat the lobster mixture and sole with the sauce. Sprinkle with freshly grated Parmesan cheese and a few drops of melted butter. Brown the dish quickly under a hot broiler, and serve. NET: 6 to 8 servings.

FILETS DE SOLES BONNE FEMME

Poached Fillets of Sole with Mushrooms and Hollandaise Sauce

4 large fillets of sole or flounder
A little lemon juice
Salt
Freshly cracked white pepper
4 large firm white mushrooms
7 tablespoons salt butter
½ cup dry white wine
¼ cup water
2 egg yolks
A few grains cayenne pepper
2 tablespoons tarragon vinegar

2 tablespoons heavy cream
6 tablespoons frozen sweet butter, cut in pieces
Optional: Thinly sliced black truffles
5 tablespoons all-purpose flour
⅔ cup light cream
Duchess potatoes (page 609)
4 firm white mushroom caps, fluted if desired, sautéed in a little butter

Preheat the oven to 350°. Wash the fillets in lemon juice and water. Dry well. Season the skin side with a little salt and pepper. Fold over lengthwise. Arrange them on a buttered baking dish. Slice the mushrooms and sauté in 2 tablespoons salt butter, 1 teaspoon lemon juice, salt, and pepper. Cook briskly 2 minutes. Add the wine and water, bring to a boil, simmer a minute or two, and spoon over the fish. Cover the fillets with buttered wax paper and poach 15 minutes in the oven. While they are cooking, prepare the sauce.

HOLLANDAISE SAUCE. Put the egg yolks in a small bowl, add salt, the cayenne pepper and vinegar, and mix well with a little whisk. Add the heavy cream. Stand the bowl in a shallow pan of hot water over low heat. Beat with the whisk until it is as thick as you want. (You must achieve the desired thickness before adding butter.) Then add the frozen sweet butter bit by bit, and 2 drops lemon juice. When the Hollandaise sauce is finished, cover the bowl with plastic wrap and stand it in a bowl of lukewarm water (not hot) and it can hold all day. (Thinly sliced truffles may be put in the Hollandaise sauce.)

When the fillets are cooked, set aside to keep warm. Strain the stock the fish was poached in and reserve the sliced mushrooms.

FISH VELOUTÉ SAUCE. Melt 3 tablespoons salt butter in a tin-lined copper pan. Remove the pan from the heat and stir in the flour, then stir in ¾ cup strained fish stock. Stir over low heat until the sauce thickens. Add the light cream and bring to a boil. Add another 2 tablespoons salt butter, bit by bit.

The proper way to serve this dish is as follows. Encircle an oval platter with piped scallops of Duchess potatoes, dot with butter, and brown under the broiler (use a pastry bag and star tube to pipe the potatoes). Arrange the cooked fillets in the center and spoon the sliced mushrooms neatly on the fillets. Spoon the fish velouté sauce over the fillets but not over the potatoes. Then spoon a wide ribbon (4 to 5 inches) of Hollandaise sauce down the center of the dish over the velouté. Brown quickly under the broiler (not too long or the Hollandaise sauce will separate). Put one fluted sautéed mushroom on top of each fillet. Serve at once. NET: 4 servings.

FILETS DE SOLES CAPRICE

Poached Fillets of Sole with Carrot and Sherry Sauce

4 fillets of sole or flounder
Juice of half a lemon
¼ cup dry white wine
¼ cup water
Bouquet garni (parsley, dill, and
    bay leaf)
4 whole peppercorns
1 slice onion
1 garlic clove, bruised
12 tablespoons salt butter
2 carrots, finely shredded
Salt
¼ cup dry sherry
1½ tablespoons all-purpose
    flour
¼ cup milk
Freshly cracked white pepper
¼ cup light cream
4 medium-size ripe tomatoes,
    cored and skinned
4 fresh button mushrooms

Preheat the oven to 350°. Wash and dry the fillets of sole. Fold them over lengthwise and place them on a buttered baking dish. Add the lemon juice, wine, water, bouquet garni, peppercorns, onion, and garlic. Cover with buttered wax paper and poach 15 minutes in the oven. Arrange the fillets on a hot serving dish and keep them warm. Strain and reserve the liquid. Leave the oven on.

SAUCE. In a saucepan melt 8 tablespoons butter. Add the shredded carrots, salt, and dry sherry. Cover the pan with the lid and cook slowly 10 minutes, or until the carrots are soft, without browning. Off the heat, stir in the flour. Mix in ¾ cup strained liquid from the sole. Stir over low heat until the sauce thickens. Add the milk with a little extra salt and pepper. Stir over low heat until the sauce comes to a boil. Add the light cream and, bit by bit, stir in 2 tablespoons butter. Cover the pan with a piece of plastic wrap and keep it warm.

TOMATOES AND MUSHROOMS. Place the tomatoes on a baking dish. Season with salt and pepper and pour over them 2 tablespoons melted butter. Place the dish in the oven 5 minutes. Wash the mushrooms, and, if desired, flute them. Place them in a small pan and just cover with water. Add a good squeeze of lemon juice, salt, and pepper. Cover and cook 5 to 6 minutes.

To serve, place a warmed whole tomato on each fillet on the serving dish. Spoon the sauce over them. Place a mushroom on each tomato. NET: 4 servings.

FILETS DE SOLES CÉCILE

Sautéed Fillets of Sole
with Asparagus Tips

4 fillets of sole or flounder
A little all-purpose flour (for
    dusting)
Salt
Freshly cracked white pepper
4 tablespoons salt butter

16 to 20 fresh asparagus tips
3 tablespoons freshly grated
    Parmesan cheese
1 small black truffle, finely
    sliced

Wash and dry the fillets of sole. Dust them lightly in flour seasoned with a little salt and pepper. Melt the butter in a sauté pan. When foaming, put in the fillets and cook on each side until golden brown. Arrange them on a hot serving dish and keep warm. Cook the asparagus tips in boiling water (or steam them) and drain. Warm the tips 3 to 4 minutes in the pan in which the fish was cooked. Scatter the tips over the fish. Sprinkle with grated Parmesan cheese and brown quickly under a hot broiler. Garnish with a few slices of truffle and serve. NET: 4 servings.

FILETS DE SOLES CENDRILLON

Poached Fillets of Sole
in Baked Potatoes with
White Wine Sauce

"Cendrillon" literally calls for hot coals, but oven-baked potatoes do very well.

4 medium-size Idaho-type
    potatoes
4 tablespoons salt butter
½ cup hot milk
Salt
Freshly cracked white pepper
4 small fillets of sole or
    flounder, and the bones of
    the fish

A little lemon juice
¼ cup water
¼ cup dry white wine
1 bay leaf
1½ tablespoons all-purpose
    flour
¼ cup milk
1 tablespoon heavy cream
4 teaspoons tomato paste

Preheat the oven to 400°. Prick the potatoes all over with a fork and bake until soft, about 45 minutes to 1 hour. Cut off the tops of the potatoes and scoop out the insides. Rub the potato meal through a strainer and beat in 2 tablespoons butter, the hot milk, salt, and pepper. Keep it warm. Reduce the oven temperature to 350°. Wash the fillets of sole in a little lemon juice and water. Dry well. Fold in half and place them on a buttered baking dish. Pour the water and wine over them. Add salt, pepper, and the bay leaf. Cover with the fish bones and buttered wax paper. Poach 15 minutes in the oven. Remove, set the fillets aside, and keep them warm. Strain the liquid and reserve.

WHITE WINE SAUCE. In a saucepan melt 2 tablespoons butter. Off the heat, stir in the flour, salt, and pepper. Add ½ cup fish stock and bring to a boil to thicken. Add the milk and bring to a boil. Add the heavy cream.

Put 1 teaspoon of tomato paste in the bottom of each potato shell.

Put a folded fillet of sole on it and 1 teaspoon white wine sauce on each fillet. Put the mashed potato meal in a pastry bag with a large star tube. Cover each potato with potato rosettes. Arrange on a hot serving dish and serve at once. NET: 4 servings.

4 fillets of sole or flounder
½ cup dry white wine
¼ cup water
1 slice onion
Bouquet garni (including oregano, bay leaf, and parsley)
Juice of half a lemon
1 garlic clove, bruised
6 whole peppercorns
4 tablespoons salt butter
1½ tablespoons all-purpose flour
Salt

A few grains cayenne pepper
¼ cup milk
1 tablespoon heavy cream
Small anchovy fillets and strips for garnish

FISH FORCEMEAT
¼ pound cooked hake or halibut
2 egg whites
Salt
A few grains cayenne pepper
2 tablespoons heavy cream
2 anchovy fillets, finely chopped

Poached Fillets of Sole Stuffed with Forcemeat of Hake and Anchovies

FISH FORCEMEAT. Skin, bone, and mince the hake or halibut. Put the minced fish in a bowl over a bowl of ice and beat the egg whites in slowly (use a wire whisk). Add salt and cayenne pepper to season. Slowly beat in the heavy cream, then the anchovy fillets. (This forcemeat can also be beaten in an electric mixer.)

Preheat the oven to 350°. Wash and dry the fillets of sole. Spread a little of the forcemeat on the skinned side of each fillet (reserve about half the forcemeat for quenelles). Roll up the fillets, tie them with thread, and place them on a buttered baking dish. Pour on the wine and water. Add the onion, herbs, a squeeze of lemon juice, garlic clove, and peppercorns. Cover with buttered wax paper and poach 20 minutes in the oven. Drain, and reserve the stock.

QUENELLES. Have ready a pan of hot, barely simmering salted water. With two teaspoons, form the remaining forcemeat into small egg shapes. Drop them into the water. Poach gently 10 minutes without boiling. Remove them carefully and drain on paper towels. Keep them warm.

WHITE WINE SAUCE. In a saucepan melt 2 tablespoons butter. Off the heat add the flour, salt, and cayenne pepper. Add ¾ cup strained liquid from the sole. Add the milk and stir over low heat until the sauce comes to a boil. Add 1 tablespoon heavy cream. Stir in, bit by bit, 2 tablespoons butter.

Arrange the paupiettes (rolled stuffed sole) on a serving dish. Put a pile of quenelles (dumplings) in the middle of the dish. Spoon over the sauce. Decorate the top of each paupiette with a small fillet of anchovy and the pile of quenelles with strips of anchovy. NET: 4 servings.

FILETS DE SOLES FARCIS AU CHAMPAGNE

Fillets of Sole Stuffed with Lobster, Champagne Sauce

2 whole Dover soles or flounder
3 tablespoons salt butter
1 cup finely chopped fresh white mushrooms
1 lemon
Salt
Freshly cracked white pepper
1 small black truffle, chopped
1 tablespoon chopped fresh chives
Meat of 1 small (about ¾ pound) boiled lobster, finely chopped
1 pint brut Champagne
2 cups heavy cream
2 tablespoons salt butter mixed with 2 tablespoons all-purpose flour

Preheat the oven to 350°. Wash the fish in a little lemon juice and water, and dry them. Skin and bone the fish (page 266). Fold back the two fillets. Melt the butter in a sauté pan. Add the chopped mushrooms, a little lemon juice, salt and pepper. Cook briskly a few minutes. Add three-quarters of the chopped truffle and the chives and lobster meat. Mix well and stuff in the belly of the soles. Reshape the fish and place on a buttered baking dish.

Open the bottle of brut Champagne and pour it over the fish. Cover with buttered wax paper and poach 25 minutes in the oven. Remove from the oven and place the fish on a flat serving dish. Strain the liquid and boil it down to 2 tablespoons. Scald the cream and add the reduced fish liquid. Then, bit by bit, stir in the mixed butter and flour. Bring the sauce to a boil, add the rest of the chopped truffle, and pour over the fish. Serve at once. NET: 4 servings.

FILETS DE SOLES COLBERT

Sautéed Fillets of Sole with Maître d'Hôtel Butter

4 fillets of sole or flounder
Juice of half a lemon
A little all-purpose flour (for dusting the fillets)
Salt
Freshly cracked white pepper
1 egg, beaten
½ cup dry breadcrumbs (page 69)
4 tablespoons vegetable oil
2 tablespoons chopped fresh parsley
Maître d'Hôtel Butter (page 57)

Wash the fillets of sole in lemon juice and water and dry well. Dust them lightly with flour seasoned with a little salt and pepper. Brush the fillets with beaten egg and roll them in the breadcrumbs. Heat the vegetable oil very hot in a sauté pan. Cook the fillets in the hot oil on each side to a golden brown. Arrange them on a hot serving dish. Garnish with chopped fresh parsley. Serve with the traditional Maître d'Hôtel Butter. NET: 4 servings.

FILETS DE SOLES À LA CRÈME

Poached Fillets of Sole with White Wine Sauce

4 fillets of sole or flounder, and the bones of the fish
Juice of half a lemon
4 whole peppercorns
1 sprig fresh tarragon
1 garlic clove, bruised
1½ cups dry white wine
2 tablespoons salt butter
Salt
Freshly cracked black pepper

½ cup heavy cream   1 teaspoon chopped fresh
                                       parsley

Preheat the oven to 350°. Wash and dry the fillets of sole. Place them
on a buttered baking dish. Add the peppercorns, tarragon, and garlic.
Cover with the fish bones and pour in the wine. Cover with buttered
wax paper and poach 15 minutes in the oven. Remove the fillets,
arrange on a hot serving dish, and keep warm. Strain the liquid, boil
down to ¾ cup, and reserve. In a saucepan melt the butter. Season
with a little salt and pepper. Add the heavy cream and slowly beat
in the reduced liquid from the sole. Bring slowly to a boil and simmer
to the consistency of cream. Add the parsley. Spoon the sauce over
the sole and serve very hot. NET: 4 servings.

FILETS DE SOLES DIEPPOISE

*Poached Fillets of Sole
with Shrimps and
Mussels, Velouté Sauce*

4 fillets of sole, flounder, or
   whiting
Juice of half a lemon plus a little
   extra for washing the fish
¾ cup dry white wine
1 cup water
1 slice onion
1 garlic clove, bruised
Bouquet garni, including parsley
   and thyme
Freshly cracked white pepper
3 cups mussels (in the shells)
1 teaspoon dry mustard
1 bay leaf
1 small onion, sliced
1 small carrot, sliced
6 whole peppercorns
Salt
¾ cup whole shrimps, shelled
   and cooked
5 tablespoons salt butter
¼ cup heavy cream
1 tablespoon chopped fresh
   parsley
3 tablespoons all-purpose flour
1 tablespoon freshly grated
   Parmesan cheese

Preheat the oven to 350°. Wash the fillets in a little lemon juice and
water and dry well. Fold the fillets lengthwise and turn under the
tail ends. Place them on a buttered baking dish. Pour over the juice
of half a lemon, ½ cup wine, and the water. Add the onion slice,
half the garlic clove, and the herbs and pepper. Cover with buttered
wax paper and poach 15 minutes in the oven. Carefully remove the
fillets to a warm serving dish. Strain and reserve the stock. Wash the
mussels well in cold water and the mustard. Put them in a pan with
the bay leaf, onion, carrot, peppercorns, salt, and the rest of the
garlic. Add ¼ cup wine and a little water. Bring slowly to a boil,
cover, and shake over moderate heat 3 to 4 minutes. Strain, shell,
and remove the beards from the mussels. Put the mussels and shrimps
in a sauté pan with 1 tablespoon butter, 2 tablespoons heavy cream,
and a sprinkling of chopped parsley and pepper. Shake over moderate
heat a few minutes.

VELOUTÉ SAUCE. Reduce the fish stock to 1 cup. In a saucepan melt
2 tablespoons butter. Remove from the heat and add the flour. Season
with a little salt and pepper and pour in the reduced fish stock. Stir
over low heat until the sauce comes to a boil. Add, bit by bit, 2 table-

spoons butter and the rest of the heavy cream. Simmer 3 to 4 minutes.

Scatter the mussels and shrimps over the warm fillets on the dish, and spoon over the sauce. Sprinkle with the grated cheese and brown under the broiler. NET: 4 servings.

FILETS DE SOLES DORIA

Deep-Fried Fillets of Sole with Buttered Cucumber

This salpicon of cucumber is also excellent with grilled sole, hake, or cod.

4 fillets of sole or flounder
A little lemon juice
A little all-purpose flour (to
    dust the sole)
Salt
Freshly cracked white pepper
1 egg, beaten
Dried white breadcrumbs for

coating (page 69)
Vegetable oil for deep-fryer
1 small cucumber
2 tablespoons salt butter
1 teaspoon chopped fresh mint
    leaves or dill
Lemon wedges

Wash the fillets of sole in lemon juice and water. Dry, dust lightly with flour, salt, and pepper, then brush them with beaten egg and roll in the dried white breadcrumbs. Deep-fry the fillets in hot (375°) fat until golden brown. Remove, drain on paper towels, and place on a hot serving dish.

SALPICON OF CUCUMBER. Cut off the top and bottom of the cucumber. Skin and seed it. Cut it into small dice. Melt the butter in a small heavy pan. Add the cucumber, salt and pepper. Cover with wax paper and the lid, and cook very slowly 7 to 8 minutes. Remove the lid and paper and add the chopped mint or dill.

Serve the fish with the cucumber and lemon wedges. NET: 4 servings.

FILETS DE SOLES DUGLERÉ

Poached Fillets of Sole with Fresh Tomatoes and Mushrooms, Velouté Sauce

4 fillets of sole or flounder
1 teaspoon lemon juice plus
    extra for washing the fish
6 tablespoons sweet butter
3 firm white mushrooms, sliced
Salt
1 cup dry white wine
½ cup water
4 whole peppercorns
3 tablespoons all-purpose flour
A few grains cayenne pepper

4 tomatoes, skinned
½ cup light cream
¼ cup heavy cream
2 teaspoons chopped fresh
    parsley
2 tablespoons dry breadcrumbs
    (page 69)
3 tablespoons freshly grated
    Parmesan cheese
A little melted salt butter

Preheat the oven to 350°. Wash the fillets in a little lemon juice and water. Dry well and place on a buttered baking dish. Melt 2 tablespoons butter in a sauté pan, and sauté the sliced mushrooms over moderate heat with 1 teaspoon lemon juice and a little salt. Cook 2 minutes. Add the wine, water, and peppercorns. Bring to a boil and pour over the fillets. Cover with buttered wax paper and poach 15 minutes in the oven. Arrange the fillets on a serving dish, and keep them warm. Strain, and reserve the liquid and the mushrooms.

VELOUTÉ SAUCE. Melt 4 tablespoons butter in a saucepan. Off the heat, stir in the flour, salt, and cayenne pepper. Add 1 cup of the reserved fish liquid. Cut the tomatoes in quarters, remove the seeds, and rub the seeds through a fine vegetable strainer to extract whatever juice there may be. Add this juice to the sauce. (Reserve the outer tomato sections.) Stir the sauce over low heat until it comes to a boil. Stir in the light cream, then the heavy cream. Cut the tomato sections into neat strips. Add these strips, the reserved mushrooms, and the chopped parsley to the sauce.

Spoon the sauce over the fillets. Sprinkle with the breadcrumbs, grated cheese, and a little melted butter. Brown under a hot broiler. NET: 4 servings.

FILETS DE SOLES DURAND

Baked Fillets of Sole on Mixed Vegetables, with Tomatoes

8 tablespoons salt butter
2 cups finely diced carrots
2 cups finely diced turnips
1 cup finely diced onions
2 cups dry white wine
2 tablespoons chopped mixed
   herbs, including parsley
   and thyme
Salt

Freshly cracked white pepper
4 fillets of sole or flounder
6 large ripe tomatoes, skinned,
   seeded, and shredded
1 teaspoon potato flour
Juice of half a lemon
½ cup heavy cream
1 tablespoon chopped fresh
   parsley

Preheat the oven to 350°. In a heavy pan melt 2 tablespoons of butter and add the carrots, turnips, onions, half the wine, and half the chopped mixed herbs. Mix well. Cover with wax paper and cook until dry, without browning. Season with a little salt and white pepper. Wash and dry the fillets of sole well. Place on a baking dish. Spoon the cooked vegetable mixture and the shredded tomatoes around the sole. Sprinkle well with the rest of the mixed herbs, moisten with the rest of the wine, and cook 25 minutes in the oven, basting frequently with the sauce in the dish. Remove from the oven, and strain off the liquid into a saucepan, and reduce it (by boiling) to half quantity (about ⅓ cup). Off the heat, mix in the flour, a little lemon juice, and 2 tablespoons water. Beat in the heavy cream very slowly and season well. Bring slowly to a boil. Add bit by bit, off the fire, 2 tablespoons of butter and the parsley. Pour the sauce over the sole. Brown under the broiler 2 to 3 minutes before serving. NET: 4 servings.

FILETS DE SOLES FLORENTINE

Poached Fillets of Sole with Lobster and Spinach Hollandaise

8 fillets of sole or flounder
½ cup dry white wine
Salt
Freshly cracked white pepper

1 bay leaf
2 small boiled lobsters (about
   ¾ pound each)
4 tablespoons salt butter

1 tablespoon Marsala wine
½ cup cut-up raw spinach
3 egg yolks

A few grains cayenne pepper
4 tablespoons heavy cream
1 tablespoon tarragon vinegar

Preheat the oven to 350°. Wash and dry the fillets. Put them on a buttered baking dish and add the wine, salt, pepper, and bay leaf. Cover with buttered wax paper and poach 15 minutes in the oven. Remove, and arrange the fillets on a serving dish. Strain the liquid, boil down to 1 tablespoon in quantity, and reserve for the sauce. Remove the meat from the tails and claws of the boiled lobsters. Cut it into small bite-size pieces. Heat 2 tablespoons butter in a sauté pan, put in the pieces of lobster, season with salt and pepper, toss over brisk heat a few minutes, then add the Marsala. Scatter the lobster over the sole.

SPINACH HOLLANDAISE SAUCE. Put the spinach through a fine meat grinder or blender. In a bowl put the egg yolks, salt, cayenne pepper, 2 tablespoons heavy cream, and the vinegar, and beat well with a wire whisk. Put the bowl in a shallow pan of hot water over low heat and continue beating until the sauce thickens. Then add, bit by bit, 2 tablespoons butter, 2 tablespoons heavy cream, the ground spinach, and the tablespoon of reduced fish stock. Season well.

Spoon the sauce over the fish, brown under a hot broiler, and serve.
NET: 4 to 6 servings.

FILETS DE SOLES GEORGETTE

Poached Sole and
Shrimps in Potato
Shells, Nantua Sauce

4 fillets of sole or flounder
1⅓ cups water
Juice of 1 lemon
Salt
Freshly cracked white pepper
4 Idaho-type potatoes
½ cup raw shrimps with shells

8 tablespoons salt butter
1 tablespoon chopped fresh
  parsley
5 tablespoons heavy cream
3 tablespoons all-purpose flour
A few grains cayenne pepper
1 cup milk

Preheat the oven to 350°. Wash and dry the fillets of sole. Fold them lengthwise with tail ends under. Place on a buttered baking dish. Pour over the water and lemon juice, and season with salt and pepper. Cover with buttered wax paper and poach 15 minutes in the oven. Drain. Scrub the potatoes well. Prick all over with a fork and bake until soft. Toss the raw shrimps in 1 tablespoon hot salt butter. Season with salt and pepper. Add the chopped parsley and 3 tablespoons heavy cream. Simmer 2 to 3 minutes.

BÉCHAMEL SAUCE. Melt 3 tablespoons butter in a pan. Off the heat, stir in the flour. Season with salt and cayenne pepper. Mix in the milk. Stir over low heat until the sauce comes to a boil. Add 2 tablespoons heavy cream.

NANTUA SAUCE. Shell the cooked shrimps and set them aside. Pulverize the shells in a blender with 2 tablespoons butter. Pass through a fine sieve. Add a little pepper and the Béchamel Sauce. Simmer 2 to 3 minutes, stirring constantly.

Cut off the top of each potato and scoop out some of the potato meal.

In a mixer beat the potato meal until smooth, then add 2 tablespoons butter, salt, and pepper. Set aside. Place some shrimps in the hollow of each potato. Place a folded fillet of sole on the shrimps. Coat with the Nantua sauce and replace the top of the potato. Put the creamed potato meal in a pastry bag with a star tube and pipe around the edge of the potatoes. Serve the stuffed potatoes on a napkin with a bouquet of parsley in the center of the dish. NET: 4 servings.

---

4 fillets of sole or flounder
Lemon juice
7 tablespoons salt butter
Meat of 1 small boiled lobster
¼ cup plus 2 tablespoons
    Cognac or good brandy
Salt
Freshly cracked white pepper
A few grains cayenne pepper
¼ pound cooked shrimps,
    shelled and sliced
¼ pound firm white mushrooms,
    sliced
1 tablespoon chopped fresh

chives or parsley
A little melted salt butter

QUICK MOUSSELINE SAUCE
12 large mussels
1 teaspoon dry mustard
1 small onion, sliced
1 small piece of celery, sliced
1 small piece of carrot, sliced
½ cup dry white wine
¼ cup water
5 egg yolks
Salt
12 tablespoons sweet butter

FILETS DE SOLES GRAND VÉFOUR EN PAPILLOTE

Fillets of Sole with Lobster Baked in Paper, Sauce Mousseline

Preheat the oven to 350°. Cut the fillets in half lengthwise. Wash in lemon juice and water and dry thoroughly. Fold the fillets lengthwise, tail end under. Cut some little diagonal slits on the fillets, and in each slit insert a thin slice of lobster tail. Sprinkle the fillets with a little brandy, salt, and white pepper, and set aside to marinate. Chop fine the rest of the lobster tail meat and the claws. Melt 4 tablespoons butter in a pan. Add the lobster, any coral there may be, the sliced shrimps, salt, and cayenne pepper. In another pan melt 3 tablespoons butter and add the mushrooms. Cook briskly, adding 1 teaspoon lemon juice, salt, and cayenne pepper. Add the mushrooms to the lobster and shrimp mixture. Add the chopped chives or parsley. In a little pan, heat 2 tablespoons brandy, ignite, and add to this mixture.

Cut heavy parchment, freezer paper, or wax paper into eight 7-inch squares. Brush the top of each square with a little melted butter. Place 1 folded fillet in the center of the square of paper and put a spoonful of the lobster and shrimp mixture on the fillet. Sprinkle with a little more melted butter and fold the paper like a package. Place the wrapped fillets on a jellyroll pan or baking dish, and bake 25 minutes.

QUICK MOUSSELINE SAUCE. Wash the mussels in cold water and the mustard. Put them in a pan with the onion, celery, carrot, wine and water. Bring to a boil, cover the pan, and cook briskly 2 minutes (until the mussels open). Strain off the liquid and boil it down to 4 table-spoons. Beat the egg yolks in an electric mixer until they are light and fluffy. Slowly add the reduced mussel stock. Add salt, if needed, and beat until very thick. Dissolve the butter and just bring it to a boil.

Remove the egg yolk mixture from the mixer, and with a wire whisk slowly beat in the melted butter. Remove the mussels from the shells and add them to the sauce.

When the fillets are cooked, cut a slit in the top of the paper so your guests can see what you are serving. Serve the sauce separately. NET: 4 servings.

FILETS DE SOLES JOINVILLE

Poached Turban of Sole with Salmon Mousse, Velouté Sauce

A Vicomtesse de Joinville doted on beautiful fish dishes, and this dish, traditionally presented in a "turban style," was created especially for her.

10 small fillets of sole or flounder
1¼ pounds fresh salmon (uncooked, finely ground)
3 egg yolks
3 egg whites
1¼ cups plus ⅓ cup light cream
Salt
Freshly cracked white pepper
¼ teaspoon ground cardamom seed
12 tablespoons salt butter
6 tablespoons all-purpose flour
½ teaspoon tomato paste
1¾ cups fish stock (page 36) or clam juice

⅓ cup plus 3 tablespoons heavy cream
2 tablespoons dry sherry
½ pound firm white mushrooms, sliced
6 whole firm white mushrooms
1 teaspoon lemon juice plus a little extra for washing the fish
¾ pound cooked shrimps, shelled
2 tablespoons chopped fresh parsley
1 black truffle, sliced
2 teaspoons salt

Preheat the oven to 350°. Generously butter an 8-inch diameter ring mold. Wash and dry the fillets of sole in a little lemon juice and water, and cut them in half lengthwise with scissors. Line the mold with the fillets, laying each one in the mold white side down, with the narrow end to the center and the wide end over the outer edge. The fillets must overlap slightly.

SALMON MOUSSE. Put the ground salmon in a mixer bowl with the egg whites and mix well. Add 1¼ cups light cream very, very slowly. Then add 2 teaspoons salt, a little pepper, and the ground cardamom seed.

Fill the mold with this mixture, and fold over the ends of the fillets to cover the mousse. Cover the mold with buttered wax paper. Stand it in a shallow pan half filled with hot water, and set it in the oven to bake 30 minutes. Remove from the oven and water bath and cool at least 8 minutes. Turn out onto a serving platter.

VELOUTÉ SAUCE. Melt 8 tablespoons butter in a saucepan. Off the heat, stir in the flour, salt, a little pepper, tomato paste, and fish stock. Return to low heat and bring to a boil, stirring constantly. Add ⅓ cup light cream, ⅓ cup heavy cream, and simmer 2 to 3 minutes. In a separate bowl, mix the egg yolks with the sherry and 3 tablespoons heavy cream. Pour a little of the hot sauce into the egg yolk mixture, stirring constantly. Then return the yolk mixture to the rest of the sauce in the pan. Reheat without boiling. Coat the mold with this sauce.

GARNISH. In a sauté pan melt 4 tablespoons butter. Add the sliced mushrooms, whole mushrooms (which can be fluted, if desired), 1 teaspoon lemon juice, salt, and a little pepper. Add the shrimps and chopped parsley. Heat a little. Remove the whole mushrooms. Fill the center of the mold with the shrimps and sliced mushrooms. Decorate the dish with the whole mushroom caps and slices of truffle. NET: 4 to 6 servings.

FILETS DE SOLES JUDIC

Poached Fillets of Sole on Braised Lettuce, Velouté Sauce

Puff pastry crescents (page 254)
2 heads Boston lettuce
Salt
Freshly cracked white pepper
½ cup fish stock (page 36)
*   or clam juice*
¼ cup hake or halibut
2 egg whites, unbeaten
4 tablespoons heavy cream
4 fillets of sole or flounder and
*   the fish bones*
Juice of half a lemon

1 garlic clove, bruised
1 slice onion
6 whole peppercorns
Bouquet garni (fresh parsley and
*   bay leaf)*
½ cup dry white wine
¼ cup water
5 tablespoons salt butter
1½ tablespoons all-purpose
*   flour*
¼ cup milk
A little melted salt butter

Make the puff pastry crescents first, and keep them warm. Clean the lettuce, remove the outside leaves, and cut each head in half. Put in a pan of cold water and bring to a boil. Drain, and dry on paper towels. Place on a buttered baking dish and sprinkle with salt and pepper. Pour the fish stock over the lettuce halves, cover with buttered wax paper, and put in the oven to braise 35 minutes. (Keep the oven on for the sole.) Skin, bone, and mince the raw hake or halibut. Put it into a bowl over another bowl of ice (or in an electric mixer) and beat in the egg whites. Add ¼ teaspoon each of salt and freshly cracked white pepper, beating constantly. Slowly add 2 tablespoons heavy cream, while continuing to beat. Set this forcemeat aside while you wash and dry the fillets of sole, then spread a tablespoon of it on the shiny (skinned) side of the fillets. Fold over lengthwise and place on a buttered baking dish. Add the lemon juice, garlic, onion, peppercorns, bouquet garni, wine, and water. Cover with the fish bones. Poach 20 minutes in the oven. Remove from the oven, and strain off and reserve the liquid.

VELOUTÉ SAUCE. In a saucepan, melt 3 tablespoons butter. Remove from the heat and add the flour, salt, and pepper. Stir until smooth. Add the strained stock from the sole. Return to low heat and stir until the sauce thickens. Add the milk and bring to a boil. Bit by bit add the rest of the butter and 2 tablespoons heavy cream.

Remove the lettuce from the baking dish, dry on paper towels, and arrange on a serving dish. Place a stuffed fillet on each lettuce half. Spoon over the sauce, dot with a little melted butter, and brown under a hot broiler. Surround with crescents of puff paste. NET: 4 servings.

FILETS DE SOLES MACONNAISE

Poached Fillets of Sole
in Red Wine Sauce
with Mushrooms and
Onions

4 fillets of sole or flounder, and
   the fish bones
Juice of half a lemon plus
   1 teaspoon
½ cup dry red wine
¼ cup water
Bouquet garni, including
   tarragon, parsley, and
   1 bay leaf
1 garlic clove, bruised
1 slice of onion

4 whole peppercorns
1 pound firm white mushrooms
6 tablespoons salt butter
Salt
Freshly cracked white pepper
1½ tablespoons all-purpose
   flour
A few grains cayenne pepper
2 tablespoons heavy cream
18 baby onions (if using fresh,
   blanch them, page 78)

Preheat the oven to 350°. Wash and dry the fillets of sole, and arrange on a buttered baking dish. Pour on the juice of half a lemon, wine, and water. Add the bouquet garni, garlic clove, onion slice, and peppercorns. Cover with the fish bones and buttered wax paper. Poach 15 minutes in the oven. Remove, arrange the fillets on a hot serving dish, and keep them warm. Strain and reserve the liquid. Wash the mushrooms and cut in quarters. Melt 2 tablespoons butter in sauté pan. Add the mushrooms, 1 teaspoon lemon juice, salt, and pepper. Cook 2 to 3 minutes and keep them warm. Put 2 tablespoons butter in a saucepan. Off the heat, add the flour, salt, and cayenne pepper. Stir until smooth. Add the strained liquid from the sole (at least ¾ cup). Bring the mixture to a boil. Over low heat, stir in 2 more tablespoons butter bit by bit, and the heavy cream. Add the baby onions to the sauce and simmer gently 5 to 6 minutes. Keep the sauce warm. To serve, scatter the mushrooms on the fillets of sole. Spoon the red wine sauce and the onions over them. NET: 4 servings.

FILETS DE SOLES MARGUERY

Poached Fillets of Sole
with Mussels and
Shrimps in Mussel
Fumet

4 fillets of sole or flounder
½ cup dry white wine
½ cup water
1 bay leaf
1 slice onion
4 whole peppercorns
2 cups large mussels (in shells)
1 teaspoon dry mustard

½ cup shelled boiled shrimps
7 tablespoons salt butter
2 tablespoons all-purpose flour
Salt
Freshly cracked white pepper
6 tablespoons heavy cream
¼ pound firm white
   mushrooms, sliced

Preheat the oven to 350°. Wash and dry the fillets of sole. Fold them lengthwise, place on a buttered baking dish, pour over the wine and water, and add the bay leaf, onion, and peppercorns. Cover with buttered wax paper and poach 15 minutes in the oven. Remove, arrange the sole on a serving dish, strain and reserve the liquid. Wash the mussels very well in cold water and the dry mustard. Put them in a pan. Pour on the liquid from the sole. Bring slowly to a boil, cover, and let simmer a few minutes until the shells are open. Remove the mussels from the shells, and remove the beards. Strain and reserve the liquid. Warm the boiled shrimps in 1 tablespoon of melted butter, salt, and a little pepper. Set aside.

SAUCE. Melt 2 tablespoons butter in a saucepan. Off the heat, add the flour, salt, pepper, and 1 cup of the mussel liquid. Stir over low heat until the sauce comes to a boil. Add the heavy cream and bring to a boil. Stir in, bit by bit, 2 tablespoons of butter.

To serve, scatter the cooked mussels and shrimps over the fillets of sole. Sauté the sliced mushrooms in 2 tablespoons butter and scatter them over the mussels and shrimps. Spoon over the sauce. Sprinkle with a little more melted butter. Brown under a hot broiler. NET: 4 servings.

FILETS DE SOLES À LA MEUNIÈRE

Sautéed Fillets of Sole with Orange and Tomato Sections

2 large navel oranges
3 large ripe tomatoes
8 tablespoons salt butter
4 fillets of sole or flounder
A little all-purpose flour (for dusting)
Salt
Freshly cracked white pepper
¼ teaspoon finely chopped

garlic
5 thin slices bacon, grilled crisp
Juice of half a lemon
¼ cup dry white wine
1 teaspoon finely chopped shallot
1 teaspoon chopped mixed fresh parsley and thyme
Thin slices of lemon

Remove the pith and rind from the oranges and cut in sections. Skin and quarter the tomatoes and remove the seeds. Shake the seeded tomato sections and orange sections over brisk heat in 1 tablespoon hot butter for 1 minute and keep them warm. Wash and dry the fillets. Lightly flour them and season with salt and pepper. Heat a sauté pan and put in 4 tablespoons butter. When it is foaming, put in the fillets. Fry until golden brown on each side, turning only once. Arrange them on a serving dish with a grilled slice of bacon between each fillet. Strew the orange and tomato sections around the serving dish. Strain the butter from the sauté pan and return it to the pan with 3 more tablespoons butter. Reheat, and when the butter is foaming, quickly add the lemon juice, wine, shallot, mixed herbs, and garlic. Season with salt and pepper. Cook 1 minute swirling the mixture around the pan with a whisk. Pour this butter over the fish and serve at once. Garnish with thin slices of lemon. NET: 4 servings.

FILETS DE SOLES MONTROUGE

Poached Fillets of Sole on a Carrot and Potato Purée, Velouté Sauce

¾ pound carrots
2 Idaho-type potatoes, peeled
Salt
Freshly cracked white pepper
10 tablespoons salt butter
2 egg yolks
4 fillets of sole or flounder, and

the fish bones
1 garlic clove, bruised
1 slice onion
1 bay leaf
Juice of half a lemon
6 whole peppercorns
½ cup water

½ cup dry white wine
1½ tablespoons all-purpose

flour
2 tablespoons heavy cream

CARROT AND POTATO PURÉE. Cut up ½ pound carrots and the potatoes, put in a pan, and cover with cold water. Add salt, pepper, and 3 tablespoons butter. Bring slowly to a boil and simmer until tender. Drain, return to the pan and dry a little over the heat. Put them in an electric mixer bowl and beat until smooth and well blended. Add 2 tablespoons butter, the egg yolks, salt and pepper to season. Arrange the purée in a mound on the bottom of a serving dish and keep it warm.

Preheat the oven to 350°. Wash and dry the fillets of sole. Fold over the tail end of each fillet and place them, white side up, on a buttered baking dish. Add the garlic, onion, bay leaf, lemon juice, peppercorns, water, and wine. Cover with the fish bones and buttered wax paper. Poach 15 minutes in the oven. Remove; arrange the fillets on the purée, strain and reserve the liquid.

SAUCE. Finely shred the remaining ¼ pound carrots. In a saucepan melt 3 tablespoons butter. Add the shredded carrots. Season with salt and pepper. Cover the pan and cook slowly until the carrots are nearly soft. Remove from the heat and add the flour. Stir in the strained liquid from the sole, return to the heat and bring to a boil. Bit by bit, add 2 tablespoons butter and the heavy cream.

To serve, spoon the sauce over the fillets and the purée. NET: 4 servings.

FILETS DE SOLES À LA MORNAY

Poached Fillets of Sole
with Cheese Sauce

4 fillets of sole or flounder, and
   the fish bones
Juice of half a lemon
2 bay leaves
1 sprig thyme
1 cup water
1 cup milk
1 slice onion
2 garlic cloves, bruised

4 whole peppercorns
4 tablespoons salt butter
2 tablespoons all-purpose flour
Salt
Freshly cracked white pepper
2 tablespoons heavy cream
4 tablespoons freshly grated
   Parmesan cheese

Preheat the oven to 350°. Wash and dry the fillets of sole and fold lengthwise, tail ends under. Place on a buttered baking dish. Add the lemon juice, 1 bay leaf, the thyme, and water. Cover with the fish bones and buttered wax paper. Poach 15 minutes in the oven.

MORNAY SAUCE. Put the milk, onion, garlic, peppercorns, and the other bay leaf in a pan. Bring slowly to a boil and strain. Melt the butter in a saucepan. Off the heat, stir in the flour and season with salt and pepper. Return the pan to low heat and cook a moment without browning. Add the strained milk mixture. Stir over low heat until the sauce comes to a boil. Simmer a few minutes and stir in 3 tablespoons grated cheese.

To serve, arrange the fillets on a serving dish. Spoon the sauce over them. Sprinkle with the rest of the grated cheese and brown under a hot broiler. NET: 4 servings.

8 small fillets of sole or flounder, and the bones
Juice of half a lemon
8 tablespoons salt butter
1 onion, sliced
1 carrot, sliced
1 stalk celery, sliced
1 sprig thyme
1 sprig parsley
1 bay leaf
6 peppercorns, black and white mixed

Salt
1½ cups water
½ cup dry white wine
Meat from 1 small crab or ¾ cup lump crab
A few grains cayenne pepper
6 tablespoons heavy cream
3 tablespoons all-purpose flour
Freshly cracked white pepper
½ cup milk
3 tablespoons freshly grated Parmesan cheese

FILETS DE SOLES NAVAROFF

Poached Fillets of Sole on Crab Meat Coated with Cheese Sauce

Preheat the oven to 350°. Wash the fillets of sole in a little lemon juice and water and dry well. Place on a buttered baking dish. Melt 2 table-spoons butter in a deep pan. Sauté the onion, carrot, and celery a few minutes. Add the fish bones, thyme, parsley, bay leaf, peppercorns, salt, water, and wine. Bring to a boil and simmer down to half the quantity. Strain the liquid (court-bouillon) and pour over the fillets. Cover with buttered wax paper and poach in the oven 20 minutes. Remove the meat from the crab with a small paring knife (or use the lump crab) and add it to 2 tablespoons melted butter in a sauté pan. Add salt, cayenne pepper, and 3 tablespoons heavy cream. Heat gently. Spread the crab on the bottom of a hot serving dish. Arrange the cooked fillets of sole on the crab. Strain and re-serve the liquid in which the sole was cooked.

CHEESE SAUCE. In a saucepan, melt 2 tablespoons butter. Off the heat, add the flour, salt, and white pepper. Stir in ½ cup of the liquid from the sole, and stir over low heat until the sauce thickens. Add the milk and bring to a boil. Stir in most of the grated cheese, 3 tablespoons heavy cream, and bit by bit, 2 tablespoons butter. Simmer very slowly 4 to 5 minutes.

Spoon the sauce over the fish. Sprinkle with a little more grated cheese. For decoration, mark a crisscross design on the coated fish with a red-hot skewer. NET: 4 servings.

8 fillets of sole or flounder
A little all-purpose flour (for dusting)
Salt
Freshly cracked white pepper
8 tablespoons salt butter

1 teaspoon finely chopped garlic
6 tomatoes, skinned and cut in thick slices
1 cup chopped raw spinach
½ cup sour cream mixed with ¼ cup light cream

SOLE NEW ORLEANS

Fried Fillets of Sole on Fresh Tomatoes, with Spinach and Cream Sauce

2 tablespoons freshly grated
  Parmiesan cheese
½ teaspoon lemon juice

1 tablespoon coarsely chopped
  fresh parsley

Wash and dry the fillets of sole, and dust with flour seasoned with salt and pepper. Heat 6 tablespoons butter in a sauté pan and cook the fillets on both sides until golden brown. Drain and keep them warm. In another pan melt 2 tablespoons butter. Add the garlic, cook 1 minute without browning, then add the tomatoes. Cook briskly 2 minutes.

SPINACH AND CREAM SAUCE. Put the raw spinach through a fine meat chopper, and transfer it to a bowl, and add the mixed sour cream and light cream. Season with salt and pepper and add the grated cheese and lemon juice.

Arrange the sautéed tomato slices on the bottom of a serving dish. Place the fillets on top. Spoon the sauce over the sole and sprinkle with chopped fresh parsley. Brown under a hot broiler and serve. NET: 4 servings.

FILETS DE SOLES NORDAISE

Poached Fillets of Sole with Cheese and Mushroom Sauce

4 fillets of sole or flounder and
  the bones
Juice of half a lemon
¼ cup water
1 slice onion
1 garlic clove, bruised
Bouquet garni, including parsley
  and celery leaf
5 tablespoons salt butter
4 ounces firm white mushrooms,

thickly sliced
Salt
Freshly cracked white pepper
2 egg yolks
¾ cup heavy cream
3 tablespoons freshly grated
  Parmesan cheese
A few grains cayenne pepper
A little melted butter

Preheat the oven to 350°. Wash and dry the fillets and place on a buttered baking dish. Add the lemon juice, water, onion, garlic, and herbs. Cover with the fish bones and poach 15 minutes in the oven. Arrange the fillets on a serving dish. Strain the stock, boil it down to 1 tablespoon, and reserve it. In a sauté pan melt 2 tablespoons butter. Add the sliced mushrooms, salt, and a little white pepper. Sauté with the lid on 5 to 6 minutes. In a saucepan melt 3 tablespoons butter. In a separate little bowl beat the egg yolks with the heavy cream, and add to the melted butter in the saucepan, stirring constantly. Add the grated cheese, salt, and cayenne pepper. Stir over low heat until the sauce thickens. Add the mushrooms and reduced fish stock and mix well. Spoon the sauce over the fillets on the serving dish. Sprinkle with a little melted butter and brown under a hot broiler. NET: 4 servings.

FILETS DE SOLES NORMANDE

Poached Fillets of Sole Normande

The poached fillets are coated with the classic Normande Sauce, made with oyster and mushroom juices, and garnished with steamed baby potatoes. The recipe is a contemporary adaptation of the very elaborate Sole Normande in its ultimate expression of haute cuisine, as given to me by Jean Lariaga, owner of Le Mistral Restaurant in New York City.

4 (or 6) fillets of sole or
  flounder
1 cup dry white wine
1 cup water
1 bay leaf
2 slices onion
8 whole peppercorns
2 cups shelled oysters in their
  juice
6 tablespoons salt butter
5 tablespoons flour
Salt
Few grains cayenne pepper
3 tablespoons mushroom juice

(cook stems and trimmings
  with a little water, lemon
  juice, and salt; strain before
  using)
2 egg yolks
2 tablespoons dry sherry
6 tablespoons heavy cream
2 teaspoons sweet butter
4 (or 6) whole firm white
  mushroom caps, lightly
  sautéed in a little butter and
  lemon juice (for garnish)
Steamed baby potatoes (page
  612)

Preheat the oven to 350°. Wash and dry the fillets of sole. Fold them lengthwise, place on a buttered baking dish, pour over the wine and water, and add the bay leaf, onion, and peppercorns. Cover with buttered wax paper and poach 15 minutes in the oven. Remove, arrange the fillets of sole on a heatproof serving dish, strain the liquid, and reserve.

Put the oysters in their juice in a pan, bring to a boil, and remove from the heat. Let the oysters stand a few minutes, then strain them, set them aside, and reserve the liquid. Melt the salt butter in a tin-lined copper pan. Off the heat, stir in the flour. Season with salt and cayenne pepper. Mix in the strained stock from the fish, ½ cup of the liquid from the oysters, and the mushroom juice. Stir over low heat until the mixture comes to a boil. In a separate bowl, mix the egg yolks with the dry sherry. Add the heavy cream. Stir a little of the warm sauce into the egg yolk mixture, then stir it all into the rest of the sauce. Simmer gently 5 to 10 minutes. (Do not allow the sauce to boil or it will separate.) Bit by bit, add the sweet butter (to make the sauce shiny).

To serve, arrange the oysters along one side of the serving dish and the baby potatoes on the other side, with the fillets of sole in the center. Spoon the sauce over the fillets. Place a whole mushroom cap on each. Quickly brown the dish under a hot broiler. NET: 4 to 6 servings.

8 fillets of sole, flounder, or bass
A little lemon juice
1 teaspoon finely chopped garlic
2 firm white mushrooms, finely
  chopped
3 tablespoons sour cream
1 tablespoon chopped mixed

herbs, including tarragon
1 egg white
A little melted butter
9 whole firm white mushrooms
About 4 tablespoons salt butter
2 tablespoons dry sherry
Salt

FILETS DE SOLES EN PAPILLOTE

Fillets of Sole and
Mushrooms Baked
in Paper

Freshly cracked white pepper
2 apples
A little granulated sugar
1 tablespoon chopped fresh

chives
2 teaspoons chopped fresh
    tarragon

Preheat the oven to 350°. Wash the fillets well in water and lemon juice and dry. Put 2 fillets through a fine meat chopper and add ½ teaspoon garlic and the chopped mushrooms, sour cream, mixed herbs, and egg white. Mix well and put a spoonful of this stuffing on each of the 6 remaining fillets. Fold them over and brush each side with melted butter. Cut 12-inch squares of wax paper and fold in half. Place each fillet on a double thickness of wax paper. Cut the whole mushrooms in thin slices, sauté them quickly in 1 tablespoon hot butter, and stir in the sherry, salt, and pepper. Put a thick layer of this on each fillet. Pare, core, and chop the apples in small pieces, sauté them in 1 tablespoon butter, and sprinkle with a little sugar to glaze. Put this over the mushrooms. Cream 2 tablespoons butter, mix in ½ teaspoon garlic, the chives, tarragon, salt and pepper. Dot each fillet generously with this mixture.

Wrap the fillets in the paper, folding it over at the center and twisting each of the three sides together to form an envelope. Place the wrapped fillets on a jelly roll pan or baking dish and bake 25 minutes. Serve in the papers, slit to show the contents. NET: 6 servings.

FILETS DE SOLES SYLVETTE

Poached Fillets of Sole Sylvette

These fillets are covered with a mirepoix and garnished with fresh tomatoes stuffed with hake or cod.

4 fillets of sole or flounder
½ cup dry white wine
¼ cup water
1 slice yellow onion
1 garlic clove, bruised
Bouquet garni, including parsley
    and tarragon
6 whole peppercorns
12 tablespoons plus 1 teaspoon
    salt butter
2 leeks (white part), finely
    chopped
¼ cup string beans, finely
    chopped

2 carrots, finely chopped
2 stalks celery, finely chopped
2 medium yellow onions, finely
    chopped
Salt
Freshly cracked white pepper
2 tablespoons Madeira
¼ pound firm white mush-
    rooms, finely chopped
4 small firm ripe tomatoes
¼ pound boiled hake or cod
8 tablespoons light cream
4 tablespoons all-purpose flour
½ cup milk

Preheat the oven to 350°. Wash and dry the fillets of sole and place on a well-buttered baking dish. Pour over the wine and water and add the onion slice, garlic, bouquet garni, and peppercorns. Cover with buttered wax paper and poach in the oven 15 minutes. Set aside the fillets. Strain the liquid, boil down to ¼ cup, and reserve. Leave the oven on.

MIREPOIX. In a heavy pan, melt 3 tablespoons salt butter. Add the chopped leeks, beans, carrots, celery, and onions, and mix. Season with salt and pepper. Cover with wax paper and the lid and cook over low heat 5 minutes. Then cook in the oven 15 minutes. Remove, and add the Madeira. Reduce the oven heat to 325°.

In a separate sauté pan, cook the mushrooms in 2 tablespoons butter 5 minutes. Add them to the vegetable mixture and keep it warm.

TOMATOES STUFFED WITH HAKE OR COD. Skin and core the tomatoes and remove the insides without breaking the outsides. Pour ½ teaspoon melted butter into each tomato and season with salt and pepper. Set them in a pan and bake 3 minutes. Skin and bone the cooked hake or cod, and chop it fine. Season with salt and pepper. Beat in 2 tablespoons light cream and 1 teaspoon butter. Fill the tomatoes with this fish mixture. Cook in the oven 2 minutes.

VELOUTÉ SAUCE. In a saucepan melt 3 tablespoons butter. Remove from the heat and stir in the flour, then the salt and pepper. Stir until smooth. Pour on the milk. Stir over low heat until the sauce comes to a boil. Then beat in 6 tablespoons light cream, 2 tablespoons butter bit by bit, and the reduced liquid from the sole.

Arrange the fillets on a serving dish. Scatter the mirepoix of vegetables over them. Surround with the tomatoes stuffed with fish and spoon the sauce evenly over the whole dish. NET: 4 servings.

FILETS DE SOLES VERDUETTE

Sautéed Fillets of Sole with Mushrooms and Fresh Herbs

8 small fillets of sole or flounder
Juice of 2 lemons
A little all-purpose flour (for dusting)
Salt
Freshly cracked white pepper
1 egg, beaten
About ½ cup dry breadcrumbs (page 69)
6 tablespoons salt butter
⅓ cup dried mushrooms, soaked in 1 cup water at least 3 hours

3 tablespoons vegetable oil
1 tablespoon chopped fresh chives
1 small white onion, finely chopped
1 tablespoon chopped fresh parsley
1 teaspoon chopped fresh tarragon
1 teaspoon chopped fresh chervil (if available)

Wash the fillets of sole in lemon juice and cold water and dry well. Dust lightly with flour seasoned with a little salt and pepper. Brush with the beaten egg and roll them in the breadcrumbs. Heat 5 tablespoons butter in a sauté pan until it is hot and clear. Sauté the fillets until golden brown on both sides. Drain. Arrange them on a hot serving platter. Strain the soaked mushrooms and chop them. Heat the vegetable oil in a little pan and add the mushrooms, chives, and onion. Cook slowly until the onion is nearly soft. Drain off the oil, add 1 tablespoon butter and the parsley, tarragon, and chervil, and cook a few minutes. Add a little lemon juice. Spoon the mixture over the sole just before serving. NET: 4 servings.

FILETS DE SOLES VÉRONIQUE

Poached Fillets of Sole with Fresh White Grapes

4 fillets of sole or flounder
A little lemon juice
2 tablespoons salt butter
2 firm white mushrooms, sliced
Salt
Fresh cracked white pepper
½ cup dry white wine
¼ cup dry sherry
¼ cup water

SAUCE
4 tablespoons salt butter
4 tablespoons all-purpose flour
Salt
A few grains cayenne pepper
Strained fish stock (from the sole)
⅔ cup light cream

2 egg yolks
1 tablespoon Cognac or good brandy
1 tablespoon tarragon vinegar
2 tablespoons heavy cream
6 tablespoons frozen sweet butter

GARNISH
1 tablespoon salt butter
¾ cup skinned and seeded fresh white grapes
1 teaspoon chopped fresh parsley
1 teaspoon Cognac or good brandy
Salt
Freshly cracked white pepper

Preheat the oven to 350°. Wash the fillets in water and a little lemon juice. Dry well and fold them lengthwise with the bone side (white) out. Put them on a buttered baking dish. Make a court bouillon as follows. Melt the butter in a sauté pan and add the mushrooms. Cook over brisk heat with ½ teaspoon lemon juice, salt, and a little pepper. Add the wine, sherry, and water. Bring slowly to a boil. Spoon this court bouillon over the fillets. Cover with buttered wax paper and poach 15 minutes in the oven. Remove from the oven and arrange the fish on a warm serving platter. Strain the stock and reserve it.

SAUCE. Melt the salt butter in a saucepan. Off the heat, stir in the flour. Season with salt and the cayenne pepper. Add the strained stock from the fish. Stir over low heat until the sauce comes to a boil. Add the light cream and simmer gently 10 minutes. Put the egg yolks in a medium-size bowl. With a wire whisk mix in the brandy, vinegar, salt, and a little cayenne pepper. Mix in the heavy cream. Stand the bowl in a shallow pan of hot water over low heat. Beat until the yolk mixture is as thick as you want it. Cut the frozen sweet butter into little pieces and beat it into the yolk mixture piece by piece. Mix this egg sauce (which is a Hollandaise) into the white wine sauce and set aside.

GARNISH. In another little pan melt the butter. Add the grapes, parsley, and brandy. Season with salt and a little white pepper. Heat gently over low heat.

To serve, scatter the grapes over the fillets. Spoon the sauce evenly over the dish. Brown quickly under a hot broiler. NET: 4 servings.

FILETS DE SOLES VIN BLANC AUX ASPERGES

Poached Fillets of Sole with White Wine and Asparagus

4 fillets of sole or flounder, and the fish bones
A little lemon juice
6 whole peppercorns

1 slice onion
1 garlic clove, bruised
1 bay leaf
¼ cup dry white wine

1/4 cup water
4 tablespoons salt butter
1 1/2 tablespoons all-purpose
  flour
Salt

A few grains cayenne pepper
1/4 cup milk
2 tablespoons heavy cream
About 12 fresh asparagus tips
A little melted butter

Preheat the oven to 350°. Wash the fillets of sole in a little lemon juice and water and dry well. Fold over the narrow end of the fillets and place them on a well-buttered baking dish. Add the peppercorns, onion slice, garlic, and bay leaf. Pour over the wine and water, cover with the fish bones and buttered wax paper, and poach in the oven 12 to 15 minutes. Remove, and arrange the fillets on a serving dish. Strain the liquid and reserve.

SAUCE. In a small saucepan, melt 2 tablespoons butter. Remove the pan from the heat and add the flour, salt, and cayenne pepper. Stir until smooth. Add the liquid from the sole and the milk. Return to low heat and stir until the sauce comes to a boil. Bit by bit, add 2 tablespoons butter and the heavy cream. Cook or steam the asparagus tips until just cooked but still crisp. Drain. Split them in half lengthwise and add to the sauce.

To serve, spoon the sauce over the fillets, dot with a little melted butter, and brown under a hot broiler. NET: 4 servings.

As created for the Comtesse Walewska, one of Napoleon's paramours.

FILETS DE SOLES WALEWSKA

Poached Fillets of Sole Stuffed with Lobster, with Cardinal Sauce

1 boiled lobster (about 1 1/2 to
  2 pounds)
1/4 cup dry sherry
1/2 cup dry white wine
1/2 cup water
4 large firm white mushrooms
Salt
Freshly cracked white pepper
4 fillets of sole or flounder
A little lemon juice
6 tablespoons salt butter
1 teaspoon lemon juice

3 tablespoons Cognac or good
  brandy
1 teaspoon chopped fresh
  parsley
1 shallot, finely chopped
1/2 teaspoon tomato paste
4 tablespoons all-purpose flour
2/3 cup light cream
2 egg yolks
1/2 cup whipped cream (1/4 cup
  heavy cream)
Optional: 1 black truffle, sliced

STOCK. Remove the lobster meat from the tail and claws, keeping the tail meat in one piece. Put the lobster shells in a pan with the sherry, wine, water, 1 mushroom (sliced), salt, and pepper, and bring slowly to a boil. Simmer about 20 minutes. Strain, and reserve the liquid (stock).

Preheat the oven to 350°. Wash the fillets of sole in a little lemon juice and water, and dry well.

STUFFING. Slice 3 mushrooms and sauté briskly 3 minutes with 2 tablespoons hot butter, 1 teaspoon lemon juice, salt, and pepper. Chop the lobster claw meat and add to the pan. In a separate little pan heat

2 tablespoons brandy, ignite, and pour over the mixture. Add the chopped fresh parsley.

Spread out the fillets of sole skin side up. Spread the stuffing on the fillets (skin side), fold them over lengthwise, and arrange on a buttered baking dish. Pour the stock over the stuffed fillets and poach 15 minutes in the oven. Remove, strain off the stock, and reserve it. Set the fillets aside to keep warm.

CARDINAL SAUCE. In a saucepan melt 3 tablespoons butter. Add the chopped shallot and cook a minute or two. Off the heat, stir in one by one the tomato paste, then the flour, then 1 cup strained stock from the fish. Return to low heat and stir until the sauce thickens, but do not boil it. Add the light cream. Bit by bit, stir in 1 tablespoon butter. In a separate bowl mix the egg yolks with 1 tablespoon brandy. Pour a little of the hot sauce into the yolk mixture, stirring constantly, then return the mixture to the saucepan and reheat, but do not boil. Fold in the whipped cream.

Arrange the fillets of sole on a flat serving platter. Cut the lobster tail meat into ½-inch slices, warm them in a little hot butter in a sauté pan, and arrange on the fillets. Spoon the sauce over, and garnish, if desired, with a few slices of truffle. The lobster head and tail shells and little claws, slightly oiled, may also be used to decorate the dish. NET: 4 servings.

MOUSSE DE SOLES, SAUCE VELOUTÉ

Mousse of Sole with Velouté Sauce

4 fillets of sole or flounder, and the bones
Juice of half a lemon
½ cup white breadcrumbs (page 69)
Milk
2 egg whites
11 to 12 tablespoons heavy cream
Salt
A few grains cayenne pepper
Optional: 1 black truffle, finely chopped
6 tablespoons salt butter
2 tablespoons all-purpose flour
¼ cup dry white wine
¾ cup water
6 peppercorns
1 bay leaf

Preheat the oven to 350°. Wash the fillets of sole in a little lemon juice and water, dry well, and put them through a fine meat grinder. Put the ground sole in a mixer bowl and add the breadcrumbs, which have been soaked in a little milk and squeezed out. Slowly beat in the egg whites. Rub the mixture through a fine strainer and put it in a bowl over another bowl of cracked ice. With a whisk beat in slowly 8 to 9 tablespoons heavy cream. Season well with salt and the cayenne pepper. Add the chopped truffle, if desired. Butter a mold and fill it with this mousse. Cover the top with buttered wax paper, place it in a pan of hot water, and put it in the oven to steam slowly 25 to 30 minutes.

VELOUTÉ SAUCE. First prepare a simple fish stock. Put the fish bones in a pan with the wine, water, salt, peppercorns, and bay leaf. Bring to a boil, simmer down to ¾ cup in quantity, and strain. In a saucepan melt 3 tablespoons butter. Off the heat, stir in the flour, then stir in the fish stock and bring to a boil. Stir in, bit by bit, 3 tablespoons butter and 3 tablespoons heavy cream.

When the mousse is cooked, turn it out onto a serving dish. Spoon the sauce over it. NET: 4 servings.

DOVER SOLE FARCI MEUNIÈRE

Soles Stuffed with Shrimp Mousse, Sautéed in Meunière Butter

The stuffed soles are garnished with anchovy tomatoes and artichoke bottoms (with a touch of gin).

2 whole Dover soles or flounders
A little lemon juice
2 tablespoons Cognac or
   good brandy
Salt
Freshly cracked white pepper
A little flour (for dusting)
4 tablespoons salt butter

SHRIMP MOUSSE STUFFING
1/2 pound raw shrimp
1 large egg white
1/2 cup light cream
2 teaspoons salt
1 teaspoon fresh tarragon
1/2 teaspoon finely chopped
   garlic
1 tablespoon finely chopped
   shallot
A few grains cayenne pepper
1 tablespoon gin
3 juniper berries, crushed
8 tablespoons salt butter

MEUNIÈRE BUTTER
2 tablespoons dry sherry

2 tablespoons dry white wine
4 tablespoons salt butter
1/4 teaspoon finely chopped
   garlic
2 teaspoons finely chopped
   shallot
1/2 teaspoon lemon juice
1 tablespoon finely chopped
   fresh parsley

GARNISH
4 artichoke bottoms (canned)
A little salt butter
1 tablespoon gin
Salt
Freshly cracked white pepper
4 small firm ripe tomatoes
   (skins on)
1/4 teaspoon garlic, finely
   chopped
4 fillets of anchovy
4 tablespoons sweet butter
Thin slices of lemon
2 to 3 tablespoons very finely
   chopped parsley
1 tablespoon paprika

Skin and bone the soles (page 266), removing the tails and heads. Wash them well in lemon juice and water, dry well on paper towels, brush the insides with brandy, and sprinkle with a little salt and pepper. Reshape the fish. Wrap each in foil, to marinate while you make the stuffing.

SHRIMP MOUSSE STUFFING. Shell and devein the shrimp and put them through a fine meat chopper. Put the ground shrimp in a small metal bowl and stand it over another bowl of crushed ice. With a small wire whisk mix in the egg white and, very slowly, beat in the light cream. When thoroughly blended, mix in the other ingredients.

Unwrap the fish. Stuff them with the mousse, dividing it evenly. Reshape and dry them again with paper towels. Dust lightly with flour. Melt the butter slowly in a large heavy sauté pan; stir it with a wooden spoon until it is golden brown. Put in one fish and shake over moderate heat until it is golden brown on one side. Turn with a spatula and brown the other side. Do the same with the other fish. Arrange them on a hot platter, and set it in a warm oven (with the door open).

MEUNIÈRE BUTTER. In the pan in which the fish were sautéed, alternately stir in a little of the sherry, white wine, and butter, over low heat, until it is a nice blend. Add the garlic and shallot, and continue stirring. At the end, add the lemon juice and parsley. Set aside until you are ready to arrange the dish.

GARNISH. Heat the artichoke bottoms in a sauté pan with a little salt butter, gin, salt, and pepper. Core the tomatoes rather deeply. Season with salt, pepper, and a bit of chopped garlic inserted in the top. Gently warm them, core side down, in a sauté pan with a little salt butter. Make an anchovy butter (crush the anchovy fillets to a paste with a mortar and pestle, cream the sweet butter in a mixer, and blend together with a little pepper), and put 1 teaspoon of it in the center of each artichoke bottom. Put a tomato, core side down, on top of the anchovy butter. With a red-hot skewer, mark the top (bottom now up) of each tomato with a square or diamond. Dip half of each lemon slice in finely chopped parsley and the other half in paprika.

Place the soles on a serving platter. Spoon the meunière butter over them. Garnish with the lemon slices, and surround with the tomatoes in artichoke bottoms. NET: 4 servings.

SOLE ALBERT

Sole with Nantua Sauce, Bouchées of Shrimps, and Mussels and Oysters

½ pound puff paste (page 723), to make 6 small bouchée cases
1 whole sole or flounder, gutted only
11 tablespoons salt butter
¼ cup freshly grated Parmesan cheese
1 onion, finely sliced
1 carrot, finely sliced
½ teaspoon finely chopped garlic
1 large sprig fresh parsley
6 whole peppercorns
Salt
1 cup dry white wine
2 cups large mussels (in the shells)
1 teaspoon dry mustard
2 bay leaves
1 cup water
Freshly cracked white pepper
8 to 10 shelled oysters
Juice of half a lemon
1 cup small firm white mushrooms
½ cup boiled shrimps (with shells on)
A little paprika
3 tablespoons all-purpose flour
½ cup milk
3 tablespoons heavy cream

BOUCHÉE CASES (or use commercial bouchées). Preheat the oven to 375°. Roll out the prepared puff paste ¼ inch thick. Cut 12 2-inch rounds with a fluted cookie cutter. With a 1-inch cutter, cut out the center of 6 rounds (to look like rings, but with the bottoms whole). Place the whole rounds on a wet baking sheet and brush them with water. Set the rings on the whole rounds. Place the prepared baking sheet in the freezer and chill thoroughly. Brush with beaten egg. Bake 30 to 35 minutes, until golden brown. Remove and carefully scoop out a little more of the center, to form a case for the shrimps that garnish the sole.

Reduce the oven to 350°. Wash the fish, dry, and place on a buttered baking dish. Pour over it 2 tablespoons melted butter and the grated cheese, and put under a hot broiler for a few minutes. Remove, and scatter over the fish the onion, carrot, and garlic. Add the parsley, peppercorns, and salt to season. Pour the wine over all. Cover with buttered wax paper and bake 30 minutes. Scrub the mussels well in water and the dry mustard. Put them in a pan with the bay leaves, water, and salt and pepper. Bring to a boil. Cover, and simmer 5 minutes. Remove from the shells, remove the beards, and keep the mussels warm in a pan with a little hot butter (1 tablespoon). Cook the oysters 3 minutes in a little lemon juice and water, 1 tablespoon butter, salt, and pepper. Sauté the mushrooms in 1 tablespoon butter, season with salt and pepper, and add the drained oysters.

NANTUA SAUCE. Strain the cooking liquid from the sole and mussels through a fine strainer and reduce it by boiling it down to 1 cup in quantity. In a saucepan melt 3 tablespoons butter. Season with salt and pepper. Off the heat, stir in the flour. Pour in the reduced fish stock and stir over low heat until the sauce thickens. Pour in the milk and bring to a boil. Add the heavy cream. Stir in, bit by bit, the following shrimp butter.

SHRIMP BUTTER. Remove the shells and tails from the shrimps. Cream 4 tablespoons butter, and season with salt, pepper and a little paprika. Add a little of the sauce and the shrimp shells and tails to the butter, and thoroughly pulverize the mixture in an electric blender.

Slice the whole shrimps, mix with a little of the sauce, and fill the bouchée cases with them. Place the baked sole on a warm serving platter. Spoon the sauce over it. Surround the dish with the bouchée cases filled with the sliced shrimps and sauce. In between the boucheé cases put little clusters of the mussels and the mixed oysters and mushrooms. NET: 4 servings.

---

1 whole sole or flounder
  (about 1½ pounds)
A little all-purpose flour (for
  coating the fish)
Salt
Freshly cracked white pepper
1 whole egg, beaten
¾ cup dry white breadcrumbs
  (page 69)
Vegetable oil for deep-fryer
1 pound firm ripe tomatoes
2 tablespoons salt butter
8 tablespoons frozen sweet

butter
2 teaspoons finely chopped
  fresh parsley
2 tablespoons tarragon vinegar
½ teaspoon finely chopped
  garlic
1 slice onion
4 whole peppercorns
2 egg yolks
1 tablespoon heavy cream
1 tablespoon finely chopped
  fresh tarragon
1 teaspoon meat glaze

SOLE ALEXANDRE

Deep-Fried Sole on
Fresh Tomatoes with
Béarnaise Sauce

Remove the bones from the sole, keeping the fish whole (see page 266). Dust it lightly with flour mixed with a little salt and pepper. Brush it with the beaten egg and roll it in the breadcrumbs. Fry it in a deep-fry basket, with the oil at 375°, until golden brown. Drain on paper towels and keep it warm. Skin, quarter, and seed the tomatoes. Put the sections in a sauté pan with the salt butter, salt, pepper, and half the parsley. Shake over low heat 3 minutes.

BÉARNAISE SAUCE. Put the vinegar in a little pan with the garlic, onion slice, peppercorns, and the rest of the parsley. Boil and reduce to half quantity. Strain. Beat the egg yolks in a small bowl; add the reduced vinegar. Stand the bowl in a shallow pan of hot water over low heat. Slowly beat in the frozen sweet butter bit by bit. Add the heavy cream, tarragon, and meat glaze.

To serve, arrange the tomatoes on a warm serving dish. Place the sole on top. Serve the Béarnaise sauce separately. NET: 4 servings.

SOLE FLORENTINE

Poached Whole Sole on Spinach and Cream, with Cheese Sauce

4 whole small soles or flounder, gutted	½ cup heavy cream
Juice of 2 lemons	3 tablespoons all-purpose flour
10 tablespoons salt butter	1½ cups milk
Salt	4 tablespoons freshly grated Parmesan cheese
Freshly cracked white pepper	¼ cup water
1½ pounds fresh spinach	

Preheat the oven to 350°. Remove and discard the heads, and wash the soles in a little lemon juice and water and dry well. Place them with skin and bones intact on a buttered baking dish. Pour on the juice of 1 lemon mixed with 3 tablespoons melted butter, salt, and pepper. Cover with buttered wax paper and poach in the oven 20 minutes. Wash the spinach well. Melt 3 tablespoons butter in a pan with a little salt and pepper. Put in the spinach, turn it a few times, and simmer 5 to 6 minutes until it is wilted. (The spinach should not be chopped.) Drain it and dry very well. Mix the spinach with ¼ cup heavy cream and a little pepper.

CHEESE SAUCE. Melt 3 tablespoons butter in a saucepan. Off the heat, add the flour, salt, and pepper. Stir in the milk and bring to a boil. Add 3 tablespoons grated cheese, ¼ cup heavy cream, and (bit by bit) 1 tablespoon butter. Simmer 5 minutes.

Place the spinach on the bottom of a flat heatproof serving dish. Drain the cooked soles and place them on the spinach. Spoon the sauce over all, sprinkle with the remaining grated cheese, and dot with a little butter. Brown under a hot broiler and serve. NET: 4 servings.

SOLE AU FOUR MAISON

Whole Sole Baked in Velouté, with Shredded Carrots and Mushrooms

1 whole sole or flounder, gutted	2 small carrots, finely shredded
Juice of half a lemon	Salt
3 tablespoons salt butter	Freshly cracked white pepper

1/4 cup finely sliced fresh
mushrooms
2 tablespoons all-purpose flour
3/4 cup fish stock (page 36)
or clam juice
1/2 cup milk
1/4 cup heavy cream

3 tablespoons freshly grated
Parmesan cheese
2 tablespoons dry breadcrumbs
(page 69)
2 tablespoons chopped fresh
parsley

Preheat the oven to 350°. Remove both skins from the sole (the dark upper skin and the white skin on the underside). Trim off the outside fins. Wash in lemon juice and water. Dry well. Place on a buttered baking dish and set aside. In a saucepan melt 2 tablespoons butter and add the shredded carrots. Season with salt and pepper and cook very slowly until the carrots are soft without browning. Add the mushrooms and cook another minute. Off the heat, add the flour and a little more salt and pepper. Pour on the fish stock. Stir over low heat until it thickens. Add the milk and bring to a boil. Add the heavy cream and 1 tablespoon grated cheese. Simmer a few minutes. Pour the sauce over the sole in the baking dish. Sprinkle with 2 tablespoons grated cheese and the breadcrumbs, dot with one tablespoon butter, and bake 25 minutes. When done, sprinkle with chopped fresh parsley, and serve. NET: 4 servings.

SOLE (OU MERLAN) AU GRATIN

Whole Sole (or Whiting) Baked in Demi-Glace with Chopped Mushrooms

2 whole soles or whitings,
cleaned, with head and tail
left on
4 tablespoons salt butter
2 carrots, sliced
2 medium-size yellow onions,
quartered
1 tablespoon all-purpose flour
1 tomato, cut in eighths
About 1/2 cup mushroom
trimmings and stems
1 teaspoon tomato paste

Salt
Freshly cracked white pepper
1 1/2 cups fish stock (page 36)
or clam juice
1/4 cup dry white wine
1/2 cup finely chopped fresh
mushrooms
1 tablespoon dry breadcrumbs
(page 69)
1 tablespoon freshly grated
Parmesan cheese
A few slices lemon

Preheat the oven to 375°. Wash and dry the two fish. Score well (cut little slits) on top. Lay the fish on a buttered baking dish.

DEMI-GLACE. Heat 2 tablespoons butter in a pan. Add the onions and carrots and brown slowly. Add the flour and brown it, also. Off the heat, add the tomato, mushroom trimmings and stems, tomato paste, salt, and pepper. Pour on the fish stock and bring slowly to a boil. Simmer 20 minutes. In a separate little pan reduce the wine to half quantity and add it to the demi-glace. In another little pan sauté the chopped mushrooms in a little butter. Strain the demi-glace onto the mushrooms.

Pour the demi-glace sauce over the sole in the baking dish. Sprinkle the top with the breadcrumbs and grated cheese, and bake 15 minutes. Remove from the oven, garnish with a few slices of lemon, and serve. NET: 4 servings.

TRUITE AU BLEU

Blue Trout (Classic Poached Live Trout)

4 small live trout
6 tablespoons tarragon vinegar
1 quart fish stock (page 36)
¾ cup melted clarified butter (page 56)

Sprigs of fresh parsley
Slices of lemon
8 to 12 baby new potatoes, steamed (page 612)

The trout must be alive, in a bucket. Heat the fish stock in a deep pan large enough to hold the 4 fish. Add 2 tablespoons of tarragon vinegar. Degut the live trout quickly. Have at hand a little pan containing 4 tablespoons of simmering vinegar. Set each fish aside in a dish and put 1 tablespoon boiling vinegar over it (this will make them a brighter blue when they are poached). As soon as all four fish are degutted, put them into the hot fish stock. (Take great care not to rub the outside of the fish, if possible, as it is the outer film that keeps the trout blue.) Poach until the fish's eye clouds or becomes opaque. Take the fish out of the stock carefully and quickly with a large slotted fish slice. Arrange them on a warm napkin on a platter and garnish with slices of lemon and parsley. Serve with melted clarified butter and steamed baby new potatoes, separately. NET: 4 servings.

TRUITE À LA MEUNIÈRE

Trout Sautéed in Meunière Butter

4 small whole trout
8 tablespoons salt butter
About 3 teaspoons lemon juice
Salt
Freshly cracked white pepper
A little milk (for coating)
A little flour (for dusting)

⅓ cup dry white wine
1 lemon, thinly sliced
2 tablespoons finely chopped parsley
A little paprika
12 baby new potatoes, steamed (page 612)

Clean the trout, wash them in water and about 2 teaspoons lemon juice, and dry on paper towels. Season the insides with salt, pepper, and a little lemon juice. Brush them all over with milk, then dust lightly in flour. Put 4 tablespoons butter in a heavy sauté pan and stir until it is a light brown color. Sauté the trout gently until golden brown on both sides. Arrange them on a hot flat serving dish. To the sauté pan add the wine and 1 teaspoon lemon juice. Bit by bit, add 4 tablespoons butter. Pour this butter quickly over the fish. Garnish with thin slices of lemon, half of each slice dipped in paprika and the other half in finely chopped parsley. At one end of the dish place the steamed baby new potatoes, or serve them separately in an earthenware potato steamer. NET: 4 servings.

4 small whole rainbow trout
Salt
Freshly cracked white pepper
A little lemon juice
A little melted salt butter
⅓ cup fish stock (page 36)
  or clam juice
4 black dried currants
1 egg, beaten
Hollandaise sauce (page 49)

SALMON MOUSSE
1 cup finely ground raw salmon

2 raw egg whites
1 cup light cream
2 teaspoons salt
A few grains cayenne pepper

PASTRY
2 cups all-purpose flour
½ teaspoon salt
6 tablespoons salt butter
2 tablespoons pure olive oil
1 egg yolk
⅓ cup ice water

Preheat the oven to 350°. Remove the scales, tails, and heads from the trout. Slit down the back and remove the bone and guts at the same time. Open them up from the back and sprinkle with salt, pepper, and a little lemon juice. Fold them over, leave about 10 minutes, then rinse in very cold water. Dry them well on paper towels, then sprinkle again with a little salt, pepper, and lemon juice, and allow to marinate.

SALMON MOUSSE. Put the ground salmon in a small metal bowl over a bowl of crushed ice. With a wire whisk stir in the egg whites. Add the light cream, drop by drop, beating all the time. Then add the salt and cayenne pepper.

Stuff this mousse into the trout. Arrange the stuffed trout on a buttered baking dish and brush them all over with melted butter. Pour the fish stock over them, cover with buttered wax paper, and cook 10 minutes in the oven. Remove the trout from the oven, drain, and chill them.

PASTRY. Reset the oven to 375°. Put the flour and salt in a bowl. Add the butter and rub it into the flour until it resembles coarse cornmeal. Then add the olive oil, egg yolk, and ice water. Work up quickly to a firm dough.

Divide the dough into 4 pieces, and roll each piece out large enough to encase a trout. Wrap each fish in pastry and secure the edges. Then, with a small knife and pastry pincers, make markings of a fish on the pastry (fins, tail, head, etc.) and dot with a black currant for the eye. Place the pastry-enclosed trout on a buttered baking sheet. Brush with beaten egg and bake until golden brown (about 20 minutes). Remove, arrange on a hot napkin on a platter, and serve with a separate bowl of Hollandaise sauce. NET: 4 servings.

6 fillets of whiting
½ cup fish stock (page 36)
  or clam juice
¼ cup dry white wine
2 cups large mussels
1 teaspoon dry mustard

1 onion, sliced
1 carrot, sliced
1 garlic clove, bruised
2 bay leaves
4 whole peppercorns
½ cup water

6 tablespoons salt butter
6 ounces fresh button
   mushrooms
1 teaspoon lemon juice
Salt
Freshly cracked white pepper

1 cup cooked shrimps, shelled
4 tablespoons all-purpose flour
¾ cup light cream
3 tablespoons heavy cream
A little melted salt butter

Preheat the oven to 350°. Skin the fillets, wash and dry them, put them on a buttered baking dish, and pour the fish stock and wine over them. Cover with buttered wax paper and poach 12 minutes in the oven. Place the fillets on an au gratin dish and reserve the liquid. Scrub the mussels in cold water with the dry mustard. Put them in a pan with the onion, carrot, garlic, bay leaves, peppercorns, and water, and strain over them the liquid reserved from the whiting. Bring slowly to a boil, cover, and simmer 4 to 5 minutes. Remove the mussels from the shells, remove the beards. Set the mussels aside. Strain and reserve the liquid. Melt 2 tablespoons butter in a sauté pan. Add the button mushrooms, lemon juice, salt, and pepper, and cook briskly a minute or two. Add the shelled shrimps and cook briskly another minute or two. Add the mussels. Scatter the shellfish and mushroom mixture over the whiting.

VELOUTÉ SAUCE. Melt 3 tablespoons butter in a saucepan. Off the heat, stir in the flour, salt, and pepper. Add ¾ cup of liquid strained from the mussels. Return to low heat and stir until the sauce thickens. Add the light cream and bring to a boil. Bit by bit, add 1 tablespoon butter and the heavy cream.

Spoon this sauce evenly over the whiting and shellfish, sprinkle with a little melted butter, and brown under a hot broiler. NET: 4 servings.

GRENOUILLES À LA PROVENÇALE

Frog Legs Provençal,
Sautéed

8 frog legs (fairly large ones, or enough legs to serve 4 persons)
A little lemon juice
A little flour (for dusting)
Salt
Freshly cracked white pepper
5 tablespoons salt butter
2 teaspoons finely chopped

garlic
2 tablespoons mixed finely chopped fresh herbs (tarragon, parsley, chives, if available)
1 tablespoon Cognac or good brandy
2 tablespoons dry white wine
Thin slices lemon

Wash the frog legs very well in lemon juice and water. Dry them on paper towels and dust lightly with flour seasoned with a little salt and pepper. Heat the butter in a saucepan until it foams, and add the garlic. Cook 1 minute. Put in the frog legs and shake until golden brown on each side. Add salt, pepper, and the mixed fresh herbs. Cook another minute. In a separate little pan, heat the brandy and wine, ignite, and pour it flaming over the frog legs. Serve at once on a very hot platter, garnished with thin slices of lemon. NET: 4 servings.

SHELLFISH

12 raw shelled clams
Vegetable oil for deep-fryer
Green Mayonnaise (page 54)
   or Tartar Sauce (page 55)

BATTER
8 tablespoons all-purpose flour

1 egg
1 egg yolk
1 tablespoon vegetable oil
5 tablespoons milk
Salt
1 teaspoon baking powder
1 egg white

CLAMS EN BEIGNETS

Clam Fritters

With a whisk, beat the flour, egg, egg yolk, vegetable oil, 3 tablespoons milk, and a pinch of salt until smooth. In a separate bowl, beat the egg white to soft peaks. Add to the flour mixture 2 tablespoons milk and the baking powder and beaten egg white. Leave the batter in the refrigerator at least 30 minutes, to set. Fill a deep frypan with vegetable oil and heat to 375°. Dip the clams one at a time in the batter, drop in the hot oil, and fry until golden brown. Remove with a slotted spoon and drain on paper towels. Serve immediately with a separate bowl of Green Mayonnaise or Tartar Sauce. NET: 4 servings.

8 small soft-shell crabs
A little all-purpose flour (for
   dusting)
Salt
Freshly cracked white pepper
6 tablespoons salt butter
8 triangular croûtons (page 69)

   about the size of the crabs
¼ cup finely chopped shallots
1 teaspoon lemon juice
2 tablespoons finely chopped
   parsley
Thin slices of lemon
Paprika

CRABES MOUS MEUNIÈRE

Sautéed Soft-Shell Crabs

Have the fishmonger clean the soft-shell crabs (which should be bought as fresh as possible). Dust them very lightly in flour mixed with a little salt and pepper. Melt the butter slowly in a heavy sauté pan. When bubbling, put in the crabs, taking care not to let them touch one another. Sauté them slowly until brown on each side. Remove them with a slotted spoon, arrange them on a hot flat serving dish on the toast triangles, and keep them warm. Add the shallots to the butter in the pan with the lemon juice. Cook 2 minutes and spoon over the crabs. Sprinkle the crabs with chopped parsley and garnish with thin slices of lemon. (For decoration, half of each lemon slice can be coated with paprika and the other half with chopped parsley.) NET: 4 servings.

CRABE À LA DIABLE

Deviled Crab in the Shells

1 cup lump crab meat, cooked,
   and shells from 4 crabs
½ teaspoon dry mustard
1 tablespoon Worcestershire

   sauce
2 tablespoons dry white breadcrumbs (page 69)
2 tablespoons heavy cream

Salt
Freshly cracked white pepper
A few grains cayenne pepper

1 tablespoon freshly grated
  Parmesan cheese
2 tablespoons pure olive oil

Preheat the oven to 400°. Put the crab meat in a bowl. Add the dry mustard, Worcestershire sauce, breadcrumbs, heavy cream, salt, white pepper, and cayenne pepper. Mix thoroughly and fill the crab shells. Sprinkle the tops with the grated cheese and a little olive oil. Bake 5 to 10 minutes. NET: 4 servings.

CRÊPES AU CRABE, SAUCE MORNAY

Crêpes Stuffed with Crab Meat, with Mornay Sauce

CRÊPES
8 tablespoons all-purpose flour
Pinch of salt
1 egg
1 egg yolk
2 tablespoons vegetable oil
1 cup milk

FILLING
4 ounces firm white mushrooms,
  thickly sliced
6 tablespoons salt butter
2 teaspoons lemon juice
Salt
Freshly cracked white pepper
1/2 teaspoon finely chopped
  garlic
1 pound lump crab meat
3 tablespoons Cognac or good
  brandy

MORNAY SAUCE
6 tablespoons salt butter

6 tablespoons all-purpose flour
1 teaspoon Dijon mustard
1 teaspoon dry mustard
1 teaspoon salt
A few grains cayenne pepper
2 cups milk
1 small piece celery
1 small slice onion
1 bay leaf
1/3 cup freshly grated Parmesan
  cheese
1/3 cup freshly grated Swiss
  cheese
1/3 cup light cream
1 tablespoon sweet butter

TO FINISH
2 tablespoons dry breadcrumbs
  (page 69)
3 tablespoons freshly grated
  Parmesan cheese
A little melted butter

CRÊPES. In a small bowl put the flour, pinch of salt, egg, egg yolk, vegetable oil, and 4 tablespoons milk. Beat with a whisk until smooth, then add the rest of the milk. The batter should be the consistency of light cream. Cover the bowl with plastic wrap and let it stand in the refrigerator at least 30 minutes, to set. (If the batter has thickened after it has chilled, thin it with a little more milk.) Heat an omelet pan very hot (a dot of butter dropped in it should sizzle and brown). Rub the inside of the pan with salt butter, using a wad of wax paper. Using a ladle, cover the bottom of the pan with a thin layer of batter. Brown the crêpe on one side, then turn it over with a spatula and brown on the other. Pile one crêpe on top of the other as you make them (there should be 10 or 11). Set them aside.

FILLING. Sauté the sliced mushrooms with 3 tablespoons butter, the lemon juice, salt, and pepper. Add the garlic and cook briskly 3 to 4 minutes. Add the lump crab meat and another 3 tablespoons butter. Cook slowly 2 minutes. In a small pan warm the brandy, ignite, and pour over the crab mixture.

MORNAY SAUCE. Melt the salt butter in a saucepan. Off the heat, stir in the flour, mustards, salt, and cayenne pepper. In a separate saucepan put the milk, celery, onion, and bay leaf. Stir until it comes to a boil, then strain and mix it into the flour and butter mixture. Stir over low heat until it comes to a boil and thickens. Add the grated Parmesan and Swiss cheeses and the light cream. Simmer about 5 minutes. Add the sweet butter, bit by bit.

Mix ½ cup of the sauce into the crab filling. Put 2 tablespoons of the filling on the "underside" of each crêpe. Spread it evenly over the crêpe, to the edge. Roll up the crêpes like fat cigars and arrange them on a buttered au gratin dish. Brush the rolled crêpes with a little melted butter, spoon over the rest of the sauce, sprinkle with breadcrumbs and grated Parmesan cheese. Sprinkle with a little more melted butter and brown under a hot broiler. NET: 4 to 6 servings.

CRÊPES AUX FRUITS DE MER

Crêpes with Seafood

The preceding recipe for Crêpes au Crabe may be prepared with other kinds of seafood. Instead of 1 pound crab meat, use 2 cups boiled lobster meat, boiled shrimps, poached scallops, or steamed clams and/or mussels.

COQUILLE DE HOMARD

Lobster and Mushrooms in Cream Sauce in the Shells, with Duchess Potatoes

3 boiled lobsters (1¼ pounds each)	3 tablespoons freshly grated Parmesan cheese
4 firm white mushrooms, sliced	1 cup milk
5 tablespoons salt butter	4 tablespoons heavy cream
3 tablespoons all-purpose flour	1 egg yolk
Salt	Duchess potatoes (page 609)
A few grains cayenne pepper	Butter and grated Parmesan
1 teaspoon dry mustard	cheese for browning

Split the boiled lobsters in half and reserve the shells. Remove the body and claw meat from the shells and cut it in ½-inch bite-size pieces. Sauté the sliced mushrooms quickly in 1 tablespoon butter and set aside. In a saucepan, melt 4 tablespoons butter. Off the heat, stir in the flour, salt, cayenne pepper, dry mustard, and grated cheese. Add the milk and stir over low heat until the sauce comes to a boil. Add 3 tablespoons of heavy cream and simmer gently 5 minutes. In a small bowl, mix the egg yolk with 1 tablespoon heavy cream and add it to the sauce. Add the lobster pieces and sliced mushrooms to the sauce. Fill the 6 shell halves with this mixture. Pipe a border of Duchess potatoes around each filled shell. Sprinkle with a little grated Parmesan cheese, dot with butter and brown under a hot broiler. NET: 6 servings.

CRÊPES DE HOMARD

Crêpes Stuffed with Lobster and Mushrooms, with Lobster Sauce

CRÊPES *(page 302)*

LOBSTER FILLING
2 tablespoons salt butter
4 ounces firm white mushrooms
Salt
A few grains cayenne pepper
A little lemon juice
1 boiled lobster (1¼ pounds)
1 tablespoon Cognac or good
    brandy

LOBSTER SAUCE
4 tablespoons salt butter
½ cup dry sherry
½ cup dry white wine
½ cup water
1 small bay leaf

1 small sprig celery leaf
5 white peppercorns
4 tablespoons all-purpose flour
Salt
A few grains cayenne pepper
⅓ cup light cream
2 egg yolks
1 tablespoon Cognac or good
    brandy
2 tablespoons heavy cream

FINISH
2 tablespoons dry breadcrumbs
    (page 69)
3 tablespoons freshly grated
    Parmesan cheese
1 tablespoon melted butter

Make up the crêpes according to the recipe for them under Crêpes au Crabe (page 302), and set aside.

LOBSTER FILLING. Put the butter in a sauté pan. Slice the mushrooms (reserve the stems) and add them. Season with salt, cayenne pepper, and a few drops of lemon juice. Cook briskly 3 minutes. Remove the meat from the lobster tail and claws (reserve the shell). Chop the lobster meat and add to the mushrooms. Add the brandy and warm a little.

SAUCE. Prepare the following stock. In another pan melt 1 tablespoon salt butter. Chop the reserved mushroom stems, add them, and cook briskly a minute or two. Cut up the lobster shell and add to the pan, then add the sherry, wine, water, bay leaf, celery leaf, and peppercorns. Bring to a boil and simmer about 10 minutes. Strain, and reserve the stock. Melt 3 tablespoons butter in a saucepan. Off the heat, stir in the flour, salt, and a little cayenne pepper. Pour in 1 cup of the strained lobster stock. Stir over low heat until it comes to a boil. Add the light cream and simmer a few minutes. In another bowl, beat the egg yolks with the brandy and heavy cream. Pour a little of the sauce onto this egg yolk mixture, beating all the time. Return it to the saucepan. Stir over low heat until it is thick, but do not boil.

Put about 2 tablespoons of this sauce in the mushroom-lobster mixture. Put 1 spoonful of the mushroom-lobster mixture on the "wrong" *under* side of each crêpe. Spread it over the crêpe, and roll up the crêpe like a little cigar. Arrange the rolled crêpes on an au gratin dish. Brush them with a little melted butter and spoon the rest of the sauce over them. Sprinkle with the breadcrumbs and grated cheese, dot with melted butter, brown under the broiler, and serve. NET: 4 to 6 servings.

2 live lobsters (about 2 pounds
    each)
4 tablespoons salt butter
2 tablespoons vegetable oil
¼ cup Cognac or good brandy
1 cup each of finely diced raw
    carrots and green beans
Salt
Freshly cracked white pepper
4 ripe tomatoes, skinned and cut
    into eighths
2 teaspoons finely chopped
    garlic
1 teaspoon tomato paste

½ cup dry white wine
¼ cup dry sherry
1 tablespoon all-purpose flour

SAFFRON RICE
4 tablespoons salt butter
1 yellow onion, finely chopped
2 cups long-grain rice
4 cups water or fish stock (page
    36)
1teaspoon leaf saffron
2 tablespoons hot water
2 teaspoons salt
A few grains cayenne pepper

HOMARD À L'ARMORICAINE

Lobster with Tomatoes
and Mirepoix in
Saffron Rice Ring

Split the lobsters in half with a large knife, starting from the little cross in the center of the head. Remove the small sac from behind each eye. Cut off the small claws and large claws. Cut the tails in 3 pieces each, leaving the shell on. Try to reserve the lobster juice that accumulates on the cutting board. If you can, cook it with the lobster. In a large heavy pan heat 3 tablespoons butter and the vegetable oil. When the butter and oil are very hot, put in all the pieces of lobster, including the head sections. Cover the pan and cook slowly 3 to 4 minutes and uncover. In a small pan warm the brandy, ignite, and pour over the lobster. Cover the pan again and cook briskly 7 to 8 minutes. The lobsters must be very bright red. Remove the lobster pieces and set aside. Strain the pan juices and put the juice back in the pan.

Cook the carrots and beans together in boiling water until a little soft but still crunchy. Drain, and put in the pan in which the lobster was cooked. Season with salt and pepper and cook very slowly 5 minutes. Add the tomatoes and chopped garlic and cook briskly 3 minutes. Stir in the tomato paste, wine, and sherry. Bring slowly to a boil. Mix 1 tablespoon soft butter with 1 tablespoon of flour. If there was any coral in the lobsters, add the coral to the butter and flour mixture. Bit by bit, add this mixture to the sauce. Simmer a few minutes.

SAFFRON RICE. Preheat the oven to 350°. Melt the butter in a heavy pan. Add the chopped onion and cook slowly until it is translucent. Add the rice and stir until it is completely coated with butter. Cover with the water or fish stock. Crush the leaf saffron with a pestle and mortar and mix with the hot water. Add this to the rice with the salt and cayenne pepper. Stir over moderate heat until the liquid comes to a rolling boil. Cover the pan with a lid and bake 30 minutes. Remove, and fluff the rice with 2 forks.

To serve, lightly butter a ring mold and fill it with the saffron rice. Press it in firmly with the back of a spoon. Turn out the ring of rice onto a hot serving dish. Loosen the meat from the pieces of lobster shell. Put the meat with the shells loosely attached in the center well of the rice ring. Spoon the sauce over the lobster pieces and around the outside of the ring. Decorate with the lobster head shells and little claws. NET: 4 to 6 servings.

HOMARD À LA BARANTE

Lobster Pieces Mixed with Mirepoix and Cream Sauce, Gratinée

Start soaking the dried mushrooms at least 3 hours before making this dish, to get the flavorful mushroom liquid.

2 live lobsters, 1¼ pounds each
2 tablespoons vegetable oil
Salt
Freshly cracked white pepper
¼ cup red Burgundy wine
A mirepoix of diced raw vegetables: ¼ cup green beans, ½ cup carrots, ½ cup turnips
3 tablespoons salt butter
1 ounce dried mushrooms,

soaked at least 3 hours in
1 cup water
2 tablespoons all-purpose flour
A few grains cayenne pepper
½ cup milk
¼ cup heavy cream
2 teaspoons chopped fresh chives
2 tablespoons freshly grated imported Swiss cheese

Wash the lobsters. Split in half with a large knife, starting from the little cross in the center of the head. Remove the small sac from behind each eye and remove the eyes. Cut off the small claws and large claws. Crack the large claws. Cut the tails in 3 or 4 pieces, according to size. In a deep heavy pan, heat the vegetable oil, and add the lobsters with a little salt and pepper. Cover, and cook until the lobster shells are bright red. Heat the wine in a little pan, ignite, and pour over the lobsters. Blanch the diced carrots, green beans, and turnips by bringing them to a boil from cold water. Drain. Return them to the pan with salt, pepper, and 2 tablespoons butter. Drain the soaked mushrooms, chop them, and add to the mirepoix. Boil the mushroom water down to 2 teaspoons and add it to the mixture. Cover, and cook slowly over low heat 15 to 20 minutes.

CREAM SAUCE. In another pan, melt 1 tablespoon butter. Off the heat, stir in the flour, salt, and cayenne pepper. Pour in the milk and heavy cream. Stir well over low heat until the sauce comes to a boil. Add the chopped chives.

Remove the meat from the lobster shells. Mix it with the vegetables and cream sauce. Arrange in a shallow, heatproof au gratin dish. Scatter the grated Swiss cheese over it and brown under a hot broiler. NET: 4 servings.

HOMARD À LA NEWBURGH

Lobster Newburgh

A chafing dish of poached lobster in egg sauce, with purée of potatoes.

1 tablespoon vegetable oil
1 small onion, sliced
1 small carrot, sliced
1 small stalk celery, sliced
4 cups water
Salt
6 peppercorns
A little paprika
1 bay leaf

2 live lobsters, about 1½ pounds each
2 tablespoons salt butter
3 egg yolks
1 cup heavy cream
1 tablespoon freshly grated Parmesan cheese
Freshly cracked white pepper
½ teaspoon dry mustard

3 tablespoons dry sherry   Potato purée (page 610)

In a large heavy pan, heat the vegetable oil. Add the onion, carrot, and celery, and cook 2 minutes. Pour on the water and bring to a boil. Add salt, the peppercorns, and paprika to season; also add the bay leaf. Reduce the heat to simmer. Wash the lobsters and put them whole into this stock. Cover, and cook very gently 15 minutes. (The stock can be strained and kept for use in chowder.) Remove the meat from the lobsters and cut it in small bite-size pieces. In the top of a double boiler put the butter, egg yolks, heavy cream, grated cheese, salt, pepper, mustard, and sherry. Stir over hot water over low heat until the mixture thickens and coats the back of a silver spoon. (Be careful that it does not curdle.) Add the lobster meat to the sauce. Serve in a hot chafing dish with a good creamy purée of potato (page 610). NET: 4 servings.

Optional: Puff pastry crescents
    (page 254, or buy
    frozen ones)
2 live lobsters, 1½ pounds each
2 tablespoons salt butter
⅓ cup Cognac or good brandy
½ pound firm white mushrooms
Salt

A few grains cayenne pepper
1 large black truffle
2 cups heavy cream
1 tablespoon sweet butter mixed
    with 1 tablespoon all-purpose
    flour (beurre manié)
2 tablespoons chopped fresh
    tarragon or parsley

HOMARD BORÉAL

Casserole of Lobster in Cream Sauce with Truffles and Mushrooms

Make the puff pastry crescents first (page 254). Then cut the heads off the lobsters, cut the tails in three pieces, split the heads in half, remove the large claws, and remove the small sac from behind each eye. Heat the salt butter in a heavy pan. Add the lobster pieces and cover the pan. Cook slowly 2 to 3 minutes with the cover on, then uncover. Heat the brandy in a little pan, ignite it, and pour it over the lobster. Cover the pan again, and cook until the shells are bright red. Remove the lobster and set aside. Slice the mushrooms. Put them in the pan in which the lobster was cooked, season with salt and the cayenne pepper, and cook briskly 3 to 4 minutes. Cut the truffle in thin slices and add to the mushrooms. Cook another minute. Pour on the heavy cream and bring to a boil. Reduce the heat to a simmer and add the flour-butter mixture (beurre manié) bit by bit. Bring the sauce to a boil.

    Remove the meat from the pieces of lobster tail and claws. Add it to the sauce. Put the lobster mixture in a casserole. Lay the 2 head shell halves (from one of the lobsters) together in the center of the casserole. Sprinkle with chopped tarragon or parsley. Surround with the crescents of puff pastry. NET: 6 servings.

HOMARD CHEZ SOI

Poached Lobster and Eel in Red Wine Sauce

1 boiled lobster (1¼ pounds)
6 tablespoons salt butter
2 tablespoons pure olive oil
1 small eel, with head and tail removed (but not boned)
1 large onion, thinly sliced
Bouquet garni, including parsley, thyme, 1 bay leaf
1 teaspoon finely chopped garlic
Salt
A few grains cayenne pepper
¾ cup dry red wine

8 firm white mushrooms
A little lemon juice
¾ cup fish stock (page 36) or the lobster stock
1 small carrot, sliced
1 stalk celery, sliced
4 tablespoons all-purpose flour
1 teaspoon tomato paste
1 bay leaf
1 tablespoon red currant jelly
2 tablespoons chopped fresh chives

Remove the lobster meat from the tail and claws and cut it into large pieces. In a large sauté pan, melt 2 tablespoons butter with the olive oil. Warm the pieces of lobster in it and set aside. Cut the eel in 6 pieces. In a heavy pan, melt 1 tablespoon butter, add three-quarters of the sliced onion, and cook 1 minute. Put in the pieces of eel, bouquet garni, chopped garlic, salt, and the cayenne pepper. Pour on the wine. Cover, and cook slowly 25 minutes. Remove the eel and add it to the lobster. Slice the mushrooms and reserve the stems. Sauté the mushroom slices in 1 tablespoon butter and a little lemon juice. Add the mushrooms to the lobster and eel mixture. Cover, and keep it warm.

Strain the liquid in which the eel was cooked. Add to it the fish stock (or the lobster stock if you boiled the lobster). In a heavy pan melt 2 tablespoons butter. Add the remaining sliced onion and the carrot and celery. Brown the vegetables slowly, then add the flour and brown to a dark color very slowly. Add a few chopped mushroom stems and cook 1 minute. Add the tomato paste. Off the heat, pour in the eel and fish stock. Stir over low heat until the mixture comes to a boil. Add the bay leaf and the currant jelly. Boil this down to a creamy consistency and strain it. Arrange the pieces of lobster and eel with the mushrooms in a shallow serving dish or au gratin dish. Pour the sauce over them. Sprinkle with chives. NET: 4 servings.

HOMARD CORDON BLEU

Lobster in Fresh Tomato Sauce, in the Shells, au Gratin

2 live lobsters, 1¼ pounds each
1 tablespoon pure olive oil
3 tablespoons salt butter
¼ cup dry sherry
½ teaspoon chopped fresh tarragon
½ teaspoon chopped fresh parsley

¼ teaspoon tomato paste
¾ cup light cream
Salt
Freshly cracked white pepper
1 pound firm ripe tomatoes
1 tablespoon freshly grated Parmesan cheese

Preheat the oven to 350°. With a large knife, split the lobsters in half, starting from the little cross in the center of the head shell. Remove the sac from behind each eye. In a large heavy pan, heat the olive oil and 2 tablespoons butter. Put the split lobsters in the pan, split side down. Cover the pan and shake over brisk heat 5 minutes. In a small pan, heat the sherry, ignite, and pour it flaming over the lobsters. Add the tarragon, parsley, tomato paste, and cream. Season with salt and pepper. Skin the tomatoes and remove the seeds. Cut the tomato pulp into shreds, and add to the lobster. Cover, and cook in the oven 15 minutes. Remove all the lobster meat from the shells and claws and chop it coarsely. Place the four half-shells on a serving platter. Mix the chopped lobster meat into the tomato sauce. Spoon the mixture into the lobster shells. Sprinkle with the Parmesan cheese and 1 tablespoon melted butter. Brown under a hot broiler and serve immediately. NET: 4 servings.

HOMARD ET CHAMPIGNONS EN CROÛTE

Lobster and Mushroom Pie with Velouté Sauce

3 boiled lobsters, ¾ to 1 pound
   each
12 medium-size firm white
   mushrooms
3 tablespoons salt butter
A little lemon juice
3 tablespoons all-purpose flour
Salt
A few grains cayenne pepper
1½ cups fish stock (page 36)
   or chicken stock (page 35)
1 teaspoon chopped fresh chives
1 egg, beaten

PASTRY
2 cups all-purpose flour
4 raw egg yolks
4 tablespoons salt butter, at
   room temperature
3 tablespoons freshly grated
   Parmesan cheese
2 hard-boiled egg yolks, rubbed
   through a fine strainer
1 teaspoon salt
1 teaspoon paprika
½ teaspoon chili powder
A few grains cayenne pepper

Remove the lobster tail and claw meat from the shells, and cut into bite-size chunks. Cut the mushrooms in half and sauté them in 1 tablespoon butter and a little lemon juice. Mix the mushrooms with the lobster pieces and put the mixture into a deep baking dish.

VELOUTÉ SAUCE. In a saucepan, melt 2 tablespoons butter. Off the fire, stir in the flour, salt, and cayenne pepper. Pour in the stock and stir over low heat until the sauce comes to a boil. Add the chives, and keep the sauce warm.

PASTRY. Preheat the oven to 400°. Put the flour on a pastry slab. Make a well in the center, put the rest of the ingredients in it, and work them to a smooth paste with the fingers. Then, with the heel of the hand, quickly work in the flour. Roll out on a lightly floured surface to a size that will cover the baking dish (not too thin).

Pour the velouté sauce over the lobster and mushrooms in the baking dish. Cover the dish with the pastry. Brush the pastry with the beaten egg, and bake 30 minutes. Serve hot. NET: 4 to 6 servings.

HOMARD FARCI SAINT-JACQUES

Lobster and Sea Scallops in Lobster Shells, Mushroom Sauce

4 boiled lobsters, ¾ to 1 pound
   each
1 pound sea scallops

½ cup dry white wine
2 tablespoons dry sherry
½ cup water

1 bay leaf
Salt
6 peppercorns
½ cup sour cream
1 tablespoon chopped fresh dill
   or parsley
Freshly cracked white pepper
6 tablespoons salt butter

3 tablespoons all-purpose flour
A few grains cayenne pepper
1 egg yolk
3 tablespoons heavy cream
½ cup sliced firm white
   mushrooms
¼ cup freshly grated Parmesan
   cheese

Split the boiled lobsters in half, remove the sac from behind each eye, and remove the lobster meat from the shell. Arrange the 8 half-shells on a heatproof serving dish and fill them with the following filling.

FILLING. Put the scallops in a pan with the wine, sherry, water, bay leaf, salt, and peppercorns. Bring slowly to a boil and cook 4 to 5 minutes (no longer or the scallops will toughen). Strain, and reserve the liquid. Slice the lobster meat and scallops, and mix them together with the sour cream and dill or parsley. Season with salt and white pepper.

SAUCE. In a saucepan, melt 3 tablespoons butter. Off the heat, stir in the flour, salt, and cayenne pepper. Strain in the stock from the scallops and stir over low heat until the sauce comes to a boil and thickens. Add, bit by bit, 1 tablespoon butter. In a separate small bowl mix the egg yolk and the heavy cream, and add to the sauce. Sauté the sliced mushrooms in 1 tablespoon butter, and add to the sauce. Blend well.

Spoon the sauce over the lobster and scallop mixture in the shells. Sprinkle with the Parmesan cheese, dot with 1 tablespoon butter, and brown under a hot broiler. NET: 8 servings.

HOMARD MARGUERITE

Lobster Marguerite

Lobster shells filled with lobster sections and fillets of sole stuffed with a cod mousse, covered with a fresh tomato and lobster sauce.

2 live lobsters, 1¼ pounds each
2 tablespoons pure olive oil
9 tablespoons salt butter
2 bay leaves
2 medium-size yellow onions,
   chopped
Salt
Freshly cracked white pepper
¾ cup sliced firm white
   mushrooms
4 to 5 teaspoons lemon juice
4 large ripe tomatoes, skinned,
   seeded, and shredded

2 tablespoons chopped fresh
   parsley
4 small fillets of sole or flounder,
   plus the bones
½ cup fresh cod (skinned,
   boned, and minced)
1 egg white
5 tablespoons heavy cream
¼ cup dry sherry
¼ cup dry white wine
5 teaspoons all-purpose flour
2 egg yolks, beaten

Preheat the oven to 325°. With a large knife, split the lobsters in half, starting from the little cross in the center of the head shell. When split, remove the sac from behind each eye. Remove and crack the large claws. In a large heavy pan, heat the olive oil and 2 table-spoons butter. When hot, put in the lobsters, split side down. Shake over brisk heat 2 to 3 minutes. Add 1 bay leaf to the lobster pan, cover, and cook in the oven 10 to 15 minutes. (When done, leave the oven on.) Remove the meat from the tail and cut it into neat scallops. Keep the lobster meat in a warm place. Reserve the juices from the pan. In another pan, melt 2 tablespoons butter. Add the onions, salt, and pepper. Cook until the onions are nearly soft. Add ½ cup sliced mushrooms and 1 teaspoon lemon juice. Cover, and cook 3 minutes. Chop the lobster claw meat and add to the pan. Add the shredded tomato pulp and chopped parsley. Cover, and keep the mixture warm.

Wash the fillets of sole or flounder in water and a little lemon juice. Dry them well and set them aside for a moment. Put the cod in a bowl and, with a wire whisk, slowly beat in the egg white. Add a pinch of salt, white pepper, and 1 tablespoon heavy cream. Chop fine ¼ cup sliced mushrooms, and add to the cod mixture. Spread a thin layer of the cod mixture on the fillets of sole. Roll them up and tie each with a piece of fine string. Place them on a well-buttered baking dish. Add 1 bay leaf and pour over them the sherry and wine. Cover with the bones of the fish and bake 12 to 15 minutes.

SAUCE. Strain the liquid the fillets were cooked in and reduce it by boiling down to ¼ cup. In the top of a double boiler, but not over any heat, beat the 2 egg yolks. Pour in the reduced fish liquid. Add 4 tablespoons heavy cream and 2 teaspoons lemon juice. Put the double boiler over hot water on low heat and stir with a wire whisk until it thickens. Mix a beurre manié of the flour and 5 tablespoons butter. Beat this in bit by bit. Stir in the juices from the lobster pan.

Wash the 4 lobster half-shells. Heat them slightly in the oven and arrange on a hot serving dish. In the head section of each shell place a stuffed fillet of sole. Arrange the lobster scallops overlapping in the tail section. Spoon the tomato and claw sauce over the shells. NET: 4 servings.

---

2 live lobsters, 1¼ pounds each
4 tablespoons vegetable oil
4 tablespoons salt butter
1 large yellow onion, finely
  chopped
½ cup dry white wine
3 tablespoons all-purpose flour
Salt

A few grains cayenne pepper
¾ cup milk
¼ cup heavy cream
1 teaspoon dry mustard
Paprika
½ cup freshly grated Parmesan
  cheese

HOMARD THERMIDOR

Lobster and Chopped Onion in Béchamel Sauce, Served in the Shells

Wash the lobsters well in cold water. Split them in half, with a large knife, starting from the little cross in the shell at the center of the head. Remove the small sac from behind each eye and remove the eyes. In a large heavy pan, heat the vegetable oil. Place the lobsters shell side down in the oil. Cover, and cook slowly 12 minutes. Remove from the heat and take the lobster meat from the shell. Cut the lobster meat coarsely and set aside. Place the four half-shells on a serving dish and keep them warm. Reserve the liquid from the pan.

Melt 2 tablespoons butter in the pan. Add the onion and cook until soft without browning. Add the wine and cook slowly until it has evaporated. In another pan, melt 2 tablespoons butter. Off the heat, stir in the flour, salt, and cayenne pepper. Stir until smooth and add the milk. Stir over low heat until the mixture comes to a boil. Add the heavy cream and combine this cream sauce with the onion mixture. Add the mustard, a pinch of paprika, and 2 tablespoons Parmesan cheese to the mixture. Reduce it to a thick, creamy consistency by adding a little of the reserved lobster liquid. Add the cut-up lobster meat to this sauce, and spoon it into the lobster shells. Sprinkle well with the rest of the grated Parmesan cheese and dot with the remaining butter. Brown quickly under the broiler. NET: 4 servings.

HOMARD VILLEROI

Salpicon of Lobster and Mushrooms, with Lobster Chunks, in the Shell

4 tablespoons vegetable oil
1 small onion, sliced
1 small carrot, sliced
1 stalk celery, sliced
2 cups water
¼ cup dry white wine
1 bay leaf
Salt
A few grains cayenne pepper

2 live lobsters, 1¼ pounds each
5 tablespoons salt butter
2 cups sliced firm white fresh
    mushrooms
A little lemon juice
4 egg yolks
1 tablespoon Dijon mustard
4 tablespoons freshly grated
    Parmesan cheese

COURT BOUILLON. In a large heavy pan, heat the vegetable oil. Add the onion, carrot, and celery, and cook 3 to 5 minutes, until the vegetables are golden brown. Pour in the water and wine, add the bay leaf, salt, and cayenne pepper, and bring to a boil. Simmer 15 to 20 minutes.

Cook the whole lobsters in this liquid 15 minutes, with the lid on the pan. Remove the lobsters and cool them a little. Split them down the center of the back through the tail shell. Remove the meat from the tails. (Reserve the coral and shells.) Cut the tail meat into neat scallops and put them in a sauté pan. Warm with 1 tablespoon butter. Add salt and a little cayenne pepper. Remove from the pan and keep the lobster warm. In the same sauté pan, melt another tablespoon of butter, add the sliced mushrooms and a little lemon juice. Remove the meat from the lobster claws and chop it. Add the claw meat and the coral, if any, to the mushrooms.

MUSTARD SAUCE. Strain the liquid the lobster was cooked in and boil it down to ½ cup. Beat the egg yolks and pour the reduced liquid onto the yolks. Put the yolk mixture in the top of a double boiler, over hot water, over low heat. Beat with a wire whisk until the sauce begins to thicken and coats the back of a silver spoon. Bit by bit, beat in 3 tablespoons butter. Then add the Dijon mustard. Strain the sauce through a fine strainer.

Mix about 2 tablespoons of the mustard sauce into the mushroom mixture. Place the four half-shells on a hot serving dish. Fill them with the mushroom mixture. On that arrange the scallops of tail meat, overlapping. Cover the filled lobster shells with mustard sauce. Sprinkle with freshly grated Parmesan cheese and brown quickly under a hot broiler. NET: 4 servings.

This strudel which combines lobster, shrimp, cod and mushrooms can be made a day before you want to serve it, and warmed in the oven.

LOBSTER STRUDEL

1 boiled lobster, 1½ pounds
¼ pound fresh cod
A little fish stock (page 36) or clam juice
¼ pound firm white mushrooms, thinly sliced
1 cup boiled shrimps, thinly sliced
9 tablespoons salt butter
¼ cup all-purpose flour
Salt
Freshly cracked white pepper
1 cup milk
6 tablespoons freshly grated Parmesan cheese

1 teaspoon dry mustard
2 tablespoons heavy cream
2 to 3 tablespoons melted salt butter
½ cup dry breadcrumbs (page 69)

STRUDEL DOUGH
2¼ cups all-purpose flour
1 egg
Vegetable oil as required
Pinch of salt
¾ cup warm water
8 tablespoons melted salt butter

You can make the filling and sauce while the strudel dough is resting for an hour.

FILLING. Remove all the meat from the lobster and chop it fine. Cook the cod 10 minutes in the fish stock or clam juice, then skin, bone, and flake it. Sauté the mushrooms 5 minutes in a little butter. Mix all together with the sliced shrimps, and keep it warm.

SAUCE. Melt 8 tablespoons butter in a saucepan. Off the heat, stir in the flour. Season with salt and pepper, and pour in the milk. Stir over low heat and bring to a boil. Add 4 tablespoons Parmesan cheese and the mustard and heavy cream. Keep the sauce warm.

STRUDEL DOUGH. Put 2 cups flour on a pastry board or marble slab. Make a well in the center and put in the egg, 1 tablespoon vegetable oil, and a pinch of salt. Work to a soft paste with the warm water. Literally slap the dough on the board until it becomes very light and elastic (about a hundred times). Place it in a floured bowl and brush with oil. Cover the bowl with a cloth and leave it 1 hour in a warm place. Then cover a table about 3 feet square (card table size) with a cloth (like a sheet) and sprinkle it with the remaining flour. Roll the dough out to a large square and brush it with vegetable oil. Roll it out as thin as possible, so that it covers the table. Brush it with vegetable oil and pull it carefully over the edge of the table until it is thin like parchment or tissue paper. Sprinkle the dough with the melted butter.

Preheat the oven to 350°. Scatter the filling mixture (lobster, shrimps, cod, and mushroom) over the strudel dough. Drop teaspoonfuls of the sauce evenly over the filling. Roll up the strudel, trimming off each end. Place it on a well-buttered baking sheet (cut it in two or bend it like a horseshoe). Brush it with the melted butter and sprinkle with 2 tablespoons Parmesan cheese and the breadcrumbs. Bake 30 to 35 minutes, until golden brown. Remove from the oven and trim off each end. NET: 6 to 8 servings.

MAYONNAISE DE HOMARD

Lobster Mayonnaise

Cold lobster on a vegetable macédoine, coated with mayonnaise and decorated with the lobster shells.

2 boiled lobsters, 1½ to 2 pounds each
1 cup long-grain rice
⅓ cup vegetable oil
2 cups water
1 teaspoon salt
A few grains cayenne pepper
1 cup each of finely diced cooked (but still crisp) green beans and carrots
1½ pounds tomatoes, skinned, seeded, and shredded

MAYONNAISE SAUCE
3 egg yolks
½ teaspoon dry mustard
1 teaspoon Dijon mustard
1 teaspoon salt
A few grains cayenne pepper
Pinch of sugar
2 tablespoons tarragon vinegar
2 cups vegetable oil
½ cup pure olive oil
A little light cream, if needed

GARNISH
2 tomatoes, skinned, quartered, and seeded
1 cucumber, thinly sliced
1 black truffle
Small bunch crisp fresh watercress

Remove all the lobster meat, keeping the lobster head and tail shells as intact as possible. Also keep 6 of the small claws. Brush the shells with a little vegetable oil and set aside.

RICE SALAD. Preheat the oven to 350°. Put the rice in a heavy pan with the vegetable oil and water. Add the salt and cayenne pepper and stir over moderate heat until it comes to a rolling boil. Cover, and cook 30 minutes in the oven. Put the cooked rice in a bowl, chill, and separate the grains with a fork. Mix in all the vegetables.

Arrange the rice salad in the general shape of a lobster on a cold oval serving platter. Cut the lobster tail into neat slices and arrange them overlapping on one end of the rice salad. Put the claws at the top. Put the second joints in the middle with any coral that may have been in the lobster.

MAYONNAISE SAUCE. Put the egg yolks in a mixer bowl. Add the mustards, salt, cayenne pepper, and sugar. Beat until very thick. Slowly add the tarragon vinegar. Add the vegetable oil and the olive oil very slowly, drop by drop until it begins to thicken. (If the mayonnaise is too thick for coating, dilute it with a little light cream.) NOTE: If you want to coat the lobster considerably ahead of the time you plan to serve, add 1 teaspoon unflavored gelatine, dissolved in 2 tablespoons warm milk, to the mayonnaise.

Coat the lobster and rice salad smoothly with this mayonnaise. Place the lobster head shell at one end of the dish on the mayonnaise, and the tail shell at the other end. Put the small claws in the middle (3 at each side), so the dish looks like a lobster resting. Cut the truffle into thin slices and arrange down the center of the dish (like the buttons on his suit). Arrange sections of tomato and thin slices of cucumber around the sides of the dish. Put 1 or 2 bouquets of fresh watercress at each end of the dish. NET: 4 to 6 servings.

PILAF DE HOMARD

Mold of Rice Pilaff Filled with Lobster

2 tablespoons vegetable oil
4 tablespoons salt butter
1 onion, finely chopped
1 teaspoon finely chopped garlic
2 cups long-grain rice
4 cups fish stock (page 36) or clam juice
Salt
Freshly cracked white pepper
1 bay leaf
4 tablespoons freshly grated Parmesan cheese
2 live lobsters, about ¾ pound each
4 tablespoons heavy cream or sour cream
Paprika
Optional: 2 teaspoons chopped fresh chives

Preheat the oven to 350°. In a medium-size heavy pan, heat 1 tablespoon vegetable oil and 1 tablespoon salt butter. Add the onion and garlic, and cook until soft without browning. Add the rice, and cook slowly 7 minutes, stirring all the time. Cover with the fish stock. Bring to a boil. Season with salt and pepper and the bay leaf. Cover with wax paper and the lid, and cook 25 minutes in the oven. Remove the cooked rice from the oven, and with a fork stir in 2 tablespoons grated cheese and 2 tablespoons butter. Butter a 1-quart mold (such as a charlotte mold) and line it with the rice mixture, leaving a well in the center. Reserve a third of the rice to cover the top later.

Wash the lobsters and split them in half. Remove the sac from behind each eye, also remove the eyes. Heat 1 tablespoon oil and 1 tablespoon butter in a large heavy pan. Put the lobster halves in the pan, split side down. Cover the pan and cook slowly until the shells are bright red. Remove the lobster meat from the shells and cut it up coarsely. (Reserve a few of the shells for decoration.) Mix the lobster meat with the remaining grated cheese and the heavy (or sour) cream, and paprika to color. Season with salt and pepper and add the chopped chives, if desired.

Put the lobster mixture into the well in the rice mold. Cover with the remaining rice. Press down gently. Turn out of the mold onto a serving dish. Decorate with a few lobster shells. NET: 4 to 6 servings.

SOUFFLÉ PLAZA ATHENÉE

Lobster and Cheese Sandwich Soufflé

This is the famous soufflé spécialité of the Hotel Plaza Athenée in Paris. No sauce is necessary with this soufflé; it is rich enough.

LOBSTER SOUFFLÉ
Meat and shells of 1 small boiled lobster (about ¾ to 1 pound)
A few mushroom trimmings and stems
6 tablespoons salt butter
½ cup dry white wine
¼ cup dry sherry
½ cup cold water
Salt
6 white peppercorns
1 sprig fresh dill, if available
Half a bay leaf
1 tablespoon finely chopped shallots
½ teaspoon finely chopped garlic
1 large firm white mushroom, finely chopped
¼ cup each of very finely diced raw green beans and carrots
Freshly cracked white pepper
½ teaspoon lemon juice

2 tablespoons Cognac or good brandy
½ teaspoon tomato paste
4 tablespoons all-purpose flour
3 egg yolks
4 egg whites

CHEESE SOUFFLÉ
4 tablespoons salt butter
4 tablespoons all-purpose flour
½ teaspoon dry mustard
1 teaspoon Dijon mustard
A few grains cayenne pepper
½ teaspoon salt
A few grains freshly grated nutmeg
1 cup milk
½ cup freshly grated Parmesan cheese
⅓ cup freshly grated imported Gruyère cheese
2 tablespoons sour cream
3 egg yolks
4 egg whites

LOBSTER STOCK. Cut up the shells of the lobster coarsely and put them in a pan with the mushroom trimmings and stems, 2 tablespoons butter, the wine, sherry, water, 1 teaspoon salt, white peppercorns, sprig of dill, and half bay leaf. Bring slowly to a boil and simmer 20 minutes, or until it has boiled down to 1 cup liquid. Strain.

LOBSTER SOUFFLÉ. In a saucepan heat 3 tablespoons butter. Add the shallots, garlic, and chopped mushroom. Cook 1 to 2 minutes. Blanch the chopped green beans and carrots, drain, and add to the saucepan. Season with salt, pepper, and the lemon juice. Cook slowly 3 to 4 minutes. Chop the lobster meat (claws and tail) very fine and add to the saucepan with 1 tablespoon butter. Stir well. Heat the brandy in a little pan, ignite, and pour it over the mixture. Stir in the tomato paste, flour, and the cup of fish stock. Stir over a low heat until it comes to a boil and thickens. Remove from the heat and mix in, one at a time, the egg yolks. Cover the pan with plastic wrap and set aside.

CHEESE SOUFFLÉ. Preheat the oven to 375°. In a saucepan melt the butter. Off the heat, stir in the flour, mustards, cayenne pepper, salt, and nutmeg. Mix in the milk. Return to low heat and stir until the mixture comes to a boil. Add 1 tablespoon Parmesan cheese and all the Gruyère cheese and sour cream. Stir over low heat and mix well. Remove from the heat and add the egg yolks one at a time, stirring each one in.

Put the egg whites for both soufflés (8 whites) in a copper beating bowl. Beat with a wire whisk to soft peaks. Fold half the beaten egg whites into the lobster soufflé mixture and the other half into the cheese soufflé mixture. Brush the inside of a 6-cup (#7) soufflé dish with melted butter. Tie a double band of buttered wax paper around the outside (the paper should be 3 to 4 inches higher than the sides of the dish). (See soufflé notes, page 787.) Dust the inside with the rest of the Parmesan cheese, reserving a little for the top of the soufflé. Spoon alternate layers of cheese and lobster soufflé into the dish, beginning and ending with cheese soufflé. Sprinkle the top with a little Parmesan cheese. Stand the filled soufflé dish in a shallow pan half-filled with hot water. Bake 1 hour and 10 minutes. (If individual soufflé dishes are used, bake 35 to 40 minutes.) Test the soufflé with a cake tester (if it comes out clean, it is cooked). Remove from the oven, peel off the wax paper, wrap a white cloth napkin around the sides, and serve immediately. NET: 4 to 6 servings.

HOMARD CARDINAL

Lobster Shells Filled with Lobster, Mushrooms, and Truffles, with Cardinal Sauce

1 cup mixed sliced onion, carrot, and celery
2 peppercorns
1 bay leaf
1 sprig fresh dill
½ cup dry white wine
3 cups water
2 live lobsters, 1½ pounds each
1 cup coarsely chopped firm white mushrooms
2 tablespoons salt butter
Salt
1 teaspoon lemon juice
2 black truffles, chopped
1 black truffle, thinly sliced
8 firm white mushroom caps

for garnish (it is nice to flute them)

CARDINAL SAUCE
3 tablespoons sweet butter
3 tablespoons all-purpose flour
Salt
A few grains cayenne pepper
1 tablespoon tomato paste
¾ cup liquid in which lobster was cooked
¾ cup light cream
2 egg yolks
2 tablespoons dry sherry
8 shelled cooked shrimps
1 tablespoon salt butter

In a large heavy pan combine the onion, carrot, celery, peppercorns, bay leaf, and dill. Pour over the dry white wine and water. Bring the liquid to a boil and put in the whole live lobsters. Cook them in this court bouillon until the shells turn red. Leave the cooked lobsters in the liquid until cool. Then split them in half, using a large French knife. Start at the star on the center of the head shell and cut down through the body and tail. Remove the meat from the tail and large claws. Cut the claw meat into coarse dice. Leave the tail meat intact. Reserve the 4 half-shells. Sauté the mushrooms in the butter with salt and the lemon juice. Add the chopped claw meat and truffles to the mushrooms. Divide this mixture among the 4 lobster shells. Cut a few slits in each of the 4 strips of tail meat and insert a thin slice of truffle in each slit. Place the tails on top of the mixture in the bottom of the shells.

CARDINAL SAUCE. Melt the sweet butter in a saucepan over low heat (do not allow it to brown). Off the heat, stir in the flour, salt, and cayenne pepper. Mix in the tomato paste, ¾ cup of the strained liquid in which the lobster was poached, and ½ cup light cream. Mix and stir over low heat until the sauce comes to a boil. In a small bowl combine the egg yolks and dry sherry and mix well. Then mix in ¼ cup light cream. Coarsely chop 4 shrimps. Mix them roughly with the salt butter and crush them with the little claws of the lobster in a blender. Rub through a fine strainer. Off the heat, add the egg yolk mixture to the sauce stirring all the time. Continue stirring and, bit by bit, add the shrimp-lobster butter. Reheat the sauce but do not boil it.

Arrange the stuffed lobster shells on a serving dish. Spoon the sauce over them. Garnish the lobsters with the remaining shrimps and the whole mushroom caps. NET: 4 servings.

HOMARD DELMONICO

Casserole of Lobster in Port Wine Sauce, with Rice

4 live lobsters, 1 pound each
2 tablespoons salt butter
Salt
1 cup good port wine
2 tablespoons heavy cream
4 egg yolks
10 tablespoons frozen sweet butter
A few grains cayenne pepper
A little chopped fresh parsley

COURT BOUILLON
1½ cups dry white wine
3 cups water
2 teaspoons salt
1 teaspoon freshly cracked white pepper
½ cup mixed sliced onion, carrot, and celery
1 sprig fresh parsley
1 sprig fresh dill (if available)
1 bay leaf
2 cups cooked rice (page 675)

Prepare a court bouillon. In a deep large heavy pan put the wine and water, and add the salt, white pepper, sliced onion, carrot, and celery, parsley, dill, and bay leaf. Bring the liquid to a rolling boil and put the live lobsters in the pan. Cover, and poach them 15 minutes over low heat. Let them cool in the stock. Then remove the meat from the large claws and tail, keeping the pieces as whole as possible. Cut the tail meat into thick slices.

Melt the salt butter in a sauté pan. Put the lobster meat in the pan, season it with a little salt, and pour over the port wine. Over fairly low heat, allow the port to cook down slowly, then light a match to the pan to let the alcohol burn out. Remove the lobster from the pan with a slotted spoon and keep it warm. Pour off the remainder of the wine into a cup and reserve it.

PORT WINE SAUCE. Combine the egg yolks with the drained port wine in a small bowl and mix well with a small wire whisk. Stand the bowl in a shallow pan half filled with hot water over moderate heat. Beat with the whisk until the mixture begins to thicken. Add the heavy cream and continue beating until the sauce is the consistency of thick, almost-whipped cream. Cut the frozen sweet butter into bits and beat it into the sauce, a piece at a time. Add a few grains of cayenne pepper, and more salt if necessary.

Arrange the pieces of lobster in a warm copper casserole. Spoon the sauce over them and sprinkle with a little chopped fresh parsley. Serve the rice in a separate bowl. NET: 4 to 6 servings.

HOMARD WASHINGTON

Lobster in Ring of Sole Mousse

4 tablespoons salt butter
½ teaspoon finely chopped garlic
Finely chopped raw vegetables: 1 medium-size onion, 2 small stalks celery, 2 medium-size carrots, 8 green beans
Salt
A few grains cayenne pepper
2 1-pound live lobsters
¼ cup Cognac or good brandy
4 teaspoons all-purpose flour
½ teaspoon tomato paste

1 cup heavy cream
1 large black truffle, cut into fine shreds
¼ cup light cream

SOLE MOUSSE
1½ pounds sole or flounder fillets
2 egg whites
1¼ cups light cream
2 teaspoons salt
⅛ teaspoon cayenne pepper

SOLE MOUSSE. Preheat the oven to 350°. Well-butter a 1-quart ring mold. Put the fish through a fine meat chopper. Transfer to a mixer bowl, add the raw egg whites, and beat until the mixture is smooth. Very slowly (literally drop by drop), add the light cream, beating all the time. Then add the salt and cayenne pepper. Beat the mixture very well. Pack the mousse into the ring mold, making sure there are no air pockets. Cover the mold with buttered wax paper, stand it in a shallow roasting pan half filled with hot water, and set the pan in the oven. Steam the mousse 45 minutes, or until it is firm to the touch.

LOBSTER. Melt the butter in a deep heavy pan big enough for the lobsters, and add the chopped garlic. Cook over low heat 2 minutes. Add the finely chopped onions, carrots, celery, and green beans. Season with salt and a little cayenne pepper, and cook slowly 3 to 4 minutes.

Split the live lobsters in half. To do this, hold a kitchen towel over the head of the lobster with the left hand. In the right hand hold a large French knife. Place the point of the knife at the star in the center of the head shell of the lobster, and cut down through the lobster body and tail. Remove the small sacs behind the eyes and the large vein. Cut off the large and small claws with kitchen shears. Put the pieces of lobster (shells with meat attached) in the heavy pan with the chopped vegetables. Cover the pan with the lid and cook briskly 3 minutes. Remove the lid. Heat the brandy in a small pan, ignite, and pour it over the lobster. Cover the lobster again and cook another 6 to 7 minutes, until the shells are red all over.

Set aside all the lobster pieces, leaving the vegetable mixture (mirepoix) in the pan. Add the flour and tomato paste, and stir until smooth. Then add the heavy cream, and stir the mixture over low heat until it comes to a boil. Add the shredded truffle. Remove all the meat from the lobster and cut it into bite-size pieces. Return the lobster meat to the sauce. Gently reheat the mixture.

To serve, turn the ring of sole mousse out onto a large round serving dish. Spoon all the lobster pieces into the center of the ring with some of the sauce. Add the light cream to the sauce left in the pan, reheat, and spoon it around the mousse. Serve at once. NET: 4 to 6 servings.

MOULES À LA BORDELAISE

Mussels in Bordelaise Sauce

2 quarts mussels
1 teaspoon dry mustard
½ cup dry white wine
½ cup water
1 onion, sliced
1 stalk celery, sliced
Bouquet garni, including fresh dill, parsley, 1 bay leaf, celery leaf
1 tablespoon all-purpose flour
1½ tablespoons salt butter
½ teaspoon finely chopped garlic
1 tablespoon finely chopped parsley
1 slice stale white bread, chopped
1 teaspoon tomato paste
Salt
Freshly cracked white pepper

Wash and scrub the mussels thoroughly in cold water and the mustard. Put them in a pan with the wine, water, onion, celery, and bouquet garni. Cover, and shake over moderate heat until the mussels open (6 to 7 minutes). Remove one shell from each mussel. Strain the liquid through a fine cloth or strainer. In a separate pan, put the butter and flour and brown the mixture. Chop the garlic, parsley, and bread together a bit and add to the butter and flour mixture with the tomato paste. Season with salt and pepper. Put the mussels in a casserole. Put in the flour and bread mixture. Pour in enough of the mussel liquid to make a sauce of syrupy consistency. Cook gently over a low flame, about 15 minutes. NET: 4 servings.

TO CLEAN AND STORE FRESH MUSSELS

(1) Roughly scrub the mussels under the cold water tap and put them in a pan. Cover them with cold water and sprinkle the water with 1 teaspoon dry mustard. Leave them about an hour. (This loosens any barnacles on the shells.) Scrub the mussels with a small firm brush, as you must remove all traces of sand and grit. Rinse again in cold water.

(2) To keep fresh mussels a day or so, put them in a bowl after they have been scrubbed. Cover with cold water and sprinkle the water with oatmeal. The fresh mussels will eat the oatmeal and become fatter in the process.

(3) The shells of raw mussels must be tightly closed. If they are open, discard them; it means the mussels are dead. After you have cooked the mussels, any that remain with the shells closed are also to be discarded, as they are not good.

<table>
<tr><td>

2 quarts mussels
1 teaspoon dry mustard
1½ cups finely chopped mixed
   celery, carrot, onion, and leek
1 bay leaf
Salt
Freshly cracked white pepper
½ cup dry white wine
1 tablespoon dry sherry

</td><td>

¼ cup water
1 tablespoon all-purpose flour
1 tablespoon salt butter
½ teaspoon finely chopped
   garlic
2 egg yolks
½ cup heavy cream
2 tablespoons coarsely chopped
   fresh parsley

</td></tr>
</table>

MOULES À LA POULETTE

Mussels in Rich Velouté Sauce

Scrub the mussels in cold water with the mustard. Blanch the chopped vegetables by bringing them to a boil from cold water. Drain them, then put them in a pan with the mussels, bay leaf, salt, pepper, wine, sherry, and water. Bring slowly to a boil, cover, and simmer about 5 minutes, until the mussel shells are opened. Remove the top shells, and arrange the mussels on a platter. Strain the chopped vegetables and scatter them over the mussels. Reserve the liquid.

RICH VELOUTÉ SAUCE. Reduce the liquid in which the mussels were cooked to two-thirds quantity. Work the flour, butter, and garlic to a smooth paste. Over low heat, stirring constantly, add this paste bit by bit to the reduced mussel stock. In a little bowl mix the egg yolks with the heavy cream. Add the yolk mixture to the sauce. Add the parsley. Reheat, but do not boil. Pour the sauce over the mussels. NET: 4 servings.

<table>
<tr><td>

1½ quarts mussels
1 teaspoon dry mustard
¾ cup water
1 onion, sliced
Bouquet garni consisting of
   oregano, parsley, chives
2 tablespoons pure olive oil
2 medium-size onions, chopped
½ teaspoon finely chopped
   garlic
¼ cup finely shredded raw

</td><td>

bacon
3 tomatoes, skinned, seeded,
   and shredded
¾ cup long-grain rice
Fish stock (page 36) or water,
   if necessary
Salt
Freshly cracked white pepper
Paprika
A little freshly grated
   Parmesan cheese

</td></tr>
</table>

MOULES EN RISOTTO

Mussels Cooked with Rice

Preheat the oven to 325°. Wash and scrub the mussels thoroughly in the water and the mustard. Put them in a pan with the water, sliced onion, and bouquet garni. Shake over the fire until the mussels open. Remove them from the shells. In a separate pan, heat the olive oil. Add the chopped onions, garlic, bacon, and tomatoes. Add the shelled mussels and sauté all together. Add the rice, the liquid from the mussels, and fish stock or water, if necessary to cover the mixture, salt, pepper, and a little paprika. Bring the liquid to a boil, cover the pan tightly, and cook in the oven 25 minutes. The rice should be soft, and the mixture creamy. Sprinkle with the Parmesan cheese and serve. NET: 4 servings.

MOULES FORESTIÈRE

Mussels Cooked by Pinecones, with Cheese Sauce

3 dozen large mussels
1 teaspoon dry mustard
Salt
Freshly cracked black pepper
2 dozen dry pinecones

4 tablespoons salt butter
½ cup light cream
2 tablespoons freshly grated
   Parmesan cheese
A few grains cayenne pepper

Wash and scrub the mussels throughly in cold water and the mustard. Put them in a pan. Sprinkle with salt and pepper. Take them outdoors and scatter the pinecones over them. Light the cones and let them burn out. By this time the mussels will have opened. Remove the top shells, and arrange the mussels in the bottom shells on a hot heatproof dish. In a separate pan, melt the butter. Add the cream, 1 tablespoon grated cheese, salt, and the cayenne pepper. Beat the sauce well and pour over the mussels. Sprinkle the top with a little more cheese and brown quickly under the broiler. Serve at once. NET: 4 servings.

MOULES MARINIÈRE

The Classic Mussels in White Wine

3 quarts mussels
1 teaspoon dry mustard
1 stalk celery, diced
2 carrots, diced
1 onion, finely chopped
¾ cup dry white wine
¾ cup water
Bouquet garni, including thyme,

   parsley, and 1 bay leaf
1 teaspoon finely chopped garlic
Salt
Freshly cracked white pepper
2 egg yolks
¼ cup heavy cream
1 tablespoon chopped fresh
   parsley

Scrub the mussels thoroughly in cold water and the mustard. Put them in a pan with the celery, carrots, onion, wine, water, bouquet garni, garlic, salt, and pepper. Bring slowly to a boil. Cover, and simmer until all the shells are open but not longer than 5 minutes. Discard any unopened mussels. Strain off the liquid and reduce it by one-third. Mix the egg yolks with the heavy cream. Off the heat, add the yolk mixture to the reduced mussel liquid. Stir over low heat until it thickens, without boiling. Add the chopped parsley. Remove one shell from each mussel. Arrange the mussels in a dish. Pour on the sauce and serve at once. NET: 4 servings.

1 quart mussels
1 teaspoon dry mustard
½ cup water
Bouquet garni, including fresh
    tarragon, parsley, chervil
    (if available)
Salt
Freshly cracked white pepper
2 extra teaspoons of the same
    herbs, chopped together

1 small onion, finely chopped
1 tablespoon salt butter
1 tablespoon all-purpose flour
1 cup light cream
A little milk, if necessary
1 drop iodine
2 tablespoons dry breadcrumbs
    (page 69) browned
1 tablespoon chopped fresh
    parsley

MOULES PANÉES

Mussels Baked in
Cream Sauce

Preheat the oven to 375°. Wash and scrub the mussels thoroughly in cold water and the mustard. Put them in a heavy pan with the water, bouquet garni, salt, and pepper. Bring to a boil and shake over moderate heat 5 to 6 minutes. Remove from the heat and discard any mussels that have not opened. Strain the liquid through a fine cloth or strainer. In a separate pan, melt the butter and add the flour. Brown a little. Add the cream, and if the sauce is too thick, add a little milk. Stir until smooth. Add the mixed chopped herbs and chopped onion, then the drop of iodine. Bring slowly to a boil and simmer gently about 5 minutes. Remove one shell from each mussel. Lay the mussels in a baking dish and cover them with the cream sauce. Sprinkle well with browned breadcrumbs and chopped parsley. Brown in the oven and serve very hot. NET: 4 servings.

5 tablespoons salt butter
2 small onions, sliced
Salt
Freshly cracked white pepper
¾ cup long-grain rice
1½ cups fish stock (page 36)
    or clam juice
2 tablespoons freshly grated
    Parmesan cheese
1 quart mussels
1 teaspoon dry mustard

½ cup dry white wine
1 cup water
Juice of half a lemon
Bouquet garni, including thyme,
    parsley, and 1 bay leaf
2 tablespoons all-purpose flour
½ cup milk
2 tablespoons heavy cream
1 tablespoon chopped fresh
    parsley

PILAF DE MOULES À L'ORIENTALE

Charlotte Mold Lined
with Rice Pilaff,
Filled with Mussels,
Velouté Sauce

RICE PILAFF. Preheat the oven to 350°. In a heavy pan, melt 2 tablespoons butter. Add the onions, salt, and pepper, and cook 2 to 3 minutes. Add the rice and cook 1 minute. Pour in the fish stock and bring to a boil. Cover the pan with wax paper and the lid and cook 25 minutes in the oven. Remove from the oven and, with a fork, stir in 1 tablespoon butter and all the grated cheese. Keep the rice warm.

MUSSELS. Wash the mussels in cold water and the mustard. Put them in a pan with the wine, water, salt, lemon juice, and bouquet garni. Bring slowly to a boil, cover, and simmer 5 minutes, shaking the pan occasionally. Remove the mussels from the shells and keep them warm. Reserve the liquid.

SAUCE. In a saucepan, melt 2 tablespoons butter. Off the heat, add the flour, salt, and pepper. Strain the liquid from the mussels into a separate pan, boil down to ¼ cup, and add the reduced mussel liquid to the saucepan. Add the milk. Stir the sauce over low heat until it boils. Add the heavy cream.

Moisten the mussels with a spoonful or two of the sauce. Butter a charlotte mold and line it with two-thirds of the rice pilaff, leaving a well in the center. Fill the center with the mussels and cover with the remaining third of the rice. Press down gently. Turn out the mold quickly onto a hot serving dish. Spoon the rest of the sauce around the mold and decorate the top with one or two mussels and a little chopped parsley. NET: 4 servings.

MOULES LARVAISES

Deep-Fried Mussels with Crab Meat Coating

24 very large mussels
1 teaspoon dry mustard
¼ cup dry white wine
3 peppercorns
1 bay leaf
Vegetable oil for deep-fryer
8 large fried croûtons (page 69)
Optional: A few crisp sprigs fresh watercress

CRAB MEAT COATING
4 tablespoons salt butter
¾ cup dry breadcrumbs (page 69)
2 tablespoons chopped fresh parsley
6 ounces fresh finely flaked

crab meat
A few drops Tabasco sauce
A few drops Worcestershire sauce
1 teaspoon finely chopped garlic
Salt
A few grains cayenne pepper
⅛ teaspoon dry mustard

BATTER
3 tablespoons all-purpose flour
1 egg, beaten
1 tablespoon vegetable oil
½ teaspoon salt
¼ cup milk
1 egg white

Soak the mussels in water and the dry mustard, and scrub them thoroughly. Put them in a deep heavy pan with the wine, peppercorns, and bay leaf. Cover the pan and cook briskly until all the shells are open (about 5 to 7 minutes). Remove the shells, cover the mussels with plastic wrap, and chill them.

CRAB MEAT COATING. Melt the butter in a sauté pan, add the breadcrumbs, and sauté until they are golden brown. Remove the pan from the heat and mix in the parsley, crab meat, Tabasco, Worcestershire, garlic, salt, cayenne pepper, and mustard. Mix all together thoroughly and set aside.

BATTER. In a small bowl combine the flour, beaten egg, 1 tablespoon vegetable oil, the salt, and 2 tablespoons of the milk. Beat with a little whisk until the mixture is quite smooth, then add the rest of the milk. Let the batter rest in the refrigerator at least 30 minutes. When it has set, beat the egg white until stiff and fold it into the batter.

Have the deep-fryer ready, half filled with vegetable oil heated to 375°. (Use a deep-fry thermometer to keep the temperature constant.) Also have a pad of paper towels ready on which to drain the fried mussels. Dip a mussel in the batter. When it is coated with batter, roll it well in the crab meat and breadcrumb mixture. Dip the mussel again in the batter and carefully, using a large spoon, lower it into the hot oil. Fry it until it is golden brown. Remove, and drain on a paper towel. Fry all the mussels in this manner. To serve, arrange the fried mussels in a warm shallow serving dish and surround them with the croûtons. A garnish of crisp fresh watercress may be added. Serve immediately. NET: 4 servings.

HUÎTRES FRITES, SAUCE BÉARNAISE

Fried Oysters with Béarnaise Sauce

3 dozen shelled oysters	Salt
1 egg	A few grains cayenne pepper
3 egg yolks	4 tablespoons frozen sweet
1 teaspoon baking powder	butter
1 tablespoon vegetable oil	2 tablespoons chopped fresh
4 tablespoons milk plus more,	herbs such as thyme, parsley,
if necessary	or chives
4 tablespoons all-purpose flour	¼ teaspoon finely chopped
1 tablespoon tarragon vinegar	garlic
2 tablespoons heavy cream	Vegetable oil for deep-fryer

BATTER. Put in a bowl the egg, 1 egg yolk, the baking powder, vegetable oil, milk, and flour. Beat until smooth, then add more milk to reduce the batter to the consistency of thick cream. Leave the batter in the refrigerator at least 30 minutes.

BÉARNAISE SAUCE. In a small bowl put 2 egg yolks and the vinegar, heavy cream, salt, and cayenne pepper. Stir well with a wire whisk. Put the bowl in a shallow pan of hot water over low heat. Beat until it becomes as thick as you want it. Add, bit by bit, the frozen sweet butter, herbs, and garlic.

Have ready a deep-fryer with hot fat at 375°. Dip the oysters in the batter and fry in the hot fat until golden brown. Pile the oysters on a hot napkin on a hot platter. Serve the sauce separately, in a sauceboat. NET: 4 servings.

COQUILLES SAINT-JACQUES À LA MORNAY

Poached Sea Scallops with Cheese Sauce

To serve, you need 4 6-inch scallop shells or 6 4-inch shells.

1½ pounds sea scallops	Freshly cracked white pepper
Juice of half a lemon	3 tablespoons salt butter
1 cup water	1 bay leaf
Salt	1½ tablespoons all-purpose

flour
¾ cup milk
2 tablespoons heavy cream
4 tablespoons freshly grated

Parmesan cheese
2 tablespoons chopped fresh
   parsley

Wash the scallops well in lemon juice and cold water. Put them in a pan and pour over the water, salt, pepper, 1 tablespoon butter, and the bay leaf. Bring slowly to a boil and simmer 5 minutes. Drain. Strain and reserve the liquid. Keep the scallops warm. In a saucepan, melt 2 tablespoons butter. Off the heat, stir in the flour, salt, and pepper. Pour on the milk and stir until smooth. Return to low heat and bring to a boil. Reduce the liquid in which the scallops were cooked to 1 tablespoon in quantity. Add to the sauce the reduced stock, heavy cream, and 3 tablespoons Parmesan cheese. Simmer 3 to 4 minutes. Mix in the sliced scallops. Fill the scallop shells with this mixture. Sprinkle with the rest of the grated cheese. Brown quickly under a hot broiler. Sprinkle with chopped fresh parsley. Serve immediately. NET: 4 to 6 servings.

COQUILLES SAINT-JACQUES PROVENÇALE

Sautéed Bay Scallops with Cèpes and Fresh Tomatoes

The mushrooms in this recipe should be soaked at least 3 hours in advance.

1½ pounds bay scallops
Juice of half a lemon
6 tablespoons salt butter
Salt
Freshly cracked white pepper
1 tablespoon chopped onion
4 to 6 diagonal fried croûtons
   (page 69)
1 tablespoon cèpes (dry wood
   mushrooms) soaked in water

at least 3 hours
2 large ripe tomatoes, skinned,
   seeded, and chopped
1 tablespoon dry white wine or
   dry vermouth
1 teaspoon chopped fresh chives
½ teaspoon finely chopped
   garlic
2 tablespoons freshly grated
   Parmesan cheese

Wash the scallops well in lemon juice and cold water. In a pan melt 3 tablespoons butter. Add the scallops, salt, pepper, and onion. Sauté very gently 5 to 6 minutes. Remove, and arrange on croûtons of fried bread on a hot serving dish (reserve the liquid). Strain the cèpes, which have been soaking and softening in water. Sauté them 10 minutes in 2 tablespoons butter with salt and pepper. Add the tomatoes, wine, a little extra salt and pepper, the chives and garlic. Simmer another 6 to 7 minutes. Add the liquid from the scallops. Stir well. Spoon the sauce over the scallops. Sprinkle with grated cheese and 1 tablespoon melted butter. Brown quickly under a hot broiler and serve. NET: 4 servings.

To serve, you need 4 6-inch scallop shells or 6 4-inch shells.

1½ pounds sea scallops
A little lemon juice
1 small onion, chopped
½ teaspoon finely chopped
    garlic
Bouquet garni, including parsley
    and tarragon
Salt
Freshly cracked white pepper
½ cup dry white wine
½ cup water

3 hard-boiled eggs, cut in
    quarters
4 tablespoons salt butter
½ pound carrots, finely chopped
2 tablespoons all-purpose flour
¼ cup heavy cream
3 tablespoons freshly grated
    Parmesan cheese
1 tablespoon dry breadcrumbs
    (page 69)

COQUILLES SAINT-JACQUES À LA SUCHET

Poached Sea Scallops with Carrots and Hard-Boiled Eggs, Velouté Sauce

Wash the scallops well in cold water and lemon juice. Place them in a saucepan with the onion, garlic, bouquet garni, salt, and pepper. Add the wine and water. Bring slowly to a boil. Simmer 5 minutes. Strain off and reserve the liquid. Place the scallops and quartered hard-boiled eggs together, and keep them warm. Melt 3 tablespoons butter in a saucepan. Remove from the heat and add the carrots, salt, and pepper. Cover the pan with buttered wax paper and the lid. Cook very slowly 10 to 15 minutes, stirring occasionally. Remove the pan from the heat. Add the flour and stir until smooth. Stir in the strained liquid in which the scallops were cooked. Stir over low heat until the mixture comes to a boil. Add the cream, mix in the scallops and hard-boiled eggs, and fill the scallop shells with the mixture. Sprinkle with grated cheese, breadcrumbs, and 1 tablespoon melted butter. Brown under a hot broiler and serve immediately. NET: 4 to 6 servings.

To serve, you need 4 6-inch scallop shells or 6 4-inch shells. In this version the scallops, with oysters and mushrooms in a white wine sauce, are covered with thinly sliced fresh tomatoes and cheese and browned under the broiler.

1½ pounds sea scallops
½ cup dry white wine
½ cup water
Bouquet garni, including parsley,
    thyme, and 1 bay leaf
Salt
Freshly cracked white pepper
8 oysters, shelled
½ cup sliced mushrooms

3 tablespoons salt butter
3 tablespoons all-purpose flour
1 egg yolk
2 tablespoons heavy cream
2 or 3 large ripe tomatoes,
    skinned and thinly sliced
4 tablespoons freshly grated
    Parmesan cheese

COQUILLES SAINT-JACQUES AU GRATIN

Poached Sea Scallops with Oysters and Mushrooms in White Wine Sauce

Put the scallops in a pan, pour on the wine and water. Add the bouquet garni, salt, and pepper. Bring to a boil and simmer 5 to 6 minutes. Drain the scallops, slice, and keep them warm. Reserve the liquid.

Put the oysters in a small pan. Pour on the reserved liquid from the scallops and bring to a boil. Strain, and add the oysters to the sliced scallops. Reserve the liquid for the sauce. Sauté the mushrooms in 1 tablespoon butter, add to the oysters and scallops, and keep them warm. In a saucepan, melt 2 tablespoons butter. Off the heat, stir in the flour. Add the strained liquid from the oysters and bring to a boil over low heat, stirring all the time. In a little bowl mix the egg yolk with the heavy cream. Pour a little of the hot sauce onto the yolk mixture, stirring constantly, then mix the yolk mixture into the sauce in the pan. Reheat, but do not boil. Mix the sauce with the scallops, oysters, and mushrooms. Fill the scallop shells. Cover with overlapping slices of tomatoes. Sprinkle well with the grated cheese and brown quickly under a hot broiler. NET: 4 to 6 servings.

COQUILLES SAINT-JACQUES CHAPON FIN

Poached Sea Scallops with Mushrooms and Tomatoes in Velouté Sauce, with Duchess Potatoes

To serve, you need 4 6-inch scallop shells or 6 4-inch shells.

1½ pounds large sea scallops
Juice of half a lemon plus
*   1 teaspoon lemon juice*
¼ cup fish stock (page 36)
*   or water*
½ cup dry white wine
Salt
Freshly cracked white pepper
1 bay leaf
1 onion, sliced
6 white peppercorns
1 sprig parsley
¼ pound firm white mush-

*   rooms, sliced*
6 tablespoons salt butter
3 tomatoes, skinned, seeded,
*   and shredded*
3 tablespoons all-purpose flour
4 tablespoons heavy cream
⅓ cup freshly grated Parmesan
*   cheese*
¼ cup dry breadcrumbs
*   (page 69)*
Duchess potatoes for garnish
*   (page 609)*

Wash the scallops well in water and the juice of half a lemon. Put them in a pan and pour over them the wine and water or fish stock. Add the salt, peppercorns, bay leaf, onion, and parsley. Bring to a boil and simmer 4 to 5 minutes. Strain and reserve the liquid. Cut the scallops in slices. Sauté the mushrooms in 2 tablespoons butter with 1 teaspoon lemon juice. Mix the scallops with the mushrooms and the shredded tomatoes. In a saucepan, melt 3 tablespoons butter. Off the heat, stir in the flour. Add the strained scallop stock and bring to a boil over low heat, stirring constantly. Add the heavy cream. Mix this sauce into the scallop mixture, fill the shells, and sprinkle with breadcrumbs, grated cheese, and 1 tablespoon melted butter. Around each shell pipe a border of Duchess potatoes through a pastry bag fitted with a star tube. Brown under a hot broiler. NET: 4 to 6 servings.

To serve, you need 4 6-inch scallop shells or 6 4-inch shells.

1½ pounds bay scallops
4 white peppercorns
1 bay leaf
½ cup dry white wine
½ cup water
Salt
1 cup sliced firm white mush-
    rooms and 4 to 6 whole firm
    white mushrooms
4 tablespoons salt butter
1 teaspoon lemon juice

Meat of a 1½-pound lobster
2 tablespoons all-purpose flour
1 tablespoon dry mustard
A few grains cayenne pepper
⅓ cup light cream
2 tablespoons dry breadcrumbs
    (page 69)
4 tablespoons freshly grated
    Parmesan cheese
A little melted butter

COQUILLES SAINT-JACQUES DE HOMARD

Poached Bay Scallops with Lobster and Mushrooms in Mustard Sauce

Put the scallops in a pan with the bay leaf, peppercorns, wine, water, and salt, bring slowly to a boil, and simmer 3 to 4 minutes. Do not cook too long or they will instantly toughen. Strain off and reserve the liquid. If the scallops are large, cut them in two. Sauté the sliced and whole mushrooms in 2 tablespoons butter with lemon juice, salt, and pepper. Set the whole mushrooms aside for garnish. Mix the sliced mushrooms with the scallops and set aside. Cut the lobster meat into 1-inch pieces and toss in 1 tablespoon hot butter in a sauté pan a few minutes. Add the lobster to the scallops and mushrooms.

MUSTARD SAUCE. Melt 1 tablespoon butter in a saucepan. Off the heat, stir in the flour, mustard, salt, and cayenne pepper. Add to the pan the strained liquid from the scallops, then add the light cream and bring to a boil over low heat, stirring constantly.

Stir the scallop mixture into the mustard sauce and fill the scallop shells. Sprinkle with the breadcrumbs, grated cheese, and a little melted butter, and brown under a hot broiler. Garnish each shell with one whole sautéed mushroom. NET: 4 to 6 servings.

To serve, you need 4 6-inch scallop shells or 6 4-inch shells.

1 pound sea scallops
Lemon juice
1 small piece celery, sliced
1 small white onion, sliced
1 bay leaf
1 small piece carrot, sliced
¾ cup dry white wine
¼ cup dry sherry
6 peppercorns, black and white
    mixed
Salt
⅓ cup water
2 tablespoons salt butter
4 ounces firm white mushrooms

Freshly cracked white pepper

WHITE WINE SAUCE
4 tablespoons salt butter
3 tablespoons all-purpose flour
Salt
A few grains cayenne pepper
Stock from the scallops
1 tablespoon sweet butter
2 egg yolks
2 tablespoons Cognac or good
    brandy
2 tablespoons heavy cream

COQUILLES SAINT-JACQUES PARISIENNE

Poached Sea Scallops with Mushrooms in White Wine Sauce, with Duchess Potatoes

GARNISH
Duchess potatoes (page 609)
2 tablespoons dry breadcrumbs
   (page 69)
3 tablespoons freshly grated

Parmesan cheese
A little melted butter
2 tablespoons chopped fresh
   parsley

Wash the scallops in a little lemon juice and water. Drain and dry, and put them in a pan with the celery, onion, bay leaf, and carrot. Pour over the wine and sherry, and add the peppercorns, ½ teaspoon salt, and the water. Bring quickly to a boil and simmer 3 to 4 minutes. Stir the scallops to turn them over. They must cook quickly so as not to toughen. Drain at once (reserve the stock). Heat the butter in a sauté pan. Slice the mushrooms and add them to the pan with 1 teaspoon lemon juice, salt, and pepper. Cook briskly 3 minutes. Cut the scallops into thick slices and add to the mushrooms.

WHITE WINE SAUCE. Melt the butter in a saucepan. Off the heat, stir in the flour. Season with salt and cayenne pepper. Stir in the strained liquid in which the scallops were cooked, and stir over low heat until the sauce comes to a boil. Stirring constantly, add the heavy cream, then the sweet butter bit by bit. In a separate bowl, beat the egg yolks and brandy. Pour a little of the hot sauce into the yolk mixture, then stir the yolk mixture into the saucepan and reheat without boiling.

Stir the scallops and mushrooms into the sauce and fill the scallop shells. Sprinkle the tops with the breadcrumbs and grated cheese. Around each filled shell pipe a border of Duchess potatoes through a pastry bag fitted with a star tube. Dot with a little melted butter. Brown under the broiler. Sprinkle with the parsley. Serve immediately.
NET: 4 to 6 servings.

COQUILLES SAINT-JACQUES DIABLE

Deviled Scallops

Poached sea scallops and crisp croûtons are coated with onion and curry sauce. To serve them, you need 4 6-inch scallop shells or 6 4-inch shells.

1½ pounds large sea scallops
A little lemon juice
A little coarse salt
Freshly cracked white pepper
½ cup mixed sliced onion,
   carrot, and celery
1 bay leaf
6 peppercorns
½ cup dry white wine
½ cup water
1 cup small fried croûtons
   (page 70)
A few dry breadcrumbs (page
   69)
A little freshly grated Parmesan
   cheese

A few crisp sprigs of watercress

SAUCE DIABLE
8 tablespoons sweet butter
2 Bermuda onions, finely
   chopped
Salt
A few grains cayenne pepper
2 tablespoons finely chopped
   fresh parsley
4 tablespoons all-purpose flour
2 teaspoons Dijon mustard
1 teaspoon curry powder
½ teaspoon Tabasco sauce
1 teaspoon Worcestershire
   sauce

Liquid reserved from the
  scallops

½ cup light cream
4 tablespoons heavy cream

Wash the scallops in a little lemon juice and water. Drain and dry them. Spread the scallops out on a platter and season with a little coarse salt and white pepper. Leave them about 10 minutes, then place them in a small heavy pan. Scatter the mixed sliced vegetables over them. Add the bay leaf and peppercorns, but no salt. Pour over the wine and water and bring to a boil quickly, turning the scallops over once or twice. As soon as the mixture boils, strain off the liquid (reserving it), remove the scallops from the vegetables, and cut the scallops into bite-size pieces or slices, depending upon size. Set aside.

SAUCE DIABLE. Melt 6 tablespoons sweet butter in the same saucepan in which the scallops were cooked. When it is melted (but not browned), add the Bermuda onions and season with a little salt and the cayenne pepper. Stir and cook the onion over low heat until it is soft but not brown. Then, off the heat, stir in the parsley and flour. Mix in the mustard, curry powder, Tabasco sauce, Worcestershire sauce, and the strained liquid reserved from the scallops. Stir over moderate heat until the sauce begins to thicken, then mix in the light cream and bring to a boil. Reduce the heat to a bare simmer and, bit by bit, stir in 2 teaspoons butter. Stir in the heavy cream.

Mix the small fried croûtons with the sliced scallops, combine with half the sauce, and fill the scallop shells. Coat the mixture in each shell with the rest of the sauce. Sprinkle with the breadcrumbs and grated cheese. Melt the rest of the butter and sprinkle it over the cheese and breadcrumbs. Brown the shells quickly under a hot broiler. Arrange them on a hot folded napkin on a hot serving platter and garnish with the watercress. NET: 4 to 6 servings.

This dish, of whole shrimps in Creole sauce, with saffron rice, is from New Orleans.

SHRIMP CREOLE

4 tablespoons salt butter
2 tablespoons pure olive oil
1 cup each of finely chopped
  raw onion, carrot, celery,
  green beans, red pepper, and
  green pepper
Salt
A few grains cayenne pepper
2 tablespoons curry powder
1 teaspoon freshly grated
  nutmeg
½ teaspoon mace
4 tablespoons all-purpose flour
3 cups sour cream
1 tablespoon paprika

4 cups raw shrimps, shelled and
  deveined

SAFFRON RICE
⅓ cup vegetable oil
3 tablespoons salt butter
1 large yellow onion, finely
  chopped
1 cup long-grain rice
2 cups chicken stock (page 35)
1 teaspoon leaf saffron, crushed
  with a pestle and mortar
2 teaspoons salt
⅛ teaspoon cayenne pepper

SAFFRON RICE. Preheat the oven to 350°. Melt the oil and butter in a small deep heavy pan. Add the chopped onion and cook over low heat, slowly, 4 to 5 minutes, until the onion becomes translucent but not brown. Add the rice and stir well to coat it with the oil and butter. Add the chicken stock, saffron, salt, and cayenne pepper. Stir over moderate heat until it comes to a boil. Then cover the pan and put it in the oven to cook 30 minutes. Fluff the rice with a fork before serving.

CREOLE SAUCE. In a heavy pot, melt the butter with the olive oil. Then put in the raw chopped vegetables in layers, in the order listed above, starting with the onions on the bottom. Sprinkle the top with salt and the cayenne pepper. Cover with buttered wax paper and the lid. Cook over moderate heat until the vegetables are soft. Remove from the heat and mix in the curry powder, nutmeg, mace, and flour. Stir until smooth, then mix in the sour cream and paprika. Cook over low heat 10 to 15 minutes.

Add the shrimps to the sauce and cook just a very few minutes over low heat, until they turn pink. Serve the Shrimp Creole in a casserole and the rice in a separate bowl. NET: 4 to 6 servings.

CURRY D'ÉCREVISSE

Shrimp Curry

The ten-boy condiments follow this recipe.

2 tablespoons salt butter
2 tablespoons pure olive oil
2 pounds raw shrimps, in the shells
Saffron rice (above)

CURRY SAUCE
2 tablespoons pure olive oil
2 tablespoons salt butter
1 cup finely chopped onion
1/4 cup finely chopped celery
1/2 cup finely chopped carrot
1 green apple (with skin on), cored and sliced
Salt
Freshly cracked white pepper
2 tablespoons curry powder
1 teaspoon tomato paste
1 teaspoon meat glaze
1 1/2 cups fish stock (page 36) or chicken stock (page 35)
2 tablespoons honey
2 teaspoons red currant jelly
2 tablespoons shredded coconut

A few grains cayenne pepper
1/2 small cinnamon stick
2 juniper berries, crushed with mortar and pestle
2 crushed coriander seeds or 1/8 teaspoon ground coriander
1 small bay leaf
Quarter of a lemon

VEGETABLE GARNISH
1 medium-size eggplant
1/4 cup pure olive oil
2 medium-size carrots, cut into thick julienne strips (matchstick size)
2 medium-size yellow onions, cut into 1/4-inch thick rings
1 heart of celery, cut into eighths across
Salt
A few grains cayenne pepper
A little curry powder
1 teaspoon finely chopped garlic
3 tomatoes, skinned and cut into eighths

2 small green peppers (blanched   boil), seeded and cut into
   in cold water brought to a   eighths

CURRY SAUCE. Warm the olive oil and butter in a small heavy pan. Add the onion, celery, carrot, and apple, and season with salt and pepper. Cover the pan and cook over low heat, stirring occasionally. When the ingredients are nearly soft, add the curry powder, mix well, and cook over low heat 5 minutes, stirring once or twice. Off the heat, mix in the tomato paste, meat glaze, and fish or chicken stock. Stir over low heat until the mixture comes to a boil, then add the honey, jelly, coconut, and salt and cayenne pepper. Also add the cinnamon stick, juniper berries, coriander seeds, bay leaf, and the quarter-lemon cut in half. Simmer this combined mixture over very low heat 45 to 50 minutes. Then remove the cinnamon stick, pieces of lemon, and bay leaf, and purée the sauce in the electric blender or put it through a very fine strainer. Set the sauce aside.

Heat the butter and olive oil in a heavy sauté pan. When hot, add the raw shrimps (in the shells). Shake the pan briskly over moderate heat until they are pink all over. Cool them a little, then shell and devein them. Add the shrimps to the curry sauce.

VEGETABLE GARNISH. Cut the eggplant into 1-inch cubes, leaving the skin on. Scatter the cubes on a platter, sprinkle with salt, and let stand 30 minutes. Then drain, wash, and dry them well. Warm the olive oil in a deep heavy pan and add the julienne carrots, onion rings, celery sections, and eggplant cubes. Season with salt and cayenne pepper, and sprinkle with curry powder. Mix in the garlic. Stir the vegetables around, cover the pan, and cook over low heat until they are just soft. Then add the tomato and pepper sections, and mix with the other vegetables in the pan.

Serve the shrimps in the curry sauce in a casserole, with the saffron rice and the vegetable garnish in two separate bowls. Accompany with a tray containing the ten-boy condiments.

TEN-BOY CONDIMENTS FOR SHRIMP CURRY. Serve each of the ten condiments separately in a little Oriental bowl. (1) Cut 1 medium-size Bermuda onion into very thin slices, separate them into rings, and sprinkle lightly with a few grains cayenne pepper and a little olive oil. (2) Skin 2 small avocado pears with a potato peeler, cut them in half to remove the large pit, then cut into small dice. Cut ¼ pound bacon into thin shreds and sauté in a heavy frypan until crisp. Drain, dry it well, and lightly mix it with the avocado. Season with salt, a few grains cayenne pepper, and a few drops lemon juice. (3) Cut 1 large green pepper into fine dice. Add the grated rind and skinned sections of 2 large navel oranges, a little salt, and a few grains cayenne pepper. (4) Freshly shredded coconut. (5) Shredded almonds. (6) Guava jelly. (7) Dried currants. (8) A small package of Bombay Duck, cut into ½-inch pieces and sautéed in a little butter. (9) Chopped fresh parsley. (10) Chopped hard-boiled egg.

SCAMPI MILANESE

This sauté of shrimps with green peppers, chives, and onions, served with saffron rice, may be prepared in advance. Before serving, reheat the rice (covered) in a warm oven and the scampi in a double boiler. Soak the mushrooms at least 3 hours ahead of preparation.

2 green peppers
1½ pounds medium-size boiled shelled shrimps
2 tablespoons pure olive oil
4 tablespoons salt butter
1 tablespoon vegetable oil
1 tablespoon finely chopped garlic
1 tablespoon dry mushrooms, soaked about 3 hours in advance in 4 tablespoons water, drained, and finely

chopped
Salt
Freshly cracked white pepper
¼ teaspoon dry mustard
A few grains cayenne pepper
A little paprika
2 tablespoons finely chopped fresh chives
2 tablespoons finely chopped red onions
Saffron rice (page 332)

Blanch the green peppers (cover them with cold water, bring it to a boil, plunge the peppers immediately into cold water, and drain them). Cut them into quarters, remove the seeds, then chop the peppers fine and set aside. Combine the olive oil, 2 tablespoons butter, and the vegetable oil in a large sauté pan and slowly warm over low heat. Add the garlic and sauté it 2 minutes without browning, then add the mushrooms and the green peppers. Season with salt, pepper, and the mustard and cayenne pepper. Sprinkle with a little paprika. Add the rest of the butter. Next add the shrimps, and shake the pan over moderate heat 5 minutes, making sure the green pepper mixture covers the shrimps well. Mix in the chives and, last, the red onions. Keep the mixture warm. Serve with a separate bowl of saffron rice. NET: 4 to 6 servings.

POULTRY

THE CONTEMPORARY chicken-in-every-pot of America is 3½ pounds of unidentifiable breed and underdeveloped flavor, the result of accelerated production. To serious cooks, therefore, the modern chicken is as the blank canvas is to the artist. The cook's art must be devoted to giving the chicken back its identity — for those who would behold it, savor it, and eat it.

The chicken may well be the mainstay of diets all around the world, but in classic French cookery the chicken enjoys the most developed and extensive repertoire. It is the family meal of the French nation — the Poule-au-Pot (chicken in the pot) — as well as established in their prideful haute cuisine — a grand Vol-au-Vent à la Reine, for example — with hundreds of masterpieces in between.

Here is a list of some of the classic chicken and poultry dishes which were most popular with the people who attended my cooking classes and which reportedly enjoyed many successful encores in their homes. Of course Poule-au-Pot (stuffed chicken in the pot) and Coq au Vin (chicken cooked in wine); also Poulet en Demi-Deuil (chicken in half-mourning, in two versions — with white velouté sauce or brown sauce), Poulet à l'Estragon (chicken with fresh tarragon), also in two versions, Poulet Sauté Grandmère (a sauté of chicken with croûtons, ham, and potatoes), Poulet à la Hongroise (chicken paprika as adopted by the French, garnished with gnocchi Parisienne), the famous Poulet Marengo (with tomatoes, lobster, and the authentic fried eggs), Poulet Provençale (the spirit of Provence — tomatoes, eggplant, and peppers), Poulet à la Kiev (a very special, delicate Kiev), Suprêmes de Volaille Archiduc (the breasts, or fillets, of the chicken stuffed with mushrooms, ham, and cheese), Ballotine de Volaille à la Régence (French mastery — boned chicken stuffed with mousse of chicken breast), and Crêpes Niçoise (thin pancakes stuffed with chicken and sauced with chicken velouté). Also duck and game fowl: Caneton à l'Orange (with fresh orange sauce and unique orange potato garnish), Faisan Vallée d'Auge (a masterwork of Normandy — pheasant braised in cream with a salpicon of apples and celery), and Cailles aux Raisins (quail with white grapes in a sauce raffinée). And cold pièces de résistance: Suprêmes de Volaille Jeanette (breasts of chicken sandwiched with pâté and coated with chaud-froid sauce and aspic), and Galantine de Faisan à la Gelée (boned pheasant stuffed with pâté and coated with chaud-froid sauce and aspic).

Though not of French origin, my own discovery, the Poulet Mallorca (with tomatoes and oranges), and the fabulous Spanish Paella interpreted in the classic manner invariably had to be included in the course by student demand. In this volume, as a special present to my friends and readers, I have included my own favorite dish, the very simple, homely Poule Farcie au Pot, and for your next party — a new Twelve-Boy Curry.

If you never cooked with me before, perhaps you might use this as a primary list from which to explore the classic culinary mastery of poultry. My suggestion would be to start with two or three of the sautées or poached dishes before addressing the ballotine, galantine, or the quail.

"Conformist" Poultry

Because poultry is an excellent protein food for mass population feeding, poultry production in the U.S. aims primarily to produce the best possible bird for the lowest possible price. The product is a chicken that combines the most useful qualities of a variety of breeds and responds to a special feed formula that accelerates growth and development so that it weighs in at 3½ pounds (the most successful commercial size) in 8 weeks instead of 3 or 4 months. A necessity of our time, but even some poultry men shake their heads in assent with James Trager's lament: "The factor least considered, it seems, is taste" (The Foodbook, 1970).

In the prevailing urban life style, most of us never meet the poultry man, either the producer or the wholesaler; for that matter, in supermarket shopping, one rarely sees a butcher. But a little understanding of his produce, as offered in today's market, added to the lore of French culinary origins, might help. One of the largest and most respected poultry wholesalers in the New York area contributes some ideas about the raisons d'être of present poultry products.

(1) CHICKENS. Wyandotte, Leghorn, Cornish, Rhode Island Red, Plymouth Rock — no longer do these names conjure meaning even to persistent gourmets. They are all different breeds of chickens, with distinct characteristics, and home cooks as well as professionals used to have their definite preferences. But rarely now can the home cook specify a stewing hen, a roasting chicken, or a plump-breasted pullet, with any vendor comprehension or response. Today there are three main breeds used to produce "meat" chickens: White Rock, Cornish Rock, Plymouth Rock. The famous Leghorn is used mostly for egg-

laying; it is too scrawny for eating. Other breeds tend to be localized or regional, with no widespread demand.

In today's poultry market, the producer (owner of the chicken farm) leases the fertilized eggs from the wholesaler. The wholesaler also supplies the producer with his own special formula of feed. The producer ultimately is paid per pound of chicken he delivers back to the wholesaler; if he loses any chicks, he is not paid for them. Therefore, economic necessity dictates that the producer raise them, fatten them, and sell them back to the wholesaler in the shortest possible amount of time.

The *grading* standard offered by the Department of Agriculture is not a law. The commercial market has its own standards of Grade A, Grade B, and culls, arrived at through competitive practices, which are mainly followed.

The most generally available *cooking types* are classified primarily by weight (except capons) and applied to culinary intentions accordingly.

WEIGHT RANGE	TRADE CONCEPT OF "USE"
1½ to 2½ pounds	Fryers
2½ to 3½ pounds	Broilers
3½ pounds plus	Roaster
5½ pounds plus	Fowl
Capons, 5 pounds plus	Large roaster

The reason that the 3½-pound chicken is the most widely available size is that 3½ pounds is commercially the most profitable slaughtering point, as previously explained. It is often difficult, if not well-nigh impossible, to buy a chicken of 4 pounds or more. The poultry trade shies from heavier chickens (except capons) because they must be kept alive longer and fed more; consequently they cost more to raise, which requires at least 10 to 20 cents more per pound in the wholesale price.

A word about the castration method for capons, which are the only nice tender plump poultry available to us of any size above 3½ pounds. There are still some people, I find, who are reluctant to serve or eat capon because the news has not yet reached them that capons are no longer fattened with hormonal injections. In fact, they haven't been since 1959; all capons must be castrated surgically (And we are informed that the tide may also be turning away from using hormonal injections for fattening beef)

For many years my basic recipe for chicken stock included a good quantity of chicken feet; they give the very best flavor, without adding any fat. No more. Not even the stockpot could defer the interstate commerce regulation prohibiting the shipment of non-eviscerated poultry across state lines. All poultry must have head, feet, and innards removed. Henceforth, if you have to rely on the average American supermarket poultry supply, the only way you can have the fine stock made with chicken feet in your sauce and the supreme garnish of cockscomb on your plate will be to raise a few chickens of your own. Although these parts are permitted in intrastate commerce, there is not enough demand to encourage many wholesalers to stock these specialties, except possibly a noble kosher butcher here and there. Again, the law of economics.

Squabs, squab chickens, and Rock Cornish game hens have specific identifications, although there is often misunderstanding, even at the meat counter, about which is which. Technically, they are as follows. Squab: A pigeon. Most are raised domestically. Squab chicken: A young chicken, sometimes called a spring chicken; in France they are called "poussins." Rock Cornish game hen: A special breed of little chicken that is a cross between the Cornish and the White Rock. It is the spring chicken (poussin) of that particular cross-breed.

(2) DUCKS. The most prevalent commercial dressed duck, distributed nationally, is the Long Island duckling, which consistently weighs in at 4 pounds, including its thick (almost ¼ inch) layer of fat between the skin and the flesh. One duck will serve two persons respectably and no more. The market settled on this fellow because the Long Island breed (a development of the Chinese Pekin duck, which has been in America for well over a hundred years) has proven to be the one that develops most easily and rapidly in and around pools, ponds, shores, and lakes. (How reassuring that the web-footed creatures must still be raised in their natural habitat!)

The quality of duck, like beef, is determined by the fat. But while the moist and tender quotient of beef is determined by the "marbling" of fat through the flesh, the duck's lean flesh is moist and tender because of its fat "wrapping" — a natural model for the culinary technique of wrapping a sheet of fatback around a veal roast or tenderloin, or lining a pâté pan with it.

There are other duck breeds which have less fat but have no market scope because they are not known; I understand that some good ones are Michigan ducks, Boston ducks, and Maryland ducks. Finally, like genuine Champagne, which must come from the Champagne country, there is the prize of gastronomy, the Rouen duck, which you must visit France to enjoy.

Culinary Methods for Cooking Delicious Poultry

Along with, before, or after the egg (I can't decide), the chicken is my favorite food. After the egg, the chicken is the most versatile food. It can be prepared in more ways than any meat — survey the chicken dishes in this book and in other good French cookbooks. The cooking and eating of chicken should never become boring.

The challenge to today's cook is an awesome one: give the chicken a personality. Again, the artist with his bare canvas, a brush and some paint — will it be a Picasso or . . . ? To the cook, a chicken, a pot, and some ingredients — will it be a statement of chicken, real or imagined, in appearance, fragrance, flavor, and texture? With an extra measure of our "tender loving care" ingredient, it will be a masterpiece! Here are a few fundamentals which account for the goodness of poultry cooked in the French manner, and will go a long way toward putting your 3½-pound conformist chicken through a charm course and stealing the show as a memorable dish.

(1) Never overcook poultry — always undercook it a little. This is true for chickens; cooked, they should still run just a little pink and succulent when pierced in the breast or thigh. It is also true of ducks, geese, and turkeys to avoid their being dry. And it is absolutely de rigueur with game fowl; game lovers insist that their *roast* partridge, pheasant, and grouse should always show pinkish flesh, although *braised* game dishes will be well done. But well-done chicken is dry and stringy.

(2) Become familiar with the range of methods by which poultry can be cooked. These basic methods of cooking chicken lead to many, many permutations and compositions with various vegetables, fruits, nuts, and other meats, in hot and cold dishes. The gamut runs from excellent plain roast chicken basted with wine for the picnic basket to the most exquisite creations of suprêmes. The chicken and the egg — the egg and the chicken — are indeed the food that sustains men all over the world.

POACH (or boil). The poultry is gently *simmered* in stock or water. Personally, I resist the term "boiling" here; it is mainly for old hens, and there are very few of them on the market.

BRAISE. Braising is usually restricted to larger or older chickens, and sometimes game (as in partridges with cabbage). The bird is browned all over, then placed in the pot with braising liquid, covered, and slowly cooked, usually in the oven, for a long time.

ROAST. The bird is tied (trussed) and cooked on a rack in a roasting pan in the oven or skewered on a spit and rotated in a rotisserie.

SAUTÉ. The whole chicken is neatly tied or cut into sections, and browned and cooked a little in hot butter. (Up to this point, this method is the same as the American interpretation of "pan-fried".) Then, if more cooking is necessary, the French method is to finish it by adding the basic sauce or liquid to the pan with the chicken and continue cooking either in the oven or on top of the stove at moderate to low heat. (This is similar to braising, the main difference being that the cooking time for the sauté dish is not nearly as long.)

GRILL OR BROIL. Small thin pieces of chicken are cooked under direct heat. (The small broiler size of chicken should be used for this method.)

DEEP-FRY. Small, delicate preparations of poultry are coated with egg and breadcrumbs and quickly cooked in deep hot fat.

BAKE. The French use this method of slow and even cooking for delicate chicken preparations such as mousses and pâtés. The pan containing the preparation is placed in a larger pan half filled with hot water. The whole assembly is placed in the oven and cooked at moderate to low heat.

(3) Prepare some homemade chicken stock, freeze it, and always

have it on hand. It may seem that I dwell on the homemade stock requirement, but so it has always been in my classes. There really is no substitute. Nowhere in the *Larousse Gastronomique* is there a suggestion of a substitute. Homemade stock should be as staple as salt, flour, and sugar in your larder. You can easily make it and make a delicious meal at the same time, as is described in the recipe for Pot-au-Feu (page 130).

(4) Learn the correct techniques for handling poultry — to tie a chicken, carve it, and bone it. They are described step by step on pages 342–344, and the tying and carving procedures are used in the majority of recipes. Please do master them; they will make the whole activity easier and much more professional. Also note that in the correct tying method nowhere does the string cross the body of the bird. With a 24-inch length of string, you will have a neat, compact, plump, easy to handle bird with no string lines marring the breast or the thighs. Unfortunately this is not always so with the butcher method.

As with meat roasts, a large turkey or capon should be allowed to "set" at least 20 minutes after it is cooked, and it will be much easier to carve, or slice.

How to Tie a Chicken

The terms "truss" and "tie" a chicken are synonymous. All poultry being cooked whole should be tied in this manner, including chicken, duck, goose, turkey, and all game fowl.

(1) Place a whole dressed chicken on the surface in front of you. If it was tied or trussed in any way by the butcher, undo it. Release the wings and the legs, so that all are free and the chicken is lying on its back.

(2) Discard any chunks of fat still clinging to the bird. Dry it with paper towels. Insert any seasonings or stuffing in the cavity. (The neck, liver, gizzard, and heart are not used. These may be reserved for the sauce.)

(3) Take a piece of white cotton kitchen cord about 24 inches long. Begin by crisscrossing the string over and under the ends of the drumsticks (the knobs), so that they are snugly together. The ends of the drumsticks should be in position just below and pushing against the bottom tip of the breastbone. This position will keep them in place.

(4) Push the thighs gently up against the sides of the breast, so that the chicken now appears to be fat and snug. Bring the two ends of the cord from the ends of the drumsticks up the crevices between the thighs and the lower sides of the breast.

(5) When you have the cord at the point of the waist of the chicken (midway), flip the chicken back side up. Bring the string from the front of the chicken through the crook of the wing (like the crook of the arm), from each side to the center back.

(6) Pull the flap of the neck skin from front to back between the wings, so that the top of the chicken will have a neat, smooth skin surface.

(7) Then tie the cord between the two wings. Pull the cord a little to tie it snugly. Flip the tips of the wings under the main part of the wings; this forms a sort of flat platform for the chicken to rest on.

(8) Turn the chicken over so that it is now resting on its back. Be sure that the legs are secure and snugly positioned against the sides of the breast.

(9) Using your thumb, firmly push the chicken's tail into the cavity. This action will snap the tail end of the vertebrae and keep the tail in this position. Pull the adjacent flaps of skin over it.

You should now have a beautiful-looking, snugly tied chicken with which to work. There are no trussing needles to mar it, nor are there any strings tied across the surface of the breast or thighs to leave marks when the chicken has been browned and cooked.

How to Carve a Chicken in the Kitchen

When it is necessary to cut chicken, or any other poultry, into serving pieces, this is how it is done.

(1) Place the chicken on a cutting board and remove the string or trussing.

(2) Using a sharp carving knife and small fork (for leverage), cut the whole legs off the chicken at the thigh and hip joint.

(3) Next, cut each leg into two pieces at the knee joint.

(4) Using kitchen shears, cut the knobs off the ends of the drumsticks — if it is a domestic fowl. If it is a game bird, such as pheasant or wild duck, the knobs are left on. This is the traditional professional procedure, so that the diner knows if the fowl is domesticated or game.

(5) With the kitchen shears, cut all the way through the center of the breastbone, from the tip at the bottom up to the throat (through the wishbone).

(6) Also with the kitchen shears, cut one-half of the breast away from the back, starting from the lower ribs around to the back of the wing. The wing should remain attached to its side of the breast. Do this to both sides of the breast.

(7) Take one-half of the breast with wing attached. Cut the breast in half diagonally (on the bias). You now have two pieces of breast from the half (actually quarters) — one piece with wing attached and the lower piece of breast only. Cut off the tip of the wing only. Cut the other side of the breast in the same manner.

(8) Cut the back in half at the small of the back. There is no meat on the upper half, and it can be discarded. There are the precious "oysters" on the lower back, on either side of the wide bone. The oysters may be removed and served as the delicacy with the rest of the chicken, or the lower half of the back may be included as an extra serving piece.

This carving procedure results in eight good serving pieces (two breast pieces with wing attached, two lower breast pieces, two thighs, two drumsticks) plus the lower back with the two oysters or the oysters served separately.

This procedure applies to the boning of all poultry — turkey, chicken, duck, pheasant, squab, partridge, quail, etc. (In quail, the leg and wing bones are not removed — only the body carcass.)

(1) Place the raw dressed chicken on a cutting board. Remove any trussing, and dry the chicken thoroughly with paper towels.

(2) With a sharp cleaver, chop the knobs off the drumsticks. Then chop off the wings between the shoulder and the elbow. Chop off the tail.

(3) Place the chicken breast side down on the board. With a small, very sharp, pointed knife, cut a slit through the skin down the center of the back, the whole length. Proceed to bone one side of the chicken in the following manner (throughout, take great care not to puncture the skin).

(4) First loosen the oyster. Slip the knife carefully under the skin on the lower, bony part of the back. Be sure to get the meat that is there over the bone. Then edge your knife along the ribs and loosen the breast meat, being very careful not to cut through the skin at the breastbone, where it is attached with a very thin membrane.

(5) Work the knife through the thigh joint, to detach the leg from the body.

(6) Work the knife through the knee joint to separate the drumstick from the thigh.

(7) Make a cut in the flesh, through to the bone, down the length of the thigh. Cut the bone away from the meat.

(8) Pull the skin back from the drumstick. With the back of the knife (the dull edge), cut the drumstick bone away from the meat.

(9) Pull the skin away from the shoulder. With the knife tip, detach the wing joint. Then, with the knife tip, work the wing bone away from the meat.

(10) One side of the chicken should now be completely boned. It should be attached to the carcass only by the skin at the center of the breastbone. Leave it there. Repeat the boning process on the other side of the chicken, just as carefully.

(11) When both sides of the chicken have been boned, hold the carcass away from the flesh and skin. It is now attached only by the thin skin at the breastbone. With great care, cut the skin away from the breastbone, right down the center.

(12) Reserve the carcass for the stockpot (it may be kept in the freezer).

(13) Spread out the boned chicken with the skin side against the board, flesh facing up, and proceed according to the recipe.

(14) When the chicken has been stuffed according to the recipe, bring the two edges of the back together and sew it with a needle and fine poultry thread.

CHICKEN

A traditional way to poach chicken is in the stockpot (as done in the Pot-au-Feu, page 130), which replenishes the stock supply (to be stored in the freezer) and also turns up a very good meal — in its honest simplicity, the best food to warm the cockles of the heart. Many of my students, in learning to prepare a vol-au-vent, or Crêpes Niçoise, adopted the poached chicken preparation as regular family fare, as it is in France. To add to its convenience, it can be prepared a day in advance, chilled in its stock in the refrigerator, and briefly reheated when you are ready to eat. In Jewish cooking, this is that wonderful dish known as "chicken in the pot."

The chicken in any poached chicken recipe may be poached in stock from the chicken stock recipe (Fonds Blancs de Volaille, page 35). When the chicken is to be prepared along with the stock preparation, be certain to cook the chicken only 30 to 45 minutes if it is unstuffed (as described in the recipe for Pot-au-Feu) and 1 to 1½ hours if stuffed (depending on size). Then continue cooking the stock as long as required.

POACHED CHICKEN IN THE STOCKPOT

Poule-au-pot is probably the "family meal" of all France. It is one of those honestly good dishes that reaches all mankind and can take its place on the bill of fare in the finest restaurants. I have eaten a superb Alsatian version of it at lunch in the Lutèce restaurant in New York. It was the plat du jour and was perfect with a bottle of Beaujolais, of which this restaurant maintains an excellent supply.

POULE-AU-POT

Poached Chicken Stuffed with Veal and Pork Mousse, with Vegetables

1 5-pound whole dressed capon
1 pound finely ground lean veal
2 raw egg whites
1 cup light cream
8 tablespoons salt butter
1½ cups dry breadcrumbs (page 69)
1½ pounds sausage meat
1 medium-size yellow onion, finely chopped
1 teaspoon finely chopped garlic
¼ pound sliced bacon, shredded, and sautéed until crisp
2 teaspoons dried thyme
½ teaspoon freshly grated

nutmeg
¼ teaspoon mace
Water
Bouquet garni (2 or 3 sprigs parsley, 1 bay leaf, a little celery leaf, and, if available, 1 sprig tarragon tied in cheesecloth)
Salt
Freshly cracked white pepper
8 small white onions
8 small carrots, scraped
8 3-inch pieces of celery
4 leeks, cleaned well and cut into ½-inch pieces

Carefully wipe the inside of the capon with paper towels, then prepare the stuffing.

STUFFING. Make a veal mousse mixture as follows. Put the ground veal in the mixer with the raw egg whites and beat well. Slowly, drop by drop, pour in the light cream, beating all the time. When all the cream has been incorporated, add 2 teaspoons salt. Set the veal mixture aside for a moment. Melt the butter in a sauté pan and cook the breadcrumbs until they are golden brown. In a large bowl combine the breadcrumbs with the sausage meat, chopped onion, garlic, and cooked bacon. Mix these ingredients with the hands and add the thyme, nutmeg, and mace. Then mix in the veal mousse gently and thoroughly.

Stuff the capon completely with this mixture. Tie the capon (page 342). Wrap it loosely in cheesecloth (or a clean kitchen towel or strip of muslin) and tie the cloth at each end. Place the capon in a deep heavy stockpot, cover it with cold water and bring the water slowly to a boil. Skim off any scum that may form on the surface. Add the bouquet garni to the pot together with 1½ tablespoons salt and 1 teaspoon pepper. Cover the pot and simmer very, very gently until the chicken is tender, about 1½ hours. After the chicken has been in the pot 1 hour, tie the whole onions, carrots, chunks of celery, and leeks in cheesecloth and put them into the pot. Cover, and continue simmering another 30 minutes.

To serve, remove the chicken from the pot. Also remove the bouquet garni and vegetables. Unwrap and untie the chicken, and place it on a hot earthenware platter. Unwrap the vegetables and arrange them in a pile at one end of the platter. Carve the chicken into serving pieces (page 343), and serve a section of chicken, a spoonful of stuffing, and a garnish of vegetables on each plate. Moisten with a little broth. (Strain the rest of the broth and reserve it for future soups or sauces or a quick Poule Farcie au Pot, below.) NET: 4 to 8 servings.

POULE FARCIE AU POT

Stuffed Chicken in the Pot

This is my own favorite Poule Farcie au Pot, poached in already prepared stock and served with braised celery.

1 whole dressed chicken, 3 to 5 pounds	6 tablespoons fresh parsley, coarsely chopped
1 pound finely ground veal	2 eggs
1 cup good white breadcrumbs (coarse)	¼ cup dry white wine
	Salt
1 cup very finely chopped mixed celery and onion	Freshly cracked black pepper
	1 to 2 quarts chicken stock (page 35)
2 teaspoons fresh thyme or 1 teaspoon dried thyme	Braised celery (page 588)

Wipe the inside of the chicken thoroughly with paper towels.

STUFFING. In a large bowl combine the raw veal, breadcrumbs, mixed celery and onion, thyme, 4 tablespoons chopped parsley, the eggs and wine. Mix thoroughly with the hands and season with salt and freshly cracked black pepper.

Stuff the chicken with this mixture, tie it (page 342), then thoroughly wrap it in cheesecloth (or clean cloth kitchen towel or piece of muslin). Tie the cloth at each end. Place the chicken in a deep heavy pot just large enough to fit it, and cover the chicken with the chicken stock (as much as is needed). If any stuffing remains, it may be securely wrapped in foil and cooked in the pot with the chicken. Bring the stock to a boil, cover the pot, and gently simmer the chicken over low heat 1 hour, or until the chicken is tender. While it is cooking, braise the celery.

To serve, remove the chicken from the pot. Pour the stock through a wire strainer lined with a damp cloth. Unwrap and untie the chicken and carve it into serving pieces (page 343). Arrange them on a hot serving platter. Cut the stuffing into slices and arrange around the chicken. Spoon a very little of the stock over the chicken (just to moisten) and sprinkle the rest of the chopped parsley over it. Serve the braised celery in a separate dish. Return the rest of the stock to the freezer. NET: 4 servings.

This is the basic method for poaching a chicken for use in a dish requiring cooked chicken. It is also a quick, easy to prepare, wholesome, and delicious dish.

POULARDE POCHÉE AUX LÉGUMES

Poached Chicken with Vegetables

1 whole dressed chicken, 3 to 4 pounds	*1 tablespoon very finely chopped fresh parsley*
Half a lemon	*Prepared vegetables (see below)*
3 to 4 cups chicken stock (page 35)	*Kosher salt*
	Freshly cracked black pepper

For the vegetables, use any one or a combination of baby new potatoes, baby carrots (or large ones cut into olive shapes), baby turnips (or large ones cut into olive shapes), fresh young whole green beans, the white part of leeks. The vegetables should be steamed or blanched until just tender and then added to the chicken during the last 5 minutes of cooking. Braised celery (page 588), without the sauce, is also excellent with poached chicken.

Rub the chicken all over with the cut lemon (to keep the skin white). Tie the chicken (page 342). Fold a 24-inch piece of foil in half lengthwise. Place the chicken on the foil, like a hammock, and place it in a heavy pan. Pour the chicken stock over it. Cover the pan and let the chicken cook over low heat 30 to 45 minutes (depending on size), until it is just tender. Drain the chicken and strain the stock. Remove the string and cut the chicken into serving pieces (page 343). Put it in a deep casserole. Add whatever vegetables you plan to serve with the chicken. Pour the strained stock over it. Gently reheat about 5 minutes. Sprinkle with the parsley. Serve with a separate bowl of kosher salt and black pepper in a pepper mill. NET: 4 servings.

POULET
EN DEMI-DEUIL

Poached Chicken in
Half-Mourning, with
Black Truffles and
Rich Velouté Sauce

1 3½ pound (or larger) whole
  dressed chicken
Salt
3 large black truffles
Water
1 carrot, sliced
2 onions, cut in quarters
1 small stalk celery, sliced
Bouquet garni (parsley, celery
  leaf, 1 bay leaf)
12 black peppercorns
Freshly cracked white pepper
10 tablespoons salt butter

4 tablespoons all-purpose flour
A few grains cayenne pepper
1¼ cups strained stock from
  cooking the chicken
6 firm white mushrooms, finely
  sliced
2 egg yolks
½ cup heavy cream
2 tablespoons Cognac or good
  brandy
24 firm white mushrooms,
  baby size, fluted if desired
1 teaspoon lemon juice

With your fingers, loosen the skin from the flesh all over the chicken. Be careful not to break the skin. Rub the outside of the chicken with a little salt. Cut 2 truffles into thin slices and slip them between the flesh and the skin. Arrange them over the drumsticks and thighs and completely cover the breast. Tie the chicken (page 342). Fold a long piece of foil vertically so that you have a long narrow piece, and place the chicken on it like a hammock. Place the hammock with the chicken in a deep heavy pot and barely cover it with water. Slowly bring the water to a boil, then reduce the heat to a simmer and skim off any scum from the surface of the water. Add the carrot, onions, leek, and celery to the pot, also the bouquet garni wrapped in cheesecloth, 1 tablespoon salt, and the peppercorns. Half cover the pot and simmer very gently until the chicken is cooked (about 45 minutes to 1 hour for 3½ to 4 pounds). Remove the chicken in its hammock and drain it carefully. Remove the string. Place the chicken on a hot serving dish and keep it hot. Strain the stock.

VELOUTÉ SAUCE. Melt 4 tablespoons butter in a saucepan. Off the heat, stir in the flour, season with a little salt and cayenne pepper, and add 1¼ cups of the strained stock. Stir over low heat until the sauce comes to a boil. Sauté the sliced mushrooms in 2 tablespoons butter and add them to the sauce. Beat the egg yolks in a little bowl and mix in the heavy cream and brandy. Pour a little of the hot sauce into the yolk mixture, stirring all the time; then return the yolk mixture and sauce to the rest of the sauce in the pan. Reheat the sauce without boiling. Slice the remaining truffle and add it to the sauce.

Flute the baby mushrooms, if desired. Sauté them in 4 tablespoons butter with the lemon juice, salt and white pepper. Spoon the hot sauce over the chicken. Garnish the dish with the mushrooms. NET: 4 servings.

This classic dish of poached chicken coated with velouté and fresh tarragon leaves, served with rice pilaff, may be made with breasts of chicken or a whole dressed chicken. If the latter, tie it (page 342), cook it whole, and carve it into serving pieces (page 343).

Poached Chicken with Velouté Sauce and Fresh Tarragon

8 chicken breasts or 1 whole
   chicken
1 yellow onion, sliced
1 carrot, sliced
1 small stalk of celery, sliced
¼ cup dry white wine
Water
Salt
1½ cup long-grain rice
3 tablespoons melted salt butter
Freshly cracked white pepper
1 to 2 teaspoons paprika

5 tablespoons salt butter
4 tablespoons all-purpose flour
A few grains cayenne pepper
1½ cups liquid in which the
   chicken was cooked
2 tablespoons heavy cream
1 egg yolk
1 tablespoon milk
3 tablespoons fresh tarragon
   leaves
3 sprigs fresh tarragon

Remove the skin from the chicken breasts and trim the bones neatly. Put the breasts in a pan with the onion, carrot, celery, and wine. Add just enough water to cover the chicken, and ½ teaspoon salt. Bring to a boil, cover, and simmer 25 minutes.

RICE PILAFF. Cover the rice with 3 cups water, add 1 teaspoon salt, bring to a boil, lower the heat and cover the pan, and cook over low heat 30 minutes without lifting the lid. When cooked, fluff the rice with two forks. Mix into it the melted butter, a little white pepper, and paprika. Set the rice aside and keep it hot.

VELOUTÉ SAUCE. Melt 4 tablespoons butter in a saucepan. Off the heat, stir in the flour and season with salt and cayenne pepper. When blended, strain in 1½ cups of the liquid in which the chicken was cooked. Stir over low heat until the sauce comes to a boil. Bit by bit, stir in another tablespoon of butter and the heavy cream. Simmer the sauce gently 5 minutes. Mix the milk and egg yolk, stir into the sauce, then add the tarragon leaves (not the sprigs).

Arrange the rice on an au gratin or shallow serving dish. Place the chicken breasts on it. Coat them with the sauce, garnish with tarragon sprigs, and sprinkle with a little paprika. NET: 8 servings.

Fricassee of Chicken (Poached Chicken in Light Velouté Sauce)

1 3½-pound whole dressed
   chicken (or larger)
Water
1 onion stuck with 4 whole
   cloves
1 carrot, sliced
1 stalk celery, sliced
1 leek, sliced
2 bay leaves
Salt

4 peppercorns
7 tablespoons salt butter
4 tablespoons all-purpose flour
Freshly cracked white pepper
12 baby white onions
½ pound firm white mushrooms
1 teaspoon plus 1 tablespoon
   lemon juice
¼ pound green beans, cut in
   small dice

3 small carrots, cut in small dice
2 egg yolks
¼ cup heavy cream, whipped
1 tablespoon chopped fresh

parsley
8 large diagonal fried croûtons
page 69)

Tie the chicken (page 342). Put it on a foil hammock in a deep heavy pot and barely cover it with cold water. Bring slowly to a boil and skim off all the scum on the surface. Add the onion stuck with cloves, the carrot, celery, leek, bay leaves, 1 teaspoon salt, and the peppercorns. Cover the pot (leaving a small opening) and simmer gently until the chicken is tender, about 45 minutes to 1 hour. Let the chicken cool a little in the stock, then remove it on its foil hammock, untie it, and cut it into neat serving pieces (page 343). Remove the skin. Strain the stock, measure out 1¾ cups, and set it aside. Keep the cut-up chicken warm in the rest of the stock.

Melt 4 tablespoons butter in a small heavy pan. Off the heat, stir in the flour and season with salt and white pepper. Pour in the 1¾ cups stock. Stir the sauce over low heat until it comes to a boil. Bit by bit, stir in 1 tablespoon butter. Cover the saucepan with plastic wrap and keep it warm.

Put the baby onions in a little pan, cover with a little of the stock, and simmer until tender. Drain, and set aside. Put 2 tablespoons butter in a sauté pan, and when it is foaming add the mushrooms with 1 teaspoon lemon juice, salt, and pepper. Cook 3 minutes. Set aside. Put the diced beans and carrots in a small pan, cover with cold salted water, and bring to a boil. Drain immediately and put the vegetables back in the pan. Add 3 tablespoons of the stock with a little salt and pepper. Cover, and cook them until barely soft. Add these vegetables to the sauce. Beat the egg yolks until they are light and creamy. Add 1 tablespoon lemon juice, salt, and pepper. Fold the whipped cream into the egg yolks. Carefully fold the yolk mixture into the sauce. (At this point, the sauce may be very, very gently reheated, if necessary, but it must not boil.)

Arrange the chicken on an au gratin dish. Spoon over it the sauce, which should be the consistency of heavy cream. Garnish the dish with the mushrooms and onions, sprinkle with the chopped parsley, and surround with the croûtons. NET: 4 servings.

CHAPON RÔTI AUX NOUILLES

Roast Capon with
Noodle and Mushroom
Dressing

This dish is extra special if you use homemade noodles (page 661). You will need two paper cutlet frills for decoration.

1 5-pound (or more) whole
   dressed capon
6 tablespoons salt butter
3 sprigs fresh parsley
1 cup dry white wine

NOODLE DRESSING
1 pound egg noodles
6 tablespoons melted salt butter
1 pound firm white mushrooms,
   sliced
1 teaspoon lemon juice
3 stalks celery, diced

1 cup heavy cream
Salt
Freshly cracked white pepper

2 tablespoons chopped fresh
   parsley
1 cup water

Preheat the oven to 350°. Put 2 tablespoons butter and the parsley sprigs into the cavity and tie the capon (page 342). Rub the capon all over with 3 tablespoons softened butter. Place it in a shallow roasting pan with ½ cup wine. Cover the pan with aluminum foil and insert a meat thermometer to check the cooking. Roast the capon 18 minutes per pound (about 1½ hours for 5 pounds). Half an hour before the finish, remove the foil so the skin can brown. Spread another tablespoon of butter on the breast and legs and add the other ½ cup of wine to the pan. While the capon is in the oven, prepare the dressing.

NOODLE DRESSING. Heat a large pan three-quarters full of salted water. When it is boiling, add the noodles and cook until just done (al dente). Drain in a colander and rinse with a little warm water. Put them in a pan, add 3 tablespoons melted butter, and keep them warm. Sauté the mushrooms 3 minutes in 3 tablespoons melted butter with the lemon juice, salt, and pepper. Cook the celery in boiling salted water until it is tender, and drain. Add the mushrooms and celery to the noodles. With a wooden spatula gently stir in the heavy cream. Season with salt and pepper.

When the capon has finished roasting, remove it from the pan and let it stand 5 minutes. Remove the string tie. Carefully cut off the whole breasts (each side). Then, with kitchen shears, cut out the large breastbone, so that the cavity is exposed. Remove the parsley, place the capon on a hot serving dish, and fill the center cavity with the noodle dressing. Slice the breast meat neatly with a very sharp knife. Arrange the slices on the noodles, reshaping the breast of the chicken. Sprinkle with the chopped parsley. Place the paper frills on the ends of the drumsticks. Put the roasting pan with the juices on the stove. Add 1 cup water, bring to a boil, boil down a little (stirring and loosening the pan glaze), and strain into a sauceboat. NET: 6 servings.

To decorate the capon you need two paper cutlet frills. It is served with deep-fried cork-shaped potatoes.

1 whole dressed capon, 7 to 8
   pounds
Half a lemon
4 tablespoons softened salt
   butter
1 cup muscatel wine, plus a
   little more for basting
2 tablespoons melted salt butter
Croquettes de Pommes de Terre

(Deep-Fried Cork-Shaped
   Potatoes, page 614)

STUFFING
1 raw egg white
½ pound finely ground lean
   veal
1 cup light cream
Salt

CHAPON VÉRONIQUE

Roast Stuffed Capon
with White Grapes,
in Velouté Sauce

Freshly cracked white pepper
1 ounce dried mushrooms,
    soaked in 1 cup water 1 hour,
    drained, and finely chopped
1 large yellow onion, finely
    chopped
A little butter

SAUCE
½ cup Cognac or good brandy
3 cups white grapes, skinned
    and seeded
2 teaspoons potato flour or
    2 tablespoons all-purpose
    flour
½ cup muscatel wine
½ cup chicken stock (page 35)

Preheat the oven to 350°. Wipe the capon inside and out with paper towels. Rub it with the cut lemon.

STUFFING. Put the ground veal in the mixer with the egg white. Slowly beat in the light cream. Season with salt and pepper. Sauté the mushrooms and onion in a little butter in a frypan until soft but not brown, and mix into the veal mixture.

Stuff the capon with this mixture. Close the vent with small skewers. Tie the bird (page 342) and place it in a roasting pan. Brush the skin with the softened butter. Cover the capon with aluminum foil. Insert a thermometer to check the cooking. Pour 1 cup of muscatel wine in the bottom of the pan. Roast the capon about 2 hours, or until it is tender. Baste every 15 minutes with 1 tablespoon muscatel wine and 1 tablespoon water. When the capon has been in the oven 1½ hours, remove the foil so that the skin can brown. Brush it with melted butter. When the capon is cooked, remove the skewers and string and place it on a hot serving dish. Leave it in the oven with the heat off.

SAUCE. Put the roasting pan over moderate heat on the stove. When it is very hot, deglaze the bottom of the pan with the brandy. Add the grapes and warm over low heat 3 minutes. Off the heat, stir in the flour. Add the wine and chicken stock. Return the pan to low heat and stir until the sauce just comes to a boil. If necessary, season with salt and pepper. Simmer gently only 2 to 3 minutes.

To serve, place paper cutlet frills on the capon legs. Remove the grapes from the sauce with a slotted spoon and put a few of them on the capon. Spoon a little of the sauce over it and serve the rest in a sauceboat. Garnish the capon with the prepared cork-shaped potatoes (Croquettes de Pommes de Terre), placed in little piles of 3 (2 on the bottom and 1 on the top), alternating with small mounds of the rest of the grapes. Serve immediately. NET: 8 to 10 servings.

POULET RÔTI AU JUS

Roast Chicken with Pan Juices

This roast chicken is also good as cold roast chicken in a picnic basket. It is given here as an entrée au jus to be served with any vegetable in season.

1 whole dressed chicken, 3½ to
    4 pounds
Half a lemon

Salt
Freshly cracked white pepper
2 tablespoons salt butter

1 bay leaf
1 piece celery leaf or fresh
   tarragon
2 tablespoons melted salt butter
About 1 cup dry white wine
Water
1 bunch crisp fresh watercress

SAUCE AU JUS
The pan juices
½ cup chicken stock (page 35)
2 tablespoons Cognac or good
   brandy
½ teaspoon tomato paste
½ teaspoon meat glaze
1 teaspoon potato flour

Preheat the oven to 375°. Wipe the chicken inside and out with paper towels. Stuff with butter, bay leaf, and celery leaf or tarragon. Tie it (page 342), rub it all over with the half-lemon, then rub with salt and pepper. Insert a thermometer to check the cooking. Place the chicken in a roasting pan (not on a rack). Brush it all over with the melted butter. Put about 2 tablespoons wine and an equal amount of water in the pan. Put the chicken in the oven and roast 30 minutes. Then reduce the heat to 325° and continue roasting another hour. Every 20 minutes during cooking add another 2 tablespoons wine and 2 tablespoons water to the pan, then baste the chicken. Turn it breast down after it has been in the oven 40 minutes. After 20 minutes more, turn it back to breast up.

When the chicken has finished roasting, remove it from the pan and let it stand a few minutes. Put the pan with the roasting juices on the stove. Stir in ¼ cup chicken stock and the brandy over low heat. Check the seasoning. Off the heat, add the tomato paste, meat glaze, and potato flour. Add another ¼ cup chicken stock. Bring the sauce to a boil and strain it. Carve the chicken (page 343). Arrange it on a hot serving platter. Pour a little of the sauce over it and serve the rest in a sauceboat. Garnish the platter with crisp fresh watercress. NET: 4 servings.

1 whole dressed chicken, 3½
   to 4 pounds
1 tablespoon softened salt
   butter
⅔ cup dry white wine
⅔ cup water
1 sprig celery leaf or fresh
   tarragon
Water
Matchstick potatoes (page 617)
1 bunch crisp fresh watercress

STUFFING
1 tablespoon salt butter

½ large yellow onion, finely
   chopped
¼ pound firm fresh mushrooms,
   finely chopped
½ pound raw sausage meat
½ teaspoon finely chopped
   garlic
5 chicken livers, sautéed in hot
   butter and chopped
1 tablespoon chopped fresh
   parsley
¼ teaspoon dried thyme
Salt
Freshly cracked white pepper

POULET RÔTI FARCI

Roast Stuffed Chicken
with Forcemeat of
Sausage, Chicken
Livers, Mushrooms

Preheat the oven to 350°. Make the stuffing: Melt the butter in a small frypan and cook the onion and mushrooms over low heat 5 minutes. Put the sausage meat in a mixer bowl, add the cooked onion and mushrooms and all the other stuffing ingredients. Mix well. Stuff the chicken with this mixture and close the opening with small skewers. Tie the chicken (page 342) and rub the skin with the softened butter. Put it in a roasting pan with ⅓ cup wine mixed with ⅓ cup water, and the celery leaf or tarragon. Roast 1 to 1¼ hours, or until the chicken is tender. Baste every 15 to 20 minutes with the remaining ⅓ cup wine mixed with an equal amount of water.

When the chicken is cooked, remove the string and skewers and place it on a hot serving dish. Garnish with the matchstick potatoes and watercress. Put the roasting pan with the pan juices on the stove over low heat. Add ½ cup water to the pan and bring to a boil, stirring quickly to pick up the glaze. Strain, and serve this sauce in a separate bowl. NET: 4 to 6 servings.

POULET RÔTI, AU MIREPOIX

Roast Chicken with Vegetables and White Grapes

1 3½-pound whole dressed chicken
5 tablespoons salt butter
1 bay leaf
1 garlic clove, bruised
Salt
Freshly cracked white pepper
¼ cup dry white wine, plus more as needed for basting
¼ cup water, plus more as needed for basting
2 carrots, diced
1 turnip, diced

1 stalk celery, diced
1 leek, diced
½ cup diced green beans
½ cup shelled green peas, fresh or frozen
Water or chicken stock (page 35) for the sauce
4 tablespoons heavy cream
1 tablespoon chopped fresh parsley
¾ cup fresh white grapes, skinned and seeded

Preheat the oven to 350°. Wipe the chicken inside and out with paper towels. In the cavity insert 2 tablespoons butter, the bay leaf and garlic clove. Tie the chicken (page 342), sprinkle with a little salt and pepper, and brush the breast with 2 tablespoons softened butter. Place the chicken in a roasting pan and pour the wine and water in the bottom of the pan. Cover the pan with foil, and roast the chicken 50 to 60 minutes. When it has been in the oven 30 minutes, turn it over, then turn it breast up again after 15 minutes. Baste frequently, adding a little more wine and water to the pan as needed. About 15 minutes before the roasting is finished, remove the foil to brown the chicken. When it is done, carve it into serving pieces (page 343) and keep it warm. Reserve the pan juices. Leave the oven on.

Put the diced vegetables and the peas all together in a pan. Barely cover them with cold water. Slowly bring to a boil, then drain. In a small heavy pan, dissolve 1 tablespoon butter. Add the blanched vegetables and season with salt and pepper. Press a piece of buttered wax paper down on the vegetables and cover the pan with the lid. Place the pan in the oven and cook until the vegetables are tender, about 30 minutes. (This can be done while the chicken is cooking, if there is room in the oven.)

WHITE GRAPE SAUCE. Strain into a little saucepan the juices from the pan in which the chicken was cooked. Add enough water or chicken stock to make 1 cup liquid in the saucepan. Season with salt and pepper. Reduce the liquid (by boiling) to half the quantity. Remove from the heat and stir in the heavy cream. Return to moderate heat, bring to a boil, and again reduce a little by boiling. Add the chopped parsley and grapes.

To serve, spread the cooked diced vegetables to form a bed on a serving platter. Arrange the chicken on the mirepoix (diced mixed vegetables). Spoon the sauce over the chicken. NET: 4 servings.

ARMENIAN RICE WITH CHICKEN LIVERS

A good buffet casserole.

12 chicken livers
8 tablespoons salt butter
2 tablespoons chopped onion
2 teaspoons finely chopped garlic
¼ cup sliced firm white mushrooms
1 green pepper, cut in thin shreds
2 cups long-grain rice
2 tablespoons tomato paste
2 teaspoons meat glaze
4 cups chicken stock (page 35)
Salt
Freshly cracked white pepper
A little chili pepper
½ teaspoon dry mustard
2 tablespoons pineapple or

peach preserve
1 medium-size eggplant, cut in ½-inch slices and sprinkled with salt
4 tablespoons vegetable oil
½ cup blanched almonds
2 apples, skinned, cored, and cut in ½-inch slices
2 Bermuda onions, cut in ½-inch slices
3 ripe tomatoes, skinned and cut in ½-inch slices
1 green pepper, finely sliced
1 pimento, sliced (canned is all right)
½ pound sliced bacon, grilled crisp

In a deep heavy pan, heat 4 tablespoons butter. When it is golden brown, brown the chicken livers in it on both sides, then remove them and add the chopped onion and garlic to the pan. Cook over moderate heat 1 minute. Add the mushrooms and green pepper and cook 2 minutes. Add the rice to the same pan. Cook it slowly 2 to 3 minutes, stirring to mix it with the vegetables. Stir in the tomato paste and meat glaze. Pour in the chicken stock. Cover the pan tightly and cook over low heat 25 minutes, until the rice is tender. Add salt, pepper, the chili pepper, mustard, and preserves, and cook another 4 to 5 minutes. Continue cooking over low heat until all the liquid is absorbed, then remove from the heat.

Drain the eggplant and dry the slices on paper towels. Heat the vegetable oil in a frypan. When it is very hot, put in the eggplant slices and fry until golden brown on both sides. Add them to the rice. Brown the almonds in the hot oil and put them in the rice. Heat 4 tablespoons butter in a frypan, brown the apple and onion slices, and add them to the rice. Cook the green pepper in the frypan 2 or 3 minutes and add it and the (uncooked) sliced tomatoes to the rice.

Cut the chicken livers in thick slices and add them and the pimento to the rice. Cover, and warm over very low heat 10 minutes. To serve, put the mixture in a hot casserole and garnish with the strips of crisp bacon. NET: 6 servings.

CHICKEN À LA KING

An American Classic

1 whole dressed chicken, 3½ to
   4 pounds
1 cup mixed sliced onion, carrot,
   and celery
1 bay leaf
6 black peppercorns
Salt
2 tablespoons salt butter
4 firm white mushrooms, thinly

sliced
Half a red pepper, finely diced
Half a green pepper, finely diced
½ teaspoon meat glaze
3 tablespoons all-purpose flour
¼ cup freshly grated Parmesan
   cheese
A little melted butter
Rice pilaff (page 675)

Wipe the chicken inside and out with paper towels and tie it (page 342). Place it in a pan and just cover it with cold water. Bring slowly to a boil and skim off all the scum. Add the mixed onion, carrot, and celery, the bay leaf, peppercorns, and about 2 teaspoons salt. Simmer very slowly 40 minutes. Remove the chicken and strain the liquid. Take the skin off the chicken, remove all the meat from the bones, and cut the meat into bite-size pieces.

Melt the butter in a deep heavy pan. Add the mushrooms and sauté 2 to 3 minutes. Add the diced red and green peppers and cook about 3 minutes. Off the heat, stir in the meat glaze and flour. Add 1½ cups of the strained liquid in which the chicken was cooked. Return to low heat and stir until the sauce comes to a boil. Add the chicken meat and warm a little over low heat, then spoon into an uncovered casserole or au gratin, sprinkle with grated cheese and a little melted butter. Brown it under the broiler, and serve with a separate bowl of rice pilaff. NET: 4 servings.

COQ AU VIN

Chicken in Wine

In France, Coq au Vin is often made in a special pot which allows the various wines to drip slowly onto the chicken while it is cooking. The pot has a little container in the cover with a small hole in it. This type of casserole is available in most American stores that sell gourmet cooking equipment.

1 3½ pound whole dressed
   chicken
14 tablespoons salt butter

⅓ cup Cognac or good brandy
2 teaspoons meat glaze
1 teaspoon tomato paste

4 teaspoons potato flour
1½ cups chicken stock
   (page 35)
½ cup dry red wine
¼ cup Madeira wine
¼ cup dry sherry wine
½ cup dry white wine
½ teaspoon red currant jelly
Freshly cracked white pepper
24 baby white onions, skinned

6 ounces boiled ham, cut in
   ¾-inch cubes (salt pork can
   be substituted)
A little granulated sugar
6 ounces firm white mushrooms,
   cut in half
1 teaspoon lemon juice
Salt
8 diagonal fried croûtons (page
   69)

Preheat the oven to 375°. Dry the chicken inside and out with paper towels, and tie it (page 342). Heat 5 tablespoons butter in a deep heavy casserole. Put in the chicken, breast down, and slowly brown it all over. Heat the brandy in a little pan, ignite, and pour it over the chicken. Remove the chicken from the pan, and stir into the same pan, off the heat, the meat glaze, tomato paste, and potato flour. When it is smooth, mix in the chicken stock, four wines, jelly, and a little pepper, but no salt. Stir over low heat until the sauce comes to a rolling boil. Remove it from the heat. Carve the chicken into serving pieces (page 343). Put them in the sauce, and set the casserole on the top shelf of the oven, without the cover. Cook 45 minutes.

While the chicken is cooking, prepare the garnishes. Put the baby onions in a pan, cover with cold water, and bring the water to a boil. Drain immediately. Heat 5 tablespoons butter in a sauté pan. When the butter is foaming, put in the onions and shake them over brisk heat until they begin to brown. Sprinkle them with a little salt and granulated sugar. Continue shaking over the heat until they are beautifully glazed. Remove them from the pan, wipe it a little with paper towels, and put in 2 tablespoons butter. When the butter is foaming, add the ham. Shake the ham over brisk heat, and when it begins to brown a little, sprinkle with granulated sugar, shake it a bit more, and remove it from the pan. Put 2 tablespoons butter in the pan and add the mushrooms, lemon juice, a little salt, and pepper. Cook over moderate heat 3 minutes.

About 5 minutes before the chicken is finished cooking, scatter the onions, ham, and mushrooms over the pieces of chicken in the casserole in the oven. When done, stick the croûtons all around the sides of the casserole, with points up, and serve. NET: 4 servings.

This is a twelve-boy curry; condiments are described after the recipe.

2 whole dressed chickens, 2 to 3
   pounds each
8 tablespoons salt butter
¼ cup dry white wine

CURRY SAUCE
4 tablespoons salt butter
½ cup pure olive oil
1 small white onion, sliced
1 small carrot, sliced

CURRY DE POULET

Chicken Curry

2 stalks celery, sliced

2 green apples, cored and sliced, but not skinned

3 tablespoons strong curry powder

4 tablespoons all-purpose flour

2 teaspoons tomato paste

1 teaspoon meat glaze

2 cups chicken stock (page 35)

1 small piece cinnamon stick

2 black peppercorns

1 large piece gingerroot

1 tablespoon shredded coconut

6 cardamom seeds, crushed with a mortar and pestle

1 tablespoon guava jelly (or red currant)

1 bay leaf

½ teaspoon freshly grated nutmeg

SAFFRON RICE

2 tablespoons salt butter

¼ cup pure olive oil

¾ cup finely chopped onion

1 cup long-grain rice

2 cups chicken stock (page 35)

1 teaspoon leaf saffron, crushed with a mortar and pestle

2 teaspoons salt

A few grains cayenne pepper

Wipe the chickens inside and out with paper towels, and tie them (page 342). Heat the butter in a deep heavy pan. When it is foaming, put in a chicken, breast down, and slowly brown it all over. Remove it, and brown the other chicken the same way. Carve them (page 343), return the pieces to the pan, skin side down, and pour the wine over them. Cover, and cook over low heat until the chicken is tender (about 30 minutes). Turn the pieces once or twice during cooking.

CURRY SAUCE. Heat the butter and olive oil in a heavy pan. Add the onion, carrot, celery, and apples. Stir well, and cook until nearly soft. Off the heat, mix in the curry powder and flour. Stir over low heat 2 to 3 minutes. Mix in the tomato paste and meat glaze and stir in the chicken stock. Stir over low heat until the sauce comes to a boil, then add the rest of the ingredients. Simmer it 45 minutes, stirring occasionally. Remove the gingerroot, cinnamon stick, and bay leaf. Blend the sauce in an electric blender until it is very smooth.

SAFFRON RICE. Preheat the oven to 350°. Heat the butter and olive oil in a small heavy pan. Add the onion and cook until it is translucent but not brown. Add the rice, chicken stock, and crushed saffron. Add the salt and cayenne pepper, and stir over moderate heat until the stock comes to a boil. Cover the pan and cook in the oven 30 minutes. Remove, and fluff with two forks.

Add the pieces of cooked chicken to the curry sauce and simmer together 4 to 5 minutes. Serve in a casserole, with the rice in a separate bowl. Surround with any or all of the following condiments. NET: 4 to 6 servings.

TWELVE-BOY CONDIMENTS FOR CHICKEN CURRY. Each condiment should be in a little Oriental bowl, and the bowls set around the curry casserole for serving. (1) Shred ½ pound bacon very fine, and sauté it in a heavy frypan until crisp. Drain, and dry it well on paper towels. Skin a large avocado, remove the pit, cut the avocado into small dice, and add a little salt and freshly cracked white pepper and the juice of half a lime. Gently mix in the bacon. (2) Remove the seeds from

2 green peppers and 1 red pepper, and cut the peppers into small dice. Mix them with 1 tablespoon lemon juice, 2 tablespoons olive oil, the grated rind of 2 navel oranges, salt, and a few grains cayenne pepper. Mix in gently the skinned sections of the oranges. (3) Cut 2 Bermuda onions into very thin slices, and separate into rings. Sprinkle them with a little olive oil and freshly cracked black pepper. (4) Freshly shredded coconut. (5) Guava jelly. (6) Mixed chopped candied fruits. (7) Sticky raisins. (8) Shredded toasted almonds. (9) A small package of Bombay Duck, cut into ½-inch pieces and sautéed in a little butter. (10) A fried pappadam for each person. (In Indian cookery, a pappadam is a parchment-thin disk of peppery lentil flour. They are fried in very hot oil.) (11) Finely chopped parsley. (12) Chopped hard-boiled egg.

What is the difference between squabs and squab chickens? Squabs are of the same family as pigeons. Squab chickens are little spring chickens. The bone structure is different, as is the species. Either variety can be used in this recipe.

PETIT POUSSIN FARCI

Boned Stuffed Squab Chicken with Forcemeat of Squab Livers, Mushrooms, Apples, Ham

2 plump squab chickens or squabs (or 4 if they are small)
8 chicken livers
2 squab or squab chicken livers
6 tablespoons salt butter
4 large firm white mushrooms, sliced
1 apple, peeled, cored, and sliced
4 ounces cooked ham or

tongue, shredded
Salt
Freshly cracked white pepper
3 tablespoons Cognac or good brandy
½ teaspoon tomato paste
1 teaspoon meat glaze
2 teaspoons potato flour
¾ cup chicken stock (page 35)
½ cup dry white wine
1 sprig fresh tarragon

Bone the squab chicken (page 344), removing the backs and breastbones only (leave the leg bones and wing bones). Spread the squab chickens out on a board.

STUFFING. Sauté all the livers quickly in 2 tablespoons hot butter. Remove them, and add another tablespoon of butter to the pan. Add the mushrooms and apple, and sauté them until lightly browned. Slice the livers and put them in the pan with the mushrooms. Mix in the shredded ham or tongue and season with salt and pepper.

Spread this stuffing over the boned squab chickens. Fold them over and sew the back seams with fine thread. Tie the stuffed squab chickens (page 342). Heat 3 tablespoons butter in a deep heavy pan. When the butter is foaming, brown the squab chickens in it, turning them on all sides. Heat the brandy in a small pan, ignite, and pour it over the squab chickens. Remove them from the pan and set them aside.

SAUCE. Off the heat, blend the tomato paste, meat glaze, and potato flour into the butter already in the pan. Pour in the stock and wine, and stir over low heat until the sauce comes to a boil. Return the squab chickens to the pan and add the tarragon. Cover the pan with wax paper and the lid. Simmer over low heat 30 minutes.

To serve, untie the squab chickens and place them on a hot serving dish. Spoon a little of the sauce over them. Serve the rest of the sauce in a sauce bowl. NET: 4 servings.

PETITS POUSSINS À LA HAMBOURG

Squab Chickens
à la Hamburg

The squab chickens are boned, stuffed with a forcemeat of chicken livers, tongue and pistachios, and served with Hamburg spinach.

4 squab chickens or squabs
⅔ cup Cognac or good brandy
Salt
Freshly cracked white pepper
4 tablespoons salt butter
4 tablespoons melted salt butter

STUFFING
6 tablespoons salt butter
6 chicken livers
2 tablespoons Cognac or good brandy
2 green apples, skinned, cored, and sliced
4 large firm white mushrooms, sliced

4 ounces cooked tongue, cut in fine shreds
¼ cup shelled, blanched pistachio nuts

HAMBURG SPINACH
3 pounds fresh spinach
3 tablespoons salt butter
Salt
1 cup ¼-inch fried croûtons (page 70)
½ cup sour cream
½ cup freshly grated Parmesan cheese
A little melted butter

Bone out the breast and back of each squab chicken (page 344). Leave the leg and wing bones attached to the flesh. Be extremely careful not to pierce the skin. Spread the boned squab chickens out on the cutting board, flesh side up. Brush them with ⅓ cup brandy. Season with salt and pepper. Fold them over and allow the flesh to marinate a little while you prepare the stuffing.

STUFFING. Heat 2 tablespoons butter in a small heavy pan. When the butter is very hot, quickly brown the chicken livers on each side. Heat the brandy in a separate little pan, ignite, and pour it over the livers. Remove them from the pan and put in another 4 tablespoons butter, then the apples and mushrooms, and cook briskly about 3 minutes. Slice the livers and put them back in the pan. Also mix in the tongue and pistachio nuts.

Preheat the oven to 350°. Spread out the squab chickens and divide the filling evenly among them. Fold each one over and sew up the back seam with fine thread. Tie them with string (page 342). Heat the butter in a deep heavy pan. When it is on the point of browning, put in the birds, breast side down, and brown them all over very, very slowly. Be careful again not to pierce the skin. When they are beautifully browned, turn them breast side up and brush them with half the melted butter. Heat ⅓ cup brandy in a little pan, ignite, and pour it over the squab chickens. Put them in the oven in this pan, uncovered, to cook 35 minutes. Baste them frequently, first putting 1 to 2 tablespoons of water in the pan. During the cooking, brush the breasts once with the rest of the melted butter.

HAMBURG SPINACH. Remove the stalks from the spinach. Wash the leaves in several changes of water and drain very well. Put the spinach in a pan with the butter and a little salt. Cover the pan and wilt the spinach very quickly over low heat (about 5 minutes). Drain it thoroughly through a colander, and press it down with a small plate to drain it even more. Chop it roughly on a cutting board and put it in a bowl. Mix in the fried croûtons. Form the mixture into 8 or so large egg shapes, using two tablespoons. Arrange them on a baking sheet and spoon a little sour cream over them. Sprinkle with grated cheese and a little melted butter, and put under the broiler for a few minutes. Remove and keep them warm.

To serve, remove the squab chickens from the cooking casserole and remove the string ties and thread. Arrange the birds on a hot serving dish. Arrange the spinach at each end of the dish. Serve at once. NET: 4 servings.

The Cornish hens are stuffed with wild rice, pine nuts, raisins and mushrooms, and garnished with buttered zucchini.

PETIT POUSSIN FARCI PARISIENNE

Stuffed Cornish Hen Parisienne

2 large or 4 small dressed
   Cornish hens
2/3 cup Cognac or good brandy
6 tablespoons salt butter
2 teaspoons potato flour
1 teaspoon meat glaze
1/2 teaspoon tomato paste
1 cup chicken stock (page 35)
1/4 cup dry white wine
1 sprig fresh tarragon
1 black truffle, chopped
1 1/2 pounds zucchini
Salt
Freshly cracked white pepper
1 bunch crisp fresh watercress

STUFFING
1 cup wild rice, washed and

   rinsed well
2 tablespoons vegetable oil
2 teaspoons lemon juice
Salt
Freshly cracked white pepper
8 tablespoons melted salt butter
2 medium-size onions, finely
   chopped
1/2 cup white raisins, soaked in
   1/2 cup dry sherry
1 tablespoon pine nuts (pignoli
   or piñon nuts)
2 firm white mushrooms,
   finely chopped
The livers of the Cornish hens,
   sautéed in hot butter and
   chopped

STUFFING. Put the wild rice in a pan and cover it with plenty of water. Add the vegetable oil, lemon juice, salt, and pepper. Bring to a boil and continue boiling over moderate low heat until the rice is soft. Drain the rice well, put it in a bowl, and mix in the melted butter, onions, raisins, mushrooms, and pine nuts. Season well with salt and pepper and add the chopped livers.

Bone the Cornish hens (page 344), leaving in the leg and wing bones. Spread the hens out on a board, skin side down. Brush the flesh with brandy. Spread each with the stuffing. (Do not try to put in too much or they will burst.) Sew the birds down the back seam. Tie them as you would unboned poultry (page 342). Heat 3 tablespoons butter in a deep heavy pan. Brown the stuffed hens in the hot butter. In a separate little pan, heat ¼ cup brandy, ignite, and pour it over the hens. Remove them from the pan and stir in, off the heat, the potato flour, meat glaze, and tomato paste. Pour in the chicken stock and wine. Stir the sauce over low heat until it comes to a boil. Return the hens to the pan with the tarragon. Cover the pan with wax paper and the lid. Simmer very gently 25 minutes over low heat. When the hens are tender, remove them from the pan, remove the string, and place them on a hot serving dish. Strain the sauce into a saucepan. Put it over low heat. Stir in 1 tablespoon butter bit by bit, the chopped truffle, and the remaining brandy. Simmer the sauce 10 minutes.

ZUCCHINI. Slice the zucchini and put it in a small heavy pan. Cover with water, bring to a boil, and drain immediately. Put the zucchini back in the pan with 2 tablespoons butter, salt, and white pepper. Cover with wax paper and the lid. Cook very gently about 5 minutes, until the zucchini is tender but still crisp.

To serve, pour the sauce over the stuffed Cornish hens. Garnish the serving dish with the zucchini and watercress. NET: 4 servings.

POULET SAUTÉ AMANDINE

Sautéed Chicken with Almonds

1 3½-pound whole dressed chicken
4 tablespoons salt butter
2 tablespoons Marsala wine
4 or 5 large ripe tomatoes, skinned and quartered
1 teaspoon tomato paste
3 tablespoons all-purpose flour
Salt
Freshly cracked white pepper
1½ cups chicken stock (page 35)
¾ cup sour cream
¾ cup slivered blanched almonds
¼ cup crushed (in a blender) blanched almonds
1 bay leaf
Butter for glazing

Preheat the oven to 350°. Tie the chicken (page 342). Heat the butter in a deep heavy pan until it is golden brown. Put in the chicken, breast side down, and slowly brown the chicken all over. In a separate little pan, heat the Marsala wine, ignite, and pour it over the chicken. Remove the chicken from the pan, and put the tomatoes in the same pan. Cook over moderate heat until they are pulpy. Off the heat, stir in the tomato paste, flour, salt, and pepper. Mix in the chicken stock. Return the pan to moderate heat and stir until the sauce comes to a boil. Reduce the heat to low and stir in the sour cream, a little at a time. Add ¼ cup slivered almonds and all the crushed almonds.

Return the chicken to the pan, breast side down. Add the bay leaf and a little more salt and pepper. Put the pan, uncovered, on the top shelf of the oven and cook 45 to 50 minutes. Occasionally baste the chicken with the sauce in the pan, and turn it once or twice during cooking. When done, remove the chicken from the pan. Carve it into serving pieces (page 343) and arrange them on a flat au gratin dish. Spoon the sauce over them and sprinkle with the remaining ½ cup slivered almonds. Dot with a little butter and put under a hot broiler until the almonds are golden brown. Serve at once. NET: 4 servings.

POULET EN CASSEROLE BONNE FEMME

Casserole of Chicken with Onions, Mushrooms, and Salt Pork

1 3½-pound whole dressed
   chicken
5 tablespoons salt butter
2 garlic cloves
1 bay leaf
Salt
Freshly cracked white pepper
4 tablespoons Cognac, good
   brandy, or dry sherry
Liver, heart, and skinned gizzard
   of the chicken
2 ounces lean salt pork, cut
   into ½-inch cubes

18 baby white onions, skinned
18 small firm white mushroom
   caps
1 teaspoon tomato paste
1 teaspoon meat glaze
2 teaspoons potato flour
1½ cups chicken stock (page
   35)
½ cup dry white wine
2 black truffles, cut in ¼-inch
   dice
2 teaspoons chopped fresh
   parsley

Put 1 tablespoon butter, half a garlic clove, and a piece of bay leaf in the cavity, add a little salt and pepper, and tie the chicken (page 342). Heat 4 tablespoons butter in a deep heavy pan. When it is foaming, put in the chicken, breast down, and brown it all over. Heat the brandy or sherry in a little pan, ignite, and pour it over the chicken. Remove the chicken, and with kitchen shears cut it in half, cut away the back, and cut the chicken in quarters. Brown the liver, heart, and gizzard in the pan the chicken was browned in, and set these aside with the chicken.

Add the salt pork to the pan and sauté it over brisk heat 3 minutes. Reduce the heat, add the onions, and slowly brown them with the salt pork. Add the mushrooms and cook 2 minutes. Off the heat, stir in the tomato paste, meat glaze, and potato flour. Add the chicken stock and wine. Stir the mixture over low heat until it comes to a boil. Then, off the heat, return the chicken to the pan, skin side down. Cover it with wax paper and the lid, and cook very gently over low heat 25 to 30 minutes, or until the chicken is tender. Remove the chicken's back from the pan. If the sauce is too thin, thicken it with a little more potato flour blended with a little water. Cut the liver, heart, and gizzard in large dice and add to the pan with the diced truffles. Serve in a casserole, sprinkled with chopped fresh parsley. NET: 4 servings.

POULET
AU CHAMPAGNE

Chicken in Champagne

1 whole dressed chicken, 3½
    to 4 pounds
Salt
Freshly cracked white pepper
6 tablespoons salt butter
½ cup Cognac or good brandy
2 splits or 1 quart brut
    Champagne

½ cup finely chopped shallots
2 teaspoons sweet butter mixed
    with 2 teaspoons all-purpose
    flour
1 cup heavy cream, whipped
2 black truffles, thinly sliced
6 puff pastry crescents (page
    724)

Preheat the oven to 325°. Dry the chicken inside and out with paper towels. In the cavity put a little salt and white pepper. Tie the chicken (page 342). Heat the butter in a deep heavy pan. When it is foaming, put in the chicken, breast down, and brown it all over. Heat the brandy in a little pan, ignite, and pour it over the chicken. Pour the Champagne over the chicken and slowly bring to a boil, then remove the chicken from the pan and reduce the heat to a simmer. Carve the chicken into serving pieces (page 343), and set it aside. Add the chopped shallots to the pan and simmer the liquid down to about 1¾ cups. Over low heat, stir in the mixed butter and flour. Then stir in the whipped cream, spoonful by spoonful. Add the truffles. Put the pieces of chicken in the pan and baste them with the sauce. Cover the chicken with wax paper and the lid. Cook it in the oven 30 minutes.

When the chicken is cooked, remove it from the pan and arrange it in a casserole. Boil the Champagne sauce down to a nice creamy consistency and coat the chicken. Garnish around the edge of the casserole with the baked puff pastry crescents. NET: 4 servings.

POULET SAUTÉ
CHASSEUR

Chicken with
Mushrooms and
Fresh Tomatoes

In this recipe the mushrooms should be soaked three hours in advance of preparation.

2 small whole dressed chickens,
    about 2½ pounds each, with
    the livers
A little lemon juice
7 tablespoons salt butter
1 garlic clove, cut in half
Salt
Freshly cracked white pepper
¼ cup Cognac or good brandy
½ teaspoon finely chopped
    garlic
¼ pound bacon, cut into small
    dice
2 ounces dried mushrooms,

soaked at least 3 hours in ¾
    cup water, drained, and
    coarsely chopped
2 ounces firm white fresh
    mushrooms, cut in quarters
4 ounces canned Polish
    mushrooms, cut in large
    pieces, and the juice
6 large, ripe tomatoes, skinned
    and cut in eighths
¼ cup dry sherry
1 tablespoon chopped fresh
    chives

Wash the chickens in lemon juice and water and dry them well with paper towels. In each cavity, put 1 tablespoon butter, half a garlic clove, salt, and pepper. Also rub a little salt on the outside of the chickens. Tie the chickens (page 342). Melt 4 tablespoons butter in a deep heavy pan. Brown the chickens in it very slowly, taking care not to break the skin. Heat 2 tablespoons brandy in a small pan, ignite, and pour over the chickens. Remove the chickens from the pan, set them aside, and add 2 tablespoons butter to the pan. Add the chopped garlic and cook over low heat 2 minutes, then the diced bacon and cook 2 minutes. Add the three kinds of mushrooms, and then the tomatoes. Season with salt and pepper and cook 3 minutes over high heat, with the lid on the pan.

In a separate little pan boil down to half quantity the juice from the canned mushrooms, the rest of the brandy, the sherry, 1½ table-spoons butter, salt and pepper. Split the chickens in half. Put the halves, split side down, on the tomatoes, pour over the reduced liquid, and cover the pan. Simmer over low heat 40 to 50 minutes, or until the chickens are just tender. To serve, spoon a little of the tomato and mushroom sauce on the bottom of a shallow casserole. Place the chicken halves on top, skin side up. Pour the rest of the sauce over them. Sauté the chicken livers quickly in ½ tablespoon hot butter. Garnish the casserole with the livers, cut in half, and chopped fresh chives. NET: 4 servings.

This dish is also very nice prepared with boned chicken breasts instead of a whole chicken. Cheese beignets (page 785) are a favorite with this recipe.

POULET SAUTÉ AU CITRON

Sautéed Chicken with Lemon

1 3½-pound whole dressed chicken	3 tablespoons all-purpose flour
8 tablespoons salt butter	1¼ cups chicken stock (page 35)
¼ cup Cognac or good brandy	1 cup sour cream
Finely grated rind of 2 lemons	1 cup heavy cream, whipped
2 teaspoons finely chopped garlic	Juice of 1 lemon
Salt	2 teaspoons granulated sugar
Freshly cracked white pepper	1 teaspoon guava jelly
1 teaspoon tomato paste	3 tablespoons freshly grated Parmesan cheese
1 teaspoon meat glaze	

Preheat the oven to 350°. Tie the chicken (page 342). Heat 5 table-spoons butter in a deep heavy pan until it is golden brown. Put in the chicken, breast side down, and slowly brown it all over. In a separate little pan, heat the brandy, ignite, and pour it over the chicken. Remove the chicken from the pan and put into the pan 3 tablespoons butter. Add the lemon rind, garlic, salt, and pepper. Cook very slowly over low heat 2 to 3 minutes. Off the heat, stir in the tomato paste, meat glaze, and flour, and mix to a smooth paste. Add the chicken stock and stir over low heat until the sauce comes to a boil. Reduce the heat to a gentle simmer.

In a separate bowl, fold the sour cream into the whipped cream. Stir the mixture into the simmering sauce with a wire whisk or wooden spatula, little by little. Then mix in the lemon juice, sugar, and jelly. Carve the chicken (page 343) into serving pieces and put them into the sauce. Put the pan, uncovered, on the top shelf of the oven, and cook about 35 to 40 minutes. Occasionally baste the chicken with the sauce in the pan. (If the sauce separates, it can be returned by stirring in a little cold sour cream.) To serve, arrange the chicken pieces in an earthenware casserole or on a flat au gratin dish. Carefully spoon the sauce over them. Sprinkle generously with grated Parmesan cheese and brown under a hot broiler. NET: 4 servings.

POULET AUX DENTS DE CHAT

Sautéed Chicken with Cat's Teeth (Slivered Almonds), with Sour Cream and Tomato Sauce

1 3½-pound whole dressed chicken
9 tablespoons salt butter
4 tablespoons melted salt butter
2 tablespoons dry sherry
¼ teaspoon finely chopped garlic
2 tablespoons finely chopped onion
5 or 6 ripe tomatoes, skinned
1 tablespoon tomato paste

3 tablespoons all-purpose flour
1½ cups chicken stock (page 35) or water
¼ cup slivered blanched almonds
Salt
Freshly cracked white pepper
1 bay leaf
1½ cups sour cream
3 tablespoons freshly grated Gruyère cheese

Preheat the oven to 350°. Tie the chicken (page 342). Heat 4 tablespoons butter in a deep heavy pan until it is golden brown. Put in the chicken, breast down, and slowly brown it all over. In a separate little pan, heat the sherry, ignite, and pour it over the chicken. Remove the chicken from the pan, and put into the pan the garlic, onion, and 3 sliced tomatoes. Cook over moderate heat 2 to 3 minutes. Off the heat, stir in the tomato paste and flour, and blend until the mixture is smooth. Pour in the chicken stock or water. Return the pan to moderate heat and stir until the sauce comes to a boil. Add the slivered almonds, salt, pepper, and the bay leaf. Put the whole chicken back in the pan, breast down. Put the pan, uncovered, on the top shelf of the oven and cook 45 to 50 minutes. Occasionally baste the chicken with the sauce in the pan, and turn it once or twice during cooking.

When the chicken is cooked, remove it from the pan, carve it into serving pieces (page 343) and arrange on a flat au gratin dish. Put the pan over low heat and stir in, little by little, the sour cream, the remaining 2 or 3 tomatoes, sliced, and some of the grated cheese. Simmer the sauce gently 3 minutes. Spoon it over the chicken. Sprinkle with the rest of the cheese, dot it with a little butter, and brown under a hot broiler. NET: 4 servings.

It is sad that giantism seems to have caught the fancy of the truck farmers of this country, for they know well the delicacy of baby-size vegetables. Even the little farm stands along country roads in summertime display huge carrots, turnips, and beets; everything is super giant size. So, with resignation, we must follow the solution of the great chefs and make "pretend" spring vegetables when we have to, by cutting them into little olive shapes.

1 3½-pound whole dressed
   chicken
4 tablespoons salt butter
2 tablespoons Marsala wine or
   dry sherry
18 small white onions, skinned
12 baby carrots, or large carrots
   cut into olive shapes
12 baby turnips, or large turnips
   cut into olive shapes
6 hearts of celery, cut in half
6 white parts of leek (well

washed)
12 firm white mushroom caps
   (small to medium size)
1 teaspoon tomato paste
2 teaspoons potato flour
1½ cups chicken stock
   (page 35)
Salt
Freshly cracked white pepper
1 bay leaf
2 tablespoons chopped fresh
   parsley

Preheat the oven to 375°. Tie the chicken (page 342). Heat the butter in a deep heavy pan. When it is foaming, put in the chicken and slowly brown it on all sides, taking care not to puncture the skin. Heat the wine in a separate little pan, ignite, and pour it over the chicken. Remove the chicken from the pan. Carve it into serving pieces (page 343) and set it aside. Put into the pan the onions, carrots, turnips, celery hearts, and leeks. Sauté them 2 to 3 minutes, then add the mushroom caps. Off the heat, stir into a corner of the pan the tomato paste and potato flour. Pour in the chicken stock. Add the bay leaf and season with salt and pepper. Stir over low heat until the sauce comes to a boil. Remove from the heat, put in the pieces of chicken, and cook 35 minutes in the oven.

When the chicken is cooked, remove it from the pan and arrange it in a casserole. Remove the vegetables with a slotted spoon and scatter them over the chicken. If the sauce is too thin, thicken it with a little more potato flour mixed with a little water. Reboil the sauce and pour it over the chicken. Sauté the liver of the chicken in a little butter and place it in the center of the casserole. Sprinkle the top with chopped fresh parsley. NET: 4 servings.

POULET
À L'ESTRAGON
AU BRUN

Sautéed Chicken in
Brown Sauce, with
Fresh Tarragon

To serve this chicken you need two white paper cutlet frills. Gnocchi à la Romana is a nice accompaniment.

1 3½-pound whole dressed
   chicken
10 tablespoons salt butter
1 sprig fresh tarragon

6 white peppercorns
⅓ cup Cognac or good brandy
1 tablespoon finely chopped
   shallot

1 teaspoon finely chopped garlic	⅓ cup dry white wine
2 tablespoons finely chopped fresh tarragon	¼ cup dry sherry
	¼ cup Marsala wine
3 firm white mushrooms, finely chopped	1 teaspoon red currant jelly
	1 chicken liver
Freshly cracked white pepper	3 firm white whole mushroom caps
½ teaspoon tomato paste	
½ teaspoon meat glaze	Salt
2 teaspoons potato flour	1 teaspoon lemon juice
1 cup chicken stock (page 35)	1 bunch crisp fresh watercress

Preheat the oven to 375°. Dry the chicken inside and out with paper towels. Insert in the cavity 2 tablespoons butter, the tarragon sprig, and 6 peppercorns. Tie the chicken (page 342). Heat 4 tablespoons butter in a deep heavy pan. When it is foaming, put the chicken in the pan, breast down, and brown it slowly all over. Heat the brandy in a little pan, ignite, and pour it over the chicken. Remove the chicken from the pan, set it aside, and put 2 tablespoons butter in the pan. Also add the chopped shallot, garlic, tarragon, and mushrooms. Season with a little pepper but no salt. Cook over low heat 2 to 3 minutes. Off the heat, mix in the tomato paste, meat glaze, and potato flour. Stir to a smooth paste, and add the chicken stock, wine, sherry, Marsala, jelly, and a little more pepper. (Taste the sauce to judge if it needs salt.) Return the pan to low heat and stir until the sauce comes to a boil. Put the chicken back in the pan with the sauce and cook, uncovered, on the top shelf of the oven about 35 to 40 minutes, until it is tender. Every 10 minutes, baste the chicken with the sauce. While the chicken is cooking, sauté the 3 mushroom caps in 1 tablespoon butter with the lemon juice and a little salt and pepper. Remove them from the pan, add another tablespoon of butter, and sauté the chicken liver. Cut it in half, and stick the pieces of liver and the mushroom caps on a small silver skewer.

The traditional way to serve this chicken is to place it whole on a serving platter (first remove the string tie). Stick the silver skewer into the throat of the chicken. Cut the knobs off the drumsticks and put on white paper frills. Garnish with crisp fresh watercress and serve the sauce in a separate bowl. If preferred, the chicken may be carved into serving pieces (page 343), arranged in a shallow au gratin dish, coated with the sauce, and garnished. NET: 4 servings.

POULET SAUTÉ GENEVRIÈRE

Chicken Sautéed with Gin and Juniper Berries

Most lunchtime martini drinkers seem to prefer drinking the martini right through lunch. For them I invented this compatible entrée. To prepare it with chicken breasts, use 6 to 8 half breasts of chicken. Follow the recipe except that the oven should be at 300° rather than 350°.

1 3½-pound whole dressed chicken	½ cup gin
8 tablespoons salt butter	2 tablespoons juniper berries, crushed with a mortar and

pestle or in a blender
½ teaspoon finely chopped
   garlic
1 teaspoon meat glaze
½ teaspoon tomato paste
4 tablespoons all-purpose flour

1 cup chicken stock (page 35)
1 cup heavy cream, whipped
3 tablespoons freshly grated
   Parmesan cheese
8 large fried croûtons (page 69)

Preheat the oven to 350°. Dry the chicken inside and out with paper towels. Tie the chicken (page 342). Heat 4 tablespoons butter in a deep heavy pan. When it is foaming, put the chicken in the pan, breast down, and brown it all over slowly. Heat the gin in a little pan, ignite, and pour it over the chicken. Remove the chicken from the pan, carve it into serving pieces (page 343), and set aside. Add another 4 table-spoons butter to the pan. Also add the crushed juniper berries and chopped garlic. Cook over low heat about 5 minutes, stirring occa-sionally. Off the heat, stir into the pan the meat glaze, tomato paste, and flour. Mix to a smooth paste and add the chicken stock. Stir over low heat until the sauce comes to a boil. Little by little, beat in the whipped cream. (If the sauce is too thick, add a little light cream.) Put the pieces of chicken back in the pan with the sauce. Cover, and bake 25 to 30 minutes, until the chicken is tender.

To serve, remove the chicken from the pan and arrange it in a shallow casserole or au gratin dish. Spoon the sauce over it and sprinkle with grated cheese. Brown under a hot broiler just before serving. Surround the edge of the dish with the large fried croûtons. NET: 4 servings.

POULET SAUTÉ GRANDMÈRE

Traditional
Grandmother's
Chicken with Croûtons,
Ham and Potatoes

1 3½-pound whole dressed
   chicken or (preferably)
   2 smaller ones (do not use a
   larger chicken)
1 sprig fresh tarragon
13 tablespoons salt butter
1 garlic clove, bruised
2 peppercorns
Salt
A little melted butter
⅓ cup Cognac or brandy
1 teaspoon tomato paste
1 teaspoon meat glaze
4 teaspoons potato flour
2 cups chicken stock (page 35)

¼ cup dry white wine
¼ cup dry sherry
2 teaspoons guava or red
   currant jelly
Freshly cracked white pepper
24 baby white onions
A little granulated sugar
1 pound boiled ham cut into
   ¾-inch cubes
12 baby white mushrooms
2 teaspoons lemon juice
Pommes de Terre Château
   (page 617)
8 diagonal fried croûtons
   (page 69)

Preheat the oven to 350°. Insert in the cavity the tarragon sprig, 2 tablespoons butter, garlic clove, peppercorns and a little salt, and tie the chicken (page 342). Brush the breast and legs with melted butter. Heat 5 tablespoons butter in a large heavy casserole. When it is foaming, put the chicken in, breast side down, and brown it all over.

Heat the brandy in a separate little pan, ignite, and pour it over the chicken. Remove the chicken from the casserole, set it aside, and add to the casserole the tomato paste, meat glaze, and potato flour. Off the heat, stir in the chicken stock, wine, and sherry. Add the jelly and a little pepper. Stir the sauce over low heat until it comes to a rolling boil, then remove from the heat. Carve the chicken into serving pieces (page 343) and put them into the sauce. Put the casserole with the chicken, uncovered, on the top shelf of the oven and cook 45 to 50 minutes.

While the chicken is cooking, prepare the Château Potatoes (Pommes de Terre Château) and set them aside. Skin the baby white onions, put them in a pan, and cover with cold water. Bring the water slowly to a boil. Immediately drain the onions and plunge them into cold water. Dry them well. Put 4 tablespoons butter in a frypan. When it is foaming, put in the onions. Shake them over brisk heat until they begin to brown, sprinkle with granulated sugar, and continue to shake them over the heat until they glaze. Lift them from the pan with a slotted spoon. Add the ham to the pan, sprinkle it with a little more sugar, and brown it. Lift out the cubes with a slotted spoon. Add another 2 tablespoons butter to the frypan. Add the baby white mushrooms with the lemon juice, salt, and pepper. Shake them over brisk heat about 3 minutes, then set aside with the ham and onions.

About 5 minutes before the chicken has finished cooking, add the potatoes, onions, ham, and mushrooms to the casserole. To serve, stick the fried diagonal croûtons all around the sides of the casserole, points up. NET: 4 servings.

POULET À LA HONGROISE

Chicken Paprika with Gnocchi Parisienne

This recipe is also superb with pheasant instead of chicken. Fried Gnocchi (page 674) may be substituted for Gnocchi Parisienne.

2 2½-pound whole dressed chickens
2 large pieces celery leaf
1 large garlic clove, cut in half
6 tablespoons salt butter
Salt
Freshly cracked white pepper
3 tablespoons Cognac or good brandy
1 green apple, sliced (with skin left on)
1 large yellow onion, sliced
1 stalk celery, sliced
1 tablespoon paprika
3 tablespoons all-purpose flour
½ teaspoon meat glaze
2 teaspoons tomato paste

1½ cups chicken stock (page 35)
¾ cup sour cream
½ cup heavy cream, whipped
2 teaspoons juniper berries, crushed with a mortar and pestle
4 tablespoons freshly grated Parmesan cheese
2 tablespoons melted salt butter
Half a red pepper and half a green pepper, blanched quickly in boiling water, seeded, and finely chopped

GNOCCHI PARISIENNE
1 cup water

1 teaspoon salt
4 tablespoons salt butter
1 cup all-purpose flour
3 eggs
1 teaspoon dry mustard
1 teaspoon Dijon mustard

A few grains cayenne pepper
Salt, if necessary
2 tablespoons melted salt butter
⅓ cup plus 4 tablespoons grated
  Parmesan cheese

Dry the chickens inside and out with paper towels. Insert in each cavity a large piece of celery leaf, half a garlic clove, and 1 tablespoon butter. Season with salt and a little pepper. Tie them (page 342). Heat 3 tablespoons butter in a deep heavy pan. When it is foaming, brown the chickens, starting with the breast, then the legs and back. Heat the brandy in a little pan, ignite, and pour it over the chickens. Remove the chickens from the pan, carve them into serving pieces (page 343), and set aside.

Preheat the oven to 375°. Add 1 tablespoon butter to the pan. Also add the apple, onion, and celery, and season with salt and pepper. Cover the pan and cook over low heat until the mixture is soft. Stir in the paprika and continue to cook another 5 minutes. Off the heat, stir in the flour, meat glaze, tomato paste, and chicken stock. Return to low heat and stir until the sauce comes to a boil. Rub the sauce through a fine strainer and return it to the pan. With a wire whisk, slowly beat in the sour cream. Put the pieces of chicken in the sauce in the pan. Cook on the top shelf of the oven 45 minutes to 1 hour, until the chicken is tender. Occasionally baste the chicken with the sauce.

GNOCCHI PARISIENNE. Put the water in a saucepan. Add the salt and butter and bring slowly to a boil. When bubbling, throw in the flour. Remove from the heat, and stir until the mixture is smooth. Transfer it to a mixer bowl. Beat in the eggs, one at a time, then mix in the mustards, cayenne pepper, salt (if necessary), and ⅓ cup grated cheese. Beat well and put the mixture into a pastry bag fitted with a plain round tube about the size of a dime. Hold the pastry tube on the edge of a pot three-quarters full of simmering salted water. Squeeze and, using a sharp paring knife, chop off 1-inch pieces of dough, letting them drop into the water. Cover the top of the water with a paper towel and poach the gnocchi 15 to 20 minutes. (When they are cooked, they rise to the top of the water.) Drain with a slotted spoon. When ready to serve, arrange them down a buttered au gratin dish. Sprinkle with the melted butter and 4 tablespoons of grated cheese. Brown under the broiler.

When the chicken is cooked, remove and arrange it in an au gratin dish. Put the pan with the sauce over low heat, and slowly beat in the whipped cream and juniper berries. Spoon the sauce over the chicken, sprinkle with the grated cheese and melted butter, and brown under the broiler. Sprinkle rows of finely chopped red and green pepper over the top. NET: 4 to 6 servings.

POULET SAUTÉ LOUISETTE

Sautéed Chicken with Ham and Tongue

2 whole dressed chickens,
    2½ to 3 pounds
6 tablespoons salt butter
1 medium-sized yellow onion,
    thinly sliced
Salt
Freshly cracked white pepper
2 tablespoons dry white wine
2 firm white mushrooms, sliced

1 ⅛-inch slice boiled ham,
    cut in fine shreds
½ cup shredded cooked tongue
½ teaspoon meat glaze
1 teaspoon potato flour
¾ cup chicken stock (page 35)
6 large diagonal fried croûtons
    (page 69)

Tie the chickens (page 342). Heat the butter in a deep heavy pan. When it is golden brown, put in the chickens, breast side down, and slowly brown them all over. Turn them onto their backs, place a few thin slices of onion on top, and season with salt and pepper. Cover, and cook slowly over low heat 35 to 40 minutes. When the chickens are cooked, remove them from the pan, and put into it the wine and mushrooms. Sauté a few minutes, add the shredded ham and tongue, and cook another minute. Off the heat, stir in the meat glaze, potato flour, and chicken stock. Mix well, and bring to a boil over low heat. Season with salt and pepper. Carve the chickens into serving pieces (page 343), and return them to the sauce in the pan. Shake over moderate heat a few minutes. Then arrange the chicken in a casserole, garnish around the sides with the fried croûtons, and spoon on the sauce. NET: 4 to 6 servings.

POULET MALLORCA

Sautéed Chicken with Tomatoes, Oranges, and Peppers

A favorite garnish is Rosemary Potatoes (page 611).

1 whole dressed chicken, 3½ to
    4 pounds
2 garlic cloves, bruised
15 tablespoons salt butter
1 sprig tarragon
3 peppercorns
Salt
⅓ cup Cognac or good brandy
Rind of 2 oranges, cut in very
    fine shreds crosswise
1 teaspoon finely chopped garlic
1 teaspoon meat glaze
3 teaspoons tomato paste
4 teaspoons potato flour
2 cups chicken stock (page 35)
½ cup dry white wine

½ cup dry sherry
2 teaspoons guava or red currant
    jelly
Freshly cracked white pepper
6 ounces firm white mushrooms,
    thickly sliced
2 teaspoons lemon juice
2 green peppers, blanched in
    boiling water, seeded, and cut
    in ¾-inch cubes
3 ripe tomatoes, skinned and
    quartered
Juice from the tomatoes
Skinned and seeded sections of
    3 oranges

Preheat the oven to 350°. Wipe the chicken inside and out with paper towels. Insert in the cavity the garlic cloves, 3 tablespoons butter, the tarragon sprig, peppercorns, and a little salt. Tie the chicken (page 342). Heat 4 tablespoons butter in a deep heavy pan until golden brown. Put in the chicken, breast side down, and slowly brown it all over. In a separate little pan, heat the brandy, ignite, and pour it over the chicken. Remove the chicken from the pan, and put into the pan 4 tablespoons butter. Melt it over low heat and add the orange rind and chopped garlic. Off the heat, stir in the meat glaze, tomato paste, and potato flour. When the mixture is smooth, add the chicken stock, wine, and sherry. Add the jelly and a little pepper (but no salt). Stir the sauce over low heat until it comes to a rolling boil, then remove from the heat. Carve the chicken into serving pieces (page 343). Put them back in the pan and cover with the sauce. Cook, uncovered, on the top shelf of the oven 40 to 45 minutes. Baste once or twice with the sauce in the pan.

While the chicken is cooking, prepare the garnish. Melt 4 table-spoons of salt butter in a sauté pan. Add the mushrooms, lemon juice, salt, and a little pepper. Cook over brisk heat 3 minutes. Add the green peppers, season with a little more salt and pepper, and cook 2 to 3 minutes (the peppers should be a little crunchy). Cut the tomatoes into quarters. Remove the seeds and press in a fine strainer to get the fresh juice. Add this juice to the pan with the sections of tomato and orange. (Do not cook further, or the sections may disintegrate.) When the chicken is cooked, arrange it in a casserole. Pour over it a little of the sauce in which it was cooked. Scatter half the vegetables on the chicken. Pour on the rest of the sauce, then scatter the rest of the vegetables over it. NET: 4 servings.

A true "Chicken Marengo" must include fried eggs! . . . A battlefield meal foraged by Napoleon's chef — some eggs, tomatoes, a chicken, and crayfish. (Here we use a lobster.)

POULET SAUTÉ À LA MARENGO

Sautéed Chicken with Lobster and Fried Eggs

1 3½-pound whole dressed chicken	2 teaspoons potato flour
12 tablespoons salt butter	1½ cups chicken stock (page 35)
½ cup Cognac or good brandy	¼ cup dry sherry
2 teaspoons finely chopped garlic	6 firm white mushrooms, sliced
4 ripe tomatoes, skinned and thickly sliced	1 boiled lobster in the shell
Salt	A little cayenne pepper
Freshly cracked white pepper	4 large fried croûtons (page 69)
1 teaspoon meat glaze	4 eggs
2 teaspoons tomato paste	1 tablespoon vegetable oil
	1 teaspoon finely chopped fresh chives

Preheat the oven to 375°. Tie the chicken (page 342). Heat 4 table-spoons butter in a deep heavy pan until it is on the point of browning, then very slowly, brown the chicken all over in the pan. Heat ¼ cup brandy in a separate little pan, ignite, and pour it over the chicken. Remove the chicken from the pan, and add to the pan, off the heat, the garlic, tomatoes, and a little salt and pepper. Cook over moderate heat fairly briskly until the tomatoes are about half cooked. Off the heat, stir in the meat glaze, tomato paste, and potato flour. Mix in 1¼ cups chicken stock and the sherry. Stir over low heat until the sauce comes to a boil. Add a little more pepper and the mushrooms. Carve the chicken (page 343), put the pieces in the sauce, and cook on the top shelf of the oven, uncovered, 45 to 50 minutes. Occasionally baste the chicken with the sauce in the pan.

While the chicken is cooking, remove the meat from the boiled lobster. Keep the claw and tail meat whole. Keep the head shell and tail shell whole. Heat 4 tablespoons butter in a sauté pan. When it is foaming, put in the lobster claw and tail meat. Over moderate heat, coat them with the butter, sprinkle with a few grains of cayenne pepper, and brown the lobster a little. In a separate little pan, heat ¼ cup brandy, ignite, and pour it over the lobster. Set the lobster aside, and prepare the fried croûtons in the same sauté pan, if you like. In a small frypan, heat 2 tablespoons butter and 1 tablespoon vegetable oil to cook the "turned" eggs. When the fat begins to foam, reduce the heat slightly and put in 1 egg. (To be sure you have no broken yolks, break the egg into a cup and slide it into the pan.) Tip the pan so that the egg cooks in the edge. When the white begins to set, fold the white over the yolk and delicately brown each side. Prepare all the eggs in this manner and carefully set them aside on paper towels.

When the chicken is cooked, arrange the pieces on a flat au gratin dish. Lay the diagonal croûtons around them and put a turned egg on each croûton. Slice the lobster tail, and arrange it and the claw meat on the chicken. Spoon the sauce in which the chicken was cooked over the lobster and chicken. Sprinkle with the chives. Rub the lobster head and tail shells with a little vegetable oil, to give them a gloss, and decorate the top of the dish with them. NET: 4 servings.

POULET SAUTÉ PARMESAN

Chicken with Parmesan Cheese Sauce

1 3½-pound whole dressed chicken
8 tablespoons salt butter
½ cup finely chopped shallots
4 tablespoons Cognac or good brandy
4 tablespoons all-purpose flour
1 teaspoon Dijon mustard

Salt
A few grains cayenne pepper
1½ cups milk
¾ cup freshly grated Parmesan cheese
⅓ cup heavy cream
3 tablespoons dry breadcrumbs (page 69)

Preheat the oven to 350°. Dry the chicken inside and out with paper towels. Tie the chicken (page 342). Heat 4 tablespoons butter in a deep heavy pan. When it is foaming, put the chicken in the pan, breast down, and brown it all over. Heat the brandy in a separate little pan, ignite, and pour it over the chicken. Remove the chicken from the pan and carve it into serving pieces (page 343), and set them aside. Add 4 tablespoons butter to the pan, then add the shallots and cook over low heat 3 minutes. Off the heat, stir in the flour and the Dijon mustard. Season with salt and the cayenne pepper. Mix in the milk and half the Parmesan cheese. Stir over low heat until the sauce comes to a boil. Add the heavy cream and mix well. Arrange the pieces of chicken in a shallow au gratin or baking dish. Spoon the Parmesan cheese sauce over them. Sprinkle with the rest of the cheese and the breadcrumbs. Bake 25 to 30 minutes, until the chicken is tender, and serve piping hot. NET: 4 servings.

1 whole dressed boiling fowl,
   5 to 5½ pounds
6 yellow onions, sliced
6 carrots, sliced
1 stalk celery, sliced
Bouquet garni (celery leaf and
   parsley)
6 black peppercorns
Salt
Water
Freshly cracked white pepper
5 tablespoons salt butter

½ teaspoon finely chopped
   garlic
2 slices raw bacon, diced
¼ cup dry red wine
2½ cups of the reserved chicken
   stock
1 teaspoon tomato paste
¼ cup chopped fresh herbs
   (such as parsley, chives,
   tarragon)
2 turnips, sliced

POULET PAYSANNE

Braised Fowl Peasant Style, with Vegetables

Tie the chicken (page 342). Put it in a deep heavy pan with about a third of the sliced onions and carrots, and the sliced stalk of celery, bouquet garni, peppercorns, and 2 teaspoons salt. Cover with cold water, bring to a boil, and simmer gently over low heat 1 to 1½ hours. Remove the chicken and cool it a little. Strain, and reserve the stock.

Preheat the oven to 325°. Melt 2 tablespoons butter in a casserole and brown the cooked chicken lightly over low heat. Remove the chicken, set it aside, and add to the casserole about a quarter of the remaining sliced onions and carrots, then the chopped garlic and diced bacon. Cook 3 minutes over low heat. Stir in the wine, 2 cups stock, the tomato paste, and half the chopped herbs. Bring the mixture to a boil, return the chicken to the pan, and cook in the oven 1 hour, or until it is tender. (Shrinking of the meat from the drumstick ends is an indication that chicken is tender.) Remove the chicken from the pan (remove the string), carve it into serving pieces (page 343), and keep it warm. Strain the mixture in the pan, put it in a saucepan, boil it down to half quantity, and set it aside. In a small heavy pan, melt 3 tablespoons butter. Add the rest of the sliced onions and carrots, then the turnips, salt, pepper, and ½ cup stock. Cover the vegetables with wax paper and the lid. Simmer over low heat until they are tender.

To serve, arrange the vegetables in the middle of a round serving dish. Place the chicken pieces on top. Spoon over a little of the reduced sauce and serve the rest in a sauceboat. Sprinkle the chicken with the rest of the fresh herbs. NET: 4 servings.

POULET PROVENÇALE

Casserole of Chicken with Eggplant, Onions, Mushrooms, Peppers, Tomatoes

1 3½-pound whole dressed chicken
3 tablespoons salt butter
¼ cup Cognac or good brandy
½ teaspoon finely chopped garlic
2 teaspoons tomato paste
1 teaspoon meat glaze
4 teaspoons potato flour
2½ cups chicken stock (page 35)
¼ cup dry white wine
1 teaspoon red currant jelly
Freshly cracked white pepper

PROVENÇALE GARNISH
1 large eggplant
Salt
⅓ cup vegetable oil
5 tablespoons salt butter
2 yellow onions, cut into eighths
1 teaspoon finely chopped garlic
Freshly cracked white pepper
1 red pepper and 1 green pepper, seeded and cut into eighths
4 firm white mushrooms, thickly sliced
2 teaspoons lemon juice
3 ripe tomatoes, skinned and cut into eighths

Preheat the oven to 375°. Dry the chicken with paper towels inside and out. Tie it (page 342). Heat the butter in a deep heavy pan. When it is foaming, put in the chicken breast down, and slowly brown it all over. Heat the brandy in a little pan, ignite, and pour it over the chicken. Remove the chicken from the pan, carve it into serving pieces (page 343), and set it aside. Add to the pan, off the heat, the garlic, tomato paste, meat glaze, and potato flour. Mix to a smooth paste. Mix in the chicken stock, wine, jelly, and a little pepper (but no salt). Stir the sauce over low heat until it comes to a boil. Simmer about 5 minutes, then put the chicken pieces in the pan and baste with the sauce. Cook, uncovered, on the top shelf of the oven about 50 minutes, until the chicken is tender. While it is cooking, prepare the garnish.

PROVENÇALE GARNISH. Cut the stalk off the eggplant. Cut the eggplant in half lengthwise, then into ¼-inch slices. Spread them out on a platter, sprinkle well with salt, and let stand 30 minutes. Rinse in clear water, drain, and dry them on paper towels. Heat the vegetable oil in a large frypan. When it is very hot, brown the eggplant slices on both sides, a few at a time, and drain on paper towels. Next add 3 tablespoons butter to the pan, and the onions and garlic. Shake the pan over brisk heat until the onions become tinged with brown. Season with salt and pepper. Add 2 tablespoons butter to the pan, and the red and green peppers, also the sliced mushrooms. Season with the lemon juice and a little more pepper. Cook briskly 3 minutes. Remove the frypan from the heat and add the tomatoes and eggplant.

About 5 minutes before the chicken has finished cooking in the oven, add the Provençale mixture to it. Serve in a large casserole (perhaps accompanied by hot garlic bread). NET: 4 servings.

1 3½-pound whole dressed
    chicken
6 tablespoons salt butter
2 Bermuda onions, finely
    chopped
Salt
Freshly cracked white pepper
1 cup light cream
3 tablespoons all-purpose flour

1 cup milk
1 tablespoon tomato paste
½ teaspoon curry powder
½ teaspoon paprika
2 teaspoons lemon juice
3 firm white mushrooms, sliced
1 large black truffle, sliced
6 large fried croûtons (page 69)

POULET À LA STANLEY

Braised Chicken with a
Curry Onion Sauce,
Garnished with
Croûtons

Carve the uncooked chicken into serving pieces (page 343). Melt 2 tablespoons butter in a deep heavy pan. Add the onions and cook slowly, without browning, 6 to 8 minutes. Add another 2 tablespoons butter to the pan. Put in the chicken pieces, season with salt and pepper, and add the light cream. Cover, and cook over low heat 30 minutes. Remove the chicken pieces and keep them warm. In a small saucepan, melt 1 tablespoon butter. Off the heat, stir in the flour and add the milk. Return to low heat and bring to a boil, stirring constantly. Stir this sauce into the onion mixture, then stir in the tomato paste and rub the mixture through a fine strainer. Return the strained sauce to the pan. Add the curry powder and paprika. Sauté the mushrooms in 1 tablespoon butter with the lemon juice, and add, with the sliced truffle, to the sauce. Bring slowly to a boil, return the chicken, and simmer very gently 10 minutes. To serve, arrange the chicken on a flat serving dish, spoon the sauce over it, and surround it with the large fried croûtons. Serve at once. NET: 4 servings.

1 3½-pound whole dressed
    chicken
3 tablespoons salt butter
8 to 12 new (baby) carrots
1 onion, finely sliced
3 firm white mushrooms or
    mushroom stems, sliced
Salt
Freshly cracked white pepper
1 teaspoon meat glaze
½ teaspoon tomato paste

2 tablespoons all-purpose flour
½ cup dry red wine
1 cup chicken stock (page 35)
1 bay leaf
1 sprig fresh tarragon
1 teaspoon lemon juice
2 tablespoons dry white wine
2 tablespoons chopped fresh
    parsley
3 tablespoons sour cream

POULET SAUTÉ À LA VICHY

Sautéed Chicken with
Carrots and Sour Cream

Preheat the oven to 350°. Dry the chicken inside and out with paper towels, and tie it (page 342). Heat 2 tablespoons butter in a deep heavy pan. When it is golden brown, brown the chicken in it on all sides. Remove the chicken and set it aside. Add to the pan 1 carrot, finely sliced, and the sliced onion, and cook slowly until they are just tender. Add the mushrooms, season with salt and pepper, and cook over low heat 3 minutes. Off the heat, stir in the meat glaze, tomato paste, and flour; mix well. Stir in the red wine and chicken stock. Return to moderate heat and stir until the sauce comes to a boil.

Return the chicken to the pan. Add the bay leaf and tarragon sprig. Cover the pan and cook on the top shelf of the oven 35 to 40 minutes.

When the chicken is done, remove it from the pan. Strain the liquid into a saucepan and boil it down to the consistency of cream. Carve the chicken into serving pieces (page 343) and keep them warm. Scrape the remaining carrots and cut into paper-thin slices. (It is best to use a mandoline to get them very thin and uniform.) Put them in a small heavy pan, cover with cold water, and bring to a boil. Drain the carrots and return them to the pan. Add 1 tablespoon butter, salt, pepper, and the lemon juice, then add the white wine. Cover with wax paper and the lid and cook until the carrots are barely soft (3 to 4 minutes). Add the chopped parsley and sour cream. To serve, spread the carrots on the bottom of a serving dish. Place the carved chicken on top. Spoon the sauce over it. Serve at once. NET: 4 servings.

POULET SAUTÉ AUX MARRONS

Chicken Sautéed with Dill, with Chestnut Croquettes

1 3½-pound whole dressed chicken
1 garlic clove, bruised
1 sprig fresh dill
2 black peppercorns
8 tablespoons salt butter
Salt
¼ cup Kirsch
½ teaspoon finely chopped garlic
¼ cup finely chopped shallots
½ teaspoon ground cardamom seed
1 teaspoon tomato paste
1 teaspoon meat glaze
2 teaspoons potato flour
1 cup chicken stock (page 35)
1 medium-size ripe tomato, skinned, quartered, seeded, and finely diced
¼ cup dry sherry
2 tablespoons dry white wine
2 tablespoons chopped fresh dill
Freshly cracked white pepper
2 marrow bones

CHESTNUT CROQUETTES
1-pound can unsweetened chestnut purée
1 cup potato purée (page 610)
2 eggs
Salt
Freshly cracked white pepper
A few dry white breadcrumbs (for coating, page 69)
Vegetable oil for deep-fryer

Preheat the oven to 350°. Insert in the cavity the garlic clove, dill sprig, peppercorns, 1 tablespoon butter, and a little salt, and tie the chicken (page 342). Heat 4 tablespoons butter in a heavy casserole over moderate heat. When it is foaming, put in the chicken, breast side down, and slowly and carefully brown it all over. Heat the Kirsch in a separate little pan, ignite, and pour it over the chicken. Remove the chicken from the casserole and set it aside. Off the heat, stir into the pan 1 tablespoon butter, the chopped garlic, shallots, and ground cardamom seed. Cook over low heat 2 to 3 minutes. Again off the heat, stir in the tomato paste, meat glaze, and potato flour. Pour in the chicken stock and add the tomato, sherry, and wine. Stir the sauce over low heat until it comes to a boil. Add the chopped dill. Keep the pan over low heat and stir in 2 tablespoons butter bit by bit. Carve the chicken into serving pieces (page 343). Put them in the sauce, and add a little salt and pepper if necessary. Add the marrow bones to the pan. Cover the chicken with wax paper and the lid, and cook in the oven 30 to 35 minutes, until the chicken is tender.

CHESTNUT CROQUETTES. Beat the chestnut purée in the mixer until it is smooth. Add the potato purée, continue beating, and blend well. Add 1 egg, salt, and a little pepper, and beat the mixture thoroughly. Form the purée mixture into cork shapes on a lightly floured board. Beat the remaining egg and brush the cork shapes with it, then coat with breadcrumbs. Fry them in 375° oil until golden brown all over. Drain well on paper towels.

To serve, arrange the chicken on a heated au gratin dish. (If the sauce is too thin, mix ½ teaspoon potato flour with 2 tablespoons cold water, add to the sauce, and reboil.) Spoon the sauce over the chicken. Pile the chestnut croquettes at each end. NET: 4 servings.

POULARDE FLAMBÉE À L'ÉCU DE FRANCE

Chicken Braised in Cream, with Artichoke Bottoms and Shredded Ham, Tongue, and Truffles

2 whole, dressed chickens, 3 to 3½ pounds each
8 tablespoons salt butter
6 tablespoons Cognac or good brandy
1 cup heavy cream
6 thin slices onion
8 sprigs fresh parsley
1 large bay leaf
1 garlic clove, bruised
1 sprig celery leaf
½ teaspoon ground juniper berries
8 canned artichoke bottoms, cut in quarters
12 fresh firm white button mushrooms, finely sliced
Salt
Freshly cracked white pepper
¼ teaspoon freshly grated nutmeg
1 cup each of shredded cooked lean ham and tongue
3 large black truffles, cut into strips
2 tablespoons chopped fresh parsley
6 large fried croûtons (page 69)

Preheat the oven to 350°. Wipe the chickens inside and out with paper towels. Tie them (page 342). Heat the butter in a deep heavy pan and brown the chickens all over in it. In a separate little pan, heat the brandy, ignite, and pour it over the chickens. When the flame burns out, remove the chickens and carve them into serving portions (page 343). Return the chicken to the pan, cover, and cook over moderate heat 10 to 15 minutes, shaking the pan frequently. Put the heavy cream, onion, parsley, bay leaf, garlic clove, celery leaf, and juniper berries in a separate little pan. Bring to a boil, and simmer gently 4 minutes. Strain this cream over the chickens.

Add the artichoke bottoms and mushrooms to the chicken and season with salt, pepper, and the nutmeg. Cover the pan tightly with the lid, and cook the chicken 30 minutes in the oven. When done, arrange the chicken in a shallow casserole. Mix the ham, tongue, and truffles into the artichoke and mushroom mixture, and spoon over the chicken. Sprinkle with chopped fresh parsley. Surround the sides of the casserole with the large fried croûtons. NET: 6 servings.

POULET SAUTÉ EN DEMI-DEUIL, SAUCE BRUNE

*Chicken in
Half-Mourning
with Brown Sauce*

In this "demi-deuil" the chicken is lined with black truffles under the skin and there is a salpicon of black and white truffles in the sauce. Served with Gnocchi à la Romana (page 672), it always seems to be a sensation — a simple and elegant dish with which to show off a fine big white wine. Advance note: It is a good idea to marinate the whole truffles in Cognac or Madeira a few hours before using. Also, once a can of truffles has been opened, the unused truffles can be stored in Cognac or Madeira in a screw-top jar and kept in the refrigerator.

1 whole dressed chicken, 3½ to
   4 pounds
2 large black truffles, thinly
   sliced
7 tablespoons salt butter
⅓ cup Cognac (including the
   Cognac or Madeira marinating the truffles)
⅓ cup finely chopped shallots
1 teaspoon finely chopped garlic
2 teaspoons finely chopped fresh
   tarragon
1 large black truffle, finely
   chopped

1 large white truffle, finely
   chopped
½ teaspoon tomato paste
½ teaspoon meat glaze
2 teaspoons potato flour
¼ cup Marsala wine
¼ cup dry sherry
¼ cup dry white wine
1¼ cups chicken stock (page
   35)
2 teaspoons red currant or grape
   jelly
Freshly cracked white pepper

Preheat the oven to 375°. With great care loosen the skin on the breast and legs of the chicken. Insert the thin slices of black truffle between the flesh and the skin; there should be a row on each side of the breastbone and on each thigh and drumstick. Tie the chicken (page 342). Heat 6 tablespoons butter in a deep heavy pan over low heat. When it is foaming, put the chicken in the pan, breast down, and slowly brown it all over. Take great care not to break the skin. In order to get the skin translucent so that the truffles show through beautifully, the chicken must be browned slowly, over low heat. When the chicken has been perfectly browned, heat the brandy in a little pan, ignite, and pour it over the chicken. Remove the chicken from the pan and set it aside. Add to the pan 1 tablespoon salt butter, and the shallots, garlic, tarragon, and chopped black and white truffles. Cook very, very slowly, stirring all the while, 2 to 3 minutes. Remove the pan from the heat and stir in the tomato paste, meat glaze, and potato flour. Mix to a paste, then add the Marsala wine, sherry, white wine, and chicken stock. Also add the jelly and stir the sauce over low heat until it comes to a boil. Add a little pepper.

Put the chicken back in the pan and baste it with the sauce. Cook, uncovered, on the top shelf of the oven 45 minutes. Reduce the temperature to 350° after the chicken has been in 10 minutes. When the chicken is cooked, remove the tie and arrange it for serving. This chicken may be served whole on a serving platter and garnished with the Gnocchi à la Romana. Spoon a little of the sauce over the chicken and serve the rest in a separate bowl. Or it may be carved in the kitchen (page 343) and arranged on an au gratin dish. Coat the pieces of chicken with the sauce and serve the gnocchi in a separate, smaller au gratin. NET: 4 servings.

8 large square or round
   croûtons, fried in butter
   (page 69)
8 tablespoons salt butter
2 chicken livers
6 firm white mushrooms, finely
   sliced
½ cup finely shredded cooked
   tongue
Salt

Freshly cracked white pepper
1 teaspoon dry thyme
2 whole dressed chickens,
   2 to 2½ pounds each
   (broilers)
3 tablespoons dry white wine
3 tablespoons water
2 tablespoons chopped fresh
   parsley

POULET SAUTÉ À LA MAINTENON

Broiled Chicken on Croûtons with Mushrooms and Tongue

Have the croûtons prepared. Heat 1 tablespoon butter in a deep heavy pan. When it is brown, put in the chicken livers and brown them on both sides quickly. Remove the livers and melt 3 tablespoons butter in the pan. Add the mushrooms, tongue, salt, pepper, and thyme, and cook 3 minutes over moderate heat. Spread a little of this mixture on each of the croûtons. Arrange them on a flat au gratin dish and set aside.

Cut the chickens in half and season with salt and pepper. Melt 4 tablespoons butter. Brush the pieces of chicken with the butter and broil them slowly under the broiler on both sides. Cut them in quarters and put a piece of chicken on each garnished croûton. Slice the chicken livers and garnish the top of the chicken. Add to the pan the wine, water, salt, and pepper. Bring it to a boil, pick up any glaze on the bottom of the pan, and strain. Spoon this sauce over the chicken. Sprinkle with chopped fresh parsley and serve immediately. NET: 8 servings.

This recipe, in which sautéed breasts of chicken are coated with brown sauce, garnished with Hollandaise, and served on broccoli purée, was created at the Drake Hotel, New York.

CHICKEN DIVAN

3 whole chicken breasts (6 sides)
½ cup Cognac or good brandy
6 tablespoons salt butter
2 teaspoons potato flour
1 teaspoon meat glaze
1 teaspoon tomato paste
1½ cups chicken stock (page
   35)
¼ cup dry white wine

Salt
3 cups broccoli purée (page 576)

HOLLANDAISE SAUCE
3 egg yolks
2 tablespoons light cream
1 tablespoon tarragon vinegar
8 tablespoons frozen sweet
   butter, cut in small pieces

First prepare the broccoli purée and set it aside. Then skin and bone the chicken breasts. Brush them with brandy and let them marinate 30 minutes, then dry with paper towels. Heat 4 tablespoons butter in a sauté pan. When it is foaming, put the 6 half breasts in the pan and brown them on each side. Put a flat lid with a weight on them, to keep them flat. When they are cooked, remove the lid and weight. Heat the rest of the brandy in a little pan, ignite, and pour it over the chicken. Set the chicken aside in the pan and keep it warm.

BROWN SAUCE. Melt 2 tablespoons butter in a small saucepan. Stir in the potato flour, meat glaze, and tomato paste. Off the heat, stir in the chicken stock and wine. Return to low heat and stir the sauce until it comes to a boil. Simmer it gently a few minutes and keep it warm.

HOLLANDAISE SAUCE. Put the egg yolks in a medium-size bowl and beat them with a little whisk. Stir in the light cream, then the vinegar. Stand the bowl in a shallow pan half filled with hot water, over low heat. Continue to beat with the whisk until the yolk mixture thickens. Beat the frozen sweet butter into the sauce, little by little.

To serve, form the broccoli purée into a bed on a hot flat serving dish. Arrange the chicken breasts on top. First spoon over the brown sauce, then spoon the Hollandaise sauce over that. Brown the dish quickly under a hot broiler and serve immediately. NET: 6 servings.

CÔTELETTES DE VOLAILLE POJARSKY

Cutlets of Chicken Breast Forcemeat

To serve this dish you need twelve little paper cutlet frills (to fit the macaroni).

3 whole chicken breasts (6 sides)	*About 1 cup dry white bread-*
8 tablespoons salt butter	*crumbs (page 69)*
¾ cup heavy cream, whipped	*6 tablespoons sweet butter*
Salt	*2 teaspoons lemon juice*
Freshly cracked white pepper	*12 pieces raw macaroni (about*
A little freshly grated nutmeg	*¼ to ½ inch diameter)*
A little flour (for dusting)	*1 bunch crisp fresh watercress*
1 egg, beaten	

Skin and bone the chicken breasts, and remove all sinew, including the long tendon running through each side. Put the breast meat and salt butter (cut in pieces) through a fine meat chopper four times. When the mixture is very fine and well blended, rub it through a fine strainer into a bowl. With a whisk, mix in the whipped cream, salt, pepper, and nutmeg. Shape a ball of the mixture with two tablespoons. Working with lightly floured hands, roll it on a lightly floured board. With a small spatula, flatten it out and form it into a cutlet shape. Brush the cutlet with beaten egg and cover it with breadcrumbs. Prepare all the chicken breast mixture in this manner (there should be 12 cutlets). If possible, put the prepared cutlets in the freezer for 1 hour.

Put the sweet butter in a sauté pan with the lemon juice and a little salt. When it is foaming and just on the point of browning, put the cutlets in the pan and brown on each side. Cover the pan and let them cook another 3 minutes on each side. Arrange the cooked cutlets on a large flat serving dish in the form of a crown. Stick a little piece of raw macaroni at the narrow end of each cutlet. Slip a paper cutlet frill over the macaroni. Spoon the butter from the pan over the cutlets. Garnish with crisp fresh watercress. Serve immediately. NET: 6 servings.

You will need 12 small cutlet molds for this dish. The cutlets are coated with Sauce Grand Vefour, and garnished with buttered cucumbers.

CÔTELETTES DE VOLAILLE VICOMTESSE

Poached Breast of Chicken Mousse in Cutlet Molds

2 whole breasts of chicken (large size)
½ cup water
4 tablespoons sweet butter
Salt
½ cup all-purpose flour
2 eggs
3 egg whites
½ cup light cream
Freshly cracked white pepper
2 tablespoons Cognac or good brandy
4 tablespoons cool melted salt butter

FILLING
1 tablespoon salt butter
2 large (or 4 small) firm white mushrooms, cut in small dice
¼ teaspoon lemon juice
Salt
Freshly cracked white pepper
2 ounces tongue, finely diced
2 teaspoons chopped fresh dill

SAUCE GRAND VEFOUR
3 tablespoons salt butter
3 tablespoons all-purpose flour
Salt
A few grains cayenne pepper
1 cup chicken stock (page 35)
⅓ cup light cream
2 egg yolks
3 tablespoons tarragon vinegar
1 garlic clove, bruised
1 small piece celery
1 small piece bay leaf
4 black peppercorns
1 sprig parsley
2 tablespoons heavy cream
6 tablespoons frozen sweet butter, cut into bits

CUCUMBER GARNISH
2 cucumbers
2 tablespoons salt butter
Salt
Freshly cracked white pepper
1 tablespoon chopped fresh dill

Skin and bone the chicken breasts, and remove all sinew. Put them through a very fine meat chopper. Prepare a paste (like a pâte à choux): Put the water in a small tin-lined copper saucepan. Add the sweet butter and a pinch of salt, and bring slowly to a boil. Literally throw in the flour. Stir the mixture with a wooden spoon, over low heat, until it is smooth. Put it in a mixer bowl, and beat in, one at a time, the eggs and 1 egg white. Remove this paste from the mixer bowl and chill it in the refrigerator a moment.

Put the ground chicken breast in the mixer bowl with the 2 remaining egg whites. Beat well. Continue beating as you slowly add the light cream (it should be a very thin stream). Add the paste and season very well with salt and pepper. In a separate little pan, heat the brandy, ignite, and pour it on the chicken breast mixture, beat the mixture well, then rub it through a fine strainer. Brush 12 cutlet molds with a little melted salt butter. Fill the molds level with the chicken breast mixture. With a damp finger, make a little indentation about the size of a teaspoon in the center of each cutlet.

FILLING. Melt the butter in a small sauté pan. When it is foaming, add the mushrooms, lemon juice, salt, and pepper. Cook briskly 2 to 3 minutes. Add the diced tongue and season with salt, pepper, and the dill.

Put a little of this filling in the hollows in the cutlets and cover with another generous spoonful of the chicken breast mixture, smoothing it out with a wet teaspoon. Fill a large pot three-quarters full with water. Season with salt. Bring the water to a boil and reduce it to a gentle simmer. Drop the cutlets in their molds into the pan of hot water. Let them poach about 20 minutes, until they come out of their molds and rise to the top of the water. Remove them with a large slotted spoon, drain carefully on paper towels, and arrange them in a crown (circle) on a flat round serving dish.

SAUCE GRAND VEFOUR. First prepare a basic velouté sauce: Melt the salt butter in a saucepan. Off the heat, stir in the flour, and season with salt and cayenne pepper. Mix in the chicken stock. Return to low heat and stir until the sauce comes to a boil. Stir in the light cream. Make the following Hollandaise sauce: Put the vinegar, garlic clove, celery, bay leaf, peppercorns, and parsley sprig in a little pan, and boil down to about 1 tablespoon liquid. Put the egg yolks in a medium-size bowl and mix with a small whisk. Continuing to beat, strain the reduced vinegar onto the yolks. Then beat in the heavy cream. Put the bowl in a shallow pan of hot water over low heat. Continue to beat with the whisk until the yolk mixture has thickened. Add the frozen sweet butter bit by bit, beating constantly and waiting until each piece has been incorporated before you add the next. Fold the Hollandaise sauce into the velouté sauce.

Carefully spoon the sauce over the cutlets. Fill the well in the center of the crown with the cucumber garnish.

CUCUMBER GARNISH. Cut off the tops and bottoms of the cucumbers, and skin them. Cut them in half lengthwise, remove the seeds, and cut the pulp into ½-inch slices. Put the slices in a small heavy pan, cover with cold water, bring to a boil, drain, and return them to the pan. Add the butter, salt, pepper, and the chopped dill. Cover with buttered wax paper and cook slowly only 3 to 4 minutes, with the cover off.

Serve immediately. (If it is necessary to rewarm this dish, do so in a low oven, about 250°–300°, so that the sauce does not separate.) NET: 6 servings.

WARNING: If the Chicken Kiev is properly sealed, avert your face when eating. The warm melted butter will spout when the chicken is cut.

POULET
À LA KIEV

Deep-Fried Chicken
Breasts Stuffed with
Herbed Sweet Butter

4 half breasts of chicken
8 tablespoons frozen sweet
    butter (preferably in a
    ¼-pound stick)
2 teaspoons chopped fresh
    tarragon or chives
1 teaspoon finely chopped garlic
Salt
Freshly ground white pepper
A little all-purpose flour (for
    dusting)
1 egg, beaten
About ¾ cup dry white bread-
    crumbs (page 69)
Vegetable oil for deep-fryer
1 bunch crisp fresh watercress
Suggested accompaniment:
    Noisette Potatoes (page 616),
    Rice Pilaff (page 675), or
    Fried Gnocchi (page 674)

Skin and bone the chicken breasts. Remove all the fat and sinew, including the long tendon running through the breast. With the palm of the hand, flatten each half breast on a cutting board. With a very sharp knife, slit the half breast in two. (You now have 2 fillets from one half breast.) Divide all the half breasts in this manner. Put the 8 fillets between two long sheets of wax paper, skin side down. Flatten them out with the side of a heavy cleaver. Beat them with the side of the cleaver until they are almost transparent. Carefully peel off the top paper.

Cut the frozen sweet butter into 8 even sticks. Place 1 stick of butter slightly diagonal on each flattened piece of chicken. Also put ¼ teaspoon chopped fresh tarragon or chives, ⅛ teaspoon chopped garlic, salt, and pepper over the butter. Roll up each piece of chicken carefully, being very careful to completely envelop the butter. Seal the ends by pressing them together or tucking them inside. (At this point the chicken may be frozen for later use.) When you wish to cook the chicken, dust each rolled fillet lightly with flour, brush it with beaten egg, and roll it in breadcrumbs. Fry them in hot oil at 350° until golden brown (about 4 to 6 minutes). Drain them on paper towels, and arrange on a hot napkin on a warm serving plate. Garnish with crisp fresh watercress. If desired, decorate by sticking into each piece a cocktail stick topped with a small paper frill. NET: 4 servings (2 pieces each).

SUPRÊMES
DE VOLAILLE
AMANDINE

Breasts of Chicken
Sautéed in Butter,
with White Wine
and Almonds

3 whole chicken breasts
    (6 sides)
Salt
A little all-purpose flour (for
    dusting)
Freshly cracked white pepper
8 tablespoons salt butter
2 tablespoons lemon juice
½ cup split blanched almonds
1 teaspoon finely chopped garlic
1 tablespoon finely chopped
    onion
¼ cup dry white wine
2 teaspoons chopped fresh
    parsley

Bring a pan of salted water to a boil and put in the chicken breasts.

Boil them 2 minutes and drain. Remove all the skin and breastbone, leaving attached the tiny tip of wing bone if there is one. Dry the six half breasts thoroughly in paper towels. Mix some flour with a little salt and pepper and dust the chicken breasts with it. Heat 4 tablespoons butter in a heavy pan. Put in the chicken breasts and brown them very slowly on each side. Add the lemon juice and season with salt and pepper. Cover the pan and sauté gently, over low heat, until the chicken is tender. Then remove it, set it aside, and add to the pan the almonds, garlic, onion, and another 2 tablespoons butter. Shake the pan over medium heat until the almonds are nicely browned. Then stir in the rest of the butter alternately with the wine. Return the chicken to the pan, reheat, and arrange it in a shallow serving dish. Spoon the almonds and sauce over the pieces, and sprinkle with chopped parsley. NET: 6 servings.

SUPRÊMES DE VOLAILLE ARCHIDUC

Sautéed Breasts of Chicken Stuffed with Mushrooms, Ham, and Cheese, with Madeira Sauce

This lovely dish could also be served on a bed of broccoli purée (page 576), in which case omit the mushroom and artichoke garnish.

3 whole chicken breasts (6 sides)
½ cup Cognac or good brandy
Salt
Freshly cracked white pepper
¼ pound firm white mush-rooms, thinly sliced
11 tablespoons salt butter
2 teaspoons lemon juice
2 ounces boiled ham or tongue, finely shredded
1 teaspoon Dijon mustard
3 ounces Gruyère cheese, finely shredded
1 tablespoon chopped fresh tarragon
2 chicken livers

1 teaspoon meat glaze
1 teaspoon tomato paste
3 teaspoons potato flour
1¼ cups chicken stock (page 35)
½ cup dry sherry
⅓ cup Madeira wine
⅓ cup dry red wine
1 teaspoon red currant jelly
6 firm white mushroom caps (fluted, if desired)
6 artichoke bottoms (canned)
6 thin slices Gruyère cheese
4 tablespoons freshly grated Parmesan cheese

Skin and bone the chicken breasts. Cut a pocket in the side of each half breast. Open up the pockets and brush them with 2 table-spoons brandy. Season with salt and pepper. Close the pockets and let the breasts marinate while you prepare the stuffing.

STUFFING. Melt 2 tablespoons butter in a sauté pan. Add the sliced mushrooms with 1 teaspoon lemon juice, salt, and pepper, and cook briskly 3 minutes. Stir in the ham, mustard, and 1 tablespoon brandy. Remove the mixture from the pan and chill it, then mix in the shredded Gruyère cheese and chopped tarragon. Put a spoonful of this stuffing in the pocket of each half breast of chicken. Stuff them as full as possible, and reshape the breasts.

Heat 5 tablespoons butter in a large heavy frypan. When it is foaming, put in the stuffed chicken breasts skin side down. Cover them with a flat lid or layer cake tin, weighted to keep them flat.

Brown them on both sides. At the same time brown the chicken livers. Heat the rest of the brandy (about ¼ cup) in a separate little pan, ignite it, and pour it over the chicken breasts and livers in the frypan. Then remove them from the pan, set aside, and add another table-spoon of butter to the pan. Off the heat, stir in the meat glaze, tomato paste, and potato flour. When the mixture is smooth, add the chicken stock, sherry, Madeira wine, red wine, jelly, and a little pepper (but no salt). Stir over low heat until the sauce comes to a boil. Slice the livers very thin and add them to the sauce. Put the chicken breasts back in the pan, cover the pan with wax paper and the lid, and cook very gently over low heat 15 to 20 minutes, until the chicken is tender. While the chicken is cooking, prepare the garnish: Heat 1 tablespoon butter in a sauté pan. Add the mushroom caps and artichoke bottoms with 1 teaspoon lemon juice and a little salt and pepper. Cook briskly 3 minutes only.

To serve, arrange the stuffed chicken breasts down a shallow au gratin dish. Place a thin slice of Gruyère cheese on each breast. Coat the chicken with the sauce. Put a mushroom cap on each artichoke bottom and arrange them on both sides of the chicken. Sprinkle the chicken with the grated Parmesan cheese and a little melted butter (about 2 tablespoons). Brown under a hot broiler and serve. NET: 6 servings.

SUPRÊMES DE VOLAILLE BÉARNAISE

Sautéed Breasts of Chicken on Sliced Eggplant and Tomatoes

An hour before you plan to prepare this dish, start soaking the dried mushrooms.

2 whole chicken breasts (4 sides)
Salt
A little all-purpose flour (for dusting)
Freshly cracked white pepper
8 tablespoons salt butter
3 tablespoons dry sherry
2 tablespoons lemon juice
2 ounces dried mushrooms, soaked 1 hour in ½ cup dry

white wine and ¼ cup water
2 small eggplants
A little vegetable oil
½ teaspoon finely chopped garlic
6 large ripe tomatoes, skinned and cut into thick slices
1 tablespoon chopped fresh chives

Bring a pan of salted water to a boil and put in the chicken breasts. Boil them 2 minutes and drain. Remove the skin and breastbone, leaving on the tiny tip of wing bone if there is one. Dry the four half breasts thoroughly in paper towels. Mix some flour with a little salt and pepper and dust the chicken breasts with it. Heat 4 table-spoons butter in a deep heavy pan. When it is foaming, put in the chicken breasts and brown them slowly on each side. Pour the sherry over them, season with salt, pepper, and the lemon juice. Cover the pan and cook 25 minutes over very low heat.

Drain the mushrooms, which have been soaking in wine and water, and reserve the liquid. Add a little of this liquid to the chicken breasts from time to time as they are cooking. Slice the eggplants into ¼-inch rounds. Spread the slices out on a large platter and sprinkle generously with salt. Let them stand 30 minutes, then drain, rinse in cold water, and dry them. Heat a little vegetable oil in a large frypan. When it is sizzling hot, fry the eggplant slices to a golden brown on each side. Arrange them to cover the bottom of a shallow serving dish.

Add 2 tablespoons butter to the pan in which the eggplant was browned. Add the garlic and cook over low heat 1 minute. Add the tomatoes and cook briskly over high heat 3 minutes. Spoon the tomatoes over the eggplant. Place the cooked chicken breasts on the tomatoes.

Chop the drained mushrooms and put them in the pan in which the chicken was cooked with the rest of the soaking liquid. Boil this down slowly to about ¼ cup. Bit by bit, stir in 2 tablespoons butter. Dribble this sauce over the chicken breasts. Sprinkle the chicken with the chopped fresh chives. NET: 4 servings.

SUPRÊMES DE VOLAILLE BOURGUIGNONNE

Sautéed Breasts of Chicken with Ham and Gruyère Cheese, on a Pea Purée

2 large whole chicken breasts (4 sides)
5 tablespoons Cognac or good brandy
4 slices cooked tongue
Salt
Freshly cracked white pepper
3 tablespoons salt butter
2 teaspoons potato flour
¼ teaspoon tomato paste

1 teaspoon meat glaze
½ cup dry white wine or dry vermouth
¾ cup chicken stock (page 35) or water
4 slices boiled ham or prosciutto
4 slices Gruyère cheese or mozzarella
Purée Saint-Germain (page 607)

Prepare the pea purée and set it aside. Skin and bone the chicken breasts. Cut a pocket in the side of each breast and brush the inside with 2 tablespoons brandy. Insert a slice of cooked tongue in each, season with a little salt and pepper, and reshape the half breast. Heat the butter in a heavy pan. When it is foaming, put in the chicken breasts. Put a flat lid or layer cake pan directly on the breasts, with a weight (such as a brick) on it to keep them flat. Brown the chicken breasts in this manner on both sides. Heat 3 tablespoons brandy in a separate little pan, ignite, and pour it over the chicken. Remove the chicken from the pan and set it aside. Off the heat, add to the pan the potato flour, meat glaze, and tomato paste. Mix it to a smooth paste, pour in the wine and chicken stock, stir over low heat until the sauce boils, then simmer until it is slightly thick. Return the chicken breasts to the pan and baste them with the sauce.

To serve, spread the pea purée on a shallow au gratin dish. Arrange the chicken breasts on the purée. Put a slice of ham and a slice of cheese on each half breast. Strain the sauce and spoon it over the chicken. Put the dish under the broiler until the cheese melts. Serve at once. NET: 4 servings.

Start soaking the dried mushrooms an hour before you expect to prepare this dish.

4 whole chicken breasts (8 sides)	2½ cups chicken stock (page 35)
4 tablespoons all-purpose flour, plus a little for dusting the chicken	½ cup chopped fresh mushrooms
Salt	8 firm white mushroom caps (fluted, if desired)
Freshly cracked white pepper	2 egg yolks
7 tablespoons salt butter	1 tablespoon tarragon vinegar
4 tablespoons dry sherry	2 tablespoons heavy cream
3 tablespoons dried mushrooms, soaked 1 hour in ½ cup water (reserve the liquid)	4 tablespoons frozen sweet butter, cut into small pieces
A few grains cayenne pepper	

Sautéed Breasts of Chicken with Mushroom Velouté Sauce, Hollandaise Sauce, and Mushrooms

Skin and bone the chicken breasts. Mix a little flour with some salt and pepper and lightly dust the 8 half chicken breasts with this mixture. Heat 4 tablespoons butter in a heavy pan. When it is foaming, put in the chicken breasts skin side down, and brown them on both sides. Heat the sherry in a little pan, ignite, and pour it over the chicken. Season the chicken with a little salt and pepper. Cover the pan with the lid and cook over low heat 15 to 20 minutes, until the chicken is tender. During the cooking, gradually moisten the chicken with the liquid in which the dried mushrooms were soaked. Drain the soaked mushrooms well and chop them. When the chicken is cooked, arrange it on a serving dish and keep it warm.

MUSHROOM VELOUTÉ SAUCE. Melt 2 tablespoons butter in a saucepan. Stir in 4 tablespoons flour and season with salt and cayenne pepper. Off the heat, pour in the chicken stock and add the chopped fresh mushrooms. Stir the sauce over low heat until it comes to a boil, then add the chopped soaked mushrooms.

HOLLANDAISE SAUCE. Put the egg yolks in a small bowl with salt, cayenne pepper, and the vinegar and heavy cream. Mix well with a small wire whisk. Put the bowl in a shallow pan half filled with hot water over low heat. Beat until the sauce thickens. Continue to beat, adding the sweet butter bit by bit.

Heat 1 tablespoon butter in a small sauté pan, and quickly warm the whole mushroom caps a minute or two. Spoon the mushroom velouté sauce over the chicken breasts already arranged in a serving dish. Over the mushroom velouté sauce, spoon the Hollandaise sauce (add this just before serving). Place a mushroom cap on each chicken breast. Serve immediately. NET: 8 servings.

3 whole breasts of chicken (6 sides)	12 thin slices cooked tongue
5 tablespoons Kirsch or good brandy	Dijon or German mustard
	4 tablespoons salt butter
	3 tablespoons sweet butter

Sautéed Breasts of Chicken with Tongue and Béarnaise Sauce on a Pea Purée

1 teaspoon finely chopped garlic
1 teaspoon tomato paste
1 teaspoon meat glaze
2 teaspoons potato flour
½ cup dry white wine
1 cup chicken stock (page 35)
1 large black truffle, finely
chopped
¾ cup Sauce Béarnaise (page 50)
2 tablespoons chopped fresh parsley
Purée Saint-Germain (page 607)

Prepare the Sauce Béarnaise and pea purée and set them aside. Skin and bone each of the 6 half breasts of chicken and remove the long tendon in each. Using a very sharp knife, cut a pocket in the side of each half breast and brush the inside with 3 tablespoons Kirsch or brandy. Insert a slice of tongue in each, spread a little mustard on the tongue, and reshape the breast. Heat the salt butter in a heavy frypan. When it is foaming, put in the chicken breasts skin side down. Set a flat cake tin with a weight (such as a brick) directly on the breasts to keep them flat, and brown them on both sides. Heat 2 tablespoons Kirsch or brandy in a little pan, ignite, and pour it over the chicken. Remove the chicken from the pan, set it aside, and melt 2 tablespoons sweet butter in the pan. Off the heat, stir in the garlic, tomato paste, meat glaze, and potato flour. Pour in the wine and chicken stock. Stir the sauce over low heat until it comes to a boil. Still over low heat, stir in another tablespoon of sweet butter bit by bit, and add the chopped truffle. Remove from the heat, and stir in the Béarnaise sauce and parsley.

To serve, spread the pea purée on the bottom of a shallow au gratin or serving dish in an oval shape. Place the chicken breasts on it, cover them with the six remaining slices of tongue, and coat evenly with the sauce. Brown quickly under a hot broiler. Serve immediately.
NET: 6 servings.

SUPRÊMES DE VOLAILLE NANETTE

Sautéed Breasts of Chicken with Crab-Stuffed Mushrooms, with Cream Sauce, Gratinée

3 whole breasts of chicken (6 sides)
2 tablespoons Cognac or good brandy
Salt
Freshly cracked white pepper
½ teaspoon ground marjoram
7 tablespoons salt butter
⅓ cup dry sherry
1½ cups light cream
3 egg yolks
1 teaspoon potato flour
½ teaspoon freshly grated nutmeg
6 slices sturdy white bread, cut in large rounds
6 large firm white mushroom caps
6 ounces fresh lump crab meat
⅓ cup freshly grated Gruyère cheese
2 tablespoons breadcrumbs, fried in 2 tablespoons melted butter (page 69)

Skin and bone the chicken breasts. Place the 6 half breasts between two long sheets of wax paper and flatten them just a little with the side of a heavy cleaver. Wipe each with a damp cloth and brush all over with brandy. Let them stand 15 minutes to mellow. Mix a little salt, pepper, and the marjoram together and rub a little of this mixture over each half breast. Heat 6 tablespoons butter in a heavy sauté pan. When it is foaming, put in the half breasts and sauté on both sides over moderate heat until they are brown and tender. Remove them, put them in a heated pan or dish, cover with foil, and keep them hot.

Add the sherry to the pan, and cook over low heat until it is almost evaporated. Mix the light cream with the egg yolks in a separate little bowl. Off the fire, stir into the pan the potato flour and the cream and egg yolk mixture. Season the sauce with salt, pepper, and the nutmeg. Toast the large rounds of bread on each side under the broiler, and set them aside. Put the lump crab meat into a small pan and warm it with a little of the sauce. Sauté the mushroom caps in 1 tablespoon butter. Fill the caps with the crab meat.

Place the toasted rounds of bread on a hot flat serving dish. On each place a mushroom cap filled with crab meat, and on the filled mushroom, place the cooked chicken breast. Over low heat, bring the cream sauce just to a boil, stirring constantly. Coat the chicken breasts with the sauce. Sprinkle the sauce with the grated cheese and buttered breadcrumbs. Brown the dish under the broiler. Serve immediately. NET: 6 servings.

SUPRÊMES DE VOLAILLE SMITANE

Sautéed Breasts of Chicken in Sour Cream Sauce, with Mushrooms and Fresh Dill

4 whole breasts of chicken
  (8 sides)
7 tablespoons salt butter
2 tablespoons Marsala wine
½ teaspoon tomato paste
1 tablespoon all-purpose flour
  plus a little for dusting the
  chicken
½ cup chicken stock (page 35)
1½ cups sour cream
Salt

Freshly cracked white pepper
1 tablespoon red currant jelly
4 tablespoons freshly grated
  Parmesan cheese
½ pound firm white mush-
  rooms, sliced
A few grains cayenne pepper
1 teaspoon lemon juice
1 tablespoon dry sherry
1 tablespoon finely chopped
  fresh dill

Skin and bone the chicken breasts, except the little wing bone at the ends (if the butcher left them in). Dust the half-breasts lightly with flour. Heat 4 tablespoons butter in a sauté pan. When it is foaming, quickly brown the chicken breasts in it (both sides), then pour over them the Marsala wine. Remove the chicken breasts from the pan, set them aside, and add to the pan, off the heat, the tomato paste and 1 tablespoon flour. Stir in the chicken stock. Return the pan to low heat and stir until the sauce thickens. With a wire whisk, stir in the sour cream, spoonful by spoonful. Season with salt, pepper, the jelly, and 3 tablespoons grated cheese. Put the chicken breasts back in the pan, cover with the sauce, and cook over low heat 15 to 20 minutes, until they are tender.

While the breasts are cooking, prepare the mushrooms. Heat 2 tablespoons butter in another sauté pan. Add the mushrooms, lemon juice, salt, and cayenne pepper. Cook briskly 3 to 4 minutes, then stir in the sherry and mix in the dill. Remove the half breasts from the pan and arrange on an au gratin dish or shallow serving dish. Spoon the sauce over them, sprinkle with 1 tablespoon grated cheese, dot with butter, and brown under a hot broiler. Serve the mushrooms in a separate little au gratin dish. NET: 8 servings.

AMERICAN CHICKEN PIE

This pie is made with poached chicken, mushrooms, and hard-boiled eggs in velouté sauce, with a pastry cover.

2 whole dressed chickens,
  2½ to 3 pounds each
1 onion, sliced
1 carrot, sliced
1 stalk celery, sliced
Salt
Freshly cracked white pepper
1 bay leaf
Water
6 tablespoons salt butter
4 tablespoons all-purpose flour
A few grains cayenne pepper
1½ cups chicken stock (page
  35)
¼ cup heavy cream
2 firm white mushrooms, finely
  chopped

2 hard-boiled eggs, cut in
  eighths
2 tablespoons chopped fresh
  herbs (parsley, chives,
  tarragon, etc.)
1 egg, beaten

PASTRY
1½ cups all-purpose flour
4 tablespoons salt butter
3 egg yolks
2 tablespoons water
3 tablespoons freshly grated
  Parmesan cheese
½ teaspoon paprika
Salt

Tie the chickens (page 342) and put them in a deep heavy pan. Add the onion, carrot, celery, salt, pepper, bay leaf, and enough water to cover them. Bring slowly to a boil, skim off any scum, and simmer 25 to 30 minutes, until the chickens are tender. Take the meat from the bones, remove all the skin, and cut the meat into small chunks or coarse shreds.

SAUCE. Melt 4 tablespoons butter in a heavy pan. Off the heat, add the flour, salt, and cayenne pepper. Pour in the chicken stock. Stir over moderate heat until the sauce comes to a boil. Add the remaining butter and the cream, little by little. Add the chopped mushrooms, and blend well.

PASTRY. Put the flour on a slab or counter top. Make a well in the center and put in it the butter, egg yolks, water, grated cheese, paprika, and salt. Work them to a smooth paste, then work in the flour. Work up to a ball of dough. Roll out on a lightly floured surface, to a size large enough to cover the top of the baking dish.

Preheat the oven to 375°. To the finished sauce add the chicken, hard-boiled eggs, and chopped herbs. Put this mixture into a deep baking dish, brush the edge of the dish with beaten egg, and cover the top with the pastry crust. Trim the edges off neatly. Make a little hole in the center to release the steam. Brush the pastry with beaten egg. Bake 30 to 35 minutes. Serve immediately. NET: 6 servings.

The chicken is boned, stuffed with breast of chicken mousse, and poached. It is served with rich velouté sauce and a garnish of mushrooms, artichoke bottoms, and green olives.

Chicken Ballotine
à la Régence

1 3½-pound whole dressed
   chicken
5 tablespoons Cognac or good
   brandy
Salt
Freshly cracked white pepper
2 whole large breasts of chicken
   (4 sides)
3 egg whites
1½ cups light cream
½ teaspoon freshly grated
   nutmeg
1 slice boiled ham, ¼ inch thick,
   cut into finger-size strips
   (or use cooked tongue)
2 black truffles, coarsely
   chopped

RICH VELOUTÉ SAUCE
6 tablespoons salt butter
6 tablespoons all-purpose flour

Salt
A few grains cayenne pepper
½ cup light cream
1¼ cups chicken stock (page
   35)
3 egg yolks
3 tablespoons Cognac
   or good brandy
4 tablespoons heavy cream

GARNISH
½ pound firm white button
   mushrooms
3 teaspoons lemon juice
Salt
Freshly cracked white pepper
3 tablespoons salt butter
6 artichoke bottoms (canned),
   cut into halves
12 pitted black olives
12 pitted green olives

Bone the chicken (page 344). Spread it out on a cutting board, skin side down. Brush the flesh with 3 tablespoons of Cognac and season it with salt and a little pepper.

CHICKEN MOUSSE. Skin and bone the two chicken breasts. Put the meat through a fine meat chopper. Transfer the ground chicken breast to a mixer bowl and add the egg whites. Beat the mixture well. Continue beating, and slowly add 1½ cups light cream. Add 2 teaspoons salt, a little pepper, 2 tablespoons Cognac, and the nutmeg. Beat very well. Spread this mousse on the boned chicken, leaving a 1-inch margin all around the edge.

Arrange the fingers of ham or tongue on the mousse; set them about 1 inch apart, vertical with the chicken. Scatter over the top the chopped truffles. Fold the edges over carefully and sew the chicken together with white kitchen thread. Roll the chicken in wax paper, then in a sheet of foil, then in a clean cloth or kitchen towel. Gather each end and tie it securely with string, leaving about 12 inches of string on each end. Tie the ballotine in two places around the middle. Lay it in a deep oval pan with a handle at each end, and with the string tie it to the handles like a hammock, so that it doesn't touch the bottom of the pan. Fill the pan halfway with cold water and bring the water to a rolling boil. Cover the pan. Reduce the heat, and very gently simmer the ballotine 50 minutes.

While the ballotine is cooking, prepare the sauce. Melt 5 tablespoons butter in a saucepan. Off the heat, stir in 4 tablespoons flour, season with salt and cayenne pepper, and mix in the chicken stock. Stir over low heat until the sauce comes to a boil. Add the light cream. Bit by bit, stir in 1 tablespoon butter. Put the egg yolks in a little bowl. Mix in the brandy and heavy cream. Pour a little of the sauce into the egg yolks, beating all the time. Return this mixture to the sauce in the pan. Mix well and reheat gently; do not allow the sauce to boil. Cover the sauce with plastic wrap and set aside.

GARNISH. Wash the mushrooms in 2 teaspoons lemon juice and water and drain well. Sauté them lightly in the butter, with 1 teaspoon lemon juice, salt, and pepper. Add to the sauté pan the halved artichoke bottoms and the pitted black and green olives. Shake the pan over low heat a minute or two to warm the garnish.

When the ballotine is cooked, let it stand 5 minutes or so, then unwrap it. Remove all the thread. Cut as many slices as needed for one serving. Arrange the slices overlapping down an oval serving platter. Place the uncut piece at the other end of the platter. Coat the ballotine with the sauce. Arrange the garnish along the sides. NET: 4 to 6 servings.

CRÊPES NIÇOISE

Pancakes Stuffed with Chicken, Velouté Sauce

This dish offers an extra dividend meal from the Pot-au-Feu since it requires only a cup of cooked chicken. Any leftover chicken or turkey can be used. Traditionally, a Niçoise preparation includes tomatoes. There are none in these crêpes stuffed with chicken, but for some reason this well-known dish has always been so termed.

CRÊPES
8 tablespoons all-purpose flour
Pinch of salt
1 egg
1 egg yolk
2 tablespoons vegetable oil
About ¾ cup milk
Salt butter (for crêpe pan)

FILLING
1 cup finely shredded cooked
 chicken
2 tablespoons Cognac or good
 brandy
Salt
Freshly cracked white pepper
¼ pound firm white mush-
 rooms, sliced
2 tablespoons salt butter
1 teaspoon lemon juice

VELOUTÉ SAUCE
4 tablespoons salt butter
4 tablespoons all-purpose flour
Salt
A few grains cayenne pepper
1 cup chicken stock (page 35)
¼ cup light cream
2 egg yolks
1 tablespoon Cognac or good
 brandy
2 tablespoons heavy cream

FINISH
2 tablespoons melted salt butter
3 tablespoons dry breadcrumbs
 (page 69)
4 tablespoons freshly grated
 Parmesan cheese

CRÊPES. Put the flour, salt, egg, egg yolk, vegetable oil, and 4 tablespoons of the milk in a small bowl. With a little whisk, beat the mixture until it is quite smooth. Then add enough milk to make the batter the consistency of light cream (it should just coat the back of a metal spoon). Cover the bowl with plastic wrap and leave it in the refrigerator at least 30 minutes. When ready to make the crêpes, heat an omelet or crêpe pan until smoking hot. Have ready a wad of wax paper, some butter, a ladle, and a spatula. If the batter has thickened, add a little more milk. Wipe the inside of the hot pan with butter, using the wad of wax paper. Ladle a little of the batter over the bottom of the pan. Brown the crêpe on one side, turn it over, and brown it on the other side. Pile the crêpes on a rack, one on top of the other.

FILLING. Put the chicken in a small bowl. Sprinkle it with the brandy and season with a little salt and pepper. Let it marinate a bit. Put the butter in a sauté pan. Add the mushrooms with the lemon juice, salt, and pepper. Shake over brisk heat 2 minutes. Mix the mushrooms into the chicken.

VELOUTÉ SAUCE. Melt 3 tablespoons butter in a tin-lined copper pan. Off the fire, stir in the flour. Season with a little salt and the cayenne pepper. Mix in the chicken stock. Return the pan to low heat and stir until the sauce comes to a boil. Add the light cream and, bit by bit, 1 tablespoon butter. Simmer gently about 5 minutes. In a little bowl, beat the egg yolks with the brandy and heavy cream. Pour in a little of the hot sauce, stirring all the time, then stir the yolk mixture into the sauce and reheat gently. Do not boil.

To finish, mix 2 tablespoons of the sauce into the chicken and mushroom mixture. Have ready a buttered flat au gratin dish. Spread each crêpe out flat, with the "wrong side" (the side cooked second) up. Spread 1 tablespoon of the chicken mixture on it, and roll it up like a small cigar. Arrange the rolled crêpes on the buttered dish. Brush the tops with a little melted butter. Spoon the sauce evenly over the crêpes, and sprinkle with the breadcrumbs, grated cheese, and melted butter. Brown under the broiler, and serve at once. NET: 4 servings.

This mousse recipe uses cooked chicken, both white and dark meat. Turkey may be substituted.

2 cups cooked white meat of chicken
1 cup cooked dark meat of chicken
⅓ cup dry sherry
8 tablespoons sweet butter
8 tablespoons all-purpose flour
Salt
A few grains cayenne pepper
2 cups milk
2 eggs
2 egg whites

RICH VELOUTÉ SAUCE
4 tablespoons sweet butter
3 tablespoons all-purpose flour
Salt
A few grains cayenne pepper
1 cup chicken stock (page 35)
⅓ cup light cream
2 egg yolks
1 tablespoon dry sherry
2 tablespoons heavy cream

GARNISH
8 ounces fresh firm white

MOUSSE
DE VOLAILLE
CHAUDE AUX
CHAMPIGNONS

Charlotte Mold of Hot Chicken Mousse with Rich Velouté Sauce and Mushrooms

mushrooms (whole if button-
size; if larger, halved or
quartered)
2 tablespoons salt butter
1 teaspoon lemon juice

Salt
Freshly cracked white pepper
Optional: 2 teaspoons chopped
fresh mint leaves

Preheat the oven to 350°. Put the chicken through a fine meat chopper
two times, then put it in a large bowl, mix in the sherry, cover with
plastic wrap, and set it aside. Melt the butter in a saucepan. Off the
heat, with a small whisk, stir in the flour. Season with salt and
cayenne pepper, and mix in the milk. Stir this cream sauce over
low heat until it comes to a boil, then cool it a little. Mix the eggs
and egg whites into it, then mix it all into the ground chicken. Put
the whole mixture in an electric blender and blend until smooth.
Generously butter a charlotte mold. Pack it firmly with the mousse
mixture, cover it with buttered wax paper, put it in a shallow roasting
pan half filled with hot water, and cook it in this pan in the oven
45 minutes.

RICH VELOUTÉ SAUCE. Melt the butter in a saucepan. Off the heat,
stir in the flour and season with salt and cayenne pepper. Mix in the
chicken stock and stir over low heat until the sauce comes to a boil.
Mix in the light cream. Beat the egg yolks in a separate little bowl.
Add the sherry and heavy cream. Mix a little of the hot sauce into
the yolk mixture, then add the yolk mixture to the sauce in the pan,
beating all the time. Reheat the sauce gently; do not allow it to boil.

MUSHROOMS. Melt the butter in a small sauté pan. Add the mushrooms, lemon juice, salt, and pepper. Sauté briskly 2 to 3 minutes.
Add the chopped mint.

When the mousse is cooked, remove it from the oven and let it
stand 5 minutes. Slide a sharp thin knife blade around the edge of
the mold, and turn the mousse out onto a hot flat serving dish. Coat
with the velouté sauce, and garnish with the mushrooms. NET: 4
servings.

MOUSSE
DE VOLAILLE
CHAUDE, SAUCE
HOLLANDAISE

Ring Mold of Hot
Chicken Mousse with
Hollandaise Sauce and
Cucumber Garnish

2 whole chicken breasts (4 sides)
3 raw egg whites
1¾ cup light cream
2 teaspoons salt
A few grains cayenne pepper
2 egg yolks
1 cup sour cream or heavy
cream

HOLLANDAISE SAUCE
2 tablespoons tarragon vinegar
2 tablespoons dry white wine
1 bay leaf
1 small piece celery leaf

2 peppercorns
2 egg yolks
12 tablespoons frozen sweet
butter, cut into small pieces
2 tablespoons heavy cream
1 or 2 drops lemon juice

CUCUMBER GARNISH
4 small thin cucumbers
2 tablespoons salt butter
Salt
Freshly cracked white pepper
1 tablespoon chopped fresh dill

Preheat the oven to 350°. Skin and bone the chicken breasts, and remove all the sinews. Put the breast meat through a fine meat chopper two times, then transfer it to a metal bowl. Put this bowl over a bowl of ice. Add the egg whites to the ground chicken and mix well with a small wire whisk. When they are thoroughly blended, beat in the light cream, drop by drop at first, until it thickens. Mix in the salt, cayenne pepper, and sour (or heavy) cream. Generously butter an 8-inch ring mold, and pack the mousse mixture into it. Cover the mold with buttered wax paper, stand it in a shallow roasting pan half filled with hot water, and place it in the oven. Bake about 40 minutes, or until the mousse is just firm to the touch.

HOLLANDAISE SAUCE. Combine the vinegar, wine, bay leaf, celery leaf, and peppercorns in a small pan. Boil the mixture down to 1½ tablespoons of liquid. Beat the egg yolks in a medium-size bowl. Strain the vinegar and wine mixture and add it to the yolks, beating all the time. Beat in the heavy cream. Stand the bowl in a shallow pan half filled with hot water, over low heat. Beat the frozen sweet butter into the sauce piece by piece, using a little whisk. Last, add the lemon juice. Cover the sauce with plastic wrap and keep it warm.

CUCUMBER GARNISH. Cut the tops and bottoms from the cucumbers, skin them, cut them in half lengthwise, and scoop out the seeds. Cut the pulp into ¾-inch slices. Put them in a pan, cover with cold water, and bring to a boil. Drain immediately, and return the cucumbers to the pan with the butter, salt, pepper, and the chopped fresh dill. Cover with buttered wax paper and the lid, and cook 3 minutes only over moderate heat, shaking the pan once or twice. The cucumbers should be slightly crisp.

When the mousse is done, remove it from the oven and let it stand 5 minutes before unmolding. Slide a thin-bladed knife around the edge of the mold, and turn the mousse out onto a hot flat serving dish. Coat it evenly with the Hollandaise sauce. Fill the center of the ring with the cucumbers. Serve at once. NET: 4 servings.

MOUSSE DE VOLAILLE, SAUCE VELOUTÉ, SIMPLE

Charlotte Mold of Simple Chicken Mousse with Velouté Sauce

This is a basic mousse with basic velouté to which you may adapt your own idea of a garnish, or enjoy it au simplicité.

3 whole chicken breasts	2 egg yolks
3 egg whites	
2½ cups light cream	
1 cup cold Béchamel Sauce (page 42)	VELOUTÉ SAUCE
	4 tablespoons salt butter
2 teaspoons salt	3 tablespoons all-purpose flour
A few grains cayenne pepper	1 cup chicken stock (page 35)
A few grains freshly grated nutmeg and allspice	⅓ cup heavy cream
	Salt
⅓ cup heavy cream	A few grains cayenne pepper

First prepare the Béchamel sauce and chill it.

Preheat the oven to 325°. Skin and bone the chicken breasts. Put the breast meat through a fine meat chopper two times. Transfer it to an electric blender. Add the egg whites, light cream, and cold Béchamel sauce. Season with salt, pepper, nutmeg and allspice. Blend the mixture until it is very smooth. Last, add the heavy cream and the egg yolks and blend again. Generously butter a charlotte mold or #6 soufflé dish and fill it with the mousse mixture. Pack it down well and cover the mold with buttered wax paper and foil. Put the mold in a shallow roasting pan half full of hot water and bake in the oven about 25 to 30 minutes, until it is just firm to the touch.

While the mousse is cooking, prepare the velouté sauce. Melt 3 tablespoons butter in a saucepan. Off the heat, stir in the flour and season with salt and cayenne pepper. Mix in the chicken stock and stir over low heat until the sauce comes to a boil. Bit by bit, stir in the remaining tablespoon of butter and the heavy cream.

When the mousse is out of the oven, let it stand 5 minutes, then turn it out onto a flat round serving dish. Spoon the velouté sauce evenly over it, and serve. NET: 4 servings.

POULET CRÉOLE

Chicken Creole

A whole roast chicken stuffed with Creole-style rice (with mushrooms, almonds, raisins, green pepper, tomatoes). The breast is boned and reshaped with alternating slices of breast and grilled bacon, glazed with Espagnole sauce. The recipe was given to me by a student from Mexico City. It is an unusual and beautiful presentation, and very good to eat.

1 whole dressed capon, 5 to 6
  pounds
Half a lemon
1 sprig fresh summer savory or
  tarragon
9 tablespoons salt butter
A little melted salt butter (to
  brush the chicken)
Salt
6 peppercorns
2 garlic cloves, bruised
1½ cups dry white wine
2 teaspoons finely chopped fresh
  parsley
1 yellow onion, finely chopped
1 tablespoon finely chopped
  shallots
2 teaspoons finely chopped
  garlic
4 firm white mushrooms, sliced
1 teaspoon lemon juice
Half a red pepper, finely diced

Half a green pepper, finely diced
½ cup browned salted almonds
⅓ cup raisins, soaked in a little
  Cognac
Freshly cracked black pepper
A few grains freshly grated
  nutmeg
1 teaspoon Dijon mustard
½ cup long-grained rice
1 cup chicken stock (page 35)
½ teaspoon leaf saffron
  (pulverized with a mortar and
  pestle and mixed with 1
  tablespoon water)
A few grains cayenne pepper
2 large ripe tomatoes, skinned,
  seeded, and shredded
About ½ pound bacon, thinly
  sliced

SAUCE
2 teaspoons salt butter

Liver from the capon
2 tablespoons Cognac or good
    brandy
1 teaspoon tomato paste
½ teaspoon meat glaze

2 teaspoons potato flour
½ cup dry white wine
1 cup chicken stock (page 35)
Pan juices (from roasting the
    capon)

Preheat the oven to 375°. Wipe the capon with paper towels. Rub it inside and out with the lemon half. Reserve the liver for the sauce. In the cavity put the summer savory or tarragon, 2 tablespoons butter, 1 teaspoon salt, and the peppercorns and garlic cloves. Tie the chicken (page 342). Place it on a rack on a roasting pan. Brush a little melted butter over the top of the chicken. Pour half the wine into the bottom of the roasting pan. Roast the capon 1½ hours, then reduce the oven to 350° and continue to roast it another 10 to 15 minutes. (You may insert a meat thermometer in the breast of the capon to check for doneness.) Every 20 minutes during roasting, put a little of the remaining wine in the bottom of the pan to pick up the glaze, then baste the capon with the pan juices. After each basting, again brush a little melted butter on the breast. When the capon has been in the oven 45 minutes, turn it over on its breast. After 20 minutes, turn it breast up again to finish cooking. When it is done, remove it from the oven and let it stand 5 minutes. Untie it and, with a very sharp knife, remove the breast meat from each side in one piece. With kitchen shears, cut out the breastbone so that the cavity is exposed.

STUFFING. Heat 5 tablespoons butter in a small heavy pan. Add the chopped parsley, onion, shallots, and garlic. Cook a minute or two over low heat. Add the mushrooms, lemon juice, and another 2 tablespoons butter. Next add the diced red and green pepper, almonds, and raisins soaked in brandy, and season with salt, pepper, and the nutmeg and mustard. Add the rice, and stir it around until it is well coated. Add the chicken stock, saffron, and a good shake of cayenne pepper. Stir the mixture over moderate heat until it comes to a boil. Cover the pan, and cook 25 minutes in a preheated 350° oven or 30 minutes over low heat on top of the stove. When the rice mixture is cooked, add the shredded tomatoes. Fluff the rice mixture with two forks.

ESPAGNOLE SAUCE. Heat 1 tablespoon butter very hot in a saucepan. Brown the chicken liver in the hot butter. In a separate little pan, heat the brandy, ignite, and pour it over the liver. Remove the liver from the pan and add another teaspoon of butter. Stir in, off the heat, the tomato paste, meat glaze, and potato flour. Add the wine, chicken stock, and juices from the roasting pan, and taste for seasoning. Stir the sauce over low heat until it comes to a boil. Return the liver to the sauce and simmer gently for 30 minutes.

Fill the cavity of the capon with the rice mixture and reshape it to look like a lovely fat chicken. With a very sharp carving knife, cut the two pieces of breast meat into long thin slices, and set aside. To grill the bacon in flat strips, put the slices on a cake rack and another rack on the slices. Place the racks with the bacon on a baking sheet, and grill it in a hot oven. Place the breast and bacon slices (first one then the other alternately) on the breast area of the capon, covering it so that the stuffing does not show. Place the prepared capon on a warm serving platter. When ready to serve, spoon a little sauce over the chicken and serve the rest separately in a sauceboat. NET: 6 servings.

TIMBALE À L'ORLOFF

Timbale Lined with Crêpes, Filled with Chicken, Ham, and Mushrooms, with Soubise Sauce

CRÊPES
8 tablespoons all-purpose flour
1 egg
1 egg yolk
2 tablespoons cool melted butter or vegetable oil
¼ teaspoon salt
About 1 cup milk
A little butter for the crêpe pan

FILLING NO. 1
3 cups chicken stock (page 35)
9 tablespoons uncooked cream of wheat or cream of farina
2 egg yolks
4 tablespoons salt butter
½ cup freshly grated Parmesan cheese

FILLING NO. 2
4 tablespoons salt butter
3 tablespoons all-purpose flour

Salt
A few grains cayenne pepper
1 cup chicken stock (page 35)
2 tablespoons heavy cream
2 egg yolks
1 cup diced cooked chicken
½ cup diced cooked ham
1 cup sliced fresh mushrooms, sautéed in a little butter and lemon juice
1 tablespoon finely chopped fresh parsley

SOUBISE SAUCE
1 Bermuda onion, sliced
1½ cups milk
1 bay leaf
Salt
A few grains cayenne pepper
2 tablespoons salt butter
2 teaspoons potato flour
2 tablespoons heavy cream

CRÊPES. Put the flour, egg, egg yolk, melted butter or oil, salt, and 4 tablespoons milk in a small bowl. Beat with a small wire whisk until the batter is quite smooth. Add the rest of the milk. The batter should be thick enough to coat the back of a silver spoon; if not, add a little more milk to make it thinner.) Put the batter in the refrigerator to set at least 30 minutes. Then heat a crêpe or omelet pan until a drop of butter sizzles and turns brown. Wipe the pan out with soft butter. Pour just enough batter into the pan to cover the bottom. Brown the crêpe on one side, then on the other. Pile the crêpes on a wire cake rack.

Lightly butter a charlotte mold, bombe mold, or round cake pan. Cut half the crêpes into 2 pieces and line the bottom and sides of the mold with them. Set aside. Preheat the oven to 350°.

FILLING NO. 1. Put the chicken stock in a pan and bring it to a boil. Add the cream of wheat, stirring all the time. Continue to cook over low heat until the cream of wheat comes away from the sides of the pan (stir it occasionally). Then beat the egg yolks into the mixture with the butter and grated cheese.

Spread a layer of the cream of wheat mixture on the crêpes in the mold, covering the bottom and sides. (Reserve about a third of this mixture.)

FILLING NO. 2. Melt 2 tablespoons butter in a saucepan. Off the heat, stir in the flour, salt, and cayenne pepper. Pour in the chicken stock and stir over low heat until the sauce comes to a boil. Mix the heavy cream with the egg yolks, stir a little of the sauce into them, then stir all back into the sauce. Cut the remaining butter into bits, and stir it into the sauce bit by bit. Mix the chicken, ham, mushrooms, and parsley in a bowl. Mix the sauce well into this mixture.

Cover the cream of wheat in the bottom of the mold with a crêpe. Spread the chicken and ham mixture on it. Cover this with another crêpe, and spread on it the rest of the cream of wheat mixture. Cover with another crêpe. Place the mold in the preheated 350° oven and bake 20 to 25 minutes. While it is baking, prepare the sauce.

SOUBISE SAUCE. Put the onion and milk in a pan with the bay leaf, salt, and cayenne pepper, and bring to a boil. Simmer very gently until the onion is quite soft. Melt the butter in a saucepan. Off the heat, stir in the potato flour with salt and cayenne pepper. Strain (or purée in a blender) the onion and milk mixture, add it to the saucepan, and stir over low heat until it comes to a boil. Stir in the heavy cream and simmer gently 4 to 5 minutes.

When the timbale is baked, turn it out onto a hot serving dish. Spoon the onion sauce over it. NET: 4 servings.

---

1 whole dressed chicken,
   2 to 2½ pounds
1 onion, sliced
1 small carrot, sliced
1 small stalk celery, sliced
1 leek, sliced
1 bay leaf
6 peppercorns
Salt
1 pair sweetbreads
1 cup chicken stock (from
   cooking the chicken)
Freshly cracked white pepper
6 ounces firm white mushrooms
3 tablespoons salt butter
2 teaspoons lemon juice
1 black truffle
2 tablespoons chopped fresh
   parsley

PUFF PASTE CASE
2 cups all-purpose flour
½ teaspoon salt
¾ cup ice water
16 tablespoons (½ pound) firm
   salt butter
1 egg, beaten

RICH VELOUTÉ SAUCE
6 tablespoons salt butter
5 tablespoons all-purpose flour
Salt
A few grains cayenne pepper
1 cup chicken stock (from
   cooking the chicken)
2 egg yolks
1 teaspoon lemon juice
¼ cup heavy cream

VOL-AU-VENT À LA REINE

Puff Paste Case with Chicken and Sweetbreads, Rich Velouté Sauce

---

PUFF PASTE CASE. Make and work the dough according to the directions on page 723, carrying it through four roll and fold procedures (the point at which the puff paste could be left in the refrigerator overnight). When you are ready to prepare the puff paste case, roll the dough out into a long strip again. Fold it in 3. Roll it next into a strip at least 6 inches wide and 18 inches long. Fold in 3 layers again. Now place a 6-inch diameter round lid on the dough and cut out a circle with a knife, cutting down on an outward slant. Brush the edges of the two inside layers with water and stick all three layers together. On the top, mark out a smaller circle, about 4½ inches in diameter. Within this smaller circle, with the tip of the knife, mark a crisscross design. Place the puff paste round on a wet baking sheet. Set the oven at 375°. Chill the puff paste shell in the freezer 30 minutes. Then brush the top with beaten egg and put the pastry immediately into the oven and bake 30 to 45 minutes, until it is golden brown all over. Cool it on a cake rack. Then cut out the lid (the 4½-inch round), and very carefully remove it and scoop out the center of the puff pastry.

Dry the chicken inside and out with paper towels and tie it (page 342). Put it in a pan, cover it with water, bring to a boil slowly, and skim off all the scum. Add the onion, carrot, celery, and leek, also the bay leaf, peppercorns, and 1 tablespoon salt. Simmer very gently 35 to 40 minutes, until the chicken is just soft. Let it cool a little in the stock, then skin it and remove all the meat from the bones. Cut the meat into bite-size squares. Pour a little of the cooking stock over the chicken and set it aside. Strain the rest of the stock, reserve 2 cups, and store (freeze) the rest.

Blanch the sweetbreads by plunging them into boiling water 2 minutes. Drain, and immediately plunge them into ice water. Carefully remove all skin and sinew. Put the sweetbreads in a pan with 1 cup of the reserved chicken stock, season with a little salt and pepper, and simmer gently 10 minutes. Drain, and reserve the stock. Cut the sweetbreads into the same size pieces as the chicken, and add them to it. Cut the mushrooms into quarters and sauté them in the butter with the lemon juice, salt, and pepper. Cut the truffle into large dice. Add the mushrooms and truffle to the chicken and sweetbreads.

RICH VELOUTÉ SAUCE. Melt 4 tablespoons butter in a saucepan. Off the heat, stir in the flour, and season with salt and cayenne pepper. Pour on 1 cup chicken stock. Return the pan to low heat and stir until the sauce comes to a boil. Simmer gently 5 minutes, stirring in the rest of the butter bit by bit. In a separate bowl, beat the egg yolks until they are light and fluffy. Stir in the lemon juice and heavy cream. Pour a little of the hot sauce into the yolk mixture, stirring all the time. Then return the yolk and sauce mixture to the sauce in the pan, and mix well. (Do not boil the sauce at this point.)

Mix the sauce into the chicken, sweetbread, and mushroom mixture. Place the puff paste case on a warm folded starched napkin on a serving platter. Fill the shell with the sauce mixture, and cover with the lid of the case. Sprinkle with chopped fresh parsley. Serve immediately. NET: 6 servings.

OTHER POULTRY

Pineapple is used in roasting the ducks, and they are served with pineapple sauce, sautéed fresh pineapple slices, and rosettes of Duchess potatoes.

2 4-pound whole dressed ducks
2 small onions, each stuck with
   1 clove
1 small can (1 pound) sliced
   pineapple and the juice
   (reserve ⅓ cup for the sauce)
2 garlic cloves, bruised
A few white peppercorns
5 tablespoons salt butter
1 cup plus 2 tablespoons dry
   white wine
1 cup water
4 tablespoons melted salt butter
½ cup apricot jam

PINEAPPLE SAUCE
3 tablespoons salt butter
Livers of the ducks
⅓ cup Cognac or good brandy
1 teaspoon finely chopped garlic
1 slice of the fresh pineapple,
   cut into tiny cubes

1 teaspoon tomato paste
1 teaspoon meat glaze
3 teaspoons potato flour
1½ cups chicken stock (page
   35)
⅓ cup pineapple juice (from
   the canned pineapple)
½ cup Marsala wine
¼ cup dry white wine
½ cup apricot jam
Freshly cracked white pepper

SAUTÉED FRESH PINEAPPLE SLICES
1 fresh pineapple
A little flour (for dusting)
4 tablespoons salt butter
A little granulated sugar

GARNISH
Duchess Potato Rosettes
   (page 609)

Prepare the fresh pineapple. Cut off the top and the bottom. With a stainless steel knife, cut off the outer skin first, cutting it down the sides. Then, with a little knife, score around the lines of the burrs. Next, cut a parallel line and lift out the strip of burrs. Continue in this manner until all the burrs have been removed. Cut the pineapple into ½-inch slices. Cut out the core with a small cookie cutter, and cut the slices into halves. Set the pineapple aside.

Preheat the oven to 350°. Dry the inside and outside of each duck thoroughly with paper towels. In the cavity of each put 1 onion stuck with a clove, 4 slices canned pineapple, 1 garlic clove, 2 or 3 peppercorns, and 1 tablespoon butter. Tie the ducks (page 342). Prick the skin on the breast and thighs so the fat can run out. Place the ducks on a rack in a shallow roasting pan. Brush the breasts with some juice from the canned pineapple and the melted butter. Pour ¼ cup wine and 2 tablespoons water around the roasting pan. Roast the ducks 2 hours, basting every 15 minutes. Each time you baste, add about 2 tablespoons each of wine and water to the pan. After each basting, brush the breasts of the ducks again with pineapple juice and melted butter. After the ducks have been in the oven about 45 minutes, turn them over on their breasts. After another 30 minutes,

CANETON
AUX ANANAS

Roast Duckling
with Pineapple

turn them back breast side up. About 10 minutes before the roasting is finished, spread the apricot jam on the breasts.

PINEAPPLE SAUCE. Heat 2 tablespoons butter in a small heavy pan. When it is brown, put in the duck livers and brown them on both sides. Heat the brandy in a separate little pan, ignite, and pour it over the livers. Remove the livers from the pan. Add another tablespoon of butter to the pan with the chopped garlic and cubed pineapple. Cook over low heat 2 to 3 minutes, until the pineapple is a little brown. Off the heat, stir in the tomato paste, meat glaze, and potato flour. Add the chicken stock, pineapple juice, Marsala wine, white wine, apricot jam, and a little pepper. Stir the sauce over low heat until it comes to a boil. Return the livers to the pan, and simmer gently 30 minutes.

SAUTÉED FRESH PINEAPPLE SLICES. Dry the fresh pineapple slices on paper towels. Dust lightly with flour. Heat the butter in a frypan. When it is foaming, put in the pineapple slices and get them golden brown on each side. Then sprinkle them with a little granulated sugar, to glaze, and continue browning another 2 to 3 minutes.

When the ducks have finished roasting, put them on a cutting board, remove the string, and carve them into serving pieces (page 343). Arrange the pieces on a serving platter. Cover with the slices of fresh pineapple, slightly overlapping. Spoon the sauce over them. Garnish with the prepared potato rosettes. (This platter may be warmed briefly in a low oven.) NET: 4 to 6 servings.

CANETON FARCI

*Roast Boned Duckling
with Sausage and
Veal Forcemeat*

*1 4-pound whole dressed duck
4 tablespoons Cognac or good
   brandy
1 pound sausage meat
4 ounces ground veal
1 egg
1 tablespoon sour cream
Salt
Freshly cracked black pepper
1 teaspoon sage
¼ teaspoon thyme
Liver of the duck
¼ cup shelled blanched*

*   pistachio nuts
2 tablespoons melted salt butter
⅔ cup dry red wine
Bunch of crisp, fresh watercress*

DEMI-GLACE SAUCE
*2 tablespoons salt butter
2 teaspoons potato flour
2 teaspoons meat glaze
1 teaspoon tomato paste
½ cup dry red wine
1¼ cups chicken stock (page
   35)*

Bone the duck carefully (page 344). Spread the boned duck out on a cutting board, flesh side up. Brush it with brandy. Preheat the oven to 375°.

FORCEMEAT FILLING. Put in a mixer bowl the sausage meat, veal, egg, sour cream, and 2 tablespoons brandy. Mix well, and season with salt, pepper, sage, and thyme. Spread the mixture on the duck. Lay the liver in the middle of the filling. Sprinkle with the pistachio nuts. Roll up the duck and sew up the back seam with strong kitchen thread. Brush the duck with the melted butter, place it on a rack in a roasting pan, and pour the wine into the pan. Roast the duck 1 hour, basting it frequently with water or more wine. Occasionally rub the top with an ice cube to keep the fat from coming out.

DEMI-GLACE SAUCE. Melt the butter in a saucepan. Off the heat, stir in the potato flour, meat glaze, and tomato paste. Pour on the wine and the chicken stock. Stir the sauce over low heat until it comes to a boil. Simmer 10 minutes.

When the duck has finished roasting, remove it from the pan and let it stand a moment, then pull out the thread from the back. Cut enough slices of duck for one serving and arrange them, overlapping, at one end of a hot flat serving dish. Put the uncut piece of duck at the other end. Spoon the sauce over the duck. Garnish with the watercress. NET: 4 to 6 servings.

CANETON AUX FIGUES

Braised Duck with Fresh Figs on a Vegetable Macédoine

Note that the figs should be soaked in the wine 24 hours ahead of time. The dish is garnished with croûtons and served with brown sauce.

2 4-pound whole dressed ducks
Salt
Freshly cracked black pepper
2 small oranges, cut in quarters
2 small onions, cut in quarters
1 garlic clove, cut in half
8 tablespoons melted salt butter
2½ cups chicken stock (page 35)
8 tablespoons salt butter
1 cup mixed sliced onion, carrot, celery, and leek
4 tablespoons all-purpose flour
2 teaspoons tomato paste
2 teaspoons meat glaze

½ cup mushroom pieces (stems, trimmings)
1 very ripe tomato, cut in eighths
12 green figs and 12 black figs (fresh, if possible), soaked 24 hours in 3 cups dry white wine
½ cup Cognac or good brandy
1 black truffle, finely chopped
2 cups each of diced raw green beans, carrots, and turnips
12 diagonal croûtons, fried in butter (page 69)

Preheat the oven to 375°. Wash the ducks inside and out and dry them thoroughly with paper towels. Season the cavities with salt and pepper, and stuff them with the orange and onion quarters and a half clove of garlic each. Tie the ducks (page 342), rub them with salt and pepper, place them on a rack in a roasting pan, and brush them with melted butter. Prick the skin in a few places on the breast and sides to release the fat. Pour about ½ cup chicken stock in the pan. Roast the ducks 20 minutes, then add a little water to the pan, baste the ducks, brush with a little more melted butter, reduce the oven to 350°, and continue roasting 30 minutes more. Remove them from the pan and let them cool a little. Leave the oven on.

BROWN SAUCE. Melt the butter in a small heavy pan. Add the mixed sliced vegetables, and cook over low heat 3 to 4 minutes. Do not brown the vegetables. Off the heat, add the flour, and continue to stir over low heat until the flour becomes nut-brown. Off the heat, stir in the tomato paste, meat glaze, mushroom pieces, and tomato sections. Pour in the chicken stock and stir over low heat until the sauce comes to a boil. Drain the figs from the wine in which they have been soaking. Cut them into quarters and set them aside. Strain the wine and add it to the sauce. Bring to a boil again, reduce the heat, and cook the sauce down to a creamy consistency.

Cut the legs off the ducks, cut them into drumsticks and thighs, and place the 8 pieces in a large heavy casserole. Arrange the quartered figs on the legs. Cut off the breast meat, keeping each side in one piece. Then cut the breasts into thin slices lengthwise. Arrange the slices, overlapping, on the layer of figs. In a separate little pan, heat the brandy, ignite, and pour it over the duck. Strain the brown sauce, add the chopped truffle to it, and pour the sauce over the duck. Cover the pan with wax paper and the lid. Cook it in the preheated 350° oven 30 to 45 minutes. Put the diced green beans, carrots, and turnips in a pan and cover them with salted water. Bring to a boil and drain immediately. Put a little melted butter in a heavy pan and add the blanched vegetables. Cover them with wax paper and the lid and cook in the 350° oven 15 minutes. When cooked, season with a little salt and pepper.

To serve, pile the diced vegetables in the center of a hot flat serving dish. Arrange the leg pieces of the duck on the vegetables. Around the edge spread a layer of the figs, and on them arrange the breast slices. Spoon the sauce over the duck. Surround the dish with the fried croûtons. NET: 6 to 8 servings.

CANETON À LA MONTMORENCY

Roast Duckling with Black Cherries and Cork-Shaped Potatoes

Pineapple may be substituted for the cherries and juice.

1 4-pound whole dressed duck
Salt
Freshly cracked white pepper
1 garlic clove
1 or 2 whole peaches, fresh or canned
2 tablespoons melted salt butter
⅔ cup dry red wine

CHERRY SAUCE
Liver, heart, and gizzard of the duck
2 tablespoons salt butter
1 teaspoon finely chopped garlic
1 onion, finely chopped
2 teaspoons potato flour
1 teaspoon meat glaze
1 teaspoon tomato paste
1 cup pitted black cherries

(canned is fine)
½ cup canned black cherry juice
¾ cup chicken stock (page 35)
¼ cup dry sherry
1 tablespoon red currant jelly
2 teaspoons sweet butter

DEEP-FRIED CORK-SHAPED POTATOES
2 large Idaho-type potatoes, peeled and cut in quarters
Salt
1 egg
4 tablespoons salt butter
A few grains cayenne pepper
A few grains freshly grated nutmeg
1 egg, beaten (for coating)

Dry breadcrumbs (for coating,   *Vegetable oil for deep-fryer*
  page 69)

Preheat the oven to 375°. Wash the duck inside and out and dry it with paper towels. Season the cavity with salt, pepper, and the garlic clove. Stuff it with the peaches, and tie it (page 342). Place the duck on a rack in a roasting pan and brush the breast with melted butter. Prick the breast and sides in a few places to release the fat as it cooks. Roast the duck 45 minutes, frequently pouring a little red wine into the pan and basting the bird with it. When the duck has finished roasting, let it rest out of the oven a few minutes, then carve it (page 343), and arrange it on a hot serving dish.

CHERRY SAUCE. Heat the salt butter in a small heavy pan. Brown the liver, heart, and gizzard quickly in the hot butter. Remove them from the pan, reduce the heat, and add the chopped garlic and onion to the pan. Cook slowly 2 minutes, without browning. Off the heat, stir in the potato flour, meat glaze, and tomato paste. When the mixture is smooth, add the cherry juice, chicken stock, sherry, and jelly. Return the pan to low heat and stir until the sauce comes to a boil. Bit by bit, stir in the sweet butter, then add the cherries. Simmer gently about 3 minutes. Spoon the sauce over the duck.

CORK-SHAPED POTATOES. Put the potatoes in a pan, cover them with water, season with salt, and bring to a boil. Simmer, covered, until the potatoes are very soft. Drain, and return them to the pan a moment to dry thoroughly. Put them in a mixer and beat until smooth. Add the egg, butter, salt, cayenne pepper, and nutmeg. Spread the potato mixture on a plate and put it in the refrigerator to chill. Then, with lightly floured hands, form the mixture into cork shapes about 1 inch in diameter and 3 inches long. Brush them with beaten egg, roll in breadcrumbs, and fry in hot oil at 375° until they are a lovely golden brown.

To serve, arrange two piles of the potato croquettes at each end of the serving dish with the duck. NET: 4 servings.

This recipe differs from Caneton à l'Bigarade, in which the duck has a crispy skin. With this recipe, the skin becomes sticky and tartly orange, and the duck is moist and defatted.

1 4-pound whole dressed
  duckling
1 orange, cut in quarters
1 garlic clove, bruised
2 peppercorns
Salt
4 tablespoons melted butter
1 cup dry red or white wine
¼ cup bitter orange marmalade

ORANGE SAUCE
2 teaspoons plus 1 tablespoon
  salt butter
Liver of the duck
2 tablespoons Cognac or good
  brandy
Finely shredded rind of 2
  oranges (shredded length-
  wise)
2 teaspoons finely chopped
  garlic

CANETON À L'ORANGE

Roast Duckling with Orange Sauce and Orange Potatoes

1 teaspoon tomato paste
1 teaspoon meat glaze
2 teaspoons potato flour
¼ cup Marsala wine
¾ cup chicken stock (page 35)
¼ cup fresh orange juice
⅓ cup sweet orange marmalade
¼ cup bitter orange marmalade
Freshly cracked white pepper
1 teaspoon guava or red currant
  jelly
Skinned sections of 2 oranges

ORANGE POTATOES
2 large Idaho-type potatoes
2 teaspoons salt
3 tablespoons salt butter
Grated rind of 1 orange
2 eggs
A few grains cayenne pepper
¾ cup dry breadcrumbs (for
  coating, page 69)
Vegetable oil for deep-fryer

Preheat the oven to 375°. Dry the duck inside and out with paper towels. Insert the quartered orange in the cavity with the garlic clove, peppercorns, and a little salt. Tie the duck (page 342). Place it on a rack in a roasting pan, brush it with a little melted butter, prick the breast and sides in a few places to release the fat while roasting, and pour a little wine into the pan. Roast the duck 1 hour and 50 minutes. Every 20 minutes, put about 4 tablespoons mixed wine and water into the pan, then baste the duck with the liquid in the pan. Once or twice brush the breast of the duck with a little more melted butter, and prick the skin again. After the duck has cooked 40 minutes, turn it over on its breast. After the next 20 minutes turn it back breast side up. Ten minutes before the duck has finished roasting, spread the bitter marmalade all over the breast.

ORANGE SAUCE. Heat (very hot) 2 teaspoons butter in a small heavy pan, and brown the liver in it on both sides. Heat the brandy in a little pan, ignite, and pour it over the liver. Remove the liver, and add to the pan 1 tablespoon butter. When it is melted, add the orange rind and garlic. Cook 2 minutes over very low heat, without browning. Off the heat, stir in the tomato paste, meat glaze, and potato flour. When the mixture is smooth, mix in the Marsala wine, chicken stock, orange juice, and the two marmalades. Add a little freshly cracked pepper (but no salt) and the jelly. Stir the sauce over low heat until it comes to a boil, then slice the liver and return it to the sauce. Simmer gently about 30 minutes. Then add the orange sections (do not cook them; they should be kept whole).

ORANGE POTATOES. Peel the potatoes, cut into quarters and put them in a pan. Cover them with salted cold water and bring to a boil. Simmer until they are very soft. Drain, return them to the pan to dry, then put them in a mixer bowl and beat until smooth. Add the butter, orange rind, 1 egg, salt, and cayenne pepper. Beat well. Form the mixture into cork shapes on a lightly floured board. Beat the remaining egg, brush the potatoes with it, and roll them in breadcrumbs. Heat the oil to 375°, and deep-fry the potatoes until golden brown.

When the duck is roasted, remove the string and carve the duck into serving pieces (page 343). Arrange on an au gratin or serving dish. Spoon the orange sauce over the duck, and arrange a pile of orange potatoes at each end of the dish. Serve at once. NET: 4 servings.

With all due respect to Aylesbury and Peking, the finest ducks in the world come from Rouen; and any duck recipe which is marked "à la Rouennaise" is well worth trying.

CANETON À LA ROUENNAISE

Roast Boned Duck Stuffed with Veal Mousse, with Soufflé Potatoes

1 4-pound whole dressed duck
Salt
Freshly cracked black pepper
6-ounce piece of boiled ham
4-ounce piece of cooked tongue
2 black truffles, cut in quarters
6 tablespoons melted salt butter
½ cup Marsala wine
About 1 cup water
¼ cup Cognac or good brandy
¼ cup cream sherry
Bunch of crisp fresh watercress

VEAL MOUSSE
¾ pound finely ground veal
4 slices white bread
2 egg whites
1 cup light cream

2 teaspoons salt
Freshly cracked black pepper

SAUCE
3 to 4 tablespoons ice water
1 teaspoon tomato paste
1 teaspoon meat glaze
2 teaspoons potato flour
1½ cups chicken stock (page 35)
½ cup dry white wine
1 tablespoon red currant jelly

SOUFFLÉ POTATOES
4 Idaho-type potatoes
Vegetable oil for deep-fryer
Salt

Dry the duck inside and out with paper towels, and bone it (page 344). Spread the boned duck on a cutting board, flesh side up. Season with salt and freshly cracked black pepper. Preheat the oven to 375°.

VEAL MOUSSE. Put the ground veal through a fine meat chopper. Soak the bread in a little water until it is quite soft and squeeze it dry in a cloth. Add the bread to the ground veal and put the mixture through the meat chopper, then into a mixer bowl and beat in the egg whites, and then into a metal bowl and put it over a bowl of ice. Gradually beat in the light cream. Season with the salt and a little pepper. (This mousse must be of firm consistency.)

Spread the mousse on the duck, leaving a margin of ½ inch all the way around. Cut the ham and tongue into ¼-inch strips. Arrange these strips in rows on the veal mousse. Between the strips of ham and tongue, place the quartered truffles. Fold the duck over and sew the back seam with strong white thread. Rub the duck all over with salt and pepper. Place it on a rack in a roasting pan. Brush the skin with melted butter. Pour the Marsala wine and ½ cup water into the pan. Roast the duck 20 minutes, then remove it from the oven. In a separate little pan, heat the brandy, ignite, and pour it over the duck. Reduce the oven to 350° and roast the duck about 1 hour, or until the duck is soft to the touch. Baste frequently, each time adding about 1 tablespoon cold water. Also, each time you baste, brush the duck with a little more melted butter. When it has finished roasting, remove it from the pan and let it stand a little while.

SAUCE. Skim the fat from the juices in the roasting pan, and place the pan over low heat. When the liquid is hot, stir in the ice water to lift off the glaze. Pour the sauce into a small saucepan. Off the heat, stir in the tomato paste, meat glaze, and potato flour. Add the chicken stock, wine, and jelly. Stir over low heat until the sauce comes to a boil. Simmer gently 10 minutes, then strain.

SOUFFLÉ POTATOES. Peel the potatoes. Cut them into thin, even slices lengthwise, about ¼ inch thick, with a potato slicer or mandoline. Soak the potatoes in ice water 15 minutes. Drain, and dry thoroughly in a cloth. Have ready vegetable oil at 350° in the deep-fryer. Cook a few slices at a time in the deep fat until nearly soft, without browning them. Remove them from the fat and dry thoroughly on paper towels. Allow the semicooked potatoes to get quite cold. (Up to this point they can be prepared ahead of time.) When ready to serve, heat the oil in the deep-fryer to 450°. Plunge a few slices of potato into the hot oil. When they have blown up and are brown all over, drain them on paper towels. Sprinkle them with a little salt before serving. Cook them all the same way, a few slices at a time.

To serve the duck, pull out the thread from the back, and cut the duck into as many slices as required for one serving. Arrange the slices, overlapping, at one end of a hot flat serving dish. Place the uncut piece of duck at the other end. Spoon the sauce over the duck. Garnish with crisp fresh watercress and the soufflé potatoes. NET: 4 to 6 servings.

POMPADOUR DE CANETON À LA MIRABEAU

Duckling with Olives

This is a handsome presentation. A charlotte mold is lined with olives stuffed with mousse of sweetbreads and veal. (The olives are split to show the outline of olive and mousse.) The center of the mold is filled with boned duck. When cooked and turned out on a serving dish, it looks like a mosaic.

4 cups large pitted green olives
1 pair sweetbreads
1¼ cups chicken stock
   (page 35)
1 pound finely ground veal
4 slices white bread, crusts
   removed
¼ cup dry white wine
2 egg whites
1½ cups light cream
Salt

Freshly cracked black pepper
4 tablespoons salt butter
1 4-pound whole dressed duck
4 tablespoons Cognac or good
   brandy
1 teaspoon tomato paste
2 teaspoons meat glaze
2 teaspoons potato flour
½ cup port wine
2 tablespoons red currant jelly

Put the sweetbreads in a little pan, cover with some of the chicken stock, and simmer 10 to 12 minutes. Drain (reserving the stock), and cool, then skin them, and add them to the ground veal. Soak the bread

in the dry white wine, squeeze dry, and add it to the sweetbreads and
veal. Put the combined mixture through a fine meat chopper two times,
then put it in a mixer bowl and beat in the egg whites. Gradually add
the light cream, beating all the time. Season well with salt and pepper.
Put a little of the mousse into a pastry bag fitted with a small round
tube. Fill all the olives with the mousse. Have ready a pan of simmering
salted water, throw in the filled olives, and poach them 4 minutes.
Remove the olives with a slotted spoon. Cut them in half and line a
plain, well-buttered deep mold (like a charlotte). Then immediately
cover the back of the olives with some of the mousse mixture. (Reserve
a little mousse for the top.) There will be a well in the center of the
mold. Put the mold in the refrigerator to set.

Preheat the oven to 375°. Wipe the duck inside and out with paper
towels, and tie it (page 342). Heat the butter in a deep heavy pan.
When it is golden brown, quickly brown the duck in it, on all sides.
Heat the brandy in a little pan, ignite, and pour it over the duck. Remove the duck from the pan and remove the string. Cut off the legs
and cut each into two pieces. Cut out the breast meat and cut each side
into long slices. Add the tomato paste, meat glaze, and potato flour to
the pan in which the duck was browned. Stir until smooth, then stir in
the port wine, chicken stock, and jelly. Stir over low heat until the
sauce comes to a boil. Strain, and return it to the pan with the pieces
of duck. Cover the pan and cook the duck in the oven 40 minutes.

Remove the bones from the legs, thighs, and breast, and fill the
well in the mold with the pieces of duck. Moisten with a little sauce,
and cover with the reserved veal mousse. Cover the mold with
buttered wax paper and put it in a shallow roasting pan half filled
with hot water. Reduce the oven heat to 350° and bake the mold (in
the pan) 20 to 25 minutes. Let it stand 5 minutes after taking it out
of the oven. Then turn it out on a flat serving dish. Reheat the sauce,
strain, and spoon it over the mold. Serve at once. NET: 4 to 6 servings.

A delicious way to use extra cooked duck, chicken, or turkey.

QUENELLES DE CANETON AUX NOUILLES

*Duck Dumplings
with Noodles*

6 tablespoons salt butter
1½ tablespoons finely chopped
 onion
1 teaspoon each of finely
 chopped fresh parsley and
 chives
1 tablespoon finely chopped
 green pepper
1½ cups chopped cooked duck
 meat
½ cup finely chopped cooked
 lean ham

½ cup soft white breadcrumbs
½ teaspoon marjoram
1 teaspoon salt
Freshly cracked black pepper
1 egg
4 cups chicken stock (page 35)
3 cups cooked egg noodles,
 mixed with melted butter
 and a little chopped fresh
 parsley and paprika, and
 kept warm

Heat the butter in a deep heavy pan. Add the onion, parsley, chives, and green pepper. Cook 3 to 4 minutes over very low heat, stirring constantly so that the vegetables do not brown. Add the duck meat, ham, breadcrumbs, marjoram, salt, and pepper. Mix well, and remove the pan from the heat. Beat the egg slightly, blend it into the duck mixture, and shape the mixture into 1-inch balls. Bring the chicken stock to a boil in a moderately deep pan. Reduce it to a gentle simmer and drop in the duck dumplings. Simmer them 10 minutes. Drain with a slotted spoon. Spread the hot noodles on a buttered au gratin dish, arrange the dumplings on the noodles, and serve at once. NET: 4 servings.

OIE À L'ALSACIENNE

Roast Goose Stuffed with Sausage Meat, on Sauerkraut

The sauerkraut is mixed with fried apple, and the dish is also garnished with bacon, sausages, and steamed new potatoes.

1 whole dressed goose, about 7 pounds
Salt
Freshly cracked black pepper
4 cups finely chopped onion, sautéed in butter until translucent
2½ pounds sausage meat
1 cup applesauce (canned or fresh)
Liver of the goose, finely chopped
1 teaspoon ground sage

¼ cup Cognac or Calvados
4 tablespoons melted salt butter (or more as needed)
8 thick slices Canadian bacon
4 cups sauerkraut, drained
2 teaspoons caraway seed
2 large apples, skinned, cored, and quartered
24 baby potatoes
2 teaspoons finely chopped fresh parsley
3 ounces small Italian sausages

Wash the goose well and dry it thoroughly, inside and out. Trim off the extra fat and reserve it. Season the cavity with salt and pepper. Preheat the oven to 375°. In a large bowl, combine the onion, sausage meat, applesauce, liver, sage, salt, pepper, and half the Cognac or Calvados. Mix very well. Stuff the goose with this mixture and tie it (page 342). Place it on a rack in a roasting pan. Rub the top with a little salt and pepper and brush with melted butter. Pour the rest of the Cognac or Calvados in the pan with a little water. Roast the goose 15 to 20 minutes per pound (about 2¼ hours). Baste it frequently, each time adding 1 to 2 tablespoons water to the pan.

While the goose is roasting, prepare the garniture. Broil the Canadian bacon and Italian sausages on a broiler rack to catch the fat. Put the sauerkraut in a heavy casserole. Add the fat from the bacon and sausage to the sauerkraut. Season the sauerkraut with a little salt, pepper, and caraway seed. Heat a little of the goose fat in a frypan, sauté the apple sections, and add them to the sauerkraut. Cover the sauerkraut with wax paper and the lid and bake in the oven 40 minutes. Peel the baby potatoes and cut them into even slices. Steam them until they are just soft, and sprinkle with chopped parsley.

To serve, arrange the sauerkraut on the bottom of a large hot serving dish. Place the whole goose on it. Garnish the dish with the broiled sausages, bacon slices, and sliced potatoes. For the sauce, skim off the fat from the juices in the roasting pan. Add approximately 1 cup cold water to the pan and bring to a boil over high heat. Stir and scrape up the glaze as it cooks. Strain, pour a little over the goose, and serve the rest in a sauceboat. NET: 8 to 10 servings.

BAKED AVOCADOS STUFFED WITH TURKEY, GRATINÉE

4 avocados, not too soft and
   ripe
Salt
4 tablespoons salt butter
4 tablespoons all-purpose flour
1 cup chicken stock (page 35)
1 cup light cream

Freshly cracked white pepper
2 cups diced cooked turkey
¾ cup freshly grated Parmesan
   cheese
1 teaspoon paprika
1 bunch crisp fresh watercress

Preheat the oven to 350°. Cut the avocados in half lengthwise, with the peel on, and remove the large pits. Sprinkle them lightly with salt, and set aside. Melt the butter in a medium-size heavy pan. Off the heat, stir in the flour. Add the chicken stock and light cream and stir over low heat until the mixture comes to a boil. Season with salt and pepper. Add the diced cooked turkey and ¼ cup grated cheese. Mix well, and fill the avocado pears with the mixture, spreading it over the entire top and doming it up in the center. Sprinkle with the remaining ½ cup grated cheese and paprika. Place the stuffed avocados on a baking sheet and bake 15 minutes. If the tops are not lightly browned, finish off with 1 to 2 minutes under the broiler. Arrange the stuffed avocados on a hot serving dish and garnish with watercress. NET: 8 servings.

DINDONNEAU EN DEMI-DEUIL

Roast Turkey in Half-Mourning

Like the chicken versions, this delectable turkey achieves its demi-deuil effect through slices of black truffle slipped under the skin. It is a handsome presentation, with a garnish of artichoke bottoms topped with rosettes of chestnut purée. For the drumsticks, you will need two paper frills.

1 small squab turkey, not more
   than 8 pounds, whole and
   dressed
Salt
Freshly cracked white pepper
About 14 to 16 tablespoons cool
   melted salt butter
2 large black truffles
1½ cups dry vermouth
10 artichoke bottoms

1¼ cups unsweetened chestnut
   purée
3 tablespoons freshly grated
   Parmesan cheese

STUFFING
½ pound finely ground veal
3 slices white bread, crusts
   removed, soaked in ½ cup
   milk

2 egg whites
1 cup light cream
¾ cup unsweetened chestnut
   purée

2 pounds pork sausage meat
2 tablespoons each of finely
   chopped onion and parsley

Wash and dry the turkey with paper towels. Season the cavity with salt and pepper and brush the inside completely with melted butter. Preheat the oven to 375°.

STUFFING. Put the ground veal twice through a fine meat chopper with the soaked bread, which has been squeezed dry. Transfer to a mixer bowl and beat in the egg whites. Beat in the light cream very gradually. Season well with salt and pepper. Mix in the chestnut purée and sausage meat. Finally, mix in the chopped onion and parsley. Set the stuffing aside.

Cut the truffles into thin slices. Carefully loosen the skin on the turkey without breaking it. Slip the slices of truffle between the skin and the flesh — on the drumsticks, thighs, a row up each side of the breast. Then pull the skin back in place and stuff the turkey. Cover the cavity opening with the flaps and fasten it with small skewers. Tie the turkey (page 342). Place it on a rack in a roasting pan. Pour 2 to 3 tablespoons vermouth in the pan. Brush the top of the turkey with melted butter. Insert a meat thermometer in the turkey to check when it is finished cooking. Roast the turkey 20 to 25 minutes per pound. After it has cooked about 1½ hours, reduce the heat to 350°. Baste frequently, adding a little vermouth to the pan each time you baste. If the top of the turkey browns too quickly, cover it with aluminum foil.

When the turkey has finished roasting, place it on a large serving platter. Remove the string and thread, and rub the skin with a little more melted butter. Cut the knobs off the drumsticks and cover the ends with paper frills. Transfer the roasting pan with its juices to the top of the stove. Add to it ½ cup vermouth and a little water. Bring to a boil and stir to pick up the glaze off the bottom of the pan. Strain the sauce, pour a little of it over the turkey, and serve the rest separately in a sauceboat. To garnish, gently warm the artichoke bottoms in a little butter. Put the chestnut purée in the mixer bowl and beat to a cream with 4 tablespoons melted butter, salt, and pepper. Put this mixture into a pastry bag with a #8 or #9 star tube. Pipe a rosette of chestnut purée on top of each artichoke bottom. Sprinkle the rosettes with a little grated cheese and a little melted butter, and brown under the broiler just before serving. Arrange them around the turkey on the platter. NET: 8 to 10 servings.

DINDONNEAU
À LA DIABLE

*Cooked Breast of
Turkey Broiled with
Deviled Sauce*

4 large neat slices cooked breast
   of turkey
2 tablespoons melted salt butter
¾ cup dry breadcrumbs
   (page 69)

½ teaspoon dry mustard
Salt
A few grains cayenne pepper
½ teaspoon curry powder
Bunch of crisp fresh parsley or

watercress for garnish

SAUCE À LA DIABLE
2 shallots or 1 small white
  onion, finely chopped
½ cup wine vinegar
8 black peppercorns, coarsely
cracked
½ teaspoon dry mustard
1 bay leaf
Salt
½ teaspoon paprika
1 cup Brown Sauce (page 38)
  or use leftover turkey gravy

Brush the slices of turkey breast with the melted butter. In a little bowl, mix the breadcrumbs, mustard, salt, cayenne pepper, and curry powder. Coat the turkey slices evenly with this mixture. Place them on a rack on a broiler pan, and broil until nicely browned on both sides. Either use a low flame or have the turkey 3 to 4 inches away from the flame so that it will brown slowly.

SAUCE À LA DIABLE. Combine in a little pan the chopped shallots or onion, vinegar, peppercorns, mustard, bay leaf, salt, and paprika, and blend well. Simmer over low heat until the mixture is reduced to half quantity, then strain it into the brown sauce or turkey gravy. Cook until the sauce is thoroughly heated. To serve, arrange the turkey slices slightly overlapping on a hot serving dish. Garnish with the parsley or watercress. Serve the sauce in a separate bowl. NET: 4 servings.

The stuffing is veal mousse encased in sausage forcemeat, with a center of chicken livers in egg whites wrapped in slices of ham, tongue, and liver sausage, and a scattering of pistachio nuts.

DINDONNEAU FARCI À L'ÉCU DE FRANCE

Roast Boned Turkey
with De Luxe Stuffing
and Brown Sauce

1 whole dressed turkey, 8 to 10
  pounds
2 pounds sausage meat
3 egg whites
1 cup sour cream
2 tablespoons chopped mixed
  herbs (such as parsley,
  tarragon, shallot)
Salt
Freshly cracked white pepper
½ pound thinly sliced boiled
  ham
½ pound thinly sliced cooked
  tongue
A few thin slices liver sausage
3 hard-boiled eggs
3 chicken livers

1 cup dry white wine
½ pound sliced bacon
Optional: A few shelled
  blanched pistachio nuts
Brown Sauce (page 38)

VEAL MOUSSE
1 pound ground veal
2 egg whites
1¼ cups light cream
1 teaspoon salt
Freshly cracked white pepper

GARNISH
Any vegetable in season, plain-
  cooked or steamed

Wash and dry the turkey inside and out with paper towels. Completely bone it (page 344). Spread the boned turkey, skin side down, on the working surface.

Preheat the oven to 375°. Mix the sausage meat, egg whites, sour cream, mixed herbs, salt, and pepper in a mixer bowl. Spread this on the turkey.

VEAL MOUSSE. Put the ground veal in the mixer bowl. Add the egg whites, mix well, and rub the mixture through a strainer. Place the strained mixture in a tin-lined saucepan over a bowl of ice. With a small wire whisk, slowly beat in the light cream. Add the salt and pepper.

Spread the veal mousse over the sausage mixture, and cover the mousse with the slices of ham, tongue, and liver sausage. Remove the yolk from each hard-boiled egg and insert in its place a small piece of raw chicken liver. Place the reassembled eggs in a row down the middle of the spread turkey. Scatter the pistachio nuts over the surface. Roll the boned turkey with its stuffing carefully, and sew the back seam with fine thread. Reshape the bird a little. Cover the top (breast) with overlapping slices of bacon. Tie each piece of bacon down with string. Place the bird on a rack in a roasting pan, and roast about 15 minutes per pound. Baste with a little white wine and water every 20 minutes. To serve, remove the strings. Carefully cut enough slices for one serving and arrange them slightly overlapping on a serving platter, so that the design in the stuffing is beautifully displayed. Put the uncut part of the turkey at one end of the platter. Garnish with the vegetables. Serve the brown sauce separately in a sauceboat. NET: 12 to 14 servings.

DINDONNEAU AU GRATIN

Cooked Turkey in Meat Sauce with Lasagna au Gratin

1 package lasagne pasta
2 tablespoons vegetable oil
3 cups cooked turkey
3 cups Sauce Bouchère (meat

sauce, page 47)
1 cup freshly grated Parmesan cheese
4 tablespoons melted salt butter

Cook the lasagne 12 minutes in an ample amount of boiling salted water. Put the vegetable oil in the water also; it keeps the pasta from sticking together. Drain the lasagne and dry with paper towels. Line an au gratin dish with some of the strips of cooked lasagne. Mix the cooked turkey with the Sauce Bouchère. Put alternating layers of sauce and lasagne on the au gratin dish until the dish is full. End with a layer of lasagne on top. Spoon a little of the meat sauce over it. Sprinkle with ½ cup grated cheese and melted butter and brown under the broiler. Serve the rest of the grated cheese in a separate bowl. NET: 4 servings.

DINDONNEAU RÔTI FARCI

Roast Turkey with Chestnut, Sausage, and Veal Stuffing

1 whole dressed turkey, 12 to 15 pounds
Salt
Freshly cracked white pepper
About 6 tablespoons sweet

butter
1 large slice or 2 thin slices of fresh fatback (enough to cover the turkey breast)
About 6 tablespoons cool melted

butter
1 cup dry Madeira wine (Sercial)
8 coarsely cracked black
   peppercorns
Bouquet garni, including parsley
   and celery leaf
2 teaspoons potato flour
1½ cups chicken stock
   (page 35)
1 or 2 bunches crisp fresh
   watercress

(page 589)
1 pound sausage meat
2½ pounds finely ground veal
1 cup dry breadcrumbs fried in
   butter (page 69)
2 teaspoons dried thyme
½ cup Cognac or good brandy
2 eggs
½ cup sour cream
Salt
Freshly cracked black pepper

STUFFING
2 1-pound cans skinned cooked
   unsweetened chestnuts, or
   cook and skin raw chestnuts

SUGGESTED GARNISH
Roast potatoes (page 610)
Corn fritters (page 590)

Preheat the oven to 500°. Wash the turkey and wipe it dry, inside and out, with paper towels. Season the inside with salt and pepper. Loosen the skin over the breast and legs and insert tiny bits of the sweet butter under the skin.

STUFFING. Mix all the ingredients in a large bowl.

Stuff the turkey and sew the flaps closed or use small skewers. Tie the turkey (page 342). Cover the breast with the fatback and tie it down. Place the turkey on a rack on a roasting pan breast side down. Brush the back of the bird with some of the melted butter. Put a meat thermometer in the bird to check when it is cooked. Allow about 20 minutes per pound. Roast 20 minutes in the oven, then reduce the temperature to 375° and add to the roasting pan the Madeira wine, peppercorns, a little salt, and the bouquet garni. Leave the turkey breast side down and continue to roast, basting frequently with the drippings and the wine. (If necessary, add more wine, mixed with an equal part of water.) After 1 hour of roasting (including the starting period at 500°), brush the bird all over with melted butter, and continue roasting. About 1 hour before the roasting time is up, remove the fatback and string, remove the rack in the roasting pan, and place the turkey breast side up directly on the pan. Continue to roast uncovered, so that the skin will be crisp and brown, and continue to baste frequently.

When the turkey has finished cooking, remove the roasting pan from the oven, turn off the heat, and leave the oven door open. Remove the string and thread or skewers, transfer the turkey to a hot serving platter, and place it in the open oven 15 to 20 minutes (to ease the job of carving and to allow the flavors to mingle.) Skim most of the fat from the liquid in the roasting pan, and strain. Place the pan on top of the stove. Off the heat, stir in the potato flour. Add the chicken stock, and mix well. Stir the sauce over low heat until it comes to a boil. Adjust the seasoning and serve separately in a sauceboat. Garnish the turkey platter with bunches of crisp fresh watercress and the potatoes or corn fritters. NET: 14 to 16 servings.

TURKEY TURNOVERS

Cooked Turkey with Fresh Herbs, Baked in Pastry

A compendium of my class recipes would not be complete without Turkey Turnovers. Incidental to the cooking lessons, the question of what to do with all the leftover turkey was perennially addressed to me during the Thanksgiving and Christmas holiday period, and Turkey Turnovers seemed to please. Yet I shall never understand why we must have such big turkeys to begin with. If there is to be a family reunion, why not have one or two small turkeys?

1½ cups chopped cooked turkey
   (white and/or dark meat)
1 tablespoon finely chopped
   fresh parsley
1 tablespoon chopped fresh
   chives
1 tablespoon finely chopped
   baby white onion
1 tablespoon chopped green
   pepper

½ cup turkey gravy
2 tablespoons dry sherry
1 egg yolk
2 tablespoons heavy cream

PASTRY
1 cup all-purpose flour
¼ teaspoon salt
6 tablespoons sweet butter
⅓ to ½ cup ice water

Mix the turkey, parsley, chives, onion, and green pepper with the turkey gravy. Add the sherry and season well to taste. Preheat the oven to 375°.

PASTRY. Sift the flour and salt into a bowl. Cut the butter into the flour and rub the mixture with the finger tips until it resembles coarse cornmeal. Add just enough ice water (the least possible) to work the ingredients up quickly to a firm dough.

On a lightly floured board, roll the dough out very thin, about ⅛ inch thick, and cut into 4-inch squares. Put 1 tablespoon of the prepared turkey filling on each square. Fold the dough over the filling, into a triangle shape. Brush the edges with a little water and seal them securely. Beat the egg yolk with the heavy cream and use it to brush the tops of the turnovers. Set them on an ungreased baking sheet and bake about 15 minutes, or until they are a golden brown. To serve, pile the freshly baked turnovers on a hot folded napkin on a warm serving plate and serve immediately. NET: 4 servings.

GAME FOWL

CANARD SAUVAGE GRANDMÈRE

Roast Wild Duck with Port Wine Sauce, Juniper Berries, and Croûtons

1 or 2 whole dressed wild ducks
   (depending on size and any
   damaged areas)
A little lemon juice
8 tablespoons salt butter
2 peaches (fresh or canned)
Salt
Freshly cracked black pepper
Enough sliced fatback to cover

the breasts of the ducks
½ cup Cognac or good brandy
Liver(s) of the duck or 2 chicken
   livers
½ cup soft white breadcrumbs
½ teaspoon meat glaze dissolved
   in 1 cup chicken stock
   (page 35)
½ cup port wine

½ cup finely chopped shallots
2 white part of leeks, finely
    chopped
1 stalk celery, finely chopped
1 carrot, finely chopped
4 firm white mushrooms, finely
    chopped
6 dried juniper berries, crushed

with a mortar and pestle
1 tablespoon black raspberry
    jam
1 cup heavy cream
Juice of 1 lime
8 diagonal croûtons, fried in
    butter (page 69)

Preheat the oven to 375°. Clean the ducks. Wash them in lemon juice and water and dry thoroughly inside and out. In the cavity of each put 1 tablespoon butter, 1 whole peach with the stone in it (if possible) and salt and pepper. Tie the ducks (page 342), and cover the breasts with slices of fatback. Put them on a rack in a roasting pan. Pour a little water and brandy into the pan. Roast the ducks 15 minutes per pound. Baste frequently, each time adding a little more brandy and water.

SAUCE. Chop the raw livers and mix them with the breadcrumbs (do this with a pestle and mortar to achieve a paste). Put this mixture in a pan with the chicken stock and stir until the liquid boils. Add the port wine. Simmer gently 5 minutes. Rub the sauce through a fine sieve. Melt 6 tablespoons salt butter in a saucepan. Add the finely chopped shallots, leeks, celery, carrot, and mushrooms, and season with salt and pepper. Cover the pan, and cook over low heat until the vegetables are soft. Add this mixture to the previous sauce. Add the juniper berries, black raspberry jam, and heavy cream. Mix thoroughly and gently reheat. Last, add the lime juice.

When the ducks are roasted, remove the ties. Carve into serving pieces (page 343). Arrange the pieces on a shallow au gratin dish. Spoon the sauce over them. Put the dish under a very hot broiler just to glaze the top. Stick the fried croûtons around the sides of the dish. Serve at once. NET: 4 to 6 servings.

We have also used this recipe with Cornish hens, in which case use 4 birds rather than 1 whole guinea hen for 4 servings. The wild rice is mixed with mushrooms, raisins, and pine nuts. The brown sauce is enriched with sour cream.

PINTADE AU RIZ
SAUVAGE

Braised Guinea Hen
on Wild Rice with
Brown Sauce
and Truffles

1 whole dressed guinea hen, 3½
    to 4 pounds, or 4 small
    Cornish game hens
6 tablespoons salt butter
¼ cup Cognac or good brandy
1 apple, peeled, cored, and
    chopped
1 stalk celery, thinly sliced
1 small onion, thinly sliced
½ teaspoon tomato paste
1 teaspoon meat glaze

3 tablespoons all-purpose flour
1½ cups chicken stock, for
    sauce (page 35)
Salt
Freshly cracked white pepper
¾ cup large white raisins,
    soaked at least ½ hour in
    ½ cup dry white wine
1 cup wild rice
About 6 cups chicken or veal
    stock or salted water (to cover

rice)
3 firm white mushrooms, thinly
  sliced
½ cup pine nuts (pignoli nuts)

1 cup sour cream
½ cup heavy cream, whipped
2 black truffles (1 sliced and
  1 finely chopped)

Dry the guinea hen, inside and out, and tie it (page 342). Heat 2 table-spoons butter in a deep heavy pan. When it is on the point of brown-ing, put in the guinea hen and brown it all over, taking care not to break the skin. Heat the brandy in a little pan, ignite, and pour it over the guinea hen. Remove the hen from the pan and set it aside. Add another tablespoon of butter to the pan. Add the apple, celery, and onion, and cook over low heat 5 minutes. Off the heat, blend in the tomato paste, meat glaze, and flour. Add the chicken stock and stir over low heat until the mixture comes to a boil. Simmer the sauce 10 minutes, strain, and return it to the pan. Carve the guinea hen into serving pieces (page 343) and put them in the sauce, skin side down. Season with salt and pepper, cover with the lid, and cook over very low heat until the bird is tender, about 40 to 50 minutes.

While the guinea hen is cooking, prepare the rice. Drain the raisins and reserve the wine in which they were soaked. Wash the wild rice in several waters. Put it in a pan and cover it with plenty of liquid (chicken stock or salted water). Bring to a boil and simmer until the rise is tender. Sauté the sliced mushrooms in 3 tablespoons butter 4 to 5 minutes. Drain the rice when it is cooked. Mix the rice with the raisins, mushrooms, the pan juices from the mushrooms, and the pine kernels. To serve, make a bed of the wild rice on a hot flat serving dish. Arrange the pieces of guinea hen on top of the rice. Add to the sauce the wine in which the raisins were soaked, then stir in the sour cream a little at a time, using a wire whisk. Stir in the whipped cream, little by little, and the chopped truffle. Spoon this sauce over the guinea hen. Garnish the pieces of guinea hen with the sliced truffle. NET: 4 servings.

SUPRÊME DE PINTADE AU JAMBON

Sautéed Breast of
Guinea Hen and
Ham on Croûtons

This dish is very special with guinea hen, but it can also be prepared with breast of chicken. It is served with a sherry sauce and garnished with mushroom caps.

4 half (2 whole) breasts of
  guinea hen
5 tablespoons salt butter
4 slices cooked smoked ham
4 large firm white mushroom
  caps

3 tablespoons dry sherry
1½ cups heavy cream
Salt
4 large croûtons fried in butter
  (page 69)

Skin and bone the breasts of guinea hen. Heat 4 tablespoons salt butter in a deep heavy pan. When it is foaming, put in the breasts. Cover the pan, and cook the breasts over low heat about 30 minutes. Turn them once or twice while cooking so that they become tender and golden brown on both sides. When cooked, remove them from the pan and keep them warm. Put another tablespoon of butter in the pan and add the ham slices and mushroom caps. Warm them slightly in the butter and keep them warm with the guinea hen breasts.

SAUCE. Pour the sherry into the pan and bring it to a boil, stirring all the while to lift the glaze from the bottom of the pan. Add the heavy cream and a little salt, and simmer over low heat about 5 minutes.

To serve, arrange the croûtons on a serving platter. Put a slice of ham on each one. On the ham, put a breast of guinea hen. On the breast, put a whole mushroom cap. Spoon the sauce over the presentation and serve immediately, while the croûton is still crisp. NET: 4 servings.

A lovely game casserole of breast and leg sections of partridges slowly braised in cream, garnished with croûtons.

PERDREAUX À LA CAMÉLIA

Partridges Cooked in Cream

4 small partridges, dressed	½ cup Cognac or good brandy
A little lemon juice	1½ cups heavy cream
A little all-purpose flour (for dusting)	1½ cups pitted prunes
	6 large diagonal croûtons, fried in butter (page 69)
Salt	
Freshly cracked black pepper	1 tablespoon chopped fresh parsley
4 tablespoons sweet butter	

Preheat the oven to 350°. Wash the partridges very well in cold water with a little lemon juice. Dry them inside and out. Cut each partridge into 4 serving pieces. Mix a little salt and pepper with some flour. Dust the partridge pieces lightly with the seasoned flour. Heat the butter in a deep heavy pan. When it is foaming, put in the pieces of partridge. Brown them evenly and slowly on both sides. Heat the brandy in a separate little pan, ignite, and pour it over the partridges. Pour the heavy cream over them, and add more salt and pepper. Cover the pan, and let the birds cook in the oven 20 to 25 minutes. Then add the pitted prunes and cook about 5 minutes more. To serve, arrange the pieces of partridge in a casserole, surround them with the diagonal croûtons, and sprinkle with the parsley. NET: 4 servings.

The casserole is garnished with bacon, sausage, and carrots, and served with a demi-glace sauce.

PERDRIX AUX CHOUX

Casserole of Partridge with Cabbage

4 whole dressed partridges	2 small white onions, with 1 whole clove stuck in each
5 tablespoons salt butter	
½ cup Cognac or good brandy	2 carrots, pared and cut in finger-size pieces
2 small green cabbages, trimmed and cut in quarters	
	1 teaspoon finely chopped garlic
1 pound bacon, in 1 piece	1 garlic sausage, cut in 1-inch

slices
2 frankfurters, cut in 1-inch
   slices
Bouquet garni, including parsley,
   thyme, and rosemary
   (wrapped in cheesecloth)
1½ cups chicken stock
   (page 35)
½ cup dry red wine
Salt
Freshly cracked black pepper
1 tablespoon chopped fresh
   parsley

DEMI-GLACE SAUCE
2 tablespoons vegetable oil
2 tablespoons salt butter
1 onion, sliced

1 small carrot, sliced
1 small stalk celery, sliced
1 leek, sliced
4 tablespoons all-purpose flour
2 teaspoons tomato paste
1 teaspoon meat glaze
½ cup mushroom stems and
   trimmings
1 ripe tomato, cut in eighths
½ cup dry red wine (preferably
   Burgundy)
1¾ cups chicken stock
   (page 35)
2 tablespoons dry sherry
1 tablespoon red currant jelly
1 bay leaf
Freshly cracked black pepper

Preheat the oven to 375°. Wipe the partridges with paper towels and tie them (page 342). Melt 4 tablespoons butter in a deep heavy casserole. When it is foaming, put in the partridges and brown them on all sides. Heat the brandy in a separate little pan, ignite, and pour it over the partridges. Rub a little butter over the breasts of the partridges. Cover the casserole with the lid, and braise the partridges in the oven 25 to 30 minutes.

    DEMI-GLACE SAUCE. Heat the vegetable oil and butter in a deep heavy pan. Add the onion, carrot, celery, and leek. Cook over low heat, without browning, 3 minutes. Add the flour, and cook it very slowly until it is dark brown, stirring frequently. Mix in the tomato paste, meat glaze, mushroom stems and trimmings, and the tomato. Cook this mixture, still over low heat, 2 minutes. Off the heat, add the wine and chicken stock. Stir the sauce over low heat until it comes to a boil. Add the sherry, jelly, bay leaf, and a little pepper. Simmer this sauce 40 minutes. When it has cooked, strain it.

    While the sauce is cooking, put the cabbage sections in a pan, cover with cold water, and bring to a boil. Drain immediately and cut the sections into coarse shreds. Cut the pound of bacon into ½-inch cubes, put them in a pan, cover with cold water, and bring to a boil. Boil about 3 minutes, and drain. When the partridges are finished braising, remove them from the oven and lower the temperature to 350°. Put the shredded cabbage in a large heavy casserole. Make a well in the center of the cabbage and put in it the bacon cubes, onions, carrots, garlic, garlic sausage, frankfurters, and bouquet garni (wrapped in a piece of cheesecloth so that it can be removed later). Pour in the chicken stock and wine (they should be about ¾ of the way to the cabbage level). Bring to a boil on the stove, then season with a little salt and pepper, cover with the lid, and cook it in the oven 1½ to 2 hours.

    After the cabbage has braised 1 hour, put the cooked partridges in the middle of the casserole with the other ingredients. Cover the casserole again and continue braising the second hour (depending on the tenderness of the partridges). Then remove the partridges, untie them, and cut them in halves or quarters. Remove the bouquet garni. Drain the cabbage well (using a large slotted spoon) and arrange it down a shallow serving dish. Arrange the partridges on the cabbage, and decorate around the edge of the dish with the bacon cubes, sliced sausages, and carrot fingers. Sprinkle the top with the parsley. Serve the demi-glace sauce in a separate bowl. NET: 4 servings.

Partridge, snipe, and grouse may be roasted in the same manner.

FAISAN RÔTI CLASSIQUE

Classic Roast Pheasant with Fried Breadcrumbs and Soufflé Potatoes

2 croustades or 8 large croûtons (see directions below)
2 whole dressed pheasants, 2 to 3 pounds each
About 1 cup Cognac
Salt
2 sprigs fresh celery leaf
2 tablespoons salt butter
2 baby white onions or 2 shallots, cut in quarters
8 white peppercorns
About 6 tablespoons cool melted salt butter
A little all-purpose flour (to dust the breast)
2 thin slices fatback, enough to cover both pheasant breasts
About ½ cup dry sherry

GARNISHES
About 8 tablespoons fried breadcrumbs (page 69)
About 4 tablespoons guava jelly
Soufflé Potatoes (page 618) or Pommes de Terre Anna or Nina (page 613)
1 bunch crisp fresh watercress

Note that all garnishes should be started in advance of roasting the pheasants.

CROUSTADES. A croustade is a fried bread platform on which the pheasant is placed when presented whole on the serving platter. To make 2 of them, cut from an unsliced white sandwich loaf 2 pieces of bread, each measuring 6 to 8 inches by 3½ inches by 2½ inches thick. Fry them in hot butter on all sides until golden brown. Croûtons (page 69) are used when a pheasant is served already carved; a section of pheasant is placed on each croûton. For this recipe, prepare 2 croustades or 8 croûtons, according to which service you use.

Preheat the oven to 350°. Dry the pheasants thoroughly inside and out with paper towels. Brush the insides with Cognac and insert in each a little salt, a sprig of celery leaf, 1 tablespoon salt butter, 1 quartered onion or shallot, and 4 peppercorns. Tie each pheasant (page 342). Brush all over the outsides with the cool melted butter (there should be a thick coating of butter all over each pheasant).

Place the pheasants on a rack in a roasting pan. Dust the tops lightly with a little all-purpose flour. Cover the breasts with the thin slices of fatback. Insert a thermometer in one to check the cooking. Be careful they do not overcook (150° is right). Pour a little Cognac into the roasting pan and roast the pheasants 55 to 60 minutes. Baste them every 10 minutes, first with 3 tablespoons Cognac, next with 3 tablespoons dry sherry, and an equal quantity of water. (Reserve ¼ cup Cognac to flame the birds after they are out of the oven.) When they have roasted 20 minutes, turn them over on their breasts and continue roasting 15 minutes. Then turn them breast up again and remove the fatback. Brush the breasts with melted butter and continue roasting for the allotted time with the breasts uncovered. (Continue to brush the breasts with a little butter after each succeeding basting.) When the pheasants are properly roasted, remove them from the oven, but leave them in the roasting pan for a moment. Heat ¼ cup Cognac in a small pan, ignite, and carefully pour it over the pheasants.

POTATOES. If you are preparing soufflé potatoes, prepare the first stage in advance of the pheasant. Then give them the second frying just before you are ready to serve. If you are preparing Pommes de Terre Anna or Nina, plan the preparation so that they will be finished baking when the pheasants are roasted.

To serve, remove the string ties from the pheasants. If they are to be served whole and carved at the table, place each pheasant on a large croustade on a warm serving platter. If they are to be carved in the kitchen, carve each pheasant into quarters. Arrange each quarter on a diagonal croûton on a warm serving platter. Garnish the platter with crisp fresh watercress. If soufflé potatoes are being served, arrange them at either end of the serving platter. Pommes de Terre Anna or Nina should be served in their own dish. (The little Nina molds could be used to garnish the pheasant platter, if desired.) The fried breadcrumbs and guava jelly are served in separate little condiment dishes. NET: 4 servings.

SCOTTISH ROAST PHEASANT

Partridge, snipe, and grouse may also be presented in this manner. The traditional garnishes for the Scottish manner are red currant jelly, fried breadcrumbs (page 69), and a delicious bread sauce (below). Roast and serve the pheasants as for Classic Roast Pheasant (above). Serve the bread sauce, fried breadcrumbs, and 4 to 5 tablespoons red currant jelly separately in little condiment dishes. Do not accompany with potatoes. If a vegetable is desired, a little buttered zucchini, broccoli purée, or deep-fried parsley are very good.

BREAD SAUCE
4 slices sturdy white bread
½ cup light cream
1 small white onion, skinned and studded with 2 whole cloves
Half a bay leaf
1 whole allspice
2 tablespoons salt butter
¼ teaspoon salt
A little freshly grated white pepper
2 small pieces celery (without leaf)

Trim all the crusts from the slices of bread. Cut the slices into 1-inch squares. Put all the other ingredients in a small tin-lined copper pan. Heat the mixture very slowly until the cream is just at the point of boiling, then put in the squares of bread. Mix and cook gently until all the cream is absorbed in the bread and the sauce is very thick. (Stir occasionally.) Remove the onion, bay leaf, and celery. Serve in a small bowl, accompanying the roast pheasant. NET: 1 cup.

FAISAN SOUVAROFF

The pheasant is boned, then stuffed with truffles, chicken livers and mushrooms, and braised. It is served with a demi-glace sauce laced with truffle juice and wine.

Pheasant Souvaroff

1 3½-pound whole dressed
    pheasant with 2 of the tail
    feathers
About ⅓ cup Cognac
8 tablespoons salt butter
Salt
Freshly cracked black pepper
10 slices raw bacon
3 ounces firm white mushrooms
    (the caps only, sliced)
3 black truffles, thinly sliced
1 whole black truffle
Bouquet garni (parsley, thyme,
    celery leaf)
1 croustade (page 70)
8 diagonal croûtons (page 69),
    fried in butter

STUFFING
2 tablespoons salt butter
6 chicken livers

6 ounces firm white mushrooms,
    finely chopped
1 black truffle, coarsely chopped
Salt
Freshly cracked black pepper
Truffle liquid from the can

DEMI-GLACE SAUCE
2 shallots, sliced
2 slices raw bacon, cut into fine
    shreds
A few mushroom trimmings
Salt
Freshly cracked black pepper
2 tablespoons all-purpose flour
½ cup dry sherry
¼ cup dry red wine (preferably
    Burgundy)
¼ cup chicken stock (page 35)
Truffle liquid from the can

STUFFING. Heat the butter in a frypan; when it is very hot, brown the chicken livers in it. Remove them, add the mushrooms to the pan, and season with salt and pepper. Cook 2 minutes. Chop the chicken livers fine. Mix the chopped liver and truffle with the mushrooms and a little of the juice from the truffles.

Bone the pheasant (page 344), then spread it out, skin side down, on a board or slab. Sprinkle it with a little brandy. Brush with melted butter and season with salt and pepper. Spread on the stuffing, then fold the pheasant over and sew it together with fine kitchen thread. Melt the rest of the butter (about 6 tablespoons) in a deep heavy pan. When it is foaming, put in the pheasant, and brown it slowly all over. Remove the pheasant and set it on the board. Completely cover it with slices of bacon, slightly overlapping. Tie each piece of bacon down with string. Set the pheasant aside. Preheat the oven to 375°.

DEMI-GLACE SAUCE. To the pan in which the pheasant was browned, add the shallots, shredded bacon, and mushroom pieces. Season with salt and pepper, and cook slowly 3 to 4 minutes. Then stir in the flour and let it brown, stirring frequently. In a separate little pan boil the sherry down to half quantity and add it to the sauce. Add the wine, chicken stock, and the rest of the liquid from the truffles. Stir the sauce over low heat until it comes to a boil, then simmer gently 4 minutes.

Place the pheasant in a heavy casserole. Strain the sauce over it and heat it a little. Heat ¼ cup brandy in a separate little pan, ignite, and pour it over the pheasant. Add to the casserole the sliced mushroom caps, sliced truffles, whole truffle, and the bouquet garni wrapped in a piece of cheesecloth. Cover the pheasant with buttered wax paper and the lid. Cook 25 minutes in the oven. Place the thick slice of fried bread (croustade) in the center of a hot shallow au gratin dish. Remove the string from the pheasant, but leave the bacon on. Also pull out the thread in the back. Place the pheasant on the croustade. Remove the bouquet garni from the sauce, boil the sauce down to a creamy consistency, and spoon it over the pheasant. Stick one or two pheasant feathers in the whole truffle and arrange it at the tail end of the pheasant. Surround with the diagonal croûtons of fried bread. NET: 4 servings.

FAISAN VALLÉE D'AUGE

Pheasant Vallée d'Auge

Pheasant with brown sauce, enriched with a salpicon of apple and celery, Calvados, and heavy cream. Even non-game-eaters have applauded this classic when prepared precisely in this manner. It is one of my favorites. It contains all the goodness of that wonderful corner of France known for the best cream and butter and apples — Normandy. This recipe can be applied to chicken with equal success.

1 3½-pound whole dressed
    pheasant (or 2 small
    pheasants)
Half a lemon
6 tablespoons butter
Liver of the pheasant
Sprig of celery leaf
Salt
Freshly cracked black pepper
¼ cup brandy (preferably
    Calvados)
1 apple, cored and sliced
2 small yellow onions, sliced
¾ cup sliced celery
½ teaspoon meat glaze
3 tablespoons all-purpose flour
1½ cups chicken stock (page
    35)
1 cup heavy cream, whipped
3 tablespoons freshly grated

Parmesan cheese
1 tablespoon melted salt butter

APPLE GARNISH
1 large apple, skinned, cut into
    4 ½-inch slices, and cored
    with a 1-inch cutter
A little flour (for dusting)
2 tablespoons salt butter
2 large stalks celery, cut into
    kitchen matchstick size

NOISETTE POTATOES
4 Idaho-type potatoes, cut into
    small balls with a melon
    scoop and soaked in cold
    water
4 tablespoons salt butter
1 tablespoon finely chopped
    fresh parsley

Preheat the oven to 375°. Rub the pheasant all over, inside and out, with the lemon half. Insert in the cavity 2 tablespoons of butter, the liver, celery leaf, and a little salt and pepper. Tie the pheasant (page 342). Heat 4 tablespoons butter in a deep heavy pan. When it is foaming, put in the pheasant, breast side down, and slowly brown it all over. Heat the brandy in a small pan, ignite, and pour it over the pheasant. Remove the pheasant from the pan, set it aside, and add to the pan the sliced apple, onions, and celery. Stir this mixture in the butter in the pan, season with salt and pepper, cover with the lid, and cook over low heat until it is quite soft. Off the heat, stir in the meat glaze and flour. When the mixture is smooth, add the chicken stock. Stir the sauce over low heat until it comes to a boil. Then rub the whole mixture through a fine strainer.

Return the strained sauce to the pan. Carve the pheasant into serving pieces (page 343) and put it in the sauce. Cook it on the top shelf of the oven, uncovered, about 30 minutes. Baste 3 or 4 times with the sauce in the pan. When the pheasant is cooked, remove it from the pan, carefully scraping off the thick sauce. Return the pan with the sauce to low heat. Beat in the whipped cream a little at a time, using a wire whisk. Arrange the pieces of pheasant on a shallow au gratin dish, coat it with the sauce, and sprinkle with the Parmesan cheese and melted butter.

APPLE GARNISH. Soak the apple slices in cold water and dry them on paper towels. Dust them lightly with a little flour. Fry them quickly in hot butter until they are golden brown. Divide the celery sticks into 4 bundles, each tied with string. Put them in a pan and cover with cold salted water. Bring to a boil and cook a little (not too soft). Drain well, and slip each bundle inside an apple ring.

NOISETTE POTATOES. Soak the potato balls in several waters, to remove the starch, and dry them very well on paper towels. In a small deep pan, heat the butter. When it is foaming, put in the potatoes and coat with butter. Cover the pan tightly with the lid and shake occasionally over moderate heat until the potatoes are golden brown. After the potatoes have browned, season with a little salt and pepper and sprinkle with chopped parsley.

When ready to serve, brown the pheasant under the broiler. Remove the string from the celery bundles and arrange the apple and celery on the pheasant. (This garnish represents the character of the sauce that accompanies the pheasant.) Put a pile of the potatoes at each end of the pheasant dish. NET: 4 servings.

SUPRÊMES DE FAISAN BERCHOUX

Breasts of Pheasant Stuffed with Truffles and Livers

A poetic creation perpetuated in the culinary repertoire of a few scholarly chefs in honor of Joseph Berchoux's *Gastronomie* (1800). It is served on a salpicon of pheasant and mushrooms, with Sauce Napolitaine.

4 small whole dressed pheasants	8 tablespoons salt butter
1½ cups red Dubonnet vermouth	1 cup finely chopped fresh mushrooms

Juice of half a lemon
Salt
Freshly cracked black pepper
¼ cup Cognac or good brandy

STUFFING
Livers of the pheasants
½ cup breadcrumbs, fried in
  butter (page 69)
1 tablespoon chopped black
  truffles
¼ cup chicken stock (page 35)
Salt
Freshly cracked black pepper

SAUCE NAPOLITAINE
Bones of the pheasants
1 carrot, finely chopped
1 onion, finely chopped
1 turnip, finely chopped
1 leek, sliced

Bouquet garni, including 1 bay
  leaf, parsley, and celery leaf
2 cups chicken stock (page 35)
2 tablespoons salt butter
3 teaspoons potato flour
2 teaspoons meat glaze
1 teaspoon tomato paste
½ teaspoon finely chopped
  garlic
1 tablespoon chutney
Pinch of freshly grated nutmeg
1 canned mango, strained

GARNISH
4 or 5 diagonal croûtons, fried
  in butter (page 69)
1 black truffle, sliced
8 firm white mushroom caps,
  quickly sautéed in a little
  butter and lemon juice

Remove the breasts from the pheasants and skin and bone them. (You should have 8 suprêmes — boned, skinned half breasts.) Also remove the meat from the legs and set it and the pheasant bones aside. (The meat from the legs will be chopped; don't bother to keep whole, neat pieces.) Put the 8 half breasts in a dish with the Dubonnet to marinate 1 hour. Drain them on paper towels and cut a pocket in each breast.

STUFFING. Chop the raw pheasant livers very fine and mix them with the breadcrumbs, truffle, and chicken stock. Season with salt and pepper.

Spoon the stuffing into the pockets of the pheasant breasts. Heat 4 tablespoons butter in a sauté pan, put in the stuffed breasts, and cook over moderate heat until they are golden brown on each side. During this process, put over the breasts a flat lid or cake pan with a weight (such as a brick) on it, to keep them flat. When the breasts are browned, remove the lid and weight and let the breasts cook over very low heat 15 minutes. Meanwhile, put the meat from the legs of the pheasants through a fine meat chopper. Melt 4 tablespoons butter in another sauté pan and add the chopped mushrooms with a little lemon juice, salt, and pepper. Add the brandy and chopped pheasant meat and cook a few minutes over moderate heat. Set this salpicon aside for a moment.

NAPOLITAINE SAUCE. Put some of the pheasant bones in a pan with the carrot, onion, turnip, leek, and bouquet garni. Add the chicken stock and simmer 15 minutes. Melt 2 tablespoons of salt butter in a saucepan. Off the heat, stir in the potato flour, meat glaze, and tomato paste, and mix to a smooth paste. Strain on the stock, add the garlic, and stir over low heat until the sauce comes to a boil. Add the chutney and nutmeg, and boil the sauce to a creamy consistency. Rub the sauce through a fine strainer with the mango.

To serve, arrange the salpicon of chopped pheasant and mushroom on the bottom of an au gratin or serving dish. Place the stuffed pheasant breasts on it. Spoon the sauce over them. Place a whole mushroom cap on each breast. Garnish with the sliced truffle. Stick the diagonal croûtons around the sides of the dish. NET: 8 servings.

SUPRÊMES DE FAISAN, RIZ SAUVAGE

Breasts of Pheasant Braised in Cream, with Wild Rice, Pine Kernels, and Raisins

2 cups uncooked wild rice
8 tablespoons salt butter
4 shallots, finely chopped
Salt
Freshly cracked black pepper
6 cups chicken stock (page 35)
½ cup pine kernels (pignoli nuts)
½ cup white raisins soaked in

¼ cup Cognac or good brandy
4 half breasts of pheasant
¼ cup Cognac or good brandy, plus a little extra to brush on the breasts
1 teaspoon meat glaze
1 tablespoon all-purpose flour
2 cups heavy cream

Preheat the oven to 350°.

WILD RICE. Wash the rice thoroughly in several changes of cold water. Drain it well. Heat 4 tablespoons of butter in a deep heavy pan. Add the chopped shallots. Cook 1 minute and add the wild rice. Cook over low heat 3 minutes, stirring all the time. Season with 1 teaspoon salt and black pepper, and pour in the chicken stock. Stir until the stock comes to a boil. Add the pine kernels and the soaked raisins with the brandy. Cover the rice with buttered wax paper and the lid. Cook it 45 minutes in the oven, or until the rice is just soft.

Skin and bone the pheasant breasts (page 344). Brush them with a little brandy. In a small heavy casserole, heat 4 tablespoons butter. When it is foaming, put in the pheasant breasts and brown them very slowly, on both sides. Heat the brandy in a separate little pan, ignite, and pour it over the breasts in the casserole. Remove the breasts, set them aside, and stir the meat glaze and flour into the casserole. Off the heat, add the heavy cream, stirring all the time. Return the pheasant breasts to the sauce. Season with a little salt and pepper. Cook very slowly, over low heat, about 35 minutes. Do not cover the pan, and turn the breasts frequently. When they are done, remove them from the sauce, boil it down to a creamy consistency, and add the chopped chives. To serve, arrange the wild rice down a shallow au gratin dish, place the pheasant breasts on it, and spoon the sauce over them. NET: 4 servings.

CAILLES À LA JUDIC

Braised Quail with Braised Lettuce

2 large carrots, pared and cut into small even matchsticks
1 large Bermuda onion, sliced
1 large stalk celery, cut into

small even matchsticks
About 5 tablespoons melted salt butter
Salt

Freshly cracked black pepper
2 or 3 heads Boston lettuce
(half head for each quail)
6 slices raw bacon
1 cup chicken stock (page 35)
4 to 6 whole dressed quail
4 tablespoons salt butter
¼ cup Cognac or good brandy

SAUCE
Liquid in which lettuce is cooked
1 teaspoon tomato paste
1 teaspoon meat glaze
1 teaspoon potato flour
1 cup chicken stock (page 35)

Preheat the oven to 350°.

BRAISED LETTUCE. Put the carrots, onion, and celery into a pan and cover with cold water. Bring to a boil and drain the vegetables at once. Return the blanched vegetables to the pan with 3 tablespoons melted butter, salt and pepper. Cover them with wax paper and the lid, and cook in the oven 10 to 15 minutes. Remove, and set them aside. Wash the lettuces really well, and drain. Cut them in half, then put them in a pan, cover with cold water, bring to a boil, remove and drain them well on paper towels. Line the bottom of an oblong baking dish with half of the sliced bacon. Scatter just a few of the cooked vegetables on top of the bacon. Place the drained lettuces (4 to 6 halves) on top. Cover them with the rest of the bacon and pour the chicken stock over them. Cover the pan and put it in the oven to cook 45 minutes.

While the lettuces are braising, prepare the quail. Tie them (page 342). Brush them with a little melted butter. Put 4 tablespoons butter in a deep heavy pan. When it is foaming, put the quail in it and carefully brown them all over. In a separate little pan, heat the brandy, ignite, and pour it over the quail. Season them with salt and pepper, cover the pan, and put them in the oven to braise 25 minutes.

SAUCE. Strain the liquid in which the lettuce was braised and set it aside. To the pan in which the quail were cooked, add the tomato paste, meat glaze, and potato flour. Stir to a smooth paste, then pour in the chicken stock and the liquid from the lettuce. Stir the sauce over low heat until it comes to a boil. Simmer 10 minutes.

To serve, make a bed of the vegetables on a flat serving dish. Remove the string from the quail and arrange them on the vegetables. Garnish around the edge of the dish with the braised lettuces. Spoon the sauce over the dish. NET: 4 to 6 servings.

CAILLES AUX MARRONS

Braised Quail with Chestnuts

Whole quail, braised in Cognac and glazed with brown sauce, served on artichoke bottoms filled with chestnut purée.

4 to 6 whole dressed quail
About 8 tablespoons salt butter
¼ cup Cognac or good brandy
1 teaspoon tomato paste
1 teaspoon meat glaze
1 teaspoon potato flour

1¼ cups chicken stock (page 35)
1 tablespoon grape jelly
8 artichoke bottoms
Salt
Freshly cracked black pepper

2 cups unsweetened chestnut
    purée

8 round croûtons, fried in butter
    (page 69)

Preheat the oven to 375°. Tie the quail (page 342). Heat 4 table-spoons butter in a deep heavy pan. When it is foaming, put in the quail and carefully brown them all over. Heat the brandy in a separate little pan, ignite, and pour it over the quail. Cover the pan and cook the quail in the oven 20 minutes, then remove from the pan and set aside. Place the pan on the stove, and put in the tomato paste, meat glaze, and potato flour. Pour in the chicken stock, add the jelly, and stir the sauce over low heat until it comes to a boil. If it is too thick, add a little more stock. Return the quail to the sauce and keep them warm.

Heat the artichoke bottoms in a little butter, salt, and pepper, and set them aside. Melt 2 tablespoons butter in a saucepan, add the unsweetened chestnut purée, salt, and pepper, and stir over low heat until the purée is hot. Arrange the fried croûtons on an oval serving platter. Fill a pastry bag fitted with a large round tube (#8 or #9) with the chestnut purée. Pipe rosettes of chestnut purée on the top of each artichoke bottom. Place each filled artichoke bottom on a round fried croûton. Untie the quail and put a whole quail on each alternate artichoke bottom, on top of the purée. Spoon the sauce over them. Serve at once. NET: 4 servings.

CAILLES À LA MILANESE

Quail with Risotto

The quail are cooked in chicken stock and rice with white truffles, and served with fresh tomato sauce.

6 whole dressed quail
6 small slices salt pork or fat-
    back (to cover each quail)
10 tablespoons salt butter
½ cup Cognac or good brandy
1 cup fresh tomato pulp (about
    ½ pound tomatoes, skinned,
    quartered, seeded and finely
    chopped
1 Bermuda onion, finely

    chopped
Salt
Freshly cracked white pepper
1 cup long-grain rice
2½ cups chicken stock (page
    35)
6 white truffles (fresh or
    canned), sliced
¾ cup freshly grated Parmesan
    cheese

Tie the quail (page 342). Place a slice of salt pork on each breast and tie again. Heat 4 tablespoons butter in a deep heavy pan. Quickly brown the quail on all sides. Add another 2 tablespoons butter, cover the pan, and cook the quail about 5 minutes. Remove them from the pan, set them aside, add the brandy to the pan, and stir to pick up the glaze. Stir in the tomato pulp and bring to a boil. Set the sauce aside and keep it warm.

Melt 4 tablespoons butter in another deep heavy pan. Add the onion and cook over low heat until it is translucent but not brown. Season with salt and pepper. Add the rice and stir over low heat a few minutes. Pour in the chicken stock and bring to a boil. Add the truffles. Cover the pan, and cook over low heat 25 minutes, then stir in the grated cheese with a fork. Remove the strings and salt pork slices and put the quail into the rice pan. Cover the pan again, and finish cooking the rice and quail together (another 10 minutes) over low heat. Remove the quail from the pan.

To serve, pile up the rice in a pyramid in the center of a hot flat serving dish. Arrange the quail around the dish. Spoon the sauce over them. Serve at once. NET: 6 servings.

CAILLES AUX RAISINS

Quail with White Grapes

The quail are boned, stuffed with foie gras and veal mousse, and braised in cream. The sauce is made with white grapes, and the dish is garnished with mushroom caps.

4 whole dressed quail
10 tablespoons brandy
  (preferably Calvados)
Salt
Freshly cracked white pepper
4 ounces ground veal
1 egg white
⅓ cup light cream
2 ounces fine liver pâté or
  foie gras
A few grains cayenne pepper
A few grains freshly grated
  nutmeg
2 black truffles, finely chopped
5 tablespoons clarified butter
  (page 56)
¼ teaspoon finely chopped
  garlic

2 finely chopped shallots
1 firm white mushroom,
  finely chopped
½ teaspoon tomato paste
½ teaspoon meat glaze
2 tablespoons all-purpose flour
¾ cup chicken stock (page 35)
¾ cup heavy cream, whipped
2 egg yolks
½ teaspoon Dijon mustard
2 tablespoons heavy cream,
  unwhipped
¾ cup skinned and seeded
  white grapes
4 to 8 firm white mushroom
  caps (fluted if desired),
  lightly sautéed in butter

First, bone the quail. Quail are almost all breast. To bone, remove the carcass only (page 344), leaving the bones in the wings and legs. Spread the boned quail out on a cutting board, skin side down. Brush the flesh with 2 tablespoons brandy. Season with a little salt and pepper.

STUFFING. Put the veal in a small metal bowl over another bowl of ice. Using a small wire whisk, beat in the egg white. Very gradually, mix in the light cream. Then mix in the liver pâté or foie gras, 1 teaspoon salt, a very few grains of cayenne pepper and grated nutmeg, 1 tablespoon of brandy, and 1 chopped truffle.

Spread each quail with stuffing, fold over the edges, and sew them together with fine white thread. Tie the quail (page 342). Heat 3 tablespoons clarified butter in a small heavy pan. When it is foaming, put the birds in the pan, breast down. Carefully brown them all over. Heat 4 tablespoons brandy in a little pan, ignite, and pour over them.

Remove them from the pan, set aside, and add another tablespoon of butter to the pan. Over low heat, stir in the garlic, shallots, mushroom, and the other truffle. Cook 1 to 2 minutes and season with salt and pepper. Off the heat, stir in the tomato paste, meat glaze, and flour. Mix in the chicken stock. Return the pan to low heat and stir until the sauce comes to a boil. Using a wire whisk, beat in the whipped cream, spoonful by spoonful. Return the quail to the pan and baste with the sauce. Cover the pan with wax paper and the lid, and simmer over very low heat about 25 minutes. When they are cooked, remove the string and thread and arrange the quail on a serving dish. Heat 2 tablespoons brandy, ignite, and pour it over them in the serving dish.

Finish the sauce as follows — if it has thinned a little, thicken it with ½ teaspoon potato flour mixed with 1 tablespoon light cream. Put the egg yolks in a little bowl. Using a small wire whisk, beat in the Dijon mustard, 1 tablespoon brandy, and the unwhipped heavy cream. Pour a little of the cooking sauce into the yolk mixture, stirring all the time, then stir the yolk mixture into the rest of the sauce in the pan. Add the grapes. Stir over low heat, without boiling, until the sauce thickens. To serve, coat the quail on the serving dish with the sauce, and garnish around the edge of the dish with the fluted mushroom caps. NET: 4 servings.

COLD POULTRY

1 whole dressed chicken,
  5 to 6 pounds
A little lemon juice
2 onions (1 whole and 1 sliced)
4 whole cloves
2 small carrots, sliced
1 stalk celery, sliced
2 leeks, sliced
Bouquet garni, including 1 bay
  leaf, 2 or 3 sprigs parsley,
  tarragon, and celery leaf
2 teaspoons salt
6 black peppercorns
6 cups chicken aspic (1½
  quantity of recipe, page 37),
  of which ¼ cup each goes
  into the ham mousse and
  chaud-froid sauce

HAM MOUSSE
1 pound lean boiled ham
4 tablespoons vegetable oil

4 tablespoons water
2 teaspoons unflavored gelatine
4 tablespoons all-purpose flour
Salt
A few grains cayenne pepper
12 tablespoons sweet butter,
  creamed in the mixer until
  light and fluffy
2 teaspoons tomato paste
¼ cup of the liquid chicken
  aspic (above)
½ cup heavy cream, whipped

CHAUD-FROID SAUCE
2 tablespoons vegetable oil
8 tablespoons water
6 tablespoons all-purpose flour
1 tablespoon unflavored
  gelatine
Salt
A few grains cayenne pepper
1½ cups milk

CHAUD-FROID DE POULARDE ROSE-MARIE

Cold Chicken Stuffed with Ham Mousse, in White Chaud-Froid Sauce, with Floral Decorations

¾ cup light cream
¼ cup of the liquid chicken
   aspic (above)

RICE SOCLE
¼ pound raw rice
Salt

DECORATION
A few stalks of chives
A few sprigs of fresh parsley
2 to 3 small red radishes
1 hard-boiled egg yolk
1 tablespoon creamed sweet
   butter
1 large black truffle

Wash the chicken in water with the lemon juice. Dry it with paper towels and tie it (page 342). Put it in a deep pan, cover with cold water, bring slowly to a boil, and skim off all the scum. Stick the cloves in the whole onion and put it in the pot with the chicken. Also add the sliced onion, carrots, celery, leeks, bouquet garni, salt, and peppercorns. Simmer very gently 1¼ hours, or until the chicken is tender. Allow the chicken to cool in the stock, then remove it, remove the string, and carefully take off all the skin. Cut off the wings and carefully cut out the breasts (meat only). Cut the breast meat into fine even slices (there should be 6). With kitchen shears, cut the breastbone from the carcass. Set aside the carcass, with the rest of the meat still attached, to cool completely.

HAM MOUSSE. Remove any trace of fat or sinew from the ham, and put it through a fine meat chopper 3 times. Prepare a panade: Heat the vegetable oil and water in a small pan. Mix the gelatine with the flour. Off the heat, stir the mixed flour and gelatine into the oil and water. Season with salt and cayenne pepper. Stir over low heat until the sauce comes to a boil, then pour it onto a plate, put it in the refrigerator, and chill it. Put the finely chopped ham in a mixer bowl. Add the creamed butter little by little, beating all the time. Then beat in the chilled panade little by little. Finally, stir in the tomato paste and liquid aspic, and fold in the whipped cream. Set the ham mousse aside to cool.

CHAUD-FROID SAUCE. Heat the vegetable oil and water in a saucepan. In a separate bowl, mix together the flour, gelatine, salt, and cayenne pepper. Off the heat, stir the flour mixture into the oil and water. Then stir in the milk, and stir over low heat until the sauce comes to a boil. Put the saucepan over a bowl of ice and stir until the sauce is cool; then add the light cream and liquid aspic. Cover the pan with plastic wrap and set the sauce aside.

RICE SOCLE (optional). Cook the rice in ample boiling water until it is very soft and mushy. Drain it, and pound it with a large pestle and mortar until it is smooth. Smooth this paste on the bottom of a flat oval silver serving platter. Form it into a long oval shape with a flat surface. Cover it with thin aluminum foil.

Have ready 5½ cups of liquid chicken aspic. Pour a little of it in a layer cake pan and put it in the refrigerator to set. Put the rest in a saucepan and set aside for a moment. Fill the chicken with some of the ham mousse. Lay the chicken breast slices on the mousse and re-form in the shape of the chicken. Set the chicken on a rack on a jelly roll pan. Stir the chaud-froid sauce over a bowl of ice until it is on the point of setting. With a large spoon, carefully coat all the chicken with this sauce. Put the chicken in the refrigerator to set for a moment to set the coating, then decorate as follows. Lay thin stalks of chives on the chaud-froid coating as stems. Stick on bits of parsley as leaves of a small rosebush. Cut the red radishes into very thin slices and arrange them on the chaud-froid to represent roses. Strain the hard-boiled egg yolk and mix with the creamed butter. Make a little wax paper cornucopia, put the egg yolk mixture in it, and cut off the tip. Using the cornucopia like a pastry bag, squeeze little yellow centers onto the roses. Put the aspic over a bowl of ice. When it is on the point of setting, spoon a little aspic over the decoration, taking great care that it does not slip down. Then coat the entire chicken with a thin coat of clear aspic. Allow it to set again in the refrigerator.

Place the chicken on the socle of rice, or on a platter without the socle. Fill 8 lightly oiled small oval (dariole) molds with the remainder of the ham mousse. Press down well, and put the molds in the refrigerator to set. When chilled, turn out the mousse. Put a round of truffle on the top, and coat with aspic on the point of setting. Pipe out a rosette of egg yolk mixture on the truffle. Turn the aspic in the layer cake tin out onto a cutting board and chop it. Put the chopped aspic in a pastry bag with a #8 or #9 round tube. Garnish the platter with chopped aspic piped around the chicken and/or edge of the platter. Place the little molds of ham mousse at intervals around the chicken. NET: 8 servings.

This galantine, made with chicken, pheasant, or duck, was the pride of many who accomplished it in our classes. It was also prepared for Mr. Craig Claiborne, the famous food and wine connoisseur and critic, who wrote about it in the New York *Times*. The galantine is a boned chicken stuffed with sausage meat, with whole egg whites filled with chicken livers, ham fingers, pistachio nuts, and truffles, the whole coated with white chaud-froid sauce and decorated with a floral design.

GALANTINE DE VOLAILLE

Galantine of Chicken

1 3½-pound whole dressed chicken and its liver
4 tablespoons brandy (preferably Cognac or Calvados)
Salt
Freshly cracked white pepper
1 pound bulk pork sausage meat
1 raw egg
2 tablespoons finely chopped shallots
½ teaspoon finely chopped

garlic
1 tablespoon chopped fresh parsley
¼ teaspoon freshly grated nutmeg
¾ cup shelled blanched pistachio nuts
¼-pound slice boiled ham, cut into ¼-inch strips
Optional: 1 black truffle, coarsely chopped
2 hard-boiled eggs
For flower decoration: hard-

boiled egg pieces, radish
slices, dill sprigs, chives and
scallions
4 cups clear chicken aspic
(page 37)
Thin slices French bread,
toasted

CHAUD-FROID SAUCE
3 tablespoons vegetable oil
6 tablespoons warm water
4 tablespoons all-purpose flour
1½ tablespoons unflavored
gelatine
1 teaspoon salt
A few grains cayenne pepper
1½ cups milk
2 tablespoons heavy cream

Bone the chicken (page 344). Place it skin side down on a cutting board, and sprinkle with 2 tablespoons brandy and a little salt and pepper. Fold the chicken and set it aside to marinate for a moment. Place the sausage meat in a mixer bowl. If necessary, season with salt and pepper. Add the raw egg, shallots, garlic, parsley, and nutmeg. Beat well. Unfold the chicken and spread this mixture on it, leaving a 1-inch margin all around the edge. Scatter the pistachios all over the stuffing and press them down lightly. Arrange the strips of ham lengthwise over the stuffing, and scatter the chopped truffle over all. Cut the hard-boiled eggs in half, and set the yolks aside for some other use. Put the whites together again around the chicken liver (half in each egg) instead of the yolks. Place the reassembled eggs lengthwise in the center of the chicken. Sprinkle the surface with salt, pepper, and the rest of the brandy.

Fold the sides of the chicken overlapping, sausage fashion, and sew up the overlapping edges with white kitchen thread. Roll the chicken in wax paper, then roll in aluminum foil. Next, roll the "package" in a clean cloth or kitchen towel. Tie each end of the cloth with string, leaving tails of string about 12 inches long. Tie two pieces of string around the center of the package about 2 inches apart. Place the wrapped chicken in a fish cooker, deep oval casserole, or dutch oven. Tie it to the handles of the pan so that it is suspended like a hammock. It should not touch the bottom of the pan. Half fill the pan with cold water and bring it slowly to a boil. Cover the pan and reduce the heat to a simmer. Cook slowly 1½ hours, and let the chicken stand in the cooking liquid until it is cold. Drain, and remove the cloth but keep the paper on. Put the galantine into a bread pan (it should be snug). Put a weight on top (such as a brick). Refrigerate overnight. Next day remove all the wrappings and string, wipe the galantine free of fat, and place it on a cake rack over a jelly roll pan ready for coating.

CHAUD-FROID SAUCE. Place the vegetable oil in a small saucepan, add the warm water, and bring to a boil. In a small bowl combine the flour, gelatine, salt, and cayenne pepper. Off the heat, blend this into the oil mixture. Stir until smooth, and stir in the milk, using a wire whisk. Then stir over low heat until the sauce comes to a boil. Stir in the heavy cream. Place the saucepan over a bowl of crushed ice, and continue stirring until the sauce just starts to set.

Remove the pan from the ice, and quickly and evenly coat the galantine with the sauce and put it in the refrigerator. When the chaud-froid coating is well set, decorate the top of the galantine with the design of a flower, using the pieces of chive or scallion for stems, dill for leaves, hard-boiled egg white and radish slices for flowers. Then put the liquid clear aspic over a bowl of ice and stir until it is on the point of setting. Carefully spoon it over the galantine. Put the galantine in the refrigerator to set. Put the rest of the clear aspic in a layer cake pan and put it also in the refrigerator to set. Then turn the aspic in the pan out onto a cutting board and chop it fine. Put the chopped aspic in a pastry bag fitted with a #8 or #9 round tube. Arrange the finished galatine on a serving dish. Pipe chopped aspic all around it. Let the prepared dish set really well. To serve, slice it, and accompany it with thin slices of plain toasted French bread, served in a separate dish. NET: 12 or more servings.

This cold mousse is actually served in the soufflé dish, the top decorated with slices of truffle and cucumber and with chopped aspic.

MOUSSE DE VOLAILLE

Cold Chicken Mousse

1 5-pound whole dressed chicken	1 tablespoon unflavored gelatine
1 small onion, stuck with 4 whole cloves	1½ cups milk
1 large onion, cut in eighths	1 tablespoon tomato paste
1 stalk celery, sliced	1½ cups heavy cream, whipped
1 large carrot, sliced	Freshly cracked white pepper
2 leeks, sliced	
Bouquet garni, including tarragon, parsley, and a bay leaf	ASPIC
	4 cups stock from cooking the chicken
7 black peppercorns	3 egg whites
Salt	½ cup dry white wine
1 cup dry white wine	¼ cup dry sherry
12 tablespoons salt butter	2 tablespoons unflavored gelatine
3 tablespoons vegetable oil	5 tablespoons tomato paste
4 tablespoons water	
4 tablespoons all-purpose flour	DECORATION
Salt	1 truffle, thinly sliced
A few grains cayenne pepper	1 cucumber, thinly sliced

Tie the chicken (page 342), and put it in a deep heavy pot. Cover it with cold water and bring to a boil. Skim off the scum. Add both onions and the celery, carrot, leeks, bouquet garni (tied in cheesecloth), peppercorns, 1 tablespoon salt, and the wine. Simmer gently 2 hours, until the chicken is quite soft. Allow it to get almost cold in the stock. When it is tepid, remove it from the stock. Strain the stock and put it in the freezer. Remove all the meat from the bones, being careful to discard any sinew or tough parts. Also discard the skin. Then put the chicken meat through a fine meat chopper three times.

Put the butter in a mixer bowl and beat until it is light and fluffy. Slowly, little by little, mix in the chicken, and set the mixture aside.

PANADE. Melt the oil and water in a saucepan. In a small bowl, mix the flour, salt, cayenne pepper, and gelatine. Stir this dry mixture into the warm oil and water until it is quite smooth. Add the milk, and stir over low heat until it comes to a boil. Pour the panade onto a platter and let it chill.

Mix the chilled panade into the chicken and put the whole mixture through a fine strainer. Mix in the tomato paste, and fold in the whipped cream. Season with salt and white pepper. Fill a #8 soufflé dish with this mousse to about ¼ inch from the top. Smooth with a spatula and put the mousse in the refrigerator to set.

ASPIC. Remove the fat that has solidified on the chicken stock in the freezer. Beat the egg whites to soft peaks. Put 4 cups stock in a pan with the white wine, sherry, gelatine, tomato paste, and beaten egg whites. Beat over low heat until it comes to a boil. Remove the pan from the heat and let it stand absolutely still 15 to 20 minutes. Then pour it through a strainer which has been lined with a damp cloth.

Put the pan of clear aspic over a bowl of ice. Stir until it is on the point of setting. Put a thin layer of aspic over the chicken mousse, and put in the refrigerator to set. Next, cover the top with alternating thin slices of cucumber and truffle. Fill the soufflé dish to the very top with more aspic jelly on the point of setting, and let it set in the refrigerator. Let the rest of the aspic set, turn it out onto a cutting board, and chop it fine. Put the chopped aspic into a pastry bag fitted with a small round tube, and pipe it around the edge of the soufflé dish. Serve on a starched white napkin on a flat silver serving platter. NET: 8 servings.

SUPRÊMES DE VOLAILLE JEANNETTE

Chicken Breasts Sandwiched with Pâté, Coated with Chaud-Froid Sauce and Aspic

3 whole chicken breasts (6 sides)
4 cups chicken stock (page 35)
Salt
Freshly cracked white pepper
2 tablespoons Cognac or good
    brandy
4 cups chicken aspic (page 37)

FILLING
12 tablespoons sweet butter
12 ounces fine liver pâté or
    foie gras
3 tablespoons Cognac or good
    brandy
Salt
Freshly cracked white pepper
1 black truffle, finely chopped

CHAUD-FROID SAUCE
7 tablespoons water
3 tablespoons vegetable oil
8 tablespoons all-purpose flour
3 tablespoons unflavored
    gelatine
Salt
A few grains cayenne pepper
1½ cups milk
1 cup light cream

GARNISH
18 perfect thin slices of firm
    white mushroom with a little
    bit of the stem
Lemon juice

Put the three whole breasts of chicken, still attached to the bone, in a heavy pan and cover them with the chicken stock. Bring to a boil, cover, and simmer gently 25 minutes. Let the breasts cool in the stock, then drain, and carefully remove the skin and bone. (From here on, each side is termed "a breast.") Wipe the breast meat with paper towels, trim off all excess fat and sinew, and with a very sharp knife slice each breast in half horizontally, making 12 pieces. Season the inside of each with a little salt, pepper, and brandy. Reassemble the two slices of each breast, and wrap each breast (both slices) in plastic wrap. Place the individually wrapped breasts between two baking sheets with a weight on top, to flatten them out a little. Set aside in a cool place. Prepare the mushroom garnish — plunge the slices into a little boiling water and lemon juice for just 1 to 2 minutes, drain, then plunge them into cold water and drain again. Dry them flat on paper towels. Set them aside.

FILLING. Cream the sweet butter in a mixer until it is light and fluffy. Add the fine liver pâté (or foie gras) and mix well. Add the brandy and season with salt (if necessary) and freshly cracked white pepper. Last, mix in the chopped truffle.

Unwrap the chicken breasts. Put the filling into a pastry bag fitted with a #7 round tube. On the bottom slice of each breast pipe a covering of pâté about ½ to ¾ inch thick. Cover it with the top slice of breast. Smooth around the edges with a small spatula. Place the filled (sandwiched) breasts on a rack on a jelly roll pan. Chill them in the freezer or refrigerator.

CHAUD-FROID SAUCE. Warm the water with the vegetable oil in a tin-lined copper saucepan. In a little bowl, mix the flour with the gelatine, season with salt and cayenne pepper, and mix it all with the water and oil in the pan. Using a small whisk, mix in the milk. Stir the sauce over low heat until it just comes to a boil. Remove from the heat and add the light cream.

Stir the chaud-froid sauce over a bowl of ice until it is on the point of setting. Using a large serving spoon, carefully coat each chicken breast evenly, with no bumps or ridges. Put them in the freezer or refrigerator a minute or two, then coat them again with chaud-froid sauce. Arrange 3 of the prepared mushroom slices in a row on each coated breast, the domed top of one overlapping the stem of the next one up. Put the six coated breasts on a rack on a clean jelly roll pan. Put the clear aspic in a pan over a bowl of ice. Stir until the aspic is on the point of setting. Using a large serving spoon, carefully coat each chicken breast with aspic. Put to set in the refrigerator. If necessary, give the breasts another coating of aspic. Put the remainder of the aspic in a layer cake pan and put it to set in the refrigerator.

To assemble, arrange the coated breasts in the shape of a fan on a silver serving platter. Turn out the aspic in the layer cake pan onto a sheet of wax paper on a cutting board. If desired, cut about a third of it into triangular shapes and set them around the edge of the platter. Chop the rest into fine cubes. Put it in a pastry bag fitted with a plain #3 tube and pipe aspic around each coated breast. Cover the rest of the surface of the platter with the chopped aspic. If there is any remaining pâté, put it into a pastry bag with a #7 star tube and pipe little scallops at both ends of the platter. Chill well in the refrigerator before serving. NET: 6 servings.

PAIN DE VOLAILLE EN GELÉE

Jellied Chicken Loaf

This is an ideal hot weather dish — simple and good, with the least bother. And it may be prepared a day ahead of time.

1 5-pound chicken or capon, or 2 3-pound chickens	Salt
6 cups cold water	6 peppercorns
1 small onion, sliced	2 tablespoons unflavored gelatine
1 stalk celery, sliced	¼ cup cold water for the gelatine
1 carrot, sliced	
1 bay leaf	Small bunch crisp fresh parsley or watercress (for garnish)
1 sprig fresh parsley	

Tie the chicken (page 342), and put it in a foil hammock in a deep heavy pot. Add 6 cups cold water, and bring slowly to a boil. Skim off all the scum on the surface. Add the onion, celery, carrot, bay leaf, parsley, salt, and peppercorns. Cover the pot (leaving a small opening) and simmer until the chicken is very tender and starts falling off the bones. (This may require about 1½ hours, or longer if the chicken is an old fowl.) Remove the chicken. Strain the stock in which it was boiled. If there is more than 4 cups, reduce it to that amount by boiling it down. Soften the gelatine in the cold water, add it to the reduced hot chicken stock, and stir until it is completely dissolved.

Skin the cooked chicken. Remove all the meat from the bones and cut it into small dice, as uniform in size as possible. Combine the chicken and the stock and taste for seasoning. Pour the mixture into a loaf pan and chill it in the refrigerator until it is well set, at least 2 to 3 hours (and much longer if you wish). Unmold onto a silver serving platter and garnish it with crisp fresh parsley or watercress. NET: 8 servings.

CANETON AUX CERISES À LA MONTMORENCY

Cold Duckling in Brown Chaud-Froid Sauce, with Cherries and Truffles

1 4-pound whole dressed duck	Freshly cracked white pepper
1 orange cut in quarters	
Salt	BROWN CHAUD-FROID SAUCE
Freshly cracked white pepper	4 tablespoons vegetable oil
3 tablespoons vegetable oil	1 cup mixed sliced onion, carrot, and celery
5½ cups chicken aspic (page 37)	4 tablespoons all-purpose flour
	1 tomato, sliced
STUFFING	A few mushroom stems or caps
3 cups fine liver pâté	2 teaspoons meat glaze
8 tablespoons sweet butter, beaten until light and fluffy	2 teaspoons tomato paste
Salt	1 tablespoon red currant jelly

2 cups chicken stock (page 35)
½ cup dry sherry
2 tablespoons Cognac or good
  brandy
1 tablespoon unflavored gelatine

GARNISH
2 cups ripe Bing cherries (fresh
  or canned), seeded

1 cup Marsala wine
¾ cup granulated sugar
1 cup ripe Bing cherries, with
  stems on
¾ cup superfine sugar
⅔ cup cold water
¼ teaspoon cream of tartar
3 black truffles

Preheat the oven to 375°. Wipe the duck inside and out with paper towels. Insert the orange quarters into the cavity and season with salt and pepper. Tie the duck (page 342). Place it on a rack in a roasting pan. Brush the top with a little vegetable oil. Prick the skin all over the breast and sides to release the fat. Pour a little water into the pan, and roast the duck 45 to 50 minutes. Baste frequently, each time adding another 1 to 2 tablespoons water to the pan and then basting the duck with the juices. Occasionally reprick the skin to release the fat. When the duck is cooked, remove it from the pan, set it aside to cool, then chill in the refrigerator.

STUFFING. Put the pâté in the mixer and beat until creamy. Add the creamed butter and season with salt and pepper. Beat again until the mixture is light and fluffy.

When the duck is chilled, remove the breasts — there should be two whole pieces, one from each side. With kitchen shears, cut away the breastbone. Remove the orange, and clean out the inside of the duck that is now exposed. Fill the cavity with the pâté mixture and reshape the top of the duck. With a very sharp knife, cut the breast pieces into very thin slices lengthwise and arrange them, overlapping, on the liver pâté. Set the duck again in the refrigerator to chill. Put the seeded Bing cherries (for garnish) in a pan with the Marsala wine and granulated sugar. Cook very gently until the cherries are swollen. Put them in the refrigerator to chill.

BROWN CHAUD-FROID SAUCE. Heat the vegetable oil in a small deep pan. Add the mixed onion, carrot, and celery, and cook very slowly until they are soft but not brown. Add the flour and continue to cook slowly until it is dark brown. Off the heat, stir in the tomato, mushroom stems or caps, meat glaze, tomato paste, and jelly. Pour in the chicken stock, sherry, and brandy. Return the pan to low heat and stir until it comes to a boil. Simmer very gently about 10 to 12 minutes. Rub the sauce through a strainer into a saucepan or metal bowl. Dissolve the gelatine in about 2 tablespoons of this sauce and then mix it back into the sauce.

Place the duck on a rack on a jelly roll pan. Put the chaud-froid sauce over a bowl of ice and stir until it is on the point of setting. Then carefully spoon the sauce over the duck, coating it smoothly all over. Drain the cooked chilled cherries well on paper towels, so they are dry. Cut the truffles into thin slices or cut out designs. Decorate the top of the duck with the thin slices of truffle and half the cherries. Put the aspic over a bowl of ice, stir until it is on the point of setting, and carefully coat the duck and decorations with·it. Put the duck in the refrigerator to set. Mix the remainder of the cherries with a little of the aspic and scatter them on a silver serving platter. Put the platter in the refrigerator to set. Put the remaining aspic in a layer cake pan and put it in the refrigerator to set.

Stir together the superfine sugar, cold water, and cream of tartar (for the garnish), and boil until the mixture just begins to turn caramel color. Glaze the stemmed cherries by dipping them into the mixture, and cool them. When the duck, cherries in aspic, and aspic in the layer cake tin are all set, arrange the duck on the cherries on the platter, and arrange the glazed cherries around the duck. Turn the clear aspic out onto a chopping board, and chop it into fine dice. Put it into a pastry bag fitted with a plain round #8 or #9 tube. Garnish the platter with a piped border of chopped aspic. Put the completed presentation in the refrigerator to set well. NET: 4 to 6 servings.

CANETON À L'ORANGE FROID

Cold Duckling in Orange Aspic, with Fresh Orange Sections and Truffle

1 4-pound whole dressed duck
1 small orange, cut in quarters
1 bay leaf
Salt
4 cups chicken stock (page 35)
1 cup mixed sliced onion, carrot, and celery
4 peppercorns
2 cups fresh strained orange juice
Grated rind and juice of 1 lime

½ cup Madeira wine
½ cup Grand Marnier
3 egg whites
3 tablespoons unflavored gelatine
1 large black truffle, thinly sliced
Skinned sections of 3 navel oranges, with all pith removed
Grated rind of 2 navel oranges
1 bunch crisp fresh watercress

Dry the duck thoroughly, inside and out, and remove all the fat. Insert in the cavity the quartered orange, bay leaf, and a little salt. Tie the duck (page 342). Wrap it in cheesecloth and put it in a small oval pan with the chicken stock, mixed onion, carrot and celery, and peppercorns. Bring to a boil slowly and simmer very gently 1 hour, or until the skin just begins to loosen around the legs. Let the cooked duck cool in the stock. When cool, remove it from the stock, and remove the cheesecloth. Take all the skin and fat off the duck, and wipe the duck very dry with a soft cloth. Put it in the refrigerator to chill thoroughly.

Strain the stock. Put it in a tin-lined copper pan with the orange juice, lime juice, Madeira wine, Grand Marnier, gelatine, and beaten egg whites. Beat with a wire whisk over low heat until the mixture comes to a rolling boil. Remove the pan from the heat and let it stand, without moving it, 15 minutes. Line a colander with a clean damp cloth and pour the mixture through into a bowl. You should now have clear orange aspic. Put half of it in a metal bowl and set it over a bowl of crushed ice. Place the chilled duck on a rack in a jelly roll pan. Stir the aspic over ice until it is on the point of setting. Then quickly and evenly coat the duck all over with the aspic. Return the duck to the refrigerator to set the aspic, then coat it with another layer of aspic in the same way. (If the aspic in the bowl has set, gently reheat it.) Decorate the top of the duck with the thin slices of truffle and skinned sections of orange (be sure the orange sections are uniform and neat). Give the duck another two coatings of aspic, refrigerating to set each time.

Mix the grated orange rind and lime rind with the remainder of the orange aspic. Put this aspic either into little oval dariole molds or into a layer cake pan and then into the refrigerator to set. When it is set, arrange the coated, decorated duck on a silver platter. Turn the molds out and arrange them around the duck. (Or turn the aspic out of the layer cake tin onto a cutting board, cut into diamond or triangular shapes, and arrange them around the duck.) In addition, garnish the platter with little sprigs of watercress. NET: 4 servings.

This recipe uses two small pheasants, which are boned and stuffed with a mousseline forcemeat, coated with chaud-froid sauce, and garnished with chopped aspic. On the presentation platter, one pheasant galantine is sliced and one is left whole. Start the recipe a day in advance.

GALANTINE DE FAISAN À LA GELÉE

Galantine of Pheasant in White Chaud-Froid Sauce and Aspic

2 whole dressed pheasants, 2½ to 3 pounds each
½ cup brandy (preferably Calvados)
Salt
Freshly cracked white pepper
6 cups chicken aspic (page 37)
Several nice sprigs of fresh tarragon to decorate the pheasants
Very thin slices of French bread, toasted

STUFFING
1 pound finely ground lean veal
1 pound finely ground lean pork
4 raw egg whites
1½ cups light cream
4 teaspoons finely chopped shallots
1 teaspoon finely chopped garlic
2 tablespoons finely chopped parsley
2 teaspoons finely chopped

tarragon
3 teaspoons salt
1 teaspoon finely ground white pepper
4 tablespoons brandy (Calvados)
⅓ cup shelled, blanched, coarsely chopped pistachio nuts
2 slices each of boiled ham and cooked tongue, ¼ inch thick and cut into fingers
2 hard-boiled eggs
Livers of the pheasants

CHAUD-FROID SAUCE
12 tablespoons warm water
4 tablespoons vegetable oil
10 tablespoons all-purpose flour
5 tablespoons unflavored gelatine
Salt
A few grains cayenne pepper
2 cups milk
⅔ cups light cream

Dry the pheasants inside and out with paper towels, and bone them (page 344). Spread them out on a cutting board, skin side down.

Brush them thoroughly with brandy and season with salt and pepper. Fold them and let them marinate.

STUFFING. Put the ground veal and pork in a mixer. Add the egg whites and beat well. Gradually mix in the light cream, at first drop by drop. Add the shallots, garlic, parsley, tarragon, salt, white pepper, and 2 tablespoons brandy. Mix thoroughly.

Spread the stuffing on the boned pheasants. Sprinkle the pistachio nuts all over the top. Cover the stuffing with alternate rows of the ham and tongue strips about ½ inch from each other. Cut the hard-boiled eggs in half, remove the yolks, and insert the pheasant livers in the egg whites. Place an egg in the center of each pheasant. Cut the yolks in half and put a half at each end of each egg. Roll up the pheasants, and sew the back with fine kitchen thread. Roll each pheasant in wax paper, then in foil, then in a clean cloth or kitchen towel. Fasten each end of the cloth securely with string, leaving 12-inch tails of string. Tie each pheasant "package" in two places around the middle, and with the extra string fasten the packages to the handles of a large pot, so that the pheasants are suspended like hammocks. Half fill the pan with water and slowly bring it to a boil. Reduce the heat to a gentle simmer and cover the pan. Simmer 50 minutes, then remove the pheasants from the pan and let them sit at least 5 minutes before unwrapping. Remove the cloth, but leave the foil and wax paper. Fit each galantine into a loaf pan rather snugly. Put a weight on top of each (such as a brick). Cool them at room temperature and then put them in the refrigerator overnight. Next day, unwrap the pheasants and remove the thread. Lightly dry them with paper towels. Remove any fat on the surface. Place them on a rack in a jelly roll pan, ready for coating.

CHAUD-FROID SAUCE. Put the warm water and vegetable oil in a large saucepan. Heat to lukewarm, and off the heat, stir in the flour mixed with the gelatine. Also mix in the salt and a little cayenne pepper. Mix in the milk, return the pan to low heat, and stir until the sauce just comes to a boil. Add the light cream.

Stir the chaud-froid sauce over a bowl of crushed ice. When it is on the point of setting, carefully and evenly coat the galantines, using a large serving spoon. Put them in the refrigerator to set. Return the sauce drippings to the pan, reheat, put over ice, and give the galantines another coating after the first has set. Select several beautiful sprigs of tarragon. Quickly dip them in boiling water and blot on paper towels. Decorate the breasts of the pheasants with the tarragon sprigs and leaves.

Have the liquid aspic ready in a pan. Pour a little in a layer cake pan and put it in the refrigerator to set. Place the coated galantines on a clean rack and jelly roll pan. Stir the clear aspic over ice until it is at the point of setting. Using a large spoon, coat the galantines with the aspic, and put them in the refrigerator to set. If necessary, give them another coating of aspic. Chill the coated galantines very well. When ready to serve, slice one galantine and place the slices, slightly overlapping, down a large silver serving platter. Place the uncut galantine at the other end. Turn out the aspic in the layer cake tin onto a piece of wax paper on a cutting board. Chop it into fine dice. Put this aspic into a pastry bag fitted with a #3 or #4 plain round tube, and pipe a border all around the galantines on the platter. Serve with very thin toasted slices of French toast. NET: About 20 servings.

The pheasants are stuffed with a purée of chestnuts and foie gras. They are coated with brown chaud-froid sauce and garnished with walnuts, truffles, and aspic.

FAISAN GLACÉ À LA MARIE-JEANNE

Cold Pheasants Stuffed with Chestnuts

2 whole dressed pheasants, 2½ to 3 pounds each
Lemon juice
6 tablespoons salt butter
¼ cup dry sherry
4 tablespoons vegetable oil
1 cup mixed sliced onion, carrot, and celery
2 apples, coarsely chopped
4 tablespoons all-purpose flour
2 teaspoons tomato paste
2 teaspoons meat glaze
1 sliced tomato
A few mushroom stems and trimmings

2 cups chicken stock (page 35)
2 tablespoons unflavored gelatine
2 tablespoons red currant jelly
2 2-pound cans unsweetened chestnut purée
1 cup foie gras or fine liver pâté
Salt
Freshly cracked white pepper
4 cups chicken aspic (page 37)
About ½ cup perfect shelled walnut halves
2 large black truffles, thinly sliced

Preheat the oven to 375°. Wash the pheasants in cold water with the lemon juice. Dry them inside and out, and tie them (page 342). Put the butter in a large deep heavy pan. When it is foaming, put in the pheasants one at a time, and brown them all over. Remove them from the pan, set them aside, and add to the pan the vegetable oil, mixed onion, carrot, and celery, and the apples. Cook the mixture slowly without browning. Stir in the flour and cook over low heat until it becomes a nut-brown color. Off the heat, add the tomato paste, meat glaze, sliced tomato, and mushroom trimmings. Pour in the chicken stock and stir the mixture over low heat until it comes to a boil. Simmer over low heat about 15 minutes, then rub it through a fine strainer. Return the pheasants to the pan, pour the strained sauce over them, cover the pan with the lid, and cook them in the oven 45 to 50 minutes. When they are done, remove them from the pan and remove the ties.

In a separate little bowl, mix the unflavored gelatine with a little of the sauce from the pan. Then put the gelatine mixed with sauce into the pan with the rest of the sauce. Stir in the jelly. Warm the sauce enough to dissolve the gelatine and jelly, then set aside to cool. Put the chestnut purée in a mixer bowl with the foie gras or fine liver pâté. Season according to taste with salt and pepper. Beat very well. Set aside half the mixture. To the half that remains in the mixer bowl, add 1 cup aspic slowly, beating all the time. Have ready 8 small baba molds, and fill them with the chestnut-pâté-aspic mixture. Put the filled baba molds to set in the refrigerator.

Carefully, with a sharp knife, remove the pheasant breasts, one from each side of each pheasant, in one piece. With kitchen shears, cut the breastbone away from each bird, exposing the cavity. Fill both cavities with the rest of the chestnut-pâté mixture. With a very sharp knife, neatly slice the breast meat. Cover the filling in both pheasants with the thin slices of breast meat. Place both filled pheasants on a rack in a jelly roll pan. Put the brown sauce in which the pheasant was cooked in a tin-lined copper pan over a bowl of ice. Stir it until it is just on the point of setting. Coat each pheasant with this sauce, and put in the refrigerator to set. When the sauce has set, remove the pheasants from the refrigerator and decorate them with the walnut halves and truffle slices. Put the clear aspic in a tin-lined copper pan over a bowl of ice. Stir it, and when it is just on the point of setting, coat the pheasants again, this time with the clear aspic. (There should be about 1 cup aspic remaining in the pan.) Put the aspic-coated pheasants to set again in the refrigerator. Unmold the baba molds, place 1 walnut half on each, cover with a little aspic on the point of setting, and put them to chill in the refrigerator. Put the rest of the aspic in a little metal pan and put it in the refrigerator to chill.

When the prepared pheasants are well chilled and set, place them on a silver serving platter. Arrange the molds of chestnut-pâté mixture around the edge. Turn out the rest of the aspic onto a cutting board and chop it fine. Put it in a pastry bag fitted with a #3 or #4 round tube, and garnish the platter. Put the "pièce montée" in the refrigerator to set really well. NET: 6 to 8 servings.

CAILLES EN ASPIC MUSCATE

Boned Quail Stuffed with Mousse de Foie Gras, in White Wine Aspic with White Grapes

4 whole dressed quail
2 cups chicken stock (page 35)
4 tablespoons sweet butter
6 ounces foie gras or fine liver pâté
2 tablespoons Cognac or good brandy
Salt
Freshly cracked white pepper
2 tablespoons whipped cream
1 tablespoon unflavored gelatine
½ cup Sauternes wine
1 teaspoon tomato paste
2 egg whites
1 cup white grapes (Muscat grapes, if available), skinned, seeded, and blotted on paper towels

Tie the quail (page 342), and put them in a small heavy pan with the chicken stock. Bring very slowly to a boil, and gently simmer 25 minutes. Let the birds chill in the stock. Then remove the quail and remove the string. Slit the skin and very carefully remove the breastbone and rib cage of each bird, leaving the wing and leg bones and backbone.

MOUSSE DE FOIE GRAS. Cream the sweet butter in a mixer until it is very light and fluffy. Add the foie gras or fine liver pâté, and cream it with the butter. Continue beating, and mix in the brandy, salt, pepper, and whipped cream. Beat until the whole mixture is light and fluffy.

Fill the cavities of the quail with the mousse, and set the rest aside. Reshape the breast meat over the mousse and put the birds in the refrigerator to chill thoroughly.

WHITE WINE ASPIC. Strain the stock in which the quail were cooked, and put it into a tin-lined copper pan with the gelatine, Sauternes wine, tomato paste, and stiffly beaten egg whites. Beat the mixture with a wire whisk over low heat until it comes to a rolling boil. Remove the pan from the heat and let it stand, without moving it, 15 minutes. Then strain it carefully through a colander lined with a damp cloth. You should now have clear wine aspic.

Put the rest of the mousse de foie gras in a pastry bag fitted with a medium-size star tube (#4 or #5), and pipe a bed on a silver serving platter. Place the quail on the mousse and chill again. Put half the wine aspic in a layer cake tin and let it set in the refrigerator. Put the pan containing the rest of the aspic over a bowl of ice and stir until it is on the point of setting. Coat the quails on the platter evenly with the aspic. Chill to set, then coat the quails again. Cover the whole platter with the grapes. Coat the grapes and the bottom of the platter with aspic. Turn the aspic in the layer cake pan onto a sheet of wax paper on a cutting board. Chop it into fine dice. Put it into a pastry bag fitted with a #3 or #4 plain round tube, and put a border of chopped aspic around the platter. Chill the prepared platter very well before serving. NET: 4 servings.

MEAT

T HERE ARE STILL TOO MANY HOMES that are in a steak-and-chops rut, not to mention the burger that totals the dietetic universe of too many children. Why? Perhaps because, as we lose our ties with rural life and more meats are prewrapped, meat takes on the image of all other prepackaged goods, losing identity.

The purpose of this introduction to the meat recipes is to present the great talent and ingenuity of French cuisine, describe in briefest terms the parts that form the whole animal and how they are cooked, and discuss some of the famous dishes in which these different meats are so good.

One of the great rewards of teaching cooking was to see the surprise and happy accomplishments of people learning new meat dishes. I refer not only to new ways of preparing meats, but often the very discovery of "new" parts of the animals. Being able to produce one really good ragoût, or a perfect roast beautifully garnished, made many heroes and heroines. I have no doubt that these dishes soon became "my special daube," or "the way I make my blanquette." But don't you wish others, where you may have dined, would be so moved to master one really good dish?

Steak is largely an American invention, and in French cuisine, the word had to be invented from the English — "*bifteck*." The French menu is so full of other good meat preparations that steak was boring by comparison . . . and much too expensive for the frugal French.

It is to the credit of modern industry that "no part of the animal is ever wasted"; but after the steaks and chops and roasts are cut out, not all the rest of the animal need go to the soap factory. Some real delicacies remain. Every bit of the flesh and bones and innards (called "offal" in culinary parlance) is edible, and mastery of French cuisine means a limitless repertoire of good dishes for all these parts.

First may we offer an explanation of the basic ways of cooking meat. Then we will describe the animal parts of each kind of meat — beef, veal, lamb, and pork, and how each of these parts is cooked in some well-known dish. When you review these charts, or the whole table of contents for the recipes in this chapter, you will quickly realize that steaks and chops, the most expensive of all meat cuts, are the least represented in classic French gastronomic creations.

Ways of Cooking Meat

(1) POACH, SIMMER, BOIL. The term "poach" is rarely applied to meat. Meats (mainly brisket, head, heart, tongue, feet, and other tough parts) are generally simmered in stock or seasoned water for a long period until the sinews are softened and broken down, and the meat is tender.

(2) BRAISE. Roast-size (fairly large) pieces of meat are quickly browned (seared) in hot fat on all sides in a heavy pan to seal in the juices. Then usually the pan glaze is loosened by pouring over flaming brandy or wine and adding a liquid or sauce mixture. The meat in the pan is then cooked slowly, generally for a long time, either in the oven or on top of the stove, most often with the cover on. This cooking process is primarily used for potentially tough cuts of meat; often the meat may be tenderized in advance by marinating (or larded for extra moisture).

(3) SAUTÉ. Small pieces of meat are browned on all sides in hot fat in a sauté pan. For certain meats such as veal scallops, chops, and steaks, this should complete the cooking.

Certain other meats are also browned in the sauté manner, then sauce or a little liquid is added, and the meat (or poultry) is allowed to continue cooking in the pan, either in the oven or on top of the stove, until done. (This procedure is not unlike braising, except that braising usually means tougher and larger cuts of meat and cooking for a long period of time.)

(4) ROAST. A large, relatively tender cut of meat is cooked either on a rack in the oven or skewered in a rotisserie. The meat is turned and basted regularly. It should maintain its texture and be moist and flavored with its own juices.

(5) GRILL. In classic culinary parlance, to grill meat is to cook it under a broiler, not on top of the stove. To "grill" slices of bacon, cook them in a preheated 450° oven (not under the broiler) this way. Lay the bacon strips on a cake rack set on a jelly roll pan, and lay a second cake rack on the strips; it will keep them flat and allow both sides to cook at once, as the fat drips into the pan beneath.

(6) BAKE. This method is used to cook pâtés and mousses. The food preparation is placed in its baking dish, which is then placed in a pan of hot water (bain marie) and baked in a moderate oven. Also certain slow-cook preparations like ham or meat encased in pastry, not basted, are baked.

(7) CASSEROLE COOKERY. The various refinements of casserole cookery — ragoût, daube, estouffade, carbonnade — are not methods per se, but rather a combination of methods, usually of sautéing and/or braising. (Please do say "ragoût," not "stew.")

BROWNING MEAT. There must be air space all around each piece in the hot fat to seal in the juices. If the pieces touch each other, they'll stew instead of sauté. It is thus better to brown a few pieces at a time than to crowd them.

As a general rule, red meats are browned quickly, uncovered, unlike poultry, which is browned slowly, covered or uncovered.

In sautéing veal scallops (which is the browning process, and often the whole cooking of this thin, delicate meat), a flat lid or pan with a weight on it should be placed directly on the meat slices to keep them flat and brown them quickly and evenly.

Handling and Storage of Meat

Here are a few tips which are helpful in knowing more about the meat you plan to cook and eat.

(1) Beef should be very bright red and well marbled with white fat. Veal should be very, very white. Pork should be pink, with as little fat as possible. Lamb should be rosy-red and not fatty.

(2) To keep raw meat fresh and odorless, rub it with oil or dip it into its own rendered fat or melted butter before refrigerating. Don't wrap it.

(3) Have meat at room temperature before cooking it, except for raw meat that has been frozen. The latter can be cooked as soon as it is soft enough for the juices to begin to run. If you allow it to thaw completely, you will lose too much of the juice.

(4) In handling meats, use tongs for pieces you're browning or for turning steaks. Never use a fork. Piercing lets the juices escape.

(5) Never carve any sizable piece of meat (or poultry) right after it comes out of the oven. Give a big roast, turkey, or capon at least 20 minutes to set into itself, and it will be much easier to slice.

MEAT CUTS AND COOKERY

SECTION	CUT	GENERAL COOKING METHOD	A CLASSIC EXAMPLE
Steer (Beef, Boeuf)			
Hindquarters	Top round Bottom round (smaller cuts include eye of round, top	Braise	Boeuf à la Mode Boeuf en Daube Boeuf Bourguignonne Paupiettes de Boeuf

SECTION	CUT	GENERAL COOKING METHOD	A CLASSIC EXAMPLE
	sirloin, rump roast or steak, round steaks, London broil}		
Midsection	Fillet (whole tenderloin)	Roast	Filet de Boeuf Wellington
		Sauté	Boeuf Stroganoff (pieces)
	Filet mignon (steak)	Grill or sauté	All the classic Tournedos combinations
	All the steaks (loin and rib)	Grill or sauté	Steak au Poivre
	Prime ribs	Roast	Côte de Boeuf Rôtie au Jus
Forequarters	Brisket	Simmer	Pot-au-Feu
	Chuck or shank	Braise	Boeuf Bourguignonne
Offal	Tripe	Braise	Tripes à la Mode
	Tail (oxtail)	Simmer	Vinaigrette or Soup
	Tongue	Simmer	Langue de Boeuf Parisienne
Lean scraps	Ground beef	Bake	Moussaka
		Simmer	Sauce Bouchère

*Calf (Veal, Veau)**

SECTION	CUT	GENERAL COOKING METHOD	A CLASSIC EXAMPLE
Hindquarters	Leg, cut as: Scallops (Fr. Escalopes, Ital. Scaloppine)	Sauté	Escalopes de Veau Valentino
		Sauté and braise	Paupiettes de Veau Fontanges
	Leg pieces	Braise	Daube de Veau
	Shanks	Braise	Osso Buco
	Knuckles and feet	Simmer	Pot-au-Feu and Fonds Blanc
Loin section	Loin (whole)	Roast	Rôti de Veau Farcie
	Loin chops	Sauté and braise	Côtes de Veau aux Fines Herbes
Forequarters	Shoulder	Braise	Gulyas de Veau à la Hongroise
Offal	Brains	Sauté	Cervelle de Veau au Beurre Noir
	Heart	Braise	Coeur de Veau Farci
	Liver	Sauté	Foie de Veau à la Moutarde
		Bake	Petites Crèmes de Foie de Veau

*Some famous dishes in grand cuisine require a whole leg or saddle of veal. These large cuts, however, are not often used in the home kitchen.

SECTION	CUT	GENERAL COOKING METHOD	A CLASSIC EXAMPLE
	Sweetbreads	Sauté	Ris de Veau Talleyrand
		Grill	Mixed Grill Bercy
	Kidney	Sauté	Rognon de Veau à la Crème
		Roast	Rognon de Veau au Four
	Head	Simmer	Tête de Veau à la Poulette
Lean scraps	Ground veal	Sauté	Fricadelles de Veau
		Various	As forcemeat or mousse

Lamb (Lamb, Agneau)

SECTION	CUT	GENERAL COOKING METHOD	A CLASSIC EXAMPLE
Whole baby lamb		Roast	
Hindquarters	Leg	Roast	Gigot d'Agneau Rôti
	Shanks	Braise	Ragoût d'Agneau
Loin	Saddle (both loins)	Roast	Selle d'Agneau Bordelaise
Rib	Rack	Roast	Carré d'Agneau Persillé
	Crown roast	Roast	Crown Roast of Lamb with Sausage Meat Stuffing
	Rib chops	Sauté and braise	Côtelettes d'Agneau Narona
		Grill	Mixed Grill Bercy
Forequarters	Breast	Braise	Poitrine d'Agneau Farcie Bordelaise
	Shoulder	Braise	Ragoût d'Agneau à la Printanière
Offal	Kidneys	Sauté	Rognons d'Agneau Turbigo

Pig (Pork, Porc; Ham, Jambon)

SECTION	CUT	GENERAL COOKING METHOD	A CLASSIC EXAMPLE
Whole suckling pig		Roast	Cochon de Lait Parisienne
Hindquarters	Ham*	Roast	Jambon en Croûte
		Boil (often commercial preparation)	Mousse Froide de Jambon

*Smoked commercially (as Virginia ham in America, Bayonne ham in France, prosciutto ham in Italy), and often precooked.

SECTION	CUT	GENERAL COOKING METHOD	A CLASSIC EXAMPLE
	Hocks and feet	Boil	Pieds de Porc Sainte Menehould
Center	Fatback	Salted (commercial preparation)	Used in wrapping roasts and encasing pâtés
	Loin	Roast	Hawaiian Pork
	Loin chops	Braise	Choucroute Garnie Côtes de Porc à la Normande
	Bacon	Grill (page 452)	for many garnish uses
	Spareribs	Roast	Spareribs Sweet and Sour
Forequarters	Shoulder	Braise	Le Cassoulet de Castelnaudary
Head	Whole	Braise	Head Cheese (more often a commercial preparation)
All parts of meat, offal, and blood			All manner of pork sausages, usually commercial preparations
Caul (stomach lining)			Often used to wrap meat or forcemeat preparations encased in dough (as could be done with Filet de Boeuf en Brioche, page 475)

BEEF

BOEUF À LA MODE

Braised Beef à la Mode

This dish should be started a day in advance. It is garnished with marrow, pieces of calf's foot, mushrooms, onions, carrots, and turnips.

3 to 4 pounds top sirloin of beef (or rump, which may need braising a little longer)
Optional: 6 ounces fatback of pork (for larding)
3 tablespoons salt butter

1 calf's foot, cut in pieces
4 marrow bones
¼ cup Cognac or good brandy
1 teaspoon meat glaze
1 teaspoon tomato paste
4 teaspoons potato flour

2½ cups chicken stock
   (page 35)
½ cup dry red wine
2 tablespoons dry sherry
2 teaspoons currant jelly
1 teaspoon freshly cracked black
   pepper
1 sprig celery leaf
1 bay leaf

MARINADE
¼ cup pure olive oil
¼ cup vegetable oil
1 cup tarragon vinegar
1 cup dry red wine
1 garlic clove, bruised
1 onion, sliced

1 stalk celery, sliced
1 bay leaf
6 whole black peppercorns

GARNISH
18 baby white onions
18 baby carrots (or large carrots
   cut in olive shapes)
18 baby turnips (or large turnips
   cut in olive shapes)
4 tablespoons salt butter
Salt
Freshly cracked white pepper
1 tablespoon granulated sugar
18 button-size fresh mushrooms
1 teaspoon lemon juice

The beef must be marinated at least 4 hours before it is cooked, and ideally longer — overnight if possible. If it is to be larded in the traditional fashion, cut the fatback into thin strips and thread them through the beef, using a long larding needle. If the roast was wrapped in fat by the butcher, remove it. Tie the beef tightly and neatly (with no fat wrapping) in several places, and place it in a deep container.

Mix all the marinade ingredients together in a saucepan, warm a little, and pour over the beef. Cover, and allow the beef to marinate at least 4 hours. When it is to be cooked, drain and dry it well. (The marinade may be kept in a tightly covered container in the refrigerator for future use.)

Preheat the oven to 375°. Heat the butter in a large heavy pan, and brown the beef on all sides. Also brown the pieces of calf's foot and marrow bones. In a separate little pan, heat the brandy, ignite, and pour it over the meat. Remove the meat and bones from the pan, set them aside, and add to the pan, off the heat, the meat glaze, tomato paste, and potato flour. Stir to a smooth paste. Stir in the chicken stock, wine, sherry, and jelly, and season with pepper. Stir over moderate heat until the mixture boils. Return the beef, calf's foot, and marrow bones to the pan and add the celery leaf and bay leaf. Cook the beef, uncovered, in the oven at least 1½ hours. (It may also be cooked on top of the stove.) Baste the meat frequently with the pan juices, and turn it over after 1 hour.

While the beef is cooking, blanch the onions, carrots, and turnips (for garnish) by bringing them (separately) to a boil from cold water, then draining. Melt 3 tablespoons butter in a sauté pan, add all the vegetables with a little salt and pepper, and shake over moderate heat until they begin to brown. Sprinkle with the sugar to glaze them a bit, and remove the vegetables from the pan. Add 1 tablespoon of butter to the pan, then the mushrooms, lemon juice, salt, and pepper, and sauté 2 minutes.

About 15 minutes before the beef is finished cooking, remove the meat from the pan and strain the sauce. Return the sauce to the pan with the marrow from the bones. (If too much fat has formed, add a little potato flour mixed with water.) Return the beef and calf's foot to the pan with the prepared vegetables. Reduce the oven temperature to 350° and cook another 15 minutes, or until the beef is tender. To serve, cut a few slices of the beef and arrange them overlapping on a platter. Place the uncut piece of beef at one end of the dish. Remove the vegetables and pieces of calf's foot from the sauce with a slotted spoon and garnish the platter. Spoon the sauce over the beef. NET: 6 to 8 servings.

BOEUF BOURGUI-GNONNE

Cubes of Beef Braised in Red Burgundy, with Salt Pork, Onions, and Mushrooms

2½ to 3½ pounds top sirloin
5 tablespoons salt butter
¼ cup Cognac or good brandy
2 teaspoons finely chopped garlic
2 teaspoons tomato paste
1 teaspoon meat glaze
4 teaspoons potato flour
2 cups chicken stock (page 35)
½ cup red Burgundy wine
¼ cup Madeira wine
¼ cup dry sherry
2 teaspoons currant jelly
Freshly cracked black pepper

GARNISH
6 ounces lean salt pork
12 baby white onions
3 tablespoons salt butter
1 tablespoon granulated sugar
Salt
Freshly cracked black or white pepper
6 ounces firm white mushrooms
1 teaspoon lemon juice
2 tablespoons chopped fresh parsley

Preheat the oven to 375°. Trim all the fat and sinew from the beef. Cut the beef into 1½-inch cubes. Heat 3 tablespoons butter in a heavy casserole over high heat. Brown the pieces of beef, a few at a time, quickly, on all sides. When all have been browned, put all the meat back in the casserole. In a separate little pan, heat the brandy, ignite, and pour it over the meat. Remove the meat, using a slotted spoon so that the juices stay. Melt 2 tablespoons butter in the casserole and add the garlic. Off the heat, stir in the tomato paste, meat glaze, and potato flour. When smooth, mix in the chicken stock, Burgundy wine, Madeira wine, sherry, and jelly. Add a little pepper but no salt. Stir over moderate heat until the mixture comes to a boil. Then put the meat back in the casserole, cover with the lid, and braise in the oven 1½ hours, basting frequently with the sauce. Reduce the oven to 350° and cook another 45 minutes, or until the meat is tender. Meantime, make the garnish.

GARNISH. Trim the rind from the salt pork and cut the pork into ¾-inch dice. Blanche it (put it in cold water, bring to a boil, drain well), then put it into a hot frypan, and shake over a hot burner until it is crisp. Drain, and set aside. Skin the onions, bring them to a boil from cold water, and drain. Melt 2 tablespoons butter in the frypan and add the blanched onions. Shake over moderate heat until they begin to brown. Sprinkle with the sugar, season with salt and pepper, and set aside. Cut the mushrooms in quarters. Melt 1 tablespoon butter in the frypan and add them with the lemon juice, salt, and pepper. Sauté briskly 3 minutes, and set aside. Mix the salt pork, onions, and mushrooms together. About 15 minutes before the beef is finished, add them to the beef in the oven. Serve in the casserole, sprinkled with chopped fresh parsley. Hot garlic bread is good with this dish. NET: 4 to 6 servings.

This recipe should not be attempted with a smaller piece of meat, which would not hold up well under the long cooking time. Any leftover meat can be served cold.

BOEUF BRAISÉ

Braised Beef (Pot Roast Braised in Tomato Sauce)

1 tablespoon salt butter	1 cup dry red wine
4 to 5 pounds bottom round of beef	Salt
	Freshly cracked white pepper
1 2-pound can tomatoes	2 tablespoons all-purpose flour
1 bay leaf	or 2 teaspoons potato flour
1 sprig parsley	¼ cup cold water
2 large yellow onions, thinly sliced	½ teaspoon dried thyme
	½ teaspoon celery salt
2 thin slices lemon	¼ cup dry sherry

Heat the butter very hot in a large deep heavy pan. Brown the beef on all sides, then add the tomatoes, bay leaf, parsley sprig, onions, and lemon slices. Cover the pan and cook over very low heat 50 minutes for each pound of meat (3 hours and 20 minutes for a 4-pound roast). Add the wine a little at a time while the meat is cooking, and turn the meat several times to ensure even cooking. When the meat has cooked 2 hours, season it with salt and pepper. When the meat is done, remove it from the pan, and finish the sauce as follows. Blend the flour with the cold water. Stir it into the sauce in the pan, then stir over low heat until the sauce thickens. Add the thyme, celery salt, and sherry. Simmer 2 minutes.

To serve, slice as much meat as needed for one serving, and arrange the slices slightly overlapping on a hot serving platter. Place the uncut piece of meat at one end of the dish. Spoon some of the sauce over the meat and serve the rest in a gravy boat. NET: 8 to 10 servings.

This dish should be started one or two days in advance of serving.

BOEUF BRAISÉ DUBARRY

Braised Beef with Cauliflower Gratinée

Marinade Crue (page 61)	6 tablespoons salt butter
4 pounds top round of beef	2 tablespoons dry sherry
¼ pound salt pork or fatback	1 teaspoon tomato paste
(for larding)	1 teaspoon meat glaze

4 tablespoons all-purpose flour
1½ cups chicken stock (page 35)
¼ cup dry red wine
Salt
Freshly cracked black pepper

1 bay leaf
2 small cauliflowers (or 1 large)
4 tablespoons freshly grated
    Parmesan cheese

Marinate the beef in the Marinade Crue preparation a minimum of 12 hours and up to two days. When the beef has been properly marinated, remove, and dry with paper towels.

Preheat the oven to 350°. Cut the salt pork or fatback into thin strips. Using a larding needle, pull the strips through the piece of beef to lard it. In a deep heavy pan, heat 4 tablespoons butter over high heat until it is light brown. Quickly brown the beef all over in the hot butter, and pour in the sherry. Remove the beef from the pan and, off the heat, add to the pan the tomato paste, meat glaze, and flour. Stir until smooth. Add the chicken stock, and stir over low heat until the mixture comes to a boil. Stir in the wine, salt, pepper, and bay leaf, and return the beef to the pan. Cover, and braise 1½ hours in the oven, basting the beef frequently with the pan sauce.

While the meat is braising, prepare the cauliflowers. Trim, and divide them into small "bouquets." Cook in boiling salted water until they are just soft and still a bit crisp. Drain, and gently squeeze them dry in a cloth. Arrange them on a baking sheet, sprinkle with the grated cheese and 2 tablespoons melted butter, and brown under the broiler. To serve, cut as many thin slices of beef as required for 1 serving. Arrange the slices overlapping on a serving dish, and place the uncut piece at one end. Strain the sauce and spoon it over the meat. Garnish each end of the dish with the cauliflower. NET: 6 to 8 servings.

BOEUF BRAISÉ À L'ITALIENNE

Braised Beef in Tomato Sauce with Fried Gnocchi

2 tablespoons pure olive oil
4 tablespoons salt butter
3-pound piece top round of beef
2 medium-size yellow onions,
    finely chopped
1 teaspoon finely chopped garlic
¼ pound salt pork, cut in ½-
    inch dice and blanched in
    boiling water
2 tablespoons all-purpose flour
¾ cup Chianti wine or red
    Burgundy
3 cups chicken stock (page 35)
Bouquet garni including parsley,
    thyme, fresh marjoram, and
    1 bay leaf (tied in cheesecloth)

4 large ripe tomatoes, skinned
    and quartered

FRIED GNOCCHI
3 cups water
6 tablespoons yellow cornmeal
2 tablespoons salt butter
2 eggs, one of them beaten
½ cup freshly grated Parmesan
    cheese
1 teaspoon Dijon mustard
Salt
Freshly cracked white pepper
About 1 cup dried white
    breadcrumbs (page 69)
Vegetable oil for deep-fryer

Preheat the oven to 375°. Heat the olive oil and butter in a large heavy casserole until they are very hot. Put in the piece of beef and brown it quickly on all sides. Remove the beef, and add to the pan the onions, garlic, and salt pork. Sauté this mixture over moderate heat 5 minutes. Off the heat, stir in the flour. Return the pan to the heat, brown the mixture slightly and again off the heat, stir in the wine and chicken stock. Stir over low heat until the sauce comes to a boil. Add the bouquet garni, return the beef to the pan, and cover the pan with wax paper and the lid. Braise the beef in the oven 2 to 3 hours, until it is tender. Add the quartered tomatoes about 30 minutes before the beef is done.

FRIED GNOCCHI. Bring the water to a boil. Stir in the cornmeal and simmer 4 minutes, stirring frequently. (The cornmeal should be quite soft and come away from the sides of the pan.) Remove the pan from the heat and beat in the butter, unbeaten egg, cheese, salt, mustard, and pepper. Beat well, and spread the mixture onto a flat platter to cool in the refrigerator. Shape the cooled mixture into balls on a floured board. Brush them with the beaten egg, roll them in breadcrumbs, and fry them in deep fat at 375° (or in a sauté pan) until they are golden brown all over. Drain the gnocchi on paper towels and keep them warm.

When the beef is cooked, remove it from the cooking pan and lay it on an au gratin dish. Cut as many slices as are needed for the first serving. Skim the fat from the sauce and remove the bouquet garni. Reduce the sauce slightly by boiling, and spoon it over and around the beef. Arrange the gnocchi at each end of the dish. NET: 4 to 6 servings.

FILET DE BOEUF BRAISÉ ORLOFF

Braised Fillet of Beef in Sour Cream Sauce

This elegant dish is garnished with mushrooms and quenelles, and served with a rice pilaff.

2 to 3 pounds fillet of beef in
   1 piece (tenderloin)
Salt
Freshly cracked white pepper
½ cup Cognac or good brandy
½ pound bacon, thinly sliced
6 tablespoons salt butter
½ pound firm fresh mushrooms,
   cut in half if large
1 teaspoon lemon juice
½ teaspoon finely chopped
   garlic
1 teaspoon tomato paste
1 teaspoon meat glaze
3 teaspoons potato flour
1¼ cups chicken stock
   (page 35)
⅓ cup dry sherry
1 teaspoon guava or currant jelly

1 cup sour cream
¼ cup freshly grated Parmesan
   cheese
2 tablespoons melted salt butter

BEEF QUENELLES
½ pound ground beef
2 egg whites
½ cup light cream
1 teaspoon salt
Freshly cracked white pepper

RICE PILAFF
3 tablespoons salt butter
1 yellow onion, finely chopped
1½ cups long-grain rice
3 cups chicken stock (page 35)
   or water
2 teaspoons salt

¼ teaspoon ground cardamom
  seed

A few grains cayenne pepper

Preheat the oven to 325°. Trim the fillet of beef of all fat and sinew from the beef. Rub the beef with salt and pepper and brush with ¼ cup brandy. Cover with slightly overlapping bacon slices, and tie each piece down neatly with string. Heat 2 tablespoons butter in a heavy pan, and brown the meat in it on all sides. In a separate little pan heat ¼ cup brandy, ignite, and pour it over the beef. Remove the beef, and add 4 tablespoons butter to the pan with the mushrooms, lemon juice, salt and pepper. Cook 3 minutes, without browning the mushrooms too much. Off the heat, add the garlic, tomato paste, meat glaze, and potato flour, and mix to a smooth paste. Add the chicken stock, sherry, and jelly, and stir over moderate heat until the mixture comes to a boil. Lower the heat so that the sauce is barely simmering, and stir in the sour cream a little at a time. Return the beef to the pan, and cook, uncovered, in the oven 45 minutes. Baste once or twice with the sauce.

BEEF QUENELLES. Put the ground beef in a mixer with the egg whites and beat well. Slowly add the light cream, and season with the salt and a little pepper. With 2 teaspoons, form this mixture into neat little dumplings. When the beef has been in the oven 30 minutes, drop them into the sauce and cook them with the beef.

RICE PILAFF. Melt the butter in a heavy pan. Add the onion and cook slowly until it is translucent but not brown. Add the rice, and stir until it is coated with the onion and butter. Cover with the chicken stock or water. Add the salt, cayenne pepper, and cardamom seed. Stir over moderate heat to a rolling boil, then cover the pan with the lid and cook over low heat 40 minutes. Fluff the cooked rice with 2 forks. (Note: The rice can be cooked (after it has come to a boil) in a 325° oven.)

When the beef is done, remove it from the pan and remove the string, but not the bacon slices. Cut the beef into ½-inch slices, and arrange overlapping down an au gratin dish. Spoon over them the sauce with the mushrooms and quenelles. Sprinkle with grated cheese and melted butter and brown under a hot broiler. Serve with a separate bowl of rice pilaff. NET: 6 to 8 servings.

FILET DE BOEUF STROGANOFF

Fillet of Beef Stroganoff

This famous preparation of sautéed fingers of tenderloin in sour cream sauce, with fresh dill, should be served with a Rice Pilaff (page 675) or Gnocchi Parisienne (page 673).

2 pounds fillet of beef (the tail
  end)
5 tablespoons salt butter
3 tablespoons Cognac or good
  brandy

½ ounce dried mushrooms,
  soaked in 1 cup water at least
  30 minutes
1 teaspoon finely chopped garlic
1 teaspoon tomato paste

1 teaspoon meat glaze
3 tablespoons all-purpose flour
⅓ cup chicken stock (page 35)

1 cup sour cream
2 tablespoons finely chopped
   fresh dill

Trim off most of the fat from the fillet of beef, and cut the meat into strips about 2 inches long and ½ inch wide. Heat 2 tablespoons butter in a heavy frypan. When it is light golden brown, brown the pieces of meat a few at a time. Each piece should be sautéed quickly, in seconds, and be a little pink inside, to retain its flavor and seal in the juices; the meat must not cook. When all of it has been browned, return the pieces to the pan. In a separate little pan, heat the brandy, ignite, and pour it over the meat. Lift the meat out of the pan again, and add to the pan another 3 tablespoons butter. Drain the mushrooms, chop them fine, and reserve the water in which they soaked. Sauté them with the garlic in the frypan over moderate heat a minute or two. Off the heat, stir in the tomato paste, meat glaze, and flour. Mix in the chicken stock and ½ cup of the mushroom water. Stir over low heat until the sauce just comes to a boil, then slowly beat in the sour cream and 1½ tablespoons chopped fresh dill.

Up to this point, this dish can be made in advance, but do not put the meat in the sauce until ready to serve. Serve in a casserole, with the sauce spooned over the meat, and the top sprinkled with the rest of the chopped fresh dill. NET: 4 to 6 servings.

BOEUF EN CASSEROLE PROVENÇALE

Casserole of Beef with Sauce of Fresh Tomatoes, Onions, and Stuffed Olives

Garlic bread is a good accompaniment.

2½ pounds eye round of beef
3 tablespoons salt butter
2 tablespoons Cognac or good
   brandy
3 yellow onions, cut in eighths
½ teaspoon finely chopped
   garlic
4 large ripe tomatoes, skinned
   and cut in eighths
½ cup green pimento-stuffed
   olives
2 teaspoons tomato paste

2 teaspoons potato flour
1 teaspoon meat glaze
½ cup red Rhone wine (such as
   Châteauneuf-du-Pape)
1 cup chicken stock (page 35)
1 teaspoon currant jelly
¼ cup dry sherry
1 sprig fresh tarragon
   or 1 bay leaf
2 tablespoons chopped fresh
   parsley

Trim the fat off the beef and cut the meat into 1½-inch cubes. In a medium-size heavy pan, brown 2 tablespoons butter. Then brown the pieces of beef in the pan a few at a time, browning each one on all sides. Remove the beef from the pan. Heat the brandy in a small pan, ignite, pour it in the pan in which the beef was browned, and loosen the glaze. Add 1 tablespoon butter to the pan, then add the onions and garlic. Sauté briskly for 5 minutes, until the onion is slightly glazed. Add the tomatoes and olives, and cook briskly 2 minutes. Off the heat, stir into the pan the tomato paste, potato flour, and meat glaze. Stir the mixture until it is smooth, then pour in the wine, chicken stock, and sherry. Return to low heat and stir until the sauce comes to a boil. Add the currant jelly.

Put the pieces of beef back in the pan. Add the fresh tarragon or bay leaf. Cover the pan with wax paper and the lid, and simmer the beef over low heat 45 minutes to 1½ hours, until the beef is tender. Serve in a casserole, sprinkled with fresh parsley. NET: 4 servings.

BOEUF EN DAUBE

Daube of Beef

Braised beef, mushrooms, and olives covered with thin slices of raw tomato and melted Parmesan cheese, bordered with Duchess potatoes.

2½ pounds top round of beef
4 tablespoons salt butter
2 tablespoons Cognac or good brandy
12 small fresh firm white mushrooms
24 pitted green olives
1 teaspoon tomato paste
3 tablespoons all-purpose flour
2 cups chicken stock (page 35)
½ cup dry red wine
1 tablespoon currant jelly
1 bay leaf

3 or 4 large ripe tomatoes, skinned and thinly sliced
½ cup freshly grated Parmesan cheese
A little melted butter

DUCHESS POTATOES
3 large Idaho-type potatoes
Salt
1 egg
2 tablespoons salt butter
Freshly cracked white pepper
Milk (if necessary)

Cut the beef in 1½-inch cubes. Heat 3 tablespoons butter over high heat in a heavy casserole. Brown the pieces of beef very quickly on all sides. In a separate little pan, heat the brandy, ignite, and pour it over the beef in the casserole. Remove the meat, and in the same casserole brown the mushrooms in 1 tablespoon butter over moderate heat. Off the heat, add the olives, tomato paste, and flour. Pour in the chicken stock. Stir over moderate heat until the mixture comes to a boil. Add the wine, jelly, and bay leaf. Put the meat back in the pan, cover, and cook over low heat until it is tender.

DUCHESS POTATOES. Cook the potatoes in boiling salted water until soft. Drain, dry, and put them in a mixer. Beat them until smooth. Add the egg, butter, salt, pepper, and a little milk (if necessary), and beat well.

Put the potato purée in a pastry bag fitted with a large (#8 or #9) star tube. When the meat is cooked, arrange it on a long flat au gratin dish. Spoon the sauce from the cooking pan over it. Cover with the thinly sliced tomatoes. Sprinkle with the grated cheese and a little melted butter, and pipe the Duchess potatoes all around the edge. Brown the dish under a hot broiler and serve. NET: 4 to 6 servings.

This beef is pounded and larded, then cut into grenadins (slices) and braised. It is served on a bed of spinach purée mixed with croûtons and sour cream.

2 pounds rump of beef
Salt
Freshly cracked white pepper
Pinch of thyme
Pinch of freshly grated nutmeg
6 ounces salt pork, cut in 18
   match-size strips
5 tablespoons salt butter
½ cup each of finely chopped
   carrots, white part of leeks,
   and celery
2 tablespoons finely chopped
   shallots or chives
1 bay leaf
1 teaspoon chopped fresh thyme
1 teaspoon chopped fresh
   tarragon

6 whole black peppercorns,
   coarsely cracked
1½ cups dry red wine
1 cup chicken stock (page 35)
2 tablespoons dry sherry
12 firm white mushroom caps
1 teaspoon lemon juice
1 bunch crisp fresh watercress

SPINACH PURÉE
2 pounds fresh spinach
2 tablespoons water
Salt
Freshly cracked white pepper
4 tablespoons salt butter
½ cup sour cream
1 cup fried croûtons (page 69)

Preheat the oven to 350°. Pound the piece of beef thoroughly with a wooden mallet. During the pounding, sprinkle it with a little salt, pepper, and the pinch of thyme and nutmeg, so that you pound the seasonings into the beef. When it is pounded down to a thickness of about 1 inch, lard it with the strips of salt pork, using a small larding needle. Trim off the ends of the larding pork neatly and cut the beef into 6 equal portions. Heat 4 tablespoons butter in a heavy casserole, and brown the beef on both sides. Add to the casserole the carrots, leeks, celery, and shallots or chives. Also add the bay leaf, fresh thyme and tarragon, and peppercorns. Pour the wine over all, cover the casserole with the lid, and braise the beef in the oven 30 minutes. When it is done, remove the pieces of beef from the casserole and keep them warm. Strain the sauce into a saucepan, and boil it down to ½ cup, add the chicken stock and sherry, boil this liquid down to half quantity, and set it aside. Wash the mushroom caps, sauté them in 1 tablespoon butter with the lemon juice, salt, and pepper, and set them aside.

SPINACH PURÉE. Wash the spinach very well. Put it in a large pan with the water, salt, and pepper, and cook it over moderate heat 5 minutes. Drain it through a colander, and press it until it is quite dry. Rub it through a fine strainer or put it through a fine meat chopper. Melt the butter in a pan, add the spinach, mix in the sour cream and fried croûtons, and warm the mixture quickly.

To serve, arrange the puréed spinach on a hot flat serving dish. Place the grenadins of beef on it. Brush the beef with the sauce, garnish with the mushroom caps, and brown quickly under a hot broiler to get a good glaze on the meat. Garnish with the fresh watercress. NET: 4 servings.

PAUPIETTES DE BOEUF À LA REINE

Stuffed Beef Birds with Pea Purée

These beef birds are stuffed with veal mousse, tongue, and truffles. Substitute broccoli purée for pea purée if you like.

2 pounds top round of beef in
   one piece
Salt
Freshly cracked white pepper
1 teaspoon lemon juice
6 slices sturdy white bread,
   crusts trimmed off
1 cup dry white wine
1 pound finely ground veal
2 egg whites
1 cup light cream
½ pound boiled tongue
   (in 1 piece)
4 black truffles
8 tablespoons salt butter
¼ cup Cognac or good brandy

1 teaspoon tomato paste
2 level teaspoons meat glaze
2 teaspoons potato flour
1½ cups chicken stock
   (page 35)
½ cup dry red wine
1 tablespoon currant jelly

PEA PURÉE
4 packages frozen peas
Salt
3 tablespoons salt butter
4 tablespoons all-purpose flour
1 tablespoon sour cream
Freshly cracked white pepper

Trim all the fat and sinew off the beef. Cut the beef into very thin slices. Place them between two pieces of wax paper, and pound with a wooden mallet until the slices are very thin (almost translucent). Remove the top piece of paper. Season the slices with salt, pepper, and a drop or two of lemon juice. Soak the slices of bread in the wine. When they are soft, press them out in a soft cloth. Mix the wine-dampened bread with the veal, and put the mixture through a fine meat chopper two times. Then put the mixture in a mixer bowl, and mix in the egg whites. Slowly beat in the light cream, and season well with salt and pepper. Spread this stuffing (which should be thick and stiff) ¼ inch thick on each slice of beef. Cut the tongue into little finger-size strips, and put 3 strips across each slice of beef on the stuffing. Cut the truffles into smaller strips, and put them between the tongue fingers (reserve a little truffle for the sauce). Roll up the stuffed slices of beef tightly and tie at each end with fine string.

Heat 4 tablespoons butter in a heavy casserole. When it is very hot, brown the beef birds all over. Warm the brandy in a separate little pan, ignite, and pour over the beef birds. When the flame is out, cover the beef, and cook over very low heat 25 to 30 minutes. Remove the beef birds from the casserole, remove the string, and keep the beef warm. Add 4 tablespoons butter to the casserole and, off the heat, stir in the tomato paste, meat glaze, and potato flour. When smooth, pour in the chicken stock and wine. Stir over moderate heat until the sauce comes to a boil. Add the jelly, and simmer over low heat 3 to 4 minutes. Strain the sauce over the beef birds and sprinkle with the reserved chopped truffle. Keep the dish warm.

PEA PURÉE. Cook the frozen peas in boiling salted water. Drain, and rub them through a fine strainer. Melt the butter in a pan. Off the heat, stir in the flour, and let it brown. Add the puréed peas, sour cream, salt, and pepper. Cook over low heat 5 minutes, mixing well.

To serve, arrange the pea purée in a bed down a long flat oval serving dish. Smooth each side with a knife, so that it looks like a mound. Cut the beef birds in half, and arrange them on the pea purée with the cut side up. Spoon the sauce over them. NET: 4 to 6 servings.

SAUERBRATEN

This dish should be started at least a day in advance.

Braised Beef,
German Style, with
Sweet-Sour Cabbage

4 pounds bottom round or side
   round of beef
2 garlic cloves
Salt
Freshly cracked black pepper
1 large Bermuda onion, sliced
4 cups water
¼ cup tarragon vinegar
4 whole peppercorns
2 slices lemon
1 bay leaf
2 whole cloves
5 tablespoons salt butter
4 medium-size yellow onions,
   coarsely chopped
A little all-purpose flour
A little paprika
2 teaspoons granulated sugar

2 teaspoons tomato paste
1 carrot, finely chopped
6 gingersnaps
1 cup sour cream

SWEET-SOUR RED CABBAGE
2 small red cabbages
2 medium-size yellow onions
2 tablespoons bacon fat or
   salt butter
2 cups sliced apples (cored and
   skinned)
½ cup brown sugar
1 cup chicken stock (page 35)
Salt
Freshly cracked black pepper
2 tablespoons vinegar

The beef must be marinated at least 24 hours. Cut the garlic cloves into small slices and insert them into the beef with a sharp knife. Rub it well with salt and pepper. Put it in an earthenware bowl, and cover it with the sliced Bermuda onion. In a separate pan, mix the water, vinegar, and peppercorns, lemon, bay leaf, and cloves, boil 3 minutes, and pour it over the meat. Cover the bowl tightly with foil, and leave it in the refrigerator at least 24 hours. After the meat has been properly marinated, drain it and dry it on paper towels. Reserve the marinade to use in the sauce (below).

Preheat the oven to 350°. In a small heavy pan, melt 2 tablespoons butter and sauté the yellow onions. Pat the roast lightly with flour. Melt 3 tablespoons butter in a deep heavy casserole and brown the roast in it, turning on all sides. Add the sautéed onions to the casserole, also the paprika, sugar, tomato paste, carrot, 1½ cups of the marinade, and the roughly crumbled gingersnaps. Cover the casserole with a tight lid and cook in the oven 3½ to 4 hours, until the meat is tender.

SWEET-SOUR RED CABBAGE. Cut the red cabbages in fine shreds. Put the shredded cabbage in cold water, bring to a boil, and drain (it is now blanched). Sauté the onions in a casserole in the bacon fat or butter. Add the cabbage, apples, brown sugar, chicken stock, salt, and pepper. Cover with wax paper and the lid, and cook in a preheated

350° oven 1½ hours. Remove from the oven, and stir in the vinegar.

When the meat is tender, transfer it to a hot platter. Taste the sauce for seasoning, and mix in the sour cream. Reheat the sauce and strain it. Spoon some of the sauce over the meat and serve the rest in a sauceboat. Serve the cabbage separately. NET: 6 to 8 servings.

ENTRECÔTE À LA FORESTIÈRE

Sautéed Steak with Rissolé Potatoes, Mushrooms, and Canadian Bacon

Rissolé potatoes are ¾-inch cubes of raw potato fried in butter.

½ pound small firm white
    mushrooms
1 teaspoon lemon juice
Salt
Freshly cracked white pepper
11 tablespoons salt butter
¼ pound Canadian bacon, sliced
4 individual steaks (shell, rib,
    or sirloin)

½ cup dry white wine
2 tablespoons finely chopped
    fresh parsley

RISSOLÉ POTATOES
4 Idaho or large Maine potatoes
3 tablespoons salt butter
Salt
Freshly cracked white pepper

RISSOLÉ POTATOES. Pare the potatoes and cut them into ¾-inch cubes. Cover with cold water and let stand 30 minutes. Drain, and dry between paper towels. Melt the butter in a sauté pan. When it is foaming, add the potatoes. Cook over moderate heat about 20 to 25 minutes, until the potatoes are cooked and nicely browned all over. Shake the pan occasionally and turn the potatoes to brown evenly. Season with salt and pepper just before serving. Set aside and keep warm.

Wash and dry the mushrooms and trim off the stems. Sauté the caps in 2 tablespoons butter with the lemon juice, salt and pepper. Set the mushrooms aside, add 1 tablespoon butter to the same pan, quickly sauté the Canadian bacon until lightly browned, and set it aside. Melt 4 tablespoons butter and brush the steaks with it. Heat another 4 tablespoons butter in a large frypan over high heat. Quickly sauté the steaks on both sides to the desired finish (rare, medium-rare, etc.). To serve, arrange the steaks on a hot serving platter, slightly overlapping. Add the wine to the pan the steaks were cooked in, bring it to a boil, gather up the pan glaze, and pour it over the meat. Surround the steaks with small alternating mounds of rissolé potatoes and mushroom caps on Canadian bacon. Sprinkle the potatoes and mushrooms with the parsley. NET: 4 servings.

MIXED GRILL BERCY

A Mixed Grill Bercy offers a rich assortment of grilled meats (the "grand platter" includes all of them) garnished with sautéed mushrooms, broiled tomatoes, potato balls in potato baskets, and fresh crisp watercress, and served with frozen balls of Bercy butter to melt over the whole. For your mixed grill, select any or all of the meats and vegetables; selection and quantity of the items to be cooked are a matter of personal preference. The recipes for Bercy Butter and

STUFFED TOMATOES AND
  MUSHROOMS
4 tablespoons salt butter
4 chicken livers
1 cup finely chopped onion
½ pound boiled ham, finely
  chopped
½ cup finely chopped
  mushrooms
1 teaspoon finely chopped fresh
  parsley

3 tablespoons sour cream
Salt
Freshly cracked white pepper
4 medium-size ripe tomatoes
½ teaspoon finely chopped
  garlic
2 tablespoons freshly grated
  Parmesan cheese
A little melted salt butter
8 firm white mushroom caps

Rub the steak with the garlic, brush it with melted butter, and season with salt and pepper. Brown the steak quickly on one side only under a hot broiler, and place it browned side down on a large wooden steak plank. Set aside.

STUFFED TOMATOES AND MUSHROOMS. Heat 2 tablespoons butter very hot in a sauté pan and brown the chicken livers. Remove the livers from the pan, chop them, and set aside for a moment. Add another 2 tablespoons butter to the pan, and cook the onion until it is translucent. Return the chicken livers to the pan, and add the ham, mushrooms, parsley, sour cream, salt, and pepper. Blend together 3 minutes over low heat. Cut the tops off the tomatoes and scoop out the pulp. Season the insides with a little chopped garlic, salt, and pepper. Fill the centers with the chopped mixture, and sprinkle with the grated cheese and melted butter. Fill 4 mushroom caps with the same mixture, cover with the other 4 mushroom caps, and sprinkle with melted butter.

MASHED POTATOES. Pare the potatoes and cook in boiling salted water about 20 minutes, or until they are soft. Drain, and return to the pan to dry a minute or so over the heat. Put them in a mixer bowl and beat in 1 egg, the hot milk, butter, salt, and cayenne pepper.

Place the mushrooms and tomatoes alternately around the steak on the plank. Put the mashed potatoes in a pastry bag fitted with a large star tube (#8 or #9). Pipe the potatoes all around the edge of the plank. Brush them with slightly beaten egg. Place the assembled plank under the broiler, not too close to the heat, to cook about 15 minutes. (The steak is cooked on one side only; therefore, it should not be more than 1 inch thick.) NET: 4 servings.

4 individual steaks (shell or rib)
4 tablespoons salt butter
Bunch of crisp fresh watercress
  or chicory

BERCY SAUCE
4 tablespoons salt butter

2 tablespoons finely chopped
  onion
2 tablespoons finely chopped
  shallots
1 cup dry white wine
1 cup chicken stock (page 35)
Salt

STEAK
À LA BERCY

Sautéed Steaks with
Bercy Sauce

Freshly cracked white pepper
2 tablespoons all-purpose flour

1 teaspoon finely chopped fresh
parsley

BERCY SAUCE. Melt 2 tablespoons butter in a saucepan. Add the onion and shallots and cook over very low heat until they are soft but not browned. Add the wine and chicken stock, season with salt and pepper, and cook over low heat 5 minutes. Blend the flour with the remaining butter. Over low heat, add the butter and flour mixture to the sauce bit by bit, stirring all the time. When the flour and butter are thoroughly blended into the sauce and it is absolutely smooth, let it simmer for 15 minutes. Just before serving, add the parsley.

STEAKS. Melt the butter in a large heavy frypan. Brush the steaks with about half of it. Heat the rest, and when it is on the point of browning, put the steaks in the pan. Brown them quickly on both sides, to the desired degree of finish. (Probably only 2 steaks will fit into the pan at one time, and more butter may be needed to cook them all.)

Arrange the steaks on a hot serving platter. Garnish with the watercress or chicory. Serve the sauce in a separate bowl. NET: 4 servings.

STEAK AU POIVRE, SAUCE BÉARNAISE

Sautéed Pepper Steak,
Béarnaise Sauce

Coarsely cracked peppercorns are pressed into one side of the steak and sautéed to form a crust.

4 individual steaks (shell or
club)
4 tablespoons salt butter
2 tablespoons white peppercorns
2 tablespoons black peppercorns
Bunch of crisp fresh watercress

BÉARNAISE SAUCE
3 egg yolks
3 teaspoons tarragon vinegar
3 tablespoons light cream
8 tablespoons frozen sweet
butter

1 teaspoon finely chopped white
onion or shallot
⅛ teaspoon finely chopped
garlic
1 tablespoon chopped fresh
parsley
1 teaspoon chopped fresh
tarragon
1 teaspoon chopped fresh chives
¼ teaspoon tomato paste
⅛ teaspoon meat glaze
1 drop lemon juice

BÉARNAISE SAUCE. Put the egg yolks in a small bowl. Beat in the vinegar and the light cream. Stand the bowl in a shallow pan half full of hot water over slow heat. Stir with a little whisk until the sauce thickens. Cut the frozen sweet butter into little pieces, and stir it into the yolk mixture bit by bit. Then stir in the rest of the ingredients. (This sauce may be made ahead of time. Cover it with foil and stand it over warm water until ready to use.)

Beat the steaks briefly with the side of a cleaver to break the fibers. Score the surface lightly (make a few crisscross slashes with a knife). Melt the butter. With half of it, brush one side of each steak. Crush the peppercorns coarsely with a mortar and pestle. Press them into the unbuttered side of the steak. Chill the steaks in the refrigerator to set the butter. When ready to serve, broil the steaks quickly on each side under a hot broiler to the desired finish. Arrange them on a hot serving platter, pepper side up. Brush them with the rest of the melted butter. Garnish with crisp fresh watercress. Serve the sauce in a separate bowl. NET: 4 servings.

TOURNEDOS HENRY IV

Broiled Filet Mignon with Béarnaise Sauce

Garnished with artichoke bottoms capped with mushrooms, accompanied by matchstick potatoes.

2½ pounds fillet of beef, in
    1 piece
4 ounces fat salt pork, cut into
    thin strips for larding
2 tablespoons Cognac or good
    brandy
Freshly cracked white pepper
6 slices bacon
¼ teaspoon finely chopped
    garlic
4 tablespoons salt butter
6 large round sturdy croûtons,
    fried in butter (page 69)
Salt

BÉARNAISE SAUCE
2 egg yolks
2 tablespoons light cream
2 tablespoons tarragon vinegar
¼ bay leaf

2 whole peppercorns
Salt
A few grains cayenne pepper
12 tablespoons frozen sweet
    butter
2 tablespoons finely chopped
    fresh parsley
2 tablespoons finely chopped
    fresh chives
¼ teaspoon tomato paste
¼ teaspoon meat glaze
2 drops lemon juice

GARNISH
6 artichoke bottoms
6 large firm white mushroom
    caps
2 cups prepared matchstick
    potatoes (page 617)
Bunch of fresh crisp watercress

BÉARNAISE SAUCE. Put the egg yolks in a medium-size bowl and mix in the light cream. Put the vinegar, bay leaf, and peppercorns in a little saucepan, and boil down to 1 tablespoon liquid. Strain, and slowly beat the reduced vinegar into the egg yolk mixture. Add a little salt and cayenne pepper. Place the bowl in a shallow pan half full of hot water over low heat. Beat the mixture until it is as thick as desired. Cut the frozen sweet butter in pieces. Continue beating the sauce and add the butter bit by bit. Then mix in the rest of the ingredients. Cover the bowl with foil and keep it warm over hot water until ready to use.

Thread a larding needle with the strips of salt pork and lard the fillet of beef. Rub the fillet with a cloth dipped in the brandy. Wrap the fillet in the cloth and let it stand 30 minutes. Then cut the fillet into 6 slices (tournedos). Put a little pepper on each slice. With fine string, tie a slice of bacon around the outside of each slice. Season with a speck of garlic. Put a little butter on each slice and broil quickly under a hot broiler, each side. Arrange the tournedos on the rounds of fried bread on a hot flat serving dish in the form of a circle. Warm the artichoke bottoms and mushroom caps in a little butter, salt, and pepper. Put a spoonful of Béarnaise sauce in the center of each artichoke bottom and cover with a mushroom cap. Fill the center of the platter with the prepared matchstick potatoes. Garnish with the watercress and serve the sauce in a separate bowl. NET: 6 servings.

TOURNEDOS MELBA

Sautéed Filet Mignon Melba

Garnished with baked tomato stuffed with chicken, mushrooms and truffle, and served on fried croûtons, with braised lettuce.

6 small tomatoes, 2 to 2½ inches in diameter
Salt
Freshly cracked black pepper
6 tablespoons salt butter
3 tablespoons all-purpose flour
A few grains cayenne pepper
½ cup chicken stock (page 35)
½ cup heavy cream
1 cup finely chopped cooked chicken
1 cup finely chopped fresh firm

white mushrooms, sautéed in a little butter and lemon juice
2 black truffles, thinly sliced
3 tablespoons dry breadcrumbs (page 69)
6 filets mignons, 1¼ inch thick
4 tablespoons sweet butter
A little melted butter
6 large round fried croûtons, fried in butter (page 69)
3 Boston lettuces, quartered and braised (page 601)

Have the braised lettuce cooked, and keep it warm.

STUFFED TOMATOES. Preheat the oven to 350°. Cut the tops off the tomatoes and scoop out the centers. In the bottom of each hollowed-out tomato, put a little salt, pepper, and a small piece of salt butter. Melt 2 tablespoons salt butter in a sauté pan. Off the heat, stir in the flour, salt, and cayenne pepper, and pour in the chicken stock. Stir the sauce over low heat until it thickens, then add the heavy cream and bring to a boil. Mix the chicken, mushrooms, and truffles into this sauce, and fill the tomatoes with it. Sprinkle them with breadcrumbs and dot with a little salt butter. Bake until the tops are a little browned (about 10 to 15 minutes). Set them aside and keep them warm.

If the butcher wrapped bacon around the filets mignons, remove it and retie them with a clean length of cord. Heat the sweet butter in a large frypan. When it is on the point of browning, put in the tournedos (filets mignons) and quickly cook them over high heat until nicely browned on each side. (Do not overcook them; fillet of beef should always be on the rare side.) Season them with salt and pepper, and brush the tops with a little melted butter. Remove the strings. To serve, arrange the croûtons of fried bread in a circle on a serving platter. Place a sautéed tournedos on each round, and a baked stuffed tomato on each tournedos. Garnish with the quartered sections of braised Boston lettuce. NET: 6 servings.

2-pound fillet of beef
½ teaspoon finely chopped
   garlic
Salt
Freshly cracked white pepper
3 tablespoons Cognac or good
   brandy
6 tablespoons salt butter
3 ounces fine liver pâté
Few grains freshly grated
   nutmeg
4 large thin slices boiled ham
1 egg, beaten

BRIOCHE
1 package yeast
¼ cup lukewarm water
2 cups all-purpose flour
10 tablespoons salt butter
3 eggs
½ teaspoon salt
2 teaspoons granulated sugar

BORDELAISE SAUCE
1 teaspoon and 1 tablespoon salt
   butter
2 chicken livers
1 tablespoon Cognac or good
   brandy
1 teaspoon tomato paste
1 teaspoon meat glaze
2 teaspoons potato flour
1¼ cups chicken stock
   (page 35)
¼ cup dry sherry
1 teaspoon currant or grape jelly
A little freshly cracked white
   pepper
2 marrow bones
1 cup dry red wine
1 bay leaf
4 whole peppercorns
1 garlic clove, bruised
1 small stalk celery, sliced
1 sprig celery leaf
2 slices onion

FILET DE BOEUF EN BRIOCHE, SAUCE BORDELAISE

Roast Fillet of Beef in Brioche, with Bordelaise Sauce

BRIOCHE. In a small bowl, dissolve the yeast in the lukewarm water. Add it to ½ cup of flour, and stir with a rubber scraper until the mixture forms a firm ball away from the sides of the bowl. Turn the ball out onto a lightly floured board. Knead it a little to get a smooth surface (on the bottom). Turn bottom side up and cut a crisscross on it. Place the ball in a bowl of lukewarm water, cut side up, and let it rise to the top of the water. Cream the butter in a mixer until it is light and fluffy. Remove it from the mixer, set aside, and put in the mixer bowl (as it is) 1½ cups flour and the eggs, salt, and sugar. Beat this mixture until it is shiny. Add the creamed butter and beat again. Lift the ball of yeast out of the water with your hand and put it in the mixer bowl. Beat until well mixed. Wipe out a large bowl with a damp cloth and dust lightly with flour. Put the brioche dough in this bowl and cover with plastic wrap and a cloth. Let the dough rise in a warm place until it is more than double in bulk (about 45 minutes). Break the rise by running a finger around the edge of the bowl, cover again, and put the bowl in the freezer.

Preheat the oven to 375°. Place the fillet of beef on a rack in a roasting pan and roast 30 minutes. Remove it from the oven (and either leave the oven on or preheat it again to 375°). Rub the beef with the chopped garlic, salt, and pepper. Brush it generously with brandy. Wrap it in foil, and let it cool a little in the refrigerator. Cream the butter in a mixer, mix in the liver pâté, 1 teaspoon brandy, salt, pepper, and nutmeg, and beat well. Spread this pâté thickly on the chilled beef. Lay out the ham slices like a sheet and wrap the pâté-spread beef in the ham. Chill the meat again for a moment.

Remove the brioche dough from the freezer, and roll out two-thirds of it about ½ inch thick. Generously butter a loaf pan and line it with the rolled-out brioche dough. Put the ham-wrapped fillet of beef in the pan and brush the edges of the dough with beaten egg. Roll out the remaining third of dough large enough to cover the top of the pan. Tuck the edges in the sides securely. Cover the pan with a cloth canopy (it must not touch the dough), and let the dough rise about 15 minutes. Brush the top with beaten egg and bake in the preheated oven 45 to 50 minutes.

BORDELAISE SAUCE. Heat 1 teaspoon butter in a saucepan. Brown the chicken livers quickly on each side. Flame with the brandy. Remove the livers from the pan, and add to the pan 1 tablespoon butter. Off the heat, stir in the tomato paste, meat glaze, and potato flour, and mix until smooth. Add the chicken stock, sherry, jelly, and a little pepper. Stir over moderate heat until it comes to a boil. Reduce to a simmer and return the chicken livers to the pan. Heat another saucepan very hot and brown the marrow bones. Pour on the wine, and add the rest of the ingredients. Bring to a boil slowly, then stir into the sauce in the first pan. Simmer the combined sauce down gently to a smooth, creamy consistency. Strain. Slice the livers and return them to the sauce. Remove the marrow from the bones, crush it, and stir into the sauce with a whisk, bit by bit.

To serve, turn the loaf of brioche containing the fillet of beef out onto a platter. Serve the sauce in a separate bowl. NET: 4 to 6 servings.

FILET DE BOEUF À LA MODE EN GELÉE

Roast Fillet of Beef à la Mode in Aspic

This dish is garnished with little clusters of onions, carrots, peas in artichoke bottoms, green beans, mushrooms, and asparagus tips. Sauce Moutarde is a good accompaniment (page 52). The dish can be made a day in advance.

2 pounds fillet of beef (top end)
1 garlic clove, bruised
¼ cup Cognac or good brandy
Coarse salt
Freshly cracked white pepper
5 cups chicken aspic (page 37)

GARNISH
1 cup chilled cooked baby white
*   onions (fresh or canned)*
1 cup chilled cooked baby
*   carrots (fresh or canned)*
A little fresh parsley or dill

1 cup chilled cooked baby green
*   peas (fresh or frozen)*
4 chilled canned artichoke
*   bottoms*
½ pound chilled cooked green
*   beans (fresh)*
8 thin strips pimento
1 cup chilled cooked button
*   mushrooms (fresh, cooked in*
*   lemon juice and boiling water)*
12 chilled cooked asparagus tips
*   (fresh)*

Preheat the oven to 350°. Trim off all fat and sinew from the fillet of beef. Tie it securely in several places with fine string. Place it on a rack in a roasting pan, and roast 35 to 40 minutes. Remove from the oven, and at once rub the fillet with the garlic clove, brush it all over with brandy, and rub the salt and pepper into it. Wrap the fillet of beef tightly in foil and chill in the refrigerator. When it is well-chilled, remove the strings and dry it well with paper towels. Cut it into ½-inch slices with a very sharp knife. Arrange the slices on a rack in a jelly roll pan. Have the aspic ready, in a pan over ice, at the point of setting. Coat the slices of meat and chill them in the refrigerator (not the freezer, or the aspic will cloud).

Pour a little of the aspic on the bottom of a cold flat metal serving platter and chill it in the refrigerator. Then arrange the coated fillets, overlapping, on the platter, and garnish all around the platter with the chilled cooked vegetables, which have been drained and thoroughly dried, as follows. (1) Little clusters of baby white onions. (2) Little clusters of baby carrots, with a tip of parsley or dill stuck in the tops. (3) The artichoke bottoms filled with the baby green peas. (4) Little clusters of button mushrooms. (5) Four little bundles of green beans, each "tied" with a strip of pimento. (6) Four little bundles of asparagus tips, also "tied" with pimento. Carefully coat all the vegetables with a little aspic, using a soft brush. Chill the rest of the aspic in a layer cake tin, and when it is firm, unmold, and chop it into fine cubes. Put the chopped aspic in a pastry bag fitted with a plain #9 tube and pipe all around the serving platter. Chill the assembled platter well before serving. NET: 6 to 8 servings.

FILET DE BOEUF WELLINGTON, SAUCE MOUTARDE

Roast Fillet of Beef in Pâté and Puff Pastry, with Bouchées of Mustard Sauce

This may also be served with Sauce Demi-Glace or Bordelaise, in which case the bouchées are not used.

4-pound fillet of beef	MUSTARD SAUCE
Optional: truffles, to stud the	2 egg yolks
fillet of beef	2 tablespoons Dijon mustard
¼ cup Cognac or good brandy	1 teaspoon dry mustard
Salt	1 teaspoon salt
Freshly cracked white pepper	A few grains cayenne pepper
9 tablespoons salt butter	2 teaspoons tarragon vinegar
6 ounces fine liver pâté	¾ cup vegetable oil
Prepared Puff Paste dough	1 tablespoon finely chopped
(page 723)	shallots
1 egg, beaten	1 tablespoon sour cream
	⅛ teaspoon meat glaze, dis-
	solved in 1 tablespoon water
	3 tablespoons whipped cream

If the fillet of beef is to be studded with truffles, cut them into small strips and, using a larding needle, insert them throughout the meat. Trim off all excess fat, and brush the meat well with brandy. Sprinkle with salt and pepper. Melt 3 tablespoons butter in a heavy pan. When it is golden brown, brown the fillet of beef in it on all sides. Remove the meat from the pan and spread it with the following pâté: Cream 6 tablespoons butter in a mixer. Add the liver pâté. Beat well, and add pepper and 1 tablespoon brandy.

Preheat the oven to 375°. Have the puff paste dough ready. Roll it out ⅜ inch thick, in a rectangle large enough to wrap up the fillet of beef. Brush the dough with beaten egg. Roll up the beef in this dough (completely encase it). Trim off the excess. Place the wrapped fillet of beef on a wet baking sheet. Brush the top with a little more beaten egg. Roll out the scraps of puff paste about ¼ inch thick. Cut some of it into crescent shapes and decorate the top of the pastry-wrapped beef with them. Brush the crescents with beaten egg. Make little bouchées with the rest of the puff pastry dough: Cut 16 1½-inch rounds with a cookie cutter, and place 8 of them on the baking sheet. With a ¾-inch cutter, cut a hole in the center of the remaining 8 rounds (to look like rings). Brush the whole rounds with water and place the rings on them. Brush with beaten egg.

Put the baking sheet with the meat and bouchées on it in the freezer to chill or freeze. (Puff paste bakes better when frozen solid.) Then bake 30 to 35 minutes.

MUSTARD SAUCE. Put the egg yolks and both mustards in a mixer bowl. Add the salt and cayenne pepper, and beat until very thick. Slowly beat in the vinegar. Then beat in the vegetable oil slowly, drop by drop until the sauce thickens. Mix in the rest of the ingredients.

When the bouchées are baked, scoop out the centers and fill them with mustard sauce. Transfer the fillet of beef to a serving platter. Surround it with the bouchées, and serve immediately. NET: 6 to 8 servings.

CÔTE DE BOEUF RÔTIE AU JUS

Roast Prime Ribs of Beef with Pan Juices

This roast may be accompanied with Yorkshire pudding or a variety of vegetable garnishes.

3-pound prime rib roast of beef (or top sirloin)
Optional: 1 garlic clove, bruised
Salt
Freshly cracked white pepper
¼ cup Cognac or good brandy
½ pound bacon or salt pork,
thinly sliced
1 cup dry sherry
1 cup dry red wine
½ cup chicken stock (page 35)
1 teaspoon potato flour
1 tablespoon salt butter

Preheat the oven to 375°. Trim all the fat from the beef. (If desired, rub the beef with a bruised clove of garlic.) Rub the beef with salt and pepper, and brush it all over with the brandy. Cover it with the slices of bacon or salt pork. Tie each piece down with a piece of string. Place the roast on a rack in a roasting pan. Pour a little sherry over it. Insert a meat thermometer, and roast it about 1 hour. Baste every 20 minutes, with the wine and sherry alternately.

When the roast has reached the desired degree of finish, remove it from the roasting pan and set it aside on a cutting board. Set the roasting pan over low heat, and slowly stir in the chicken stock and a little more sherry into the pan juices. Mix 2 tablespoons brandy with the potato flour, and stir it into the sauce. Bring the sauce slowly to a boil and stir in the butter. Strain the sauce. To serve, cut as many slices of the meat as needed for one serving and arrange them, overlapping, down a hot serving platter. Put the uncut piece of meat at one end. Spoon a little of the juice over the meat. Serve the rest in a sauceboat. NET: 4 to 6 servings.

ROAST BEEF WITH YORKSHIRE PUDDING AND ROAST POTATOES

If two ovens are not available, one for the lower temperature (meat and potatoes) and one for the higher (Yorkshire pudding), it is possible to bake the pudding in a "top-of-the-stove oven," using a round baking dish with a cover.

2 pounds fillet of beef (or rib roast)
4 ounces salt pork, cut into ¼-inch strips (for larding)
4 tablespoons melted salt butter
Salt
Freshly cracked black pepper
½ cup dry red wine

ROAST POTATOES
1 to 2 potatoes per serving

Salt
8 tablespoons salt butter
A few grains cayenne pepper

YORKSHIRE PUDDING
1 cup all-purpose flour
1 teaspoon salt
1 cup milk
2 eggs, beaten
8 to 12 tablespoons hot vegetable oil

Preheat the oven to 350°. If you are using a fillet of beef, lard the beef throughout with the strips of salt pork. (This is not necessary with a well-marbled rib roast.) Tie the roast (either fillet or rib) in several places with fine string. Place the meat on a roasting pan, brush the top with melted butter, and season with salt and pepper. Pour a little red wine over the meat. Roast it 45 to 50 minutes, using a meat thermometer. Baste frequently with the wine mixed with cold water. If necessary, use more wine and water. Each time the meat is basted, also brush the top with more melted butter.

ROAST POTATOES. Pare the potatoes, score them with a fork, and cook them in boiling salted water 2 minutes. Drain and cool them. Put them in a shallow baking dish. In a separate little pan, melt the butter, season it with the cayenne pepper, and pour it over the potatoes. Roast the potatoes in the 350° oven until nearly soft, turning them frequently. Just before serving, put them under a hot broiler to make them crusty. (Roasting potatoes this way, instead of with the meat, allows them to retain their delicate flavor.)

YORKSHIRE PUDDING. Preheat the oven to 425°. Put the flour and salt in a mixer bowl and stir in the milk with a whisk. Add the beaten eggs and beat in the mixer 10 minutes. Let the batter stand in the refrigerator at least 30 minutes. Heat popover pans or baba molds;

have them very hot. In each mold put 1 tablespoon hot vegetable oil. Half fill these pans with the batter, and bake 25 to 30 minutes. Remove from the oven, turn out of the molds, and serve at once.

When the meat is cooked, remove it from the oven and cut it into thin slices. Arrange them, overlapping, on a hot flat serving platter. Surround with the roast potatoes. Serve the Yorkshire pudding either separately or around the platter of meat. NET: 4 servings.

FILET DE BOEUF À LA FLAMANDE

Roast Fillet of Beef with Braised Belgian Endive

2 pounds fillet of beef, in 1 piece
2 ounces salt pork, cut into
    ¼-inch strips (for larding)
½ cup dry red wine
Salt
Freshly cracked black pepper

SAUCE
1 tablespoon salt butter
2 teaspoons potato flour
1 teaspoon tomato paste
1 teaspoon meat glaze
½ cup dry red wine
1 cup chicken stock (page 35)
1 teaspoon currant jelly

Freshly cracked black pepper
1 bay leaf

BRAISED BELGIAN ENDIVE
6 stalks Belgian endive
3 tablespoons tarragon vinegar
4 slices bacon
½ cup mixed sliced onion,
    carrot, and celery
1 cup chicken stock (page 35)
½ teaspoon meat glaze
½ teaspoon potato flour
2 tablespoons cold water
1 tablespoon chopped fresh
    parsley

BRAISED BELGIAN ENDIVE. Preheat the oven to 400°. Remove the outside leaves from the endive, put the endive in a pan, and cover with cold water. Add the vinegar and bring to a boil. Drain at once. Put 1 or 2 slices bacon on the bottom of a loaf pan. On it, put the mixed onion, carrot, and celery. On the vegetables, put the blanched endive. Cover with more slices of bacon. Warm the chicken stock, dissolve the meat glaze in it, and pour over the endive. Cover the pan with buttered wax paper. Braise the endive in the oven 40 minutes. Remove it from the pan. Strain the liquid. Mix the potato flour and cold water and stir into the endive liquid. Set aside and keep it warm.

Reduce the oven heat to 375°. Using a larding needle, lard the fillet of beef with the salt pork strips in many places. Rub the beef all over with salt and pepper. Neatly tie it in several places with string and place it in a roasting pan. Pour over a little of the wine. Roast it 40 minutes, basting frequently with the rest of the wine and a little water.

SAUCE. Melt the butter in a small heavy pan. Off the heat, stir in the potato flour, tomato paste, and meat glaze. Add the wine, chicken stock, jelly, and pepper. Stir the sauce over low heat until it comes to a boil. Add the bay leaf and simmer 10 minutes over low heat. Add the strained juices from the roasting pan, and pour the sauce through a fine strainer.

To serve, slice as many pieces of the roast as required for one serving. Arrange the slices, overlapping, down a hot serving platter, and put the uncut piece at one end. Spoon a little of the sauce over the meat and serve the rest separately in a sauceboat. Arrange the endive in a separate vegetable dish. Pour over it the gravy in which it was braised. Sprinkle it with the parsley. NET: 4 servings.

The vegetables are mushrooms, fresh peas, baby carrots, baby turnips, green beans, cauliflower bouquets, broiled tomatoes, and Noisette Potatoes.

During the time of our Petit Cordon Bleu Restaurant and School in London, King Edward VIII became engaged to Wallis Simpson. By royal request we cooked a special dinner for His Royal Highness every Thursday. In the early evening a Daimler with two butlers came to our shop to pick up the food. They would bring with them the most magnificent silver serving dishes from his summer palace, Belvedere, on which to arrange it. Generally he specified lobster, but sometimes he asked for fillet of beef, and once we were requested to lard the fillet with his coat of arms. It meant larding the entire fillet through, so that each slice presented the complete coat of arms. It was a terrible session.

FILET DE BOEUF À LA BOUQUETIÈRE

Roast Fillet of Beef with Brown Sauce and Clusters of Vegetables

3½ pounds fillet of beef, in
   1 piece
Salt
Freshly cracked black pepper
¼ cup Cognac or good brandy
Thin piece of beef fat (enough
   to wrap the fillet)
6 ounces salt pork, cut into long
   ¼-inch strips
½ cup dry red wine

BROWN SAUCE
2 tablespoons vegetable oil
2 tablespoons salt butter
½ cup mixed sliced onion,
   carrot, and celery
3 tablespoons all-purpose flour
2 firm white mushrooms, sliced
1 tomato, sliced
1 tablespoon tomato paste
1 teaspoon meat glaze
3 cups chicken stock (page 35)
1 tablespoon currant jelly
½ cup Madeira wine

VEGETABLE GARNISH
12 large firm white mushrooms

10 tablespoons melted salt
   butter
Salt
Freshly cracked white pepper
1 teaspoon lemon juice
2 cups shelled fresh peas
   or 1 package frozen
2 cups carrots, cut in olive
   shapes
2 cups turnips, cut in olive
   shapes
1 pound green beans, tied in
   6 little bundles with string,
   and the ends trimmed off
   even
3 tablespoons chopped fresh
   parsley
1 small cauliflower
3 firm ripe tomatoes
A little granulated sugar
6 thin slices yellow onion
½ teaspoon finely chopped
   garlic
3 tablespoons freshly grated
   Parmesan cheese
2 cups Noisette Potatoes (page
   616)

Preheat the oven to 375°. Rub the fillet of beef all over with salt and pepper, and brush it generously with the brandy. Let it stand 30 minutes to marinate. Then wrap it in the beef fat and tie it around in several places with string, neatly. Using a larding needle, lard the fillet with the salt pork. Place it in a roasting pan and pour in a little of the wine. Insert a meat thermometer to ensure the desired degree of cooking. Roast the fillet 20 minutes per pound (about 1 hour for a 3-pound fillet). Baste every 10 minutes, using the rest of the wine and a little water.

BROWN SAUCE. Heat the butter with the vegetable oil in a small heavy pan. Add the mixed onion, carrot, and celery. Cook slowly, over low heat, 5 minutes. Stir in the flour, and continue to cook over low heat. Off the heat, add the mushrooms, tomato, tomato paste, and meat glaze. Stir in the chicken stock and bring the sauce to a boil over moderate heat, then simmer over low heat 30 minutes. Rub the sauce through a fine strainer, return it to the pan, and stir in the jelly and the Madeira wine. When the fillet is cooked, strain the pan juices into this sauce. Simmer to reheat it when you are ready to use it.

VEGETABLE GARNISH. (1) Sauté the mushroom caps in 1 tablespoon butter, salt, pepper, and 1 teaspoon lemon juice. (2) Boil the peas, carrots, turnips, and green beans (separately) until they are just soft and still a little crisp. This can be done in one large pan by wrapping each vegetable in a foil package and setting the packages in boiling salted water or in a steamer. As each vegetable is properly cooked, remove and drain it. Mix each vegetable with 1 tablespoon melted butter and chopped parsley. (3) Separate the head of cauliflower into little bouquets, put them in a pan, cover with cold salted water, bring to a boil, and cook until just soft. Drain well, and sprinkle with 2 tablespoons melted butter. (4) Core and cut the tomatoes in half horizontally. Sprinkle the top of each half with sugar, salt, and pepper. Place a slice of onion on each, add a speck of garlic, sprinkle with grated cheese and 2 tablespoons melted butter. Brown the tomatoes under the broiler. (5) Prepare the Noisette Potatoes, using 4 tablespoons melted butter.

When the fillet of beef is done, remove it from the oven and remove the string. (Strain the pan juices into the brown sauce and reheat it.) Cut as many thin slices as required for one serving. Arrange the slices overlapping down a hot flat serving platter. Place the uncut piece at one end. Spoon a little of the sauce over the meat and serve the rest separately in a sauceboat. Arrange the tomato halves and mushroom caps around the beef, with separate little clusters of the peas, carrots, turnips, beans, cauliflower, and potato balls. Serve at once. NET: 6 servings.

LANGUE DE BOEUF FLORENTINE

Poached Beef Tongue with Spinach Purée and Sweet and Sour Sauce

This dish should be started a day in advance.

1 smoked beef tongue, 3 to 4 pounds	*1 onion, sliced*
	1 carrot, sliced

1 stalk celery, sliced
1 bay leaf
12 whole peppercorns
2 garlic cloves, bruised

SPINACH PURÉE
2 pounds fresh spinach
Salt
Freshly cracked white pepper
4 tablespoons salt butter
4 tablespoons all-purpose flour
½ cup sour cream

SWEET AND SOUR SAUCE
3 tablespoons salt butter
2 teaspoons potato flour

1 teaspoon tomato paste
2 teaspoons meat glaze
2 tablespoons red currant jelly
1½ cups tongue stock
¾ cup white raisins, soaked in
    ¼ cup tarragon vinegar
2 tablespoons dry sherry
1 red onion, finely chopped
3 ounces firm white mushrooms,
    finely chopped and sautéed
    in a little butter
1 green pepper, seeded and
    finely chopped
1 red pepper, seeded and finely
    chopped

Cover the tongue with cold water and soak it a minimum of 6 hours or overnight. Drain the tongue, place it in a heavy pan, and cover it with cold water. Add the onion, carrot, celery, bay leaf, peppercorns, and garlic cloves. Bring it slowly to a boil, remove any scum, and simmer over low heat 3 hours, or until the tongue is tender. Let it cool in the stock. When it is cool enough to handle, remove it, and strain the stock, reserving 1½ cups for the sauce. Remove from the tongue the skin, gristle, and little bones at the thick end.

SPINACH PURÉE. Wash the spinach very well and drain it. Put it in a large pan with salt, pepper, and 2 tablespoons butter. Cook briskly 5 to 8 minutes, until it is wilted. Drain, press it very dry, and put it through a fine meat chopper. Melt 2 tablespoons butter in a pan. Off the heat, add the flour, then cook over low heat until the mixture is golden brown. Mix in the spinach purée and sour cream, season to taste, and warm the mixture.

SWEET AND SOUR SAUCE. Melt the butter in a saucepan. Off the heat, stir in the potato flour, tomato paste, meat glaze, and jelly, and mix to a smooth paste. Add the reserved tongue stock, the raisins with vinegar, and the sherry. Stir over low heat until the mixture comes to a boil. Then add the onion, mushrooms, and peppers, and gently simmer about 10 minutes.

To serve, spread the spinach purée on a warm serving platter. Slice the tongue and arrange it on the purée. Spoon the sauce over the tongue. NET: 6 to 8 servings.

LANGUE DE BOEUF PARISIENNE

Braised Beef Tongue with a Puréed Vegetable Sauce

This dish should be started a day in advance.

1 3-pound smoked beef tongue
12 small white onions
1 cup diced carrots

½ cup diced celery
¼ pound firm white mushrooms,
    chopped

4 tablespoons salt butter
2 cups strained tongue stock
2 tomatoes, skinned and cut in
  ½-inch slices
Salt

Freshly cracked white pepper
2 tablespoons chopped fresh
  parsley
2 tablespoons all-purpose flour
¼ cup cold water

Cover the tongue with cold water and soak it a minimum of 6 hours or overnight. Then drain, and place the tongue in a deep heavy pan. Barely cover it with cold water and bring it slowly to a boil. Remove the scum and simmer the tongue 2 hours. Remove it from the stock and remove the skin, gristle, and bones at the thick end. Reserve the stock.

Preheat the oven to 350°. Sauté the onions, carrots, celery, and mushrooms in 3 tablespoons butter until the mixture is lightly browned. Place the vegetables on the bottom of a deep, heavy covered casserole just large enough to hold the tongue. Add the tomatoes and season with salt and pepper. Lightly brown the tongue in the pan the vegetables were browned in, adding a little more butter if necessary, then place it in the casserole on the vegetables. Pour over 2 cups strained tongue stock. Cover the casserole and cook in the oven 1½ hours, until the tongue is tender. To serve, place the tongue on a hot serving dish and sprinkle with the chopped parsley. Thicken the sauce in the casserole with flour mixed with the cold water. Purée it to a smooth consistency in an electric blender and serve in a separate bowl. NET: 6 to 8 servings.

QUEUE DE BOEUF VINAIGRETTE

Hot Braised Oxtail with
Cold Vinaigrette Sauce

3 pounds oxtail, cut into
  uniform chunks
1 cup mixed sliced onion, celery,
  and carrot
Bouquet garni, including
  parsley, thyme, and bay leaf
  (tied in cheesecloth)
4 cups chicken stock (page 35)
  or water
½ cup dry white wine
Salt
Freshly cracked black pepper
Optional: 3 tablespoons salt
  butter
4 tablespoons chopped fresh
  parsley or chives

VINAIGRETTE SAUCE
1 teaspoon salt
½ teaspoon freshly cracked
  black pepper
¼ teaspoon dry mustard
¼ teaspoon sugar
1 hard-boiled egg, finely
  chopped
1 tablespoon finely chopped
  fresh parsley
1 tablespoon finely chopped
  green olives
1¼ cups vegetable oil
¼ cup pure olive oil
¼ cup tarragon vinegar
3 drops lemon juice
1 raw egg

Put the pieces of oxtail in a deep heavy pan and cover with cold water. Bring slowly to a boil, and drain. Add to the pan the onion, celery, and carrot, and the bouquet garni, stock or water, wine, salt, and pepper. Bring to a boil, cover the pan, and simmer over low heat about 2½ to 3 hours, until the oxtail is very tender.

VINAIGRETTE SAUCE. Put all the ingredients into a 1-pint screw-top jar. Shake very well, and chill a few hours. Shake again before serving.

When the oxtail is cooked, drain and dry it well. Then, if you prefer the color and flavor of browned meat, brown the pieces quickly in the heated butter. Arrange them on a hot serving dish and sprinkle well with the parsley or chives. Serve the cold vinaigrette sauce in a separate sauce bowl. NET: 6 servings.

This is the French classic preparation of tripe. According to *Larousse Gastronomique*, it should include all parts of the mesentery, composed of "the honeycomb or reticulum, the psalterium or manyplies, rennet or reed, and the belly." Its devotees require very white tripe cooked very, very slowly in very good brandy. This dish should be started a day in advance.

TRIPES À LA MODE DE CAEN

Tripe à la Mode de Caen

3 pounds fresh cleaned honeycomb tripe
½ pound fatback or bacon,
  thinly sliced
3 carrots, thinly sliced
3 medium-size onions, thinly
  sliced
3 leeks, well washed and thinly
  sliced
3 stalks celery, thinly sliced
2 small green peppers, seeded
  and cut into very thin strips
3 calf's feet, sawed in medium
  pieces by the butcher
2 tablespoons chopped fresh
  parsley
¼ teaspoon each of thyme,
  marjoram, and mace
3 bay leaves
3 whole cloves

10 black peppercorns
2 teaspoons salt
An ample amount of Calvados
  (or cider or white wine) to
  cover the ingredients in the
  pot
Flour and water (enough to
  seal the lid)
½ cup finely chopped shallots
4 tablespoons salt butter
2 cups chopped fresh tomato
  pulp (about 4 large tomatoes,
  skinned, seeded, and chopped)
½ cup brandy (preferably
  Calvados)
3 tablespoons chopped fresh
  parsley
12 puff paste crescents (page
  724) or buy ready made

Tripe is usually already cleaned and blanched when sold; nevertheless, wash it again in several changes of cold water. Cut it into strips 2 inches by ½ inch.

Preheat the oven to 200°. Line the bottom of a large heavy enamel pan or earthenware casserole with the sliced fatback or bacon. Mix together lightly the carrots, onions, leeks, celery, and green peppers, and arrange them on the fatback in the form of a bed. Place the strips of tripe on the vegetables, and the pieces of calf's feet on the tripe. Season with the parsley, thyme, marjoram, mace, bay leaves, cloves, peppercorns, and salt. Then cover the ingredients in the pan with good brandy, cider, or white wine. Mix the flour and water to a stiff paste and use it to seal the lid of the pan. Cook overnight (12 to 18 hours) in the very slow oven.

Sauté the chopped shallots in the butter, and mix with the tomato pulp. When the tripe is cooked, uncover, add the tomato pulp mixture and ½ cup Calvados, and mix a little. Sprinkle the top with chopped fresh parsley and surround with crescents of crisp puff pastry. NET: 6 to 8 servings.

HACHIS À LA LANGUE-DOCIENNE

Hash with Eggplant and Tomatoes

A baked mold lined with eggplant skins and filled with ground cooked beef and mushrooms, with tomato sauce and broiled tomato garnish. It is good too made with veal or lamb.

2 medium-size eggplants
2 tablespoons pure olive oil
1 cup finely chopped onion
3 tablespoons salt butter
3 cups finely ground cold
  cooked beef (or veal or lamb)
2 ounces firm white mushrooms,
  finely chopped
1 tablespoon each of chopped
  fresh parsley and dill
1 green pepper, seeded and
  finely chopped
2 tablespoons fried breadcrumbs
  (page 69)
2 tablespoons sour cream
1 egg
Salt
Freshly cracked white pepper
A few grains freshly grated
  nutmeg
If using lamb: ½ teaspoon
  finely chopped garlic

BROILED TOMATO GARNISH
3 small ripe tomatoes
1 teaspoon granulated sugar
½ teaspoon finely chopped
  garlic
Salt
Freshly cracked white pepper
6 thin slices onion
2 tablespoons dry breadcrumbs
  (page 69)
2 tablespoons freshly grated
  Parmesan cheese
2 tablespoons melted salt butter

TOMATO SAUCE
2 tablespoons salt butter
1 tablespoon all-purpose flour
2 tablespoons tomato paste
1¼ cups water
2 teaspoons sweet butter
¼ teaspoon finely chopped
  garlic

Preheat the oven to 375°. Brush eggplants with the olive oil. Wrap each eggplant in foil, and bake 45 minutes. Melt the butter in a heavy pan and sauté the chopped onion until golden brown. Add the ground meat, mushrooms, parsley, dill, and green pepper. Cook over low heat 3 minutes, then add the breadcrumbs, sour cream, and egg. Season with salt, pepper, nutmeg, and (if using lamb) garlic, and set aside. When the eggplants are done, unwrap them and cut in quarters from the top down. Scoop out some of the pulp, chop it roughly, and mix it with the hash.

Line a shallow layer cake tin with the quartered eggplants, with the skin side against the pan. Fill with the hash, and fold the ends of the eggplant sections over the hash. Cover the pan with a piece of wax paper. Reduce the oven temperature to 350°, and bake 25 minutes.

BROILED TOMATO GARNISH. Core and cut the 3 tomatoes in half, horizontally, leaving the skins on. Season the tops with the sugar, garlic, salt, and pepper. Put a thin slice of raw onion on each and sprinkle with breadcrumbs, grated cheese, and melted butter, and brown under the broiler.

TOMATO SAUCE. Melt the butter in a saucepan. Off the heat, stir in the flour and tomato paste. Pour in the water. Stir over low heat until the sauce comes to a boil. Stir in the sweet butter bit by bit, and then add the garlic. Simmer over low heat 5 minutes.

When the hash is baked, turn it carefully out of the pan onto a hot round serving dish. Spoon the sauce over the hash, and garnish the dish with the broiled tomato halves. NET: 6 servings.

Terribly English and terribly good.

STEAK AND KIDNEY PIE

3 or 4 lamb kidneys
1¼ pounds beefsteak
3 tablespoons salt butter
2 teaspoons tarragon vinegar
2 tablespoons all-purpose flour
2 teaspoons tomato paste
Salt

1½ cups chicken stock (page 35)
Freshly cracked white pepper
Puff Paste (½ pound of recipe on page 723, or commercial)
1 egg, beaten

Skin the kidneys, cut them in half and remove the cores; then cut each half in 4 pieces. Cut the steak in bite-size chunks. Heat the butter in a heavy pan. Brown the steak and kidney pieces very quickly over high heat. Pour the vinegar over them. Remove the meat from the pan. Off the heat, add the flour and tomato paste to the pan and work it to a smooth paste. Pour in the chicken stock, and season with salt and freshly cracked white pepper. Stir over low heat until the mixture boils, then return the steak and kidneys to the pan and simmer over low heat 1 hour.

Preheat the oven to 400°. Have ready a deep pie dish. Roll out the puff paste ¾ inch thick. Put the cooked steak and kidneys in the pie dish. Cover with the puff paste. Trim the pastry and make a little hole in the top for the steam to escape. Make a few leaves with the scraps of puff paste and decorate the top of the pie. Brush with beaten egg and put the pie in the freezer for a few minutes. Bake 15 minutes. NET: 4 servings.

*Coulibiac of Meat Loaf
in Homemade Bread,
with Brown Sauce*

The meat loaf is excellent with or without the homemade bread, served hot or cold. This dish can be completely baked and frozen.

White bread dough (page 706)
½ pound ground lean beef
½ pound ground lean veal
¼ pound ground lean pork
3 eggs, beaten
⅓ cup sour cream
*1 medium-size yellow onion,
  very finely chopped*
*½ teaspoon finely chopped
  garlic*
*½ teaspoon freshly grated
  nutmeg*

1 pinch mace
1 teaspoon salt
*1 teaspoon freshly cracked
  black pepper*
*3 slices sturdy white bread,
  crusts removed*
¼ cup milk
*About ½ pound bacon, thinly
  sliced*
3 tablespoons melted salt butter
Brown Sauce (page 38)

Prepare the bread dough first, and while it is rising, prepare the meat loaf.

Preheat the oven to 325°. Put the ground beef, veal, and pork in a large bowl. Add 2 of the beaten eggs, and the sour cream, onion, garlic, nutmeg, mace, salt, and pepper. Soak the trimmed slices of bread in the milk and add to the ground meat. Work all these ingredients together with the hands. Wet a piece of foil with water. Make a few little holes in the foil so that the fat can drain out. On the foil, form the ground meat mixture into a nice meat loaf shape with wet hands (slightly smaller than the loaf pan in which you plan to bake the coulibiac). Cover the meat with overlapping slices of bacon. Tuck the ends of the bacon under the meat loaf. Wrap the meat loaf in the foil, place it on a rack in a pan, and bake 1 hour. When it is baked, unwrap and let it cool, then chill it.

Brush the loaf pan with a little cool melted butter. When the bread dough has risen, run a finger around it to break the rise, and slap it on the board a few times. Lightly flour the board and roll half the dough out about ¾ inch thick. Flour the top of the dough a little and line the loaf pan with it, patting it out so that the bottom and sides of the pan are lined and a little dough hangs over the top. Brush the dough with a little melted butter, and place the meat loaf in the lined pan. Pat the edges of the dough against the meat loaf and brush them with some of the remaining beaten egg. Raise the oven heat to 375°. Roll out the remainder of the dough, cover the top of the coulibiac with it, and pat it in place neatly. Make a few slashes on top of the dough (but not all the way through) and brush it with beaten egg (like a loaf of bread). Cover with a cloth and allow the loaf to rise in a warm place about 15 minutes before baking. Bake 45 minutes at 375°, then reduce the heat to 350° and bake another 20 minutes.

To serve, turn the coulibiac out onto a serving platter (it will look like a plain loaf of bread). Slice and serve with a simple brown sauce.
NET: 4 to 6 servings.

A baked mold lined with eggplant skins, filled with ground beef and tomatoes, with tomato sauce.

Minced Beef and
Eggplant,
Turkish Style

4 medium-size eggplants
¼ cup pure olive oil
3 cups water
Salt
½ cup cream of farina
½ cup freshly grated Parmesan
  cheese
1 teaspoon dry mustard
12 tablespoons salt butter
A few grains cayenne pepper
1 cup finely chopped onions
1 teaspoon finely chopped garlic
1 pound ground lean beef
2 medium-size ripe tomatoes,
  skinned and chopped

1 tablespoon tomato paste
1 teaspoon meat glaze
Freshly cracked black pepper

TOMATO SAUCE
2 tablespoons salt butter
2 tablespoons all-purpose flour
3 tablespoons tomato paste
1¼ cups chicken stock
  (page 35)
½ teaspoon finely chopped
  garlic
Salt
Freshly cracked black pepper

Preheat the oven to 350°. Brush the eggplants with olive oil. Wrap each one individually in foil and bake them until they are very soft to the touch, about 45 minutes. Remove them from the oven (leave it on or preheat it to 350° again later), unwrap, and chill them thoroughly. Then cut them in quarters lengthwise and scrape out the pulp without breaking the outer skin. Brush a layer cake pan with a little olive oil and completely line it with two-thirds of the eggplant skins (reserve the rest for the top). Set aside the lined pan and the eggplant pulp.

Put 3 cups water in a heavy pan with 2 teaspoons salt. Bring the water to a rolling boil. Continue boiling and slowly add the cream of farina, stirring all the time. Stir until the farina is thick and comes away from the sides of the pan. Mix in the grated cheese, dry mustard, cayenne pepper, and 4 tablespoons butter. Spread half this mixture on the eggplant skins in the pan, and set the rest aside for a moment.

Heat 8 tablespoons butter in a heavy pan. Add the onions and garlic, and cook over low heat until the onions are translucent. Add the ground beef and cook 2 minutes. Add the tomatoes, tomato paste, and meat glaze. Season with salt and black pepper. Add the eggplant pulp. Mix thoroughly, and cook 2 minutes. Spread this mixture in the eggplant mold on the layer of farina. Cover it with the remaining farina, and cover the farina with more eggplant skins. Put the pan in the preheated 350° oven and bake the moussaka 30 minutes.

TOMATO SAUCE. Melt the butter in a saucepan. Off the heat, stir in the flour and tomato paste, and mix until smooth. Add the chicken stock, garlic, and a little salt and pepper. Stir over moderate heat until the sauce comes to a boil. Reduce the heat and simmer very gently 10 minutes. Strain.

When the moussaka has finished baking, remove it from the oven and let it stand 5 minutes. Turn it out onto a hot flat serving dish, and spoon the tomato sauce around it. NET: 8 servings.

BLANQUETTE DE VEAU

Poached Veal in Rich Velouté Sauce, Garnished with Baby Peas, Carrots, and Onions

3 pounds loin of veal (whole, rolled, and tied with string) or shoulder of veal (cut into uniform 1½-inch cubes)
1 large yellow onion, cut in eighths
1 small carrot, sliced
2 stalks celery, cut in chunks
Bouquet garni (2 sprigs parsley, 1 bay leaf, some celery leaf, and 1 sprig tarragon if available)
2 teaspoons salt
12 black peppercorns
½ teaspoon granulated sugar
Rice Pilaff (page 675)

VELOUTÉ SAUCE
8 tablespoons salt butter
4 tablespoons all-purpose flour

Salt
A few grains cayenne pepper
1½ cups veal stock (liquid in which the veal is cooked)
⅓ cup light cream
4 tablespoons sweet butter
2 teaspoons lemon juice
2 egg yolks
2 tablespoons Cognac or good brandy
¼ cup heavy cream

GARNISH
1 package frozen baby green peas or 1½ cups shelled fresh peas
1 cup baby carrots or large carrots cut in olive shapes
18 baby white onions, skinned

Put the veal in a deep, heavy pan, Barely cover the meat with cold water and bring it slowly to a boil. Skim off all the scum. Add the onion, carrot, celery, bouquet garni (tied in a cloth), salt, pepper-corns, and sugar. Simmer very slowly until the meat is tender. Remove the meat, and pour a little of the stock over it to keep it moist while the sauce and garnishes are prepared.

VELOUTÉ SAUCE. Strain the stock in which the veal was cooked. Melt the salt butter in a saucepan. Off the heat, add the flour, salt, and cayenne pepper, and mix until smooth. Pour in 1½ cups of the strained veal stock. Return to low heat and stir until the sauce comes to a boil. Add the light cream and simmer gently 3 minutes. Still over low heat, stir the sweet butter into the sauce bit by bit. Add the lemon juice. Beat the egg yolks in a little bowl. Mix in the brandy and heavy cream. Pour some of the sauce onto this yolk mixture, beating all the time, then return it to the rest of the sauce in the pan and mix well. Reheat the sauce very gently, but do not boil it or it will separate.

GARNISHES. Boil the peas, carrots, and onions (separately) in salted water until just soft. Drain.

To serve, remove the string from the loin of veal, slice it, and arrange the slices, slightly overlapping, down a shallow au gratin dish. If shoulder of veal was used, pile the pieces in the center of the dish. Spoon the sauce over the veal, and arrange the cooked peas, carrots, and onions around it. A true blanquette de veau is served with a rice pilaff, either as a bed under the veal or served separately. NET: 4 to 6 servings.

4 thick veal chops (¾ to 1 inch)
3 tablespoons salt butter
12 small white onions, peeled
½ teaspoon finely chopped
    garlic
8 medium-size firm white
    mushrooms, quartered
1 teaspoon all-purpose flour

½ teaspoon tomato paste
¾ cup dry white wine
½ cup chicken stock (page 35)
Salt
Freshly cracked white pepper
1 bay leaf
2 tablespoons chopped fresh
    parsley

CÔTES DE VEAU À LA BONNE FEMME

Braised Veal Chops with Mushrooms and Onions

Preheat the oven to 375°. Heat the butter in a heavy casserole and brown the veal chops quickly on each side. Remove the chops from the casserole and brown the onions in it. Add the garlic and mushrooms and cook 2 minutes. Off the heat, add the flour, tomato paste, wine, and chicken stock. Season with salt and white pepper and bring the mixture to a boil. Return the chops to the casserole. Add the bay leaf, cover the casserole with the lid, and cook in the oven 25 minutes. When the cooking is finished, sprinkle the chops with the parsley and serve in the casserole. NET: 4 servings.

This dish may be made with veal scallops instead of chops.

4 veal chops, trimmed and fat
    removed
2 tablespoons all-purpose flour
6 tablespoons salt butter
½ teaspoon meat glaze
¼ cup dry white wine
½ teaspoon lemon juice
¼ teaspoon tomato paste
2 tablespoons water

1 teaspoon chopped shallots
Salt
Freshly cracked black pepper
1 tablespoon finely chopped
    mixed fresh herbs (such as
    tarragon, parsley, chives)
A few sprigs crisp fresh
    watercress

CÔTES DE VEAU AUX FINES HERBES

Sautéed Veal Chops with Fresh Herbs

Dust the veal chops lightly with the flour. Heat 3 tablespoons butter in a heavy frypan and brown the chops quickly on both sides. Then cover the pan and cook the chops very slowly 15 to 20 minutes, turning them once or twice. (If veal scallops are being used, cook only 5 minutes.) Remove the chops from the pan, keep them warm, and add to the pan the meat glaze, wine, lemon juice, tomato paste, water, and shallots. Season with salt and pepper, and simmer over low heat 4 minutes. Stir in 3 tablespoons butter with the chopped mixed herbs. Arrange the chops on a hot platter. Spoon the sauce over them. Garnish with fresh watercress. Serve immediately. NET: 4 servings.

This dish may be made with veal scallops instead of chops.

4 veal chops, trimmed and fat
    removed

3 tablespoons salt butter
3 tablespoons dry sherry

CÔTES DE VEAU AU MARSALA

Sautéed Veal Chops with Marsala Wine

½ teaspoon finely chopped
  garlic
½ teaspoon tomato paste
½ teaspoon meat glaze
2 teaspoons potato flour or 2
  tablespoons all-purpose flour
1 cup chicken stock (page 35)

or water
¼ cup Marsala wine
¼ cup dry white wine
Salt
Freshly cracked white pepper
4 large ripe tomatoes, skinned
  and sliced ½ inch thick

Heat 2 tablespoons butter in a large heavy frypan. Quickly brown the veal chops on both sides. In a separate little pan, heat the sherry, ignite it, and pour it over the chops. Remove the chops from the pan, and add to it 1 tablespoon butter and the garlic and cook a half-minute. Off the heat, add the tomato paste, meat glaze, and potato flour, and mix to a smooth paste. Add the chicken stock or water, Marsala wine, and white wine. Stir over moderate heat until the mixture comes to a boil. Season with salt and pepper. Return the chops to the pan and cook slowly until they are tender, about 40 minutes. (If using veal scallops, cook gently 10 minutes.) Add the tomatoes to the pan and cook slowly for another 5 minutes. Arrange the chops on a hot serving dish and spoon the sauce over them. NET: 4 servings.

DAUBE DE VEAU

*Braised Veal with
Quenelles and Olives*

This, frankly, is my interpretation of the classic daube. Made with chunks of veal, with little veal quenelles and olives, it has always been one of the favorites in my classes. I do not agree that to be authentic this daube must contain orange.

2½ pounds veal, cut from
  center of leg
5 tablespoons salt butter
3 tablespoons Cognac or good
  brandy
1 teaspoon tomato paste
1 teaspoon meat glaze
4 teaspoons potato flour
2½ cups chicken stock (page
  35)
½ cup dry sherry or dry white
  wine
1 teaspoon currant jelly
Freshly ground white pepper
Salt
1 small bay leaf
Rice Pilaff (page 675)

QUENELLES
½ pound ground raw lean veal

2 raw unbeaten egg whites
¾ cup light cream
1 teaspoon salt
½ teaspoon freshly cracked
  white pepper
A few grains cayenne pepper
1 tablespoon Cognac or good
  brandy
½ teaspoon finely chopped
  garlic

GARNISH
6 ounces fresh white baby
  mushrooms (if larger, cut in
  halves or quarters)
2 tablespoons salt butter
1 teaspoon lemon juice
Salt
Freshly cracked white pepper
6 large pitted black olives

6 large pitted green olives

1 tablespoon chopped fresh
chives or parsley

Preheat the oven to 350°. Trim all the skin, sinew, and fat from the veal. Cut it into 1½-inch cubes. In a deep heavy pan, heat 3 tablespoons butter. Brown the pieces of meat a few at a time over high heat (they must not touch each other). When all the meat has been browned, put it back in the pan. In a separate little pan, heat the brandy, ignite, and pour it over the browned veal. Remove the meat from the pan, and melt in the pan 2 tablespoons butter. Off the heat, add the tomato paste, meat glaze, and potato flour. Stir to a smooth paste; then mix in the chicken stock, sherry or wine, and jelly. Add a little pepper and taste the sauce for salt. Stir the sauce over moderate heat until it comes to a boil, then return the veal to the pan with 1 small bay leaf. Cook, uncovered, on the top shelf of the oven about 55 minutes, until the veal is tender.

QUENELLES. Put the ground veal and egg whites in a mixer bowl, and beat well. Continue beating, and slowly add the light cream. Season with the salt, white pepper, and cayenne pepper. Mix in the brandy and chopped garlic. About 15 minutes before the daube has finished cooking, remove it from the oven. Form the ground veal mixture into small quenelles (dumplings), shaping them with 2 teaspoons. Drop them directly into the sauce with the veal. Baste the quenelles gently with the sauce and return the pan to the oven for 15 minutes.

While the veal is cooking, briskly sauté the mushrooms 2 minutes in the butter with the lemon juice. Season with salt and pepper. Add the mushrooms and olives to the veal. Serve the daube in a casserole. Sprinkle it with chopped fresh chives or parsley. Accompany it with a fluffy rice pilaff. NET: 4 to 6 servings.

In this preparation two thin slices of veal, sandwiched with a salpicon of mushrooms, prosciutto ham, white truffle, and mozzarella and Parmesan cheeses, are served in a white wine sauce. The dish is one of my favorites. The veal scallops can be prepared a day or two ahead of time, up to the point of cooking them. Keep them well refrigerated.

ESCALOPES DE VEAU À LA PIÉMONTAISE

Sautéed Veal Scallops with White Truffles

12 very thin slices loin of veal
3 tablespoons plus ⅓ cup
  Cognac or good brandy
Salt
Freshly cracked white pepper
10 tablespoons salt butter
¼ pound firm white mush-
  rooms, very thinly sliced
½ teaspoon lemon juice
2 ounces prosciutto ham, very

finely shredded
1 large white truffle (or 2 small),
  cut in fine shreds
2 tablespoons juice from the
  truffle can
Half 1 small mozzarella cheese,
  cut in shreds
1 tablespoon freshly grated
  Parmesan cheese
1 whole egg, beaten

A little flour (to dust the veal
   slices)
A few grains cayenne pepper
3 tablespoons dry white wine
2 teaspoons finely chopped
   shallots
½ teaspoon finely chopped
   garlic

BOILED RICE
4 tablespoons salt butter
1 small onion, finely chopped
1½ cups long-grain rice
3 cups water
2 teaspoons salt
A few grains cayenne pepper

Place the very thin slices of veal between two pieces of wax paper and pound them with the flat side of a cleaver until they are translucent. Remove the top paper and brush them with 3 tablespoons brandy. Season them lightly with salt and pepper, and allow to marinate this way for a moment. Melt 1 tablespoon butter in a small sauté pan. Add the mushrooms with the lemon juice, salt, and pepper. Cook briskly over moderate heat 3 minutes, then add the prosciutto ham, white truffle, and truffle juice. Mix and chill this mixture. When it is thoroughly chilled, add the mozzarella and Parmesan cheeses. Divide the mixture among 6 of the veal slices; put it in the middle of each slice. Brush the edges of these slices with the beaten egg, cover with the remaining 6 slices, and press down firmly. Mix about ½ cup flour with a little salt and cayenne pepper, and dust the stuffed veal scallops lightly with it.

Put 2 tablespoons butter in a large heavy frypan. Stir over moderate heat until it is golden brown. Brown the stuffed veal scallops quickly on each side (only 2 or 3 at a time, so that they do not touch each other while browning). When all the veal has been browned, put it all back into the pan, cover, and cook slowly, over low heat, about 7 minutes on each side. When it is cooked, remove from the heat. In a separate little pan, heat ⅓ cup brandy, ignite, and pour it over the veal. Remove the veal from the pan and keep it warm. Over high heat, reduce the liquid in the pan almost to a glaze. Lower the heat to moderate, and slowly stir in 4 tablespoons butter, then stir in the wine, shallots, and garlic. Cook this down a bit, and then add 3 more tablespoons butter, stirring all the while. (The butter must be well blended with the wine.)

BOILED RICE. Preheat the oven to 350°. Melt the butter in a deep heavy pan over moderate heat. Cook the onion until it is translucent, but not brown. Add the rice, and stir to cover it with butter. Stir in the water, and season with the salt and cayenne pepper. Bring to a rolling boil, cover, and cook in the oven 30 minutes. Remove from the oven, and fluff with two forks.

To serve, arrange the stuffed veal scallops down a hot flat serving platter. Spoon the sauce around the side (not over the top of the meat). Serve the rice separately. NET: 6 servings.

6 to 8 thin slices veal
½ cup Cognac or good brandy
Salt
Freshly cracked white pepper
6 tablespoons salt butter
2 teaspoons tomato paste
1 teaspoon meat glaze
2 teaspoons potato flour
1 cup chicken stock (page 35)
¾ cup dry white wine
1 teaspoon red currant jelly
1 sprig celery leaf

1 small eggplant (or half a
   large one)
¼ cup pure olive oil
3 tablespoons vegetable oil
2 large ripe tomatoes, skinned
   and sliced ½ inch thick
1 teaspoon finely chopped garlic
6 to 8 slices mozzarella cheese
   about ¼ inch thick
¼ cup freshly grated Parmesan
   cheese
2 tablespoons melted salt butter

Sautéed Veal Scallops with Eggplant, Tomatoes, and Mozzarella

Place the veal slices between two pieces of wax paper and flatten them very thin with the side of a heavy cleaver. Remove the top piece of paper. Brush the veal with ¼ cup brandy and season with salt and pepper. Heat 2 tablespoons butter in a frypan. Brown the slices of veal in the hot butter, on each side (press them down with a flat lid and a weight on top so that they stay flat). When all the slices are browned, return them to the pan. In a separate little pan, heat ¼ cup brandy, ignite, and pour it over the veal. Set the veal aside. Melt another 2 tablespoons butter in the pan and (off the heat) add the tomato paste, meat glaze, and potato flour. Mix to a smooth paste, and add the chicken stock, wine, and jelly. Stir the sauce over moderate heat until it comes to a boil. Return the veal to the pan with a piece of celery leaf. Keep this warm until ready to serve.

Remove the stem from the eggplant and cut the eggplant in half lengthwise. (Do not skin it.) Cut it in ½-inch slices, put them in a bowl, sprinkle liberally with salt, and let stand 30 minutes. Rinse them several times in cold water and dry thoroughly on paper towels. In a separate frypan heat the olive oil and vegetable oil. Brown the eggplant slices quickly on each side, and set them aside. Add 2 tablespoons butter to the pan, then add the tomatoes, garlic, salt, and pepper. Cook only 2 minutes (the tomato slices should not disintegrate). Return the eggplant slices to the pan with the tomatoes and carefully mix them together.

To serve, spoon the eggplant and tomato mixture on the bottom of a serving dish. Arrange on it the slices of veal and the mozzarella slices, alternating and overlapping. Strain the sauce from the veal and spoon it over the dish. Sprinkle with the grated Parmesan cheese and the melted butter. Brown under a hot broiler, and serve at once. NET: 4 to 6 servings.

Sautéed Veal Scallops with Tomatoes and Cheese

The veal scallops are on a bed of spinach and sour cream, and are covered with fresh tomatoes and Gruyère cheese.

6 to 8 thin slices veal
7 tablespoons salt butter

¼ cup dry sherry
1 teaspoon tomato paste

1 teaspoon meat glaze
1 teaspoon potato flour
1 cup chicken stock (page 35)
¼ cup dry white wine
1 bay leaf
2 pounds fresh spinach
Salt
Freshly cracked white pepper

½ cup sour cream
2 shallots, finely chopped
½ teaspoon finely chopped
    garlic
6 ripe tomatoes, skinned and
    sliced
6 thin slices Gruyère cheese

Put the veal slices between two pieces of wax paper and flatten them with the side of a cleaver until they are very thin. Melt 4 tablespoons butter in a sauté pan, and brown the slices quickly on each side. In a separate little pan, heat the sherry, ignite, and pour it over the veal. Remove the veal, and set it aside. Off the heat, add to the pan the tomato paste, meat glaze, and potato flour, and mix until smooth. Stir in the chicken stock and wine. Return the pan to moderate heat, and stir until the sauce boils. Add the bay leaf, put the veal in the sauce, and keep it warm.

Melt 2 tablespoons butter in a large pan. Wash the spinach very well, drain, and cook it in the pan with the butter 6 minutes, stirring occasionally. Season with salt and pepper. Drain the spinach well and press it dry. Chop it coarsely, mix it with the sour cream, and set it aside. Melt 1 tablespoon of salt butter in a heavy pan and gently cook the chopped shallots and garlic 1 minute. Add the sliced tomatoes and season with salt and pepper. Cook briskly 5 minutes.

To serve, spread the spinach mixture as a bed on an au gratin dish. Arrange the veal scallops on it, spoon the cooked tomatoes over them, and on top of that place slices of Gruyère cheese. Strain the sauce the veal was cooked in and spoon it over the cheese. Brown under a hot broiler just before serving. NET: 4 to 6 servings.

ESCALOPES DE VEAU VALENTINO

Sautéed Veal Scallops with Asparagus Tips

6 to 8 thin slices veal
½ cup dry sherry
Salt
Freshly cracked white pepper
5 tablespoons salt butter
4 firm white mushrooms, sliced
1 teaspoon lemon juice
1 teaspoon tomato paste
1 teaspoon meat glaze

3 teaspoons potato flour
2 cups chicken stock (page 35)
¼ cup dry white wine
1 teaspoon currant jelly
24 fresh or frozen asparagus tips
    (trimmed)
3 tablespoons freshly grated
    Parmesan cheese
1 tablespoon melted salt butter

Put the slices of veal between two pieces of wax paper and flatten them with the side of a cleaver. Remove the top paper, brush the veal with ¼ cup sherry, and season with a little salt and pepper. Heat 2 tablespoons butter in a heavy frypan. Brown the pieces of veal on both sides a few at a time; press them flat while they cook with a flat lid and a weight on top. When all the veal has been browned, return it to the pan. In a separate little pan, heat ¼ cup sherry, ignite, and pour it over the veal. Remove the veal from the pan and set it aside. Add 3 tablespoons butter to the pan with the mushrooms, lemon juice, salt, and pepper. Cook briskly 3 minutes. Off the heat, add the tomato paste, meat glaze, and potato flour. Mix well, and add the chicken stock, wine, and jelly. Stir this over low heat until it comes to a boil. Put the veal in the sauce and keep it warm.

Cook the asparagus in a little boiling salted water until just soft (it must be crisp; the cooking time will depend on whether it is fresh or frozen). To serve, place the slices of veal, overlapping, down an au gratin dish. Arrange the asparagus tips neatly on the veal. Spoon the sauce over them, sprinkle with grated cheese and melted butter, and brown under a hot broiler. NET: 4 to 6 servings.

This goulash may be prepared with beef instead of veal.

GULYAS DE VEAU À LA HONGROISE

Hungarian Veal Goulash (Braised)

2 pounds boned veal (from shoulder or leg), cut in 1½-inch squares
2 tablespoons salt butter
2 onions, sliced
2 carrots, sliced
1 stalk celery, sliced
½ teaspoon finely chopped garlic
1 green pepper and 1 red pepper, seeded and cut in shreds
1 tablespoon tomato paste
3 tablespoons all-purpose flour
1 tablespoon paprika
2 cups chicken stock (page 35)
Salt
Freshly cracked white pepper
1 bay leaf
½ cup sour cream

Preheat the oven to 350°. In a heavy casserole, on top of the stove, heat the butter and quickly brown the pieces of veal on all sides. Remove the veal from the pan and add the onions, carrots, celery, and garlic. Cook slowly 5 minutes. Add half the shredded green and red peppers. Off the heat, stir in the tomato paste, flour, paprika, and chicken stock. Stir over moderate heat until the mixture comes to a boil. Season with salt and pepper, and add the bay leaf and the veal. Cover, and cook in the oven 45 minutes, or until the veal is tender.

Remove the pan from the oven and remove the veal from the sauce. Strain the sauce and return it to the pan. Add the rest of the shredded green and red peppers, and gently cook the sauce down to a thick consistency. Stir in the sour cream, return the veal to the casserole, and serve. NET: 4 to 6 servings.

OSSO BUCO

Italian Braised Veal Shins with Risotto

2½ pounds veal shins or knuckle, cut in 4 pieces (the meat should be very white, and the bone should contain marrow)
1 garlic clove, cut in half
¼ cup dry sherry
Freshly cracked white pepper
16 tablespoons salt butter (½ pound)

½ cup Cognac or good brandy
2 large Bermuda onions, finely chopped
2 teaspoons finely chopped garlic
6 ounces firm white mushrooms, thinly sliced
¾ cup pine kernels (pignoli nuts

Salt
1½ cups long-grain rice
3 cups chicken stock (page 35)
1 teaspoon leaf saffron
3 tablespoons cold water
4 tablespoons frozen sweet butter
½ cup freshly grated Parmesan cheese

Rub the veal with the cut halves of garlic clove. Brush it with the sherry, and sprinkle with pepper. Let the veal marinate this way about 30 minutes.

Preheat the oven to 350°. Heat 3 tablespoons salt butter in a large deep heavy pan. When it is golden brown, brown the pieces of veal on all sides very well (almost cook it). In a separate little pan, heat the brandy, ignite, and pour it over the veal. Remove the veal from the pan, and set it aside. In the same pan, melt the rest of the salt butter (13 tablespoons), but do not let it brown. Add the onions and garlic, cook until the onions are translucent, then add the mushrooms and pine kernels. Stir in the rice, then the chicken stock. Crush the leaf saffron with a small mortar and pestle, mix it with the cold water, and add it to the rice. Add 1½ teaspoons salt and freshly cracked pepper. Stir the rice mixture over moderate heat until it comes to a boil. Put the pieces of veal in the pan and cover them with the rice. Cover the pan, and cook in the oven 45 minutes.

Remove the pan from the oven and serve the veal and rice in a casserole, garnished with 4 lumps of frozen sweet butter. Serve with a bowl of freshly grated Parmesan cheese. NET: 4 servings.

PAUPIETTES DE VEAU FONTANGES

Braised Veal Birds on Pea Purée, with Brown Sauce

6 thin slices veal (about 8 by 4 inches)
½ cup plus 1 tablespoon Cognac or good brandy
Salt
Freshly cracked white pepper
½ pound ground lean veal
2 egg whites
¾ cup light cream
1 shallot, finely chopped
1 teaspoon chopped fresh tarragon
About 4 slices cooked tongue, ¼ inch thick (enough to make 12 finger-size strips about 4 inches long)
6 green olives stuffed with pimento (or 6 pieces black truffle)
5 tablespoons salt butter
1 teaspoon tomato paste
1 teaspoon meat glaze
2 teaspoons potato flour
1¼ cups chicken stock (page 35)
¼ cup dry white wine
1 teaspoon red currant jelly
½ teaspoon finely chopped garlic
3 packages frozen green peas or 4 cups fresh shelled peas
½ cup water
2 teaspoons sugar
2 tablespoons all-purpose flour
2 tablespoons sour cream

Put the slices of veal between two pieces of wax paper and flatten them very thin with the side of a cleaver. Remove the top paper, brush the veal with ¼ cup brandy, and season with a little salt and pepper.

VEAL MOUSSE. Put the ground veal in a mixer bowl with the egg whites and beat well. Very gradually beat in the light cream. Add the shallot, tarragon, 1 tablespoon brandy, ½ teaspoon pepper, and 1 teaspoon salt.

Spread the mousse about ¼ inch thick on each slice of veal, and on it, on each slice, place 2 fingers of tongue about ½ inch apart. Between the tongue strips put 1 pimento-stuffed green olive or a piece of truffle. Roll up each slice carefully, and tie with string in two places.

Preheat the oven to 375°. Heat 2 tablespoons butter in a heavy pan and brown the veal birds on all sides. In a separate little pan, heat ¼ cup brandy, ignite, and pour it over the veal birds. Remove them from the pan and add to it 1 tablespoon butter. Off the heat, stir in the tomato paste, meat glaze, and potato flour, and mix to a smooth paste. Add the chicken stock, wine, jelly, garlic, and a little pepper (no salt). Stir this mixture over moderate heat until it boils. Return the veal birds to the pan, and cook in the oven 25 minutes. During the cooking, baste the meat a few times with the sauce.

While the meat is cooking, cook the peas in a pan with the water, sugar, and 1 teaspoon salt until they are just soft. Drain, and rub through a fine strainer. Melt 2 tablespoons butter in the pan and stir in the flour. Brown the mixture a little, then add the puréed peas and sour cream. Correct the seasoning and gently warm over low heat.

To serve, form a bed of pea purée on an au gratin dish. Remove the veal birds from the sauce, remove the string, and cut the veal birds exactly in half (through the middle of the olive). Arrange the halves in two rows on the pea purée. Strain the sauce, and spoon it over the veal birds. NET: 6 servings.

An unusual and delicious variation of paupiettes.

PAUPIETTES DE VEAU À LA GRECQUE

Braised Veal Birds Stuffed with Hard-Boiled Eggs and Fresh Herbs

10 long, narrow, very thin slices veal
½ cup Cognac, brandy, or whiskey
Salt
Freshly cracked white pepper
8 tablespoons salt butter
2 large yellow onions, finely chopped
3 hard-boiled eggs, finely chopped
2 tablespoons dry breadcrumbs (page 69)

4 tablespoons chopped fresh chives
1 tablespoon chopped fresh parsley
A few grains freshly grated nutmeg
⅛ teaspoon mace
1 teaspoon tomato paste
1 teaspoon meat glaze
3 teaspoons potato flour
1¾ cups chicken stock (page 35)
⅓ cup dry sherry

1 teaspoon red currant jelly　　　　*Rice Pilaff (page 675)*

Lay the slices of veal between 2 sheets of wax paper, and flatten them with the side of a heavy cleaver until they are almost translucent. Remove the top paper. Brush the veal with ¼ cup brandy or whiskey, and season with a little salt and pepper.

STUFFING. Melt 3 tablespoons butter in a sauté pan and slowly cook the onions until they are translucent and soft, but not brown. Put them in a bowl with the hard-boiled eggs, breadcrumbs, 2 tablespoons chives, and the parsley, nutmeg, and mace. Mix, and season well with salt and pepper.

Spread a spoonful of stuffing in the middle of each slice of veal. Roll up the stuffed slices and tie each in two places with fine string. Heat 3 tablespoons butter in a heavy pan. When it is on the point of browning, put in the veal birds and brown them quickly all over. In a separate little pan, warm ¼ cup brandy or whiskey, ignite, and pour it over the meat. Remove the meat from the pan and set aside for a moment.

Preheat the oven to 375°. Add 2 tablespoons butter to the pan. Off the heat, stir in the tomato paste, meat glaze, and potato flour. Add the chicken stock, sherry, and jelly, and stir over moderate heat until the sauce boils. Put the veal birds in the sauce and cook them on the top shelf of the oven 25 minutes, basting once or twice with the sauce. Have the rice pilaff prepared, and mix 2 tablespoons chopped fresh chives in it.

To serve, pack the cooked rice into an oiled shallow layer cake pan. Turn it out onto a round serving dish. Remove the veal birds from the sauce and remove the strings. Arrange the veal birds on top of or around the rice. Strain the sauce, and spoon it over the veal birds. NET: 4 to 5 servings.

RAGOÛT DE VEAU AUX CHAMPIGNONS

Veal Ragoût with Mushrooms

2½ pounds veal, cut from the shoulder, in 1 piece
Salt
Freshly cracked white pepper
1 garlic clove, cut in half
¼ pound strip beef fat
4 tablespoons salt butter
2 tablespoons dry sherry
1 medium-size onion, finely chopped
½ teaspoon finely chopped garlic
½ cup raisins, soaked 30

minutes in ½ cup dry white wine
½ pound small fresh mushrooms, cut in halves or quarters (depending on size)
1 teaspoon meat glaze
1 teaspoon tomato paste
2 teaspoons potato flour
1¼ cups chicken stock (page 35)
1 bay leaf
2 tablespoons chopped fresh parsley

Spread out the piece of veal. Season it with salt, pepper, and rub it with the cut clove of garlic. Place a strip of beef fat on the veal, roll up the veal, and tie it like a roast, in several places.

Preheat the oven to 350°. Heat 2 tablespoons of butter in a heavy pan, and brown the veal quickly in the hot butter. Heat the sherry in a separate little pan, ignite, and pour it over the veal. Remove the veal from the pan, set aside, and add to the pan another 2 tablespoons butter and the onion, garlic, and the raisins (reserve the wine the raisins were soaked in). Add a little salt and pepper and cook over low heat 5 minutes. Add the mushrooms and cook another 2 minutes. Off the heat, stir in the meat glaze, tomato paste, and potato flour. Pour in the chicken stock and the wine from the raisins, and stir the mixture over low heat until it comes to a boil. Return the veal to the pan with the bay leaf. Cook in the oven 45 to 50 minutes, uncovered. Baste with the pan sauce occasionally.

Remove the veal from the pan and remove the strings. Cut as many slices as required for one serving. Arrange them overlapping down a serving dish. Spoon the sauce over them, and sprinkle with chopped parsley. NET: 4 servings.

---

2 pounds veal (from shoulder
    or leg), boned and cut into
    1½-inch squares
6 tablespoons salt butter
⅓ cup Cognac or good brandy
2 small onions, finely chopped
3 ounces fresh firm white mush-
    rooms, sliced
1 teaspoon lemon juice
Salt
Freshly cracked white pepper

Optional: 1 cup white raisins
    soaked in ½ cup dry sherry
1 teaspoon finely chopped garlic
2 teaspoons tomato paste
1 teaspoon meat glaze
3 tablespoons all-purpose flour
1 cup chicken stock (page 35)
1 cup sour cream
½ cup heavy cream, whipped
2 tablespoons chopped fresh
    chives or parsley

SAUTÉ DE VEAU À LA CRÈME

Veal Casserole with Cream Sauce, Mushrooms, and Raisins

Preheat the oven to 350°. Heat 3 tablespoons butter in a heavy pan, and quickly brown the pieces of veal in it. When all the meat has been browned, return it to the pan. In a separate little pan, warm the brandy, ignite, and pour it over the veal. Remove the meat from the pan, set it aside, and add to the pan another 3 tablespoons butter with the chopped onions. Cook them 2 minutes, add the mushrooms, lemon juice, salt, and pepper, and cook slowly 3 minutes more. (If desired, at this point add the raisins and sherry.) Add the chopped garlic, cover the pan, and cook very slowly 5 more minutes, stirring once or twice. Off the heat, add to the pan the tomato paste, meat glaze, and flour. Mix well, and add the chicken stock. Stir over low heat until the mixture comes to a boil. Slowly mix in the sour cream little by little. Put the veal back in the pan, and cook 45 minutes on the top shelf of the oven.

When the veal is done, remove it from the oven and stir in the whipped cream. Serve in a casserole, sprinkled with the chopped chives or parsley. NET: 4 to 6 servings.

VEAU EN CASSEROLE

Veal Casserole with Mushrooms and Black Olives, in Beer and Sour Cream Sauce

2-pound rolled boned veal roast (loin or shoulder)
7 tablespoons salt butter
3 tablespoons Cognac or good brandy
2 medium-size yellow onions, coarsely chopped
1 teaspoon finely chopped garlic
1 teaspoon dry mustard
2 teaspoons Dijon mustard
1 teaspoon tomato paste
½ teaspoon meat glaze
4 tablespoons all-purpose flour
1 cup beer
½ cup sour cream
12 baby white fresh mushrooms (if larger, cut in halves or quarters)
½ teaspoon lemon juice
Salt
Freshly cracked white pepper
2 tablespoons dry breadcrumbs (page 69)
1 hard-boiled egg, finely chopped
1 tablespoon finely chopped fresh parsley
12 pitted black olives
Rice Pilaff (page 675)

Preheat the oven to 350°. Over high heat, melt 3 tablespoons butter in a deep heavy pan. Brown the veal roast quickly in this butter, turning it on all sides. In a separate little pan, heat the brandy, ignite, and pour it over the veal. Remove the veal from the pan, set it aside, and add to the pan another 2 tablespoons butter. Add the onions and garlic, and cook them slowly, over low heat, until the onions are golden brown. Off the heat, add the two mustards, tomato paste, meat glaze, flour, and beer. Stir this mixture over low heat until it comes to a rolling boil. Rub it through a fine vegetable strainer. Return the strained sauce to the pan, put it over low heat, and beat in the sour cream a little at a time. In a separate little pan, sauté the mushrooms in 1 tablespoon butter with the lemon juice, salt, and pepper. Add them and the black olives to the sauce.

Return the veal to the pan and baste it with the sauce. Cook the veal, uncovered, on the top shelf of the oven 1 hour, basting it frequently with the sauce in the pan. For the garnish, fry the breadcrumbs in 1 tablespoon of butter until golden brown. Mix them with the finely chopped hard-boiled egg and parsley. To serve, remove the veal from the pan, remove the string ties, and cut into ¾-inch slices. Arrange the slices, slightly overlapping, down an au gratin dish. Spoon the sauce over them. Sprinkle with the breadcrumb and hard-boiled egg mixture, and serve with the Rice Pilaff. NET: 6 servings.

ESCALOPES DE VEAU MAINTENON

Sautéed Loin of Veal Scallops Maintenon

The veal scallops are domed with ham, mushrooms, and Béchamel sauce, and served with Brown Sauce and Parisienne Potatoes.

Parisienne Potatoes (page 617)
3 veal loin chops, 1 inch thick
6 tablespoons salt butter
4 chicken livers
5 firm white mushrooms, sliced
Salt
Freshly cracked white pepper
5 thin slices smoked cooked ham, cut in shreds
3 tablespoons all-purpose flour
A few grains cayenne pepper
1 cup milk

3 tablespoons freshly grated
  Parmesan cheese
½ teaspoon dry mustard
2 tablespoons melted salt butter

½ teaspoon tomato paste
2 tablespoons dry sherry
6 tablespoons chicken stock
  (page 35)

Make the Parisienne potatoes first, and keep them warm. Then carefully cut out the piece of meat from each chop. Cut the pieces into thin slices (about 12). Place the little slices between two pieces of wax paper and beat the meat with the side of a heavy cleaver until it is very thin. Heat 3 tablespoons butter in a frypan and brown the veal scallops on one side only. Set them aside. In another pan, melt 1 tablespoon butter. When it is golden brown, brown the chicken livers quickly on both sides. Remove the livers, add to the pan the mushrooms, salt, and pepper, and cook briskly 3 minutes. Dice the livers, add them and the ham to the mushrooms, and cook 1 minute. Arrange the veal scallops on a baking sheet. Dome a spoonful of the ham, mushroom, and liver mixture on each scallop.

Melt 2 tablespoons butter in a saucepan. Stir in the flour, salt, and cayenne pepper, and cook 1 minute. Off the heat, add the milk. Return the sauce to low heat and stir until it comes to a boil. Add 2 tablespoons grated cheese and the mustard, and simmer gently until the sauce is thick. Pour 1 spoonful of this sauce over each domed slice of veal. Sprinkle with the rest of the grated cheese and dot with butter. Brown the prepared veal scallops under a hot broiler. Arrange them on a hot serving dish. Add to the pan in which the veal was browned the tomato paste, sherry, chicken stock, and salt and pepper. Bring this mixture to a boil, strain, and spoon it around the veal in the serving dish. Pile the Parisienne potatoes at each end of the veal platter. NET: 4 servings.

SCALOPPINE CON SALSA DI POMODORO

Sautéed Veal Scallops with Fresh Tomato Sauce

8 thin slices veal
4 tablespoons salt butter
4 tablespoons dry sherry
¼ cup chicken stock (page 35)
¼ cup dry white wine
1 cup shredded tomatoes (2 or
  3 medium-size ripe tomatoes,
  skinned, seeded, and
  shredded)

1 tablespoon tomato paste
1 teaspoon finely chopped garlic
1 tablespoon chopped fresh
  parsley
½ teaspoon potato flour mixed
  with 2 tablespoons water
Salt
Freshly cracked white pepper
Thin slices lemon

Put the veal slices between two pieces of wax paper and flatten them with the side of a cleaver until they are very thin. Melt the butter in a sauté pan, and brown the slices of veal quickly on each side. In a separate little pan, heat the sherry, ignite, and pour it over the veal. Turn the heat to low, remove the veal, and set it aside. Off the heat, add to the pan the chicken stock, wine, tomatoes, tomato paste, 1 teaspoon garlic, and parsley. Mix these ingredients, then stir in the potato flour mixed with water. Bring the mixture to a boil over low heat, stirring all the while. Season with salt and pepper. To serve, arrange the veal slices on a warm serving platter. Spoon the fresh tomato sauce over them. Garnish with thin lemon slices. NET: 4 servings.

RÔTI DE VEAU FARCI

Roast Loin of Veal
Stuffed with
Veal Mousse,
Sauce Espagnole

2½ pounds loin or shoulder of veal
5 tablespoons Cognac or good brandy
1 garlic clove, cut in half
Salt
Freshly cracked white pepper
6 ounces ground veal
2 egg whites
¾ cup light cream
2 teaspoons finely chopped shallots

1 teaspoon finely chopped fresh tarragon (if available)
2 tablespoons dry breadcrumbs (page 69), mixed with 3 tablespoons melted salt butter
½ pound thinly sliced raw bacon
1 cup dry white wine, mixed with 1 cup water
1 cup Sauce Espagnole (page 38)

Spread out the piece of veal and rub it with the cut garlic clove, salt, and pepper. Brush it with 3 tablespoons brandy. Fold it, and set aside to marinate.

VEAL MOUSSE. Put the ground veal in an electric mixer bowl with the egg whites and beat very well. Slowly add the light cream, beating constantly. Add the shallots, tarragon, 1 teaspoon of salt, 2 tablespoons brandy, and the breadcrumbs mixed with the melted butter, and mix well.

Preheat the oven to 350°. Spread out the veal again (if necessary cut a pocket for the stuffing) and spread it with the veal mousse. Roll it up tightly, cover the roll with slightly overlapping slices of bacon, and tie each piece of bacon down neatly with string. Place the veal on a rack in a roasting pan. Pour a little of the wine and water mixture over the roast, enough to cover the bottom of the pan. Place the roast on the top shelf of the oven and cook 1½ hours, basting at least every 20 minutes with the wine and water mixture (use more if necessary). Turn the meat over after it has cooked 45 minutes, and after another 30 minutes turn it back and complete the last 15 minutes of cooking.

To serve, remove the string ties, but not the bacon. Place the roast whole or sliced on a warm platter. Serve the Sauce Espagnole separately in a sauceboat. NET: 6 to 8 servings.

RÔTI DE VEAU À L'ANGLAISE

Veal Roast with
Yorkshire Pudding,
Demi-Glace Sauce

Veal roast cut from the leg (2 to 3 pounds)
Salt
Freshly cracked white pepper
¼ teaspoon finely chopped

garlic
2 tablespoons Cognac or good brandy
2 tablespoons melted salt butter
Dry white wine and water,

for basting as needed
Yorkshire Pudding (page 479)

DEMI-GLACE SAUCE
2 tablespoons salt butter
1 teaspoon tomato paste

1 teaspoon meat glaze
2 teaspoons potato flour
1¼ cups chicken stock (page 35)
½ cup dry white wine
2 teaspoons red currant jelly

Preheat the oven to 350°. Rub the veal roast with salt, pepper, and chopped garlic. Brush it with the brandy. Tie it with string neatly in several places, and place it on a rack in a roasting pan. Brush it with the melted butter, and pour some of the mixed wine and water in the bottom of the pan. Roast 1½ hours, turning the meat over once or twice during the roasting, and basting frequently with the wine and water.

Make the Yorkshire pudding to finish when the roast does — it takes about an hour and a quarter to mix and bake. If you do not have two ovens to accommodate the veal and Yorkshire pudding at different temperatures, the Yorkshire pudding may be cooked on top of the stove in a covered casserole dish.

SAUCE. Melt the butter in a saucepan. Off the heat, stir in the tomato paste, meat glaze, and potato flour. Add the rest of the ingredients, and stir over moderate heat until it boils. Simmer gently 10 minutes. When the roast has finished cooking, strain the pan juice and add it to the sauce.

When the roast is done, let it rest a few minutes out of the oven, then remove the string ties and slice enough meat for one serving. Arrange the slices, overlapping, on a serving platter, with the uncut piece of meat at one end. Spoon the sauce around or over the meat. Garnish the platter with the Yorkshire pudding. NET: 4 to 6 servings.

This is an elegant main course for very special sit-down dinners, especially with its garnishes of baby carrots and artichoke bottoms stuffed with chestnut purée. It can, but really should not, be made in smaller quantity.

Loin of veal, 4 to 5 pounds, boned
Kosher (or table) salt
Freshly cracked white pepper
5 tablespoons Cognac or good brandy
2 whole chicken breasts (4 sides), skinned and boned
1 pound ground lean veal
½ cup egg whites
¾ cup light cream
1 tablespoon finely chopped

fresh tarragon (if available)
1 tablespoon shallots, finely chopped
½ pound thinly sliced raw bacon (you need enough to wrap around the roast)
1½ cups dry red wine
1½ cups water
A few sprigs dill or parsley
2 cups baby carrots, cooked or canned, or large carrots cut in olive shapes and cooked

RÔTI DE VEAU À LA FOYOT

Roast Loin of Veal Stuffed with Breast of Chicken Mousse, Sauce Espagnole

1 cup chestnut purée (page 589)
8 artichoke bottoms (canned),
    lightly sautéed in a little
    butter
8 medium-size fresh mushroom
    caps, fluted, and lightly
    sautéed in a little butter and
    lemon juice

2 cups Sauce Espagnole (page
    38)

PANADE
¾ cup water
6 tablespoons salt butter
¾ cup all-purpose flour
3 small eggs

PANADE. Put the water and butter in a saucepan and bring to a boil. Throw in the flour and stir until smooth. Remove from the heat and beat in the eggs. Spread the mixture out on a plate and chill.

Spread out the loin of veal, season it with salt (preferably coarse kosher salt) and pepper. Brush it with 3 tablespoons brandy. Allow the meat to marinate this way while you prepare the mousse.

BREAST OF CHICKEN MOUSSE. Put the skinned boned chicken breasts through a fine meat chopper. Combine them with the ground veal in the bowl of an electric mixer and mix well. Add the egg whites and beat until smooth. Slowly add the light cream, beating all the while. Mix in the panade. Season with salt, pepper, 2 tablespoons of brandy, and the shallots and tarragon.

Preheat the oven to 350°. Spread the mousse preparation on the veal (reserving about 2 tablespoons of mousse for the chestnut purée). Roll up the veal. Cover it neatly with strips of bacon, slightly overlapping. Tie each piece of bacon with string. Place the veal on a rack in a roasting pan. Mix the wine and water. Pour enough of the mixture over the roast to cover the bottom of the pan. Reserve the rest to baste the veal as it cooks. Roast the veal 2 hours, basting frequently. Use more wine and water if needed.

Have the vegetable garnishes ready when the veal is finished roasting. Put a tiny sprig of fresh dill (or parsley) in the top of each baby carrot to represent the top. Mix a little of the chicken breast mousse into the chestnut purée. Fill the artichoke bottoms with this purée, mounding the tops with a small spatula. Set a fluted mushroom on the chestnut purée. Remove the veal from the oven when the roasting is completed. Remove the string but not the bacon. Slice enough veal for one serving. Place the slices, slightly overlapping, on a serving platter, with the uncut piece of veal at one end. Surround the veal with alternating clusters of baby carrots and stuffed artichoke bottoms. Serve the Sauce Espagnole separately in a sauceboat. NET: 8 servings.

RÔTI DE VEAU À LA PROVENÇALE

Roast Veal Stuffed with Veal Mousse, with Tomato and Olive Garnish

The tomatoes are filled with poached green olives stuffed with veal mousse.

2 pounds boned rolled veal roast
Salt
Freshly cracked white pepper

½ teaspoon finely chopped
    garlic
2 tablespoons salt butter

2 tablespoons Cognac or good
    brandy
Dry white wine and water,
    mixed in equal parts, as
    needed for basting
2 tablespoons melted salt butter

VEAL MOUSSE
½ pound ground lean veal
1 egg white
¾ cup light cream
Salt
Freshly cracked white pepper

2 teaspoons finely chopped
    fresh parsley
2 teaspoons finely chopped
    onion

TOMATO GARNISH
6 small ripe tomatoes
Salt
Freshly cracked white pepper
Sugar
4 tablespoons salt butter
2 cups small pitted green olives
6 firm white mushrooms, fluted

Preheat the oven to 375°. Untie and spread out the veal roast. Season well with salt, pepper, and the garlic.

VEAL MOUSSE. Put the ground veal and egg white in a mixer and beat well. Slowly, drop by drop, beat in the light cream. Season with pepper and 1 teaspoon salt, and mix in the parsley and chopped onion.

Spread two-thirds of the mousse on the veal (reserve one-third for the olives). Reroll the roast tightly and tie it securely with string in several places, about 1 inch apart. Heat 2 tablespoons of salt butter in a heavy casserole and carefully brown the stuffed roast all over. Heat the brandy in a separate little pan, ignite, and pour it over the roast. Cook the roast, uncovered, 50 to 60 minutes. Baste it frequently with the wine and water. When it has cooked 25 minutes, turn it over, and sprinkle a little salt and pepper in the pan juices. (Each time you baste, brush the roast with a little melted butter.)

When the roast is cooked, remove it from the pan and allow it to stand about 5 minutes in a warm place. Remove the string. Reheat the sauce in the pan and add a little more dry white wine and water, with a little salt and pepper. Stir with a wooden spoon to lift up all the glaze. Strain.

TOMATO GARNISH. Cut the tops off the tomatoes and carefully scoop out the inside. Reserve the caps. (The pulp can be strained and the juice added to the sauce.) In the bottom of each tomato, put a little salt, pepper, pinch of sugar, and about ½ tablespoon butter. Place the tomatoes and their caps on a baking dish and bake in a 350° oven 5 minutes. Put the reserved veal mousse in a pastry bag fitted with a small plain tube (about #3), and stuff a little into each pitted olive. Drop the stuffed olives into a pan of hot salted water and allow them to poach gently without boiling for 5 minutes. Drain, and mix the olives with a little butter. Fill the tomatoes with these olives, cover with the tomato caps. Sauté the mushrooms in a little butter, and place one mushroom cap on top of each tomato.

To serve, cut as many slices of the roast as required for one serving. Arrange them, overlapping, on a warm serving platter, with the uncut piece at one end. Spoon the sauce over or around the veal. Garnish the platter with the olive-stuffed tomatoes. NET: 4 to 6 servings.

CERVELLE DE VEAU AU BEURRE NOIR

Calf's Brains in Brown Butter

1 pound calf's brains
1 tablespoon lemon juice
2 tablespoons all-purpose flour
2 tablespoons salt butter
10 baby new potatoes, plain-
    boiled and skinned (page 612)
1 tablespoon finely chopped
    fresh parsley

BEURRE NOIR
The pan butter plus 3 more
    tablespoons salt butter
1 tablespoon lemon juice
1 tablespoon tarragon vinegar
Salt
Freshly cracked black pepper
¼ cup capers

Soak the calf's brains 1 to 2 hours in cold water with the lemon juice. Drain. With a small knife, remove the skin and veins. Dry well on paper towels. Dust the brains very lightly and evenly with the flour. Melt the butter in a large frypan. When it is at the point of browning, put in the prepared brains. (Do not let the pieces touch each other, or they will not brown properly.) Brown the brains on both sides. Place them slightly overlapping on a hot serving dish, and keep them warm in the oven at very low temperature while you prepare the sauce.

BEURRE NOIR. Add 3 tablespoons butter to the pan in which the brains were cooked. Allow the butter to darken very slowly (this may take 10 minutes). Then stir the rest of the ingredients into the browned butter.

Spoon the sauce over the brains. Pile the potatoes at each end of the dish, and sprinkle them with the parsley. NET: 4 servings.

COEUR DE VEAU FARCI

Braised Veal Heart Stuffed with Sausage Meat

2 veal hearts
A little milk and all-purpose
    flour (for coating)
2 tablespoons salt butter
1 cup dry red wine
1 cup water
1 tablespoon all-purpose flour

STUFFING
¼ pound pork sausage meat
½ cup finely chopped onion
½ cup chopped fresh
    mushrooms
½ cup soft breadcrumbs
Salt
Freshly cracked white pepper
1 tablespoon chopped fresh
    parsley

Preheat the oven to 325°. Wash the veal hearts well in several changes of water to remove all the blood. Cut out the veins and arteries, making a pocket for the stuffing. Dry the hearts well with paper towels.

STUFFING. Cook the sausage meat in a sauté pan until it is brown and crisp. Remove the meat from the pan with a slotted spoon. In the same pan, with the fat from the sausage meat, slowly sauté the chopped onion and mushrooms, over low heat, until they are lightly browned. Add the onions and mushrooms to the cooked sausage meat, and mix in the breadcrumbs, salt, pepper, and chopped parsley.

Stuff the veal hearts with this mixture. Secure the stuffed hearts with skewers and string. Brush them with a little milk and dust lightly with flour. Heat 1 tablespoon butter in a heavy pan. Brown the hearts in this pan and pour over them the wine and water. Cover the pan, and cook in the oven 2 hours, until tender. Baste occasionally with the liquid in the pan.

When tender, remove the hearts from the pan. Remove the skewers and string. Cut the hearts into slices, crosswise. Arrange them slightly overlapping on a hot serving dish. Mix 1 tablespoon flour with 1 tablespoon butter and stir it into the liquid the hearts were cooked in. Spoon this sauce over the slices of heart. NET: 4 to 6 servings.

FOIE DE VEAU À LA MOUTARDE

Sautéed Calf's Liver in Mustard Cream Sauce

This dish can also be prepared with veal kidneys or chicken livers. The sauce is a simple demi-glace to which heavy cream, shallots, and mustard are added to give it a unique character. With the chicken livers, served in a chafing dish, it is a very good menu item for a buffet.

4 thick slices calf's liver
½ cup Cognac or good brandy
4 tablespoons salt butter
1 teaspoon tomato paste
1 teaspoon meat glaze
2½ cups heavy cream
2 teaspoons finely chopped shallots
1 teaspoon finely chopped garlic

1 egg yolk
½ teaspoon potato flour
1 teaspoon dry mustard
2 teaspoons Dijon mustard
2 tablespoons light cream
1 tablespoon chopped fresh tarragon (if available)
Optional: 4 to 6 large fried croûtons (page 69)

Dry the slices of liver with paper towels. (If you are using veal kidneys, remove the fat and core and cut the kidney into ¾-inch slices.) Brush them with a little brandy, and allow to marinate a moment. Heat 3 tablespoons butter in a large frypan until it is on the point of browning. Brown the slices of liver on each side and cook to the desired degree. Heat the rest of the brandy in a separate little pan, ignite, and pour it over the liver in the frypan. Remove the slices of liver from the pan and keep them warm. To the pan in which the liver was cooked, add another tablespoon butter, the tomato paste and meat glaze. Very slowly, over low heat, stir in the heavy cream. When all the cream has been blended, add the chopped shallots and garlic. In a small bowl mix the egg yolk with the potato flour, two mustards, and light cream. Off the heat, stir this mixture into the sauce. Add the chopped tarragon, if available. Gently reheat the sauce.

To serve, arrange the slices of liver on a shallow serving dish. Spoon the sauce over them. Garnish with the large fried croûtons. NET: 4 servings.

PETITES CRÈMES DE FOIE DE VEAU PARISIENNE

Molded Liver Creams
with Mushroom and
Fresh Tomato Sauce

¾ pound calf's liver
3 tablespoons salt butter (plus
    butter for the molds)
3 tablespoons all-purpose flour
Salt
Freshly cracked white pepper
¾ cup chicken stock (page 35)
1 egg
1 egg yolk
½ cup heavy cream
6 firm ripe tomatoes, skinned
    and quartered
1 tablespoon chopped fresh
    parsley

1 tablespoon melted salt butter

SAUCE
2 tablespoons salt butter
4 ounces firm white mushrooms,
    sliced
Salt
Freshly cracked white pepper
1 teaspoon lemon juice
1 tablespoon all-purpose flour
2 teaspoons tomato paste
1 cup chicken stock (page 35)
    or water

Preheat the oven to 300°. Put the liver through a fine meat chopper two times. Melt the butter in a pan. Over low heat, stir in the flour, salt, and pepper, and let cook 1 minute without browning. Off the heat, add the chicken stock. Stir over low heat until it comes to a boil. Remove from the heat, cool a little, and mix into the ground liver. With a small whisk, beat into the liver mixture the egg, egg yolk, and heavy cream. Rub the mixture through a fine strainer. Butter 4 to 6 cabinet pudding molds (little custard crème molds) and fill them with the liver mixture. Place the molds in a shallow roasting pan half filled with hot water. Cover them with buttered wax paper and bake them 20 minutes, or until firm to the touch. Meanwhile, remove the seeds from the tomato quarters, rub the seeds through a strainer, and reserve the juice for the sauce.

SAUCE. Melt the butter in a sauté pan and add the mushrooms, lemon juice, salt, and pepper. Cover the pan and cook over low heat 4 minutes. Off the heat, stir in the flour and tomato paste. When the mixture is smooth, pour in the chicken stock or water. Stir over low heat until the sauce comes to a boil, and allow to simmer gently 4 minutes. Add the reserved strained tomato juice to the sauce. Set the sauce aside.

Put the tomato sections in a pan with the melted butter, parsley, salt, and pepper. Shake over brisk heat 1 minute; they should not disintegrate. To serve, first spoon the sauce onto a round shallow serving dish. Then turn the liver creams out of the molds and arrange them around the dish. Put the tomato sections in a mound in the middle. NET: 4 to 6 servings.

PETITES CRÈMES DE FOIE DE VEAU, SAUCE FOYOT

Molded Liver Creams
with Fresh Green Peas,
Foyot Sauce

These liver creams might be described as "liver custard creams" because they actually are calf's liver prepared in the custard cream formula. Garnished with fresh garden peas and a piquant Foyot sauce, they are an elegant first course or luncheon dish.

½ pound ground calf's liver

2 eggs, beaten

½ cup light cream
2 tablespoons heavy cream
Salt
A few grains cayenne pepper
A little melted salt butter (to
  brush the molds)

Sauce Foyot (page 52)
2 cups fresh shelled green peas
1 tablespoon sweet butter
1 teaspoon chopped fresh mint
  or parsley

Preheat the oven to 350°. Either have the calf's liver finely ground by the butcher or put it through a fine meat chopper two times. Then combine the ground liver with the eggs, light cream, heavy cream, salt, and cayenne pepper in the mixer bowl, and beat well. Rub the whole mixture through a fine strainer. Generously butter 6 to 8 individual custard molds, such as used for custard creams or cabinet pudding molds. Fill them with the liver cream. Place the molds in a shallow baking pan and half fill the pan with hot boiling water. Cover the molds with wax paper, and bake them 20 minutes.

Prepare the Sauce Foyot. Then cook the shelled green peas in boiling salted water until they are just soft. Drain, and toss them in the sweet butter and fresh mint or parsley. To serve, remove the liver creams from the oven, when they are finished cooking, and unmold them on a hot serving dish. Spoon the Foyot sauce over each liver mold. Garnish the serving dish with the fresh garden peas. NET: 6 to 8 servings.

---

6 slices calf's liver
4 tablespoons salt butter
2 tablespoons dry red wine
1 tablespoon chopped onion
2 teaspoons finely chopped
  garlic
1 tablespoon chopped fresh
  parsley
3 tablespoons chicken stock
  (page 35)
1 large navel orange, cut horizontally into 6 slices, with
  skin on

3 tablespoons vegetable oil
2 tablespoons granulated sugar
Rice Pilaff (page 675)
Optional: ¼ cup freshly grated
  Parmesan cheese (for pilaff)

DUSTING MIX
All-purpose flour
Salt
Freshly cracked white pepper
Dry mustard
Chili powder

FOIE DE VEAU SAUTÉ À L'ORANGE

Sautéed Calf's Liver
with Orange

Dry the slices of liver on paper towels; then dust them very lightly with a little flour seasoned with a pinch of salt, white pepper, dry mustard, and chili powder. Heat 2 tablespoons butter in a large frypan and brown the slices of liver very quickly, on both sides. Set the liver aside and keep it warm. In the same pan, heat the red wine and 2 tablespoons butter. Add the onion and cook 1 minute, then the garlic and cook 1 minute, then the parsley and chicken stock. Arrange the sautéed slices of liver on a serving dish, spoon over the sauce, and keep the dish warm.

In same frypan, heat the vegetable oil very hot. Brown the orange slices quickly in the oil on both sides, then sprinkle with the sugar to glaze them. Garnish the liver with these orange slices. Serve with the rice pilaff, into which you could mix ¼ cup of freshly grated cheese, for a variation. NET: 6 servings.

RIS DE VEAU ET FOIE DE VOLAILLE EN BROCHETTE

Grilled Sweetbreads and Chicken Livers on Skewers

1 pair large calf's sweetbreads
6 to 8 slices bacon
6 to 8 chicken livers
8 to 10 firm white mushroom caps
1 tablespoon salt butter

1 teaspoon lemon juice
Salt
Freshly cracked black or white pepper
4 tablespoons melted salt butter
1 bunch fresh crisp watercress

Put the sweetbreads in a pan, cover them with cold water, and slowly bring to a boil. Simmer 2 minutes, and drain. Plunge them into cold water. Remove the skin and membrane. Cut the sweetbreads into pieces about the size of half a chicken liver. Roll the pieces of sweetbread in half slices of bacon. Cut the chicken livers in half and roll each of them in a half slice of bacon. Sauté the mushroom caps in the butter, lemon juice, salt, and pepper. Thread the sweetbreads, chicken livers, and mushrooms on the skewers, in alternating fashion. Place the skewers on a rack on a broiler pan and brush them with some of the melted butter. Season with salt and pepper. Brown quickly under a hot broiler (about 4 minutes on each side). Brush them again with melted butter. Arrange them on a hot serving platter, garnished with sprigs of watercress. NET: 4 servings.

RIS DE VEAU GISMONDO

Sautéed Sweetbreads on Spinach and Sour Cream

3 large pairs calf's sweetbreads
A little all-purpose flour (to dust)
6 tablespoons salt butter
2 tablespoons dry sherry
1 teaspoon tomato paste
3 teaspoons potato flour

2 cups chicken stock (page 35)
Salt
Freshly cracked white pepper
1 bay leaf
2 pounds fresh spinach
2 tablespoons sour cream

Put the sweetbreads in a pan, cover with cold water, and slowly bring to a boil. Drain, and rinse in ice water. Dry the sweetbreads well, and place them between two baking sheets with a weight on top to flatten them, and chill. Skin them and remove the membrane. Split them in half lengthwise, and dust them lightly with flour. Heat 4 tablespoons butter in a heavy sauté pan and brown the sweetbreads quickly. Heat the sherry in a little pan, ignite, and pour it over them. Remove them from the pan. To the same pan, off the heat, add the tomato paste and potato flour and stir to a smooth paste. Pour in the chicken stock and stir over low heat until the mixture boils. Season with salt and pepper and add the bay leaf and sweetbreads. Cover the pan and cook over low heat 10 minutes.

Wash the spinach very well. Melt 2 tablespoons butter in a large pan and add the spinach, salt, and pepper. Cook quickly, stirring occasionally, for 7 minutes. Drain, press dry, and chop the cooked spinach very fine in a wooden bowl. Mix in the sour cream and correct the seasoning. To serve, arrange the spinach in the form of a loaf or mound on a serving dish. Put the sweetbreads on the spinach. Spoon the sauce over them. NET: 6 servings.

RIS DE VEAU SAUTÉ CLAMART

Sautéed Sweetbreads
on Pea Purée
with Brown Sauce

2 pairs calf's sweetbreads
4 tablespoons salt butter
2 tablespoons Cognac or Scotch whisky
4 thin slices of ham (to wrap around the sweetbreads)

BROWN SAUCE
2 tablespoons salt butter
1 small white onion, finely chopped
½ teaspoon finely chopped garlic
1 teaspoon meat glaze
1 teaspoon tomato paste
2 teaspoons potato flour
1 cup chicken stock (page 35)

¼ cup dry white wine
¼ cup dry sherry
1 teaspoon red currant jelly
Salt
Freshly cracked white pepper
1 medium-size firm white mushroom, chopped

PEA PURÉE
2 packages frozen peas or 3 cups shelled fresh peas
3 tablespoons salt butter
3 tablespoons all-purpose flour
Salt
A few grains cayenne pepper
2 tablespoons heavy cream

Put the sweetbreads in a pan, cover with cold water, and bring to a boil. Simmer 2 minutes. Drain. Put the sweetbreads between 2 flat plates, and flatten them with a weight. Dry the sweetbreads, split them, and remove the skin and membrane. Heat 2 tablespoons butter in a frypan. Brown the sweetbreads quickly on each side. In a separate little pan, heat the Cognac or Scotch, ignite, and pour it over the sweetbreads. Remove them from the pan, wrap each piece in a ham slice, and set aside.

BROWN SAUCE. Heat the butter in the same frypan. Add the onion and garlic. Stir over low heat, but do not brown. Off the heat, stir in the meat glaze, tomato paste, and potato flour. Stir in the chicken stock, wine, sherry, and jelly. Season with salt and pepper. Stir over low heat until the sauce comes to a boil, then add the chopped mushroom.

Place the ham-wrapped sweetbreads in the sauce and gently sauté over low heat 15 to 20 minutes.

PEA PURÉE. Boil the peas in water until just soft. Drain them well and rub through a fine strainer. Melt the butter in a pan. Off the fire, stir in the flour. Season with a little salt and cayenne pepper, and brown gently over low heat. Add the pea purée and heavy cream. Mix well.

To serve, arrange the pea purée in a mound on the bottom of a hot flat serving dish. Place the cooked sweetbreads on it, and spoon the sauce over them. NET: 4 servings.

RIS DE VEAU TALLEYRAND

Sweetbreads Braised in Rich Brown Sauce on a Purée of Peas and Broccoli

2 large pairs calf's
   sweetbreads
A little flour (for dusting)
5 tablespoons salt butter
¼ cup Cognac or good brandy
½ teaspoon finely chopped
   garlic
2 teaspoons finely chopped
   tarragon
1 teaspoon tomato paste
½ teaspoon meat glaze
2 tablespoons all-purpose flour
1 cup chicken stock (page 35)
1 cup heavy cream, whipped
1 teaspoon Dijon mustard
2 tablespoons Madeira wine
3 tablespoons freshly grated
   Parmesan cheese

1 tablespoon melted salt butter
6 firm white fresh mushroom
   caps (fluted, if desired),
   sautéed in a little salt butter
   and lemon juice

PURÉE OF PEAS AND BROCCOLI
2 packages frozen green peas
   or 4 cups shelled fresh peas
1 package frozen broccoli
1 cup water
2 teaspoons granulated sugar
Salt
Freshly cracked white pepper
3 tablespoons salt butter
3 tablespoons all-purpose flour
1 tablespoon sour cream

Put the sweetbreads into a pan, cover with cold water, and bring slowly to a boil. Drain, and plunge the sweetbreads into cold water. Drain again, place them between two flat plates or pans with a weight on top to flatten them, chill them, then skin them, remove the membrane, and cut them in half horizontally. Dry them well on paper towels, and dust lightly with flour. Heat 3 tablespoons butter in a sauté pan. Brown the sweetbreads in the hot butter, quickly, over high heat. Brown only 2 or 3 pieces at a time; they will not brown if they touch each other. Also, put a weighted flat lid on the sweetbread when it is first put into the sauté pan, so that it remains flat. When the sweetbread is turned over, the lid and weight are not required. When all the pieces are browned, return them to the pan. In a separate little pan, heat the brandy, ignite it, and pour it over the sweetbreads. Remove them from the sauté pan, and stir into the pan, off the fire, another 2 tablespoons butter and the garlic, tarragon, tomato paste, meat glaze, and flour. Mix to a smooth paste and add the chicken stock. Stir over low heat until the mixture comes to a boil. Reduce the heat to a gentle simmer, and with a wire whisk beat the whipped cream into the sauce. In a separate little bowl, mix the Dijon mustard with the Madeira wine. Stir this and 1 tablespoon grated cheese into the sauce. Put the sweetbreads into the sauce and simmer them, uncovered, 25 minutes very gently over the lowest heat. Stir occasionally, so that they don't stick to the pan.

PURÉE OF PEAS AND BROCCOLI. Put the frozen peas and broccoli in a pan with the water, sugar, and 1 teaspoon salt. Bring very slowly to a boil and cook 5 minutes, stirring once or twice. Drain thoroughly, and rub the vegetables through a fine strainer. (If using fresh vegetables, the cooking time will be longer.) Melt the butter in a pan. Off the fire, stir in the flour. Put the pan over low heat and stir until the butter-flour mixture is light brown. Add the pea and broccoli purée. Mix in the sour cream, and correct the seasoning with salt and freshly cracked white pepper. Stir over low heat to warm the mixture.

To serve, arrange the purée in a low mound on the bottom of an au gratin dish. With the side of a wooden spoon, make little ridges or indentations down the top of the purée. Place the sweetbreads down the top of the purée. Spoon the sauce over them. (If it has become too thick, thin it with a little light cream.) Sprinkle the top with the rest of the grated cheese and a little melted butter, and brown the dish under a hot broiler. Garnish with the mushroom caps. NET: 4 servings.

4 veal kidneys	½ teaspoon dried thyme	**ROGNON**
2 tablespoons Cognac or good brandy	Salt	**DE VEAU**
4 tablespoons salt butter	Freshly cracked white pepper	**À LA CRÈME**
2 shallots, finely chopped	1 teaspoon meat glaze	
½ teaspoon finely chopped garlic	1 tablespoon all-purpose flour	
½ ounce dried mushrooms, soaked at least 30 minutes in 4 tablespoons water, drained and chopped (reserve water)	¼ cup chicken stock (page 35)	*Veal Kidney in Sour Cream Sauce*

4 veal kidneys
2 tablespoons Cognac or good
  brandy
4 tablespoons salt butter
2 shallots, finely chopped
½ teaspoon finely chopped
  garlic
½ ounce dried mushrooms,
  soaked at least 30 minutes
  in 4 tablespoons water,
  drained and chopped (reserve
  water)

½ teaspoon dried thyme
Salt
Freshly cracked white pepper
1 teaspoon meat glaze
1 tablespoon all-purpose flour
¼ cup chicken stock (page 35)
1 cup sour cream
2 tablespoons dry breadcrumbs
  (page 69)
2 tablespoons freshly grated
  Parmesan cheese
A little melted butter

*ROGNON
DE VEAU
À LA CRÈME*

---

*Veal Kidney
in Sour Cream Sauce*

Cut all the fat away from the kidneys. Cut a slit down the center of each kidney with a sharp knife and remove the core. Cut the kidneys into ¾-inch slices. Mix with the brandy and allow to marinate about 30 minutes. Then heat the butter in a sauté pan. Add the shallots, garlic, mushrooms, and thyme. Season with salt and pepper, and cook over low heat 5 minutes. Add the kidney slices over moderate heat, brown them quickly on each side, and remove them from the pan. Off the heat, stir the meat glaze and flour into the pan. Add the chicken stock and reserved water from the mushrooms, and stir over low heat until the sauce boils. Continuing over low heat, slowly stir in the sour cream. (If the sauce is too thick, add a little plain light cream.) Simmer gently 4 minutes.

Return the sliced kidneys to the sauce, and spoon them with the sauce into a shallow au gratin dish. Sprinkle with the breadcrumbs, grated cheese, and melted butter, and brown quickly under a hot broiler. NET: 4 servings.

ROGNON DE VEAU AU FOUR, MAÎTRE D'HÔTEL

Baked Veal Kidney with Maître d'Hôtel Butter

4 veal kidneys in their fat
4 slices bread, crusts removed
1 bunch fresh crisp watercress

MAÎTRE D'HÔTEL BUTTER
8 tablespoons sweet butter
   (room temperature)

1 tablespoon lemon juice
Salt
Freshly cracked white pepper
1 tablespoon finely chopped
   fresh parsley
Optional: 1 teaspoon chopped
   fresh tarragon

MAÎTRE D'HÔTEL BUTTER. Cream the butter in a mixer until it is very light and fluffy. Add the lemon juice drop by drop. Season with salt, white pepper, and the parsley and tarragon. Chill in the refrigerator or freezer.

Preheat the oven to 425°. Trim some of the fat off the kidneys, leaving about ¼ inch of fat all over. Place the kidneys on a rack in a roasting pan and roast about 30 minutes. Put the fat from the roasting pan into a frypan, and fry the bread slices in this fat until golden brown on each side. Arrange the fried bread down a hot, flat serving dish. Peel off the fat from the kidneys. Make an incision down the center of each kidney with a small sharp knife, and remove the core. Arrange the baked kidneys on the slices of fried bread. Just before serving, fill the center of each kidney with the Maître d'Hôtel Butter. Garnish the dish with clusters of fresh crisp watercress. NET: 4 servings.

TÊTE DE VEAU À LA POULETTE

Poached Calf's Head (Meat, Tongue, Brains) with Poulette Sauce

When I first came to this country during World War II, I had a restaurant on East 60th Street. Because of my business I was able to get meat wholesale. A collection of English families who had taken refuge in America because of the war were my friends, and they had congregated on a rented farm near Morristown, New Jersey. My contribution to their general welfare was to bring them meat once a week from New York. I did this after I closed the restaurant on Friday nights.

One particular Friday night I finished quite late and left the restaurant about 2 A.M. for Morristown. I had with me a duffle bag full of fresh meat, including a calf's head with the skin on it and its long curly lashes.

To get to New Jersey from New York, one had to take the Hudson tube under the Hudson River to Hoboken and the Lackawanna train from there to Morristown. When I came out of the tube at Hoboken, I was suddenly so tired I could not lift the duffle bag full of meat. There was one man walking rather unsteadily along the platform. I stopped him and asked him to help me get the bag onto the train. He tried and couldn't. Then, suddenly, he ran away, and I couldn't imagine why.

When I arrived at the Morristown station (I finally managed to drag the bag on the train), I was met by four policemen and two police cars. This was at about 4 A.M. They put me in one car and my purse and the duffle bag in another car and took me to the police station. When we arrived I asked the sergeant why I was being arrested. He said, "We had a telephone report that you asked somebody to lift your duffle bag." "And what is wrong with that?" I asked. "Nothing," he replied, "but when he lifted it, there was blood coming out of it!" I asked for the duffle bag, opened it, and out fell the calf's head, complete with curly lashes. I thought the sergeant was going to faint. (You see, they assumed I had murdered someone and was trying to get the body across the state line.) Then he said, "Oh, my God, you are Dione Lucas, and I watch you every week on TV!" So we became great friends, and he took me to my friends' farm escorted by not one but two police cars, the sirens blaring all the way.

The reason I had the calf's head was that I was planning to prepare a Tête de Veau à la Poulette for them, the recipe for which follows.

1 calf's head, skinned and split in half (with tongue left whole)
8 large fried croûtons, cut diagonally (page 69)
Optional: 5 or 6 very thin slices Gruyère cheese

COURT BOUILLON
4 quarts water
1 large carrot, sliced
1 medium-size onion, sliced
1 slice lemon
2 bay leaves
2 whole cloves
2 sprigs fresh dill
2 garlic cloves, bruised

1 tablespoon salt
12 white peppercorns

SAUCE POULETTE
3 tablespoons salt butter
3 tablespoons all-purpose flour
1½ cups strained court bouillon (from the calf's head preparation)
Salt
A few grains cayenne pepper
2 teaspoons Cognac or good brandy
2 egg yolks
½ cup heavy cream
2 tablespoons chopped fresh parsley

The butcher should skin the calf's head and split it, taking care not to split the tongue. The head should then be soaked in plenty of cold water several hours; change the water occasionally. Remove the brains and tongue, and soak them in ice water 30 minutes. Put all the ingredients for the court bouillon in a large kettle, then bring slowly to a boil and simmer 10 minutes. Put in the calf's head and tongue and simmer 1½ to 2 hours, until the meat is tender. Remove the head from the court bouillon, put in the brains, and simmer them in the court bouillon 15 minutes. Meanwhile, trim all the meat off the cooked head and dice it. Skin the tongue; remove the little bones and gristle, and slice the rest of the tongue. Remove the brains when cooked and dice them. Set the meats aside while you prepare the sauce.

POULETTE SAUCE. Melt the butter in a medium-size saucepan. Off the heat, blend in the flour. Add 1½ cups strained court bouillon from the kettle in which the meats were cooked. Stir the sauce over moderate heat until it comes to a boil. Season with salt and the cayenne pepper. Add the brandy. In a separate little bowl, beat the egg yolks and add the heavy cream. Remove the saucepan from the heat and add the yolk mixture, blending it in carefully. Put all the meat in the sauce with the parsley. Gently reheat; do not boil.

To serve, spoon the calf's head meats and sauce into a casserole. Surround the casserole with the diagonal croûtons. The top of the dish may be covered with a few very thin slices of Grúyère cheese. NET: 6 to 8 servings.

FRICADELLES DE VEAU SUÉDOISE

Swedish Meat Balls on Spaghetti with Dill and Sour Cream Sauce

1½ pounds ground meats
  (½ pound each of veal,
  beef, and pork)
1 small onion, finely chopped
  and sautéed in a little butter
2 large slices white bread, crusts
  removed, soaked in light
  cream
½ teaspoon freshly grated
  nutmeg
½ teaspoon paprika
1 tablespoon finely chopped
  fresh parsley
½ teaspoon finely chopped
  garlic
2 eggs, slightly beaten
2 teaspoons salt
1 teaspoon freshly cracked
  white pepper
4 tablespoons salt butter
½ cup freshly grated Parmesan
  cheese

2 tablespoons chopped fresh
  dill, parsley, or chives

DILL AND SOUR CREAM SAUCE
2 tablespoons salt butter
3 tablespoons all-purpose flour
1 cup chicken stock (page 35)
1 teaspoon meat glaze
2 teaspoons tomato paste
1½ cups sour cream
Salt
Freshly cracked white pepper
1 teaspoon finely chopped white
  onion
¼ teaspoon finely chopped
  garlic
1 tablespoon chopped fresh dill

SPAGHETTI
½ pound spaghetti
2 teaspoons salt
2 tablespoons vegetable oil

Put the ground meats through a fine meat chopper 3 or 4 times, and put the mixture in a large bowl. Add the sautéed onion and the bread (squeezed damp), nutmeg, paprika, parsley, garlic, and eggs. Season with salt and pepper. Mix the ingredients very well with your hands. Then dip your hands in cold water (to prevent sticking), and roll 1 teaspoonful of the meat mixture into a little ball. Make all the meat into balls in this manner. Heat the butter in a sauté pan. Over high heat, fry all of the meat balls. Brown them on one side, turn over, and brown on the other. Put them in a bowl and set aside.

DILL AND SOUR CREAM SAUCE. Leave in the pan the butter in which the meat balls were fried. Add another 2 tablespoons butter and melt it. Off the heat, add the flour, and stir it into the butter until smooth. Add the chicken stock, a little at a time, over low heat, then stir in the tomato paste and meat glaze. Continue to stir over low heat until the sauce is smooth and thick. Raise to moderate heat and bring to a boil, then lower the heat and stir in the sour cream, a little at a time. Correct the seasoning, and add the onion, garlic, and dill.

SPAGHETTI. Cook the spaghetti in boiling salted water, with the vegetable oil in the water, about 12 minutes, until al dente (just tender but still firm, with body). Drain well.

Reheat the meat balls in the sauce over very low heat for 10 minutes. Put the spaghetti in a mound on a warm earthenware platter, and sprinkle it with the grated cheese. With a slotted spoon, arrange the meat balls over the spaghetti. Spoon the sauce over the meat balls and spaghetti, and sprinkle with the dill, parsley, or chives. NET: 4 to 6 servings.

PAIN DE VEAU FERMIÈRE

Farmer's Veal Loaf

This loaf, cooked in a charlotte mold and served with velouté sauce, can be prepared in exactly the same way with fish, chicken, ham, or other meats. If ham is used, it must be boiled ham. It is garnished with shredded cabbage, sliced carrots, tomatoes, and baby onions.

4 tablespoons salt butter
3 tablespoons all-purpose flour
Salt
Freshly cracked white pepper
¾ cup milk
1 pound raw ground veal
2 large (or 3 small) eggs
½ teaspoon freshly grated
   nutmeg
½ cup light cream

VELOUTÉ SAUCE
4 tablespoons salt butter
3 tablespoons all-purpose flour
1 cup chicken stock (page 35)
2 teaspoons lemon juice
Salt
A few grains cayenne pepper
1 egg yolk
3 tablespoons heavy cream

2 tablespoons heavy cream,
   whipped

GARNISH
1 small firm head of green
   cabbage, finely shredded
8 tablespoons salt butter
Salt
Freshly cracked white pepper
2 large carrots, peeled and cut
   into paper-thin rounds
1 teaspoon lemon juice
1 tablespoon chopped fresh
   parsley
3 large ripe tomatoes, skinned,
   quartered, and seeded
2 teaspoons chopped fresh dill
18 baby white onions, skinned
2 tablespoons chopped fresh
   parsley

PANADE. Melt the butter in a small heavy pan. Off the heat, stir in the flour, salt, and pepper. When smooth, pour in the milk, and stir over low heat until the mixture comes to a boil and thickens. Pour onto a plate and chill well.

Preheat the oven to 350°. When the panade has chilled, mix it into the ground veal and beat well in a mixer. Beat the eggs until light and fluffy, and add them to the mixture with a little more salt, pepper, and the nutmeg. Rub the mixture through a fine strainer. Return to the mixer and slowly add the light cream. Butter a charlotte mold and fill it with the mixture. Cover with buttered wax paper and place in a shallow roasting pan half filled with hot water. Put it in the oven to cook 30 to 40 minutes, until it is firm to the touch. Remove from the oven and keep it warm.

VELOUTÉ SAUCE. Melt 2 tablespoons butter in a small saucepan. Off the fire, stir in the flour. When smooth, pour in the chicken stock. Stir over low heat until the sauce comes to a boil, simmer gently 5 minutes, and remove it from the heat. In a separate bowl, mix the egg yolk with the plain heavy cream, and stir into the sauce. Add the lemon juice, and season with salt and cayenne pepper. Stir in 2 tablespoons butter bit by bit, blend well, then fold in the whipped cream. Keep the sauce warm, but do not boil it.

GARNISH. Put the cabbage in a pan, cover with cold water, bring to a boil, simmer 5 minutes, and drain well. Melt 2 tablespoons butter in the pan, return the cabbage to the pan with a little salt and pepper, and keep it warm. Put the carrots in a pan, cover with water, bring to a boil, and drain. Return them to the pan with 2 tablespoons butter, the lemon juice, salt, and pepper. Cover with wax paper and the lid, and cook gently until the carrots are just soft. Then add the chopped parsley, cover, and keep them warm. Melt 2 table-spoons butter in a sauté pan, put in the tomato sections, and add salt, pepper, and the dill. Cook over low heat only 3 minutes, cover, and keep them warm. Put the skinned baby white onions in a little pan, cover with cold water, bring to a boil, boil 5 minutes, and drain. Add 2 tablespoons butter to the pan, return the onions to it, season with salt and pepper, and cook until just soft. Sprinkle with the parsley, and keep them warm.

Let the cooked veal mold stand a minute or two, then turn it out onto a hot flat serving dish by sliding a thin knife around the edge. Spoon a little of the sauce over the veal and serve the rest separately in a bowl. Arrange the bouquet of vegetables neatly around the veal. NET: 6 servings.

TERRINE MAISON

Cold Meat Loaf with Liver, Sausage Meat, and Veal Strips

Any meat or game can be used instead of veal. This dish was always a spécialité in my restaurants. It should be prepared a day in advance of serving.

About 10 thin slices bacon
    (to line the terrine)
1 pound raw liver (calf's, beef,
    or pork)
2 small white onions, finely
    chopped
½ teaspoon finely chopped
    garlic
1 pound pork sausage meat
Salt
Freshly cracked white pepper

1 teaspoon mixed finely chopped
    fresh thyme and marjoram
    (if not available use ½
    teaspoon dried)
2 hard-boiled eggs, finely
    chopped
1 pound lean veal (1 piece)
1 bunch fresh crisp watercress
Flour and water mixed to a
    stiff paste (to seal the cover)

Preheat the oven to 350°. Line a small earthenware terrine (the shape of a bread tin) with the bacon (lay it crosswise). Put the liver through a fine meat chopper, then put it through again with the onions and garlic. Mix it with the sausage meat, season with salt, pepper, and the thyme and marjoram. Add the hard-boiled eggs. Spread a third of this mixture on the bottom of the terrine. Cut the veal into fine strips. Place half the veal strips on the layer of liver and sausage meat. Add another third of the liver and sausage meat. Cover it with the remaining strips of veal. Cover the top with the remaining third of the liver and sausage meat.

Cover the top of the terrine with well-buttered wax paper and the lid. Seal the edges with the flour and water paste. Stand the terrine in a roasting pan half filled with hot water, and cook it in the oven 2½ hours. When it is cooked, remove the cover, place a clean piece of double wax paper on the terrine, and place a weight on the wax paper (about 2 pounds). Chill the mold in the refrigerator for 24 hours. To serve, turn out of the mold onto a small flat serving dish. Slice, if desired, and garnish with fresh watercress. NET: 6 to 8 servings.

VITELLO TONNATO

Cold Veal and Tuna Salad

This variation of the Italian classic is a platter presentation, convenient for buffet service as well as a sit-down meal. It may be prepared a day in advance.

1 cup long-grain rice
2 cups water
¼ cup plus 2 tablespoons
    vegetable oil
Salt
A few grains cayenne pepper
1 cup finely diced carrots,
    cooked until just soft
½ pound green beans, finely
    diced, cooked until just soft
1 cucumber, skinned, seeded,
    and finely diced
2 firm ripe tomatoes, skinned,
    seeded, and shredded
1½-pound boned loin of veal
Freshly cracked white pepper
3 tablespoons Cognac or good
    brandy
12 tablespoons sweet butter
    (room temperature)
8 ounces canned white tuna fish

8 juniper berries, crushed with
    a pestle and mortar
¼ teaspoon mace

MAYONNAISE
2 egg yolks
1 teaspoon salt
½ teaspoon dry mustard
1 teaspoon Dijon mustard
A few grains cayenne pepper
1 tablespoon tarragon vinegar
1½ cups vegetable oil
⅓ cup light cream
1 package (1½ tablespoons)
    unflavored gelatine
4 tablespoons milk

GARNISH
2 firm ripe tomatoes, skinned,
    quartered, and seeded
1 bunch fresh crisp watercress

MACÉDOINE OF VEGETABLES. Preheat the oven to 350°. In a heavy pan with a lid, put the rice, water, ¼ cup vegetable oil, 2 teaspoons salt, and a few grains of cayenne pepper. Stir this mixture over moderate heat until it comes to a boil. Cover, and cook in the oven 30 minutes. Fluff the rice with two forks, and chill in the refrigerator. When it has chilled, sprinkle it with 2 tablespoons vegetable oil and mix in the carrots, beans, cucumber, and shredded tomatoes. Season, if necessary, with more salt and cayenne pepper, and mix with 1 cup (half) of the mayonnaise below. Brush a layer cake pan with vegetable oil and pack the rice mixture into it. Put it in the refrigerator to set.

MAYONNAISE. Put the egg yolks in an electric mixer bowl. Add the salt, two mustards, and cayenne pepper, and beat very well. Slowly add the vinegar and the vegetable oil, literally drop by drop, until the mayonnaise has thickened. Add the light cream. Put the gelatine in a little pan with the milk. Stir over low heat until the gelatine has dissolved. Cool it a moment, and mix it slowly into the mayonnaise.

Maintain the oven heat at 350° after the rice is removed. Spread out the boned loin of veal and rub it with a little salt and pepper. Brush it with the brandy. Reroll and retie it neatly with string, place it on a rack in a small roasting pan, and roast it 1 hour. After it has cooked 30 minutes, turn it over, then after 20 more minutes turn it back. Wrap the veal in foil, and chill it thoroughly. Beat the sweet butter in an electric mixer until it is very light and creamy. Slowly add the rest of the mayonnaise (1 cup). Drain the canned tuna, flake it a little, and very slowly add it to the creamed butter and mayonnaise. Season with salt (to taste) and the crushed juniper berries and mace. Put this mixture into a pastry bag with a plain #7 tube.

Remove the string ties from the roast veal, pat it dry with paper towels, and cut it into very thin slices. Sandwich each 2 slices together with a generous dollop of the tuna mixture, forced through the pastry tube. Turn out the macédoine of vegetables onto a round serving platter. Arrange the tuna-sandwiched veal around the macédoine. Between each veal "sandwich" put a quarter of tomato that has been skinned and seeded. Garnish the top of the macédoine and around the platter with little sprigs of crisp fresh watercress. NET: 6 to 8 servings.

LAMB

Lamb is considered a most elegant meat in France and Italy, and is gradually becoming more accepted in the United States. It is a superb meat with which to enjoy the regal austere character of great Bordeaux wines. Mutton is less favored in America. In France there are special quality grades of mutton (mouton), and it is highly regarded.

There are three categories of lamb, all now available year round. (1) Baby lamb (agneau de lait), 3 to 9 weeks old, preferably not more than 6, and unweaned. It must usually be ordered in advance from a specialty butcher, and is most available during March and April (because of its popularity as an Easter meat, not because all lambs are born in January or February). Milk-fed baby lamb is a very special delicacy, but has very little flavor; therefore, unlike other lamb, it should be cooked a little beyond the pink stage. (2) Spring lamb, 3 to 6 months old. (3) Lamb, 6 months to a year old. (After a year, it is a young sheep.)

Lamb is so delicate in flavor and texture that (except for baby lamb as noted) it should be only pink when cooked. Never overcook lamb.

1 complete rack of lamb, chined
  (vertebrae cracked)
4 tablespoons salt butter
¼ cup dry sherry
2 onions, sliced
2 carrots, sliced
1 tablespoon all-purpose flour
2 firm white mushrooms, finely
  chopped
1 teaspoon finely chopped garlic
1 teaspoon meat glaze
½ cup dry red wine
1½ cups chicken stock
  (page 35)

Salt
Freshly cracked black pepper
Bouquet garni, including
  2 sprigs parsley, 2 sprigs
  fresh thyme or ½ teaspoon
  dried, 1 sprig fresh mint
2 thin cucumbers
4 large ripe tomatoes, skinned,
  quartered, and seeded
2 teaspoons finely chopped
  fresh mint
14 baby new potatoes, steamed
  (page 612)
A little melted salt butter

CARRÉ
D'AGNEAU
FRANÇAISE

Braised Rack of Lamb
in Brown Sauce,
with Fresh Mint,
Cucumbers, Tomatoes,
and New Potatoes

Preheat the oven to 375°. Trim the excess fat from the lamb, but do not trim out the rib bones. Heat the butter in a large heavy pan, put in the meat, and brown it well all over. Heat the sherry in a little pan, ignite, and pour it over the meat. Remove the meat from the pan, set it aside, and add to the pan the sliced onions and carrots. Cook slowly 2 minutes over low heat. Off the heat, add the flour. Brown it carefully over the heat. Again off the heat, add the mushrooms, garlic, and meat glaze. Stir in the wine and chicken stock, and season with salt and black pepper. Stir the sauce over low heat until it comes to a boil. Add the bouquet garni, return the meat to the pan, and let it braise, uncovered, on the top shelf of the oven, 35 to 40 minutes.

Cut the top and bottom off the cucumbers and split them lengthwise, but do not peel them. Cut them across in ¼-inch slices. Put them in a pan, cover with cold water, bring to a boil, simmer them 3 minutes, and drain them. Cut the tomato sections into shreds and add to the cucumber. When the meat is cooked, remove it from the pan and boil the sauce down to two-thirds quantity. Strain, and return it to the pan. Add the cucumbers, tomatoes, and 1 teaspoon chopped mint to the sauce. Divide the rib chops with a sharp knife. Lay them down a hot flat serving dish. Spoon the sauce over the chops. At each end of the dish put a little pile of the steamed new potatoes, which have been mixed with a little melted butter and 1 teaspoon chopped fresh mint. NET: 4 servings.

CÔTELETTES D'AGNEAU FARCIES

Baked Lamb Chops Stuffed with Veal Mousse

6 double-rib lamb chops,
   trimmed
2 garlic cloves, cut in thin strips
4 tablespoons salt butter
¼ cup dry white wine
1 teaspoon meat glaze
1 teaspoon tomato paste
2 teaspoons potato flour
1¼ cups chicken stock
   (page 35)

VEAL MOUSSE
1 cup ground lean veal
2 egg whites, unbeaten
1½ cups light cream
1½ teaspoons salt
Freshly cracked white pepper

GARNISH
6 diagonal fried croûtons
   (page 69)
6 broiled tomatoes (page 624)

VEAL MOUSSE. Put the ground veal in a mixer bowl. Add the unbeaten egg whites and beat well. Very slowly add the light cream, beating constantly. Then add the salt and pepper.

Preheat the oven to 375°. Make a pocket incision in each double-rib chop, and spoon in the stuffing. Make a few tiny incisions in the tops of the chops and insert the thin strips of garlic. Heat the butter in a heavy pan. Quickly brown the stuffed chops in the hot butter. Pour 2 tablespoons wine into the pan, and place the pan, uncovered, on the top shelf of the oven. Cook 20 to 25 minutes, turning the chops occasionally. When they are cooked, remove them from the pan, set them aside, and add to the pan the meat glaze, tomato paste, and potato flour. Mix to a smooth paste, then add the chicken stock and the rest of the wine. Stir the sauce over low heat until it comes to a boil, and simmer gently 10 minutes.

To serve, arrange the fried croûtons down a hot flat serving dish. Place a stuffed lamb chop on each croûton. Surround the dish with the broiled tomatoes. Strain the sauce and spoon it over the chops. Serve immediately. NET: 6 servings.

CÔTELETTES D'AGNEAU NARONA

Braised Rib Lamb Chops with Deep-Fried Forcemeat Balls, Brown Sauce

8 rib lamb chops, 1 inch thick
Freshly cracked black pepper
2 tablespoons salt butter
1 medium-size yellow onion,
   finely sliced
1 carrot, sliced
1 mushroom, sliced
Salt
1 tablespoon all-purpose flour
¼ cup dry sherry
½ cup dry red wine
¼ cup chicken stock (page 35)
1 teaspoon tomato paste
¼ cup water
2 tablespoons chopped fresh
   parsley

FORCEMEAT BALLS
3 ounces boiled ham
3 ounces boiled tongue
1 small garlic sausage (about
   3 ounces), uncooked
1 hard-boiled egg, finely
   chopped
1 cup coarsely chopped fresh
   white mushrooms
Salt
Freshly cracked black pepper
1 tablespoon chopped fresh
   parsley
½ teaspoon finely chopped
   garlic
1 egg yolk

1 egg, beaten
About ¾ cup dry breadcrumbs

(page 69)
Vegetable oil for deep-fryer

Preheat the oven to 375°. Trim the rib lamb chops neatly, and season with pepper only. Heat the butter in a shallow heavy pan, and brown the chops over high heat in it. Remove them from the pan, set them aside, and add to the pan the onion, carrot, and mushroom. Season with a little salt and pepper, cover the pan, and cook over low heat 3 minutes. Remove the cover, sprinkle the vegetables in the pan with the flour, and place the chops on the vegetables. In a separate little pan, heat the sherry, ignite, and pour it over the chops. Pour on the red wine and chicken stock, and bring to a boil over low heat. Cover the pan, and place it in the oven to cook 25 minutes. Baste the chops occasionally with the liquid in the pan.

FORCEMEAT BALLS. Put the ham, tongue, and sausage meat through a fine meat chopper. Mix in the hard-boiled egg and the mushrooms and put the combined mixture through the meat chopper. Season with salt, pepper, and the parsley. Add the garlic and egg yolk, and mix thoroughly. With floured hands, shape the mixture into balls about 1 inch in diameter. Brush them with beaten egg and roll them in breadcrumbs. Heat the vegetable oil in the deep-fryer to 375° and fry the balls in the hot oil until they are golden brown. Remove from the oil with a slotted spoon and drain on paper towels.

To serve, arrange the chops down a hot au gratin dish. Cover, and keep them warm for a moment. Add the tomato paste and water to the pan in which they were cooked, and mix well. Cook over high heat for a few minutes, until the sauce is reduced to a creamy consistency. Quickly rub it through a fine strainer and spoon it over the chops. Arrange a pile of the forcemeat balls at each end of the dish. Sprinkle the chops with the parsley, and serve. NET: 4 to 8 servings.

POITRINE D'AGNEAU À LA PORTUGAISE

Poached Stuffed Breast of Lamb Portuguese Style

The lamb is served with caper sauce, and garnished with tomatoes stuffed with rice and mushrooms.

2 small boned breasts of lamb (2 to 3 pounds each) and the bones separately
Salt
Freshly cracked white pepper
¼ teaspoon dried thyme
A few grains freshly grated nutmeg
1 cup finely chopped boiled ham
½ cup finely chopped fresh parsley
¼ cup finely chopped celery

1 cup finely chopped green pepper
Bouquet garni (2 sprigs parsley, 1 bay leaf, 1 piece celery leaf)
2 medium-size yellow onions, sliced
1 cup mixed sliced celery, leek, carrot, and white turnip
1 garlic clove, bruised
1 whole clove
8 mixed black and white peppercorns

2 tablespoons melted butter

SAUCE
4 tablespoons salt butter
3 tablespoons all-purpose flour
Salt
Freshly cracked white pepper
A few grains freshly grated
    nutmeg
½ cup dry vermouth
1 cup stock from the lamb
1 tablespoon chopped fresh
    chives (if available)
1 tablespoon finely chopped
    shallots
1 tablespoon capers

GARNISH
8 small firm, ripe tomatoes,
    skinned
2 tablespoons salt butter
½ cup finely chopped onions
¼ cup dried mushrooms,
    soaked at least 30 minutes in
    1 cup water
½ cup long-grain rice
¼ cup water
Salt
Freshly cracked white pepper
½ cup freshly grated Parmesan
    cheese

Spread out the boned breasts of lamb and sprinkle them with salt, pepper, and the thyme and nutmeg. In a bowl, mix together the ham, parsley, green pepper, and celery, and season with salt and pepper. Spread the mixture on the lamb. Roll up each stuffed breast of lamb tightly, tie securely with string in several places, and wrap tightly in cheesecloth. Put the lamb in a large heavy pot with the lamb bones and the bouquet garni. Add the onions, the mixed vegetables, and the garlic and whole clove. Add enough water to cover the lamb breasts, 1 teaspoon salt, and the peppercorns. Bring to a boil, and skim off the scum. Simmer very gently over low heat 2 to 2½ hours, until the meat is tender (but not falling apart). Allow the meat to cool a little in the stock, then remove it from the stock, and remove the cheesecloth and string. (Strain and reserve the stock.) Keep the meat warm.

SAUCE. Melt 2 tablespoons butter in a saucepan. Off the heat, add the flour, salt, pepper, and the nutmeg. Still off the heat, add the vermouth and 1 cup of the strained stock in which the lamb was cooked. Stir the sauce over low heat until it comes to a boil. Add the chives, shallots, and capers, and simmer 5 minutes.

STUFFED TOMATOES. Preheat the oven to 350°. Melt 2 tablespoons butter in a small heavy pan. Add the chopped onions and cook over low heat until they are translucent. Drain the mushrooms and reserve the water in which they were soaked. Chop them fine and add them to the onions in the pan. Add the rice and mix well. Add the water and the reserved mushroom water, ½ teaspoon salt, and pepper. Stir over moderate heat until the liquid comes to a boil. Cover the pan, and cook it in the oven 25 minutes. When it is done, fluff with two forks, and mix in the grated cheese. Cut the tops off the tomatoes, scoop out the insides, and sprinkle a little salt and pepper in the tomatoes. Gently stuff the rice mixture into the tomatoes, and cover them with their caps.

When ready to serve, brush both lamb breasts with a little melted butter and brown them very quickly under a hot broiler. Slice one of the breasts and arrange the slices, overlapping, down a warm serving platter. Place the uncut breast at one end of the platter. Spoon the sauce over the lamb, and arrange the stuffed tomatoes around it. NET: 6 to 8 servings.

This dish could also be served on a bed of pea purée instead of the broiled tomato garnish.

Roast Breast of Lamb Stuffed with Veal Mousse, Bordelaise Sauce

2 boned breasts of lamb
¼ cup Cognac, good brandy, or whiskey
Salt
Freshly cracked white pepper
1 teaspoon finely chopped garlic
½ pound ground lean veal
2 egg whites
⅔ cup light cream
2 ounces finely diced boiled ham
1 large firm white mushroom, finely chopped
1 teaspoon salt butter
½ teaspoon lemon juice
2 shallots, finely chopped
1 teaspoon finely chopped fresh tarragon (if available)
About ½ pound thinly sliced bacon
1½ cups dry red wine
1½ cups water

BORDELAISE SAUCE
1 teaspoon and 2 tablespoons salt butter
2 chicken livers
¼ cup Cognac or good brandy
2 teaspoons tomato paste
1 teaspoon meat glaze
2 teaspoons potato flour
1¼ cups chicken stock (page 35)
¼ cup dry sherry
2 tablespoons dry red wine
1 teaspoon red currant jelly
2 marrowbones
1 cup dry white wine
1 small piece celery with leaf
1 slice onion
1 bay leaf
2 peppercorns
2 whole allspice

GARNISH
Broiled tomatoes (page 624)

Preheat the oven to 350°. With a very sharp meat knife, slit the breasts carefully, but not all the way through, so that you have a pocket. Brush the meat all over (outside and inside the pocket) with the brandy or whiskey, rub it with salt and pepper, and spread half the garlic on it. Roll up the meat tightly to marinate while you prepare the stuffing.

VEAL MOUSSE. Put the ground veal in a small metal bowl over another bowl of ice. With a wire whisk, mix in the raw egg whites. Slowly add the light cream, beating with the whisk all the time. Mix in 1½ teaspoons salt and the ham. In a little sauté pan, cook the mushroom 2 minutes with the butter, lemon juice, salt, and pepper, then add the shallots, tarragon, and the rest of the garlic. Add this mixture to the veal mousse.

Carefully stuff this mousse into the pockets of the lamb breasts, and roll up the breasts. Cover each breast with slightly overlapping slices of bacon. Tie each slice down with string neatly and securely. Place the breasts on a rack on a roasting pan. Mix the wine with the water, and pour some of it over the meat — just enough to cover the bottom of the roasting pan. Roast the meat 50 to 60 minutes, basting frequently with wine and water (use more if necessary). After the meat has been in the oven 20 minutes, turn the breasts over, then after another 15 minutes, turn them back again.

BORDELAISE SAUCE. Heat 1 teaspoon butter in a small heavy saucepan. When it is golden brown, put in the chicken livers and quickly brown them on both sides. In a separate little pan, heat the brandy, ignite, and pour it over the livers. Remove them from the pan, set them aside, and add to the pan 2 tablespoons butter. Stir in, off the heat, the tomato paste, meat glaze, and potato flour. When the mixture is smooth, pour in the chicken stock, sherry, and red wine. Add the jelly. Stir the sauce over low heat until it comes to a boil, then remove from the heat. Heat another small heavy pan, with nothing in it. Put in the marrowbones and brown them on both sides. Pour in the white wine, and add the rest of the ingredients. Bring this mixture to a boil slowly, then add it all to the first sauce. Also return the chicken livers to the saucepan. Simmer the sauce down, over low heat, until it attains a creamy consistency. Remove the marrowbones and livers, and set them aside, strain the sauce, and return it to the pan. Slice the livers neatly and put them in the sauce, and crush the marrow and add it. Taste for seasoning.

To serve, remove the strings from the roast breasts of lamb. Slice one rolled breast of lamb and arrange the slices, slightly overlapping, down a warm serving platter. Place the uncut breast of lamb at one end of the platter. Spoon a little of the sauce over the meat and serve the rest separately in a sauceboat. Garnish the platter with the broiled tomatoes. NET: 6 servings.

RAGOÛT D'AGNEAU À LA PRINTANIÈRE

Ragoût of Lamb with Spring Vegetables

This ragoût recipe is also superb with trimmed lamb shanks, in which case, allow 1 shank per serving.

3 pounds boned shoulder of lamb
14 tablespoons salt butter
3 tablespoons Cognac or good brandy
1 teaspoon tomato paste
½ teaspoon meat glaze
1 teaspoon potato flour
3 cups chicken stock (page 35)
½ cup dry red wine
¼ cup Marsala wine or dry sherry

1 teaspoon red currant jelly
Freshly cracked white pepper
1 small bay leaf
12 small firm white mushrooms
1 teaspoon lemon juice
Salt
Optional: 2 Idaho potatoes, peeled and cut in olive shapes
2 large carrots, cut in olive shapes
2 tablespoons granulated sugar
12 baby white onions, skinned

½ package frozen baby peas
½ pound green beans, topped
   and tailed
3 small ripe tomatoes, skinned
and quartered
2 tablespoons chopped fresh
   parsley

Preheat the oven to 350°. Trim off all the extra fat, sinew and skin from the lamb. Cut the meat into 1½-inch squares. (If using shanks, leave them whole.) Heat 3 tablespoons butter in a large deep heavy pan, and stir until it is golden brown. Brown the meat quickly, a few pieces at a time, on all sides in the hot butter (do not let them touch each other or they will not brown). When all the meat is browned, return it to the pan. In a separate little pan, heat the brandy, ignite, and pour it over the meat. Remove the meat from the pan, set it aside, add to the pan 3 tablespoons butter, and melt it. Off the heat, add the tomato paste, meat glaze, and potato flour. Stir until the mixture is smooth. Still off the heat, stir in the chicken stock, wine, Marsala or sherry, and jelly. Stir this sauce over moderate heat until it comes to a boil. Add a little pepper (but no salt) and the bay leaf. Put the lamb in the sauce, and baste it with the sauce.

Cover the pan, put it on the top shelf of the oven, and cook the lamb 1½ hours or until the meat is tender. After it has cooked 30 minutes, remove the cover. Baste with the sauce in the pan once or twice after the cover has been removed. While the lamb is cooking, prepare the vegetables.

Heat 2 tablespoons salt butter in a small sauté pan. When it is foaming, add the mushrooms with the lemon juice, salt, and pepper. Cook briskly 3 minutes. Remove the mushrooms from the pan and set aside. Cook the potatoes in a little boiling salted water until half done, and drain them. Add 2 tablespoons butter to the sauté pan the mushrooms were cooked in, then add the potatoes with a little salt and pepper. Cook slowly 5 minutes, remove from the pan, and set them aside.

Cook the carrots in a little boiling salted water until half done, and drain them. Add 2 tablespoons butter to the sauté pan, then add the carrots with 1 tablespoon sugar, salt, and pepper. Cook slowly 5 minutes, remove from the pan, and set them aside. Put the onions in a pan, cover with cold water, bring to a boil, and drain. Add 2 tablespoons butter to the sauté pan, add the onions, and shake over moderate heat until they begin to brown. Sprinkle them with 1 tablespoon granulated sugar and a little salt and pepper. Shake over the heat until they begin to glaze. Remove the onions and set them aside. Boil the frozen baby peas in plain water until just soft, and the green beans in salted water until just soft.

Five minutes before the ragoût is finished cooking, add all the vegetables and the uncooked quartered tomatoes to the pan. When it is finished cooking, sprinkle it with the chopped fresh parsley, and serve. NET: 4 to 6 servings.

IRISH STEW

This stew is made with mutton. Use lamb if you wish.

4 pounds boned shoulder of
  mutton
1 pound white onions, skinned
  and thinly sliced
2½ pounds old potatoes,
  skinned and sliced (these
  supply thickening for the
  stew)
Salt

Freshly cracked white pepper
Bouquet garni (parsley, thyme,
  1 bay leaf)
1½ pounds baby new potatoes,
  skinned
2 tablespoons chopped fresh
  parsley
2 teaspoons Worcestershire
  sauce

Cut the meat into pieces, about 3 inches square. Put them in a pan, cover with cold water, bring to a boil, and simmer 6 minutes. Drain, and rinse them under cold water. Have ready a deep heavy pan with a cover. Put the onions on the bottom of the pan, and the old potatoes on the onions. Season with salt and pepper. Place the meat on the potatoes. Tie the bouquet garni in cheesecloth and put it in the pan. Barely cover the ingredients in the pan with cold water. Bring to a boil slowly, cover, and simmer very gently about 1½ hours. By this time the mutton should be about three-quarters cooked.

At this point in cooking, remove the meat and bouquet garni from the pan with a slotted spoon. Put everything else in the pan into an electric blender, and blend until smooth. Return the meat to the pan, pour the puréed mixture over it, and add the new potatoes. Simmer very gently until the meat is tender and the potatoes are cooked. Serve this stew in a deep casserole, with the parsley and Worcestershire sauce sprinkled over the top. NET: 6 to 8 servings.

LE CASSOULET DE CASTELNAUDARY

Bean Stew with Lamb, Goose (or Pork) and Garlic Sausage

This provincial dish must be started at least 24 hours in advance of serving.

2 pounds (4 cups) dry white
  kidney beans
Water or stock or both (for
  cooking beans)
2 medium-size yellow onions,
  cut in quarters
4 carrots, cut in quarters
2 garlic cloves, bruised
¾ pound fatback
2½ pounds breast of lamb
  (bones in)
6 ounces goose fat
3 cups finely chopped onions

1 teaspoon finely chopped garlic
1 cup tomato purée
Salt
Freshly cracked black pepper
Half a small goose, uncooked,
  leftover cooked goose, or
  3 pounds pork breast
  (bones in)
1 good-size garlic sausage
  (Italian or Polish type)
A few dry breadcrumbs (page
  69)

Cover the dry white kidney beans with plenty of cold water and let them soak overnight. At any time, you may plain-roast the goose or breast of pork in a preheated 350° oven, turning it occasionally to cook on all sides, until it is cooked through. The day after you put the beans to soak, drain them, put them in a large pan, and cover them again with plenty of cold water or stock or both. Add to the pan the quartered onions and carrots, and the garlic cloves. Roll up the fatback and breast of lamb and tie the roll tightly with string. Put them in the pan with the beans and vegetables. Cover, and cook very gently until the beans are about half cooked.

While the beans are cooking, melt the goose fat in a large sauté pan. Add the chopped onions and the finely chopped garlic and sauté the mixture 3 to 4 minutes, then add the tomato purée, season with salt and pepper, and set aside. When the beans are half cooked, remove the breast of lamb and fatback from the bean mixture, cut them into large pieces (not boned), and add to the chopped onion mixture. Cut the goose or pork breast into serving pieces, slice the garlic sausage into chunks, and add these to the beans. If necessary, add a little more water or stock to the beans. Allow the beans to simmer another 30 minutes with the goose and sausage.

Preheat the oven to 350°. Take a large casserole, big enough to contain all the ingredients. Cover the bottom with half the beans, removing them from the cooking pan with a slotted spoon. Put all the meats (serving pieces of goose or pork, chunks of garlic sausage, lamb and fatback with onion mixture) in the center. Then cover with the rest of the beans. Spoon a little of the bean liquid into the casserole. Cover the casserole with buttered wax paper and the lid, and place it in the oven. Cook it 1½ hours, adding from time to time a little liquid in which the beans were cooked. Serve the cassoulet from the casserole. Sprinkle the surface with a few dried breadcrumbs before serving. NET: 6 servings.

BROCHETTE D'AGNEAU CAUCASIENNE

Caucasian Lamb on Skewers with Rice Pilaff

This Mid-East rendition takes a little time and effort. Start it a day in advance of serving. You will need six long skewers.

2½ pounds boned leg or
    shoulder of lamb
¼ cup pure olive oil
8 tablespoons vegetable oil
1 red onion, finely sliced
3 garlic cloves, sliced
2 shallots, sliced
1 small piece celery, sliced
8 mixed black and white
    peppercorns
2 bay leaves
1 cup dry red wine
2 tablespoons tarragon vinegar
6 lamb kidneys
6 chicken livers

½ pound thinly sliced raw
    bacon
1 large eggplant (or 2 small)
Salt
A little all-purpose flour (to
    dust eggplant)
¾ pound firm white mushrooms
8 tablespoons salt butter
1 teaspoon lemon juice
Freshly cracked white pepper
6 medium-size firm ripe
    tomatoes
6 medium-size white onions
2 fresh sweet red peppers
2 fresh green peppers

½ teaspoon finely chopped
    garlic
1 bunch crisp fresh watercress

RICE PILAFF
4 tablespoons sweet butter
2 tablespoons vegetable oil
1 Bermuda onion, finely
    chopped
Salt
Freshly cracked white pepper
1 teaspoon leaf saffron
1 tablespoon hot water

1 cup long-grain rice
2 cups chicken stock (page 35)
¼ teaspoon ground cardamom
    seed
½ cup blanched, split almonds
½ cup white raisins, soaked in
    warm water
½ cup black raisins, soaked in
    warm water
2 tablespoons each of finely
    chopped candied orange peel
    and lemon peel

Remove all the fat, skin, and sinew from the lamb. Cut it into
1½-inch cubes. Put the pieces in a large bowl, and pour over them
the olive oil and 4 tablespoons vegetable oil. Thoroughly coat the
lamb with the oil. Add the red onion, garlic cloves, shallots, celery,
peppercorns, and broken-up bay leaves. Mix all this thoroughly with
the lamb. Cover the bowl and let it stand 1 hour, then pour on the
red wine and tarragon vinegar. Allow the lamb to marinate in this
mixture at least 6 hours and overnight if possible. When you are
ready to prepare the skewers, start by making the rice pilaff.

RICE PILAFF. Preheat the oven to 350°. Heat the sweet butter and
vegetable oil in a deep heavy pan on top of the stove. Add the
Bermuda onion, 1 teaspoon salt, and ½ teaspoon white pepper. Cover,
and cook over low heat until the onion is translucent. Crush the leaf
saffron with a pestle and mortar, dissolve it in the hot water, and
mix it with the onion in the pan. Stir the rice also into the pan. Cover
with the chicken stock, and stir over moderate heat until it comes
to a boil. Then mix in the cardamom seed, almonds, raisins, orange
peel, and lemon peel. Cover the pan with wax paper and the cover,
and cook in the oven 30 minutes. When done, remove the wax paper
and fluff the rice with two forks.

Drain the lamb thoroughly, strain the liquid, and set both aside.
Skin the lamb kidneys, cut them in half, and remove the core. Roll
each half in half a slice of bacon. Cut the chicken livers in half and
wrap each piece in half a slice of bacon. Cut the eggplant (unpeeled)
in 1½-inch cubes. Sprinkle them with salt and let stand 30 minutes.
Wash and dry them well, dust lightly with flour, and brown on all
sides in 4 tablespoons vegetable oil heated in a sauté pan. Remove
from the pan and set aside. Trim the stems from the mushrooms. Add
1 tablespoon butter to the sauté pan, melt it, and cook the mushroom
caps in it 3 minutes with the lemon juice, salt, and pepper. Core the
tomatoes and cut them in quarters. Skin the onions and cut them in
half. Cut the red and green peppers in half and remove the seeds.
Cut the peppers into 1½-inch squares.

Have ready 6 long skewers. Sort out the meats and vegetables into
6 uniform groups, and thread the skewers: a piece of lamb, 2 vegetables, chicken liver, 2 vegetables, lamb kidney, 2 vegetables, etc.

a separate bowl. NET: 2 to 4 servings (a rack of lamb can be planned for two people, depending on the rest of the menu).

CARRÉ D'AGNEAU PERSILLÉ

Roast Parslied Rack of Lamb, Garnished with Baby New Potatoes or Cherry Tomatoes

1 rack of lamb, French-trimmed
    and chined (vertebrae
    cracked)
2 garlic cloves, cut in half
¼ cup Cognac or good brandy
¾ cup dry red wine

GARNISH
1 bunch crisp fresh watercress
12 baby new potatoes, steamed
    and skinned, or 2 cups cherry
    tomatoes, skinned and

warmed in a little butter
A little melted butter
2 tablespoons chopped fresh
    parsley

EXTRA-PARSLIED MAÎTRE D'HÔTEL
    BUTTER
4 tablespoons sweet butter
Salt
Freshly cracked white pepper
½ cup finely chopped fresh
    parsley

EXTRA-PARSLIED MAÎTRE D'HÔTEL BUTTER. Cream the butter in an electric mixer until it is light and fluffy. Add salt and pepper. Beat in the parsley. Chill it a little, then place it on a sheet of foil and mold it into a roll like a sausage. Put it in the freezer until ready to use.

Preheat the oven to 375°. Trim most of the fat from the lamb. Rub it all over with the cut cloves of garlic, salt, and pepper, brush it with the brandy, and allow it to marinate this way 30 minutes to 1 hour. Then place the lamb on a rack in a roasting pan, and pour into the pan enough of the wine to cover the bottom of the pan. Insert a meat thermometer into the thickest part of the meat (to ensure removing the meat at the desired stage; it should be only pink when finished). Roast the meat on the top shelf of the oven about 45 minutes. (For rare, remove when thermometer reaches 140°.) Baste it frequently with the rest of the wine. After it has cooked 20 minutes, turn it over for 10 minutes and then turn it up again. When the lamb is finished roasting, remove it from the pan and let it stand for a moment.

To serve, carve the rack into individual rib chops and arrange them slightly overlapping down a serving platter. Slice the maître d'hôtel butter, and put a slice on each chop. Garnish with clusters of watercress and a pile of the new potatoes or cherry tomatoes sprinkled with a little melted butter and parsley. Serve immediately. NET: 2 to 4 servings (depending on the rest of the menu).

ÉPAULE D'AGNEAU FARCIE, SAUCE AUX CÂPRES

Roast Stuffed Shoulder of Lamb with Spicy Caper Sauce

1 boned shoulder of lamb, about
    5 to 6 pounds
½ teaspoon finely chopped
    garlic
3 tablespoons dry sherry

STUFFING
½ pound sausage meat
¼ pound ground lean veal
1 medium-size onion, finely
    chopped

½ teaspoon finely chopped
  garlic
1 tablespoon finely chopped
  parsley
2 tablespoons sour cream
1 egg
Salt
Freshly cracked white pepper
½ teaspoon freshly grated
  nutmeg
½ teaspoon dried thyme
⅛ teaspoon ground cloves
⅛ teaspoon mace
½ teaspoon ground cinnamon
2 tablespoons dry breadcrumbs
  (page 69)
About ½ pound sliced bacon
1 cup dry red wine

CAPER SAUCE
1 tablespoon pure olive oil
2 tablespoons plus 2 teaspoons
  sweet butter
½ teaspoon tomato paste
½ teaspoon meat glaze
1 teaspoon tarragon vinegar
3 tablespoons all-purpose flour
1 teaspoon dry mustard
1¼ cups light cream
2 tablespoons plain whipped
  cream
2 tablespoons capers
1 egg yolk mixed with 1 tablespoon dry sherry
1 tablespoon light cream or milk
½ teaspoon ground cardamom
  seed

GARNISH
8 broiled tomatoes (page 624)

Preheat the oven to 375°. Spread out the shoulder of lamb and beat it with the side of a cleaver to even it out — it should be about 1½ inches thick. Press the garlic into the top of the meat and brush it with the sherry.

STUFFING. Put into a large bowl the sausage meat, veal, onion, garlic, parsley, sour cream, and egg. Season well with salt and pepper, and add the nutmeg, thyme, cloves, mace, cinnamon, and breadcrumbs. Work the mixture together thoroughly with your hands.

Spread the stuffing on the lamb and roll it up tightly. Cover it with slightly overlapping slices of bacon and tie each slice with string, neatly and securely. Place the lamb on a rack in a roasting pan, pour a little of the wine into the pan, and roast the lamb on the top shelf of the oven 50 minutes. Mix the rest of the wine with an equal part of water and baste the roast frequently with this mixture. When the lamb is cooked, remove it from the oven and let it stand at least 10 minutes before slicing.

CAPER SAUCE. Heat the olive oil and 2 tablespoons sweet butter in a saucepan. Off the heat, add the tomato paste, meat glaze, vinegar, flour, and mustard. Mix to a smooth paste. Still off the heat, add the light cream. Stir over low heat until the sauce comes to a boil. Stir in the 2 teaspoons sweet butter bit by bit, then the whipped cream, capers, mixed egg yolk and sherry, light cream or milk, and ground cardamom seed. Gently reheat but do not boil.

To serve, slice enough for one serving and arrange the slices, slightly overlapping, down a warm serving platter. Place the uncut piece of lamb at one end of the platter. Serve the sauce separately. Garnish the platter of lamb with the broiled tomatoes. NET: 8 servings.

When the saddle of lamb is cooked, remove it from the oven, put it on a carving board and let it rest 5 minutes. Then, with a sharp knife, trim out the fillet, in one neat section, from each side of the long bone. Cut each fillet into thin slices lengthwise. Place the saddle bone on a warm platter. Arrange the slices of fillet over the bone, overlapping. Pour a little of the sauce over or around the meat, and serve the rest in a sauceboat. (If there are some good juices in the roasting pan, not too fatty, skim, strain, and add them to the sauce.) Arrange a pile of Parisienne potatoes at each end of the saddle of lamb, and two stuffed tomatoes on each side. NET: 4 servings.

For this impressive dish you need ten paper frills for the bones. The baked potato shells are filled with Duchess potatoes and topped with the broiled kidneys.

CROWN ROAST OF LAMB WITH CHESTNUT FILLING AND STUFFED POTATO GARNISH

1 10-bone crown lamb roast
10 1-inch cubes salt pork
2 tablespoons all-purpose flour
Salt
Freshly cracked white pepper
12 slices bacon
1 cup dry red wine

STUFFING
2 teaspoons salt butter
6 chicken livers
1 pound unflavored chestnut purée (canned)
½ pound boiled ham, finely diced
¼ pound cooked tongue, finely diced
¼ pound sausage meat
¼ pound fresh mushrooms, sliced and sautéed in a little

butter and lemon juice
2 tablespoons dry sherry
¼ cup dry breadcrumbs (page 69)

GARNISH
5 even-sized Idaho potatoes
Duchess Potatoes (page 609)
2 eggs
A little hot milk
Salt
A few grains cayenne pepper
4 tablespoons salt butter (and a little for browning)
10 lamb kidneys
A little melted salt butter
4 tablespoons sweet butter
2 tablespoons chopped fresh parsley
2 teaspoons lemon juice

GARNISH. Preheat the oven to 350°. Bake the potatoes until soft, then cut each one in half lengthwise. Scoop out the potato meal (reserve the skins), put it in a mixer bowl, and beat it until smooth. Add the Duchess potatoes to the mixer bowl, then beat in the eggs, hot milk, salt, cayenne pepper, and salt butter. Put the mashed potatoes in a pastry bag fitted with a large star tube, and refill the potato skins in attractive mounds. Dot with a little butter and keep them warm. Skin the lamb kidneys and remove the cores by slitting them down the bottom, but keep them whole. Put them on a broiler rack, brush with a little melted salt butter, sprinkle with a little salt and pepper, and set aside. Cream the sweet butter in a mixer. Mix in the chopped parsley, lemon juice, salt, and cayenne pepper. Chill in the refrigerator. (This garnish will finish cooking when the roast is done.)

Maintain the oven temperature at 350°. Have the butcher prepare the crown of lamb in a circle and trim out the chops. Cover each bone tip with a salt pork cube to prevent its burning while the meat is roasting. Mix the flour with salt and pepper and rub the meat with this mixture. Wrap the bacon slices around the lower part of the crown. Place the crown directly on a roasting pan.

STUFFING. Heat the butter in a small heavy pan. Brown the chicken livers very quickly in it, on both sides. Remove the livers, dice, and mix them into the chestnut purée. Also add the ham, tongue, sausage meat, and mushrooms to the chestnut purée, and mix well. Mix in the sherry. Season with salt and white pepper.

Put this mixture into the center of the crown of lamb. Cover the top evenly with the breadcrumbs. Sprinkle a little of the wine around the bottom of the pan. Place the lamb roast in the oven and roast 25 to 30 minutes per pound. Baste frequently with the wine and water (use more if necessary). When the roast is cooked, remove it from the oven and let it stand 5 minutes. While it is resting, brown the potatoes and broil the kidneys quickly under a hot broiler. Place a kidney on each potato, and put in each kidney 1 teaspoon of the chilled parslied butter. Remove the salt pork and bacon from the roast, place the roast on a warm serving platter, and put a paper frill on the end of each chop bone. Surround with the garnish of stuffed baked potatoes. Serve immediately. NET: 10 servings.

CROWN ROAST
OF LAMB
WITH SAUSAGE-
VEAL FILLING
AND
MUSHROOM
GARNISH

The center is filled with veal mousse and sausage meat, garnished with stuffed mushrooms.

1 10-bone crown lamb roast,
   and the finely ground
   trimmings
½ teaspoon finely chopped
   garlic
Freshly cracked white pepper
¼ cup Cognac or good brandy
Salt
10 1-inch cubes salt pork
2 cups dry red wine
Bordelaise Sauce (page 39)

STUFFING
½ pound ground lean veal
3 egg whites
1 cup light cream
½ teaspoon finely chopped
   garlic

½ teaspoon dried thyme
½ teaspoon freshly grated
   nutmeg
¼ teaspoon mace
1½ teaspoons salt
½ teaspoon freshly cracked
   white pepper
¼ pound sausage meat
¼ cup dry breadcrumbs (page
   69)
3 tablespoons freshly grated
   Parmesan cheese

GARNISH
20 medium-size firm white
   mushrooms
4 tablespoons salt butter
Salt

Freshly cracked white pepper
Duxelles (page 71)
1/4 cup dry breadcrumbs (page
    69)

1/2 cup freshly grated Parmesan
    cheese
2 tablespoons melted salt butter

Preheat the oven to 375°. Remove the ground lamb trimmings that the butcher puts in the center of the crown and reserve them for the stuffing. Between each chop of the crown roast put a bit of finely chopped garlic and a little pepper. Brush with the brandy. Rub the roast all over with salt (preferably coarse salt).

STUFFING. Put the ground veal in a mixer bowl. Add the egg whites and beat well. Very slowly add the light cream, beating all the time. Add the thyme, garlic, nutmeg, mace, salt, and pepper. Add the sausage meat and ground trimmings of the roast. Mix well.

Fill the center of the crown roast with this stuffing. Sprinkle the top with breadcrumbs and Parmesan cheese. Stick a cube of salt pork on the tip of each rib bone (to prevent their burning in the oven). Place the meat on a roasting pan and pour a little of the wine around the bottom of the pan. Insert a meat thermometer in the thickest part of the roast to ensure cooking it to the desired degree (140° for rare or pink). Roast the meat about 1 hour and 10 minutes. Baste every 20 minutes with the rest of the wine mixed with an equal amount of water.

STUFFED MUSHROOMS. Remove the stems from the mushrooms. Place the caps top down in a sauté pan with 1 tablespoon hot salt butter. Put a dot of butter in the center of each mushroom. Season them with a little salt and pepper, and cook slowly only a minute or two. Remove the mushrooms, chill them a little, then stuff with the prepared duxelles (chopped mushroom filling). Sprinkle the tops with the breadcrumbs, grated cheese, and melted butter.

When the meat is finished, remove it from the roasting pan and let it stand 5 minutes, while you brown the mushrooms under a hot broiler. Place the roast in the center of a warm round serving platter. Surround it with the mushrooms, and serve the garnished, stuffed crown roast with a separate bowl of Bordelaise sauce. NET: 10 servings.

GIGOT D'AGNEAU FARCIE NAPOLEON I

Roast Boned Leg of
Lamb Stuffed with Veal
and Ham Mousse,
with Flageolets,
Bordelaise Sauce

A large white paper frill to represent the leg bone is traditional. Use a skewer or uncooked macaroni for the bone.

1 whole leg of lamb, about
    7 pounds
2 tablespoons Cognac or good
    brandy
1/2 teaspoon finely chopped
    garlic
Freshly cracked white pepper
1 1/2 cups dry red wine

1 pound thinly sliced bacon,
    minus 6 slices for the stuffing
Bordelaise Sauce (page 39)
Flageolets (small green French
    kidney beans, page 599)
6 diagonal fried croûtons (page
    69)

STUFFING
1/2 pound ground lean veal
2 ounces ground boiled ham
1/2 teaspoon chopped fresh
    tarragon
2 egg whites
2/3 cup light cream
1/2 teaspoon finely chopped

garlic
4 tablespoons Cognac or good
    brandy
6 juniper berries, crushed with
    a mortar and pestle
6 chicken livers
6 thin slices bacon (from the
    pound above)

Preheat the oven to 375°. Bone the leg of lamb, removing all the bone but leaving the meat as whole as possible. Cut the meat into several layers (like the leaves of a book), about 1 to 1½ inches thick. Do not cut all the way through. Brush between each layer of meat with brandy, and sprinkle with the garlic and pepper.

STUFFING. Put the veal, ham, tarragon, and egg whites in a mixer bowl and beat well. Slowly beat in the light cream. Add ¼ teaspoon chopped garlic, 2 tablespoons brandy, the crushed juniper berries, and a generous sprinkling of freshly cracked white pepper. Set the mixture aside. Remove the fat from the chicken livers, brush them with 2 tablespoons brandy, and sprinkle with pepper and ¼ teaspoon chopped garlic. Wrap each liver in a bacon slice, arrange them on a rack on a baking sheet, cook them in the preheated oven 7 minutes, and cool them a little.

Spread the veal and ham mixture between the layers of lamb. Arrange the chicken livers down the inside center of the lamb. Roll up the stuffed lamb carefully, cover the top with slightly overlapping bacon slices, and over each bacon slice tie a piece of string around the meat. Then tie one string lengthwise around the lamb. Put the meat on a rack on a roasting pan. Pour ⅔ cup dry red wine in the bottom of the pan. Insert a meat thermometer in the thickest part of the meat, to ensure the correct degree of cooking (175° for done through). Roast the meat in the preheated oven 1 hour and 25 minutes (for a 7-pound roast), basting every 15 minutes with the rest of the wine mixed with an equal amount of water. When the meat has cooked 30 minutes, turn it over; then turn it topside again after another 30 minutes. When the meat has finished roasting, remove it from the oven immediately.

Remove the strings from the stuffed leg of lamb, but not the bacon strips. Cut as many slices from the thick end as required for one serving and arrange them down a warm large flat serving dish. Place the uncut part at one end of the dish. Fasten a white paper frill on a skewer or piece of macaroni and stick it into the uncut end of the lamb. Spoon a little sauce around the meat, and serve the rest of the sauce separately in a sauceboat. Arrange the flageolets down one side of the lamb, and the fried croûtons around the sides of the dish. NET: 6 to 8 servings.

8 lamb kidneys
4 tablespoons salt butter
½ teaspoon finely chopped
   garlic
1 cup sliced firm white fresh
   mushrooms
1 tablespoon Dijon mustard
½ teaspoon dry mustard

½ teaspoon tomato paste
½ teaspoon meat glaze
2 tablespoons all-purpose flour
½ cup dry red wine
1 cup chicken stock (page 35)
1 bay leaf
1 tablespoon chopped fresh
   chives or parsley

ROGNONS D'AGNEAU, SAUCE MOUTARDE

Lamb Kidneys with Mustard Sauce

Skin the kidneys. Cut them in half and remove the cores. Heat 3 tablespoons butter in a sauté pan and brown the kidneys quickly on both sides. Remove the kidneys, set them aside, and add the garlic to the pan. Stir it around a minute over low heat, then melt 1 tablespoon butter in the pan. Add the mushrooms and sauté them 4 minutes, then the Dijon mustard and cook 1 minute. Remove the pan from the heat and stir in the dry mustard, tomato paste, meat glaze, and flour. Mix well. Still off the heat, add the red wine and chicken stock. Simmer over low heat 5 minutes. Add the bay leaf and return the kidneys to the pan. Continue to cook over low heat 15 minutes. To serve, place the mixture in a casserole and sprinkle the top with fresh chives or parsley. NET: 4 servings.

8 lamb kidneys
8 tablespoons salt butter
2 shallots, finely chopped
½ teaspoon finely chopped
   garlic
¼ pound firm white mush-
   rooms, sliced
1 tablespoon chopped fresh
   parsley
1 tablespoon chopped fresh
   chives

½ cup dry white wine
½ cup chicken stock (page 35)
Salt
Freshly cracked white pepper
1 tablespoon all-purpose flour
4 tablespoons vegetable oil
3 large ripe tomatoes, skinned,
   quartered, and seeded
4 diagonal fried croûtons (page
   69)

ROGNONS D'AGNEAU SAUTÉ AUX TOMATES

Sautéed Lamb Kidneys with Fresh Tomatoes

Skin the kidneys. Remove the cores and cut each one across into 6 slices. Set aside. Melt the butter in a shallow heavy pan. Put the shallots and garlic in the pan and cook 3 minutes over very low heat. Add the sliced kidneys and cook 5 minutes over moderate heat, shaking the pan briskly. Remove the pan from the heat and add the mushrooms, parsley, chives, wine, chicken stock, salt, and pepper. Return the mixture to low heat and bring slowly to a boil. Blend the flour with 1 tablespoon vegetable oil, and stir this, off the heat, into the kidney mixture. Simmer the mixture very gently, over low heat, 5 minutes. Add the tomato sections to the pan and warm them in the mixture 2 minutes.

To serve, turn the contents of the pan into a shallow casserole. Stick the fried croûtons around the sides of the dish. Serve immediately. NET: 4 servings.

ROGNONS D'AGNEAU TURBIGO

Sautéed Lamb Kidneys with Mushrooms

8 lamb kidneys
4 tablespoons salt butter
12 small white onions, skinned
8 medium-size firm white mushrooms, cut in quarters
½ teaspoon meat glaze
½ teaspoon tomato paste
3 teaspoons potato flour
1½ cups chicken stock (page 35)
¼ cup dry red wine
1 sprig parsley
Salt
Freshly cracked white pepper
2 tablespoons chopped fresh parsley

Skin the kidneys. Cut them in half and remove the cores. Heat 3 tablespoons butter in a sauté pan and brown the kidneys quickly on both sides. Remove the kidneys and set them aside. Put the onions in a pan, cover with cold water, and bring to a boil. Drain, and add the onions to the sauté pan in which the kidneys were browned. Cook the onions a few minutes until they are fairly soft. Add the quartered mushrooms and cook 2 minutes. Remove the sauté pan from the heat and add the meat glaze, tomato paste, and potato flour. Mix well. Still off the heat, add the chicken stock and wine. Stir the mixture over low heat until it comes to a boil. Simmer very gently 10 minutes. Add the sprig of parsley, adjust the seasoning, and return the kidneys to the pan. Continue to cook over low heat 15 minutes.

Serve in a casserole. Sprinkle the top with the chopped fresh parsley. NET: 4 servings.

PORK

CHOUCROUTE GARNIE

Sauerkraut Garnished with Pork Chops and Sausages

8 frankfurters
6 small lean loin pork chops
3 tablespoons salt butter
8 smoked pork sausages
2 large yellow onions, finely chopped
½ cup finely chopped carrots
2 teaspoons finely chopped garlic
2 teaspoons tomato paste
2 teaspoons meat glaze
4 teaspoons potato flour
3 cups beer
½ cup chicken stock (page 35)
2 bay leaves
4 juniper berries, crushed with a mortar and pestle
1 teaspoon freshly cracked black pepper
Thick slices bacon (to cover bottom and top of cooking pot)
½ cup pure olive oil
1 tablespoon caraway seeds
A few grains cayenne pepper
2 quarts sauerkraut, rinsed in cold water and drained dry
16 thick slices garlic sausage

Blanch the frankfurters (put them into cold water, bring to a boil, remove and drain them). Heat the butter in a large sauté pan and quickly brown the pork chops on each side. Remove them from the pan. Brown the sausages and frankfurters in the same pan, remove, and set them aside. Add to the pan all but 1 tablespoon of the chopped onion, also add the carrots and 1 teaspoon chopped garlic. Cook these vegetables 5 minutes over low heat. Off the heat, mix in the tomato paste, meat glaze, and potato flour. When the mixture is smooth, pour in the beer and chicken stock. Stir the mixture over low heat until it comes to a boil. Add the bay leaves, juniper berries, and black pepper. Return the meats to this pan and let stand a moment.

Preheat the oven to 375°. Line the bottom of a large round heavy pot with half the bacon slices. Mix together, in a little bowl, the olive oil, caraway seeds, cayenne pepper, and the other tablespoon of chopped onion and teaspoon chopped garlic. Put this mixture on the bacon. Spoon a little of the brown sauce (from the pan with the meats) over the bacon, and add a layer of sauerkraut about 1½ inches thick. Then put in a layer of the browned meats, then a layer of garlic sausage slices. Alternate in this fashion until all the ingredients have been used, ending with the rest of the bacon on top. Cover with the lid and bake 1½ hours. Serve from the pot. NET: 6 servings.

COCHON DE LAIT PARISIENNE

Roast Suckling Pig Parisienne

If possible, this dish should be started a day in advance of serving.

1 whole suckling pig, about 10 pounds
1 garlic clove, cut in half
¼ cup Cognac or good brandy
8 tablespoons melted salt butter
1 cup hot water
8 tablespoons melted sweet butter

STUFFING
3 cups soft white breadcrumbs
1 cup apple cider
2 tablespoons each of chopped fresh parsley and chives
½ teaspoon finely chopped garlic
3 tablespoons finely chopped onion
1 pound sausage meat, cooked
2 teaspoons salt
½ teaspoon freshly cracked white pepper
½ teaspoon thyme
A few grains each of ground nutmeg, mace, and clove
2 eggs, beaten

GARNISH
1 small red apple (for pig's mouth)
Raw cranberries (enough to string a necklace for the pig)
2 bunches fresh crisp watercress

SAUCE
2 tablespoons salt butter
Liver of the suckling pig
2 tablespoons Cognac or good brandy
2 green peppers, seeded and finely chopped
¼ cup finely chopped shallots
2 teaspoons meat glaze
1 teaspoon tomato paste
2 teaspoons potato flour
1¼ cups chicken stock (page 35)
½ cup dry red wine (preferably Beaujolais)
2 tablespoons finely chopped parsley
2 tablespoons sweet sherry

BAKED APPLES
6 small green or tart apples
Butter
1 cup granulated sugar
½ cup sweet sherry

1 cup apricot jam
2 cups cranberries, cooked

whole with a little sugar (or
canned), and drained

Wash the pig in several changes of cold water. (If possible, it is a good idea to soak it overnight in the bathtub.) Dry it well with a cloth. Rub the inside with the cut garlic clove and brush the inside all over with brandy.

Preheat the oven to 350°.

STUFFING. Soak the breadcrumbs in the apple cider, put them in a cloth, and squeeze them dry. Put the crumbs in a large bowl and add the parsley, chives, garlic, onion, and sausage meat. Season the mixture with the salt, pepper, thyme, nutmeg, mace, and cloves. Add the beaten eggs to the mixture and mix well, with your hand, until the stuffing is thoroughly blended.

Stuff this loosely into the belly of the pig. Fasten the belly with skewers and lace it with string. Truss (tie with string) the forelegs and the hindlegs close under the body of the pig. Wipe the pig with a damp cloth and brush it with the melted salt butter. With a sharp-pointed knife make a number of slashes all over the top of the pig so the fat will drip down into the roasting pan. Place a block of wood in the pig's mouth to brace it for the apple that will be inserted later. Cover the ears with brown paper bags or foil to keep them from burning. Place the pig on a rack in a large roasting pan, and roast it 3 to 3½ hours, until the meat is tender and thoroughly cooked. Cover the body of the pig with brown paper or foil if it is browning too fast during roasting. Baste it frequently with the fat from the pan to which should be added the hot water.

SAUCE. Heat the butter in a heavy pan. When it is foaming and about to brown, brown the pig's liver in it. In a separate little pan, heat the brandy, ignite, and pour it over the liver. Remove the liver, set it aside, and add to the pan the peppers and shallots. Cook them slowly, over low heat, 2 minutes. Off the heat, stir in the meat glaze, tomato paste, and potato flour. Then add the chicken stock, wine, and sherry. Return to low heat, and stir until the sauce comes to a boil. Slice the liver, return it to the sauce, and add the parsley.

BAKED APPLES. Remove the apple cores with a corer. Place the apples on a buttered baking dish. In a separate little pan, mix the sugar, sherry, and jam, and cook over low heat until it is well mixed, like a syrup. Pour this syrup over the apples. Bake them in a preheated 350° oven, basting frequently with the syrup in the dish. Cook them until they are just soft. When done, fill the centers with the cooked cranberries.

When the pig is roasted, transfer it to a large hot platter. Remove the block of wood from its mouth and replace it with the red apple. Brush the skin all over gently with the melted sweet butter (the skin should be shining and crisp). Garnish all around the platter with the cranberry-stuffed baked apples. Put a necklace of raw cranberries around the pig's neck. Stick one or two raw cranberries on toothpicks for earrings. Garnish the platter with fresh crisp watercress. Serve the sauce separately, in a bowl. NET: 8 to 10 servings.

6 pork chops, 1 inch thick
4 tablespoons salt butter
⅓ cup finely chopped shallots
⅓ cup tarragon vinegar
2 teaspoons potato flour
1 teaspoon tomato paste
1 teaspoon meat glaze
¼ cup dry sherry
¼ cup dry white wine
1 cup chicken stock (page 35)

6 small sour gherkins
Salt
Freshly cracked white pepper
6 large green or tart (cooking)
   apples
¼ cup water
2 tablespoons lemon juice
A little granulated sugar
Grated rind of 1 lemon

CÔTES
DE PORC À LA
NORMANDE

Braised Pork Chops
with Applesauce

Preheat the oven to 350°. Trim the excess fat from the pork chops. Heat the butter in a heavy pan and, over moderate heat, quickly brown the chops on each side. Remove them from the pan, set aside, and add the chopped shallots to the pan. Cook slowly, over low heat, 2 minutes, then add the vinegar and boil it down until the pan is almost dry. Remove the pan from the heat, and add the potato flour, tomato paste, meat glaze, sherry, wine, and chicken stock. Stir until smooth, return the pan to low heat, and stir until the sauce comes to a boil. Cut the gherkins into thin slices and add them to the sauce. Season it with salt and pepper. Return the pork chops to the pan, coat them with the sauce, and put them, uncovered, on the top shelf of the oven to braise 35 to 40 minutes.

Cut the apples in quarters and trim out the cores. (Do not skin them.) Cut the quarters into thick slices. Put the apples into a heavy pan, sprinkle with the water and lemon juice, and cook over moderate heat until the apples are mushy. Stir them occasionally. Rub the cooked apples through a fine strainer. Mix the puréed apples with the sugar and grated lemon rind to taste.

Serve the finished pork chops in a casserole, with the applesauce in a separate bowl. NET: 6 servings.

This dish was taught to me by a pupil of mine who lived in Hawaii.

1 loin of pork, 2 to 3 pounds,
   chined (cracked between the
   rib joints)
Salt
Freshly cracked white pepper
¼ cup Cognac, good brandy,
   or sweet sherry
2 tablespoons melted salt butter
½ cup unsweetened pineapple
   juice (from can)

FRIED PINEAPPLE
6 slices canned or fresh
   pineapple

3 tablespoons salt butter
2 tablespoons granulated sugar

SAUCE
2 tablespoons salt butter
1 medium-size onion, finely
   chopped
1 teaspoon finely chopped garlic
1 green pepper, seeded and
   finely diced
Finely shredded rind of
   1 orange
1 teaspoon tomato paste
1 teaspoon meat glaze

HAWAIIAN
PORK

Party Roast Pork,
with Fried Pineapple

2 teaspoons potato flour
¼ cup sweet sherry
¼ cup dry white wine

1 cup chicken stock (page 35)
Skinned sections of 2 large
  oranges

Preheat the oven to 375°. Trim the excess fat from the pork. Cut a slit between each rib bone (where you will eventually carve the chops). Season the inside with salt and pepper, and brush with the brandy or sherry. Tie the roast securely with string. Place it on a rack in a roasting pan, brush the top with the melted butter, and pour ¼ cup pineapple juice over it. Roast the pork 45 to 50 minutes, basting it frequently with the pan juices, adding 1 more tablespoon of pineapple juice each time you baste.

FRIED PINEAPPLE SLICES. Dry the pineapple slices between paper towels. Heat the butter in a frypan. When it is foaming, on the point of browning, put in the pineapple slices. Sprinkle them with granulated sugar and brown quickly on both sides.

SAUCE. Put the salt butter in a small heavy pan with the onion, garlic, and green pepper. Cook slowly, over low heat, 5 minutes, without browning the vegetables. After the first 2 minutes of cooking, add the shredded orange rind. Off the heat, stir in the tomato paste, meat glaze, and potato flour. Pour in the sherry, wine, and chicken stock. Stir over low heat until the sauce comes to a boil, and simmer it slowly 10 minutes. Add the skinned orange sections, and gently reheat without boiling.

When the pork is finished roasting, remove it from the oven, cut it into slices, and arrange them overlapping down a hot serving dish. Between each slice, put a fried pineapple slice. Spoon the sauce over the pork and pineapple. NET: 4 to 6 servings.

SPARERIBS SWEET AND SOUR

4 to 5 pounds meaty spareribs
¼ cup soy sauce

SWEET AND SOUR SAUCE
1 cup granulated sugar
1 cup wine vinegar
¼ cup Madeira wine
2 tablespoons soy sauce
1 green pepper, seeded and
  finely shredded

1 tablespoon cornstarch or
  potato flour
2 firm white mushrooms, sliced
1½ ounces sliced crystallized
  ginger
½ cup pineapple chunks (fresh,
  if possible)
¼ cup thinly sliced sweet
  pickles

Preheat the oven to 350°. Brush the spareribs well on both sides with the soy sauce. Place them in a shallow roasting pan, and roast 1½ hours, or until they are brown and crisp all over. Turn them over once during the roasting period.

SWEET AND SOUR SAUCE. In a deep heavy pan heat the granulated sugar, vinegar, Madeira, soy sauce, and green pepper to the boiling point. Mix the cornstarch with a little cold water, stir it into the sauce mixture, and continue to stir, over low heat, until the sauce becomes thick and clear. Then add the rest of the ingredients, and gently simmer 10 to 15 minutes.

When the spareribs are properly roasted, cut them into neat finger-sized pieces and arrange on a hot platter. Spoon the sweet and sour sauce over the spareribs, and serve. NET: 6 servings.

4 pig's feet	2 pounds raw chestnuts (in
1 garlic clove, cut in half	the shells)
⅓ cup pure olive oil	2 cups chicken stock (page 35)
Salt	4 tablespoons sweet butter
Freshly cracked white pepper	2 tablespoons sour cream

PIEDS DE PORC AUX MARRONS

Roast Pig's Feet with Chestnut Purée

Preheat the oven to 400°. Remove the outer skin and any sinew from the pig's feet (if the butcher has not already done so). Rub the feet with the cut pieces of garlic and brush them with the olive oil. Place them in a pan and roast 25 to 30 minutes, turning them once. Remove from the oven, and drain thoroughly.

CHESTNUT PURÉE. To shell the chestnuts, put them in a pan, cover with cold water, bring to a boil, and cook 2 to 3 minutes. Remove from the heat, but leave each one in the water until you skin it. Use a small sharp knife to remove the outer and inner skins. When all the chestnuts are shelled, discard the water, and put the chestnuts back in the pan with the chicken stock. Simmer very gently until they are soft (they should have absorbed all the chicken stock). Rub them through a fine strainer. Put the chestnut purée in a mixer, and beat in the sweet butter and the sour cream. Season to taste with salt and pepper.

Shape the chestnut purée in the form of a bed down a hot flat serving dish, and arrange the baked pig's feet on it. Warm in the oven, if necessary, and serve very hot. NET: 4 servings.

4 pig's feet	4 whole cloves
6 cups water	Salt
1 onion, sliced	12 black peppercorns
1 carrot, sliced	2 tablespoons melted salt butter
1 garlic clove, bruised	½ cup dry breadcrumbs
Bouquet garni (1 sprig thyme,	(page 69)
2 sprigs parsley, 1 bay leaf)	Dijon mustard

PIEDS DE PORC SAINTE-MENEHOULD

Pig's Feet Simmered and Broiled with Dijon Mustard

Remove the outer skin and sinew from the pig's feet (if the butcher has not already done so). Put the water in a pot with the onion, carrot, garlic, bouquet garni, cloves, salt, and peppercorns. Bring this court bouillon to a boil, and simmer 30 minutes. Then add the pig's feet and let them simmer very, very gently 4 to 5 hours (they should become very tender). Cool the pig's feet in the court bouillon. (If you wish to make sure the skin does not break, tie each foot tightly in cheesecloth before putting it into the pot.

When the pig's feet have cooled, brush each foot with melted butter and roll it in the breadcrumbs. To finish, either broil them slowly until golden brown all over, or roast them in a hot oven (preheated to 450°) until they are well browned. Serve the pig's feet with a little pot of Dijon mustard. NET: 4 servings.

HAM

CHRISTMAS HAM BAKED IN A CRUST

In Yorkshire, England, this ham is served at Christmastime, with sprigs of holly stuck in it. If you use a raw smoked ham, start the dish a day in advance of serving.

1 ham, 10 to 12 pounds
4 bottles beer
1 teaspoon crushed black peppercorns
4 crushed cloves
¾ cup dry red wine (preferably Burgundy)
½ cup Cognac or good brandy
3 tablespoons honey

CRUST
6 cups all-purpose flour
3 dried juniper berries, pulverized with a mortar and pestle
4 teaspoons baking powder
½ teaspoon powdered sage
1 teaspoon dry mustard
2 teaspoons salt
1 cup chilled lard or shortening
1½ cups ice-cold milk
1 egg, beaten

If the ham is a raw smoked one, scrub it well with a brush and cold water. Soak it in fresh cold water 24 hours, changing the water every 6 to 8 hours. Drain, and dry it.

Put the ham in a deep pan. Boil the beer in a separate pan and pour it over the ham. Add the crushed peppercorns and cloves, bring the beer to a boil, reduce the heat to low, and simmer the ham very gently 1½ hours. Replenish the beer, if necessary, to keep it covered with liquid. Then remove the ham, drain it, and dry it thoroughly with paper towels.

Preheat the oven to 375°. Place the ham in a deep roasting pan. Pour the wine and brandy over it. Roast the ham 2½ to 3 hours, basting frequently with the pan juices. Add more wine if necessary. When the ham is roasted, remove it from the oven and lay it on a wooden board. Carefully carve it into thin slices. Replace the slices on the bone and reshape the ham. In a little bowl mix 3 tablespoons pan juices with the honey, and brush this mixture all over the ham. Set the ham in the refrigerator to firm.

CRUST. Sift the flour, juniper berries, baking powder, sage, mustard, and salt together in a bowl. Add the lard or shortening and rub it into the flour mixture until it resembles coarse cornmeal. Add the cold milk and quickly work up to a firm dough. Turn the dough out onto a pastry board and knead it 1 to 2 minutes until it is quite smooth on top.

Preheat the oven to 400°. Roll the dough out about ¼ inch thick on a lightly floured surface. The piece should be large enough to cover the ham. Set the ham on the rolled-out dough, and fold the dough over it, encasing the ham. Trim off the edges of the dough, roll out the scraps, and cut out little leaves or flowers for decoration. Embellish the ham with these cutouts. Brush the dough with beaten egg, and carefully transfer the ham to a baking sheet. Bake it 10 minutes to set the pastry, then reduce the temperature to 350° and bake 15 to 25 minutes more. During this time, brush the crust once or twice with cold milk.

This ham may be served hot or cold. It can be accompanied with applesauce, chilled cranberry sauce, horseradish sauce, or black raspberry sauce. To serve, loosen the crust so that it can be lifted off. Slice the ham and give each person a slice of ham and a piece of the crust. NET: 18 servings.

This dish should be started a day in advance of serving. It needs a paper frill for the ham bone.

JAMBON EN CROÛTE AU CHAMPAGNE

Ham in Pastry with Champagne

1 uncooked ham, 8 to 10 pounds
½ cup sweet Madeira (Bual or Malmsey)
Half-bottle of Champagne (minus ½ cup for the sauce)
¾ cup granulated sugar

LINING PASTRY
2 cups all-purpose flour
1 teaspoon salt
12 teaspoons salt butter
⅓ cup ice water
1 egg, beaten

DEMI-GLACE SAUCE
4 tablespoons fat from the ham
1 medium-size onion, sliced
1 carrot, sliced
1 stalk celery, sliced
3 tablespoons all-purpose flour
1 large ripe tomato, sliced
About ¼ cup mushroom stems and trimmings
2 teaspoons tomato paste
2 teaspoons meat glaze
2 cups chicken stock (page 35)
½ cup Champagne (from the half-bottle above)
1 bay leaf
Salt
Freshly cracked white pepper
¼ teaspoon finely chopped garlic
Optional: 1 black truffle, sliced or shredded, or 4 firm white mushrooms, sliced

Scrub the ham well with a brush and cold water. Soak it 24 hours in fresh cold water. Then remove the ham and rub it all over with a clean cloth. Loosen the skin around the end of the bone. Place the ham in a large kettle and cover it completely with cold water. Bring to a boil and simmer it 20 minutes per pound. Remove the ham, remove the skin while the ham is hot, and, if there is too much fat, slice off the excess.

Preheat the oven to 375°. Place the ham in a roasting pan and sprinkle with the Madeira. Pour a little of the Champagne around the bottom of the pan, reserving ½ cup for the sauce. Sprinkle the ham with half of the granulated sugar. Glaze the ham in the oven 45 minutes. Baste it frequently, adding more Champagne and granulated sugar each time. The ham should be shiny all over and completely browned (like a roast). Remove it from the oven, let it cool awhile, and then chill it. When the ham is chilled, cut it into very thin slices. Pile one slice on the next, so they can be replaced on the lower half of the ham in their exact shape. Reshape the ham in this manner. Set the ham aside and keep it cool.

DEMI-GLACE SAUCE. Heat the ham fat in a small heavy pan. Add the onion, carrot, and celery, and cook very slowly without browning them. Then add the flour and brown the mixture very slowly. Off the heat, stir in the tomato and the mushroom trimmings and stems. Cook this mixture over low heat 2 to 3 minutes. Add the tomato paste and meat glaze. Pour in the chicken stock and Champagne. Stir the sauce over low heat until it comes to a boil. Add the bay leaf and season with salt and pepper. Simmer gently 30 to 45 minutes. Remove the fat from the pan in which the ham was glazed (skim it off). Add the stock remaining in this pan to the demi-glace sauce. Strain the sauce. (This sauce may be served either plain, or with a garnish of sliced truffle, or the white part of sliced mushrooms, or shredded tomato pulp.)

LINING CRUST. Put the flour and salt in a bowl. Cut the butter in pieces and work it into the flour with the fingertips until it resembles coarse cornmeal. Add barely ⅓ cup ice water and work up to a firm dough. Leave the dough in the refrigerator at least 30 minutes to set. Then roll it out to a piece big enough to encase the ham. Place the ham on the pastry and completely cover it. Place the pastry-covered ham on a baking sheet and brush it all over with the beaten egg. Roll out the scraps of pastry, cut out little pastry leaves and flowers, and decorate the top of the ham. Brush the decorations with beaten egg.

Put the encased ham in the refrigerator and chill at least 30 minutes. Preheat the oven to 375°. Bake the ham about 1 hour, watching to see that the crust does not become too brown. If it does, lower the heat. When the pastry has baked, remove the ham from the oven and place it on a hot serving platter. Cover the bone with a frill. Serve the sauce in a separate bowl. Loosen the crust around the edge, so that the whole crust can be lifted off at the table. Serve a slice of ham and a little of the crust with the sauce. The proper wine to drink with this dish is, of course, iced Champagne. NET: 16 to 18 servings.

Puff paste dough (page 723, or
  equal commercial quantity)
1 small boned cooked ham
3 tablespoons Cognac or good
  brandy
8 tablespoons sweet butter
4 ounces fine liver pâté
1 teaspoon chopped fresh
  tarragon
2 teaspoons finely chopped
  black truffle
Salt
Freshly cracked white pepper
1 egg, beaten
Sauce Duphot (white truffle
  sauce, page 51)

JAMBON EN CROÛTE SAUCE DUPHOT

Ham, Sandwiched with
Liver Pâté, Baked in
Puff Pastry, with
White Truffle Sauce

Have the prepared puff paste dough ready. Cut the ham in half like
a sandwich. Prick it with the tines of a fork all over and sprinkle
with brandy.

FILLING. Put the butter in a mixer and cream it until it is very light
and fluffy. Add the liver pâté and beat well. Add the tarragon, black
truffle, salt, and pepper, and mix very well.

Spread the filling on the lower half of the ham, sandwich it with
the top, and put the ham in the freezer. Roll the puff paste dough
about ½ inch thick. Remove the ham from the freezer, cut it in slices
about ¾ inch thick, and reshape. Wrap the ham in the puff paste.
Seal the edges with a little beaten egg. Decorate the top with cut-out
leaves of puff-paste. Stick them on with beaten egg. Place the ham
on a wet baking sheet. Put it to set in the freezer at least 30 minutes.
(The more frozen puff paste is, the better it will bake.) Preheat the
oven to 375°. When the puff paste around the ham is well frozen,
brush it all over with beaten egg and bake it 40 to 45 minutes, until
the pastry is well risen and golden brown all over. Serve hot, with
a separate bowl of Sauce Duphot. Serve each ham slice with its
surrounding crust. NET: 6 to 8 servings.

For this dish you need ten cornucopia molds.

5 paper-thin rectangular slices
  lean boiled ham, about
  8 by 4 inches
12 tablespoons sweet butter
6 ounces fine liver pâté
2 tablespoons Cognac or good
  brandy
Salt
Freshly cracked white pepper
1 black truffle, cut into thin
  slices
Chicken aspic (page 37)

VEGETABLE MACÉDOINE
1½ cups each of finely diced
  young turnips and carrots
1½ cups fresh shelled peas
1½ cups each of finely diced
  green beans and asparagus
  tips (about ½-inch)
Salt
Freshly cracked white pepper
1 teaspoon lemon juice

MAYONNAISE
2 egg yolks
½ teaspoon dry mustard
1 teaspoon Dijon mustard
½ teaspoon salt
A few grains cayenne pepper
2 tablespoons tarragon vinegar
¾ cup vegetable oil
¼ cup pure olive oil
⅓ cup light cream

CORNETS DE JAMBON LUCULLUS

Ham Cornucopias
Stuffed with Liver Pâté
on a Vegetable
Macédoine (cold)

| | 1½ tablespoons unflavored gelatine | 5 tablespoons milk |

Try to get lean slices of ham that will not fall apart. Cut the rectangles exactly in half so that you have two 4-inch squares from each slice of ham. Line 10 cornucopia molds with the ham. Trim the ends off neatly. Put the sweet butter in a mixer bowl and beat until it is light and fluffy. Add the pâté and the brandy. Season with salt and pepper. Put this filling in a pastry bag fitted with a large (#8 or #9) plain tube. Pipe the pâté into the cornucopia molds. Smooth over the open ends. With a small round cutter, cut 10 even rounds (about the size of a nickel or penny) out of the truffle slices. Put a round of truffle on the pâté at the open end of each cornucopia. Chill the filled cornucopias in the freezer. Put a little aspic in a small pan, dissolve it (if it has set), and stir it over ice until it is at the point of setting. Coat the open ends of the molds with this aspic. Put whatever aspic is left in a layer cake pan, and let it set in the refrigerator. (When set, it will be used for garnish.)

VEGETABLES MACÉDOINE. Wrap each of the five vegetables separately in foil, and put all the packages in a large saucepan. Barely cover with cold water, add a little salt, bring to a boil slowly, and cook until the vegetables are soft. Remove each vegetable as it is cooked (the asparagus will be cooked first). Drain each as it is removed, and when they are all cooked, put them in a bowl and mix together. Season with salt, pepper, and the lemon juice, and set aside for the vegetables to marinate.

MAYONNAISE. Put the egg yolks in a mixer bowl. Add the two mustards, salt, and cayenne pepper. Beat well. Slowly add the vinegar, vegetable oil, and olive oil, beating constantly. Add the light cream. Mix the gelatine with the milk in a little pan. Put the pan over low heat and stir until the gelatine is dissolved. Let the gelatine cool a little and then beat it into the mayonnaise.

Mix this mayonnaise with the vegetables. Rinse a layer cake pan with cold water and pack the vegetables into it. Put it to set in the refrigerator or freezer. When it is set, turn it out onto a serving dish. Remove the cornucopias from the molds and arrange them in a cartwheel shape on the macédoine. Turn out the aspic in the layer cake tin onto a cutting board, chop it fine, and put it in a pastry bag with a large plain tube. Pipe the chopped aspic between each cornucopia mold and pipe a rosette in the center of the macédoine. Allow it to set in the refrigerator, or serve immediately. NET: 4 to 5 servings.

JAMBON À LA SAINT-GERMAIN

Ham Slices on Pea Purée, Demi-Glace Sauce

This dish requires a ham bone, and the dried peas must be started overnight. It is a good way to use leftover ham.

2 tablespoons sweet butter	12 thin slices ham
3 tablespoons Cognac or good brandy	Salt
	Freshly cracked white pepper

PEA PURÉE
4 cups dried peas
1 onion, studded with 3 cloves
1 carrot, sliced
1 leek, sliced
2 heads Boston lettuce, cut in
    half
1 ham bone
Salt
Freshly cracked white pepper
1 teaspoon granulated sugar
2 sprigs fresh parsley
8 tablespoons salt butter

DEMI-GLACE SAUCE
4 tablespoons ham fat or
    salt butter

1 medium-size onion, sliced
1 carrot, sliced
1 piece celery, sliced
3 tablespoons all-purpose flour
1 large ripe tomato, sliced
¼ cup mushroom trimmings
    and stems
2 teaspoons tomato paste
2 teaspoons meat glaze
2 cups chicken stock (page 35)
½ cup Sauternes
1 bay leaf
1 garlic clove, bruised
2 tablespoons Cognac or good
    brandy
Salt
Freshly cracked white pepper

PEA PURÉE. Soak the dried peas overnight in cold water. The next day, drain, rinse, and wash them again in clear water. Put them in a large pan and barely cover with water. Add the onion, carrot, leek, lettuces, and ham bone. Then add salt, pepper, and the sugar and parsley sprigs. Bring to a boil, cover, and cook over low heat until the peas have absorbed all the liquid and are very mushy. Remove the ham bone and parsley, and rub the rest through a fine strainer. Mix in the salt butter, a little at a time. Keep the purée warm.

Put the sweet butter in a large frypan and slowly melt it. Add the brandy, and warm over moderate heat. Heat the ham slices and keep them warm.

DEMI-GLACE SAUCE. Melt the ham fat in a saucepan. Add the onion, carrot, and celery, and cook them very slowly without browning them. Then add the flour, and brown the mixture slowly. Off the heat, mix in the tomato and mushroom peelings and stems, and cook slowly 2 to 3 minutes. Add the tomato paste and meat glaze, and mix well. Pour in the chicken stock and Sauternes, and stir over moderate heat until the sauce comes to a boil. Add the bay leaf, garlic clove, brandy, salt, and pepper. Simmer the sauce 30 to 45 minutes, and strain it.

To serve, shape the pea purée into a bed down a long flat warm serving dish. Place the warmed slices of ham on the pea purée, overlapping each other. Spoon the sauce over all. NET: 6 servings.

Start this recipe a day ahead of serving. You will need a large paper frill for the ham bone.

1 uncooked ham, 8 to 10 pounds
1 split Champagne

½ cup Bual Madeira (fairly
    sweet)

JAMBON BRAISÉ, SAUCE DEMI-GLACE

Braised Glazed Ham
with Demi-Glace Sauce

¾ cup granulated sugar

DEMI-GLACE SAUCE
4 tablespoons ham fat from the
    braising pan
1 medium-size onion, sliced
1 carrot, sliced
1 stalk celery, sliced
3 tablespoons all-purpose flour
1 large ripe tomato, sliced
A few pieces of mushroom
    stems and trimmings
2 cups chicken stock (page 35)
½ cup dry red wine

2 teaspoons tomato paste
2 teaspoons meat glaze
1 bay leaf
Salt
Freshly cracked white pepper
1 garlic clove
Optional: 1 large black truffle,
    sliced, or 4 firm white mush-
    room caps, sliced, or 2 large
    tomatoes, skinned, seeded,
    and shredded
2 tablespoons Cognac or good
    brandy

Scrub the ham with a brush and cold water. Rinse it, cover it with cold water, and soak it 24 hours. Then dry it well with a clean cloth. Loosen the skin a little around the bone. Place the ham in a large kettle, cover it completely with cold water, and bring to a boil. Reduce the heat to low, and simmer the ham 20 minutes per pound. When it is done, remove it from the water, and carefully remove the skin while it is hot. If there is too much fat, trim off the excess.

Preheat the oven to 375°. Place the ham in a roasting pan. Sprinkle it with the Madeira. Pour a little of the Champagne around the bottom of the roasting pan and sprinkle the ham with about half the granulated sugar. Braise it in the oven 1¾ hours. Baste frequently, each time adding a little more Champagne to the pan and sprinkling a little more sugar on the ham. The ham should be shiny all over and completely brown.

DEMI-GLACE SAUCE. Put the ham fat in a saucepan. Add the onion, carrot, and celery, and cook very slowly, without browning, until the onion is translucent. Off the heat, add the flour and brown the mixture slowly, over low heat. Remove from the heat and stir in the sliced tomato and mushroom pieces. Cook slowly 2 to 3 minutes. Pour in the stock and wine and add the tomato paste and meat glaze. Stir the sauce over low heat until it comes to a boil. Add the bay leaf, salt, pepper, and the garlic clove, and simmer gently 45 minutes. Skim the fat from the pan juices in the roasting pan. Then add these juices (with fat removed) to the sauce. Strain the sauce through a fine strainer. It can be served either plain or with a garnish of sliced truffle, or sliced mushrooms, or shredded tomatoes.

When the ham has finished cooking, place it on a warm flat oval serving dish. Cover the end bone with a large paper frill, and serve the sauce in a separate bowl. Just before serving the sauce, heat the brandy in a little pan, ignite, and pour it onto the sauce. NET: 14 to 16 servings.

This is a classic New Orleans Creole dish, with sausage and ham.

½ cup water
½ pound link sausages
1 large Bermuda onion, finely
    chopped
1 green pepper, seeded and
    diced
1 pound smoked ham, diced
½ teaspoon finely chopped
    garlic
1½ cups long-grain rice
1 medium-size ripe tomato,
    skinned and chopped

3 cups chicken stock (page 35)
    or water
Salt
Freshly cracked white pepper
2 sprigs fresh thyme (or ½
    teaspoon dried)
1 tablespoon chopped fresh
    parsley
12 raw oysters, shelled, and/or
    12 cooked shrimp, shelled
    and deveined

Put the water into a deep heavy pan with a cover. Cook the sausages in it (uncovered) over moderate heat, until they are well browned and the water has disappeared. Remove them from the pan, cut them in half, and set aside. Add to the pan the onion, green pepper, and ham. Cover, and cook over moderate heat until they are lightly browned, stirring frequently so that they will brown evenly. Add the garlic and cook 1 minute more. Next, add the rice and tomato, and cook for another minute. Pour in the stock or water and bring the mixture to a boil, stirring all the while. Season with salt, pepper, thyme, and the chopped parsley. Return the sausage to the pan. Cover, and cook the mixture over very low heat 30 to 35 minutes, until the rice is tender but not mushy.

A minute or two before serving, add the oysters and/or shrimps, and gently reheat just until the edges of the oysters curl. Serve in a hot casserole. NET: 6 to 8 servings.

This charlotte mold of ham mousse is coated with aspic and decorated with diamonds of black truffle and white of hard-boiled egg. It is recommended that it be prepared a day in advance of serving.

Cold Ham Mousse

2 pounds lean boiled ham
12 tablespoons sweet butter
3 tablespoons vegetable oil
6 tablespoons water
4 tablespoons all-purpose flour
1 tablespoon unflavored gelatine
1 tablespoon tomato paste
A few grains cayenne pepper
1 cup milk
2 cups heavy cream
Salt

Freshly cracked white pepper
1 black truffle
2 hard-boiled eggs

ASPIC
3 egg whites
4 cups chicken stock (page 35)
3 tablespoons unflavored
    gelatine
1 tablespoon tomato paste
⅓ cup sweet sherry or Madeira

Put the boiled ham through a fine meat chopper two times. Cream the sweet butter in a mixer until it is light and fluffy. Slowly add the ground ham, mix well, and chill it thoroughly.

PANADE. Put the vegetable oil and water in a small saucepan over moderate heat. Mix the flour and gelatine together, and when the oil and water mixture comes to a boil, remove them from the heat and stir in the flour and gelatine. Add the tomato paste, cayenne pepper, and milk. Return the pan to low heat, and stir the mixture until it comes to a boil and thickens. Pour it onto a plate and chill it.

Put the ham in a mixer bowl and slowly mix in the chilled panade. Then slowly beat in the heavy cream. Season with salt and freshly cracked white pepper. Beat the mixture well, until it is very smooth. Set it in the refrigerator, and chill an empty charlotte mold in the freezer.

ASPIC. Beat the egg whites to stiff peaks. Put the chicken stock in a large tin-lined copper pan with the gelatine, tomato paste, sherry or Madeira, and beaten egg whites. Beat with a wire whisk over low heat until the mixture comes to a rolling boil. Remove the pan from the heat, and let the mixture stand absolutely still 15 minutes. Line a colander with a damp cloth, and slowly pour the mixture through the colander. This is clear aspic.

Pour the aspic into a clean saucepan and stand it over a bowl of crushed ice. Stir it until it is on the point of setting. Pour it quickly into the frozen empty charlotte mold. Tip the mold all around so that it is completely coated with aspic. Have the aspic slightly thicker on the bottom of the mold. Slice the truffle and cut the slices into diamond shapes. Dip a diamond in liquid aspic and place it on the aspic in the center of the bottom of the mold. Dip the other truffle diamonds in aspic and place them at even intervals around the sides of the mold. Cut some very thin slices of hard-boiled egg white and cut them into crescent shapes. Dip the white crescents in liquid aspic and place them between the truffle diamonds. Put a thin layer of aspic (on the point of setting) over the decorations. Set the mold in the refrigerator to set (not the freezer, or the aspic will cloud).

Reheat the aspic if it has solidified. Allow it to cool a little and mix a little of the liquid aspic into the ham mousse, enough to reduce the ham mousse to the consistency of whipped cream. Fill the aspic-lined charlotte mold with this mousse, and put it to set in the refrigerator. When the mousse is set, remove it from the refrigerator and pour liquid aspic, at room temperature, over the top of the mousse to fill in all the spaces. Then return the mold to the refrigerator to get very firm. (This is more assured if it can be left overnight.) Put the rest of the aspic in a layer cake pan to set for garnish.

When you are ready to serve, slide the tip of a thin-bladed knife around the top edge of the mousse and turn the mold over onto a flat chilled serving platter. Wipe the mold with a cloth wrung out in hot water, if necessary, to release the mousse. Unmold the aspic from the layer cake pan onto a sheet of wax paper. Cut it into crescent shapes with a round cutter, or chop it fine. Garnish the platter with this aspic. NET: 4 to 6 servings.

A Greek culinary expression with ham, tongue, mushrooms, rice. Apricot oil is available in Greek food shops.

24 edible grape leaves (in cans
    or jars)
¼ cup pure olive oil

STUFFING
4 tablespoons apricot oil or
    pure olive oil
2 tablespoons salt butter
2 tablespoons finely chopped
    yellow onion
2 teaspoons finely chopped
    garlic
2 tablespoons diced cooked ham
2 tablespoons diced cooked
    tongue
2 tablespoons finely chopped
    firm white mushrooms
1 tablespoon finely chopped
    green pepper
2 teaspoons sesame seeds
Pinch of dried thyme
Salt

A few grains cayenne pepper
¾ cup long-grain rice
1½ cups chicken stock (page
    35)

SAUCE
1 teaspoon and 1 tablespoon
    salt butter
1 chicken liver, gizzard, or neck
1 teaspoon tomato paste
1 teaspoon meat glaze
2 teaspoons potato flour
1 teaspoon finely chopped garlic
½ cup dry red wine
1 cup chicken stock (page 35)
¼ cup red currant jelly
2 tablespoons Cognac, good
    brandy, or dry sherry
Salt
Freshly cracked white pepper
1 cup pitted fresh (or sour
    canned) cherries

Preheat the oven to 375°. Remove the leaves from the jars and dry them spread out flat on paper towels.

STUFFING. Heat 3 tablespoons apricot oil and 1 tablespoon butter in a heavy pan (reserve the other tablespoon of butter for the top). Add the rest of the ingredients. Stir the mixture over low heat until it comes to a boil. Dot the top with butter and cover the pan with the lid. Reduce the heat to a gentle simmer and cook without lifting the cover 25 minutes. When the rice is soft, stir in the rest of the apricot oil.

Spoon this mixture onto the leaves, about 2 teaspoons per leaf. Roll them, tucking in the ends neatly. Pour the olive oil in the pan and pack the stuffed, rolled-up leaves in it. Cover with the lid and cook in the preheated oven 40 minutes.

SAUCE. Heat 1 teaspoon salt butter very hot in a saucepan. Brown the liver, gizzard, or neck in it (to glaze the bottom of the pan). Remove, and use it for something else. Add 1 tablespoon butter to the pan. Off the heat, stir in the tomato paste, meat glaze, potato flour, and chopped garlic. Stir till smooth, then pour in the wine, chicken stock, jelly, and brandy. Season with salt and pepper. Return to low heat, and stir until the sauce comes to a boil. Simmer gently 5 minutes. Add the cherries and simmer another 5 minutes.

When the stuffed grape leaves are cooked, arrange them down a shallow serving dish. Spoon the sauce over them. NET: 6 servings.

CÔTELETTES DE CHEVREUIL PROVENÇALE

Braised Venison Chops Provençal with Steamed New Potatoes

This dish should be started a day in advance of serving.

6 venison loin chops
4 tablespoons salt butter
1½ teaspoons finely chopped garlic
2 tablespoons finely chopped shallots
2 teaspoons potato flour
1 teaspoon meat glaze
½ cup chicken stock (page 35)
1¼ cups heavy cream
½ teaspoon dried thyme
Salt
Freshly cracked white pepper
1 tablespoon finely chopped fresh parsley

1½ pounds baby new potatoes, steamed and skinned (page 612)
A little freshly grated nutmeg

MARINADE
½ cup pure olive oil
½ cup Madeira wine
1 teaspoon finely chopped garlic
12 mixed black and white peppercorns
1 small bay leaf
1 tablespoon coarsely chopped fresh parsley
Salt

The meat takes at least 12 hours to marinate. Remove the excess fat and trim the chops. Put them in a deep earthenware bowl or crock. Pour the olive oil and Madeira over them. Add the chopped garlic, peppercorns, bay leaf, parsley, and a little salt. Turn the chops a few times, so they can be evenly covered with this marinade. Cover the container and leave it in a cool place overnight. Next day remove the chops and wipe them dry with paper towels (reserve the marinade). Heat the butter in a heavy pan. When it is on the point of browning, put in the chops a few at a time and brown them on both sides. (They must not touch each other or they will not brown.)

Preheat the oven to 350°. Remove the chops from the sauté pan, and add to the pan the finely chopped garlic and shallots. Reduce the heat to low, and cook the vegetables slowly 2 minutes, without browning them. Off the heat, stir in the potato flour and meat glaze. Strain the marinade and pour it into the pan, also add the chicken stock. Stir the mixture over low heat until it thickens, then slowly stir in the heavy cream little by little. Add the thyme and season to taste with salt and pepper.

Return the venison chops to the pan, cover the pan with wax paper and the lid, and put the pan on the top shelf of the oven. Cook the chops 45 minutes, basting them once or twice during the cooking with the sauce in the pan. When they are cooked, arrange them on a hot flat serving dish. (If the sauce has separated a little, mix ½ teaspoon potato flour in a small cup with 2 tablespoons water and stir it into the sauce. Reboil the sauce and it will come together again.) Add the finely chopped parsley to the sauce and spoon the sauce over the chops. Serve the skinned baby new potatoes separately, on a hot napkin, sprinkled with the nutmeg. NET: 6 servings.

This dish should be started the day before serving it.

5 pounds boned shoulder of
    venison
2 quarts Marinade Crue (page
    61)
1 ounce dried mushrooms
2 cups chicken stock (page 35)
5 tablespoons salt butter
½ cup Madeira wine
1 teaspoon finely chopped garlic
2 teaspoons meat glaze

2 teaspoons tomato paste
5 teaspoons potato flour
1 cup dry red wine
1 tablespoon red currant jelly
Salt
Freshly cracked black pepper
1 cup pitted black olives
2 tablespoons chopped fresh
    parsley

The meat must be marinated overnight. First trim all the skin and fat from the meat. Cut the meat into 2-inch cubes, and put them into an earthenware crock or bowl. Pour the marinade crue over the meat, cover, and let it stand overnight, stirring it once or twice. Soak the dried mushrooms overnight in the chicken stock. After the meat is marinated, drain, and dry it on paper towels (strain and reserve the marinade.) Drain the mushrooms and chop them fine.

Preheat the oven to 350°. Heat the butter in a deep heavy pan. When it is hot, put the meat in the pan and brown it, a few pieces at a time. In a separate little pan, heat the Madeira wine, ignite, and pour it over the meat. Remove the meat, set it aside, and add to the pan the mushrooms and garlic. Reduce the heat to low, and cook 4 minutes. Off the heat, stir in the meat glaze, tomato paste, and potato flour. When the mixture is smooth, add the chicken stock, ⅓ cup of the strained marinade, the red wine and jelly. Return to low heat, and stir until the sauce comes to a boil. Season to taste with salt and pepper. Return the venison to the pan. Cover, and put on the top shelf of the oven. Cook 1½ hours, or until the venison is tender. After about 45 minutes, remove the cover.

When the meat is cooked, add the black olives. Transfer the ragoût to a casserole and sprinkle with the parsley. NET: 8 to 10 servings.

1 4-pound rabbit, dressed
2 tablespoons lemon juice or
    vinegar
½ cup all-purpose flour mixed
    with salt and freshly cracked
    black pepper (for dusting)
3 tablespoons salt butter
1 medium-size onion, finely
    chopped
1 teaspoon finely chopped
    garlic
4 firm white fresh mushrooms,
    sliced

3 tablespoons all-purpose flour
1 teaspoon meat glaze
1 teaspoon tomato paste
1½ cups chicken stock
    (page 35)
½ cup dry white wine
Salt
Freshly cracked black pepper
2 tablespoons dry mustard
½ cup sour cream
2 sprigs fresh tarragon
1 teaspoon chopped fresh
    tarragon

Cut the rabbit into neat small pieces. Soak it 2 hours in cold water with the lemon juice or vinegar. Drain and dry the pieces of rabbit on paper towels, and dust the pieces lightly with the flour mixed with a little salt and pepper. Heat the butter in a deep heavy pan. When it is sizzling hot, brown the rabbit. Remove the rabbit from the pan, set it aside, and add to the pan the onion and garlic. Cook over low heat 3 minutes, then add the mushrooms and cook 2 minutes longer. Off the heat, add 3 tablespoons flour and the meat glaze and tomato paste. Stir until the mixture is smooth. Add the chicken stock and wine. Season with salt and pepper. Stir the mixture over low heat until it comes to a boil. Mix the mustard into the sour cream and stir this into the sauce. Return the pieces of rabbit to the pan with the leaves from the tarragon. Cover with the lid and cook slowly, over very low heat, 1 hour, or until the rabbit is quite tender.

To serve, put the rabbit in a deep casserole. If the sauce is too thin, boil it down until it is thicker. Spoon the sauce over the rabbit. Sprinkle the top with the chopped fresh tarragon. NET: 4 servings.

LAPIN SAUTÉ CHASSEUR

Sautéed Rabbit Hunter's Style

1 rabbit, 3½ to 4 pounds
½ cup all-purpose flour mixed with salt and freshly cracked black pepper (for dusting)
2 tablespoons pure olive oil
2 tablespoons salt butter
2 small yellow onions, finely chopped
½ teaspoon finely chopped garlic
1 teaspoon tomato paste
1 tablespoon all-purpose flour
2 teaspoons meat glaze

½ cup dry red wine
1 cup chicken stock (page 35)
Bouquet garni (1 bay leaf, 2 sprigs tarragon, 2 sprigs parsley, tied in cheesecloth)
Salt
Freshly cracked black pepper
4 ounces firm white mushrooms, sliced
6 to 8 large croûtons, fried in olive oil (page 69)
1 tablespoon chopped fresh parsley

Cut the rabbit into neat small pieces. Wash them well in salted water and dry very well. Dust lightly with flour mixed with a little salt and pepper. Heat the olive oil and butter in a heavy pan. When the pan is very hot, brown the pieces of rabbit. Remove the rabbit from the pan, set it aside, and add the chopped onions and garlic to the pan. Cook 3 minutes over low heat, then stir in, off the heat, the tomato paste, 1 tablespoon flour, and the meat glaze. When the mixture is smooth, pour in the wine and the chicken stock. Stir over low heat until the sauce comes to a boil. Return the pieces of rabbit to the pan with the bouquet garni, salt, and pepper. Simmer gently, over low heat, 30 to 40 minutes, until the meat is quite tender. Ten minutes before it is finished, add the mushrooms.

To serve, remove the bouquet garni and place the rabbit in a deep hot earthenware dish. Stick the fried croûtons around the sides of the dish. Sprinkle the top with the parsley. NET: 4 servings.

VEGETABLES
AND GARNISHES

GARDEN :

"We have an ancient gardener who works on it with great joy, and the produce is just fine. We have tomatoes, and pumpkins, and delicious cucumbers, and summer squash, the yellow straight-neck squash, and butternut squash. We have carrots and beets and romaine and Bibb, and delicious broccoli. Lots of string beans."

"And herbs, too?"

"We're just now planting the herb garden, so that they will be ready for next year. But the early results have been extremely good."

"It must be a lovely garden. I can't imagine anything more marvelous."

"It's nice and large, and it's quite sufficient. We also have an asparagus bed that is longer than this room. The garden has been there about thirty years. It is in wonderful condition. At least twice a week, if not three times, during asparagus season, whatever the meal, we simply eat a piece of toast, asparagus, and butter or Hollandaise. Now we're getting tomatoes that have the most luscious flavor; they're beautiful, red and ripe and juicy."

Several years ago I had this conversation with Bill Perry, television producer, playwright, and connoisseur of good things to eat, telling me about his garden in a suburb just north of New York City. Victims we may be of the plastic-wrapped and waxed produce offered in supermarket bins, but I believe our young people are going to bring about a rediscovery of the real nature of vegetables and fruits. Maybe it will be only a little but genuine taste from the yield of a hobby garden, or a summer of country goodness from a vacation group garden. Or perhaps (wishfully) there will be a kitchen garden revival within the national drive to rebeautify and "renaturalize" America.

There is indeed, in classic French cooking, a fine precedent and reference point for cultural appreciation of vegetables and fruits in their natural eloquence.

Classic French cooking honors the natural vegetable. It is given very special attention in its role in the menu and equally in its preparation. Vegetables are important enough to have a course of their own, always. A vegetable appears with the fish, meat, or poultry course only when it is an integral part of that particular dish. Served in that way, a vegetable is a garnish and must always blend with the flavor of the basic dish; garnishes provide the harmony, not the melody.

There are many, many definitive and traditional garnishes in classic cookery. In this book, the recipe for a garnish traditional to a certain dish is given with the recipe for the basic dish; for example, the pea purée with veal birds (Paupiettes de Veau Fontanges) or the tomatoes and mushrooms with Filets de Soles Dugleré. And, like many another cook, chef, and gastronome devoted to the classic art, I have invented a few garnitures which I believe add special enhancement to the character of a dish. It is necessary to comment that a garnish is not merely a decoration: it must always be edible, it must always play a complementary role (not the starring role), it should always be beautifully prepared, and it should taste like what it really is.

Fresh vegetables are magnificent when given the honor of a course on their own. If your eating attitude is in the doldrums, why not entertain a new-old idea — a separate vegetable course, with a lovely fresh vegetable, correctly and carefully prepared to release a beautiful natural fragrance and flavor you may never have known the vegetable possessed. (Carefully followed, any of the recipes in this chapter will do just that.)

Possibly contributing to some people's lack of interest, if not downright dislike, for vegetables is the English-American cliché of serving "meat and two vegetables," marshaled without regard for compatibility. A national gastronomic disaster is the result. The custom may arise from the effort to round out very simple fare that is characteristic of English and American cuisines — looking for something to eat with plain roast beef or plain roast chicken. The result is that our national use of vegetables is neither as a complementary garnish nor as an interesting separate dish.

The vegetable as a separate course can fit into various places on the menu. Usually, in the French manner, it is served after the entrée. But it might also be served as the first course; for example, a spinach tart or asparagus vinaigrette. Flexibility in integrating vegetables into a menu is also illustrated in the menu discussion on page 7. When a vegetable is served as a separate course, the salad course is invariably eliminated.

This method of menu organization offers the maximum scope for your culinary expertise and palate cultivation. If you have beautifully broiled lamb chops, for example, with watercress, and a lovely cauliflower mousse, you would not want to dissipate the goodness of each by eating them together, not even with one as a "side dish"

— another New World invention. Enjoy the delicate and subtle pink juices of the lamb with a proper wine; then move on to the next act — a different food flavor and texture.

Proper Cooking of Vegetables

Extra tender loving care. So many people put all their care in cooking, whatever there may be of it, into the meat course. The vegetables are just thrown into a pot of cold water and — hope for the best. The truth is that vegetables should be cooked with extreme care. You can't neglect them at all.

To taste their best, vegetables should be a little undercooked, so that they will still be firm, a little crunchy, but cooked.

A frequent technique in vegetable cookery is to blanch the vegetable and then finish cooking it in butter. That's the classic way of cooking peas, green beans, and most other vegetables.

To blanch vegetables, cover cleaned vegetables with cold water and bring it to a boil quickly. Then drain, and finish cooking them in the manner of the recipe. (Simply to plunge a vegetable in boiling water is not enough. Putting it in cold water, then bringing it to a boil and draining, draws out all the bitter juices.)

Often all that is needed after blanching is to cook the vegetable just a little in a little lemon juice, butter, and maybe a few tablespoons of cold water. Then one can really taste the vegetable. By blanching properly you also maintain the color of vegetables. For example, green beans — if you slice them very fine, blanch them, return them to the pot with a lot of butter, cover them with buttered wax paper and the lid, and cook them briskly 5 to 6 minutes, shaking them occasionally, they'll be perfect and as bright a green as they grow. Blanching keeps the natural color of all fresh vegetables. Vegetables lose their color the minute they're overcooked. That's the test. They are then over the hill; they can't be saved. (See blanching procedure on page 571.)

Another acceptable way of cooking vegetables is "au vapeur," by steam. (I do not mean using a pressure cooker. I don't think they are used much any more, because they can be dangerous. But to me it is the most dreadful way to cook anything; everything tastes the same in a pressure cooker and loses its texture and vitality.) By cooking vegetables with steam I mean using a pan like an asparagus cooker, where the vegetables sit on a little platform and do not touch the water. This method cooks very quickly and also keeps the vegetables very firm and crisp. It is especially good for cooking asparagus (only 4 minutes), baby potatoes, red beets, cauliflower, and corn on the cob.

"demoisturizing" vegetables. Rather than being blanched, eggplants and cucumbers often should be demoisturized before cooking or adding other ingredients. (For some recipes, summer and zucchini squash should be demoisturized too.) To drain some of the excess moisture and eliminate any bitter character, the vegetable should be cut, either split or sliced, and the pieces spread out on a platter. Then generously salt the vegetable and allow it to stand 20 to 30 minutes. In that time, water globules will form. Then rinse the vegetable in clear water and thoroughly dry it before proceeding with the preparation.

Proper Chopping and Cutting of Vegetables

As an example of chopping, this is how to chop an onion. Cut the onion in half vertically. Place one half on the chopping board with the flat cut surface down. Cut the onion into slices, vertically, with the grain of the onion, holding the sliced onion together with your left hand. Then give the sliced onion one quarter-turn (90 degrees) and slice it against the grain, so that now you have, actually, finely diced onion. This procedure is all that is necessary to chop an onion. How finely it is diced depends on how thinly it is sliced — both with the grain and against the grain. You never really "chop" an onion; that would pound out all of the juices, leaving them on the chopping board instead of in the onion.

(Before you begin to chop the onion, sprinkle the cut surfaces of the two halves with a little lemon juice, and your tear ducts will be unaffected.)

Most vegetables are chopped in this manner, with judgment as to the shape and structure of the particular vegetable. If "finely chopped" is desired, then proceed to chop in a mincing fashion until it is as tiny as you want it. This procedure also applies to tiny little shallots and garlic cloves, as well as parsley and other leaf herbs.

CUTTING VEGETABLES INTO OLIVE SHAPES. Frequently in French culinary processes, certain vegetables (generally potatoes, carrots, or turnips) are cut into olive shapes. To make an olive shape, cut the vegetable into pieces or chunks approximating the size of a large olive. Then, with a paring knife, trim off the sharp corners, rounding off a little at the top and bottom.

Other techniques for preparing and cooking vegetables are explained with each recipe as needed.

LÉGUMES AU BEURRE

Plain-Cooked Fresh Vegetables with Butter

The following vegetables may be cooked by first blanching them, then cooking them in a covered pan with butter and only a few tablespoons of water. The vegetables should be "just" cooked, to retain a crisp quality when served; the whole cooking process should take only a few minutes, exactly how many depending on the type, size, and quantity of vegetable.

VEGETABLES. Haricots verts (green beans), whole or French-cut; petits pois (green peas), shelled; pois mange-tout (snow peas), whole; carottes (carrots), whole, sliced thin (à la Vichy) or in olive shapes; brocoli (broccoli), trimmed; concombres (cucumbers), skinned, cut in half lengthwise, seeded, and cut into ½-inch slices; chou-fleur (cauliflower), trimmed, whole, or broken into clusters; courgettes (zucchini), with skin left on, cut into good ½-inch slices.

Vegetables (any quantity of any
  of the above, cleaned and
  prepared as noted)
Lump of salt butter (about 3
  tablespoons to 1 pound
  vegetables)
Salt

Freshly cracked white pepper
3 or 4 drops lemon juice
4 tablespoons cold water
Optional: Any appropriate
  chopped fresh herb (parsley,
  dill, chives, Italian parsley,
  etc.)

Blanch the vegetable (cover with cold water, bring to a boil, drain). Return it to the pan with a little salt, pepper, and the lemon juice and butter. Add the cold water. Lightly press a piece of buttered wax paper on top of the vegetable and cover the pan with the lid. Place the pan over low heat and cook slowly only a few minutes, according to the particular vegetable and quantity. Test for doneness with an ice pick (not the tines of a fork, which could split the piece of vegetable). Serve in a warm vegetable dish. Sprinkle with chopped fresh herbs, if desired.

Globe artichokes grow like big flowers on a bush, as distinguished from Jerusalem artichokes, which are roots. In this recipe the choke is removed and replaced with a duxelles mixture, and the artichokes are served hot.

ARTICHAUTS BARIGOULE

Globe Artichokes
Stuffed with Duxelles

4 globe artichokes
2 tablespoons fresh lemon juice
4 tablespoons salt butter
1 cup finely chopped firm white
  mushrooms
4 tablespoons shredded cooked
  ham
4 tablespoons shredded cooked
  tongue
2 small onions, finely chopped
3 teaspoons tomato paste
3 tablespoons finely chopped
  fresh parsley

3 tablespoons dry breadcrumbs
  (page 69)
2 tablespoons melted salt butter
4 slices bacon
2 tablespoons vegetable oil
½ cup dry white wine
½ cup chicken stock (page 35)
1 tablespoon dry sherry
2 tablespoons all-purpose flour
Salt
A few grains cayenne pepper
½ teaspoon finely chopped
  garlic

Boil the artichokes in salt water with the lemon juice until they are tender, about 15 to 20 minutes. Drain them, pull out the small center leaves, and remove the choke (thistle-like center). Set the artichokes aside while you prepare the stuffing. Preheat the oven to 350°.

DUXELLES. Melt 3 tablespoons butter in a sauté pan. Put in the mushrooms, ham, and tongue, and cook over low heat 4 minutes. Add the onions, 2 teaspoons tomato paste, 1 tablespoon parsley and 1 tablespoon breadcrumbs, and cook 2 minutes.

Spoon the stuffing into the center of each artichoke, and sprinkle the top with the remaining 2 tablespoons breadcrumbs and a few drops of melted butter. Tie a slice of raw bacon around each artichoke. Stand the artichokes in a buttered baking dish. Brush them with the vegetable oil. Put them in the preheated oven, cook 2 minutes, and remove them. Add the wine, chicken stock, sherry, and 1 teaspoon tomato paste to the bottom of the baking dish. Cover the artichokes with buttered wax paper, return them to the oven, and cook 40 minutes. Remove them from the oven, reserve the cooking liquid, and keep them warm.

SAUCE. Melt 1 tablespoon salt butter in a saucepan. Off the heat, add the flour, with salt and cayenne pepper to taste. Stir the mixture until it is smooth. Strain the liquid in which the artichokes were cooked and add it to the saucepan. Stir the sauce over low heat until it comes to a boil. Add the finely chopped garlic and simmer the sauce 2 minutes.

To serve, pour the sauce on the bottom of a hot serving dish. Remove the bacon around each artichoke. Arrange the artichokes on the serving dish. Sprinkle with the remaining parsley. NET: 4 servings.

FONDS D'ARTICHAUTS ARGENTEUIL

Artichoke Bottoms (Hearts) Stuffed with Asparagus Tips

6 large cooked artichoke bottoms (fresh or canned)
2 tablespoons fresh lemon juice
4 tablespoons salt butter
4 tablespoons all-purpose flour
Salt
A few grains cayenne pepper
1 teaspoon Dijon mustard

1 cup milk
½ cup freshly grated Parmesan cheese
⅓ cup heavy cream
2 cups cooked fresh asparagus tips
6 thin slices imported Swiss cheese

Drain and dry the cooked artichoke bottoms on paper towels. Sprinkle them with lemon juice and set aside. Melt the salt butter in a small pan. Off the heat, stir in the flour and season with salt and the cayenne pepper. Stir in the Dijon mustard, milk, and ¼ cup grated cheese. Stir this mixture over low heat until it comes to a boil. Then add the heavy cream. Reserve 6 asparagus tips for garnish, and stir the rest of the asparagus tips into the sauce. Fill the artichoke bottoms with this sauce. Place a thin slice of imported Swiss cheese on each. Brown them under a hot broiler, lay an asparagus tip on each one, and serve immediately. NET: 6 servings.

FONDS D'ARTICHAUTS FARCIS

Artichoke Bottoms (Hearts) Stuffed with Ham and Celery

6 large cooked artichoke bottoms (fresh or canned)
2 tablespoons fresh lemon juice
Salt
Freshly cracked white pepper

6 tablespoons salt butter
½ cup each of finely chopped onion and celery
1 cup finely ground boiled ham or cooked tongue

1 tablespoon chopped fresh
   parsley
2 tablespoons chicken stock
   (page 35)

2 tablespoons dry breadcrumbs
   (page 69)
3 tablespoons freshly grated
   Parmesan cheese

Sprinkle the artichoke bottoms with a little lemon juice, salt, and pepper. Melt 3 tablespoons butter in a sauté pan. Add the onion and celery, and cook 5 minutes without browning. Remove the pan from the heat, and add the ham or tongue and parsley. Season to taste with salt and pepper, moisten with the chicken stock, and mix well. Fill the artichoke bottoms with this mixture, shaping it like a dome with a spoon. Sprinkle them with the breadcrumbs and Parmesan cheese. Melt the rest of the butter and sprinkle it over the tops. Brown the stuffed artichoke bottoms under the broiler, and serve. NET: 6 servings.

Jerusalem artichokes are quite different from globe artichokes. Their taste and consistency is more like a water chestnut, and they look rather like a water chestnut in color but not in shape. They are lovely on the outside, with bright scales. When you peel them, they look just like a water chestnut. Delicious — and topinambour is such a marvelous name.

TOPINAMBOURS ROUXELANE

Jerusalem Artichokes in Brioche

2 pounds Jerusalem artichokes
¼ cup vinegar
2 quarts water
2 tablespoons fresh lemon juice
6 tablespoons salt butter
5 tablespoons all-purpose flour
1 cup sour cream
Salt
Freshly cracked white pepper

¼ cup finely chopped onion
½ cup freshly grated Parmesan
   cheese
8 small (individual) brioches
   (best for this if they are a
   few days old and a little
   dried)
2 tablespoons pure olive oil

Skin the Jerusalem artichokes and set them in the mixed vinegar and water to keep their color. Bring a deep pan of salted water and lemon juice to a boil, plunge the artichokes into it, and cook until they are quite soft. Drain them very well, and rub through a fine strainer. Melt 2 tablespoons butter in a pan. Off the heat, add the flour. Return to low heat and stir until the flour and butter mixture is light brown. Add the artichoke purée and sour cream, and season with salt and pepper. Cook over low heat 5 minutes; then add the chopped onion. Mix in the grated cheese and keep the mixture warm.

   Preheat the oven to 350°. Carefully cut off the tops of the brioches. Scoop out all the inside without damaging the outside crust. Spread the inside with the rest of the butter, and fill it with as much artichoke purée as possible. Cover the brioche with its top, and brush it all over with the olive oil. Prepare each brioche in this fashion. Wrap each one in foil, and bake them 10 to 15 minutes, until warmed through. To serve, spread a bed of the remaining artichoke purée on a hot flat serving dish. Unwrap the little stuffed brioches and place them on the purée. Serve at once, very hot. NET: 8 servings.

ASPERGES MALTAISE

Asparagus with Orange Hollandaise Sauce

24 medium-size spears fresh asparagus (or 6 to 8 spears per serving, depending on size)
2 egg yolks
1 tablespoon dry sherry
1 tablespoon heavy cream

¼ teaspoon salt
A few grains cayenne pepper
8 tablespoons sweet butter
Grated rind of 1 large orange
4 slices white toast, crusts removed

Cut off the tough ends of the asparagus. Scrape off the scales with a sharp little knife. Wash the asparagus well in cold water. Tie the spears into a bunch with fine string, stand it in an asparagus cooker or tall pan, and cook in boiling salted water until the asparagus is barely tender. (Do not overcook; asparagus very quickly loses its bright green color and becomes mushy and stringy.)

SAUCE MALTAISE. Put the egg yolks and sherry in a small bowl and beat well. Add the heavy cream, salt, and the cayenne pepper and beat again. Put the bowl in a shallow pan half filled with hot water over low heat. Beat the yolk mixture steadily until it thickens. Then, continuing to beat, add the sweet butter bit by bit, and the grated orange rind. Thin the sauce with a little cream if it is too thick. (If the sauce is not to be used immediately, cover it with plastic wrap and leave it in the bowl, standing in tepid water.)

To serve, arrange the cooked asparagus spears on the slices of toast. Spoon the sauce over them, and lightly brown them under the broiler just before serving. NET: 4 servings.

TARTE AUX ASPERGES

Asparagus Tart with Hollandaise Sauce

2 pounds asparagus spears
6 tablespoons salt butter
5 tablespoons all-purpose flour
1¾ cups milk or light cream
4 tablespoons freshly grated Parmesan cheese
¼ pound boiled ham, cut in fine shreds
½ pound fresh mushrooms, thinly sliced and lightly sautéed in butter
Salt
Freshly cracked white pepper
2 tablespoons dry breadcrumbs (page 69)

PASTRY
2 cups all-purpose flour
1 teaspoon salt
12 tablespoons salt butter (room temperature)
⅓ cup ice water
2 cups raw rice (to anchor the pastry)

HOLLANDAISE SAUCE
2 egg yolks
Salt
A few grains cayenne pepper
1 tablespoon tarragon vinegar
1 tablespoon heavy cream
8 tablespoons sweet butter

PASTRY. Preheat the oven to 375°. Put the flour and salt in a bowl. Cut the butter into pieces, put it in the flour, and work the flour and butter together with your fingertips until the mixture resembles coarse cornmeal. Add the ice water and gather the dough into a ball. Wrap it in wax paper and leave it in the refrigerator 15 minutes. Have ready a flan ring 10 or 11 inches in diameter, standing on a baking sheet. Roll the pastry dough out on a lightly floured surface. Line the flan ring with the dough, and trim the edges off neatly. Line the pastry shell with a piece of buttered wax paper and hold the paper down with the raw rice. Bake the pastry shell 25 minutes. Remove the rice and wax paper and bake another 5 to 10 minutes. Remove from the oven and cool.

HOLLANDAISE SAUCE. Put the egg yolks, salt, and cayenne pepper in a small bowl and beat well. Add the vinegar, then the heavy cream, and beat well. Put the bowl in a shallow pan half filled with hot water over low heat. Continue to beat the yolk mixture until it is thick. Cut the sweet butter into pieces and add it, bit by bit, to the sauce, beating all the time. (If the sauce is not to be used immediately, cover it with plastic wrap and leave it in the bowl, standing in tepid water.)

Cut off the tough ends of the asparagus and scrape off the scales. Tie the spears in a bundle and cook them upright in a deep pan or asparagus cooker, in boiling salted water, until they are barely tender. Drain immediately, and set aside. Melt the butter in a pan. Off the heat, blend in the flour, then stir in the milk or light cream. Return to low heat and bring the sauce to a boil, stirring constantly. Add 2 tablespoons grated cheese, and the ham and mushrooms. Add salt and pepper to taste. Sprinkle the bottom of the baked pastry shell with the breadcrumbs and 2 tablespoons grated cheese. Next, spread the ham and mushroom mixture over the bottom. Arrange the cooked trimmed asparagus spears on the filling, and spoon the Hollandaise sauce over all. Place the tart under the broiler for a minute or two, until it is nicely browned. (Watch it carefully to prevent overbrowning, since Hollandaise browns very quickly.) Serve immediately. NET: 6 to 8 servings, depending on the rest of the menu.

Artichokes, endive, green beans, and leeks can be prepared in the same manner. Any of these vegetables should be quickly cooked in boiling salted water or a steamer (until soft but still crisp) and cooled. With artichokes, the center leaves and choke are removed and 2 or 3 tablespoons of vinaigrette sauce are put in the center well.

About 24 medium-size spears
   of asparagus

VINAIGRETTE SAUCE
2 teaspoons salt

1 teaspoon freshly cracked
   mixed black and white
   peppercorns
½ teaspoon finely chopped
   garlic

ASPERGES VINAIGRETTE

Warm Asparagus with Cold Vinaigrette Sauce

¼ teaspoon sugar
½ teaspoon dry mustard
1 teaspoon Dijon mustard
⅛ teaspoon cayenne pepper
Dash of Worcestershire sauce
Dash of Tabasco sauce
3 tablespoons tarragon vinegar

10 tablespoons vegetable oil
2 tablespoons heavy cream
1 hard-boiled egg, finely
   chopped
2 teaspoons chopped fresh
   parsley

VINAIGRETTE SAUCE. Put all the sauce ingredients in a large screw-top jar. Close it tightly, and shake until the sauce is well blended. Keep the sauce in the refrigerator.

Cut off the tough ends of the asparagus and scrape off the scales. Tie the spears into a bundle with fine string. Put the bundle in a vegetable steamer or stand it upright in an asparagus cooker, and cook in boiling salted water until the asparagus is just tender. (In a steamer, this will require only about 4 minutes. Do not overcook.) Drain the asparagus and remove the string. Cool, and arrange the spears neatly on individual serving plates. Pour the vinaigrette sauce over the tips only. NET: 4 servings.

BETTERAVES À L'ESTRAGON

Beets with Tarragon

These baby beets are served in a sauce made with puréed beet tops, sour cream, and tarragon.

24 fresh baby beets with green
   tops
4 tablespoons salt butter
Salt
Freshly cracked black pepper
1 teaspoon granulated sugar

2 tablespoons tarragon vinegar
1 tablespoon all-purpose flour
4 tablespoons sour cream
1 tablespoon chopped fresh
   tarragon

Cook the baby beets in boiling salted water until they are soft. Skin them carefully, and leave them whole. Wash the beet tops well, put them in a pan with a little water and salt, and cook until they are wilted. Drain them well, press dry, and rub through a fine strainer.

Melt 2 tablespoons butter in a heavy pan. Add the skinned baby beets with salt, pepper, sugar, and vinegar. Shake over moderate heat until the beets are hot. Add the other 2 tablespoons butter and melt it. Remove the pan from the heat and mix in the flour. Then add the strained beet tops, sour cream, and tarragon. Put the beets in a hot serving dish, and serve. NET: 4 to 6 servings.

PURÉE DE BROCOLI

Broccoli Purée

1 bunch fresh broccoli (about
   1½ pounds)
2 tablespoons lemon juice

2 tablespoons salt butter
3 tablespoons all-purpose flour
2 tablespoons sour cream

Boil the broccoli in salted water with the lemon juice until it is soft.

(Lemon juice helps preserve the green color.) Drain well. Rub the cooked broccoli through a fine strainer to make a plain purée. Melt the butter in a pan. Off the heat, stir in the flour. Return the pan to low heat and stir until the mixture is light brown. Add the strained broccoli and sour cream. Stir over low heat until the purée has a nice thick consistency. Serve as a vegetable accompaniment in a separate serving dish, or on the bottom of an au gratin dish as a bed for the entrée with which it is to be served. NET: About 1 cup purée.

---

1 bunch fresh broccoli (to
    produce about 1 cup cooked
    and strained for a plain purée)
2 tablespoons lemon juice
3 tablespoons salt butter
3 tablespoons all-purpose flour
Salt
A few grains cayenne pepper

¾ cup milk
2 tablespoons freshly grated
    Parmesan cheese
1 teaspoon dry mustard
3 egg yolks
4 egg whites
A few curls of cold sweet butter
    (for garnish)

SOUFFLÉ DE BROCOLI

Broccoli Soufflé with Curls of Sweet Butter

Boil the broccoli in salted water with the lemon juice until it is soft. (The lemon juice helps preserve the green color.) Drain well. Rub the cooked broccoli through a fine strainer. This should produce about 1 cup of strained broccoli. Set it aside.

Preheat the oven to 400°. Butter the inside of a 4-cup (#6) soufflé dish and tie a piece of double wax paper, which has also been brushed with butter, around the outside. The wax paper collar should rise about 3 inches above the top of the dish. Melt the salt butter in a tin-lined copper pan. Off the heat, add the flour, salt, and the cayenne pepper. When this is well blended, stir in the milk. Stir over low heat until the mixture thickens. Add the grated cheese, mustard, egg yolks, and strained broccoli. Stir 2 to 3 minutes over low heat until the mixture is blended well. Beat the egg whites to soft peaks. Fold them into the broccoli mixture, and spoon into the prepared soufflé dish. Place the soufflé dish in a shallow baking pan half-filled with hot water, and bake 30 minutes. When it is done, remove it from the oven and from the water bath. Remove the paper collar. Put a few curls of sweet butter on top. Serve immediately. NET: 4 servings.

---

1 bunch fresh broccoli
2 tablespoons fresh lemon juice
2 tablespoons vegetable oil
4 or 5 medium-size firm ripe
    tomatoes, skinned and sliced
    ½ to ¾ inch thick
2 tablespoons chopped fresh
    marjoram or ½ teaspoon
    dried marjoram with 2 table-

spoons chopped fresh parsley

SAUCE
2 egg yolks
Salt
A few grains cayenne pepper
1 tablespoon tarragon vinegar
1 tablespoon heavy cream
1 teaspoon tomato paste

BROCOLI À LA PROVENÇALE

Broccoli with Sautéed Tomatoes

4 tablespoons frozen sweet
  butter
½ teaspoon meat glaze

1 tablespoon fresh herbs
  (marjoram, parsley, or other)
2 drops fresh lemon juice

Cut off the tough ends and leaves of the broccoli. Boil the trimmed broccoli in salted water with the lemon juice until it is soft. Drain well, set aside, and keep it warm.

SAUCE. Put the egg yolks in a small bowl. Add a little salt and the cayenne pepper, tarragon vinegar, heavy cream, and tomato paste, and beat well with a wire whisk. Place the bowl in a shallow pan half filled with hot water over low heat. Continue to beat the mixture until it thickens. Cut the frozen sweet butter into pieces and add it bit by bit, beating all the while. Last, beat in the meat glaze, herbs, and lemon juice. Cover with plastic wrap and leave it in the bowl, standing in tepid water, until needed.

Heat the vegetable oil in a sauté pan and cook the thick tomato slices over high heat. Sprinkle them with the marjoram or dried marjoram and parsley. Arrange the tomato slices on a hot au gratin dish. Place sprigs of cooked broccoli on top. Pour the sauce over the dish and serve immediately. NET: 4 servings.

BROCOLI BÉARNAISE

Broccoli with Béarnaise Sauce

2 bunches fresh broccoli (about 3 pounds)
2 tablespoons fresh lemon juice

BÉARNAISE SAUCE
3 egg yolks
1 tablespoon tarragon vinegar
2 tablespoons heavy cream
Salt
A few grains cayenne pepper
8 tablespoons frozen sweet

butter
2 tablespoons mixed chopped fresh herbs (such as parsley, tarragon, chives, thyme, basil)
¼ teaspoon very finely chopped garlic
1 teaspoon very finely chopped onion
1 teaspoon very finely chopped green olives
¼ teaspoon meat glaze

Cut off the tough ends of the broccoli and trim off any leaves. Cook the broccoli in boiling salted water with the lemon juice until it is just soft. Drain well, set aside, and keep it warm.

BÉARNAISE SAUCE. Put the egg yolks in a little bowl and mix in the vinegar, heavy cream, a little salt, and the cayenne pepper. Place the bowl in a shallow pan half filled with hot water over low heat. Beat the mixture with a whisk until it thickens. Cut the sweet butter in pieces, and beat them into the mixture bit by bit. Last, mix in the mixed fresh herbs, garlic, onion, olives, and meat glaze.

Arrange the cooked broccoli in a hot serving dish. Spoon the Béarnaise sauce over it, and serve at once. NET: 4 servings.

The English invariably overcook brussels sprouts. But brussels sprouts can be a beautiful vegetable dish. They should be barely cooked, "just" cooked, and they will have enough crunch and stay very bright green. Believe me, they are especially delicious with braised chestnuts.

Casserole of Brussels
Sprouts and Chestnuts

1 pound chestnuts	2 teaspoons potato flour
2 tablespoons salt butter	1 cup chicken stock (page 35)
2 tablespoons dry sherry	1 bay leaf
1 teaspoon meat glaze	1 quart firm brussels sprouts
1 teaspoon tomato paste	2 tablespoons lemon juice

Cover the chestnuts with cold water, bring to a boil, and boil 3 minutes. With a small sharp knife, shell and skin the chestnuts, leaving each one in the water until you are ready to shell it. When all the chestnuts have been shelled, put them in a heavy pan with the butter. Melt the butter in the pan and pour the sherry over the chestnuts. Coat the chestnuts with the liquid, remove them with a slotted spoon, and set them aside. Off the heat, add to the pan the meat glaze, tomato paste, and potato flour. Stir until the mixture is smooth, and pour in the chicken stock. Return the pan to low heat and stir until the sauce comes to a boil. Put the chestnuts in this sauce with the bay leaf. Simmer gently over low heat until the chestnuts are just soft.

While the chestnuts are cooking, clean and trim the brussels sprouts, and cook them until tender in boiling salted water with the lemon juice. Drain them well. Just before serving, mix the cooked brussels sprouts with the chestnuts and sauce. Serve in a casserole. NET: 4 servings.

Sautéed Brussels
Sprouts with Fresh
Chives

1 quart firm fresh brussels sprouts	Salt
1 small onion, sliced	4 tablespoons salt butter
1 bay leaf	Freshly cracked white pepper
2 whole cloves	2 tablespoons chopped fresh chives

Clean and trim the brussels sprouts, discarding the wilted leaves. Soak them 10 to 15 minutes in well-salted lukewarm water. Drain, put them in a pan, and cover them with boiling water. Add the sliced onion, bay leaf, cloves, and 1 teaspoon salt. Simmer the brussels sprouts 10 to 15 minutes, or until barely tender. Drain them well. Melt the butter in a sauté pan. Add the brussels sprouts and sauté them over low heat, shaking the pan frequently, until they are covered with butter and warmed. Sprinkle with a little salt and pepper, if necessary. Sprinkle the chives over them. NET: 4 servings.

CHOU FARCI

Stuffed Cabbage

This cabbage, stuffed with ground meats and green apples, and served with fresh tomato sauce, is an entrée, or main course.

1 large Savoy or green cabbage
Salt
½ pound sliced bacon
12 prunes, pitted
1 cup dry white wine

STUFFING
6 tablespoons salt butter
3 green apples, peeled, cored, and chopped
2 cups finely chopped onion
1 tablespoon finely chopped garlic
1½ pounds ground lean pork
¾ pound ground boiled ham
1 pound ground lean veal
2 tablespoons chopped fresh sweet basil
Salt
Freshly cracked white pepper

½ teaspoon freshly grated nutmeg
2 eggs, beaten
⅓ cup chicken stock (page 35)
⅓ cup milk
1 cup coarse dry white bread-crumbs (page 69)

FRESH TOMATO SAUCE
3 tablespoons salt butter
2 large, very ripe tomatoes, skinned and coarsely chopped
½ teaspoon finely chopped garlic
2 tablespoons tomato paste
2 tablespoons all-purpose flour
1½ cups chicken stock
Salt
Freshly cracked white pepper

Trim the damaged or wilted leaves from the cabbage. Put it in a large kettle and completely cover it with cold water. Add 2 tablespoons salt. Bring to a boil slowly. Remove from the heat immediately and allow the cabbage to cool about 30 minutes in the cooking liquid. Carefully remove the cabbage from the pot, and just as carefully loosen (but do not detach) the leaves, all the way down to the heart. (The cabbage heart should be no larger than a small orange.) The whole cabbage should still be intact. Set it aside while you prepare the stuffing.

STUFFING. Melt the butter in a pan. When it is foaming, add the apples, onion, and garlic. Cook until they just begin to brown. Then add the pork, ham, veal, and sweet basil. Blend this mixture well and season it with salt, pepper, and nutmeg. Mix in the beaten eggs and chicken stock. In a separate little pan, scald the milk, and pour it over the breadcrumbs, then mix the soaked breadcrumbs into the stuffing. Adjust the seasoning with salt and pepper.

Preheat the oven to 350°. Put a little of the stuffing on each cabbage leaf, starting from the center and spreading it up to the edge of the leaf. Then gently push the whole cabbage into shape again and cover it with slices of bacon. Carefully and securely tie the cabbage with fine string. Place it in a heavy casserole. Place the prunes around the edge of the cabbage in the pan. Pour the wine over it. Cover the pan and cook the cabbage in the oven 2½ to 3 hours.

FRESH TOMATO SAUCE. Heat 2 tablespoons butter in a saucepan. Add the tomatoes and garlic. Cook over low heat 4 minutes. Off the heat, stir in the tomato paste and flour. Add the chicken stock. Season with salt and pepper. Return to low heat, and stir until the sauce comes to a boil. Simmer gently 5 minutes. Rub the sauce through a fine strainer and finish off by stirring in 1 tablespoon butter.

Remove the cabbage from the oven when it is cooked. Carefully remove the string. Place the stuffed cabbage on a hot serving dish and surround it with the cooked prunes. To serve, cut in wedges. Serve the fresh tomato sauce separately. NET: 6 to 8 servings.

---

1 firm green or white cabbage, cut in quarters or eighths, according to size
2 tablespoons salt butter
Salt
Freshly cracked white pepper
¼ cup dry white wine
½ cup chicken stock (page 35) or water
2 tablespoons heavy cream
¼ cup freshly grated Parmesan cheese

SALPICON
½ pound ripe tomatoes, skinned and quartered
4 tablespoons salt butter
2 small onions, thinly sliced
½ teaspoon finely chopped garlic
1 teaspoon tomato paste
1 teaspoon potato flour
1 tablespoon mixed chopped fresh herbs (such as parsley, chives, basil)
Salt
Freshly cracked white pepper

CHOU DE LORRAINE

Braised Cabbage with Salpicon of Tomatoes, Onions, and Herbs

Cut the cabbage into quarters or eighths, according to the size. Boil in salted water 5 to 10 minutes. Drain well. Melt the butter in a heavy pan with a lid. Lay the wedges of cabbage carefully in this pan. Add a little salt, pepper, and the wine and stock or water. Cover, and simmer over low heat until the cabbage is tender but firm.

SALPICON. First, remove the seeds from the tomato quarters and set the pulp aside. Rub the seeds through a fine strainer and reserve the juice. Cut the quarters of pulp in half and set them aside. Melt the butter in a pan. Add the onions and garlic, and simmer gently until they are just soft. Off the heat, stir in the tomato paste and potato flour. Add the reserved strained tomato juice, the tomato pulp, and half the mixed herbs. Season with salt and pepper, and simmer gently 2 minutes.

Lay the wedges of cooked cabbage on one half of a hot serving dish. Reduce the wine and stock mixture in which they were cooked by boiling it down to about 3 tablespoons, and add it to the salpicon. Spoon the salpicon on the other half of the dish. Sprinkle the remaining fresh herbs over the cabbage, and spoon the heavy cream over it. Serve the grated cheese in a separate bowl. NET: 4 servings.

DOLMAS DE CHOUX

Cabbage Leaves Stuffed with Meat, Rice and Tomato

1 large green or white cabbage

STUFFING
2 tablespoons pure olive oil
1 tablespoon salt butter
1 medium-size yellow onion,
    finely chopped
1 large firm white mushroom,
    chopped
½ pound ground beef
1 teaspoon tomato paste
2 tablespoons chicken stock
    (page 35) plus a little more
    for baking
1 tablespoon chopped fresh dill
    (or 2 teaspoons dried)
2 hard-boiled eggs, finely
    chopped

½ cup long-grain rice, boiled
    13 minutes in 1 cup salted
    water and drained
1 large ripe tomato, skinned and
    chopped
Salt
Freshly cracked white pepper
A little flour (for dusting)

TOMATO SAUCE
2 tablespoons pure olive oil or
    salt butter
1 tablespoon tomato paste
1 tablespoon all-purpose flour
½ teaspoon finely chopped
    garlic
1½ cups chicken stock (page
    35)

Put the whole cabbage in a large deep pot, cover it with salted water, and slowly bring to a boil. Remove the cabbage, and pour cold water over it to cool it. With a sharp pointed knife, carefully remove the leaves from the core. With scissors, cut off the thick ribbed part at the base of the leaves. Set aside while you prepare the stuffing. (There should be about 8 good leaves, not too small to stuff and roll securely.) Preheat the oven to 350°.

STUFFING. Heat the olive oil and butter in a heavy sauté pan. Add the onion and cook until it is translucent. Add the mushroom and ground beef. Mix, and cook over moderate heat 6 to 7 minutes. Then add the tomato paste, 2 tablespoons chicken stock, dill, hard-boiled eggs, cooked rice, and tomato. Season with salt and pepper.

Put a generous tablespoonful of this stuffing on each of the 8 (or more) leaves. Fold the leaf over (from the right and from the left). Then roll up the stuffed leaf to form a small "sausage" or roll. Dust the cabbage rolls with a little flour and pack them in a deep heavy pan or casserole. Spoon over a little more stock to moisten the pan, cover the pan with buttered wax paper and the lid, and put the pan in the oven to cook the stuffed cabbage rolls 40 minutes.

TOMATO SAUCE. Heat the olive oil or butter in a saucepan. Off the heat, stir in the tomato paste and flour. Add the garlic and chicken stock. Return the pan to the heat and stir until the sauce comes to a boil. Reduce the heat and simmer gently 10 minutes.

Remove the stuffed cabbage rolls from the oven when they are cooked, and drain them well. Arrange them on a serving dish. Spoon the tomato sauce over them, and serve. NET: 8 servings.

HOT CABBAGE STRUDEL

The strudel may be prepared a few hours ahead of time and warmed in a slow oven when you want to serve it.

Strudel dough (page 729)
¾ cup melted salt butter
2 cups breadcrumbs, lightly
    fried in butter (page 69)

FILLING
2 small firm green or white
    cabbages
10 slices bacon
1 large Bermuda onion, finely
    chopped
1 teaspoon finely chopped
    garlic
Salt
Freshly cracked white pepper
4 hard-boiled eggs, finely
    chopped
2 tablespoons chopped fresh dill
1 cup freshly grated Parmesan
    cheese

Make and stretch the strudel dough according to the instructions in the master strudel recipe (Apfelstrudel, page 729), using only a cup of water unless you need more.

FILLING. Preheat the oven to 375°. Cut the cabbages into very fine shreds, put the shredded cabbage in a pan, cover it with cold salted water, and bring quickly to a boil. Drain the shredded cabbage and dry it well. Cut the bacon into fine shreds and cook in a frypan until it is crisp. Drain, reserving the fat. Put half the bacon fat in large heavy pan and, over low heat, cook the onion and garlic in it a minute or two. Add the blanched shredded cabbage, salt, and pepper. Cover the pan with wax paper and the lid. Put it in the oven and cook the cabbage 30 minutes. When it is done, lightly mix in (with a fork) the hard-boiled eggs, fried bacon, and dill.

Reduce the oven heat to 350°. Sprinkle all over the top of the dough with about ¼ cup melted butter and cover it with the fried breadcrumbs. Spread the shredded cabbage mixture evenly over the top of the breadcrumbs. Sprinkle the surface with another ¼ cup of the melted butter. Carefully roll up the strudel like a jelly roll. Put it on a baking sheet, either bend it (like a horseshoe) or cut it to make it fit on the pan. Brush the top well with more of the melted butter. Sprinkle the top generously with the grated cheese. Bake the strudel 45 minutes. While it is baking, sprinkle it frequently with the rest of the melted butter and grated cheese. Remove from the oven, cut in individual serving sections, and serve hot. NET: 8 or more servings.

This dish is for springtime . . . a casserole of new carrots with sweet butter, sugar, egg yolks, and heavy cream. Very good!

CAROTTES À LA FLAMANDE

Flemish-Style Carrots

1 pound fresh baby carrots
¼ cup cold water
6 tablespoons salt butter
Salt
Pinch of granulated sugar
3 egg yolks
½ cup heavy cream
2 tablespoons melted sweet
    butter
1 tablespoon finely chopped
    fresh parsley
3 drops lemon juice

Scrape the baby carrots (do not pare them), and leave them whole. Put them in a pan, cover with cold water, bring to a boil, and drain.

Generously butter a casserole and put in the carrots. Add ¼ cup cold water and the salt butter, and season with salt and the granulated sugar. Cover the casserole and bring to a boil. Reduce the heat, and continue to cook at a gentle simmer until the carrots are tender (about 25 minutes). Shake the pan every 5 minutes so they do not burn. In a separate little bowl mix the egg yolks with the heavy cream and the cool melted sweet butter. Add the parsley and lemon juice. Carefully stir the yolk mixture into the casserole with a wooden spoon. Serve at once. NET: 4 servings.

CAROTTES À LA POULETTE

Carrots in a Rich
Velouté Sauce

6 large carrots
2 tablespoons lemon juice
2 tablespoons salt butter
3 tablespoons all-purpose flour
Salt
A few grains cayenne pepper
2 cups chicken stock (page 35)

½ cup heavy cream
2 teaspoons sweet butter
2 egg yolks
1 tablespoon chopped fresh
   parsley
1 teaspoon chopped fresh chives
2 tablespoons milk

Pare the carrots, cut them in small thick pieces (olive shapes or chunks), cook them in boiling salted water with the lemon juice until just tender. Drain, and set aside.

POULETTE SAUCE. Melt the salt butter in a saucepan. Off the heat, stir in the flour, salt, and cayenne pepper. When it is blended, pour in the chicken stock. Return to low heat, and stir until the sauce thickens. Stir in the heavy cream. Then stir in the sweet butter bit by bit. In a separate bowl, mix together the egg yolks, parsley, chives, and milk, and off the heat, stir this into the sauce.

Add the carrots and gently reheat, but do not boil. Serve in a small vegetable dish. NET: 4 servings.

CAROTTES NOUVELLES GLACÉES

Glazed Young Carrots

1 pound fresh baby carrots
6 tablespoons salt butter
Salt
Freshly cracked white pepper

⅓ cup honey
1 teaspoon lemon juice
⅓ cup granulated sugar

Scrape the baby carrots (do not pare them), and leave them whole (or, if they are longer than 2 to 3 inches, cut into olive shapes). Put them in a pan and cover with cold water. Bring to a boil, and drain. Melt the butter in a heavy sauté pan. Add the blanched carrots and shake the pan over moderate heat until the carrots begin to get soft. Add salt and pepper, pour the honey over the carrots, and sprinkle them with the lemon juice. Cook over low heat until they are almost cooked but still crunchy. (Shake the pan frequently.) Then sprinkle the granulated sugar over the carrots and shake the pan over high heat until the carrots are beautifully glazed all over. Serve in a small vegetable dish, or as a garnish. NET: 4 servings.

1 pound carrots (preferably
   young)
Salt
Freshly cracked white pepper
Pinch of granulated sugar
¼ cup Vichy water or plain

water
5 tablespoons salt butter
¼ cup finely chopped fresh
   parsley
1 tablespoon lemon juice

CAROTTES VICHY

Carrots Cooked
in Vichy Water

Scrape the carrots, then soak them in ice water 1 hour. Drain, and dry well. Cut the carrots into paper-thin slices. (This is best done with a mandoline.) Put the sliced carrots in a pan, cover with cold water, and slowly bring to a boil. Drain immediately. Generously butter a heavy casserole. Put the blanched carrots in the casserole. Season them with salt, pepper, and granulated sugar. Sprinkle the Vichy (or plain) water over them. Dot them with 4 tablespoons butter, and sprinkle the lemon juice over them. Cover them with wax paper and the lid. Cook very slowly, over low heat, until the carrots are just tender. They should still be crispy, or crunchy. Uncover, and mix in the parsley, a little more sugar, and 1 tablespoon butter. Serve in a small warm vegetable dish. NET: 4 servings.

2 small cauliflowers (or 1 large)
2 tablespoons lemon juice
8 tablespoons sweet butter
4 tablespoons dry breadcrumbs
   (page 69)
1 tablespoon finely chopped
   onion

3 hard-boiled eggs, finely
   chopped
Salt
Freshly cracked white pepper
2 tablespoons chopped fresh
   parsley

CHOU-FLEUR À LA POLONAISE

Cauliflower
with Brown Butter
and Hard-Boiled Egg

Remove the outer leaves from the cauliflowers and trim the core. Put them (whole) in a pan and cover with salted water and the lemon juice. Bring to a boil, and simmer until they are just tender. Carefully drain them.

POLONAISE SAUCE. Melt the sweet butter in a little pan. Add the breadcrumbs and chopped onion, and brown a little. Add the hard-boiled eggs and season with a little salt and pepper. Cook gently 1 minute. Mix in the parsley.

Place the cauliflowers on a hot serving dish and spread the sauce over them. Serve immediately. NET: 4 servings.

Cauliflower makes an excellent mousse.

1 large cauliflower
1 tablespoon lemon juice
4 tablespoons salt butter
4 tablespoons all-purpose flour
Salt
A few grains cayenne pepper

1 cup milk
¼ cup heavy cream
3 eggs, well beaten
A few dry breadcrumbs (page
   69)

MOUSSE DE CHOU-FLEUR, SAUCE MOUSSELINE

Cauliflower Mousse
with Mousseline Sauce

MOUSSELINE SAUCE
1 egg
2 egg yolks
8 tablespoons frozen sweet
    butter

2 tablespoons tarragon vinegar
Salt
A few grains cayenne pepper
¾ cup heavy cream, whipped

Trim off any outside leaves on the cauliflower. Cut the cauliflower into large bouquets and put them with the lemon juice into a pan of boiling salted water. Cook the cauliflower until it is just tender. Drain it thoroughly, chill, put it through a coarse meat chopper.

Preheat the oven to 350°. Melt the salt butter in a medium-size saucepan. Stir in the flour, and season with a little salt and the cayenne pepper. Cook gently 1 minute. Off the heat, add the milk, then stir the sauce over low heat until it comes to a boil. Add the heavy cream, and chill the sauce. When it is chilled, mix it into the ground cauliflower. Add the well-beaten eggs, and taste for seasoning. Generously butter a plain charlotte mold. Dust the inside lightly with a few dry breadcrumbs. Fill the mold with the cauliflower mixture, and cover with buttered wax paper. Stand the mold in a shallow roasting pan half filled with hot water, and put it in the oven to cook about 30 minutes, or until the mousse is just firm to the touch.

MOUSSELINE SAUCE. Put the egg and egg yolks in a small bowl, and stand the bowl in a shallow pan half full of hot water over low heat. Beat the eggs with a rotary beater until they are thick. In a separate little pan, boil the vinegar and add it to the yolk mixture, beating all the time. Cut the sweet butter into pieces, and beat it into the sauce bit by bit. Season to taste with salt and a little cayenne pepper. Fold in the whipped cream.

When the mousse is done, remove it from the oven and let it stand at least 5 minutes before turning it out onto a hot flat serving dish. Serve with the mousseline sauce in a separate bowl. NET: 4 servings.

SOUFFLÉ DE CHOU-FLEUR, SAUCE TOMATE

Cauliflower Soufflé with Fresh Tomato Sauce

¼ cup dry breadcrumbs
    (page 69)
1 cauliflower, about 2 pounds
3 tablespoons salt butter
3 tablespoons all-purpose flour
Salt
A few grains cayenne pepper
1 cup milk
3 egg yolks
¼ teaspoon freshly grated
    nutmeg
5 egg whites

TOPPING
2 tablespoons melted salt butter

1 cup dry breadcrumbs, fried in
    butter (page 69)
2 hard-boiled eggs, finely
    chopped
2 tablespoons finely chopped
    parsley
Salt
A few grains cayenne pepper

FRESH TOMATO SAUCE
3 tablespoons salt butter
2 tablespoons all-purpose flour
2 tablespoons tomato paste
Salt
A few grains cayenne pepper

*1½ cups chicken stock
    (page 35)
½ teaspoon finely chopped*

*garlic
2 tomatoes, skinned, seeded, and
    shredded*

Butter the inside of a #8 soufflé dish. Tie a band of buttered wax paper around the outside of the soufflé dish. The wax paper should rise about 3 inches above the top of the dish. Dust out the inside of the prepared soufflé dish with a few breadcrumbs.

Preheat the oven to 375°. Trim off the outside leaves of the cauliflower and slightly hollow out the core. Cook the cauliflower in a pot of boiling salted water. Drain it, cut it into smaller pieces, and rub it through a coarse strainer. Melt the butter in a saucepan. Off the heat, stir in the flour, salt, and cayenne pepper. Add the milk. Return the pan to low heat, and stir until the mixture comes to a boil. Stir in the egg yolks one by one, and add the nutmeg. Remove the pan from the heat and add the egg mixture to the puréed cauliflower. Beat the egg whites to soft peaks. Carefully fold the beaten egg whites into the cauliflower mixture. Fill the soufflé dish with the cauliflower mixture. Place it in a shallow roasting pan half filled with hot water, and put the whole assembly in the oven to bake 55 minutes.

TOPPING. In a little bowl, mix the melted butter with the fried breadcrumbs, hard-boiled eggs, and parsley. Season with salt and cayenne pepper.

TOMATO SAUCE. Melt 2 tablespoons butter in a pan. Off the heat, stir in the flour, tomato paste, salt, and cayenne pepper. Add the chicken stock, and return the pan to low heat. Stir until the sauce comes to a boil. Stir in the remaining 1 tablespoon of butter bit by bit. Then add the finely chopped garlic and, at the very last, the shredded tomatoes.

Remove the soufflé from the oven when it is baked. Scatter the crumb topping over the top, and remove the wax paper collar. Serve the sauce in a separate bowl. NET: 4 servings.

---

*6 hearts of celery (or 3 bunches
    celery cut in half)
Salt
2 teaspoons lemon juice
2 teaspoons tarragon vinegar
4 large ripe tomatoes, skinned
    and thickly sliced
12 anchovy fillets
4 very thin slices imported
    Swiss cheese
3 tablespoons sweet butter
6 pitted ripe olives*

*DRESSING
1 teaspoon salt
½ teaspoon freshly cracked
    white pepper
1½ teaspoons tarragon vinegar
¼ cup pure olive oil
¼ cup vegetable oil
1 teaspoon finely chopped garlic
1 tablespoon anchovy oil (from
    the anchovy tin)*

CÉLERI PROVENÇALE

*Baked Celery
with Cheese,
Anchovies,
Black Olives,
on Fresh Tomatoes*

Preheat the oven to 375°. Trim off the leafy top section of the celery and the damaged outside stalks. Wash the celery well. Put it in a large pan, cover with cold water, salt, and the lemon juice and tarragon vinegar, and bring to a boil. Simmer very gently until the celery is nearly soft. Drain it very well.

DRESSING. Put all the dressing ingredients in a screw-top jar and shake vigorously.

Arrange the sliced tomatoes on a buttered au gratin dish. Arrange the celery on the tomatoes, and the anchovy fillets on the celery. Spoon the dressing over the dish, and cover with slices of Swiss cheese. Dot with the sweet butter, and bake 15 to 20 minutes. Remove from the oven, scatter the pitted black olives over the top, and serve hot. NET: 6 servings.

CÉLERI BRAISÉ

Braised Celery

Braised celery is a classic vegetable preparation. It makes a perfect companion to almost any poultry, game, or meat dish, and seems to be liked by most people. Unfortunately, it is often overlooked or incorrectly prepared. It should always be gently braised in stock, taking great care not to overcook it, and it should be served with just a little of the thickened stock to moisten. This recipe can also be followed for braised endive, leeks, or fennel.

2 bunches celery
Salt
2 teaspoons tarragon vinegar
4 slices bacon
½ cup mixed sliced onion, carrot, and celery
Freshly cracked white pepper
1 small bay leaf

1¼ cups chicken stock (page 35)
½ teaspoon meat glaze
1 teaspoon potato flour
3 tablespoons water
1 tablespoon chopped fresh parsley

Preheat the oven to 350°. Trim off the leafy top section of the celery and the damaged outside stalks. Keep the rest of the celery whole. Put both prepared celery bunches in a pot, and cover with cold water, salt, and the vinegar. Bring to a boil, and immediately drain the celery. Put 2 slices bacon in a small deep baking dish. Scatter half the mixed onion, carrot, and celery on the bacon. Season with a little salt and pepper. Cut the blanched celery in half lengthwise (or in quarters, if very large) and place the 4 halves on the vegetables. Scatter the rest of the vegetables on the celery, and cover them with the bay leaf and the 2 remaining slices of bacon. Pour the chicken stock over them, and cover the dish with buttered wax paper and the lid. Braise in the oven 1 hour.

After the celery is braised, remove it carefully from the baking dish and arrange it on a small flat vegetable dish. Strain the stock from the baking dish and put it in a saucepan. Off the heat, stir in the meat glaze. Mix the potato flour with the water and stir it into the stock. Correct the seasoning with salt and pepper. Put the saucepan over low heat and stir until the sauce comes to a boil. Allow it to simmer about 4 minutes. Spoon this sauce over the celery, sprinkle with the parsley, and serve. NET: 4 servings.

<table>
<tr><td>

3 large hearts of celery
6 slices bacon
2 small onions, thinly sliced
2 small carrots, thinly sliced
Salt
Freshly cracked black pepper
1 teaspoon meat glaze
Grated rind and juice of 2

</td><td>

large navel oranges
2 teaspoons tarragon vinegar
2 tablespoons salt butter
½ teaspoon potato flour
1 cup chicken stock (page 65)
1 tablespoon chopped fresh
  parsley

</td><td>

*CÉLERI
À L'ORANGE*

Braised Celery
with Orange

</td></tr>
</table>

Preheat the oven to 375°. Remove the outside stalks of the celery and cut off enough of the tops to leave stalks about 4 inches long. Place the trimmed celery hearts in a large saucepan, cover with cold water, and very slowly bring to a boil. Drain, and cut them in half lengthwise. In the bottom of an oblong baking dish arrange a bed of 3 bacon slices, and on the bacon put half the onion and carrot slices. Season with a little salt and pepper, and place the 6 halves of celery on the vegetables. Scatter the remaining vegetables on the celery, and cover with the other 3 bacon slices. Mix together the meat glaze, orange juice, orange rind, and vinegar, and pour the chicken stock over the celery. Cover the baking dish with buttered wax paper, and put it in the oven to braise the celery 45 to 55 minutes, or until it is quite soft.

When the celery has finished cooking, place it in an earthenware serving dish. Strain the stock in which it was braised. Melt the butter in a small saucepan. Off the heat, stir in the potato flour and pour in the strained stock. Stir the sauce over low heat until it comes to a boil. Simmer 3 minutes, then pour it over the celery in the serving dish. Sprinkle with the parsley. Serve at once. NET: 6 servings.

<table>
<tr><td>

This recipe may also be prepared with 1 to 1½ cups canned unsweetened chestnut purée, in which case eliminate the chicken stock and the procedure in the first paragraph.

</td><td>

*PURÉE
DE MARRONS*

Fresh Chestnut Purée

</td></tr>
</table>

2 pounds raw chestnuts
2 cups chicken stock (page 35)
4 tablespoons sweet butter

2 tablespoons sour cream
Salt
Freshly cracked white pepper

To remove the shells and skins in the easiest way, put the chestnuts in a pot, cover with cold water, and bring the water to a boil. Boil 4 minutes and remove from the heat. Leave the chestnuts in the water. With a small sharp knife, remove the outer and inner skins. When all the chestnuts have been shelled and skinned, pour out the water. Return the chestnuts to the pan, cover them with the chicken stock, and simmer very gently until the chestnuts are soft (by this time they should have absorbed all the stock). Rub them through a fine strainer.

Transfer the chestnut purée to a mixer, and beat in the sweet butter bit by bit, and the sour cream. Season to taste with salt and pepper. NET: 4 to 6 servings.

CORN FRITTERS

"Corn fritters" may sound un-French, but fritters are a classic preparation with all manner of fillings. Their French name is "beignets"; if you will, then, here are Beignets de Maïs . . . very delicate, light little corn fritters as a garnish with a simple chicken sauté. This recipe is best if fresh uncooked corn is used: just grate the kernels from the raw ear of corn.

1 egg	butter
1 egg yolk	1½ cups fresh or cooked corn
8 tablespoons all-purpose flour	kernels, well-drained
6 tablespoons milk	A little salt butter for the
Salt	frypan
A few grains cayenne pepper	Sprigs of fresh parsley
2 tablespoons cool melted salt	

Put the egg, egg yolk, flour, and milk in a small deep bowl. Beat them with a small wire whisk until the mixture is quite smooth. Add the salt, cayenne pepper, and cool melted butter. Last, mix in the corn kernels. Heat a large frypan. Test it with a speck of butter. When it sizzles, rub it out with more butter. Put the corn batter in the frypan in tablespoonfuls. Brown each fritter on one side, then turn it to brown the other side. Drain them on paper towels. When all the fritters are fried, arrange them, overlapping, on a hot serving platter and garnish with a bouquet of fresh parsley. NET: 4 servings.

FRESH BAKED CORN

À la Grace and Nicholas Roosevelt

Mr. Nicholas Roosevelt was one of my very best pupils. (He is also the man who started radio station WQXR when he was editor of the New York *Times*.) It was my privilege to stay with the Roosevelts in California whenever I went to Australia. (The last time, there was a white rose tree, with a hummingbird's nest in it, outside my window, and in the nest were baby hummingbirds.) Nicholas also introduced me to sweet lemons. A man of many achievements, to the gastronomic world he is the inventor of garlic soup — an absolutely delicious soup that nobody realizes has garlic in it. The Roosevelts are two of my favorite people and fine cuisiniers. Mr. Roosevelt shares their culinary pleasure in his own book, *Creative Cooking*. During the fresh corn season, they generously permitted me to pass this excellent dish on to other interested students. It couldn't be more delicious. It's simple, as you can see, and awfully good. You can get the "corn grater" at any of those old-fashioned shops in Vermont, and in specialized cooking utensil shops. The alternative is to trim the kernels off the ears with a sharp paring knife, but it is not quite so efficient.

4 cups grated fresh corn kernels	Salt
3/4 cup melted sweet butter (12 tablespoons)	Freshly cracked white pepper

Preheat the oven to 350°. Remove the outer leaves and silk from very fresh ears of corn. Grate the ears carefully with a special corn grater. (It is a good idea to do this into a dish so that none of the precious liquid from the corn is lost.) Mix the melted butter into the corn, leaving a little to sprinkle over the top. Season well with salt and pepper. Butter a #8 soufflé dish or similar baking dish. Fill it with the corn mixture. Sprinkle the top with the remaining melted butter. Bake 25 to 35 minutes, until the top is golden brown and crispy. NET: 4 servings.

---

*MAÏS FRAIS
AU NATUREL*

*Corn on the Cob:
The Best Way to Cook It*

Ideally, the corn should be picked only a few minutes before it is cooked. If this is impossible, try to buy it from a farm stand and rush it to the kettle. Above all, enjoy corn in season. Out-of-season corn obviously must be *days* old, and even frozen corn loses the blush of nature.

Remove the outer leaves and the silks from the ears. Put half the leaves and silk in the bottom of a deep kettle. Sprinkle these well with boiling water. Put the ears of corn on top and cover them with the rest of the leaves and silk. Pour a little more boiling water over them; it is not necessary to cover or fill the pan with water. Cover the kettle with the lid and cook briskly 5 to 6 minutes.

Have ready melted clarified sweet butter (page 56). Remove the corn and insert a pair of holders in each ear. Brush each ear with clarified butter.

Never add sugar or other seasoning to corn, as it has plenty of its own, and all the vitamins are destroyed if this is done.

Cook 1 or 2 ears per person, as desired.

---

*CONCOMBRES À
LA NAPOLITAINE*

*Cucumbers
with Tomatoes*

4 thin cucumbers	3 tablespoons all-purpose flour
3 tablespoons salt butter	1/2 cup chicken stock (page 35) or water
1 finely chopped onion	1 tablespoon chopped fresh mint
1 bunch scallions (about 12), coarsely chopped	4 large ripe tomatoes, skinned, quartered, and seeded
Salt	
Freshly cracked white pepper	

Cut off the tops and bottoms of the cucumbers, then skin and cut them in half lengthwise. Remove the seeds, and cut the cucumber in ½-inch slices. Melt the butter in a heavy casserole. Add the onion, scallions, and the sliced cucumbers. Season with salt and pepper. Cover the casserole with the lid, and simmer over very low heat 7 minutes, stirring occasionally. Remove the pan from the heat and stir in the flour. Add the stock or water and the mint. Cover the pan and simmer again, over very low heat, 15 minutes. At the very last, add the quartered seeded tomatoes, and cook another 1 to 2 minutes to warm them. Serve in the casserole. NET: 4 servings.

CONCOMBRES À LA TOSCANA

Cucumbers with Mushrooms in Rich Cream Sauce

3 thin cucumbers
4 tablespoons salt butter
2 tablespoons all-purpose flour
Salt
A few grains cayenne pepper
1 cup liquid from cooking cucumbers
2 firm white mushrooms, finely sliced
1 egg yolk
¼ cup heavy cream
2 teaspoons chopped fresh mint
2 slices sturdy white bread (crusts removed, toasted, cut in finger-size pieces, and brushed with butter)

Cut off the tops and bottoms of the cucumbers. Peel 2 of them and cut all 3 of them into slices 1 inch thick. Put them in a pan, cover with cold water, and bring to a boil. Drain immediately, and reserve the liquid. Melt 2 tablespoons butter in a heavy casserole. Remove the pan from the heat and stir in the flour, salt, and cayenne pepper. Stir until the mixture is smooth, and pour in 1 cup of the strained cucumber liquid. Return the pan to low heat, and stir until the mixture comes to a boil. Add the mushrooms, blanched cucumbers, and a little more salt and cayenne pepper. Simmer gently, over low heat, until the cucumbers are just soft. In a little bowl, mix the egg yolk with the heavy cream. Remove the cucumber casserole from the heat and stir in the yolk and cream mixture. Add the chopped mint. Serve in the casserole, surrounded by the toast fingers. NET: 4 servings.

AUBERGINES À LA MEUNIÈRE

Eggplant Slices Sautéed in Butter

2 medium-size eggplants
Salt
8 tablespoons salt butter
Juice of 1 lemon
Freshly cracked white pepper
Thin half-slices from 1 whole lemon
A little all-purpose flour (to dust the eggplant)

Skin the eggplants with a potato peeler, and cut off the stems. Cut them lengthwise into ½-inch slices. Sprinkle the slices well with salt, spread them out on a platter, and let stand 20 minutes. Drain the water and salt that forms, dry the slices well on paper towels, and dust them lightly with flour. Heat some of the butter in a sauté pan, and brown the eggplant slices on each side to a golden brown. Do a few at a time, adding more butter as needed. Drain the fried slices on paper towels, and arrange them on a flat serving dish. When all the slices have been browned and arranged on the serving dish, sprinkle with the lemon juice and pepper. Reheat the butter left in the frypan, dribble it over the eggplant in the serving dish. Place half a slice of lemon on each eggplant slice. NET: 4 servings.

Chopped eggplant, sliced mushrooms, and sliced onions are mixed with cheese sauce and served in the eggplant shells.

AUBERGINES À LA BOSTON

Eggplant with Mushrooms and Cheese Sauce

2 medium-size eggplants
Salt
3 tablespoons all-purpose flour, and a little for dusting the eggplants
4 tablespoons vegetable oil
6 tablespoons salt butter
2 medium-size onions, sliced
Freshly cracked white pepper

6 firm white mushrooms, sliced
A few grains cayenne pepper
¾ cup milk
4 tablespoons freshly grated Gruyère and Parmesan cheeses, mixed
3 tablespoons heavy cream
½ teaspoon dry mustard

Cut the eggplants in half lengthwise and make a few cuts in the pulp with a sharp knife. Sprinkle the pulp well with salt and let the eggplants stand 30 minutes. Squeeze the water and salt out of the eggplant halves, and dry them on paper towels. Dust the tops lightly with flour. Heat the vegetable oil in a large frypan. Put the eggplants cut side down in the hot oil. Cover the frypan with a lid and cook slowly 5 minutes. Turn them over and cook slowly for another 5 minutes. Remove the eggplants from the frypan and set them aside. Add 2 tablespoons butter and the onions to the same frypan, and cook slowly until the onions are soft but not brown. Season with a little salt and pepper. Remove the onions and set them aside. Add another tablespoon of butter to the pan and lightly sauté the mushrooms.

Melt 2 tablespoons butter in a saucepan. Off the heat, add the flour, salt, and cayenne pepper. Still off the heat, add the milk. Return to low heat and stir until the mixture boils. Then stir in 2 tablespoons grated cheese, and the heavy cream and mustard. Add the cooked onions and mushrooms. Scoop out the pulp from the fried eggplants. Chop the pulp coarsely on a wooden chopping board, and add it to the onion and mushroom mixture. Carefully fill the eggplant skins with this mixture. Arrange them on a flat baking dish or platter, and sprinkle with the rest of the grated cheese. Melt the last tablespoon of butter and pour it over the tops. Brown the stuffed eggplants under the broiler and serve. NET: 4 servings.

AUBERGINES À L'AUVERNAISE

Sautéed Eggplant Slices with Tomatoes and Mushrooms

This dish should be started a few hours in advance.

4 tablespoons dried mushrooms
(or 4 firm white fresh mushrooms)
3 tablespoons salt butter
1 teaspoon finely chopped garlic
Salt
2 medium-size eggplants
A little all-purpose flour
(for dusting)
8 tablespoons vegetable oil

6 large firm ripe tomatoes,
skinned and thickly sliced
1 teaspoon chopped fresh
tarragon
Freshly cracked white pepper
2 Bermuda onions, cut in thick
(½-inch) rings
Vegetable oil for deep-fryer
1 teaspoon chopped thyme

If using dried mushrooms, soak them for about 3 hours in 1 cup water. When they are well soaked, drain, squeeze them in paper towels. Shred the mushrooms. Heat the butter in a frypan. Add the garlic and a little salt and cook 1 minute. Add the mushrooms, cover with a lid, and cook very slowly 10 minutes. Cut the eggplants in half lengthwise, then cut the halves in ¼-inch slices. Arrange the slices on a flat platter, sprinkle well with salt, and let them stand 20 minutes. Drain off the water and salt, and dry the slices on paper towels.

Preheat the oven to 375°. Dust the eggplant slices lightly in flour. Heat 8 tablespoons vegetable oil in the frypan and fry a few of the eggplant slices until golden brown on both sides. Remove them from the pan immediately. Fry all the slices in this manner, and set them aside. Fry the sliced tomatoes a minute or two in the same oil. Sprinkle the tarragon over them as they cook. Season with a little salt and pepper. Arrange layers of eggplant slices, tomatoes, and mushrooms on an au gratin dish or a shallow ovenproof serving dish, and bake 6 minutes. Heat the vegetable oil in the deep-fryer to 375°. Dust the onion rings lightly with flour and deep-fry them until golden brown and crisp. Drain well on paper towels.

Remove the eggplant dish from the oven when it is cooked. Arrange the onion rings on top, sprinkle with the thyme, and serve piping hot. NET: 4 to 6 servings.

AUBERGINES À LA PROVENÇALE

Eggplant Stuffed with Eggplant, Tomato, and Onion

2 medium-size eggplants
Salt
4 tablespoons vegetable oil
2 tablespoons salt butter
4 medium-size onions, sliced
4 large ripe tomatoes, skinned
and coarsely chopped
Freshly cracked white pepper

¼ cup freshly grated Parmesan
cheese
2 tablespoons dry breadcrumbs
(page 69)
6 anchovy fillets
A little melted salt butter
2 tablespoons chopped mixed
fresh herbs

Cut the eggplants in half lengthwise and make a few cuts in the pulp (meat) with a sharp knife. Sprinkle the cut surfaces of the eggplants well with salt and let stand 30 minutes. Squeeze out the water and salt, and dry them on paper towels. Heat the vegetable oil in a frypan. Place the eggplant halves cut side down in the hot oil, cover with the lid, and cook 10 minutes. Turn them over skin side down, cover the pan, and cook another 10 minutes. Add more vegetable oil if necessary. When they are cooked, scoop out the pulp and chop it coarsely on a chopping board. Reserve the eggplant skins. Melt the butter in a sauté pan. Add the onions, and cook over low heat until they are soft but not brown. Add the tomatoes and eggplant pulp. Cover with the lid, and cook over very low heat 5 minutes. Season with salt and white pepper.

Carefully fill the eggplant skins with the eggplant and tomato mixture. Sprinkle the tops with the grated cheese and breadcrumbs. Cut the anchovy fillets into thin strips and arrange them like a lattice on the top of each stuffed eggplant. Dot the tops with a little melted butter. Place the stuffed eggplants on a flat ovenproof serving dish, brown them well under the broiler, and sprinkle with chopped fresh herbs. NET: 4 servings.

This recipe should be started a few hours in advance of serving.

AUBERGINES À LA BORDELAISE

Sautéed Eggplant Slices with Tomatoes, Mushrooms, and Shallots

2 or 3 medium-size eggplants
Salt
About ½ cup pure olive oil
1 ounce dried mushrooms,
   soaked in ½ cup water at
   least 2 hours
½ cup finely chopped shallots
   or baby white onions
2 teaspoons finely chopped
   garlic

1 tablespoon Dijon mustard
Freshly cracked black pepper
½ cup chopped fresh Hamburg
   or Italian parsley
6 medium-size firm ripe
   tomatoes, skinned and cut in
   3 slices each
¼ cup melted salt butter
1 cup dry breadcrumbs, fried
   in a little butter (page 69)

Peel the eggplants, and cut off the stems. Cut them into slices a little less than half an inch thick. Spread the slices on a platter, sprinkle well with salt, and let stand 30 minutes. Rinse the slices under cool water and dry them well on paper towels.

Preheat the oven to 400°. Heat a little of the olive oil in a shallow heavy frypan. Fry the eggplant slices a few at a time until golden brown on each side. Remove from the frypan, arrange on a hot flat ovenproof serving dish, and keep them warm. Drain the mushrooms, chop, and cook them in olive oil in the same frypan. Then add the shallots, garlic, mustard, salt, and black pepper. Cook this mixture over low heat 5 to 6 minutes. Then add the parsley.

Arrange the uncooked tomato slices on the eggplant slices. Add the melted butter to the shallot mixture in the frypan, warm it a little, and spoon it over the tomatoes. Sprinkle the breadcrumbs over the top. Bake 10 minutes, and serve hot. NET: 4 to 6 servings.

AUBERGINES À L'ITALIENNE

Eggplant Stuffed with Ham and Vegetables

With the diced ham, this stuffed eggplant can be a main course for a luncheon or supper. Or it is nice to make with baby-size eggplants for a first course, in which case use 3 or 4 eggplants, depending on size.

2 medium-size eggplants
Salt
About 6 tablespoons vegetable oil
3 tablespoons salt butter plus a little melted butter
2 medium-size onions, finely chopped
1 carrot, finely chopped
12 fresh green beans, finely chopped
Freshly cracked white pepper
1 cup finely chopped firm white

mushrooms
1 teaspoon tomato paste
12 tablespoons diced boiled ham (about ¾ cup)
3 tablespoons dry breadcrumbs (page 69)
3 large ripe tomatoes, skinned and coarsely chopped
4 tablespoons freshly grated Parmesan cheese
2 tablespoons chopped fresh chives or parsley

Cut the eggplants in half lengthwise and make a few cuts in the pulp with a sharp knife. Sprinkle the cut surfaces of the eggplants well with salt, and let stand 30 minutes. Squeeze out the water and salt, and dry them on paper towels. Heat the vegetable oil in a sauté pan. Put in the eggplant halves cut side down, cover, and cook 10 minutes over low heat. Turn the halves over skin side down, cover, and cook another 10 minutes. Remove them from the pan, scoop most of the pulp out (being careful not to break the skins), and chop the pulp fine on a chopping board. Reserve the skins. Melt 3 tablespoons butter in a heavy pan. Add the onions, carrot, and green beans. Season with a little salt and pepper. Cook over very low heat until the vegetables are quite soft. Add the mushrooms and cook 3 minutes. Then stir in the tomato paste, ham, breadcrumbs, and a little extra salt and pepper. Cover the pan with the lid and cook slowly 5 minutes.

Add the tomatoes and eggplant pulp to the mixture in the pan and mix well. Fill the eggplant skins with this mixture, sprinkle the tops with the grated cheese and a little melted butter, arrange on a flat ovenproof serving dish, and brown under the broiler. Sprinkle with chopped fresh chives or parsley, and serve. NET: 4 servings.

AUBERGINES À LA PIÉMONTAISE

Eggplant Stuffed with Tomato, Rice and Red Pepper

3 medium-size eggplants
Salt
⅓ cup pure olive oil
8 tablespoons salt butter
½ cup finely chopped onion
½ teaspoon finely chopped garlic

½ cup long-grain rice
4 large ripe tomatoes, skinned and cut into eighths
1 cup chicken stock (page 35)
Freshly cracked white pepper
1 sweet red pepper, seeded and cut into thin strips

6 tablespoons freshly grated
imported Swiss cheese

1 tablespoon chopped fresh
parsley

Skin the eggplants with a potato peeler, and cut off the stems. Cut them in half lengthwise, and carefully scoop out the center, leaving a ½-inch thick shell of eggplant. Spread the scooped-out pulp on a platter, and sprinkle it and the shells with salt. Let stand 15 minutes, then drain the salt and water from the eggplant and dry well on paper towels.

Preheat the oven to 350°. Heat the olive oil in a large sauté pan and fry the eggplant shells until they are nearly cooked but still firm. Remove, and arrange them in a baking dish. Heat butter in a heavy casserole. Put in the onion and garlic, and cook over low heat 2 minutes. Dice the raw eggplant pulp and add it to the casserole. Cook another 2 minutes. Add the rice and chicken stock. Stir the mixture over low heat until it comes to a boil. Add the tomatoes. Season with salt and pepper. Cover the casserole, and bake it 30 minutes.

Remove the casserole from the oven, add the sweet red pepper, season to taste, and fill the eggplant shells with this mixture. Sprinkle them with the Swiss cheese. Melt the rest of the butter and dribble it over them. Brown them under a hot broiler, sprinkle with the chopped fresh parsley, and serve. NET: 6 servings.

---

8 Belgian endive
2 teaspoons vinegar
¼ pound sliced bacon
½ yellow onion, sliced
1 stalk celery, sliced
1 small carrot, sliced
1 teaspoon meat glaze
1 cup chicken stock (page 35)

1 small bay leaf
2 teaspoons chopped fresh
parsley
½ teaspoon potato flour
2 tablespoons cold water
Salt
Freshly cracked black pepper

ENDIVES BRAISÉES

Braised Belgian Endive

Preheat the oven to 350°. Remove the dry outside leaves and wash the endive well. Fill a pan three-quarters full of water, add the vinegar, bring to a boil, and plunge the endive into it. Leave them 2 to 3 minutes, and drain. Line a deep baking dish with two-thirds of the bacon. Scatter half the sliced onion, celery, and carrot on the bacon. Place the blanched endive on the vegetables, and cover with the rest of the bacon. Mix the meat glaze with the chicken stock, pour it over the dish, and place the bay leaf on top. Cover the dish with the lid, and braise in the oven 1 hour.

When the endive are cooked, arrange them on a flat vegetable dish. Strain the braising liquid and put it in a small saucepan. Mix the potato flour with the water, and stir this into the braising liquid. Adjust the seasoning with salt and pepper. Bring the liquid to a boil. Spoon it over the endive. Sprinkle with the chopped parsley, and serve. NET: 4 servings.

ENDIVES FLAMANDES

Endive Braised in Sweet Butter, with Fresh Lemon and Lime

8 Belgian endive
1 tablespoon tarragon vinegar
½ cup melted sweet butter
Juice of half a lemon
Juice of half a lime
Salt
Freshly cracked black pepper

2 teaspoons granulated sugar
1 cup chicken stock (page 35)
1 teaspoon meat glaze
4 slices bacon
1 tablespoon chopped fresh
   parsley

Preheat the oven to 375°. Wash the endive very well and place in a deep heavy pan. Cover with cold water, add the vinegar, bring slowly to a boil, and simmer 15 minutes. Drain, and dry the endive thoroughly on paper towels. Arrange them on a buttered baking dish and set aside. Melt the sweet butter in a pan and mix in the juices. Season well with salt and pepper, and add the sugar. Add the chicken stock and meat glaze. Warm this a little over low heat. Cover the endives with the bacon and pour the stock and butter mixture over them. Place them uncovered in the oven and bake 1 hour.

When the endive are done, remove the bacon, dot the dish with a little more sweet butter, and brown under a hot broiler. Sprinkle with the parsley, and serve. NET: 4 servings.

FENOUIL À LA MOUTARDE

Braised Fennel in Mustard Sauce

Fennel is frequently available in supermarkets, and especially in Italian markets. In Italian it is called "finocchio," and is a favorite in that cuisine. Fennel resembles a bunch of celery, except that its base is ballooned, or bulbous. It has a distinct flavor and aroma of anise. The green tops are used both in fresh and dried form as seasoning, and the stems and base (like celery) are eaten as a vegetable.

2 bunches fennel, braised (see
   method for Braised Celery,
   page 588)
Strained braising liquid
Chicken stock (page 35) or
   water
1 tablespoon salt butter
1 tablespoon all-purpose flour

1 tablespoon dry mustard
Salt
Freshly cracked white pepper
1 teaspoon chopped fresh dill
1 tablespoon heavy cream
¼ cup freshly grated Parmesan
   cheese

When the fennel is braised, remove it from the braising pan and place it on a shallow serving dish. Strain the stock and add enough chicken stock or water to make 1 cup.

MUSTARD SAUCE. Melt the butter in a saucepan. Off the heat, stir in the flour, mustard, salt, and pepper. Pour in the cup of stock. Stir over low heat until the sauce comes to a boil. Add the dill and heavy cream.

Spoon the sauce over the fennel in the serving dish. Sprinkle it with the grated cheese and brown under a hot broiler. NET: 4 servings.

Flageolets are a favorite garnish with roast lamb. If you are cooking dried flageolets (for this recipe or to serve otherwise), see the instructions at the end of this recipe and start a day in advance of serving.

2 large shallots, finely chopped
Half a small white onion, finely chopped
1/4 teaspoon finely chopped garlic
4 tablespoons salt butter
1/4 cup whole salted almonds
1/4 cup sliced water chestnuts
Salt

Freshly cracked white pepper
1/4 teaspoon ground ginger
1/4 teaspoon ground cardamom seed
4 cups cooked or canned flageolets (to cook, see below)
1/2 bunch fresh scallions, finely sliced

Melt 2 tablespoons butter in a deep heavy pan over low heat. Add the shallots, onion, and garlic. Cook very slowly until the mixture is soft but not brown. Add the almonds and water chestnuts, then another 2 tablespoons butter. Season with salt and pepper. Add the ginger, cardamom seed, and 4 cups cooked flageolets. Heat the mixture very gently, over low heat. Stir once or twice. Just before serving, add the scallions (they should be barely cooked, still crispy). NET: 4 servings.

TO COOK DRIED FLAGEOLETS. Put 2 cups dried beans in a bowl and wash them very well. Cover with cold water, add half a lemon cut in quarters, and soak the beans overnight. Change the water once or twice during the process. Next day, preheat the oven to 300°. Drain the beans and rinse them in clear water. Put them in a pan and cover with chicken stock. Add a split pig's foot, a bay leaf tied with several sprigs of parsley, salt, and a few peppercorns. Cook very gently in the oven until the beans are soft, about 2½ hours. Turn them carefully, once in a while, with a wooden spoon. When they are cooked, remove all the meat from the pig's foot, dice it, and put it back in the beans. Serve as is, or continue with the recipe above. NET: 4 cups.

1 pound young fresh green beans
1 teaspoon lemon juice
4 tablespoons salt butter

Salt
Freshly cracked black pepper
1/4 cup slivered blanched almonds

Top and tail the green beans and cut them lengthwise into thin slivers (French-cut). Put them in a heavy pan, cover with cold water, and bring to a boil. Boil 2 minutes and drain the beans (but not too dry). Melt 2 tablespoons butter in the same pan. Return the beans to the pan with the lemon juice, salt, and a little pepper. Cover them with buttered wax paper. Cover the pan tightly with the lid. Put it over low heat and cook 10 to 15 minutes, shaking it occasionally. Melt 2 tablespoons butter in a little pan. Add the slivered almonds, and brown the almonds and butter over low heat. Arrange the cooked beans on a flat warm vegetable dish. Spoon the almonds and butter over them. Brown under a hot broiler 1½ minutes. NET: 4 servings.

PURÉE DE HARICOTS VERTS ET PETITS POIS

Purée of Green Beans and Green Peas

Adding green peas gives the right consistency — green beans by themselves are too watery for a true purée.

3 pounds young green beans
2 cups shelled peas, fresh or
    frozen
6 tablespoons salt butter

½ cup finely chopped onion
¼ cup sour cream
Salt
Freshly cracked white pepper

Top and tail the green beans and cut them in half horizontally. Put them in a large pot. Add the shelled fresh peas. (If you are using frozen peas, cook them separately, according to package instructions.) Cover the vegetables in the pot with cold water. Add a little salt and pepper. Cook over moderate heat until the vegetables are soft but still a little crunchy. Drain thoroughly. Melt 3 tablespoons butter in a little pan. Add the onion, and cook over low heat until it is soft but not brown. Add it to the beans and peas. Put the cooked vegetables in the electric blender, and blend until you have a smooth purée. (Or you can rub them through a fine strainer.) Return the purée to the pan. Mix in the rest of the butter (not melted) and the sour cream. Reheat gently if necessary. Serve in a small warm vegetable dish. NET: 2 cups purée.

POIREAUX BRUXELLOISES

Leeks with Ham

Leeks, of the onion family but not so strong, are a favorite flavoring in the classic stockpot. Usually only the white to light yellow-green part is used in cooking; the darker green top is discarded or used in salads. Leeks are difficult to clean, so even though you clean them thoroughly before blanching, check also after they have been blanched and drained, and remove any traces of grit by rinsing them in water. Leeks ought to be better known and used more — not only in Vichyssoise or Potage Bonne Femme, but also in recipes like this, or served cold with a vinaigrette dressing. Perhaps if more good cooks demand them, they will appear in more of our markets. In this recipe, the poached leeks are wrapped in ham, spread with Dijon mustard, and braised.

8 fresh fat leeks
2 tablespoons tarragon vinegar
8 thin slices boiled ham
2 teaspoons Dijon mustard
¼ cup freshly grated Parmesan
    cheese

2 tablespoons melted salt butter

SAUCE
2 tablespoons salt butter
2 tablespoons all-purpose flour
Salt

1½ cups chicken stock (page 35)   *A few grains cayenne pepper*
4 tablespoons heavy cream

Preheat the oven to 375°. Cut off the green tops of the leeks, trim off any damaged skin, and wash them very well. Be certain that all sand between the layers is removed. Then put the leeks in a pan, cover with cold water, and add the vinegar (vinegar in the water helps keep the flavor and whiteness of leeks). Bring to a boil, and simmer until the leeks are just tender but still firm. Drain, plunge them into ice water, drain again, and dry them on paper towels. Spread each slice of ham with a little Dijon mustard, lay a leek on it, and wrap the leek in the ham. Arrange them down a buttered baking dish.

SAUCE. Melt the butter in a saucepan. Off the heat, stir in the flour and season with salt and cayenne pepper. Add the chicken stock and stir the sauce over low heat until it comes to a boil. Add the heavy cream and simmer gently 5 minutes.

Cover the leeks with this sauce, and sprinkle the top with the grated cheese and melted butter. Bake 15 to 20 minutes, until the top is golden brown. NET: 4 servings.

This is one of the most delicious ways to eat lettuce. It is a favorite on French menus.

LAITUES BRAISÉES AU JUS

Braised Lettuce in Stock

4 medium-size heads Boston lettuce (or 8 heads Bibb)   *¼ teaspoon meat glaze*
2 slices raw bacon   *Salt*
1 small onion, finely chopped   *Freshly cracked white pepper*
1 small carrot, finely chopped   *3 tablespoons salt butter*
¾ cup chicken stock (page 35)   *2 tablespoons chopped fresh parsley*

Preheat the oven to 350°. Remove the damaged leaves of the lettuce and wash the heads very well. Be certain that all sand is removed from the inside leaves. Place the heads in a pan, cover with cold water, and bring to a boil. Remove them immediately, plunge them into ice water, and dry on paper towels. Cut the heads in half if they are Boston lettuce; leave whole if Bibb. Butter a baking dish and place the bacon in it. Sprinkle the onion and carrot over it. Fold under the tops of the lettuces neatly (so that they look neat and trim), and place them on the bacon and vegetables. Mix the meat glaze with the chicken stock and pour it over them. Season with salt and pepper. Cover with buttered wax paper and the lid, and braise in the oven 45 minutes.

To serve, arrange the braised lettuce neatly on a hot serving dish. Strain the braising liquid and put it into a saucepan. Reduce the liquid a little by boiling it down. With a whisk, gradually beat in the butter. Spoon this over the lettuce, and sprinkle with the parsley. NET: 4 servings.

HARICOTS DE LIMA À LA POULETTE

Lima Beans in Rich Velouté Sauce

Lima beans are strictly American and very good. They are not raised in France. There this dish is made with broad white beans (les fèves), which are not available in America except occasionally in Italian grocery shops. Broad beans are marvelous. When you open them up, the inside is lined with what looks like soft white cotton, in which the beans rest; they look like rather pudgy hearts. They are the most delicious bean that exists.

3 pounds young lima beans	¾ cup chicken stock (page 35)
Salt	2 tablespoons heavy cream
2 tablespoons salt butter	1 egg yolk
1 tablespoon all-purpose flour	1 tablespoon finely chopped
Freshly cracked white pepper	fresh parsley
1 teaspoon lemon juice	

Shell the beans. Put them in a pan, cover with cold water and a little salt, bring to a boil, and simmer about 15 minutes, or until they are just soft. Drain, and return them to the pan. Melt the butter in a saucepan. Off the heat, stir in the flour and season with salt, pepper, and the lemon juice. Add the chicken stock, return the pan to low heat, and bring the sauce to a boil. In a separate little bowl, mix the heavy cream with the egg yolk and parsley. Pour a little of the hot sauce into the yolk mixture, stirring all the while. Then stir the yolk and sauce mixture into the sauce in the pan. Adjust the seasoning, and pour the sauce over the cooked beans. Gently reheat the beans in the sauce, but do not let it boil. Serve in a warm vegetable dish. NET: 6 servings.

CHAMPIGNONS AU XÉRÈS

Mushrooms with Sherry

Always use firm white fresh mushrooms. Do not hesitate to select them from the greengrocer's assortment with that standard of quality. Those with dried, spotted brown skins have lost their mushroom bouquet, and it is, indeed, one of the loveliest when truly fresh.

Mushrooms should not be peeled. Wash them in a little lemon juice and cool water, then dry with paper towels. To use whole or in halves or quarters, trim the stem even with the bottom of the cap, then cut into sections. (The bits of stem can go into the next stockpot or sauce.) To "chop" a mushroom, trim the stem even with the cap, set the cap on its bottom on the chopping board, cut it in slices — thin or thick as required for fine or coarse dice — then give it a quarter turn and slice it crosswise to make the dice. Actual chopping would simply pound a mushroom and leave all the delectable juices on the chopping board.

These mushrooms with sherry are a good touch with any chicken dish.

1 pound firm white mushrooms	Salt
3 teaspoons lemon juice	2 tablespoons finely chopped
4 tablespoons salt butter	fresh dill

Freshly cracked white pepper   2 to 3 tablespoons dry sherry

Wash the mushrooms in cold water and 2 teaspoons lemon juice. Drain them, trim off the stems even with the caps, and cut the caps into thin slices. Melt the butter in a sauté pan. When it is foaming but not brown add the mushrooms and 1 teaspoon lemon juice, season with salt and pepper, and cook briskly 2 to 3 minutes over moderate heat. Stir in the sherry and dill, toss lightly, and serve as a garnish or in a separate little heated vegetable dish. NET: 4 servings.

These interesting herbed mushrooms are served in a toasted bread shell (croustade).

CHAMPIGNONS EN CROÛTE

Mushrooms in a Crust (Croustade)

1 loaf sturdy white bread
   (whole, not sliced)
3 teaspoons fresh lemon juice
Vegetable oil for deep-fryer
1 cup finely chopped mixed
   fresh herbs (parsley, tarragon, chives, thyme, etc.)

2 pounds firm white fresh
   mushrooms
12 tablespoons salt butter
Salt
Freshly cracked white pepper
1/4 cup finely chopped shallots

Carefully trim the crust from all six sides of the loaf of bread. Gently hollow out the inside like an open box, leaving a 1/4-inch shell. Take great care that it does not break. Half fill a large frypan with vegetable oil, and heat it to 350°. Carefully deep-fry the bread shell in the hot fat a side at a time, until it is golden brown all over. (Turn it carefully to fry the sides.) Remove the croustade from the hot oil and drain it well on paper towels. Cover it all over with the chopped fresh herbs (outside and inside), and keep it warm.

Wash the mushrooms in cold water and 2 teaspoons lemon juice. Drain, and trim the stems even with the caps (save the stems for a stockpot). Set aside 4 whole mushroom caps for garnish, and flute them. Cut all the remaining caps in half. Melt 6 tablespoons butter in a sauté pan. When it is foaming, add the mushrooms (including the whole fluted caps), 1 teaspoon lemon juice, salt, and pepper. Shake the mushrooms briskly over moderate heat 2 to 3 minutes. Then stir in the remaining 6 tablespoons butter bit by bit. Adjust the seasoning, remove the 4 whole mushrooms, and add the finely chopped shallots. Place the croustade on a hot napkin on a serving platter, fill it with the mushrooms, and garnish with the whole mushrooms. To serve, spoon out the mushrooms on each plate, then cut a piece of the croustade for each serving. NET: 4 servings.

CHAMPIGNONS AU BEURRE

Mushrooms Sautéed in Butter

1 1/2 pounds firm white fresh
   mushrooms
2 teaspoons fresh lemon juice

8 tablespoons salt butter
Salt
Freshly cracked white pepper

2 tablespoons chopped fresh herbs (parsley, dill, mint,	thyme, or a mixture of any two)

Wash the mushrooms in cold water and 1 teaspoon lemon juice. Dry them on paper towels. Cut the stems even with the caps (save the stems for a stockpot). Cut the mushroom caps into thick slices or quarters. Heat the butter in a heavy sauté pan until it is foaming but not brown. Put the mushrooms in the pan and coat them with the butter. Add 1 teaspoon lemon juice, salt, and pepper. Sauté the mushrooms over moderate heat 4 to 5 minutes. Mix in the herbs. Serve in a small warm vegetable dish. NET: 4 servings.

SOUFFLÉ DE CHAMPIGNONS

Mushroom Soufflé

½ pound firm white mushrooms, washed	Salt
5 tablespoons freshly grated Parmesan cheese	A few grains cayenne pepper
	1 cup light cream
4 tablespoons salt butter	4 egg yolks
1 teaspoon fresh lemon juice	¼ cup sour cream
3 tablespoons all-purpose flour	6 egg whites

Preheat the oven to 375°. Prepare a #7 (1½-quart) soufflé dish as described on page 787, using half the grated Parmesan cheese for dusting the inside of the buttered dish. Put the mushrooms through a coarse meat chopper, or chop them very fine. Heat 1 tablespoon butter in a sauté pan. Add the mushrooms with the lemon juice. Sauté briskly over high heat 2 to 3 minutes. Season with salt and cayenne pepper. Set aside.

Heat the remaining 3 tablespoons butter in a saucepan until foaming but not brown. Off the heat, stir in the flour, season with salt and the cayenne pepper, and mix in the light cream. Return the mixture to low heat and stir until it comes to a boil. Off the heat, beat in, one at a time, the egg yolks. Add the cooked mushrooms and sour cream. Season to taste. Mix in 1 tablespoon grated cheese. Beat the egg whites to soft peaks. Pour all the mushroom mixture on top and fold it into the egg whites very carefully with a rubber scraper.

Fill the prepared soufflé dish with the mixture. Sprinkle the remaining 1½ tablespoons grated cheese on top. Stand the filled soufflé dish in a shallow roasting pan half filled with hot water, and bake 1 hour. As soon as it is properly baked, remove it from the oven, carefully remove the paper collar, and place the soufflé on a serving tray. Serve at once. NET: 4 servings.

OIGNONS FARCIS

Onions Stuffed with Spinach, in Mushroom Sauce and Gruyère Cheese, Gratiné

6 small Bermuda onions	¼ cup freshly grated Gruyère cheese
Salt	
Freshly cracked white pepper	¼ cup freshly grated Parmesan cheese
About 2 tablespoons salt butter	

¼ cup dry breadcrumbs (page
   69)
1 tablespoon chopped fresh
   parsley

STUFFING
¼ cup water
A little lemon juice
1 pound fresh spinach or
   1 package frozen
¼ pound sorrel or an additional
   ¼ pound fresh spinach
   sprinkled with lemon juice
4 tablespoons salt butter
4 tablespoons all-purpose flour

¼ cup sour cream
Salt
Freshly cracked white pepper

SAUCE
2 tablespoons salt butter
4 firm white fresh mushrooms,
   coarsely chopped
1 cup heavy cream
Salt
Freshly cracked white pepper
1 egg yolk
1 teaspoon potato flour
1 tablespoon Cognac or good
   brandy

Skin the onions. Put them in a pan, cover with water, bring to a
boil, and drain. Remove the centers, and season the insides with salt,
pepper, and a small piece of butter. Set them aside.

STUFFING. Wash the fresh spinach and sorrel leaves thoroughly.
Put them in a pan with the water and lemon juice, cover, and cook
until they are wilted. Put them through a fine meat chopper. Melt
the butter in a pan. Off the heat, stir in the flour. Return the butter
and flour mixture to low heat, and brown it a little. Add the spinach
and sorrel purée. Mix in the sour cream, salt, and pepper. Cook gently
over low heat 5 minutes.

SAUCE. Melt the butter in a saucepan. Add the mushrooms. Stir in
the heavy cream and season with salt and white pepper. Over moderate heat, bring the mixture to a boil. In a separate little bowl, mix
the egg yolk with the potato flour and brandy. Off the heat, pour the
yolk mixture into the saucepan, stirring all the while. Return it to
low heat and stir until the sauce thickens, but do not let it boil.

Carefully fill the onions with the spinach mixture and arrange
them on a flat ovenproof serving dish. Spoon half the sauce over the
onions. Sprinkle with the Gruyère cheese, then spoon over the rest
of the sauce and sprinkle with the Parmesan cheese and breadcrumbs.
Dot the top with butter. Brown under a hot broiler, sprinkle with the
parsley, and serve at once. NET: 6 servings.

3 large Bermuda onions
All-purpose flour
1 egg, beaten
About 1 cup dry white bread-

crumbs (page 69)
Vegetable oil for deep-fryer
Salt

OIGNONS
EN FRITOT

*French-Fried
Onion Rings*

Skin the onions and cut them very evenly into ¼-inch slices. Separate them into rings. (Do not use the very small ones.) Dust each
onion ring separately in flour. Brush it all over with the beaten egg,
taking great care to coat the whole ring, and dip it in breadcrumbs.

Then fry one or two rings at a time in the deep-fry basket in hot oil at 375°. When the rings are golden brown all over, drain them on paper towels. Sprinkle with salt before serving. NET: 4 servings.

PERSIL EN FRITOT

French-Fried Parsley

This is an excellent garnish for most deep-fried entrées.

2 large bunches fresh crisp parsley	*Vegetable oil for deep-fryer*

Remove the parsley leaf clusters from the stems. (If it is necessary to wash the parsley, thoroughly dry it in paper towels; even roll the parsley in several layers of paper towels and leave in the refrigerator overnight. The parsley must be absolutely dry.) Half fill a deep-fryer with vegetable oil and heat it to 350°. Put the parsley in the frying basket and plunge it into the hot fat. Remove it the instant it is crisp. Do not leave it in too long, or it will become black. Drain the fried parsley carefully and well on paper towels.

PANAIS À LA CRÈME

Parsnips with Cheddar Cheese in Cream Sauce

Parsnips are in great favor in French cooking, but so few Americans seem to know or like them. Try this for a very tasty vegetable dish — young parsnips covered with cream and large thin slices of sharp Cheddar cheese, glazed to a golden brown.

2 pounds young parsnips	*1 bay leaf*
Salt	*2 black peppercorns*
4 tablespoons melted sweet butter	*Freshly cracked white pepper*
2 tablespoons all-purpose flour	*2 tablespoons sour cream*
1 cup light cream	*4 large thin slices sharp Cheddar cheese*

Clean and pare the parsnips. Cut them into small finger-size sticks, as for French-fried potatoes. Put them in a pan, cover with cold water and a little salt, bring to a boil, and simmer until they are just tender, about 10 minutes. Drain well, and keep them warm.

Preheat the oven to 375°. Melt 2 tablespoons sweet butter in a saucepan. Off the heat, stir in the flour. Return to low heat, and stir until the mixture is golden brown. In a separate little pan, bring the cream to a boil with the bay leaf and peppercorns. Strain and stir it, off the heat, into the flour and butter mixture. Season with salt and pepper, and stir over low heat until the sauce comes to a boil. Simmer gently 5 minutes, then carefully mix in the sour cream. Arrange the parsnips down a buttered au gratin dish. Cover them with the Cheddar cheese slices, and spoon the sauce over all. Melt the remaining 2 tablespoons butter and sprinkle it over the top. Bake 15 to 20 minutes, until the top is golden brown. NET: 4 servings.

This is one of the great classic vegetable dishes and should really be served as a separate course after the entrée.

2 cups shelled fresh spring peas
    or 2 packages frozen baby
    peas
Salt
1 bunch fresh scallions, cut in
    half (also use green tops)
1 head Bibb or Boston lettuce,

trimmed and quartered
2 tablespoons granulated sugar
¼ cup cold water
¼ teaspoon baking soda
6 tablespoons salt butter
3 teaspoons all-purpose flour

*Casserole of
Fresh Baby Peas
with Lettuce
and Scallions*

Put the fresh peas (omit this step for frozen peas) in a pan, cover with cold water and a little salt, bring to a boil quickly, and drain immediately. Put the blanched fresh peas or the frozen peas into a small heavy casserole with a cover. Add the scallions, lettuce, sugar, 1 teaspoon salt, and water and baking soda. Cover the pan and cook very slowly until the peas are almost tender, 15 to 25 minutes. (Or, if you have the time, cook them the best way — put the casserole in a roasting pan half filled with hot water, and cook in a preheated 350° oven 45 to 50 minutes.) Cream the butter with the flour (beurre manié). When the vegetables are cooked, stir in the beurre manié bit by bit. Cover the pan and cook another 4 to 5 minutes. NET: 4 servings.

4 cups shelled fresh green peas
    (or 3 packages frozen)
Salt
2 teaspoons granulated sugar

2 tablespoons salt butter
3 tablespoons all-purpose flour
2 tablespoons sour cream

*PURÉE
SAINT-GERMAIN*

Purée of Green Peas

Put the peas (fresh or frozen) in a pan and barely cover with cold water. Add 1 teaspoon salt and the granulated sugar. Cover the pan, bring to a boil, lower the heat, and simmer gently until the peas are just soft. Drain them thoroughly, and rub them through a fine strainer or blend in an electric blender until they are smooth. Melt the butter in a pan. Off the heat, stir in the flour, then return to low heat and brown the mixture a little. Off the heat, add the pea purée and sour cream. Adjust the seasoning. Cook for 2 to 3 minutes over low heat, stirring all the while. Serve in a little flat warm vegetable dish, or use as a garnish for fish, meat, or poultry. NET: 2 cups.

Snow peas are becoming more readily available. They are delicate and sweet, and are eaten whole, pod and all.

*POIS
MANGE-TOUT
AU BEURRE*

1½ pounds fresh snow peas
Salt
2 tablespoons granulated sugar

4 tablespoons melted clarified
    butter (page 56)

Snow Peas with Butter

Top and tail the snow peas and cut off the edge with a pair of kitchen scissors. Half fill a pan with water and add the salt and sugar. Bring to a boil and put in the snow peas. Cook them until they are just becoming tender but are still slightly crunchy (about 10 to 12 minutes). Drain, and put them in a warm vegetable dish. Brush the melted clarified butter over the top. NET: 4 servings.

PIMENTS DOUX FARCIS

Stuffed Sweet (Green or Red) Peppers

6 small green or red sweet
   peppers
Salt
Freshly cracked white pepper

SAUCE
2 tablespoons salt butter
1 tablespoon all-purpose flour
2 tablespoons tomato paste
Salt
Freshly cracked white pepper
1½ cups chicken stock (page
   35)
¼ teaspoon finely chopped
   garlic

STUFFING
¼ cup pure olive oil

4 tablespoons sweet butter
½ cup each of finely chopped
   celery and carrot
1 cup finely chopped onion
½ ounce dried mushrooms,
   soaked 2 hours in 1
   cup water, drained, and
   chopped
2 teaspoons finely chopped
   garlic
Salt
Freshly cracked white pepper
½ cup long-grain rice
1 cup water
2 hard-boiled eggs, finely
   chopped
¼ teaspoon oregano

Put the peppers in a pot, cover with cold water, and bring slowly to a boil. Drain immediately, and plunge the peppers into ice water. When they are chilled, carefully cut off the tops at the stalk end and remove all the insides without breaking the pepper shells. Reserve the tops. Season inside the peppers with salt and pepper.

STUFFING. Heat the olive oil and 2 tablespoons sweet butter in a heavy pan. Add the celery, carrot, onion, mushrooms, and garlic. Season with salt and pepper. Cook over low heat 5 minutes, but do not let them get brown. Add the rice and water, and continue to stir over low heat until it comes to a boil. Cover the pan, reduce the heat to a simmer, and cook 25 minutes (without lifting the lid). Then fluff the rice with a fork, and mix in the chopped hard-boiled eggs. Also mix in the rest of the sweet butter and the oregano.

Fill the peppers with this mixture, replace the tops, and arrange the peppers on a buttered baking dish. Preheat the oven to 350°.

SAUCE. Melt the salt butter in a saucepan. Off the heat, stir in the flour and tomato paste. Season with salt and white pepper. Add the chicken stock. Return the pan to low heat and stir until the sauce comes to a boil. Simmer 4 minutes, then add the garlic.

Pour the sauce over the peppers. Put them in the oven and bake them 20 to 25 minutes. Serve them hot. NET: 6 servings.

After raw potatoes have been peeled and cut into the prescribed shape, they should be soaked in several changes of cool water to remove excess starch. They can soak in the water all day this way, if you want to start them ahead of time. When they are to be cooked, drain them and dry them thoroughly in paper towels. Potatoes which are to be French-fried, especially, should be soaked and dried in this manner.

To cook old potatoes, put them in cold water and bring the water to a boil. To cook new potatoes, plunge them into already boiling water. Cook until just soft.

POTATOES

Duchess potatoes are mashed potatoes enriched with egg and butter. The mixture is fairly firm, so that it can be shaped or piped for a variety of garnitures. These potatoes may be prepared ahead of time.

POMMES DE TERRE DUCHESSE

Duchess Potatoes

3 large Idaho-type potatoes
Salt
1 egg
1 egg yolk (optional)

3 tablespoons salt butter
A few grains cayenne pepper
2 tablespoons melted salt butter

Peel the potatoes with a parer. Cut them in quarters or eighths. Put them in a pan and cover them with cold water. Add 1 teaspoon salt to the water and bring it to a boil. Simmer over low heat until the potatoes are soft. Drain them and return them to the pan to dry a moment. Cool a little, then put them in a mixer bowl and beat until they are smooth. Then beat in the egg, egg yolk, and butter, and season well with salt and cayenne pepper. Beat the potato purée until it is well mixed and smooth.

To serve (various ways), put the potato purée in a pastry bag with a #8 or #9 star tube. You may pipe rosettes of duchess potatoes on a baking sheet to surround a roast or fowl or you may pipe a scallop design around a serving platter in which to serve a fish dish with its sauce. Either way, after the potatoes have been piped out of the pastry bag, brush them with the melted butter and brown under the broiler. NET: 2 cups.

POMMES DE TERRE MONTROUGE

Potato and Carrot Purée

4 medium-size potatoes
4 large carrots
Salt
1 egg
3 tablespoons freshly grated
   Parmesan cheese

2 tablespoons vegetable oil
2 tablespoons sour cream
A few grains cayenne pepper
1/2 teaspoon dry mustard
A little melted salt butter

You want to have close to equal parts of potato and carrot for this recipe. Peel the potatoes and carrots with a parer. Cut them into large slices. Put them together in a pan and cover them with cold water.

Add 1 teaspoon salt and cook until they are soft. Drain, and rub them together through a strainer. Put the potato and carrot purée in a mixer bowl. Beat in the egg, grated cheese, vegetable oil, sour cream, salt, cayenne pepper, and mustard. Put the purée in a pastry bag fitted with a #8 or #9 star tube. Pipe the mixture in rosettes on a baking sheet or simply mound with a spoon in a small warm vegetable dish. Dot with the melted butter and brown under the broiler. NET: 4 servings.

POMMES DE TERRE MOUSSELINE

Potato Purée (Light Mashed Potatoes)

3 pounds potatoes
Salt
1 egg
1 egg yolk

4 tablespoons sweet butter
A few grains cayenne pepper
A little hot light cream or milk

Peel the potatoes (leave them whole). Put them in a pan and cover them with cold water. Add 1 tablespoon salt to the water, bring slowly to a boil, and boil until the potatoes are quite soft. (Test them with a sharp knife or an ice pick, not a fork. The tines of a fork will break or waterlog the potatoes.) Drain the potatoes, return them to the pan to dry for a moment over low heat, then rub them through a strainer. Put them in a mixer bowl and beat in the egg, egg yolk, sweet butter, salt, cayenne pepper, and enough hot milk to reduce the potato purée to a light consistency. Beat the mixture very well. Serve these potatoes in a hot au gratin dish. NET: 4 servings.

POMMES DE TERRE RÔTIES

Roast Potatoes

8 medium-size new potatoes (about 1½ to 2 inches in diameter)

¾ cup roast drippings
Salt
Freshly cracked white pepper

Peel the potatoes with a parer (leave them whole). Put them in a pan, cover them with cold water, and bring to a boil. Boil 2 minutes only, then drain them. Plunge them immediately into cold water. Prick each potato with the tines of a fork. Put them in the roasting pan around the bird or meat, or roast them separately (heat some of the roast drippings in a saucepan, season with salt and pepper, coat the potatoes with the drippings and roast them until they are golden brown). NET: 4 servings.

POMMES DE TERRE AUX MARRONS

Potato and Chestnut Purée

This potato recipe may be prepared several hours ahead of time.

2 Idaho-type potatoes
Salt
8 tablespoons unsweetened

chestnut purée (canned is suitable)
4 tablespoons salt butter

1 egg yolk
1 egg
1 tablespoon sour cream

A few grains cayenne pepper
2 tablespoons cool melted butter

Peel the potatoes with a parer and cut them in halves or quarters. Put them in a pan and cover them with cold water. Add 2 teaspoons salt and bring the water to a boil. Simmer until the potatoes are soft. Drain them and return them to the pan to dry for a moment. Then put them in a mixer bowl and beat until they are light and fluffy. Beat in the chestnut purée, butter, egg yolk, egg, sour cream, salt, and cayenne pepper. Beat the mixture until it is smooth. Put the potato and chestnut purée in a pastry bag fitted with a #8 or #9 star tube. Pipe rosettes on a buttered baking sheet (or into artichoke bottoms). Sprinkle the tops with a little cool melted butter. Brown under the broiler. NET: 4 servings.

4 or 5 medium-size potatoes
1 tablespoon salt butter
1 tablespoon paprika
2 tablespoons tomato paste
1 tablespoon all-purpose flour
2 cups water

½ teaspoon finely chopped garlic
1 sprig fresh tarragon
Salt
Freshly cracked white pepper

POMMES DE TERRE HONGROISE

Braised Potatoes in Tomato Sauce with Paprika

Peel the potatoes with a parer and cut them into rather thick slices (about ¼ inch). Soak them in cold water while you prepare the sauce.

TOMATO SAUCE. Melt the butter in a heavy pan and stir in the paprika. Cook a few minutes over low heat. Off the heat, add the tomato paste and flour. Blend well, then stir in the water and garlic. Season with salt and pepper. Return the pan to the heat and stir until the sauce comes to a boil. Remove from the heat and keep it warm.

Drain the potatoes and dry them on paper towels. Add the potatoes to the sauce with the sprig of fresh tarragon. Cover, and simmer very gently until the potatoes are soft. NET: 4 servings.

3 Idaho-type potatoes
6 tablespoons salt butter
Salt
Freshly cracked white pepper

2 teaspoons rosemary leaves, crushed with a mortar and pestle (fresh or dried)

POMMES DE TERRE AU ROMARIN

Rosemary Sautéed Potatoes

Peel the potatoes with a parer (leave them whole). Put them in a pan and cover them with cold water. Bring slowly to a boil, then drain. Cut them in half lengthwise, then cut each half into slices about ¼ inch thick. Heat the butter in a large sauté pan until it is foaming. Add the potatoes to the pan and shake them over moderate heat until they are golden brown all over. (Do not add seasoning, or they won't become brown.) Then season the potatoes with salt, pepper, and the crushed rosemary. NET: 4 servings.

GNOCCHI DE POMMES DE TERRE

Potato Dumplings with Grated Cheese

2 pounds potatoes
4 tablespoons salt butter
Salt
2 eggs
1 egg yolk
¾ cup all-purpose flour

Freshly cracked white pepper
½ cup clarified butter (page 56)
½ cup freshly grated Parmesan cheese

Peel the potatoes with a parer and cut them in half. Put them in a pan and cover them with cold water. Add 1 teaspoon salt to the water and bring to a boil. Simmer the potatoes until they are really soft. (Test them with an ice pick or a knife, not a fork, to avoid puncturing the potatoes and making them waterlogged.) Drain the potatoes and return them to the pan to dry over low heat, then transfer them to a mixer bowl and beat until they are smooth. Add the butter, eggs, egg yolk, flour, salt, and pepper, and beat really well. Cool the potato mixture in the refrigerator.

Lightly flour a board and roll the potato mixture into long sausage shapes, 1½ inches in diameter. Have ready a large pot of hot (not boiling) salted water. Pinch off ½-inch pieces of the potato rolls with your thumb and finger, and throw the pieces into the hot water. Simmer the gnocchi gently (the water must not boil) 25 minutes, until they are firm. When they have finished cooking, remove them from the water with a slotted spoon and drain on paper towels. Arrange the gnocchi on an au gratin dish. Carefully mix them with the clarified butter. Sprinkle the dish with the Parmesan cheese, and serve. NET: 4 servings.

POMMES DE TERRE NOUVELLES AU VAPEUR

Steamed or Boiled New Potatoes

Tiny new potatoes, enough for 4 servings

Melted clarified salt butter
Chopped fresh dill or parsley

Scrub the potatoes, but do not peel them. *To steam*, put them in the upper part of a vegetable steamer with the bottom half filled with boiling water, and steam until they are just done (about 5 to 12 minutes, depending upon the size of the potatoes. (Test them with an ice pick, not a fork; the tines of the fork will break them.) *To boil*, bring a pan of salted water to a boil, put in the new potatoes, cover the pan, and boil about 20 minutes, or until the potatoes are tender.

Drain the potatoes, and either remove the skins (with your fingers, not a knife) or leave the skins on. Place the potatoes in a hot vegetable dish or covered casserole. Pour a little melted clarified butter over them and sprinkle with chopped fresh dill or parsley. Serve immediately. NET: 4 servings.

3 or 4 Idaho-type potatoes   Salt
12 tablespoons salt butter   Freshly cracked white pepper

Generously butter a deep round baking dish. Preheat the oven to 375°. Peel the potatoes with a parer and cut them in half. Cut through each half with a long cylinder cutter about 1½ inches in diameter. (Or use a similar size round cookie cutter.) Then, using a mandoline, cut these uniform cylinders of potato into very thin slices, about ⅛ inch thick. (This is the "formal" version. For the informal version just cut the potatoes into very thin slices with a mandoline — do not cut a cylinder first for uniform slices.)

Cover the inside of the buttered baking dish with overlapping slices of potatoes. Dot with little bits of butter, and season with salt and pepper. Fill the center of the dish with more thin slices of potato in layers. At about 1-inch levels, dot with more bits of butter, salt, and pepper. Cover the last layer with buttered wax paper and a weight. Bake about 40 to 50 minutes, until the edges of the potatoes are golden brown and the center potatoes are tender when pierced with an ice pick. Remove from the oven. Slide a thin knife around the edge of the dish and give the dish a sharp knock. Turn out, bottom side up, onto a serving dish. NET: 4 servings.

Pommes de Terre Nina are prepared and cooked exactly like Pommes de Terre Anna, except that Nina potatoes are baked in individual-size buttered custard cups instead of one large baking dish. Bake them in the preheated 375° oven until the edges are golden brown and the potatoes are just soft. Use them as a garnish for a roast or appropriate entrée.

POMMES
DE TERRE NINA

Individual Molds of
Sliced Potatoes
Baked in Butter

4 large Idaho-type potatoes   Freshly cracked white pepper
1 large yellow onion, finely   6 tablespoons salt butter
   chopped   Salt

POMMES
DE TERRE RÖSTI

Swiss-Style
Sautéed Potatoes

Peel the potatoes with a parer. Grate them raw through the coarse side of a hand cheese grater. Put them in a bowl of cold water and let them soak 1 hour. When you are ready to cook, drain them. Rinse them again, drain, and dry them thoroughly on paper towels. Then mix in the chopped onion and a little pepper. Heat a heavy sauté pan, dry. Then add the butter. When the butter is foaming and at the point of turning brown, add the grated potatoes and onion. Smooth the mixture over the bottom of the pan (it should be about ¾ inch thick). Pat it down flat with a spatula. Brown it on one side. Then slide it from the pan onto a plate. Flip it over from the plate back into the sauté pan so that the uncooked side will brown. When both sides are brown, slide it onto a serving plate. Sprinkle with a little salt and serve immediately, while the brown surface is still crisp. NET: 4 servings.

POMMES DE TERRE LORETTE

Potatoes with Cream Puff Dough, Deep-Fried

2 pounds potatoes, peeled and
  cut in half
Salt
Vegetable oil for deep-fryer

CREAM PUFF DOUGH
1 cup water

4 tablespoons salt butter
Pinch of salt
A few grains cayenne pepper
1 cup all-purpose flour
3 eggs
½ teaspoon baking powder
1 egg white

Cook the potatoes in boiling salted water until they are very soft. Drain, and dry them thoroughly in the pan over low heat. Rub them through a fine strainer, and set aside.

CREAM PUFF DOUGH. Put the water, butter, salt, and cayenne pepper in a saucepan. Bring to a boil as the butter melts. When the water is bubbling, throw in the flour. Beat the mixture until it is smooth, and remove from the heat. Beat in the eggs one at a time, then add the baking powder. Beat the egg white to soft peaks and fold it into the dough.

Mix the mashed potatoes into the cream puff dough and blend well. Heat the vegetable oil in the deep-fryer to 350°. Form the mixture into little egg shapes with two teaspoons and drop them into the hot fat. Deep-fry them until they are golden brown all over. Remove them with a slotted spoon and drain them well on paper towels. Serve either in a separate warm vegetable dish or as a garnish. NET: 4 servings.

CROQUETTES DE POMMES DE TERRE

Deep-Fried Cork-Shaped Mashed Potatoes

6 to 8 medium-size potatoes
Salt
2 whole eggs
2 tablespoons freshly grated
  Parmesan cheese

2 tablespoons salt butter
½ teaspoon dry mustard
Dry white breadcrumbs (to
  coat the potatoes, page 69)
Vegetable oil for deep-fryer

Peel the potatoes, cut them in half, put them in a pan, and cover with cold water. Add 1 teaspoon salt to the water and bring it to a boil. Simmer the potatoes until they are really soft. (Test them with an ice pick or knife, not a fork, to avoid puncturing the potatoes and making them waterlogged.) Drain the potatoes and return them to the pan to dry over low heat. Then put them in a mixer bowl and beat until they are smooth. Beat in one of the eggs, and the grated cheese, butter, and mustard. Form the potato mixture into cork shapes (about 3 inches long and 1-inch diameter) with lightly floured hands. Beat the remaining egg and brush the potato shapes with it. Roll the potatoes in breadcrumbs.

Heat the vegetable oil in the deep-fryer to 375° temperature. Drop the prepared potatoes into the hot fat and fry them until golden brown. Drain them on paper towels. Serve the croquettes on a warm napkin on a serving dish, or as a garnish. NET: 4 to 6 servings.

In France, whenever they find a particularly good dish that is simple to make and nourishing, it is invariably called "the good woman's dish." This is just such a good way to prepare potatoes.

POMMES DE TERRE BONNE FEMME

"Good Woman" Potatoes, with Bacon, Onions, and Parsley

3 Idaho-type or large potatoes
3 tablespoons salt butter
4 slices bacon, cut in shreds
1 medium-size yellow onion, thinly sliced

Freshly cracked white pepper
1 tablespoon chopped fresh parsley or a sprinkle of paprika, for garnish

Peel the potatoes with a parer. Cut them in half lengthwise and then cut into scant ¼-inch slices. Put the butter in a deep heavy pan, then put the bacon over it, the onions over the bacon, and the potatoes over the onions. Sprinkle with a little pepper, but no salt. Cover the pan, set it over low heat, and cook 20 to 25 minutes. Shake the pan once or twice, but do not stir. When the potatoes are cooked, mix them a little and transfer them to a hot serving dish. Sprinkle with the parsley or paprika. NET: 4 servings.

Orange potatoes are an especially good garnish with Duck à l'Orange.

POMMES DE TERRE À L'ORANGE

Croquettes or Rosettes of Orange Mashed Potatoes

2 pounds potatoes
Salt
Grated rind of 1 large orange
1 egg
Freshly cracked white pepper
2 tablespoons salt butter
2 tablespoons hot milk

FOR CROQUETTES
A little all-purpose flour (for dusting)
1 beaten egg
Dry white breadcrumbs (for coating, page 69)
Vegetable oil for deep-fryer

Peel the potatoes with a parer, cut them in half, put them in a pan, and cover with cold water. Add salt and bring the water to a boil. Simmer the potatoes slowly until soft. Drain, and return them to the pan to dry for a moment. Then rub them through a strainer or beat them until smooth in a mixer. Add the grated orange rind, 1 egg (unbeaten), salt, pepper, and the butter and hot milk. Beat thoroughly.

FOR ROSETTES. Preheat the oven to 400°. Put the potato mixture in a pastry bag fitted with a #8 or #9 star tube. Pipe out small rosettes onto a buttered baking sheet, and bake until they are golden brown. When they are done, slide them off the baking sheet with a spatula.

FOR CROQUETTES. With lightly floured hands, form the potato mixture into small cork shapes about 3 inches long and 1 inch in diameter. Roll them in flour, brush them with the beaten egg, and roll them in the breadcrumbs. Heat the vegetable oil in the deep-fryer to 375° and fry the croquettes in the hot oil until golden brown. Remove them with a slotted spoon and drain on paper towels.

Arrange the rosettes or croquettes on a hot serving dish or around an entrée as garnish. NET: 4 servings.

POMMES DE TERRE SAUTÉES

Sautéed Potatoes

2 pounds potatoes
Salt
6 tablespoons salt butter

Freshly cracked white pepper
1 tablespoon chopped fresh
  parsley

Peel the potatoes with a parer and put them in a pan. Cover them with cold water, add salt, bring to a boil and boil 2 minutes, then drain. Dry them in paper towels and cut the potatoes in slices about ¼ inch thick. Melt the butter in a heavy sauté pan. When it is foaming, add the sliced potatoes. Shake them over moderate heat until they begin to brown. Season with salt, pepper, and some of the parsley, and continue to sauté until all the slices are cooked and golden brown. Pile them on a hot serving dish, sprinkle with more parsley, and serve. NET: 4 servings.

POMMES DE TERRE NOISETTE

Noisette Potatoes (Sautéed Potato Balls)

"Noisette" in culinary terms means anything the size of a smallish nut such as a hazelnut or walnut. Both Noisette Potatoes and Parisienne Potatoes (below) are favorite garnitures.

2 pounds mature potatoes or 1
  pound new potatoes no larger
  than 1½ inches
4 tablespoons salt butter

Salt
Freshly cracked white pepper
1 tablespoon chopped fresh
  parsley

Peel the potatoes with a parer. With a 1¼-inch melon scoop, scoop out potato balls. (If you are using the small new potatoes, scrape them; do not try to shape them with the baller. Soak the potato balls or scraped new potatoes before cooking; see page 609.) Put the potatoes in a pan, cover them with cold salted water, and bring the water to a boil. Drain immediately, and dry the potatoes on paper towels or a cloth. Heat the butter (without browning) in a deep heavy pan. Put in the potatoes and cover the pan with the lid. Shake the pan over moderate heat until the potato balls are brown all over and just tender but not mushy. Season with salt and pepper. Drain them from the butter with a slotted spoon. Put them in a warm serving bowl or garnish an entrée with them. Sprinkle with fresh parsley, and serve. NET: 4 servings.

POMMES
DE TERRE
PARISIENNE

Parisienne Potatoes
(Little Sautéed
Potato Balls)

Parisienne Potatoes are made exactly like Noisette Potatoes above, but are smaller. Use the smaller-size baller, about 1 inch in diameter, and use only older potatoes (unless you have marble-size new ones, in which case scrape but do not shape them). Like Noisette Potatoes, these may be served separately or arranged as a garnish with an entrée.

POMMES FRITES
ALLUMETTES

French-Fried
Matchstick Potatoes

1 pound new potatoes
4 tablespoons salt butter
Salt

Freshly cracked white pepper
2 tablespoons chopped fresh
parsley

To cut the potatoes into olive shapes, cut them in half or quarter them, peel, and pare off the sharp edges (shape them no larger than olive size); then soak them (page 609). Heat the butter in a heavy sauté pan. When it is foaming, add the potatoes. Shake over moderate heat until the potatoes are tender and golden brown all over. Season with salt and pepper. Transfer the potatoes to a warm serving dish or garnish an entrée with them. Sprinkle with the parsley. NET: 4 servings.

POMMES
DE TERRE
CHÂTEAU

Château Potatoes
(Sautéed Olive Shapes)

2 large Idaho-type potatoes

Vegetable oil for deep-fryer

Peel the potatoes with a parer. Cut them into very thin slices, about ⅛ inch thick. Then cut the slices into very thin sticks, the size of a kitchen match, about 3 inches long. Put the potato sticks in a bowl and cover with cold clear water. Soak at least 15 minutes, changing the water several times, to remove some of the starch. Dry the sticks thoroughly in paper towels. Heat the vegetable oil in the deep-fryer to 375°. Fry the potato sticks in the deep fat, a few at a time, until they are golden brown all over. Remove, and drain well on paper towels. These potatoes are usually served as a garnish with grilled meats, fish, or poultry. NET: 4 servings.

POMMES
DE TERRE
FARCIES

Stuffed Baked Potatoes

Directions for stuffed baked potatoes are given in recipes for Oeufs Pochés Georgette (Poached Eggs in Baked Potatoes with Shrimp Sauce, page 194), Filets de Soles Cendrillon (Poached Fillets of Sole in Baked Potatoes with White Wine Sauce, page 272), Filets de Soles Georgette (Baked Potato Shells with Shrimps, page 278), and Crown

Roast of Lamb, with Baked Potatoes Garnished with Lamb Kidneys (page 541).

If you wish to serve baked potato shells stuffed with potato only, follow any of these recipes for puréeing and seasoning the potato, or adapt Pommes de Terre Mousseline (Potato Purée, page 610) to the quantity of cooked potato that you have. Sprinkle the lightly mounded filled potatoes with melted butter and freshly grated Parmesan cheese before browning under the broiler.

POMMES DE TERRE SOUFFLÉES

Soufflé Potatoes

Puffy souffléed slices of potato are deep-fried twice. The first time they are half-cooked in 350° oil. Then they must be cooled, after which they are plunged into very hot 450° oil. This process results in the pillow-shaped potatoes. Needless to say, they must be served at once.

4 Idaho-type potatoes
Vegetable oil for deep-fryer (if you have it, clarified beef fat is even better)

Salt
Bunch of crisp fresh watercress or parsley

Peel the potatoes. With a potato slicer or mandoline, cut them lengthwise into even slices about ¼ inch thick. Soak them in ice water 15 minutes. Drain, and dry them thoroughly in a cloth. Have ready vegetable oil heated to 350° in the deep-fryer. Cook a few potato slices at a time in the deep fat until they are nearly soft. Do not let them brown. Remove them from the fat, dry them thoroughly on paper towels, and let them get quite cold. (Up to this point they can be prepared ahead of time.)

When you are ready to serve the potatoes, heat the oil in the deep-fryer to 450°. Plunge a few potato slices into the hot oil. When they have blown up (as if inflated) and are brown all over, drain them gently on paper towels. Sprinkle them with a little salt, arrange them on a hot napkin on a hot serving dish, garnish with crisp fresh watercress or parsley, and serve immediately. NET: 4 servings.

SALSIFIS ITALIENNE

Salsify (Oyster Plant) with Tomatoes and Cheese

In the United States, salsify (oyster plant) can be found in the spring, usually in the Western states.

8 sticks salsify (oyster plant)
Salt
Juice of half a lemon
2 tablespoons salt butter
1 medium-size yellow onion, chopped
2 firm white fresh mushrooms, chopped

2 tablespoons chopped boiled ham
1 tablespoon all-purpose flour
1 teaspoon tomato paste
Salt
Freshly cracked white pepper
¼ cup dry white wine
1 cup chicken stock (page 35)

2 large firm ripe tomatoes,
   skinned and quartered
1 teaspoon chopped fresh tarragon or chives or 1 table-

spoon chopped fresh parsley
1 cup freshly grated Parmesan
   cheese

Wash the salsify thoroughly. Trim, scrape, and cut it into 1½-inch pieces. Put it in a pan, cover with cold water, add a little salt and lemon juice, and bring to a boil. Simmer over low heat until the salsify is tender (about 45 to 50 minutes). Melt the butter in a heavy casserole. Add the onion, mushrooms, and ham. Cook this mixture slowly, over low heat, 7 to 10 minutes, stirring frequently. Off the heat, mix in the flour, tomato paste, salt, pepper, wine, and chicken stock. Return the pan to low heat, bring the mixture to a boil, and simmer 15 to 20 minutes (uncovered). Add the cooked salsify and the quartered tomatoes to the casserole, and cook gently 5 minutes. Sprinkle the casserole with the chopped fresh herbs. Serve with a separate bowl of grated Parmesan cheese. NET: 4 servings.

If you are fortunate enough to have a resource for sorrel, you can offer a most delicious and unique vegetable treat. Sorrel is also called sour grass. It grows wild and, I understand, is grown domestically by a few specialists. Because it is so rare these days, in dishes where sorrel is a complementary rather than a main ingredient, spinach with a little lemon juice may be substituted, as in the soups. The following purée, however, has to be made with genuine sorrel.

PURÉE D'OSEILLE

Sorrel Purée Glazed
with Whipped Cream,
with Croûtons

2 pounds sorrel
Juice of half a lemon
Salt
Freshly cracked black pepper
4 tablespoons salt butter

3 tablespoons all-purpose flour
½ cup sour cream
½ cup heavy cream, whipped
4 to 6 large fried croûtons
   (page 69)

Wash the sorrel thoroughly in several waters. Drain, but not too well. Put it in a pan with the lemon juice, a little salt, and pepper. Cover the pan and cook briskly 5 minutes, to wilt the leaves. Then drain it thoroughly to remove all the moisture. Put the wilted sorrel in a colander and press it down with a small plate, then put it through a fine vegetable strainer or a fine meat chopper. Melt the butter in a saucepan. Add the flour and brown it slowly. Add the sorrel purée, sour cream, salt, and pepper, and cook slowly 4 to 5 minutes. Arrange the sorrel purée in the form of a bed on the bottom of a hot flat serving dish. Spoon the whipped cream over it and brown quickly under a hot broiler. Surround the dish with the large fried croûtons. NET: 4 servings.

PAIN D'ÉPINARDS À LA CRÈME

Spinach Mold (Ring or Dome), Glazed with Cream, with Croûtons

Spinach is a popular vegetable, and in Pain d'Épinards you may have an exciting new way to serve it. Very finely ground spinach is mixed with eggs, egg yolk, and cream — like a custard — and baked in a ring mold, glazed with heavy cream, and garnished with croûtons. The flavor and texture are exquisite.

1½ pounds fresh spinach
4 tablespoons salt butter
Salt
Freshly cracked white pepper
3 tablespoons all-purpose flour
¾ cup chicken stock (page 35)

½ cup heavy cream
2 eggs
1 egg yolk
1 cup small cubed croûtons
   fried in butter (page 70)

Wash the spinach thoroughly in several waters. Drain, and put it in a pan with 2 tablespoons butter, salt, and pepper. Cover, and cook 3 to 4 minutes, stirring occasionally, until the spinach is wilted. Drain thoroughly, reserve the liquid, and return the spinach to the pan to dry over heat for a moment. Rub the wilted spinach through a fine strainer or put it through a fine meat chopper. Melt the remaining 2 tablespoons butter in a large saucepan. Off the heat, add the flour, salt, and pepper. Strain in the liquid drained from the spinach. Return the pan to low heat and stir until the mixture thickens. Add 2 tablespoons heavy cream, bring the sauce to a boil, then cool it a little. In a separate bowl, beat the eggs and egg yolk, and mix in the strained spinach and sauce. Add 1 more tablespoon of heavy cream and a little extra salt and pepper.

    Preheat the oven to 350°. Generously butter a ring mold or a dome mold. Fill it with the spinach mixture. Cover the top with buttered wax paper and stand the mold in a roasting pan half filled with hot water. Place it in the oven and bake 20 minutes, or until the spinach is firm to the touch. Remove it from the oven and water bath, and let it stand in the mold about 5 minutes. Slide a thin-bladed knife around the edge of the mold, and turn the spinach out onto a hot serving dish. Spoon the remaining heavy cream over it and surround it with the fried croûtons. NET: 4 servings.

ÉPINARDS EN BRANCHE PARMESAN

Spinach in Cheese Sauce, with Croûtons

2 pounds fresh spinach
5 tablespoons salt butter
Salt
Freshly cracked black pepper
2 tablespoons all-purpose flour
A few grains cayenne pepper
½ cup heavy cream

5 tablespoons freshly grated
   Parmesan cheese
½ teaspoon dry mustard
2 tablespoons sour cream
4 to 6 diagonal croûtons, fried
   in butter (page 69)

Wash the spinach thoroughly in several waters. (To remove all the grit, first plunge the spinach leaves into cold water, then into warm salted water, and last, into cold water again.) Drain, and put the spinach in a pan with 2 tablespoons butter, salt, and pepper. Cover, and cook slowly 5 to 6 minutes, until the spinach is wilted, stirring occasionally. Drain in a colander, reserving the liquid. Press the spinach down firmly with a small plate to extract all of it. Return the spinach to the pan and dry it a little longer over low heat. Keep it warm.

Melt 2 tablespoons butter in a large saucepan. Off the heat, add the flour, salt, and cayenne pepper. Stir until the mixture is smooth. Strain in the reserved liquid from the spinach, and add the heavy cream. Return the pan to low heat, and stir until the mixture comes to a boil. Add the grated cheese little by little. Then stir in the remaining tablespoon of butter and the mustard. Let it simmer over low heat a few minutes, then mix in the spinach. Arrange the spinach mixture on a hot vegetable dish and spoon the sour cream over it. Surround the dish with the fried croûtons. NET: 4 servings.

This recipe can be made with broccoli as well.

2 pounds fresh spinach	4 tablespoons seedless raisins
2 tablespoons salt butter	4 tablespoons pine kernels
3 tablespoons pure olive oil	(pignoli nuts)
1 teaspoon finely chopped garlic	3 tablespoons freshly grated
Salt	Parmesan cheese
A few grains cayenne pepper	2 tablespoons melted butter

Wash the spinach thoroughly in several waters. Drain it well and cut it in coarse shreds. Bring a pot of water to a boil, put in the shredded spinach, wilt it, and drain thoroughly. Heat the butter and the olive oil in a deep heavy pan. Add the garlic, salt, and cayenne pepper. Cook over moderate heat 2 to 3 minutes. Add the raisins and pignoli nuts, and cook 2 minutes. Add the spinach and mix well. Arrange the spinach mixture on a hot au gratin dish. Sprinkle the grated cheese over the top, then the melted butter. Brown the dish quickly under a hot broiler. NET: 4 servings.

ÉPINARDS À L'ITALIENNE

Spinach with Pignoli Nuts, au Gratin

2 pounds fresh spinach	3 tablespoons freshly grated
4 tablespoons salt butter	Parmesan cheese
Salt	2 tablespoons freshly grated
Freshly cracked black pepper	Gruyére cheese
2 tablespoons all-purpose flour	3 tablespoons heavy cream
A few grains cayenne pepper	1 cup small cubed croûtons,
1 cup milk	fried in butter (page 70)
½ teaspoon dry mustard	

Wash the spinach thoroughly in several waters. (To remove all the grit, first plunge it into cold water, then into warm salted water, and last, into cold water again.) Drain the spinach well. Put it in a pan with

ÉPINARDS À LA HAMBOURG

Spinach with Croûtons and Mornay Sauce

1 tablespoon butter, salt, and pepper. Cover the pan and cook slowly 6 to 7 minutes, until the spinach is wilted, stirring occasionally. Drain it well through a colander, pressing it down with a small plate to extract all the liquid. Coarsely chop the spinach in a wooden bowl or on a chopping board. Transfer it to a bowl and set it aside.

MORNAY SAUCE. Melt 2 tablespoons butter in a saucepan. Off the heat, stir in the flour, salt, and cayenne pepper. Add the milk. Return the pan to low heat, and stir until the sauce comes to a boil. Mix in the mustard, 2 tablespoons Parmesan cheese, all the Gruyère cheese, and the heavy cream. Simmer the sauce slowly 8 minutes.

Mix the fried croûtons into the spinach and arrange it on an au gratin dish. Spoon the Mornay sauce over it. Sprinkle the remaining Parmesan cheese on the sauce. Dot with the remaining tablespoon of butter and brown quickly under a hot broiler. NET: 4 servings.

BAKED ACORN SQUASH MARTINIQUE

Baked halves of acorn squash filled with slices of poached marrow and sprinkled with a little brandy and butter.

2 medium-size acorn squashes
    (or 3 or 4 small)
4 tablespoons salt butter, melted
Salt
Freshly cracked white pepper
¼ teaspoon ground ginger
1½ cups warm chicken stock
(page 35)
2 large beef marrow bones
    (each 6 inches)
¼ cup Cognac or good brandy
1 tablespoon salt butter,
    creamed and mixed with 1½
    teaspoons hot mustard

Preheat the oven to 350°. Wash the acorn squashes but do not peel them. Cut them in half and remove the seeds. Coat the insides heavily with melted butter and season with salt, pepper, and the ground ginger. Put the squash halves cut side up in a shallow baking dish or roasting pan, and pour the warm chicken stock around them. Bake 1 hour, or until the squash is very tender and brown. While it is baking, cook the marrow bones in boiling salted water 20 minutes. Cool them quickly in the freezer, remove the marrow, and cut it into 1-inch slices.

About 8 minutes before the squash is finished, put a few slices of marrow in the hollow of each half. Pour in a little brandy and sprinkle with a little more salt and pepper. Return the squash to the oven and finish baking. Just before serving, dot the squash halves with the creamed butter mixed with hot mustard. Serve very hot. NET: 4 servings.

SOUFFLÉ AUX PATATES

Sweet Potato Soufflé

2 cups mashed cooked or canned
    sweet potatoes
1 cup sour cream
¼ cup Cognac or good brandy
4 tablespoons melted salt butter
¼ teaspoon cayenne pepper
¼ teaspoon freshly grated
    nutmeg

½ teaspoon salt
Grated rind of half a lemon

4 egg yolks
5 egg whites

Preheat the oven to 400°. Butter the inside of a #7 (1½-quart) soufflé dish. Tie a collar of doubled wax paper, buttered, around the outside of the dish so it rises about 2 inches above the rim. Put the sweet potatoes in a mixer bowl and gradually mix in the sour cream and brandy. Slowly add the melted butter and beat until the mixture is smooth. Beat in the cayenne pepper, nutmeg, salt, and lemon rind. Then mix in the egg yolks one by one. With a wire whisk, beat the egg whites to soft peaks, and fold them into the sweet potato mixture. Spoon the mixture into the prepared soufflé dish, and place the filled dish in a shallow roasting pan half filled with hot water. Put the whole assembly in the oven and bake 25 to 30 minutes, until the soufflé is lightly browned. Gently remove the dish from the oven and from the water bath. Peel away the paper collar and serve at once. NET: 4 servings.

FRESH TOMATOES

Did you know that the tomato is a relatively new arrival on the menu of the Western world? Although it was discovered in Peru by the Spanish, it was not really accepted by the French until the mid-nineteenth century, nor by Americans until just before 1900. Then it was the "tiger milk" of the day — nutritionists discovered it bursting with vitamins, sugars and proteins, and the tomato zoomed into prominence as America's third largest crop!

The tomato does have medicinal qualities. If you should feel faint and eat a tomato, you will feel revived at once. It is from the same botanical family as the potato. If a tomato plant is grown on top of a potato plant, better tomatoes and potatoes will result. I have seen this done in England. Also, the blossom and the leaf of the potato and the tomato are closely the same.

The tomato is without rival as a garnish or salad ingredient. Here are ways to prepare it for serving raw as well as for cooking.

TO CORE AND SKIN A TOMATO. There are two methods. (1) Cover the tomato with boiling water, count to 10, drain it, cover with cold water, then remove the core and slip off the skin, using a small sharp paring knife only if necessary. (2) Impale the tomato at the core on a fork. Hold it over a hot burner for a moment, turning it so that the skin is loosened all around. Cut out the core and remove the skin, picking it up with a small paring knife if necessary.

TO SECTION A SKINNED TOMATO. Set it stem end down on the chopping board. For *quarters*, cut it vertically into 4 equal wedges. For *eighths*, cut each quarter in half, vertically for decorative thin wedges, and horizontally for cubes.

TO CHOP A SKINNED TOMATO. Cut it in half vertically. Lay each half on the chopping board cut side down and follow the same cutting pattern as for chopping an onion — first slice in one direction, then slice across the first cuts to make dice. Make the slices thick or thin for coarse or fine dice.

TO REMOVE SEEDS FROM A TOMATO. Core and skin the tomato, and cut it into quarters. With a small sharp paring knife cut the inner pith out of each quarter, exposing the seeds. Slide them out with your finger. Reserve the skinned pulp section in one dish and the pith and seeds in another. Use the seeded tomato pulp either in quarter sections, as above, or cut into narrow shreds, or chopped coarse or fine as required. The pith and seeds can be rubbed through a fine strainer to produce fresh tomato juice to use in the recipe or store in the refrigerator.

TO HOLLOW OUT A WHOLE TOMATO. Remove the core and skin. With a narrow sharp paring knife, loosen the pith in the center of the tomato. Then scoop out the pith and seeds with a small spoon, being careful not to break the tomato shell.

TOMATES PROVENÇALE

Tomatoes with Onions, Garlic, and Herbs

6 tablespoons sweet butter
6 large ripe tomatoes, skinned
   and cut in ½-inch slices
2 teaspoons finely chopped
   garlic
Salt
Freshly cracked white pepper
A little granulated sugar

¾ cup dry white wine
1 tablespoon chopped fresh
   parsley
2 teaspoons chopped fresh dill
1 tablespoon all-purpose flour
2 tablespoons finely chopped
   white onion

Melt 3 tablespoons butter in a large frypan. Add the garlic, salt, and pepper, and cook for half a minute. Lay the tomato slices in the pan and season again with salt, pepper, and the sugar. Cover the frypan and cook 3 minutes over low heat. Remove the cover, pour the wine over the tomatoes, and sprinkle them with the parsley and dill. Work the remaining 3 tablespoons butter with the flour and chopped onion to form a paste. Stir this into the sauce at the side of the frypan, bit by bit. Reheat the tomato mixture and carefully spoon it into a shallow copper casserole. Serve at once. NET: 4 servings.

TOMATES GRILLÉES

Broiled Tomatoes with Onions, Breadcrumbs, and Parmesan Cheese

These tomatoes are a popular, versatile garnish and a very good way to put flavor into lackluster hothouse tomatoes. They may be prepared hours in advance and broiled just before serving.

4 medium-size firm ripe
   tomatoes

Salt
Freshly cracked white pepper

2 teaspoons granulated sugar
1 teaspoon finely chopped garlic
8 wafer-thin slices of onion,
    the same diameter as the
    tomatoes
½ cup dry breadcrumbs (page

69)
½ cup freshly grated Parmesan
    cheese
4 tablespoons melted salt butter
1 tablespoon chopped fresh
    parsley

Carefully remove the core from the tomatoes (but do not skin them). Cut the tomatoes in half horizontally. Sprinkle the cut sides with salt, pepper, and ¼ teaspoon sugar. Put a speck of garlic on each tomato, and lay an onion slice on it. Sprinkle the tops with the breadcrumbs, grated cheese, and the melted butter. Place the tomato halves on the broiler tray and brown them under the broiler. Sprinkle the tops with the parsley, and serve at once. NET: 4 servings.

4 large firm ripe tomatoes, cored
    and skinned
Salt
Freshly cracked white pepper
6 tablespoons melted salt butter
5 tablespoons solid salt butter
2 medium-size yellow onions,
    thinly sliced
½ cup finely chopped firm
    white fresh mushrooms
¾ cup chopped boiled ham
½ cup chopped cooked tongue
1 small frankfurter

3 tablespoons chopped fresh
    parsley
½ cup mixed freshly grated
    Parmesan and Gruyére
    cheeses
½ cup dry breadcrumbs (page
    69)
2 tablespoons all-purpose flour
2 tablespoons tomato paste
1½ cups chicken stock (page
    35) or water
½ teaspoon finely chopped
    garlic

TOMATES FARCIES À LA BAYONNE

Tomatoes Stuffed with Ham and Tongue, with Tomato Sauce

Preheat the oven to 350°. Cut a thin slice off the tops of the skinned tomatoes and carefully scoop out the seeds and pith. Set the seeds and pith aside. Dry the hollowed-out tomatoes well with a soft cloth and place them on a shallow baking dish. Season the inside of each with a little salt and pepper and pour in 1 tablespoon melted butter. Warm the tomato shells in the oven 4 minutes.

STUFFING. Melt 3 tablespoons butter in a sauté pan. Add the onions, salt, and pepper, and cook a few minutes over low heat. Add the mushrooms, cook 3 minutes, then add the ham and tongue. In a separate little pan, simmer the frankfurter in water 6 minutes, chop it fine, and add it to the mixture in the sauté pan. Mix the stuffing thoroughly, adding a little extra salt and pepper and 1 tablespoon chopped parsley. Simmer the mixture a few minutes over low heat.

Carefully stuff the tomatoes with this mixture. Sprinkle the tops with the grated cheese and breadcrumbs. Then sprinkle each stuffed tomato top with 1½ teaspoons melted butter. Brown the tomatoes under the broiler, then arrange them on a warm flat serving dish.

SAUCE. Melt 1 tablespoon butter in a saucepan. Off the heat, stir in the flour, salt, pepper, and tomato paste. Add the chicken stock or water. Return the saucepan to low heat and stir until the sauce comes to a boil. Add the garlic and 1 tablespoon butter and simmer 10 to 15 minutes.

Strain the sauce and pour it around the tomatoes. Sprinkle them with the remaining parsley, and serve immediately. NET: 4 servings.

TRUFFLES, BLACK AND WHITE

My favorite idea for a stocking stuffer at Christmastime is a big fat truffle, either fresh frozen (if available) or in a tin. I truly love truffles, and this is the loveliest jewel of which I can conceive to give my friends.

The truffle appears to be one of the original secrets of the universe. How does it get into the ground? Why should such diverse creatures as pregnant pigs and psychic dogs be the exclusive communicators for finding them for us? Only nature holds the keys to the mystery of the truffle.

As we all know, there are black truffles and white truffles, and the best of both come from southwestern France and northern Italy, although they are found in various other spots around Europe. But the fragrance, texture, and certainly the appearance of the black and the white truffle are different. Sometimes it is possible to purchase fresh frozen truffles in the United States. Fresh, unquestionably, is the best. If fresh frozen truffles are bestowed upon you, keep them frozen, cutting off only as much as you require when you use them. Most often in the United States we can buy only canned truffles, which are excellent. After you open the tin, if you do not use them all, store those that remain in an airtight screw-top jar, sprinkled with a little light Madeira or Cognac if there is not enough juice. The truffle juice mixed with Madeira or Cognac should be used in the sauce for the dish with the truffles, so as not to lose a whiff.

The fragrance of truffles is impossible to explain — like great perfumes, they are what they are. A truffle smells like . . . a truffle. Learn it, and become addicted. Like rarest pure jasmine, the truffle is individual, it is fine, and it is properly rare in its fragrance. But beyond its perfume, the truffle has a visual quality which adds to its mystique . . . the black ones — black, flat, deep. The black punctuation of the truffle makes a statement about any dish it adorns — that here is a dish with elegance.

One of my favorite dishes with white truffles is Escalopes de Veau Piémontaise (page 493). Black truffles are almost the hallmark of classic French cuisine. Among many dishes, the one in which I think cooks and chefs of the French school most often pay homage to the truffle is the Poulet en Demi-Deuil (see the index for our versions of this dish).

"The" first course, served alone, with very dry Champagne. It is one of the superlative dishes of classic cuisine, and despite the cost of truffles, it is a good idea to know of it, just in case there comes a good year in truffles, or if they find a lode of truffles in Texas or somewhere, and the prices go down.

SAUTÉ DE TRUFFES

Sautéed Black Truffles in Puff Pastry Case

Puff pastry case (page 401)
½ pound fresh frozen or canned
   black truffles
1 teaspoon finely chopped garlic
Salt
Freshly cracked black pepper
4 tablespoons pure olive oil

¼ cup very dry white wine
¼ cup Cognac
8 tablespoons sweet butter
2 teaspoons chopped fresh
   tarragon
Juice of half a lemon

Make the puff pastry case first (page 401).

Cut the truffles into slices about ¼ inch thick. Lightly mix them with half the garlic, a little salt, and pepper. Set them aside. Heat the olive oil in a small sauté pan with the remaining garlic and the wine and Cognac. Season with a little more salt and pepper, and boil the sauce down to about 2 tablespoons. Cut the sweet butter into pieces and, using a wire whisk, beat it into the sauce in the sauté pan bit by bit. Then add the sliced truffles. Mix them gently with the sauce, and let them warm over low heat 2 minutes. Mix in the chopped tarragon and lemon juice.

Warm the puff paste case a little in the oven if it has cooled. Set it on a warm serving platter. Spoon the truffles into the center well. Tilt the lid on the top. Serve immediately. NET: 4 servings.

NAVETS NOUVEAUX GLACÉS

Glazed New Turnips

12 to 16 new baby turnips (or
   large ones cut in olive shapes,
   page 570)
1 tablespoon fresh lemon juice
1 tablespoon tarragon vinegar

4 tablespoons salt butter
Salt
Freshly cracked black pepper
¼ cup granulated sugar
2 tablespoons honey

Peel the turnips and wash them in lemon juice and cold water. Bring to a boil a pan of water with the tarragon vinegar. Add the turnips, simmer them gently until they are just soft (they should still be a little crispy), then drain them. Melt the butter in a shallow sauté pan. When it is foaming, add the turnips. Season with salt and pepper, sprinkle with the sugar, and add the honey. Shake the turnips over high heat until they are glazed and golden brown all over. Serve very hot in a small shallow casserole, or as a garnish. NET: 4 servings.

COURGETTES À LA PROVENÇALE

Casserole of Zucchini with Tomatoes, Green Pepper, and Cheese

2 pounds small firm zucchini
6 tablespoons salt butter
¼ cup finely chopped shallots
6 small ripe tomatoes, skinned, quartered, and seeded
2 tablespoons pure olive oil
Salt

Freshly cracked white pepper
1 teaspoon finely chopped garlic
1 green pepper, finely chopped
½ cup freshly grated Parmesan cheese
2 tablespoons chopped fresh parsley

Wash the zucchini and cut them into horizontal slices about ½ inch thick. Put them in a pan, cover with cold water, and bring to a boil. Drain immediately, and set them aside. Melt 2 tablespoons butter in a casserole. Add the shallots and cook over low heat until they are just turning brown. Spread the tomato sections on the shallots and pour the olive oil over them. Sprinkle with salt and pepper, and add the garlic and green pepper. Cover the casserole and cook the mixture over low heat 10 minutes.

Uncover the casserole and arrange the blanched zucchini on the tomato mixture. Melt the remaining 4 tablespoons butter and sprinkle it over the zucchini. Cover the casserole and cook gently over low heat until the zucchini is just tender. (This requires only 2 to 3 minutes, as the zucchini must not become mushy.) Remove the casserole from the heat. Sprinkle the zucchini with the grated cheese and chopped parsley. Serve in the casserole. NET: 4 servings.

SALADS

WHAT'S A SALAD?

The history of a salad is a hodgepodge. Thanks to such social chroniclers as Homer and Daniel, we know that the salad is as old as civilization. It was one of the many indulgences of the Greek gods and a remarkable refinement in the feastings of Belshazzar and the Babylonians during their stay in Mesopotamia ("a salad of cress, lettuce, and endive").

Salads were very much present in the gourmandise of the Renaissance . . . "the 'first service' from the credenza consisted of salads decked out with various fantasies such as animals made of citron, castles of turnips, high walls of lemons; and variegated with slices of ham, mullet roes, herrings, tunny, anchovies, capers, olives, caviar, together with candied flowers and other preserves" (*The Horizon Cookbook and Illustrated History of Eating and Drinking Through the Ages*, New York, 1968).

Whereupon the French began to organize the salad into the developing national cuisine. Brillat-Savarin finally declared its singular purpose in dining pleasure was to freshen the palate, and Dumas underscored the subtle artistry and purpose required of a proper salad by preparing the salads himself, instead of leaving them to his chef, for his famous dinners.* This French achievement was saluted by Richard Ford in 1846: "The salad is the glory of every French dinner and the disgrace of most in England" (*Gatherings from Spain*).

In America in the 1890's, the beautiful calligraphy of Louis Sherry, caterer to New York society's famous Four Hundred, records in his ledger great Belle Époque menus with salads such as "salade dandelion, demi-deuille [sic], fines herbes, Russe, lettuce and tomato," of

---

* One of the most delightful pieces of French culinary literature is Alexander Dumas's letter to his friend Jules Janin in the late 1860's, part of which is a thesis on the salad and detailed instructions for one of his own successful renditions. If you haven't, I think you will enjoy reading it; it has a refreshing ring of truth.

which the first two seem to have been the most frequent. By the mid-twentieth century everyone dabbled in salad-making, including the drugstore counter short-order cooks, whose national spécialité became the infamous "American luncheon salad": Iceberg lettuce with canned pineapple rings, apricots or peaches. Soggy cottage cheese and a ghastly dressing, topped, of course, with a cherry. (This seems to be the ultimate in eating pleasure — to get a cherry on top of a dish!)

Meanwhile the French had refined the art of the salad to two classifications, with which most gastronomers seem to agree, from Pellaprat and Escoffier to the contemporary school:

(1) A simple bowl of tossed greens with a simple oil and vinegar dressing is the daily classic accompaniment to refresh the palate after a savory main course (see Salade Française, Tossed Green Salad, page 635).

(2) Combination (or compound) salads represent a separate and special course, either as an hors d'oeuvre or following the entrée (instead of the tossed green salad).

Any salad is only as good as the care given the preparation of the vegetables and dressing. Here are some guidelines for making a "decent salad."

The Greens

(1) These lettuce and leaf vegetables are usually available in the markets of this country the year round:

Arugula	and curly endive)
Bibb lettuce	Purslane
Boston lettuce	Romaine lettuce
Chicory (curly endive)	Salad bowl lettuce
Dandelion leaves	Spinach
Belgian endive	Watercress
Escarole (also called chicory	

Never use iceberg lettuce! There is no need to eat it. It is tough, fibrous, and unflavorful in comparison with any of the available greens listed above — and there are more local types to choose from. Eating iceberg lettuce is like eating the bare dressing diluted with water. The only reason it's used in airline and restaurant salads is that it keeps reasonably well for a long time. I think all iceberg lettuce should be put in the Atlantic Ocean with the other icebergs.

(2) Little young spinach leaves are absolutely delicious.

(3) Beet greens are not used much in salads. They are too strong.

(4) In my opinion the best greens for salad are Bibb, romaine, Boston, salad bowl, and — best of all from a flavor point of view — blanched dandelion leaves.

(5) Blanched dandelion greens are a classic salad ingredient. (In

Louis Sherry's elegant menus they follow such entrées as Saddle of Lamb Chartreuse, Double Entrecôte aux Morilles, Bordelaise, and Filet de Boeuf Jardinière and Pain de Bigier St. Hubert.) I don't know where you could buy blanched dandelion greens today, although in season some Italian greengrocers do carry green dandelion leaves. But if you have a garden or a lawn, I will tell you how you can raise your own exclusive delicacy. In the spring, when the "unwanted" dandelions are tiny, cover them, every one, with a flower pot. Leave them in the ground to grow, but covered to keep out the sun, the way white asparagus is raised in Europe. When the leaves have developed but are not too large, prepare a salad of blanched dandelion leaf with a simple vinaigrette. It will be the most delicious salad you have ever had in your life. The young leaves of green dandelion make a very good salad too.

(6) How many kinds of lettuce or greens would you put in a salad? There should not be too many — certainly not more than two or three — because they counteract each other. They all have a rather delicate taste. See the Salade Française recipe (page 635) for my favorite combinations.

(7) Celery in a tossed salad? No, never.

(8) Avocado? Never in a salad. The best way to really enjoy the avocado is by itself, perfectly ripe, with a little lemon juice, salt, and freshly cracked pepper.

(9) When you buy lettuce, wash the individual leaves thoroughly in many waters (salt and clear), shake them in a salad basket or a salad dryer, and wrap them in paper or cloth towels. Then put them to crisp in the refrigerator several hours at least. If they are to be kept for a longer period, place them in a plastic bag, completely dried, and store in the refrigerator. All greens should be cleaned immediately, before they are stored in the refrigerator. Then they will be properly clean, crisp, and ready for instant use.

(10) Never use a knife to cut lettuce leaves; break them gently by hand. Lettuce is only cut if you are cutting a whole head of lettuce in half.

Combination Salads

My teacher, M. Pellaprat, offered the best description and advice for combination salads: "They may be made of a mixture of different vegetables, meat, fish, shellfish, poultry, game, or fruit, or a combination of these with vegetables. All ingredients for salads must be cut neatly, never chopped beyond recognition, and arranged with taste. They must be well seasoned and served very cold. A warm salad tastes insipid."

This chapter contains the recipes for preparing some classic combination salads. They are beautiful taste combinations when prepared correctly, and ought to be rediscovered. They can usually be made well in advance and may be served as an hors d'oeuvre, the main dish for a luncheon or supper, or as a separate course after the entrée. The Salade Niçoise is probably the best known of the French combination salad types. The simple Mixed Raw Vegetable Salad arranged in a colorful cartwheel is a revelation of natural vegetable textures and flavors.

Tomatoes are always a salad favorite, but unfortunately are often a little anemic in appearance and flavor when marketed. Let them sit on a sunny windowsill awhile; it will help bring out the flavor as well as the color. Another way to bring out flavor is to marinate the tomatoes with a few grains of sugar, salt, and freshly cracked pepper a little while before using them.

This chapter contains recipes for the excellent French and German types of potato salads. Both use only oil, mustard, salt, cracked pepper; and the German type uses no vinegar. Neither use mayonnaise. The habit of mixing mayonnaise with potato salad is total discord in my opinion. With mayonnaise, the consistency is wrong and the flavor is wrong.

Dressings

(1) There are six classic salad dressing bases, which are adapted as needed to the salad to be dressed. Their basic ingredients are as follows.

VINAIGRETTE. A simple vinaigrette is 3 parts oil with 1 part vinegar, seasoned with salt and pepper. This very simple salad dressing is used with tossed greens and a variety of combination vegetable salads, and as a sauce or marinade in other dishes.

MAYONNAISE. The mayonnaise dressing is beaten egg yolk, vinegar, and oil. It is used to bind combination salads and as a sauce over cold egg, fish, poultry, and meat dishes. Its use in a salad is exemplified in the recipe for Salade Russe or Cold Chicken Salad.

EGG. Hard-boiled egg yolk and/or raw egg yolk are beaten with vinegar and oil, as in the dressing for Salade Belle Hélène, and as in the Sauce Gribiche.

CREAM. Heavy cream is mixed with a little vinegar and oil, as in the recipe for Salade de Betteraves.

MUSTARD AND CREAM. Mustard and heavy cream are combined with vinegar and oil for a dressing traditionally used with shredded celery root (Salade de Céleri-Rave).

BACON FAT. This dressing is a rather specialized one for strong greens and cabbages. Shredded bacon is fried very crisp. The bacon fat is added to a little hot wine vinegar and olive oil, which are then added to the salad with the crisp shreds of bacon.

(2) Occasionally a Roquefort dressing is a nice change of pace on a tossed salad, and the recipe for one is given in the Sauce chapter. But I prefer to serve cheese separately, with good French bread, rather than in a cheese dressing.

(3) Not of the French school but the Scandinavian, sweet vinegar dressing is very good. It is given here with Finnish Cucumber Salad. It also goes well with beet salads.

(4) The addition of either heavy cream or a raw egg to a vinaigrette dressing binds it, stops it from separating.

(1) It is preferable to serve a salad (tossed or combination) as a separate course to enjoy it fully. The practice of eating meat, vegetables, and salad all at once desensitizes the taste buds. If you should desire to serve a salad with the entrée, it should be tossed salad with a vinaigrette dressing, never a combination salad. The vinaigrette dressing for tossed salad that is to accompany the entrée should be adapted to complement the course. Here are some practices that are followed in France:

If you're serving a red wine with the meat, then use a little of the wine instead of vinegar in your salad dressing. Or use some of the juice from the roasting pan in the dressing instead of vinegar. At any rate, avoid using vinegar in the dressing when the salad is to be eaten with a course at which wine will be drunk. Another alternative would be to use fresh lemon juice instead of vinegar in the dressing.

(2) Do wash out salad bowls. The old maxim about never washing out salad bowls is wrong, and only results in a rancid salad bowl. The French preference is to make salads in porcelain, glass, silver, or enamel bowls, which are scrupulously clean. The cleaner the bowl, the better the salad.

(3) Always toss a salad at the table and always with wooden spoons. Metal spoons bruise the lettuce.

Properly introduced to them, children usually love salads, and you will think of ways to help develop your child's palate in this as in other directions. One idea is to use romaine lettuce leaves, the larger ones, as "boats" and spread a little cream cheese in them. That's fun. It makes a marvelous way of giving children a snack, and they usually end up eating a great deal more salad than they might otherwise.

This is the classic bowl of fresh garden greens, the "salade simple." The selection, care, and preparation of the greens, dressing, and salad are extremely important in achieving the beautiful crisp fresh clean taste that is the pleasure of this dish, so please read carefully the introduction to this chapter. The pointers there require no additional effort; it's just a matter of making this salad the right way instead of the wrong way.

This recipe gives suggested combinations of greens, suggested garnishes, and one more version (see also pages 62 and 63) of a

SALADE FRANÇAISE

Tossed Green Salad

basic vinaigrette dressing (in this case made in the salad bowl) for your daily bowl of greens.

GREENS. The quantities of greens represent about 4 to 6 servings.

GROUP 1
2 small heads Boston lettuce
    or 4 small heads Bibb lettuce
Half a head of escarole
1 large head endive or 2 small
Handful of young spinach
    leaves
2 tablespoons chopped fresh
    parsley
¼ cup whole chervil leaves, if
    available

GROUP 2
1 head Boston lettuce
Half a head of romaine lettuce
2 tablespoons chopped fresh
    parsley or ¼ cup fresh
    chervil

GROUP 3
4 or 5 small heads Bibb lettuce
    or about ½ pound tender

dandelion leaves
2 tablespoons chopped fresh
    parsley or ¼ cup fresh
    chervil

GROUP 4
1 bunch salad bowl lettuce or
    4 heads Bibb lettuce
2 large heads endive
2 tablespoons chopped fresh
    parsley

GROUP 5
2 or 3 large heads endive
Half a head of escarole

GROUP 6
2 small heads Boston lettuce
Handful of young spinach
    leaves
2 tablespoons chopped fresh
    parsley

GARNISHES. These garnish suggestions are strictly optional. Most of the time you may prefer to serve a combination of greens only.

CROUTONS AND SHREDDED BACON
1 cup small fried croûtons
    (page 70)
4 slices bacon, shredded, fried
    until crisp, and thoroughly
    drained

RAW CAULIFLOWER
About 1 cup thin little slices of

cauliflower (detach the florets
    and slice paper-thin with a
    mandoline)

RAW MUSHROOMS
About 1 cup thin slices of fresh
    raw firm white mushrooms
    (in salads they really must be
    firm, white, and fresh)

VINAIGRETTE DRESSING. The basic simple and compound vinaigrette recipes are in the Sauce chapter (pages 62 and 63). Use one of them or this one, which is yet another variation to permit you to compare differences in choosing "your" vinaigrette. This dressing is made in the bottom of the salad bowl. The recipe makes ½ cup of dressing.

1 bruised clove garlic
1 teaspoon kosher salt
½ teaspoon freshly cracked
    white pepper

½ teaspoon dry mustard
1 teaspoon Dijon mustard
2 tablespoons pure olive oil
1 teaspoon fresh lemon juice

2 tablespoons tarragon or wine   4 tablespoons vegetable oil
  vinegar

Wash all the greens thoroughly in salted water, then in clear ice
water. Dry them very well in a salad dryer or with paper or cloth
towels. Put them in a large plastic bag, bury the bag in a pan of
crushed ice, and place it in the refrigerator (this should be done at
least several hours ahead of serving; the best time is when you bring
the greens home — then they will be ready to use as needed).

To mix the dressing, rub the inside of the salad bowl with the
bruised garlic clove. Put in the salt, pepper, two mustards, and olive
oil. Stir vigorously with a wooden spoon. Slowly add the vinegar
and lemon juice. Last, add the vegetable oil drop by drop, stirring
constantly.

TO ASSEMBLE. Place the clean well-dried salad greens on the dressing, including chopped parsley and/or chervil if they are being used
(sprinkle the herbs over the greens). If you are using a garnish,
scatter it over the greens also. (Your salad may sit in the refrigerator
several hours this way.) When you are ready to eat the salad, only
then toss it and serve. NET: 4 to 6 servings.

2 pounds celery root (celeriac)
½ pound pine kernels (pignoli
  nuts)
4 medium-size beets, plain-
  cooked
12 shelled walnut halves
Optional: 1 black truffle, sliced
Optional: 4 hard-boiled egg
  whites, cut into thin shreds

DRESSING
4 hard-boiled egg yolks
1 raw egg yolk

3 tablespoons tarragon vinegar
2 teaspoons Dijon mustard
¼ teaspoon salt or ½ teaspoon
  kosher salt
½ teaspoon freshly cracked
  white pepper
¼ cup pure olive oil
¼ cup vegetable oil
Optional: 1 to 2 tablespoons
  heavy cream
2 tablespoons chopped fresh
  basil leaves

SALADE BELLE HÉLÈNE

*Beet and Celery Root
Salad*

Peel the celery root, cut it into very thin uniform matchsticks, and
cook in boiling salted water 4 to 5 minutes. Drain it, rinse in cold
water, and dry in a cloth or on paper towels.

DRESSING. Strain the hard-boiled egg yolks and put them into a
mixer bowl with the raw egg yolk. Mix well. Add half of the
vinegar, and all of the Dijon mustard, salt, and pepper, and mix.
Then, continuing beating, add the olive oil and vegetable oil drop
by drop. Beat in the rest of the vinegar and, if desired, the heavy
cream. Last, mix in the basil.

Mix together the celery root, pine kernels, and dressing. Dome the
mixture in a shallow glass salad bowl. Peel the beets, cut them into
very thin slices, and trim with a fluted cookie cutter. Arrange the

beet slices around the salad, slightly overlapping each other. Decorate the center with split walnuts and (if wished) the truffle and egg white. (If the truffle is not being used, use more sliced beet in the center.)

SALADE DE BETTERAVE

Beet Salad

This is a favorite French salad. I love fresh garden beets, but they should be little — no more than 1 to ½ inches in diameter; they are the most delicate and flavorful. Use the tops, too — not in salad but cooked (like spinach). They can be awfully good.

8 medium-size beets
½ cup finely chopped scallions

DRESSING
½ cup heavy cream, whipped
3 teaspoons dry mustard

2 teaspoons lemon juice
Salt
A few grains cayenne pepper
2 tablespoons tarragon vinegar
2 teaspoons granulated sugar
¼ cup pure olive oil

Wash the beets well, and cook in a steamer or in boiling salted water until they are just tender. Cool and skin them, and cut them into julienne strips (matchsticks). Put them in a salad bowl and sprinkle the scallions over them.

DRESSING. Put all the ingredients into a 1-pint screw-top jar and shake vigorously.

Just before serving, pour the dressing over the beet salad and mix lightly. NET: 4 servings.

CAESAR SALAD

2 heads romaine lettuce
⅓ cup chopped parsley
¼ cup freshly grated Parmesan
    cheese
6 slices bacon, cut into fine
    shreds, fried crisp, and
    drained (reserve the fat)
1 cup small crisp croûtons,
    made of bread, fried in the
    strained bacon fat (above)
2 hard-boiled eggs
12 anchovy fillets

DRESSING
½ teaspoon salt or 1 teaspoon

kosher salt
½ teaspoon freshly cracked
    white pepper
¼ teaspoon freshly cracked
    black pepper
¼ teaspoon dry mustard
½ teaspoon Dijon mustard
A few grains granulated sugar
1 teaspoon lemon juice
1 teaspoon finely chopped garlic
2 tablespoons tarragon vinegar
3 tablespoons pure olive oil
½ cup vegetable oil
1 raw egg

Wash the lettuce thoroughly, dry it well, and chill it several hours.

DRESSING. Put all the ingredients in the bottom of a large salad bowl. Mix well with a wooden spoon.

With the hands, break the romaine lettuce into ½-inch pieces and put them in the salad bowl on the dressing. Sprinkle the fried croûtons on the lettuce. Scatter the crisp-fried shredded bacon over the croûtons, then sprinkle the cheese and parsley over all. Cut each egg into 6 wedges and arrange them around the salad. Drape an anchovy fillet across each wedge of egg.

When ready to eat it, toss the salad, picking up the dressing from the bottom, and serve. NET: 4 servings.

SALADE DE CÉLERI-RAVE

Celery Root Salad

2 or 3 celery roots (celeriac)

DRESSING
1 tablespoon Dijon mustard
2 tablespoons dry mustard
¼ cup pure olive oil

½ cup vegetable oil
1 tablespoon tarragon vinegar
¼ cup heavy cream
Salt
A few grains cayenne pepper

Wash and peel the celery root. Cut it into fine even matchsticks. Put it in a pan, cover with cold salted water, bring it to a boil, boil 4 to 5 minutes, and drain. Plunge the celery root into cold water, drain, and dry thoroughly.

DRESSING. Mix the two mustards together in a little bowl. With a small wire whisk, slowly beat in the olive oil and vegetable oil drop by drop. Add the vinegar, then the heavy cream, and season with salt and cayenne pepper. Mix the celery root with the dressing, making sure it is thoroughly coated. Serve well chilled in a crystal salad bowl. NET: 4 servings.

COLD CHICKEN SALAD

Ham, cold poached salmon, shrimps, crabmeat, or other seafood may be substituted for chicken.

¾ cup long-grain rice
1½ cups chicken stock (page 35) or water
¼ cup vegetable oil
Salt
A few grains cayenne pepper
2 cups cold cooked chicken (white and dark meat), cut in chunks or bite-size pieces
1 cup shelled baby peas, plain-

cooked
1 cup diced carrots, plain-cooked
2 cups Basic Mayonnaise (page 52)
A little light cream (to thin the mayonnaise)
½ bunch crisp fresh watercress
2 fresh sweet red peppers, finely diced

Preheat the oven to 350°. Put the rice in a deep heavy pan and add the chicken stock or water. Mix in the vegetable oil and season with 1 teaspoon salt and a little cayenne pepper. Stir over moderate heat until it comes to a boil, then cover tightly with the lid and put the pan in the oven to cook 30 minutes. When cooked, separate the grains with two forks and chill it thoroughly.

Remove any skin and sinew from the chicken. Mix the peas and carrots into the rice and arrange the mixture as a bed on a cold flat serving dish. Arrange the chicken pieces on the rice and vegetables. Mix enough light cream into the mayonnaise to permit coating the chicken without marks or ridges. Carefully coat the chicken. Garnish the dish with red pepper and sprigs of watercress. NET: 4 servings.

WINTER COLESLAW

Coleslaw, the omnipresent American salad! There seem to be as many ways of making it as there are cooks who make it. I was given this version and found it especially good with baked beans and baked ham on a cold winter's evening.

1 medium-size green cabbage
3 large carrots, pared and grated
1 large Bermuda onion, finely chopped
⅓ cup dark raisins, softened in warm water and drained

1 medium-size apple (with skin on), cored and cut into small dice
½ cup Rich Mayonnaise (page 53)

Trim any wilted or damaged leaves from the cabbage. Cut it into very thin shreds (done best with a mandoline). Cover the cabbage with ice water and let it stand about 30 minutes to 1 hour in the refrigerator. Then drain, dry it thoroughly, and mix it with the carrots, onion, raisins, and apple in a large bowl. With two forks, blend in the mayonnaise. Chill well before serving. NET: 4 servings.

SALADE DE CONCOMBRES ET ANETH

Cucumber and Dill Salad (with oil)

4 small cucumbers
1½ teaspoons salt
¼ cup finely chopped shallots
¼ cup finely chopped fresh dill

DRESSING
2 teaspoons granulated sugar

3 tablespoons tarragon vinegar
1 tablespoon pure olive oil
1 teaspoon Dijon mustard
1 teaspoon freshly cracked white pepper
½ teaspoon salt

Cut the tops and bottoms from the cucumbers. Skin, and cut them into very thin slices (a mandoline is best to get them paper-thin and uniform). Arrange them down a flat dish and sprinkle with the salt. Cover, and chill 30 minutes. Then drain the cucumbers, wash them in cold clear water, and dry them on paper towels. Put them in a salad bowl and add the shallots and dill.

DRESSING. Mix all the ingredients together in a little bowl.

Pour the dressing over the cucumbers, toss lightly with two wooden forks, and serve well chilled. NET: 4 servings.

6 small cucumbers
4 tablespoons vinegar mixed
   with 1 tablespoon granulated
   sugar
Salt

A few grains cayenne pepper
¼ cup heavy cream, whipped
½ cup sour cream
2 tablespoons chopped fresh dill

FINNISH
CUCUMBER
SALAD

Cut the tops and bottoms from the cucumbers. Skin, and cut them in half lengthwise. Remove the seeds and cut the pulp into thin slices. Put the sliced cucumbers into a bowl and mix with the vinegar and sugar, salt, and cayenne pepper. Let them marinate 1 hour in the refrigerator. Mix the whipped cream into the sour cream. Add the dill, and stir the mixture into the cucumbers. Serve this salad ice cold in a little bowl. NET: 4 servings.

6 thin cucumbers
¼ cup water
1 large bunch of fresh dill
Salt
Freshly cracked white pepper
2 tablespoons unflavored
   gelatine
1 teaspoon lemon juice mixed
   with 2 teaspoons water
4 egg whites, beaten to soft
   peaks
3 cups heavy cream, whipped

Extra slices of cucumber for
   cornucopias
Sprigs of dill for decoration

CUCUMBER MAYONNAISE
1 egg white
1 cup Basic Mayonnaise (page
   52)
½ cup heavy cream, whipped
1 small cucumber, skinned,
   seeded, and very finely diced

MOUSSE
DE CONCOMBRES

Cold Cucumber Mousse

Chill an attractive 2-quart mold in the freezer. Remove the tops and bottoms of the cucumbers. Leave the skin on three of them and skin the other three. Cut all six into fairly thick chunks and put them into a heavy pan with the water, bunch of dill, and salt and pepper. Cover, and cook over low heat until the cucumbers are soft. Drain the cucumbers and dill thoroughly, rub through a fine strainer, and chill in the refrigerator. Then, in an electric blender, purée them until smooth. Dissolve the gelatine in the lemon juice and water, and add this to the cucumber and dill purée. Fold in the stiffly beaten egg whites, then fold in the whipped cream. Pour the mousse into the chilled mold and put it to set in the refrigerator.

CUCUMBER MAYONNAISE. Beat the egg white to soft peaks and fold it into the mayonnaise. Also fold in the whipped cream and diced cucumber pulp. Chill thoroughly.

Unmold the cucumber mousse onto a silver serving platter. Decorate it with little sprigs of dill and little cucumber cornucopias. (For each cornucopia, make a radial cut, from center to edge, in a thin slice of cucumber. Overlap the cut edges to make a cone. Press the edges together and place on the mousse.) Serve the sauce in a separate sauceboat. NET: 4 to 8 servings (depending on the rest of the menu).

SALADE D'OEUFS DURS

Hard-Boiled Egg Salad

In this salad, the eggs are stuffed with cream cheese and tuna fish, and served on a macédoine of vegetables and rice. It makes an excellent luncheon entrée.

1½ cups long-grain rice
3 cups water
Salt
6 hard-boiled eggs
16 tablespoons (½ pound) sweet butter, creamed in a mixer until it is light and fluffy
6 ounces cream cheese, beaten in a mixer
2 teaspoons tomato paste
A few grains cayenne pepper
1 cup canned white tuna fish
1 cup each of diced cooked fresh green beans and fresh carrots
1 cup diced cucumber pulp (skin, cut lengthwise, seed, and dice)
1 cup diced tomato pulp (skin, quarter, seed, and dice)
1 bunch crisp fresh watercress
3 small sour gherkins
A little canned pimento

DRESSING
½ cup vegetable oil
2 tablespoons tarragon vinegar
1 teaspoon salt
½ teaspoon freshly cracked pepper
½ teaspoon lemon juice
1 egg, beaten

Put the rice in a deep heavy pan with the water and 1 teaspoon salt. Bring to a rolling boil, cover tightly with the lid, reduce to a simmer, and cook over very low heat 30 minutes without lifting the lid. Fluff the rice with forks and chill it in the refrigerator. Shell the eggs, cut them in half lengthwise, and remove the yolks. Place the whites in a bowl of clear cold water, and set aside. Rub the yolks through a fine strainer. Add them to the butter and beat together until light and fluffy. Divide the mixture into two bowls. To one bowl, add the cream cheese and tomato paste, mix well, season with salt and cayenne pepper, and set aside. Rub the tuna fish through a fine strainer, mix it into the second bowl, season with salt and cayenne pepper, and set aside.

DRESSING. Put all the dressing ingredients into a screw-top jar and shake well.

Mix the dressing into the rice, then combine the rice with the green beans, carrots, cucumber, and tomato in a large bowl and mix them together lightly. Arrange the mixture in a large salad bowl. Make a well in the center and stick a bunch of watercress in it. Drain the egg whites and dry them on paper towels. Put the cream cheese mixture in a pastry bag fitted with a large star tube, and the tuna fish mixture in another pastry bag fitted with a large plain tube. Pipe rosettes of cream cheese into six of the egg white halves, and pipe domes of tuna fish into the remaining six. Decorate the stuffed egg halves with sliced gherkins and bits of pimento. Arrange them around the rice and vegetable mixture, alternating cream cheese and tuna fish. Chill thoroughly, and serve. NET: 6 servings.

These eggs are stuffed with cream cheese and liver pâté. The macé-doine of rice and vegetables which is a part of this dish is also a wonderful base for Lobster Mayonnaise, Salmon Mayonnaise, or any such cold entrée.

Stuffed Eggs on a Macédoine of Rice and Vegetables

½ cup long-grain rice
1 cup water
1 teaspoon salt
½ cup each of diced cooked
    fresh carrots and green beans
½ cup diced cucumber (skin,
    cut in half lengthwise, seed,
    and dice)
½ cup diced tomato pulp (skin,
    seed, and dice)
1 small bunch crisp fresh
    watercress

STUFFED EGGS
4 hard-boiled eggs
8 tablespoons sweet butter,
    creamed in a mixer until

    light and fluffy
4 ounces fine liver pâté
4 ounces cream cheese
2 teaspoons tomato paste

FRENCH DRESSING
6 tablespoons vegetable oil
1 tablespoon tarragon vinegar
½ teaspoon salt
¼ teaspoon freshly cracked
    white pepper
¼ teaspoon dry mustard
A little granulated sugar
Half a raw egg or 2 tablespoons
    heavy cream or 1 tablespoon
    sour cream (to bind the
    dressing)

DRESSING. Put all the ingredients into a 1-pint screw-top jar and shake vigorously. Chill in the refrigerator.

MACÉDOINE OF RICE AND VEGETABLES. Put the rice in a small heavy pan with the water and salt. Stir over medium heat until it comes to a boil. Reduce the heat to a simmer, cover the pan with a tight lid, and cook (without lifting the lid) 25 minutes. Let the rice cool in the pan, then put it into a large bowl and fluff it with your fingers. Add the carrots, green beans, cucumber, and tomatoes (the carrots and green beans should have been cooked in a little boiling salted water until just tender, then thoroughly chilled). Add the French dressing and stir with two forks until the mixture is well blended. Arrange this mixture in a salad bowl. Make a well in the center and stand the watercress in it.

STUFFED EGGS. Shell the eggs, cut in half lengthwise, and remove the yolks. Rub the yolks through a strainer, beat together with the creamed butter, and divide the mixture in half. Add the liver pâté to one half of the yolk and butter mixture, the cream cheese and tomato paste to the other half. Mix each filling well.

Put the cream cheese mixture in a pastry bag fitted with a #3 or #4 star tube and fill four of the egg white halves with rosettes of cream cheese. Put the pâté mixture in a pastry bag fitted with the same size plain round tube, and pipe mounds on the other four halves. Arrange the filled egg whites around the macédoine, alternating cream cheese and liver pâté fillings. Chill thoroughly. NET: 4 servings.

SALADE D'ENDIVE MARGUERITE

Mixed Vegetable Salad with Endive

1 celery root (celeriac)
Salt
1½ pounds endive
2 Idaho-type potatoes
½ pound green beans
4 beets
4 small firm ripe tomatoes
½ pound firm white mushrooms, sliced
Freshly cracked white pepper
1 cup Basic Mayonnaise (page 52)
⅓ cup dry white wine
2 tablespoons wine vinegar
¼ cup pure olive oil

Pare the celery root and cut it into very thin julienne strips (match-stick size). Plunge them into boiling salted water and boil 4 minutes. Drain, rinse in ice water, and dry on paper towels. Cut the endive into pieces 1 inch long. Cook the potatoes in boiling salted water until just tender, and drain. Cool, skin, and cut them into medium-size dice. Top and tail the green beans and break them in half. Cover with cold water, add salt, and boil until they are just tender but still crunchy. Drain and chill. Steam the beets until tender. Chill, skin, and cut them into thin slices. Skin the tomatoes and cut them into slices as thin as the beets.

Put the celery root, endive, potatoes, beans, and mushrooms in a bowl, and sprinkle with salt and pepper. Pour over them the wine, vinegar, and olive oil. Mix lightly with two wooden forks, then mix in the mayonnaise. Arrange the salad in a crystal salad bowl. Decorate the top with alternate rounds of sliced beet and sliced tomato. Serve well chilled. NET: 4 to 6 servings.

SALADE À LA GRECQUE

Greek Salad

6 small fresh sweet green peppers
4 small fresh sweet red peppers
6 medium-size firm ripe tomatoes
4 medium-size Bermuda onions
½ cup pure olive oil
2 tablespoons tarragon vinegar
2 teaspoons lemon juice
½ teaspoon granulated sugar
1 teaspoon dry mustard
Salt
Freshly cracked white pepper

Preheat the oven to 375°. Chill a salad bowl in the refrigerator. Wrap the green and red peppers individually in aluminum foil, and bake until just soft. Remove the foil, cut them into eighths, and remove all the seeds. Core and skin the tomatoes and cut them into slices ½ inch thick. Cut the Bermuda onions into thin rings and separate them. Warm the olive oil in a sauté pan over low heat. Add the peppers, tomatoes, and onions, and simmer gently 5 to 6 minutes. In a small bowl mix the vinegar, lemon juice, sugar, dry mustard, and a little salt and pepper, and stir the mixture into the salad. Chill the salad thoroughly. Serve it in the chilled salad bowl. NET: 4 servings.

2 quarts large mussels
1 teaspoon dry mustard
½ cup dry white wine
¼ cup water
1 small onion, sliced
2 1-inch pieces celery
1 small carrot, sliced
1 bay leaf
5 peppercorns
4 large Idaho-type potatoes
Salt
Freshly cracked white pepper

DRESSING
Mussel stock (above), boiled

down to 3 tablespoons
1 tablespoon Dijon mustard
½ teaspoon dry mustard
1 teaspoon salt or 2 teaspoons
    kosher salt
1 teaspoon freshly cracked
    white pepper
¼ cup pure olive oil
½ cup vegetable oil
3 tablespoons tarragon vinegar
1 egg, beaten
3 tablespoons heavy cream
2 tablespoons chopped fresh
    parsley

*Mussel and Potato Salad
(Vinaigrette Dressing)*

Scrub the mussels thoroughly in cold water with the dry mustard (see notes on mussels, page 320). Put them in a pan with the wine, water, onion, celery, carrot, bay leaf, and peppercorns. Cover, and bring to a boil. Reduce the heat a little, and simmer 5 to 6 minutes, until the shells have opened, shaking the pan once or twice during the process. Remove the mussels (with shells) from the pan. Boil the stock down to 3 tablespoons, strain, and reserve it for the dressing.

POTATOES. Put the potatoes in a pan, cover with water, add a little salt, and boil until soft. Chill them a little, skin, and cut them in half lengthwise and then into thick slices (about ½ inch). Sprinkle with a little salt and pepper.

DRESSING. Put all the ingredients in a 1-pint screw-top jar and shake vigorously.

Reserve about 12 mussels in their bottom shells, and discard all the other shells. Put the shelled mussels into a bowl with the sliced potatoes. Set 2 to 3 tablespoons dressing aside for the garnish. Pour the rest over the potatoes and mussels, and let them marinate in the dressing about 1 hour. Then arrange them in a shallow glass bowl. Loosen the 12 mussels in their shells and spoon a little of the dressing on each. Garnish the bowl around the edge with these mussels. NET: 4 servings.

2 quarts large mussels
1 teaspoon dry mustard
Bouquet garni, including sprigs
    of parsley, celery leaf, and
    1 bay leaf
5 peppercorns
1 small onion, sliced
1 small carrot, sliced
2 1-inch pieces celery
1 cup water

4 large Idaho-type potatoes
½ cup dry white wine
2 or 3 sour gherkins, thinly
    sliced

MAYONNAISE DRESSING
2 egg yolks
½ teaspoon salt or 1 teaspoon
    kosher salt
A few grains cayenne pepper

*Mussel and Potato Salad
(Mayonnaise Dressing)*

½ teaspoon Dijon mustard
¾ cup vegetable oil
1 teaspoon lemon juice
1 teaspoon chopped fresh

tarragon
1 teaspoon finely chopped
fresh parsley
1 sour gherkin, finely chopped

Scrub the mussels thoroughly in cold water with the mustard (see notes on mussels, page 320). Put them in a pan with the bouquet garni, peppercorns, onion, carrot, celery, and water. Cover, and bring to a boil. Reduce the heat a little, and shake the pan briskly over it 5 to 6 minutes, until the mussel shells have opened. Remove them (with shells) from the pan. Discard all the shells, beard the mussels, and set aside. Steam or boil the potatoes in their skins and peel while they are still hot. Cut them into thick chunky slices and sprinkle with the wine.

MAYONNAISE. Put the egg yolks, salt, pepper, and mustard in a mixer bowl and mix well. Drop by drop, add the vegetable oil and lemon juice, beating constantly. Then mix in the tarragon and parsley, and finally the chopped gherkins.

Arrange alternate layers of potatoes, mussels, and mayonnaise in a salad bowl. Finish with a layer of mayonnaise, and decorate with the sliced gherkins and a few mussels. NET: 4 servings.

SALADE DE CHAMPIGNONS

Raw Mushroom Salad

1 pound firm white fresh
mushrooms
Juice of 1 lemon
Any vinaigrette dressing (pages
62, 63, and 636)

½ cup very thinly sliced celery
1 teaspoon chopped fresh chives
or parsley
1 small bunch crisp fresh
watercress

Wash the mushrooms in cold water with the lemon juice, and dry well. Trim the stems off even with the caps, and slice the caps rather thickly (save the trimmed stems for other uses). Put the mushrooms in a bowl and pour the vinaigrette dressing over them. Mix carefully, and let the mushrooms marinate in the dressing in the refrigerator at least 30 minutes. When ready to serve, mix the celery and chives with the mushrooms and vinaigrette. Transfer to a salad bowl and garnish generously with little sprigs of the watercress. NET: 4 servings.

SALADE NIÇOISE

Salad of Tuna Fish,
Tomatoes, Anchovies
and Olives

A true Salade Niçoise should contain all these ingredients, which are characteristic of the Nice area. One friend and former student of mine loves this salad with a summer passion. With hot French bread and a chilled bottle of Moselle wine, it's a frequent hot weather meal for him — but without its anchovies because with equal passion he hates anchovies. Whatever the variation on the Niçoise theme, this salad is a delicious and wholesome meal in itself. It can also be a first course, a separate salad course, or a buffet dish. My salad-eating friend even keeps any that is left over . . . for a late snack.

1 head Boston lettuce
2 cups diced cooked Idaho
   potatoes
2 cups cooked green beans,
   cut in half
Optional: 1 cup diced love
   apples or crab apples
1½ cups drained canned white
   tuna fish, broken into chunks
2 large tomatoes or 3 medium-
   size, skinned and cut into
   slices or wedges
4 hard-boiled eggs, cut into
   wedges
8 anchovy fillets
¾ cup pitted black olives

¼ cup chopped fresh parsley

VINAIGRETTE DRESSING
1 teaspoon salt or 2 teaspoons
   kosher salt
1 teaspoon freshly cracked
   white pepper
¼ teaspoon granulated sugar
1 teaspoon Dijon mustard
½ teaspoon dry mustard
1 teaspoon lemon juice
2 tablespoons tarragon vinegar
8 tablespoons vegetable oil
2 tablespoons pure olive oil
1 egg

Thoroughly wash, drain, and dry the lettuce leaves. Put them in a plastic bag and chill them in the refrigerator.

VINAIGRETTE DRESSING. Put all the ingredients into a 1-pint screw-top jar and shake thoroughly.

Put the potatoes, green beans, love apples, and tuna fish into a large mixing bowl. Pour the vinaigrette over them, mix lightly with two wooden spoons, and let the mixture marinate about an hour. Line a large salad bowl with the crisp lettuce leaves. Arrange the marinated mixture on them, including any dressing that may have settled in the bottom of the bowl. Put the tomato slices or wedges in a row around the outer edge of the salad bowl. Between or in front of the tomatoes, put a circle of the hard-boiled egg wedges. Over each wedge of egg, lay an anchovy fillet. Scatter the olives over the salad. Sprinkle the top with the parsley. To serve, toss it lightly. NET: 4 servings.

4 large navel oranges
6 heads of endive
⅓ cup vegetable oil
1 tablespoon tarragon vinegar
½ teaspoon dry mustard

½ teaspoon salt or 1 teaspoon
   kosher salt
Freshly cracked black pepper
¼ teaspoon cayenne pepper
½ teaspoon granulated sugar

SALADE D'ORANGE ET ENDIVE

Orange and Endive Salad

Cut the rind from one orange with a potato parer, and cut it crosswise into very fine shreds. Plunge it into boiling water, remove from the heat, let stand 3 to 4 minutes, and drain. Skin all the oranges and cut into sections, making certain no pith is attached. Put the sections in a bowl. Cut the endive into halves, wash thoroughly, drain, and separate the leaves. Add them to the orange sections and chill thoroughly. Put the vegetable oil, vinegar, mustard, salt, black pepper, sugar, and cayenne pepper in a screw-top jar and shake vigorously. Just before serving, pour the dressing over the endive and orange sections. Toss together lightly with two spoons and serve in a small crystal salad bowl. NET: 4 servings.

SALADE DE FENOUIL, SCAROLE ET L'ORANGE

Fennel, Escarole, and Orange Salad

4 fennel stems
2 bunches escarole
A few young spinach leaves
Skinned sections of 6 large navel oranges
3 tablespoons chopped fresh parsley
2 teaspoons chopped fresh dill

DRESSING
2 teaspoons salt

½ teaspoon freshly cracked black pepper
1 teaspoon Dijon mustard
½ teaspoon lemon juice
¼ teaspoon granulated sugar
1 egg
2 tablespoons sour cream
3 tablespoons tarragon vinegar
½ cup vegetable oil
¼ cup pure olive oil
Grated rind of 1 orange

DRESSING. Put all the ingredients into a 1-pint screw-top jar. Shake vigorously, and chill before using.

Wash the fennel stems, escarole, and spinach leaves thoroughly in ice water, dry well, roll up in paper towels, and chill them at least 1 hour in the refrigerator. Break the escarole and spinach leaves into 1-inch pieces and arrange them in a salad bowl. Coarsely chop the fennel stems and add to the bowl. Decorate with the sections of orange. Sprinkle with the parsley and dill. Just before serving, pour the dressing over all, and toss lightly. NET: 4 servings.

SALADE DE POMMES DE TERRE

French Potato Salad

5 or 6 Idaho-type potatoes
½ cup hot chicken stock (page 35)

VINAIGRETTE DRESSING
½ teaspoon salt or 1 teaspoon kosher salt
½ teaspoon freshly cracked white pepper
¼ teaspoon coarsely ground black pepper
¼ teaspoon granulated sugar
½ teaspoon dry mustard
1 teaspoon Dijon mustard
⅛ teaspoon mace

A few grains cayenne pepper
2 teaspoons lemon juice
2 tablespoons tarragon vinegar
1 tablespoon red wine vinegar
4 tablespoons pure olive oil
8 tablespoons vegetable oil
3 teaspoons finely chopped shallots
⅛ teaspoon finely chopped garlic
2 tablespoons finely chopped fresh parsley
1 tablespoon chopped chives
1 finely chopped hard-boiled egg

VINAIGRETTE DRESSING. Put all the dressing ingredients into a screw-top jar, and shake it thoroughly.

Boil the potatoes in their skins in salted water until just soft. Drain, and return them to the pan to dry over heat for a minute. Cool them a little, skin them (using your fingers, not a knife), and cut them into quarters lengthwise, then into slices (this method gives little chunks). Put them in a bowl, pour the hot chicken stock over them, and toss with two large wooden spoons (these help keep the potatoes from breaking). Then pour the vinaigrette sauce over the potatoes (it is important to add it while they are still hot), and mix it in with the wooden spoons. NET: 4 to 6 servings.

<table>
<tr><td>

2 pounds new potatoes
¾ cup finely chopped yellow onion
1 teaspoon finely chopped garlic
½ cup mixed fresh herbs, such as chopped parsley, celery leaf, chervil
1½ teaspoons salt

</td><td>

½ teaspoon freshly cracked black pepper
½ teaspoon freshly cracked white pepper
3 tablespoons pure olive oil, warmed
½ cup vegetable oil, warmed

</td></tr>
</table>

HOT GERMAN POTATO SALAD

Cook the potatoes in their skins in boiling salted water until just tender. Drain, wrap them in a cloth, and let them sit 15 minutes. Warm a large wooden salad bowl in the oven at very low heat with the door open, to avoid damage to the bowl. Then put in it the onion, garlic, and herbs. Add the salt and black and white pepper. Skin the warm potatoes and cut them into the bowl in medium-size pieces. Pour the warm oils over them and, with two large wooden forks, toss all the ingredients together. Serve at once. If the salad has to wait, cover it with a cloth and set it in the warm oven. NET: 4 servings.

<table>
<tr><td>

¾ cup long-grain rice
¼ cup pure olive oil
2 teaspoons salt
¼ teaspoon cayenne pepper
1½ cups water
1½ cups shelled baby peas, cooked in a little salted water and chilled

</td><td>

¼ pound boiled ham, cut into matchsticks
½ pound firm white fresh mushrooms, sliced
1 cup Basic Mayonnaise (page 52)
½ cup Vinaigrette I (page 62)
1 cup shelled walnut halves

</td></tr>
</table>

DERBY SALAD

Rice Salad
with Ham and Peas

Preheat the oven to 350°. Put the rice in a deep heavy pan with the olive oil, salt, cayenne pepper, and water. Stir until the mixture comes to a boil. Cover firmly with the lid, and cook 30 minutes in the oven. When the rice is cooked, fluff it with two forks, chill it thoroughly, then lightly mix with it the peas, ham, and mushrooms. Mix the mayonnaise and the vinaigrette dressings together, pour them over the salad, and again lightly toss. To serve, pile the salad in a dome shape in a shallow salad bowl. Garnish with the walnut halves. NET: 4 servings.

SALADE RUSSE

Russian Salad

A traditional Russian Salad is always composed of a macédoine of cooked vegetables with a mixture of boiled shellfish and ham or beef.

1 cup fresh shelled green peas,
  plain-cooked
1 cup each of diced fresh green
  beans, carrots, and turnips
1 cup shredded boiled ham or
  cooked tongue
1 cup chopped boiled lobster
  meat
2 tablespoons capers plus
  ¼ cup
6 sour gherkins, sliced

12 anchovy fillets, sliced
A little light cream
1 cup Basic or Rich Mayonnaise
  (pages 52, 53)
½ cup red caviar
1 or 2 large fresh beets for
  garnish
3 hard-boiled eggs, cut into
  eighths
Optional: 1 black truffle, sliced

Cook the peas, green beans, carrots, turnips, and beet separately in boiling salted water until barely tender and still crunchy. Chill them thoroughly. Then put the peas, green beans, carrots, and turnips into a large bowl. Add the ham or tongue, lobster, 2 tablespoons capers, gherkins, and anchovy fillets, and mix all the ingredients together lightly with two wooden spoons. Pile the mixture in a dome shape in a shallow glass bowl. Mix a little light cream into the mayonnaise and spoon it over the vegetables. Cut the beet into thin slices and decorate the salad with a border of beet slices all around it. On alternate slices of beet put 1 teaspoon red caviar, and on the other slices ½ teaspoon capers. Decorate the center of the salad with the thin wedges of hard-boiled egg and the truffle slices. NET: 4 servings.

SALADE D'ÉPINARDS AU LARD

Spinach Salad with Bacon

2 to 3 pounds fresh spinach
1 pound sliced bacon
4 anchovy fillets
⅓ cup pure olive oil
2 tablespoons dry white wine
2 tablespoons lemon juice

1 teaspoon salt
1 teaspoon freshly cracked
  black pepper
1 teaspoon dry mustard
¼ teaspoon granulated sugar

Wash the spinach in several waters and drain it. Have ready a large pot one-quarter full of boiling water. Plunge the spinach into the boiling water for 1 minute. Stir once so that all the leaves are blanched. Drain, and rinse it in clear cold water. Dry it as much as possible. Put it in the refrigerator to chill a little. Cut the bacon slices across into thin shreds. Cook in a frypan until crisp. Drain through a strainer, then on paper towels.

DRESSING. Crush the anchovy fillets with a mortar and pestle until you have a smooth paste. Slowly mix the olive oil into the anchovy paste. Mix in the wine and lemon juice drop by drop. Then mix in the salt, pepper, mustard, and sugar.

When ready to serve, put the spinach in a large salad bowl and sprinkle the bacon over it. Mix it lightly with the dressing. Serve the salad very cold. NET: 4 to 6 servings.

6 large firm ripe tomatoes or
   3 ripe beefsteak tomatoes
2 medium-size yellow onions
1 teaspoon granulated sugar
1 tablespoon chopped fresh
   parsley

DRESSING
2 teaspoons Dijon mustard
½ teaspoon salt or 1 teaspoon

kosher salt
1 teaspoon freshly cracked
   black pepper
½ teaspoon lemon juice
½ teaspoon finely chopped
   garlic
2 tablespoons tarragon vinegar
¼ cup pure olive oil
¼ cup vegetable oil

Tomato Salad

Put the tomatoes in a large bowl and cover with boiling water. Count to 10 slowly. Drain off the water and plunge them immediately into ice water. Remove the core and skin, and cut the tomatoes into slices ¼ to ½ inch thick. Arrange the slices in straight rows, overlapping, on a shallow oblong salad dish. Peel the onions and slice them very thin. Separate the slices into rings. Cover the tomatoes with the thin onion rings. (The appearance should remind you of a heavy fall of snow.) Sprinkle the salad with the sugar.

DRESSING. Put all the ingredients in a 1-pint screw-top jar and shake vigorously.

Pour the dressing over the tomatoes. Sprinkle the top with the parsley. NET: 4 servings.

2 pounds firm ripe tomatoes
   (either large or beefsteak
   type)
1 Bermuda onion
1 or 2 sprigs fresh basil or dill,
   for garnish

DRESSING
½ teaspoon dry mustard
1 teaspoon Dijon mustard

½ teaspoon salt or 1 teaspoon
   kosher salt
½ teaspoon freshly cracked
   white pepper
¼ teaspoon finely chopped
   garlic
¼ teaspoon granulated sugar
¼ cup pure olive oil
1 tablespoon lemon juice
1 tablespoon tarragon vinegar
⅓ cup chopped fresh basil or dill

*Tomato and Fresh
Basil Salad (or Dill)*

Core and skin the tomatoes, and cut them into ¼-inch slices. Arrange them on a flat salad platter and chill.

DRESSING. Put the two mustards, salt, pepper, garlic, and sugar in a small bowl. Slowly mix in the olive oil. Then mix in the lemon juice and vinegar. Mix the chopped herb into the dressing (basil or dill).

Pour the dressing over the tomatoes. Cut the Bermuda onion into wafer-thin slices. Separate the rings and scatter them over the tomatoes. Garnish with the sprigs of basil leaf or dill. NET: 4 servings.

MACÉDOINE DE LÉGUMES

Salad of Mixed Cooked Vegetables

1 cup fresh shelled young peas
1 cup each of diced fresh young
   green beans, carrots, and
   turnips
1 cup fresh or frozen baby lima
   beans
3 tablespoons chopped fresh
   parsley

FRENCH DRESSING
1 teaspoon salt or 2 teaspoons

kosher salt
1 teaspoon freshly cracked
   white pepper
1/4 teaspoon granulated sugar
1 teaspoon Dijon mustard
1/4 teaspoon dry mustard
1 teaspoon lemon juice
2 tablespoons tarragon vinegar
8 tablespoons vegetable oil
2 tablespoons pure olive oil
2 tablespoons heavy cream

Cook the vegetables separately in a little boiling salted water until just tender; they should still be crunchy. Mix them all together in a bowl. Chill them thoroughly.

FRENCH DRESSING. Put all the ingredients in a 1-pint screw-top jar and shake it vigorously.

When the vegetables are well chilled, pour the dressing over them and mix them lightly with two forks. Serve the macédoine in a round salad dish, sprinkled with the chopped fresh parsley. NET: 4 servings.

SALADE DE LÉGUMES MAISON

Mixed Raw Vegetable Salad

1 cup coarsely grated raw beets
1 cup very finely shredded raw
   carrots
1 cup finely shredded raw
   cabbage
1 cup finely shredded cucumber
   pulp (cucumbers peeled and
   seeded)
1 cup shredded tomato pulp
   (tomatoes skinned, quartered,
   seeded, and shredded)
1 cup raw shredded zucchini
   (not peeled)
1 cup finely diced heart of

celery

FRENCH DRESSING
1 teaspoon salt or 2 teaspoons
   kosher salt
1 teaspoon freshly cracked
   white pepper
1/4 teaspoon granulated sugar
1 teaspoon lemon juice
2 tablespoons tarragon vinegar
8 tablespoons vegetable oil
2 tablespoons pure olive oil
2 tablespoons heavy cream

FRENCH DRESSING. Put all the ingredients into a 1-pint screw-top jar and shake vigorously.

Mix a little of the dressing into each vegetable. Keep the vegetable groups separate, and chill thoroughly. To serve, arrange the separate vegetables in the form of a cartwheel on a large shallow crystal salad bowl. NET: 4 to 6 servings.

Prepare the vegetables and eggs well in advance of serving, so they can be completely chilled.

2 cups diced raw cucumbers
  (skin and seed before dicing)
2 cups each of diced cooked
  fresh carrots, green beans,
  young turnips, and beets
2 cups diced ripe tomatoes
  (skin, quarter, and seed
  before dicing)
2 cups chopped hard-boiled
  eggs
4 small bunches crisp fresh
  watercress

DRESSING
1 teaspoon salt or 2 teaspoons
  kosher salt
½ teaspoon freshly cracked
  black pepper
½ teaspoon finely chopped
  garlic
1 teaspoon lemon juice
¼ teaspoon granulated sugar
1 raw egg
2 tablespoons sour cream
2 tablespoons tarragon vinegar
½ cup vegetable oil
¼ cup pure olive oil

*Carmen Salad
(Brightly Colored
Cartwheel of Cold
Cooked Vegetables)*

Have all the vegetables and the eggs prepared and well chilled. Rinse the watercress in ice water, drain thoroughly, and chill.

DRESSING. Put all the ingredients into a 1-pint screw-top jar, and shake vigorously.

Mix each vegetable with a little of the dressing. Arrange the vegetables in sections in a large shallow bowl, in the shape of a cartwheel (a section of cucumber, another of carrot, etc.). Arrange the chopped eggs in the middle. Garnish around the edge of the wheel with the watercress. NET: 4 to 8 servings, depending on the rest of the menu.

The Mimosa Salad is a lovely salad, a good salad, and a very French salad. It has an interesting rich egg-base dressing which gives a special flavor to this simple array of vegetables and eggs.

6 firm ripe tomatoes
1 teaspoon sugar
Salt
Freshly cracked white pepper
2 cucumbers
4 celery roots (celeriac)
½ pound green beans
4 large beets
6 hard-boiled eggs

DRESSING
2 raw egg yolks
2 tablespoons tarragon vinegar
Salt

A few grains cayenne pepper
1½ cups vegetable oil
1 tablespoon chopped fresh dill
2 teaspoons chopped fresh
  chives
1 teaspoon Tabasco sauce
3 tablespoons fresh tomato
  juice (strained from the seeds
  of the tomatoes used in the
  salad)
1 teaspoon Worcestershire
  sauce
1 cup heavy cream, whipped

Mimosa Salad

When each vegetable is prepared, set it in the refrigerator. Have them all well chilled before making the salad. Chill the eggs too.

Skin the tomatoes, cut into quarters, and remove the seeds. Rub the seed parts through a fine strainer and reserve the juice for the dressing. Cut the pulp into shreds and sprinkle with the sugar, salt, and pepper. Cut the tops and bottoms from the cucumbers, skin with a potato peeler, cut into very thin slices (best done with a mandoline), and sprinkle with a little salt. Peel the celery root with a potato parer, cut into thin slices, then into very thin shreds. Put it in a pan, cover with cold water, bring to a boil, boil 3 minutes, drain, and sprinkle with a little salt.

Top and tail the beans, cut into small dice, put in a pan, cover with cold water, bring to a boil, and drain. Cook the beets in a steamer or in boiling salted water until soft. Skin, and cut them into matchsticks. Remove the yolks from the hard-boiled eggs, rub them through a coarse strainer, and set aside. Cut the whites into shreds.

DRESSING. Beat the egg yolks in the mixer until light and fluffy. Add the vinegar, salt, and cayenne pepper, and beat again. Very slowly, drop by drop, add the vegetable oil. When the dressing begins to thicken like mayonnaise, the oil can be poured in a little faster. When all the oil has been added, mix in the rest of the dressing ingredients, folding in the whipped cream last.

This salad should be presented on a shallow round platter. Arrange wedge-shaped sections of individual vegetables in a cartwheel: a section of tomatoes, of cucumbers, of beets, of egg whites, of green beans, of egg yolks, of celery root. Keep the salad arrangement chilled until ready to serve. Serve the dressing in a separate bowl. NET: 4 to 6 servings.

SALADE DE MÂCHE ET BETTERAVES

Arugula and Beet Salad

Arugula has long been favored on European tables and is now available at some greengrocers in this country. It has a unique combination of slight bitterness and pungency that is kept in perfect balance when combined with the sweet character of beets and walnuts (as in this salad), or with a good wine vinaigrette if served alone. This recipe comes from La Boule d'Or in Paris.

4 medium-size fresh beets
Enough arugula leaves for a
*   salad for 4 persons*
½ cup walnut halves

Vinaigrette dressing with
*   tarragon or red wine vinegar*
*   (page 62)*

Cook the beets in a steamer or in boiling salted water until soft. Cool, skin, and cut them into matchsticks. Thoroughly wash and dry the arugula leaves and crisp them in the refrigerator. Marinate the prepared beets in a little vinaigrette dressing for 30 minutes to an hour before serving. When ready to serve, combine the beets, arugula leaves, and walnut halves in a large salad bowl with vinaigrette dressing. Toss, and serve immediately. NET: 4 servings.

2 firm cucumbers, skinned and
    thinly sliced
6 medium-size firm tomatoes,
    skinned and quartered
A little granulated sugar
Salt
Freshly cracked white pepper
4 celery roots, peeled and cut
    into very thin shreds
1 very small green cabbage,
    very finely shredded
4 large cooked fresh beets,
    skinned and cut into match-
    sticks
6 hard-boiled eggs, yolks
    rubbed through a fine
    strainer and whites cut into
    fine shreds

GREEN DRESSING
2 egg yolks
2 tablespoons tarragon vinegar
Salt
A few grains cayenne pepper
1¼ cups vegetable oil
1 tablespoon chopped fresh dill
2 tablespoons very finely
    chopped fresh parsley
2 teaspoons chopped fresh
    chives
Generous sprinkling of
    Tabasco sauce
1 tablespoon strained fresh
    tomato juice (from tomatoes
    in the salad)
1 teaspoon Worcestershire
    sauce
¾ cup heavy cream, whipped

INSALATA VERDE

Italian Vegetable Salad with Green Dressing

Sprinkle the sliced cucumbers with salt and set them in the refrigerator. Remove the seeds from the tomatoes, rub the seed parts through a fine strainer, and reserve the juice. Cut the pulp sections into shreds, sprinkle them with a little sugar, salt, and pepper, and chill. Put the celery root in a pan, cover with cold water, bring to a boil, and cook 5 minutes. Drain, sprinkle with salt, and set it in the refrigerator. Put the cabbage in a pan, cover with cold water and a little salt, bring to a boil, and drain. Sprinkle with a little salt, and set it in the refrigerator. Chill the beets.

DRESSING. Beat the egg yolks in the mixer until light and fluffy. Add the vinegar, salt, and cayenne pepper, and beat well. Very slowly, literally drop by drop (until the dressing thickens like mayonnaise) pour in the vegetable oil, beating constantly. Then mix in the rest of the ingredients, folding in the whipped cream last.

When all of the vegetables have been thoroughly chilled, arrange them and the egg yolks and whites in separate wedge-shaped sections forming a colorful cartwheel on a shallow round platter. Serve the green dressing in a separate bowl. NET: 6 servings.

PASTA AND GRAINS

P ASTA, PASTACIUTTA, GNOCCHI, RISOTTO are Italian words for which there seem to be no translations in either French or English. The French culinary term pâte (paste), as in Pâte à Chou, refers to a different food category. The United Nations of gnocchi cookery has no synonym in English or French to match the Russian varenyky and German knöderl. Indeed, the subject of pasta deserves a treatise (such as Raymond Oliver's scholarly summation of the bouillabaisse) to record its history or legend and bless its presence in many national cuisines. That would, indeed, be a great tribute to the Italian table, which succored the Latin spirit to produce its great art in paintings, sculpture, and music. (If this sounds a little native, it's probably the touch of Italian in me from my early childhood in Venice and many return visits to this wonderful land.)

Pasta is an important food in the French national diet; France is the third largest consumer of pasta per capita in the world, with 14 pounds per person per year, exceeded only by Italy, of course, and Switzerland.

The most accurate culinary classification of pastas is the rather broad one of "farinaceous preparations." This unfortunate term is avoided by most classic gastronomers. M. Pellaprat wrote in *Modern French Culinary Art:*

"*Pasta:* Pastes made from the wheaten semolina in a variety of shapes and dried. Among the best known are macaroni, spaghetti, vermicelli, noodles, ravioli (which are stuffed with finely minced meat or vegetable), etc. The credit for first making macaroni belongs to the Chinese. They were copied by the Germans, and finally it became an Italian industry. The name is said to be of Greek derivation, meaning the blessed bread, an allusion to the ancient custom of eating it at feasts of the dead."

Pastaciutta became the hallmark of Italian cuisine, whether it truly originated as such from the Chinese, or from the Greco-Roman culture. This wonderful story is told about the great operatic composer

Rossini — who, of course, was a gourmet of considerable magnitude. He was approached by a rather boorish fellow at a party, who said, "Signor Rossini, I am so delighted to see you again," and started to strike up a conversation. Rossini was obviously bored, and the man finally said, "You must remember me, I sat next to you in Genoa. We had that marvelous macaroni dish — it must have been five or six years ago." "Ah, yes," Rossini said. "I remember that macaroni dish very well, but I don't seem to remember you."

The purpose of this chapter is to show how to cook some of the best and favorite pasta and grain dishes in the home kitchen. Whole grains and ground meals have provided an important food since the beginning of time. They include, from America, the cornmeal of the American Indians, and their wild rice — unique to one region in Minnesota. Pastas in the form of fresh noodles and gnocchi, and risotto variations, are as established in French cuisine as the use of Italian Parmesan cheese in the au gratin.

Gathered in this chapter are favorite dishes from my cooking classes. They represent a variety of techniques, which are described in the individual recipes in adequate detail. The only general pointer needed here is to emphasize our plea for the correct cooking of all pastas *al dente, please*. Meaning, cooked pasta should still require some chewing, and not be a pulp. The method and time for cooking various pastas al dente are shown with each recipe.

The critical import of "al dente" is illustrated by Luigi Velpicelli, vice president of the Italian Academy of Good Cooking, in this little tale. "When I was a young man teaching in a Roman liceo I remember a corpulent classics master who devoured pastaciutta as Xenophon and his army devoured parasangs. If it should happen once a year that the Head called us for some special staff meeting lasting half an hour after the lesson, he would rush to the telephone like a man calling the fire brigade. 'Caterina, wait — don't throw it in the water!' he would shout in an agitated voice. When the meeting was over and greetings past, he would return to the telephone and say one crisp word, 'Throw!' Not a word more. This left him exactly the time to go down into the street, go to the corner, turn right, walk fifty yards, go up two flights of stairs, take off his hat, and sit down at the table. Caterina, his wife, who had heard the door open, arrived immediately with the steaming bowl of spaghetti, which was a sufficient greeting to her returning husband."

SEMOLINA AND SEMOLINA FLOUR. Because it may be difficult to buy semolina flour unless you have access to a good Italian grocery shop, I have formulated the recipes for noodles and pastas in this chapter with all-purpose unbleached flour. For granular semolina, as called for in Gnocchi à la Romana, you can use cream of farina, which is also used by many American-Italian cooks.

EQUIPMENT. There is a piece of equipment which will increase your joy in making and eating pasta at home, so much so that it may become standard fare as did happen with many of my former students. That equipment is a "pasta machine" — a roller and cutter to roll the dough down to the proper thinness and cut it into wide and/or narrow noodles (fettucini).

Buon appetito!

Homemade buttered noodles can be a surprise variation (instead of potatoes or rice) to garnish a roast, or with a Boeuf Bourguignonne, a daube, or a ragoût. With a pasta roller and cutter, delicious home-made noodles and pasta can be convenience foods.

NOODLE DOUGH
1⅓ cups all-purpose flour
1 egg
1 egg yolk
½ teaspoon salt
1 tablespoon pure olive oil
¾ cup semolina (or cream of
  farina mixed with a little
  rice flour or all-purpose flour)

TO COOK AND SERVE
3 tablespoons vegetable oil
6 tablespoons sweet or salt
  butter, creamed in a mixer
  until light and fluffy
Salt
Freshly cracked white pepper

NOODLE DOUGH. Put the all-purpose flour in a mound on the pastry board. Make a well in the center. In a little bowl, beat the egg, egg yolk, salt, and olive oil together with a rotary beater. Put the mixture in the well in the flour, and work up the flour with the egg mixture to form a firm dough. Knead it a little to get a shiny surface. Wrap it in plastic and refrigerate it at least 2½ hours.

TO CUT THE NOODLES. Cut the refrigerated dough in half. With a rolling pin, roll out each piece of dough to a strip roughly 12 to 18 inches long. Have ready a jelly roll pan with the semolina spread in it. Roll one piece of dough through the wide flat rollers of the machine three times, each time setting the rollers at a thinner position. When you have the thinnest sheet of dough (which is now very long), roll it through the cutting rollers, either the wide or the narrow cutters, depending on the width you want. When the noodles have been cut, lift them gently with your hands and let them straighten out, so that they don't stick together. Lay them in folds the length of the jelly roll pan and sprinkle with the semolina. Roll, cut, and lay out the rest of the dough in the same way.

When all the noodles have been cut and dusted in this manner, they can be used immediately, or they can be left to dry and kept for a week or so.

TO COOK THE NOODLES. Fill a large pan three-quarters full of water. Add the vegetable oil and 1 tablespoon salt. Bring to a rolling boil, put in the noodles, and simmer them 6 to 7 minutes. Drain immediately through a colander and put them in a hot serving dish. Using two forks, lightly toss the creamed butter with the noodles a little at a time. Season with salt and pepper. Serve immediately. NET: 4 servings.

FETTUCINI

Italian Noodles

This "recipe" was invariably a "fun" lesson in my classes. It offers basic Italian noodles (fettucini) in white, red, and green doughs, and describes the proper way to cook fettucini, with serving suggestions. This classic pasta is a perfect accompaniment for many favorite French as well as Italian dishes. For an understated soup course, save a few broken scraps when you make fettucini. Warm a little chicken stock, which you always have on hand in the freezer. Cook the noodles in it until they are just soft. Sprinkle with a little chopped fresh parsley. Serve!

PLAIN EGG NOODLE DOUGH (WHITE). This dough for the classic plain white noodles, which are wonderful themselves, is also the base for red and green noodle doughs (below).

2 cups all-purpose flour	1 egg yolk
1 teaspoon salt	2 tablespoons pure olive oil
1 egg	A little water (barely ¼ cup)

Sift the flour with the salt into a bowl. Make a well in the center. In a separate little bowl, beat the egg, egg yolk, and olive oil. Put the mixture in the well in the flour, add the water, and work up all the ingredients quickly to a stiff dough (the dough must be very hard). Turn it out onto a lightly floured board and knead it with the tips of the fingers until it has a nice shiny surface. Wrap the dough in plastic and chill it in the refrigerator at least 30 minutes, longer if possible. NET: This recipe will deliver about 2 quarts cooked noodles, enough for 4 servings as a main course, more as a garnish.

TOMATO DOUGH (RED NOODLES). To make this dough you need all the ingredients for plain noodle dough (above) except the water, which is replaced by the tomato glaze.

Noodle dough ingredients, except water	*chunks (leave skin on)*
	2 tablespoons tomato paste
	2 tablespoons Chianti wine
TOMATO GLAZE	*Salt*
3 very ripe large tomatoes, cored and cut into coarse	*Freshly cracked white pepper*

TOMATO GLAZE. Put all the ingredients for the glaze into a saucepan, and cook until the mixture is thoroughly amalgamated into a tomato sauce. Rub it through a fine strainer to make a tomato purée, then return it to the saucepan and boil it down to about ½ cup concentrated tomato glaze. Chill.

Prepare the recipe for plain egg noodle dough (above), using ½ cup tomato glaze instead of ¼ cup water. If more liquid is needed to hold the dough together, add a very few drops of water. Knead, wrap, and chill the tomato dough as for plain egg noodle dough.

SPINACH DOUGH (GREEN NOODLES). Spinach noodle dough requires all the ingredients for the plain egg noodle dough (page 662) except the water; the spinach purée is used instead of water.

Noodle dough ingredients,
*   except water*

SPINACH PURÉE
1 pound fresh spinach
2 tablespoons salt butter
Salt
Freshly cracked white pepper

SPINACH PURÉE. Wash the spinach leaves thoroughly in several waters, and drain (not too well). Put the spinach in a pan with the butter, salt, and pepper, and cook it briskly, turning it over with a wooden spoon, until it is just wilted. Drain the spinach through a colander into a bowl to reserve the juice. Press it down with a plate to squeeze out all the juice. Purée the spinach in an electric blender at low speed until it is smooth. Chill.

Prepare the recipe for plain egg noodle dough (above), but use ½ cup spinach purée instead of ¼ cup water. If more liquid is needed to hold the dough together, add a very few drops of spinach juice. Knead, wrap, and chill the spinach dough as for plain egg noodle dough.

TO ROLL, CUT, AND COOK THE NOODLES. For this you need the following ingredients:

¾ cup fine semolina (or cream
*   of farina) mixed with a little*

rice flour (or all-purpose flour)
3 tablespoons vegetable oil

Have the pasta machine ready. Cut the chilled dough in half. With a rolling pin, roll out each piece of dough to a strip about 12 to 18 inches long. Have ready a jelly roll pan and the semolina and flour mixture (or cream of farina and flour). Roll one piece of dough through the wide flat rollers of the machine three times, each time setting the rollers at a thinner position. When you have the thinnest sheet of dough (which is now very long), roll it through the cutting rollers. (For Italian fettucini, use the wide cutters; for a noodle garnish or accompaniment to a ragoût, you may wish to use the narrow cutters.) Lift the cut noodles gently with your hands, and let them straighten out so they don't stick together. Lay them in folds the length of the jelly roll pan and sprinkle with the semolina and flour mixture. Roll, cut, lay out, and dust the rest of the dough in the same manner.

Fill a large pan three-quarters full of water. Add salt and the vegetable oil (the oil keeps the noodles from sticking together). Bring to a boil, put in the quantity of noodles you require, stir them with a fork to separate them, and simmer briskly over medium heat 7 minutes, *no longer*. Noodles, like all pasta, should be served al dente. Drain the noodles in a colander.

TO SERVE PLAIN FETTUCINI. This is a simple and wonderful way to serve fettucini.

8 tablespoons sweet butter
1 teaspoon finely chopped
   garlic
1 teaspoon freshly cracked
   white pepper

Salt
1 cup freshly grated Parmesan
   cheese
Optional: Finely chopped clams
   or tiny little cooked shrimps

Cream the butter in a mixer until it is light and fluffy. Continue beating, and add the garlic, pepper, and a little salt. Put the hot cooked fettucini in a hot casserole. At the table or in the kitchen, using two forks, toss the garlic butter and the cheese alternately into the fettucini. Toss quickly so that the butter stays creamy and does not get oily. If desired, the shrimps or chopped clams may also be tossed into the fettucini.

TO SERVE THE THREE TYPES OF FETTUCINI. For a more dramatic salute to Italian cuisine, present three hot bowls of fettucini on the table or buffet, as follows:

White (plain) noodles tossed with garlic butter and Parmesan cheese, as above.

Red (tomato) noodles tossed with garlic butter, Parmesan cheese, and tiny cooked shrimps.

Green (spinach) noodles tossed with garlic butter, Parmesan cheese, and chopped clams.

CANNELLONI À LA TOSCANA

Cannelloni Stuffed with Chicken or Veal, with Velouté Sauce

CANNELLONI DOUGH
1⅓ cups all-purpose flour
1 egg
1 egg yolk
½ teaspoon salt
1 tablespoon pure olive oil
3 tablespoons vegetable oil and
   1 tablespoon salt
   (for cooking)
A little melted butter

FILLING
3 tablespoons salt butter
6 chicken livers
1 large onion, finely chopped
½ teaspoon finely chopped
   garlic
1½ cups diced cooked chicken

   or veal
2 eggs
½ teaspoon thyme
Salt
Freshly cracked white pepper

VELOUTÉ SAUCE
4 tablespoons sweet butter
4 tablespoons all-purpose flour
1 cup chicken stock (page 35)
Salt
A few grains cayenne pepper
½ cup light cream

GARNISH
½ cup freshly grated Parmesan
   cheese
3 tablespoons melted salt butter

Put the flour in a mound on the pastry board. Make a well in the center. Beat the egg, egg yolk, salt, and olive oil together in a small bowl with a rotary beater, put the mixture in the well in the flour, and work up all the ingredients to a firm dough. Knead a little to get a shiny surface on the dough. Wrap it in plastic wrap and chill in the refrigerator 2½ hours. Then roll it out very, very thin (the thinnest setting on the pasta machine). With a large straight-bladed French knife, cut it into 3½-inch squares. Fill a large pan three-quarters full of water, add the vegetable oil and salt, and bring to a boil. Put in the squares of dough and simmer them briskly over medium heat 8 minutes (until tender but somewhat firm). Drain the cooked cannelloni on paper towels or a cloth.

FILLING. Heat 1 tablespoon butter in a deep heavy pan. When it is foaming, brown the livers quickly on each side. Remove them from the pan, set aside, and add 2 tablespoons butter to the pan. Then add the onion and garlic, and cook over low heat until soft but not browned. Return the livers to the pan and add the chicken or veal. Mix the contents of the pan together and put the whole mixture through a fine meat grinder. Beat the eggs in a mixer, add the chicken or veal mixture, and season with the thyme, salt, and pepper.

Spread a little filling on each cannelloni square, roll them up into tubes, and arrange them side by side on a flat baking dish. Brush the tops with a little melted butter.

VELOUTÉ SAUCE. Melt the butter in a saucepan. Off the heat, stir in the flour, then the chicken stock, and season with salt and the cayenne pepper. Stir over low heat until the sauce comes to a boil, then stir in the light cream.

Spoon the sauce over the cannelloni in the baking dish. Sprinkle with the cheese and melted butter, and brown under the broiler. NET: 4 servings.

Cannelloni (page 664)
4 tablespoons melted sweet
    butter
1 cup freshly grated Parmesan
    cheese
1 tablespoon chopped fresh
    parsley

FILLING
4 ounces cream cheese
2 cups ricotta cheese
1 small egg
1 teaspoon finely chopped garlic
Salt
Freshly cracked white pepper

VEAL AND TOMATO SAUCE
2 tablespoons pure olive oil
1 cup finely chopped onion
1 teaspoon finely chopped garlic
6 medium-size firm ripe
    tomatoes, skinned and sliced
2 tablespoons tomato paste
2 teaspoons potato flour
1½ cups ground lean veal
3 tablespoons chopped fresh
    parsley
½ cup chicken stock (page 35)
Salt
Freshly cracked white pepper

CANNELLONI
STUFFED WITH
RICOTTA AND
CREAM CHEESE

Prepare the cannelloni (page 665) through cooking and draining the squares.

FILLING. Cream the cream cheese in the mixer until it is smooth and light. Add the ricotta cheese, egg, garlic, salt, and pepper, and mix well.

Spread some of this filling in the center of each cooked cannelloni square. Roll them up into tubes and arrange on a buttered baking dish. Brush them with the melted butter and sprinkle with some of the cheese.

VEAL AND TOMATO SAUCE. Warm the olive oil in a sauté pan and add the onion and garlic. Cook slowly 2 minutes, then add the tomatoes and cook briskly 3 minutes. Mix the potato flour with the tomato paste and, off the heat, stir it into the sauté pan. Add the veal, parsley, and chicken stock, and stir over moderate heat until the mixture comes to a boil, then simmer gently 5 to 6 minutes. Season with salt and pepper.

Preheat the oven to 350°. Spoon the sauce over the cannelloni in the baking dish. Sprinkle with more Parmesan cheese and the parsley, and bake 15 minutes. Serve piping hot with a separate bowl of freshly grated Parmesan cheese. NET: 4 to 6 servings.

RAVIOLI À LA BOLOGNESE

Ravioli Stuffed with Spinach and Meat, with Fresh Tomato Sauce

RAVIOLI DOUGH
1½ cups all-purpose flour
½ teaspoon salt
3 egg yolks
2 tablespoons pure olive oil
    or vegetable oil
¼ cup lukewarm water
1 egg, beaten
¼ cup fine semolina or cream
    of farina mixed with a little
    flour

FILLING
1 pound fresh spinach
2 tablespoons salt butter
Salt
Freshly cracked white pepper
1 egg
3 ounces ground beef
3 ounces ground veal
1 small white onion, finely
    chopped
½ teaspoon finely chopped
    garlic
A few grains freshly grated

nutmeg
⅛ teaspoon mace

FRESH TOMATO SAUCE
4 tablespoons salt butter
4 large ripe tomatoes, skinned
    and cut into ½-inch cubes
1 teaspoon finely chopped garlic
Salt
Freshly cracked white pepper
2 tablespoons tomato paste
2 teaspoons potato flour mixed
    with 2 tablespoons water
2 cups chicken stock (page 35)
    or water
1 teaspoon sugar

GARNISH
3 tablespoons dry breadcrumbs
    (page 69)
2 tablespoons melted salt butter
1 cup freshly grated Parmesan
    cheese
2 tablespoons chopped fresh
    parsley

Sift the flour and salt into a mound on the pastry board. Make a well in the center. In a small bowl, beat the egg yolks with the oil, using a rotary beater. Put the mixture in the well in the flour, add the water, and work it all up into a firm dough. Knead it a little until it is a smooth satiny ball, wrap it in plastic, and chill it in the refrigerator 2½ hours.

FILLING. Wash the spinach thoroughly in several changes of water and drain, but not too well. Put it into a pan with the butter and a little salt and pepper. Cook the spinach over high heat 4 to 5 minutes, just until it wilts (stir to turn it). Drain it through a colander, pressing it with a small plate to squeeze it as dry as possible. Cool it a little, and put it through a coarse meat grinder. Beat the egg in a mixer. Add the spinach and all the other filling ingredients. Mix thoroughly with the hands.

Have the pasta machine ready. Cut the ravioli dough in two, with one piece a bit larger than the other. Roll out the smaller piece of dough very thin, about ⅛ inch thick. (Roll it out on a board with a rolling pin, then through the pasta machine down to the thinnest sheet.) Brush it all over with beaten egg and mark it into 2-inch squares with the dull side of a large straight knife. Roll the filling into marble-size balls and place a ball in the center of each square. Roll out the larger piece of dough to the same thickness as the first. Cover the little marbles of filling with this piece of dough. With the dull back of the knife, press down between the rows of filling to seal each little square.

Either cut the ravioli into squares as marked, with the sharp side of a long, straight-bladed knife, or cut them into 2-inch rounds with a plain or fluted cookie cutter. Sprinkle half the semolina and flour mixture on a jelly roll pan and set the cut ravioli in it. Sprinkle them with the rest of the mixture. If possible, let the ravioli dry overnight.

FRESH TOMATO SAUCE. Heat the butter in a tin-lined copper pan. Add the tomatoes, garlic, and a little salt and pepper. Cook briskly over high heat 3 to 4 minutes. Off the heat, stir in the tomato paste, and the potato flour mixed with water. Add the chicken stock or water, sugar, and a little more salt and pepper if necessary. Stir over moderate heat until the sauce comes to a boil, then simmer gently 15 to 20 minutes.

Have ready a large pan three-quarters full of boiling salted water. Drop in the ravioli, cook 10 minutes, remove with a slotted spoon, and drain them on paper towels. Arrange the cooked ravioli on a buttered baking dish. Spoon the fresh tomato sauce over them. Sprinkle with the breadcrumbs, melted butter, and a little of the Parmesan cheese, and brown under the broiler. Sprinkle the top with the parsley and serve with a separate bowl of grated cheese. NET: 4 servings.

RAVIOLI ITALIENNE

Ravioli Stuffed with Spinach, Chicken (or Prosciutto), and Cheese

Ravioli dough (page 666)

FILLING
1 pound fresh spinach
2 tablespoons salt butter
Salt
Freshly cracked white pepper
1 cup cooked chopped white meat of chicken or chopped Prosciutto
4 egg yolks
½ cup ricotta cheese
½ teaspoon freshly grated nutmeg
½ teaspoon finely chopped garlic

FRESH TOMATO SAUCE
3 tablespoons salt butter
1 medium-size onion, finely chopped
1 teaspoon finely chopped garlic
2 large ripe tomatoes, sliced (not skinned)
2 tablespoons tomato paste
3 teaspoons potato flour mixed with 4 tablespoons water
2 cups chicken stock (page 35)
¼ teaspoon curry powder
Salt
Freshly cracked white pepper

GARNISH
3 tablespoons dry breadcrumbs (page 69)
1 cup freshly grated Parmesan cheese
2 tablespoons melted salt butter
2 tablespoons chopped fresh parsley

Please follow the procedure for preparing the dough, rolling, assembling, and cutting it as given for Ravioli à la Bolognese on pages 666-667.

FILLING. Follow the procedure for the Bolognese filling through the step of draining the cooked spinach as dry as possible. Cool it a little. Mix it loosely with the chicken or prosciutto and put the whole mixture through a fine meat grinder twice. Beat the egg yolks and ricotta cheese in a mixer. Add the ground spinach and chicken or prosciutto, nutmeg, and garlic, and season with salt and pepper. Mix lightly.

Prepare the ravioli dough in the manner prescribed in Ravioli à la Bolognese, and put the little balls of filling on it. Cover with the top piece of dough and cut as desired in squares or rounds. Set aside on a jelly roll pan sprinkled with semolina and flour.

FRESH TOMATO SAUCE. Heat the butter in a tin-lined copper pan. Add the onion and cook until it is soft and lightly browned. Add the garlic and tomatoes, and cook over moderate heat 2 to 3 minutes. Off the heat, stir in the tomato paste and mixed potato flour and water. Add the chicken stock and stir over low heat until the sauce comes to a boil. Season with the curry powder, salt, and pepper. Simmer gently 5 minutes, and strain.

Have ready a large pan three-quarters full of boiling salted water. Drop the ravioli in the water and cook 10 minutes. Remove them with a slotted spoon and drain on paper towels. Arrange them on a buttered baking dish.* Spoon over them the fresh tomato sauce, sprinkle with breadcrumbs, a little freshly grated Parmesan cheese, and melted butter. Brown under the broiler. Sprinkle the top with chopped fresh

*An alternative is to serve the plain ravioli in the buttered baking dish, sprinkled with Parmesan cheese and melted butter, and serve the sauce in a separate bowl.

parsley and serve with a separate bowl of grated cheese. NET: 4 servings.

Ravioli dough (page 666) or
  commercially prepared
  lasagne strips
2 tablespoons vegetable oil, or
  olive oil and 1 tablespoon
  salt (for cooking)

FILLING
8 tablespoons salt butter
1 pound cottage cheese
½ pound cream cheese
½ pound ricotta cheese
⅓ cup freshly grated Parmesan
  cheese
½ teaspoon finely chopped
  garlic
1 teaspoon freshly cracked
  white pepper
½ teaspoon salt (or 1 teaspoon
  kosher salt)
⅛ teaspoon freshly grated
  nutmeg
⅛ teaspoon ground mace

FRESH TOMATO AND MEAT SAUCE
4 tablespoons salt butter
4 tablespoons pure olive oil
2 medium-size yellow onions,
  finely chopped
1 teaspoon finely chopped garlic
3 large ripe tomatoes, skinned
  and cut into eighths
3 tablespoons tomato paste
1 pound ground lean beef
½ cup chicken stock (page 35)
1 teaspoon meat glaze
2 tablespoons dry breadcrumbs
  (page 69) mixed with 1
  tablespoon all-purpose flour
Salt
Freshly cracked white pepper
3 tablespoons Chianti wine

GARNISH
3 tablespoons melted salt butter
1 ball mozzarella cheese (enough
  for 12 thin slices)
1 cup freshly grated Parmesan
  cheese

LASAGNE

*Lasagne with
Cheese Filling, with
Fresh Tomato and
Meat Sauce*

LASAGNE STRIPS. If you are making the dough, please follow the dough recipe for Ravioli à la Bolognese (page 666). Roll the dough as thin as possible, then cut it into strips 2 inches by 8 inches. You should have at least 12 of these pieces of uncooked pasta. Fill a large pan three-quarters full of water. Add the oil and salt for cooking. Bring to a rolling boil and put in the lasagne. Cook briskly 12 minutes, no longer. Stir once, gently, to make sure that they do not stick together. Drain the cooked lasagne in a colander, rinse with cold water, and spread them out on paper towels to dry.

FILLING. Beat the butter in a mixer until it is light and fluffy. Add the cottage cheese and beat well, then the cream cheese and beat well, then the ricotta cheese. Continue beating and add the Parmesan cheese, garlic, pepper, salt, nutmeg, and mace. Blend the mixture thoroughly, and spread it generously on each strip of lasagne. Roll them up individually (individually stuffed and rolled strips instead of layers are easier to serve). Arrange the stuffed rolled lasagne on a well-buttered au gratin dish.

FRESH TOMATO AND MEAT SAUCE. Heat the butter with the olive oil in a saucepan. Add the onions and garlic and cook over low heat 1 to 2 minutes, without browning. Add the tomatoes and tomato paste. Continue to cook over low heat until the tomato pieces are almost disintegrated into a sauce. Crumble the ground beef over the sauce and stir it in. Mix the meat glaze with the chicken stock and stir it in. Sprinkle the breadcrumbs mixed with the flour over the sauce and stir them in. Season with salt and pepper, mix in the wine, and simmer the sauce gently, over low heat, 30 minutes.

Preheat the oven to 350°. Brush the lasagne in the au gratin dish with melted butter. Spoon a little of the sauce over the lasagne. Cut the ball of mozzarella cheese into 12 thin slices, and put a slice on each of the lasagne. Spoon the rest of the sauce over the dish, sprinkle with melted butter and a little of the Parmesan cheese, and warm in the oven 10 minutes. Then brown the lasagne under the broiler and serve it with a separate bowl of freshly grated Parmesan cheese. NET: 4 to 6 servings.

SPAGHETTI À LA BOLOGNESE

Spaghetti with Fresh Tomato and Meat Sauce

1 pound spaghetti
¼ cup pure olive oil and
   1 tablespoon salt (for cooking)
1 cup freshly grated Parmesan
   cheese

SAUCE BOLOGNESE
8 tablespoons salt butter
2 cups finely chopped yellow
   onion
1 teaspoon finely chopped garlic

1 pound ripe tomatoes, skinned
   and cut into eighths
1½ pounds ground lean beef
2 tablespoons tomato paste
1 tablespoon chopped fresh
   parsley
1 tablespoon chopped fresh
   oregano or 1 teaspoon dried
Salt
Freshly cracked black pepper
¼ cup Chianti wine

SAUCE BOLOGNESE. Heat the butter in a heavy sauté pan. When it is foaming, add the onion and garlic, and cook over low heat until the onion is lightly brown. Add the tomatoes to the pan and simmer gently until they are slightly mushy. Crumble the ground beef over the pan and stir it in until it blends with the other ingredients. Mix in the tomato paste, parsley, and oregano, season with salt and pepper, then stir in the Chianti wine. Simmer the sauce very gently, over low heat, 45 minutes.

Fill a large pan three-quarters full of water. Add the olive oil and salt, bring to a rolling boil, cook the spaghetti 10 to 12 minutes, depending on size, until it is al dente. Drain well, and arrange it in a buttered baking dish. To serve, cover the spaghetti with the sauce. Sprinkle a little of the Parmesan cheese over the sauce and serve the rest in a separate bowl. NET: 4 to 6 servings.

Spaghetti, vermicelli, macaroni, or any nonfilled types of pasta may be used in this simple and excellent dish.

½ pound spaghetti or other pasta	Freshly cracked black pepper
Salt	1 cup freshly grated Parmesan cheese
2 tablespoons vegetable oil	½ cup heavy cream, whipped
6 tablespoons sweet butter	¼ cup sour cream

Fill a large pan three-quarters full of water. Add 1 tablespoon salt and the vegetable oil. Bring to a rolling boil, and cook the spaghetti 10 to 12 minutes, until it is al dente. (If you are using another type of pasta, the cooking time may vary.) Drain well, and put it into an earthenware or copper casserole. Melt the sweet butter and cool it a little. Using two forks, lightly mix it and the cheese, whipped cream, and sour cream into the spaghetti. Season with salt and pepper. NET: 4 servings.

SPAGHETTI
À L'ITALIENNE

Spaghetti with Sweet Butter, Parmesan Cheese, and Cream

6 tablespoons salt butter	and chopped coarsely
12 chicken livers	1 tablespoon all-purpose flour
1 teaspoon finely chopped garlic	½ teaspoon meat glaze
2 large onions, finely chopped	3 tablespoons tomato paste
8 firm white fresh mushrooms, finely chopped	¼ cup chicken stock (page 35)
Salt	2 tablespoons mixed chopped fresh green herbs
Freshly cracked white pepper	1 cup freshly grated Parmesan cheese
¼ teaspoon dry mustard	
5 large ripe tomatoes, skinned	

CHICKEN LIVER
AND FRESH
TOMATO SAUCE
FOR SPAGHETTI

Heat 1 tablespoon butter in a heavy pan. Brown the chicken livers on both sides quickly, remove and set them aside, and melt the remaining butter in the pan. Add the garlic and cook 1 minute over moderate heat, then the onions and cook over high heat until they begin to brown. Reduce the heat to low, add the mushrooms, and cook 5 minutes. Season with salt, pepper, and the mustard. Add the tomatoes and cook 2 minutes. Off the heat, stir in the flour, meat glaze, and tomato paste. Add the chicken stock and stir over low heat until the sauce comes to a boil. Simmer gently 4 minutes, and add the herbs. Chop the chicken livers fine, add them to the sauce, and simmer 2 minutes. Serve this sauce on spaghetti cooked al dente, with the Parmesan cheese in a separate bowl, for each person to mix into the sauce after it is served. NET: 4 servings.

LINGUINE
PIEMONTESE

Linguine with Clams, Garlic, Butter and Cream

½ pound linguine (very thin spaghetti)	2 tablespoons vegetable oil
Salt	6 tablespoons sweet butter
	1½ cups freshly grated

Parmesan cheese
¼ cup pure olive oil
1½ cups finely chopped
   Bermuda onion
2 teaspoons finely chopped
   garlic
¼ cup finely chopped fresh

chives
½ pound can minced clams
   (reserve the juice)
½ teaspoon potato flour
Freshly cracked white pepper
¾ cup heavy cream

Fill a large pot three-quarters full of water and add 1 tablespoon salt and the vegetable oil. Bring to a boil, add the linguine, and boil 10 to 12 minutes, until just cooked, al dente. Drain well and arrange in an au gratin dish. Melt half the sweet butter and mix it into the linguine with two forks. Sprinkle with grated Parmesan cheese and set it aside to keep it warm.

Heat the olive oil in a sauté pan, add the onion and garlic, and cook over low heat 5 minutes without browning them. Add the minced clams and chives, then stir in the potato flour mixed with ¼ cup clam juice from the can. Season with a little salt and pepper, and stir over low heat until the sauce comes to a boil. Stir in the rest of the butter bit by bit, then the heavy cream. Simmer the sauce very slowly 3 minutes, and spoon it over the linguine. Serve at once with the rest of the cheese in a separate bowl. NET: 4 servings.

GNOCCHI À LA ROMANO

This gnocchi, made with semolina or cream of farina, is the perfect garnish with so many meat and poultry dishes.

3 cups cold water
½ teaspoon salt
½ cup semolina or cream of
   farina
2 tablespoons salt butter
⅔ cup freshly grated Parmesan

cheese
½ teaspoon dry mustard
1 teaspoon Dijon mustard
A few grains cayenne pepper
2 tablespoons melted salt butter

Put the water in a pan with the salt. Bring to a rolling boil and slowly stir in the semolina or cream of farina. Continue to stir until it thickens and comes away from the sides of the pan. Remove from the heat and mix in the butter, half the Parmesan cheese, the two mustards, and the cayenne pepper. Cook 2 to 3 minutes over low heat. Rinse a layer cake or jelly roll pan with cold water. Spread the mixture on the pan about ½ inch thick, and put it in the refrigerator to set. When it is chilled, cut it into 1½-inch rounds with a cookie cutter. Butter a small au gratin dish. Arrange the gnocchi down the dish slightly overlapping. Sprinkle with the melted butter and the rest of the grated cheese, and brown under a hot broiler. NET: 4 servings (as a garnish).

6 cups cold water
1 teaspoon salt
1 cup semolina or cream of
  farina
1/2 teaspoon dry mustard
1 teaspoon Dijon mustard
A few grains cayenne pepper
1/2 cup freshly grated Parmesan
  cheese
6 tablespoons sweet butter

GARNISH
1 cup freshly grated Parmesan
  cheese
2 tablespoons melted salt butter

FRESH TOMATO SAUCE
3 tablespoons salt butter
6 large ripe tomatoes, skinned
  and cut into eighths
1 teaspoon finely chopped garlic
Salt
Freshly cracked white pepper
2 tablespoons tomato paste
1/2 teaspoon potato flour mixed
  with 2 tablespoons water
1/2 cup chicken stock (page 35)
  or water
1 tablespoon chopped fresh
  parsley

GNOCCHI À LA NAPOLITANA

Semolina-type Gnocchi
with Fresh Tomato
Sauce and Cheese

Put the water in a pan with the salt, bring to a rolling boil, and slowly stir in the semolina or cream of farina. Continue to stir until it thickens and comes away from the sides of the pan, then remove from the heat and mix in the two mustards, cayenne pepper, Parmesan cheese, and butter. Cook 2 to 3 minutes over low heat, stirring all the while. Rinse a jelly roll pan with cold water. Spread the mixture on the pan about 1/2 inch thick, and put it in the refrigerator to set.

FRESH TOMATO SAUCE. Heat the butter in a large saucepan. When it is foaming, add the tomatoes and garlic. Season with salt and pepper and cook briskly, over moderate heat, 5 to 6 minutes. Off the heat, add the tomato paste, the mixed potato flour and water, and chicken stock. Mix well and simmer 6 minutes. Add the chopped parsley, and season with more salt and pepper if needed.

When the semolina mixture is chilled, cut it into 1 1/2-inch rounds with a cookie cutter. Butter a large oval au gratin dish. Arrange the rounds of gnocchi in rows, slightly overlapping, on the dish. Sprinkle with half the Parmesan cheese and the melted butter for garnishing. Brown the gnocchi under a hot broiler, and serve with separate bowls of sauce and grated cheese. NET: 4 to 6 generous servings.

1 cup cold water
Salt
4 tablespoons salt butter
1 cup all-purpose flour
4 eggs
1 teaspoon dry mustard
1 teaspoon Dijon mustard
1/4 cup freshly grated Parmesan
  cheese

1/8 teaspoon freshly grated
  nutmeg
A few grains cayenne pepper

GARNISH
1/4 cup freshly grated Parmesan
  cheese
2 tablespoons melted salt butter

GNOCCHI PARISIENNE

Cream Puff Paste
Dumplings, with
Parmesan Cheese

Put the water in a saucepan with 1/2 teaspoon salt and the butter, and bring the water slowly to a boil. (The butter should dissolve as the water comes to a boil, so that both arrive at the same point together.) When the mixture is at a rolling boil, throw in the flour. Over low heat, stir the mixture with a wooden spoon until it thickens and comes away from the sides of the pan. Put it in a mixer bowl, beat in the eggs one at a time, then beat in the two mustards, ½ teaspoon salt, and the Parmesan cheese, nutmeg, and cayenne pepper. Put the mixture into a pastry bag with a #9 plain round tube. Have ready on the stove a large pan three-quarters full of boiling water seasoned with 1 tablespoon salt. Reduce the heat to a simmer.

Rest the pastry tube on the edge of the pan and squeeze out the paste, cutting it off at 1-inch lengths with a small knife, and letting them drop into the water. When all the gnocchi are cooking, lay a paper towel on the water and let the gnocchi simmer, without boiling, 20 minutes. (They can be left in the water longer, an hour or so, if you wish.) When ready to serve, generously butter an au gratin dish. Remove the gnocchi from the water with a slotted spoon, drain on paper towels, and arrange in the au gratin dish. Sprinkle with the Parmesan cheese and melted butter for garnishing. Brown under a hot broiler. NET: 4 servings.

FRIED GNOCCHI

This is a variation of Gnocchi Parisienne, tiny cream puff paste dumplings, poached, coated with egg and breadcrumbs, and fried in butter.

1 cup water	½ cup freshly grated Gruyère
Salt	cheese
A few grains cayenne pepper	1 teaspoon Dijon mustard
9 tablespoons salt butter	A little all-purpose flour (for
1 cup all-purpose flour	dusting)
3 eggs	1 whole egg, beaten
¾ cup freshly grated Parmesan	A few dry white breadcrumbs
cheese	(page 69)

Put the water, ½ teaspoon salt, cayenne pepper, and 3 tablespoons butter in a small heavy pan. Bring slowly to a boil, throw in the flour, remove from the heat, and beat until the mixture is smooth. Beat in 3 eggs one at a time. Stir in half the Parmesan cheese, all the Gruyère cheese, and the mustard. Put the mixture into a pastry bag fitted with a #9 plain round tube. Have a pot three-quarters full of barely simmering salted water on the stove. Rest the pastry tube on the edge of the pan and squeeze out the paste mixture, cutting it off at 1-inch lengths and letting them drop directly into the water. Cover the water with paper towels and poach the gnocchi gently 20 minutes, until firm to the touch. Remove them from the water with a slotted spoon. Drain thoroughly on paper towels. Roll them lightly in flour, brush with beaten egg, and roll them in breadcrumbs.

Heat 6 tablespoons butter in a large frypan. When it is foaming and light brown, put in the gnocchi and fry them until golden brown. Turn them gently with a spatula to brown all sides. Drain on paper towels.

Garnish an entrée with them, or serve separately on a warm vegetable dish. NET: 4 to 6 servings.

VARENYKY

Russian Cream Cheese Dumplings (Gnocchi) with Sweet Butter and Fresh Dill

½ *pound cream cheese*
2 eggs, beaten
Salt
Freshly cracked white pepper
A little all-purpose flour

DILL BUTTER
6 tablespoons sweet butter
⅛ *teaspoon cayenne pepper*
1 teaspoon lemon juice
1 tablespoon chopped fresh dill

Beat the cream cheese in the mixer until it is very light and creamy. Continue beating and slowly add the beaten eggs. Season with salt and pepper, and mix in just enough flour to bind the mixture (a light dumpling dough consistency). Half fill a sauté pan with water, season it with salt, bring to a boil, then reduce to a gentle simmer. Drop a teaspoonful of the cream cheese mixture into the water, then put it all in teaspoonful by teaspoonful. Let the varenyky cook in the simmering (not boiling) water until firm. Remove them with a slotted spoon and arrange on a hot baking dish. Melt the butter in a little pan over low heat so that it does not brown. Add ½ teaspoon salt and the cayenne pepper. Mix in the lemon juice and dill. Pour this butter over the varenyky and serve. NET: 4 servings.

PLAIN COOKED RICE

Generally for use in a salad or in a mold.

2 cups long-grain rice
4 cups water

2 teaspoons salt

Preheat the oven to 350°. Put the rice in a deep heavy pan with the water and salt. Stir over moderate heat until it comes to a rolling boil. Cover the pan firmly with the lid and cook 30 minutes in the oven. Then remove it from the oven, fluff it with two forks, and it is ready for use. NET: 6 cups or more, fluffed; 5 cups, firmly packed.

RIZ PILAF

Rice Pilaff

A pilaff is rice cooked in stock with onion and seasonings.

4 tablespoons salt butter
1 medium-size yellow onion,
   finely chopped
Optional: ½ *teaspoon finely*
   chopped garlic
1 cup long-grain rice
2 cups chicken stock (page 35)

   or water
1 teaspoon salt
½ *teaspoon freshly cracked*
   white pepper
Optional: ½ *teaspoon ground*
   cardamom seed

If you plan to cook the rice in the oven, preheat it to 350°. Melt the butter in a small heavy pan. When it is foaming, add the onion and garlic. Cook slowly, over low heat, until the onion is translucent but not brown. Add the rice and stir until it is coated with butter. Cover with the chicken stock or water. Season with the salt, pepper, and cardamom seed. Stir over moderate heat until it comes to a rolling boil. Cover firmly with the lid. Put it in the oven to cook 25 minutes, or, if preferred, cook it on top of the stove over very low heat 25 minutes, without lifting the lid. When the rice is cooked, fluff it with two forks, and serve in whatever manner the menu calls for. NET: 4 servings.

RIZ AU SAFRAN

Saffron Rice

8 tablespoons salt butter
3 tablespoons pure olive oil
1 cup finely chopped yellow onion
2 cups Carolina rice (slightly fluffier than regular long-

grain rice)
Salt
A few grains cayenne pepper
4 cups chicken stock (page 35)
1 teaspoon leaf saffron, crushed with a mortar and pestle

Preheat the oven to 350°. Heat the butter with the olive oil in a deep heavy pan. When it is foaming, add the onion and cook over low heat until it is translucent but not brown. Add the rice and stir over low heat 2 minutes to thoroughly coat it with the butter, then add 2 teaspoons salt and the cayenne pepper. Add the chicken stock and stir over moderate heat until it comes to a boil. Add the crushed saffron, and stir until the mixture is thoroughly blended with the saffron color. Cover the pan firmly with the lid and cook 30 minutes in the oven. When the rice is cooked, remove it from the oven immediately and fluff it with two forks. NET: 4 to 6 servings.

RISOTTO WITH CHICKEN LIVERS, LAMB KIDNEYS, AND TOMATO SAUCE

For the Italian risotto, stock is gradually added to the rice as it is absorbed. Carolina rice is used here, which is a little fluffier than the regular long-grain.

½ pound chicken livers
6 lamb kidneys
4 tablespoons salt butter
1 large onion, sliced
6 firm white mushrooms, sliced
1 tablespoon tomato paste
1½ cups Carolina rice
3 cups chicken stock (page 35)

6 large ripe tomatoes, skinned and sliced
Salt
Freshly cracked white pepper
¾ cup freshly grated Parmesan cheese
2 tablespoons melted salt butter

Preheat the oven to 325°. Cut the livers and kidneys in half. Heat the butter in a deep heavy pan. When it is foaming, brown the livers and kidneys on both sides. Remove them from the pan with a slotted spoon, set aside, and add the onion to the pan. Brown it slowly, add the mushrooms, cook the mixture a little, then add the tomato paste and rice. Barely cover the contents of the pan with chicken stock and cook slowly over low heat, stirring, until the rice has absorbed the liquid. Add more chicken stock from time to time and continue to stir until the rice is nearly cooked and the stock absorbed. Cut the livers and kidneys into coarse dice, add to the rice with the tomatoes, and season with salt and pepper. Put the whole mixture in an earthenware baking dish, sprinkle with some of the grated cheese and the melted butter, and bake 15 minutes. Sprinkle with more grated cheese and serve. NET: 4 servings.

---

10 tablespoons salt butter	Freshly cracked white pepper	## RISOTTO MILANESE
6 chicken livers	2 cups Carolina rice	
1 cup finely chopped yellow onions	6 cups chicken stock (page 35)	
1 cup firm white fresh mushrooms, chopped	4 white truffles, thinly sliced	*Risotto with White Truffles, Mushrooms, and Chicken Livers*
Salt	1½ cups freshly grated Parmesan cheese	

Heat 2 tablespoons butter in a deep heavy pan. When it is foaming and golden brown, quickly brown the livers in it on each side. Remove them from the pan and set aside. Add the rest of the butter to the pan, let it melt, add the onions, and cook over low heat 2 minutes. Add the mushrooms and continue cooking 4 minutes. Season with a little salt and pepper, add the rice, and stir until it is well coated with the other ingredients. Cook 2 to 3 minutes. Add a little chicken stock and continue to stir the mixture over low heat until the stock is absorbed. Continue to add chicken stock little by little, always stirring until it is absorbed by the rice before adding more. Cut the livers into rather thick strips, and when the rice is just tender but firm (not mushy), add them to the rice with the white truffle slices. Cook 1 to 2 minutes longer. Pile up the rice in a warm earthenware casserole and serve with a separate bowl of freshly grated Parmesan cheese. NET: 6 servings.

---

3 tablespoons pure olive oil	shrimps	## RISOTTO CON SCAMPI ALLA MILANESE
8 tablespoons sweet butter	3 white truffles, sliced	
½ cup finely chopped onion	4 ounces firm white fresh mushrooms, thinly sliced and sautéed in a little butter and lemon juice	
2 teaspoons finely chopped garlic		
3 cups Carolina rice	Salt	*Saffron Rice with Shrimps, White Truffles, and Parmesan Cheese*
1 teaspoon leaf saffron	Freshly cracked black pepper	
1 tablespoon hot water	2 cups freshly grated Parmesan cheese	
7½ cups chicken stock (page 35)		
2 cups thinly sliced cooked		

Preheat the oven to 350°. Heat the olive oil with 4 tablespoons butter in a large deep heavy pan. Add the onion and garlic and cook over low heat 2 minutes. Add the rice and cook slowly another 2 minutes. Pulverize the leaf saffron with a small mortar and pestle. Dissolve it in the hot water and add it to the rice. Cover the rice with the stock, add the shrimps, truffles, and mushrooms, season with a little salt and pepper, and bring to a boil. Cover the pan with the lid firmly and cook the rice mixture in the oven 25 minutes. Then remove it from the oven, fluff the rice with two forks, add 4 tablespoons butter and ½ cup grated cheese, and mix lightly. Serve in a warm casserole with the rest of the grated cheese in a separate bowl. NET: 6 servings.

PAELLA

Spanish Rice with Meat,
Poultry, and Seafood

This paella is an accumulation of many recipes which I have put together myself, using the best of each. The frequency with which it was requested in my classes would indicate much interest in this Spanish "las ultimas" in the gourmet kitchens of America. Ideally, you should serve the paella in a traditional large round metal paella pan, but a large casserole is fine.

MEAT AND POULTRY
1 pound boned shoulder of
   lamb, cut into 1-inch cubes
9 tablespoons salt butter
1 2½-pound whole dressed
   chicken, with its liver
⅓ cup Cognac or good brandy
2 teaspoons meat glaze
2 teaspoons tomato paste
4 teaspoons potato flour
2 cups chicken stock
   (page 35)
¼ cup dry sherry
½ cup dry white wine
2 teaspoons red currant jelly
Freshly cracked white pepper
2 very hot Spanish or Italian
   sausages

MUSSELS, CLAMS, LOBSTER
24 mussels (reserve the stock)
1 teaspoon dry mustard
12 cherrystone clams
4 cups water
1 cup dry white wine
1 cup mixed sliced onion,
   carrot, and celery
1 bay leaf

2 or 3 sprigs fresh dill
7 black peppercorns
1 live lobster, about 1½
   pounds
4 tablespoons salt butter
2 tablespoons pure olive oil
¼ cup Cognac or good brandy

RICE AND SHRIMPS
4 tablespoons salt butter
2 tablespoons pure olive oil
2 small yellow onions, finely
   chopped
1 teaspoon finely chopped garlic
2½ cups long-grain rice
4 cups stock from the mussels
2 teaspoons leaf saffron,
   crushed with a pestle and
   mortar and mixed with 2
   tablespoons cold water
2 teaspoons salt
¼ teaspoon cayenne pepper
1 pound raw shrimps, shelled
   and deveined

VEGETABLES
3 tablespoons pure olive oil
5 tablespoons salt butter

2 or 3 medium-size yellow
   onions, cut into eighths
½ teaspoon chopped garlic
6 ounces firm white fresh mushrooms, cut in thick slices
2 teaspoons lemon juice
Salt

Freshly cracked white pepper
1 red and 1 green pepper
   (sweet), seeded and cut into
   eighths
3 or 4 large firm ripe tomatoes,
   skinned and cut into eighths
A little granulated sugar

MEAT AND POULTRY. Preheat the oven to 350°. Heat 3 tablespoons butter in a large deep heavy pan. When it is golden brown, quickly brown the lamb cubes in it on all sides, then remove them from the pan and set aside. Dry the chicken inside and out with paper towels. Tie it (page 342). Add another 3 tablespoons butter to the pan and brown the chicken and its liver slowly. Heat the brandy in a separate little pan, ignite, and pour it over the chicken and liver. Then remove them from the pan, melt the remaining 3 tablespoons butter in it and, off the heat, stir in the meat glaze, tomato paste, and potato flour. Mix to a smooth paste, then mix in the chicken stock, sherry, wine, jelly, and a little pepper (but no salt). Stir the sauce over moderate heat until it comes to a rolling boil. Carve the chicken into serving pieces (page 343), and add it and the sliced liver to the sauce with the lamb and sausages. Cook in the oven without a cover 45 to 50 minutes, basting fairly frequently with the sauce in the pan. When done, cut the sausages into 1-inch lengths. Keep the pan warm.

   MUSSELS, CLAMS, LOBSTER. Clean the mussels in cold water mixed with the mustard. Scrub well, put them into a deep pan with the clams, and pour in the water and wine. Add the onion, carrot, celery, bay leaf, dill, and peppercorns. Bring very slowly to a boil, covered, and boil gently 3 minutes, until the shells are open wide. Strain off and reserve the liquid. Remove the top shells of the mussels and clams and keep the pan warm. With a large sharp pointed knife, split the live lobster in half, starting from the star in the center of the head shell and cutting down through the tail. Remove the sac from behind each eye and the large vein down the tail. Heat the butter and olive oil very hot in a large deep heavy pan, put in the lobster shell side down, with the claws (in their shells) on the head and tail sections. Cover, and cook slowly 3 minutes. Heat the brandy in a separate little pan, ignite, and pour it over the lobster. Remove the lobster from the pan and loosen the meat from the shells but leave them attached. Keep it warm.

   RICE AND SHRIMPS. Add the butter and olive oil to the same pan, add the onions and garlic, and cook over low heat 3 to 4 minutes. Mix in the rice, and stir until it is coated with butter and oil. Cover with the strained mussel stock, add the saffron and water, salt, and cayenne pepper, and stir over low heat until the mixture comes to a rolling boil. Add the shrimps, cover the pan, and cook in the oven 30 minutes. Remove from the oven and immediately fluff the rice with two forks.

VEGETABLES. Heat 3 tablespoons olive oil in a large frypan, add the butter, and when it is melted add the onions and garlic. Cook slowly until the onions begin to brown a little, mix in the mushrooms, lemon juice, salt, and pepper, and cook a minute or two. Add the red and green peppers and 2 tablespoons olive oil and cook 2 to 3 minutes. Then add the tomatoes with a little more salt and pepper and a sprinkling of sugar. Cook just a minute or two (the tomatoes should not soften or disintegrate).

ASSEMBLY. Either in a paella pan or a large casserole, arrange each category of ingredients in a layer, one on top of the other, so that each individual serving will reach down into a little of everything. Garnish with the meat and shells of the lobster (cut the lobster tail into individual pieces). Serve immediately, or the dish may be re-warmed in a slow oven. NET: 8 to 10 servings.

WILD RICE

Like the truffles of France and Italy, wild rice is a mystery; no one knows how it originated. It is unique to one region in Minnesota, and is found nowhere else in the world. This plain cooked wild rice is for use in stuffings or other garnishes.

1 cup wild rice   1 teaspoon salt
6 cups water

Wash the wild rice in several waters until it is thoroughly clean. Put it in a large heavy pan and pour the water over it. Add the salt, cover the pan, and cook over low heat until the water starts to boil. Then remove the cover and let the water boil, without stirring the rice, until it is tender (about 30 minutes).

Preheat the oven to 300°. When the rice is cooked, drain it and put it in a shallow baking dish. Cover it with cheesecloth and bake it 10 to 15 minutes. The rice is now ready to incorporate into any recipe you wish to use. NET: 3 cups.

WILD RICE WITH CHICKEN LIVERS

2 cups wild rice
4½ cups chicken stock
   (page 35)
Salt
Freshly cracked black pepper
Bouquet garni, including
   oregano, chives, parsley,
   celery leaf, tied in cheesecloth
½ cup pure olive oil
2 tablespoons dried black
   currants

8 tablespoons salt butter
1 pound chicken livers
1 cup finely chopped onion
4 tablespoons finely chopped
   sweet green pepper
½ pound firm white fresh
   mushrooms, sliced
1 tablespoon chopped fresh
   sweet basil or ½ teaspoon
   dried
1 cup pine kernels (pignoli
   nuts)

Wash the wild rice thoroughly in several cold waters and drain. Put it in a deep heavy pan with the chicken stock, add salt, pepper, and the bouquet garni, and stir over moderate heat until it comes to a boil. Stir in the olive oil and black currants, put the lid on the pan, and cook over low heat until the rice has absorbed the stock and is tender.

While the rice cooks, heat 2 tablespoons butter in a sauté pan. When it is foaming and turning brown, add the chicken livers and brown quickly on both sides. Remove them from the pan, and put into it the rest of the butter. Melt it, add the onion, and cook 3 minutes without browning. Mix in the green pepper and mushrooms, season with salt and pepper, and add the basil and pine kernels. Slice the chicken livers, return them to the sauté pan, and cook 3 minutes over low heat. When the rice is cooked, remove the bouquet garni and stir the chicken liver mixture into the rice. Pile it in an earthenware casserole and serve. NET: 4 to 6 servings.

CHEESE

CHEESE IS OMNIPRESENT in good cooking and good eating. It is as basic and universal to man's diet as bread and wine. Like wine and like bread, cheese needs to be understood, and also like wine and bread, it has a life within itself. All three foods develop by fermentation.

Because the place of cheese in cooking and the menu was always important in my teaching, we have included a dissertation "On Cheese" (pages 687–697) written by a devoted connoisseur, who also gives detailed instructions for preparing and serving that wonderful French institution "le plat de fromage," the cheese tray, where cheese in its natural form has its own place in the daily meal.

In this chapter we include recipes for the classic cheese soufflé, cheese omelet, and cheese tart, because they can be singular main-course dishes. Dishes in other chapters in which cheese is a major ingredient are listed under Cheese in the index. Please check the list — it is our repertoire of fine cheese dishes.

3 tablespoons salt butter
3 tablespoons all-purpose flour
½ teaspoon dry mustard
1 teaspoon Dijon mustard
1 teaspoon salt
A few grains cayenne pepper
1 cup milk
2 tablespoons sour cream
⅓ cup freshly grated imported
   Swiss cheese
¼ cup freshly grated Parmesan
   cheese
2 tablespoons dry sherry
4 egg yolks
7 egg whites

TO LINE SOUFFLÉ DISH
A little cool melted butter
2 to 3 tablespoons freshly
   grated Parmesan cheese
2 tablespoons dry breadcrumbs
   (page 69)

SOUFFLÉ AU FROMAGE

Cheese Soufflé (Main Course Soufflé) with Swiss and Parmesan

Preheat the oven to 325°. Prepare a 4-cup #6 soufflé dish according to the detailed instructions on page 787. To line it, brush it with the cool melted butter and dust it with the Parmesan cheese and breadcrumbs. Have ready a shallow pan half filled with hot water.

Melt the butter in a saucepan over low heat (do not let it brown). Off the heat, stir in the flour, the two mustards, salt, and cayenne pepper. Pour the milk over it and mix well. Return the pan to low heat and stir until the mixture is smooth and thick. Again off the heat, mix in the sour cream, Swiss cheese, Parmesan cheese, and sherry. Then stir in the egg yolks one at a time. Beat the egg whites in a heated bowl with a piano wire whisk until they are so stiff you can turn the bowl upside down without spilling them. Pour the egg yolk sauce on the whites. Carefully pass the sauce through the beaten egg whites with a rubber scraper. Take great care not to break down the egg whites any more than necessary, yet the soufflé should be evenly mixed.

Spoon the mixture into the prepared soufflé dish. Set the dish in the pan of hot water, put the whole assembly in the oven, and bake 1 hour. When the soufflé is baked, carefully take off the paper collar, and serve at once. (NOTE: This recipe will accommodate 4 individual-size #3 soufflé dishes. Bake these smaller soufflés 35 to 40 minutes.) NET: 4 servings.

OMELETTE AU FROMAGE

Cheese Omelet

Basic Savory Omelet Mixture (3 eggs, 1 teaspoon cold water, ¼ teaspoon salt)
1 tablespoon salt butter
A little melted sweet butter

FILLING
½ cup freshly grated Gruyère

cheese

GARNISH
1 tablespoon freshly grated Parmesan cheese
A few grains cayenne pepper
A little paprika

Prepare and cook the omelet according to the procedure on page 210. Just before you are ready to fold it, put the grated Gruyère cheese in the middle. (Take care that none of the cheese touches the pan or it will stick.) Then fold the omelet over and turn it out onto a hot serving dish.

There are two ways to serve this cheese omelet. (1) Have a metal skewer red-hot by the time you have finished cooking the omelet and turned it out. Mark a crisscross on the top of the omelet with the skewer (traditionally, any dish with cheese should be browned). Sprinkle with a little grated Parmesan cheese and serve at once. (2) Brush the omelet with a little melted sweet butter, sprinkle with the Parmesan cheese, cayenne pepper, and paprika. Serve at once. NET: 1 serving.

1 baked 10-inch tart shell (page
   726)
3 eggs
2 egg yolks
2 teaspoons Dijon mustard
½ teaspoon freshly grated
   nutmeg
½ teaspoon salt
A few grains cayenne pepper

½ pound cream cheese
¼ pound ricotta cheese
¾ cup sour cream
⅓ cup freshly grated imported
   Swiss cheese
1 cup milk, scalded
½ cup freshly grated Parmesan
   cheese

TARTE
AU FROMAGE

Cheese Tart (Hot)

Preheat the oven to 350°. Have the baked shell ready on a baking sheet. Mix the eggs and egg yolks together with a wire whisk. Add the mustard, nutmeg, salt, and cayenne pepper. In a mixer beat the cream cheese until light and fluffy, stir it into the egg mixture, then stir in the ricotta cheese and sour cream. Mix in the grated Swiss cheese and scalded milk. Pour the mixture into the shell, sprinkle with the Parmesan cheese, and bake 30 minutes. Serve piping hot. NET: Serves 4 to 6.

ON CHEESE

BY LIONEL H. BRAUN

Cheese in Civilization

I don't remember who told me that "cheese is the adult form of milk," but I have loved cheese all my life, and not having had to wait and grow up to appreciate cheese, I may perhaps have missed the liquid part of my youth. I make up for it now with good wines and great cheeses.

The word cheese is derived from the Latin "caseus," which in German, Dutch, Welsh, and English came out kaw, kaas, caws, cyse. Around 1100 in England it became caese (cease), and by the late sixteenth century the English had changed it to ches, chiese, and schese.

In France, where things are always different, the word "fromage" derives from the old French "formos," essentially a Greek word. A formos is a tiny basket made of rushes and was used as a nest for curdled milk, which eventually took the form of a small cream cheese. (Like a Coeur à la Crème in its basket?)

In those far-off days cheese was an end-of-the-meal dish and something taken to help mop up evidences of heavy imbibing. In Nero's and Caesar's time, we know, along with olives and dried raisins the legions traveled with cheese. Both epicure and pleb liked cheeses that were green, or smoked, to eat with special bread seasoned with coriander. Other cheese specialties available during this period in the Eternal City were cheese cakes called glycinas and tuniai. They were made of cheese, sweet white wine, and olive oil.

Whenever the subjects of food and taste arise, the great Brillat-Savarin stands out as "le professeur de gastronomes." However, the real genius of the time was Alexander Balthazar Grimod de la Reynière. This man ate his way through the French Revolution, Empire, Restoration, and beyond, until he died in 1838, his eighty-first year. In his *Almanach des Gourmands* Grimod wrote: "Cheese, we have already said, is the biscuit of drunkards; that is, of course, the salted cheeses which like Gruyère, Roquefort, Sassenage, and Geraramer, provoke thirst and make all pedestrian wines taste good. But between these cheeses and fresh cheese there is such a difference that one would hardly believe that they were of the same family. The four we have quoted hold a high place among the first group and to these we can add those of Mont d'Or, Franche-Comté, Maroilles (or Marolles), and above all these cheeses is Brie, one of the best that is eaten in Paris."

I often wonder what many dishes and ingredients passed down to us over centuries were really like in their legendary days. We know that the eggs Carême used when he held culinary court for Talleyrand and Emperor Alexander of Russia were smaller than those of today. Therefore, why can't we question the butterfat content of a cheese made two hundred years ago in relation to the "same" cheese made today, or the pungency of a Parmesan when Alexander Dumas produced *Le Grand Dictionnaire de Cuisine* a hundred years ago?

The Contemporary Aspect

In America, of course, we have depended more upon imported taste than upon things we have developed ourselves in our relatively young country. France has been the major supplier of great imports for the table. Camembert, Pont l'Évêque, Brie, Neufchâtel, and almost any cheese made in France now reaches us in almost any season or region of America, which gives us endless opportunity to add the flavor, interest, and balance to a meal that cheese supplies. In a Frenchman's menu, cheese finds its way to the table in soufflés, omelets, and the ever-present au gratin garnish. It may be the main course at lunch or start the evening dinner. It is an essential ingredient in many sauces, or may top a soup, a vegetable, or enhance a salad. It is a mainstay of every Frenchman's diet, and the Frenchman who dines à table or carries a lunch box to his travail may even enjoy it as dessert — a sugared Petit Suisse or a Reblochon with some fresh fruit of the season.

Types of Cheeses

Excellent books have been written on this fascinating subject, including detailed catalogues and descriptions of most cheeses of the world. In French cuisine we are concerned with soft, semi-soft, blue, firm, hard, and crème cheeses. The following table covers a small representation of some of the more readily available French cheeses of each type as well as some Swiss, Italian and American representatives:

TYPE OF CHEESE	NAME	CURRENT SOURCE
Hard (firm, almost brittle)	Parmesan	Italy: Parmigiano
	Asiago	Vicenza
	Cheddar	U.S.A.: Vermont
		Wisconsin
		California (Monterey Jack)
	Sapsago	Switzerland
Firm (firm but not brittle or crumbly)	Comté (French Gruyère)	France: Jura
	Beaufort	Savoy
	Cantal	Auvergne
	Gruyère	Switzerland: Emmenthal
	Appenzeller	Appenzelle
	Saanen	Saanen Valley
	Edam	Holland: North
	Gouda	South
	Provolone	Italy: Palermo
		Calabria
Blue (firm to creamy, with fissures of blue mold)	Roquefort	France: Aveyron
	Bleu de Bresse	Lyon
	Mont Clarat Bleu	
	Gorgonzola	Italy: Cremona
		Milan
	Stilton	England
Semi-Soft (soft but resilient; not runny)	Tête de Moine	France: Jura
	Maroilles	Maroilles
	Port du Salut	Mayenne
	Munster	Alsace
	Reblochon	Savoy
	Tomes de Savoie	Savoy
	Fontina	Italy: Val d'Aosta (Piedmont)
Soft (delicate, creamy, or runny consistency)	Brie	France: Meaux
		Coulommiers
	Camembert	Normandy
	Vendôme	Vendôme
	Neufchâtel	Normandy
	Livarot	Normandy
	Pont l'Évêque	Normandy
	Beaumont	Savoy

TYPE OF CHEESE	NAME	CURRENT SOURCE
	Saint-Nectaire	Auvergne
	Valençay	Berry
	Vacherin Mont d'Or	Switzerland: Vaud Fribourg
	Vacherin Fribourg	
Fromage Fraîche (Fresh Cheese)		
Simple Cream: less than 50 per cent fat	Ricotta	Italy and U.S.A.
	Mozzarella	Italy and U.S.A.
	Cottage cheese and pot cheese	U.S.A.
Double Crème: 60 per cent fat	Rollot	France: Picardy
	Fromage Monsieur	
	Chèvre St. Maure	
	St. Marcellin	Isère
Triple Crème: 75 per cent fat	Petit Suisse	France: Normandy
	Magnum	
	Une Friandise or Le Morinet	Meaux area
	Brillat-Savarin	

Wine and the Cheese

The classic accompaniment to cheese is wine, but oddly, French districts noted for cheese usually produce little wine, and vice versa. Even so, a cheese is best with a wine from its own natural background — a Swiss Gruyère, for example, has a perfect companion in a light white Swiss wine; sherry or port would be alien to it. And I wouldn't serve a fine Corton with a country goat cheese, but rather a coarser wine whose bite will refresh the palate and cut the goat taste. With sherry or port I would pair Stilton.

I think the wine guides for cheese can be easily remembered if one keeps in mind the simple general criteria of wine selection: white wines with chicken or veal, fish or shellfish; red wines with red meat. (This rule is by no means sacred, but it will never lead one astray.) By the same token, light dry wines are served with delicately flavored cheeses, and full-bodied red wines with stronger cheeses. Here is a simple guide to follow.

Delicate cheeses (such as double and triple crèmes, Munster, Brillat-Savarin, Tome au Marc de Raisin, Bel Paese). Dry white wines such as Pouilly-Fuissé, Pouilly Fumé, even to the less dry Moselle or Alsatian.

Cheeses more developed in flavor (such as Gruyère, Dunlop, Appenzeller, or Port Salut). Dry red Bordeaux or such Burgundies as Nuit St. George or Chateauneuf-du-Pape, and sometimes enjoyed with tawny port.

Brie, Camembert, Bleu de Bresse. The Brie harmonizes particularly well with Nuit St. George. For the others, Volnay and a white Corton-Charlemagne. Côte de Beaune and St. Émilion wines are also recommended for such cheeses.

Strong soft-ripening cheese (such as Pont l'Évêque, Livarot, Maroilles, or blue-veined cheese) are best with big red wines — Bordeaux, Burgundy, for example Clos Vougeot, Chambolle Musigny, and Côtes du Rhône bottlings.

This list is by no means complete, and new experiences of taste, smell, and texture may be had by keeping in mind that cheese and wine in general marry well, and rewarding tastes come from experimenting with all wines. Also, though we consider French wines the best for French cheeses, they are not the ultimate with all cheeses. A Valpolicella, Bardolino, Lugano, Soave, or Verdicchio will go best with mild Italian cheeses such as Fontina, Bel Paese, or a young Provolone, and the lustier Italian reds — Chianti, Nebbiolo, Barolo, or Barbaresco — will mate perfectly with highly seasoned or rich cheeses like Romano, Gorgonzola, or Asiago.

How to Serve Cheese

In my trips to the cheese-making districts of France and the shires of England, I find the most appeal in the presentation of cheeses in the shops. In France you often see cheese displayed on chestnut leaves, the young cool green ones in springtime and the gold and russet leaves in the fall; it reminds us that cheese, like wine, is nature's child and is most attractive in its own elements. There is more serving harmony when cheese is displayed on a simple wooden board or marble slab (with a few grape leaves or a garnish of parsley and watercress) than in more elaborate service.

While cheese grows in popularity as a snack or hors d'oeuvre with drinks, our acceptance of the European custom of serving cheese as a last course is also increasing. At all the wine tastings taking place here in America, one finds cheese sitting in the center of the table, as many as three or four varieties, with biscuits or French bread.

Cheese harmonizes with so many kinds of food that at the end of a meal it enhances almost any luncheon or dinner — except, of course, it would not be suitable following such rich meats as pork or roast duck, or if a cheese soufflé had been served before. It is interesting, however, that cheese seems to go well with almost any menu from countries that are major cheese producers. Can you imagine a Swiss, French, or Italian meal without some cheese during or after?

TEMPERATURE. All cheese should be served at room temperature. When the weather is warm, an hour out of the refrigerator is sufficient to adjust the cheese; if it is hot, 30 minutes should be enough. But a soft cheese like Camembert takes only one-third the time a firmer cheese like Gruyère does to arrive at perfection, so let the harder cheeses leave refrigeration before the softer ones.

MODUS OPERANDI. (1) Arrange your cheese board or serving tray so that mild cheeses are away from strong cheeses. (2) Provide a separate knife for each cheese. (3) Provide ample room on the board to cut the cheese. (4) Prepare only as much cheese as you expect to use. Any cheese that has been at room temperature several hours will not gain by being refrigerated again. (5) Strike a balance between strong and mild cheeses (see cheese tray combinations, page 696). This means having alternatives unless you are completely familiar with your guests' tastes.

THE CHEESE COURSE AFTER THE ENTRÉE. There are two kinds of dinner cheese: (1) The cheeses that "talk back" — cheeses of character, of personality, like Brie, Stilton, Gorgonzola. These cheeses may be followed by a sweet dessert. (2) Cheeses specifically known as dessert cheeses, usually delicate and creamy like a double or triple crème — a Crème Chantilly, which is luxurious, rich, and meant to be eaten in small bits. In France I always enjoy a Petit Suisse (now also available in America) or Fontainebleau, with a sprinkling of sugar, and with strawberries or raspberries in season.

The lighter and more delicate double and triple crèmes are ideal luncheon cheeses when the main course is some shade of aspic or an omelet. But the big meat courses require the heartier cheeses, perhaps something with a dry astringent character like a Stilton.

HORS D'OEUVRES AND OTHER SUSTENANCES. Cheeses that allay hunger pangs or that may be used in a main dish are by themselves satisfying. Good Cheddar, Appenzeller, Gruyère cheeses may in themselves be a meal, with a loaf of bread and a modest bottle of red wine.

When it comes to hors d'oeuvres, the variety of cheeses to be served depends upon the drink served immediately before dinner or at an extended dinner party. If your pre-prandial beverage is quickly followed by dinner, it is considerate to serve something a little perky like a Bleu de Bresse from France, a Maytag Blue from Maytag, Iowa, U.S.A., or anything not bland. But when it comes to cocktailing, sustenance is a necessity. I like to recommend four or more good cheeses at different taste levels. One of my favorites is Fontina, a full Italian cheese, slightly yellowish and made like Gruyère, but with ewe's milk. A big Edam cheese is my second selection, and my third pick, of course, a creamy Gorgonzola, which spreads very well, or the popular Bresse Bleu. Two cheeses to round out the party are a Camembert or triple crème such as Caprice des Dieux, and a French Port Salut.

It is perhaps wiser to program an ample supply of fewer cheeses than to serve many kinds that you never see again as the tray returns for the second and third voyage of the party.

Buying and Storing Cheese

Watch what you're doing! Know your cheesemonger — the less

familiar you are with the cheese you are buying, the more critical this becomes. I would rather follow the example of the White House and order by mail from a reliable shop than to buy some of the fast-ripening supermarket imports that are probably over the hill.

Sampling is the first important step before you buy. It will tell you more about the cheese than any individual can. Many better specialty food shops are glad to give sample plugs, and people knowledgeable about cheese do ask for them. I always take my business to a store that is obliging and takes an interest, answers questions, and doesn't rush me.

Of equal importance is how cheeses are kept by the retailer. All cheeses should be kept covered with a tight plastic film. Strong cheeses should be kept away from mild cheeses. A ham or liverwurst should not be side by side with a Swiss cheese. A mild cheese, like chocolates or butter, will absorb the surrounding smells and flavors of stronger foods. Remember, too, that most cheeses should be refrigerated, and only as much cheese should be displayed on a counter as seems likely to sell during a day.

The art of buying cheese starts with a relatively simple idea: Cheese that is good looks good! A few cheeses like goat cheese never look good by ordinary standards, but such cheeses have their own following, and they will look good to you if your experience with them is good. Too many imported cheeses are found in improper condition, and a hapless buyer will be told "that's the way they're supposed to be."

When buying a piece of cheese from the bulk, you run less risk of making a bad decision because you view an entire cheese. But supermarkets and delicatessens rarely encourage "a taste," so sampling is an awkward activity.

BUYING CHEDDAR. A Cheddar, or any hard pressed cheese, need not look moist, but if it looks crack-laden or obviously dry or shows flecks of white mold in the body of the cheese, it probably has been around too long and has been improperly cared for.

BUYING BLUE. Roquefort has risen from humble beginnings to its place among the bluebloods of all cheesedom. Today there are more than fifty varieties of great blue-veined cheeses, but one taste of Roquefort explains why it has been so widely recognized as the king of cheeses. Some people refer to this noble cheese as effervescent — its prickly flavor can make almost any wine taste better — but its essence is captured by Bunyard, who speaks of the "tingling Rabelaisian pungency of Roquefort."

Exported Roquefort is salted more liberally than Roqueforts made for French consumption, and the flavor may be uneven, which makes it essential to sample Roquefort before you buy. Any blue-veined cheese must always look moist and not granular, with a marbling attractive to the eye. Gorgonzola, an Italian veined cheese, or Stilton from England, are two other outstanding blue-veined delicacies. Examine the Italian and English blues carefully. If within a half-inch of the rind there is a darkening, it probably is getting old and you should try it before you buy it. If it has fissures or black streaks while the body shows graying or yellowing, the cheese has become cakey and old.

Bleu de Bresse, another French blue which may arrive here in late spring, is a cheese that can have the consistency of a thick cream, like a ripening Brie in texture, and the blue is suspended somewhat like nuggets.

BUYING SWISS. In my observations, most neighborhood stores will feature a domestic Swiss and an imported variety. But "imported" doesn't mean it comes from Switzerland, and many a Finnish Swiss passes at a higher price than is justified for Switzerland Swiss. Try buying Swiss in bulk, and look for the country of origin — "Switzerland" stamped in red all over the rind. If you buy it pre-packaged in plastic wrap, read the label carefully.

BUYING PARMESAN. Unless you live in an Italian neighborhood, much of the Parmesan in stores is pre-grated and probably bears the name of one of America's big dairy companies. This cheese cannot compare in flavor with the Italian Parmesan, particularly Parmigiano-Reggiano. There is no substitute for "freshly grated Parmesan cheese." Buy it in a 1-pound or 2-pound chunk; it will keep for a long time in a plastic bag in the refrigerator. The flavor is infinitely better and the cheese will go a longer way toward tastier food preparation and good economy.

BUYING MEDIUM-FIRM CHEESES. Cheeses such as Fontina, Reblochon, Munster, Gouda, Edam, and the Scandinavian cheeses ending in "bo" are usually the best-keeping cheeses you will find. Munster can vary a great deal in its color or creaminess. Make certain that it bends away from a blade when cutting.

Usually any of these cheeses will be good if they look good. However, when it comes to Fontina, which is Italy's version of Emmenthal, look for the same color as the Swiss Emmenthal, and a rind the color of an almond skin. (This cheese makes an excellent fondue and should not be confused with a cheese called Fontine or Fontinella.)

BUYING SOFT CHEESES. All soft cheeses should feel pleasingly plump in their wrappers. A Camembert or Brie should fill the thin wooden box, and show no depression in the center. They should be soft and white, not hard or brown. When you have eaten as many "moon-faced" cheeses as I have and cried in despair, you'll agree that Brie is the most difficult of all cheeses to find at its peak. But Brie is one of the very few soft ripening cheeses which may be bought in bulk. My favorite source for this queen of cheeses is the little village of Meaux. The Meaux Brie is a large white pancake-like cheese and only about a half-inch high. Look for a Brie that is glossy throughout, without a dry cakey center (a dry center means that the cheese will not ripen evenly if the center is to catch up at all). This superb cheese should be eaten only at perfection.

Storing Cheese

A cheese well wrapped in plastic will not lose its moisture. But it is the type of cheese that dictates the amount of moisture present, so perhaps it is better to think in terms of degrees of firmness and flavor type. A firm Cheddar has had considerably more moisture removed than a softer cheese like Port-Salut, while a fresh cheese like ricotta or a soft ripening Brie has been allowed to keep its moisture. But regardless of its texture, a cheese must be properly covered to maintain its own level of moisture.

Firmer cheeses will usually keep longer than soft and semi-soft cheeses — a Parmesan longer than a Munster, for example. Plastic wrap is ideal for these firmer cheeses. Another way is to keep them encased in a dampened cloth that is wetted regularly with a solution of ½ cup water, 1 teaspoon vinegar, and ½ teaspoon salt.

Regardless of how beautiful a big oversize piece of cheese looks on the table, cut only what is required, wrap and return the rest to the refrigerator.

If your cheese develops a mold (which it may if it hasn't been properly wrapped), remember that under the mold the cheese is perfectly good, so cut away only the top and use the rest.

The secret of keeping a blue cheese is to have air around the cheese. This need for air is peculiar to the blues, as it is the relation of bacterial spores and cool air currents during the curing stage that creates the blue veining. Therefore, even with a lengthy period of refrigeration, a blue cheese will sharpen in flavor. Before refrigerating a blue, wrap it in a damp cloth and cover with a glass or plastic dome. The dome permits some air while preventing the moisture from escaping. The damp cloth helps to replace the dissipating moisture.

Of the three kinds of soft ripening cheeses (free-flowing like Brie, thick like double and triple crèmes, and firmer like Reblochon), the free-flowing cheeses are the most perishable. The surest way of keeping them is to buy them in small quantities. Remember, once a good Brie starts to flow freely, don't stop the action by refrigerating. It will never come back again, so make the most of it.

All whole uncut soft ripening cheeses should stay in their original boxes until several hours before they are served. Even refrigeration won't stop the ripening, only retard it! So the only thing to do with any free-flowing cheese is to wrap it in plastic, leave it at room temperature overnight, and eat it the following day.

The firmer cheeses like Pont l'Évêque or Maroilles will also mature steadily under refrigeration. It is best to wrap leftovers in foil or plastic, leave at room temperature, and eat as soon as possible.

The double or triple crème soft cheeses appear to hold flavor and texture longer. These cheeses may be opened, held to room temperature, and returned in plastic wrap to the refrigerator — and still survive. The high cream content in these cheeses acts as a stabilizer to keep the cheese from deteriorating too quickly.

We are here suggesting combinations of cheeses to have on hand for your cheese course at home, whether for a family meal or for guests. Each combination represents a group of distinctive flavor contrasts. Far beyond these modest suggestions, you will discover and create a thousand more wonderful cheese offerings — to finish off your bottle of wine or to taste a new wine. (Cheese and bread are the preferred sop for serious wine tasting.)

The only other foods served in the cheese course are breads and fruits. With the bread, little curls of sweet butter may be offered, even though the French have long been against eating butter with cheese. Frankly, I find it a matter of personal taste. The soft ripening and richer cheeses don't seem to need butter, but the drier and more crumbly types — including the salty Roquefort exported to us — remain totally enjoyable if eaten with biscuits or bread spread with butter.

BREADS. Skinny French and Italian breads that are mostly crust go well with French and Italian cheeses, while a good rye bread or pumpernickel goes perfectly with the Swiss, Dutch, and German varieties. Bland crackers such as water biscuits go well with all cheeses, but try wheat wafers with Gruyère or a creamy blue, and you will find a different and pleasant taste to lead you to experiment. The bread server may include any or several of: French bread (the narrow baguettes preferred), French dinner rolls, Italian bread, rye bread, pumpernickel bread, biscottes or melba toast, rusks, water crackers, and any other crackers you like (except saltines).

FRUITS. The fresh fruit offering with the cheese course is an excellent but optional idea. The fruit should be appropriate to the cheese and served in an attractively arranged fruit bowl. Any one kind or a combination may be served.

With hard, semi-soft, and soft cheeses that have a sturdy character and flavor, the complementary fruits are pears, apples, grapes, plums, and fresh figs. Also, nuts in shells (with a nutcracker) accompany this group of fruits and cheese very well.

With double and triple crèmes and fromages fraîches (fresh cheeses), these fruits complete the romance: strawberries, raspberries, peaches, apricots, nectarines. Serve these fruits cleaned (and peeled) in a crystal bowl.

PLATS DES FROMAGES

Some Suggested Plats des Fromages (Cheese Trays)
for Hors d'Oeuvres

CHEESE (AND TYPE)	BREAD	FRUIT
(A) Saanen (firm) Tête de Moine (semi-soft) Appenzeller (firm) Sainte-Nectaire (soft) Beaumont (soft)	Assorted small pieces	None

Cheese Trays

(B) Vacherine Mont d'Or (soft, avail-   Assorted small pieces   None
       able Nov.-Feb. only)
     Chèvre Chabichou (soft goat
       cheese)
     Pont l'Évêque (soft)
     Reblochon (semi-soft)
     Munster (semi-soft)

Some Suggested Plats de Fromage (Cheese Trays)
For After the Entree

CHEESE (AND TYPE)	BREAD	FRUIT
(A) Chèvre Montrachet (soft creamy goat cheese) Bleu de Bresse or Gorgonzola (semi-soft creamy blue)	Any type on page 696	Pear/apple group (optional)
(B) One or two of these double crèmes: Rollot, Magnum, Fromage Monsieur, Le Morinet, or Chèvre St. Maure (a double crème from goat's milk) Brie (soft runny) Emmenthal (firm Swiss)	Water biscuits	Berries/peaches group (optional)
(C) A double crème from the Tray B list Le Beau Pasteur (soft white cream cheese with herbs) Mont Clarat Bleu (buttery creamy blue)	French bread	Pear/apple group (optional)
(D) Brie (soft) Stilton (English blue, firm) Vacherin Fribourg (soft and buttery; available Nov.-Feb. only)	French bread	Pear/apple group (optional)
(E) Petit Suisse (white fresh triple crème), dusted with confectioners sugar (this cheese is rarely served without fresh fruit)	None	Berries/peaches
(F) Roquefort (blue) Camembert (soft creamy)	French bread	Pear/apple group (optional)

BREADS, PASTRY, CAKES, OTHER DOUGHS

THE MYSTIQUE of baking has always, I think, had a Svengali-like hold over me. Maybe it is the ripe promise of a life-pull one feels in the touching, kneading, beating, and shaping of flour, yeast, eggs, sugar, and rich cream as they are transformed into breads and pastries of superb taste and texture.

This attraction is so strong that one summer, to be near my son in Vermont, I spent my days as a "pastry chef" at a restaurant free of chic in a big converted Victorian house. My special kitchen was the cool airy basement, well equipped with an enormous Blodgett baker's oven, two grand work tables, and a gas burner for the relatively small amount of surface cooking a baker has to do. Three large windows looked out on a country garden with a superb population of birds, squirrels, and adorable chipmunks, big handsome trees, and air! . . . air so sweet it always gave me the same sensation as eating honey. I wished I could send some to my friends in the grim and vast hot city.

In my New England boulangerie-pâtisserie, I worked entirely alone, and anything that even faintly suggested flour or yeast came from my kitchen. This meant daily making of all the breads, brioches, croissants, light dinner rolls, small and large vol-au-vents, tarts, and as many different desserts as possible, ten to twelve different kinds each day! In addition, a lot of time went into basic preparations, such as making chocolate rounds, glazes, and creams; and with no helper to ask to whip this, or stir that, I often felt it was a test of my devotion to my profession, not to mention my sheer physical endurance. Anyhow, I tried to do everything with tender loving care, and although this seems to take longer, the breads and pastries were beautiful, and it was a great joy to behold the products of my hands.

My Vermont kitchen was indeed a far cry from what may be the most magnificent pastry kitchen in the world, aboard the SS *France*. Here was a vision I shall always remember. Never in all my life have

I seen such a kitchen, large but very compact, and not a spatula out of place. What order, color, and balance, a wonderful atmosphere! In the boulangerie (bakery) there was a wooden table about the size of a ballroom floor, which had been so well scrubbed that it looked like satin. On one wall were racks full of long and short French loaves just out of the ovens, baskets of corkscrew rolls, croissants, and brioches, and long shelves with sandwich bread. On a smaller shelf were handy boxes filled with rusks, fairy toast, and three sizes of croûtons. In the next kitchen on the *France* the pastry chef and his assistant were just finishing off the most elaborate sugar baskets and flowers for a gala dinner that evening.

In yet another kitchen of my experience, the most remarkable cakes, chocolate rolls and fruit tarts were made by children around twelve years old. This was always my favorite class in my teaching curriculum, the "young gourmet" as one editor called it. Children are so receptive and have no preconceived notions. "Instead of cookies, they are making the world's gooiest Maple Cake, 80 percent frosting and 20 percent cake," is the way *Look* described our efforts in a delightful picture story. In no way were these classes fun-and-games; these young bakers, whom I called Les Enfants Boulangers, pursued each recipe seriously, performing all the main actions themselves — measuring the flour, mixing the pastry dough with their fingers, rolling out the crust, and easing it into a flan ring on a baking sheet. One pair of young hands would finish off the edges and prick the shells all over with the tines of a fork, while another would beat the heavy cream in a round-bottomed bowl nested in ice. These young chefs even learned to use the whisk in the French manner.

In recent years my regular adult classes have included a growing representation of young career people, both women and men — a model, a research assistant, a couple of lawyers, a teacher, young people like that. They want to learn how to bake — how a common ordinary loaf of bread comes into being, luscious fresh fruit tarts, and what makes a cream puff puff.

In this section we have organized the recipes into those main types of French baking and pastry-making which can be accomplished successfully in the home kitchen; and, as is the pattern of this compendium, there are also some favorite dough preparations from other cuisines.

The primary methods are given in "basic recipes," in which each step is numbered. We hope this will enable those who have hesitated to attempt a baking adventure to do so. Proceed slowly, surely, carefully, and correctly with much "tender loving care" through the basic recipe, and you will be rewarded with the best brioche you have ever eaten, or become the heroine of Crêpes Suzette! Then, buoyed by your success, keep right on surprising yourself and impressing your guests as you master more baking marvels.

Here is a résumé of the organization of this chapter:

BREADS: FRENCH YEAST DOUGHS. Basic recipes are given for the most frequently used doughs: Pain Français (ordinary steam-baked French bread), Petits Pains au Lait (milk-dough French dinner rolls and bread), Brioche, Savarin, and Baba.

BREADS: SPÉCIALITÉS. These other interesting breads are described in the recipes. It might be rather special to offer homemade bread sticks at your next party. Also included are a garlic bread and a hot herb bread, both delicious, and one of my favorites — the Swedish coffee bread (a Danish pastry type), with 20 pounded cardamom seeds.

PASTRY. Basic recipes are given for the most frequently used doughs: Pâte Feuilletée (puff paste or flaky pastry), Croissants de Boulanger (croissants made of yeast puff paste), Pâte à Foncer (short pastry shell, for tarts and quiche), Pâte à Choux (cream puff dough). In addition to dozens of desserts composed of these basic French pastry doughs — such as the Napoleon, the fresh fruit tarts and tartlets, the profiteroles and croquembouche — there are other delicious pastries made possible for the home, including strudels (which are such fun to make), baklava, and rather extraordinary renditions of American apple pie and lemon meringue pie.

CAKES. Cakes? Or concoctions? In the French school, cake-making is pure sorcery as various doughs are put together with pastry creams, butter creams, fondants, fruits, meringues, bavaroises, et cetera. The whole universe of imagination and fancy are the pastry chef's palette. Thus, under the stars of a summer night in the Adirondacks I first encountered the Chocolate Roll (a "cake" with no flour at all). Perhaps the little cakes of savarin dough became the little rum-soaked "granny" cakes (more glamourously called Babas au Rhum) because some chef idolized his grandmother (baba). Was it the majesty of a royal command that inspired the crowning achievement of Crêpes Suzette?

This section does not offer master cake recipes. Even the basics, such as the genoese and the biscuit (sponge), are used in very different ways from cake to cake. For the home pastry chef, therefore, who may not plan to whip up ten to twelve different desserts a day as I did in Vermont, these recipes are generally independent. In most cases, like the traditional French Christmas cake (Bûche de Noël) or the Viennese Doboschtorte, which may seem complicated, you can concentrate on your single recipe and avoid the distraction of having to refer to other recipes for the component parts. With any recipe, and especially the capricious cakes, it is a good idea to study the formula and get a clear picture of the composition and preparatory processes that are unique to it.

OTHER DOUGHS: CRÊPES, BEIGNETS, SOUFFLÉS, PETITS FOURS. A basic recipe is given for Crêpes (one of the easiest of all dough preparations), which can be cooked days ahead of time and frozen. Beignets are actually made of cream puff dough (the dough for these little puffs of wind — in France they are referred to as "pets de nonne" — can be prepared in advance and will keep a day or two in the refrigerator). If there still lurks a mystery about the Soufflé, perhaps the notes on page 787 will help. It is the most spontaneous dessert you can make, and one of the simplest! Petits Fours are a delightful froufrou of the pastry-making art. This section includes recipes for many types of Petits Fours Secs plus a very elementary guide to making some of the Fours à la Crème Glacés and Fruits Déguisées of haute pâtisserie.

Who would want to bother? Well, in creative menu planning, if you are having guests, why not give your meal the most stunning touch with a silver tray of your own glazed fruits and demitasse, after the cheese? Or homemade ice cream and your own homemade Cigarettes, or — most elegant and welcome — a simple basket of just two or three kinds of Petits Fours Secs such as Tuiles aux Amandes, Langues de Chat, or Madeleines?

Come join me in the wonderland of baking and pastry-making!

FRENCH YEAST DOUGHS

A slice of crusty homemade bread spread with homemade sweet butter is one of the elixirs of life. Bread is not difficult to make, nor is butter (page 56). This is the most genuine living experience as your hands touch and knead the dough, encouraging the growth of the yeast; then the heady aroma of the baking, and the delicious panic as you slice the warm homemade loaf and spread it with cool sweet butter.

French bread is always baked in a steam oven or with steam in the oven (usually from a large pan of hot water in the bottom) because that is the only way a good crust will form around those long French loaves (see the recipe for Pain Français, page 705). American-type homemade bread is similar to French dinner rolls, in which the yeast is dissolved in milk. The recipe formula is quite different, and steam heat is not required (page 706).

Advice on Baking with Yeast

YEAST. Be very careful not to kill the yeast by dissolving it in water that is too hot. The liquid should be the same heat as milk or formula you would feed to a baby.

KNEADING. It is always best to knead dough by hand, never with a machine or a spoon. When I was a child, our cook baked bread about twice a week; it was the only bread I knew. But when she prepared the dough, she always disappeared. Discreet investigation by my mother exposed the reason for the disappearance — Cook would retire to her quarters to knead the dough on her bare chest. Her method made the most delicious bread, because yeast is alive and needs life and warmth to touch it.

RISING. Rising is the growth of the yeast culture in the dough before it is baked. It must be allowed its own given time to rise (or grow) properly. If it over-rises, it becomes too bubbly and will have large holes inside when it is baked. If it under-rises, it might resemble a bagel in texture and consistency. Correctly risen yeast dough should double its original size.

Never make yeast dough rise too many times. Follow the steps of your recipe precisely.

When you set the dough aside to rise, be certain that it is not in a draft and that the temperature is warm enough. To rise properly, the dough must be kept warm; use a blanket if necessary (the warmth of a baby blanket is just right).

When the dough is put to rise, brush the top of it with vegetable oil so that a hard crust doesn't form on the rising dough.

PROVING. Proving is the term for the last rising, after the dough is put in the pan and before it is put into the oven. The dough should prove to double its size, no more. Twenty percent of the final growth of the dough takes place in the oven.

GLAZING. Brushing the formed dough with milk, beaten egg, egg mixed with milk or water, melted butter, or other glazing ingredients, should be done just before the dough goes into the oven. Use a very soft brush (a badger hair shaving brush is perfect if it hasn't been used for shaving). Brush very gently so that the shape of the loaf is not damaged.

BAKING. The oven must be fully preheated to the specified temperature when the dough enters it. The immediate heat of the oven sets the rise that has taken place thus far. Don't bang the oven door or hit the tin. (I have known bread or brioche dough to fall when someone has shouted while standing near the bowl!)

WHEN IS THE DOUGH BAKED? Turn the loaf out of the pan and tap it with your knuckles. If it is baked, it should sound hollow. Most breads should have a hard crust, except for brioche and Scandinavian breads, which should be wrapped at once in a hot cloth to preserve the soft crust. Place hard-crust breads and rolls on a wire rack so that the air can circulate about and cool them.

---

1 cup lukewarm water
1 package dry yeast
1 tablespoon granulated sugar
1½ teaspoons salt
2 tablespoons sweet butter
   (soft, at room temperature)
3 cups all-purpose flour
¼ cup cornmeal

GLAZE
1 raw egg white
1 tablespoon water
½ teaspoon salt
Optional: 1 teaspoon crushed
   rock salt, sesame seeds, or
   poppy seeds

PAIN FRANÇAIS

French Bread

STEP 1. Put the water in a large warm mixing bowl and slowly mix in the yeast. Cover the bowl with a cloth and let the yeast rise 5 minutes.

STEP 2. Mix the granulated sugar, salt, and butter into the water and yeast mixture. Stir well and add 2 cups flour. Beat the dough thoroughly with the hand or electric mixer.

STEP 3. Add another cup of flour to the dough (or, just enough to make the dough stiff) and mix well.

STEP 4. Sprinkle the pastry board or marble slab with a little flour and put the dough on it. Cover the dough with a cloth and let it rise 10 minutes.

STEP 5. Knead the dough very well. Cover it with the cloth and let it rise again 10 minutes.

STEP 6. At this point, punch the dough down, cover it with the cloth, and let it rise again until it doubles in size. (The reason for punching down the dough is to allow all gases to escape from the yeast.)

STEP 7. Divide the dough into 2 or 3 pieces, cover, and let them rest another 10 minutes.

STEP 8. With a rolling pin, roll out each piece of dough about ¼ inch thick. Roll up each piece of dough lengthwise and tight, to make a long slender loaf. (If you divided the dough into 2 pieces, you should now have 2 rolls about 18 inches long and 2 inches thick.) Press the dough firmly along the rolled edge to seal.

STEP 9. Sprinkle a jelly roll pan or baking sheet with the cornmeal, and put the rolls of dough (loaves) on it. Allow at least 3 inches between each loaf (so the bread will be crusty all over when baked). With a sharp knife, cut diagonal slashes across the top of each loaf, about ¼ inch deep.

STEP 10. Beat the egg white, water, and salt for the glaze. Brush the loaves with this glaze (save some for step 14). If desired, sprinkle the tops with crushed rock salt, or sesame or poppy seed.

STEP 11. Let the loaves rise, uncovered, until double in bulk, approximately 1 hour.

STEP 12. At this point turn on the oven to 425°, to preheat.

STEP 13. Put a large roasting pan of boiling water on the bottom shelf of the oven. Place the pan with the bread on the rack above the hot water. Bake the bread 10 minutes at 425°.

STEP 14. Quickly brush the loaves again with the egg white mixture. Reduce the oven temperature to 375° and continue to bake the bread 25 to 30 minutes longer, or until it sounds hollow when you tap it.

STEP 15. Remove the bread from the oven and let it cool on a wire rack.

NET: Two 18-inch loaves.

PETITS PAINS AU LAIT

French Dinner Rolls or a Fine Loaf of White Bread

1 cup milk
2 tablespoons granulated sugar
2 teaspoons salt
5 tablespoons sweet butter
1 cup lukewarm water
1 package dry yeast
5½ cups sifted all-purpose flour

About 4 to 5 tablespoons cool melted sweet butter (to brush the dough)
1 egg, beaten
Optional: Coarse salt, poppy seed, caraway, or sesame seed

STEP 1. Put the milk, sugar, salt, and butter in a pan. Stir over moderate heat until the mixture comes to a boil. Cool the mixture.

STEP 2. Put the water in a large bowl. (Be sure it is no hotter than lukewarm, or the heat will kill the yeast action.) Sprinkle the yeast over the top of the water. Using a wooden spoon, stir it into the water until it dissolves.

STEP 3. Add the cooled milk mixture to the water and yeast, and mix thoroughly.

STEP 4. Stir 3 cups sifted flour into the liquid and beat it thoroughly with a wooden spoon. Then stir in the remaining 2½ cups.

STEP 5. Turn the dough out onto a lightly floured board or marble slab. Knead until it is shiny and satin-smooth (about 10 minutes).

STEP 6. Wipe out a large bowl with a damp cloth, dust the bowl lightly with flour, and put in the dough. Brush all over the top of the dough with cool melted butter. Cover the bowl with plastic wrap and a warm cloth.

STEP 7. Put the bowl with the dough in a warm place (ideally 80°) and let it rise 1 hour and 20 minutes.

STEP 8. Break the rise, by running your finger around the edge of the bowl, and turn the dough out onto a lightly floured board or slab. (Do not knead it again.)

STEP 9. Start to preheat the oven at 375°. (For Dinner Rolls, proceed with step 10. For Loaf Bread, skip to step 10-a.)

STEP 10. Butter a jelly roll pan or baking sheet. Take little fistfuls of dough. (You should have 18 to 24 of them, for the number and size rolls you wish to make.) On a lightly floured board, knead them a little to form a smooth surface. Then pat them out into an oval shape about 4 inches long by 2½ inches wide. With a knife, make two 3-inch cuts in the length of the dough, so that they are still connected at one end. The piece of dough should now have three 3-inch tails.

STEP 11. Braid the three tails on each piece of dough, and you should now have the shape of a braided roll. Set the roll out on the buttered pan. Cut and braid all the pieces of dough in this manner.

STEP 12. When all of the rolls have been braided and set on the baking pan, put them in a warm place and let them prove (rise in the pan) about 15 minutes. Keep dough covered with a cloth supported by water glasses (the cloth should not touch the dough).

STEP 13. Brush each roll with the beaten egg. If desired, sprinkle some or all of the rolls with coarse salt, poppy seed, caraway, or sesame seed. Put them in the preheated 375° oven and bake 15 to 20 minutes, until they sound hollow when you tap them.

STEP 14. Cool the rolls on a wire rack.

For Loaf Bread, proceed as follows:

STEP 10-a. Butter 1 large or 2 small loaf pans. With the hands, form the dough into 1 large or 2 small loaves and put it in the pan(s). Make a few diagonal incisions with a knife on top of the dough. Brush with the beaten egg.

STEP 11-a. Put the pan(s) in a warm place and let the dough prove (rise in the pan) about 15 minutes before baking. Keep the dough covered with a cloth supported by water glasses (the cloth should not touch the dough).

STEP 12-a. Set the pan(s) on a baking sheet or jelly roll pan and bake 45 minutes.

STEP 13-a. Reduce the oven temperature to 350° and bake another 20 minutes. (Test the bread by knocking the side. If it sounds hollow, it is completely baked.)

STEP 14-a. Remove the bread from the loaf pan and let it cool on a wire rack.

NET: 18 to 24 dinner rolls, or 1 large or 2 small loaves.

BRIOCHE

This recipe gives directions for baking brioche in either large or small fluted molds. You will need 2 large (8-inch) molds, or 18 to 24 small (2-inch) molds, or 32 to 48 tiny (1-inch) molds, or any combination of these. Brioche dough may be prepared several days in advance and frozen, or extra dough may be frozen if you don't require the whole quantity. To freeze, after the dough has been in the refrigerator and has set (step 9), wrap the extra dough in plastic and store it in the freezer.

½ cup lukewarm water
2 packages dry yeast
4 cups all-purpose flour
20 tablespoons (5/8 pound)
 sweet butter
6 large eggs or 7 small

2 tablespoons granulated sugar
2 teaspoons salt
Melted salt butter (to grease
 molds)
1 egg, beaten (for glaze)

STEP 1. Dissolve the yeast in the water.

STEP 2. Put 1 cup flour into a small bowl. Add the yeast mixture and stir with a spoon until the contents form a firm ball.

STEP 3. Turn the ball of dough out onto a lightly floured pastry board and knead it a little to get a smooth surface on the bottom. Then cut a cross on the surface, like a hot cross bun. Open the cut a little. Literally drop the yeast cake (ball of dough) into a small bowl of plain lukewarm water. Let it stand until it rises to the top of the water.

STEP 4. Meanwhile, put the sweet butter in a mixer and beat it until it is very light and fluffy. Remove the creamed butter from the mixer bowl and set it aside on wax paper. (No need to wash the mixer bowl.)

STEP 5. Put 3 cups flour in the mixer bowl. Add the eggs, sugar, and 1 teaspoon salt. Beat until the mixture is very shiny.

STEP 6. Add the creamed butter to the mixer bowl and beat well.

STEP 7. Lift the yeast ball out of the water with your hand, so that it drains through your fingers, and add it to the mixer bowl. Beat the dough thoroughly.

STEP 8. Wipe the inside of a large bowl with a damp cloth and dust it lightly with flour. Put the brioche dough in this bowl. Cover the bowl tightly with plastic wrap and a warm cloth. Put it in a warm place (ideally 80°) and let the dough rise until double its bulk.

STEP 9. When the dough has risen, put it as is — in the bowl — into the freezer. (With brioche, do not break the rise of the dough, as is done with other yeast doughs.) If possible, after the dough has set — become workable, more firm, less loose — transfer it to the refrigerator and let it continue to rest at least 6 hours or overnight. (If the time is not available, just proceed with the recipe after the dough has become set in the freezer.)

STEP 10. Move the dough from the bowl onto a lightly floured board. TO FILL TWO 8-INCH MOLDS: Brush the molds with melted butter. Divide the dough in half. Take one half of the dough and cut off about a quarter of it. Fill the brioche pan with three-quarters of the dough. Roll the little piece of dough into a ball, then continue rolling it into a cone shape. Insert the small end of the ball into the center of the brioche in the pan so that the larger part sticks out like a cap. Prepare the second pan the same way. TO FILL 18 TO 24 2-INCH MOLDS: Brush the molds with melted butter. Divide the dough in half. Roll each half of the dough into a long roll like a sausage, about 1½ inches in diameter. Cut three-quarters of each roll into 1½-inch pieces. Roll the pieces into balls on the lightly floured board; then cup your hands and roll each ball so the bottom is smaller than the top. Place them in the brioche molds small end down. Roll the remaining quarter of each roll a little narrower, cut into ¾-inch pieces, and roll them into balls in the same manner. With your finger forming a well, stick a smaller ball in the center of each brioche to form the cap. TO FILL 32 TO 48 1-INCH MOLDS: Brush the molds with melted butter. Follow the same procedure as for 2-inch molds, using smaller pieces of dough.

STEP 11. Place the molds on a jelly roll pan or baking sheet. Put them in a warm place and cover them with a cloth, supported by water glasses, like a canopy. Let the dough rise 30 minutes, or until it about doubles in bulk.

STEP 12. When you leave the dough to rise, start to preheat the oven to 375°.

STEP 13. Remove the cloth and lightly brush the tops of the brioches with a little well-beaten egg. (Do not let the egg dribble to touch the mold, or the brioches will not rise as well in the oven.)

STEP 14. Put the brioches on the baking sheet in the oven and bake until well risen and nicely browned. The baking time will be about 35 to 45 minutes for 8-inch molds, 25 to 30 minutes for 2-inch molds, 15 to 20 minutes for 1-inch molds. Check the baking progress in any case.

STEP 15. Remove the brioches from the oven and turn them out of the molds at once. If they are to be served immediately, wrap them in a heavy warm cloth napkin and serve hot (brioches should have soft crusts, and covering them with a napkin keeps them soft). If they are to be served within a few hours, wrap them in a warm cloth and warm them in a preheated 350° oven a few minutes just before you serve them. If they are to be served next day, store them in a plastic bag and warm them as above before serving.

SAVARIN À LA CRÈME

Savarin with Rum and Pastry Cream

This recipe contains the basic recipes for two basic items in pastry-making, Savarin Dough and Pastry Cream (Crème Pâtissière). Savarin dough is a light yeast dough baked in a ring mold. The dough is also used for babas. In this recipe, the savarin is soaked with rum, with pastry cream in the center. You will need an 8-inch ring mold for the savarin and a bowl of ice for the pastry cream.

SAVARIN DOUGH
¼ cup lukewarm water
1 package dry yeast
1 "heaping" cup all-purpose flour (about 1 cup and 2 tablespoons)
⅛ teaspoon salt
3 eggs, well beaten
2 tablespoons sweet butter
1 tablespoon superfine sugar
2 tablespoons currants (optional for Savarin Dough, basic for Babas)
2 tablespoons cool melted salt butter

RUM SYRUP
¾ cup light rum
1¼ cups granulated sugar
¼ teaspoon cream of tartar

¾ cup water

GLAZE AND DECORATION
¾ cup apricot jam
2 tablespoons rum
Candied cherries
Leaf cutouts from angelica

PASTRY CREAM (CRÈME PÂTISSIÈRE)
2 eggs
2 egg yolks
6 tablespoons granulated sugar
6 tablespoons all-purpose flour
⅛ teaspoon salt
2 tablespoons unflavored gelatine
2 cups milk
2 egg whites
2 cups heavy cream, whipped
2 teaspoons vanilla extract

SAVARIN DOUGH

STEP 1. Dissolve the yeast in the lukewarm water.

STEP 2. Put the flour and salt in a medium-size bowl. Add the beaten eggs and the dissolved yeast. Beat the mixture with the hand until light and plastic (slightly cup your hand and use it like a whisk).

STEP 3. Cover the bowl with plastic wrap and a cloth. Let it rise in a warm place (ideally about 80°) 45 minutes.

STEP 4. Cream the butter and sugar together in the mixer. After the dough has risen, mix them into it, using a rubber scraper. Also mix in the currants.

STEP 5. Preheat the oven to 375°.

STEP 6. Brush the ring mold with the cool melted butter. Put the dough in the mold. (An 8-inch ring mold should be about a quarter full.) Cover the mold with a cloth and let the dough stand in a warm place until it rises to the top of the mold.

STEP 7. Bake the savarin cake 35 minutes, until it is well risen and beautifully brown all over.

STEP 8. Turn the cake out of the mold onto a wire cake rack.

RUM SYRUP. Put the four ingredients in an unlined copper pan. Stir with a metal spoon over moderate heat until the sugar dissolves. Boil about 3 minutes, to the consistency of a light syrup.

Place the wire rack with the savarin cake on a jelly roll pan. Spoon the hot rum syrup over the cake. Pour the syrup that collects in the jelly roll pan back into the syrup pan, and keep spooning it over the cake until all the syrup is absorbed.

GLAZE AND DECORATION. In a little pan, mix the apricot jam with the rum. Warm the mixture over low heat and put it through a wire strainer. Brush the savarin cake all over with this apricot glaze. Cut the candied cherries in half and cut little green leaves from a thin strip of angelica. To decorate the savarin, arrange about 6 half cherries cut side down on it, with two green leaves attached to each.

PASTRY CREAM (CRÈME PÂTISSIÈRE)

STEP 1. Put the eggs and egg yolks in a bowl with the flour, sugar, and salt. Beat with a wire whisk or electric mixer until the mixture is a light lemony color. Stir in the gelatine.

STEP 2. Put the milk into a small pan and bring it to a boil. Add it gradually to the egg mixture, stirring all the time.

STEP 3. Transfer the whole mixture to a large saucepan. Over low heat, stir it until it just comes to a boil.

STEP 4. Put the saucepan over a bowl of ice and continue stirring until the sauce begins to cool.

STEP 5. Beat the egg whites to soft peaks, and with a small wire whisk stir them into the pastry cream over ice.

STEP 6. Have the whipped cream ready. Very gradually, almost teaspoon by teaspoon, add it to the pastry cream, beating it in thoroughly with the small whisk. Mix in the vanilla.

ASSEMBLY. Carefully transfer the savarin cake to a handsome serving platter. Pile the crème pâtissière in the middle of the ring. Serve the Savarin à la Crème at once, or it can be chilled until ready to serve. NET: 6 to 8 servings.

BABAS AU RHUM

These light yeast cakes are baked in little round molds, and soaked with rum. You will need 16 baba molds, 2¼ inches across and 2¼ inches high. Babas prepared this way can be kept in a screw-top jar in the refrigerator for quite a long time.

Savarin dough (page 710)

RUM SYRUP
¾ cup light rum

1¼ cups granulated sugar
¼ teaspoon cream of tartar
¾ cup water

Prepare the savarin dough through step 5. Preheat the oven to 375°.

STEP 6. Brush 16 baba molds with the cool melted salt butter. Fill each little mold barely a quarter full with dough. Set the molds on a jelly roll pan. Cover them with a cloth and let the dough rise at room temperature until it just reaches the tops of the molds.

STEP 7. Bake the molds on the jelly roll pan 15 to 20 minutes, until the babas are well risen and beautifully brown.

STEP 8. Turn them out of the molds and set them on a wire rack.

RUM SYRUP. Put the rum, sugar, cream of tartar, and water in an unlined copper pan. Stir with a metal spoon until the sugar dissolves. Boil about 3 minutes, to a light syrup consistency.

Place all the little babas, which may be still warm from the oven, in a large wire strainer. Place the strainer over a large bowl. Spoon the hot syrup over the babas. Return the syrup in the bowl to the pan and continue to pour syrup over the babas until all of it is absorbed. Turn the babas over in the strainer basket to be sure they are soaked on all sides. To serve, place the babas on a shallow dessert dish and sprinkle them with a few drops of rum. NET: 16 little babas.

KUGELHUPF

Alsatian Raised Cake

This cake is baked in the traditional kugelhupf mold.

About 6 to 8 tablespoons soft
    (not melted) salt butter
⅓ cup slivered blanched
    almonds
¼ cup lukewarm water
1 package dry yeast
3 eggs
1 "heaping" cup all-purpose
    flour (about 1 cup and
    2 tablespoons)
3 tablespoons sweet butter
2 tablespoons granulated sugar

¼ teaspoon salt
1 tablespoon finely chopped
    angelica
Grated rind of 1 lemon
1 tablespoon finely chopped
    candied cherries
1 tablespoon finely chopped
    candied pineapple
¼ cup white raisins
About ½ cup confectioners
    sugar (to dust the cake)

Using a piece of wax paper, generously butter the inside of a kugelhupf mold with the salt butter. Be sure that all the ridges are covered. Then stick the slivered almonds all around the inside of the mold on the butter, and set the mold aside. Dissolve the yeast in the water. Put the eggs in a little bowl and beat them well. Put the flour in a warm bowl. Add the yeast and water and the beaten eggs to the flour. Beat the ingredients lightly with a cupped hand until the dough is plastic. Wipe out a large bowl with a damp cloth and dust it lightly with flour. Put the dough in this bowl, cover it with plastic wrap and a warm cloth, and put it in a warm place (ideally 80°) to rise until it is double in bulk. Cream the sweet butter in a mixer until it is very light and fluffy. Add the sugar and salt to the butter.

Preheat the oven to 375°. When the dough has properly risen, gently, using a rubber scraper, mix in the creamed butter mixture and the angelica, grated lemon rind, candied fruit and raisins. Put the dough into the buttered mold. Cover the mold with plastic wrap and a warm cloth and leave it in a warm place until the dough almost rises to the top of the mold. Bake about 35 to 45 minutes, until it is well risen and a good golden brown color on the top. Test it with a cake tester; it should come out clean. When the kugelhupf is done, immediately and with great care turn it out onto a wire cake rack. When it has cooled a little, dust it generously with confectioners sugar. NET: 6 to 8 servings.

BREADS: SPÉCIALITÉS

APPLE BREAD

The origin is English. Apple bread is a rich quick-to-prepare fruit bread for breakfast, with a cup of tea. If you have no sour milk, see page 78.

8 tablespoons sweet butter or vegetable shortening	2 cups all-purpose flour
½ cup granulated sugar	1 teaspoon baking soda
2 eggs, beaten	½ teaspoon salt
1 cup ground green cooking apples (put cored apples through a fine meat grinder with some of the skin)	1½ tablespoons sour milk
	½ cup coarsely chopped nuts
	1 teaspoon freshly grated orange rind
	1 teaspoon vanilla

Preheat the oven to 350°. In a mixer bowl, cream the butter or shortening with the sugar. Mix in the beaten eggs, then the ground apples. In a separate bowl, sift the flour with the baking soda and salt. Stir them gradually into the egg mixture and mix well. Mix in the sour milk. Last, stir in the nuts, orange rind, and vanilla. Mix the dough thoroughly. Brush a 10-inch loaf pan with butter or vegetable shortening. Line it with wax paper, and brush the paper with butter or shortening. Dust the lined pan lightly with flour. Put the dough into the lined pan and bake it 50 to 60 minutes. Turn it out of the pan immediately. Peel off the wax paper and serve at once or let it cool. NET: 1 10-inch loaf.

BISCOTTES DE SEIGLE

Rye Rusks

2 packages dry yeast	½ cup molasses
2½ cups warm milk	⅓ cup granulated sugar
2 tablespoons cool melted bacon fat (preferred) or vegetable oil	¼ teaspoon salt
	Grated rind of 3 navel oranges
8 tablespoons cool melted sweet butter	2 cups rye flour
	6 cups all-purpose white flour
	About ¼ cup warm water

Dissolve the yeast in ½ cup lukewarm milk. Put the bacon fat and

BREADS: SPÉCIALITÉS / 713

sweet butter into a large bowl and mix it with the rest of the milk (2 cups). Add the molasses, sugar, salt, yeast and milk mixture, and orange rind. Sift the flours together, gradually add them to the other ingredients, and beat until the dough is smooth and firm. Sprinkle it with a little white flour, cover the bowl with a cloth, and put it in a warm place for the dough to rise until double in bulk. Turn the properly risen dough out onto a lightly floured board and knead it until it is smooth and satiny.

Preheat the oven to 375°. Divide the dough into 6 parts and form it into little loaves. Place them on buttered baking sheets, let rise to double in bulk, then bake 15 to 20 minutes. When done, place them on a towel, brush the tops with the warm water, and let the loaves cool.

When the loaves have cooled, cut them in half lengthwise, then cut each half into ½-inch slices. Put the slices on baking sheets to dry in a slow oven (275°) to a light brown. Turn off the oven heat, open the oven door, and leave the rusks in the oven until dry and crisp. They may be served immediately or stored in a tightly closed metal container. NET: 24 small rusks.

CHEESE BREAD

This French bread spread with a cheese butter is good with soups or salads.

1 long loaf French bread or	2 ounces cream cheese
2 short loaves	¼ cup freshly grated Parmesan cheese
	⅓ cup freshly grated Cheddar
CHEESE BUTTER	cheese
8 tablespoons sweet butter	Salt
¼ teaspoon dry mustard	A few grains cayenne pepper
1 teaspoon Dijon mustard	

Preheat the oven to 375°. Put the butter in a mixer bowl and beat until it is very light and fluffy. Add the rest of the ingredients, and beat well. Cut the French bread diagonally in thick or thin slices, but do not cut it all the way through the bottom crust. Spread a generous dollop of cheese butter between the slices (reserve about 1 tablespoon to spread on the top crust). Press the slices together so that the loaf is "reunited." Brush the reserved butter on top. Wrap the loaf tightly and securely in aluminum foil. Bake it about 10 minutes. Serve very hot. NET: 1 long loaf French bread with cheese butter.

CORN BREAD

Among dishes that contribute to the profile of an "American cuisine," the daily bread of the South has an established place.

¾ cup white or yellow cornmeal	⅓ cup granulated sugar
1 cup all-purpose flour	1 teaspoon baking soda

2 teaspoons cream of tartar
¾ teaspoon salt
1 cup sour cream or yoghurt
¼ cup milk

1 egg, beaten
2 tablespoons cool melted
 sweet butter

Preheat the oven to 425°. Put the cornmeal, flour, sugar, baking soda, cream of tartar, and salt in a mixer bowl and mix well. Add the sour cream or yoghurt and milk, and mix again. Stir in the beaten egg and melted butter. Generously butter a shallow 8-inch square pan or 12 corn muffin molds. Bake 20 minutes. NET: 4 to 6 servings.

A unique bread, and uniquely American, for Thanksgiving dinner or with a cup of tea. It is fairly tart.

CRANBERRY BREAD

2 cups all-purpose flour
1 cup granulated sugar
½ teaspoon baking soda
1½ teaspoons baking powder
1 teaspoon salt
Juice of 1 orange

Boiling water
1 egg, beaten
1 cup chopped fresh cranberries
 (put through a coarse meat
 chopper)
1 cup finely chopped nuts

Preheat the oven to 350°. Sift the flour, sugar, baking soda, baking powder, and salt together into a large bowl. Mix the orange juice with enough boiling water to make ¾ cup liquid. (Or use ¼ cup frozen orange juice with ½ cup boiling water.) Add the orange juice mixture to the ingredients in the bowl and mix well. Stir in the beaten egg and the chopped cranberries and nuts. Butter a 10-inch loaf pan, put in the dough, and bake the bread 1 hour. When it is baked, turn it out of the pan and serve when desired. NET: 1 10-inch loaf.

Originally of English origin, hot cross buns are now the traditional bread for Good Friday and the Lenten period.

HOT CROSS BUNS

1 cup lukewarm milk
1 package dry yeast
¼ cup superfine sugar
¼ teaspoon salt
6 tablespoons salt butter,
 creamed until light and fluffy
2 eggs
1 egg yolk
About 2½ cups all-purpose flour
½ teaspoon cinnamon
¼ cup chopped seeded raisins

About 4 tablespoons cool
 melted sweet butter

FROSTING
4 tablespoons sweet butter
¼ cup heavy cream
¾ cup confectioners sugar
Flavoring (vanilla, or a little rum,
 or grated rind of 1 orange
 with 1 teaspoon orange
 essence)

Put the milk in the mixer bowl and slowly mix in the yeast. Cover the bowl with a cloth and let it stand in a warm place 5 minutes. Then add the superfine sugar, salt, and creamed salt butter. With a rotary beater, beat the eggs and egg yolk until light and fluffy. Mix them into the yeast mixture, add the cinnamon and raisins, and beat the whole mixture thoroughly. Gradually beat in 1½ cups of flour. Remove the bowl from the mixer base, cover it with a cloth, and set it in a warm place for the dough to rise to double its bulk, which may require about 40 minutes. When the dough has properly risen, mix in about 1 cup flour. (Use just enough flour to make the dough firm enough to handle. It should be soft.) Cover the bowl and chill the dough in the refrigerator.

When the dough is thoroughly chilled, turn it out onto a lightly floured board. Knead it well, until it is smooth and satiny. Have ready a buttered baking sheet. Shape the dough into round buns, arrange them on the sheet, and brush the tops with the melted butter. Cover the baking sheet with a cloth canopy (drape it over water glasses so that it does not touch the dough). Let the rolls rise until double in bulk, approximately 1 hour.

Preheat the oven to 400°. When the buns are risen, bake them until delicately brown, about 12 to 20 minutes, depending on the size of the buns.

FROSTING. Melt the sweet butter in a small heavy pan. Off the heat, slowly stir in the heavy cream. Beat in enough confectioners sugar so the frosting holds its shape, then beat until smooth and flavor as desired.

When the buns are baked, while they are still hot make an X on the top of each with the frosting. NET: 24 medium-size buns.

HOT GARLIC BREAD

1 long loaf French bread or
  2 short loaves
A little pure olive oil

GARLIC BUTTER
8 tablespoons salt butter

3 teaspoons finely chopped
  garlic
¼ teaspoon salt
1 teaspoon freshly cracked
  black pepper
2 teaspoons Dijon mustard

Preheat the oven to 350°. Put the butter in the mixer bowl and cream it until very light and fluffy. Add the garlic, salt, and pepper, and continue to beat. Add the Dijon mustard and beat well. Cut the French bread diagonally into 1½-inch slices, but do not cut all the way through to the bottom crust. Put a generous dollop of garlic butter between each slice. (Reserve about 1 tablespoon to brush on top.) Press the slices together to "reunite" the loaf. Brush all over the crust with olive oil, then brush it with the reserved garlic butter. Wrap the loaf tightly and securely in aluminum foil, and bake it 10 to 15 minutes. Serve it piping hot. NET: 1 long loaf French bread with garlic butter.

As a variation, just before you put the bread sticks in the oven, they may be brushed with a little water and sprinkled with sesame or poppy seed, or with coarse salt.

1 cup lukewarm milk or sour milk (page 78)	1 teaspoon salt
1 package dry yeast	1 egg white
4 tablespoons soft salt butter	About 2½ cups all-purpose flour
1 tablespoon granulated sugar	

Put the milk in a large warm bowl and slowly mix in the yeast. Cover, and let the mixture stand 5 minutes. Then add the soft butter, sugar, salt, and egg white. Mix well. Gradually add the flour, beating thoroughly between each addition of flour. (This can be done by hand or with the electric mixer at a slow speed.) Then beat the dough 5 minutes. Add enough flour to make the dough just barely firm enough to handle (it should not be too stiff). Knead it well, about 10 minutes.

Preheat the oven to 425°. Shape the dough into bread sticks as follows: Roll out the dough to a rectangular shape, approximately 8 by 12 inches. Cut it in half to get two pieces 8 by 6 inches. Then cut each piece into approximately 16 6-inch strips. (Use a long straight-blade French knife to cut them straight.) Roll each strip of dough between two lightly floured hands to make smooth even sticks 8 to 10 inches long and thin as a pencil. Lightly flour (but do not grease) a baking sheet. Arrange the strips 1 inch apart. Cover, and let them rise at room temperature, about 15 minutes. Bake them 5 minutes, reduce the oven to 350°, and bake another 15 minutes. (Slower baking makes the bread sticks more crisp.) Remove from the oven, cool, and use when desired. NET: 32 bread sticks.

This bread was created as an alternative to garlic bread for Mrs. Alexander H. Cohen (Hildy Parks), when she gave a beautiful opening night party for Peter Ustinov's *Unknown Soldier and His Wife* at Lincoln Center, for which I was privileged to prepare the supper.

1 loaf of bread (thinly sliced square rye or pumpernickel or long loaf of French bread)	fresh thyme or ½ teaspoon dried thyme, soaked in a little water
	2 tablespoons finely chopped fresh parsley
HERB BUTTER	¼ teaspoon powdered sage
6 tablespoons sweet butter	¼ teaspoon powdered rosemary
2 teaspoons very finely chopped white onion	½ teaspoon salt
1 tablespoon finely chopped fresh tarragon	¼ teaspoon freshly cracked black pepper
1 teaspoon finely chopped	½ teaspoon Dijon mustard

Preheat the oven to 350°. Cream the butter in the mixer until very light and fluffy. Add all the rest of the ingredients, and beat well. Spread this butter evenly between slices of bread. Reshape the loaf and wrap it securely in aluminum foil. (If using French bread, cut it diagonally in about 1½-inch slices, but do not cut through the bottom crust.)

Warm the foil-wrapped loaf in the oven 10 to 12 minutes. Serve this bread hot. NET: 1 loaf.

SWEET CREAM DOUGHNUTS

1¾ cups cake flour (without baking powder in it)
2 teaspoons baking powder
¼ teaspoon freshly grated nutmeg
⅛ teaspoon cinnamon
½ teaspoon salt
1 egg

1 egg yolk
4 tablespoons melted sweet butter
½ cup heavy cream
½ cup superfine sugar
Vegetable oil for deep-fryer
Confectioners or granulated sugar (for dusting)

Sift all the dry ingredients together (flour, baking powder, nutmeg, cinnamon, and salt). Beat together the egg, egg yolk, 2 tablespoons cool melted sweet butter, and heavy cream. Add them to the dry ingredients and beat well. Then add enough more flour to make the dough just firm enough to handle, but keep it as soft as possible. Cover the bowl and let the dough chill in the refrigerator at least 1 hour. When chilled, put a third of the dough on a lightly floured board. Knead it lightly and roll it out about ⅓ inch thick. Cut out doughnuts with a doughnut cutter, set them aside, add the dough trimmings to another third of the dough, knead it lightly, roll it out ⅓ inch thick, and cut the doughnuts. Repeat the procedure with the last third of the dough. (Handling it in small quantities avoids overkneading, which results in toughness.)

Place the cut-out doughnuts on a sheet of lightly floured wax paper. Let them stand 5 to 10 minutes at room temperature before deep-frying. Have ready on the stove a deep-fryer three-quarters full of vegetable oil. Insert a frying thermometer and heat the oil to 360°. (It is important to maintain the fat at this temperature; therefore keep the thermometer in the fat while frying the doughnuts. At lower temperatures they absorb too much fat, and at higher temperatures brown too quickly.) Lower each doughnut slowly into the hot oil and let it cook gently; make 3 or 4 doughnuts at a time. When they are a lovely brown on both sides, remove them from the fat and drain on paper towels (put the handle of a cooking utensil through the hole of the doughnut and lift it out).

When all of the doughnuts have been fried and cooled just a little, dust them with sugar. Place a good amount of granulated or confectioners sugar in a bag and shake 2 or 3 doughnuts at a time in it gently until well coated. NET: About 24 doughnuts.

This is a very rich nut bread, to be served for breakfast or with tea.

NUT BREAD

1 package dry yeast
½ cup lukewarm water
1¾ cups lukewarm pineapple
  juice
3 tablespoons vegetable oil
½ cup molasses
1½ teaspoons salt
6 cups sifted all-purpose flour

A little melted sweet butter or
  vegetable oil
2 cups pitted dates, coarsely
  chopped
1 cup nuts, coarsely chopped
  (pecans and almonds or
  pecans and cashews)

Dissolve the yeast in the water in a large bowl. Add the pineapple juice, vegetable oil, molasses, and salt, and mix together. Add enough flour (about 4 cups) to make a stiff dough. Mix it well and brush the surface very lightly with the melted butter or oil. Cover the bowl with a cloth, put it in a warm place (ideally 80°), and let it double in bulk, about 2 hours. Then turn it out onto a lightly floured board. Dredge (dust) the dates with a little flour, combine them with the nuts, and knead the mixture into the dough on the board. Knead the dough about 10 minutes, or until it is smooth and satiny, adding as much of the remaining cups of flour as necessary to achieve a firm elastic dough.

Divide the dough into two equal portions and mold each into a ball. Cover them on the board with a cloth and let them rest 10 minutes. Brush two 10-inch loaf tins with melted butter. Shape the balls of dough into loaves, put them into the pans, and brush the tops with melted butter or vegetable oil. Cover them with a cloth draped over water glasses so it doesn't touch the dough. Let the dough rise 1 hour, or until double in bulk.

Preheat the oven to 375° and bake the loaves 45 to 55 minutes. Serve hot or when desired. NET: 2 10-inch loaves.

This is a Scottish recipe.

OATMEAL
MUFFINS

1 cup cooked stone-ground
  oatmeal
1 cup sour milk (page 78)
6 tablespoons sweet butter or
  vegetable shortening (room
  temperature)

½ cup brown sugar
1 egg, beaten
1 cup all-purpose flour, sifted
1 teaspoon baking powder
½ teaspoon baking soda
½ teaspoon salt

Preheat the oven to 350°. Put the oatmeal in a bowl and stir in the sour milk. In a large bowl, mix the sweet butter or shortening with the sugar, then add the beaten egg. Sift together in a separate bowl the flour, baking powder, baking soda, and salt. Add a little of the oatmeal and milk mixture to the butter mixture, then a little of the flour mixture, and continue adding alternately until all the ingredients are combined. Butter 12 muffin tins, fill with the dough, and bake 20 minutes. Turn out of the tins and serve warm. NET: 12 muffins.

DARK RYE BREAD WITH MOLASSES AND RAISINS

1 package dry yeast
2 cups lukewarm water
2 cups sifted rye flour
1 tablespoon vegetable oil
1 tablespoon molasses
1 cup muscat (white) raisins,
    soaked in lukewarm water
    20 minutes and drained
2 cups unsifted rye flour
About 2 cups sifted all-purpose
    white flour resifted with 1
    teaspoon salt

Prepare a sponge with the yeast, as follows. Put the yeast in a large bowl with ½ cup lukewarm water, stir until it is dissolved, then little by little add to the yeast 1 cup lukewarm water alternately with the sifted rye flour. Beat the dough with a wooden spoon until it is quite smooth. Cover the bowl with a cloth and let the sponge rise in a warm place about 1½ hours, until it is light and bubbly. Mix the molasses and vegetable oil with ½ cup lukewarm water and blend well. Mix this into the sponge, then the drained raisins, then add the unsifted rye flour and mix thoroughly. Turn the dough out onto a lightly floured board. Knead it about 5 minutes with closed fists, adding as you go along the white flour resifted with salt (knead in about ½ cup at a time).

Place the dough in a lightly buttered large bowl. Cover the bowl with a cloth and leave it in a warm place 1 hour, or until the dough doubles in bulk. When it has risen, turn it out onto a lightly floured board and knead it again. Use quick strokes of the fists to prevent it from sticking. If it does, sprinkle a little more flour on the board. Divide the dough in half. Knead each half until smooth, shape into a loaf form, and put into a buttered 10-inch loaf pan. Allow them to rise again, until double in bulk. Preheat the oven to 350° and, when the loaves are risen, bake them 1 hour, or until the loaf sounds hollow when you tap it. Turn the loaves out of the pan and cool on a wire rack. NET: 2 10-inch loaves.

SAFFRON BREAD

This is not of the French repertoire, but it is a very good bread in my opinion. I love saffron. Serve it for breakfast, or with a big cup of hot Darjeeling tea. Actually the "bread" is rolled up like a jelly roll, sliced, and then baked.

2 packages dry yeast or 2 yeast
    cakes
2½ cups milk, warmed
1 teaspoon leaf saffron
1 tablespoon Cognac or good
    brandy
1½ cups granulated sugar
¼ teaspoon salt
2 eggs, beaten until frothy
16 tablespoons (½ pound) cool
    melted sweet butter
8 cups all-purpose flour

TOPPING
½ cup ground (pulverized)
  almonds
1 cup white seedless raisins
½ cup finely chopped citron
  peel
½ cup finely chopped orange
  peel

Grated rind of 1 lemon
Granulated sugar

GLAZE
2 tablespoons granulated sugar
  dissolved in ¼ cup of warm
  milk

Dissolve the yeast in ½ cup lukewarm milk. Put the saffron in a mortar with the brandy and pound it with the pestle until smooth. In a large bowl, mix the rest of the milk (2 cups) with the saffron and brandy, sugar, salt, beaten eggs, half (½ cup) of the sweet butter, and a little of the flour. Mix in the dissolved yeast and, gradually, the rest of the flour. Beat the dough with a wooden spoon until smooth and firm. Sprinkle it with a little flour, cover it with a warm cloth, and put it in a warm place (ideally 80°) to rise. It should double in bulk, which may require about 2 hours.

Turn out the dough onto a lightly floured board and knead until it has a smooth surface. Cover the dough on the board with a cloth and leave it 30 minutes. Then roll it out into a long sheet. Brush it with the rest of the butter. Mix together the almonds, raisins, citron and orange peels, and lemon rind, and sprinkle evenly over the dough, pressing them well in with the back of a wooden spoon. Then sprinkle the whole surface generously with granulated sugar. Roll up the dough like a jelly roll, very tightly. Wrap it in a cloth and chill it in the refrigerator or freezer at least 1 hour.

Preheat the oven to 375°. Liberally butter two baking sheets. When the dough is chilled, cut it into ¾-inch slices. Place them on the baking sheets and let them rise in a warm place 15 to 25 minutes. Mix the milk and sugar for a glaze together, brush each roll lightly with it, and bake them 15 to 20 minutes, or until lightly browned. Serve warm.
NET: About 24 slices saffron bread.

A hearty brown (whole wheat) bread.

SOUR CREAM BREAD

1½ packages dry yeast or
  1½ yeast cakes
½ cup lukewarm water
½ cup milk
1 cup sour cream
1 tablespoon granulated sugar
1½ teaspoons salt

1 tablespoon melted sweet
  butter or vegetable
  shortening, or vegetable oil
1¼ pounds whole wheat flour
  and white flour (half of each),
  sifted together
A little cool melted butter

In a warm bowl, dissolve the yeast in the water. Add the milk and sour cream and stir until blended. Add the sugar, salt, and butter or shortening and mix well. Add the flour and beat until smooth. Wipe out a large bowl with a damp cloth and dust it lightly with flour. Transfer the dough to this bowl. Cover the bowl with a cloth, set it in a warm place, and let the dough rise until double in bulk. Then turn it out onto a well-floured board or pastry slab and knead it down. Return it to the bowl, brush the top with the melted butter, cover the bowl, and let the dough rise to double in bulk again. Again turn it out onto a well-floured board and knead it down, working in a little more flour if necessary.

Preheat the oven to 400°. Divide the dough in half. Grease 2 loaf pans (8 by 4 by 3 inches) with butter and dust them out with flour. Put half the dough in each pan, patting it into a loaf shape. Let it rise in the pans 20 minutes in a warm place, then bake 30 to 35 minutes, or until the bread is firm and sounds hollow when you tap it. Cool the bread on a wire rack. NET: 2 small loaves.

SWEDISH COFFEE BREAD

A traditional Swedish braided coffee cake.

2 packages dry yeast or
  2 yeast cakes
2½ cups lukewarm milk
16 tablespoons (½ pound) cool
  melted sweet butter
1 cup granulated sugar
½ teaspoon salt
20 cardamom seeds, crushed
  with a mortar and pestle, or

about ½ teaspoon ground
  cardamom
2 cups all-purpose flour
1 egg, beaten
½ cup blanched browned
  almonds, finely chopped
½ cup crystal sugar (coarse
  sugar granules, available in
  specialty food shops)

Dissolve the yeast in ½ cup of lukewarm milk. In a large bowl, mix the melted sweet butter with the rest of the milk (2 cups), the sugar, salt, and cardamom seeds, and a little of the flour. Beat until it is quite smooth. Add the yeast, mix well, and gradually add the rest of the flour, beating with a wooden spoon until the dough is smooth and firm. Sprinkle it with a little flour, cover it with a cloth, and leave it in a warm place (ideally 80°) to rise to double its bulk, which may require about 2 hours. When the dough has risen, turn it out onto a lightly floured board and knead it until smooth.

Divide the dough in half on the board, and each half into three pieces. Roll each piece into a long rope. Braid three of the ropes into a loaf, and do the same with the remaining three. Place the loaves on a buttered baking sheet. Cover them with a cloth canopy draped over water glasses so it doesn't touch the dough. Let the loaves rise until double in size. Preheat the oven to 375°.

When the loaves have risen, brush the tops lightly with the beaten egg and sprinkle them with the almonds and sugar granules. Bake 35 to 45 minutes, or until the loaves are well risen and firm to the touch. Serve immediately or when desired. NET: 2 large braided loaves.

2 tablespoons sweet butter
1 cup clear honey
1 egg, well beaten
1½ tablespoons grated orange
    rind
2 tablespoons finely chopped
    citron
2½ cups sifted all-purpose flour
2½ teaspoons baking powder

½ teaspoon baking soda
½ teaspoon salt
¼ cup chopped blanched
    almonds
½ cup finely chopped Brazil
    nuts
¾ cup unstrained orange juice
1 or 2 tablespoons melted
    sweet butter

Preheat the oven to 350°. Cream the butter and honey together in the mixer until light and fluffy. Add the beaten egg, orange rind, and citron. In a separate bowl, mix the flour, baking powder, soda, and salt together and sift twice. Gradually mix them with the butter and honey mixture, then add the chopped nuts and the orange juice and mix well. Butter a loaf pan, put in the batter, brush the top with the melted butter, and bake until bread is brown on top and has shrunk a little from the sides of the pan, about 40 to 50 minutes. Let this bread become quite cold before using it. It is best sliced very thin and buttered before serving. NET: 1 loaf.

PASTRY

Whenever you have scraps of puff pastry after preparing a recipe, freeze them to use for crescents for garnishes or various forms of hors d'oeuvres. Ideally, puff paste is prepared in a very cool room.

PÂTE FEUILLETÉE

*Puff Paste
(Flaky Pastry)*

2 cups all-purpose flour (not
    sifted)
1 teaspoon salt

¾ cup ice water
½ pound (16 tablespoons) salt
    butter

STEP 1. Put the flour and salt in a bowl. Add the ice water and work the mixture quickly to a firm dough (which at this point will look crumbly and stringy).

STEP 2. Turn the dough out onto a lightly floured board and roll it out to a 12-inch square.

STEP 3. Knead the butter a little with the fingers, until it is the same consistency as the dough, and shape it into a 4-inch square. Set the butter square in the middle of the dough.

STEP 4. Fold the dough like a package (with the butter in the center). Wrap the dough in plastic wrap or wax paper and a cloth (a small kitchen towel is just right). Let the dough chill 30 minutes in a cold refrigerator.

STEP 5. (a) Remove the dough from the refrigerator, unwrap it, and place it on a lightly floured board. Roll the dough out into a long strip. Fold it in three equal folds. (This is the first "turn"; in making puff paste, one rolling and folding action is a "turn," and proper puff paste must be given a total of six turns to achieve the "layers" or leaves implied by its name.)

(b) With the folded dough still on the floured board, turn it so that open edges are facing you. Proceed with the second "turn": roll out the dough into a long strip and fold it in three equal folds. Wrap it in wax paper or plastic wrap and a cloth, and chill it in the cold refrigerator 30 minutes.

STEP 6. (a) Make the third turn: unwrap the dough, roll it out into a long strip, and fold it in three equal folds.

(b) Turn the dough so that a folded edge is facing you and proceed with the fourth turn: roll out the dough into a long strip and fold it in three equal folds. Wrap it again in wax paper or plastic wrap and a cloth and chill it in the cold refrigerator at least 30 minutes.

NOTE. After four turns, the puff paste may be stored in the refrigerator several days, or longer in the freezer. Keep it wrapped in wax paper or plastic wrap and a cloth.

Whenever you plan to use the puff paste, the next action is to give it the final two turns as follows.

STEP 7. (a) Unwrap the dough. Roll it out into a long strip, and fold it in three equal folds (fifth turn).

(b) Turn the dough so that an open edge is facing you, roll out the dough into a long strip, and fold it in three equal folds (sixth turn).

The dough is now ready to roll out and use for any recipe requiring puff paste, such as Napoleon, Vol-au-Vent, Pastry Cases, Boeuf Wellington, Pithiviers, Croissants. NET: 1 pound puff paste.

CROISSANTS DE PÂTISSERIE

Croissants Made of Puff Paste

1 pound Puff Paste (page 723)   *1 egg, beaten*

Prepare the puff paste through the sixth turn (Step 7). Then proceed as follows. Roll the dough out to a long strip about ¼-inch thick. With a large straight-bladed French knife cut the dough into 4-inch squares. Brush each square with the beaten egg and cut it in half diagonally, to make two triangles of dough from one square. Roll up each triangle, starting from the wide base and rolling toward the point. Curve the rolled dough into a half-moon shape, with the point facing the center inside. Prepare as many croissants as you wish (any leftover dough can be stored in the freezer). Place them on a wet jelly roll or baking pan, and set them in the freezer until firm or even frozen.

Preheat the oven to 375°. Brush the tops of the croissants with beaten egg and bake 30 minutes, or until they are puffy and golden brown. NET: About 24 croissants.

CROISSANTS DE BOULANGER

Croissants Made of Yeast Puff Paste

1 cup lukewarm milk
1 package dry yeast
1 tablespoon granulated sugar

1 teaspoon salt
1 tablespoon vegetable oil or soft lard

2½ cups all-purpose flour	*sweet butter*
½ pound (16 tablespoons)	*1 egg, beaten*

STEP 1. Put the milk in a bowl and mix in the yeast. Cover the bowl with plastic wrap and let stand 5 minutes.

STEP 2. Stir the mixture well and mix in the sugar, salt, and vegetable oil or lard.

STEP 3. Very gradually add 1 cup flour and beat thoroughly. Mix in a second cup of flour.

STEP 4. Turn the dough out onto a lightly floured board or marble slab. Roll and knead it into a ball. Sprinkle about ½ cup flour on the board and roll the dough lightly into the additional flour. Leave it on the board, cover it with a bowl, and let stand about 5 minutes.

STEP 5. Knead the dough well, until it is quite elastic. Butter a large bowl, put the dough in it, cover the bowl, and let the dough rise until double in bulk, about 1 hour.

STEP 6. Punch down the risen dough in the bowl, cover it with plastic wrap, and chill it in the refrigerator at least 1 hour (longer if possible).

STEP 7. Beat the butter into a firm cream — spreadable, but not so soft it is oily and runny.

STEP 8. (a) Put the chilled dough on a lightly floured board and roll it into a long rectangle about ¼ inch thick. Spread a quarter (4 tablespoons) of the creamed butter over the dough. Fold the dough into 3 equal folds.

(b) Turn the folded dough so that an open edge faces you. Roll it into another long strip about ¼ inch thick. Spread with 4 more tablespoons creamed butter, and fold the dough in three equal folds. Wrap the dough in plastic wrap and a cloth. Chill it in a cold refrigerator at least 30 minutes.

STEP 9. (a) Proceed with the third turn. Unwrap the dough, roll it out into a long strip, spread it with 4 tablespoons creamed butter, and fold it in three equal folds.

(b) Turn the folded dough so an open edge faces you. Proceed with the fourth turn. Roll out the dough into a long strip, spread it with the last 4 tablespoons creamed butter, and fold it in three equal folds. Wrap it in plastic wrap and the cloth, and chill it at least 30 minutes in a cold refrigerator.

STEP 10. (a) Unwrap the dough and proceed with the fifth turn. Roll it out into a long strip and fold it into three equal folds.

(b) Turn the folded dough so that an open edge faces you. Proceed with the sixth and final turn. Roll out the dough into a long strip and fold it in three equal folds.

STEP 11. Wrap the dough in plastic wrap and the cloth and return it to the cold refrigerator to chill at least 2 hours.

STEP 12. To cut out and shape the croissants, roll the dough out to a strip ¼ inch thick, cut it into 4-inch squares, and cut each square diagonally, into two triangles. Roll each triangle tightly, starting from the wide base and rolling toward the point, and place it on a wet baking sheet, turning the ends in to form a crescent.

STEP 13. Chill the croissants on the baking sheet in the freezer 20 minutes.

STEP 14. Preheat the oven to 400°.

STEP 15. Brush the top of each croissant with a little beaten egg (do not let the egg dribble down and touch the pan, or the croissant will not rise as well in the oven). Bake them 10 minutes, then decrease the heat to 350° and continue to bake another 20 minutes. NET: About 24 croissants.

PÂTE À FONCER

Short Pastry Shell

This basic pastry shell can be used for savory or sweet tarts and quiches. Usually, however, a recipe will call for some variation in ingredients to complement the particular dish.

2 cups all-purpose flour	1/4 teaspoon salt
12 tablespoons sweet butter	1/3 cup ice water
(room temperature)	A little melted butter

Have the following equipment ready: a 10-inch flan ring on a jelly roll pan or baking sheet, a French rolling pin, wax paper, raw rice or dried beans or rock salt to anchor the paper lining, and pastry pincers.

STEP 1. Preheat the oven to 375°.

STEP 2. Put the flour and salt in a bowl. Put in the butter, cut it into pieces, then rub it into the flour, using your fingertips, until the mixture resembles coarse cornmeal in texture.

STEP 3. Add the ice water, and quickly gather the mixture into a firm ball of dough. Put the dough on a lightly floured board.

STEP 4. Roll the dough out into a round large enough to line the flan ring. (The round of dough should measure roughly 13 to 14 inches across.)

STEP 5. Lay the dough over the rolling pin and transfer it to the flan ring, laying it loosely over the ring. With the fingers, shape it firmly against the ring and bottom of the pan. Roll the rolling pin over the top rim of the ring to trim off the excess dough. Shape the top edge of the dough evenly and trim all around with pastry pincers.

Prick all over the bottom of the dough with a fork. (If the shell is for a liquid filling like a quiche, don't prick all the way through it.)

STEP 6. Brush the bottom of the pastry with a little melted butter. Line the pastry shell with wax paper (the butter will help to hold it down). Also to keep the paper down, put the rice, beans, or rock salt on the paper.

STEP 7. Bake the pastry shell on the jelly roll pan in the preheated oven 30 minutes.

STEP 8. Remove the rice, beans, or salt with the wax paper. Return the shell to the oven and bake another 10 to 15 minutes, until it is golden brown all over.

The pastry shell is now ready for use. NET: 1 10-inch pastry shell.

1 cup water

⅛ teaspoon salt

8 tablespoons sweet butter

1 cup all-purpose flour

4 eggs

PÂTE À CHOUX

Cream Puff Dough

Have ready a pastry bag fitted with a plain round tube (the size of the tube depends on what you will make with the cream puff dough), and a jelly roll pan or baking sheet.

STEP 1. Preheat the oven to 350°.

STEP 2. Put the water and salt in a small heavy pan. Cut the butter into small pieces and add it to the water. Set the pan over low heat and stir with a wooden spoon until the mixture comes to a rolling boil (the butter should become totally melted at the moment the water boils).

STEP 3. Throw in the flour all at once. Stir until it is blended with the liquid and the mixture comes away from the sides of the pan. Transfer the dough to the mixer bowl.

STEP 4. Add 3 eggs one at a time, beating thoroughly each time. Break the fourth egg into a small bowl, beat it well with a little whisk, add half of it to the mixer bowl, and reserve the rest for glaze. Beat the cream puff dough until it is very shiny.

STEP 5. Chill the dough in the refrigerator at least 30 minutes.

STEP 6. Put the dough into the pastry bag fitted with the required size of plain round tube. For small cream puffs (about 2 inches in diameter) use a #6 or #7 plain round tube (½-inch opening). Pipe little balls about ½ inch high on the baking sheet. Try not to leave any points on the tops of the balls as you pipe out the paste.

STEP 7. With the reserved beaten egg, brush the tops of the balls. Do not let any of the egg touch the baking sheet, or the puff won't rise as well.

STEP 8. Bake the cream puffs in the preheated oven 20 minutes.

STEP 9. Lower the oven temperature to 325° and continue baking until they are golden brown all over. The baking time, of course, will vary with the size and shape of the cream puff dough being baked.

STEP 10. Remove the baked puffs from the oven and let them cool.

The cream puffs are now ready to use in whatever recipe you are making. NET: 18 to 24 cream puffs.

Serve this pie warm with cold sour cream sauce.

AMERICAN TWO-CRUST APPLE PIE

PASTRY

3 cups all-purpose flour

2 tablespoons granulated sugar

1 teaspoon salt

Grated rind of 1 lemon

18 tablespoons (½ pound plus 2 tablespoons) sweet butter (room temperature)

½ cup ice water mixed with 1

tablespoon lemon juice

A little melted butter and 2 cups raw rice for anchoring the pastry

1 egg, beaten

CRUMB MIXTURE

2 tablespoons dry breadcrumbs (page 69)

2 tablespoons granulated sugar
⅛ teaspoon freshly grated
  nutmeg
⅛ teaspoon ground cinnamon

APPLE FILLING
2 no. 2 cans unsweetened sliced
  pie apples
Grated rind of 1 lemon
12 ounces apricot jam
Grated rind of 1 orange
2 tablespoons chopped browned
  almonds
¼ cup brown sugar

1 teaspoon cinnamon
½ teaspoon freshly grated
  nutmeg

COLD SOUR CREAM SAUCE
1 cup sour cream
3 tablespoons sifted
  confectioners sugar
½ teaspoon freshly grated
  nutmeg
⅛ teaspoon cinnamon
Grated rind of 1 lemon
¾ cup heavy cream, whipped

PASTRY. Preheat the oven to 375°. Have ready a 9-inch or 10-inch pie tin.

Sift the flour into a bowl with the sugar and salt. Add the lemon rind. Cut the butter into the flour and rub them together with the fingertips until the mixture resembles coarse cornmeal in texture. Work it up quickly to a firm dough with the mixed ice water and lemon juice. Wrap half the dough in wax paper and store it in the refrigerator. Roll the rest out on a lightly floured board, line the pie tin with it, trim the edges off neatly, and prick all over the bottom with a fork. Brush the pastry with a little melted butter and line it with wax paper. Put the rice on the paper to keep it down, and bake the shell 25 minutes.

CRUMB MIXTURE. In a little bowl mix the breadcrumbs, sugar, nutmeg, and cinnamon, and set aside.

APPLE FILLING. In a large bowl, mix the apples, lemon rind, apricot jam, orange rind, almonds, and brown sugar. Then add the cinnamon, and freshly grated nutmeg.

SOUR CREAM SAUCE. Put in a bowl the sour cream, sugar, nutmeg, cinnamon, and lemon rind. Mix lightly with a rubber scraper, then fold in the whipped cream. Chill until it is very cold.

When the pastry shell has baked 25 minutes, remove it from the oven (leave the oven on). Remove the rice and wax paper, sprinkle the crumb mixture over the bottom of the shell, fill the shell with the apple mixture (dome it up a little in the center), and brush the edges of the shell with beaten egg. Save a little of the reserved pastry dough for decoration, and roll out the rest to a sheet large enough to cover the pie. Lay it over the pie and trim all around the edge with pastry pincers. Make a few cuts on top with a sharp knife, and make a little hole in the center (for the steam to escape). Roll out the dough saved for decoration and cut out petal shapes (with fluted cutters, if you have some). Brush them with a little water and arrange them around the hole in the center, like a rosette. Brush the whole top of the pie with beaten egg. Sprinkle generously with granulated sugar.

Bake the filled pie 30 minutes, until it is a lovely golden brown. Serve immediately, or when ready to serve warm it a few minutes in a 225° oven. Serve the ice cold sour cream sauce in a separate bowl. NET: 8 to 12 servings.

PASTRY
2 cups all-purpose flour
4 egg yolks
8 tablespoons sweet butter
   (room temperature)
4 tablespoons granulated sugar
1/8 teaspoon salt
2 cups raw rice (to anchor
   pastry)

MERINGUE
4 egg whites

12 tablespoons superfine sugar
A little granulated sugar

APPLE FILLING
5 or 6 large apples
2 teaspoons lemon juice
Grated rind of 1 lemon
4 tablespoons apricot jam
4 tablespoons granulated sugar
2 tablespoons sweet butter
1/4 teaspoon ground cinnamon

PASTRY. Preheat the oven to 375°. Have ready a 10-inch pie tin. Put the flour on a board or slab. Make a well in the center and put in it the egg yolks, butter, sugar, and salt. Work them with the fingers to a smooth paste, then work in the flour quickly. Roll the pastry out on a lightly floured board and line the pie tin. Trim the edge neatly and prick all over the bottom with a fork. Line it with wax paper and anchor the paper with the rice. Bake the pastry shell about 30 minutes, until it is golden brown. Remove it, and reset the oven to 325°.

APPLE FILLING. Peel and core the apples, cut into thick slices, and put them in a deep heavy pan with the lemon juice, rind, jam, sugar, and butter. Cook over low heat until the apples begin to form a sauce but are still a little chunky. Cool the mixture a little, put it into the shell, and sprinkle it with the cinnamon.

MERINGUE. In a mixer bowl, beat the egg whites to soft peaks, slowly adding the sugar while beating. Continue to beat until the whites are very stiff. Put them into a pastry bag with a #8 or #9 star tube, and pipe scallops all over the pie. Sprinkle a little granulated sugar over the meringue.

Place the pie in the oven and bake until the meringue is golden brown. Let it cool a little, or chill it, and serve. NET: 1 10-inch pie.

Serve this Viennese strudel warm, with icy cold sour cream sauce.

STRUDEL DOUGH
4 cups all-purpose flour plus
   a little extra
1/2 teaspoon salt
1 egg
2 tablespoons vegetable oil
   plus a little extra

1 1/2 to 1 3/4 cups lukewarm water

APPLE FILLING
2 cups dry breadcrumbs
   (page 69)
2 cups granulated sugar
1 teaspoon freshly grated nut-

meg
1 teaspoon cinnamon
1/2 teaspoon ginger
1/4 teaspoon mace
1 1/4 pounds sweet butter,
    melted and cooled
2 no. 2 cans (20 ounces) sliced
    pie apples
3/4 cup white seedless raisins
1/2 cup dried currants
1 cup black seedless raisins
1/2 cup chopped pecans

Grated rind of 1 lemon

SOUR CREAM SAUCE
1 cup sour cream
1/3 cup superfine sugar
Grated rind of 1 lemon
1/4 teaspoon freshly grated
    nutmeg
1/4 teaspoon cinnamon
3/4 cup heavy cream, whipped

TOPPING
A little confectioners sugar

STRUDEL DOUGH. Sift the flour and salt together into a bowl. Make a well in the center and put the egg and vegetable oil in it. Begin to work up to a soft dough by adding lukewarm water, between 1½ and 1¾ cups. Turn the dough out onto a counter top or firm table and beat it a hundred times (to beat the dough means to pick it up and throw it down with force). Then dust it lightly with flour and knead it until it has a smooth surface on the bottom. Place the dough on a lightly floured plate and brush all over the top with vegetable oil. Cover it with a large inverted bowl and let it stand 1 hour at room temperature.

Then cover a table (preferably a little larger than a card table) with a sheet. Sprinkle flour all over the top, putting a little more in the center than at the edges. Rub the flour into the sheet. After the strudel dough has stood an hour, put it in the center of the sheet and roll it out to about an 18-inch square. Brush the square with vegetable oil and begin to stretch it. First lift the dough with the back of your hand to pull from the center out toward the edge of the table. Work like this all the way around the table little by little. Pull the dough out thin enough so you can read a newspaper through it. Cut the thick edges off with kitchen scissors. Let the thin sheet of dough dry on the table about 10 to 15 minutes (a little longer if the weather is damp), until it is somewhat like parchment.

APPLE FILLING. Combine in a bowl the breadcrumbs, 1 cup granulated sugar, the nutmeg, cinnamon, ginger, and mace. Mix in two-thirds of the cool melted butter. Have the pie apples ready in another bowl. In a third bowl mix the raisins, currants, pecans, and lemon rind. Also have ready the other cup of granulated sugar.

Preheat the oven to 375°. Sprinkle a little of the remaining third of the melted butter all over the top of the dough. Cover two-thirds of the dough area with the breadcrumb mixture. Spread the apples on the crumbs. Sprinkle them with a little melted butter, then with the reserved granulated sugar, then with the raisin and nut mixture, and again with a little melted butter. Fold three sides of the dough a few inches over the filling to hold it in, and sprinkle the folded edges with melted butter. Then, working with the sheet, roll the strudel like a jelly roll toward the fourth side.

Place the rolled strudel on a jelly roll pan, bending it like a horseshoe to fit. Brush the top with melted butter, and bake it about 45 to 50 minutes, until the top is golden brown and it is baked through. During baking, brush the strudel once or twice more with melted butter.

SOUR CREAM SAUCE. Put the sour cream in a bowl with the sugar, lemon rind, nutmeg, and cinnamon. Mix well with a rubber scraper, then fold in the whipped cream. Chill the sauce until it is icy cold.

When the strudel is baked, let it cool a little and serve, or let it cool entirely and, when you are ready to serve, warm it a few minutes in a preheated 325° oven. Dust it heavily with confectioners sugar. Serve the warm strudel with the ice cold sour cream sauce. NET: 10 to 12 servings.

Whole little apples baked in pastry, dusted with nuts, and garnished with whipped cream.

APPLE DUMPLINGS

1 egg, beaten
A little granulated sugar (for dusting)
1 cup browned blanched almonds, chopped
1 cup heavy cream
2 tablespoons confectioners sugar
1 teaspoon vanilla extract

DUMPLING DOUGH
1⅔ cups all-purpose flour
¼ teaspoon salt
16 tablespoons (½ pound) sweet butter

4 tablespoons ice water

FILLING
12 small sour green apples
A little lemon juice
1 cup granulated sugar
12 tablespoons cool melted sweet butter
½ cup light brown sugar
2 teaspoons cinnamon
1 teaspoon freshly grated nutmeg
½ cup honey
Grated rind of 2 lemons

DUMPLING DOUGH. Sift the flour and salt into a large bowl. Cut the butter into the flour, then rub it in lightly with the fingertips until the texture resembles coarse cornmeal. Add the ice water and work the dough lightly and quickly until it is mixed. Wrap the dough in wax paper and chill it 1 hour.

Peel and core the apples. Soak them in ice water with the lemon juice 1 hour. Drain and dry each apple well. Roll the chilled dough out to a thin sheet on a lightly floured board. Cut it into 5-inch squares (or bigger if necessary for the size apple you are using).

Preheat the oven to 425°. Place an apple in the center of each pastry square. Combine in a bowl the other filling ingredients, saving a little butter for the tops, stuff the mixture into the apples, and dot the tops with butter. Fold the corners of the dough up over the apples, pinching the edges together. Brush the dumplings well with beaten egg, and sprinkle them liberally with the granulated sugar and chopped almonds. Set the dumplings on an ungreased baking sheet and bake them 5 minutes, then reduce the oven to 350° and continue baking until the apples are tender and the pastry is crisp and a nice light brown, about 35 to 45 minutes.

While the dumplings are baking, whip the heavy cream over a bowl of ice. When it is half whipped, add the confectioners sugar and vanilla extract, and continue to beat until the cream is stiff. Serve the baked dumplings hot or cold with the sweetened whipped cream. NET: 6 servings of 2 dumplings each.

BAKLAVA

Syrian Honey and Nut Cake

2 cups all-purpose flour plus
    extra for dusting
1 egg
2 tablespoons vegetable oil
    plus extra for brushing dough
¼ teaspoon salt
¾ cup lukewarm water

¾ cup cool melted sweet butter
1 cup finely chopped blanched
    almonds or blanched
    pistachio nuts
1 egg, beaten
2 cups warmed honey

Put the flour in a bowl and make a well in the center. In the well put the egg, vegetable oil, and salt. Work them together a little, then add the water and work up all the ingredients to a soft dough. Turn the dough out onto a lightly floured board, knead it a little, and then beat it a hundred times (to beat dough is to pick it up and throw it down with force). Then brush the dough all over with a little vegetable oil, cover it with a large bowl, and let stand 45 minutes.

Cover a table (on which to stretch the dough) with a clean cloth (a sheet, for instance) and dust it all over with flour, putting a little more flour in the center. Put the dough in the center of the cloth, roll it out to about an 18-inch square, and brush it with vegetable oil. Proceed to pull it out to the thinness of tissue paper, working from all sides of the table and being very careful not to get any holes in the dough. It should be pulled to a sheet at least 33 by 34 inches (for at least three layers about 11 by 17 inches, to fit in a jelly roll pan), and larger if possible. When it is tissue-paper thin, let it dry a little. Then sprinkle it with melted butter, cut 1 layer, and put it on the jelly roll pan. Sprinkle it with a layer of chopped nuts, and continue to build layers of dough and chopped nuts, ending with dough on top. Properly, there should be 6 to 8 layers of dough.

Brush the top layer with melted butter and beaten egg, and bake the baklava 35 to 40 minutes, until it is golden brown. Then thoroughly chill it. To serve, cut the chilled baklava into serving pieces and pour the warm honey over them. NET: 24 to 36 servings.

BANANA CREAM PIE

PASTRY SHELL
2 cups all-purpose flour
4 egg yolks
8 tablespoons sweet butter
    (room temperature)

4 tablespoons granulated sugar
⅛ teaspoon salt
A little cool melted sweet butter
    (to brush the dough)
2 cups raw rice (to anchor

the pastry)

BANANA CREAM FILLING
5 egg yolks
7 tablespoons granulated sugar
1½ tablespoons unflavored
   gelatine
1½ cups light cream, scalded
5 egg whites

2½ cups heavy cream, whipped
2 teaspoons vanilla essence
1 cup crushed bananas (mashed
   with a fork)
2 whole bananas

APRICOT GLAZE
½ cup apricot jam
1 tablespoon dry sherry

Have ready a 10-inch flan ring on a jelly roll pan.

PASTRY. Preheat the oven to 375°. Put the flour on a board or slab. Make a well in the center and put in it the egg yolks, sweet butter, sugar, and salt. Work them with the fingers to a smooth paste, then work in the flour quickly. Roll out the dough a little larger than the flan ring, lift, and lay it over the ring. Shape it with your fingers to line the flan firmly, and neatly trim off the edges. Shape a little thicker rim around the top edge, and trim the rim with pastry pincers. Prick all over the bottom of the shell with a fork, brush the dough with cool melted butter, line it with wax paper, and fill the paper with raw rice. Bake the shell for 30 minutes. Remove the rice, paper, and flan ring, and return the shell to the oven to bake another 10 minutes, to brown the bottom a little. Chill the pastry shell.

BANANA CREAM FILLING. Combine the egg yolks in the mixer with the sugar and beat until light and fluffy. Stir in the gelatine. Slowly pour in the light cream, stirring all the time. Transfer the mixture to a saucepan and continue stirring over low heat until it coats a metal spoon. Put the saucepan over a bowl of ice and beat the mixture (custard) with a small wire whisk until it cools a little. Beat the egg whites to soft peaks and stir them into the custard over a bowl of ice. Then very gradually, almost teaspoon by teaspoon, beat half the whipped cream into the custard over ice (reserve the rest of the whipped cream). Add the vanilla and mix in the crushed bananas.

Fill the chilled pastry shell with the banana cream and chill it in the refrigerator. When the banana cream is firm enough, cover it with the reserved whipped cream, saving about a third of it. Cover the whipped cream with thin slices of banana.

APRICOT GLAZE. Put the apricot jam in a little pan with the sherry. Melt the jam, strain, and cool it.

Brush the glaze over the pie. Decorate around the edge with the remaining whipped cream, piped through a pastry bag with a large star tube. Chill the pie well before serving. NET: 1 10-inch pie.

CROQUEM-BOUCHE

This famous dessert is a caramel-glazed pyramid of cream puffs filled with chocolate pastry cream.

Double quantity of Cream Puff
   Dough (page 727)

A little vegetable oil
Confectioners sugar

CHOCOLATE PASTRY CREAM
2 eggs
2 egg yolks
6 tablespoons all-purpose flour
6 tablespoons granulated sugar
⅛ teaspoon salt
4 tablespoons unflavored
    gelatine
6 ounces dark sweet chocolate

2½ cups milk
4 egg whites
2 cups heavy cream, whipped

CARAMEL GLAZE
3¾ cups granulated sugar
1½ teaspoons cream of tartar
2 cups water

CREAM PUFFS. Prepare and bake little cream puffs about 2½ inches in diameter, according to the directions on page 727. The doubled recipe should net about 24 to 30 of them.

CHOCOLATE PASTRY CREAM. Put the eggs and egg yolks in a bowl with the flour, sugar, and salt. Beat with a wire whisk until the mixture is well blended and frothy. Stir in (don't beat) the gelatine. Break the chocolate in small pieces, put it in a saucepan with the milk, and stir over low heat until the chocolate melts. Let it cool a little, then mix it into the egg mixture and transfer it all to a saucepan. Stir over low heat until it thickens, then put the pan over a bowl of ice and continue to stir until the sauce is cool. Beat the egg whites to soft peaks, and with a small wire whisk stir them into the pastry cream. Then very gradually, almost teaspoonful by teaspoonful, beat in the whipped cream.

With the point of a small knife, make a hole in the bottom of each cream puff. Put the pastry cream in a pastry bag with a #3 or #4 (¼ inch) plain round tube. Fill the cream puffs with pastry cream through the little hole in the bottom. Chill them in the refrigerator to set the pastry cream.

CARAMEL GLAZE. Put the sugar, cream of tartar, and water in an unlined copper pan over moderate heat and stir with a metal spoon until the sugar dissolves. Then let it boil just until the syrup is a pale caramel color (if it reaches too dark a stage it will not coat the puffs well). Have a bowl of cold water at hand to set the caramel pan in and stop any further browning.

Have ready two or three baking sheets or jelly roll pans brushed with vegetable oil, and a metal bombe mold or any similar conical shape around which to build the pyramid. Dip the cream puffs into the caramel and coat them neatly. Place them on the oiled baking sheets. Brush the mold with vegetable oil, and stick the caramel-coated cream puffs around it in rows, tapering up toward the top. (Use a little dissolved caramel syrup to stick them together.) Dust the whole pyramid with confectioners sugar. Place the croquembouche on a serving platter. Serve with a large fork and spoon, to remove cream puffs for individual servings. NET: 24 to 30 small cream puffs (12 to 15 servings).

How does a Gâteau Favori differ from a Paris Brest? The crown of the Gâteau Favori is lavishly encrusted with shredded almonds.

Cream Puff Dough (page 727)
1 cup shredded blanched
   almonds
¾ cup heavy cream
1 teaspoon vanilla extract
Confectioners sugar

CHOCOLATE RUM PASTRY CREAM
2 eggs
2 egg yolks

6 tablespoons all-purpose flour
6 tablespoons granulated sugar
⅛ teaspoon salt
4 tablespoons unflavored
   gelatine
2 cups milk
3 ounces dark sweet chocolate
3 tablespoons light rum
4 egg whites
1 cup heavy cream, whipped

Prepare the cream puff dough (page 727) through step 5. Put the chilled dough into a pastry bag fitted with a large plain round tube (#9). Mark a 7-inch circle on a jelly roll pan. (Use a pan cover about 7 inches in diameter and lightly mark around it with an ice pick.) Pipe out a ring of cream puff dough on the circle you have marked. Then carefully pipe out another ring of cream puff dough on top of the first one.

Preheat the oven to 375°. Let the piped dough stand at room temperature 30 minutes. Then brush the top of the cream puff ring with the remaining half of beaten egg (saved from the dough preparation). Do not let the egg drip down and touch the pan, which might prevent the dough from rising nicely. Completely cover the top of the dough with the shredded almonds, and put the ring in the oven to bake 45 minutes. Reduce the oven to 350° and bake another 15 minutes. Remove the ring from the oven and let it cool.

CHOCOLATE RUM PASTRY CREAM. Put the eggs and egg yolks in a bowl with the flour, sugar, and salt. Beat with a wire whisk until the mixture is well blended and frothy. Stir in the gelatine. Bring the milk to a boil in a saucepan. Slowly pour it into the egg mixture, stirring all the while, then transfer it all to a saucepan and stir over low heat with a wooden spoon until the sauce thickens. Remove it from the heat immediately. Break the chocolate into pieces and put them in a little pan with the rum. Stir over very low heat until the chocolate dissolves, then add it to the pastry cream and stir with a whisk over a bowl of ice until it cools a little. Beat the egg whites to soft peaks and beat them into the pastry cream over the ice. Then very gradually, almost teaspoon by teaspoon, beat in the whipped cream. Flavor the pastry cream with a little more rum if desired.

Carefully cut the baked cream puff ring in half horizontally, so that the top lifts off like a lid. Place the bottom half on a white paper doily on a flat serving platter. Set the top aside. Whip the heavy cream over ice. When it is almost stiff, add 2 tablespoons confectioners sugar and the vanilla, and continue to beat until stiff. Put the whipped cream into a pastry bag fitted with a #6 or #7 star tube and the pastry cream into another pastry bag fitted with a large plain round tube (#9). Pipe little mounds of chocolate rum pastry cream all around the base

GÂTEAU FAVORI

Cream Puff Ring
with Chocolate Rum
Pastry Cream
and Almonds

(on the bottom) of the ring (the mounds should look like little beehives). Pipe rosettes of whipped cream between each mound of pastry cream.

Liberally dust the top of the cream puff ring with confectioners sugar. Very carefully place it on the pastry cream filling. Serve the pastry at once or chill it in the refrigerator. NET: 6 servings.

GÂTEAU NORMAND

Apple Cake from Normandy

PASTRY
3 cups all-purpose flour
1 cup plus 2 tablespoons
    granulated sugar
1 teaspoon ground cardamom
    seed
1 tablespoon plus 1 teaspoon
    grated orange rind
1 tablespoon plus 1 teaspoon
    grated lemon rind
12 tablespoons sweet butter,
    cut into little pieces
2 eggs, beaten
2 tablespoons dry breadcrumbs
    (page 69), mixed with
    2 tablespoons granulated
    sugar
1 beaten egg for brushing the
    pastry

APPLE FILLING
1 cup canned apple butter
1 cup canned applesauce
½ cup apricot jam
    (superior quality)
1 cup coarse dry breadcrumbs
    (page 69)
⅓ cup cool melted sweet butter
½ teaspoon ground cinnamon
½ teaspoon freshly grated
    nutmeg
½ cup granulated sugar
Grated rind of 1 lemon

ROYAL ICING
1 egg white
About 1 cup confectioners sugar

TOPPING
½ cup shredded blanched
    almonds
Confectioners sugar

Have ready an 8-inch flan ring on a baking sheet. Preheat the oven to 425°.

PASTRY. Sift the flour into a large bowl. Add the sugar, cardamom seed, orange and lemon rinds, and butter. Work the butter into the dry ingredients with the fingertips until the mixture resembles coarse cornmeal in texture. Add the beaten eggs and work them in to form a light pastry. Roll out two-thirds of the dough on a floured board, and line the flan ring with it. (Wrap the reserved dough in plastic wrap and set it in the refrigerator.) Make a rim around the edge of the flan ring, trim off the excess dough, prick all over the bottom with a fork, and sprinkle with the breadcrumbs and sugar mixture.

APPLE FILLING. Combine the apple butter, applesauce, apricot jam, and breadcrumbs in a bowl. Stir in the melted butter. Mix in the cinnamon, nutmeg, sugar, and lemon rind. Blend thoroughly and spread the mixture on the pastry shell.

Brush the rim of the pastry shell with some of the beaten egg. Roll out the remaining third of the pastry to fit the top of the flan, and cover it (it should be about ½ inch thick). Press the edges together and trim off the excess.

ROYAL ICING. Put the egg white in the mixer bowl. As you start to beat it, add enough confectioners sugar to make a thick but spreadable paste.

Spread the icing with a spatula on the dough cover. Cover it with the blanched almonds. Set the baking sheet with the prepared cake in the oven and bake 30 minutes. Then cool it a little, remove the flan ring, and arrange the cake on a flat serving dish. Dust the top liberally with confectioners sugar, and serve. NET: 6 to 8 servings.

<table>
<tr><td>

Puff Paste (page 723, prepared
   through step 7)
1 egg, beaten
A little confectioners sugar

RUM ALMOND FILLING
4 tablespoons sweet butter
½ cup dry breadcrumbs
   (page 69)
10 ounces almond paste

</td><td>

(commercial)
2 egg whites
2 tablespoons opaque
   (crystallized) honey
½ cup finely ground un-
   blanched almonds (these can
   be ground in a blender)
¼ cup light rum
2 tablespoons browned
   shredded almonds

</td><td>

GÂTEAU
PITHIVIERS

Puff Paste Cake with
Rum Almond Filling

</td></tr>
</table>

Prepare the puff paste (page 723) through the sixth turn (step 7). For the Pithiviers, roll out the folded puff paste at the end of step 7 to a sheet ½ inch thick. Cut out a round of dough 8 inches in diameter and set it aside. Roll out the rest of the puff paste a little thinner and cut out another 8-inch round of dough. Wet a baking sheet with cold water, put the thinner round of dough on it, and set it aside.

RUM ALMOND FILLING. Melt the butter in a small sauté pan. When it is foaming, put in the breadcrumbs, and shake over moderate heat until they are crunchy. Put the almond paste in a bowl. Add the fried breadcrumbs and the unbeaten egg whites and stir these with a wooden spoon until the mixture is well blended. Mix in the honey, unblanched almonds, and rum. Then mix in the shredded almonds.

Brush the edges of the puff paste round on the baking sheet with cold water. Put the almond filling in the center of the pastry. With the tip of a knife, mark out a pinwheel design on the thicker (½-inch) round of puff paste and set it on the almond filling. Press the edges down and mark a ridge all around with pastry pincers.

Preheat the oven to 375°. Put the prepared pastry on the jelly roll pan in the freezer to set at least 30 minutes. Then brush the top with beaten egg (do not let any egg dribble onto the baking sheet, or the puff paste may not rise as well). Bake the Pithiviers 35 to 40 minutes, until it is well risen and golden brown in color. When it is baked, dust the top with confectioners sugar, and serve. NET: 8 to 12 servings.

GÂTEAU SAINT HONORÉ

A lavish composition of cream puffs and pastry cream.

Double quantity of Cream Puff
   Dough (page 727), prepared
   through step 5
A few candied cherries
A little angelica

SHORT PASTRY
1 cup all-purpose flour
⅓ cup granulated sugar
¼ teaspoon salt
4 tablespoons sweet butter
   (room temperature)
Grated rind of 1 lemon
1 whole egg, beaten

CARAMEL GLAZE
2 cups granulated sugar
¼ teaspoon cream of tartar

¾ cup water

PASTRY CREAM
2 eggs
2 egg yolks
6 tablespoons all-purpose flour
6 tablespoons granulated sugar
⅛ teaspoon salt
4 tablespoons unflavored
   gelatine
2 cups light cream
4 egg whites
2 cups heavy cream, whipped
Scraping of 2 inches vanilla
   bean or 2 teaspoons vanilla
   extract
2 tablespoons light rum

Prepare the double quantity of cream puff dough (page 727) through step 5. Chill the dough in a pastry bag fitted with a #8 plain round tube. While it is chilling, prepare the short pastry.

SHORT PASTRY. Put the flour, sugar, and salt in a bowl. Cut in the butter, and rub it into the flour mixture with the fingertips. Mix in the lemon rind and beaten egg, then turn the dough out onto a lightly floured board and knead it a little until it is smooth.

Preheat the oven to 375°. Have ready a baking sheet or jelly roll pan. Roll out the short pastry ½ inch thick. Cut out a round 8 inches in diameter, place it on the jelly roll pan, and prick it all over with a fork. Pipe a ring of cream puff paste around the round of short pastry, then pipe another ring around the first one. On another jelly roll pan pipe about 15 or 16 little balls of cream puff paste (to make little 1½-inch cream puffs). Bake both pans of pastry in the preheated oven; the large round should bake 1 hour, until it is well-risen, golden brown, and set, and the small cream puffs 35 to 40 minutes. When the pastry is baked, remove it from the oven and set it aside to cool.

PASTRY CREAM. Put the eggs and egg yolks in a bowl with the flour, sugar, and salt. Beat with a wire whisk until the mixture is well blended and frothy. Stir in the gelatine. Put the light cream in a pan and bring it to a boil. Slowly pour it into the egg mixture, stirring all the time, then transfer the custard mixture to a saucepan and stir over low heat until it thickens (but does not boil). Instantly remove it from the heat, put it over a bowl of ice, and continue to stir until the sauce is a little cool. Beat the egg whites to soft peaks, and stir them with a small wire whisk into the pastry cream, over ice. Next, very gradually, almost teaspoon by teaspoon, beat in the whipped cream (still over ice), and last, stir in the vanilla and rum.

With the point of a small paring knife, make a hole in the bottom of each little cream puff. Put half the pastry cream in a pastry bag fitted with a #3 or #4 (¼ inch) plain round tube. Fill each cream puff with pastry cream through the hole in the bottom. Chill the filled cream puffs in the refrigerator.

CARAMEL GLAZE. Put the sugar, cream of tartar, and water in an unlined copper pan over moderate heat. Stir with a metal spoon until the sugar dissolves. Then stop stirring and let the syrup cook. When it reaches a medium caramel color, set the pan in a pan of cold water to prevent further cooking.

Have ready the baked round pastry base and the filled cream puffs. Dip each cream puff in caramel glaze to coat it. Stick the caramel-coated cream puffs all around the edge of the round pastry base. Fill the center of the cake with the remaining half of the pastry cream. Cut out a few little leaves from the angelica and cut the cherries in half, and stick little cherry-and-leaf designs on the cake for garnish.

The prepared Gâteau Saint Honoré can be kept in the refrigerator for a few hours. If the cream puffs seem to turn a little soggy, crisp the cake in a warm oven before serving. NET: 6 to 8 servings.

The lemon curd used in this pie is based on a recipe I found in an old English cookbook printed in 1682. It has been most favorably received in the second half of the twentieth century.

LEMON MERINGUE PIE

PASTRY SHELL
2 cups all-purpose flour
½ teaspoon salt
12 tablespoons sweet butter
   (room temperature)
Grated rind of 1 lemon
2 tablespoons granulated sugar
⅓ cup iced lemon juice and
   water (equal quantities)
A little cool melted sweet butter
2 cups raw rice (to anchor
   pastry)

CRUMB MIXTURE
2 tablespoons granulated sugar
2 tablespoons dry breadcrumbs

(page 69)
¼ teaspoon ground cardamom
   seed

LEMON CURD
Grated rind and juice of
   2 lemons
1 cup granulated sugar
3 eggs, well beaten
16 tablespoons sweet butter

MERINGUE
6 egg whites
1 cup plus 2 tablespoons
   granulated sugar
Granulated sugar for sprinkling

Preheat the oven to 375°. Have ready a 10-in flan ring on a baking sheet.

PASTRY. Put the flour and salt in a bowl. Put the butter into the bowl and rub it into the flour with the fingertips until the texture resembles coarse cornmeal. Add the lemon rind and sugar. Pour in the lemon juice and water and quickly work the mixture up to a firm dough. Turn it out on a lightly floured board and roll it out a little larger than the flan ring. Carefully lift the pastry, lay it over the flan ring, and line the ring firmly. Trim off the edges and with the fingers shape a slightly thicker rim around the top. Trim the rim with pastry pincers, prick all over the bottom of the shell with a fork, brush the dough with cool melted butter, line it with wax paper, and put in the raw rice to anchor the paper. Bake the pastry shell 30 minutes. Remove the rice, paper, and flan ring, and return the shell on the jelly roll pan to the oven to bake 10 minutes more.

Leave the oven on when the shell is removed. In a little bowl mix the sugar, breadcrumbs, and cardamom seed for the crumb mixture, and dust it over the bottom of the pastry shell while the shell is still warm.

LEMON CURD. Heat a double boiler with water in the bottom. In the top put the lemon rind and juice, sugar, eggs, and butter. Stir with a wooden spoon until the mixture is the consistency of thick cream sauce. Pour it into a shallow layer cake pan and put it into the freezer to set.

When the lemon curd is firmly set, put it into the pastry shell. Use a rubber scraper to scrape it out of the pan and pat it evenly into the shell.

MERINGUE. Beat the egg whites to soft peaks in a mixer bowl, slowly adding the sugar while beating. Continue beating until the whites are stiff.

Fill a pastry bag, fitted with a #8 or #9 star tube, with the meringue. Pipe out large scallop shapes to cover the lemon curd completely. Sprinkle the meringue with granulated sugar and bake the pie 10 to 15 minutes, until the meringue is a delicate golden brown. Then place it in the freezer to chill about an hour before serving. NET: 1 10-inch pie.

LINZERTORTE

Linzer Tart

A raspberry tart with spiced pastry shell.

PASTRY
2 cups all-purpose flour
12 tablespoons salt butter
  (room temperature)
1 teaspoon freshly grated
  nutmeg
Grated rind of 1 lemon
1 teaspoon ground cinnamon
¼ teaspoon ground cardamom
  seed
2 teaspoons (powdered) instant
  coffee
2 hard-boiled egg yolks, rubbed
  through a fine wire strainer
4 egg yolks, beaten until fluffy
2 tablespoons ice water

*A little cool melted sweet butter
  (to brush the pastry)*
2 cups raw rice (to anchor
  pastry)

FILLING
8 tablespoons sweet butter
½ cup dry breadcrumbs
  (page 69)
¼ teaspoon cinnamon
¼ teaspoon freshly grated
  nutmeg
⅛ teaspoon ground cardamom
  seed
2 12-ounce jars red raspberry
  jam (superior quality)

Grated rind of 1 lemon

CRUMB MIXTURE
A little granulated sugar
2 tablespoons dry breadcrumbs
(page 69)

GLAZE
1 12-ounce jar red currant jelly
2 tablespoons Framboise
(raspberry brandy)

FOR PASTRY SURFACE
1 egg, beaten
Granulated sugar
Confectioners sugar

Preheat the oven to 375°. Have ready an 8-inch flan ring on a jelly roll pan or baking sheet.

PASTRY. Put the flour in a bowl. Cut the butter into the flour and rub it between the fingers until the texture resembles coarse cornmeal. Mix in lightly by hand the nutmeg, lemon rind, cinnamon, cardamom seed, coffee, and strained egg yolks. Make a well in the center, put the beaten egg yolks and ice water into it, and with one hand work the mixture up into a firm dough. Set aside about a third of the dough for the lattice top, and turn the rest out on a lightly floured board or slab. Roll it out about ¼ inch thick, carefully lay it over the flan ring, line the ring firmly, and trim the edges neatly. With the fingers, shape a slightly thicker rim around the edge and trim the rim with pastry pincers. Prick all over the bottom of the shell with a fork. Brush it with melted butter, cover with wax paper, put in the rice to anchor the paper, and bake the shell 20 to 25 minutes.

Remove the pastry shell from the oven and remove the paper and rice, but leave it on the jelly roll pan, and leave the oven on.

FILLING. Melt the butter in a saucepan. Add the breadcrumbs, cinnamon, nutmeg, and cardamom seed. Cook over low heat until the crumbs are crisp. Cool the mixture a little, and mix in the raspberry jam and grated lemon rind.

Sprinkle the bottom of the baked shell with the breadcrumb and sugar crumb mixture, then fill the shell with the raspberry mixture. Brush the outside rim of the pastry with beaten egg. Roll out the reserved third of the pastry dough to the same thickness as the shell. Cut it into strips long enough to cross the top of the flan, and about ½ inch wide. Arrange them over the tart in a crisscross (lattice) fashion. Press them down at the rim, and pinch off the excess. Sprinkle the tart with granulated sugar, and return it to the oven for about 35 minutes. Remove it and cool it a little.

GLAZE. Put the red currant jelly in a small pan with the Framboise. Melt the jelly over low heat, pour it through a fine wire strainer, and cool it a little.

Brush the glaze all over the top of the tart, including the pastry lattice, but leave a small margin around the edge. Dust liberally all around the perimeter with confectioners sugar. Serve when desired. This tart can be wrapped in foil and kept in the refrigerator 2 to 3 weeks. NET: 1 8-inch tart (6 servings).

MINCEMEAT PIE

The Italians brought pastry to France. The English brought pies to the Colonies, among which mincemeat pie was and is still the favorite Christmas dinner dessert. The mincemeat portion of this recipe should be prepared well in advance of using it. Ideally, it should be made in late summer (when the first greenings are picked) for the Christmas season. It will keep as long as three years in an airtight crock in a cool place. At the very least, make it a month prior to putting it in a pie. The quantity of mincemeat in the recipe will fill several pies.

PASTRY
3 cups all-purpose flour
½ teaspoon salt
18 tablespoons sweet butter
½ cup ice water
2 tablespoons dry breadcrumbs
    (page 69)
1 tablespoon granulated sugar
    plus extra for topping
1 teaspoon cornstarch
A little beaten egg (for brushing
    the crust)
Confectioners sugar

MINCEMEAT
½ pound beef suet (fat,
    preferably kidney fat), finely
    chopped and dredged with a
    little flour (to produce 2 cups,
    lightly packed)
2 cups sticky black raisins
2 cups dried currants
2 cups moist brown sugar
4 cups finely chopped peeled
    and cored apples
1½ cups mixed candied peels
    (lemon, orange, citron)
1 cup seedless white raisins
1 cup seedless black raisins,
    blanched, finely chopped
½ teaspoon freshly grated
    nutmeg
½ teaspoon cinnamon
Finely grated rind and strained
    juice of 2 lemons
1 cup Cognac or other good
    brandy, plus ⅓ cup more for
    after the pie is baked

MINCEMEAT. Preheat the oven to 325°. Put all of the ingredients in a deep heavy pan (such as a casserole) except the brandy, and warm them in the oven 30 minutes. Remove from the oven, mix thoroughly with 1 cup brandy, and put the mincemeat in a crock with a tight cover. Set it in a cool place and let the mincemeat marinate several months.

PASTRY. Sift the flour and salt into a large bowl. Cut the butter into the flour and rub it with the fingertips until the texture resembles coarse cornmeal. (Do this quickly so that the butter will not be held in the hands too long and melt with the flour.) Add the ice water and work the ingredients up quickly into a firm dough. Turn it out on a lightly floured board and knead it a little. Wrap it in wax paper and chill it about 30 minutes.

Preheat the oven to 375°. Roll a third of the dough out to a thin sheet on a lightly floured board. Lay it over and line a 9-inch pie pan, trim the edges off neatly, and prick all over the bottom with a fork. Mix the breadcrumbs with the sugar and cornstarch, and dust the bottom of the pastry shell with this mixture.

Fill the pastry-lined pie pan with the mincemeat, doming it up in the middle. Brush the rim with a little beaten egg. Roll out the remainder of the dough and cover the mincemeat. Trim the edges off neatly and mark them with pastry pincers to seal them well. Brush all over the top lightly with beaten egg. Roll out the dough scraps, cut out a few leaf shapes, and arrange them in a rosette in the top center of the pie. Brush the decorations with a little more beaten egg. Make a small hole in the center of the pie to allow the steam to escape while it is baking. Sprinkle the crust with granulated sugar.

Bake the pie 45 minutes, or until the top crust is nicely browned all over. When it is baked, cool it a little at room temperature, then pour as much brandy as possible (up to $\frac{1}{3}$ cup) in the hole in the center of the pie. Dust all over the top with confectioners sugar. The pie is ready to serve. NET: 6 servings (1 9-inch pie), plus mincemeat for at least 2 more pies.

NESSELRODE PIE

Short Pastry Shell (baked 10-inch shell, page 726)

WHIPPED CREAM
1½ cups heavy cream
3 tablespoons confectioners sugar
1 teaspoon vanilla

BAVARIAN CREAM
5 large (6 small) egg yolks
10 tablespoons granulated sugar

1½ tablespoons unflavored gelatine
1½ cups light cream, scalded
2 raw egg whites
4 ounces mixed candied fruit, finely chopped and soaked in 3 tablespoons dark rum
8 ounces coarsely grated dark sweet chocolate
2 tablespoons confectioners sugar

Have the baked pastry shell ready.

WHIPPED CREAM. Beat the heavy cream in a metal bowl over another bowl of ice. When it begins to thicken, add the confectioners sugar and vanilla. Continue beating until the cream is stiff. Store in the refrigerator until needed.

BAVARIAN CREAM. Beat the egg yolks and sugar in a mixer bowl until light and fluffy. Stir in the gelatine. Slowly pour in the scalded light cream, stirring all the time, then transfer the mixture to a saucepan. Continue stirring over low heat until it thickens and coats the back of a metal spoon. Remove from the heat, set it over a bowl of ice, and beat with a small wire whisk until the mixture is a little cool. Beat the egg whites to soft peaks and stir them into the egg yolk mixture over ice. Then mix in the candied fruits and a little of the grated chocolate, then add half the whipped cream preparation very gradually, beating all the time.

Fill the pastry shell with this mixture, chill it in the refrigerator, then cover the top with coarsely grated chocolate and sprinkle confectioners sugar over the chocolate. Put the rest of the whipped cream in a pastry bag fitted with a #4 or #5 star tube and pipe rosettes around the edge of the pie. Chill well before serving. NET: 1 10-inch pie.

NAPOLEON

*Puff Paste and Pastry
Cream Sandwich Cake*

*Puff Paste (page 723, prepared
    through step 7)*
A little confectioners sugar

PASTRY CREAM
2 whole eggs
2 egg yolks
6 tablespoons all-purpose flour
6 tablespoons granulated sugar
⅛ teaspoon salt

2 cups milk
*4 tablespoons unflavored
    gelatine*
*2 tablespoons sweet butter,
    frozen*
4 raw egg whites
2 cups heavy cream, whipped
3 tablespoons light rum or
2 teaspoons vanilla extract

PUFF PASTE. Preheat the oven to 425° after the sixth turn (step 7, page 724). Roll the folded dough out very thin and large enough to cut into four strips each 4 by 10 to 12 inches. Cut the strips and place them (and also the rolled-out scraps) on wet baking sheets. Bake until each strip is well risen and golden brown on top, about 35 to 40 minutes. Then set the four strips on a wire rack to cool. Crumble the baked scraps to coarse crumbs and set them aside.

PASTRY CREAM. Put the eggs and egg yolks in a bowl with the flour, sugar, and salt. Beat with a wire whisk until well blended and frothy. Stir in the gelatine. Bring the milk to a boil and slowly pour it into the egg mixture, stirring all the time. Transfer the custard mixture to a saucepan. Over low heat stir it until it thickens (but does not boil). Cut the butter into four pieces and stir them into the sauce one by one. Instantly remove the pan from the heat, set it over a bowl of ice, and continue to stir until the sauce is cool. Beat the egg whites to soft peaks and stir them into the pastry cream, then very gradually, almost teaspoon by teaspoon, beat in the whipped cream (still over the bowl of ice). Last, stir in the rum or vanilla.

Sandwich the four strips of baked puff paste with the pastry cream, and spread the top and sides with it. Sprinkle the crumbled puff paste scraps over the top, and dust the top liberally with confectioners sugar. Chill the Napoleon at least 30 minutes in the refrigerator. Serve on a white paper doily on an oblong serving platter. Cut it with a sharp knife. NET: 6 servings.

PROFITEROLES AU CAFÉ, SAUCE AU CHOCOLAT

Little cream puffs filled with coffee pastry cream and served with hot chocolate sauce.

*Cream Puff Dough (page 727),
    through step 5*
*Confectioners sugar (for
    dusting)*

COFFEE PASTRY CREAM
1 egg

1 egg yolk
3 tablespoons all-purpose flour
3 tablespoons granulated sugar
Tiny pinch of salt
*Coffee essence (2 tablespoons
    instant coffee dissolved in
    2 tablespoons hot water)*

2 tablespoons unflavored
  gelatine
1 cup milk
3 tablespoons sweet butter
2 egg whites
1 cup heavy cream, whipped

HOT CHOCOLATE SAUCE
8 ounces dark semisweet
  chocolate
3 tablespoons light rum
⅔ cup light cream

Finish making and baking the cream puffs. Use a #6 or #7 tube as on page 727 for little cream puffs about 2 inches in diameter when baked.

COFFEE PASTRY CREAM. Put the egg and egg yolk in a bowl with the flour, sugar, and salt, and beat with a wire whisk until well blended and frothy. Stir in the coffe essence and gelatine. Bring the milk to a boil and slowly add it to the egg mixture, stirring all the while. Transfer the mixture to a saucepan, and stir over low heat until it thickens. Stir in the butter bit by bit. Instantly remove the saucepan from the heat, set it over a bowl of ice, and continue stirring until the sauce is cool. Beat the egg whites to soft peaks, and with a small wire whisk, stir them into the pastry cream, then very gradually, almost teaspoon by teaspoon, beat in the whipped cream still over ice.

Using the point of a small paring knife, make a small hole in the bottom of each cream puff. Put the pastry cream in a pastry bag fitted with a #3 or #4 (¼-inch diameter) plain round tube. Fill the cream puffs with pastry cream through the hole. Chill them in the refrigerator (they should be very cold to contrast with the hot sauce).

HOT CHOCOLATE SAUCE. Break the chocolate into little pieces and put it into a small saucepan. Add the rum and light cream and stir over very very low heat until the chocolate dissolves.

To serve, dust the cream puffs (profiteroles) with confectioners sugar and serve them on a white paper doily on a flat silver platter. Serve the sauce in a separate bowl. NET: 6 servings of 3 profiteroles each.

PROFITEROLES AU CHOCOLAT

Little cream puffs filled with vanilla pastry cream, served with rich chocolate sauce.

Cream Puff Dough (page 727),
  through step 5
Confectioners sugar (for
  dusting)

PASTRY CREAM
1 egg
1 egg yolk
3 tablespoons all-purpose flour
3 tablespoons granulated sugar
Tiny pinch of salt

2 tablespoons unflavored
  gelatine
1 cup milk
2 teaspoons vanilla extract
2 egg whites
1½ cups heavy cream, whipped
  (minus 4 tablespoons for the
  sauce)

RICH CHOCOLATE SAUCE
8 ounces dark sweet chocolate

½ ounce bitter chocolate
⅓ cup light rum
¾ cup light cream

4 tablespoons whipped cream
(from the whipped cream
prepared for the pastry cream)

Finish making and baking the little cream puffs exactly as in the preceding recipe for Profiteroles, and cut the hole for filling each baked cream puff as directed there.

PASTRY CREAM. Put the egg and egg yolk in a bowl with the flour, sugar, and salt, and beat with a wire whisk until well blended and frothy. Stir in the gelatine. Bring the milk to a boil and slowly add it and the vanilla to the egg mixture, stirring all the time. Transfer the whole mixture to a saucepan. Over low heat, stir the mixture (custard) until it just comes to a boil. Instantly put the saucepan over a bowl of ice, and continue to stir until the sauce has cooled a little. Beat the egg whites to soft peaks, and with a small wire whisk, stir them into the pastry cream, still over ice. Set aside 4 tablespoons of the whipped cream for the chocolate sauce, then very gradually, almost teaspoon by teaspoon, add the whipped cream to the pastry cream over ice, beating thoroughly with the small whisk.

RICH CHOCOLATE SAUCE. Break the sweet chocolate into little pieces and put them in a small saucepan. Grate the bitter chocolate and add it. Mix in the rum and stir over very, very low heat until the chocolate is dissolved and smooth. Mix in the light cream and simmer very gently 5 or 6 minutes, until the sauce has a nice creamy consistency. Off the heat, mix in the whipped cream.

Fill each cream puff with pastry cream just as in the preceding Profiteroles recipe, and chill them. When ready to serve, dust them with confectioners sugar and serve on a white paper doily on a flat silver platter. Serve the chocolate sauce (hot or cooled) in a separate bowl. NET: 6 servings of 3 profiteroles each.

TARTE AUX FRAISES

Fresh Strawberry Tart

The strawberry is a favorite fruit in the French culinary repertoire, and the strawberry tart is invariably a sensation. It is representative of the classic tart — whole fresh fruit (in this case bright red strawberries) glistening under a glaze of currant jelly, atop fluffy crème pâtissière in a crisp flan shell.

Short Pastry Shell (baked, page 726)
2 tablespoons dry breadcrumbs (page 69)
2 tablespoons granulated sugar
1 teaspoon ground cardamom seed
4 cups whole perfect strawberries, hulled
Confectioners sugar

PASTRY CREAM
1 egg
1 egg yolk
3 tablespoons all-purpose flour
3 tablespoons granulated sugar
Tiny pinch of salt
2 tablespoons unflavored gelatine
1 cup milk
2 egg whites

1 cup heavy cream, whipped
2 tablespoons Framboise
    (raspberry brandy)

GLAZE
1 cup red currant jelly
2 tablespoons Framboise

When the short pastry shell is baked and ready (page 726), leave it on the jelly roll pan. Mix the breadcrumbs, granulated sugar, and cardamom seed in a small bowl. Sprinkle them all over the bottom of the pastry shell.

PASTRY CREAM. Put the egg and egg yolk in a bowl with the flour, sugar, and salt. Beat with a wire whisk until the mixture is well blended and frothy. Stir in the gelatine. Bring the milk to a boil in a little pan. Slowly pour it into the egg mixture, stirring all the while. Transfer the whole mixture to a saucepan. Over low heat, stir it with a wooden spoon until it thickens. Immediately remove the pan from the heat, put it over a bowl of ice, and continue to stir until the mixture has cooled a little. Beat the egg whites to soft peaks and stir them into the pastry cream. Then very gradually, almost teaspoon by teaspoon, beat in the whipped cream. Last, stir in the Framboise.

GLAZE. Put the jelly in a small saucepan with the Framboise. Dissolve the jelly over low heat and pour it through a fine wire strainer.

Spread the pastry cream on the bottom of the baked (and crumbed) pastry shell. Cover it with whole strawberries (stand them in the cream stem end down). Brush the currant jelly glaze all over the strawberries, coating each one well. Dust liberally with confectioners sugar all around the edge of the tart. Transfer it to a flat serving platter. Serve at once, or the tart may be chilled several hours in the refrigerator. NET: 1 10-inch tart (6 to 8 servings).

Short Pastry Shell (baked,
    page 726)
A little granulated sugar
1 cup heavy cream, whipped
    with 2 tablespoons confec-
    tioners sugar and 1 teaspoon
    vanilla extract
A little cocoa (for dusting)

MERINGUES
6 egg whites
1 cup superfine sugar
½ teaspoon cream of tartar

⅛ teaspoon salt

CHESTNUT BUTTER CREAM
3 egg yolks
1 cup granulated sugar
¾ cup water
¼ teaspoon cream of tartar
¾ pound sweet butter,
    creamed in a mixer until light
    and fluffy
1-pound can unsweetened
    chestnut purée
2 to 3 tablespoons light rum

TARTE AUX MARRONS

Chestnut Butter Cream Tart Decorated with Meringues and Whipped Cream Rosettes

Have the baked short pastry shell ready.

MERINGUES. Preheat the oven to 275°. Have ready two jelly roll pans covered with wax paper. Beat the egg whites in the mixer until they form soft peaks. Sift the sugar with the cream of tartar and slowly add to the egg whites, beating all the time. Add the salt, and beat the egg whites until stiff. Put this meringue into a pastry bag fitted with a #9 plain round tube. Pipe a bit of it under the corners of the wax paper in the pans to hold the paper down, then pipe it on the paper in the shape of half eggs (small oval mounds). Sprinkle them with granulated sugar, and bake them 30 minutes. Let them cool, then remove them from the wax paper by sliding a spatula under each one.

CHESTNUT BUTTER CREAM. Beat the egg yolks in the mixer until stiff. Put the sugar, water, and cream of tartar in a small heavy pan, and cook until the sugar syrup forms a thin thread between the finger and thumb. Slowly pour the hot syrup over the beaten yolks, beating all the while and continuing to beat until the mixture is thick and quite cold. Still beating, add the butter bit by bit, then the chestnut purée bit by bit. Last, beat in the rum.

Put the chestnut butter cream in a pastry bag fitted with a #9 star tube. Pipe it all over the bottom of the baked pastry shell, filling the shell to the top. Put the whipped cream in another pastry bag fitted with a star tube and pipe rosettes all around the edge of the tart. Place the meringues around the top of the chestnut purée. Dust them with a little cocoa. Chill this confection at least 2 hours, and serve. NET: 1 10-inch tart (6 to 8 servings).

TARTE AU MIEL

Honey Tart
with Cream Cheese
in Rich Pastry Shell

2 tablespoons dry breadcrumbs
  (page 69)
1 tablespoon granulated sugar
A little confectioners sugar

PASTRY SHELL
2 cups all-purpose flour
2 hard-boiled egg yolks, rubbed
  through a fine wire strainer
3 raw egg yolks
5 tablespoons granulated sugar
5 tablespoons sweet butter
  (room temperature)

1/8 teaspoon salt
Grated rind of 1 lemon

FILLING
4 ounces cream cheese
1/2 cup cottage cheese
2 tablespoons granulated sugar
5 tablespoons honey
2 tablespoons raisins, soaked
  in 2 tablespoons warm water
  (to soften) and drained
2 tablespoons sour cream

Have ready a shallow 8-inch pie tin or flan ring on a baking sheet.

PASTRY SHELL. Put the flour on a board or slab. Make a well in the center and put in it all the rest of the ingredients. Work them into a smooth paste, then quickly work in the flour. Roll out two-thirds of the dough a little larger than the pie tin or flan ring, not too thin. Lift the pastry, lay it over the pan, line the pan firmly, and trim off the edges. With the fingers, shape a little thicker rim, and trim the edge with pastry pincers. Prick all over the bottom of the pastry with a fork.

Sprinkle the shell with the breadcrumbs and set it in the refrigerator while you prepare the filling. Preheat the oven to 350°.

FILLING. Beat the cream cheese in a mixer until smooth and creamy. Add the rest of the ingredients and beat well.

Spoon the filling into the pastry shell. Roll out the remaining dough to the same thickness as the shell. Cut it into strips long enough to go across the shell and about ½ inch wide. Lay them over the tart in a crisscross (lattice) fashion. Press them down where they meet the rim and pinch off the excess. Sprinkle the top of the tart with the granulated sugar, and bake it in the preheated oven 35 to 40 minutes. Then put it in the refrigerator to cool thoroughly. To serve, remove the flan ring from the tart (or lift the tart from the pie dish) and arrange the tart on a flat serving platter or wooden board. Dust the top with confectioners sugar. NET: 1 8-inch tart (4 to 6 servings).

---

1 pound fresh peaches or pears, ripe (not bruised)
Soaking solution: juice of 1 lemon in a bowl of water
3 tablespoons peach or apricot jam (superior quality)
2 tablespoons apricot liqueur or water
1 cup heavy cream, whipped, flavored with 1 teaspoon vanilla extract
½ cup shredded blanched almonds, browned in the oven

PASTRY SHELL
2 cups all-purpose flour
4 egg yolks
4 tablespoons granulated sugar
⅛ teaspoon salt
4 tablespoons sweet butter (room temperature)
A little cool melted sweet butter (to brush the dough)
2 cups raw rice (to anchor the pastry)

TARTE AUX PÊCHES OU TARTE AUX POIRES

Tart of Fresh Peaches or Fresh Pears

PASTRY SHELL. Preheat the oven to 375°. Have ready a 10-inch flan ring on a jelly roll pan or baking sheet. Put the flour on a board or marble slab. Make a well in it and put in the egg yolks, sugar, salt, and butter. Work them with the fingers to a smooth paste, then work up with the flour quickly. Roll out the dough a little larger than the flan ring. Lay it over the ring and line the ring firmly. Trim the edges, with the fingers shape a little thicker rim, and trim the rim with pastry pincers. Prick all over the bottom of the pastry with a fork. Brush the surface of the dough with a little cool melted butter and line it with wax paper. Put in the rice to anchor the paper. Bake the shell 30 minutes, then remove the rice, paper, and flan ring. Return the shell (on the baking sheet) to the oven to bake another 10 minutes, to brown the bottom a little. Chill the pastry shell in the refrigerator.

If you are using peaches, pour boiling water over them, count to 20, rinse them in cold water, and remove the skins. Cut them in half and remove the pits. If you are using pears, peel them with a potato parer, cut them in quarters, and remove the core sections. Keep either peaches or pears in the lemon juice solution until time to use them, to preserve their color. To make the glaze, put the jam and liqueur or water in a little pan and cook to a syrupy consistency. Rub the mixture through a fine wire strainer and cool it.

Spread the whipped cream over the bottom of the baked pastry shell. Drain the peach or pear halves on paper towels, arrange them in circular rows on the whipped cream, and brush them with the glaze. Sprinkle all over the top with the almonds. Place the tart on a white paper doily on a flat serving dish. Serve at once (or it may be chilled in the refrigerator for a little while). NET: 1 10-inch tart (6 to 8 servings).

TARTE AUX QUETSCHES

Fresh Plum Tart

Pastry shell (10 inches, page 726), baked 20 minutes only
2 tablespoons dry breadcrumbs (page 69)
1½ pounds fresh purple or green sweet plums (split and pitted)

8 tablespoons red currant jelly (or apricot jam for green plums)
1 tablespoon plum brandy (Quetsch, with purple plums, or Mirabelle, with green plums) or water

When the pastry shell (page 726) has baked 20 minutes, remove it from the oven and remove the paper and rice, but leave it on the jelly roll pan and leave the oven on at 375°.

Sprinkle the breadcrumbs on the bottom of the pastry shell, and fill the shell with the split and pitted plums. Return the pastry to the oven to bake another 20 to 25 minutes, then remove it from the oven, remove the flan ring, and cool the tart. For the glaze, cook and stir the jelly or jam and the brandy or water in a little pan over low heat until the jelly melts. (If apricot jam is used, strain the glaze.) Cool the glaze a little and brush it all over the top of the tart. Chill the tart, and serve. NET: 1 10-inch tart (6 to 8 servings).

TARTELETTES AUX AMANDES

Almond Tartlets

A little granulated sugar
A little confectioners sugar

PASTRY
1½ cups all-purpose flour
3 egg yolks
3 tablespoons sweet butter (room temperature)
3 tablespoons granulated sugar

Tiny pinch of salt

ALMOND FILLING
1 egg
3 tablespoons granulated sugar
1 cup browned blanched almonds, chopped
2 tablespoons light rum
1 egg white

Preheat the oven to 350°. Have ready 8 3¼-inch tartlet molds set out on the counter in a cluster, touching each other.

PASTRY. Put the flour on a board or slab. Make a well in the center and put the other ingredients in it. Work them with the fingers to a smooth paste, then work in the flour quickly. Roll out the dough very thin to a sheet about the area of the cluster of molds. Carefully lift the sheet of dough on the rolling pin and lay it loosely over the molds.

Gently but firmly run the rolling pin over it, which will automatically cut the correct size round of dough for each mold. With the fingers, firm the dough against the bottoms and sides of the mold.

ALMOND FILLING. Beat the egg and sugar, and mix in three-quarters of the chopped almonds and all the rum. Beat the egg white to soft peaks, and with a rubber scraper fold it into the almond mixture.

Spoon the filling into the pastry shells. Sprinkle the tops with a little granulated sugar. Bake the tartlets 30 minutes, or until they are golden brown. Then cool them a little and dust the tops with confectioners sugar and the remaining chopped almonds. Serve when desired. NET: 8 tartlets.

An elegant dessert — to serve a selection of homemade fresh fruit tartlets. It is best not to fill the shells until an hour or two before serving, or they might lose their crispness. Keep them in their molds up to serving time, to protect the delicate pastry shell.

Short Pastry Shell dough (page 726; through step 3)
A little melted sweet butter
2 cups raw rice (to anchor pastry)
Confectioners sugar (for dusting)

CRUMB MIXTURE (FOR 12 TARTS)
4 tablespoons dry breadcrumbs (page 69)
4 tablespoons granulated sugar
½ teaspoon ground cardamom seed
Few grains freshly grated nutmeg

FRUIT FILLINGS (EACH FOR 6 TARTS)
Strawberry: 2 cups whole fresh perfect strawberries, hulled
Raspberry: 1½ cups whole fresh raspberries
Grape: 1½ cups fresh white grapes, peeled and seeded
Apple: 2 large ripe apples, 2 teaspoons lemon juice, ½ cup peach jam, grated rind of 1 lemon, granulated sugar

RED CURRANT JELLY GLAZE
    (for 6 tarts with red fruit)
½ cup red currant jelly
1 tablespoon Framboise (raspberry brandy)

APRICOT JAM GLAZE
    (for 6 tarts with white fruit)
½ cup apricot jam
1 tablespoon Cognac, good brandy, or ary sherry

TARTELETTES AUX FRUITS (FRAISES, FRAMBOISES, RAISINS, ET POMMES)

Fruit Tartlets (Strawberry, Raspberry, White Grape, and Apple)

Have ready the Short Pastry Shell dough and 12 3¼-inch metal tartlet molds. Preheat the oven to 375°.

PASTRY. Roll out the dough very thin. Have the tartlet molds set in a cluster, touching each other. Carefully lift the sheet of dough on the rolling pin and lay it over the molds. Run the rolling pin over it, to cut automatically the correct size round of dough for each mold. With the fingers, firm the dough against the bottoms and sides of the molds. Brush the dough with a little melted butter. Set aside the molds you will use for apple filling (which bakes with the shell). Press a piece of wax paper about 4 inches square against the buttered pastry in each of the other molds, and pour in the raw rice to anchor the paper. Set the molds on a jelly roll pan and bake them about 25 minutes, or until they are golden brown.

CRUMB MIXTURE. Mix all the ingredients together (breadcrumbs, sugar, cardamom seed, and nutmeg).

Sprinkle a little of this mixture in each pastry shell, including those for apple tartlets (still unbaked).

CURRANT JELLY GLAZE (FOR RED FRUITS). Melt the jelly with the Framboise over low heat. Pour it through a strainer into a small bowl. Let it cool a little.

APRICOT JAM GLAZE (FOR WHITE FRUITS). Melt the jam with the Cognac, brandy, or sherry over low heat. Rub it through a strainer into a small bowl. Let it cool a little.

TARTELETTES AUX FRAISES (STRAWBERRY TARTLETS) OR TARTELETTES AUX FRAMBOISES (RASPBERRY TARTLETS). Fill 6 baked tartlet shells, sprinkled with the crumb mixture, with the strawberries (stand them hulled end down) or raspberries. Brush the fruit with the currant jelly glaze, and sprinkle confectioners sugar around the edges.

TARTELETTES AUX RAISINS (WHITE GRAPE TARTLETS). Fill 6 baked tartlet shells, sprinkled with the crumb mixture, with the white grapes. Brush the grapes with apricot jam glaze, and sprinkle confectioners sugar around the edges.

TARTELETTES AUX POMMES (APPLE TARTLETS). Peel, core, and cut both apples in half. Cut one into tiny dice and sprinkle with lemon juice. Slice the other very thin and sprinkle with lemon juice (the slices should be paper-thin). Mix the diced apple with the peach jam and lemon rind. Preheat the oven to 375° and have ready 6 unbaked tartlet shells sprinkled with the crumb mixture. Fill the shells with the diced apple mixture and arrange the thin apple slices on it in a pinwheel pattern. Sprinkle with granulated sugar, put them on a jelly roll pan, and bake 25 minutes, or until they are a golden brown around the outside. Run them under a hot broiler for a moment just to singe the edges of the sliced apple. Brush them with apricot jam glaze and let them cool in the molds.

When ready to serve the tartlets, remove them from the metal molds and arrange them on a white paper doily on a serving platter. NET: 12 tartlets. (NOTE: The recipe supplies extra filling, since each of the four fillings will fill 6 tartlets. The two glazes each cover 6 tartlets.)

The pastry and lemon curd for Lemon Meringue Pie (page 739) can also be made into tasty little tartlets.

Prepare the pastry dough and line 12 tartlet molds according to the technique described for Tartelettes aux Fruits (page 751). Prepare the lemon curd the same as for Lemon Meringue Pie. Set the curd in the freezer and leave it there. When you are ready to serve, have the tartlet shells ready. Put a couple of tablespoons of lemon curd in each. It is not necessary to use a meringue on the tartlets, and the lemon curd need not be smoothed over. Serve them on a white paper doily.

TARTELETTES AU CITRON

Lemon Tartlets

Strudel dough (page 729)
1 cup cool melted sweet butter
A little confectioners sugar
Sour Cream Sauce (page 67)

CHERRY FILLING
2 cups coarse dry breadcrumbs
*   (page 69)*
1¼ cups light brown sugar
1 teaspoon cinnamon
1 teaspoon freshly grated

nutmeg
1 cup seedless white raisins
½ cup dried currants
½ cup mixed chopped candied
*   peel*
⅓ cup chopped glacé cherries
1 cup shredded blanched
*   almonds*
Grated rind of 2 lemons
3 cups black Bing cherries, fresh
*   or canned (drained), pitted*

KIRSCHEN-STRUDEL

Cherry Strudel

When the strudel dough is mixed (as for Apfelstrudel, page 729), follow the Apfelstrudel procedure through the step of stretching the dough out over the table top. Then brush cool melted butter all over the dough and let it stand 10 to 15 minutes.

CHERRY FILLING. Mix in a little bowl the breadcrumbs, ½ cup light brown sugar, and the cinnamon and nutmeg. In another bowl mix the raisins, currants, candied peel, glacé cherries, almonds, ½ cup brown sugar, and lemon rind. Have the black cherries ready in a third bowl.

Preheat the oven to 375°. Sprinkle the breadcrumb mixture all over the strudel dough. Sprinkle a little more melted butter on the bread-crumbs. Scatter the black cherries all over the breadcrumbs. Then sprinkle the raisin and candied peel mixture over the cherries. Sprinkle the surface with a little more melted butter and the remaining ¼ cup brown sugar.

Liberally butter a jelly roll pan. Roll the strudel up like a jelly roll and trim off the thick ends. Bend it like a horseshoe and place it on the pan. Bake it 45 to 50 minutes, until the strudel crust is a beautiful golden brown all over. Cool the strudel a little before serving. Sprinkle it generously with confectioners sugar, and serve it with a separate bowl of cold sour cream sauce. NET: 8 to 10 servings.

SHREWSBURY TARTS

Strangely enough, in Shrewsbury the pronunciation is "Shrowsberry," but only in Shrewsbury. Elsewhere, it is pronounced Shrewsbury. For these excellent tartlets, filled with creamy cream cheese and glazed with apricot jam, you will need 18 tiny (1½-inch) tartlet molds.

SHORT PASTRY
2 cups all-purpose flour
⅔ cup granulated sugar
¾ teaspoon salt
8 tablespoons sweet butter
2 eggs, beaten well

4 ounces cream cheese
¼ teaspoon salt
¼ teaspoon freshly grated
  nutmeg
1 tablespoon orange juice
½ teaspoon grated orange rind

CREAM CHEESE FILLING
8 tablespoons sweet butter
½ cup granulated sugar
2 egg yolks

GLAZE
1 cup strained apricot jam
  (superior quality)

Have ready 18 1½-inch tartlet molds, set together in a cluster.

PASTRY. Sift the flour, sugar, and salt together. Cut in the butter and rub it into the flour mixture until it resembles coarse cornmeal in texture. Add the well-beaten egg and work the ingredients up quickly to a firm dough. Roll it out ¼ inch thick, and carefully lift and lay it over the little tartlet molds. Lightly roll the rolling pin over the dough, which will cut the dough for each mold. Press the pastry firmly into each mold. Prick it with a fork, and set the molds on a baking sheet. Preheat the oven to 450°.

CREAM CHEESE FILLING. Cream the butter in an electric mixer. Add the sugar and beat until light and fluffy. Then beat in the rest of the ingredients.

Fill the tarts with the cheese mixture and bake them 10 minutes, then reduce the heat to 325° and bake until the shells are golden brown and the filling is firm. Invert the tarts on paper to cool. Then turn them upright, glaze them with the strained apricot jam and chill. Serve 2 or 3 per person. NET: 18 tartlets.

CAKES

THE ORIGINAL "CHOCOLATE ROLL LÉONTINE"

This unique chocolate roll recipe was given to me on my first visit to New York in 1939 by a French cook named Léontine. When I arrived in New York the temperature was 101, and a cousin took me by train to the cool air of the Adirondacks, where we stayed in a little cottage. Léontine was cooking there. The dinner she prepared the night we arrived consisted of a bass freshly caught from the lake, corn about one minute from having been picked, and this superb dessert, which is a chocolate roll made without any flour. And we ate all this under the stars in the Adirondacks. I will never forget it!

8 ounces dark sweet chocolate
⅓ cup water
8 egg yolks
1 cup superfine sugar
⅛ teaspoon salt
8 egg whites

½ cup bittersweet cocoa
1¾ cups heavy cream
2 tablespoons confectioners
 sugar
Scraping of ⅓ vanilla bean
A little vegetable oil (to oil pan)

Cut the chocolate into little pieces. Put them in a small heavy pan with the water and stir over low heat until the chocolate is melted and smooth. Do not let it get too hot or it will separate. Set the chocolate aside for a moment and let it cool a little.

Preheat the oven to 350°. Brush a jelly roll pan (11 by 17 inches) with vegetable oil. Line it with a piece of wax paper, leaving about 3 inches of paper hanging over each end. Carefully fold the overhang back to form a handle. Beat the egg yolks with the superfine sugar and salt, using a large wire whisk or a mixer, until they are very light and fluffy. Mix in the melted chocolate. Beat the egg whites to soft but firm peaks. Fold the yolk and chocolate mixture smoothly and quickly into the whites, using a rubber scraper. Spread the chocolate mixture evenly on top of the wax paper. Put the pan in the preheated oven and bake 17 minutes.

Take a strip of 4 paper towels, fold the strip in half, and wring it out in cold water. When the chocolate roll is baked, remove it immediately from the oven and gently place the damp towels on it. Cover the wet towels with one thickness of dry paper towels. Let the chocolate roll stand at room temperature until lukewarm, then remove both sets of paper towels. Slide a little knife down each side of the pan to loosen the roll. Sprinkle all over the top of the roll with bittersweet cocoa. Cover the chocolate roll with two pieces of wax paper. Hold them firmly with the ends of the jelly roll pan, and carefully but quickly flip the pan over so that the chocolate roll is now lying on the fresh wax paper and the lining of wax paper is now on the top. Remove the jelly roll pan. Carefully and immediately peel the wax paper lining off the chocolate roll.

WHIPPED CREAM FILLING. Put the heavy cream in a large metal bowl over another bowl of ice. Beat with a large whisk until it begins to hold its shape. Add the confectioners sugar and the vanilla bean scraping. Continue beating the cream until it holds its shape.

As the chocolate roll is so delicate and can become broken so easily, the best way to spread the cream on the top is to divide it into 3 rows of 3 heaping tablespoons each. Then very gently spread it out evenly with a spatula. Carefully roll it up like a jelly roll and serve on a long wooden board. (NOTE. This chocolate roll will keep well a few hours in the refrigerator, covered with foil or wax paper, and it keeps very well for longer periods in the freezer.) NET: 1 17-inch chocolate roll (8 to 10 servings).

DIONE LUCAS'S NUT ROLL

This is my own invention; in a way, it is a permutation of the Chocolate Roll Léontine.

8 egg yolks
1 cup superfine sugar
8 ounces walnuts, pulverized
  in a blender
1½ teaspoons baking powder
8 egg whites
2 tablespoons confectioners
  sugar
2 tablespoons granulated sugar

MAPLE FILLING
1½ cups pure maple syrup
½ cup egg whites

WHIPPED CREAM FILLING
  (ALTERNATE)
1¾ cups heavy cream
2 tablespoons confectioners
  sugar
⅓ scraping of vanilla bean

Preheat the oven to 350°. Butter a jelly roll pan (11 by 17 inches). Line it with a piece of wax paper, leaving about 3 inches hanging over each end. Fold the overhang to form a handle, then butter the wax paper liberally. Beat the egg yolks with the superfine sugar, using a large wire whisk or mixer, until they are light and fluffy. Mix the baking powder with the walnuts, and stir them into the egg yolk mixture, using a rubber scraper. Beat the egg whites to soft but firm peaks. Mix the egg yolk mixture into the egg whites vigorously but lightly with a rubber scraper. Spread the mixture evenly on the buttered wax paper in the jelly roll pan, and bake 12 to 15 minutes, until it is well risen and golden brown all over.

When the nut roll is baked, loosen each end and side by sliding a little knife around the pan. Mix the confectioners sugar and granulated sugar together and sift about half of it lightly on the nut roll. Place a clean cloth or kitchen towel on the table or counter. Beside the towel place a sheet of wax paper about the same length. Sprinkle the towel with the rest of the sugar mixture. Turn the nut roll out onto the cloth (not the paper). Peel off the wax paper (pan lining) now on top of the nut roll. Spread this surface of the nut roll evenly with either maple filling or whipped cream.

MAPLE FILLING. Put the maple syrup into a small pan, bring it to a boil slowly over low heat, and boil it 2½ minutes. Beat the egg whites to soft peaks in a mixer bowl. Slowly pour the hot maple syrup over the egg whites, beating all the time. Continue until it holds its shape.

WHIPPED CREAM FILLING (ALTERNATE). Put the heavy cream in a large metal bowl over another bowl of ice. Beat with a large whisk until it begins to hold its shape. Add the sugar and vanilla bean scraping. Continue beating until the cream holds its shape.

After the nut roll has been gently spread with either filling, roll it up like a jelly roll on the cloth. Then slide it gently onto the piece of wax paper that is alongside the cloth. Chill, and serve on a long wooden board. NET: 1 17-inch nut roll (8 to 10 servings).

CRUMB CRUST
2 cups fine Zwieback crumbs
1 teaspoon cinnamon
¾ cup superfine sugar
¾ cup cool melted sweet butter

CHEESE FILLING
3 tablespoons unflavored
   gelatine
¼ cup cold water
3 egg yolks
¾ cup granulated sugar

½ cup hot water
½ cup sweet butter
1 pound cream cheese,
   softened at room temperature
Grated rind of 1 lemon
1 teaspoon lemon juice
1 teaspoon freshly grated
   nutmeg
3 egg whites
1 cup heavy cream, whipped
Confectioners sugar

DIONE LUCAS'S ORIGINAL ICEBOX CHEESECAKE

CRUMB CRUST. Preheat the oven to 350°. Generously butter a 9-inch springform cake pan. Mix the crumbs in a bowl with the sugar and melted butter. Set about a quarter of the mixture aside for the top, and press the rest firmly on the bottom and sides of the pan. Bake the crust 10 minutes, remove it from the oven, and let it cool.

CHEESE FILLING. Soak the gelatine in the cold water 5 minutes. Put the egg yolks in a medium-size bowl with the sugar and hot water and blend them well. Set the bowl in a shallow pan half full of hot water over low heat and continue to beat with a little whisk until the mixture is thick. Add the softened gelatine and stir until it is thoroughly dissolved. Set the mixture aside to cool a little. Cream the butter in a mixer bowl until it is light and fluffy. Add the softened cream cheese and beat well. When the yolk mixture has cooled, stir the butter and cream cheese mixture into it, add the lemon rind, lemon juice, and nutmeg, and strain the whole mixture through a fine wire sieve. Beat the egg whites to soft peaks and lightly fold them into it, using a rubber scraper, then fold in the whipped cream.

Pour the filling into the prepared crust. Sprinkle the top with the remaining crumb mixture. Let the cheesecake stand in the freezer 30 minutes, or longer in the refrigerator, to become well set. About a half-hour before serving, turn the cheesecake out onto a paper doily on a serving dish. Place a stencil or round cake rack on the top (for a pattern) and sprinkle liberally with confectioners sugar. (Or the top of the cake can be decorated with more whipped cream.) NET: 10 servings.

1 cup vegetable shortening
1 cup granulated sugar
1 egg
3 egg yolks
1½ cups sifted cake flour
   (without baking powder)
½ cup milk
2 teaspoons baking powder
3 egg whites

CHOCOLATE FUDGE FILLING
8 ounces dark sweet chocolate
5 tablespoons rum or water
6 tablespoons sweet butter
2 tablespoons sour cream

CHOCOLATE FUDGE FROSTING
8 ounces dark sweet chocolate
6 tablespoons rum or water

AMERICAN CHOCOLATE FUDGE CAKE

1 teaspoon vegetable oil

DECORATION
6 tablespoons sweet butter,

creamed in the mixer until
light and fluffy
½ cup shelled pecan halves

Preheat the oven to 350°. Butter two 8-inch layer cake pans. Line the bottoms with rounds of wax paper and butter the wax paper. Beat the shortening in a mixer bowl until it is light and fluffy. Add the sugar and again beat until it is very light and fluffy. Continue beating and, one by one, add the egg and the egg yolks. Gradually add the flour, alternating with the milk, and mix well. Beat the egg whites to soft peaks in a separate bowl, using a wire whisk or rotary beater. Fold the egg whites into the cake mixture, also the baking powder. Divide the cake mixture evenly between the two pans, and bake them 30 minutes. Turn them out of the pans at once. Cool them on wire cake racks brushed with a little butter.

CHOCOLATE FUDGE FILLING. Cut the chocolate into pieces, put them in a small heavy pan with the rum or water, and stir over low heat until the chocolate melts. With a little whisk, beat in the sweet butter bit by bit, then beat in the sour cream. Set the pan over a bowl of ice and stir until it is on the point of setting.

Sandwich the cake layers with the filling and set the cake in the refrigerator to chill a little.

CHOCOLATE FUDGE FROSTING. Cut the chocolate into pieces, put them in a small heavy pan with the rum or water and the vegetable oil, and stir over low heat until the chocolate melts.

Place the sandwiched cake on a wire rack on a jelly roll pan. Pour the chocolate frosting over it.

DECORATION. Cream the sweet butter in a mixer until light and fluffy. Add to it the remainder of the chocolate frosting which you have scraped up from the jelly roll pan. Beat the mixture well. Put it into a pastry bag fitted with a small star tube and pipe rosettes around the top edge of the cake. Garnish the rosettes with the pecans. Chill the cake very well in the refrigerator and serve.

NET: 6 to 8 servings.

BAQUET DE CHAMPIGNONS

"Bucket
of Mushrooms"

This cake is an exercise of pastry skills for the accomplished artist, resulting in a very charming, albeit very rich "bucket of mushrooms." The "bucket" is a layer cake sandwiched and spread with chocolate rum butter cream. The bucket effect is achieved by sticking Cat's Tongue cookies (Langues de Chat) vertically around the sides of the cake, like barrel staves. The little bucket concoction is then filled to overflowing with meringue mushrooms — some right side up, some upside down, others sideways. For the handles you will need two satin ribbons a foot long and ½ inch wide.

Langues de Chat (Cat's
  Tongues) batter (page 796);

see instructions below
A little cocoa

CAKE
½ cup vegetable shortening
½ cup granulated sugar
1 egg
2 egg yolks
¾ cup all-purpose flour
¼ cup milk
1 teaspoon baking powder
2 egg whites

MERINGUES
4 egg whites
12 tablespoons superfine sugar

A little coarse granulated sugar

CHESTNUT RUM BUTTER CREAM
3 egg yolks
1¼ cups granulated sugar
½ teaspoon cream of tartar
¾ cup water
½ to ¾ pound sweet butter
½ pound canned unsweetened
   chestnut purée
2 tablespoons crème de cacao
   or light rum

LANGUES DE CHAT. Bake 24 langues de chat (page 796), making two of them about twice as large as the others (these will be the handles for the bucket). When they are baked, set the little biscuits aside.

CAKE. Preheat the oven to 350°. Butter an 8-inch layer cake pan. Line the bottom with a round of wax paper. Beat the shortening in the mixer bowl until it is light and fluffy. Add the sugar and beat again until the mixture is light and fluffy. One at a time, beat in the egg and egg yolks. Gradually add the sifted flour alternately with the milk. Beat the combined ingredients very well. Beat the egg whites to soft peaks in a separate bowl, using a wire whisk or a rotary beater. Fold the egg whites and baking powder into the cake mixture. Fill the pan and bake the cake 30 minutes. Then turn it out onto wax paper and let it cool.

MERINGUES (MUSHROOM SHAPES). Adjust the oven temperature to 300°. Beat the egg whites to soft peaks in a mixer. Slowly add the sugar and continue beating until the mixture is stiff. Line a jelly roll pan with wax paper or baking liner paper. Stick the corners down with a little of the meringue. Put the meringue in a pastry bag fitted with a #7 plain round tube. Pipe out 18 baby button mushroom caps and 18 baby stems. Sprinkle the meringues liberally with coarse granulated sugar and bake them 25 to 30 minutes, or until they are just firm to the touch. Remove them from the oven, slide a spatula under to loosen them, and set them on a rack to cool.

CHESTNUT RUM BUTTER CREAM. Beat the egg yolks in the mixer until stiff. Combine the sugar, cream of tartar, and water in an unlined copper pan and cook until the syrup is thick enough to form a thin thread between the finger and the thumb (225°). Slowly pour the hot syrup over the egg yolks, beating all the time. Continue beating until the mixture is thick and cool. Add the sweet butter bit by bit to the yolk and syrup mixture (until the mixture comes back to butter). Then add the chestnut purée, also bit by bit. Last, add the rum or crème de cacao.

Slice the cake in half horizontally and sandwich it with a little butter cream. Place it on a serving platter. Put the butter cream in a pastry bag fitted with a #3 star tube. Have the langues de chat ready, and cut a round hole in one end of each of the two larger ones. Put a dab of butter cream on the back of each langue de chat and stick it vertically to the side of the cake. Arrange them evenly all the way around, with the larger "handles" opposite each other. (When the pastry is all assembled, tie a little ribbon bow in each "handle.")

Cover the top of the cake with about half the remaining butter cream. Then pipe a little rosette on the flat part (bottom) of each little meringue mushroom cap, and dust it with cocoa, like the underside of a mushroom. Stick the stem in the center of the mushroom. Dust the top of the mushroom with a few specks of cocoa. Fill the bucket with some mushrooms upright and some with the underside showing. Put the whole composition in the refrigerator to chill and set the butter cream, at least 2 hours. (This pastry can be stored in the freezer.) Admire and serve! NET: 6 to 8 servings.

BISCUIT ROULÉ (AU CONFITURE)

Basic Sponge Cake Roll with Jelly Filling

This sponge cake can be filled with any jelly or butter cream. With or without the preserves filling, it may be kept in the freezer several weeks, wrapped in foil.

4 eggs
¼ teaspoon salt
¾ cup granulated sugar
¾ cup sifted all-purpose flour
1 teaspoon vanilla extract
A little confectioners sugar and granulated sugar (about ½ cup mixed)

RED CURRANT JELLY FILLING
½ cup red currant jelly
1 tablespoon Framboise (raspberry brandy) if desired

APRICOT JAM FILLING (ALTERNATE)
¾ cup apricot jam
1 tablespoon Kirsch (cherry brandy) if desired

Preheat the oven to 350°. Butter a jelly roll pan 11 by 17 inches. Line it with wax paper, leaving about 3 inches hanging over at each end. Fold the overhang to form a handle, then butter the wax paper liberally. Beat the eggs in the mixer with the salt and sugar until they are very light and stiff. With a rubber scraper, fold in the flour, then lightly mix in the vanilla. Spread this mixture evenly in the jelly roll pan, and bake 15 minutes, until it is just set.

Have ready a cloth (such as a clean kitchen towel) spread out and liberally sprinkled with mixed granulated and confectioners sugar. (When the cake is baked, if the edges look so crisp that they might crack when rolled, trim them off with a sharp little knife before turning the cake out of the pan.) Turn the cake out onto the cloth and peel off the lining paper now on top. Sprinkle the cake with a little more granulated sugar. Delicately roll it up like a jelly roll, wrap and cool it in the cloth, and keep it that way until you are ready to fill it.

RED CURRANT JELLY FILLING. Heat the jelly in a little pan over low heat until it melts. Mix in the Framboise if desired. Pour the mixture through a fine wire strainer and cool it a little.

APRICOT JAM FILLING (ALTERNATE). Heat the jam in a little pan, mixed with Kirsch if desired. When it is melted, press it through a wire strainer and cool it a little. To fill, unroll the cake carefully. Spread it with the filling, just a thin coating, and roll it up again, tightly. NET: 1 17-inch sponge cake roll (8 to 10 servings).

Sponge Cake Roll (page 760)
½ cup coarsely shredded sweet
   chocolate
A little confectioners sugar

CHOCOLATE FILLING
6 ounces dark sweet chocolate
½ ounce bitter chocolate
3 tablespoons cold water
3 tablespoons sweet butter
2 tablespoons light rum

Sponge Cake Roll
with Chocolate

Have the Sponge Cake Roll (page 760) rolled up and ready, wrapped in the cloth.

CHOCOLATE FILLING. Cut the dark sweet chocolate in pieces and put it in a small heavy pan with the bitter chocolate and cold water. Stir over low heat until the chocolate melts. Off the heat, stir in the sweet butter bit by bit, and the rum. Stir the chocolate over a bowl of ice until it begins to cool.

Unroll the sponge cake and spread most of the chocolate filling over the surface. Roll it up tightly and cover the top with the remaining chocolate. Cover the roll all over with the coarsely shredded sweet chocolate, and dust with confectioners sugar. Serve at once, or chill in the refrigerator. NET: 1 17-inch sponge cake roll (8 to 10 servings).

3 large eggs
½ cup granulated sugar
⅓ cup rice flour
1 teaspoon baking powder
2 tablespoons cocoa
Tiny pinch of salt
A little superfine sugar
½ cup apricot jam, warmed
   and rubbed through a fine
   wire strainer

BUTTER CREAM FROSTING
3 egg yolks
1½ cups granulated sugar

¾ cup water
16 tablespoons (½ pound)
   sweet butter, creamed in the
   mixer until light and fluffy
2 tablespoons dark rum
2 teaspoons instant coffee
1 tablespoon hot water
6 ounces dark sweet chocolate
2 tablespoons water

DECORATION (OPTIONAL)
A little green almond paste for
   leaves, or chocolate curls
   for bark

Christmas (Yule) Log,
with Chocolate
and Coffee Butter
Creams

Preheat the oven to 375°. Generously butter a jelly roll pan (11 by 17 inches), line it with wax paper, and heavily butter the paper. Combine the eggs and granulated sugar in a mixer bowl and beat until thick and lemony. Sift the rice flour, baking powder, cocoa, and salt together and fold them into the egg mixture, using a rubber scraper. Spread the cake mixture evenly in the pan and bake 7 minutes, or until it is just firm.

Slide a little knife along the sides of the pan to loosen the cake. (If the edges look as though they might crack, trim them with the knife before turning the cake out of the pan.) Turn the cake out onto a cloth (such as a clean kitchen towel). Peel off the wax paper that is now on top. Sprinkle the top with a little superfine sugar, then carefully spread with the apricot jam. Working with the cloth the cake is resting on, carefully roll the cake into a long jelly roll shape.

BUTTER CREAM FROSTING. Beat the egg yolks in the mixer until light and fluffy. In an unlined copper pan, cook the sugar with the water until the syrup forms a light thread (225°). Pour the hot syrup onto the egg yolk mixture, beating all the while. Continue beating until the mixture is thick and cold. Add the creamed sweet butter and rum and beat well. For the Coffee Butter Cream, dissolve the instant coffee in the hot water. When it has cooled, stir it into 4 tablespoons of the butter cream. For the Chocolate Butter Cream, break the chocolate into small pieces and put it into a bowl with the water. Stand the bowl in a shallow pan half filled with hot water over low heat. Melt the chocolate, stirring all the time. When it has cooled, stir it into the rest of the butter cream.

Cut a diagonal slice from each end of the jelly roll and put them at random on top of the roll (these represent the stumps of cut-off branches). Frost the roll all over with the chocolate butter cream frosting. Frost the "cut" ends of the roll and stumps with coffee butter cream frosting (this represents white wood inside the dark bark). To achieve the rough effect of the outside bark, draw a fork jaggedly through the chocolate frosting several times from end to end. If desired, the log may be further decorated with a few leaves shaped from green-tinted almond paste (which may be purchased in specialty food shops). Curls of dark sweet chocolate may also be placed on top to represent rougher bark. (To make chocolate curls, use a sharp heavy knife. On a board, shave a thick piece of chocolate with downward strokes, as thin as possible.) Keep the Bûche de Noël chilled in the refrigerator or freezer until ready to serve. NET: 1 17-inch roll (8 to 10 servings).

CHECKERBOARD CAKE

Plain and chocolate cakes in a checkerboard pattern, with checkerboard frosting.

8 tablespoons sweet butter	1/8 teaspoon salt
1/2 cup vegetable shortening	1/2 cup milk
1 cup granulated sugar	2 teaspoons baking powder
5 eggs, separated	6 ounces dark sweet chocolate
1 1/2 cups cake flour (without baking powder)	3 tablespoons water
	Confectioners sugar

CHOCOLATE BUTTER CREAM
5 ounces dark sweet chocolate
4 tablespoons rum, coffee, or
 water
4 egg yolks
¾ cup granulated sugar
½ teaspoon cream of tartar
¼ cup water

8 tablespoons sweet butter with
 8 tablespoons vegetable
 shortening, creamed in a
 mixer until light and fluffy

CHOCOLATE SQUARES
6 ounces dark sweet chocolate

Preheat the oven to 350°. Butter two 9-inch layer cake pans. Line both pans with wax paper and butter them again. With strips of folded buttered wax paper, make two circles 5 inches in diameter and two 7-inch circles. Secure them with paper clips. Put a small and a large circle in each pan.

Beat the butter and vegetable shortening in a mixer bowl until very light and fluffy. Add the sugar and continue beating until very light. Beat in the egg yolks one by one. Sift the flour and salt together and add them gradually to the mixture, alternating with the milk (begin and end with flour). In a separate bowl beat the egg whites to soft peaks with a wire whisk or rotary beater. Fold the beaten whites and baking powder into the cake mixture.

Cut the chocolate into little pieces and put it into a small heavy pan with the water. Stir over low heat until the chocolate is just melted (do not cook it, or it will separate). Cool the chocolate. Put half the cake mixture into another bowl and add the cooled chocolate to it. Fill one cake pan with chocolate batter in the middle, plain batter around it, and chocolate batter in the outside circle. In the second pan put plain batter in the middle, chocolate around it, and plain batter in the outside circle. Just before putting the pans in the oven, very gently lift out the paper separators (the batter should be thick enough not to run). Place the pans immediately in the preheated oven and bake the cakes 20 to 25 minutes. When they are baked, turn them out onto wax paper to cool.

CHOCOLATE BUTTER CREAM. Break the chocolate into little pieces and put them in the previously used chocolate pan with 4 tablespoons of rum, coffee, or water. Stir over low heat until the chocolate is just melted, and cool it a little. Beat the egg yolks in the mixer until stiff. Cook the sugar, cream of tartar, and water in a small unlined copper pan until the mixture spins a light thread between the finger and the thumb (225°). Slowly pour the hot sugar syrup over the egg yolks, beating all the time. Continue to beat until the mixture is very stiff and cool. Beat in the creamed butter and shortening, then beat in the cooled melted chocolate.

CHOCOLATE SQUARES. Have ready a jelly roll pan and about 18 2-inch squares cut out of wax paper. Cut the chocolate into small pieces and put them on a plate or shallow dish over a pan of hot simmering water. Turn the chocolate with a spatula continually until it has melted. Spread a little coating of chocolate over each wax paper square, and lay them on the jelly roll pan. Put them in the refrigerator to set. Peel off the paper when they are hard.

Sandwich and frost the cake with the chocolate butter cream, reserving a little for decoration. Dust the top of the cake almost white with confectioners sugar, then arrange the chocolate squares on it in a checkerboard design. Put the reserved butter cream in a pastry bag with a #4 or #5 star tube and pipe rosettes around the top of the cake. Chill it well and serve. NET: 6 to 8 servings.

GÂTEAU AU CHOCOLAT

Chocolate Butter Cream Cake

1 cup granulated sugar
¾ cup vegetable shortening
4 egg yolks
1½ cups sifted cake flour
   (without baking powder)
½ cup milk
4 tablespoons coffee or water
4 egg whites
1 tablespoon baking powder
4 ounces dark sweet chocolate
A little confectioners sugar

CHOCOLATE BUTTER CREAM
   FROSTING
8 ounces dark sweet chocolate
¾ cup water
1 cup granulated sugar
4 egg yolks
8 tablespoons sweet butter with
   8 tablespoons vegetable
   shortening, creamed in a
   mixer until light and fluffy

CHOCOLATE ROUNDS
4 ounces dark sweet chocolate

Preheat the oven to 350°. Brush two 8-inch layer cake pans with butter. Fit a circle of wax paper in the bottom of each pan and butter the pans again. Beat the sugar and shortening in a mixer bowl until very light and fluffy. Continue beating and, one at a time, add the egg yolks. Gradually beat in the sifted cake flour, 2 to 3 tablespoons at a time, alternating with the milk. Break or cut the chocolate in little pieces into a small heavy pan. Add the coffee or water to it, and stir over low heat until the chocolate is just melted (do not boil or cook, or it may separate). Cool the chocolate a little. In a separate bowl, beat the egg whites to soft peaks, using a wire whisk or rotary beater. Fold the chocolate into the flour mixture, using a rubber scraper, until it is well blended. Then sprinkle the baking powder over the mixture, and with the rubber scraper carefully and smoothly stir in the baking powder and beaten egg whites. Divide this mixture between the two pans and bake 35 minutes. Test with a cake tester; if it comes out clean remove the cakes from the oven and let them sit for a moment, then turn them out on wire cake racks brushed with a little vegetable oil.

BUTTER CREAM FROSTING. Break the chocolate in little pieces and put them in the previously used chocolate pan with 4 tablespoons water. Stir over low heat until the chocolate is just melted, then let it cool. In an unlined copper pan, cook the sugar and ½ cup water together until the mixture spins a light thread between the finger and thumb (225°). Beat the egg yolks in the mixer until stiff. Slowly pour the hot sugar syrup over them, beating all the time. Continue to beat until the mixture is very stiff and cool. Beat in the creamed butter and shortening, then the cooled dissolved chocolate.

CHOCOLATE ROUNDS. Cut the chocolate into small pieces, set them on a shallow plate over a pan of simmering water, and turn the chocolate with a spatula until it is melted. Cut out 24 to 30 rounds of wax paper 1½ inches in diameter. Have ready a jelly roll pan. Spread a little coating of melted chocolate over each wax paper round and set it on the jelly roll pan. Set the pan in the refrigerator so the chocolate rounds will harden. When you are ready to decorate the cake, peel off the paper.

To assemble the cake, first place four strips of wax paper on the serving plate to keep it clean. Keep the cake with the best shape for the top layer. Set the other layer on the serving plate, cover it with butter cream frosting, then put on the top layer. Cover the entire cake with the frosting, reserving about ¾ cup, which you put in a pastry bag with a large round star tube. Pipe rosettes all over the top of the cake. Stick the chocolate rounds against the frosting all around the sides of the cake. Dust the top with confectioners sugar. Chill the cake in the refrigerator at least 1 hour; it should be served well chilled. NET: 1 8-inch layer cake (8 servings).

A chocolate rum genoese cake with chocolate rum butter cream icing, created by Dione Lucas.

CHOCOLATE RUM BUTTER CREAM CAKE

4 ounces dark sweet chocolate
3 tablespoons rum, coffee, or
  water
6 eggs
1 cup granulated sugar
Grated rind of 1 lemon
¼ cup cool melted sweet butter
1 cup cake flour (without baking
  powder)
A little confectioners sugar

CHOCOLATE RUM BUTTER CREAM
8 ounces dark sweet chocolate
¾ cup water
3 tablespoons dark rum
3 egg yolks
1¼ cups granulated sugar
¼ teaspoon cream of tartar
24 tablespoons (¾ pound)
  sweet butter, creamed until
  light and fluffy

CHOCOLATE ROUNDS
4 ounces dark sweet chocolate

Preheat the oven to 350°. Butter a 9-inch springform cake pan with cool melted butter. Cut wax paper to fit the bottom, put it in, and butter the whole pan again. Dust the pan lightly with flour. Break the chocolate into a small heavy pan. Add the rum, coffee, or water, and stir over very low heat until the chocolate is just melted. Let it cool. Beat the eggs and sugar in a mixer until they hold their shape. Fold the cooled melted chocolate into this egg mousse, using a rubber scraper. Sprinkle the grated lemon rind on the mousse, and pour the melted butter over it. Fold them carefully into the mousse, then sift the flour over the top, and fold it in very, very carefully with the rubber scraper. Fill the pan with this cake mixture and bake it 50 minutes. When it is done, turn it out at once onto a wire cake rack to cool.

CHOCOLATE RUM BUTTER CREAM. Cut the chocolate into pieces and put it in a small heavy pan with 4 tablespoons water and the rum. Stir over low heat until the chocolate is melted (do not cook any longer). Let the chocolate cool. Beat the egg yolks in the mixer until stiff. In an unlined copper pan, cook the sugar, cream of tartar, and ½ cup water until the syrup forms a thin thread between the finger and thumb (225°). Slowly pour the hot syrup over the beaten yolks, beating all the while, and continue beating until the mixture is thick and cool. Add the creamed butter and beat well. Then beat in the cooled melted chocolate.

CHOCOLATE ROUNDS. Make these just like the chocolate rounds in Gâteau au Chocolat (page 765). Use 18 2-inch circles of wax paper.

To assemble the cake, cover it with the butter cream. Stick the chocolate rounds, overlapping, around the sides, and place a few on top. Chill the cake in the refrigerator at least an hour. Just before serving, dust the top with confectioners sugar. NET: 8 servings.

CHRISTMAS CAKE

Also a Traditional Wedding Cake

The best wedding present of all to give a bride and her groom must be the wedding cake. It was my privilege to prepare the wedding cake for the daughter of the artist Paul Feeley and his wife Helen (who was with Bennington College for many years and my good friend). For this occasion I especially enjoyed baking and decorating this beautiful cake, infusing it with an extra-special measure of the most important ingredient in cookery and in life — tender loving care. This cake must be made at least two days before serving, and preferably much longer (see the note at the end of the recipe).

1 pound sweet butter
1 pound brown sugar
6 ounces finely ground almonds
7 eggs
1 pound mixed candied orange, lemon, and citron peel, finely chopped
½ pound glacé cherries, cut in half
1 pound white seedless raisins
1 pound black raisins
1 pound dried currants
1 pound all-purpose flour
1 teaspoon salt
½ cup good cream sherry
1 teaspoon baking powder
A little milk

½ cup red currant jelly
Generous sprinkling of Cognac

ALMOND FONDANT ICING
3 pounds granulated sugar
½ teaspoon cream of tartar
3 cups water
1 pound finely ground blanched almonds
1 teaspoon almond essence

ROYAL FROSTING
4 egg whites
About 5 pounds confectioners sugar
About ½ cup lemon juice

Preheat the oven to 350°. Butter a 12-inch springform pan. Cut wax paper to fit the bottom, put it in, and butter the whole pan again. Beat the butter in the mixer bowl until light and fluffy. Slowly beat in the brown sugar, and beat again until the mixture is light and fluffy. Beating constantly, mix in the ground almonds, then the eggs one at a time, then gradually mix in the salt and ¾ pound flour. In a separate bowl combine the candied peels, cherries, raisins, and currants. Dredge them with the remaining ¼ pound flour. Transfer the batter from the mixer bowl to a large mixing bowl and mix in the prepared fruits, then the sherry, and then the baking powder. At this point the mixture should just drop from a spoon. If necessary, add a little milk to it. Fill the pan and bake the cake 1½ hours. If a cake tester or ice pick comes out clean, it is properly baked. Let the cake cool in the pan at room temperature 30 minutes, then turn it out. When it is completely cooled, turn it upside down on a cake rack and peel off the wax paper. Spread the bottom with the jelly, pressing it into the cake with the spatula.

ALMOND FONDANT ICING (made of equal quantities of fondant and pulverized almonds). Put the sugar, cream of tartar, and water in an unlined copper pan, stir over low heat until the sugar dissolves, then let the syrup boil gently without stirring until it makes a fine thread between the finger and thumb (225°). Have ready a jelly roll pan brushed with cold water, or a wet marble slab. Pour the hot syrup on the pan or slab. Let it stand until you can just touch it with your finger without its sticking. Then work the syrup briskly with a wooden spoon, turning and moving it around until it is quite opaque and white. Shift it to a cutting board or marble slab and knead it until it is soft and pliable. Mix the ground almonds into it, then the almond essence. Roll out the almond fondant a good ½ inch thick and cut a round to fit on top of the cake exactly (should be about 12 inches in diameter). Set it on the cake. Roll out the rest of the fondant and cut it to fit the sides of the cake exactly. Chill the cake in the refrigerator.

ROYAL FROSTING. Beat the egg whites in the mixer to soft peaks. Beating all the time, slowly add the confectioners sugar and lemon juice, and beat well. (The frosting should be thick-spreading. The quantity of sugar and lemon juice varies according to the size of the egg whites.)

Completely cover the cake with royal icing over the fondant, and chill the cake 2 hours in the refrigerator. Then decorate with the rest of the frosting in a pastry bag piped through a star tube. Allow the cake to stand in the refrigerator at least 48 hours before serving. NET: One 12-inch cake.

NOTE. This cake, without the jelly, icing, or frosting, and stored in an airtight container, will keep as long as four years, and it improves with aging. Therefore it is wise to make it several months before using. Turn it upside down every two weeks, make slits in it with a sharp knife, and sprinkle well with Cognac. If the cake is made in advance, do not ice or frost it, or spread it with jelly, until within two weeks before it is to be served.

DOBOSCHTORTE

Dobostorte
(Rich Seven-Layer
Viennese Pastry)

4 eggs
½ cup granulated sugar
Tiny pinch of salt
¾ cup all-purpose flour
1 cup coarsely grated dark
    sweet chocolate

CARAMEL
1 cup granulated sugar
½ teaspoon cream of tartar
½ cup water

CHOCOLATE RUM BUTTER CREAM
4 ounces dark sweet chocolate
5 tablespoons light rum
1¼ cups granulated sugar
½ teaspoon cream of tartar
¾ cup cold water
3 egg yolks
24 tablespoons (¾ pound)
    sweet butter, creamed in a
    mixer until light and fluffy

Preheat the oven to 350°. Butter 4 jelly roll pans and coat them lightly but definitely with flour. Mark 7 rounds 8 inches in diameter on these pans. (Put a plate or lid that size on the pan and run your finger around the edge in the flour.) Beat the eggs in the mixer with the sugar and salt until the mixture is stiff. Sift the flour over the top and fold it into the mixture carefully, using a large rubber scraper. Divide the mixture equally on the 7 rounds marked on the jelly roll pans, and spread it out evenly with a spatula. Bake until the rounds are golden brown, about 15 minutes. Remove them immediately from the oven and instantly loosen them from the pan with a spatula. With a sharp little knife, trim the rounds to uniform size (they spread quite a bit when baked, so use as a guide a pot cover close to the size of all the rounds).

CHOCOLATE RUM BUTTER CREAM. Cut the chocolate in pieces and put it in a small heavy pan with the rum. Stir over low heat until the chocolate is melted (do not cook any longer). Let the chocolate cool. Beat the egg yolks in the mixer until stiff. In an unlined copper pan, cook the sugar, cream of tartar, and cold water together until the syrup forms a thin thread between the finger and thumb (225°). Slowly beat the hot syrup into the beaten yolks, continuing to beat until the mixture is thick and cool. Beat in the sweet butter bit by bit, then beat in the cool melted chocolate.

Set aside the best-shaped cake layer for the top. Sandwich the rest of the layers with the butter cream, and spread it on the top and on the sides (reserving a little to decorate the top). Stick the coarsely grated chocolate around the sides. Place the layer of cake reserved for the top on a well-oiled jelly roll pan.

CARAMEL GLAZE. Put the sugar, cream of tartar, and water in an unlined copper pan. Stir the mixture with a metal spoon over very low heat until the sugar dissolves. (Have nearby a pan or bowl of cold water big enough to set the caramel pan in.) Let the sugar syrup cook to a lovely amber color, then immediately set the pan in the cold water, so that it doesn't darken any more.

Pour the caramel over the cake layer on the jelly roll pan. Let it cool a little and trim off the edges. With the back of an oiled knife, mark the top into wedges for serving (so you can cut the cake after the caramel has hardened). Chill the caramel-coated layer before setting it on the cake. Put the reserved butter cream into a pastry

3 tablespoons red currant jelly

FILLING
4 cups coarse macaroon crumbs
1½ cups mixed candied fruits
    (cherries, citron, orange,
    lemon peel), finely chopped
1 cup dark rum

FONDANT ICING
5 cups granulated sugar

1 teaspoon cream of tartar
2 cups water
Juice of 1 orange
A few drops red vegetable
    coloring

DECORATION
A few crystallized violets
A few small cutouts of angelica
    for leaves

Preheat the oven to 350°. Butter an 8-inch springform cake pan. Cream the vegetable shortening in the mixer until it is light and fluffy. Add the sugar and again beat until light and fluffy. One at a time, beat in the egg and egg yolks. When the mixture is very light, alternately beat in the sifted flour and milk little by little. In a separate bowl, beat the egg whites to soft peaks with a wire whisk or rotary beater. Fold them into the flour mixture, then fold in the baking powder. Put the mixture into the pan and bake 30 minutes, or until the cake is firm to the touch and just begins to shrink away from the sides of the pan. Remove the cake from the oven. Turn it out of the springform mold and cool it on a wire rack.

FILLING. Combine the macaroon crumbs and candied fruits in a bowl with the rum. Let the mixture stand until all the rum is absorbed.

Lightly butter an 8-inch springform cake pan. Slice the cake horizontally into ½-inch layers. Put a layer in the bottom of the springform mold. Cover it with a little of the filling. Sandwich the whole cake, alternating layers of cake with filling, and ending with a layer of cake on the top. Cover the cake with foil and put a gentle weight on the top. Chill the assembled cake in the freezer 2 hours, then turn it out onto a cake rack. Melt the jelly in a little pan, and brush it all over the cake.

FONDANT ICING. (1) Combine the sugar, cream of tartar, and water in an unlined copper pan, and cook until the syrup forms a fine thread between the finger and thumb (225°). (2) Brush a jelly roll pan with cold water and pour the hot syrup on it. Let it stand just until you can touch it without sticking. Then work the syrup briskly with a wooden spoon, turning and moving it around on the pan, until it is quite opaque and white. (3) Put it on a cutting board or marble slab and knead it until it is soft.

Put this fondant in a heavy saucepan with the strained orange juice and a few drops of red vegetable coloring, and stir over very low heat until it is the consistency of heavy cream (it must never get too hot). Cover the top and the sides of the cake with the fondant. Chill the iced cake in the refrigerator at least 30 minutes. Place it on a serving platter and decorate the top with crystallized violets and angelica leaves. NET: 1 8-inch cake (8 to 10 servings).

GINGER ROLL

This lovely cake roll is a bouquet of mixed spices, very good and very economical. It can be filled with whipped cream, as for the Chocolate Roll Léontine, instead of the filling here.

1 cup all-purpose flour
1 teaspoon ground ginger
1 teaspoon cinnamon
1 teaspoon freshly grated
   nutmeg
1 teaspoon ground allspice
1 teaspoon baking soda
1/3 cup cool melted sweet butter

1/3 cup molasses
1/3 cup granulated sugar or light
   corn syrup
1 egg, well beaten
1/2 cup hot water
Confectioners sugar
1/2 cup corn syrup
2 egg whites

Preheat the oven to 350°. Butter a jelly roll pan, 11 by 17 inches. Line it with wax paper, leaving about 3 inches of the paper hanging over each end. Carefully fold the overhang to form a handle. Then butter the wax paper liberally. Mix the flour, ginger, cinnamon, nutmeg, allspice, and baking soda in a bowl. Add the melted butter, molasses, sugar or light corn syrup, beaten egg, and hot water. Mix all together thoroughly, using a whisk. Spread the mixture evenly in the jelly roll pan, and bake 12 to 15 minutes, until it is just set.

Fold in half a strip of 4 paper towels, and wring it out in cold water. When the ginger roll is baked, remove it from the oven immediately and gently place the damp towels on it. Cover them with a single layer thickness of dry paper towels. Cool the ginger roll in the refrigerator. When it is chilled, dust the top liberally with confectioners sugar. Cover the ginger roll with 2 strips of wax paper. Hold them firmly with the ends of the pan, and carefully but quickly flip the pan over so that the ginger roll is lying on the wax paper, and the lining of wax paper is on the top. Peel the lining wax paper off the ginger roll.

FILLING. Cook the corn syrup in a little pan to a light thread stage (the syrup should be thick enough to form a thread between the finger and thumb, about 225°). Beat the egg whites to soft peaks in a mixer bowl. Slowly pour the hot syrup over the beaten egg whites, beating all the time. Continue beating the mixture until it holds its shape. Gently spread this mixture on the ginger roll, and roll it up like a jelly roll. Serve it on a long wooden board. (It can be stored in the refrigerator, covered with a piece of foil or wax paper.) NET: 1 17-inch-long cake roll, about 8 to 10 servings.

MAPLE CAKE WITH MAPLE FROSTING

This cake seems to have such a regal quality. It was always a spécialité on my restaurant menus, and proud was the student who made it in cooking class.

1 cup vegetable shortening
1 cup granulated sugar
1 egg

3 egg yolks
1 1/2 cups sifted cake flour
   (without baking powder)

½ cup milk
2 teaspoons baking powder
3 egg whites

MAPLE FROSTING
3 cups maple syrup
¾ cup egg whites

Preheat the oven to 350°. Brush two 8-inch layer cake pans with butter. Cut wax paper to fit the bottom of each pan, put in the wax paper, and butter the pans again. Beat the vegetable shortening and sugar in a mixer until very light and fluffy. One at a time, add the egg and egg yolks. Continue to beat as each is added. Gradually beat in the sifted cake flour, 2 or 3 tablespoons at a time, alternating with the milk. Beat the egg whites in a separate bowl with a wire whisk or rotary beater until they have soft peaks. Sprinkle the baking powder over the flour mixture. Stir the baking powder and beaten egg whites into the flour mixture, using a rubber scraper. Divide this mixture between the two pans, and bake for 30 minutes. Test with a cake tester; if it comes out clean, the cake is baked. Remove the cakes from the oven and let them sit a moment, then turn them out to cool on wire racks brushed with a little vegetable oil.

MAPLE FROSTING. Put the maple syrup in a small saucepan, and bring it slowly to a boil over low heat. Let it boil for 5 minutes. Beat the egg whites in a mixer until they form soft peaks. Slowly pour the hot maple syrup over the egg whites, beating all the time. Maintain the beating until the frosting holds its shape (it should become very light and puffy).

Set the bottom layer bottom side down on a plate. Spread a little of the frosting on the top of this layer. Set the second layer of cake top side down on the frosting. Cover the whole cake with the frosting — use it all. With the flat tip of a spatula, make peaks all over the frosting. Serve when desired. (This cake can be chilled in the refrigerator. Be careful not to mar the frosting. NET: 1 8-inch layer cake (8 servings).

Coffee-flavored cake with coffee butter cream and meringue mushrooms.

5 eggs
½ cup granulated sugar
2 tablespoons instant coffee
4 tablespoons hot coffee
    or water
⅔ cup sifted cake flour
    (without baking powder)

MERINGUE
3 egg whites
8 tablespoons granulated sugar
A little cocoa
A little superfine sugar

COFFEE BUTTER CREAM
3 egg yolks
2 cups granulated sugar
¾ cup water
½ tablespoon cream of tartar
24 tablespoons (¾ pound)
    sweet butter, creamed until
    light and fluffy
2 tablespoons instant coffee
4 tablespoons hot coffee or
    water
2 tablespoons dark rum

GÂTEAU MERINGUE AU CAFÉ

Coffee Meringue Cake

Preheat the oven to 350°. Butter a 9-inch springform cake pan. Cut wax paper to fit inside the bottom of the pan, and put it in. Butter the whole pan again. Stir the eggs and sugar together in a mixer bowl and beat until very light and thick. Dissolve the instant coffee in the hot coffee or water. Cool it a little and add it to the egg mixture, beating all the time. Gradually add the sifted cake flour — sprinkle it little by little on the egg mixture and mix it in lightly with a rubber scraper. Put the cake mixture into the pan and bake 40 to 45 minutes. Test with a cake tester; if it comes out clean, it is done. Turn out of the springform mold and let it cool. Turn the oven down to 250° for the meringues.

COFFEE BUTTER CREAM. Beat the egg yolks in a mixer bowl until very light and fluffy. Cook the sugar, water, and cream of tartar in an unlined copper pan until the syrup forms a light thread between the finger and thumb (225°). Pour the hot syrup slowly over the beaten yolks, beating all the time. Continue beating until the mixture is thick and cold. Add the butter bit by bit, beating constantly. Dissolve the instant coffee in the hot coffee or water and cool it. Slowly add the coffee essence to the butter cream. Then slowly pour in the rum, beating thoroughly.

MERINGUE. Beat the egg whites in a mixer bowl until they nearly hold their shape. Slowly add the sugar and continue beating until the egg whites firmly hold their shape. Put the meringue in a pastry bag fitted with a #6 plain round tube (½-inch opening). Cover a baking sheet with wax paper. Pipe out the parts of mushrooms: small balls of meringue for the mushroom caps and narrow long pieces for the stems. Put a little sugar and cocoa (half and half) in a sugar shaker. Shake a little of this on the balls (not stems) of meringue. Bake the meringues in the preheated 250° oven about 4 minutes. Remove them from the oven and let them cool, then take them up from the paper.

Split the cake in half horizontally and sandwich it with some of the coffee butter cream. Cover it with more butter cream. Set in the refrigerator. Put the rest of the butter cream in a pastry bag fitted with a #3 star tube. Pipe a small rosette of butter cream on the backs of *half* of the meringue balls. Sprinkle the rosette with a little cocoa and stick a little meringue stalk in the middle of each. Remove the cake from the refrigerator. Stick the mushrooms with stems and mushroom caps without stems in a scattered or piled fashion on top of the cake. Pipe a row of butter cream rosettes around the top edge. Keep the cake chilled in the refrigerator until ready to serve. NET: 1 9-inch cake (8 to 10 servings).

GÂTEAU DE MERINGUE AUX FRAISES

Strawberry Meringue Cake

This luscious meringue cake can be made several days in advance, as it keeps well.

8 egg whites
22 tablespoons (1¼ cups plus 2 tablespoons) granulated sugar

FILLING
2 cups heavy cream
6 tablespoons confectioners sugar

| 3 tablespoons Cognac or good brandy | 3 cups large fresh ripe strawberries, hulled |
| 3/4 cup red currant jelly | 1/4 cup Kirsch (cherry brandy) |

Preheat the oven to 200°. Beat 6 egg whites in a mixer until they nearly hold their shape. Add slowly 1 cup granulated sugar and continue beating until the egg whites are stiff. Fill a pastry bag, fitted with a #5 star tube (medium size), with the stiffly beaten egg whites. Brush a baking sheet with vegetable oil, cover with wax paper, and brush it again with vegetable oil. Pipe out half-egg shapes of meringue (oval-shaped mounds). Sprinkle them with a little more granulated sugar, and bake until firm to the touch. Then cool them at room temperature and remove them from the wax paper.

Clean the mixer bowl. Put the remaining 2 egg whites in it and proceed as with the others, slowly adding 6 tablespoons granulated sugar. Brush another baking sheet with vegetable oil, line it with wax paper, and oil again. On this wax paper mark a circle 8 inches in diameter (use a lid or plate of that size as a guide). Spread a thin layer of meringue to cover the circled area. Then build a crown of little meringues around the outside edge of the circle of meringue. To do this, stick the little cooked oval-shaped meringues together, using some of the remaining uncooked meringue as a mortar to stick them together. Fill the center of the crown with the remaining oval-shaped meringues, including broken ones. Decorate around the top of the crown with more uncooked meringue piped through the pastry tube. Sprinkle the crown with a little granulated sugar and bake it 45 minutes. Then let it cool at room temperature.

FILLING. Whip the heavy cream in a metal bowl over a bowl of ice. When it just begins to hold its shape, add the confectioners sugar and brandy. Continue beating until the cream is stiff. Put it in the refrigerator until ready to use. Put the jelly in a little pan with the cherry brandy and melt it over low heat. Pour it through a fine wire strainer and cool it. Pour the currant jelly sauce over the hulled strawberries, reserving a few perfect strawberries for decoration. Put about three-quarters of the whipped cream in the center of the meringue crown on the little scrap meringues, and put the strawberries on the whipped cream. Decorate the top with rosettes of whipped cream (piped through a pastry bag with a #8 or #9 star tube) and the reserved strawberries. NET: 8 servings.

The most beautiful sponge cake! This cake is in perfect balance because all the primary ingredients are weighed.

GÂTEAU MILANAISE

The weight of 4 eggs in granulated sugar	The weight of 1 egg in potato flour
The weight of 1 egg in all-purpose flour	4 eggs plus 2 egg yolks
	2 egg whites

Grated rind of 1 lemon
1/4 cup dried currants

Confectioners sugar

Preheat the oven to 350°. Butter a 9-inch springform cake pan and dust it lightly with flour. Put the eggs and egg yolks in a mixer bowl. Add the sugar and the two flours and beat them 15 minutes. Beat the egg whites to soft peaks in a separate bowl with a wire whisk. Using a rubber scraper, fold the egg whites, lemon rind, and currants into the first mixture. (The final mixture should be smooth and light, with no lumps of egg white.) Put the mixture into the springform mold and bake 45 to 50 minutes. When baked, put the cake (still in the pan) upside down on a cake rack and let it cool. Then turn it out of the pan. Place a stencil or the round wire cake rack on the cake. Sprinkle confectioners sugar liberally on the top. Transfer the cake to a cake plate and serve when desired. (This cake is never frosted.) NET: 1 9-inch cake, 6 to 8 servings.

MILLE-FEUILLE

Thousand-Leaf Cake

Sandwiched with apple purée and vanilla cream.

MILLE-FEUILLE DOUGH
1 2/3 cups all-purpose flour
16 tablespoons cold sweet
   butter
4 tablespoons ice water
A little granulated sugar

APPLE PURÉE
1 1/2 cups canned applesauce

VANILLA CREAM
2 egg yolks
1 1/2 tablespoons sweet butter
3/4 tablespoon potato flour
1 cup heavy cream

2 tablespoons granulated sugar
1 teaspoon vanilla extract

ICING
1 cup confectioners sugar
1 1/2 tablespoons water
1/2 tablespoon lemon juice

GARNISH
Candied orange peel, cut in
   fine strips
Shredded almonds
1 cup heavy cream, whipped
   with 1 teaspoon confectioners
   sugar

MILLE-FEUILLE (THOUSAND-LEAF) PASTRY. Sift the flour on a pastry board or slab. Cut in the butter, using two knives or a pastry blender, or work it together with the fingertips. Transfer it to a bowl, and gradually work in the ice water, using a wooden spoon, until the dough is smooth. Cover the bowl with plastic wrap and chill it at least 30 minutes in the refrigerator.

Preheat the oven to 450°. When the dough is chilled, divide it into 6 or 7 portions. Put each piece of dough between sheets of wax paper and roll out the dough very, very thin. Peel off the top papers and cut the dough into circles 8 inches in diameter or in uniform rectangles. Prick the dough all over, gently, with a fork. Put the pieces of dough (with wax paper underneath) on baking sheets. Brush them with ice water, sprinkle with granulated sugar, and bake 6 to 8 minutes, until the pastry is golden brown. Let it cool on the wax paper at room temperature. When it is cold, peel off the papers.

VANILLA CREAM FILLING. Heat water in the bottom of a double boiler to a simmer. Off the heat, stir together in the top the egg yolks, butter, potato flour, heavy cream, and sugar. Cook the mixture over the simmering water, stirring constantly, until it is smooth and thick. Then again off the heat, add the vanilla extract, and beat the mixture occasionally until it is cold.

ICING. Put the confectioners sugar, water, and lemon juice in a bowl and stir until smooth.

Build up the pastry in layers, spreading the bottom layer with applesauce, the next with vanilla cream, and so on alternately with these fillings until all of the layers of pastry are used. Cover the top of the cake with icing. Garnish the top and sides of the cake with thin pieces of candied orange peel, shredded almonds, and rosettes of whipped cream, piped from a pastry bag with a #6 or #7 star tube. Serve immediately or chill. NET: 1 8-inch cake (6 to 8 servings).

This is a very nice sponge cake with an unusual butter cream icing.

GÂTEAU PISTACHE

Pistachio Nut Cake

5 eggs (3 whole, 2 separated)
Granulated sugar to equal the
    weight of 4 eggs (use a scale)
All-purpose flour to equal the
    weight of 1 egg
Potato flour to equal the
    weight of 1 egg
Grated rind of 1 lemon
A few whole shelled blanched
    pistachio nuts
Confectioners sugar

PISTACHIO BUTTER CREAM
    FROSTING
3 egg yolks
1¼ cups granulated sugar
¾ cup water
24 tablespoons (¾ pound)
    sweet butter, creamed until
    light and fluffy
½ cup finely chopped shelled
    and blanched pistachio nuts
A few drops green vegetable
    coloring (if necessary)

Preheat the oven to 300°. Grease a 9-inch springform pan with vegetable shortening. Cut a round of wax paper to fit the bottom of the pan, put it in, and grease the whole pan again. Put 3 eggs and 2 egg yolks in a mixer bowl. Add the sugar and both flours, and beat until the mixture is very light and fluffy, about 15 minutes. In a separate bowl, using a wire whisk or rotary beater, beat 2 egg whites to soft peaks. Add the egg whites and lemon rind to the egg yolk mixture and mix carefully but well. Put the mixture in the mold and bake about 45 minutes, until it is fairly firm to the touch. Test with a cake tester; if it comes out clean, the cake is done. Let it cool in the pan a few minutes, then turn it out onto a cake rack.

PISTACHIO BUTTER CREAM FROSTING. Beat the egg yolks in a mixer bowl until they are stiff. Boil the sugar and water in an unlined copper pan until the syrup forms a light thread between the finger and thumb (225°). Slowly pour the hot syrup over the beaten egg yolks, beating all the while. Beat until the mixture is stiff and cold. Then beat in the butter and pistachio nuts. (If at this point the butter cream is not "pistachio green," add a few drops of green vegetable coloring.)

Cover the cake with pistachio butter cream frosting. Sprinkle the whole pistachio nuts on the frosting. Dust with confectioners sugar. NET: 1 9-inch cake (6 to 8 servings).

SALLY LUNN CAKE

Hot Lemon Tea Cake

Sally Lunn was an enterprising young lady who hawked tea cakes through the streets of Bath, England, in the late eighteenth century. The cakes which bear her name are now popularly served at tea in Yorkshire, and there is, perhaps, nothing more satisfying after a long walk on the moors than to come home to a tea of cucumber sandwiches, rich plum cake, and gay Sally Lunns served with tea around a blazing log fire. They were the cakes served for tea in *Wuthering Heights*. For a more simple but interesting interlude, simply serve a few home-baked Sally Lunns with big cups of hot smoky-flavored Lapsang Soochong tea.

8 tablespoons (4 ounces) sweet butter
4 ounces granulated sugar
2 eggs, separated
4 ounces all-purpose flour, sifted
Grated rind of 1 large lemon
1 teaspoon baking powder

LEMON BUTTER FILLING
4 tablespoons sweet butter
1 ounce superfine sugar
2 teaspoons lemon juice
Grated rind of ½ lemon
A little granulated sugar (for topping)

Preheat the oven to 350°. Butter a shallow cake pan 7 inches in diameter and dust it lightly with flour. Put the butter and sugar in the mixer bowl and beat until white and fluffy. Beat in the egg yolks and lemon rind. Beat the egg whites in a separate bowl, with a wire whisk or rotary beater, until they form soft peaks. Fold them into the butter mixture. Gradually stir in the flour, a very little at a time. Sprinkle the baking powder on top, and mix it in. Put the batter in the pan, and bake 30 to 35 minutes, or until the cake just shrinks away from the sides of the pan. When the cake is baked, turn it out of the pan and slice it in half, horizontally, at once.

FILLING. In the mixer, beat the butter and sugar until light and fluffy. Beat in the lemon juice and rind. Quickly sandwich the cake with this filling, reshape it, and sprinkle the top with a little granulated sugar. Serve hot, immediately (don't let it sit, or the lemon butter filling will dissolve). NET: 1 7-inch cake (4 to 6 servings).

This cake is as American as the Fourth of July!

*1 cup raw egg whites (about
   10 large or 12 medium-size
   eggs)
1 cup superfine sugar sifted
   with 1 teaspoon cream of
   tartar
1 cup cake flour (without
   baking powder) sifted with
   ½ cup superfine sugar and
   ½ teaspoon salt*

*1 teaspoon vanilla extract
2 cups fresh ripe strawberries,
   hulled
¾ cup red currant jelly*

WHIPPED CREAM
*3 cups heavy cream
3 tablespoons confectioners
   sugar
2 tablespoons vanilla extract*

Preheat the oven to 350°. Have ready an unbuttered angel food cake pan. Beat the egg whites in a mixer to soft peaks. Slowly add the sifted sugar and cream of tartar, beating all the time, and continue to beat until stiff. Remove the egg whites from the mixer and fold in the sifted flour, sugar, and salt, using a large rubber scraper. (Don't break down the egg whites too much. Tip the bowl each time you stir.) Carefully add the vanilla flavoring. Put the cake mixture in the tin. Press it down with the flat side of the rubber scraper so that there are no air holes. Make tiny indentations in the top so the cake will rise evenly. Bake it 1 hour. Turn it upside down on a cake rack (still in the pan) and let it cool thoroughly. Then carefully remove it from the pan.

WHIPPED CREAM. Put the heavy cream in a large metal bowl over a bowl of ice and beat it with a large whisk until it begins to thicken. Then add the confectioners sugar and vanilla, and beat until the cream is stiff.

Place the cake on a serving platter. Reserve about 6 perfect strawberries for decoration, cut the rest in half, mix them with the jelly, and fill the well in the cake with them. Cover the whole cake with whipped cream, reserving for decoration a little that you put in a pastry bag with a star tube (#4 or #5). Pipe rosettes around the edge of the cake. Decorate the top of the cake with the reserved strawberries dipped in the jelly. When the cake is thus assembled, it should be served immediately. NET: 8 servings.

This is similar to a vacherin, which is layers of baked meringue, but I think the use of a macaroon-type layer with ground nuts, enriched with butter, is a little more unusual and less sweet. Peaches or pears may be substituted for the strawberries.

MACAROON LAYERS
   *(weigh the first five ingredi-
   ents for perfect balance)*
7 ounces superfine sugar

*3 ounces all-purpose flour
3 ounces ground blanched
   almonds or filberts
2 ounces cool melted sweet*

*Macaroon Layer Cake
Sandwiched with Fresh
Strawberries and
Whipped Cream*

butter
4 egg whites
3 tablespoons cool melted sweet
butter (for baking sheets)
Flour (for baking sheets)

WHIPPED CREAM AND STRAWBERRY
FILLING
2 cups heavy cream
Scraping of half a vanilla bean
3 tablespoons confectioners
sugar

3 egg whites
2 cups cleaned fresh strawberries, sliced

GARNISH
A little confectioners sugar (for
dusting top of cake)
Whole perfect fresh strawberries, or chocolate rounds
and cornucopias as in
Marquise Alice aux Fraises
(page 814)

Preheat the oven to 350°. Have ready three baking sheets brushed
with 3 tablespoons sweet butter and dusted lightly with flour. With
the tip of the finger, using an 8-inch plate or lid as a guide, mark a
circle 8 inches in diameter in the middle of each pan. Sift the flour
and superfine sugar together several times. Beat the egg whites to
soft peaks. Sprinkle the sifted sugar and flour mixture on the beaten
egg whites and fold it in, using a rubber scraper. Sprinkle the ground
nuts over the mixture and fold them in lightly. Dribble the sweet
butter over the mixture and fold it in. Divide the mixture evenly into
the circles marked on the baking sheets. With a rubber scraper,
spread the mixture evenly within each circle. Bake each layer individually about 15 minutes, until it is a lovely golden brown all over.
When a layer is removed from the oven, let it sit for a minute, then
loosen it from the pan carefully with a spatula. When the layer has
been removed from the baking sheet, put the same dish or lid on
top (lightly!) and trim the sides evenly. Cool all the layers at room
temperature.

WHIPPED CREAM STRAWBERRY FILLING. Put the heavy cream in a large
metal bowl over a bowl of crushed ice. Beat it with a large whisk
until it begins to thicken. Add the vanilla bean scraping and confectioners sugar. Continue beating until the cream holds its shape. Beat
the egg whites to soft peaks and fold them into the whipped cream.
(Set aside 2 cups of this mixture for garnish.) Drain the sliced strawberries of any liquid, then fold them into the mixture.

Sandwich the macaroon layers with the strawberry mixture. Do
not spread any strawberry mixture on the top layer. Place a stencil or
round wire cake rack on the top layer and sprinkle it with confectioners sugar. Coat the sides of the cake with the reserved whipped
cream and pipe a few rosettes on the top with a pastry bag and #7
star tube. Place a whole fresh strawberry on each rosette. Or use
the alternate chocolate garnish, chocolate rounds and cornucopias as
for Marquise Alice aux Fraises, and decorate this cake like the
Marquise Alice. NET: 6 servings.

CRÊPES AND BEIGNETS

Crêpes can be prepared and frozen and will hold very well. They should be securely wrapped in plastic film.

With vegetable oil in the batter, crêpes are less likely to stick than with butter. Butter, however, gives a more delicate crêpe.

If you accidentally tear a crêpe, return it to the hot pan, pour a tiny bit of batter on the tear, and let it cook a moment. It will unite the crêpe.

To make crêpes you will need an omelet pan (7-inch base), wad of wax paper, ladle, spatula, and wire cake rack.

CRÊPES

Thin Pancakes

8 tablespoons all-purpose flour
1 egg
1 egg yolk
2 tablespoons vegetable oil or
   cool melted sweet butter

⅛ teaspoon salt
4 tablespoons milk plus about
   ¾ cup milk
Soft salt butter for greasing
   the pan

STEP 1. In a small bowl combine the flour, egg, egg yolk, vegetable oil or melted butter, salt, and 4 tablespoons milk. Beat the mixture with a little wire whisk until very smooth.

STEP 2. Stir in about ¾ cup milk. The batter should be brought to the consistency of light cream — use only as much milk as needed.

STEP 3. Cover the bowl with plastic wrap and put it in the refrigerator to set. You can leave it a minimum of 30 minutes to a maximum of 1 week.

STEP 4. When you are ready to use the crêpe batter, add a little more milk if the mixture is too thick. It should just coat the back of a metal spoon.

STEP 5. Heat the omelet pan. Test the pan with a speck of butter, which should brown the moment it touches the pan. Have the crêpe batter, ladle, soft butter, a wad of wax paper, a spatula, and wire cake rack ready on the adjacent work area.

STEP 6. When the omelet pan tests hot enough, rub it out with a little salt butter, using the wad of wax paper. With the ladle, pour about ½ cup of the crêpe batter into the pan. Tilt the pan around so that a thin layer of batter quickly covers the bottom (there should be no holes or open areas).

STEP 7. When the crêpe is brown on one side, lift it with a spatula and turn it over to brown the other side.

STEP 8. When the second side (sometimes called the "wrong side") is browned, remove it from the pan with the spatula and lay it on the cake rack.

STEP 9. Prepare all of the crêpes in this manner, piling them one on top of the other on the wire rack when they are finished.

NET: 11 to 12 crêpes 6 inches in diameter.

CRÊPES SUZETTE

Crêpes with Orange Butter and Grand Marnier Sauce

Crêpes Suzette means with "orange," and the dessert should not be overwhelmed with brandy. In this composition, I have tried to refine the essence of orange throughout much as a parfumeur seeks to compose a citrus top note in certain fragrances.

Crêpes (page 781); see below for quantity

ORANGE BUTTER
6 tablespoons sweet butter
3 tablespoons superfine sugar
Grated rind of 1 orange
2 tablespoons Grand Marnier

GRAND MARNIER SAUCE
Grated rind of 1 orange
¾ cup granulated sugar
6 lumps sugar
8 tablespoons sweet butter
Juice of 2 oranges
⅓ cup Grand Marnier
Skinned sections of 3 large navel oranges

CRÊPES. Have ready one and one-half times the quantity of the Crêpes recipe (page 781), which will net about 18 6-inch crêpes, to serve 6. Adjust the recipe according to the number of crêpes that will be required.

ORANGE BUTTER. Cream the butter in a mixer. When it is very light and fluffy, add the sugar and beat until well mixed. Continue beating and add the orange rind and Grand Marnier.

Spread a little of this butter on the "wrong" (second) side of each crêpe. Then fold the crêpes into triangles and set them aside.

GRAND MARNIER SAUCE. (This sauce may be made in a sauté pan on the stove, or it may be made in a chafing dish at the table, in which case have the ingredients neatly assembled on an adjacent tray.) Remove the rind of 1 large orange with a potato parer. Cut the rind into very thin shreds crosswise. Rub the lumps of sugar on the grated orange. Use both these oranges plus another to prepare the orange sections. Be very sure that there is no pith left on them. Put into the sauté pan or chafing dish the shredded and grated orange rind and the granulated sugar, lumps of orange-rubbed sugar, butter, orange juice, and Grand Marnier. Stir the mixture over very low heat until the orange rind is translucent, then let it simmer very gently about 5 minutes. Add the skinned orange sections.

Lay the folded crêpes in the pan with the sauce. In a separate little pan, heat a little more Grand Marnier, ignite, and pour it over the crêpes in the large pan. Use a large spoon to serve the individual portions of crêpes and sauce. NET: 6 servings.

CRÊPES FOURRÉES SAUCE ABRICOT

Very Thin Pancakes Layered with Apple Purée, with Apricot Sauce

Crêpes (page 781)

APPLE PURÉE
4 pounds green apples, skinned, cored, and thickly sliced, sprinkled with the juice of 1 lemon

Grated rind of 1 lemon
18 ounces apricot jam, superior quality (1½ 12-ounce jars)
½ teaspoon freshly grated nutmeg
1 cup light brown sugar

APRICOT SAUCE
18 ounces apricot jam, superior
    quality (1½ 12-ounce jars)
Juice of 2 lemons
½ cup superfine sugar

TOPPING
Confectioners sugar
½ cup shredded browned
    almonds

For this dish, have ready 10 to 12 crêpes (page 781).

APPLE PURÉE. Put the sliced apples in a heavy pan with the lemon rind, and cook slowly over low heat until the apples are soft. Continue cooking until most of the liquid has evaporated. Mix in the apricot jam, nutmeg, and brown sugar.

APRICOT SAUCE. Combine the apricot jam, lemon juice, and sugar in a pan. Stir over low heat until well blended. Strain the sauce through a fine wire strainer.

Stack the crêpes one on top of the other, with the apple purée spread between them but not on the top. Dust the top liberally with confectioners sugar, sprinkle with the shredded almonds, and place the assembled crêpes on a shallow serving dish. Pour the apricot sauce around the edge of the dish. This dish may be chilled until serving time. NET: 4 to 6 servings.

CRÊPES MAXIM

*Very Thin Pancakes
Filled with Candied
Fruit Soufflé, with
Sauce Sabayon*

Crêpes (page 781)
2 tablespoons melted sweet
    butter
A little granulated sugar
½ cup coarsely chopped
    browned almonds

CANDIED FRUIT SOUFFLÉ FILLING
3 tablespoons sweet butter
3 tablespoons all-purpose flour
¾ cup milk
6 tablespoons granulated sugar

3 egg yolks
½ cup finely chopped mixed
    candied fruits, soaked in ¼
    cup Cognac
4 egg whites

SABAYON SAUCE
3 egg yolks
¼ cup Cognac
¼ cup Cointreau
6 tablespoons granulated sugar

For this dish, have ready 12 crêpes (page 781).

CANDIED FRUIT SOUFFLÉ FILLING. Melt the butter in a saucepan over low heat. Off the heat, stir in the flour. Pour in the milk and stir over low heat until the mixture comes to a boil. Off the heat, mix in the granulated sugar, egg yolks, and candied fruit with Cognac. Beat the egg whites to soft peaks and fold them into the flour and yolk mixture. NOTE: You may prepare this filling in advance up through adding the candied fruit with Cognac, and finish it when you are ready to fill the crêpes (about 45 minutes before the crêpes are to be served).

Preheat the oven to 350°. Brush a large shallow glass baking platter with the melted butter and dust it with granulated sugar. Put 2 tablespoons of the soufflé filling in the center of the wrong side of each crêpe. Fold each crêpe like a small package, and arrange them on the baking dish. Sprinkle them with the almonds and granulated sugar, and bake 15 to 20 minutes, or until the crêpes are puffed up like small pillows. Make the sauce while they are baking.

SABAYON SAUCE. Put the egg yolks in a bowl with the sugar, Cognac, and Cointreau. Stand the bowl in a shallow pan half filled with hot water over low heat. Beat the egg mixture with a rotary beater until it is very light, thick, and fluffy. NOTE: This sauce should hold up about 15 to 30 minutes.

When the crêpes are baked, remove them from the oven and serve at once with the sauce. NET: 12 crêpes (6 servings).

CRÊPES SOUFFLÉES PRALINÉES

*Very Thin Pancakes
Filled with Praline
Soufflé, with a
Mousseline Sauce*

Crêpes (page 781)
4 tablespoons melted sweet
   butter
Praline powder (from preparation below)
A little confectioners sugar

PRALINE POWDER
1 cup whole blanched almonds
1¼ cups granulated sugar
½ teaspoon cream of tartar

PRALINE SOUFFLÉ FILLING
3 tablespoons sweet butter
4 tablespoons all-purpose flour
Tiny pinch of salt
¾ cup milk

4 egg yolks
4 tablespoons granulated sugar
3 tablespoons Grand Marnier
¾ cup praline powder (from
   preparation above)
6 egg whites

MOUSSELINE SAUCE
1 egg
2 egg yolks
4 tablespoons superfine sugar
Tiny pinch of salt
2 tablespoons Grand Marnier
Praline powder (from preparation above)
4 tablespoons plain whipped
   cream

For this recipe, have ready 12 crêpes (page 781).

PRALINE POWDER. Make the praline powder, using the above quantities, according to the method on page 77. NOTE: This praline powder will keep indefinitely in the refrigerator in a screw-top jar, and can be made well in advance.

PRALINE SOUFFLÉ FILLING. Melt the butter in a saucepan over low heat. Stir in the flour and salt off the heat. Pour in the milk, and stir the mixture over low heat until it comes to a boil. Off the heat, mix in the egg yolks one at a time, the sugar, and the Grand Marnier. Then mix in the praline powder. Beat the egg whites to soft peaks and fold them into the flour and yolk mixture. NOTE: This filling may be prepared in advance up through mixing in the praline powder, and finished when you are ready to fill the crêpes (about 45 minutes before they are to be served).

Preheat the oven to 350°. Have ready a large shallow glass baking dish, brushed with melted sweet butter. Put 2 tablespoons of the soufflé filling in the center of the wrong side of each crêpe. Fold each crêpe like a small package, and arrange them on the baking dish. Brush the crêpes with melted sweet butter, sprinkle half the remaining praline powder over them, and bake 25 minutes, or until the crêpes are puffed up like small pillows. While they are baking, prepare the sauce.

MOUSSELINE SAUCE. Put the egg and egg yolks in a small bowl with the sugar and salt. Stand the bowl in a shallow pan half filled with hot water over low heat. Beat the mixture with a rotary beater until it holds its shape. Beat in the Grand Marnier. Remove the bowl from the hot water and fold in the rest of the praline powder and the whipped cream.

When the crêpes are baked, dust them with a little confectioners sugar and serve them immediately, with the sauce in a separate bowl. NET: 12 crêpes (6 servings).

Beignets are made with very light deep-fried cream puff paste.

BEIGNETS SOUFFLÉS AUX FRAMBOISES NOIRES OU À LA SAUCE D'ABRICOT

Very Light Fritters with Black Raspberry Sauce or Apricot Sauce

BEIGNET DOUGH
½ cup cold water
Pinch of salt
4 tablespoons sweet butter, cut in little pieces
½ cup all-purpose flour
2 small eggs or 1½ large eggs
2 egg whites
1 teaspoon sugar
½ teaspoon baking powder
Vegetable oil for deep-fryer
A little confectioners sugar

BLACK RASPBERRY SAUCE
1 jar (12 ounces) seedless

black raspberry jam
(superior quality)
3 teaspoons lemon juice
5 tablespoons Framboise
(raspberry brandy)

APRICOT SAUCE
1½ jars (18 ounces) apricot jam
(superior quality)
Juice of 1 lemon
Grated rind of 1 lemon
½ cup granulated sugar
⅓ cup Sauternes (sweet white wine)

Put the cold water in a small heavy pan with the salt and butter. Bring the water to a boil as the butter melts. When it is boiling, throw in the flour. Stir the paste over low heat until smooth. Put it in the mixer bowl and beat in the eggs one by one, then continue to beat until the mixture is shiny. In a separate bowl beat the egg whites to soft peaks. Remove the flour mixture from the mixer, sprinkle it with sugar and baking powder, fold them in, then fold in the beaten egg whites.

Chill the dough in the refrigerator at least 30 minutes, or leave it there until you are ready to serve the beignets. (Beignets must be fried immediately before serving and should always be eaten piping hot. If left to wait after cooking, they may deflate.) While the dough is chilling, make the sauce.

BLACK RASPBERRY SAUCE. Combine the jam, lemon juice, and 4 tablespoons Framboise in a saucepan. Stir over very low heat until the jam melts. Just before serving, flame the sauce with another tablespoon of Framboise.

APRICOT SAUCE. Combine the ingredients in a saucepan and stir over low heat until the jam melts. Simmer the sauce 15 minutes. Rub it through a fine wire strainer. (This sauce may be served either hot or cold.)

To cook the beignets, half fill a deep-fryer with vegetable oil and heat it to 375°. Drop teaspoonfuls of the dough into the hot fat and let them cook until golden brown on both sides and well puffed. (When one side is cooked, they will flip over in the hot fat by themselves.) Drain them on paper towels. To serve, pile them in a mound on a flat serving plate and sprinkle with confectioners sugar. Serve immediately with a separate bowl of sauce. NET: 4 servings.

BEIGNETS SOUFFLÉS À LA ROYALE

Very Light Fritters Stuffed with Candied Fruits, with Mousseline Sauce

Beignet dough (page 785)

MOUSSELINE SAUCE
1 egg
2 egg yolks
4 tablespoons superfine sugar
Tiny pinch of salt
2 tablespoons light rum
3 tablespoons whipped cream
Vegetable oil for deep-fryer
Confectioners sugar

CANDIED FRUIT FILLING
1 egg
1 egg yolk
Tiny pinch of salt
3 tablespoons all-purpose flour
3 tablespoons granulated sugar
½ cup milk
2 tablespoons heavy cream
4 tablespoons finely chopped mixed candied fruits (such as cherries, pineapple, angelica, lemon and orange peel), soaked at least 15 minutes in 2 tablespoons light rum

Prepare the beignet dough (page 785). After the beaten egg whites have been added, spread the dough out on a plate and chill it thoroughly at least 30 minutes.

CANDIED FRUIT FILLING. Put the egg and egg yolk in a small bowl with the pinch of salt and stir until well blended. Mix in the flour and sugar and beat well with a wire whisk. Add the milk, transfer the mixture to a saucepan, and stir over moderate heat until it is thick. Off the heat, add the candied fruits with the rum in which they have been soaking. Stir in the heavy cream, and spread this mixture out on a plate to chill thoroughly.

About 15 to 20 minutes before you are ready to serve, prepare the sauce and cook the beignets, as follows.

MOUSSELINE SAUCE. Put the egg and egg yolk in a small bowl with the sugar, salt, and rum. Mix until blended. Stand the bowl in a shallow pan of hot water over low heat, and beat with a rotary beater until it is thick enough to hold its shape. Remove it from the water and fold the whipped cream into the sauce.

Half-fill a deep-fryer with vegetable oil and heat it to 375°. Take 1 tablespoon of the beignet dough, and with the back of a wet teaspoon make an indentation in it. Put a tiny coffee spoon of the candied fruit filling in the hollow. Completely cover the filling with a little more mixture. Carefully drop the stuffed beignet into the hot fat. Cook only

5 or 6 stuffed beignets at a time, and leave them in the hot oil until they are well puffed out and golden brown all over. Remove them with a slotted spoon and gently place them on paper towels to drain.

To serve, arrange a cluster of the stuffed beignets on a napkin on a serving plate, sprinkle liberally with confectioners sugar, and serve the mousseline sauce in a separate bowl. NET: 4 servings.

SOUFFLÉS

There is no witchcraft involved in soufflé making. So long as you follow a few simple guides, your soufflés will come up to your expectations — barring the usual catastrophic limitation clause, "riots, strikes, and acts of God." Ever since the great soufflé disaster on one of my television shows, I have felt compelled to thus qualify the guaranteed success of soufflé making. What happened to me . . .

As with all television programs, demonstration timing must be tight, and three soufflés were at different stages of preparation for this particular show. The mixing of the soufflé went smoothly, the soufflé went into the oven with great correctness, and then the camera zoomed in for a closeup of the baked wonder which was to be removed from the oven. With a performer's élan, I grandly removed the soufflé from the oven. It did have a lovely golden brown top, and had beautifully risen. I gently removed the paper collar — whereupon the soufflé completely collapsed in full camera view. I mustered all my English aplomb to finish the show, and thought my career was finished. Someone had raised the oven thermostat. A bad prank — but it turned out to be one of the great experiences of my life. A deluge of mail poured in for weeks from viewers delighted to know that Dione Lucas could make a mistake!

Advice on Baking Soufflés

THE PREPARED SOUFFLÉ DISH. (1) Brush the inside of the soufflé dish with melted sweet butter. Then outfit the dish with a paper collar, as follows. (2) Tear off a sheet of wax paper that will encircle your soufflé dish at least 1½ times. Fold it in half lengthwise. Brush the whole folded length on one side with melted butter. (3) Wrap the folded wax paper around the outside of the soufflé dish, with its buttered side touching the side of the dish; the wax paper collar should rise 3 to 4 inches above the top of the dish. (4) Tie a piece of kitchen string around the paper and dish to hold the collar on.

THE WATER BATH (BAIN-MARIE). Have ready a shallow roasting pan to set the filled soufflé dish in when you are ready to bake it. The roasting pan should be half filled with hot water. The water bath with the filled soufflé dish in it is placed in the properly preheated oven to bake the soufflé.

BAKING THE SOUFFLÉ. If a soufflé cooks too quickly, it will rise well but collapse when removed from the oven. Therefore, it is important that the soufflé cook as it rises. Cooked in that way, the soufflé will stand up about 30 minutes. An oven temperature between 325° and 350° is ideal for baking soufflés. (This section does include a couple of recipes for soufflés baked at 375°, which indicates that the soufflé can be baked in a slightly shorter time but must be served instantly; it will stand up only about 10 to 15 minutes.)

Test the soufflé with a cake tester to determine if it is properly baked. The tester should come out dry.

Generally, dessert soufflés should bake at a higher temperature than savory soufflés, as the dessert mixtures tend to be more liquid.

TO SERVE THE SOUFFLÉ. (1) Have the sauce ready, if one is to be served. (2) Have your individual plates and silver ready. (3) Carefully remove the soufflé and water bath from the oven, then set the soufflé dish on a flat platter or large plate. (4) Dust the top with a little confectioners sugar or Parmesan cheese, if called for in the recipe. (5) Carefully remove the string tie and very gently peel away the paper collar. (6) Serve the soufflé quickly! Each serving should include a portion of the top crust and some of the creamy inside. Spoon the sauce on the side.

If you want to be very classic, wrap a white linen napkin around the soufflé after the paper collar is off. Fasten it securely with a small straight pin. But this is not really necessary; the main thing is to get the soufflé "to the church on time."

SOUFFLÉ AUX ABRICOTS

Hot Apricot Soufflé

Please read Advice on Baking Soufflés (page 787).

Granulated sugar (for dusting)
3 tablespoons sweet butter
4 tablespoons all-purpose flour
1 cup milk
4 egg yolks
7 egg whites
2 teaspoons lemon juice

¾ cup apricot jam (superior quality) or 1 cup strained cooked sweetened apricot pulp
Confectioners sugar (for dusting)

Preheat the oven to 350°. Brush a #7 (1½-quart) soufflé dish with butter. Fold a long piece of wax paper in half lengthwise. Butter it, wrap it around the soufflé dish, and tie a string around it (the collar should rise at least 3 inches above the rim of the dish). Sprinkle the dish generously inside with granulated sugar, so that the dish and collar are well coated. Have ready a shallow roasting pan and hot water.

Melt the butter in a small heavy pan. Off the heat, stir in the flour. Then stir in the milk. Stir the mixture over low heat until it just comes to a boil. Off the heat, add the lemon juice and apricot jam or pulp. Then mix in the egg yolks one at a time and set the apricot sauce aside. Put the egg whites in a large metal bowl. Beat them vigorously with a large wire whisk until they are stiff enough to stay in the bowl held upside down. Pour the apricot sauce on the egg whites and fold it in very carefully with a rubber scraper. Spoon the mixture into the soufflé dish, stand the dish in the roasting pan, and half fill the pan with hot water. Set the whole assembly on the bottom shelf of the oven and bake 1 hour, until the soufflé is just firm to the touch. (Do not open the oven door until it has been in 45 minutes.) When it is cooked, remove the string, loosen the paper with a thin-bladed knife, peel the paper off, dust the soufflé heavily with confectioners sugar, and serve at once. NET: 4 servings.

Please read Advice on Baking Soufflés (page 787).

SOUFFLÉ AU CAFÉ, SAUCE SABAYON

Hot Coffee Soufflé with Sabayon Sauce

Granulated sugar (for dusting)
3 tablespoons sweet butter
4 tablespoons all-purpose flour
Tiny pinch of salt
1 cup light cream
4 tablespoons granulated sugar
2 tablespoons instant coffee
  dissolved in 2 tablespoons
  hot water
2 tablespoons Cognac

4 egg yolks
7 egg whites
Confectioners sugar (for
  dusting)

SABAYON SAUCE
1 egg
2 egg yolks
4 tablespoons superfine sugar
2 tablespoons Cognac

Preheat the oven to 375°. Prepare a #6 (1-quart) soufflé dish (page 787). Sprinkle the inside of the buttered and collared dish generously with granulated sugar, so that the inside of the dish and the collar are well-coated. Have ready a shallow roasting pan and hot water.

Melt the butter in a small heavy pan. Off the heat, stir in the flour, then the salt, then the cream. Stir over low heat until the mixture thickens and is very smooth. Off the heat, stir in the sugar, coffee, Cognac, and (one at a time) the egg yolks. Set the coffee sauce aside. Beat the egg whites vigorously in a large metal bowl with a large wire whisk until they are stiff enough to stay in the bowl held upside down. Distribute the coffee sauce evenly over the beaten whites and very carefully fold it in, using a rubber scraper. Spoon the mixture into the soufflé dish, stand the dish in the roasting pan, and half fill the pan with hot water. Set the whole assembly on the bottom shelf of the oven and bake 1 hour, or until a cake tester comes out dry.

SABAYON SAUCE. Put the egg and egg yolks in a small bowl and mix with the sugar and Cognac. Stand the bowl in a shallow pan half filled with hot water over moderate heat. Beat with a rotary beater until it holds its shape.

When the soufflé is out of the oven, dust the top with sifted confectioners sugar, carefully remove the paper collar, and serve immediately with the sabayon sauce. NET: 4 servings.

SOUFFLÉ AU CHOCOLAT, SAUCE VANILLE

Hot Chocolate Soufflé
with Cold Vanilla Sauce

Please read Advice on Baking Soufflés (page 787). This soufflé can also be served with a warm sabayon sauce (page 67). For chocolate lovers, this is a very chocolaty soufflé.

Granulated sugar (for dusting)
1 cup light cream
Pod of 1 vanilla bean (reserve the scraping for the sauce)
3 tablespoons sweet butter
4 tablespoons all-purpose flour
6 ounces dark sweet chocolate
4 tablespoons rum or Cognac
3 tablespoons superfine sugar, and more for sprinkling the soufflé
4 egg yolks

7 egg whites
Confectioners sugar (for dusting)

VANILLA SAUCE
4 egg yolks
4 tablespoons superfine sugar
Scraping of 1 vanilla bean
1¼ cups light cream
Pod of 1 vanilla bean (same pod as for soufflé)
1 cup heavy cream, whipped

Make the vanilla sauce first.

VANILLA SAUCE. Beat the egg yolks in a mixer until very light and fluffy. Add the sugar and beat again until thick, light, and fluffy. Mix in the vanilla bean scraping. Put the light cream in a little pan with the vanilla pod, bring to a boil, and remove from the heat. Remove (and reserve) the pod. Pour the hot cream slowly over the yolk mixture in the mixer, beating all the time. Transfer the sauce to a tin-lined copper pan over low heat, and cook until the sauce coats the back of a metal spoon, stirring all the time. Remove it from the heat, cool it a little, and fold in the whipped cream. Chill the sauce thoroughly.

Preheat the oven to 375°. Prepare a #6 (1-quart) soufflé dish (page 787). Sprinkle the dish generously with granulated sugar, so that the inside of the dish and the collar are well coated. Have ready a shallow roasting pan and hot water.

Put the light cream in a saucepan with the vanilla bean pod, bring the cream to a boil, and remove it from the heat. Melt the butter in a small heavy pan. Off the heat, stir in the flour, then the scalded cream. Stir the mixture over low heat until it just comes to a boil (it must not really boil). Remove the pan from the heat. Cut the chocolate into little pieces and put them into a small heavy pan with the rum or Cognac. Stir over very low heat until the chocolate is just dissolved and quite smooth. Mix the dissolved chocolate into the sauce. Add the sugar. Stir in the egg yolks, one at a time. Cover this chocolate sauce with plastic wrap and set it aside. Beat the egg whites vigorously in a large metal bowl with a large wire whisk until they are stiff enough to stay in the bowl held upside down. Put the chocolate sauce over the egg whites and fold it in carefully with a rubber scraper. Spoon the mixture into the soufflé dish and sprinkle with superfine sugar. Stand the dish in the roasting pan and half fill the pan with hot water. Set the whole assembly on the bottom shelf of the oven and bake about 50 minutes, or until a cake tester comes out dry.

Remove the soufflé from the oven, dust the top with sifted confectioners sugar, remove the paper collar, and serve immediately with the vanilla sauce. (If the soufflé is properly cooked, it should stand up about 10 to 15 minutes.) NET: 4 servings.

Please read Advice on Baking Soufflés (page 787). This soufflé may be served with a lemon sabayon sauce (Sabayon Sauce II, page 67, with Kirsch and the finely grated rind of a lemon added).

Granulated sugar
A few dry breadcrumbs (page
  69)
3 tablespoons sweet butter
4 tablespoons all-purpose flour
Tiny pinch of salt
1 cup milk

Grated rind of 2 lemons
Juice of 2 lemons
½ cup superfine sugar
4 egg yolks
7 egg whites
Confectioners sugar

SOUFFLÉ AU CITRON

Fresh Lemon Soufflé

Preheat the oven to 350°. Prepare a #6 (1-quart) soufflé dish (page 787). Sprinkle the dish generously with a mixture of granulated sugar and dry breadcrumbs, so that the inside of the dish and the collar are well coated. Have ready a shallow roasting pan and some hot water.

Melt the butter in a small heavy pan. Off the heat, stir in the flour, then the salt, then the milk. Stir the mixture over low heat until it just comes to a boil. Off the heat, add the lemon rind and juice. Mix in the sugar, and stir in the egg yolks one at a time. Beat the egg whites vigorously in a metal bowl with a large wire whisk until they are stiff enough to stay in the bowl held upside down. Distribute the lemon sauce over the egg whites and fold it in gently with a rubber scraper. Spoon the mixture into the soufflé dish and sprinkle it with a little confectioners sugar. Stand the dish in the roasting pan and half fill the pan with hot water. Set the whole assembly on the bottom shelf of the oven and bake 1 hour, or until a cake tester comes out dry. (Do not open the oven door until the soufflé has been in at least 40 minutes, and then only for a fleeting moment.)

When the soufflé is cooked, remove the string, loosen the paper with a thin-bladed knife, and peel it off. Dust the top heavily with confectioners sugar and serve at once. NET: 4 servings.

Please read Advice on Baking Soufflés (page 787). This sauce may be prepared in advance and served chilled, instead of being prepared while the soufflé is baking and served warm.

SOUFFLÉ AUX FRAISES, SAUCE MOUSSELINE

Hot Fresh Strawberry Soufflé with Hot Mousseline Sauce

Granulated sugar
1 cup cleaned and hulled fresh
  strawberries
⅓ cup Framboise (raspberry

brandy)
3 tablespoons sweet butter
4 tablespoons all-purpose flour
1 cup milk

½ cup superfine sugar
4 egg yolks
7 egg whites
Confectioners sugar

MOUSSELINE SAUCE
1 egg

2 egg yolks
4 tablespoons superfine sugar
Tiny pinch of salt
2 tablespoons Framboise
  (raspberry brandy)
1 cup heavy cream, whipped

Preheat the oven to 350°. Prepare a #7 (1½-quart) soufflé dish (page 787). Sprinkle the dish generously with granulated sugar, so that the inside of the dish and collar are well coated. Have ready a shallow roasting pan and hot water.

Slice the strawberries thinly, and sprinkle them with the Framboise. Melt the butter in a small heavy pan. Off the heat, stir in the flour, then stir in the milk. Stir the mixture over low heat until it just comes to a boil. Off the heat, add the sugar and the sliced strawberries with the brandy. Mix in the egg yolks one at a time, and set the strawberry sauce aside. Beat the egg whites vigorously in a large metal bowl with a large wire whisk until they are stiff enough to stay in the bowl held upside down. Pour the strawberry sauce over the egg whites and fold it in very carefully with a rubber scraper. Spoon the mixture into the soufflé dish, stand the dish in the roasting pan, and half fill the pan with hot water. Set the whole assembly on the bottom shelf of the oven and bake 1 hour and 15 minutes, until it is just firm to the touch. (Do not open the oven door until the soufflé has been in 45 minutes.)

MOUSSELINE SAUCE. Put the egg and egg yolks in a small bowl. Add the sugar, and raspberry brandy, and mix well. Stand the bowl in a shallow pan half filled with hot water over moderate heat, and beat the mixture with a rotary beater until it holds its shape. Remove the bowl from the water and fold in the whipped cream (this can be done when the egg mixture is still warm).

When the soufflé is cooked, remove the string, loosen the paper with a thin-bladed knife, and peel it off. Dust the soufflé heavily with confectioners sugar and serve at once, with a separate bowl of mousseline sauce. NET: 4 servings.

SOUFFLÉ AU GRAND MARNIER

Grand Marnier Soufflé with Grand Marnier Sauce

Please read Advice on Baking Soufflés (page 787).

Granulated sugar
3 tablespoons sweet butter
4 tablespoons all-purpose flour
Tiny pinch of salt
1 cup light cream
4 tablespoons granulated sugar
⅓ cup Grand Marnier
4 egg yolks
Optional: 2 slices glazed pine-

apple, cut into fine dice
7 egg whites
Confectioners sugar

GRAND MARNIER SAUCE
1 egg
2 egg yolks
4 tablespoons superfine sugar
2 tablespoons Grand Marnier

Preheat the oven to 375°. Prepare a #6 (1-quart) soufflé dish (page 787). Sprinkle the dish generously with granulated sugar, so that the inside of the dish and collar are well coated. Have ready a shallow roasting pan and hot water.

Melt the butter in a small heavy pan. Off the heat, stir in the flour, then the salt, then the cream. Stir the mixture over low heat until it thickens and is very smooth. Off the heat, stir in the sugar, Grand Marnier, and, one at a time, the egg yolks. (Also stir in the pineapple if it is being used.) Beat the egg whites vigorously in a metal bowl with a large wire whisk until they are stiff enough to stay in the bowl held upside down. Distribute the sauce evenly over the beaten egg whites and very carefully fold it in, using a rubber scraper. Spoon the mixture into the soufflé dish. Stand the dish in the roasting pan and half fill the pan with hot water. Set the whole assembly on the bottom shelf of the oven and bake 1 hour, or until a cake tester comes out dry.

GRAND MARNIER SAUCE. Combine the egg, egg yolks, sugar, and Grand Marnier in a small bowl. Stand the bowl in a shallow pan half filled with hot water over moderate heat, and beat the mixture with a rotary beater until it holds its shape.

When the soufflé is cooked, dust the top with sifted confectioners sugar, carefully remove the paper collar, and serve immediately. Spoon a little of the Grand Marnier sauce over each serving. NET: 4 servings.

SOUFFLÉ ROTHSCHILD

Hot Soufflé with Mixed Candied Fruits, with Mousseline Sauce

Please read Advice on Baking Soufflés (page 787). This sauce may be prepared in advance and served chilled, rather than being prepared while the soufflé is baking and served warm.

Granulated sugar (for dusting)
½ cup finely chopped mixed candied fruits (an assortment of glacé cherries, candied orange, lime, or lemon peel, candied pineapple, melon, or angelica)
½ cup light rum or, ideally, Danziger Goldwasser (a German wine with flecks of gold in it)
3 tablespoons sweet butter
4 tablespoons all-purpose flour
Tiny pinch of salt
1 cup milk
Half a bay leaf

½ cup sour cream
5 tablespoons granulated sugar
5 egg yolks
7 egg whites
Confectioners sugar (for dusting)

MOUSSELINE SAUCE
1 egg
2 egg yolks
Grated rind of 1 lemon
Grated rind of 1 orange
5 tablespoons superfine sugar
3 tablespoons light rum
1 cup heavy cream, whipped

Preheat the oven to 325°. Prepare a #7 (1½-quart) soufflé dish (page 787). Sprinkle the dish generously with granulated sugar, so that the inside of the dish and collar are well coated. Have ready a shallow roasting pan and hot water.

Put the candied fruits in a little bowl. Warm the rum or Danziger Goldwasser and pour it over them. Stir them a little and let them soak at least half an hour. Put the milk in a pan with the bay leaf half, bring it to a boil, and strain it. Melt the butter in a small heavy pan. Off the heat, stir in the flour. Slowly blend the scalded milk into the flour mixture, and stir over low heat until it just comes to a boil. Mix in the sour cream, sugar, egg yolks (one by one), and last, the fruits and rum. Beat the egg whites vigorously in a metal bowl with a large wire whisk until they are stiff enough to stay in the bowl held upside down. Distribute the candied fruit sauce evenly over the egg whites, and fold it in, using a rubber scraper. Spoon the mixture into the soufflé dish, sprinkle with confectioners sugar, stand the dish in the roasting pan, and half fill the pan with hot water. Set the whole assembly on the bottom shelf of the oven and bake 1½ hours, or until the risen soufflé is just firm to the touch. While it is baking, make the sauce.

MOUSSELINE SAUCE. Combine the egg and egg yolks in a bowl with the lemon and orange rind, sugar, and rum, and mix well. Stand the bowl in a shallow pan half filled with hot water over moderate heat. Beat with a rotary beater until the mixture holds its shape. Remove the pan from the water and fold in the whipped cream.

When the soufflé is baked, dust the top with sifted confectioners sugar, remove the paper collar, and serve immediately. Spoon a little of the mousseline sauce over each serving. NET: 4 to 6 servings.

SOUFFLÉ À L'ORANGE, SAUCE SABAYON

Fresh Orange Soufflé with Sabayon Sauce

Please read Advice on Baking Soufflés (page 787).

3 tablespoons sweet butter
4 tablespoons all-purpose flour
Tiny pinch of salt
¾ cup milk
5 tablespoons granulated sugar
Grated rind and juice of 1
   large navel orange
4 egg yolks
7 egg whites

A little confectioners sugar

ORANGE SABAYON SAUCE
4 egg yolks
6 tablespoons superfine sugar
¼ cup dry sherry
½ teaspoon arrowroot
Grated rind of 1 large navel
   orange

Preheat the oven to 350°. Prepare a #6 (1-quart) soufflé dish, but do not butter it or dust it with sugar. Have ready a shallow roasting pan half filled with hot water.

Melt the butter in a saucepan over low heat, without browning it. Off the heat, add the flour and salt. Pour in the milk, and stir the mixture over low heat until it just comes to a boil. Off the heat, mix in the sugar and the orange juice and rind. Beat the egg yolks until light and fluffy and mix them into the flour mixture. Beat the egg whites vigorously in a metal bowl with a large wire whisk until they are stiff enough to stay in the bowl when you turn it upside down.

Pour the egg yolk mixture over the whites and fold it in with a large rubber scraper. Spoon the mixture into the soufflé dish, place the dish in the roasting pan with the hot water, put the whole assembly in the oven, and bake the soufflé 1 hour, or until a cake tester comes out dry. While it is baking, make the sauce.

ORANGE SABAYON SAUCE. In a small bowl, beat all the ingredients with a rotary beater. Stand the bowl in a shallow pan half filled with hot water over low heat. Continue beating with the rotary beater until the sauce is very thick.

Remove the soufflé from the oven as soon as it is baked, and carefully peel away the paper collar with the aid of a sharp knife. Place the soufflé on a serving dish, and serve it immediately, with a separate bowl of the sauce. NET: 4 servings.

PETITS FOURS

Petits fours secs are little cookies without icing (the translation of "sec" is "dry"). Iced little cookies and cakes are identified as petits fours glacés.

For chocolate leaves, you need a leaf stencil, available in culinary specialty shops. The first four ingredients should be weighed for maximum accuracy and balance.

*FEUILLES
AU CHOCOLAT*

*Petits Fours Secs:
Chocolate Leaves*

2¼ ounces sweet butter
2¼ ounces granulated sugar
1¼ ounces ground almonds
1 egg

2¾ ounces all-purpose flour
A few drops rum
4 ounces dark sweet chocolate

Preheat the oven to 350°. Cream the butter in an electric mixer. Add the sugar and beat until the mixture is light and fluffy. Add the ground almonds. Then beat in the egg, flour, and rum. Butter and flour two baking sheets. Put the mixture through the leaf stencil by patting it carefully in with a spoon and smoothing it off with a spatula. Bake the leaves until the edges are well browned. Cut the chocolate into small pieces, put it on a plate over a pan of simmering water, and work it with a spatula until it is melted and smooth. Let it cool until it is almost set, then spread a thin coat of it on the backs (the underside that was against the baking sheet) of the cooled leaves. Mark the veins on each leaf with a sharp-pointed knife. NET: About 18 cookies.

GAUFRETTES

Petits Fours Secs:
Wafers

With this kind of batter, it is always safer to bake one test cookie. If it spreads too much, add a little flour; if it does not spread, add a little unbeaten egg white.

2 egg whites
½ cup granulated sugar
⅓ cup all-purpose flour

3 tablespoons cool melted
sweet butter

Preheat the oven to 375°. Beat the egg whites and sugar in an electric mixer until the mixture is white and fluffy. Remove the bowl from the mixer, sprinkle the flour over the mixture, and fold it in with a rubber scraper. Then sprinkle the cool melted butter over the mixture and carefully but thoroughly fold it in. Brush two baking sheets with butter and dust lightly with flour. Spread the mixture on the baking sheets in thin rounds 4 inches in diameter. Allow enough space between the rounds so they do not run together. Bake the wafers 3 to 4 minutes, or until golden brown. Remove them at once from the baking sheet and quickly roll each one around a pencil or the end of a wooden spoon. Chill the wafers and store them in an airtight container. NET: 18 wafers.

LANGUES DE CHAT

Petits Fours Secs:
Cat's Tongues

4 tablespoons sweet butter
¼ cup granulated sugar
½ teaspoon vanilla extract

2 egg whites
¼ cup all-purpose flour

Preheat the oven to 350°. Butter two jelly roll pans and dust them lightly with flour. Have ready a pastry bag fitted with a #3 plain round tube. Cream the butter in the electric mixer. Add the sugar, beat until very light and fluffy, then mix in the vanilla. Add the egg whites one at a time, and beat well. Sift the flour over the mixture, mix it carefully into the other ingredients, and put the batter in the pastry bag. Pipe it out on the pans in strips about the size of a little finger and slightly larger at the ends than in the middle. When the batter has been piped out, violently bang the pans down on the table top to flatten it. Bake until the cookies are brown around the edges. Loosen them immediately with a spatula and cool on a cake rack. When cool, they should be very crisp. Store them in an airtight container. NET: 20 cookies.

MADELEINES

Petits Fours Secs:
Little Molded Genoese
Cakes

For these you need 12 madeleine molds.

10 tablespoons cool melted
clarified sweet butter
(page 56)
1 lump of sugar
A grated orange

¾ cup granulated sugar
1¼ cups sifted cake flour
(without baking powder)
3 eggs
2 egg yolks

1 tablespoon Cognac
⅛ teaspoon salt

1 egg white
Confectioners sugar

Preheat the oven to 350°. Set 5 tablespoons of the clarified butter aside for the batter. Butter the madeleine molds with the rest — brush them with butter, set them in the freezer a few minutes, then brush them with more butter. The butter in the molds should be very thick and solid.

Rub the lump of sugar on the grated orange, crush it with a mortar and pestle, and add it to the granulated sugar and cake flour. Put the egg and egg yolks in a copper bowl. Stir them with a whisk (they should be well blended but not frothy). Gradually stir in the flour and sugar mixture. Add the Cognac and salt. Stir with the whisk until the mixture is quite smooth. Let it stand 4 minutes, then beat it vigorously 1 minute. Gradually stir in the reserved 5 tablespoons butter (be careful not to let any foam from the butter enter the batter). Put the bowl containing the batter over very low heat, and lightly beat the batter until it is heated through and has the consistency of a very thick sauce. Spoon it into the molds; they should be not quite full. Place them on a jelly roll pan and bake 15 to 20 minutes, until they are golden brown all over. When they are baked, turn them out on a rack, let them cool a little, and while they are still warm brush the ridges very lightly with a little unbeaten egg white and dust them with confectioners sugar. NET: 12 small cakes.

The first four ingredients should be weighed for maximum accuracy and balance. With this kind of batter, it is safer to bake a test cookie. If it spreads too much, add a little flour. If it does not spread, add a little more unbeaten egg white.

2¼ ounces sweet butter
  (room temperature)
2¼ ounces granulated sugar
1½ ounces dried currants (for
  Palais de Dames) or ground

almonds (for Viscontis)
2¾ ounces all-purpose flour
1 egg
A few drops rum

PALAIS DE DAMES OU VISCONTIS

Petits Fours Secs:
Little Cookies with
Currants or Almonds

PALAIS DE DAMES. Preheat the oven to 375°. Cream the butter in the mixer. Add the sugar and beat until the mixture is light and fluffy. Add the currants. Beat in the egg, flour, and rum. Butter two baking sheets. Pat out the mixture in spoonfuls and bake until the edges are golden brown. Remove from the pans, let cool, and store in an airtight container.

VISCONTIS. Use the almonds, not the currants. Viscontis are traditionally shaped into ovals with a stencil, and either left plain or sandwiched with honey, jam, or a butter cream frosting. NET: 24 cookies.

MACARONS RUSSE

Petits Fours Secs:
Russian Macaroons

7 egg whites
1 pound granulated sugar
2 cups ground blanched
  almonds (put them through

a meat chopper)
1 cup all-purpose flour
About 12 blanched almond
  halves

Preheat the oven to 375°. Have ready a buttered and floured baking sheet. Combine the egg whites, sugar, and ground almonds in a heavy pan and stir over low heat until it is just possible to bear holding your finger in the mixture. Remove the pan from the heat and stir in the flour at once. Put teaspoonfuls of the mixture on the baking sheet and pat them out a little. Bake 15 to 20 minutes. Remove the macaroons from the oven, and when the macaroons begin to be firm, place a blanched almond half on each one. NET: About 12 cookies (serves 4 or more adults, 1 or 2 children).

SABLÉS

Petits Fours Secs:
Sand Tarts

2 cups all-purpose flour
8 tablespoons sweet butter
  (room temperature)
½ cup granulated sugar
4 egg yolks

4 hard-boiled egg yolks, rubbed
  through a fine wire strainer
Tiny pinch of salt
Grated rind of 2 lemons

Preheat the oven to 350°. Have a baking sheet ready, unbuttered. Put the flour in a bowl and cut in the butter, then rub it in with the fingertips until the mixture resembles coarse cornmeal in texture. Mix in the sugar and the hard-boiled egg yolks. Beat the raw egg yolks until light and fluffy. Add them to the flour mixture and work all the ingredients up quickly to a firm dough. Roll it out ¼ inch thick on a lightly floured board and cut it into 1-inch rounds with a cookie cutter. Place them on the baking sheet, mark the tops crisscross with the back of a knife, and bake them 25 minutes. They can then be chilled and stored in an airtight container. NET: 18 cookies.

TUILES AUX AMANDES

Petits Fours Secs:
Almond Tiles

2 egg whites
4 ounces granulated sugar
Tiny pinch of salt
½ cup sifted all-purpose flour
4 tablespoons cool melted

clarified sweet butter
  (page 56)
1½ ounces shredded blanched
  almonds

Preheat the oven to 350°. Butter a jelly roll pan or baking sheet (do not dust it with flour). Have ready two French rolling pins. Put the egg whites in a bowl with the sugar. Beat with a whisk until the mixture is literally white. Add the salt, then mix in the flour and cool melted clarified butter. Add the shredded almonds. Put little mounds of dough on the baking sheet (about 1 teaspoonful). Do not place them too close together (allow about 6 to a baking sheet because they spread quite a bit). With the back of a teaspoon, spread out the mound to the size of a silver dollar (2 inches in diameter). Bake until they are delicately brown all over. The minute the cookies are baked, remove them from the oven. Instantly loosen them from the pan, and curl them around the rolling pins. Let them cool and crisp in this shape, then remove from the rolling pins and keep them in an airtight container. NET: About 18 cookies.

CIGARETTES

Petits Fours Secs: Plain and with Chocolate Nut Coating

CIGARETTES TO SERVE WITH ICE CREAM (PLAIN). Prepare the dough for Almond Tiles (page 798), leaving out the shredded almonds. Spread the dough on the baking sheets in thin rectangles. Bake as prescribed. As soon as they are removed from the oven, roll each one around a pencil (instead of the rolling pin for tiles) to get the shape of a cigarette.

CIGARETTES TO SERVE AS PETITS FOURS SECS (CHOCOLATE NUT). Have ready 2 ounces dark sweet chocolate that has been melted, and a few chopped pistachio nuts. Prepare the cigarettes as above. Then dip both ends of each cigarette in cool melted chocolate. When the chocolate is nearly set, dip the chocolate-coated tips in chopped pistachio nuts. NET: About 18 cookies.

CROISSANTS VIENNOISE

Petits Fours Secs: Viennese Vanilla Crescents

½ cup Vanilla Sugar (page 77)
12 tablespoons sweet butter
4 tablespoons confectioners sugar

Tiny pinch of salt
2 cups sifted all-purpose flour
½ cup ground blanched almonds or hazelnuts

Prepare the vanilla sugar at least 2 hours before starting to prepare these cookies. Then mix the cookie dough, as follows. Cream the butter in an electric mixer. Add the confectioners sugar and salt slowly, while beating. Work in the flour a little at a time. Fold in the ground nuts. Chill the dough 2 hours in the refrigerator. When ready to bake, preheat the oven to 350°. Then roll the dough on a floured board to a strip the thickness of a pencil. Cut off 3-inch lengths, curve them into a crescent shape, set them on a lightly floured baking sheet, and bake 10 to 15 minutes. Put the vanilla sugar in a bowl, and as soon as the crescents are baked, toss them gently in the sugar until they are covered. NET: About 24 crescents.

FOURS À LA CRÈME GLACÉS

Petits Fours Glacés: Little Frosted Genoese Cakes

This recipe and the following recipe for Fruits Déguisés comprise a small but lovely selection of the classic petits fours glacés. Both this and the fruit type are traditionally served in little paper pastry cases on a flat serving plate. They are exquisite to behold and equally so to eat.

GENOESE CAKE
1 cup vegetable shortening
1 cup superfine sugar
1 egg
3 egg yolks
1 tablespoon vanilla extract
1½ cups sifted cake flour
    (without baking powder)
½ cup milk
3 egg whites
2 teaspoons baking powder

BUTTER CREAM FILLING
3 egg yolks, beaten
1¼ cups granulated sugar
½ teaspoon cream of tartar
⅔ cup cold water
12 tablespoons sweet butter
Flavorings (see below)

FLAVORINGS FOR BUTTER CREAM
Coffee: A little Cognac, and 1
    tablespoon coffee essence
    or 2 teaspoons instant coffee
    dissolved in 2 tablespoons
    boiling water
Rum: 2 tablespoons light rum
Chocolate: 4 ounces dark sweet

chocolate, 3 tablespoons
water, and 1 tablespoon light
rum

OPTIONAL: ADDITIONAL FILLINGS
Brandied cherries, glacé cherries,
    orange peel, pistachios, jam,
    or jelly

FONDANT COATING
6 cups granulated sugar
2 cups water
1 teaspoon cream of tartar
The reserved few drops of
    coffee, rum, and chocolate
    flavorings

DECORATION
Reserved portions of flavored
    butter cream
Optional: food colorings
Tiny black currants soaked in
    rum
Candy coffee beans
Crystallized violets or other
    candied fruits or flowers
Blanched green pistachio nuts

GENOESE CAKE. Preheat the oven to 350°. Butter a jelly roll pan 11 by 17 inches. Line it with wax paper and butter it again. Cream the shortening in the electric mixer until light and fluffy. Add the sugar and beat the mixture again until very light and fluffy. One at a time, beat in the egg and egg yolks, then add the vanilla extract. Gradually mix in the flour, alternating with the milk. In a separate bowl, beat the egg whites to soft peaks. Sprinkle the baking powder over the flour mixture, add the beaten egg whites, and fold them into the batter carefully and smoothly with a rubber scraper. Spread the batter out over the pan and bake it 30 minutes. When it is baked, turn it out of the pan. Cut it into little (no more than 1 inch) rounds, squares, or ovals. Put the cakes in the freezer to chill thoroughly.

BUTTER CREAM FILLING. Beat the egg yolks in the mixer until light and fluffy. Combine the sugar, cream of tartar, and water in an unlined copper pan. Cook until the syrup forms a thin thread between finger and thumb. Pour the hot syrup over the beaten egg yolks, and continue beating until the mixture is thick and cool. Then add the sweet butter bit by bit, beating all the time. Divide the butter cream into three equal portions, to provide coffee, rum, and chocolate butter creams. Reserve a few drops of each prepared flavoring for the fondant. *Coffee:* Beat into one portion of butter cream the coffee essence or dissolved instant coffee, then add the Cognac. *Rum:* Beat the rum into the second portion. *Chocolate:* Break the chocolate into small pieces, put them in a small heavy pan with the water, and melt over low heat, stirring all the time. Mix in the rum. Cool the chocolate and beat it into the third portion of butter cream.

Set aside a little of each of the three flavored portions of butter cream to be used in the decoration. Put one flavor of butter cream into a pastry bag fitted with a #3 plain round tube. Pipe little domes (no more than half an inch high) on a third of the little pieces of cake. Do the same with the other two portions of butter cream. Return the cakes to the freezer.

ADDITIONAL FILLINGS (OPTIONAL). A brandied cherry, a piece of a glacé cherry, orange peel, or pistachio may be set on top of each butter cream dome. Or the cake may be split in two layers and sandwiched with a fruit jam or jelly.

FONDANT COATING. Combine the sugar and water in a large unlined copper pan and stir over low heat until the sugar dissolves. Add the cream of tartar and cook the syrup over moderate heat to 240°. (Have handy a bowl with cold water and a damp cloth to clean off the sides of the pan as the bubbles stick.) Remove the syrup from the heat, let the bubbles settle, and pour the hot syrup onto a marble slab, jelly roll pan, or large china platter. Let it set until you can touch it without its sticking. Then work the syrup quickly with a spatula until it becomes opaque white (crystallized), then work it with the heel of the hand until it is soft like heavy pastry dough. (At this point the fondant can be stored almost indefinitely in a crock or bowl covered with a damp cloth, or in an airtight jar. Otherwise it will become hard and brittle.)

Coat the petits fours as follows. (If you plan to prepare some Fruits Déguisés (below) reserve about ¾ cup fondant for the filling.) Put a small amount of fondant into a tin-lined copper pan with the reserved coffee flavoring. Stir it over low heat until it is the consistency of a thick sauce. Have ready a wire rack on a jelly roll pan. Hold the cake on the tip of a spatula over the pan of fondant. Pour fondant over the little cake with a tablespoon. Set the iced cake on the wire rack. (The cakes iced with coffee fondant will of course be coffee-colored.) Add the reserved rum to another small amount of fondant, and proceed in the same way to coat some of the cakes with rum fondant (these cakes will be white). Continue with the reserved chocolate flavoring in the same way, and coat some of the cakes with chocolate fondant (these cakes will be chocolate-colored). If desired, other food colorings can be added to the fondant in the same way, for a larger assortment of colors.

DECORATION. When all the cakes have been coated with fondant, decorate the tops with any of the following: (1) Tiny rosettes of the reserved butter creams, piped through a little paper cornucopia. (b) Tiny black currants soaked in rum (for the white petits fours). (c) Candy coffee beans. (d) Crystallized violets or other candied fruits or flowers. (e) Blanched green pistachio nuts.

Keep these exquisite Four à la Crème Glacés in the freezer or refrigerator until ready to serve. Serve them in little paper pastry cases. NET: 100 to 120 little filled, iced, and decorated cakes.

FRUITS DÉGUISÉS

Petits Fours Glacés: Candied Fruits

Little stuffed and glazed fruits for petits fours are assembled in the following manner.

Pitted prunes and dates
Shelled walnut and pecan
    halves
Pink and green food colorings
A little rum, gin, coffee essence, and Cognac

NOUGAT FILLING
Fondant (reserved from Petits

Fours à la Crème, pages 800, 801)
Equal quantity of almond paste (commercial)

GLAZE
1¼ cups granulated sugar
½ teaspoon cream of tartar
⅔ cup cold water

NOUGAT FILLING. Mix together the almond paste and fondant. When thoroughly mixed, divide the nougat into three portions. Color one portion pink and flavor it with rum, color another portion green and flavor it with gin, and color the third portion coffee brown with the coffee essence and flavor it with Cognac.

Stuff these pastes into the prunes and dates, and sandwich halves of walnuts or pecans together with them, letting a little of the colors show through the opening. Make little crisscrosses on the nougat that is exposed, using the back of a knife.

GLAZE. Cook the sugar, cream of tartar, and water in an unlined copper pan until it reaches the hard ball stage (275°).

Have ready a wire rack on a jelly roll pan that has been brushed with vegetable oil. Dip the stuffed fruits and nuts in the syrup and lay them on the wire rack for the glaze to set. Trim off any drippings neatly. Put the Fruits Déguisés in little paper pastry cases to serve.

DESSERTS

A s if the wonderful world of French pastries weren't enough
to steal the show, there's still another company of stars in the
dessert repertoire. In the French culinary vernacular they're
generalized as "entremets," which originally meant "interlude between dishes" but today means sweets . . . the most gentle crèmes and
custards, the richest chocolate infusions, and not only the apple,
but nature's whole cornucopia of sweet pulps and nectars.

In my restaurant days we had a large walk-in refrigerator room
where I loved to admire the wares for next day's dessert menu: custards
and crèmes — Crème Renversée Caramel and Petits Pots de Crème,
La Charlotte Malakoff, and all the fresh fruit-flavored bavarois; the
most royal Marquises Alice — aux Fraises and au Praliné; the tip-
pling Savoy Trifle and molded Flummery, so shimmery white, soon to
be bathed in the brilliance of fresh raspberry syrup; cloud puffs of
cold soufflés — caramel, rum, coffee, chocolate, strawberry, citron.
On another wall of this great refrigerator paraded the charming
Coeurs à la Crème in their little wicker baskets, great crystal bowls
with chunks of fresh fruit for the macédoine, and baskets of fresh
peaches, cherries, and plums; also the Apple Charlotte, pristine
Poires Sauternes, and my beloved Chocolate Normandy Mousse . . .
While in the colder depths lodged drums of homemade French
custard ice cream, which the French literally term "iced custard"
(crème glacée), a whole rainbow of flavors: vanilla, strawberry, raspberry, blackberry, peach, apricot, pistachio, yes — brown bread and
rum ice cream, extra rich chocolate ice cream, plus coffee and praline,
with many of these repeated in zesty sorbets.

Entremets comprise the jewels of French cuisine. And like glittering
diamonds and rubies, they ought not to be for every day. These
desserts are for a special meal, perhaps once a week, Saturday or
Sunday, when you have more time and will enjoy preparing one of
these dreams, or an anniversary dinner — any anniversary — or to
celebrate a hard-won achievement.

In the French concept of menu balance, fresh fruit with or after the cheese, or just fresh fruit, is the "daily" dessert. And with special marketing effort on your part (an important function of good cooking), it is the best dessert, and the French favorite. Besides being so good to eat, fruit actually aids digestion. But it must be *fresh*. Train yourself to be constantly on the lookout for the freshest fruit in town. Buy it whenever you find it, and serve it au naturel — the plain fruit, with no trimmings. Your efforts will be applauded.

I believe so strongly that fresh fruit au naturel must be restored to the American daily menu that I have prepared a separate discussion on serving it. I love chilled fresh fruit eaten à table, especially a Comice pear, the most esteemed pear of all, with its cool sweet syrup. After a dinner of style and sensation, the faintly scented, glowing fresh fruits of the season help to punctuate a meal by restoring balance to the mind and sweetness to the palate. As Mrs. Beeton said: "If there be any poetry at all in meals, or in the process of feeding, there is poetry in the dessert . . . pines, melons, grapes, peaches, nectarines, plums, strawberries, apples, pears, oranges, almonds, raisins, figs, walnuts, filberts, medlars, cherries, etc., all kinds of dried fruits and choice and delicately flavoured cakes and biscuits make up the dessert, together with the most costly and recherché wines." (*Mrs. Beeton's Book of Household Management*, 1892 edition.)

CUSTARDS, MOUSSES, PUDDINGS, FRUITS

CRÈME CARAMEL AU RHUM

Rum Caramel Custard

2 eggs
4 egg yolks
½ cup confectioners sugar
2 cups light cream
¼ cup light rum

CARAMEL LINING
1 cup granulated sugar
⅜ cup water

¼ teaspoon cream of tartar

RUM CARAMEL SAUCE
1 cup sugar
⅜ cup water
¼ teaspoon cream of tartar
½ cup chopped mixed candied
   fruit
⅓ cup light rum

Preheat the oven to 350°.

CARAMEL LINING. Combine the sugar, water, and cream of tartar in an unlined copper pan, and stir over low heat with a metal spoon until the sugar dissolves. Then let the syrup cook without stirring until it is a nice caramel color. Have ready a bowl of cold water and a 1-quart (#6) soufflé dish. When the syrup is a caramel color, set the pan instantly in the cold water to stop the cooking. Pour the caramel into the soufflé dish. Tip it around so that it completely coats the inside. Set the dish aside.

CUSTARD. Put the eggs and the egg yolks in a bowl with the confectioners sugar. Stir with a whisk until it is very well blended (stir in a circular motion so that no bubbles form). Put the cream in a pan, bring it to a boil, and slowly pour it into the egg mixture, stirring all the time. Add the rum. Pour the custard through a fine wire strainer into the caramel-lined dish. Stand the dish in a shallow roasting pan half filled with hot water. Put the whole assembly in the oven and cook 2 hours. Test the custard with a cake tester; if it comes out dry, the custard is done. Let it chill thoroughly in the refrigerator.

RUM CARAMEL SAUCE. Put the sugar, water, and cream of tartar in an unlined copper pan, and stir over low heat until the sugar is dissolved. Increase the heat and cook to a light caramel. Set the pan instantly in the cold water and stir in the rum and fruit. Cool the sauce before using. If it is too thick, thin it with a little water or rum.

To serve, invert the custard on a serving dish, to show the caramel. Serve the sauce in a separate bowl. NET: 4 to 6 servings.

The original recipe came from Kings College, Cambridge, England, two hundred years ago. It was then served in shallow crystal dishes and a gold hammer was passed around to crack the clear caramel. This dish was served in Great Hall on special occasions. You should start it a day in advance of serving.

2 cups thick cream	4 egg yolks
½ inch vanilla bean	1 cup granulated sugar

Put the cream in a pan with the piece of vanilla bean, slowly bring it just to a boil, and remove it from the heat. Beat the egg yolks in a bowl with 4 tablespoons sugar until very creamy and light. Very carefully and slowly pour the warm cream over the egg yolks, stirring all the while. Transfer the egg and cream mixture to a heavy pan, and stir it over low heat until it coats the back of a metal spoon. Pour it into a shallow glass heatproof serving dish and chill it overnight in the refrigerator. Next day cover the top completely with granulated sugar, so that none of the cream shows through. Place the dish on a bowl of crushed ice and set it under a hot broiler to caramelize the sugar. When it has caramelized, return the custard to the refrigerator for at least 3 minutes before serving it. NET: 4 to 6 servings.

CRÈME BRÛLÉE

Burnt Custard

5 whole eggs	1 cup milk
4 egg yolks	
1 cup superfine sugar	CARAMEL
3 inches vanilla bean or	1½ cups granulated sugar
3 teaspoons vanilla extract	Barely ¾ cup water
1 cup light cream	½ teaspoon cream of tartar
1 cup heavy cream	½ cup warm water

CRÈME RENVERSÉE AU CARAMEL

Cream Custard Coated with Caramel

Preheat the oven to 350°.

CARAMEL. Put the sugar, water, and cream of tartar in an unlined copper pan, and stir over low heat with a metal spoon until the sugar dissolves. Then let the syrup cook without stirring until it is a nice caramel color. Have ready a bowl of cold water and a 1½-quart (#7) soufflé dish. When the syrup is a rich caramel color, set the pan instantly in the cold water to stop the cooking. Pour the caramel into the soufflé dish, and tip it around so that it completely coats the inside. Pour any excess back into the pan. Set the dish aside. Add the warm water to the caramel returned to the pan, and stir over low heat until it is dissolved. Chill it.

CUSTARD. Put the eggs and egg yolks in a bowl with the sugar. Stir with a whisk until very well blended (stir in a circular motion so there are no bubbles). Put the light cream, heavy cream, and milk in a tin-lined copper pan with the vanilla bean or extract, bring it slowly to a boil, and slowly pour it into the egg mixture, stirring all the time. Pour the egg and milk mixture through a fine wire strainer into the caramel-lined dish. Stand the dish in a shallow roasting pan half filled with hot water. Put the whole assembly in the oven and cook it 1½ hours. Test with a little cake tester; if it comes out dry, the custard is done. Let it chill thoroughly in the refrigerator.

To serve, invert the custard on a serving dish and turn it out so that there is now a caramel-covered surface. Serve with the extra caramel sauce in a separate bowl. NET: 6 servings.

ÎLE FLOTTANTE

Floating Island

The islands are poached egg whites floating in custard sauce, with caramel. There is the story that this dish was improvised for a royal French Louis who would eat only liquids when he was a child. To make the custard sauce more interesting, the cook made islands of poached beaten egg whites.

CUSTARD SAUCE
6 egg yolks
1 vanilla bean, scraping and
   pod
6 tablespoons superfine sugar
1 cup heavy cream
1 cup light cream
½ cup milk

POACHED MERINGUE
3 egg whites
5 tablespoons superfine sugar
About 1 quart milk
About 1 cup water

CARAMEL
¾ cup granulated sugar
¼ teaspoon cream of tartar
¼ cup water

CUSTARD SAUCE. Put the egg yolks in a mixer with the sugar and scraping of the vanilla bean. Beat until very light and fluffy. Combine the heavy cream, light cream, and milk in a pan with the vanilla bean pod. Bring to a boil, then slowly stir it into the yolk mixture, beating all the while. (Reserve the vanilla pod.) Transfer the mixture to a saucepan and stir it with a metal spoon over low heat until it coats the back of the spoon. Pour the sauce into a large shallow crystal serving bowl and let it chill in the refrigerator.

POACHED MERINGUE. Beat the egg whites to soft peaks in the mixer. Slowly add the sugar and continue beating until the mixture holds its shape. Half fill a large sauté pan with the milk and water mixture. Add the vanilla bean pod. Bring slowly to a boil, reduce the heat to a simmer, then with two tablespoons form the meringue into large egg shapes and carefully place them in the hot milk. Simmer them very gently about 3 minutes, then turn them over to poach another 2 to 3 minutes (do not let them boil). They should be firm. Let them cool in the milk. When they are cool, lift them out with a large slotted spoon, drain on paper towels, and arrange them on the chilled custard. Return the dish to the refrigerator.

CARAMEL. Put the sugar, water, and cream of tartar in a small unlined copper pan over low heat. Stir it until the sugar dissolves, then cook without stirring until the syrup is amber-colored.

With the custard dish at hand, dip a fork in the caramel and make small streamers of it over each island. Chill the dish thoroughly in the refrigerator before serving. NET: 4 to 6 servings.

Poached meringue (Île
    Flottante, above)
Caramel (Île Flottante,
    above)

PRALINE CUSTARD SAUCE
Custard sauce (Île Flottante,
    above)
3 tablespoons praline powder
    (page 77)

1 cup heavy cream, whipped
2 to 3 tablespoons Kirsch

PINEAPPLE
About 4 tablespoons salt butter
A little granulated sugar
1 small fresh pineapple,
    skinned, cored, and cut into
    ½-inch slices

ÎLE FLOTTANTE AUX ANANAS

Floating Island with Praline Custard Sauce, Caramel, and Sautéed Fresh Pineapple

PRALINE CUSTARD SAUCE. Prepare the custard sauce as for Île Flottante, then cool it quickly by setting it over a bowl of ice and stirring. When it is well chilled, fold in the praline powder, whipped cream, and Kirsch. Pour it into a large shallow crystal bowl and set it in the refrigerator.

Prepare the egg whites, place them on the custard, decorate with caramel, and chill the dish, all exactly as for Île Flottante.

PINEAPPLE. Heat the butter in a sauté pan and add a little granulated sugar to make a glaze. Fry the pineapple slices until golden brown on each side. Cut them in half and arrange around the edge of the serving bowl.

When the pineapple has been added to the bowl, it should be served at once. NET: 4 to 6 servings.

PETITS POTS DE CRÈME: VANILLE, CHOCOLAT, CAFÉ, AMANDE

Baked Custard Cups: Vanilla, Chocolate, Coffee, Almond

The quantities in this recipe are for 8 small custard cups of *one* flavor. If several flavors are desired, adjust the recipe according to the quantity to be made of each flavor.

VANILLA CUSTARD
2 cups milk
1 inch vanilla bean (not needed for coffee or almond custard)
6 egg yolks
½ cup granulated sugar

FOR CHOCOLATE
4 ounces dark sweet chocolate
3 tablespoons water

FOR COFFEE
2 teaspoons instant coffee
2 tablespoons hot water

FOR ALMOND
2 cups light cream (instead of milk)
½ teaspoon almond extract
½ cup chopped browned almonds or 3 tablespoons chopped blanched pistachio nuts
Confectioners sugar

VANILLA CUSTARD. Preheat the oven to 250°. Have ready 8 individual custard cups and a covered baking pan in which all 8 cups will fit. Put the milk in a pan with the vanilla bean, bring it slowly to a boil, and remove it from the heat. Beat the egg yolks and sugar in the mixer until light and fluffy. Slowly pour the scalded milk over the egg yolk mixture, beating all the time. Strain the mixture through a fine wire strainer and pour it into the custard cups. Set them in the baking pan and pour hot water around them up to about half their height. Cover the pan and set it in the oven to poach them 45 minutes. Let them cool in the water, then chill thoroughly in the refrigerator.

CHOCOLATE CUSTARD. Break the chocolate in pieces and put them in a small heavy pan with the water. Stir over low heat until it is dissolved and quite smooth. Remove from the heat and cool a little. Add it before straining and pouring the custard into the cups.

COFFEE CUSTARD. Dissolve the instant coffee in the hot water and add it to the scalded milk. Omit the vanilla bean.

ALMOND CUSTARD. Substitute the light cream for the milk in the basic recipe, and omit the vanilla bean. Add the almond extract with the scalded cream. When the custards are cooked and cooled, cover the tops with the almonds or pistachio nuts. Then let them chill, and sprinkle them with a little confectioners sugar just before serving. NET: 8 servings.

BAVAROIS À LA VANILLE

Vanilla Bavarian Cream

This dish can be set in a mold and turned out on a platter, or set and served in a bowl. If it is to be served in a bowl, use half the quantity of gelatine. For Lemon, Strawberry, or Praline Bavarian

Cream served this way, use the Bavarian Cream portions of Bavarois au Citron (page 812), Marquise Alice aux Fraises (page 814), or Marquise Alice au Praline (page 816).

6 egg yolks
9 tablespoons granulated sugar
2 inches vanilla bean, scraping
    and pod
2½ tablespoons unflavored
    gelatine (or 1¼ tablespoons
    for serving in a bowl)
¾ cup heavy cream mixed with
    ¾ cup milk
6 egg whites
¾ cup heavy cream, whipped

2 tablespoons light rum

DECORATION
¾ cup heavy cream
2 tablespoons confectioners
    sugar
1 tablespoon light rum
3 glazed cherries, cut in half
About 12 leaf cutouts of
    angelica

Have ready a 1½-quart mold lightly brushed with vegetable oil. Put the egg yolks, sugar, and the vanilla bean scraping into a bowl and beat with a whisk or in a mixer until light and fluffy. Mix in the gelatine. Put the mixed cream and milk in a pan with the vanilla bean pod and bring to a boil over low heat. Then slowly pour it into the egg yolk mixture, stirring all the time. Transfer the mixture to a saucepan and stir with a metal spoon over low heat until it thickens enough to coat the back of the spoon, no more. Then remove the vanilla pod, set the mixture over a bowl of ice and stir to cool it a little. Beat the egg whites to soft peaks and fold them into the cooled custard. Next, carefully and smoothly fold in the whipped cream. Add the rum, and continue to stir the mixture over ice a little more. When it is on the point of setting, pour it into the mold and leave it in the freezer about 1 hour, to set.

When you are ready to serve, turn the Bavarian cream out onto a serving plate. Decorate as follows. Beat the heavy cream over a bowl of ice. When it is almost stiff, add the sugar and rum, and continue beating until it is stiff. Fill a pastry bag, fitted with a #5 or #6 star tube, with the whipped cream and decorate the top of the Bavarian cream. Garnish with arrangements of half a glazed cherry with two angelica leaves. NET: 6 servings.

If the Bavarian cream is to be served in a bowl rather than molded, use half the quantity of gelatine.

3 egg yolks
5 tablespoons superfine sugar
1½ tablespoons unflavored
    gelatine (or ¾ tablespoon for
    serving in a bowl)
1 tablespoon instant coffee
1 tablespoon boiling water

1 cup light cream
3 egg whites
¾ cup heavy cream, whipped
2 tablespoons rum

GARNISH
½ cup heavy cream

BAVAROIS AU CAFÉ

Coffee Bavarian Cream

1 tablespoon confectioners
 sugar
½ inch scraped vanilla bean

Narrow (¾ inch) strips of
 angelica

With a whisk, beat the egg yolks and sugar together in a bowl until light and fluffy. Stir in the gelatine. Dissolve the instant coffee in the boiling water, add it to the light cream, and bring to a boil over low heat. Slowly pour this into the egg mixture, beating all the time. Transfer the custard mixture (eggs and cream) to a saucepan and stir it over very low heat until it coats the back of a metal spoon, then cool it in the refrigerator. Beat the egg whites to soft peaks and fold them smoothly into the cooled custard. Then fold in the whipped cream, and last, stir in the rum. Brush the mold lightly with a little vegetable oil (set it upside down on a paper towel to let excess oil drain out). Fill the mold with the Bavarian cream and leave it in the freezer about one hour. Then turn it out of the mold onto a serving dish, and decorate it as follows.

Whip the heavy cream in a metal bowl, set over another bowl of ice, until it is almost stiff. Add the confectioners sugar and vanilla bean scraping and beat until stiff. Put the whipped cream in a pastry bag fitted with a #6 or #7 star tube and pipe all around the edge of the mold. Decorate the surface of the Bavarian cream with little strips of green angelica. NET: 4 servings.

BAVAROIS AU CITRON

_Fresh Lemon Bavarian
Cream with Sponge Roll_

A very lemony Bavarian cream, garnished with apricot sponge roll (or, for a still more lemony accent, spread the roll with lemon curd instead of apricot jam; see the lemon curd recipe below). This Bavarian cream is served in a large shallow crystal bowl. If you wish to set it in a mold and turn it out, add another tablespoon of gelatine. The apricot or lemon sponge roll may be prepared in advance and frozen.

6 egg yolks
9 tablespoons superfine sugar
Tiny pinch of salt
2 tablespoons unflavored
 gelatine
1½ cups light cream
Grated rind of 3 lemons
1 cup fresh lemon juice
6 egg whites
1 cup heavy cream, whipped

APRICOT SPONGE ROLL
Sponge Cake Roll (page 760)
¾ cup apricot jam
2 tablespoons Kirsch

GARNISH
2 tablespoons confectioners
 sugar
1 tablespoon Kirsch
Skinned sections of 1 lemon
Skinned sections of 1 lime
1 strip candied orange peel
1 cup heavy cream

APRICOT SPONGE ROLL. Prepare 1 Basic Sponge Cake Roll according to the recipe on page 760, and spread it with the following apricot jam:

Mix the apricot jam with the Kirsch and dissolve the jam over low heat. Strain and cool it a little. Spread the jelly roll with the jam, roll it up, wrap it in foil, and set it in the freezer until you are ready to use it.

BAVARIAN CREAM (LEMON). Beat the egg yolks, sugar, and salt in the mixer until very light and fluffy. Reduce the speed and add the gelatine. Bring the light cream to a boil over low heat, then slowly pour it into the egg yolk mixture, beating all the time. Transfer the mixture to a saucepan and stir over low heat until it coats the back of a metal spoon. Off the heat, stir in the lemon rind and juice. Cover the saucepan with foil and set it in the refrigerator to cool a little. Beat the egg whites to soft peaks and fold them smoothly into the cooled custard, using a rubber scraper. Then fold in the whipped cream. Pour the mixture into a large shallow glass serving bowl and leave it in the refrigerator at least 2 hours, and preferably longer, to set.

When the Bavarian cream is well set, garnish it as follows. Beat the heavy cream until it is almost stiff. Add the confectioners sugar and Kirsch and continue beating until stiff. Cut the apricot sponge roll into ¼-inch slices and set them in rows around the top of the Bavarian cream, starting at the outside edge. The roll will probably cover the top, but it doesn't matter if the center area is open. In the center arrange a flower, using the skinned lemon and lime sections alternately for the petals and the orange peel for the stem. Pipe rosettes of whipped cream all around the edge of the dish, using a pastry bag with a #6 or #7 star tube. The Bavarian cream is now ready to serve, but if you can, return it to the refrigerator to chill another hour or two. NET: 6 to 8 servings.

LEMON CURD FILLING FOR SPONGE ROLL

Grated rind and juice of 2 lemons	16 tablespoons (½ pound) sweet butter, cut into small pieces
1 cup granulated sugar	
3 eggs, well beaten	Pinch of salt

Combine all the ingredients in the top of a double boiler. Stir the mixture and cook it over hot water until it thickly coats the back of a wooden spoon. To spread it on cake, pour the lemon curd in a shallow dish or layer cake pan and set it in the freezer at least 30 minutes. Then work it with a spatula until it is smooth, and spread it.

EMILY'S TEETH

A very good old-fashioned English dessert, this Bavarian cream trifle has almonds sticking out of it to suggest "Emily's teeth." I don't know who Emily was.

6 egg yolks   1 cup superfine sugar

1 tablespoon unflavored
gelatine
1½ cups milk
Sponge cake (leftover or commercial sponge cake, or an
unfilled, unrolled, Sponge

Cake Roll, page 760)
⅓ cup sherry or Madeira
2 cups heavy cream, whipped
1 cup split blanched almonds
4 egg whites

Beat the egg yolks and sugar in the mixer until very light and creamy. Mix in the dry gelatine. Bring the milk to a boil in a saucepan. Slowly pour it into the egg yolk mixture, stirring all the time. Transfer the mixture to a saucepan and stir with a metal spoon over low heat until the sauce coats the back of the spoon. Then, off the heat, cover the custard with plastic wrap (so that it does not form a skin), and let it cool at room temperature. Cut the cake into little squares and sprinkle them with the sherry or Madeira. Put the custard saucepan over a bowl of ice and stir the custard until it is on the point of setting. Beat the egg whites to soft peaks, and stir them into the custard. Fold in half the whipped cream, and blend well. Spoon half the custard into a crystal serving bowl, scatter the soaked sponge cake over it, cover with the rest of the custard, and put the dish in the refrigerator to set.

When the custard is well set, stick the split almonds all over the top like porcupine quills. Put the rest of the whipped cream in a pastry bag fitted with a #6 or #7 star tube, and pipe large rosettes around the edge of the bowl. NET: 6 servings.

MARQUISE ALICE AUX FRAISES

Strawberry Marquise Alice

A spectacular — strawberry Bavarian cream, coated with whipped cream and currant jelly, and garnished with chocolate rounds and cornucopias and glazed strawberries.

STRAWBERRY BAVARIAN CREAM
6 egg yolks
9 tablespoons superfine sugar
3 tablespoons unflavored
gelatine
1½ cups light cream
6 egg whites
1½ cups heavy cream, whipped
1½ cups puréed (in a blender)
fresh strawberries
⅓ cup Framboise (raspberry
brandy)

CHOCOLATE ROUNDS AND
CORNUCOPIAS
6 ounces dark sweet chocolate

GARNISH
1½ cups heavy cream
3 tablespoons confectioners
sugar
Scraping of a 3-inch piece of
vanilla bean
¼ cup red currant jelly
About 12 large perfect fresh
strawberries (with stems on
if possible)

GLAZE
¾ cup granulated sugar
¼ teaspoon cream of tartar
⅔ cup water

STRAWBERRY BAVARIAN CREAM. Have ready a 9-inch springform mold brushed lightly with vegetable oil. Beat the egg yolks and sugar in a mixer until very light and fluffy. Reduce the speed and add the dry gelatine. Bring the light cream to a boil over low heat, and slowly pour it into the egg mixture, beating all the time. Transfer the mixture to a saucepan and stir over low heat until it coats the back of a metal spoon. Set the saucepan over a bowl of ice and stir until the custard is cool but not set. Beat the egg whites to soft peaks and fold them smoothly into the custard, using a rubber scraper. Then fold in the whipped cream. Mix the strawberries with the Framboise and carefully fold them into the Bavarian cream. Pour the mixture into the mold and leave it in the refrigerator at least 2 hours, preferably more, to set.

CHOCOLATE ROUNDS AND CORNUCOPIAS. Have ready 8 4-inch squares of wax paper, each folded in half to form a triangle. Roll the double-thick triangle into a cornucopia (the point is in the middle of the folded edge), and secure it with a staple or tape. Also have ready 24 rounds (1½ inches in diameter) of wax paper. Cut the chocolate in small pieces and put them on a plate over a pan of hot simmering water. Remove the dish just before the chocolate is melted and work it smooth with a spatula. Line the cornucopias with chocolate, using a small spoon (cover every bit of the paper inside to avoid breakage later). Put the molds on a jelly roll pan and place them in the freezer or refrigerator to set. (If the chocolate begins to solidify while you are working, melt it again.) Spread melted chocolate on each of the 24 rounds of wax paper, set them in the freezer or refrigerator on another jelly roll pan. (Later, the wax paper is easily peeled off the hardened chocolate.)

Beat the heavy cream for the garnish, and when it is almost stiff add the confectioners sugar and vanilla bean scraping. Continue beating until the cream is stiff, and store it in the refrigerator until you are ready to decorate the dish.

When the Bavarian cream is well set, turn it out on a large flat serving dish. Spread the top and sides with some of the whipped cream.

TREE PATTERN. Whip the currant jelly with a fork until it is quite smooth. Make a little cornucopia of doubled wax paper and cut off a tiny piece at the tip. Put the currant jelly in the cornucopia and pipe straight lines of currant jelly on the whipped cream about 1 inch apart. Then make a tree pattern as follows. Lay the back of a knife on top of the whipped cream at a right angle to the lines of currant jelly, and lightly pull it across the mold. Do this in lines 2 inches apart, going across the whole mold. Then turn the mold around completely and make another series of lines with the knife between the first lines, going in the opposite direction. You should now have a tree pattern with the lines of currant jelly.

Remove the wax paper from the hardened rounds of chocolate and stick them around the sides of the Bavarian cream. Put a dab of whipped cream on the back of each, if necessary, to stick it to the mold. Carefully remove the wax paper from the chocolate cornucopias and arrange them on top of the mold. Put the remaining whipped cream into a pastry bag fitted with a #4 or #5 star tube, and pipe a swirl of cream coming out of each little cornucopia.

GLAZED STRAWBERRIES. Have ready an oiled jelly roll pan. Put the sugar, cream of tartar, and water in an unlined copper pan. Stir with a metal spoon until the sugar dissolves, then cook until the syrup just begins to color (it must be almost caramel to harden on the berries). Dip the strawberries, holding them by the stems (or small tongs) into the hot syrup, and put them on the jelly roll pan to set (it takes only a minute or so).

When all of the strawberries are glazed and the glaze has set, arrange them around the sides of the Bavarian cream. Chill the dish in the refrigerator thoroughly before serving. NET: 6 to 8 servings.

MARQUISE ALICE AU PRALINÉ

Praline Marquise Alice

Praline Bavarian cream, coated with whipped cream and currant jelly, garnished with chocolate rounds.

PRALINE BAVARIAN CREAM
6 egg yolks
9 tablespoons superfine sugar
3 tablespoons unflavored gelatine
2 cups milk
6 egg whites
1½ cups heavy cream, whipped with 3 tablespoons confec-

tioners sugar and 1½ teaspoons vanilla extract
1 cup praline powder (page 77)
2 tablespoons dark rum
2 ounces red currant jelly

CHOCOLATE ROUNDS
3 ounces dark sweet chocolate

PRALINE BAVARIAN CREAM. Have ready a 9-inch springform mold, lightly brushed with vegetable oil. Beat the egg yolks and sugar in the mixer until very light and fluffy. Reduce the speed and add the dry gelatine. Bring the milk to a boil over low heat, and slowly pour it into the egg yolk mixture, beating all the time. Transfer the mixture to a saucepan and stir over low heat until it coats the back of a metal spoon. Then set the saucepan over a bowl of ice and stir until the custard is cool but not set. Beat the egg whites to soft peaks and fold them smoothly into the custard, using a rubber scraper. Then fold in ¾ cup of the flavored whipped cream. Last, fold in the praline powder and rum. Pour the Bavarian cream into the mold and leave it in the refrigerator at least 2 hours to set.

Prepare the chocolate rounds as in the preceding recipe, using 12 rounds of wax paper about 2 inches in diameter. When the Bavarian cream is set, turn it out onto a flat serving dish. Spread the top and sides with some of the reserved whipped cream.

TREE PATTERN. Whip the currant jelly with a fork until it is quite smooth, and decorate the top of the mold with it exactly as for Marquise Alice aux Fraises (above).

Peel the wax paper from the hardened chocolate rounds, and place them around the top edge of the mold. Decorate the top of each round with little rosettes of the remaining whipped cream, piped through a pastry bag fitted with a #3 or #4 star tube. Chill the assembled Marquise Alice thoroughly before serving. NET: 6 to 8 servings.

This Bavarian cream and sponge cake, laced with rum and Madeira, is an authentic English trifle, as served at the Savoy Hotel in London. This recipe, which is my interpretation of the great Savoy trifle, was published in the New York *Times* in 1968, with this story about a permutation of the trifle: "The trifle was the Victorian way for ladies to get an occasional nip. When they summered in Italy, they tried to instruct the Italian chefs how to make it, and they did come up with a similar dish. But the Italians had a sense of humor. They called it *zuppa Inglese*, or English soup."

Sponge Cake Roll made with currant jelly (Biscuit Roulé au Confiture, page 760)
4 tablespoons Madeira wine
1 cup heavy cream
1 tablespoon confectioners sugar
1 teaspoon vanilla extract
Candied cherries and angelica for decoration

BAVARIAN CREAM
4 egg yolks
4 tablespoons superfine sugar
1 tablespoon unflavored gelatine
1½ cups light cream
4 egg whites
1 cup heavy cream, whipped
2 tablespoons light rum

When the sponge cake roll with currant jelly is made, cut slices of it about ½ inch thick and completely line a crystal serving bowl with them (reserve about a third of the slices for the top). Sprinkle the cake with the Madeira and chill the cake-lined bowl.

BAVARIAN CREAM. Beat the egg yolks and sugar in a mixer until very light and fluffy. Reduce the speed and add the dry gelatine. Bring the light cream to a boil over low heat, and slowly pour it into the egg mixture, beating all the time. Transfer the mixture to a saucepan and stir it over low heat until it coats the back of a metal spoon. Set the saucepan over a bowl of ice, and stir until the custard is cool but not set. Beat the egg whites to soft peaks and fold them smoothly into the custard, using a rubber scraper. Then fold in the whipped cream, then the rum.

Spoon the Bavarian cream into the cake-lined bowl and put it in the freezer to set quickly. When it is set, cover the top with the reserved slices of sponge roll. Beat the heavy cream until half whipped, add the confectioners sugar and vanilla, and whip until stiff. Put the whipped cream in a pastry bag fitted with a #7 or #8 star tube, and garnish the top of the dish with rosettes of whipped cream decorated with little berry-and-leaf cutouts made from the candied cherries and angelica. Chill the dish thoroughly and serve. NET: 6 to 8 servings.

CHARLOTTE MALAKOFF

This charlotte mold of almond and whipped cream mousse is nice to serve with a bowl of fresh strawberries or raspberries.

24 ladyfingers or other crisp
   sweet finger-length biscuits
12 tablespoons sweet butter
  (room temperature)
¾ cup superfine sugar
¾ cup ground blanched

almonds
Generous ¼ cup Kirsch
2½ cups heavy cream
5 tablespoons confectioners
  sugar

Have ready a charlotte mold and 2 feet of ¼-inch satin ribbon. Cut wax paper to fit the bottom of the mold and put it in. Line the sides of the mold with the ladyfingers (put a speck of sweet butter on the back of each to stick it to the mold). Chill the mold. Cream the sweet butter in the mixer. Add the sugar and beat until light and fluffy. Slowly mix in the almonds and Kirsch. Whip the heavy cream with a pinch of salt in a metal bowl over a bowl of ice. When the cream begins to thicken, add the confectioners sugar, and continue beating until the cream is stiff. Reserve about 1 cup of it for decoration, and fold the rest into the mousse, using a rubber scraper. Fill the charlotte mold with the mousse. Chill it in the refrigerator at least 2 hours. To serve, unmold it on a large serving platter and remove the round of paper that is now on top. Put the reserved whipped cream in a pastry bag fitted with a #7 star tube and decorate the top of the mousse. Tie the ribbon with a bow around the middle. NET: 8 servings.

MOUSSE AU CHOCOLAT

Chocolate Mousse

I have always liked to serve this chocolate mousse in little custard cups topped with a big rosette of whipped cream. Sometimes grated chocolate is sprinkled over the whipped cream. This is the Mousse au Chocolat that was always popular on my restaurant menus.

8 ounces dark sweet chocolate
Barely ½ cup water
5 egg yolks
5 egg whites
3 tablespoons light rum

½ cup heavy cream, whipped
  with 1 tablespoon confectioners sugar and ½ teaspoon
  vanilla extract (or scraping
  of 1 inch vanilla bean)

Have ready 6 chocolate mousse pots or custard cups, or 3¼-inch ramekins may be used. Cut the chocolate into little pieces and put them in a small heavy pan with the water. Stir over very low heat until the chocolate dissolves. Remove from the heat immediately. Using a small wire whisk, beat the egg yolks one at a time into the warm chocolate. Stir in the rum. In the mixer or a large copper bowl, beat the egg whites to soft peaks. Add the chocolate mixture to the egg whites, and beat well with a whisk; this mixture should be very smooth and shiny, well blended, and of a pouring consistency. Pour the mousse into a pitcher and slowly fill each of the little pots with the mousse. Put them in the refrigerator or freezer to set. When the mousse is set, put the whipped cream in a pastry bag fitted with a #8 or #9 star tube and pipe a big rosette on each one. Return the pots to the refrigerator until ready to serve. NET: 6 servings.

MOUSSE
AU CHOCOLAT
NORMANDIE

This dessert should ideally be made with fresh butter, eggs, and cream from Normandy. If that is not possible, get the very best and freshest you can, and, prepared with an extra measure of tender loving care, your Normandy Chocolate Mousse will be a sensation.

*Normandy
Chocolate Mousse*

24 ladyfingers or other crisp
   sweet finger-length biscuits
   (enough to line a charlotte
   mold)
8 ounces dark sweet chocolate
⅓ cup water
16 tablespoons (½ pound) sweet
   butter (room temperature)
10 tablespoons granulated sugar
3 egg yolks

3 egg whites
4 ounces salted blanched
   almonds
1 cup heavy cream, whipped

DECORATION
1 cup heavy cream, whipped
   with 1 tablespoon con-
   fectioners sugar and ½ teaspoon vanilla

Have ready a charlotte mold and 2 feet of ¼-inch satin ribbon. Cut a round of white paper to fit the bottom of the mold, and put it in. Line the sides of the mold with the ladyfingers.

CHOCOLATE MOUSSE. Cut the chocolate into small pieces, put them in a pan with the water, and stir over low heat until the chocolate melts. Immediately take it off the heat and let it cool a little. Put the butter in a mixer bowl with the sugar and beat until light and fluffy. One at a time, beat in the egg yolks. Pulverize the almonds in the blender and mix them into the butter and egg mixture. Mix in the cool melted chocolate, then beat the egg whites to soft peaks and fold them in, using a rubber scraper. Last, carefully and smoothly fold in the plain whipped cream.

Fill the mold, cover it with plastic wrap, and put it in the freezer to set. When the mousse is well set, carefully turn it out onto a flat serving plate. Put the flavored whipped cream in a pastry bag fitted with a #6 or #7 star tube, and pipe rosettes and scallops on top of the mousse. Tie the ribbon around the middle of the mousse, with a little bow, and serve. NET: 6 servings.

MOUSSE
AU CHOCOLAT
VÉNITIEN

Rich chocolate mousse encased and layered in delicate chocolate genoese cake. Chocolate heaven!

*Venetian
Chocolate Mousse*

CHOCOLATE GENOESE CAKE
6 eggs

1 cup superfine granulated sugar
4 ounces dark sweet chocolate

4 tablespoons liquid coffee
1 cup sifted cake flour (without
  baking powder)
4 tablespoons cool melted sweet
  butter (and extra for the cake
  pan)
A little rum or liqueur

CHOCOLATE MOUSSE
6 ounces dark sweet chocolate
5 tablespoons frozen sweet

butter
3 egg yolks
2 tablespoons rum or any
  desired liqueur or brandy
3 egg whites
1 cup heavy cream, whipped

DECORATION
2 cups shredded dark sweet
  chocolate
A little confectioners sugar

CHOCOLATE GENOESE CAKE. Preheat the oven to 350°. Brush a 9-inch springform cake pan with cool melted sweet butter. Cut wax paper to fit the bottom of the pan, put it in, butter the pan again, and dust it lightly with flour. Beat the eggs and sugar in the mixer until very light and fluffy. Break the chocolate into small pieces. Put it in a little pan with the coffee and melt it over very low heat. Cool it a little, and fold it into the egg yolk mixture. Fold in the flour a little at a time. Sprinkle the melted butter over the top and mix it into the batter. Pour the mixture into the pan and bake 50 minutes. When it is baked, slide a sharp knife around the edge to loosen the cake and unmold it at once, very carefully, onto a wire cake rack. Allow it to cool a little.

Clean the springform pan, brush it lightly with vegetable oil, and invert the pan on a paper towel to drain excess oil. Line it with slices of the cake, as follows:

Cut one complete round of cake for the bottom of the pan, and set it in. Cut fingers (strips) of the cake to fit around the edge of the pan, and line the whole pan in this manner (reserve about a third of the cake for the layers). Sprinkle the cake with a little rum or liqueur. Set the cake aside.

CHOCOLATE MOUSSE. Cut the chocolate into pieces and put them on a glass ovenproof dish over a pan of simmering water. Work the chocolate with a spatula until it is melted, then take it off the heat and work in the sweet butter (cut in pieces) and the egg yolks (one at a time) in the same manner, with the spatula. Flavor with the rum or liqueur, and add a little warm water if the mixture is too thick. Beat the egg whites to soft peaks. Add the chocolate mixture to them and fold it in well, then fold in the whipped cream.

Spread a layer of the mousse in the cake-lined springform mold, then a layer of cake slices. Sprinkle the cake with more rum or liqueur, and continue to layer with the chocolate mousse and cake slices until the pan is full. Cover the mold with wax paper and put it in the refrigerator for about 2 hours, or in the freezer, to set. To serve, carefully turn the mousse out onto a cold flat serving platter. Sprinkle the top with the shredded chocolate, also stick some around the sides. Dust the top with a little confectioners sugar. NET: 6 servings.

Of course, the raspberry seeds are removed.

½ cup superfine sugar	2 tablespoons unflavored
1 cup water	gelatine
2½ cups cleaned fresh	3 egg whites
raspberries	1 cup heavy cream, whipped
½ cup cold water	

MOUSSE AUX FRAMBOISES

Raspberry Mousse

Have ready a mold that has been rinsed out in cold water. Put the sugar and water in a heavy saucepan. Stir until the mixture comes to a boil and then let it cook to a thin syrup (250°). Reserve about ½ cup whole raspberries for garnish and add the rest to the syrup. Let them cook slowly until they are soft. Rub the mixture through a very fine sieve to remove the raspberry seeds. Soften the gelatine in the cold water and add it to the hot raspberry purée, stirring constantly to dissolve the gelatine thoroughly. Cool the purée a little in the refrigerator. Beat the egg whites to soft peaks and fold them into the cooled purée. Also fold in half of the whipped cream and blend well. Fill the mold with the mousse and put it in the refrigerator to set. When it is well set, turn it out on a flat serving platter (wrap a hot cloth around the mold and lift it off carefully). Decorate the mousse with the rest of the whipped cream and the reserved whole raspberries. NET: 4 servings.

3 eggs	Juice of 1 large navel orange
2 egg yolks	2 tablespoons whipped cream
3 tablespoons granulated sugar	Skinned sections of 2 large
Grated rind of 1 large navel	oranges
orange	3 tablespoons red currant or
2 tablespoons unflavored	apple jelly
gelatine	2 tablespoons water

MOUSSE À L'ORANGE

Orange Mousse

Put the eggs and egg yolks with the sugar in a mixer and beat until very thick and frothy. Mix in the grated orange rind. Put the gelatine and orange juice in a small pan and stir over low heat until the gelatine is dissolved. Sprinkle this over the egg mousse and mix it in carefully. Fold in the whipped cream. Pour the mousse into a crystal serving bowl and place it in the refrigerator to set. Put the jelly in a little pan with the water and cook to a syrupy consistency. Make sure the orange sections are perfect, with all pith removed, and when the mousse is set, arrange them on it and glaze them with the jelly syrup. NET: 4 servings.

MOUSSE AUX POMMES CALVADOS

Apple Brandy Mousse

2 pounds apples, peeled, cored
    and sliced
Grated rind of 1 lemon
2 tablespoons brown sugar
2 tablespoons apricot jam
2 tablespoons sweet butter
3 eggs
2 egg yolks
3 tablespoons granulated sugar
1 tablespoon unflavored
    gelatine

1 tablespoon hot water
Juice of 1 lemon
2 tablespoons whipped cream
¼ cup Calvados (apple brandy)
Skinned sections of 2 oranges
1 apple for decoration, peeled,
    cored, and thinly sliced

APRICOT SYRUP
3 tablespoons apricot jam
3 tablespoons water

Cook the sliced apples with the lemon rind, brown sugar, and apricot jam in a deep heavy pan over low heat until the mixture is a purée. Stir in the sweet butter, rub the mixture through a fine strainer, and cool it. Put the eggs and egg yolks in a mixer bowl with the sugar. Beat until the mixture is thick and light. Dissolve the gelatine in the lemon juice and hot water, and mix it into the egg mixture. Then fold in the cooled apple purée, whipped cream, and last, the apple brandy. Pour the mousse into a serving bowl and put it in the refrigerator to set.

APRICOT SYRUP. Cook the apricot jam with the water until it melts. Boil it a minute or two, then strain and cool it.

Make sure the orange sections are perfect, with no pith. When the mousse is firm, decorate it with them and with thin slices of raw sweet apple. Glaze the top with a little clear apricot syrup. NET: 4 servings.

MOUSSE PRALINÉ

Praline Mousse

When you have some extra praline powder stored in the refrigerator, here is a good way to use it.

4 eggs
3 egg yolks
4 tablespoons granulated sugar
2 tablespoons unflavored
    gelatine
5 tablespoons hot water
2 tablespoons whipped cream

4 tablespoons praline powder
    (page 77)
1 tablespoon light rum

GARNISH
Whipped cream
Chopped almonds

Beat the eggs, egg yolks, and sugar in the mixer until stiff. Dissolve the gelatine in the hot water in a little pan over low heat. Cool it a little and stir it into the egg mixture. Then add the praline powder, whipped cream, and rum. Spoon the praline mousse into a crystal serving bowl and put it in the refrigerator to set. When it is set, garnish the top with whipped cream and sprinkle with chopped almonds. Thoroughly chill the mousse before serving. NET: 4 servings.

The origin of this dessert is Italian, and the traditional Italian zabaglione is made with Italy's great dessert wine, the Sicilian Marsala. Zabaglione is an inspired, simple concoction of eggs and a little sweet wine, beaten to a frothy mousse over low heat. It is quickly made and should be served immediately, because it cannot last more than ten minutes in its frothy state. This recipe contains no sugar; the sweetening comes from the Marsala, which is also the flavor and character of the dish.

To ensure the success of this dessert of the uncertain, this recipe includes arrowroot, the most delicate of all starch thickening agents. It will help keep the zabaglione frothy and avoid its separating.

4 egg yolks *2 teaspoons arrowroot*
1 egg *¼ cup Marsala wine*

Combine the egg yolks, egg, and arrowroot in a bowl. Stand it in a shallow pan of hot water over low heat and beat the egg mixture with a wire whisk or rotary beater until it becomes very thick and frothy. It should almost triple in volume. Heat the Marsala in a small pan. Slowly add it to the egg mixture, beating constantly to maintain the froth. Serve immediately in tall stemmed crystal dessert glasses. NET: 2 servings.

French cuisine was quick to adopt and adapt the zabaglione. In the French culinary repertoire, the sabayon is also a favorite dessert sauce, its character ever changed through the various wines, brandies, liqueurs, or zests substituted for the traditional Marsala. As a dessert, this version has particular appeal with its top note of fresh lemon zest. The Sauce section includes recipes which show how sabayon can be adapted as a sauce for soufflés, crêpes, and various puddings.

2 eggs *4 teaspoons grated lemon rind*
4 egg yolks *9 tablespoons granulated sugar*
2 tablespoons lemon juice

Combine the eggs, egg yolks, lemon juice, lemon rind, and sugar in a bowl. Stand it in a shallow pan half filled with hot water over low heat. Beat the mixture with a rotary beater until it is frothy and holds its shape, then spoon it into tall stemmed dessert glasses. Serve immediately because the sabayon cannot hold its frothy state more than 10 minutes. NET: 2 servings as dessert; 4 as a sauce.

ZABAGLIONE

Warm Egg
and Marsala Froth

SABAYON
AU CITRON

Lemon Sabayon

SOUFFLÉ FROID AU CARAMEL

Cold Caramel Soufflé

4 eggs
3 egg yolks
¼ cup granulated sugar
2 tablespoons unflavored gelatine
Juice of 1 lemon
½ cup heavy cream, whipped

¾ cup chopped blanched almonds or other nuts

CARAMEL
½ cup granulated sugar
1 tablespoon corn syrup
½ cup water

Prepare a 3-cup (#5) soufflé dish as follows. Fold a long piece of wax paper in half lengthwise, brush it with vegetable oil, wrap it around the soufflé dish, and tie it on with string. The paper collar should rise 3 to 4 inches above the dish.

CARAMEL. Put the sugar in a small unlined copper pan or heavy pan with the corn syrup and ¼ cup water. Stir over low heat until the sugar has dissolved, then raise the heat to moderate and let the syrup cook to a good dark caramel color. Remove it from the heat, stir in ¼ cup cold water, and cool the mixture a little.

Combine the eggs and egg yolks in a mixer bowl with the sugar and beat until light and stiff. Dissolve the gelatine in the lemon juice and mix it into the egg mixture, then pour in the cooled caramel syrup and blend it in. Last, fold in 2 tablespoons whipped cream. Pour the mixture into the soufflé dish (it should come above the top of the dish). Place it in the refrigerator to set (at least 2 hours). When it is well set, remove the wax paper collar, dust the sides of the soufflé with the chopped nuts, and decorate the top with the remaining whipped cream forced through a pastry bag with a star tube. NET: 4 servings.

SOUFFLÉ FROID AU RHUM

Cold Rum Soufflé

5 eggs
4 egg yolks
8 tablespoons granulated sugar
8 tablespoons dark rum
2 tablespoons unflavored

gelatine
1 cup heavy cream, whipped
½ cup finely chopped blanched almonds
¼ cup red currant jelly

Prepare a 1-quart (#6) soufflé dish exactly as for Cold Caramel Soufflé above.

Put the whole eggs, the egg yolks, sugar, and 4 tablespoons rum in the mixer bowl and beat until light and stiff. Mix the gelatine with 4 tablespoons rum and dissolve it over very low heat. Cool it a little, pour it over the egg mixture, and carefully blend it in. Reserve enough whipped cream for a thin layer on top of the soufflé and fold in the rest, using a rubber scraper. Fill the soufflé dish with the mixture. Place it in the refrigerator or freezer to set. When it is firm, remove the wax paper collar and coat the sides with the chopped almonds. Spread the reserved whipped cream over the top, and make a tree pattern on it with the red currant jelly (see the instructions under Marquise Alice aux Fraises, page 814). NET: 4 to 6 servings.

3 eggs
2 egg yolks
6 tablespoons granulated sugar
Tiny pinch of salt
2 tablespoons instant coffee
    dissolved in 2 tablespoons
    boiling water

1½ tablespoons unflavored
    gelatine
1 tablespoon lemon juice
4 tablespoons water
1 cup heavy cream, whipped
2 tablespoons strained seedless
    black raspberry jam

SOUFFLÉ FROID AU CAFÉ

Cold Coffee Soufflé

Prepare a 3-cup (#5) soufflé dish exactly as for Cold Caramel Soufflé (page 824).

Put the whole eggs, egg yolks, and sugar in the mixer bowl and beat until light and stiff. Add the salt, then the cooled dissolved coffee, and blend well. Mix the dry gelatine with the lemon juice and water, dissolve it over low heat, cool it a little, then blend it into the egg mixture. Last, fold in three-quarters of the whipped cream lightly and smoothly, using a rubber scraper. Fill the soufflé dish with the mixture and leave it in the freezer about 1 hour to set. (Or let it set in the refrigerator, about 2½ hours.) When the soufflé is firm, spread the remaining whipped cream on the top. Cut the wax paper down to just below the whipped cream. Make a tree pattern on the whipped cream with the jam, following the instructions under Marquise Alice aux Fraises (page 815). Carefully remove the rest of the paper collar and serve. NET: 4 servings.

This is another glamorous chocolate dessert — cold chocolate soufflé rising out of the white soufflé dish, the sides of the soufflé crusty with chilled grated chocolate, the top patterned with whipped cream and currant jelly.

SOUFFLÉ FROID AU CHOCOLAT

Cold Chocolate Soufflé

3 eggs
2 egg yolks
6 tablespoons superfine sugar
6 ounces dark sweet chocolate
4 tablespoons light rum
2 tablespoons unflavored
    gelatine
2 tablespoons lemon juice

3 tablespoons water
2 cups heavy cream
2 tablespoons confectioners
    sugar
2 teaspoons vanilla extract
2 tablespoons red currant jelly
¾ cup coarsely grated dark
    sweet chocolate

Prepare a 3-cup (#5) soufflé dish as for Cold Caramel Soufflé (page 824).

Put the eggs, egg yolks, and superfine sugar in the mixer bowl and beat until the mixture is light and holds its shape (about 10 minutes). Break the chocolate into small pieces, put them in a little pan with the rum, and stir over low heat until it is dissolved. Mix the dry gelatine in a little pan with the lemon juice and water, and stir over very low heat until it too is dissolved. Beat the heavy cream in a metal bowl over a bowl of ice, using a large whisk. When it is almost stiff, add the confectioners sugar and vanilla extract. Continue beating until stiff. When the egg mousse is stiff, remove it from the mixer and carefully fold in the dissolved chocolate, then the dissolved gelatine, and last, fold in two-thirds of the whipped cream. Fill the prepared soufflé dish with this mixture (it should come at least 2 inches above the top of the dish) and put it in the freezer to set (about 1 hour). (Or let it set in the refrigerator, about 2½ hours.)

When the mixture is firm, take off the wax paper collar. Spread the top of the soufflé with the remaining whipped cream, and make a tree pattern on it with the jelly (see the instructions under Marquise Alice aux Fraises (page 814). Carefully stick the coarsely grated chocolate all around the sides of the soufflé. Chill thoroughly and serve. NET: 4 servings.

SOUFFLÉ FROID AUX FRAISES

Cold Fresh Strawberry Soufflé

This soufflé is garnished with whole strawberries set in rosettes of whipped cream.

5 eggs	3 tablespoons unflavored
4 egg yolks	gelatine
8 tablespoons granulated sugar	Juice of 1 lemon
Scraping of 1 inch of vanilla	4 tablespoons water
bean	1 cup fresh mashed strawberries
1½ cups heavy cream	¾ cup finely chopped walnuts
2 tablespoons confectioners	or pecans
sugar	2 tablespoons red currant jelly
Scraping of another inch of	10 to 12 whole perfect fresh
vanilla bean, for the whipped	strawberries for garnish
cream	

Prepare a 1-quart (#6) soufflé dish as for Cold Caramel Soufflé (page 824).

Put the eggs, egg yolks, sugar, and vanilla bean scraping in the mixer bowl and beat until the mixture is light and holds its shape (about 10 minutes). Beat the heavy cream in a metal bowl over a bowl of ice, using a large wire whisk. When it is almost stiff, add the confectioners sugar and the other vanilla bean scraping. Mix the gelatine with the lemon juice and water. Stir the mixture over low heat until the gelatine is dissolved. When the egg mousse is stiff, remove it from the mixer and fold in the mashed strawberries, then fold in the dissolved gelatine, and last, fold in about ¾ cup whipped cream. Fill the soufflé dish and leave it in the freezer about 1 hour to set. (Or let it set in the refrigerator, about 2½ hours.)

When the soufflé is firm, carefully take off the wax paper collar. Coat the sides of the soufflé with the walnuts or pecans. Spread the top with some of the remaining whipped cream. Make a tree pattern with the red currant jelly on the whipped cream (see under Marquise Alice aux Fraises, page 814). Put the remaining whipped cream in a pastry bag fitted with a #6 or #7 star tube and pipe rosettes of whipped cream all around the top of the soufflé. Place a whole fresh strawberry on each rosette. Chill thoroughly and serve. NET: 6 servings.

Avec le zest de citron . . . beaucoup!

4 eggs
6 egg yolks
1½ cups superfine sugar
Tiny pinch of salt
Grated rind and juice of
   2 lemons

2 tablespoons unflavored
   gelatine
1¼ cups heavy cream, whipped
Very thin slivers of candied
   lemon peel for garnish

SOUFFLÉ FROID AU CITRON

Cold Fresh
Lemon Soufflé

Prepare a 1-quart (#6) soufflé dish exactly as for Cold Caramel Custard (page 824).

Put the whole eggs, egg yolks, sugar, and salt in the mixer bowl and beat until the mixture is light and holds its shape (about 10 minutes). Add the grated lemon rind. Dissolve the gelatine in the lemon juice over very low heat. When the egg mousse is stiff, remove it from the mixer. Fold in carefully the dissolved gelatine and lemon juice, and then the whipped cream. Fill the soufflé dish with this mixture and leave it in the refrigerator at least 2½ hours to set. Then remove the paper collar and decorate around the top of the soufflé with twists of thin slivers of candied lemon peel. NET: 6 servings.

1½ tablespoons unflavored
   gelatine
Juice of 1 lemon
¼ cup cold water
1 cup raw egg whites (about
   9 egg whites)
¾ cup superfine sugar

2 teaspoons vanilla

DARK CARAMEL SAUCE
1 cup granulated sugar
¾ cup cold water
¼ teaspoon cream of tartar

SOUFFLÉ MONTE CARLO

Cold Egg White Soufflé
with Dark Caramel
Sauce

Brush the inside of a 6-cup (#7) soufflé dish with vegetable oil. Dissolve the gelatine with the lemon juice and water over low heat. Cool it slightly. Beat the egg whites in a copper beating bowl with a large piano wire whisk until they are light and fluffy and just hold their shape. Little by little, beat in the sugar. Then carefully fold in the dissolved gelatine, blend well (using a rubber scraper), then blend in the vanilla flavoring.

Fill the soufflé dish with the mixture and place it in the refrigerator to set.

DARK CARAMEL SAUCE. Combine the sugar, ½ cup cold water, and cream of tartar in an unlined copper pan. Stir over low heat until the sugar is dissolved, then raise the heat to moderate and let the sauce cook without stirring until it is a good dark caramel color. Take it instantly off the heat, stir in ¼ cup cold water, and let it cool.

When the egg white soufflé is firmly set, carefully turn it out onto a cold flat serving plate. Pour the cooled caramel sauce around it, and serve. NET: 4 servings.

MOSCOVITE AUX FRAISES

Mold of Egg White Soufflé (Baked and Chilled) with Strawberries and Port Wine

A little cool melted sweet butter
A little granulated sugar
6 egg whites
12 tablespoons vanilla sugar
   (page 77)

STRAWBERRY AND PORT WINE
  SAUCE
½ cup ruby port wine
1 cup strained red currant jelly
2 cups fresh strawberries,
   hulled and cut in quarters

Preheat the oven to 350°. Brush the inside of a 4-cup (#6) soufflé dish with cool melted sweet butter and dust it out with granulated sugar. Have ready a shallow roasting pan half filled with hot water. Beat the egg whites (with a large whisk or in an electric mixer) until nearly stiff. Gradually add the vanilla-flavored sugar and continue beating until the egg whites hold their shape. Put the mixture in a large pastry bag fitted with a large star tube (#9), and pipe it into the soufflé dish. Cover the dish with buttered wax paper, set it in the water bath (pan with hot water), put the whole assembly in the oven, and bake about 25 to 30 minutes, or until it is firm to the touch. When the soufflé is set, let it chill in the refrigerator until cold. Then turn it out onto a flat serving dish.

STRAWBERRY AND PORT WINE SAUCE. Warm the port wine and jelly together over low heat until the jelly is melted. Strain and cool this sauce, then add it to the quartered strawberries.

Spoon the sauce around the soufflé. NET: 4 servings.

CHOCOLATE SPONGE

Crock Mold of Rich Chocolate

Chocolate sponge differs from chocolate mousse in that the sponge is set with gelatine and is much firmer than the mousse.

8 ounces dark sweet chocolate
2 tablespoons sweet butter
½ cup evaporated milk
4 egg yolks

4 egg whites
1 teaspoon unflavored gelatine
¼ cup warm water
3 tablespoons whipped cream

Have ready a deep brown crock mold (about 1 quart) or terrine. Break the chocolate into small pieces. Melt it over low heat in a small saucepan with the butter and evaporated milk. Off the heat, mix in the egg yolks, then cook the mixture 1 minute very slowly. Beat the egg whites to soft peaks. Dissolve the gelatine in the warm water. Fold the chocolate mixture into the beaten egg whites, then pour the dissolved gelatine over them and mix it in lightly but well. Pour the mixture into the mold and set it in the refrigerator to chill. Serve the chocolate sponge in the crock, garnished with a few dollops of whipped cream. NET: 4 servings.

If you don't have time for the brioche, prepare Sponge Cake Roll (page 760), but do not roll or fill it. I think, however, that brioche gives this classic dish more character.

Brioche dough (page 708)
6 ounces mixed candied fruits
    (pineapple, cherries, orange,
    lemon, citron)
3 ounces seedless white raisins
1/2 cup light rum
3 tablespoons soft sweet butter
A little granulated sugar
2 1/2 cups light cream
6 eggs
1 cup superfine sugar mixed
    with the scraping of half a
    vanilla bean

CUSTARD SAUCE
1 egg
3 egg yolks
1 1/2 cups light cream
1/3 cup superfine sugar
Pod of half a vanilla bean

GARNISH
4 whole candied cherries
16 thin pieces of angelica, cut in
    3/4-inch leaf shapes

BRIOCHE. Instead of the usual 8-inch fluted brioche pans, bake the brioche dough in two small loaf pans. When they are baked, turn them out of the pans and chill them in the freezer.

PUDDING. Have ready a 2-quart charlotte mold and a shallow roasting pan. Preheat the oven to 350°. Coarsely chop the candied fruits and raisins. Warm the rum, pour it over them, and let them marinate. Cut the brioche loaves into slices, lay them on jelly roll pans, and let them brown lightly in the oven. Then reduce the oven heat to 300°. Butter the charlotte mold with the butter and dust it out with the sugar. Drain the candied fruits (reserve the rum). Put a layer of brioche slices in the mold, then a layer of candied fruits, another layer of brioche, a layer of fruits, and so on until the mold is filled, ending with brioche. Warm the light cream. Beat the eggs and slowly pour them over the cream, beating all the time. Add the reserved rum and the sugar mixed with vanilla bean scraping. Slowly pour this into the mold (which should absorb all the liquid without overflowing). Cover the mold with buttered wax paper, place it in the roasting pan half filled with hot water, and put the whole assembly in the 300° oven to cook the pudding until it is just firm to the touch, about 1 hour.

CUSTARD SAUCE. Mix the egg and egg yolks in a bowl with the sugar, and stir with a wire whisk until the mixture is well blended but not frothy. Put the cream in a saucepan with the vanilla bean pod and bring it to a boil, then remove the pod and pour the cream slowly into the egg mixture, stirring all the time. Put the mixture back into the saucepan and stir over low heat until it coats the back of a metal spoon. Chill this sauce before serving it.

When the pudding is out of the oven, let it stand about 5 minutes. Then slide a thin-bladed knife around the mold and turn the pudding out onto a flat serving dish. Decorate with 8 arrangements of a candied cherry half with 2 green angelica leaves, placed on top all around the edge. Serve the chilled custard sauce in a separate bowl. NET: 8 servings.

This pudding should be prepared at least 4 weeks in advance of serving. You will need two 1-quart closed pudding molds for it, and a pot big enough to boil them in.

1 pound finely chopped beef
 suet (fat)
½ teaspoon salt
1½ cups dry breadcrumbs, fried
 in 6 tablespoons salt butter
 (page 69)
1 pound dark brown sugar
½ pound each of black raisins,
 white seedless raisins, candied
 lemon peel, candied orange
 peel, and candied cherries,
 all finely chopped
4 ounces each of citron and
 dates, both finely chopped
1 pound all-purpose flour
Grated rind of 2 lemons
½ pound dried currants
½ pound chopped blanched

almonds
½ teaspoon freshly grated
 nutmeg
½ teaspoon allspice
1 teaspoon cinnamon
1 teaspoon ginger
5 large eggs or 6 small
¾ cup Cognac or good brandy
Sprigs of holly

HARD SAUCE
½ pound sweet butter
½ pound confectioners sugar
Tiny pinch of salt
½ cup Cognac or good brandy

FOR FLAMING
¾ cup Cognac or good brandy

Mix the beef suet with the salt, fried breadcrumbs, and brown sugar. Dust the finely chopped fruits with a little of the flour, together with the lemon rind and dried currants. Put these two mixtures in a large pan or bowl with the rest of the flour. Add the almonds and spices (nutmeg, allspice, cinnamon, ginger). Mix it all together with your hands or a large wooden spoon. Beat the eggs until frothy and stir them in, then add the brandy. Continue to stir; the more this is stirred, the better it will be. Fill the pudding molds, making sure the covers are on tight. Put them into a large pot of boiling water and boil, uncovered, 8 hours (add more boiling water as it boils away). Then let the puddings cool and store them in the molds in a cool place at least 4 weeks.

HARD SAUCE. Cream the butter in the mixer until it is light and fluffy. Add the confectioners sugar and salt, and slowly mix in the brandy. Beat the mixture about 5 minutes in an electric mixer. Thoroughly chill it before serving.

On the day you plan to serve the puddings, steam them again in the molds in the same way at least 3 hours. Then turn them out onto a hot flat serving dish. Decorate the tops with sprigs of holly. Heat the Cognac for flaming in a little pan, ignite, and pour it over the plum puddings (traditionally they were carried blazing into the dining room, but you can flame them at the table). Serve the hard sauce in a separate bowl. NET: 18 to 24 servings.

5 tablespoons sweet butter
2 apples, peeled, cored, and cut
   into small wedges
¾ cup milk
2 inches of vanilla bean,
   scraping and pod
3 tablespoons all-purpose flour
4 tablespoons granulated sugar

3 egg yolks
3 egg whites

SABAYON SAUCE
1 egg
1 egg yolk
2 tablespoons sherry
2 tablespoons granulated sugar

Heat 2 tablespoons butter in a little sauté pan and fry the apples until they are golden brown. Set them aside. Heat the milk in a saucepan with the vanilla bean pod. Bring it to a boil, then set it aside. Melt 3 tablespoons butter in a medium-size heavy pan. Off the heat, stir in the flour, blend well, and pour in the warmed milk (lift out the vanilla pod). Stir over low heat until the mixture thickens, but do not boil it. Remove it from the heat and mix in the sugar, egg yolks (one by one), and apples. Beat the egg whites to soft peaks and carefully fold them into the egg yolk mixture. Grease a large (10-inch) loaf pan with butter and dust it out with granulated sugar. Fill the pan with the pudding mixture. Set the filled pan carefully in a large casserole half filled with hot water. Cover the casserole with a piece of wax paper and the lid, and gently steam the pudding on top of the stove over very low heat for 30 to 45 minutes, until it is firm to the touch.

HOT SABAYON SAUCE. Put the egg and egg yolk in a small bowl with the sherry and granulated sugar. Mix them with a small wire whisk (or a rotary beater) and set the bowl in a shallow pan half filled with hot water over low heat. Continue to beat until the mixture is stiff.

When the pudding is cooked, remove it from the water bath and let it stand 5 minutes. Then turn it out of the pan onto a hot serving dish. Pour the hot sauce over it and serve immediately. NET: 4 servings.

Lightest, fluffiest rice custard, with candied fruit and glazed fresh strawberries. Many a man has said, "Rice pudding was never like this!"

½ cup rice (preferably
   Carolina type)
4 cups milk (and more during
   cooking)
1½ inch of vanilla bean,
   scraping and pod
Optional: ½ cup finely chopped
   mixed candied fruit, peels,
   and angelica
¼ cup Kirsch, Grand Marnier,
   or any desired liqueur or
   brandy
3 egg yolks

1 cup superfine sugar
2 tablespoons unflavored
   gelatine
1 tablespoon lemon juice with
   a little water
2 egg whites
2 cups heavy cream, whipped

GLAZED STRAWBERRIES
About 12 large perfect strawberries, with stems on if
   possible
¾ cup granulated sugar

¼ *teaspoon cream of tartar* ⅔ *cup water*

Put the rice in a large heavy pan with the milk and the vanilla bean pod. Cook it over low heat uncovered, until it has absorbed all the milk (the slower it is cooked, the better). When all the milk has been absorbed, add a little more. Continue to stir and add milk until the rice is soft and mushy. Be careful that the milk and rice do not scorch. The slower the milk is added, the creamier the rice will be. Let the mixed candied fruit marinate in the liqueur or brandy. Put the egg yolks in a mixer bowl, add the sugar and scraping from the vanilla bean, and beat well. Dissolve the gelatine in the lemon juice and water over low heat, and add it to the yolk mixture.

When the rice is cooked, put it in a bowl over a bowl of crushed ice, and stir in the egg yolk mixture. Stir this rice custard over ice until it is just beginning to cool. Beat the egg whites to soft peaks and carefully fold them into the rice. Mix in the candied fruit mixture with the liqueur, then add three-quarters of the whipped cream slowly, spoonful by spoonful. Spoon the rice custard into a crystal serving bowl. Put the remaining whipped cream in a pastry bag fitted with a #6 or #7 star tube and pipe rosettes on the rice — one rosette for each whole strawberry you plan to glaze. Put the rice in the refrigerator to chill and set. Just prior to serving, prepare the glazed strawberries exactly as for Marquise Alice aux Fraises (page 814). Put one glazed strawberry on each whipped cream rosette, and serve at once. NET: 6 servings.

ENGLISH
SUMMER
PUDDING

This dish is a classic English summer dessert, and this is my mother's recipe. In the summer, when there was any stale bread on hand, she used to slice it and soak it in the fresh fruit and juices, press the "pudding" down with a weight, and let it stand in a cool place over-night. The next day, for dessert, it was turned out of the bowl and served with a lovely fresh custard. Blackberries, blueberries, or what-ever you fancy may be substituted for the raspberry-currant combi-nation given here. Make the pudding the day before you will serve it.

4 cups fresh raspberries
4 cups fresh red currants
2 cups granulated sugar
¾ cup water
About 2 loaves of thinly sliced
  stale white bread

ENGLISH CUSTARD SAUCE
4 egg yolks
8 tablespoons sugar
1½ cups milk
2 teaspoons vanilla extract
½ cup heavy cream, whipped

Clean the fresh raspberries and red currants. Combine the sugar and water in a pan and cook over moderate heat until it is a light syrup (215°). Add the fruit, and cook it in the syrup about 5 minutes over low heat. Stir it gently; do not break it up too much. Taste it, and add more sugar if necessary. Trim the crusts from the stale bread. Line a round bowl with about a fourth of the slices. Spoon some of the fruit and syrup over the bread, then add another layer of bread, and continue with alternate fruit and bread layers until all the ingredients are used (finish with a bread layer). Cover the pudding with a double piece of wax paper and a flat plate. Place a heavy weight (like a brick) on the plate, and leave the pudding in the refrigerator overnight.

ENGLISH CUSTARD SAUCE. Put the egg yolks in a mixer bowl with the sugar and beat until light and fluffy. Heat the milk and vanilla in a saucepan and bring it just to a boil. Slowly pour the milk into the egg yolk mixture, stirring all the time. Return the mixture to the saucepan, and stir it over low heat until it thickens and coats the back of a metal spoon. Chill the sauce, then fold in the whipped cream.

The following day turn the pudding out onto a flat serving dish. Serve the custard sauce in a separate bowl. NET: 6 to 8 servings.

Apples	*Oranges*
Bananas	*Peaches*
Berries	*Pears*
Cantaloupe	*Persimmons*
Cherries	*Plums*
Figs	*Pomegranates*
Grapes	*Watermelon*
Nectarines	

FRESH NATURAL FRUIT FOR DESSERT

How to Serve It and How to Eat It (When You Find It)

A basket or épergne of fresh natural fruit on the table for the dessert, tout seul, is the favorite dessert of the French — the routine daily dessert; pastries and composed desserts are for special occasions. The common sense that is the acid test of French cuisine recognizes how much the contrasts between the texture and zest of whole natural fruit and the creamy and crusty composé desserts contribute to the maximum appreciation of each.

Is it possible we are hesitant about how to serve and eat fresh fruit au naturel at the table with ease and grace? It is sad that fresh fruit is so rarely offered in a restaurant meal. I am sure many people who decline a dessert when dining out would accept a cluster of good grapes or a plate of orange sections cut at the table. But in spite of that, customs and habits are still formed in our homes. Make fresh fruit your "routine" dessert for the sake of your palate and body. Intersperse the yen for chocolate and creams with a dessert of cold ripe unwaxed Northern Spy apples in November, or the first picking of local strawberries in June.

Here we address the place of fruit as a dessert. For information on what fruits go best with what cheeses, please refer to Plats des Fromages (page 697). Fruits may also be served as dessert after the cheese, or if no cheese is served at all. The following notes may serve as a guide on serving and eating each type of fruit, whether served with cheese or separately. If you, the host or hostess, lead the way with the peeling of a big ripe peach impaled on the end of a fork, you will reassure the others, and you will all enjoy the ambience of a Roman banquet.

APPLES. Cool the apples and wipe them with a cloth. Serve in a basket or bowl with individual service of a dessert plate and dessert knife and fork. (The dessert or fruit knife is usually a sharp-bladed knife for peeling and coring.) To eat, anchor the fruit with a fork. On the plate, cut it in half, then in quarters. Peel and core the quarters, then slice each quarter crosswise for eating.

BANANAS. Serve the whole fruit, firm and unbruised, but ripe yellow. To eat, peel the skin off the whole banana. Cut bite-size slices crosswise, and eat.

BERRIES. Strawberries and raspberries should be picked over and hulled or stemmed. If they are gritty, they should be lightly rinsed and gently dried in a clean cloth towel. Chill, and serve the whole berries in a crystal bowl or little basket on fresh grape leaves. Individual service should include a dessert plate and dessert spoon and fork. (If you don't have dessert spoons, use tablespoons, but no teaspoons.) If the berries are small, eat them whole; if large, cut each with the side of the spoon, anchoring it with the fork.

CANTALOUPE (and all melon except watermelon). Cut the melon into narrow wedges, with the rind either left on or cut away. Serve the melon wedges on individual dessert plates, with a dessert fork and spoon. Or, if the cantaloupes are small, they may be served as halves and eaten with a spoon. To eat, cut off bite-size pieces with the side of the spoon; eat with the fork.

CHERRIES (sweet). Serve them whole, ideally with stems on. Eat them with the fingers.

FIGS. Fresh figs are an especially good dessert, and a pleasant surprise when you find them. Serve them whole. In addition to the dessert fork and knife, supply a small spoon. There are two options in eating figs. If you prefer not to eat the skin, cut a cross in the skin at the stem end. Gently peel back the skin on each section (4 quarters), starting at the stem end, and scoop out the seeds and flesh with the spoon. Otherwise, simply cut the fig in quarters lengthwise and eat.

GRAPES. Serve grapes whole, in full clusters. They are generally eaten in the hand, directly from the stem.

NECTARINES. Serve them whole, chilled, and with the skin on. A dessert knife and fork are required. If you wish to peel the nectarine, firmly impale it on the tines of the fork and peel. To slice, place the nectarine (peeled or not) stem end down on the plate, and slice it slightly off center to avoid the stone. Continue slicing around the nectarine until all the fruit is eaten.

ORANGES. Buy full round oranges with moist perfumy rind. Oranges are served whole in a fruit bowl or basket. The individual table service required is a plate and dessert knife and fork. To eat, anchor the fruit with the fork and cut a slice of rind off the top and bottom. Then stand the orange on one flat end and proceed to pare the rind away from the sides, cutting down, in vertical strips. When the orange has been peeled, cut it in half horizontally. Then cut out each section with the point of the knife, as you eat it.

PEACHES. Serve and eat like nectarines (above).

PEARS must be ripe but firm and unbruised. They must not be served if hard and dry like wood pulp. When you possess some beautiful juicy pears, cool them and serve them whole in a fruit basket or bowl. The individual service includes a plate, and fruit knife and fork. To eat, anchor the pear with a fork. On the plate, cut it in half vertically, then into vertical quarters. Peel and core each quarter, then slice crosswise for eating.

PERSIMMONS. Serve them whole in the fruit basket or bowl. A fruit knife, spoon, and fork are required. Eat them in much the same way as the fig (above) if you wish to peel them. If the skin is to be eaten, simply cut the persimmon in quarters; then slice each quarter crosswise.

PLUMS. Serve them whole, in a mixed fruit basket or bowl. Eat them with the fingers.

POMEGRANATES. Pomegranates are a challenge, but unique and so good that they are worth it. The pomegranate is the ubiquitous fruit of the table in the warm countries such as Spain, North Africa, the Mid-East. For eating at the table, I suggest the Spanish method. Prepare them in advance. Quarter the raw ripe fruit and scoop the pulp (insides) into a serving bowl. Bring the bowl to the table with a large spoon and serve portions on individual plates. The diner uses a fork and spoon to eat bite-size mouthfuls, seeds and all. Then one delicately spits the seeds out into the same spoon; this is perfectly permissible.

WATERMELON. Cut individual serving portions into wedge shapes with the rind and serve them on individual dessert plates with a fruit knife and fork. To eat, run the knife between the rind and the flesh. Then cut the flesh at right angles into bite-size pieces. Remove the seeds with the fork.

ABRICOTS À LA BOURDALOUE

Rice Custard Mold with Apricots and Almonds

2 cups milk
4 tablespoons rice (preferably sticky Carolina-type)
½ cup granulated sugar
1½ tablespoons unflavored gelatine
4 tablespoons hot water
2 teaspoons vanilla extract
2 egg yolks

2 egg whites
1 cup heavy cream, whipped
12 large ripe or canned apricots

APRICOT GLAZE
¾ cup apricot jam
¾ cup granulated sugar
¾ cup water
24 whole blanched almonds

Have ready a round layer cake pan (8 or 9 inches diameter), lightly brushed with vegetable oil. Cook the rice with the milk in a heavy pan over low heat until quite soft and very creamy. Then stir in the sugar. Soften the gelatine in the hot water and stir it into the rice. Set the pan over a bowl of ice and stir constantly until the mixture is nearly cool. Then mix in the vanilla and egg yolks. Beat the egg whites to soft peaks and fold them into the rice, then carefully fold in the whipped cream. Fill the layer cake pan with the rice mixture and leave it in a cold refrigerator 2 hours to set.

APRICOT GLAZE. Put the apricot jam, sugar, and water into a small pan. Boil the mixture 5 minutes, and strain.

If the apricots are fresh, plunge them into boiling water, count to 10, remove, and skin them. Cut them in half and remove the stones. Pour the glaze over the apricot halves and chill them in it. When the rice custard is well chilled, turn it out onto a flat serving dish. Place the apricot halves around it, cut side up, and spoon a little of the jam glaze over each. Place a blanched almond in the center of each apricot half. NET: 6 servings.

ANANAS À L'IMPÉRIALE (PINEAPPLE À LA SINGAPOURE)

Rice Cream Ring with Fresh Pineapple and Kirsch

1 cup rice (Carolina type)
5 cups milk
2 tablespoons unflavored gelatine
¼ cup water
1 teaspoon vanilla extract
1 cup granulated sugar

½ teaspoon salt
1¼ cups heavy cream, whipped
1 large fresh Hawaiian pineapple
¼ cup Kirsch (cherry brandy)
½ cup confectioners sugar

Have ready a 1½-quart ring mold lightly brushed with vegetable oil. Put the rice in a heavy pan with the milk. Bring slowly to a boil and reduce to very, very low heat. Cover the pan tightly with the lid and cook without stirring until the rice is soft and mushy, then rub the rice through a very fine strainer. Mix the gelatine with the water, dissolve it over low heat, and mix it into the rice. Add the vanilla, sugar, and salt, and mix well. Put the mixture in the refrigerator to chill to lukewarm, then fold in the whipped cream. Fill the ring mold with the rice mixture and put it in the refrigerator to set. Peel and core the pineapple. Cut three-quarters of it into fine dice (there should be about 3 cups), put it in a bowl, pour the Kirsch over it, and let it marinate. Slice the remaining pineapple for garnish.

When the rice ring is well set, turn it out onto a serving dish. Fill the center with the Kirsch-marinated pineapple. Decorate with the pineapple slices. Sprinkle the top liberally with the confectioners sugar. NET: 4 to 6 servings.

CHARLOTTE AUX POMMES

Apple Charlotte with Sour Cream Sauce

About 12 tablespoons soft sweet
  butter
A little granulated sugar
  (for mold)
1 loaf sturdy white sandwich
  bread, sliced
6 to 8 large green cooking apples
1 12-ounce jar apricot jam
  (superior quality)
Grated rind of 1 large lemon
  (or 2 small)
1/3 cup granulated sugar
2 tablespoons Calvados (apple
brandy)

SOUR CREAM SAUCE
1 cup heavy cream
2 tablespoons confectioners
  sugar
1 cup sour cream
1/4 teaspoon ginger
1/2 teaspoon freshly grated
  nutmeg
1/2 teaspoon cardamom
Grated rind of 1 lemon

Butter a charlotte mold with a little of the soft sweet butter and dust it out lightly with granulated sugar. Trim the crusts from the bread slices, and cut each slice into 3 equal strips. Melt some sweet butter in a large frypan and fry the bread strips on one side only until they are golden brown. Use more butter as necessary. Completely line the mold with strips of bread (croûtons), with the fried side against the mold. (Reserve a quarter of the croûtons for the top.) Melt some of the butter and sprinkle the inside of the mold (the unfried side of the bread) with it and with a little granulated sugar.

Preheat the oven to 375°. Skin and core the apples and cut them into thick slices. Put them into a heavy pan with the jam, lemon rind, sugar, Calvados, and 4 tablespoons sweet butter. Cover, and cook briskly over moderate heat until the apples are just mushy and in bits. Pack them into the mold, cover with the reserved croûtons (fried side up), and bake the charlotte 40 minutes.

SOUR CREAM SAUCE. Put the heavy cream in a metal bowl and stand it over a bowl of crushed ice. Beat it with a wire whisk until it begins to thicken. Add the confectioners sugar and continue beating until it is stiff. Then fold in the rest of the ingredients with a rubber scraper, and chill thoroughly.

When the charlotte is out of the oven, let it stand 15 to 30 minutes in the mold (it will hold its shape better if cooled completely at room temperature; it bulges a little anyway because there is no gelatine to hold it firm). When it is cool, turn it out on a flat serving dish. Serve the warm charlotte with the ice cold sour cream sauce. NET: 4 to 6 servings.

CLAFOUTI LIMOUSIN

A kind of baked custard pancake with fruit. It is usually made with Bing cherries, but is as good with fresh small purple plums. It is so simple that it can usually be made while preparing the rest of the meal, and it's "homely good"!

5 tablespoons granulated sugar
⅛ teaspoon cardamom seed
1 to 1½ pounds fresh or canned
    Bing (dark red) cherries
    (traditionally with pits left in)

3 eggs
5 tablespoons all-purpose flour
2 cups milk or light cream
Tiny pinch of salt
A little confectioners sugar

Preheat the oven to 375°. Lavishly butter a round shallow baking dish 8 to 10 inches in diameter.

Sprinkle over the bottom a mixture of 2 tablespoons granulated sugar and the cardamom seed. Put the cherries into the dish. (The provincial way is to leave the pits in, but the clafouti will taste almost as good if you remove them.) Put the eggs in the mixer bowl. Mix in the flour, then the milk, and add the salt. Beat the mixture at least 5 minutes in the mixer, slowly adding 3 tablespoons granulated sugar. Pour it over the cherries, then bake the clafouti 30 to 40 minutes (it should start to be a little puffy and brown). Sprinkle it heavily with confectioners sugar, and serve it warm or cold, cut in wedges. NET: 4 to 6 servings.

COEURS À LA CRÈME

Cream Cheese Hearts

The three fresh fruit sauces are for variation from menu to menu. Each will suffice for the six little hearts, and only one sauce is usually served at a time. To make the hearts, you need six 3-inch coeur à la crème wicker baskets or china molds and a length of cheesecloth (see below).

Ice water, baking soda, and
    lemon juice (for cheesecloth)
½ pound cream cheese
⅔ cup confectioners sugar
Scraping of half a vanilla bean
1¼ cups heavy cream, whipped
Optional: 6 large fresh grape
    leaves (for serving)

STRAWBERRY SAUCE
2 cups fresh strawberries
¼ cup Framboise (raspberry
    brandy)

1 cup seedless black raspberry
    jam

RASPBERRY SAUCE
2 cups fresh raspberries
1 cup red currant jelly
¼ cup light rum

PEACH SAUCE
3 cups thinly sliced fresh
    peaches
1 cup strained apricot jam
¼ cup Drambuie

Prepare six 3-inch coeur à la crème wicker baskets or china molds as follows. From a length of 4 thicknesses of cheesecloth, cut 6 squares, each large enough to line a mold plus a 2-inch margin all around. Mix a bowl of ice water with 1 tablespoon lemon juice and a pinch of baking soda. Soak the cheesecloth squares in this liquid until you are ready to fill the molds. Put the cream cheese in a mixer bowl and beat until it is light and fluffy. Add the confectioners sugar and vanilla bean scraping and continue beating. Fold the mixture carefully into the whipped cream. Wring the squares of cheesecloth damp-dry and line the little molds, leaving the 2-inch overhang all around. Spoon the cream mixture into the molds and fold the extra cheesecloth over the tops. Stand them on a rack in a jelly roll pan and chill them in the refrigerator at least 2 hours. To serve, unmold and unwrap each cream heart onto a large fresh grape leaf on a crystal dessert plate. Serve with a separate bowl of one of the sauces.

If wicker basket molds are used, serve them on the grape leaf, with each person unwrapping his own.

STRAWBERRY SAUCE. If the strawberries are large, cut them in halves or quarters. Put them in a bowl and sprinkle with the Framboise. Melt the jam over low heat and strain it over the strawberries. Chill at least 1 hour.

RASPBERRY SAUCE. Melt the jelly over low heat. Mix in the rum, and strain. Chill the sauce and raspberries separately at least 1 hour. Mix just before serving.

PEACH SAUCE. Pour the Drambuie over the peaches. Melt the jam over low heat and rub it through a fine wire strainer (if it is too thick, add a little boiling water). Mix the apricot sauce with the peaches, and chill at least 1 hour.

NET: 6 servings.

FLUMMERY

Flummery — semolina cream with fresh raspberry sauce — is a very old English dish; Tom Jones ate a flummery. It looks quite dramatic, with the dark red raspberry sauce against the shimmering white semolina cream, and is a beautiful way to enjoy fresh raspberries in season.

1 cup dry white wine
1 cup water
Tiny pinch of salt
8 tablespoons cream of farina
  (semolina)
¾ cup granulated sugar
2 teaspoons vanilla extract
4 egg whites
1½ tablespoons unflavored
  gelatine

2 teaspoons lemon juice
2 tablespoons water
¾ cup heavy cream, whipped

FRESH RASPBERRY SAUCE
1 cup raspberry jelly (or red
  currant jelly)
½ cup Cointreau
1 cup ripe fresh raspberries

Have ready a ring mold (or any mold) lightly brushed with vegetable oil. Put the wine and water in a heavy pan with the salt, bring to a boil, and throw in the cream of farina. Stir until the mixture is smooth, and let it cook slowly until it comes away from the sides of the pan. Off the heat, mix in the sugar and vanilla. Set the mixture over a bowl of ice and continue to stir until it begins to cool. Beat the egg whites to soft peaks and (over ice) fold the cream of farina mixture into them. Mix the dry gelatine with the lemon juice and water. Dissolve it over low heat in a little pan. Cool it a little and blend it into the cream of farina mixture. Last, fold in the whipped cream. Fill the mold with the mixture and place it in the refrigerator to set.

FRESH RASPBERRY SAUCE. Combine the jelly in a pan with the Cointreau and warm them a little. Pour this syrup over the raspberries and chill thoroughly.

To serve, turn the semolina cream out onto a flat serving dish. Spoon the raspberry sauce over it. NET: 4 servings.

FONDUE AUX POIRES

Poached Fresh Pears Stuffed with Rum Pastry Cream

4 large firm ripe pears
¾ cup granulated sugar
3 tablespoons apricot jam
½ cup water
1 teaspoon lemon juice

RUM PASTRY CREAM
1 egg

1 egg yolk
3 tablespoons granulated sugar
3 tablespoons all-purpose flour
1 tablespoon unflavored gelatine
¾ cup milk
3 egg whites
2 tablespoons heavy cream
2 to 3 tablespoons light rum

Peel the pears with a potato parer, cut them in half, and remove the cores. In a large heavy pan, combine the sugar, apricot jam, water, and lemon juice. Cook until the mixture is a thin syrup (215°). Simmer the pears in this syrup over low heat 7 to 8 minutes, then cool and arrange them, cut side up, on a serving dish (reserve and chill the syrup).

RUM PASTRY CREAM. Put the egg, egg yolk, sugar, and flour in a bowl and beat very well with a wire whisk. Stir in the dry gelatine. Bring the milk slowly to a boil, slowly pour it into the egg mixture, beating all the time, then transfer the mixture to a saucepan and stir over low heat until it just comes to a boil. Set the pan over a bowl of ice and stir until the mixture is cold. Then beat the egg whites to soft peaks and fold them in. Also fold in the heavy cream and rum.

Put the pastry cream in a pastry bag fitted with a #6 or #7 star tube, fill the pears, and chill thoroughly. Spoon the reserved syrup over them before serving. NET: 4 servings.

The citrus syrup in this recipe can be kept in an airtight container in the refrigerator indefinitely, ready for a great instant fresh fruit bowl.

*Fresh fruits (any mixture of
three or more; see below)*

CITRUS SYRUP
2 oranges

*2 lemons
2 limes
2 cups granulated sugar
½ teaspoon cream of tartar
3 cups water*

CITRUS SYRUP. Peel the oranges, lemons, and limes with a potato parer. Cut the rinds into fine shreds across (not lengthwise), and put them in a pan with the sugar, cream of tartar, and water. Stir over low heat until the sugar dissolves, then let the mixture cook without stirring until it is a light syrupy consistency. Chill it thoroughly.

Assemble a fresh fruit bowl of any quantity of three or more kinds of fruit, such as:

Apples, peeled and cut into bite-size chunks.
Apricots, skinned and quartered or sliced.
Blueberries, whole.
Cherries, halved and pitted.
Grapes, white or black, halved and seeded.
Grapefruit, white or pink, skinned sections.
Melon (cantaloupe, honeydew, watermelon), cut into balls with a melon scoop.
Oranges, skinned sections.
Peaches, skinned and sliced.
Pears, peeled and sliced or cut in chunks (use pears only if perfect, and cut them at the last minute to avoid discoloring).
Pineapple, peeled and cut into chunks.
Plums, halved or quartered and pitted.
Strawberries, hulled, whole or cut depending on size.

Have the fruit and syrup well chilled. Just before serving, pile up the fruit in a chilled crystal or silver bowl and spoon the syrup over it. Or hollow out a watermelon half (or any melon half large enough) cut lengthwise, leaving a strip of rind over the top like a handle, and pile the fruit in the shell.

Fresh peaches in raspberry and port wine sauce, with vanilla ice cream, whipped cream, and shredded almonds, presented on a silver platter.

*4 large perfect ripe peaches
1 tablespoon ruby port wine
1 tablespoon hot water*

*1 cup raspberry jelly
2 cups heavy cream
3 tablespoons confectioners*

sugar
Scraping of 1 inch of vanilla
    bean

1 quart vanilla ice cream
¼ cup browned shredded
    blanched almonds

The peaches should be skinned without cutting into the flesh. If necessary, pour boiling water over them, let them sit in it a few seconds, then pour off the water and skin them. Cut them in half carefully and remove the stones (you want 8 beautiful perfect peach halves for this dish).

MELBA SAUCE. Mix the port wine, hot water, and raspberry jelly together and rub the mixture through a fine strainer. Let the peaches marinate in this mixture 1 hour in the refrigerator. At the same time, thoroughly chill a silver platter for serving. Beat the heavy cream in a metal bowl over a bowl of ice until it is almost stiff. Add the confectioners sugar and vanilla bean scraping and continue beating until the cream is stiff. Arrange scoops of vanilla ice cream down the center of the chilled platter, and peach halves down each side. Coat the peaches with the raspberry and port wine sauce. Put the whipped cream in a pastry bag fitted with a #8 or #9 star tube and lavishly decorate the whole platter. Scatter the almonds over the top. NET: 8 servings.

POIRES MERINGUÉES AU CHOCOLAT À LA FOYOT

Stuffed Poached Pears in Meringue with Chocolate Sauce

6 beautiful ripe but firm pears
2½ cups granulated sugar
½ teaspoon cream of tartar
½ cup Cognac or light rum
1 cup water
Scraping and pod of half a
    vanilla bean
6 cloves

STUFFING
2 ounces finely chopped angelica
2 ounces finely chopped glazed
    pineapple
2 ounces finely chopped glazed
    cherries

1 ounce finely chopped mixed
    citron and orange peel
A little Cognac or light rum

MERINGUE
4 egg whites
12 tablespoons granulated sugar
Granulated sugar for
    sprinkling

CHOCOLATE SAUCE
5 ounces dark sweet chocolate
2 to 3 tablespoons Cognac or
    light rum
¼ cup heavy cream

Peel the pears neatly from top to bottom with a potato parer, keeping the stem on. With the potato parer, remove the core from the bottom, taking care not to pierce the top. (If the pears are peeled ahead of time, cover them with plastic wrap so they won't discolor.) Insert 1 clove in each pear next to the stem. In a large heavy pan combine the sugar, cream of tartar, Cognac or light rum, water, and the vanilla bean scraping and pod. Stir with a metal spoon over low heat until the sugar dissolves, then let the syrup cook until it forms a light thread between the finger and thumb (225°). Stand the pears in the syrup, baste them with it, and simmer them very, very gently, basting frequently, about 30 minutes (or less if the pears are not firm at the start).

STUFFING. Sprinkle the finely chopped candied fruits with Cognac or light rum, the same as is being used in the poaching syrup. Stir them gently to mix them.

MERINGUE. Preheat the oven to 325°. Beat the egg whites in a mixer bowl to soft peaks. Very slowly add the granulated sugar, continuing beating until the whites are stiff.

When the pears are poached, stuff them with the fruit mixture and arrange them upright in a baking dish. Put the meringue in a pastry bag fitted with a #9 star tube. Pipe a spiral of meringue coating around each pear, starting about three-quarters of the way down and working to the top, leaving the stem showing. Sprinkle the meringue liberally with granulated sugar, and bake the pears in the preheated oven until the meringue is golden brown.

CHOCOLATE SAUCE. Break the chocolate into little pieces and put them in a small heavy pan with the Cognac or rum (the same as used in the poaching syrup). Stir over very low heat until the chocolate is dissolved. Mix in the heavy cream and continue to stir over low heat until the sauce is of the desired consistency.

To serve, arrange the baked pears upright on a shallow serving dish. Carefully spoon the chocolate sauce around them (not on them). This dessert should be served warm. (It can be prepared a few hours ahead of time and warmed briefly in a 300° oven before pouring in the chocolate sauce.) NET: 6 servings.

---

3 cups milk
1 cup rice (Carolina type)
6 tablespoons granulated sugar
¼ teaspoon salt
1 inch of vanilla bean, split
1 tablespoon sweet butter
3 egg yolks

APPLE MERINGUES
6 large green cooking apples
2 cups cold water
1 cup granulated sugar
1 inch of vanilla bean
Juice of half a lemon
3 egg whites
¾ cup superfine sugar
Granulated sugar for sprinkling
A little red currant jelly

POMMES
MERINGUÉES
AU RIZ

Meringue-Coated
Poached Apples with
Rice Custard and
Currant Jelly

Bring the milk to a boil in a saucepan, then set it aside. Put the rice in a heavy pan, cover with cold water, and bring to a boil. Immediately take it off the heat and let it stand 5 minutes, then drain and rinse it in cold water, return it to the pan, and cover it with the scalded milk. Add the sugar, salt, and inch of vanilla bean (pulp and pod), and bring the mixture to a boil. Stir in the sweet butter, cover the pan, and simmer gently over low heat 30 minutes, or until the rice is quite soft and has absorbed the milk. (If necessary, add more milk until the rice is soft.) Remove the vanilla pod and toss the rice with a fork to separate the grains. Beat the egg yolks a little and mix them into the rice. Spread the prepared rice on a baking dish to cool.

Preheat the oven to 325°. Peel and core the apples, and leave them whole. Combine the water, granulated sugar, inch of vanilla bean, and lemon juice in a large heavy pan, stir over low heat until the sugar is dissolved, bring to a boil and cook about 5 minutes. Gently poach the apples in the syrup over low heat until they are just soft. Lift each one out with a large slotted spoon, let it drain, and arrange them on the rice. Beat the egg whites to soft peaks. Add the superfine sugar and continue beating until the whites are stiff. Put the mixture (meringue) in a pastry bag fitted with a #6 or #7 star tube and pipe meringue around each apple to cover it completely. Sprinkle the meringue-covered apples with a little more granulated sugar and put the dish in the oven to bake until the meringues have browned a little. When they are done, put a little dollop of currant jelly on each apple, and serve. NET: 6 servings.

POIRES SAUTERNES

Pears Poached in Sauternes Wine

This simple, exquisite dessert, in which the Sauternes wine (the "syrup" of the grape) enhances the glorious essence of the fruit, was created for the Wine Institute of America, one of the first sponsors of my television show. The recipe was published in *Cue* magazine (September 1971) as an example of the classic method of poaching fruit in wine. (You may substitute apples for pears in this dish.)

4 lovely fresh pears (not too ripe)
Juice of 1 lemon with cold water (for soaking pears)
2 cups good Sauternes wine
1 cup granulated sugar

¼ cup honey
½ teaspoon salt
4 cardamom seeds, crushed
4 cloves
Optional: ½ cup Sour Cream Sauce (page 67)

Preheat the oven to 325°. Skin the pears carefully with a potato parer, leaving the stem on. Remove the core (from the bottom) with the potato parer, without piercing the top. Soak the peeled pears in lemon juice and cold water while preparing the syrup.

SAUTERNES SYRUP. In a heavy pot (with a lid) combine the wine, sugar, honey, and salt. Simmer the mixture very gently until it becomes a light syrup (225°), then mix in the crushed cardamom seeds.

Stick a clove next to the stem of each pear. Place the pears in the syrup, baste them with it, cover the pot, and bake the pears until just soft (about 45 minutes, depending on their ripeness). Serve them hot or cold, with a glass of the same Sauternes wine, chilled. If you like, serve them in a crystal dessert bowl, with a separate bowl of sour cream sauce. NET: 4 servings.

8 ounces dark sweet chocolate
8 small paper cupcake cases
8 whole fresh strawberries
8 leaf cutouts of angelica

PASTRY CREAM FILLING
½ cup finely chopped mixed
    candied pineapple and
    cherries
¼ cup dark rum

1 egg
1 egg yolk
3 tablespoons all-purpose flour
3 tablespoons granulated sugar
Tiny pinch of salt
1 tablespoon unflavored gelatine
¾ cup milk
2 egg whites
1½ cups heavy cream, whipped

Chocolate Cups with
Pastry Cream, Candied
Fruits, and a Fresh
Strawberry

CHOCOLATE CUPS. Cut the chocolate into little pieces and put them on a heatproof plate over a pan of hot, barely simmering water. Stir the chocolate around the plate with a spatula until it is melted. When it is dissolved and smooth, take it off the pan and let it cool a little. Completely coat the insides of the paper cupcake cases with this chocolate. Set them on a jelly roll pan and put them in the freezer or refrigerator to chill. When they are hardened, carefully peel off the paper.

PASTRY CREAM FILLING. Mix the chopped candied fruits with the rum and let them marinate. Put the egg, egg yolk, flour, sugar, and salt in a bowl and beat with a whisk until smooth. Stir in the dry gelatine. Bring the milk to a boil in a saucepan and pour it into the egg mixture, stirring all the time. Transfer the egg mixture to the saucepan and stir over low heat until it just comes to a boil, then cool it a little. Beat the egg whites to soft peaks and fold them smoothly into the egg yolk mixture. Then fold in ¾ cup of the whipped cream. Gently stir in the mixed fruits and the rum in which they were soaking.

Set the pan over a bowl of crushed ice and stir until it is well chilled and almost on the point of setting. Fill a pastry bag, fitted with a #8 or #9 plain round tube, with the pastry cream and pipe it into the chocolate cups, not quite to the tops. Fill another pastry bag, fitted with a #8 or #9 star tube, with the remaining whipped cream and pipe a large rosette on each chocolate cup. Put a large fresh strawberry and a leaf of angelica in the center of the rosette. Chill the cups thoroughly, and serve. NET: 8 servings.

8 ounces dark sweet chocolate
8 small cupcake paper cases
1½ cups heavy cream
2 tablespoons confectioners
    sugar
1 teaspoon vanilla extract
8 fresh whole strawberries,
    with stems

A little red currant jelly

RUM, FRUIT, AND CAKE FILLING
2 cups stale cake
½ cup dark rum
½ cup finely chopped mixed
    candied fruits

Chocolate Cups with
Rum-Soaked Fruit and
Cake and a Glazed
Fresh Strawberry

Make the chocolate cups exactly as in the preceding recipe.

RUM, FRUIT, AND CAKE FILLING. Crumble the cake, soak it in the rum, and mix in the candied fruits.

Fill the chocolate cups (on a jelly roll pan) half full with this filling. Return them to the refrigerator. With a large whisk, beat the heavy cream in a metal bowl over a bowl of ice until it is nearly stiff. Add the confectioners sugar and vanilla, and continue beating until the cream is stiff. Put the whipped cream in a pastry bag fitted with a large star tube (#8 or #9) and pipe a very large rosette on each chocolate case. Melt the jelly over low heat, dip the strawberries in it, and place one in the center of each rosette. Chill the cups thoroughly, and serve. NET: 8 servings.

MONT-BLANC AUX MARRONS

Meringues with Chestnut Purée, Whipped Cream, and Grated Chocolate

This is my own version of a Mont-Blanc. The chestnut purée is drizzled over baked meringues to give this Mont-Blanc some definite crunch.

MERINGUES
3 egg whites
10 tablespoons granulated sugar
Granulated sugar for sprinkling

CHESTNUT PURÉE
1 pound chestnuts (in the shell)
Cooking liquid (half milk and half water)

1 inch of vanilla bean, split
1 cup corn syrup
2 tablespoons light rum

GARNISH
¾ cup heavy cream, whipped
½ cup coarsely grated dark sweet chocolate

MERINGUES. Preheat the oven to 225°. Beat the egg whites to soft peaks in a mixer. Gradually add the sugar, continuing to beat until the egg whites are stiff. Put the mixture in a pastry bag with a #9 plain round tube. Cover a baking sheet with wax paper. Pipe out 6 mound-shaped meringues on the paper, sprinkle them with granulated sugar, and bake them until they are firm and light golden brown. Let them cool out of the oven.

CHESTNUT PURÉE. Put the chestnuts in a pan, cover them with water, bring to a boil, boil the chestnuts 4 minutes, and remove the pan from the heat. Remove the chestnuts one by one from the water as you shell them. With a small sharp knife, remove the outer and inner skins. Put the shelled and skinned chestnuts in a saucepan, cover them with the cooking liquid, add the split piece of vanilla bean, and simmer the chestnuts until soft. Drain, remove the bean, rub the chestnuts through a fine strainer, and set them aside. Cook the corn syrup until it makes a fine thread between the fingers and thumb (225°). Stir in the rum. In the mixer, slowly beat the syrup into the chestnuts until the purée is the consistency of mashed potatoes.

Put the chestnut purée in a pastry bag fitted with a very small round tube (#2 or #3, the size of spaghetti). Pipe the chestnut purée carelessly in a mound on each meringue. Put the whipped cream in another pastry bag fitted with a #6 or #7 tube, and pipe a rosette on each chestnut mound. Sprinkle the chestnut mounds and whipped cream with the coarsely grated dark sweet chocolate. Arrange the meringues on a serving dish, and serve. NET: 6 servings.

Homemade chocolate truffles and demitasse . . . the perfect finale to a perfect dinner party.

8 ounces dark sweet chocolate
5 tablespoons water
8 tablespoons sweet butter,
   cut into pieces
3 tablespoons light rum
½ cup coarse praline powder
   (page 77)

COATING
½ cup sifted cocoa
¾ cup coarsely grated dark
   sweet chocolate
6 ounces dark sweet chocolate

Cut the chocolate into little pieces, put them in a small heavy pan with the water, and stir over low heat until the chocolate melts. Stir in the sweet butter bit by bit, then stir in the rum and cool the mixture a little. Add the praline powder and chill the mixture until firm.

COATING. Put the cocoa and grated chocolate each in a shallow little dish (to roll and coat the truffles). Cut up the 6 ounces of chocolate in little chunks, put them on a platter, and set it over a pan of barely simmering water. Stir the chocolate with a spatula until it is melted and smooth. Take it off the pan and let it cool at room temperature.

Working with two teaspoons, shape a little of the praline-chocolate mixture into a ball about ¾ inch in diameter (it should not be perfectly round, because real truffles never are). Drop the ball in the melted chocolate and coat it. Lift it out with a little spatula and drop it in either the grated chocolate or cocoa (dust half the truffles with grated chocolate and half with cocoa). Roll the coated ball in the dish to dust it, and set it on a piece of wax paper on a jelly roll pan. When all the praline-chocolate mixture is prepared in this way, put the truffles (on the jelly roll pan) in the freezer to set them. Serve them in tiny paper candy cups. NET: 50 to 60 truffles.

FROZEN DESSERTS

Ice cream (glace) made in the French manner, with good custard cream sweetened with sugar syrup and properly frozen in a churn type of freezer, is an easy but all too rare treat. You can enchant your family and guests with a simple homemade churned custard ice cream garnished with fresh fruit of the season.

We have included a few recipes for sherbets, rather than basic ices. The sherbet (sorbet) contains beaten egg white (meringue) which gives a nice finish.

(1) Ice cream, can, of course, be made in a refrigerator tray, but it simply cannot compare with ice cream which has been churned in a freezer (either electric-powered or hand-powered). Constant churning is the only way to a light, smooth, creamy consistency. The thrill of eating this quality of ice cream today is available only through home-made ice cream, which is well worth the little trouble required. All our ice cream and sherbet recipes are in terms of churn freezing.

(2) Fill the freezer drum only three-quarters full to allow for expansion of the cream during freezing.

(3) Pack the drum in the freezer bucket with a mixture of 4 parts ice to 1 part rock salt. More salt would give faster freezing but not so creamy an ice cream.

(4) Churn the ice cream until the paddles slow down and stop. The ice cream is now beginning to set. Open the drum (make sure no ice-salt drip gets in), and remove the paddles. (NOTE: This is the point at which to add fruit or other ingredients in the recipes which call for such additions before packing down the ice cream.) Pack down the ice cream, cover the drum with a piece of doubled wax paper and the lid, and seal the lid with a heavy coating of vegetable shortening or lard. Then cover the drum with more ice and salt. Wrap the whole freezer thickly with newspapers to insulate it, and let the ice cream set (ripen or mellow) for a few hours.

(5) If the basic ice mixture is too sweet, it will not set. Therefore, if liqueur (which is very sweet) is to be used in the ice cream, add it after the ice cream has set. Also, if there is an ingredient that you want to keep crisp, such as praline or breadcrumbs, add it also after the churning is finished.

GLACE À LA VANILLE

French Vanilla Custard Ice Cream

This is the basic vanilla custard ice cream, excellent as is or with other flavorings added. It is made in the French manner, with a sugar syrup added to a rich custard, to ensure creamy smoothness. You need a churn-type freezer, ice, and rock salt.

1 cup granulated sugar	*Pinch of salt*
⅛ teaspoon cream of tartar	*Scraping of half a vanilla bean*
½ cup water	*4 cups heavy cream (not*
8 egg yolks	*whipped)*

Combine the sugar, cream of tartar, and water in a small saucepan, stir with a metal spoon over low heat until the sugar dissolves, then let it cook at moderate heat until the syrup forms a thin thread between the finger and thumb (225°). Beat the egg yolks in a mixer until very light and fluffy. Slowly pour in the hot syrup, beating all the time. Continue beating until the mixture is thick and cold. Add the salt and vanilla bean scraping. Mix in the heavy cream. Freeze the mixture in a churn freezer according to the manufacturer's instructions, reading also the Notes (page 848). NET: A generous 2 quarts.

Ingredients for French Vanilla Custard Ice Cream (page 848), except the vanilla bean	*Grated rind of 1 lemon* *3 cups crushed fresh strawberries*	**GLACE AUX FRAISES**

GLACE AUX FRAISES

Fresh Strawberry Ice Cream

Purée the berries in a blender if you want them absolutely smooth. Mash them with a potato masher if you want a few pieces of pulp in the ice cream. Make French Vanilla Custard Ice Cream, substituting the lemon rind for the vanilla bean. Before packing down the ice cream, mix in the strawberries thoroughly, down to the bottom of the drum. NET: About 3 quarts.

GLACE AUX FRAMBOISES OU AUX MÛRES

Fresh Raspberry or Blackberry Ice Cream

Follow the Strawberry Ice Cream recipe above, using for the fruit 2 cups raspberries or blackberries puréed in an electric blender to crush the seeds, or strained through a fine sieve. NET: About 3 quarts.

Ingredients for French Vanilla Custard Ice Cream (page 848) *1 teaspoon almond extract*	*A little green vegetable coloring* *1½ cups finely chopped shelled blanched pistachio nuts*

GLACE AUX PÊCHES OU AUX ABRICOTS

Fresh Peach or Apricot Ice Cream

Make French Vanilla Custard Ice Cream up to the point when it is ready to be packed down. Transfer the frozen ice cream from the drum to a chilled metal bowl. Thoroughly and quickly mix in the almond extract and green vegetable coloring, then the pistachio nuts. Return the ice cream to the drum and proceed to pack it down and let it set, according to the instructions. NET: About 2½ quarts.

GLACE À LA PISTACHE

Pistachio Ice Cream

Follow the Strawberry Ice Cream recipe above, using for the fruit 2 cups skinned and thinly sliced ripe peaches or apricots. NET: About 3 quarts.

A very good and unusual ice cream from England.

Ingredients for French Vanilla Custard Ice Cream (page 848) *1½ cups good whole wheat breadcrumbs, toasted dry*	*and crisp in the oven or a dry frypan* *¼ cup light rum*

BROWN BREAD AND RUM ICE CREAM

Make French Vanilla Custard Ice Cream, but before packing it down, mix in the toasted breadcrumbs and rum thoroughly, down to the bottom of the drum. NET: About 2½ quarts.

GLACE AU CHOCOLAT

Rich Bittersweet Chocolate Ice Cream

12 ounces dark sweet chocolate
1 ounce bitter chocolate
6 tablespoons cold water
4 cups heavy cream
4 teaspoons instant coffee

dissolved in 4 teaspoons hot water
8 egg yolks
1 cup superfine sugar
Pinch of salt

Cut all the chocolate into small pieces and put it in a pan with the water. Stir over low heat until the chocolate melts and is quite smooth. Put the heavy cream in a pan with the dissolved coffee and bring it slowly to a boil. Beat the egg yolks with the sugar and salt in a mixer until light and fluffy. Stir in the melted chocolate, then stir in the scalded cream and coffee. Freeze this mixture in a churn-type freezer according to the manufacturer's instructions, noting also the comments on page 848. NET: A generous 2½ quarts.

GLACE AU CAFÉ

Coffee Ice Cream

Ingredients for French Vanilla Custard Ice Cream (page 848)
¼ cup light rum

3 tablespoons instant coffee dissolved in 3 tablespoons boiling water

Make French Vanilla Custard Ice Cream, but before packing down the ice cream, mix in the dissolved coffee and the rum. Mix thoroughly, down to the bottom of the drum. NET: A generous 2 quarts.

GLACE AU PRALINÉ

Praline Ice Cream

Ingredients for French Vanilla Custard Ice Cream (page 848)

1 to 1½ cups praline powder (page 77)

Make French Vanilla Custard Ice Cream, but before packing down the ice cream, mix in the praline powder thoroughly, down to the bottom of the drum. NET: About 2½ quarts.

BOMBE GLACÉE

Vanilla Custard and Praline Ice Cream Mold

This bombe is lined with vanilla custard ice cream and filled with praline ice cream. Turned out on a chilled serving dish, it is garnished with whipped cream and candied cherries and angelica leaves. Any combination of ice cream flavors or sherbets can be molded in the same way.

½ cup praline powder (page 77)

A little vegetable shortening, to seal the mold

VANILLA CUSTARD ICE CREAM
1 cup granulated sugar
⅛ teaspoon cream of tartar
½ cup water
3 egg yolks
Scraping of 1 vanilla bean
3 cups heavy cream

GARNISH
¾ cup heavy cream
1 tablespoon confectioners
  sugar
½ teaspoon vanilla extract
A few candied cherries, cut in
  half
A few leaf cutouts of angelica

Have ready a 1½-quart bombe mold with a lid, thoroughly chilled in the freezer.

VANILLA ICE CREAM. Combine the sugar, cream of tartar, and water in an unlined copper pan or heavy pan, and stir with a metal spoon over low heat until the sugar dissolves, then let it cook at moderate heat until the syrup forms a thin thread between finger and thumb (225°). Beat the egg yolks in a mixer until very light and fluffy. Slowly pour in the hot syrup, beating all the time. Continue beating until the mixture is thick and cold. Mix in the vanilla bean scraping and heavy cream. Freeze the mixture in a churn freezer according to the manufacturer's instructions, nothing also the comments on page 848, up to the point of packing it down. Instead of packing the ice cream in the usual manner after it has stopped churning, let it stand 3 minutes. Then open the drum, remove half the vanilla ice cream, and completely line the chilled mold with it. Set the lined mold in the freezer. Next, quickly mix the praline powder into the ice cream in the drum. Fill the center of the lined mold with the praline ice cream. Cover the mold with wax paper, put on the lid, and seal it with vegetable shortening. Pack the filled bombe mold in the freezer bucket with the same proportion of ice and salt, or put in the freezer, to become firm. At the same time, set a silver or metal serving platter in the freezer to chill thoroughly.

Just before serving, whip the heavy cream for garnish. Put it in a metal bowl over a bowl of crushed ice and beat with a large whisk until it is almost stiff. Add the confectioners sugar and vanilla, and continue beating until it holds its shape. Fill a pastry bag, fitted with a #8 or #9 star tube, with the whipped cream. Remove the lid of the mold, and invert the mold on the cold serving platter. Wrap a hot damp cloth around it and lift it off the ice cream. Decorate the bombe with piped whipped cream and little cherry-and-leaf arrangements. Serve without procrastination! NET: About 1½ quarts.

2 cups superfine sugar
4 cups water
2 cups fresh orange juice
¼ cup lemon juice

Finely grated rind of 2 large
  oranges
1 egg white

SORBET À L'ORANGE

Fresh Orange Sherbet

Combine the sugar and water, bring slowly to a boil, boil it 5 minutes, then cool it slightly before adding the orange juice, lemon juice, and grated orange rind. Cool the mixture thoroughly and pour it through a fine wire strainer. Freeze the sherbet in a churn freezer according to the manufacturer's instructions, noting also the comments on page 848.

When the sherbet has just set, beat the egg white until stiff. Open the drum, fold in the beaten egg white, and then pack down the sherbet, and proceed. The beaten egg white gives the sherbet a nice consistency. NET: About 2 quarts.

SORBET AUX ABRICOTS (OU AUX FRAISES OU AUX FRAMBOISES)

Apricot Sherbet (or Strawberry or Raspberry)

½ cup superfine sugar
2 cups water
2 tablespoons lemon juice
1 small egg white or half a

large one
1½ cups puréed fresh apricots
  (or strawberries or
  raspberries)

Make sure the fruit purée is absolutely smooth. It should be made in an electric blender or by rubbing the fruit through a fine strainer. Combine the sugar and water, bring slowly to a boil, boil 5 minutes, then add the fruit purée and lemon juice. Cool the mixture, pour it into the freezer drum, and freeze the sherbet in a churn freezer according to the manufacturer's instructions, noting also the comments on page 848. When the sherbet has just set, beat the egg white until stiff. Before packing down the sherbet, fold the beaten white into it (it gives the sherbet a nice consistency), then proceed to pack the sherbet in the drum and let it set as instructed. NET: About 1½ quarts.

FROMAGE GLACÉ À L'ANANAS

Bombe Mold of Fresh Pineapple Ice Cream

The bombe is garnished with slices of fresh pineapple and berries.

1 large ripe pineapple
4 egg yolks
½ cup granulated sugar
Juice of half a lime
1 tablespoon unflavored gelatine
  soaked in 2 tablespoons water

2 egg whites
1¼ cups heavy cream, whipped
A few canned whole lingonberries or sweetened
  cranberries

Have ready a 1½-quart bombe mold with a lid, well chilled in the freezer. Skin and core the pineapple. Put half the pulp through a coarse meat chopper and set it aside. Dice the other half of the pineapple until you have 1 cup, then slice the rest for garnish. Beat the egg yolks and sugar in the mixer until thick and fluffy. Remove the mixture from the mixer, and fold in the lime juice and chopped pineapple. Slowly add the soaked gelatine to the egg mixture, blend well, set the mixture over a bowl of ice, and stir until it is thick. Beat the egg whites to soft peaks and fold them into the egg yolk mixture, then fold in the whipped cream, and last, the diced pineapple.

Rinse the chilled bombe mold with cold water and fill it with the pineapple mixture. Chill it in the freezer at least 3 hours. Chill a metal serving plate thoroughly.

When ready to serve, remove the lid and invert the mold on the serving plate. Wring out a cloth in very hot water, wrap it around the mold, and lift it off the Pineapple Fromage Glacé. Garnish it with the pineapple slices and a few lingonberries or sweetened cranberries. NET: About 1½ quarts.

<table>
<tr><td>

This is a simple and attractive presentation of an unpeeled pineapple with its leafy headpiece lying on its side, filled to overflowing with creamy frozen fresh pineapple mousse. The dish is garnished with whipped cream rosettes and chopped pistachio nuts.

</td><td>

MOUSSE
À L'ANANAS

Frozen Fresh
Pineapple Mousse

</td></tr>
</table>

1 small ripe pineapple	*2 tablespoons confectioners*
3 cups heavy cream	*sugar*
1 cup superfine sugar	*¼ cup chopped blanched*
2 teaspoons lemon juice	*pistachio nuts*

Cut the pineapple in half lengthwise, a little off center. With a small sharp knife, trim out the pulp from both halves, being careful not to break the shell and skin of the larger half of the pineapple. Then remove the center cores and put the pineapple pulp through a coarse meat chopper. Beat 2 cups heavy cream in a metal bowl over ice. When it is almost stiff, add the superfine sugar and continue beating until the cream holds its shape. Fold in the chopped pineapple and lemon juice. Cut the leaf end from the larger half of the pineapple shell and save it for decoration. Pack the pineapple cream into the larger shell and set it in the freezer for 3 hours (do not stir it).

To serve the frozen pineapple mousse, replace the leaves on the shell, securing them with a few toothpicks. Beat the remaining cup of heavy cream. When it is almost stiff, add the confectioners sugar and continue beating until stiff. Put the whipped cream in a pastry bag with a #7 or #8 star tube, and pipe large rosettes of whipped cream around the edge of the shell. Sprinkle chopped pistachio nuts over the top. NET: 4 to 6 servings.

<table>
<tr><td>

This Italian ice cream mold is made of raspberry ice cream and pistachio nuts with a center of frozen whipped cream. Turned out on a serving platter, it is decorated with more whipped cream.

</td><td>

SPUMONE
LAMPONE

Raspberry Spumone

</td></tr>
</table>

½ cup granulated sugar	*orange*
¼ cup fresh orange juice	*3 cups heavy cream*
6 egg yolks	*2 egg whites*
1 cup puréed fresh raspberries	*⅛ cup coarsely ground*
Grated rind of 1 large navel	*blanched pistachio nuts*

3 tablespoons confectioners   1 tablespoon vanilla extract
    sugar

Have ready a well-chilled 1½-quart ice cream mold or bombe with lid. Combine the sugar and orange juice in a heavy pan, and cook to the light syrup stage (225°, or forming a thin thread between the finger and thumb). Beat the egg yolks in the mixer until light and fluffy. Slowly pour the hot syrup into them, beating all the time. Beat until the mixture is stiff and cool, then fold in the raspberry purée and orange rind. Beat 1½ cups heavy cream in a metal bowl over a bowl of crushed ice until stiff, and fold it into the raspberry mixture. Pour the mixture into the drum of a churn freezer, and freeze according to the manufacturer's instructions, noting also the comments on page 848.

When the raspberry mixture has just set, beat the egg whites to soft peaks. Carefully open the drum, fold the egg whites and pistachio nuts into it, mixing well all the way to the bottom of the drum. Proceed to pack down the mixture and let it set according to instructions. Beat the remaining 1½ cups heavy cream. When it begins to thicken, add the confectioners sugar and vanilla extract. Continue beating until it holds its shape. Carefully open the drum. Line the ice cream mold with the raspberry spumone (reserving some for the top) and fill the center with flavored whipped cream (reserving some for garnish). Cover the whipped cream with the reserved raspberry ice cream, and cover that with wax paper and the lid. Seal the lid with vegetable shortening, and leave the filled mold in the freezer at least 2 (and better 3) hours.

When you are ready to serve, remove the lid of the mold, invert the mold on a cold metal serving plate, wrap it in a hot cloth, and lift it off the ice cream. Put the remaining whipped cream in a pastry bag fitted with a #6 star tube, and decorate the mold. Serve at once. NET: 1½ quarts.

BEVERAGES
THE CORRECT BEVERAGE WITH GOOD FOOD

I f you possess this book, it is probably because you are interested in the art of good dining — eating and drinking. If you are really to enjoy the dishes you cook, there must be a correct selection of the accompanying beverage. Escoffier said it most succinctly: "To know how to eat is to know how to live."

This rather unusual beverage section is designed to help you choose the correct beverage to complement your beautiful cooking. It is organized in three main parts — on wine, on coffee, and on other classic beverage specialties.

"A day without wine is a day without sun" (Omar Khayyám, *The Rubáiyát*). In the little discussion about wine in cooking (page 79), we see wine as the lifeblood that courses through all French cuisine, in the food and with it. Wine has always been important in my classes and presentations; however, the "recipe" for choosing wine for the meal can be arrived at only through assimilation of the philosophy of wine and information about serving wines. This is the purpose of the following section on wine prepared by Lionel Braun.

The other beverage attached to the meal is coffee. Here is basic information about coffee which may help achieve that "perfect cup of coffee," as well as recipes for the classic potions.

Wine and coffee are usually the only beverages with a meal in the French manner, and each has its distinct place. Other beverages — tea, chocolate, a superb fresh fruit juice, a summer pitcher of freshly made sangría — are interludes which contribute interest, charm, festivity, or (in the case of the hot toddy), downright recovery of one's well-being.

WINE
The First Beverage of French Cuisine
BY LIONEL H. BRAUN

The wonder of wines, the great ones and the small, is so overwhelming that every true gourmet tries to describe and talk or write about it. When Alexandre Dumas said, "Burgundy should be drunk kneeling and bareheaded," he was not referring so much to the wine as to his own emotion about a particular wine. If you are anxious to understand and enjoy wines, you are more likely to succeed by being honest with yourself. Start with a glass of simple dry wine at lunch or dinner, and you will have begun to form a basis for judging quality. In order to enjoy wine, it really isn't necessary in the beginning to have knowledge of vineyards or vintages.

Wine is a mysterious liquid, always in a state of change, and the concepts governing the selection of wines to harmonize with food have a wide range of variation. One should always maintain the right to an individual opinion, whether about wine or fine art. Wine may contrast with and emphasize flavors at some cost to its own character, or it can blend with and add another taste dimension to many dishes. There is too much confusion about the conditions necessary to enjoy wine. Wine and soda can be mixed as a "cooler," or wine can be carefully presented with a meal and in the proper glass. For purposes of this essay at least we must begin with the fundamental thesis that table wines are better when served with good food. And good food is best when served with wine.

There are tangible advantages in developing the wine habit. First of all, the physiological benefits of wine are many, primarily as an aid to digestion. Wine, unlike spirits, is taken into the bloodstream at a slow pace and helps the mind and body to relax. Wine, as proven throughout centuries, is indispensable to the complete appreciation of a good repast, lovingly and well prepared.

The drinking of wine is not a secret art to be practiced by the few. It is a beverage for those who believe in the enjoyment of life, and it is for all of us who have a normal desire to keep problems in perspective and maintain ourselves in good health.

Generally speaking, wine is never better than when it is served with the appropriate food. A dinner may begin with Champagne as the apéritif, sherry with the soup, a Moselle wine with fish, a glass of red Burgundy with a partridge. Then, to conclude, a glass of Sauternes with a bombe.

As between wine and food, with wine the more vulnerable, you should always select a wine that complements food and will not be overwhelmed by it. For example, spicy foods will mutilate a Burgundy or Bordeaux; they require an Alsatian like Gewürztraminer. Often a sweet wine like Sauternes will harmonize with spicy foods or pâté. Eggs are known to neutralize the taste of most wines, but an omelet tastes fine with any medium quality red or white wine.

The table is finally set, the food is being prepared, and of course the accompanying wine should be ready on or near the table.

What shall I serve before dinner? How many times have you asked yourself that question? A Scotch on the rocks? A simple gin martini? — a bit more difficult, because martini drinkers will tell you they make their own best martini, from 3-to-1 to 15-to-1, with twists (lemon or orange), an olive, onion, no vermouth, cracked pepper.

It is not easy to decide upon an especially satisfying apéritif. Where is the something beyond the pedestrian horizon? That first drink, like the first mouthful, must satisfy the tastes of one's guests. But even more important, it should brighten the appetite and begin the conversation.

What is the purpose of an apéritif? It is the sergeant-at-arms who brings to attention your taste buds above and calls up your gastric reserves below.

There are a few simple but major points to consider for the drink before dinner, and point number one is: Serve nothing sweet — get rid of the grenadine and the ginger ale. Point number two: Don't look for liquor bargains. Buy quality brands and you'll feel secure. (Scotch and Canadian should do it. Scotch drinkers want Scotch and a bourbon drinker will not be offended by Canadian. No blends, no straights. Buy vodka American in the highest price range and imported English gin.)

While many Americans I know are inclined to go with a "spirited" apéritif or cocktail before dinner, let us consider a more companionable beverage, and one that will run to 20-proof compared to the 94-proof cocktail. The French will often consider Pernod, Scandinavians prefer aquavit, Hungarians drink Szamorodni. There are perhaps half a dozen well-known apéritifs which I will cover briefly, but for me, Champagne is first.

Champagne is the champion of all wine apéritifs. It "revs up" the palate and guests as quickly as any spirit, but in a gentle fashion, leaving the palate clean and cleared and refreshed. Champagne is festive above all, and it performs the extra task of preparing the mind to enjoy the food, your company, and the whole occasion.

Sherry. The real sherries are grown in the area of Jerez, Spain, and should not be confused with the products of some who, armed with a printer, place a label with the word "sherry" on their bottle. Sherry is a blended fortified wine available in four main categories. Fino: Light, very dry, very pale. Ideal apéritif. Amontillado: Dry, pale. A fine apéritif. Manzanilla: Light and pale, dry without the finesse of the Fino, it has a slightly bitter aftertaste. An apéritif. Oloroso: Deeper in color, with a nutty flavor. Probably better after dinner.

Vermouth is made with aged, blended white wines infused with two dozen or more herbs. It may be fortified with brandy. Vermouth is said to be as old as wine itself. In Roman times spices and herbs considered to have tonic properties were infused into wine by herbalists to make them more palatable. Italy has the strongest claim to being the home of vermouth, thanks to the eighteenth century firm of Carpano, who produced vermouth on a commercial scale.

Vermouth is made with aged, blended white wines infused with many variations, chilled, or with a lump of ice, or with a squeezed sliver of lemon rind. Because of its clean taste and bitter aroma, it makes an excellent long drink. With a little black currant liqueur, Cassis, it becomes Vermouth Cassis, or Kir. A glass of chilled dry vermouth is excellent with seafood, particularly crustacea.

Generally speaking, vermouth will keep unopened as long as a half dozen years, and certainly remain drinkable after its character has changed. Opened and corked, and half filled or more, it can remain in good condition a month or so. It is best kept refrigerated, if possible.

(Here is a tip for those of you who have searched for years hoping to find a wine for drinking with asparagus. I believe the vermouth from Chambéry will turn the trick. This vermouth from Chambéry is allowed the "appellation d'origine" and is extremely dry and light.)

Other favored vermouth apéritifs are: Dubonnet, a careful blend of aged wines with ingredients including extract of Peruvian bark, which I like for its rich flavor and mild liqueur-like qualities. Byrrh, a mixture of sweet and dry grapes passed over a series of aromatic plants and Peruvian bark, which gives it a stimulating taste. Lillet, a golden vermouth flavored with the clean dry taste of bitter oranges, from Southern France. Campari and Punte Mes, which although not strictly vermouths are particularly good apéritifs with soda, leaving a clean dry taste in the mouth.

Very often I like to find an apéritif that is away from the ordinary. The Fendant dry white wine of Switzerland, when well chilled, is very appealing. Coming from the upper reaches of the Rhône, it is made of the early ripening Fendant grapes, which have a Chasselas rootstock. It is a delicate wine, very well suited for summer picnics, too. I enjoy this wine for its crispness in the mouth, or piquancy, as well as its smooth finish on the palate. It is more easily obtainable than many Swiss wines outside of Switzerland, and very modestly priced.

Even less well known than the Fendant is a wine from the Savoy region of France known as Apremont, a mountain wine with good dryness and crispness on the palate, and surprisingly enough, it has a light "spritz" or tingle on the tongue. In the glass it will come up with a slight amber tinge. Remember this petillant de Savoie on a warm and sunny day. Chill it well and enjoy its crisp, refreshing taste — delicious!

Wines with the Meal

All the rules connected with wine drinking require nothing more than common sense, and you should be guided by personal taste. The simple rule is to serve dry wine (white or red) before a sweet wine, and in general a dry white before a dry red, (the whites prepare the palate for the more complex reds).

Here is a compendium of wines to help you with your potable planning. The suggested wines are identified by area and/or type which will be understood by any retail wine dealer. For an explanation of these identifications and more specific information about the wines they represent, check a good wine reference — two fine examples are Alexis Lichine *Encyclopedia of Wines and Spirits* and Hugh Johnson *Wonderful World of Wines.*

HORS D'OEUVRE DISHES. Champagne, Fino or Amontillado sherry, dry vermouth, dry Moselle, dry Alsatian, Muscadet, or Loire Valley wine go with most hors d'oeuvre dishes. Many, however, contain a vinaigrette sauce for piquancy, and vinegar is at swords' points with wine. A glass of sherry, vermouth, or Champagne will perhaps do more to set up your taste buds properly than something else. *Caviar* may be served with dry Champagne, chilled vodka, or iced aquavit; *melon* with tawny port or light white wine; *oysters* with Chablis, Muscadet, or Pouilly Fuissé — a dry white wine; *foie gras* or *pâté de foie gras* with Sauternes, Barsac, well-chilled Champagne, a full-bodied white wine — Alsatian or German; *artichokes* with Chateauneuf-du-Pape, Hermitage, a full red Italian wine, or a very dry rosé; *smoked salmon* with dry sherry, dry Moselle such as Brauneberger Juffer, or dry Graves.

SOUP (CLEAR). Fino sherry or Sercial Madeira (in or with).

FISH AND SHELLFISH. With *shrimp*, a dry full white wine, Fino sherry, dry Italian wines (Soave, Verdicchio); with *Lobster*, Champagne, dry full-bodied white Burgundy, or a dry white from the Rhône or Bordeaux; with *salmon*, a rich full white wine, Champagne, or a dry light red Bordeaux; with *eel*, red Bordeaux or full white Burgundy; with *nonfatty fish* such as sole, flounder, or striped bass, a dry white wine such as Chassagne Montrachet, Meursault, Pouilly Fumé.

MEAT. With *beef*, any Bordeaux from St. Estèphe through Pomerol, Burgundy's Pommard and wines from the Côte de Nuit, and California Cabernet Sauvignon. Italian choices are Barolo, Gattinara and Barbaresco. (Ragoûts and braised dishes should ideally be cooked with the same wine that will be drunk with the meal.) With *veal*, wines of the Beaujolais district as well as California Zinfandel and Italian Bardolino, Chianti and Valpolicella. With *lamb*, St. Emilion or any red Bordeaux are superb beverages, as well as Burgundies from the Côte de Beaune. With *pork*, white wines like Riesling or the dry white Graves. A rich pork dish should be accompanied by an Alsatian wine or a German Rheingau (vineyards producing good to great wines are Hattenheim, Eltville, Hallgarten). With *ham*, light reds like Volnay, Beaujolais, or even rosé and Traminer with baked ham.

POULTRY. With *chicken, Cornish hens, turkey,* both red and white wines, full or light bodied, depending upon the richness or delicacy of the dish. A better Bordeaux is perfect with roast chicken. Chicken prepared in a rich sauce may call for Chassagne Montrachet (red or white) or a white Corton Charlemagne. With *cold fowl*, Meursault or Moselle wines. With *duck*, full-bodied reds — Pomerol, St Estèphe, St. Emilion. With *goose*, spicy Alsatian white wines or a full-bodied red.

GAME. With *partridge, pigeon (squabs), quail*, the same selection as for chicken. With *pheasant, grouse*, the finest red Burgundy. With *venison*, full-bodied reds.

CHEESE. Red wine. The bigger and more flavorful the cheese, the fuller the wine (see advice in the Cheese section, page 685).

DESSERT. With *ice cream* (if you must), Champagne. With *fruit desserts, pastries and petits fours*, Champagne, Tokay, Sauternes, Trockenbeerenauslese.

After the Meal: Cognac, Brandies, and Fortifieds

You've had your meal and your wine, and now you are ready for the great healer, the archangel of forgiveness and generosity, the after-dinner drink of luxury — *Cognac*. André Simon called Cognac "the living soul of good grape wine, one of the purest of spirits, a ministering angel without wings, yet visible, always ready to act and to help."

While Cognac is brandy, not all brandy is Cognac. Brandy is the distillate of grapes, apricots, apples, cherries, pears, raspberries — almost any fruit. Cognac is made from grape wine from the Cognac region of France — about ten casks of wine to make one cask of this noble spirit. The various Cognac firms use several names within two categories to help identify their products: (a) Proprietary terms. Names like Cordon Bleu, Anniversaire, or Bras d'Or are coined by such firms as Martell, Monnet, and Hennessey. They are trademarks used only by the firm which created them. (b) Quality terms. These are used by a majority of Cognac shippers to denote quality. For example, three-star is usually a firm's youngest blend, made from blends with an average age of five to ten years. V.S.O.P. indicates an older blend — say fifteen years, although the actual age may vary with each house.

To test a good Cognac, one must simply empty a glass after it has been thoroughly wetted inside with the brandy. If the Cognac is good or better quality, the glass will maintain its aroma for days, and certainly for hours.

While Cognac and brandy have been given strong support by the medical profession, their primary use has been for after-dinner drinks, with or in the coffee.

Armagnac is a brandy second only to Cognac and is produced southeast of Bordeaux in the département of Gers. Armagnac is produced by continuous distillation, while Cognac is distilled in two steps. Armagnac casks are black oak, and Cognac casks Limousin oak. Armagnac has a drier and somewhat harder taste than Cognac.

Marc (known as "grappa" in Italy) is brandy produced from the pulpy mass in the wine press after juice is extracted from grapes.

Spanish brandy is heavier and sweeter than Cognac or Armagnac because it is distilled from sherry. Pedro Domecq and Fundador are probably the best foreign brandies produced outside of France.

Metaxa, Greek grape brandy, is sweet, heavy, and slightly resin-flavored.

Ouzo is a Greek grape brandy flavored with anise. When served with ice and water, it acquires a milky and opalescent look.

Calvados is a wonderful apple brandy distilled from cider or the pulp of small apples grown in Normandy, then aged ten years in wood before bottling. American applejack usually is aged from two to five years only.

Grand Marnier, made with a Cognac base and oranges, is usually considered a liqueur, although its predominant brandy base gives it all the drinking and flaming advantages of brandy.

Fruit brandies are always colorless, like clear alcohol, and known as "eau de vie" (water of life). They are distilled from various fruits — a fermented mash of cherries for Kirschwasser, a variety of plums for Quetsch and Mirabelle, strawberries for Fraise, raspberries for Framboise, and pears, sometimes called Williams Pear brandy. The finest of these fruit brandies usually come from Switzerland, Alsace, and the Black Forest area of Germany.

FORTIFIED WINES. Whenever I dine in London, it seems that the final beverage served is a sweet wine, and this calls forth an appraisal of the "fortified" wines: sherry from Spain, port from Portugal, Madeira from the island of the same name, and Marsala from Sicily. They are properly called fortified because alcohol has been added to them either to raise the alcoholic content, as with Madeira and sherry, or to end the fermentation in the vats, as with port.

Sherry was probably the first fortified wine well known in England, even though port and Madeira were also developed to suit English tastes. The name was derived from the Spanish town Jerez, but in Shakespearean times it was referred to as "Sherris sack," the word "sack" meaning "export" in Spanish (sacar). The Spanish people are much more in love with sherry than the Portuguese are with port, but it is the British who consume the most, probably as a bracer for the damp climate that prevails.

At the end of the meal, we are concerned with the sweet and medium sweet (the olorosos) sherries, or "full" sherries ("full" is used in such markings as "old full pale," and means soft and sweet). Paleness here is an exception to the rule that the darker the sherry, the sweeter. Bristol Cream sherry is a light-colored sweet oloroso. Amoroso (from the Spanish word meaning amorous) is medium dry but an oloroso. Brown sherry, also an oloroso and sometimes referred to as East India sherry, is rich in taste, heavily sweetened, dark, and stronger in alcohol than other sherries, and probably has more in common with Malmsey Madeira.

There are sherries made outside Spain (as in America and South Africa) that may challenge comparison. South African vineyards in particular have a coastal climate comparable to that of Andalusia, and very few people can distinguish between the best of South African sherry and ordinary Spanish sherry of the same character.

Port was invented by the British sometime around the mid-eighteenth century as a desperate measure when French wines were excluded during wartime. When Portuguese wine went to England, it was liked very little. It was decided that it might travel better if it were treated with brandy to stop fermentation. Port has always been a foundling of the British palate, and enterprising British wine lodges contain about one-half of the port at the mouth of the Duoro River. Also, most of the large estates (quintas) are owned by British shippers.

Madeira is a cousin to port and sherry; that is, brandy was added to the "shipping" wines which moved from Madeira to England in 1753 and gave Madeira wine its character and excellence. British traders carried Madeira wines to the Indies, where they were greatly appreciated. These wines seemed to improve in the holds of ships, and it became practice to store wines in "estufas" or hot rooms. Of course it is the solera system now that makes it possible to enjoy the old, outstanding vintages of 1806 Malmsey, 1815 Bual, or 1844 Verdelho. Madeira, like port, will keep its freshness only a few days once opened and should be consumed fairly quickly. The main Madeira types that are popular as dessert or after-dinner wines are Bual (Boal), a medium sweet wine, and Malmsey, a honey-like delicious wine, perfect for after-dinner.

Marsala, produced on the island of Sicily, tastes somewhat like sherry, although it is mellower and richer. This wine is dark and has a taste of burnt sugar, or caramel. Another Englishman, John Woodhouse, introduced Marsala into England in the late 18th century.

Storing Wines

If you don't have a wine cellar or a wine "library," which is generally an assortment of wines, you are missing one of life's great treasures.

Many people who have started wine cellars like to keep a record of the wines they drink, and one of my favorite record-keeping systems is the use of the labels themselves, with notes that I have made on the back of each label.

Your "cellar," even a modest one, gives you complete access to wines for any occasion. A "cellar" (in the generic sense) enables you to plan your own assortments and take advantage of any wine sale. Furthermore, newly arrived wines always need "rest" for a few days after being shipped even the most modest distance.

If you have air conditioning, you have a head start on keeping wines cool and in reasonably good condition. Ideally, of course, you should have a roomy, consistently cool and dry place away from light and vibration, with a temperature range of 50° to 60° F. Temperatures above 70° F. will accelerate maturation and may cause wines to turn before their time. Therefore, if you have enough room, build a cellar related to your own consumption level as well as budget.

An apartment dweller with an extra closet not hit by sunlight, that is air-conditioned, will be fortunate indeed. However, with some ingenuity, it is possible to convert a section of a room into a store for wines that are to be consumed relatively soon. This modest arrangement may not enable you to buy the great wines when they are young and store them for future drinking; yet enough wines can be kept on hand for current and short-term drinking. (Many wine stores can arrange storage facilities on wines that need aging, as well as give you special prices on full cases.)

One of the simplest ideas for building a cellar is to obtain metal or wooden racks from a local wine shop. But even a whiskey carton resting on its side is a good beginning. The cross-hatching or honeycombing will keep the bottles from rolling or weighing on each other. Wines always keep better when they can rest, and don't have to be shaken while you're trying to locate a special bottle at the bottom of a stack. Once you have your racks in place, all you need is a notebook for wine notes, some tags, and a thermometer. The functions of these items are obvious: The notebook is your own history book for the wines you've consumed and opinion of each one; the tags are to identify the wines so you don't have to pull the bottles out to read labels; and the thermometer enables you to maintain a temperature proper for the normal aging of the wine.

Wherever you decide to lay down your wines, the first consideration is to arrange to store them lying on their sides, front label side up, so the wine can reach the cork and keep it moist and expanded. Bottles kept in this position are less likely to have excessive air enter and damage the wine.

Buying Wine

I have always found it relatively easy to buy wines. There always seems to be at least one local liquor store that carries the standard brands in both domestic and imported bottlings. You can usually judge a store by its wine stocks. Some stores jumble their wines together, offer a few cheaper regionals and a couple of the more famous and expensive wines. A good store will make available a wide selection of logically arranged table wines from all the great regions. The better store will offer bottlings from the Loire, Rhône, Alsace, Rhine, and Moselle, Italy, California, Bordeaux, and Burgundy regions.

The purchase and selection of wines varies little from the thinking that goes into meat selection or the purchase of any worthwhile item for the home. The phrase "Know your wine merchant" is as much valid as the phrase "Know your jeweler." A trustworthy, well-informed wine man is the key to sensible planning and wine investment.

My favorite wine retailer seems to always enjoy chatting about his wares, is informative, and never loses his patience. I am provided with catalogues, vintage charts, and — more important — he inspires enthusiasm for every bottle of wine I buy. Wine price depends upon the quality of bottling and availability of the wine. Rapid price increases have become the rule for wine since the late 1960's, continuously adjusting to demand upward. The approximate retail price for Château Palmer 1970 in October 1971, was $4.25 per bottle. This same wine, which is a long way from drinking, sold for $5.50 to $6 per bottle in the spring of 1972. Investors in wine may be rewarded by a steady increase in price as the quality of many wines (particularly red Bordeaux) develops with age and stocks diminish.

Selections for a $100 Wine Cellar

Based on costs in the U.S. January-June 1973, and selected on the basis of availability as well as quality.

WHITE BORDEAUX
2 bottles, vintages '67 or '69

Dry:
Pavillon Blanc
Ch. Olivier
Ch. Loudenne
Ch. Haut-Brion Blanc
Mouton-Cadet

Sweet:
Ch. Climens
Ch. LaTour-Blanche
(Sauternes)
Ch. d'Yquem (Sauternes)
Ch. de Suduiraut (Sauternes)

RED BORDEAUX
4 bottles of any of these vineyards, '66, '67, '69

Ch. Gruaud-Larose
Ch. Lascombes
Ch. Palmer
Ch. Pichon-Longueville

Ch. Léoville-Las-Cases
Ch. Talbot
Ch. Lynch-Bages
Ch. Beycheville

RED BURGUNDY
2 bottles of any of these vineyards '67, '69*

Aloxe-Corton
Beaune
Gevrey-Chambertin
Nuits-St.-Georges

Morey St. Denis
Volnay
Vosne-Romanée

WHITE BURGUNDY
2 bottles of any of these vineyards, '69, '70, '71

Chablis
Chassagne-Montrachet
Corton-Charlemagne

Meursault
Pouilly Fuissé
Puligny-Montrachet

VIN ROSÉ
2 bottles

From California, such as Almaden, Beaulieu Vineyards, Louis Martini, or Mirassou

*Shippers of Burgundy wines are as much a criterion as vintage and area. Some major shippers are Lebeque-Bichot, Bouchard, Chanson, Joseph Drouhin, Georges de Vogüe, Faiveley, Louis Jadot, Louis Latour, Patriarche, Thorin.

FRENCH "COUNTRY" WINES
4 bottles, '69, '70, '71, '72*

Red:
  Beaujolais
  Provence
  Rhône
  Hermitage

White:
  Alsatian Riesling
  Muscadet
  Pouilly-Fumé
  Ch. de Sancerre
  Vouvray

AMERICAN WHITE WINES
2 bottles of any of these varieties

Sauvignon Blanc
Chenin Blanc
Pinot Chardonnay

Johannisberg Riesling
Semillon
Traminer

GERMAN WHITE WINES
2 bottles, '69 or '70

Moselle (green bottle)
  Bernkastel
  Brauneberg Juffer
  Graach
  Piesport
  Wehlen
  Zeltingen

Rhine (brown bottle)
  Hattenheim
  Johannisberg
  Nierstein
  Oppenheim
  Rauenthal
  Schloss Vollrads

ITALIAN WINES
4 bottles

Red:
  Bàrbaresco
  Barolo
  Chianti Classico
  Valpolicella

White:
  Soave
  Verdicchio

By doubling the above quantities you can easily increase the size of your cellar; however, these wines are good starters, and any expansion should consist of other wines from these categories. For example, you can upgrade your Burgundy selection by trying Clos de Vougeot or a Bonne Mares (both reds). Clos de Vougeot is a full-bodied wine with a big nose (aroma), and the Bonne-Mares is a rich wine with great strength and elegance.

When stocking a new cellar, I find it desirable to lay in a few special wines in addition to the majority complement of dry table wines. This case would include a bottle of Fino (dry) sherry, one of port (tawny), a dessert Madeira (Malmsey), one each of French and Italian vermouth, and at least two bottles of sparkling wine, perferably a dry imported non-vintage champagne.

*Modestly priced wines and best drunk at 3 years of age or less.

PLANNING THE WINE SERVICE. Wine is a living thing and, like most living things, needs some air after a long sleep before its vitals come alive. The younger red wines for everyday drinking stand to gain a bit by contact with the air — although the popular wines of Beaujolais are meant to be drunk young and consumed as soon as they are poured from the bottle. Except for Beaujolais, young (less than 3 years) red Burgundies can take 30 minutes or so of air time. Older wines may completely fade unless drunk soon after the cork is removed, although it usually takes 30 years or more to reach such condition. If at any time you are in doubt and haven't a handy consultant, then it is a safe rule that, generally speaking, Bordeaux wines need more breathing time than wines from Burgundy. When it comes to the very old table wines, of course, there is the possibility and annoyance of opening a superb wine and having it fade before you serve it. However, many of these older wines will last a good deal longer if you decant them before dining and keep them en carafe until you are ready to serve them. (See below, on *decanting*.)

Most dry white wines should be drunk fairly young, as many of them lose freshness and begin to oxidize after 5 years. They are generally served at once after opening, and well chilled. Some big white and dry Burgundies of great vintage years can last longer. Of course, Sauternes do last longer and may be opened just prior to serving of the dessert. This sweet wine must be served well chilled.

If you have managed to collect any fine red Bordeaux 10 years of age or more, from the great vintages of 1959 or 1961, for example, breathing time of 2 to 4 hours may be required. Any fine red Burgundy of 6 to 9 years of age can use up to 2 hours of breathing.

When planning the wine service, it is critical to allow time for the meal, and since your guests should work themselves up to a very fine wine, it is best to give them time to eat and drink during their first course. This approximate dining time of a meal is especially needed if you are planning to serve Burgundies that are 10 to 15 years of age, or Bordeaux wines of 15 to 20 years old, that have been decanted and are waiting in a decanter.

OPENING A BOTTLE OF WINE. Use a knife to cut the tinfoil capsule below the lip of the bottle to prevent the wine from coming in contact with the metal. Use a clean cloth to remove any mold which may have formed under the capsule and sediment around the mouth of the bottle. Then withdraw the cork and carefully clean the inner lip of the bottle.

For removal of the cork, the best corkscrew is the double-action type. If you can, buy one with a long flat stem. Insert the screw downward, center it over the cork, and turn the screw so it penetrates deeply into the cork. As you turn the screw gently, the arms will rise like a pair of wings. By depressing the wings you force the cork upward and out of your bottle. From time to time you may find a defect in a cork — a vein or fissure will, with age, cause deterioration or mold and give a corky taste and smell to the wine.

DECANTING. Decanting is generally for red wines, although the question is sometimes raised with regard to white wines even though sediment or deposits are not evident. Some people choose to decant all finer white wines, noting that the aeration rounds the flavor of the wine more quickly than normal bottle opening does. If you decide to decant a finer white wine, it is important to remember that the decanter as well as the bottle itself should be chilled.

The important fact about decanting old red wines is that the bottle must rest long enough for the sediment to settle in one place in the bottle. To "settle" a bottle requires that it remain either in an upright position or in a recumbent position. Ideally, the old wine should be stood upright about 48 hours before decanting, so that deposits on the sides can drift to the bottom.

COOLING A BOTTLE OF WINE. The cooling of wines is a simple, but necessary procedure if one is to enjoy the elusive bouquet of white or rosé wines. I always prefer that these wines be well chilled rather than just cooled, and the sweeter the wine the colder. Usually 1½ hours is enough time in the refrigerator to bring dry white wines to the right serving temperature, and 2 hours for a Sauternes or Barsac. Wines should not be kept refrigerated longer than necessary, and unopened remaining bottles should be placed in the least cool place in the refrigerator. Chilling wines in an ice bucket is quicker than in a refrigerator; you can cool a bottle in 30 minutes. Your ice bucket must contain enough water and ice to cover that part of the bottle containing the wine, and the bottle must be twirled periodically to cool evenly.

Cooling German wines requires some dexterity unless you have the special longer German wine buckets. Proper cooling in a regular wine bucket requires that the tall green or brown bottle be inverted, with the neck thrust down toward the bottom. This technique chills the wine in the upper portion of the bottle so that when it is returned to a standing position the wine poured first will be cool. Return the bottle to the bucket right side up after pouring, since the ice and water should be high enough to cool the remainder.

There are some exceptions to the rules concerning temperature. For example, while Beaujolais within a year of its vintage date is preferred slightly cool, the Italian sparkling wine Lacrima Christi may be served at room temperature and will be found most pleasant.

A red wine that has been overcooled can be warmed easily by holding the bowl of the glass in the palm of your hand. If necessary, you may place a bottle into a tub of lukewarm water for a few minutes to speed up the process of raising the temperature. The temperature of the water should be just above the level to which you desire to bring the wine.

THE WINE GLASS. Much too much has been said and written about the correct glass for the proper wine. Some of us have shelves laden with glasses for our cases of wine, and yet almost always we can do as well with one basic glass.

The wine glass should always be of clear thin crystal. An important step in the full comprehension of your wine is beholding its "robe" or color. This must not be diffused through amber, or green, or any color whatsoever, or through carved patterns in the glass.

The fundamental glass should be a thin one that stands 6 inches high, with a stem of about 2½ inches and a round base 2¾ inches in diameter. The bowl may be more or less tulip-shaped and have a depth of 3½ inches with a drinking diameter of 2½ to 2¾ inches at the mouth. This glass may be used for all types of wine, including fortified wines like port or sherry, and is acceptable for brandy, too! It would not be incorrect to drink Champagne from such a glass, but the experts usually prefer a narrower and more cone-shaped bowl. The glass should stand about 8¼ inches high with a stem of 3 inches. The bowl tapers at the lip to 2¼ inches. The special shape of a Champagne glass lends a very festive appearance to the table and is very much preferred to the coupe-shaped and hollow-stemmed glasses we see in motion pictures and at catered receptions.

Very large glasses may be used for fine wines; their purpose is to concentrate the bouquet. The larger bowl permits more aeration of the wine, thereby enhancing the bouquet and flavor of the bottling. I would not recommend oversize glasses for very old wines, which are vulnerable to massive doses of air and could break down quickly at the table. Such larger glasses are more common in a restaurant, where they symbolize the serving of a great older bottle. Actually a big-bowl glass is ideal for young wines and brings special attention to a small wine like Beaujolais, as is often done in Beaujolais country.

POURING THE WINE. What could sound simpler than the word "pour"? However, as we know, it is not that simple. One major cause of concern always is the little drop of wine that goes where it is not intended after each glass is filled. If it is a red wine, the staining of the tablecloth is an unsightly result. Therefore, keep a cloth in the left hand to wipe the bottle as necessary. The napkin is also very useful if a chilled white wine is being served, as a bottle of wine that has been in an ice bucket will drip water. The only caution in using the napkin is to remember that it must never hide the label, for at least part of the pleasure of drinking wine is knowing what you are tasting.

Pour a wineglass only one-third full, so that there is ample room in the bowl for the bouquet to collect and greet you as you lift your glass to drink.

All this discussion of special glasses, the right temperature, certain years and special vineyards may tend to scare some people away from becoming familiar with wines, when really it is much easier than all the foregoing might suggest. The best way to start is to drink a glass now and then during mealtimes, maybe three or four times a week — plunge right in, like the great number of people who now take an interest in wine and have acquired a taste for it with their meals. Among young people today, there is more than an appreciation of wine; there is a realization that wine can and does add to the joie de vivre. One delight of this present wine era is the greater variety of wines available from all countries, and especially the lesser-known wines now arriving from France. Today's improved transport and better wine making techniques are helping slake the thirsts of many of us. There are no longer any "bad travelers" among them — In vino veritas!

COFFEE
The Second Beverage of French Cuisine

I can't imagine anything more exasperating than, having wined and dined well, not being allowed the crown of a good meal — coffee!

Because coffee is one of the most adaptable flavors in the world, it is the perfect after-dinner beverage. Unlike the all too frequent practice of plunking a cup of coffee on the table while the meal is being served, in French cuisine it never accompanies the meal, but is served afterward in a small cup and very black.

The reason a Frenchman will ignore coffee during his meal is simply that he prefers it strong, and obviously the "wine of Islam" will not fraternize with his own wine. Unlike the confirmed coffee drinker in Brazil or Colombia, who drinks it as soon as he gets up and all day long, the Frenchman thinks about it at breakfast with hot milk only.

Coffee as a beverage was supposedly introduced to Mecca by the dervishes of Ethiopia around 1500, and its popularity grew to such proportions that coffee houses became popular in Constantinople by about 1550. The appeal of the coffeehouse over the mosque caused the Moslem holy men to enact a series of restrictions against coffee, hoping to return the people to the mosque. But eventually, coffee moved out of the "underground" and became accepted. It traveled from Constantinople to Venice in 1615, and in 1669 Suleiman Aga, Turkish ambassador to Louis XIV, introduced coffee as a beverage of high fashion at dinner parties in Paris. Some two hundred years later the great Disraeli wrote of them: "The brilliant porcelain cups in which it was poured, napkins fringed with gold, and Turkish slaves on their knees, presenting it to the ladies seated off the ground on cushions, turned the heads of the Parisian dames."

Today most readily available coffee is a blend of many coffees, and, as with other beverages, the skill of a blender or taster is required to achieve the flavor characteristics in a high-quality coffee. A blend may contain coffees from South America, Mexico, Hawaii, Africa. With his knowledge of flavors the taster can anticipate the taste any coffee will have when beans are submitted for the "cup test."

As in wine making, the quality of a particular harvest may vary from season to season, and often there is an insufficient quantity of a given bean. If this happens, the taster must find other coffees with similar characteristics to maintain the continuity of a blend. It is only by the constant tasting method that the aroma and flavor characteristics of a blend can have continuity.

(1) Begin with a totally clean coffee pot rinsed well with hot water before using. Thorough cleanliness is essential, because an invisible film of coffee oil will gather on the surface of any coffee maker, quickly become rancid, and contaminate the flavor of successive brewings. Ideally, after each brewing, every part of the coffee pot or brewer should be washed with a very mild detergent or baking soda. Always rinse well.

(2) Use absolutely fresh cold water.

(3) If possible, buy and brew freshly ground coffee. Once opened, coffee should be stored in a screw-top jar or the can in the refrigerator.

(4) Brew to the full capacity of your coffee maker, and in any case no less than three-quarters of capacity. For smaller amounts, use a smaller coffee maker.

(5) Don't boil coffee! It causes an undesirable change in taste and character.

(6) Serve coffee as soon as possible after it has been brewed. If your freshly brewed coffee must sit, let it sit in a pan of hot water over low heat.

AMERICAN COFFEE

To make the best American coffee, I prefer the cone-shaped filter type of drip coffee maker. My main reasons for this preference are that the coffee is never cooked, the water filters through it at its own speed, the glass container and paper are the least injurious materials to the sensitive essence of the coffee bean, and the water, taken boiling from the stove, has already cooled a couple of degrees below boiling before it touches the coffee. Here is the way coffee was made in all of my restaurant operations, using this type of maker.

Cold fresh water in the desired quantity

1 rounded tablespoon of freshly ground French-roast coffee per 6-ounce cup water

(1) Read and follow the Basic Guide for Making a Perfect Cup of Coffee (above).

(2) Measure the water into a pan and set it over high heat to come just to a boil. (In a standard U.S. measuring cup, 6 ounces water is ¾ cup.)

(3) Rinse out the coffee maker with another supply of hot water.

(4) Insert the paper filter and measure the ground coffee into it.

(5) When the water comes to a boil, slowly pour a little over the coffee to dampen it, making sure you reach it all.

(6) Then slowly pour in the rest of the water.

(7) Serve the coffee immediately in warm coffee cups (8 ounce size), with separate containers of cream and sugar if desired.

(8) If you made extra coffee for second cups, keep the coffee warm in a water bath over very low heat.

Café filtre is twice the strength of American coffee, and is also best made in a cone filter type of drip maker, for the reasons already stated in the recipe for American coffee (above).

To make café filtre, follow the recipe for American coffee, doubling the strength (use 2 rounded tablespoons freshly ground French-roast coffee per 6-ounce cup water). Serve it immediately in warm demi-tasse cups. Café filtre is usually drunk black, but may be served with little sugar cubes and cream. French coffee is *never* served with lemon peel.

This delicious coffee essence must be made in a special coffee pot — an espresso maker. The specially constructed equipment forces steam or very hot water under pressure through the finely ground coffee.

The coffee must be special "Italian espresso roast." It should be finely ground for espresso, and ideally it should be ground in your kitchen just before making the coffee. Avoid use of commercially ground espresso coffee if possible; once it is opened, the flavor evaporates even more quickly than regular grind because it is almost a powder.

Cold fresh water in the desired quantity
1 heaping tablespoon freshly ground Italian espresso roast

coffee per 6-ounce cup cold water
Optional: Twists of lemon peel

Espresso makers vary, so it is best to carefully study and follow the instructions of the manufacturer. After making the coffee this way a few times, you may wish to adjust the procedure to your own preferences.

Serve the coffee in warm demi-tasse cups, with twists of lemon peel if desired. Sugar and cream are not served with espresso.

The primary ingredient for this mild, nonbitter coffee is "lead time." It takes at least overnight, and preferably 24 hours. Brewing the coffee by infusion at room temperature, rather than harsh heat, draws out only the absolute essence of the coffee, and none of the bitterness. To many people, it is the touch of bitterness which gives coffee its character, but for others, here is a most marvelous mild cup of coffee. This is how it is done in Scotland, and they make very good coffee in Scotland.

Cold fresh water in the desired quantity

1 heaping tablespoon ground French-roast coffee per 6-ounce cup water

Tie the ground coffee in a cheesecloth bag. Put it in the coffee pot or a jar, cover it with the cold water, and let it soak overnight or longer (24 hours if possible). When you wish to serve it, remove the bag and heat the coffee slowly over low heat. Do not allow it to boil. Serve it hot immediately.

For iced coffee, simply add ice and serve.

CAFÉ AU LAIT

Hot Coffee with Hot Milk

This is the traditional French breakfast coffee.

4 cups strong fresh hot coffee	*Tiny pinch of salt*
2 cups whole milk	*Granulated sugar, if desired*

Have ready 4 large coffee cups, warmed. The fresh hot coffee should be kept warm in a little pan or pot over hot water while the milk with the salt is warmed in a separate little pan. Bring it just to a boil, stirring all the while. Pour the coffee and milk simultaneously into each cup. Season with granulated sugar, if desired. Serve at once. NET: 4 to 6 servings, depending on size of cups.

CAFÉ DIABLE

An after-dinner coffee with citrus and spices, flamed with Grand Marnier. If you have no chafing dish, start it in the kitchen, but contrive to flame and mix it at the table.

6 half-slices of orange	*A few grains ground allspice*
4 half-slices of lemon	*4 teaspoons sweet butter*
6 lumps sugar	*4 cups very hot Café Filtre*
4 cloves	*(page 873)*
A few grains freshly grated	*1 cup Grand Marnier*
* nutmeg*	

Have warmed demi-tasse cups ready. Into a chafing dish put the orange and lemon slices, sugar, cloves, nutmeg, allspice, and butter. Warm them slowly over the flame, turning them around in the pan a little. Add the hot coffee (with a little more sugar if desired), and continue warming the mixture. When the coffee is thoroughly hot, heat the Grand Marnier in a separate little pan. Ignite it, and carefully add it to the chafing dish. Mix the coffee and Grand Marnier, and serve at once. NET: 8 demi-tasse servings.

IRISH COFFEE

For each serving:

¾ cup hot strong coffee	*1½ ounces Irish whiskey*
About 2 teaspoons sugar	*1 tablespoon whipped cream*

Steam-heat a glass or cup (6 to 8 ounces). (Heat in a steamer pan or the dishwasher. The cup should be really hot.) Pour in the hot strong coffee, add sugar to taste, then add the Irish whiskey. Float a dollop of whipped cream on the top. Do not stir. Drink. NET: 1 serving.

CAFÉ ROYALE

Coffee with Cognac

1 cup (6 ounces) hot strong coffee
2 small sugar cubes

2 tablespoons plus 2 teaspoons Cognac

Have the ingredients ready, with 2 well heated demi-tasse cups; then pour the coffee and let each person "make" his own Café Royale. Float a tablespoon of Cognac on the filled demi-tasse cup. Put a sugar cube in a teaspoon and fill the spoon with more Cognac. Hold the spoon just above the coffee. The heat from the coffee will (or should) warm the Cognac so that it may be ignited. Light the Cognac in the spoon. As it blazes, lower it gently into the coffee. Swish the spoon back and forth in the cup until the flame burns out. NET: 2 servings.

CAFÉ TURC

Turkish Coffee

4 teaspoons sugar
1½ cups cold fresh water (12 ounces)

4 tablespoons finely ground coffee

Have ready 4 warmed demi-tasse cups. Bring the sugar and water to a boil in a heavy saucepan. Slowly add the coffee. By raising and lowering the heat, allow the coffee to froth (boil up) about three or four times in the pan; then remove the coffee from the heat. Pour it through a fine wire strainer into the warm cups. (Do not at any time stir the coffee in the pan). NET: 4 demi-tasse cups.

CAFÉ VIENNOIS

Viennese Coffee with Chocolate Ice Cream

For serving, use 8-ounce or larger cups.

2 cups double strength fresh hot coffee
2 cups whole milk
Pinch of salt
1 cup (½ pint) chocolate

ice cream
4 tablespoons whipped cream (2 tablespoons unwhipped heavy cream), flavored with ¼ teaspoon vanilla extract

The coffee should be in a pan, fresh, strong, and hot. In another pan, heat the milk with the salt until it just comes to a boil. Pour the hot coffee and hot milk together, in equal quantities, into each cup. Divide the ice cream into 4 portions and add it to each cup. Top each cup with a dollop of whipped cream. Serve at once. NET: 4 servings.

CAFÉ GLACÉ

Iced Coffee

When in Paris, do as the Parisians do! Ask for Café Mazagran. It's the name for iced coffee, and the name must be traced back to French colonial days when France maintained legionnaires at Fort Mazagran in Algeria. A simple drink of coffee syrup mixed with cold water made the heavy desert heat more easy to endure. The habit was carried back to Paris, where this drink, conceived in desperation, survives after all these years.

ICED COFFEE METHOD I. Prepare your regular coffee double strength (Café Filtre, page 873). Pour it over ice cubes.

ICED COFFEE METHOD II (PRECOOLED). Brew coffee in your regular way (American Coffee, page 872), and let it cool in a covered non-metal container 2 to 3 hours. Then pour it over ice cubes.

ICED COFFEE METHOD III (COFFEE ICE CUBES). Freeze freshly brewed regular-strength coffee in ice cube trays. Pour hot, freshly brewed regular-strength coffee over the coffee cubes. The coffee cubes and regular coffee are equivalent to a double-strength brew, which is necessary for the best iced coffee.

CAFÉ GLACÉ VIENNOIS

Viennese Iced Coffee with Coffee Ice Cream

8 ice cubes made with coffee
1 small cinnamon stick
2 quarts very hot Café Filtre
   (page 873)
1 cup heavy cream
4 tablespoons confectioners
   sugar

2 teaspoons vanilla extract
2 cups (1 pint) coffee ice cream
2 cups light cream
A few candy coffee beans
1 teaspoon powdered instant
   coffee or freshly ground
   coffee

Have ready 6 to 8 cold crystal or silver goblets. Put the cinnamon stick in the hot coffee, then chill thoroughly. Put the heavy cream in a metal bowl over a bowl of ice. Beat it with a large wire whisk until it begins to thicken. Add the confectioners sugar and vanilla extract, and continue beating until the cream holds its shape. Remove the cinnamon stick from the chilled coffee. Using a wire whisk, mix in the coffee ice cream, then the light cream. Pour the coffee mixture into the chilled goblets. Float a coffee ice cube in each goblet, top with a large tablespoon of whipped cream, and garnish the whipped cream with a sweet candy coffee bean and a sprinkling of instant or ground coffee. Serve at once. NET: 6 to 8 servings, depending upon size of goblets.

OTHER BEVERAGES, CLASSIC AND SPÉCIALITÉS

What to Know About Tea

Legend says that tea has been grown and drunk in China for more than four thousand years. Tea was prescribed by Confucians and Buddhists as a beverage of moderation, in line with their philosophy of calm and temperance.

I have always marveled at the English, who built such a demand for tea that during the eighteenth century smuggled tea was consumed in greater quantities and available at lower prices than tea coming through legitimate channels. Yet in the light of England's consumption of 2,000 cups per capita each year, the thing really to marvel at is that the English probably never really taste their tea. When I say taste, I really mean look at its color, sniff the aroma, enjoy and comment on the brew. They do all this with their wines; why not tea?

There are tea experts, as there are wine experts, who can often identify by tasting the actual vicinity and gardens where the leaves come from. And much like the vintners, they too have special words to describe what their noses and taste buds tell them. Bright, brisk, flat, fruity, malty, sweaty are but a few of the adjectives used in describing teas. Like the vintner who talks about a wine as having "bottle stink," the tea man will refer to a tea being "chesty" — he can taste the environment of the tea chest.

BUYING TEA. Buy your tea (like perfume) in small quantities. It should be stored in a tin container away from dampness and strong-smelling elements. Tea acquires alien odors and picks up moisture very easily.

While Chinese teas may soon be available again, most of the teas today still come from India or Ceylon and have such pretty names as Assam, Darjeeling, Lapsang Soochong, Orange Pekoe, Earl Grey's (a tea artificially scented with bergamot). China teas are delicate teas and are usually preferred plain and simple. These fine teas should be approached in much the same way as one selects better wine. Probably the main teas to arrive will be Keemun, Lapsang Soochong, with its tar-like flavor and particularly delightful in summer, as well as the scented teas.

Preparation of a cup of tea is simple enough, but people often forget the one or two little things that ensure really great tea service, such as warming the pot or allowing the tea to infuse. Here are the perfect steps for perfect tea made with whatever kind of tea you like.

LE THÉ

A Good Cup of Tea

*1 teaspoon loose tea per cup
   plus 1 teaspoon for the pot*

*Cold fresh water in the desired
   quantity*

(1) Put the water over high heat to come to a boil. Heat extra hot water separately to warm the pot.

(2) Warm the teapot by rinsing it out with hot water. (Warm cups don't hurt either.)

(3) Put the tea in the pot.

(4) When the water is at a racing boil, pour it directly into the teapot (move the teapot near to the pan so the water will be as hot as possible).

(5) Let the tea steep at least 5 minutes. For some teas, such as China tea, let it brew a little longer.

THÉ GLACÉ

Iced Tea

1 heaping teaspoon of your favorite tea, China or Indian, per cup	quantity
	Plenty of ice cubes
	Fresh lemon or lime
Boiling water in the desired	Granulated sugar

Boil the water. When it is at a rolling boil, rinse out the teapot to warm it, and put the tea into the hot teapot. Fill the pot with boiling water and let it stand 5 minutes. Fill tall glasses with ice cubes. Pour the hot fresh tea over the ice, taking care to pour through the ice so the glass will not crack. (The ice will partially melt; therefore, put in more ice.) Serve with wedges of lemon or lime and granulated sugar.

LE CHOCOLAT

Classic Hot Chocolate

8 ounces dark sweet chocolate	¾ cup heavy cream
1 ounce bitter chocolate	1 tablespoon confectioners sugar
1 cup water	
Tiny pinch of salt	1 teaspoon vanilla extract or scraping from 1 inch of vanilla bean
2 teaspoons sweet butter	
1½ cups light cream	

Have ready 4 tall china chocolate cups, warmed. Cut all the chocolate into little pieces. Put them into a heavy pan with the water and salt. Stir over low heat until the chocolate is dissolved. Beat the sweet butter into the chocolate bit by bit, with a small wire whisk. Mix in the light cream and beat with the whisk over low heat until the mixture just comes to a boil. Then let it simmer very gently 5 to 6 minutes. Beat the heavy cream with a large whisk in a metal bowl over a bowl of ice. When it begins to thicken, add the confectioners sugar and vanilla (extract or scraping) and continue beating until it holds its shape. Pour the hot chocolate into the warm cups. Top with a large spoonful of whipped cream. Serve at once. NET: 4 servings.

CHOCOLAT À LA VIENNOISE I

Simple Viennese Chocolate, with Coffee Ice Cream

8 ounces dark sweet chocolate	unwhipped heavy cream)
1 ounce bitter chocolate	1 cup (½ pint) coffee ice cream
2½ cups light cream	½ teaspoon powdered instant coffee
4 tablespoons whipped cream (about 2 tablespoons	

Cut the sweet and the bitter chocolate into little pieces. Put them in a small saucepan with the light cream and stir over very low heat until the chocolate is dissolved. Beat the chocolate well with a whisk. Have ready 4 tall china chocolate cups. Pour the chocolate and cream mixture into the cups. Then put a quarter of the ice cream into each cup, top it with a tablespoon of whipped cream, sprinkle the top with powdered coffee, and serve at once. NET: 4 cups.

CHOCOLAT À LA VIENNOISE II

Rich Viennese Chocolate, with Coffee Ice Cream

8 ounces dark sweet chocolate
1 ounce bitter chocolate
¾ cup fresh hot Café Filtre (page 873)
Pinch of salt
1½ cups light cream
¾ cup heavy cream
1 tablespoon confectioners
sugar
1 teaspoon vanilla extract or scraping from 1 inch of vanilla bean
2 cups (1 pint) coffee ice cream
½ teaspoon powdered instant coffee

Cut both the sweet and bitter chocolate into little pieces and put them in a saucepan with the coffee and salt. Stir over very low heat until the chocolate is dissolved. Add the light cream and stir again over low heat until the mixture just comes to a boil. Reduce the heat to the barest simmer and let the chocolate warm over this heat 5 to 6 minutes.

Beat the heavy cream with a large whisk in a metal bowl over a bowl of ice. When it begins to thicken, add the confectioners sugar and vanilla, and continue beating until it holds its shape. To serve, half-fill tall chocolate cups with the hot chocolate and cream mixture. Add 2 small scoops of the ice cream, top with a generous dollop of whipped cream, sprinkle a little powdered coffee over the whipped cream, and serve at once. NET: 4 servings.

CHOCOLAT CHAUD À L'ESPAGNOLE

Hot Spanish Chocolate

A rich spicy hot chocolate poured over egg mousse, it is a superb drink, particularly on a cold winter's day.

6 ounces dark sweet chocolate
2½ ounces bitter chocolate
¾ cup hot Café Filtre (page 873)
¼ teaspoon salt
3½ cups hot milk
1½ cups heavy cream
1 teaspoon ground cinnamon
½ teaspoon freshly grated nutmeg
½ teaspoon ground allspice
2 eggs
2 egg yolks
6 tablespoons granulated sugar
2 teaspoons vanilla extract

Cut the sweet and bitter chocolate into little pieces. Put them into a heavy pan with the coffee and salt. Stir the chocolate over very low heat until it is dissolved, then mix in the hot milk and heavy cream. Add the three spices and simmer over very, very low heat 25 to 30 minutes, beating well with a wire whisk occasionally. Beat the eggs and egg yolks in a mixer bowl with the sugar and vanilla extract until they are very light and fluffy and hold their shape.

When ready to serve, slowly pour the hot chocolate into the egg mousse, stirring well all the time. Serve in warm tall chocolate cups. NET: 4 to 6 servings, depending upon size of cups.

BEST FRESH FRUIT JUICE (ORANGE-LIME-GRAPEFRUIT)

There really are not many drinkable drinks. I think most composition drinks result in a combination of rather horrible tastes. People mix things too much, on the whole. In my judgment, drinks should be very simple and cool, such as lovely fresh orange juice, or my favorite drink, which is this one.

Juice of 2 oranges
Juice of 1 lime

Juice of 1 grapefruit

Mix well and chill thoroughly. Pour into a tall glass filled with crushed ice. Absolutely delicious!

MULLED RED WINE (HOT WINE CUP)

6 ounces lump sugar
1 bottle (fifth) good red
   Burgundy wine
Grated rind of half a lemon
   and half a lime
2 cloves

A sprinkle of mace
A small piece of cinnamon stick
6 tablespoons sweet butter
¼ cup moist brown sugar
½ cup Cognac or good brandy

Have ready 4 to 6 warm goblets. Put the lumps of sugar into a scrupulously clean saucepan. Pour the red wine into the pan and let the sugar dissolve in it. Then add the grated lemon and lime rind and the cloves, mace, and cinnamon stick. Warm the mixture over low heat. Cream the butter in a mixer until light and fluffy. Add the brown sugar, and beat well. Strain the hot wine into the goblets. Float a large teaspoon of the butter and sugar mixture on top of the wine in each glass. Pour Cognac over it. NET: 4 to 6 servings, depending upon size of glasses.

SANGRÍA

Spanish Wine Pitcher

1 lemon, sliced
1 orange, sliced
½ cup Cognac or good brandy
¼ cup granulated sugar

2 tablespoons lemon juice
2 cups soda water
1 bottle (fifth) Spanish dry red
   wine (Rioja)

Drop the lemon and orange slices in a large pitcher (3 to 4 quarts). Add the brandy and sugar and stir well with a long wooden spoon. Let the mixture stand at room temperature about 1 hour. When ready to serve, add the wine and lemon juice. Stir the mixture well and add ice cubes, then add the soda water. Stir the contents of the pitcher briskly, adding more ice if necessary, until the pitcher is well-frosted. Serve in chilled glasses. NET: About 2 quarts.

As a change of pace from the traditional Spanish sangría, try the Italian version of this wine cooler, made with fresh peaches.

Ingredients for Sangría (above)
4 to 6 fresh peaches

4 to 6 tablespoons Grand Marnier or Aurum (Italian orange liqueur)

Peel the peaches, prick them all over with the tines of a fork, and let them marinate in Grand Marnier or Aurum (1 tablespoon for each peach). The peaches should marinate a minimum of 4 hours, and overnight if desired. Be sure the container is tightly covered and refrigerated. When ready to serve, add the peaches and liquid to a big pitcher of sangría before adding the ice and soda. Serve the sangría at the meal, and the cold wine-soaked peaches for dessert. NET: About 2 quarts plus 4 to 6 dessert servings.

SANGRÍA (ITALIAN VERSION)

Every pub in England serves a shandygaff; even minors are allowed to drink it. With both beers very cold, it's a marvelous refresher for a hot day. Now that English ginger beer is available in the United States, I think more people will enjoy the shandygaff.

To make it, pour equal quantities of very cold ginger beer and lager beer into a tall chilled glass. Quaff.

SHANDYGAFF

Old-fashioned, but often effective.

2 teaspoons granulated sugar
2 ounces whiskey (your favorite)
1 stick cinnamon

Twist of lemon peel studded with 3 cloves
Boiling water

Have ready a 12-ounce glass or mug. Rinse it with hot water. Then put in the sugar and dissolve it with 3 tablespoons boiling water. Add the whiskey and fill the glass or mug with more hot water. Garnish with a stick of cinnamon and the twist of lemon peel. NET: 1 serving.

HOT TODDY

Cranberry crush, frosted with raspberry ice and soda, this is as American as the Fourth of July, and as cool and refreshing on that holiday as on Thanksgiving.

CRANBERRY PUNCH

1½ cups granulated sugar
3 cups boiling water
2 cups cranberry sauce (homemade or canned), rubbed
  through a fine strainer
⅓ cup fresh lemon or lime juice

½ cup sour cherries (fresh or
  canned), pitted
4 cups (1 quart) raspberry
  sherbet or ice
4 cups (1 quart) cold soda water
A few fresh whole cranberries

Combine the sugar and boiling water in a heavy pan, and stir over moderate heat until the sugar is dissolved. Mix in the cranberry sauce and chill the mixture thoroughly in the refrigerator. When it is well chilled, add the lemon or lime juice and the cherries. Just before serving, mix in the raspberry sherbet or ice and the soda water. Serve the punch in tall cold glasses. Top with 1 or 2 fresh whole cranberries. Serve at once. NET: 8 tall servings.

FISH HOUSE PUNCH

The principal party drink in England and America during the days of the hoopskirt was the "flowing bowl," or punch bowl. In most drink mixing, there are always different viewpoints, such as Rum? Yes! Rum? No! There is wine, Champagne, tea . . . in fact almost limitless are the recipes that will make a party a reeling success. Here is an interpretation of the original English Fish House Punch. It was a great New England favorite and will make things wondrously beautiful in the old tradition.

2 tablespoons simple sugar
  syrup (equal parts water and
  granulated sugar boiled 5
  minutes and chilled)
2 tablespoons fresh lime juice
  or 3 tablespoons lemon juice
1 bottle (fifth) Cognac or good

brandy
1 cup peach or apricot brandy
1½ bottles (fifths) Jamaica rum
3 quarts non-vintage
  Champagne
Several chunks of ice (ice cubes
  are too small)

Put the simple syrup and lime or lemon juice into a large (at least 8 quarts) punch bowl. Add the rest of the ingredients, and stir well. Serve in punch cups. NET: 6 quarts.

HOLIDAY EGGNOG

12 egg yolks
¾ cup superfine sugar
1½ quarts (fifths) good
  bourbon whiskey
1 cup apricot brandy

¾ cup Jamaican rum
1½ quarts milk
2 cups heavy cream, half
  whipped
A little freshly grated nutmeg

Have ready a 6-quart punch bowl and lots of crushed ice. Beat the egg yolks in the mixer until light and thick. Slowly beat in the sugar, and continue beating until this mixture is light and thick. Transfer the mixture to the punch bowl and fold in, with a large spoon or rubber scraper, the bourbon, brandy, and rum. Next mix in the milk, and last, fold in the half-whipped cream. Continue to fold in and out until the mixture is smooth. Embed the punch bowl in a bowl of crushed ice. Serve the eggnog in little glasses, topped with a sprinkling of freshly grated nutmeg. NET: About 5 quarts.

A MINT JULEP PUNCH BOWL

3 to 4 dozen fresh mint sprigs
1½ cups clear, cold water
¼ pound confectioners sugar

2 bottles (fifths) of good
    bourbon plus 1 cup

Half fill a large punch bowl with chipped or shaved ice. Put into a smaller bowl (in this order) the mint sprigs, water, cup of bourbon, and sugar. Macerate the mint leaves thoroughly with the back of a spoon, or a pestle if you have one. When the leaves are well infused, strain the mixture through a wire strainer onto the ice. Be sure none of the mashed mint leaves or stems fall in the ice. Then pour the bottles of bourbon over the ice, give all your guests a straw, and have them gather around the bowl. (Or serve in tall chilled glasses, garnished with a fresh sprig of mint.) Sip. NET: 10 to 15 servings.

WEDDING BREAKFAST PUNCH, WITH CHAMPAGNE AND ROSÉ WINE

This recipe should be started the day before serving it.

3 cups fresh pineapple chunks
1 bottle (fifth) rosé wine
1 cup Cognac or good brandy
½ cup fresh lemon juice
½ cup granulated sugar
¼ cup peach brandy
¼ cup Cointreau

3 quarts non-vintage Cham-
    pagne or sparkling Burgundy
2 cups fresh pineapple cubes
    (about ½-inch)
1 perfect orange and 1 perfect
    lemon, thinly sliced
A few sprigs of fresh mint

Purée the pineapple chunks in an electric blender, adding a few chunks at a time. Pour the pineapple purée into a large bowl or container (about 4-quart size) and slowly add the rosé wine, brandy, lemon juice, and sugar. Mix well. Add the peach brandy and Cointreau, and stir the entire slurry. Cover, and let it remain overnight in the refrigerator. On the following day, have ready a large punch bowl with a big block of ice in it. Strain the mixture through three or four thicknesses of cheesecloth, squeezing all the pulpy mass to extract the juice. Pour the strained mixture into the bowl over the block of ice. Very slowly stir in the Champagne. Decorate the punch bowl with the pineapple cubes, float the thin slices of lemon and orange on the punch, and scatter the sprigs of mint over it. NET: About 6 quarts.

INDEX

Ecrevisse(s), *see* Shrimp(s)
à l'Écu de France
  Poularde, 379
  Turkey (Dindonneau), 415–416
Eel, Anguille
  and Lobster (Homard Chez Soi),
    307–308
  Stewed in Dark Brown Sauce
    (Matelote à la Bourguignonne),
    247
Egg(s), Oeuf(s), 173–229
  Alice, 199
  Andalouse, 188
  Argenteuil, 186–187
  and Asparagus
    à la Polonaise, 107
    Purée (Mollet Argenteuil), 186–
     187
  in Aspic, 192–193
    with Tarragon, 193–194
  Auguste, 200
  Avgolemono Soup (Egg and
    Lemon), 156–157
  Baked or Shirred (sur le Plat;
    Miroir), 179
    Flamenco, 198
    à la Grecque, 198–199
    on Lima Beans with Tomatoes,
     197–198
  Baked in Water Bath (en Cocotte),
    180–181
    Lorraine, 203–204
    Sagan, 203
  Benedict, 189
  au Beurre Noir (with Brown Butter),
    189–190
  Boulangère, 181–182
  à la Bourguignonne, 86
  Brouillés, *see* Scrambled, *below*
  du Carême, 182–183
  and Chicken
    Marengo, 373–374
    à la Reine, 185
  Clamart, 190–191
  en Cocotte, *see* Baked in Water
    Bath, *above*
  Coddled (à la Coque), 176–177
  Cressfield, 200
  Durs, *see* Hard-boiled, *below*
  à l'Espagnole, 197
  Flamenco, 198
  Florentine, 191
    en Savarin, 192
  au Foie Gras, 85–86
  Française, 201–202
  Fried (Frits)
    American Style, 178–179
    with Brown Butter, 196–197
    in Chicken Marengo, 373–374
    French Style, 179
    and Ham (à l'Espagnole), 197
  en Gelée, 192–193
    Jellied, à la Russe, 86–87
    with Tarragon, 193–194
  Georgette, 194–195
  Greek (à la Grecque), 198–199
  Green Pea Tartlets (Clamart),
    190–191

Egg(s) (*contd.*)
  and Ham
    Boulangère, 181–182
    a l'Espagnole, 197
    Farcis Maison, 184
  Hard-boiled (Durs), 175–176; *see
    also* Stuffed (Farcis), *below*
    Asparagus with (à la Polonaise), 107
    Boulangère, 181–182
    du Carême, 182–183
    with Onions (à la tripe), 186
    à la Parisienne, 84–85
    à la Polonaise, 107
    Salad, 642
    à la Talleyrand, 185–186
  aux Haricots de Limas, 197–198
  Jellied, on Russian Salad, 86–87
  and Lemon Soup, Greek, 156–157
  Lorraine, 203–204
  Maltaise, 202
  Mariette, 202–203
  Miroir, *see* Baked or Shirred, *above*
  Molded (Moulis) or in Timbales
    (en Timbales), 181
    Cardinal, 204–205
  Mollet, *see* Soft-boiled, *below*
  Omelets, *see* Omelet; Omelette
    Nature; Omelette Soufflée
  à la Parisienne, 84–85
  sur le Plat, *see* Baked or Shirred,
    above
  Poached (Pochés), 177–178
    Andalouse, 188
    in Aspic, 192–193
     with Tarragon, 193–194
    Benedict, 189
    au Beurre Noir, 189–190
    à la Bourguignonne, 86
    Cheese Soufflé with (en Surprise),
     123–124
    Clamart, 190–191
    Florentine, 191
     en Savarin, 192
    en Gelée, 192–193
     à la Russe, 86–87
     with Tarragon, 193–194
    Georgette, 194–195
    à la Russe, 86–87
    Soubise, 196
    en Surprise, 123–124
    on Vegetable Macédoine, 195–196
  à la Polonaise, 107
  à la Printanière, 643
  Purée of Asparagus and (Argenteuil),
    186–187
  à la Reine, 185
  à la Russe, 86–87
  Sagan, 204
  Salad, 642
  in salad dressings, 634
  Sauce, 185
  Scrambled (Brouillés)
    Alice, 199
    Auguste, 200
    Cressfield, 200
    Française, 201–202
    Maltaise, 202
    Mariette, 202–203